RAND in
Southeast Asia

A History of the Vietnam War Era

MAI ELLIOTT

 INVESTMENT IN PEOPLE AND IDEAS

This book results from the RAND Corporation's continuing program of self-initiated research. Support for such research is provided, in part, by the generosity of RAND's donors and by the fees earned on client-funded research. RAND is a nonprofit institution that helps improve policy and decisionmaking through research and analysis. Opinions expressed in this book are those of the author and do not reflect positions taken by RAND, its board, or its clients.

Library of Congress Cataloging-in-Publication Data

Elliott, Duong Van Mai, 1941–
    RAND in southeast Asia : a history of the Vietnam War era / Mai V. Elliott.
    p. cm.
    Includes bibliographical references.
    ISBN 978-0-8330-4754-0 (pbk. : alk. paper)
    1. Rand Corporation—Influence. 2. Vietnam War, 1961-1975—Research—United States—History. 3. Counterinsurgency—Research—United States—History—20th century. 4. Military planning—United States—History—20th century. I. Title.

DS558.2.E44 2010
959.704'3—dc22

2009025271

The RAND Corporation is a nonprofit research organization providing objective analysis and effective solutions that address the challenges facing the public and private sectors around the world. RAND's publications do not necessarily reflect the opinions of its research clients and sponsors.

RAND® is a registered trademark.

Cover design by Eileen La Russo

Published 2010 by the RAND Corporation
1776 Main Street, P.O. Box 2138, Santa Monica, CA 90407-2138
1200 South Hayes Street, Arlington, VA 22202-5050
4570 Fifth Avenue, Suite 600, Pittsburgh, PA 15213-2665
RAND URL: http://www.rand.org/
To order RAND documents or to obtain additional information, contact
Distribution Services: Telephone: (310) 451-7002;
Fax: (310) 451-6915; Email: order@rand.org

Foreword

James A. Thomson

I celebrated my 20th anniversary as president of the RAND Corporation in August 2009, and this is my 29th year at RAND. But I joined the organization well after RAND had concluded its work in connection with the Vietnam War.

I certainly knew of that work, and when I joined the organization I had many colleagues who had worked on analyses of the war. Some had worked in Vietnam, where RAND opened and operated an office in a villa at 176 Rue Pasteur, Saigon. Today one would be hard pressed to find someone with this firsthand experience walking the hallways of RAND. Over the past three decades, most of these men and women have retired, and sadly some have passed away.

In preparing for what would be our first visit to Vietnam, as tourists in 2001, my wife and I began to explore RAND's history in Saigon. Upon arriving in Ho Chi Minh City, I set out to find 176 Rue Pasteur. I was surprised to learn that Rue Pasteur is the only street that retains its name from before the fall of Saigon in 1975. The villa is now a nursery school.

In preparing for that same trip, my wife, Darlene, came across *The Sacred Willow*, by Duong Van Mai Elliott. We enjoyed her comprehensive account of four generations of her own family and their experiences living as a part of the political elite of Vietnam. That narrative includes Elliott's own experiences, including her time working with RAND at Rue Pasteur. Those readers who are familiar with *The Sacred Willow* will agree that the book was carefully researched and clearly and compellingly written by Ms. Elliott. Her family's story is a complex one that reveals a great deal about the experience of the Vietnamese during a period that many Western readers know only from the perspective of America's Vietnam War.

Upon my return to Santa Monica, I sought out Ms. Elliott with a proposition: I wanted her help recording the stories of those who had been a part of RAND's work on Vietnam, including Ms. Elliott herself.

There are many accounts of the Vietnam War that claim to describe RAND's work there. And too often uninformed speculation or persistent but incorrect information has made its way to print and film. I didn't approach Ms. Elliott to set that record straight, or to undertake a comprehensive history. I approached her because I didn't want to lose the narratives of the men and women who worked together at Rue Pasteur or who conducted their analyses only in the United States.

This book is for RAND, and the people who want to understand what the alumni of this organization remembered about their experiences working for the U.S. government on research and analysis of what remains some of the most controversial foreign and military policy of the 20th century. I hope readers will approach Ms. Elliott's work with this in mind—and of course that they will enjoy the journey.

Preface

An insurgency is an armed rebellion against a constituted authority . . . when those taking part in the rebellion are not recognised as belligerents. . . . When insurgency is used to describe a movement's unlawfulness by virtue of not being authorized by or in accordance with the law of the land, its use is neutral. However, when it is used by a state or another authority under threat, "insurgency" often also carries an implication that the rebels' cause is illegitimate, whereas those rising up will see the authority itself as being illegitimate (Wikipedia, "Insurgency," Web page, 2009).

Whereas in ordinary war the objective is to destroy the enemy and occupy his territory, the guerrilla's aim [is] to control the population. This, therefore, must be the aim of the counter-guerrilla as well (Col. David Galula, French Marine Corps, former commander of Kabylie District, Algeria, 1956–1958, quoted in S. T. Hosmer and S. O. Crane, *Counterinsurgency: A Symposium, April 16–20, 1962*, Santa Monica, Calif.: RAND Corporation, R-412-ARPA, November 1962, p. 3).

. . . the insurgent starts out with nothing but a cause and grows to strength, while the counterinsurgent often starts with everything but a cause and gradually declines in strength to the point of weakness (Col. David Galula, in Hosmer and Crane, *Counterinsurgency: A Symposium*, 1962, p. 7).

Prepared at the request of Jim Thomson, President of RAND, to capture the story of RAND's involvement in insurgency and counterinsurgency research in Vietnam, Laos, and Thailand during the Vietnam War era, most of this document revolves around Vietnam, the main theater of warfare, and around RAND's most extensive research effort there—the Viet Cong Motivation and Morale Project—a project that was undertaken in two main phases: the first one under the direction of Joe Zasloff and John Donnell in 1964, and the second under Leon Goure from 1965 to 1967.

The insurgency in the south of Vietnam was started by the Viet Cong, a pejorative designation given by the South Vietnamese government to the insurgents to emphasize their affiliation with the Communist Party, in the early 1960s. The objective of the insurgents was to destabilize the South Vietnamese government, which they viewed as illegitimate, with military and political activities designed to gain control over the population. Their ultimate aim was to bring about the collapse of the government and replace it with a government committed to reunifying divided Vietnam and enacting political, social, and economic reforms. The insurgency evolved eventually into a combination of guerrilla warfare and conventional attacks involving large units of the North Vietnamese Army, the allies of the Viet Cong, and American troops. To combat the efforts of the Viet Cong, the South Vietnamese government, aided by the United States, launched a counterinsurgency campaign combining military and political actions to recapture control over the population and reestablish its authority in areas undermined by the insurgency.

My goal in undertaking this effort was not to write a typical RAND report but to produce a narrative that combines the tenor of the times and the personal stories, experiences, and attitudes and thinking of RAND staff members engaged in research in this region, along with the substance of the works they produced in this period. This book is based on the hundreds of papers produced by RAND analysts; on personal interviews with many staff members who played important roles in RAND's research programs in these countries; and on outside sources, such as archival materials, books, articles, and interviews with people who dealt with RAND or were familiar with its work in those times. As with personal recollections in general, not all of those gathered for this book could be corroborated by documentary evidence. With the exception of a few conducted over the telephone, the interviews, were done face-to-face, taped, and transcribed. Broad questions on issues to be discussed were provided in advance so that, prior to the conversations, the people interviewed could reach back in memory to events that happened decades earlier. Transcripts were provided to those who requested them for review. If the interviewee responded and asked for revisions, the changes were incorporated in the final transcripts. In a couple of instances, the persons interviewed declined to be taped and allowed only note taking.

Unfortunately, several limitations make a complete record impossible to assemble. With the exception of the precious few pieces that were kept by some former RAND staff members, RAND correspondence—at least those items that are unclassified, such as memoranda, letters, and notes—was discarded in a file-clearing effort, according to a former RAND administrative assistant. Without a security clearance, I was unable to gain access to the parts of the record that remain classified. Many of the key protagonists—Guy Pauker, John Donnell, Paul Langer, Bill Jones, and Oleg Hoeffding among them—have passed from the scene, and their personal recollections could not be gathered. Others, including Doug Scott and the Vietnamese interviewers for the Viet Cong Motivation and Morale Project, could not be traced or were unwilling to talk, or, as with George Tanham, were in such bad health that they were unavailable. Fortunately, three key analysts—Leon Goure, Konrad Kellen, and Tony Russo—were in good health and were willing to grant interviews before they passed away. Wherever possible, personal recollections were checked against documentary evidence.

❧ ❧ ❧

From the 1950s onward, RAND produced over five hundred documents on the subject of Vietnam, about sixty on Laos, and over one hundred on Thailand. Whether these represent the sum total of all RAND's works produced on these countries is unclear. Perhaps some were lost with the passage of time. Those that still exist range from Reports (Rs) and Research Memoranda (RMs), the top end of the document hierarchy, to Documents (Ds), Papers (Ps), and Working Notes (WNs). Although not as authoritative as Rs and RMs, Ds, Ps, and WNs were nonetheless important in the sense that they are preliminary thoughts or concepts that would later be incorporated into more-complete reports, or were even distributed to clients to serve as interim reports or to circumvent the more stringent review process required to turn them into RMs. To tell a coherent narrative, I selected only those deemed most relevant and the most important to the main story. As formal publications, Rs and RMs are usually accessible, whereas Ds, Ps, and WNs retain designations such as "For RAND Use Only" or "For Official Use Only."

During the war, RAND was perceived in some quarters as a monolithic, hard-line, progovernment think tank, a sort of "enabler" of a military in pursuit of destructive operations in Vietnam. The record clearly shows, however, that RAND was and still is similar to a university—a community of thinkers with disparate views, ranging from the supportive to the critical of U.S. government policies in Vietnam. There were people who worked to make weapons or technology more lethal. But there were also those who took issue with the destructive use of American power in Vietnam, as well as those who advocated U.S. withdrawal from the war. In short, many voices existed at RAND.

To place the RAND story in a historical context and describe the background against which RAND's work unfolded, I consulted books and articles. They were also used, whenever possible, to capture reaction to RAND's works or activities, or events at RAND, such as the Pentagon Papers affair. Through these books and articles, and especially through archival materials and interviews, I have attempted to assess the effect of RAND's work on U.S. policies and on the thinking of government officials tasked with dealing with Vietnam.

RAND had the most influence from 1965 through 1967, when American military efforts were ramped up to achieve a military solution. Three government officials who were most influenced by RAND during this period were Assistant Secretary of Defense John McNaughton, Defense Secretary Robert S. McNamara, and Walt Rostow, who eventually became President Lyndon Baines Johnson's National Security Advisor. I attempted to interview Mr. McNamara, but the former Defense Secretary declined, saying that he did not remember RAND's Vietnam research or Leon Goure, who used to brief him regularly. Unfortunately, John McNaughton and Walt Rostow had passed away. Rostow's personal papers were unavailable because they had not yet been processed by the Lyndon B. Johnson Archives at the University of Texas at Austin. In addition, many documents in the National Archives were reclassified as "Secret" by the second Bush Administration. Without access, it was not possible to determine whether they might contain any information relevant to RAND's work.

Despite all these limitations, I strongly believe that this book has captured the main threads of the RAND story in Vietnam, Laos, and Thailand during the Vietnam War era. Even when all the classified information becomes available, the new evidence will not change the story in a major way—although it would undoubtedly add many more interesting elaborations.

In assessing the effect of RAND's research, I found it difficult to trace a cause-and-effect link. At its most influential, RAND's research reinforced what policymakers were already inclined to do, encouraged them to believe that they were on the right track, and motivated them to persist in doing what they were doing or to do more of the same. The research also served as an additional arrow in their quivers to persuade the president or their colleagues that the course of action they proposed or were undertaking was correct and would produce results. At their most optimistic, some of RAND's research works on Vietnam fed their belief that success was possible, and by providing the cloak of expertise and objectivity that social science research is perceived to convey, reinforced and legitimized their policies. On the whole, however, if RAND's research was taken into account, it was simply one of several sources of data—and not always the most instrumental—in the mix for policy formulation. Sometimes, even frequently in the view of some RAND analysts, it was commissioned to demonstrate that careful consideration had been given to policy formulation and that all viewpoints had been consulted before decisions were made.

According to Seymour Deitchman, a senior official of the Advanced Research Projects Agency in the Department of Defense in the 1960s, the types of studies on Vietnam that garnered the most attention were those that "generally fit the pattern of operations and philosophy for prosecution of the war that were common among the military and civilian authorities in both Washington and Saigon."[1] By the same token, the research results that challenged how things were done or indicated failure in a program to which important officials were committed, were not usually accepted. Even when research results were accepted because they provided what the system was looking for and produced a practical outcome, it was difficult to measure the long-term effect. For example, RAND's study on the American military advisor and his

---

[1]   Seymour J. Deitchman, *The Best-Laid Schemes: A Tale of Social Research and Bureaucracy*, Cambridge, Mass.: The MIT Press, 1976, p. 342.

South Vietnamese counterpart[2] was made required reading for the Military Assistance Command Vietnam (MACV) staff, but modifications to the selection, training, and assignment of American advisors were not discernible.

RAND prided itself on its quality analysis, strategic thinking, and conceptual scope, and its staff members generally felt that their influence should be greater than it was. Whether it was Vietnam or other issues, the RAND research staff—as Gus Shubert (who took over as manager of the Viet Cong Motivation and Morale Project in 1967 and who later became a RAND vice president) has observed—were usually "disappointed to see that their research results did not have the kind of impact they thought they ought to have," and that there were some who never felt "sufficiently appreciated."[3] In his view, however, such expectations were unrealistic, because "RAND very often fails to recognize that there are other forces at play beyond its work, which will push with its results or against its results. And that those considerations like judgment, or politics . . . may have equal or even larger influence than the kind of intellectual exercise we go through here. . . . We're living in a dynamic world, and RAND strives to produce permanent solutions. It's just unrealistic . . . to expect to have that kind of profound and final effect on the big picture."[4]

In general, Deitchman's assessment of social science research conducted for the government could be applied to the work RAND performed in Vietnam—and to a lesser extent in Laos and Thailand—although not all his comments concerned RAND in particular. In his view, the value of social science field research lay in helping "all groups involved to guide themselves by something better than seat of the pants navigation" and in providing intuitive insights.[5] As an example, Deitchman cited the insights gained by Joe Zasloff, John Donnell, and Guy Pauker, the authors of the first Viet Cong Motivation and Morale study.[6] In his view, their insights were valuable and revealing, although a rigorous statistical analysis of their data might not back up their conclusions because they were circumscribed by the limitations of field research in a war zone.

Despite the problems of conducting social science field research in wartime, the knowledge gained was instructive. In Saigon, the research gave American military and civilian authorities "information and understanding they did not have and were glad to gain."[7] From such research, Deitchman believed that "a picture of the revolutionary

---

[2] Gerald C. Hickey and W. P. Davison, *The American Military Advisor and His Foreign Counterpart: The Case of Vietnam*, Santa Monica, Calif.: RAND Corporation, RM-4482-ARPA, March 1965.

[3] Martin Collins, interview with Gus Shubert, session of January 17, 1991, p. 107.

[4] Collins, 1991, interview with Gus Shubert, p. 107.

[5] Deitchman, *The Best-Laid Schemes*, p. 389.

[6] John C. Donnell, Guy J. Pauker, and Joseph J. Zasloff, *Viet Cong Motivation and Morale in 1964: A Preliminary Report*, Santa Monica, Calif.: RAND Corporation, RM-4507/3-ISA, March 1965.

[7] Deitchman, *The Best-Laid Schemes*, p. 337.

movements . . . began to emerge, with details of what motivated their members, how these movements made their way through the peasant populations, gaining or forcing adherents, and destroying the writ of the existing order and government. . . . The actions of government could be put in perspective, and it became possible to predict which actions would be effective and which ones would exacerbate the situation."[8]

With regard to research on military operations, Deitchman felt that the researchers tried to manipulate statistical data collected by the military to find patterns of enemy activity in order to point military operations in directions in which they could succeed. However, the military statistical system was not set up "to permit detailed analysis of events and their causes," and this approach produced results that were "dry" and "told the military nothing that they couldn't sense intuitively."[9] Here, Deitchman cited the study done by George Young of RAND, which analyzed dozens of operations only to prove that the Viet Cong operated mostly at night and that their activities related to the waxing and waning of the moon.

According to Deitchman, another limitation on the effect of research was that often reports did not reach the official who was truly interested and was in a position to act, or they arrived too late to have an impact. Sometimes, the official who was interested had left his position, or the reports had been overtaken by events, which made a reversal of course too difficult, if not impossible. The conclusions reached by a small number of analysts from their research data could not change the situation. In the case of Vietnam, it took a momentous event such as the Tet Offensive to make the United States change course.

On the whole, RAND research rarely advocated drastic changes, and RAND followed rather than led, and was usually behind the curve rather than ahead of it. The comment that Gus Shubert made regarding RAND's work in the domestic arena could be applied to RAND's work in Southeast Asia as well: ". . . what we were seeking was to make positive contributions at the margin. We were very unlikely to be revolutionary. . . ."[10] The trajectory of RAND's research in Vietnam paralleled the evolution of American involvement. It reached its highest mark when American intervention was at its peak, declined as the United States began to disengage, and then folded after the Paris Accords were signed in 1973—not surprising, since research was undertaken when there was interest and support in Washington or Saigon, and such interest and support were at their strongest when the U.S. commitment was intensifying. However, the decline in RAND's Vietnam field research could also be traced to disillusionment with the second phase of the Viet Cong Motivation and Morale Project and to the apprehension that the project leader's optimistic predictions had not been borne out and that RAND's reputation might have been damaged in the process.

---

[8]   Deitchman, *The Best-Laid Schemes*, pp. 386–387.

[9]   Detichman, *The Best-Laid Schemes*, p. 378.

[10] Martin Collins, interview with Gus Shubert, session of July 17, 1992, p. 82.

RAND's influence on U.S. Vietnam policy was limited, but the impact of the war on RAND itself was deep. At the beginning of the war, most people at RAND were united in a Cold War consensus and agreed that the United States was right to take a stand in Vietnam to stop communist expansion. But as the United States got bogged down and the war seemed unwinnable, and as the nature of the conflict became clearer, many analysts began to question the validity of not just American policies—but of American involvement. Eventually, some even came to question the morality of that involvement. Reflecting the mood of the country at large, RAND, too, fell prey to the same division that was splitting American society. The war and the breakup of the Cold War consensus left a lingering bitterness at RAND.

Among the analysts who went to Vietnam to perform field research, many came with support for the war and with the hope that they could make U.S. efforts more successful; ultimately, they left the country with serious doubts about the wisdom of American intervention. The war was a life-changing event for some, most especially for two analysts: Daniel Ellsberg and Tony Russo. The division at RAND eventually exploded with the unauthorized publication of the Pentagon Papers by Daniel Ellsberg, whose hope was that the revelation of what he perceived as duplicity by several presidential administrations would bring the war to an end. The furor over the Pentagon Papers led the Air Force, RAND's main sponsor, to tighten its funding, a move that might have accelerated RAND's diversification into domestic research.

According to Gus Shubert, RAND never formally evaluated the impact that Vietnam had on the organization. This book is an attempt, within limits, to tell the story of RAND's involvement in the Vietnam War and to assess what this conflict might have meant for RAND.

Contents

Photos

Maps

Acknowledgments

This book could not have been written without the generosity and assistance of many people. I am most grateful to Jim Thomson for giving me the chance to undertake this work. I appreciate immensely his patience and, above all, his willingness to give me the intellectual freedom to pursue my research and to write the book in the best way I believe it could be written. Many people were gracious in granting me interviews and in sharing their recollections. Without such personal memories, my book would be devoid of the rich details that enliven the narrative. All these people are cited in the text, and to them all I would like to extend my heartfelt gratitude. In particular, I would like to thank Joe and Tela Zasloff, and Joe Carrier for their hospitality, their insights, and the documents and photos they provided. I would like to express my deep gratitude to Vivian Arterbery, Ann Horn, Caroline Casey, and Karen Treverton for their support and patient assistance. I would also like to thank the RAND Library staff, who secured copies of innumerable reports for me. I would also like to thank Marian Branch and James Torr, who edited my manuscript; Todd Duft, who oversaw the production process; and Peter Hoffman, who directed the publication.

RAND Corporation Organization Chart, 1963

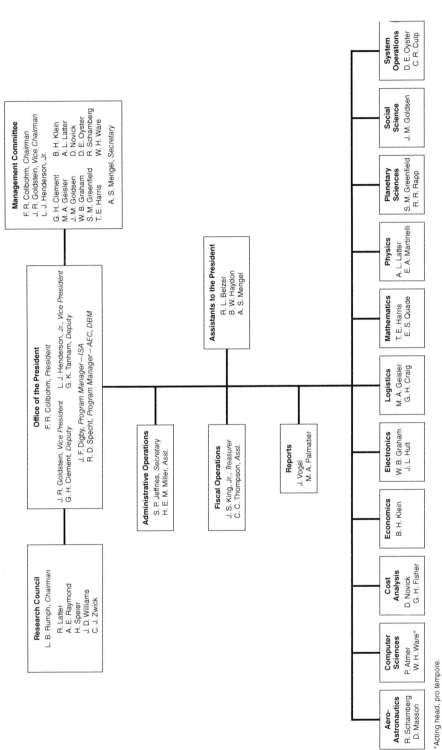

Management Committee
F. R. Collbohm, *Chairman*
J. R. Goldstein, *Vice Chairman*
L. J. Henderson, Jr.

G. H. Clement	B. H. Klein
M. A. Geisler	A. L. Latter
J. M. Goldsen	D. Novick
W. B. Graham	D. E. Oyster
S. M. Greenfield	R. Schamberg
T. E. Harris	W. H. Ware

A. S. Mengel, *Secretary*

Office of the President
F. R. Collbohm, *President*
J. R. Goldstein, *Vice President*   L. J. Henderson, Jr., *Vice President*
G. H. Clement, *Deputy*   G. K. Tanham, *Deputy*
J. F. Digby, *Program Manager—ISA*
R. D. Specht, *Program Manager—AEC, DBM*

Research Council
L. B. Rumph, *Chairman*

R. Latter
A. E. Raymond
H. Speier
J. D. Williams
C. J. Zwick

Assistants to the President
R. L. Belzer
B. W. Haydon
A. S. Mengel

Administrative Operations
S. P. Jeffries, *Secretary*
H. E. M. Miller, *Asst.*

Fiscal Operations
J. S. King, Jr., *Treasurer*
C. C. Thompson, *Asst.*

Reports
J. Vogel
M. A. Palmatier

Aero-Astronautics
R. Schamberg
D. Masson

Computer Sciences
P. Atmer
W. H. Ware*

Cost Analysis
D. Novick
G. H. Fisher

Economics
B. H. Klein

Electronics
W. B. Graham
J. L. Hult

Logistics
M. A. Geisler
G. H. Craig

Mathematics
T. E. Harris
E. S. Quade

Physics
A. L. Latter
E. A. Martinelli

Planetary Sciences
S. M. Greenfield
R. R. Rapp

Social Science
J. M. Goldsen

System Operations
D. E. Oyster
C. R. Culp

*Acting head, pro tempore.

RAND Corporation Organization Chart, 1970

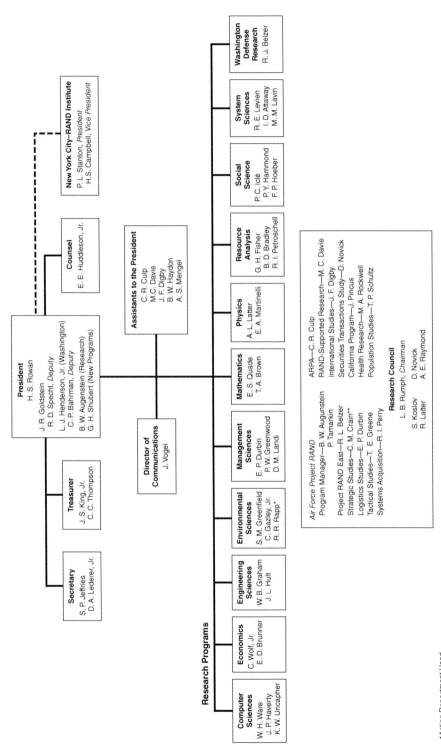

Research Programs

President
H. S. Rowan

J. R. Goldstein
R. D. Specht, *Deputy*
L. J. Henderson, Jr. (Washington)
C. P. Bahrman, *Deputy*
B. W. Augenstein (Research)
G. H. Shubert (New Programs)

New York City–RAND Institute
P. L. Stanton, *President*
H.S. Campbell, *Vice President*

Counsel
E. E. Huddleson, Jr.

Secretary
S. P. Jeffries
D. A. Lederer, Jr.

Treasurer
J. S. King, Jr.
C. C. Thompson

Director of Communications
J. Vogel

Assistants to the President
C. R. Culp
M. C. Davie
J. F. Digby
B. W. Haydon
A. S. Mengel

Computer Sciences
W. H. Ware
J. P. Haverty
K. W. Uncapher

Economics
C. Wolf, Jr.
E. D. Brunner

Engineering Sciences
W. B. Graham
J. L. Hult

Environmental Sciences
S. M. Greenfield
C. Gazley, Jr.
R. R. Rapp*

Management Sciences
E. P. Durbin
P. W. Greenwood
D. M. Landi

Mathematics
E. S. Quade
T. A. Brown

Physics
A. L. Latter
E. A. Martinelli

Resource Analysis
G. H. Fisher
B. D. Bradley
R. I. Petroschell

Social Science
P. C. Iclé
P. Y. Hammond
F. P. Hoeber

System Sciences
R. E. Levien
I. D. Attaway
M. M. Lavin

Washington Defense Research
R. J. Belzer

Air Force Project RAND
Program Manager—B. W. Augenstein
P. Tamarkin
Project RAND East—R. L. Belzer
Strategic Studies—C. M. Crain**
Logistics Studies—E. P. Durbin
Tactical Studies—T. E. Greene
Systems Acquisition—R. I. Perry

ARPA—C. R. Culp
RAND-Supported Research—M. C. Davie
International Studies—J. F. Digby
Securities Transactions Study—D. Novick
California Program—J. Pincus
Health Research—M. A. Rockwell
Population Studies—T. P. Schultz

Research Council
L. B. Rumph, *Chairman*
S. Koslov   D. Novick
R. Latter   A. E. Raymond

*Acting Department Head.
**In the absence of A. W. Marshall.

Vietnam, Laos, Cambodia, and Thailand

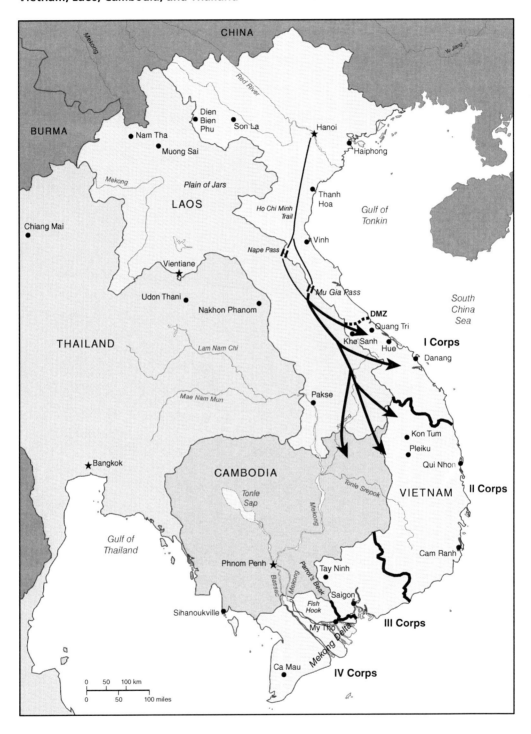

RAND: The Beginning

RAND is one of the nonprofit corporations staffed with civilian researchers and strategists that emerged in the years following World War II to advise the U.S. military, on a contractual basis, on a wide range of important issues.[1] Modern science and technology had rendered warfare so complex that the services recognized that, to remain on the technological cutting edge, they needed to enlist the advice of civilian scientists and technologists on planning, operations, and weapon development.[2]

The services began to seek the advice of civilian scientists and technologists in World War II, when the military undertook operations research, mostly in radar and anti-submarine warfare, and set up operations-analysis sections staffed with civilian scientists and mathematicians. Using a quantitative, interdisciplinary approach combining applied mathematics and formal science and relying on "methods such as mathematical modeling, statistics, and algorithms to arrive at optimal or near optimal solutions to complex problems,"[3] operations researchers and analysts facilitated military decisionmaking. Later, civilians were brought in to assist in military planning, a practice epitomized by the B-29 Special Bombardment Project. The project originated in 1944 with Dr. Edward L. Bowles, then special consultant to General H. H. "Hap" Arnold, the Army Air Force Chief, with the objective of forming a study team to work closely with the Army Air Force to increase the effectiveness of the B-29 as a strategic bomber. The idea for Project RAND emerged from the project.

Among the people Bowles brought into the project were Arthur C. Raymond, chief engineer of the Douglas Aircraft Corporation, and his aide, Frank Collbohm.

---

[1] This introduction is based mainly on the information gathered by Bruce Smith, a former professor in the Department of Government at Harvard University and member of the RAND Social Science Department, in his book *The RAND Corporation: Case Study of a Nonprofit Advisory Corporation*, Cambridge, Mass.: Harvard University Press, 1966.

[2] So many American research organization representatives were roaming "through the corridors of the Pentagon" that one foreign observer was prompted to say that they resembled the Jesuits who thronged "the courts of Madrid and Vienna three centuries ago." Cited in Bruce Smith, *The RAND Corporation*, 1966, p. 1.

[3] Wikipedia, "Operations Research," Web page, 2009.

Frank Collbohm

The project succeeded beyond expectations, and the Army Air Force accepted the team's recommendations.[4] In late 1944, there were informal discussions in the War Department and the Office of Scientific Research, which was coordinating the efforts of researchers in the military, industry, and academic laboratories on how to preserve the partnership between the military and civilian scientists—a partnership that had proved so effective—once the war ended and the scientists returned to their former positions. The technical evolution and complexity of modern warfare rendered the assistance of these scientists even more crucial to the military. Out of this discussion came the idea of contracting with a private organization to assist the military in planning, especially in coordinating planning with research and development decisions. This idea led to the conception of what would become Project RAND, mainly through the initiative of the Douglas Company, to which Raymond and Collbohm had returned in mid-summer 1945.[5]

Collbohm made several trips to Washington to pursue the concept, and, in fall 1945, he proposed to house a group of civilians at Douglas who would assist the

[4]   The team suggested "stripping away much of the heavy defensive armor" that weighed down the bomber, thereby increasing its "range, speed, and bomb load." Bruce Smith, *The RAND Corporation*, 1966, p. 37.

[5]   In the view of Bruce Smith, "It would be a mistake . . . to say simply that an evolving military technology 'required' the creation of a RAND. What can be said is that the complexity of modern warfare made it highly desirable, and probably essential, for the military to obtain scientific advice on numerous aspects of planning, operations, and weapons-development policies." Bruce Smith, *The RAND Corporation*, 1966, p. 31.

Army Air Force in planning for weapon development. General Arnold was impressed with Collbohm's proposal, and on October 1, 1945, at Hamilton Airfield outside of San Francisco, he and Dr. Bowles met with a group from Douglas Aircraft, including Donald Douglas, Arthur Raymond, Frank Collbohm, and Fred Conant, to set up the framework for an organization that would become known as Project RAND— although there were "different views . . . as to the exact form the partnership should assume and the precise objectives that it would pursue.[6]

The concept was further defined and solidified by General Curtis LeMay, who headed the newly created office of Deputy Chief of Air Staff for Research and Development, in December 1945. Shortly after LeMay's appointment, at a meeting held with representatives from the Air Staff and the Wright Field Materiel Command, the Wright Field delegation objected that RAND would encroach on its prerogatives.[7] LeMay overruled their objections, saying that the aim of Project RAND was to conduct "long-range research that might form the basis for a future military requirement" and that it was not for the Air Force to specify a requirement and tell Project RAND people what to do.

From the meeting, a work statement was issued, directing Project RAND to carry out a broad research program on "intercontinental warfare, other than surface, with the object of advising Army Air Forces on devices and techniques."[8] This broad mandate in essence gave RAND the freedom to develop its own research programs.[9] Thus began RAND's association with the Air Force. This relationship expanded and strengthened after the Air Force became a separate branch of the military in 1947. Being the youngest of the three services, the Air Force did not have the traditional internal organization made up of technical bureaus that the Army and Navy had developed. It therefore had to depend more heavily on outside experts, and it was more open to the ideas that RAND could offer.

On March 2, 1946, the Army Air Force signed a contract with Douglas Aircraft to create Project RAND with an initial staff of four housed at the company but sealed off from the rest of the personnel. Frank Collbohm was selected to head the project, pending the appointment of a permanent director. The Army Air Force was to provide

---

[6]   Bruce Smith, *The RAND Corporation*, 1966, p. 43.

[7]   Bowles in particular feared that if RAND fell under the control of the Wright Field materiel people "with their traditionalist and 'requirements approach' type of thinking," this domination would stultify the long-range research effort. Bruce Smith, *The RAND Corporation*, 1966, p. 45.

[8]   Bruce Smith, *The RAND Corporation*, 1966, p. 47. According to Smith, "The phrase, 'other than surface' was included to avoid offense to the Navy. And the words 'devices and techniques' strongly suggest that the research effort was supposed to emphasize the physical sciences. This lends support to the view that few people associated with Project RAND foresaw at this early stage the enormous impact that social science thinking later was to make on the character of the RAND research effort." Bruce Smith, *The RAND Corporation*, 1966, p. 48.

[9]   LeMay would, in general, work to protect RAND's independence. Bruce Smith, *The RAND Corporation*, 1966, p. 46.

initial financial support for several years without requiring any immediate and concrete results.

Although this transition phase enabled RAND to get established, the association with Douglas Aircraft immediately created the perception of a conflict of interest. Competitors were reluctant to share information with Project RAND out of fear that it might be passed along to their rival. The Army Air Force itself felt uneasy about the connection of RAND with the company and was concerned that it might be criticized for favoring Douglas in awarding its procurement contracts. At the same time, RAND had difficulties recruiting and retaining high-quality staff because of the antipathy harbored by academics toward industry in general. Also, many RAND people felt that RAND would have a hard time developing a reputation for truly objective research as long as it remained connected to Douglas.

For its part, Douglas wanted to be rid of RAND. Entering a difficult period due to drastically reduced government orders following the end of World War II, which left a surplus of aircraft and led to a severe workforce reduction, the company thought that RAND was putting it at a disadvantage in winning new business because, in its view, the Air Force was being forced to go to extremes in awarding procurement and development contracts to avoid the perception of favoritism toward Douglas. In May 1947, RAND moved out of Douglas and into rented quarters in downtown Santa Monica.

RAND's staff became restive about the continuing link with Douglas. To achieve maximum flexibility in RAND's operations, in late 1947, Frank Collbohm, now permanent director, asked H. Rowan Gaither, a San Francisco lawyer and friend, to help establish RAND as an independent nonprofit corporation. The Air Force, now a separate branch of service, consented to the transfer of its contract only when it became "satisfied that the new corporation is *in existence and is capable of discharging the contract obligations as effectively as the Douglas Company.*"[10]

To finance the new corporation, Collbohm and Gaither decided that it needed $1 million in working capital to ensure that it could function as a separate entity and to persuade the Air Force that it would be able to discharge its contractual obligations. To secure lines of credit from several San Francisco banks, RAND had to show that it had funds as working capital. In summer 1948, three RAND people learned that Dr. Karl Compton, a Ford Foundation trustee, was going to be on a train traveling from New York to Boston. They arranged to have seats in the same compartment. On the way to Boston, they convinced Compton to back RAND. Henry Ford II subsequently agreed to give RAND an interest-free loan of $100,000 and to guarantee $300,000 in bank credit. This arrangement allowed RAND to obtain a loan from Wells Fargo. With the

---

[10] Bruce Smith, *The RAND Corporation*, 1966, p. 68. According to Bruce Smith, this stipulation was important because it allowed RAND to become completely independent of the Air Force, since "the corporation was organized and set up independently of the Air Force—in short, came into existence *first*—and entered into the contractual relationship with the Air Force only *after* it was already established." Bruce Smith, *The RAND Corporation*, 1966, p. 69.

financing secured, Frank Collbohm recruited an impressive Board of Trustees to add prestige to the corporation and to convince the Air Force that it had "competent direction" and the support of the "scientific and industrial communities."[11]

On November 4, 1948, the Air Force officially announced a contract with RAND. By 1950, RAND had matured and had built up a competent research staff. Its efforts reached a "critical mass," and research productivity began to accelerate.[12] The relationship with the Air Force—which has endured for decades—was firmly established. Under the terms of this relationship, the Air Force would provide RAND with financial support to ensure continuity while giving RAND independence to choose its own research activities. In return, RAND would fulfill Air Force requests to conduct special research projects and to provide other forms of assistance. In practice, this arrangement meant that RAND would perform background research to identify future military requirements and assess the implications of developments at the cutting edge of science and technology to enhance national security, which at the time was dominated by the Air Force with its sole possession of nuclear weapons. By 1957, RAND's personnel would grow to about 1,000.

At the beginning in 1946, RAND's studies were geared toward "hardware" research, and were either "engineering science of a theoretical nature" or designed to address problems similar to those carried out by operations researchers in World War II.[13] During the 1950s, however, RAND evolved into a strategic think tank, producing studies that integrated "a number of complex variables, some qualitative in nature, into a broad context of some future 'system'" for decisionmaking.[14] A number of outstanding strategic thinkers—among them Herman Kahn, Albert Wohlstetter, William W. Kaufman, Bernard Brodie, and Thomas C. Schelling—emerged at RAND, and "strategic thought" became "an important part of RAND's research program."[15] RAND researchers revolutionized systems analysis by developing it "from a narrowly technical product into a novel application of numerous professional skills "for optimal allocation of resources to achieve policy goals.[16]

A good illustration was the Strategic Base Study conducted in the early 1950s to determine the most efficient basing system for Strategic Air Command (SAC) bombers for a future five-year period. This study "became involved in such important strategic

---

[11] Bruce Smith, *The RAND Corporation*, 1966, p. 72.

[12] Bruce Smith, *The RAND Corporation*, 1966, p. 91.

[13] Bruce Smith, *The RAND Corporation*, 1966, pp. 50–51.

[14] Bruce Smith, *The RAND Corporation*, 1966, p. 103

[15] Bruce Smith, *The RAND Corporation*, 1966, p. 104.

[16] Bruce Smith, *The RAND Corporation*, 1966.

issues as the vulnerability of overseas bases to enemy nuclear attack" and called into question "certain fundamental assumptions of existing Air Force strategic doctrine."[17]

However, the number of "true generalists"—"those concerned with integrating the fruits of specialized research into a broad policy context"—never exceeded 15 percent of the RAND professional staff at any given time.[18] Most of RAND's work remained research and technical advisory services of a more "traditional" nature. But the "strategic consciousness" of these generalists distinguished RAND from some of the other advisory organizations.[19]

It is this mix of operations research and strategic studies that RAND carried into its work in Southeast Asia in the 1960s and 1970s.

---

[17] Bruce Smith, *The RAND Corporation*, 1966, pp. 104–105.

[18] Bruce Smith, *The RAND Corporation*, 1966, p. 105.

[19] Bruce Smith, *The RAND Corporation*, 1966.

CHAPTER ONE

A Remote Corner of the World: The Beginning in Vietnam

The story of RAND's involvement in the Vietnam War is bound up in RAND's search for influence and funding beyond the Air Force, still its main sponsor and source of funding in the early 1960s, when the war began to emerge as an important foreign policy issue for the United States. It is also bound up in America's shift in strategic thinking from the 1950s' massive thermonuclear retaliation against the Soviet Union, the main adversary of the United States during the Cold War, to a more "flexible response" to counter what was perceived as the communist insurgency threat in Third World countries in the 1960s. It is the story of how RAND, in order to become relevant to a dominant national security issue of the time, decided to engage in research on a new type of warfare to address an insurgency in a remote country. It is a decision that would lead to mixed results. As the following narrative will show, most of the studies commanded respect, but a few others—while they fleetingly made RAND's star shine in Washington—ultimately cast a shadow over RAND's reputation.

With the exception of Communist China, which was the subject of some study during the 1950s, Asia did not loom large at RAND, and counterinsurgency was not a main focus of research. Among the works on Asia was the influential study by Alexander L. George on the cohesiveness of fighting units based on interviews with Chinese Communist prisoners of war during the Korean War.[1] A specialist in political-military studies, George, a modest man with a quiet demeanor, commanded respect for the power of his intellect and analytic insights. He held a doctorate in political science from the University of Chicago and would become the head of RAND's Social Science Department in winter 1960. This study would inspire a similar interview project with communist defectors and prisoners of war in Vietnam. The Economics Department at this time also produced a small number of studies on Asia.

Among these, the most salient were the works produced by Charles Wolf, Jr., a Harvard-trained economist who had served in the U.S. State Department, and his Eco-

---

[1] The report was submitted to the Air Force in July 1952. In 1965, Alex George revised it with new materials that had become available and added a chapter summarizing how the Chinese Communist Army had evolved since the end of the war. Columbia University Press published the revised study in 1967 with the title *The Chinese Communist Army in Action: The Korean War and Its Aftermath*.

nomics Department colleagues at RAND. Wolf would become a controversial figure at RAND, at least in the opinion of some of his colleagues, for what they perceived as "hawkish" views on the war in Vietnam. Using a systems analysis approach, Wolf and his colleagues produced in the mid-1950s a series of studies on the U.S. economic assistance program. Appearing in 1956, the first report that the group produced proposed a mathematical model intended to help policymakers make decisions about targeting foreign aid to achieve political stability; the model helped determine the necessary amounts and types of aid for various recipients. The report's analysis of the relationship between "political vulnerability" and three variables—economic aspirations, standards of living, and economic expectations—would later lead to another study of the correlation between economic aspirations and political rebellion.[2]

Wolf and his colleagues then shifted their research to the effectiveness of U.S. military aid in less developed countries in South and Southeast Asia. Research results from the first study, on the effectiveness of U.S. military assistance programs using a systems analysis approach, were published in 1956. The study had the objectives of optimizing military performance so that communist invasion or insurrection could be deterred, and of enhancing the beneficial economic and political effects of military aid. Iran and Vietnam were used as case studies.[3] This work would later inspire studies by RAND for the U.S. Agency for International Development (USAID) in Vietnam to coordinate economic aid with military assistance.

These studies aside, the focus at RAND at the time was on the Soviet Union and a thermonuclear confrontation in which Europe would be the main theater and in which the Air Force would play a central and strategic—rather than a supportive and tactical—role. However, the Korean War led some RAND analysts to shift their thinking to limited wars, which, they believed, would be the wave of the future, as the Communist Bloc resorted to such warfare to challenge American power while avoiding the massive retaliation and assured mutual destruction that would ensue in a thermo-

---

[2] Charles Wolf, Jr., *Economic Development and Mutual Security: Some Problems of U.S. Foreign Assistance Programs in Southeast Asia*, Santa Monica, Calif.: RAND Corporation, RM-1778-RC, 1956. Wolf would later recall that the first project he undertook at RAND in 1956 was a study carrying the somewhat pretentious title "The Theory and Practice of Foreign Aid." It set forth "a theory of aid as an instrument for reducing the gap between the economic aspirations of people in developing countries and the poverty they experienced in their actual living conditions. The theory further reflected the view that the greater the rate of progress in reducing this gap, the better the chances for democracy in developing countries. This theory was expressed in a model [Wolf] applied to the amount of U.S. economic aid, the rates of economic growth in South and Southeast Asia, and the outcomes of provincial elections in these countries in the 1950s." Frank Collbohm, who was not in favor of foreign aid to begin with, "did not find the case convincing, and perhaps too mechanical. But he did not interfere with the study's progress through RAND's review process, and its publication by Princeton Press in 1960." See Charles Wolf, Jr., "Frank: Few Words, Strong Character," in James Digby, ed., "Early Personalities and Projects as Recalled in the *Alumni Bulletin*," Santa Monica, Calif.: RAND Corporation, P-8055, March 2001.

[3] Charles Wolf, Jr., *Evaluation of Military Assistance in Underdeveloped Countries: A Case Study of Vietnam*, Santa Monica, Calif.: RAND Corporation, RM-2571, April 1960; and Paul G. Clark, *Military Assistance Policy in an Underdeveloped Country: Iran*, Santa Monica, Calif.: RAND Corporation, RM-2416, April 1959.

nuclear confrontation with the United States. It was anticipated that this type of conflict would occur, not in Europe, but in the less developed areas of the world: Asia and the Middle East. In limited wars, the Air Force would not be the strategic force; it would play only a supporting role.

To explore the tactical role that the Air Force might be called upon to play in limited wars, Ed Paxson of the Mathematics Department led a series of war games called Project SIERRA. (Alex George described Paxson as a star at RAND, who, however, lacked the type of persona and flamboyance that would make him a superstar in the manner of strategists Herman Kahn and Albert Wohlstetter.[4]) Starting in 1954 and lasting for several years, these war games focused on Southeast Asia, South Asia, and the Middle East, and on the tactical role that the Air Force might play in such a war in conjunction with the Army and Navy. Among various scenarios, Paxson's SIERRA simulated guerrilla warfare fighting, such as the struggles then being waged by the Viet Minh against the French in Vietnam and by Chinese insurgents against the British in Malaya. Other scenarios included Thailand and Burma.

George Tanham, a military historian and a consultant who would later head RAND's Washington office, observed that, for Vietnam, the war games were unrealistic because the Project SIERRA team was assuming that the Viet Minh guerrillas were fighting similarly to the U.S. Army. Ed Paxson acknowledged this deficiency and accepted Tanham's offer to write a handbook on Viet Minh strategy and tactics.

A Princeton graduate and a highly decorated World War II veteran who had fought in Europe, Tanham was a congenial person who combined intellect with managerial skills and could move back and forth with ease from the top rungs of RAND's administration to influential government positions. As a veteran of the Air Force, Tanham retained an affection and a loyalty for this branch of service.[5] After the war, Tanham obtained a doctorate in history from Stanford University. A year after joining RAND full-time in 1955, Tanham was sent to Paris to research the Viet Minh, who had vanquished the French. He spent eight months studying French records of the war.[6] By the time he finished the promised manual in 1957, the war games were concluding and it was no longer needed. RAND published the manual as a classified document. It was ignored until 1961, when President John Kennedy's interest in guerrilla warfare suddenly turned it into a topical document. Praeger published it in

---

[4]   Author interview with Alex George, 2004.

[5]   Author interview with Gus Shubert, 2004 and 2005.

[6]   Harvey Neese and John O'Donnell, eds., *Prelude to Tragedy: Vietnam, 1960–1965*, Annapolis, Md.: Naval Institute Press, 2000, p. xvi.

George Tanham

a declassified version, which became one of RAND's best-selling books[7] and the first work on communist insurgency by a U.S. author.[8]

A year after he completed his manual, George Tanham became the first person from RAND to visit Vietnam, but not in an official capacity. In 1958, he detoured from a RAND trip to Asia and spent several weeks traveling through a peaceful South Vietnam, to familiarize himself further with a country he had studied. In several out-of-the-way villages, he saw with discomfort pictures of communist leader Ho Chi Minh hung in homes, a sign that allegiance to the Viet Minh persisted four years after the partition of the country into a communist North and a noncommunist South.[9] American policy in Vietnam would underestimate this deep-rooted loyalty, which would translate into support for the Viet Cong in subsequent years.

The first person from RAND to visit Vietnam in an official capacity was Charlie Wolf, as part of a presidential commission under General William H. Draper to survey the situation in Southeast Asia in the early 1960s. The commission also included

---

[7]   George Tanham, "Defeating Insurgency in South Vietnam: My Early Efforts," in Neese and O'Donnell, *Prelude to Tragedy,* 2000, p. 164.

[8]   Neese and O'Donnell, *Prelude to Tragedy,* 2000, p. xvi. Nonetheless, one of SIERRA's Vietnam war-game scenarios involving large-scale guerrilla warfare by the communists very nearly anticipated the circumstances of U.S. direct involvement, as well as the brutal stalemate of the conflict. (David Jardini, "The Wrong War: RAND in Vietnam, 1954–1969," pp. 17–18, paper presented at Carnegie Mellon University Colloquium on "Cold War Science & Technology," 1998. Jardini presented this paper at a colloqium panel on "Policymaking in a Cold War Quagmire: RAND and Vietnam, 1954–1972" with Gus Shubert of RAND as a discussant, November 5, 1998. Copy of Jardini paper provided to author courtesy of Joseph Zasloff.

[9]   Tanham, "Defeating Insurgency in South Vietnam: My Early Efforts," 2000, p. 164.

General "Lightning" Joe Collins, former Chief of Staff of the Army, and Ed Lansdale, a legendary counterinsurgency expert who had helped President Ramon Magsaysay of the Philippines defeat the Hukbalahap insurgency and had played a key role in establishing Ngo Dinh Diem as the first president of an independent South Vietnam. In his interview with the author, Wolf remembered that he served as the economic expert on this commission,[10] which visited the Philippines, Indonesia, Burma, and Vietnam.

In Vietnam, the commission had several closed sessions with President Ngo Dinh Diem around a table.[11] Wolf remembered Diem spreading out a map and talking about where the communist insurgents—called pejoratively *Viet Cong* by the South Vietnamese government—were and where he had deployed his forces, and discussing his plans. Wolf was immensely impressed with Diem and thought he was intelligent, dignified, retentive, and that he had stature and gravitas.

These sessions convinced the entire commission that supporting Diem was the correct course of action for the United States, because Diem was a leader who could compete with Ho Chi Minh in stature, despite his shortcomings: being a Catholic in a mostly Buddhist country; his reliance on his autocratic brother, Ngo Dinh Nhu, for advice and governance; and his tolerance of the meddling of Nhu's arrogant wife in government affairs. Both Nhus evoked fear and loathing among many South Vietnamese. Wolf would remain supportive of Diem, later opposing the internal machinations that deposed the president with U.S. consent.

SIERRA and other studies on limited war and tactical air operations revealed that the Air Force—and the United States as a whole—was ill-prepared to fight this kind of warfare. However, they had little influence on RAND and the Air Force, which was still concentrating on strategic warfare. As a result, RAND's interest in limited war remained at a low level. Among studies on limited war were the projects conducted by Alex George and a group of social scientists, whose aim was to persuade the Air Force to take limited war more seriously. To them, one of the lessons of Korea was that, as Alex George recalled, "like it or not, we'll have to face the possibility of limited wars in the future."[12] They performed a detailed military analysis, as well as a political analysis, to determine how such a war was fought, and focused on the question of how to avoid unwanted escalation and on the challenge of how to use force for limited objectives with limited means.

In George's summary, the aim in general wars, such as World War II, is to overwhelm your opponent, achieve unconditional surrender, and occupy his country, as was

---

[10] Author interview with Charlie Wolf, 2003.

[11] For Vietnamese names, the last name comes first and the first name last. Vietnamese refer to one another by their first name even in formal address. For example, Ngo Dinh Diem is referred to as President Diem. His brother Ngo Dinh Nhu and his wife are referred to as Mr. Nhu and Mrs. Nhu. There is an exception in the case of Ho Chi Minh, which is the adopted name of Nguyen Chi Thanh: He is referred to as Uncle Ho. However, in Sino-Vietnamese fashion, the last name is used in formal designations—i.e., President Ho or President Ngo.

[12] Author interview with Alex George, 2004.

done in Germany and Japan. In limited wars, however, the objectives are restricted: They can vary from avoiding defeat, as the United States did in Korea; to preventing the opponent from achieving his aims and forcing him to stop; to giving him a debilitating blow so that he will not pose a threat in the future. Since keeping the war within bounds is crucial, limitations have to be put on the forces employed, on the targets to attack, on the weapons to use and not use, and on the geographical extent of the conflict—for example, in the Korean War, the United States fought in North Korea but avoided going into China. These limitations would later apply in Vietnam. Another issue of interest for Alex George was sanctuary in limited war, and his work would later lead other RAND analysts to research such topics as border control and the role of North Vietnam in the insurgency in the South.

It was in 1961 that RAND became involved in research on the insurgency in South Vietnam. This was a critical year during which several events and factors converged to push Vietnam to the forefront of concern in Washington and to make RAND more amenable to doing work for clients other than the Air Force. RAND's decision had as much to do with its desire not to be left out of the policy loop on an issue that was gaining importance in America's national security considerations as it did with RAND's re-evaluation of its relationship with the Air Force and the shift of power within the Department of Defense.

The event that shook RAND's placid relationship with the Air Force took place in 1959, when the Air Force froze the Project RAND budget for fiscal year 1960 and kept it at the same level as in the previous year, citing tightening research and development funding. The freeze brought home to RAND the vulnerability of its utter dependence on one major client. To make up the budget gap, RAND negotiated a contract with the Advanced Research Projects Agency (ARPA) and began work on satellite communication systems.[13] This relationship would expand as the Vietnam War intensified. ARPA had been created in the Defense Department in 1958 in response to the 1957 launching of the Sputnik satellite by the Soviet Union. The surprise launching created anxiety in the United States that the Soviets had surpassed it in space technology. The establishment of ARPA was, therefore, meant to exceed the Soviets' as well as other enemies' advance in military technology development and application, prevent similar surprises in the future, and maintain America's technological edge.

Another impetus for RAND's search for more sponsors was the growing tension between RAND and the Air Force. During the Eisenhower Administration, the Strategic Air Command under General Curtis E. LeMay was the dominant power in national defense; it alone possessed the long-range manned bombers that could unleash an atomic strike against the Soviet Union in case of a nuclear attack. SAC, in essence,

---

[13] RAND's acquisition of new clients did not violate the Air Force Policy Statement, which said that RAND "will be free to undertake supplementary work for agencies other than the Air Force, or jointly for the Air Force and other agencies, provided suitable financial arrangements are made and the work does not interfere with Air Force studies." Bruce Smith, *The RAND Corporation*, 1966, p. 82.

was the linchpin in Eisenhower's strategy of massive retaliation. In its famous basing study, led by Albert Wohlstetter, RAND demonstrated that SAC's strategic deployment of its bombers in overseas bases was flawed in that its forces could be wiped out by the Soviet Union in a preemptive attack, thus stripping the United States of most of its nuclear retaliatory capability and leaving it vulnerable. This study represented a condemnation of SAC's strategic planning and was met with great resistance—especially among the "promoters of overseas bases," according to Frank Collbohm, RAND's first president.[14]

In 1958, the Navy was developing a submarine-based intercontinental nuclear missile system known as Polaris, thus threatening the Air Force's monopoly on atomic-weapons delivery. Hoping to find weaknesses that would bolster its fight against this rival weapon system, the Air Force commissioned RAND to perform a study of Polaris. To the Air Force's dismay, RAND analysts found that Polaris was virtually invulnerable to Soviet attack. In 1959, another RAND analysis performed as part of the Strategic Offensive Force Study irked General LeMay and the Air Force. The aim of that study was to determine the force composition and force mix for the Air Force of the future. Gus Shubert, a Korean War Air Force veteran and a graduate of Yale with a degree in sociology and of Columbia University with a master's degree in English literature, who joined RAND in 1959 and became a vice president in 1968, would later recall that the findings of that study attacked some of the "great holy cows" of the Air Force and, in particular, challenged the effectiveness of the B-70 triple sonic bombers favored by General LeMay. The study concluded that the B-70 was not "justifiable on any rational basis" and should be canceled.[15]

Around the same time that the relationship with the Air Force became strained, the centralization of authority in the Department of Defense led RAND to shift toward this new source of power. In 1961, after he became Secretary of Defense, Robert S. McNamara set about instituting the rational management methods that he had employed in the automobile industry. In the process, he concentrated budget and military policymaking power in his Office of the Secretary of Defense and drastically changed the way in which the Department of Defense operated. The concentration of authority in his office further diminished the power of the Air Force in particular, a power that was already being eroded. Besides seeing its monopoly on atomic-weapons delivery challenged by the emergence of the Navy's intercontinental missiles with nuclear payloads, the Air Force was also losing its luster under Kennedy's flexible response, which aimed to build up America's conventional capabilities and give the Army a more prominent role. Flexible response would enable the United States to deal

---

[14] Martin J. Collins, *RAND's Oral History Project (RAND)*, Washington, D.C.: Department of Space History, National Air and Space Museum, containing interviews with 29 RAND individuals and covering the period from 1945 to the early 1960s. Collins interview with Frank Collbohm, 1987, p. 64.

[15] Collins, interview with Gus Shubert, 1991, pp. 55–56.

with a range of threats, from guerrilla warfare to nuclear confrontation, and give it the capabilities to fight insurgencies and other types of limited warfare in which the use of nuclear weapons, the mainstays of America's arsenal and the core of its strategy, would be inappropriate. This strategy upset General LeMay, who wanted to prepare for general wars in which total resources would be deployed to destroy an opponent and to focus on massive retaliation.

For what became known as the McNamara Revolution, the new Secretary of Defense recruited several RAND staff members, including economists Charles Hitch, Harry Rowen, and Alain Enthoven,[16] who joined the group dubbed the "Whiz Kids" to implement the changes he wanted through the systems analysis and program budgeting that had been developed first at RAND in the 1940s and 1950s. This Planning-Programming-Budgeting system sought to achieve, through systematic analysis of alternative allocation strategies—a more efficient distribution and use of resources to maximize U.S. military power and national security.[17] In addition to rationalizing defense management, the group was to engage in a wide-ranging review of general war, limited war, and counterinsurgency strategies. Since power was migrating from the Air Force to the Office of the Secretary of Defense, RAND began to forge a relationship with OSD, in particular with its Office of International Security Affairs (ISA). In the Kennedy Administration, ISA had become the leading national security policymaking body, superseding the State Department and the National Security Council. RAND also developed a broader relationship with ARPA. RAND's relationship with ISA and the expanded work for ARPA would lead it to become involved in research on counterinsurgency in Vietnam.

Whereas limited warfare had evoked little interest in the Eisenhower Administration, it assumed great importance in the administration of President John F. Kennedy. In January 1961, the formation of the National Liberation Front for South Vietnam (the NLF) was announced. The NLF's objective was to overthrow the government of President Ngo Dinh Diem and establish a coalition government, which would then negotiate with Hanoi to reunify the country. In the same month, Premier Nikita Khrushchev announced that the Soviet Union would support wars for national liberation. Communist China would later declare that all communist nations had the duty to support such wars.

---

[16] This move of RAND's strategists into McNamara's Office of the Secretary of Defense gave RAND a good deal of publicity, which displeased Frank Collbohm. One of his overriding concerns was to keep RAND out of the limelight because he felt that close scrutiny would make it difficult for RAND to carry out its mission. A low profile, he believed, would prevent RAND from becoming a target of attacks by "90 percent of the press and 90 percent of the educators" in America, who, in his view, were "liberals" wishing to keep "our military down." Collins, 1987, interview with Frank Collbohm, p. 58.

[17] For further details, see David R. Jardini, *Out of the Blue Yonder: The RAND Corporation's Diversification into Social Welfare Research, 1946–1968*, doctoral dissertation, Carnegie Mellon University, May 1966, pp. 163–170.

President Kennedy and his advisors believed that, in view of this new challenge, the Eisenhower Administration's strategy of massive nuclear retaliation against the Soviet Union, regardless of where a nuclear attack occurred, and its concomitant threat of mutual destruction, made American military power too inflexible to respond to the type of insurgency warfare that the communists were espousing. Throughout the Third World, Kennedy and his men saw many situations that could be exploited by the Communist Bloc, which was still viewed as monolithic, although the Sino-Soviet split had already occurred. In Southeast Asia and Africa, the departure of Western colonial powers and the weakness of the governments that came into being in the wake of independence created an unstable situation, rife for subversion by the Communist Bloc. In Latin America, Fidel Castro had won power in Cuba after waging a guerrilla war, and instability threatened many countries in which poverty, corruption, and oppression seemed the norm.

Fear of such subversion by Kennedy and his staff led to the belief that, if such brushfire wars were not defeated, the Communist Bloc would continue to nibble away at the periphery of the Western Bloc and eventually threaten the security of the United States and of its core Western European allies, in a domino-like fashion. This concern radiated out of Washington and pervaded RAND itself. Because of the threat of subversion in Latin America, in February 1961 Joseph Kershaw, the head of the Economics Department, expressed his desire to have a specialist on this region in his department.[18]

While continuing to build up U.S. nuclear capabilities, Kennedy and Defense Secretary McNamara began to address the issue of how to fight insurgencies under the rubric of "flexible response." Kennedy believed that, besides military means, counterinsurgency would also require economic, diplomatic, and psychological-warfare activities combined into a multipronged approach. He assigned the State Department the responsibility of dealing with diplomatic and political issues, and coordinating the efforts of other key agencies. USAID was given the task of *nation-building*, turning economic aid into a tool of counterinsurgency by strengthening recipient countries against subversion. The United States Information Agency (USIA) was assigned psychological warfare. The Central Intelligence Agency would support irregular forces not belonging to a country's central army, and the Defense Department would broaden its role in its foreign operations to include activities to influence the attitudes of the local population—undertakings, such as "military civic action," that would become known as "winning hearts and minds."[19]

---

[18] J. A. Kershaw, "The Research Program of the Economics Department," Santa Monica, Calif.: RAND Corporation, February 28, 1961 (not available to the general public).

[19] Seymour J. Deitchman, *The Best-Laid Schemes: A Tale of Social Research and Bureaucracy*, Cambridge, Mass.: The MIT Press, 1976, pp. 7–9.

In August 1961, Deputy Secretary of Defense Roswell L. Gilpatric wrote to Frank Collbohm, RAND's president, offering RAND a substantial contract with ISA (which would greatly increase RAND's non–Air Force activities). The contract would include research on potential conflicts in regions referred to as "third areas"—countries that were "allies, satellites, or neutral to the main Cold War powers."[20] The Air Force objected strongly to this contract, resenting the growing power of ISA, which had taken over much of the policy decisionmaking that used to belong to the Joint Chiefs of Staff.[21]

According to Larry Henderson, the head of RAND's Washington office, the Air Force "felt that their position as decisionmakers was being threatened, and that if we wrote a report that they didn't like, and it went to the Assistant Secretary for International Security Affairs, the next thing they knew, the Secretary of Defense would be ramming it down their throats."[22] Also, many Air Force officers feared that some of the civilians in ISA looked down on them as professional soldiers and would attempt to downgrade their status. Alex George recalled that the Air Force was angry with the RAND staff who had gone to work for McNamara, and wanted to punish RAND. But every time the Air Force "made a serious move in that direction," RAND would ask Philip Graham, the publisher of *The Washington Post* and the head of RAND's Air Force Advisory Group, who had a good relationship with Kennedy, to go see the president—and Kennedy "would force the Air Force to stop its efforts to bring RAND under control."[23]

Frank Collbohm himself had reservations about this contract, and he feared that it would embroil RAND in the civilian-military conflict in the Department of Defense.[24] However, the Executive Committee of the Board of Trustees thought that the contract with ISA would protect RAND against future budget cuts by the Air Force and decided to accept it. The Executive Committee was also swayed by the strong support for the contract within RAND, many of whose analysts recognized that, if RAND hoped to play a role in national security beyond issues of airpower, it would have to forge a closer relationship with McNamara and his staff. Many analysts

---

[20] David Jardini, "The Wrong War," 1998, p. 24.

[21] David R. Jardini, *Out of the Blue Yonder: The RAND Corporation's Diversification into Social Welfare Research, 1946–1968*, Doctoral Dissertation, Carnegie-Mellon University, College of Humanities and Social Sciences, Pittsburgh, Pa., 1996, pp. 173–178.

[22] Martin Collins, interview with Lawrence Henderson, 1989, p. 50.

[23] Author interview with Alex George, 2004.

[24] Ed Barlow recalled that Collbohm "also felt that we should have only one client, the Air Force. He didn't think the Department of Defense was here to stay, as it was made up of civilians who came and went. Neither did he think we should work for the Army or the Navy. He wanted the Air Force to trust us to be devoted solely to its mission with no conflict of interest. It was understood that we would not discuss our findings outside of Air Force circles." See Ed Barlow, "Frank and RAND's Culture in the 1950s," "Early Personalities and Projects," *Alumni Bulletin*, ed. James Digby, Santa Monica, Calif.: RAND Corporation, P-8055, March 2001, p. 11.

also were tempted by the allure of working on current policy problems, although doing so would be a departure from research on issues of long-term and strategic significance that had been RAND's forte. In the end, the Air Force remained RAND's main sponsor because RAND failed to secure a contract from the Office of the Secretary of Defense, or ARPA, or ISA, or any other Department of Defense (DoD) agency that was as long-lasting and as large as the contract that it had with the Air Force.

♣ ♣ ♣

After he took over as director of Research and Engineering at the Department of Defense, Harold Brown created Project AGILE at ARPA in 1961. The name AGILE was chosen to denote the project's ability to respond quickly to urgent requests for research. Its mission was to support U.S. counterinsurgency activities in Southeast Asia through the research and development of weapons, equipment, and techniques, as well as through social science research—with the assistance of anthropologists, psychologists, sociologists, political scientists, and economists—to improve knowledge of such foreign cultures. At the time, the social science community in the United States had not yet become disillusioned with the war in Vietnam or with American efforts to fight insurgencies in other parts of the world. *Insurgency* and *wars of liberation* were perceived as communist subversion using coercion and terrorism, and *counterinsurgency* had not acquired the sinister connotation of suppressing legitimate social and economic transformation in the Third World, so social scientists had no problem undertaking this kind of research on behalf of the Defense Department. In response to Kennedy's request, Congress approved $120 million to expand research and development programs related to limited war.[25]

In August 1961, Harold Brown sent RAND a classified letter asking for assistance in setting up the Combat Development and Test Center (CDTC) in Saigon, which was being established by ARPA's Research and Development Field Unit.[26] The CDTC's mission was to test weapons already in existence or new weapons being developed in American laboratories, including herbicides, and such equipment as communication gear for their usefulness in counterinsurgency. The creation of the center was DoD's response to President Kennedy's approval of Deputy Secretary of Defense Gilpatric's proposal to help the government of South Vietnam devise new counterinsurgency techniques.[27] The CDTC was staffed with U.S. military and civilian personnel, who worked closely with the local military personnel assigned by the government of South Vietnam. In June–July 1961, George Tanham accompanied the Defense Department

---

[25] Deitchman, *The Best-Laid Schemes,* 1976, p. 26. See also Jardini, "The Wrong War," 1998, pp. 12–13.

[26] Jardini, "The Wrong War," 1998, p. 24.

[27] William A. Buckingham, Jr., *Operation Ranch Hand: The Air Force and Herbicides in Southeast Asia 1961–1971,* Washington D.C., Office of Air Force History, United States Air Force, 1982, pp. 10–11.

Research and Development Task Force to Saigon to establish the CDTC. After returning to Washington, Tanham briefed some high-level officials at the State Department, the Department of Defense, the Central Intelligence Agency, and the White House on his own observations, conclusions, and recommendations on the situation in Vietnam, based on what he had discovered during his stay in Saigon and during trips to the countryside.[28]

The United States had put a great deal of faith in President Ngo Dinh Diem and had supported his government with economic and military aid, including dispatching pilots to provide close support for the Army of the Republic of Vietnam (ARVN), as long as the fiction was maintained that the United States was only playing a secondary role, by having a Vietnamese—dubbed a "sandbag"—flying among the crew. At this early stage, President Kennedy did not want to alarm the American public that the United States was engaging in an active war. Yet, despite all the resources that had been poured into South Vietnam, the insurgency had grown stronger and the guerrillas now numbered about 17,000, increasing from a force of 2,000 in early 1957.

In his report, Tanham wrote that the situation was getting increasingly serious.[29] However, Tanham observed that the U.S. team in Vietnam was not responding effectively to this worsening situation. Although the U.S. team now understood that the immediate danger was subversion and insurgency, rather than an invasion from North Vietnam as they had previously expected, their effort was flawed by a lack of coordination among the agencies. It was also hobbled by a military team that was saddled with a heavy administrative structure, burdened with paperwork, and ineffective at advising, assisting, and training the Vietnamese whom, for the most part, they did not understand or appreciate, and whom they could not inspire by their own example to carry out a very difficult task.

Turning to the Vietnamese civilians and military, Tanham observed that they lacked motivation and had no loyalty or devotion to President Diem. Although official American reports stated that the South Vietnamese Army was performing well, their claims could not be substantiated. For example, there were persistent reports of engagements in which the South Vietnamese Army suffered no casualties but had some of their weapons captured, whereas the Viet Cong suffered casualties but disappeared leaving no bodies on the battlefield.

Tanham did not recommend a change of leadership in Vietnam, nor a change in U.S. policy. Such recommendations would have been unthinkable at this stage in the war, when the prospect of failure seemed improbable. He advocated only technical

---

[28] George Tanham, "Trip Report—Vietnam," Santa Monica, Calif.: RAND Corporation, October 6, 1961 (not releasable to the general public).

[29] In a report on another trip made in 1963, Tanham would add that, during this 1961 visit, he had found near panic in Saigon and that there had been "a great deal of talk about evacuating the city and, indeed, losing the entire war." George K. Tanham, "Trip Report: Vietnam, January 1963," Santa Monica, Calif.: RAND Corporation, March 22, 1963.

measures that he felt would improve the situation, such as providing more helicopters. Tanham's report reflected the American belief at the time that more and improved weapons would reverse the situation, and that the issue was only to figure out how to fight the war better. In not questioning whether the United States should get involved further in Vietnam, it also implicitly reflected the Cold War consensus that the United States was making the morally right decision to meet the communist challenge wherever it occurred. This belief in the necessity to confront the communist threat anywhere was so strong that no one at RAND at the time—and no RAND strategists who had joined McNamara's staff at the Defense Department—was loudly raising the alarm and cautioning the Kennedy Administration against deepening American involvement in Vietnam. Finally, by not questioning continued U.S. support for President Diem, Tanham's report mirrored Washington's belief that the United States had no option other than to keep and strengthen Diem, and that it would have to "sink or swim" with him.

A 1969 internal RAND review of its Vietnam research performed by Alfred Goldberg of the Social Science Department concluded that "RAND did not attempt a major study and analysis, pro and con, of U.S. policy in Vietnam, particularly of U.S. goals and objectives."[30] It could have done so as early as 1961–1962, "when the growing U.S. involvement in Vietnam indicated the significance of this conflict for the United States."[31] RAND's managers did not initiate such a study, nor was RAND asked by any of its clients to do so. The commitment in Vietnam was viewed by RAND analysts as part of the struggle against the Soviet Union and, as Alex George recalled, "most people at RAND, with some degree of difference," thought that this struggle was very serious. "There were no pacifists at RAND," he said.[32] According to Gus Shubert, there was almost a missionary zeal at RAND. People felt a strong sense of urgency about their work because they were convinced that the Soviet threat was dominant and imminent and because they believed that what they were doing at RAND was "laying the groundwork for countering that threat."[33]

In November 1961, with the situation in Vietnam not improving and President Diem asking for more aid, ARPA convened several meetings attended by people from various commercial concerns and nonprofit organizations similar to RAND to discuss Project AGILE and to enlist their support. The meetings revolved around what the United States should do in Vietnam (as well as in Laos, where the communist Pathet Lao were about to take over the capital of Vientiane and defeat the right-wing government of Phoumi Nosavan, who was supported by the United States through

---

[30] Alfred Goldberg, "RAND and Vietnam, II. Some Questions from the Record," Santa Monica, Calif.: RAND Corporation, May 12, 1969, p. 14 (not available to the general public).

[31] Goldberg, "RAND and Vietnam, II," 1969, p. 14.

[32] Author interview with Alex George, 2004.

[33] Collins, interview with Gus Shubert, May 20, 1992, p. 47

the intermediary of the Central Intelligence Agency). Steve Hosmer, who had joined the Social Science Department[34] in August 1961 as a specialist in Far Eastern studies, paramilitary and guerrilla warfare, and intelligence operations, and was working out of the RAND Washington office, attended this meeting. He recalled that most of the emphasis was on the development of hardware: "Indeed during the early days ARPA was heavily into hardware."[35]

A large man with an unflappable manner, Steve Hosmer was a Southeast Asia specialist who had received his degrees from Yale University. After completing his undergraduate degree in 1953, he obtained his masters' degree in Southeast Asia studies in 1955 and his doctorate in international relations in 1961. As a fellow of the Ford Foundation, he spent the years 1953–1956 doing field research in Indonesia on the election of 1955—the first ever held in that country following independence from the Dutch. The research provided materials for his doctoral dissertation at Yale. From 1957 until 1960, he served in the United States Air Force, working in the Office of the Assistant Chief of Staff, Intelligence. At the time he came to RAND in 1961, he was one of a handful of staff members who had made a trip to Vietnam and seen it firsthand. On his way to Indonesia in 1955, he arrived in Saigon just as the French were withdrawing from Vietnam and Americans were coming in to replace them. Like other Americans who saw the city in this period, he thought it was a wonderful place, "The Paris of the East." The French were repatriating many of their units, and he recalled being caught "in a little Citroen in the middle of [a] French convoy of tanks and everything," and thinking that his vehicle was going to get crushed.[36]

These meetings with ARPA in 1961 sowed the seeds for RAND's involvement in Southeast Asia. A committee at RAND, chaired by George Clement, then vice president, and Bob Bucheim, the head of the Aero-Austronautics Department from the former Engineering Division, put together a research proposal. Jack Ellis, who worked in this department, remembered that they finalized the proposal on a Sunday at Bucheim's house and sent it off to ARPA.[37] RAND's reputation for quality research and intellectual independence ensured approval, and in November 1961 RAND was funded by Project AGILE to assign personnel to work in the Research and Development Field Unit, Combat and Development Test Center, in Saigon and in the Technical Field Unit in Bangkok, which ARPA had also set up at the same time to collabo-

---

[34] RAND was reorganized in October 1960, and the five divisions of Engineering, Mathematics, Economics, Physics, and Social Science were split into eleven smaller departments. As RAND grew in size, the divisions became too large for the division heads to manage efficiently. This was especially true for the Engineering Division, which had grown to account for 40 percent of the professional personnel at RAND. Bruce Smith, *The RAND Corporation,* 1966, p. 177.

[35] Author interview with Steve Hosmer, 2004 and 2005.

[36] Author interview with Steve Hosmer, 2004 and 2005.

[37] Author interview with Jack Ellis, 2003 and 2004.

rate with the CDTC in Saigon to test weapons, equipment, and counterinsurgency techniques.

In addition, RAND was to employ its personnel in Santa Monica and Washington to identify the main counterinsurgency problems in Southeast Asia and to recommend solutions. According to Ellis, these guidelines delineated RAND's work throughout the four years he ran the program. Thus began RAND's tentative involvement in Vietnam, devoid of a clear understanding of how far such involvement would lead and to what consequences. This uncertain entrance mirrored that of the American government itself and would evolve more or less in tandem with the steps taken by Washington—in general, following rather than leading and, with a few exceptions, facilitating or criticizing rather than attempting to change policies.

To formulate a research program for ISA, RAND's Research Council, consisting of six senior researchers, established a Third Area Conflict Board, made up of Albert Wohlstetter, Charles Wolf, Terry Greene, and consultant Guy Pauker. The board's purpose was to identify and research conflicts other than the strategic confrontation between the United States and the Soviet Union, which could occur in other regions of the world, to determine ways to further U.S. interests in such conflicts.[38] It appears that this board developed no integrated, comprehensive research program, however. The Logistics Department also got involved in research for ISA to address the possibility of communist military intervention in Southeast Asia, and produced a report comparing the logistics capabilities of the United States and of the Communist Bloc countries for supporting large-scale limited wars in Laos and South Vietnam. It concluded that distance did not place the United States at a disadvantage because, after 40 days, it could deliver more troops and materiel to potential combat zones than could the communists.

As a contribution to the field of counterinsurgency, Steve Hosmer convened a symposium of military and civilian experts in Washington in April 1962 for an exchange of ideas and experiences in fighting guerrilla warfare. According to him, the main criterion was that the attendees be people who had been successful "counter insurgents." Attendees included such people as David Galula, who had commanded a French company in Algeria in 1956 and succeeded in clearing the district of Kabylie of insurgents during his tenure there. Ed Lansdale also attended. The purpose was to bring together those experts who had gained firsthand experience in counterinsurgency in such countries as Malaya, the Philippines, Kenya, and Algeria for informal exchanges of information that might lead to fresh insights and be assembled into a detailed body of expert knowledge.

---

[38] The Research Council acted as an advisory body to the president, and provided "general direction and planning of the RAND research effort and, in particular, to assist project leaders in carrying out interdisciplinary projects." Bruce Smith, *The RAND Corporation,* 1966, p. 178.

The subjects discussed included patterns and techniques of counterinsurgency, effective organizational and operational approaches, political action, psychological warfare, intelligence and counterintelligence, and requirements for victory. The contents of these discussions were published as a RAND report and given wide circulation.[39] "We literally papered Washington with it," Hosmer recalled, but "it was as though you'd dropped it into a bottomless pit. . . . It was given short shrift."[40] As a follow up later in 1963, RAND issued separate reports on six counterinsurgency campaigns. According to Alfred Goldberg, these reports were intended only "as a compendium of information and informed views and insights on counterinsurgency conflicts."[41] There was no direct follow-up by either RAND or ARPA.

In view of the technical nature of the support being sought by ARPA/AGILE, Frank Collbohm assigned Jack Ellis to manage the AGILE contract. Ellis had joined the Engineering Division at RAND in 1947, when it was still part of the Douglas Aircraft Company, and had been working on tactical warfare issues dealing with the defense of Europe. Ellis had studied mechanical engineering at the University of California at Berkeley (UC Berkeley). From 1942 to 1944, he was on inactive duty in the Navy, but, after the war, went on active duty in the Philippines, sweeping mines in Batangas Bay, south of Manila. After his demobilization in summer 1946, he resumed his studies for a year. He had worked at Douglas Aircraft Company in Long Beach between his junior and senior years at Berkeley, so he went back to Douglas looking for a job. They told him, "We don't have any jobs, we're demobilizing, too, after the war, but we have a little outfit in Santa Monica, called RAND, and it's hiring, so why don't you go see them." So Ellis went to RAND and got a job in the old aircraft division, which was then known as the Airborne Vehicle Section. Ellis remembered that there were many reorganizations over the years, and he ended up in the large Engineering Division.[42]

After securing the contract, Jack Ellis traveled to Vietnam and Thailand in February 1962, spending a month looking at the situation firsthand and consulting with the military and civilian personnel so that he could build a research program. ARPA was managing many operations, and the contract with RAND was relatively

---

[39] S. T. Hosmer, Chairman, S. O. Crane, *Counterinsurgency: A Symposium*, Santa Monica, Calif.: RAND Corporation, R-412-ARPA, November 1962.

[40] Some years later, Hosmer was talking with a senior military officer about what needed to be done in Vietnam when the man asked him what he might read about insurgency. Hosmer pulled out a copy of the report and handed it to him. He called Hosmer the next day and said, "I've read this report. This is absolutely wonderful. This is exactly what we are talking about, what we want to do in Vietnam." Hosmer replied, "Lots of luck." But the U.S. military "went on their own way" and did not embrace counterinsurgency in Vietnam. Author interview with Steve Hosmer, 2004 and 2005.

[41] Alfred Goldberg, "RAND and Vietnam," Santa Monica, Calif.: RAND Corporation, April 23, 1969, pp. 8–9 (not available to the general public).

[42] Author interview with Jack Ellis, 2003 and 2004.

small, so it did not devote a great deal of attention to RAND's activities. Ellis recalled that there was no formal arrangement, such as the one RAND had with the Air Force, and there was no oversight committee similar to the Air Force Steering Group (AFSG) that the Air Force had established.[43] However, between RAND and ARPA there was a common understanding about what work RAND could best perform; consequently, there was no disagreement over what activities RAND would undertake for ARPA/AGILE.

Over the four years Ellis ran the program, the funding averaged about $1 million per year. To recruit RAND staff for these ARPA/AGILE projects, Ellis had to go to various department heads and persuade them to allocate the staff members who were interested in Southeast Asia, were willing to go there for fieldwork if necessary, and were qualified to perform the studies.

Among these requirements, going to Southeast Asia and living there for an extended period was the hardest to meet. Most RAND staff members were reluctant to uproot themselves and, if they had families, to leave their wives and children for months at a time. Vietnam might be exotic, but it was far away and had the reputation of being a hardship post, and RAND staff members did not relish the idea of living in conditions that they believed were substandard. Later, when the war intensified, Vietnam became dangerous, and qualified RAND people were even more reluctant to relocate there. In the end, most of RAND's work on Vietnam was performed by people in Santa Monica, using mainly data that had been gathered by RAND's research team in the field. RAND analyst Konrad Kellen, for example, authored many studies on Vietnam, but he had no desire to go there; some members of his family had perished in World War II, and "one war was enough," he later explained.[44]

Although Jack Ellis would make occasional trips to Vietnam and Thailand to look over the situation and consult with military and civilian personnel there, so that he could gather ideas for building a list of possible projects, the studies that were undertaken in Vietnam at that time were disparate, short-term, and not integrated into a comprehensive, planned, research program. If ARPA/AGILE, or the R&D Field Unit in Saigon, or RAND individual researchers identified a problem that needed a solution, and RAND was in a position to provide that solution, the project would get under way. The exigencies of fighting an insurgency resulted in projects that tended to deal with operational and technical issues and that attempted to provide answers that could be applied to the immediate problems at hand.

Looking back on the studies that were undertaken under his stewardship of the ARPA/AGILE program, Jack Ellis thought that most of the work that was performed

---

[43] The AFSG is chaired by the Vice Chief of Staff and "includes senior representatives from the Air Force Secretariat and the Air Staff." See RAND Corporation, "Project AIR FORCE: Air Force Oversight," Web page, 2009.

[44] Author interview with Konrad Kellen, 2002.

was "at the fringes of the problems" and that projects were low-level activities that did not have or could not have a major impact on Vietnam policy.[45] Even less-operational research, such as the projects dealing with the Strategic Hamlet Program, a population relocation effort to cut access to villagers by the insurgents, was short-term and intended to provide quick answers to an ongoing problem. In 1963, Jack Ellis attempted to broaden his research program by proposing a prisoner-interrogation study to glean tactical information but also to gain important insights into communism—in particular, to determine what motivated the insurgents to fight, as shown in RAND consultant Lucian Pye's 1957 book *Guerrilla Communism in Malaya*. His proposal was not taken seriously. Ellis believed that the rejection was because he was an engineer, not a social scientist possessing the right credentials to manage such research. It was true that Ellis himself was more comfortable dealing with technical data, such as bomber sorties, than with social science issues. In 1964, Ellis proposed to move away from the "nuts and bolts" approach that had characterized RAND's work in Vietnam toward a more systematic and broader look at counterinsurgency. Although ARPA expressed interest, nothing came of this proposal, and the research components under his overall management remained unintegrated.

When RAND first became involved in Vietnam, it did not have an extensive background for developing long-range studies because it lacked a level of political and military expertise on counterinsurgency comparable to its expertise on strategic nuclear war. For that matter, very few people in the United States had that expertise. Nor did RAND have in-house analysts who had acquired expertise on Vietnam, with the exception of George Tanham. This was understandable, since Vietnam was a poor, small country, of no intrinsic strategic value to the United States, and it did not merit the attention, time, and energy of RAND analysts.

One of RAND's major strengths was that it could attract outside experts, usually from academia, to work on projects when the need arose, thus freeing the think tank from having to sustain a big staff to cover a wide variety of fields that may or may not become significant. So, when the time came to plunge into Vietnam, this lack of internal expertise was not an insurmountable problem. The first two RAND researchers who went to Vietnam under contract for ARPA were consultants Gerry Hickey and John Donnell. RAND could not have found two more qualified American experts. Both were familiar with Vietnam, and both were fluent in Vietnamese. Hickey, then teaching at Yale, was an anthropologist specializing in the ethnography of Vietnam, and he had conducted social/economic research in a village in the Mekong Delta. Hickey was full of Irish charm and a great raconteur with a sardonic wit. He graduated from De Paul University in 1950 and received his master's degree and doctorate from the University of Chicago. Before coming to RAND, he served as a member of the Michigan State University Group, which assisted President Diem's government in

---

[45] Author interview with Jack Ellis, 2003 and 2004.

administration; as a research associate in the Anthropology Department at Michigan State and later at Yale; and also as a consultant to the Mekong River Project of the Ford Foundation in 1961.

Like Gerry Hickey, John Donnell, an assistant professor at Dartmouth College at the time, had extensive experience in Asia. Donnell learned Vietnamese—then called Annamese—while at Berkeley in 1943–1944. Whereas Hickey was outgoing and talkative, Donnell was more of an introvert. After serving in the Army for three years, he joined the U.S. Information Agency, which later became the U.S. Information Service (USIS), in 1949 and in this capacity opened the USIA branch in Hanoi in the early 1950s. In 1961, he spent six months in South Vietnam under a Ford Foundation Foreign Area Training Fellowship. He received his doctorate degree in political science from Berkeley in 1964 and wrote his thesis on "Politics in South Vietnam: Doctrines of Authority in Conflict." Donnell's other Asia experience included work for the Army in the Philippines and Japan during and after World War II, and stints for USIA in Malaya and Taiwan. In addition to Vietnamese, Donnell also knew Chinese, which he studied at Yale and Cornell. Besides RAND, Donnell also consulted for the State Department on North Vietnam affairs.[46]

Late in 1961, RAND asked Hickey and Donnell to go to the Central Highlands of South Vietnam to conduct a study for ARPA of Montagnard leaders, to determine what they expected from the government in Saigon. *Montagnard*, or "Mountain People," was a catch-all name that the French had given to the ethnic minorities living in the highland area, a region that had become strategically important as an infiltration route for former Viet Minh from the South who had relocated to the North following the Geneva Accords of 1954 and who were now making their way through the jungle, back into the South to reinforce the insurgency. In response, the South Vietnamese government and the American Mission had devised new strategies to retain control. But if they were to succeed, they would have to win the support of the local people—a difficult task, since President Diem's policy of forced assimilation to integrate the Montagnards into Vietnamese culture was causing a great deal of disaffection. Hickey and Donnell's study was implicitly designed to uncover the wants and needs of the Montagnard leaders in order to satisfy them and win their allegiance.

From his own viewpoint, Hickey thought of himself as an arbiter between the Montagnards and the powers in Saigon, and he believed that this project held for him "the possibility of helping the highlanders by playing the role of an intermediary between their leaders and the American Mission (and perhaps the Saigon government as well)."[47] Events, however, prevented the two consultants from carrying out their research. As part of the new strategy to cope with infiltration, the Central Intelligence

---

[46] *RANDom News*, May 1965.

[47] Gerald C. Hickey, *Window on a War*, Lubbock, Tex.: Texas Tech University Press, 2002, p. 91.

Agency was then organizing village defense in the Central Highlands, and the American in charge did not "want any anthropologists running around . . ."[48]

Unable to go into the Central Highlands, Hickey and Donnell decided to study the Strategic Hamlet Program, which was part of the strategy to win the war by restoring security in the countryside. Under this program, peasants from Viet Cong–controlled or –contested areas would be forcibly relocated into fortified hamlets to separate them from the guerrillas. The belief was that, once they were isolated from the villagers and had their access to the people cut off, the Viet Cong would become vulnerable to annihilation in a general offensive and subsequent mopping-up phase that were being planned. The program was underwritten by USAID and had been endorsed by Sir Robert Thompson, a counterinsurgency expert and the head of the British Mission to Vietnam.

Thompson was a veteran of the British fight against insurgents in Malaya, where a similar approach based on the strategic hamlet concept had brought success, albeit in a radically different situation. In Malaya, the insurgents had been ethnic Chinese who had no support among the native Malays and who could easily be identified and isolated from the rest of the population. In South Vietnam, where the guerrillas were indistinguishable from the peasants, had personal ties to them, or enjoyed their support, separating them from the rest of the population would be a different matter. Thompson, who would later serve briefly as a RAND consultant, believed that, as the strategic hamlets spread, government control would expand farther and farther, allowing security to be restored to the countryside. The French had used a similar strategic concept of expansion, which they called the *tache d'huile* or oil spot, when they were fighting the Viet Minh, and they had been defeated. However, it was believed that U.S. power and smarts would prevail where the French had failed.

Thompson's credentials endowed him with an aura that impressed people who were searching for a solution to an intractable problem. Originally, Thompson promoted a program called the "Delta Plan" and came to Washington in March 1962 to present and discuss his "Thompson Report," which laid out measures for clearing the Mekong Delta of communists and eventually pushing them back into the mangrove swamps where they could do little harm and could be starved out. Viewing the insurgency as a security problem, the plan advocated the restoration of security by police and mobile military units as a priority, before the initiation of social improvement programs provided as a reward to the villagers for cooperating with the government. Under this plan, the regrouping of people into "strategic hamlets" was only one component of the strategy, along with the creation of "prohibited areas," in which the government could shoot anyone on sight; and the adoption of control measures, such as curfews, identification cards, and checkpoints, to screen people entering and leav-

---

[48] Hickey, *Window on a War*, 2002, p. 91.

ing the zones undergoing pacification.[49] Although Thompson's plan was adopted as the basis for operations in the Mekong Delta, it got swallowed up in the rush to construct strategic hamlets, which became the key strategy for pacification while the other elements got sidetracked. Thompson was initially disappointed, but would come to be an enthusiastic advocate of the Strategic Hamlet Program and told President Kennedy in 1963 that he believed the insurgency could be defeated.

In March 1962, the pilot for the Strategic Hamlet Program, under the name Operation Sunrise, was launched in an area near Saigon, and, as part of this pacification drive, the hamlets were being constructed at breakneck speed. Gerry Hickey and John Donnell heard about Operation Sunrise and decided to study it as an alternative to their aborted research on Montagnard leaders. Instead of getting the official viewpoint, they talked to villagers to get their perspective on how Operation Sunrise was affecting their lives. The Operation Sunrise region targeted the Cu Chi District as the pilot area. This district had been under Viet Cong control from at least as far back as 1945, and it was here that the Viet Minh and, later, the Viet Cong had dug a formidable network of tunnels—part of which eventually reached under an American base at Dong Du in the area. The affected area had poor, sandy soil and was located between the lush Mekong Delta and the luxuriant jungles of the Central Highlands. Peasants here lived at a subsistence level.

In talking to villagers affected by the Strategic Hamlet Program, Hickey and Donnell found that there was widespread dissatisfaction about the forced relocation, and resentment over the way the program was being implemented.[50] Villagers complained that funds had not been disbursed as promised to feed them lunch and pay them for the labor they were required to provide for building the strategic hamlets. They resented that they had not been paid for the land they had lost in their former hamlets and for the bamboo they had to contribute for the construction of fortifications, and that they had been asked to pay for the concrete fenceposts and the barbed wire that ringed the strategic hamlets. In addition, they were suffering from a precipitous drop of income because they had to neglect work in the fields to build the strategic hamlet.[51] Political and economic reforms had not been implemented, and the promised benefits had not materialized, so they were not getting anything in return for their hardships. Hickey and Donnell reached the conclusion that the program could potentially bring

---

[49] Terrell E. Greene, "Notes on the Thompson Report on South Vietnam, and Discussion with R.G.K. Thompson," Santa Monica, Calif.: RAND Corporation, April 9, 1962 (not available to the general public). Thompson preferred to call the insurgents "bandits," because if they were captured they would have no rights. If they were called prisoners of war when captured, "you'll have people from Geneva all over the place." Greene, 1962, p 14.

[50] John C. Donnell and Gerald C. Hickey, *The Vietnamese "Strategic Hamlets": A Preliminary Report*, Santa Monica, Calif.: RAND Corporation, RM-3208-ARPA, September 1962.

[51] Hickey, *Window on a War*, 2002, pp. 93–95.

security to the villages, but that it would not be effective if it imposed "economic and social burdens on the population."[52]

Their negative evaluation, flying in the face of official optimism, provoked critical, if not hostile, reaction in American official circles in Saigon and in the United States. When they briefed Harold Brown at the Pentagon, he turned his back on them and looked out the window as they talked. Marine General Victor "Brute" Krulak pounded his fist on the desk and told them that "we" would force the peasants "to do what's necessary for the strategic hamlets to succeed."[53] Among senior officials, Krulak was a hawk, along with Walt Rostow at the State Department. Krulak was then serving as Special Assistant for Counterinsurgency and Special Activities (SACSA) and overseeing the conflict in Vietnam for the Joint Chiefs and McNamara. When Hickey and Donnell's report was circulated in Washington, ARPA objected to its pessimistic evaluation and wanted to attach a two-page rebuttal to each copy.[54]

RAND President Frank Collbohm had always insisted on RAND's freedom and strenuously resisted any attempt to encroach on its independence to publish and disseminate its research findings. Steve Hosmer recalled that he and Larry Henderson, the vice president in charge of RAND's Washington office,[55] attended a meeting called by ARPA to discuss this proposal. According to Hosmer, Henderson told ARPA that if it insisted on this approach, RAND would cease to conduct research for it in the future. ARPA relented, and the matter was dropped.[56] The reaction at the Pentagon reflected a general pattern that was to prevail throughout the Vietnam War: When RAND's research conclusions contradicted official thinking, they usually elicited strong objection and were ignored, or were dismissed outright. For Steve Hosmer, this episode

---

[52] Hickey, *Window on a War*, 2002, p. 99.

[53] Hickey, *Window on a War*, 2002, p. 99.

[54] Hickey, *Window on a War*, 2002, pp. 100–101.

[55] RAND's Washington office served as liaison between RAND and its clients. It kept clients abreast of RAND's work and, perhaps most important, kept tabs on developments at the Pentagon and the Air Force. Frank Collbohm said that Henderson "had his ear to the ground as far as what was happening in the Air Force and what would be of interest to RAND in working on its programs, and he'd let us know about that." Henderson's office also reviewed important RAND reports that had policy implications, to make sure that they were clear and could be easily understood by the clients. According to Henderson, the goal of this vetting process was not to avoid controversy, because "the whole lifeblood of RAND is controversy" as long as the controversy "is a real controversy and not a controversy about the way something had been written." His staff also arranged for analysts to brief the right people in Washington and for their reports to be distributed in the right places to achieve the most effect as well as to avoid ruffling feathers. Henderson's role as a link between RAND and the national-security establishment was quite different and separate from the function of the office itself, which was primarily to conduct research. Martin Collins, interview with Frank Collbohm, July 28, 1987, p. 45, and interview with Larry Henderson, August 30, 1989, pp. 55–57.

[56] Hickey, *Window on a War*, 2002, p. 101. See also Steve Hosmer, "Frank: Some Personal Glimpses," "Early Personalities," ed. James Digby, *Alumni Bulletin*, P-8005, March 2001, p. 13.

demonstrated the problems associated with research that countered prevailing policy and that was perceived as posing a threat to what Washington wanted to do.[57]

Bad as Operation Sunrise was proving to be, the construction of the strategic hamlets in the Mekong Delta as the operation unfolded would create even more widespread dislocation and popular discontent. In this region, the people lived in houses strung along rivers, canals, and arroyos, rather than in concentrated hamlets. As the program expanded, it herded peasants from Viet Cong–controlled or –contested areas who were living along these waterways into the strategic hamlets in a massive relocation. Some of those forced to move had their houses torn down, burned, or bombed. Province chiefs[58] were erecting strategic hamlets on a large scale to impress and please President Diem with the progress they were making. The irony was that the government of Viet Nam succeeded mostly in alienating the peasants without achieving security, because control rotated with the rising and setting sun: The government controlled the hamlets during the day, and underground Viet Cong cadres emerged to take charge during the night.

While Hickey's and Donnell's work achieved visibility and notoriety in Washington, the projects undertaken by a team under Jack Ellis ground on. According to Ellis, their work pertained mostly to combat operations and equipment—the kind of research that Gus Shubert would later describe as having practical value but lacking the intellectual heft for which RAND was known. The researchers, who came from the technical side of RAND, would spend a few weeks or months in Vietnam before returning to the United States to prepare reports on the information they had gathered in the field. They included Vic Sturdevant from Systems Analysis; George Young from Aero-Astronautics; Jim Farmer from Electronics; Jim Wilson from Systems Operations; and Joe Carrier from Cost Analysis.

The work they performed ranged from border control to the kind of radio that would be more suitable to small South Vietnamese units operating under thick jungle canopies, to the effectiveness of radio communication. Typically, the work consisted of analyzing reams of technical data—for example, evaluating the number of messages that the South Vietnamese Army could send, and the time it took to broadcast them and transcribe them. The main advantage the researchers derived from being in Vietnam was gaining ready access to relevant data. Most did not feel that it was necessary for them to acquire an understanding of the country, its people, the Viet Cong, or the insurgency to carry out their tasks. Furthermore, Vietnam and Southeast Asia were not within their professional field of work, and in general were only of mild interest

---

[57] Author interview with Steve Hosmer, 2004 and 2005.

[58] The most notorious was Colonel Pham Ngoc Thao, who headed Kien Hoa Province. Later, it was revealed that Thao was a secret Viet Cong cadre and was deliberately pushing the program in his area to cause widespread dissatisfaction with the Saigon government. At the time, however, his accomplishments made him famous, and he was hailed as the most energetic and successful province chief. He would later pay visits to RAND in Santa Monica and to the RAND office in Saigon.

to them, so they made little attempt to get a broader perspective or to delve into the complexities of the situation.

The most substantive work was performed by Vic Sturdevant, who arrived in Vietnam in mid-March 1962, after ARPA asked RAND to assist the Combat Development Test Center in Saigon in studying ways to reduce infiltration of supplies and men from the North into the South. According to Jack Ellis, the work on border control by Vic Sturdevant "died of its own weight" as ARPA shifted its attention elsewhere.[59] Perhaps there was no follow-up because it was realized that effective border control would be an impossible task—as Sturdevant himself concluded. He found that without the required resources, and even with the likely assistance from the United States and other foreign governments, South Vietnam would be incapable of sealing its extensive land and sea borders. The most cost-effective method would be to aim for less than total control through a partial sea blockade and a network of bases near the land border, from which random patrols could be launched to detect, ambush, and destroy groups of infiltrators.

Sturdevant went beyond the issue of border control, however, and suggested that the ultimate aim should be to restore security to the entire country. He expressed a belief in the efficacy of the strategic hamlets and a concept he called "inside-out" security—similar to the "oil spot" concept. He argued that government control should begin at the city, village, and hamlet and spread outward. Eventually these safe areas would be linked into larger and larger zones until the entire country was secure.[60] With the restoration of security, villagers would be more forthcoming with information about insurgent activities, without fearing retaliation from the Viet Cong. This flow of intelligence would enable the government to conduct more-effective anti-guerrilla operations, which, in turn, would bring more security and an even more voluminous flow of intelligence, and the situation would feed on itself and snowball.

Furthermore, Sturdevant believed that the restoration of security would allow the government to address the basic social, economic, and political problems that were stoking the insurgency, and that, by improving the life of the peasants and giving them a chance to choose their own leaders through democratic elections, the strategic hamlet would induce the villagers to switch their allegiance to the government. Denied access to the population and stymied by lack of popular support, the insurgency would find it difficult to survive. This view assumed that peasants in South Vietnam were neutral and would lean toward whichever side could protect them. It was a perception held by many in the South Vietnamese elite as well, who maintained that the peasants were

---

[59] Author interview with Jack Ellis, 2003 and 2004.

[60] C. V. Sturdevant, "Selected Papers on Border Control, Vietnam, 1962," Santa Monica, Calif.: RAND Corporation, D-10095-ARPA, May 28, 1962, and "The Border Control Problem in South Vietnam," Santa Monica, Calif.: RAND Corporation, D-10959-1-ARPA, Revised March 8, 1963.

apolitical and did not care who governed them as long as they could till their plots of land in security and peace.

Among the types of data-intensive research RAND performed at this time for ARPA was a study George Young conducted using statistics to describe when, how often, and what kind of Viet Cong activities took place during a lunar cycle. The objective was to look for ways to predict when Viet Cong activities would likely occur, so that countermeasures could be taken beforehand to foil them. A Chinese-American from San Francisco with a master's degree in chemistry from UC Berkeley, obtained in 1944, Young joined what would become RAND's Aero-Astronautics Department in March 1948 after working as a member of the research staff at Berkeley's Engineering Department. At RAND, he worked on projects dealing with missile design, aerodynamics, thermodynamics, nuclear propulsion, and Chinese technology.[61] Young came to Saigon in July 1962 to become RAND's first permanent representative at the R&D Field Unit.

Young's analysis showed that the dark of the moon was the most likely time of the month for insurgents to conduct operations, because they could avoid detection.[62] As Seymour Deitchman of ARPA/AGILE pointed out in his book *The Best-Laid Schemes*, this kind of research produced dry results that "told nothing the military couldn't sense intuitively."[63] He added, "Strangely enough, no one had previously demonstrated these facts with assembled and integrated data; but once demonstrated it was so obvious that the analysis did not appear significant."[64]

Of more interest, perhaps, was what these RAND people experienced in Vietnam in the days when the war had not reached its destructive phase. Joe Carrier, who had spent time in India under a Fulbright grant, actually volunteered to go to Saigon to escape from the boredom of his work in Cost Analysis. He was "dying to do something different."[65] Having been to India, he was not deterred by the prospect of living in Vietnam. Being a bachelor, he did not have a family to worry about back in the United States. Carrier had the modesty, gentleness, and kindness that the Vietnamese found attractive, and his affinity and empathy for Asia and Asians allowed him to relate easily with the locals. With his India experience, and with the curiosity and the interest in foreign cultures of an anthropologist—which he would later become—he found Vietnam absorbing rather than bewildering.

Carrier recalled that, when he arrived in Saigon in July 1962, the ARPA R&D Field Unit was located in a South Vietnamese Navy base near the Saigon River. The

---

[61] *RANDom News*, May 1965, pp. 14–15.

[62] G. B. W. Young, "Notes on Vietnam," Santa Monica, Calif.: RAND Corporation, D-11629-1-ARPA, August 16, 1963 (revised August 28, 1963).

[63] Deitchman, *The Best-Laid Schemes*, 1976, p. 378.

[64] Deitchman, *The Best-Laid Schemes*, 1976.

[65] Author interview with Joe Carrier, 2003.

nominal head was a South Vietnamese Army colonel advised by an American colonel. Carrier recalled that the R&D Field Unit was testing new weapons, such as the lighter AR15 with high muzzle velocity, to replace the M1 of World War II and Korean War vintage, which was too unwieldy for Vietnamese soldiers, whose average height was around 5'2". Other weapons being tested were the CBU—the anti-personnel cluster bomb—and defoliants. One afternoon, an American Chemical Corps major asked Carrier whether he would like to go for a ride. He immediately said, "yes," although he did not know what the purpose was. To his surprise, he was taken on a test run of chemicals to defoliate an area in the Mekong Delta. Carrier remembered that no one at the time suspected how toxic Agent Orange, or dioxin—a main component—was, and he recalled seeing South Vietnamese personnel handling the chemicals without any protective gear.[66]

The herbicide program was approved in mid-1961, and the CDTC was given the task of evaluating the effectiveness of the chemicals. The first test spraying by helicopter was conducted in August 1961 along a road in the Central Highlands, followed by a test spraying by fixed-wing aircraft along Route 13 in an area about 80 kilometers north of Saigon. Subsequently, Secretary McNamara picked December 1961 as the date for the launch of the program under the code name TRAIL DUST. The objective was to improve detection of enemy base camps and of enemy forces moving along communication lines and infiltration routes, and to destroy their crops. The use of herbicides expanded in 1965 and 1966, and reached its peak from 1967 to 1969. The U.S. Air Force dispensed a large amount of the herbicides under its Operation RANCH HAND by using C-123 cargo and transport planes. In all, 19.4 million gallons of herbicides were sprayed in South Vietnam, with dioxin accounting for 60 percent of the total, or 11.7 million gallons.[67]

Joe Carrier would work on radio communications[68] and collaborate with Vic Sturdevant on a statistical analysis covering hamlet incidents initiated by the Viet Cong, from December 1962 to September 1963, in response to the Strategic Hamlet Program.[69] While Hickey and Donnell had presented a highly negative analysis of the

---

[66] Author interview with Joe Carrier, 2003. Dioxin is a byproduct formed in the production of the defoliants.

[67] Lindsey H. Arison III, "Executive Summary: The Herbicidal Warfare Program in Vietnam, 1961–1971, *Operations Trail Dust/Ranch Hand,*" is an article posted online by Arison that is based on Buckingham, 1982, and on Paul Frederick Cecil, *Herbicidal Warfare—The RANCH HAND Project in Vietnam*, New York: Praeger, 1986.

[68] From the research, Joe Carrier would publish *Vietnamese Army Communication Support Requirements and Practices,* Santa Monica, Calif.: RAND Corporation, RM-3622-ARPA, 1963, which focuses on the support costs related to the three field radios that were most widely used in South Vietnam: the AN/PRC-6, the AN/PRC-10, and the AN/GRC-87.

[69] C. V. Sturdevant, J. M. Carrier, and J. I. Edelman, *An Examination of the Viet Cong Reaction to the Vietnamese Strategic Hamlet Program (12 December 1962 through 2 September 1963),* (Draft for Proposed RM), RAND D-11871-ARPA, November 19, 1963.

program, Sturdevant and Carrier offered a more "balanced" view. Carrier recalled that they did not want to "shoot down" a program that had high-level backing.[70] But they did caution about the consequences of the program. To Sturdevant and Carrier, the rise in Viet Cong incidents, as well as the tapering off of such incidents, indicated that the program was having an impact. Incidents, such as acts of terror, propaganda, and actual attacks, peaked in the later stages of the Strategic Hamlet Program as the Viet Cong made a last-ditch effort to stop the government from regaining control of the population, but began to decline after 50 to 60 percent of the population in a given zone had been relocated into strategic hamlets.

Despite such encouraging signs, Sturdevant and Carrier recommended a more patient approach: Although the data indicated the military success of the program, it also revealed that the population had to pay a heavy price, and these Viet Cong incidents represented the cost—or the "blood, sweat, and tears"—that the population had to bear in the course of program implementation. For this reason, and in light of the difficulties encountered in the rapid implementation of Operation Sunrise, they suggested that the program be carried out slowly to avoid exacting a high cost that could break the morale of the peasants. Security would be best achieved by moving patiently, and by expanding the program gradually, outwardly, from the pacified zones, they wrote. Looking back on this program, Carrier would say that the mere fact that the Viet Cong were hard to distinguish and to isolate from the rest of the population "should have shot [the program] down right then and there."[71] But many people at the time were blinded by their faith and hope in the program as the solution to the insurgency.

The Strategic Hamlet Program continued at a rapid pace, however, and by November 1963 when Sturdevant and Carrier's report was published, it was reaching full implementation. Sturdevant and Carrier's experience would prove to be the norm rather than the exception for RAND's research during the war. By the time a report appeared, its conclusions and recommendations were often overtaken by events, either because a course had been set and could not be reversed or because policies had proceeded too far along to be corrected or halted.

By the time George Young came to Saigon in July 1962, President Diem had survived the bombing of his presidential palace by two disgruntled Vietnamese Air Force pilots, an incident that revealed the disaffection within his own military. To shore up Diem's government, President Kennedy had decided to commit more U.S. military power by increasing the number of American advisors from 3,200 to 11,300; establishing the Military Assistance Command Vietnam (MACV) under General Paul D. Harkins; and sending more equipment, such as helicopters, light planes, and small ships. Despite these measures, the guerrillas continued to grow and to retain the ini-

---

[70] Author interview with Joe Carrier, 2003.

[71] Author interview with Joe Carrier, 2003.

tiative as the Saigon army showed little inclination to go on the attack. However, in Saigon, General Harkins and his staff were not concerned, exhibiting an arrogance born of America's victory over Nazism and Fascism in World War II. To them, the guerrillas were only "raggedy-ass little bastards" who would be defeated by the power of the United States.

Harkins had developed a four-phase strategy, based on his concept of the "Three M's: men, money, and materiel," which he believed would defeat the communists. Phases I and II would be to plan and prepare for Phase III—a coordinated campaign involving all branches of the South Vietnamese military, to be launched in mid-February 1963 and to be continued until the guerrillas were ground down. In Phase IV, mop-up operations would be conducted to eliminate the remaining guerrillas and to restore the Saigon government's control in the entire country. The war would be won in a year from the launch of Phase III. At a strategy conference in Honolulu in July, at the urging of McNamara, who wanted to interject more realism into the projection, Harkins amended the time it would take to defeat the Viet Cong to three years instead of one. The projection of victory led McNamara to instruct Harkins to develop a plan to phase out American military presence in Vietnam and to reduce it to 1,500 by December 1965.

In January 1963, George Tanham returned to Vietnam. It had been more than a year since he had last come to help set up the Combat Development and Test Center in Saigon. Although he found great optimism, he was concerned. In his trip report, he wrote that there was talk among senior American officials about "successfully concluding the war in two or three years or even less,"[72] and one even told him that, "Given a little luck we can wind this one up in a year."[73] Even Sir Robert Thompson shared this enthusiasm and optimism. Tanham found that the optimism was fed by the rapid expansion of the strategic hamlets. Flying over the northern and central regions of South Vietnam, he could see these hamlets—with their distinctive ditches, bamboo fences, and barbed wire—dotting the countryside.

The optimism was also fed by the belief that the rural development program undertaken by the United States Operations [Aid] Mission was beginning to bring social and economic improvements to the villages, and that democracy was taking hold at the grassroots level through local elections of hamlet chiefs and hamlet councils. In a political vision of the "oil spot" concept, senior officials argued that this grassroots democracy would expand to the districts and provinces and eventually to the central government. On the military side, American officials believed that the introduction of helicopters, massive U.S. aid, and the assignment of advisors to the battalion and district levels had made a huge difference. The South Vietnamese army had regained the

---

[72] Tanham, "Trip Report: Vietnam, January 1963," 1963, p. 1.

[73] Tanham, "Trip Report: Vietnam, January 1963," 1963, p. 5.

initiative and was putting the Viet Cong on the defensive, forcing them to pull back on the large engagements that they had been pushing to build toward a final offensive.

However, when Tanham talked to the press and lower-level civilian and military officials, he got a different perspective. Whereas the senior officials had a strong faith in the strategic hamlets, the lower ranks believed that the Vietnamese government may be able "to establish a garrison state," but that, in the long run, these fortified enclaves would not bring final victory, because this was a political—not a military—war. And in this political war, they did not see much change in the peasants' attitudes toward the government or any improvement in the government that would win popular support. In Tanham's own opinion, the Strategic Hamlet Program was a good concept, but its importance in winning the war had been exaggerated and it was too often relied on to solve all problems. Finally, Tanham concluded that little had changed in the political situation since his 1961 visit, that there was still no enthusiasm for President Diem among the people, and that, therefore, the United States could not hope to win the war with him. In short, Tanham found that the official optimism was unwarranted and he feared that it might prove disastrous for Vietnam and for the United States.

Since the Air Force remained RAND's major client, it was natural that George Tanham, who at one point had served as RAND's liaison with the Air Force, would pay a visit to General Rollen "Buck" Anthis, commander of the 2nd Air Force Division headquartered at Tan Son Nhut Airport. Vietnam was a war in which the Army dominated and the Air Force played only a tactical, supporting role, and Anthis reported to General Harkins. Most of the missions flown by the Air Force involved providing air support for attacks, escorting convoys, and targeting Viet Cong bases, supply points, and assembly areas in interdiction sorties. In addition, the 2nd Air Force Division also flew supply missions ferrying personnel and equipment.

It was a role that the Air Force, which had been focusing on strategic air warfare and building its nuclear capability to fight in Europe against the Soviet Union, did not relish. Insurgency was not its kind of war. Besides, the Army had built up its own air force, and in Vietnam had its own helicopters and could fly its own air missions, except for close support and other operations requiring the use of fighters and fighter bombers. Nevertheless, the presence of the Air Force had grown and its personnel in Vietnam had increased from 400 in 1961 to 2,000 in 1962. The Air Force had its own fleet of about 60 aircraft in the air commando squadron at Bien Hoa and in other units, which were painted with Vietnamese Air Force insignia to disguise the fact that the United States was directly participating in the war. The number of its sorties was growing, and so was the tonnage of bombs, rockets, and napalm dropped on the countryside.

In his meeting with Tanham, Anthis claimed that the U.S. Air Force was responsible for one-third of Viet Cong casualties in the past year, and that the Vietnamese Air Force, which Anthis was building up, was responsible for another third. (As part of Harkins's plan to reduce the American presence by the end of 1965, the U.S. military was to train the South Vietnamese to fly the fighter bombers and helicopters and to man other equipment that the Americans would leave behind.) Anthis said that he knew how many Viet Cong were killed by airpower because the Army confirmed the number and even told him that it was conservative.

Measuring progress by tracking statistics was the general tendency of the U.S. military in Vietnam. In a war without a front line, in which the enemy's objective was not to capture and hold territory and in which the U.S. goal was to grind down the enemy, the key measure of progress was the number of enemy killed in action—known as the *kill ratio* or, later, as the *body count*. Tanham deplored the Air Force inclination to measure its achievement by numbers—"So many huts were demolished; so many dwelling places were burned up; so many Viet Cong were killed; so many types of missions were flown"[74]—and believed that a more sophisticated assessment of the Air Force contribution was needed.

On the whole, he thought that General Anthis and the other Air Force generals he met during his visit were doing a good job and understood the problem in Vietnam. "The Air Force is proud of its contribution to the war in Vietnam," Tanham wrote, "though they are a little miffed that their role has not received public recognition."[75] During the meeting with Tanham, General Anthis mentioned some areas in which research would be helpful to the Air Force in Vietnam, such as the effect of air operations on "friend, foe, and neutral," night operations, improvements in surveillance, and air support for the strategic hamlets. Tanham thought that the issue of the effect of air operations would be a "good RAND-type job."[76] RAND would later perform research in all these areas, but it is not clear whether this conversation with Anthis provided the impetus for the work.

During his stay in Vietnam, Tanham visited Phuoc Binh Thanh Special Zone, encompassing areas in these three provinces near the Cambodian border that had been created in November 1962 to disrupt Viet Cong activities and eliminate the threat posed by their base located in this region—known as War Zone D. This region had been designated as an "enemy zone." As such, it was a free-fire zone, where anything that moved was fair game. Tanham found it a dangerous practice to designate an entire area an "enemy zone" and to resort to indiscriminate bombing and shooting on the assumption that anybody who lived there was either a Viet Cong or a hard-core supporter and, therefore, a legitimate target.[77]

At this time, the issue of civilian casualties from artillery and air strikes had not acquired the moral urgency that it later would when the tremendous firepower that American troops brought with them wrought havoc in the countryside. But it was being raised, nonetheless, by some American officers who were concerned that this

---

[74]   Tanham, "Trip Report: Vietnam, January 1963," 1963, p. 25.

[75]   Tanham, "Trip Report: Vietnam, January 1963," 1963, p. 24.

[76]   Tanham, "Trip Report: Vietnam, January 1963," 1963, p. 26.

[77]   Tanham, "Trip Report: Vietnam, January 1963," 1963, p. 19.

indiscriminate destruction was driving the peasants into the arms of the Viet Cong. General Harkins, who planned to quadruple the sortie rate of fighter bombers as part of his strategy to win the war, refused to discuss the issue, saying that he was tired of hearing about civilian casualties. General Anthis thought the complaints he heard were exaggerated or only concerned isolated incidents. For General Anthis, responsibility for civilian casualties should rest with the South Vietnamese, because the air strikes were all flown at the request of the ARVN, and of the province and district chiefs.[78]

It was during George Tanham's January 1963 visit that the battle of Ap Bac took place in the Mekong Delta, marking a turning point in the insurgency. Until Ap Bac, the guerrillas had been intimidated by the armored personnel carriers, the M113, and the helicopters that had been introduced into Vietnam in 1962. But on January 2, 1963, in a hamlet 40 miles southwest of Saigon, the 350 guerrillas dug in foxholes along a canal and protected by trees and shrubs defeated an attack mounted by a South Vietnamese force four times their number, which was supported by armored personnel carriers, helicopters, artillery, and fighter aircrafts dropping napalm, bombs, and rockets on their positions. They inflicted heavy casualties on the South Vietnamese attackers, killed three Americans and wounded another eight, and shot down five helicopters.

Ap Bac demonstrated that Harkins' "Three Ms" strategy was not working. Money, men, and materiel were not sufficient to turn the South Vietnamese Army into an effective fighting machine, nor could they replace the lack of leadership in an army that was used by President Diem to protect him against coups d'etat and keep him in power rather than to fight the Viet Cong aggressively. Yet Ap Bac did not disturb General Harkins, who now planned to launch his general offensive by the end of January 1963, moving up the date from mid-February. On January 19, he sent to Admiral Harry Felt, Commander in Chief Pacific, in Honolulu, the final draft of his strategy for achieving victory at the end of 1965, as McNamara had requested. (By the time Harkins left Vietnam in June 1964, his offensive would remain a pipe dream.)

Ap Bac did not dampen the official optimism in Saigon, but it worried Washington. Back in the United States, Ap Bac made front-page news and was featured in

---

[78] Alex Harding Peterson, an engineer from RAND who performed work for ARPA in Vietnam, would later say that the strikes were guided by Vietnamese airborne forward controllers and that it was not clear how often the strikes killed or injured friendly people, and he speculated whether a lot of the strikes were doing more harm than good. "If the U.S. pilot thinks it is a bad target (such as if he sees children outside a building he is to hit), he can refuse to go in but he cannot pick a target of his own," Peterson wrote. He also questioned the efficacy of the interdiction missions, because no ground force could go in to inspect the damage and confirm the inflated results. In exasperation, Peterson would ask, "How did we get ourselves into a situation like this in which we have so much at stake but no direct control over actions? Should we commit ourselves in a like manner next time?" His question encapsulated the conundrum of America's advisory role in Vietnam at that time: Despite its massive aid, the United States did not hold complete control over the prosecution of the war, nor did it possess the power to compel the South Vietnamese to do whatever it wanted. See A. H. Peterson, "Trip Report—Work with OSD/ARPA R&D Field Unit Vietnam," Santa Monica, Calif.: RAND Corporation, D-12378-ARPA, April 17, 1964.

evening television broadcasts, alerting the American people of their country's involvement in a war in a remote corner of the world. President Kennedy and Defense Secretary McNamara wanted a new appraisal of the situation, and a mission of senior officers was dispatched to Vietnam to answer the question posed by the Joint Chiefs of Staff, "Are we winning or losing?" The mission returned with an optimistic report and, reflecting the thinking in Saigon, concluded that the situation had been turned around in the space of a year and a half from "near desperation to where victory is now a hopeful prospect," and that there was no need to make a drastic change of course. The report reassured Kennedy and McNamara.

In the meantime, the Strategic Hamlet Program continued unabated. By mid-June 1963, when George Young left the R&D Field Unit and returned to the United States, 67 percent of the rural population was already living in 6,800 fortified hamlets. When all 11,246 strategic hamlets were constructed toward the end of 1963—so ran the belief in Saigon—the Viet Cong would be completely isolated. In spite of Ap Bac, whose importance was not appreciated in Saigon, it looked as though the situation was changing for the better, and a sense of optimism continued to prevail among Vietnamese province, district, and hamlet officials; and Americans in various agencies, such as the aid mission, MACV, and the embassy, with whom Young spoke about the program. In a report written upon his return to the United States, Young reflected this official optimism.[79]

He reported that the success of military operations, combined with the effectiveness of the Strategic Hamlet Program, had turned the tide in October–December 1962 and that victory was in sight. Young defined *victory* as the stage when the Viet Cong would no longer be able to conduct operations of company size or larger and would have to revert to small-size terrorism and guerrilla activities. What was even more impressive, in his view, was how quickly the tide had turned—in just one short year. The cause of the breakthrough was the restoration of security, which encouraged the villagers to come forward with intelligence, allowing the government to effectively target the insurgents. In the next phase, military operations would roll back the Viet Cong and force them to revert to guerrilla warfare, until the insurgents were "ground to a pulp."[80]

Young often quoted from an interview with Colonel F. P. (Ted) Serong, which had appeared in an English-language newspaper in Saigon on March 18, 1963. Serong was an Australian expert in counterinsurgency and special advisor to General Harkins, as well as commander of the team of 30 Australians in Vietnam who were aiding the anti-guerrilla effort. Serong had earned a reputation as a counterinsurgency specialist when he served as Strategic Advisor to the Armed Forces of Burma and assisted them

[79] G. B. W. Young, "Notes on Vietnam," Santa Monica, Calif.: RAND Corporation, D-11629-1-ARPA, August 16, 1963.

[80] Young, "Notes on Vietnam," 1963, pp. 5–6.

in their counterinsurgency. However, he was not as prominent or as respected as Sir Robert Thompson, the acknowledged preeminent expert.

In 1968, Marv Schaffer, from RAND's engineering side, arranged for Serong to become a consultant to RAND. Schaffer first met Serong in 1966, when he was working on a RAND project in Vietnam, and would say in 2004 that he did not know then that Serong was employed by the Central Intelligence Agency (CIA).[81] In fact, according to Anne Blair, Serong's biographer, he had been recruited by the CIA in 1965 and given the public cover as an employee of the State Department, where he had been seconded from the Australian Army. In 1968, the CIA instructed Serong to secure a contract with RAND to acquire a "suitable cover for his continuing operations in Vietnam," and Serong retired from the Australian Army.[82]

Serong did not make significant contributions at RAND. In Saigon, he would appear occasionally at the RAND office, and the staff used to wonder what he was really doing and for whom he was really working, and some would speculate—correctly, it turned out—that he was in the pay of the CIA. Since Serong was using RAND as a cover, he preferred to leave people guessing about what he was in fact doing. George Tanham, who met Serong in Saigon and later in Bangkok, would recall that "Serong was always very busy, but it was not always clear what he was up to."[83]

In his March 1963 interview with the Saigon newspaper, Serong exuded optimism and confidence. He said that the Viet Cong (VC) had no answer to the Strategic Hamlet Program, and that, besides, they were being challenged by a growing South Vietnamese Army bolstered by American personnel and equipment. The war would not end quickly, but "the end is in sight," he said.[84] Asked about the perception that the communist guerrillas possessed fierce determination, Serong said, "There is a lot of wool[l]y thinking and talking about dedication. It is true that some of the VC have dedication—but it doesn't go down far beyond the hard-core elements. . . . The ordinary Viet Cong province and hamlet guerrilla—these people are simply what we call in many countries juvenile delinquents. They are of the same age group."[85] According to Serong, the Viet Cong had lured these juvenile delinquents in the countryside with an aura of romantic adventure and by convincing them that their movement was something good. This dismissive view of the guerrillas as juvenile delinquents showed the same contempt that MACV officials had toward the Viet Cong at the time. Asked

---

[81] Author interview with Marv Schaffer, 2004.

[82] Anne Blair, "'Get Me Ten Years': Australia's Ted Serong in Vietnam, 1962–1975," Texas Tech University, 1996 Symposium on "After the Cold War: Reassessing Vietnam," p. 5.

[83] Blair, Anne, *There to the Bitter End: Ted Serong in Vietnam*, New South Wales, Australia: Allen & Unwin, 2001, p. 188.

[84] "The Tide Has Turned," *Times of Vietnam*, March 18, 1963 (attached as Appendix A in George Young's "Notes on Vietnam," 1963, p. 16).

[85] Young, "Notes on Vietnam," 1963, p. 18.

about the estimated duration of the war, Serong said, "This war will end when . . . the threat will no longer be a major danger to government and order: It will no longer be insurgency, but simply roving bands of bandits. And it will be a policing problem and not a military problem."[86]

Optimistic predictions aside, the situation in South Vietnam was actually worsening. By May 1963, the long-simmering political tension exploded when President Diem's police attacked Buddhist demonstrators in Hue, the former imperial capital, and killed a woman and five children in the melee. Angry Buddhists, who constituted the majority of the population and who resented Diem's favoritism toward the Catholic minority—his co-religionists—poured into the streets in the major cities, and riots erupted. Brutal repression by the government aggravated the situation. By August 1963, as Washington and Saigon were being distracted by the crisis, the Viet Cong began to dismantle the strategic hamlets. They destroyed the outposts and overwhelmed the militia, who were supposed to provide security and protection. In an ironic twist to the "inside-out" concept of pacification, they engaged in what they called a *bung ra*, or "bursting out" movement, by tearing up the fortifications and telling the people that they were free to return home to their former villages.

Harkins' strategy and the high kill ratio he thought he was achieving had not weakened the Viet Cong. They were now better armed, and equipped with weapons infiltrated from the North and with the superior weapons supplied by the United States to the South Vietnamese Army, which they had captured. And the assumption that the casualties inflicted on their ranks would deplete their fighting forces turned out to be false: The Viet Cong showed a surprising ability to replenish their ranks with new recruits.

Looking back, the RAND researchers who worked under the ARPA/AGILE contract in Vietnam in the period leading up to the overthrow of President Ngo Dinh Diem in November 1963, remembered a relatively peaceful period. There were signs of growing violence, but the war was still just an adventure, thrilling enough to add a frisson of excitement for anyone who ventured far away from Saigon, and yet not deadly enough to maim and kill indiscriminately. On one of the periodic trips Jack Ellis made to Vietnam to check on the progress of various projects and ferret out new research possibilities, he visited an outpost in the central region—just to get a firsthand look at what was happening in the countryside. He remembered that he flew out of Danang in a Marine helicopter and was dropped off at an outpost by the side of a little river in the late afternoon. He knew he was in for something different when he saw villagers bathing in the river after a long hot day.[87]

That night, he had trouble going to sleep, tense at the thought that Viet Cong territory began just across the river. To make matters worse, artillery shells were going

---

[86] Young, "Notes on Vietnam," 1963, p. 19

[87] Author interview with Jack Ellis, 2003 and 2004.

off all night long, fired at random in an exercise known as *harassment and interdiction* to keep the Viet Cong off balance. Despite Ellis's worst fears, the Viet Cong chose not to attack that night.

For Joe Carrier, this combination of exoticism and adventure in a place that, paradoxically, was still "laid back and coasting on good times," and the fascination of dealing with a variety of issues as opposed to the routine of cost analysis, got him "hooked" on Vietnam.[88] When his projects ended, he did all he could to extend his stay, but failed. Upon his return to Santa Monica, Carrier was determined to remain involved with research on Vietnam and eventually made his way back to Saigon.

Jim Wilson still has fond memories of his brief stay in Saigon. Wilson had found his niche as an engineering associate at RAND, which he joined in 1947, when the RAND staff included about 150 people. He had no reason to leave Santa Monica. But Asia had its lure, and he was interested in discovering it. When he was offered a job in Vietnam, he agreed immediately without knowing what awaited him there. He boarded a Pan Am flight and landed at Tan Son Nhut Airport one night.[89]

Life in Saigon turned out to be quite pleasant, and although it was a culture shock, Wilson enjoyed every moment of it. Vietnam was still secure for the most part, and he could travel to such places as Danang and Hue. He did not get caught in any fighting, and he never thought that he was in danger among the Vietnamese, whom he found kind and non-threatening. Yet, a war was going on in parts of the country and it provided an element of excitement. Living on salaries that were a king's ransom by Vietnamese standards, Americans could afford the "colonial" life that the French used to lead, separated from the locals not only physically in hotels or apartments that were too expensive for the Vietnamese but also in style and comfort. This lifestyle separation, along with language and cultural barriers, created a social distance that the Americans, most of whom were there only for a few months, were unable to bridge.

As with Jim Wilson, the only Vietnamese the Americans got to know were those with whom they interacted at work. Wilson's social circle included fellow expatriates: Clancy Briggs, an American colonel, and George Young, who also lived in the same hotel on Tu Do, the main street in downtown Saigon. The hotel was owned by a Frenchman, probably one of the Corsicans who had properties and roots in Vietnam that were too deep to keep them from going home after the French colonial presence ended in 1956. Wilson had a maid who would have food ready for him when he came home for a leisurely two-hour lunch, accompanied by the local beer called 33—which later would become as familiar to American GIs as Budweiser. Then, in the late afternoon, when they got home from work, the three men would gather and have drinks in their hotel rooms. Pleasant though life could be, the men had to endure loneliness and separation from home and family, and after a few months, most were ready to leave.

---

[88] Author interview with Joe Carrier, 2003.

[89] Author interview with Jim Wilson, 2004.

Jim Wilson coped by writing frequently to his wife, Berniece, who was the secretary for Frank Collbohm.

Among the RAND people in Saigon at this time, the person who perhaps enjoyed his stay the most was Gerry Hickey. But he was dismayed by the change that he saw taking place. While Jim Wilson had no time reference for evaluating Saigon, Hickey could remember the city as it was in 1956, when he arrived for the first time as a member of the Michigan State University Group (MSUG). The MSUG had a U.S. government contract to help transform the newly created South Vietnam into a modern state by improving the efficiency of the police and various ministries—part of the nation-building effort then being undertaken in the Third World to strengthen allies against a communist threat. Saigon in 1956 was still a charming city, with ornate French buildings, streets and boulevards shaded by tamarind and flame trees, villas surrounded by lush gardens, boutiques lining its main street, sidewalk cafes, restaurants serving good French food, and elegant soirees held at the Sports Club and other establishments at which the social elite gathered. Saigon well deserved its affectionate names, Pearl of the Orient and Paris of the East. President Diem had not yet ordered the French to leave, so Legionnaires were still strolling down the main street and patronizing the cafes—another sight of the mingling of East and West that gave Saigon a special atmosphere.[90] To this day, Hickey retains a nostalgia for what to him was a golden time for Vietnam.

When Hickey came back in 1962 with John Donnell, he was shocked to see how the insurgency had changed Saigon. On the road into town from the airport, American-supplied military vehicles crowded the street. From the rooftop of the Caravelle Hotel in downtown Saigon at night, he could see flares floating over the countryside near the city and he could hear the sound of exploding mortars. Then, in February, while he was getting ready to leave on a fieldtrip, he heard a loud explosion. He rushed out of the house to see plumes of smoke and an airplane swooping down over the tall trees. Tanks and military trucks filled with soldiers were rolling down the street toward the Independence Palace, the official residence of President Diem. What Hickey was witnessing was the aftermath of the bombing of the presidential palace by two disgruntled Vietnamese Air Force pilots. The bombing destroyed the imposing Second Empire structure built by the French for the former Governor General of Indochina, but President Diem survived.

The American influence that Hickey detected was changing Vietnam. By 1962, 20,000 Americans were already living there. In a small country like Vietnam, their presence was very much in evidence. They were occupying the big homes and the finest apartments, living in hotels that had been transformed into BOQs, Bachelor Officers' Quarters, and driving big American cars. Their affluent lifestyle and the glimpses of the outside world through magazines, radio broadcasts, and movies were fueling Viet-

---

[90] Hickey, *Window on a War*, 2002, pp. 21–22.

namese aspirations to achieve the same standard of living. At the same time, the sight of the Americans taking over the best of everything also reminded the Vietnamese of the colonial period, when the French lorded it over them. In their minds, they began to lump the Americans together with the French.

Young Vietnamese were the most taken with U.S. culture, and it was feared that their adoption of American mores and values would undermine Vietnamese society and traditions. Madame Ngo Dinh Nhu, President Diem's formidable sister-in-law—nicknamed the Dragon Lady by the American press—was issuing legislation to stem this influence and protect the Vietnamese family from disintegration.[91]

In the ensuing chaos following the overthrow of President Diem by a military junta in November 1963, the Viet Cong, with the willing participation of villagers, would reduce the strategic hamlets to shambles, and the existence of these fortified enclaves would eventually be obliterated. With Diem's downfall, American involvement in the war would escalate and RAND's role in Vietnam would expand, along with that of the United States.

---

[91] James Farmer, "Counter-Insurgency: Viet-Nam 1962–1963," Santa Monica, Calif.: RAND Corporation, D-11385-ARPA, June 19, 1963.

CHAPTER TWO

"What Makes the Viet Cong Tick?"

It was with the rank of general that Joe Zasloff arrived in Saigon with his wife Tela in summer 1964 to run a new RAND research project called "Viet Cong Motivation and Morale." Harry Rowen in the Pentagon had agreed to fund the project. As did other civilians attached to the Defense Department in Vietnam, Zasloff had to carry a military rank roughly the equivalent of what he would have qualified in civil service status. Before Zasloff's departure, an aide to Harry Rowen telephoned RAND and asked what rank Zasloff should have. Since Zasloff was going to depend on the U.S. Military Assistance Command in Vietnam for support for everything from obtaining living quarters to securing transport for his field study, the reply was, "Do the very best you can, it's a difficult project, and the higher we can get, the better."[1] The Pentagon obliged and gave Zasloff the rank of general to facilitate his work in Vietnam.

Traveling to a war zone required more than getting a ticket and boarding a plane. First, the Zasloffs had to obtain theater clearance from the Department of Defense. This did not pose a problem since the Viet Cong Motivation and Morale Project had been approved by the International Security Affairs within the Office of the Secretary of Defense. For Joe Zasloff, who knew French, the language most of South Vietnam's elite still spoke, going to Vietnam was not as novel as it had been in 1959, when he was selected to teach at the University of Saigon. He had applied for a grant simply to teach abroad, destination unspecified, and when he was informed that he had been assigned to a place called Saigon, he ran to a map to see where it was located.[2]

Zasloff had learned French in high school and college. His fluency had improved while he served in France during World War II and subsequently while studying at the University of Geneva for his doctorate degree. In Saigon, he taught as a visiting professor at the Faculty of Law, lecturing in French, and collaborated with the University of Michigan Group on a study of provincial administration in Vinh Long in the Mekong Delta. Zasloff thus belonged to a small group of Vietnam experts who possessed first-

---

[1] David Landau, "Behind the Policy Makers: RAND and The Vietnam War," *Ramparts*, November 1972, pp. 31–32.

[2] Author interview with Joe and Tela Zasloff, 2003.

hand knowledge of the country and who could communicate in a limited fashion with the locals. From his experience in Vietnam, he wrote an article that was published in the journal *Commentary*.

The article caught the attention of Guy Pauker at RAND. Born in 1916 in Romania, Pauker fled the country when he learned through word of mouth that his name had been placed on a list of anti-Soviet and anti-communist dissidents who were going to be purged. He made his way to Austria and then, eventually, to Harvard, where he had been accepted prior to his flight. From this personal experience, he was convinced that communism was a political system that was intolerant of independent thought. At Harvard, he specialized in Southeast Asia because he did not want to have anything to do with Eastern Europe, which would have seemed a more natural area expertise for someone of his background. After spending a summer on a Navajo reservation with an anthropologist from Harvard, he became fascinated by how an ancient culture coped with change. This experience kindled an interest in Indonesia, which had just freed itself from Dutch colonial rule and was going through a wrenching transformation.[3]

After he obtained his doctorate at Harvard, the Political Science Department at Berkeley offered him a job, which he immediately accepted. One summer, RAND invited him to spend a sabbatical there. Pauker found RAND exciting and dynamic, and he thought that its interdisciplinary approach was stimulating. According to his wife Ewa, her husband remembered that "at lunchtime, practically every day, somebody would give a lecture in the auditorium on various topics, from astronomy to physics to politics. You could broaden your mind there." For two to three years, he commuted between his job at Berkeley and his work at RAND as a consultant—a difficult undertaking in those days. Besides, his RAND work also required overseas travel. So, in 1963, Pauker resigned from Berkeley and joined RAND permanently as a Southeast Asia specialist in the Social Science Department.

The Social Science Division was set up in 1948, with Hans Speier as its chairman. Speier was born in Berlin in 1905. He received his doctorate in Heidelberg, with sociology and economics as majors and philosophy and history as minors—at age 23. He emigrated to the United States in 1933 and became a member of the New School for Social Research in New York. In 1948, Speier was invited to a RAND conference in New York City to which many prominent social scientists—economists, demographers, statisticians, sociologists, political scientists, psychologists, and anthropologists—were also invited. Speier recalled later that the objective of the conference was "to look the field over as to who might be useful as a contributor in the field of the social sciences, to be hired by RAND" and to find a head of an Economics Division and a head of a Social Science Division.[4] Frank Collbohm was interested in recruiting "various social scientists" to work with the physicists, engineers, and other

---

[3]   Author interview with Ewa Pauker, 2004.

[4]   Collins, interview with Hans Speier, April 1988, p. 24.

scientists—the initial staff at RAND—on national-security issues since, in his view, one could not predict which aspect of a problem "is going to be important in the long run."[5] Even before this conference was organized, RAND—mostly at the prodding of John D. Williams, a mathematician—had concluded that the contribution of social science had become crucial as its work expanded beyond the World War II–type of operations research, centering on mathematics, physics, and engineering, to include complex problems that required a more systematic analytic approach.[6] To Speier, the conference was "an imaginative way of going about exploring the possibility of adding something they [RAND] didn't know anything about."[7]

The addition of social scientists was deemed important because as Hans Speier recalled, the "mathematicians and logicians and physicists and engineers . . . all of a sudden discovered that you cannot talk about weapon systems without talking about the cost of weapon systems; you have to know something about economics. You cannot talk about war without knowing something about the potential enemy. You have to know something about foreign policy."[8] By adding social scientists to its professional staff, RAND was a pioneer among think tanks in instituting a broad approach to the analysis of policy issues.[9]

At first, Speier and most of the Social Science Division worked out of the Washington office, because Speier wanted to have quick access to government documents and to cultivate contacts in various agencies in order to obtain the documents. In 1957, Social Science was concentrated in Santa Monica, to facilitate synergy with other divisions so that, as Speier put it, "the talents that are there in the organization get utilized better if everybody can walk into the office of anybody else whenever he needs him.

---

[5]   Collins, interview with Frank Collbohm, 1987, p. 19.

[6]   It was John Williams who persuaded the Air Force to accept the addition of social science. In late 1946, Williams traveled to Washington to meet with General Curtis LeMay, then the Air Force Deputy Chief of Staff for Research and Development. After initially resisting the idea of spending taxpayers' money on anything other than operational weapons, LeMay—showing foresight—gave his approval, adding that if RAND was going to do this, it should "do it on a meaningful scale." Bruce Smith, *The RAND Corporation*, Cambridge, Mass.: Harvard University Press, 1966, pp. 61–62.

[7]   Collins, interview with Hans Speier, 1988, p.24

[8]   Collins, interview with Hans Speier, 1988, p. 24.

[9]   Over time, however, there was disillusionment among the hard scientists at RAND. Alex George, who took over as department chairman from Hans Speier in 1961, remembered that social scientists became unpopular with "the people who [had] insisted that they should have economics as well as social science," because social scientists "didn't think the same way that they thought." As an illustration, George told the story of one of the leading physicists who came to see him one day, "out of the blue." The physicist wanted to sound him out on an issue and was apparently expecting to get support for his own view. George told him, "Well, it's very difficult to have a simple view of this. It could be this, it could be that—we can identify three possibilities, but we can't say which one is the most likely one." The physicist was "disgusted" and said, "In other words, all you can deal with is pure opinions. My opinion is just as good as yours." George also remembered that, despite its congeniality, interdisciplinary approach, and team work, RAND was not immune to arguments, conflicts, and even bitterness over issues. Author interview with Alex George, 2004.

You have to be able to just open the door and walk in, as we walked in on Frank . . . whenever we wanted to."[10]

As chief of the Social Science Division, Speier found that it was easy to recruit people but difficult to retain them. The books his staff members published and RAND's reputation itself made those people attractive to universities, which came knocking on their doors with many offers. Under Speier's leadership, Social Science extended research beyond strategy into area studies, such as Soviet and Chinese studies. The division would include well-known experts: Alex George, Herbert Goldhamer, Myron Rush, Nathan Leites, and Paul Kecskemeti.

Pauker enjoyed the open, sharing, collegial atmosphere at RAND. Ewa Pauker, who also joined the Social Science Department at RAND (the division became a department in 1960), remembered that, "You could wander into someone's office and talk about what you were doing, what he/she was doing, and see whether there was any synergy, or pick up ideas. Frank Collbohm's attitude fostered this atmosphere. If you had a good idea, Frank would find the money for you to pursue it, and you could take as long as you needed. There was no "bottom line" and no deadline. Frank was rarely in his office. He would walk around the building, and he could stop in to talk to you, or you could stop in to see him in his office. He would even stop in an office and chat with a secretary. Everybody was the same, whether you were a janitor or the president of RAND."[11]

This description of Collbohm's accessibility to the staff, of the open atmosphere, and the absence of hierarchy at RAND has been corroborated by many RAND staff members in their reminiscences about the organization. Collbohm himself confirmed his habit of going around the building and dropping in to chat with the RAND staff, saying, "I visited all around the building very regularly. Stop in and talk to different people, how are they doing, what are they doing. Yes, I think that's something that's important. You have to do that."[12]

So Guy Pauker was not surprised when Collbohm "scratched" on the door of his office in April 1964 and asked if he had a little time. Vietnam was on his mind. Since Pauker was then RAND's foremost expert on Southeast Asia, he was the obvious choice for Collbohm to discuss the issue. According to Pauker, Collbohm said, "We are not pulling our weight" in Vietnam "where so much of the national interest is at stake."[13] In fact, Vietnam was only one area where RAND was expanding its reach, Latin America being another. During a combined Air Force Advisory Group and Board of Trustees meeting that same month, Collbohm had discussed how RAND was evolving

---

[10] Collins, interview with Hans Speier, 1988, p. 34.

[11] Author interview with Ewa Pauker, 2004.

[12] Collins, interview with Frank Collbohm, 1987, p. 53.

[13] Guy Pauker, "What Makes the Vietcong Tick," "Early Personalities and Projects," *Alumni Bulletin*, James Digby, ed., Santa Monica, Calif.: RAND Corporation, P-8055, March 2001.

from strategic bomber problems, defense and logistics studies, to other issues facing the nation. According to the minutes of that meeting, "This led some Board members to worry about RAND's studying Latin America, South Africa, Vietnam, etc. Collbohm replied that the Board, RAND Management, and the clients should carefully watch the quality of the RAND output—if it falls, it would indicate we were spreading too thin; further[,] our clients want and expect help on a large variety of problems."[14] Still uneasy, "The Board asked for a written statement prior to the next meeting[,] presenting the rationale for our undertaking new areas of research, such as Latin America." Despite the Board's misgivings, RAND did broaden its reach, and Vietnam, which was becoming an important issue, seemed to be a logical extension of RAND's focus on national security problems.

Pauker would later recall that he told Collbohm that he had "visited South Vietnam a couple of times during the previous decade," and that he "thought that an American involvement would be a big mistake, and wanted to keep RAND out of it."[15] Considering Pauker's view, it is surprising that he would help set up RAND's largest research effort in Vietnam. People who knew Pauker at the time would later say that he was a person who "liked to be where the action was" or that he was intellectually flexible enough to be on either side of an issue. Regardless of what his motive was, Pauker went along with Collbohm's wishes. As he remembered, "Frank rejected my argument and told me to find ways to make the Political Science Department useful with regard to Vietnam. I replied that, in that case, I wanted him to come with me to Washington to get something started." Collbohm agreed.[16]

In Washington, they went to see Bill Sullivan at the State Department. Sullivan was the head of the Interagency Task Force on Vietnam, which included representatives from the principal government agencies. The task force had been set up at the suggestion of McGeorge Bundy, the National Security Advisor to President Lyndon B. Johnson, to study the Vietnam situation, recommend solutions, and build consensus within the administration at a time when there was wide disagreement regarding what policy to pursue in Vietnam. Sullivan, who would later become U.S. ambassador to Laos, had prepared a list of about 25 topics "on which the interagency would have welcomed RAND research."[17] According to Pauker, "Most of the items on the list involved psychological warfare, in which I did not believe and, therefore, had no interest. The item, way down on the list, caught my attention: 'Who are the Vietcong? What makes them tick?' I asked Bill where this question came from, and he replied. 'Directly from McNamara, who keeps asking that question.' Frank and I agreed on

---

[14] Management Committee Meeting, minutes of meeting held on April 14, 1964, RAND Archives, Santa Monica, Calif.

[15] Pauker, "What Makes the Vietcong Tick," 2001.

[16] Pauker, "What Makes the Vietcong Tick," 2001.

[17] Pauker, "What Makes the Vietcong Tick," 2001.

the spot that RAND would try to answer the Defense Secretary's question."[18] Pauker thought that the work Lucian Pye of the Massachusetts Institute of Technology had performed on the Chinese Communists in Malaya during the insurgency there could serve as a model for the RAND project.

With the research topic chosen, Collbohm left Pauker to make the necessary arrangements to get the project off the ground. Pauker went to the Pentagon to see Harry Rowen, who was then Deputy Assistant Secretary of Defense for International Security Affairs, responsible for the Asia-Pacific region and reporting to John McNaughton. Rowen immediately promised to arrange for the funding of the project and reportedly told Pauker, "Why, what a splendid idea for you to go to Vietnam."[19] ISA itself did not have money to pay for the research, so the funding ultimately came from the budget of ARPA/AGILE.[20] With the funding secured, Pauker visited William Colby, at that time the Central Intelligence Agency's director of the Asia-Pacific Division, and asked for assistance in gaining access to Viet Cong prisoners and defectors in Vietnam.[21] The CIA had a detention center in Saigon, and RAND's researchers were given access to Viet Cong imprisoned at that location.

At Harry Rowen's urging, Guy Pauker and Steve Hosmer went to Saigon to scout out the possibilities of conducting interviews with enemy prisoners of war (POWs). The project had to be communicated to MACV and its commander, General William C. Westmoreland, who had replaced General Paul Harkins. To smooth the way, John McNaughton wrote to Westmoreland to inform him of the RAND study, explaining that it had been sponsored by ISA and cleared with William Sullivan at the State

---

[18] Pauker, "What Makes the Vietcong Tick," 2001.

[19] Landau, "Behind the Policy Makers," 1972, p. 31.

[20] At this time, ARPA/AGILE was itself beginning "to become concerned with the human problems" of counterinsurgency warfare, according to Seymour Deitchman, former head of Project AGILE. Deitchman recalled that, in 1964, ARPA "increased its efforts in the 'soft' sciences related to Vietnam and counterinsurgency. One [such effort] . . . under contract to the RAND Corporation and jointly sponsored with ISA, was the 'Viet Cong Motivation and Morale Study.'" Deitchman, *The Best-Laid Schemes*, 1976, p. 68. According to Deitchman, this project was "conceived and begun" at a time when almost nothing was known about the "nature of the Viet Cong revolutionary movement, including answers to such questions as what strata of society its adherents came from; why they were adherents; how group cohesiveness was built into their ranks; and how they interacted with the populace." Deitchman, *The Best-Laid Schemes*, 1976, p. 235.

[21] The defector, or *Chieu Hoi* ("Open Arms" in English), program began in 1963. It was based on the successful amnesty program in the Philippines to induce defection by the Hukbalahap insurgents, and on the British experience in Malaya, and was pushed by Rufus Phillips and C. R. Bohannan on the American side and by Sir Robert Thompson, then serving with the British Advisory Mission in Vietnam. President Diem at first was reluctant to offer any kind of amnesty to the Viet Cong, but subsequently initiated the program. Despite some success at the beginning, with 5,000 defectors in the first three months, by mid-1964 it was still a relatively modest undertaking, lacking adequate funding and personnel, and suffering from internal problems. See Jeannette A. Koch, *The Chieu Hoi Program in South Vietnam, 1963–1971*, Santa Monica, Calif.: RAND Corporation, R-1172-ARPA, January 1973.

Department, and that it was of interest to Sullivan as well to Colby at the CIA, and General Hall of the Defense Intelligence Agency.[22]

McNaughton hoped the study would not burden Westmoreland's staff and encouraged Westmoreland to follow it or participate in it in any way he saw fit. Also, McNaughton added, he would appreciate any guidance, advice, and assistance to the RAND team. In his reply of May 28, 1964, Westmoreland, while appearing neutral about the project, assured McNaughton that the study would not create a burden for his staff and expressed the hope that it would produce some practical results.[23] General John K. Boles, head of MACV's Joint Research and Test Activity, later would say that Westmoreland himself was in fact favorably disposed toward social science research because he "recognized the need and desirability" for it.[24] In answer to a query from ARPA/AGILE, Boles added that the U.S. military itself would welcome such research, since it would be important to explore "the psychology and motivation of the Vietnamese" through interviews with prisoners and defectors. The military, he said, had come to realize that "hardware research alone would not provide the answers to the war in Vietnam."[25] The Pauker project was conceived, therefore, at an opportune moment, because the military was becoming more open to this kind of proposal.

It also came at a time when the South Vietnamese government itself had become less sensitive to research by Americans under the pressure of war.[26] Until then, it had resisted permitting Americans to conduct research out of concern that they would uncover information that would reflect badly on the regime. In fact, the idea of doing a Viet Cong interrogation program had been floated by Robert H. Johnson during his tenure on the Policy Planning Council of the Department of State, a post he held beginning in 1962. In a later interview, Johnson remembered that he had recommended this idea during the Diem period to find out "why people joined the Viet Cong, what their motivations were, how were they hurting, how were the Viet Cong exploiting grievances, and so on"—as a way of studying political grievances in South Vietnam. His model was Lucian Pye's study of the insurgency in Malaya. His suggestion was not pursued because it would involve using American interrogators to get at the answers, and it was well known that President Diem would resist the idea unless he was heavily pressured by the United States—something that U.S. Ambassador Frederick Nolting was reluctant to do at a time when the relationship with Diem was already becoming strained. According to Robert Johnson, such an interrogation program would expose

---

[22] John McNaughton, Letter to General William Westmoreland, May 18, 1964. Westmoreland personal papers, Lyndon Baines Johnson Archives, Austin, Tex.

[23] Westmoreland reply to McNaughton, 28 May, 1964, Westmoreland personal papers, Lyndon Baines Johnson Archives, Austin, Tex.

[24] Deitchman, *The Best-Laid Schemes*, 1976, p. 99.

[25] Deitchman, *The Best-Laid Schemes*, 1976, p. 99.

[26] Deitchman, *The Best-Laid Schemes*, 1976, p. 98.

very politically sensitive issues and uncover "things that Diem would rather not have outsiders find out about."[27]

Joe Zasloff recalled that Guy Pauker approached him sometime in 1963 to carry out an interrogation program similar to the one Robert Johnson had alluded to, and he took a leave of absence from the University of Pittsburgh to do so. Pauker and RAND thought that clearance had been secured from the Diem government, but, at the last minute, Saigon rescinded the permission. Zasloff thought that the reason might have been that Diem "didn't want Americans to poke around in what amounts to intelligence matters, getting access to Viet Cong prisoners and defectors."[28] So RAND assigned Zasloff temporarily to its Washington office, where he performed a number of studies, including one on the role of North Vietnam in the insurgency, using RAND materials and whatever classified documents RAND could obtain for him. His RM, *The Role of North Vietnam in the Southern Insurgency*, was published in July 1964.[29]

The removal of President Diem and the advances made by the Viet Cong changed the attitude of the South Vietnamese government. In November 1963, as the Buddhist crisis escalated in the wake of Diem and Nhu's brutal repression and South Vietnam appeared on the brink of chaos, President Kennedy—acting on the recommendation of his newly appointed ambassador to the country, Henry Cabot Lodge—authorized the overthrow of Diem. In a secret cable to Kennedy, Lodge had told Kennedy that the United States could not shrink from this course of action because, "There is no possibility, in my view, that the war can be won under Diem."[30] Through Lou Conein in the CIA, Lodge gave the go-ahead to a group of disgruntled South Vietnamese generals who wanted to get rid of Diem because they feared the war was being lost. In allowing Lodge to proceed with a coup d'etat, Kennedy "asked only that Lodge guarantee him a successful coup, that he not be forced to endure the disgrace of another Bay of Pigs."[31] The generals struck on November 1, 1963. Diem and Nhu managed to flee from the presidential palace but were later caught in a church in Cholon, the Chinese section of Saigon. They were transported to the Joint General Staff headquarters in a personnel carrier but were executed on the way. Within a week of Diem's overthrow, the Viet Cong launched an offensive in the Mekong Delta and in some of the provinces near Saigon. The Delta seemed on the verge of falling into enemy hands.

Guy Pauker and Steve Hosmer left for Saigon in May 1964 to arrange for the project to proceed. According to Steve Hosmer, he and Pauker "talked to many people who had an interview effort already out there and who were familiar with Vietnam-

---

[27] Johnson, Robert H., Oral History, John F. Kennedy Presidential Library, Boston, Mass.

[28] Author interview with Joe and Tela Zasloff, 2003.

[29] This study attracted a great deal of interest in Washington. See Chapter Three.

[30] Neil Sheehan, *A Bright Shining Lie: John Paul Vann and America in Vietnam*, New York: Random House, 1988, p. 360.

[31] Sheehan, *A Bright Shining Lie*, 1988, p. 367.

ese interview issues. As a result of that, we concluded that indeed we could, and that the issues that we would be interested in weren't being adequately covered in the interrogations."[32] With the arrangements in place, Pauker decided to recruit Lucian Pye to run the project, because he himself did not want to spend time in Vietnam, preferring to focus on Indonesia, his true area of interest. Lucian Pye had other commitments, so Pauker recruited Joe Zasloff and John Donnell.

We do not know what prompted McNamara to ask the question, "Who are the Viet Cong and what makes them tick?" At a talk sponsored by the Asia Society in Los Angeles in 1999 to promote his book *Argument Without End: In Search of Answers to the Vietnam Tragedy,* McNamara said in reply to a question from the audience that he did not remember the RAND study nor in fact the question itself. But one can infer why he was curious about—if not puzzled by—the enemy he was fighting in Vietnam. Instead of crumbling under American pressure, the Viet Cong had turned out to be much tougher and much more resilient. Contrary to the widespread assertion in Saigon that the insurgents were no more than an "ill-disciplined band of terrorists and kidnappers of young boys whose hit-and-run tactics had no appeal to the peasantry"[33]—as Joe Zasloff remembered—the Viet Cong were showing incredible cohesion and strength and were taking advantage of the chaotic situation following the overthrow of Diem to expand their control. As Lyndon Baines Johnson's "oracle" for Vietnam, McNamara had assumed primary responsibility for fighting this elusive enemy and might have wished to know more about his opponents.

On the other hand, the question might have reached him from another source. According to David Morell, at the time a Second Lieutenant assigned to the J-2 Intelligence Branch at MACV and project officer for the RAND study, it was General Paul D. Harkins, Westmoreland's predecessor at MACV, who had asked the question during his debriefings at the Pentagon after being recalled from his post: "Why does the other side fight with such spirit? What morale and motivation do they have as opposed to the ARVN, Ruff Puffs (Regional and Popular Forces), and all the various friendly forces who didn't fight with the same spirit?" Harkins, according to the story that Morell heard, had recommended "that we take a good, hard look at this."[34]

With the launching of Pauker's Viet Cong Motivation and Morale Project, which would become RAND's largest research study in Vietnam, RAND's Social Science Department stepped to the fore.[35] While continuing to be conducted, the technical

---

[32] Author interview with Steve Hosmer, 2004.

[33] Author interview with Joe and Tela Zasloff, 2003.

[34] Author interview with David Morell, 2004.

[35] According to Deitchman, RAND's Social Science Department had an "excellent reputation." However, in his view, the members of this department were "'lone wolves' who preferred to pursue their own interests and ends, and it was a constant struggle to assure that the different parts of their work remained related to each other and relevant to our needs." Some "interesting and useful" research was nonetheless performed when the analysts'

and operational studies that had dominated RAND's work on Vietnam would diminish in importance and acquire a lower profile. Social Science itself was interested in conducting research in Vietnam and helping RAND "pull its weight" in the war effort. Alex George, who had become chair of the department, would later recall that, "Frank Collbohm was interested to send people over there, and many people went from other departments, so the question became, 'What will the Social Science Department do?' So it became the question of doing the interviews with prisoners of war, how would they be analyzed, who would conduct the interviews, and so on and so forth. So it became a big project." Alex George, however, adamantly refused to be drawn into it because he was already busy with his own studies of limited war.[36]

When the Viet Cong Motivation and Morale Project began in 1964, President Johnson had not committed himself to a definite course of action with regard to Vietnam. His main concern was to avoid making a mistake that would jeopardize his domestic agenda and cost him the presidential election, and he was therefore inclined to defer the hard decisions until after November 1964. The policy choices remained open. According to William Sullivan, his Vietnam Interagency Task Force was given the responsibility of considering all options, ranging from disengagement to large-scale military intervention. Within this gamut, the Joint Chiefs of Staff favored "get in" and fight to win or "get out." McNamara favored a middle position and advocated using graduated pressure to communicate resolve and to dissuade the Viet Cong and North Vietnamese from pursuing the war. McNamara's belief in using military escalation to send signals to an adversary reflected the influence of Thomas C. Schelling, a Harvard economist, developer of game theory, co-winner of the 2005 Nobel Prize for Economics, a consultant at RAND during the late 1950s and 1960s, and author of an influential book on bargaining and strategic behavior entitled *The Strategy of Conflict*. Schelling argued that warfare is essentially a particular form of bargaining in which rational opponents used signals to communicate with each other. In limited warfare, violence could be unleashed and held back in a calibrated fashion as part of a process of bargaining that could be managed.[37] John McNaughton, whom Schelling recommended for the position of Assistant Secretary of Defense, was greatly influenced by him, as was McNamara, for whom the concept that warfare could be managed much as was the Ford automobile plant must have held a great deal of appeal. The graduated-pressure strategy they pursued in Vietnam reflected Schelling's influence.

Schelling's strategic behavior and bargaining theory assumed that the opponents on both sides of a conflict behave as rational decisionmakers. For Vietnam, McNamara

---

interests "coincided with those of the DoD." This happened mainly in the years 1964–1967, when the Viet Cong Motivation and Morale Project was "at its full swing." Deitchman, *The Best-Laid Schemes*, 1976, pp. 320–321.

[36] Author interview with Alex George, 2004.

[37] McNamara would say of the bombing of North Vietnam, "It's something you can stop. It's a bargaining chip." Cited in Daniel Ellsberg, *Secrets: A Memoir of Vietnam and the Pentagon Papers*, New York: Viking, 2002, p. 52.

thought that, as the United States ratcheted up its military pressure, the North Vietnamese and the Viet Cong would rationally come to the conclusion that they could not win and would desist. Newton Minow, Chairman of the Federal Communications Commission under President Kennedy and a member of the RAND Board of Trustees, remembered "very clearly" running into this assumption during a briefing given by one of several generals who came to brief the board on a regular basis. Minow, who had reached only the rank of Army sergeant in World War II and who was new to the board, was intimidated by the general "with a lot of stars." Finally, he summoned up his courage and told the general that his analysis of Vietnam was based on the assumption that, "we're dealing with a rational enemy, a rational opponent" since the general's argument was that "if we do this, then they'll do that. And if we do that, then they'll do this." Minow pointed out to him, "You're assuming that you're dealing with someone who thinks rationally and makes rational decisions. Has it ever occurred to you maybe you're dealing with fanatics who would just as soon die as give up? They don't care; they don't think rationally; they are committed to a cause and they're so committed that they're not going to give up. You've got people who'd just as soon give up their own lives for what they are fighting for and they are not going to proceed in a rational, thoughtful way." Minow remembered that he "didn't get very far with that approach."[38]

President Johnson, who wanted to appear as a moderate in the upcoming presidential campaign, leaned toward McNamara's strategy of gradual escalation because it looked like it would not lead to a wider war and it would keep South Vietnam from sinking—a position that was described as "hold until November." Graduated pressure began with covert operations, such as seaborne strikes and raids against North Vietnamese naval and port facilities along the coast, dropping teams of South Vietnamese saboteurs into the North, and sending U.S. destroyers to patrol along the North Vietnamese coast. The Viet Cong Motivation and Morale Project was not expected to support or refute any policy options, or to make any policy recommendations. However, in this atmosphere in Washington, where official attitudes had not hardened, it could have influenced the direction of U.S. policy toward Vietnam.

The project was scheduled to last only six months. When Joe Zasloff prepared to go to Saigon in July 1964, he stopped in Santa Monica to talk to Alex George, one of his "intellectual heroes." While Pauker had thought of Lucian Pye's study of the Chinese Communists in Malaya as a model for the project, Zasloff considered the work that Alex George had performed with Chinese Communist prisoners of war during the Korean War very relevant. Zasloff recalled that Alex George gave him invaluable advice. "He was very helpful in his guidance," Zasloff remembered. "The simple thing he told me made a mark on me. He said, 'What you should do is draw on your own experience in the army in World War II.' It gave me a feel for how soldiers operate

---

[38] Author interview with Newton Minow, 2005.

Tela Zasloff in the living room of the RAND villa at 176 Pasteur, Saigon.

and what it is that motivates them, the buddy relationships, small-unit relationships. I remember Alex told me to read . . . a study of the Wermacht in World War II, and the crux of the study was that what kept the German army fighting was the small-unit cohesion and the role of the non-com, the squad leaders and the platoon leaders, the small-unit leaders. That was very helpful in my study of the Viet Cong."[39] George's Korea study dealt as well with the role of criticism and self-criticism, which the Viet Cong also used and referred to as *kiem thao*, and this alerted Zasloff to the importance of this control mechanism.

Zasloff and his wife, Tela, reached Saigon first, before John Donnell. Among the many arrangements Zasloff had to make was to find housing and office space and to recruit interviewers. He decided to take one of the big houses that MACV offered, a villa at 176 Rue Pasteur that was large enough to serve both as living quarters and as an office. Over time, the former French villa would become synonymous with RAND's presence in Vietnam. The two-story house was surrounded by a ten-foot-tall concrete wall. For security reasons, barbed wire was strung across the top. An iron gate protected the entry to the driveway. The small front yard had "a narrow strip of grass, hanging plants, a hibiscus tree and flowers."[40] There were a balcony on the second floor facing the street and verandas in the front and back. The occupants of the house hardly ever ventured out onto the balcony because of the traffic noise and fumes, and humidity and heat. A tall tree shaded the side yard and, according to the household help, its intertwining branches and dense foliage harbored some ghosts. The servants believed that the ghosts haunted the villa at night, and they refused to set foot in it then. Gerry

---

[39] Author interview with Joe and Tela Zasloff, 2003.

[40] Tela Zasloff, *Saigon Dreaming: Recollections of Indochina Days*, New York: St. Martin's Press, 1990, p. 5.

Hickey himself said that he always felt "bad vibes" whenever he entered the villa and thought that it might indeed be haunted. He had the uneasy feeling that there was something wrong [with the villa], that something lurid had occurred there."[41]

The villa was a square, concrete building with an open and large interior, appropriate for a hot and tropical climate. The windows had grillwork and shutters, and ceiling fans were usually turned on throughout the day, until the sun went down, to circulate the warm, moist air.[42] Typical of French villas in Vietnam, the inside was not designed for efficient use of space but rather for airiness and for comfort. The ground floor was a large open space—the size of a hotel lobby—which was made into a living room and a dining area, separated by a bamboo divider hung with potted plants. Red tiles covered the floor for coolness. To complement the tropical atmosphere, the housing office of MACV had furnished the living room with standard rattan furniture. One could picture French colonialists sipping *apperitifs* under the rotating ceiling fan in the living room and then repairing to the dining area for a multicourse evening meal, waited on by attentive servants. A pantry and a side room occupied the rest of the ground floor. The side room became the office for the Viet Cong Motivation and Morale Project—M&M for short. For the duration of the project under Zasloff and then under other managers, the ground floor would become the setting for receptions and dinners. In time, as the staff grew and space became a premium, a desk would be set up in a corner of the living room by the front entrance for an American secretary.

Toward the back of the dining area, a curved staircase lined with long windows covered with purple stained glass led to the upper floor where the Zasloffs used the back bedroom and bathroom as their private quarters while the rest of the rooms were turned into offices for the twenty interviewers who came and went and a staff of typists and translators. The house came furnished down to the kitchen utensils. The only thing Tela Zasloff had to do was hire the servant staff. She found a temperamental chief maid, Chi Hai, who supervised another maid on whose shoulders fell most of the tedious housework, such as mopping the tile floor every day. Tela also found a great cook, Anh Ba, who had worked for a French general and who rarely failed to remind the Zasloffs of his credentials, especially when he wanted a pay raise.

John Donnell joined the Zasloffs in September. Soon after, Donnell and Zasloff hired Susan Morell, the wife of David Morell, to be their administrative assistant. Susan Morell remembered John Donnell as a very tense, quiet man, and an old-fashioned, very detail-oriented scholar. She was young and was intimidated by Donnell, who seemed to be "concerned with very small things. The condition of the batten of the typewriter was important to him, and if I put a piece of paper without a backup piece behind it, he thought that would ruin the batten and he'd get quite upset with

---

[41] Hickey, *Window on a War*, 2002, p. 109.

[42] Author interview with Joe and Tela Zasloff, May 2003.

Clockwise from bottom: Mai Elliott, David Elliott, David Morell,
Guy Pauker, Tela Zasloff, Joe Zasloff, Susan Morell, and
John Donnell.

that."[43] Both she and her husband remembered that Donnell spoke formal, high-tone Vietnamese, which was hard for the prisoners and defectors, most of whom were of peasant background, to understand.

David Morell recalled that Zasloff played a more dominant role and took care of the practical details of the project—"how to get enough interviews done . . . how are we going to do all the things that need to be done"—while Donnell was the "ethereal intellectual."[44] According to David Morell, Donnell was "fascinated with the opportunity to be back," and having been in Hanoi at the time of Dien Bien Phu in 1954, he "probably saw the National Liberation Front and the Viet Cong as the successor to the Viet Minh more clearly than most Americans. He brought his personal history as well as his studied knowledge of the situation. . . . He even [saw] more than Joe saw . . . that there was something terribly wrong with the American involvement and with Diem and with the post-Diem structure we created."[45] The Morells remembered that Zasloff and Donnell got along well and in a way complemented each other.

For interviewers, Joe Zasloff recruited his former colleagues at the Faculty of Law and the Institute of National Administration. He thought he got very qualified people who were interested not just in the pay but also in the project. The drawback was that most only knew French. They would translate their interviews from Vietnamese into French, which did not pose a problem for Zasloff and Donnell, but when the French version was turned into English for other readers, a few things would get lost in the

[43] Author interview with Susan Morell, 2004.

[44] Author interview with David Morell, 2004.

[45] Author interview with David Morell, 2004.

Joe and Tela Zasloff and John Donnell with Vietnamese staff.

translation back and forth. Zasloff found the professors knowledgeable and intelligent, and he learned a lot from them. At first, these academics knew little about the aspirations of the peasants and the nature of the Viet Cong movement. As did the rest of the Saigon elite, they believed that the peasants only wanted to own a small plot of land and to be left in peace. But as the project developed and their knowledge of the situation deepened, they were shocked to discover what really sustained the insurgency: the grievances the peasants held against the Saigon government and the ardent aspirations they had for education, economic opportunity, equality, and justice for themselves and their descendants. Zasloff found this transformation fascinating.

Zasloff and Donnell did not have a formal questionnaire. Except for a standard set of questions to obtain demographic information, he and Donnell "had a series of areas which we wanted to explore, but my own approach was to arrange a set of questions that were relevant" to the source, according to Zasloff.[46] For example, a young Viet Cong recruit who had been in the military for three months would get a different set of questions from that for a guerrilla. The questions and answers for each interview were recorded. The interviews were done privately, one on one, with just the Vietnamese interviewer and the respondent, or with an American interviewer and a Vietnamese translator and the respondent. No Vietnamese or American official was present, so the respondent would feel free to talk.

To determine which sources were available for interviewing, Zasloff and Donnell would talk to their American contacts who "knew the lay of the land." The contacts would, in turn, put them in touch with the appropriate Vietnamese authorities to gain access.[47] At the beginning, they interviewed respondents in Saigon, but then decided

---

[46] Author interview with David Morell, 2004.

[47] Author interview with David Morell, 2004.

to go into the provinces to talk to prisoners and defectors at local holding centers, thereby obtaining a wider and more diverse sample in geographical distribution and types of cadres and soldiers in the movement. The pool included Viet Minh who had stayed behind in the South after 1954; Viet Minh who had regrouped to the North and then returned to the South; North Vietnamese who had infiltrated down the Ho Chi Minh Trail, beginning in late 1963; local cadres and guerrillas; and suspects who were unlucky enough to get caught in the dragnet.

Traveling by road was unsafe—especially at night, when ambushes and mines made driving hazardous—and the local airline did not go to many places, so they had to rely on military air transport. But even this form of transportation was not devoid of danger. Zasloff remembered that one time, after landing, they saw bullet holes in the fuselage of the small aircraft in which they had flown and realized that they must have been shot at while in the air. Military transport was not entirely reliable, and it might not be available when they needed it. On a trip to the Mekong Delta, they could not get a military aircraft to take them back to Saigon, so they went to the central market to rent a car. The only thing they could find was an old, big, red, American sedan that could be spotted for miles around and would make a tempting, DayGlo kind of target. John Donnell and some of the interviewers held their heads and said, "Do we have to drive back in this?" Zasloff remembered that there was a "certain sense of danger" during his stay in Vietnam, but that he was "never terribly frightened."[48]

Although the Vietnamese authorities were generally cooperative, the choice of sources for interviewing was limited in the sense that they could select only from the pool of POWs and defectors made available by the South Vietnamese authorities. It was not possible to choose a representative sample—as could be done in American opinion surveys—nor was it possible to know what the total pool of Viet Cong recruits and guerrillas was at large and, therefore, what a representative sample should look like. The best Zasloff and Donnell could do to obtain more current information was to try to get recent defectors and POWs.

Zasloff's best source was a senior captain who had infiltrated from the North. He had cooperated in the interrogation with a South Vietnamese intelligence officer, with the understanding that he would receive favorable treatment when the interrogation was over. But the South Vietnamese authorities reneged, and he was kept in Chi Hoa, the main prison in Saigon. Angry over this betrayal, he refused to salute the flag during the morning playing of the South Vietnamese national anthem. To punish him, the prison officials bound him in his cell so that he could not stand up. Zasloff heard about him and asked to see him. The day of the interview, the prisoner had to be carried down by his fellow inmates because he had become bent over from being tied up in this posture.

---

[48] Author interview with Joe Zasloff, 2003.

From left to right: interviewers Ninh and Que,
Joe Zasloff, John Donnell, administrative assistant
Hanh, and interviewer Thang.

Mistreatment of POWs—and of suspects—was rampant, and RAND interviewers and team leaders would often hear tales of torture from the detainees. According to Zasloff, "When we got out into the provinces, the closer we got to the period when they were just captured, systematic brutalization was something common in the intelligence operation in Vietnam."[49]

Zasloff and Donnell told Guy Pauker about what they had heard, and on December 8, 1964, Pauker sent a letter to John McNaughton, Assistant Secretary for International Security Affairs in the Department of Defense, relaying these observations as well as information on the mistreatment of prisoners, defectors, and suspects that had been gleaned from the 120 interviews conducted to that time.[50] Pauker did not raise the moral issue of torture but, rather, appealed to McNaughton from a practical, counterinsurgency standpoint, perhaps believing that such an appeal would have more of an effect in Washington. He wrote that the finding required McNaughton's immediate attention, since the brutal treatment of Viet Cong prisoners, defectors, and suspects would undoubtedly discourage insurgents from defecting. Pauker mentioned the accounts of execution of prisoners by senior ARVN officers and the brutal interrogation methods, among them prolonged torture used repeatedly. Pauker contrasted this situation with the Viet Cong's own politically more astute and more benign treatment of prisoners under the slogan of "increasing the number of friends and reducing the number of enemies." Pauker urged the Defense Department to obtain more

---

[49] Author interview with Joe Zasloff, 2003.

[50] Guy Pauker, "Treatment of POWs, Defectors, and Suspects in South Vietnam (U)," Santa Monica, Calif.: RAND Corporation, D(L) 13171-ISA, December 8, 1964.

information and to consider the implications of what was going on. It is not clear whether McNaughton tried to do something about the brutal treatment of prisoners and suspects, and the mishandling of defectors, but the fact remains that mistreatment and torture continued and that few improvements were made in the program for *chieu hoi.*

As the project progressed, the issue of methodology emerged. When Zasloff told people about the study, they would question whether it was possible to get the truth from prisoners and defectors—especially defectors—since they would tell you what you wanted to hear. In reply, Zasloff would say that survey research is not a science, and would insist that you could get at the truth, "If you just ask them to tell their stories, and as they tell their stories, you get a lot of information about the political structure, the organization, and how they react to events." Zasloff would further explain, "I guess the word 'morale' often suggests that you're studying current morale, but that's not what you're going to do, the point is to learn about the current situation, the political organization, operations, the sociology, the way that they managed morale."[51]

Alex George also had to deal with the issue of methodology in his study of Chinese Communist prisoners of war in Korea. His solution was to look at the people he interviewed "not as members of a scientific sample, but rather each one as an informant in the sense that what can I learn from each one about his unit."[52] Just as in Vietnam, there were many enemy units in Korea, and it was not possible for George to distribute the interviews evenly between all the units because "in some cases I had quite a few people from the same company or the same battalion, and some cases I didn't. So, I had to juggle my interviews to see what they could tell me about the nature of their units. . . . I felt that the best way to use the prisoners was as informants about their units, very different from using them as members of a sample: It was not at all public-opinion-survey research. The opposite."

With regard to the issue of whether one could trust what the POWs—and, for Vietnam, defectors—said, George remembers that, in Korea, the kinds of questions he was asking "were not questions where they would dissemble." Just as Joe Zasloff and John Donnell did in Vietnam, he was asking questions about such things as what was going on in the POWs' units, about their attitude toward the self-criticism sessions, and he felt that the prisoners were not misrepresenting their experience. He found that "there was a great deal of convergence of views of prisoners with regard to what life was like in the unit to which they belonged, and how they reacted to the severe punishment of military combat and so on. . . . If you have a good schedule of questions to ask and if you have good interviewers, you can get a lot of useful information from them, including some that is surprisingly frank. . . . I didn't find it a problem to get what I

---

[51] Author interview with Joe Zasloff, 2003.

[52] Author interview with Alex George, 2004.

thought was useful hard intelligence about what life was like in their system, how it worked, and so on."[53]

Seymour Deitchman himself acknowledged the problem of obtaining scientific samples in the interview projects sponsored by ARPA/AGILE in a country at war like Vietnam. The war "restricted access to subjects, . . . [impacted] control of comparative situations, stability of situations," or other elements required for "careful scientific work."[54] It was not possible to have "before and after control groups" built into the research design.[55] The data on the Viet Cong were gathered after they defected or were captured, and since it was not possible to access them before "separation," "there was no baseline data for comparison."[56] In Deitchman's assessment, in these wartime conditions, it was not possible to "integrate quantitative and nonquantitative disciplines in social science in the field." Although social scientists tried hard to be quantitative, it was clear that the main value of their research came from the "fascinating and instructive" insights they reached, even if it might be difficult "to prove by rigorous analysis of the data" that these insights were generally "valid or true."[57] He concluded, however, that such insights added new and valuable knowledge and understanding of the revolutionary movement in Southeast Asia, and allowed decisionmakers to formulate policies "by something better than seat of the pants navigation."[58]

To try to inject some scientific rigor into the project, a few months into the study, Guy Pauker sent David Himmelman to Saigon to devise a new approach to the interviews. Zasloff disagreed with Himmelman, considering his approach inappropriate to the circumstances of Vietnam, where the kind of random sampling and scientific rigor Himmelman wanted to achieve could not be applied.[59] Himmelman developed a lengthy set of questions that the interviewers were supposed to ask of every respondent, regardless of whether or not they were relevant to each particular interviewee, with multiple answers for the interviewers to tick off. The objective was to obtain extensive socioeconomic background information from the prisoners and defectors under study. Susan Morell remembered that making up this lengthy questionnaire took a lot of time. Applying the extensive questions on socioeconomic background consumed a lot of time and diverted attention from the other issues that needed to be explored. In November, Pauker traveled to Saigon to review the project and concluded that

[53] Author interview with Alex George, 2004.

[54] Deitchman, *The Best-Laid Schemes*, 1976, p. 343.

[55] Deitchman, *The Best-Laid Schemes*, 1976, p, 366.

[56] Deitchman, *The Best-Laid Schemes*, 1976, p. 365.

[57] Deitchman, *The Best-Laid Schemes*, 1976, p. 377.

[58] Deitchman, *The Best-Laid Schemes*, 1976, p. 389.

[59] Author interview with Joe and Tela Zasloff, 2003.

Himmelman's effort at quantifying the interview data was not suitable. The structured questionnaire was abandoned, and Himmelman left the project.

Zasloff recalled that, with the exception of the Himmelman disruption, the project ran smoothly. Absorbed in his work, fascinated by what was happening, he took living in Vietnam in stride. Their villa was an oasis in a city that no longer had the romantic aura that he remembered. The colonial setting was still there, but Saigon had become a bit decayed and crowded. Traffic was heavy and chaotic, and the air was polluted. Beggars accosted his wife in the street, and Vietnamese who disliked Americans openly expressed their hostility to her. Signs of instability were not far beyond the wall of 176 Pasteur. There were antigovernment demonstrations and terrorist bombings. Like the traffic fumes, pessimism hung thick in the air. The bright side of their life in Saigon was represented by the social whirl of receptions and dinners among the expatriate and diplomatic community; the contacts they established with members of the foreign press, such as François Sully, the famous foreign correspondent of *Newsweek*— and the contacts with some people among the Vietnamese elite.

Despite McNaughton's effort to interest Westmoreland in the RAND study, the general neither followed it as it unfolded nor participated in it in any way. His disinterest was shared by the top brass at MACV, and the job of facilitating and monitoring the study fell to David Morell, a second lieutenant. A year out of graduate school, Morell believed in the importance of the project, which, in his view, represented "classic intelligence in the best sense of knowing your enemy." He was amazed that senior officers at MACV would put him in charge of this potentially important study. His main role was to make sure that the project ran smoothly and that the information got relayed to MACV. He himself was curious about what motivated the enemy, and he wanted to obtain answers to such questions as, "What was the motivation for joining? What was the motivation for undergoing such hardships once they joined and [for] continuing to be so enthusiastic?"[60]

As he would explain later, "It's one thing to join. You watch Civil War movies in the United States, and the boys are off to war, and then stuff starts to happen—your buddies get killed, you're in the mud for forty-eight hours with nothing to eat. The remarkable phenomenon we were probing was why did they keep slugging it out so incredibly ?"[61] This was the kind of information that he and J-2 were not getting from the reams of translated captured VC documents and from the prisoner interrogations that flooded their office—and that he expected the RAND study to provide.

He thought that RAND would get at the profound issue of why the Viet Cong "fight and die for a cause, what was this cause, and why did they eschew the goodies that we were trying to give—economic development and all the things that Americans viewed as [helping to] win hearts and minds . . . and they just go and breathe under the

---

[60] Author interview with David and Susan Morell, 2004.

[61] Author interview with David and Susan Morell, 2004.

water from a reed for six months or so, live in the tunnels in Cu Chi. They fight for a cause, so if we can get some understanding of this, my belief . . . was certainly that we can do a better job of defeating them."[62]

Morell noted that the Vietnamese government and army played practically no part in this project. MACV never sent him to talk to the General Staff of the ARVN or to keep them informed of the progress of the study. As he put it later, "Here we are as Americans presumptively in an advisory role, we didn't have American troops there until 1965, and yet we were running this whole profoundly political study in their country. There was no coordination, no communication with the Vietnamese General Staff. It didn't bother me then, but in retrospect it's shocking, it's classic colonialism. . . . Who cares what they know, what they think?"[63] (It is worth noting that the RAND team later in fact did brief South Vietnamese General Staff officers about the findings. It is not clear what their reaction was.)

While Zasloff was busy that summer getting his project started, a study he had done earlier for RAND in 1963 and published in July 1964, *The Role of North Vietnam in the Southern Insurgency*, caught the attention of General Curtis LeMay. The report had been distributed widely. It was sent to the Air Force in July, and Air Force Secretary Eugene Zuckert forwarded personal copies of the study to McNamara and William Bundy, Assistant Secretary of State for Far Eastern Affairs. Copies also went to officers in the Intelligence Community, as well as to General Westmoreland, to members of his staff, and to the ranking Air Force and Embassy officers in Saigon. The study was also briefed to officers of Intelligence and Plans at Air Force Headquarters, at ISA, and at the State Department. At the suggestion of General Richard Yudkin, Deputy Director of Plans at Air Force Headquarters, General LeMay sent personal copies of the report to the Chairman and other members of the Joint Chiefs of Staff.

Since February 1964, General LeMay, the Air Force Chief of Staff—who dismissed the covert operations against North Vietnam favored by McNamara as ineffective "pinpricks"—had been advocating the bombing of the North to destroy its will and capacity to support the insurgency. On August 2, reports reached Washington that North Vietnamese torpedo boats had attacked the U.S. destroyer *Maddox* in the Tonkin Gulf, and then on August 4 there were reports of another attack, this time against the destroyers *Maddox* and *Turner Joy*.[64] Although the commander of the

---

[62] Author interview with David and Susan Morell, 2004.

[63] Author interview with David and Susan Morell, 2004.

[64] In 2001, Robert J. Hanyok, the National Security Agency (NSA) historian, concluded that mid-level agency officers had falsified North Vietnamese communications intercepted by the NSA to cover up earlier errors and "made it look as if North Vietnam had attacked American destroyers on August 4, 1964." *The New York Times* issue of October 31, 2005, which reported on Mr. Hanyok's classified in-house history of the NSA and Vietnam, entitled, "Spartans in Darkness," wrote that Mr. Hanyok concluded that DoD officials and President Johnson, who used the August 4 attack to get the Tonkin Gulf Resolution passed in Congress, did not know of this falsification. Mr. Hanyok, the *Times* article said, believed the NSA officers' initial misinterpretation of the intercepts

destroyer task force said in his review that the attacks were doubtful and urged further evaluation, President Johnson, wishing to defuse his Republican opponent Barry Goldwater's charges that he was irresolute and soft in foreign policy, ordered reprisal strikes against North Vietnam. The fact that threatening activities, such as naval raids against the North and the Desoto patrols by the U.S. destroyers themselves, might have provoked the attacks—if the attacks indeed did occur—was not a mitigating factor in the furor erupting in the aftermath of the reports. In the reprisal strikes, U.S. naval pilots carried out 64 sorties against North Vietnamese naval vessels and the oil storage facility at Vinh, identified as the staging area for infiltration into South Vietnam. Two American planes were shot down. One pilot was killed, and the other was captured and would be held in captivity for eight-and-one-half years. However, the air strikes were not sustained following this reprisal.

It was in this climate that, on August 17, 1964, LeMay sent a memo and an executive summary of Zasloff's report to General Earle "Bus" Wheeler, Chairman of the Joint Chiefs of Staff, to persuade him and the JCS that the bombing should continue until all 94 targets in North Vietnam that the JCS had identified as crucial were destroyed. LeMay argued that airpower offered the United States "the best chance" for winning the war without requiring the dispatch of American ground troops or Marines to South Vietnam, and tried to use the report to persuade his colleagues that it was necessary to bomb the North in order to defeat the insurgency in the South.[65]

In his report, Zasloff argued that North Vietnam was the mastermind of the insurgency and its main supporter, and its aim was to cause the collapse of the South Vietnamese government and to discourage the United States into withdrawing. One of his key conclusions was that, "Much of the strength and sophistication of the insurgent organization in South Vietnam today is attributable to the fact that North Vietnam plans, directs, and coordinates the over-all campaign and lends material aid, spiritual leadership, and moral justification to the rebellion."[66] Yet, Hanoi had so far been safe from attack and ran little risk of counteraction. Zasloff viewed the study as a factual description and did not make any recommendation.[67] Washington officials perusing his report could have reached two opposite conclusions: to disengage because the strong commitment of North Vietnam to the insurgency could lead to a bigger war or to attack North Vietnam to persuade it to abandon its goal. General LeMay chose to use the report to build a case for bombing the North.

---

was an honest mistake which they discovered immediately. However, they decided to cover it up and "doctored documents so that they appeared to provide evidence of an attack."

[65] H. R. McMaster, *Dereliction of Duty: Lyndon Johnson, Robert McNamara, The Joint Chiefs of Staff, and the Lies That Led to Vietnam,*" New York: Harper Perennial, 1997, p. 143.

[66] Joseph Zasloff, *The Role of North Vietnam in the Southern Insurgency,* Santa Monica, Calif.: RAND Corporation, RM-4140-PR, July 1964, p. v.

[67] Author interview with Joe Zasloff, 2003.

Within the U.S. military services, there was agreement that stronger action was needed but disagreement over what that action should be. Each service believed that it alone could provide the answer. The Air Force, and especially its Chief of Staff, believed that the insurgency could be defeated by bombing North Vietnam and the infiltration routes rather than by building a stable government in Saigon and winning the loyalty and support of the population in the South. The Army believed that the war would have to be won on the ground through military action and pacification, and that bombing the North would not defeat the insurgency and would instead intensify the war in the South. General LeMay dismissed the Army's approach, saying that the combination of political, economic, and psychological actions with military operations would not produce results, and that trying to build a stable South Vietnam would lead nowhere. Unable to offer a unified strategy to President Johnson, the Joint Chiefs of Staff went along with his policy of graduated pressure in the belief that more-forceful measures would be undertaken if this approach failed to produce the desired results in Vietnam.

On August 10, Congress passed the Tonkin Gulf Resolution, giving President Johnson the power to take all necessary actions, including the use of armed force to defend South Vietnam's freedom. Although he now enjoyed wide latitude in prosecuting the war in Vietnam and although his poll numbers surged after the reprisal strikes against North Vietnam, Johnson preferred to forgo a policy of sustained bombing against North Vietnam so that Vietnam would not be made a dominant issue as the Democratic National Convention approached on August 24. The Tonkin Gulf incident focused attention on the role of North Vietnam and, as the situation in South Vietnam worsened, the circle of Johnson's civilian advisors began to think of increasing pressure on the North as a way to induce Hanoi to negotiate. Drawing a lesson from the Cuban Missile Crisis, during which confrontation with Khrushchev brought about a capitulation, they believed that a confrontation with Ho Chi Minh would force Hanoi to give up its aims in the South. Since it was vulnerable to American firepower to a degree that the elusive guerrillas were not—so the reasoning went—Hanoi could be induced to negotiate if threatened with the full force of American military might. William Bundy at the State Department and John McNaughton at the Defense Department, now the key planners for Vietnam, would coordinate this coercive diplomacy. Along with McNamara, they would control and calibrate the use of force to produce results without escalating the conflict into a confrontation with the Soviet Union and China.

It was at about this time that Frank Collbohm handed to Alex George, chairman of RAND's Social Science Department, a letter from a very high-ranking Air Force general. George remembered that Collbohm walked down the hall one day and accosted him, saying very casually, "Alex, I think you might be interested in seeing this letter." George replied, "Yes, I'd like to see it." He took it as a hint from Collbohm that he should draft a reply, which he did. The letter from the Air Force general said, in brief, that airpower had not been used properly in Vietnam and asked RAND what could be done to prevent criticism of the Air Force. The letter implied a belief that, if properly used in Vietnam, airpower could force the enemy to capitulate.

The letter reminded George of the Cuban Missile Crisis, which he had been studying, during which coercive diplomacy worked effectively for the United States. He believed, however, that coercive diplomacy would fail in Vietnam because there were important differences between the two cases. According to him, "One of the problems was that people over-generalized from the Cuban Missile Crisis, thinking that if we could use coercive diplomacy to force the Russians to back away . . . , which we did, why couldn't we do it with a much lesser power? Surely what worked against the Russians should work against the North Vietnamese. So I took issue with that as best I could at that time."[68] He made these points in his reply to the general, and Frank Collbohm sent it along.

Subsequently, Alex George was asked to give a briefing to the Air Force Advisory Group that came to RAND twice a year, and to the Board of Trustees, on the problem of comparing the Cuban Missile Crisis with Vietnam, and on the reasons why the two situations were different and "why the lessons of the Cuban Missile Crisis did not apply to Vietnam."[69] According to him, one critical difference was relative motivation. "In the Cuban missile crisis," he said, "Kennedy's job[,] among other things[,] was to convince Khrushchev that we—the United States—were more highly motivated by what was at stake in Cuba than the Russians were, that we had the advantage of superiority of motivation. This was critical in eventually getting Khrushchev to stop— which he started doing very quickly, as soon as we got in. But in the Vietnam case, one cannot say that we were more highly motivated by what was at stake than the North Vietnamese were—quite the opposite. . . . This was the gist of my talk, and the Air Force didn't like it at all, because it was critical of the Air Force."[70]

---

[68] Author interview with Alex George, 2004.

[69] Author interview with Alex George, 2004. The presentation was later edited and expanded a bit into *Some Thoughts on Graduated Escalation*, Santa Monica, Calif.: RAND Corporation, RM-4844-PR, December 1965. In this research memorandum, Alex George pointed out that, in addition, Vietnam offered U.S. policymakers a more complicated and difficult problem than earlier crises, such as the Korean War and the Cuban Missile Crisis, because the United States now had to deal, not in a bipolar world, but in a world where the communist movement was no longer monolithic. Instead of having to pressure only either the Soviet Union or Communist China, the United States in Vietnam had to deal with four independent communist protagonists: the Viet Cong, Hanoi, China, and the Soviet Union.

[70] Author interview with Alex George, 2004. Later, after he left RAND and joined the faculty of Stanford University, he wrote a book on coercive diplomacy, comparing the Vietnam case, the Laos case, and the Cuban Missile Crisis, in which he tried to "indicate how they were different from each other" and to identify the critical variables that influenced the outcomes, "to get away from the notion that coercive diplomacy was a simple tool. It isn't at all simple. It's a beguiling strategy in the sense that a strong power thinks that because we're much stronger than the opponent we should be able to coerce the opponent, and that's a very naive and overly simple view of the potential of coercive diplomacy." In the case of Vietnam, Alex George would prove to be correct on this score.

In spring 1964, the Joint Chiefs of Staff had organized a war game called SIGMA I to test the assumption that airpower would destroy North Vietnam's capacity to support the insurgency in the South. The outcome suggested that bombing would *not* achieve this objective. Walt Rostow, chairman of the State Department's Policy Planning Committee, questioned this conclusion and argued that, for airpower to work, it would only have to coerce North Vietnamese leaders to desist from supporting the Viet Cong—and that, to be effective, it would not have to destroy the North's capacity. To test his thesis, the War Games Division of the Joint Chiefs of Staff conducted another war game, called SIGMA II. Harry Rowen, who was then Deputy Assistant Secretary of Defense reporting to John McNaughton, was one of the participants. Other senior officials took part in the game, including the two Bundy brothers—McGeorge Bundy, LBJ's National Security Advisor, and William Bundy of the State Department—John McNaughton, and the Joint Chiefs of Staff. Robert McNamara, Secretary of State Dean Rusk, and Walt Rostow observed the game and were briefed on its conclusions.

Rowen remembered that, at the time the game was played, the situation in South Vietnam was deteriorating and the issue facing the United States was whether or not to bomb the North. He recalled that, in the game, the North was bombed and that he played Ho Chi Minh. According to Rowen, "The North Vietnamese faced a difficult situation. But our conclusion, which was very clear, was to proceed unchanged, we were sending supplies and people into the South, and we didn't relent at all. This went on for several months—that's when the game ended. . . . In the review afterwards, I remember being attacked for having represented the situation of North Vietnam in a very implausible way, unconvincing way. But that was the way we thought the North Vietnamese saw it. And we sort of just pressed on."[71]

SIGMA II raised serious doubts about Walt Rostow's assumption. As the game progressed, American bombing escalated, destroying all industrial targets in North Vietnam, and the ports in the North were mined. But the destruction of its industrial base had little impact on the agrarian economy of the North. The air attacks, rather than making Hanoi cease and desist, actually stiffened its resistance and led it to escalate the war in the South. Meanwhile, the Viet Cong were able to continue the insurgency by resorting to their stockpiles of weapons and ammunition and by relying on the civilian population for other needs. Frustrated in its strategy, the United States was forced to introduce ground troops into South Vietnam. But the situation in the South remained unstable, and popular support in the United States began to erode to the point where the American public favored withdrawing over fighting a protracted war. The conclusions of SIGMA II were prescient, but they had no influence over U.S. policy in Vietnam.

The debate among U.S. policymakers unfolded against the backdrop of a deteriorating situation in the South. Only a few months after the overthrow of President

---

[71] Author interview with Harry Rowen, 2005.

Diem, General Nguyen Khanh staged a coup d'etat and took over the government in January 1964. In the wake of this coup, province chiefs and commanders of major units were replaced with people deemed more loyal to the new government, and these changes further undermined the government of Viet Nam's control in the countryside and sapped the morale of the army. Desertion rates rose alarmingly. The prospects for stabilization looked dim, because many South Vietnamese generals were preoccupied with intrigue against Khanh. Public disorder mounted, with street riots against the unpopular new government and sectarian fights between Catholics and Buddhists.

In Saigon, as Zasloff and Donnell completed the interviews, they would send them to Guy Pauker in Santa Monica. Then, in about December 1964, after 145 interviews had been obtained, Pauker concluded that the information was valuable and decided to come to Saigon as the project was drawing to a close. Zasloff recalled that Pauker said, "Let's put out a briefing. I'll push the pencil."[72] They worked late into the night in the study at 176 Pasteur and collaborated amicably with each other. Pauker had great analytic skills and would take notes and make out index cards. He jotted down his favorite quote about the peasants only wanting a little plot of land and being left in peace. At the end, each came up with his own observations, which Pauker sorted out in a logical order, and then they performed the analysis, which was enlarged later for a RAND report entitled *Political Motivation and Morale.*[73]

Before leaving Vietnam in December, Zasloff and Donnell gave a series of briefings, starting with General Westmoreland. They presented a summary of their findings, focusing on the reasons the Viet Cong joined the movement, why they fought against the GVN [the Government of the Republic of Vietnam], and how their organization maintained morale and inner cohesion. The Viet Cong movement, the RAND analysts said, ranged from the "casual peasant supporter who occasionally bought supplies for the VC on a trip to the local market, to the most deeply dedicated cadre in the main forces."[74] These cadres were usually Viet Minh who had remained underground in the South or who had gone to North Vietnam in 1954 and had infiltrated back into the South sometime after 1959. These veterans of the war for independence against the French—men now in their 30s—whose commitment had deepened with time and experience in the movement, formed the backbone of the insurgency, and many were members of the Lao Dong or Communist Party. They saw the insurgency in the South as a nationalist struggle, a continuation of the fight for Vietnamese independence, and believed that they were fighting to bring about social justice, to eradicate poverty, and to redistribute land to the peasants.

---

[72] Author interview with Joe and Tela Zasloff, 2003.

[73] John C. Donnell, Guy J. Pauker, and J. Joseph Zasloff, *Viet Cong Motivation and Morale in 1964: A Preliminary Report*, Santa Monica, Calif.: RAND Corporation, RM-4507/3-ISA, March 1965.

[74] John C. Donnell, Guy J. Pauker, and Joseph J. Zasloff, *Viet Cong Motivation and Morale in 1964: A Preliminary Report*, Santa Monica, Calif.: RAND Corporation, RM-4507/3-ISA, March 1965, p. vii.

The younger Viet Cong—Zasloff and Donnell pointed out—joined for a variety of reasons, ranging from anger against social injustice, disaffection with the lack of educational and job opportunities in their villages, resentment against being drafted into the ARVN—which, in their view, was the army of a government that represented "the rich, the landowners, the city" while the Viet Cong were "for the poor"—a desire to escape unpleasant personal situations or to seek adventure, and a wish to protect the country from "the American imperialists and their lackeys, the GVN."[75] Once in the movement, these younger Viet Cong were controlled and motivated through a number of techniques borrowed from the Chinese Communists. The most effective were the formation of three-man cells within each squad to enforce discipline and solidarity, and the *kiem thao*—the criticism and self-criticism session—held daily to stimulate motivation and morale, deal with loneliness, and provide political indoctrination and after-action assessment. Zasloff and Donnell also pointed out that, after expanding their control, the Viet Cong had become the "effective government in a significant area of the countryside" and that the insurgency now had to be seen, not as a "jungle insurgency led by a band of committed Communist cadres," but as "as a war waged by an alternative government."[76]

General Westmoreland listened to their briefing with great interest. Zasloff thought that the MACV commander "was pleased to hear about the seriousness of the Viet Cong. At the time, there was still this widespread assertion that the Viet Cong were kidnapping their recruits for their units, and the story that we told [was] . . . that the Viet Cong saw themselves as patriots [who were] fighting to liberate the country and redistribute the land. We described their control mechanisms, the *kiem thao*, the three-man cell, and the role of indoctrination. It was the story of a really cohesive band of soldiers. . . . This description of the Viet Cong is old stuff by now, but in 1964 it was very fresh and new."[77]

Zasloff thought that the reason Westmoreland listened with tense attention was because the findings offered a "solid insight into the nature of the enemy" and explained why he was "having trouble with the Viet Cong." One of the questions Westmoreland asked has stuck in Zasloff's mind, "Do they believe in God?" Zasloff does not know why the general asked the question, and he does not remember how he answered. "I don't think I knew the answer," he recalled.[78]

Westmoreland asked them to brief General Maxwell Taylor, who had replaced Henry Cabot Lodge as U.S. ambassador, and Westmoreland sat in on that briefing. Zasloff recalled that Taylor listened with great attention. In the briefing, Zasloff and Donnell "didn't spare anything . . . including our account of the brutalization of

[75] Donnell, Pauker, and Zasloff, Viet Cong *Motivation and Morale in 1964*, 1965, pp. viii–ix.

[76] Donnell, Pauker, and Zasloff, *Viet Cong Motivation and Morale in 1964*, 1965, p. 23.

[77] Author interview with Joe Zasloff, 2003.

[78] Author interview with Joe Zasloff, 2003.

prisoners."[79] They mentioned the case of the senior captain at Chi Hoa prison who had been bound until he became deformed, and talked about the physical abuse that was endemic in the intelligence operation in Vietnam. The account of torture brought a reaction, and Zasloff remembered, "I can see Westmoreland blanching at that and Taylor blanching."[80] Whether, following the briefing, Westmoreland and Taylor tried to put an end to the physical abuse of prisoners, the fact remains that mistreatment and torture continued. According to Zasloff, the reference to prisoner brutalization later "got sanitized in the report" when it was publicly released in July 1968.[81]

Before this briefing, at the end of November, General Maxwell Taylor had sent a pessimistic evaluation of the situation in South Vietnam to Washington. What Zasloff and Donnell had to say probably reinforced his sense of gloom about the prospects for South Vietnam and his feeling that he was dealing with a formidable foe. In early November, the Viet Cong had staged a daring attack on the air base at Bien Hoa, near Saigon, to which McNamara had dispatched a B-57 bomber unit after the Gulf of Tonkin incidents, to show U.S. determination. Four Americans were killed and 72 were wounded. Seventeen of the 36 B-57 aircraft were destroyed. The Viet Cong escaped. In his November assessment, Taylor had expressed surprise over the strength and resiliency of the Viet Cong, who were demonstrating the "recuperative powers of the phoenix" and an "amazing ability to maintain morale." He had also concluded that the prospect for improving the GVN was remote and had stated his belief that only direct attacks against North Vietnam would provide a glimmer of hope in boosting the morale in South Vietnam and might keep a moribund GVN alive.

After briefing General Westmoreland and Ambassador Maxwell Taylor, Zasloff and Donnell presented their findings to Westmoreland's senior staff at MACV head-quarters. David Morell arranged the meeting. He recalled that a couple of generals were there, including Westmoreland; Richard Stillwell, Commander of U.S. Army XXIV Corps; Carl Youngdale, Chief of Staff for Intelligence; Colonel Jack T. Young, the head of J-2 (intelligence); and Colonel B. Ward, "a tough-minded colonel" from J-3 (operations.).[82] According to Morell, the presentation "burst like a bombshell," and as the RAND analysts spoke, "it became increasingly clear that the military people were getting very discomfited. What they were hearing was very different from what they wanted to hear. It didn't make any sense in the context of American strategy," which was widening U.S. military presence in the South and getting more aggressive toward the North. According to Morell, it was a shock for the senior officers at MACV "to have this presentation[,] which was basically set in the context of Vietnamese modern history," describing the Viet Cong as the successors to the Viet Minh—"peasants who

---

[79] Author interview with Joe Zasloff, 2003.

[80] Author interview with Joe Zasloff, 2003.

[81] Author interview with Joe Zasloff, 2003.

[82] Author interview with David Morell, 2004.

had something to fight for" and who had joined the guerrillas with "some voluntarism," especially among the best elements of the VC.[83] The RAND team was painting a discouraging picture—one that was different from what these officers had come to believe about the enemy—at a juncture when American commitment was deepening.

Morell recalled that the senior officers were unhappy, unbelieving, and critical, but it was "less what they said than the sense of a kind of a pall falling [on] the room."[84] They would point out the complexities of Vietnam to rebut the conclusions that the Viet Cong were committed and dedicated; that the United States was dealing with peasant nationalism; that there was great anger against government exploitation and official corruption, and against the Strategic Hamlet Program, which had forced peasants to move from their homes and abandon the tombs of their ancestors; and that the villagers perceived Saigon and the Americans as their enemies.

The senior MACV staff could not bring themselves to believe this last point, because to them the Americans were "the good guys" in Vietnam. They would ask questions along the lines of, "How could this be?" "How could they [the peasants] be so angry at us when we're offering . . . roads, and we're going to give them electricity and running water?" "Aren't they [the Viet Cong] evil? Don't they kill village chiefs? Don't they kill civilians?" "Are you sure they [the prisoners and defectors] were telling the truth?" "It can't be true . . ." that the Americans were not being looked upon as the "good guys" fighting on the right side.[85] Judging from the reaction of the top officers at MACV, Morell believed that if they had known beforehand where the project was leading, they would have tried to put a stop to it.

Following this series of briefings in Saigon, Zasloff and Donnell left for Washington, stopping in Hawaii to present their findings to the Commander in Chief of the Pacific (CINCPAC). Toward the end of January 1965, they made their first briefing to John McNaughton, who had sponsored the study. This was the highest level they reached in Washington. Zasloff remembered sitting in a big Pentagon room with green and red lights that would light up and messages would come in, interrupting them, about one operation or another. Harry Rowen remembered that he was present at the meeting, although he was now dealing with NATO issues. Working for McNaughton, he "couldn't help but be exposed to some of this stuff [on Vietnam] because it was so important and it was happening." He recalled that he and the other people in the audience found the presentation powerful. According to him, the description of the "character of the [Viet Cong] organization, the background, the nature of the organization, the resilience . . . provided a new insight" and made an impression on him. He remembered that the briefing lasted about 45 minutes, and, when it concluded, "there was a silence in the room. . . . McNaughton and I looked at each other, and I said,

---

[83] Author interview with Joe Zasloff, 2003.

[84] Author interview with Joe Zasloff, May 2003.

[85] Author interview with Joe Zasloff, 2003.

'John, I think we're signed up with the wrong side—the side that's going to lose this war.' And he agreed. What we had heard was such a description, and from what we can tell a very accurate description, of such a strong institution, the Viet Cong, that we were in deep trouble."[86]

Zasloff remembered a comment John McNaughton made in response to the description of the solidarity of the Viet Cong and the *kiem thao*, "They sound like monks," McNaughton said, because to someone like him who was not familiar with Asian communism the austerity and discipline reminded him of a "religious order."[87] Although Zasloff and Donnell did not make any policy recommendations, their description of the Viet Cong implied that the United States was facing a strong and dedicated enemy who "could only be defeated at enormous costs, if at all." The reaction of Harry Rowen and John McNaughton indicated that they had reached the same conclusion.

Asked about McNaughton's reaction to the Zasloff-Donnell briefing, Daniel Ellsberg, a RAND analyst who was serving as John McNaughton's assistant in that period, said that, privately, John McNaughton "wanted us out of that war . . . [regardless of] whether [or not] the NLF was highly motivated. . . . He wanted out of the war. . . . That was little known. His colleagues in the government didn't know that because he carried McNamara's water; he took McNamara's line, and that was 'bomb, get in there.'"[88] According to Ellsberg, McNaughton neither believed in bombing the North nor in sending U.S. ground combat troops to the South, but he went along with his boss, Robert McNamara, out of loyalty.

Zasloff recalled that Daniel Ellsberg was at the briefing—although Ellsberg remembered that he was in the next room, and talked to Zasloff after the presentation. According to Zasloff, Ellsberg was moved by the description of the guerrillas as "selfless, cohesive, dedicated Viet Cong soldiers who saw themselves as patriots, particularly within the context of a corrupt South Vietnam and a disintegrating army." Zasloff recalled that Ellsberg came up to him afterward and asked, "Do they deserve to win?" Zasloff thought that it was a romantic question and was a bit taken aback by it. Ellsberg did not ask questions such as, "What would be the implications of a Communist victory?" or "What would it mean for the Vietnamese interests, and what would it mean for American interests?" Instead, he posed a moral question. Zasloff speculated that, at that point, Ellsberg who had been a hawk "must have been in his transition phase; he was beginning to question his own views."[89]

After the Pentagon, Zasloff and Donnell repeated their briefing for the Vietnam Task Force—now headed by Leonard Unger—and other State Department officials.

---

[86] Author interview with Harry Rowen, 2005.

[87] Author interview with Joe Zasloff, 2003.

[88] Author interview with Daniel Ellsberg, 2004.

[89] Author interview with Joe Zasloff, 2003.

The comment from the State Department audience that Zasloff remembered best came from Evelyn Colbert, the head of the Southeast Asia section of Intelligence Research. Zasloff describes her as "an old pro," because she had served in the Office of Strategic Services—the precursor of the CIA —during World War II and was a long-time State Department professional. Zasloff recalled that she said, "Your report reminds me of Foreign Service officers coming out of China for the first time, reporting on the Chinese Communists"—referring to people like John Stewart Service and John Paton Davies, who had returned with stories about the Chinese Communists similar to what he and Donnell were saying about the Viet Cong. According to Zasloff, she was saying in effect "you're really bringing a fresh perspective on the Viet Cong just as these Foreign Service officers came out and gave us rich materials on the Chinese Communists. Up until then, people were saying that the Chinese Communists were kidnapping their recruits and dragooning them into their military force. We were saying that the Viet Cong was a revolutionary army, and there was a great component of nationalism—that's what we learned about the Viet Cong: They saw themselves as Vietnamese patriots and nationalists and saw their enemies as imperialists."[90]

The RAND team also presented their findings to the Joint Chiefs of Staff, the Defense Intelligence Agency, the Air Staff, and ARPA. However, according to Pauker, McNaughton never delivered the results to the Defense Secretary, and McNamara did not ask to talk to the RAND analysts. It is not clear why McNaughton did not forward the findings to him or arrange for him to be briefed. Perhaps McNaughton thought that, even if McNamara found out the answers to his questions "Who are the Viet Cong?" and "What makes them tick?" this knowledge would come too late, because the United States was already too deeply involved in Vietnam to back out, regardless of how strong and cohesive the Viet Cong were.

In fact, by the end of 1964, McNaughton and William Bundy had concluded that American "international prestige" and influence were "directly at risk" in South Vietnam and that withdrawing without first taking strong military action would damage American credibility in Asia. Back in September 1964, McNaughton had advanced the theory of the United States as "the good doctor" who tended to the patient (South Vietnam) to the extent of being "willing to keep promises, be tough, take risks, get bloodied, and hurt the enemy badly." Even if it failed in its efforts, it would demonstrate its "willingness to go to the mat" and in so doing "bolster allied confidence in the U.S. as an ally."[91] In short, the United States had staked its credibility and would have to press on. To this, McNaughton added that what was at stake in Vietnam was the need to secure the "buffer real estate near Thailand and Malaysia" and "our reputa-

---

[90] Author interview with Joe Zasloff, 2003.

[91] Cited in Frederick Logevall, *Choosing War: The Lost Chance for Peace and the Escalation of War in Vietnam*, University of California Press, Berkeley, Los Angeles, London, 1999, p. 272.

tion." Ensuring "a better, freer way of life" for the people of South Vietnam was only a secondary objective.

According to official records, McNaughton and William Bundy agreed with George Ball, the Under Secretary of State, who argued that, although Saigon had "the smell of death," the United States should make this attempt in order to hold the line in Thailand, but that it should be prepared to accept defeat. Since failure was a possible and acceptable outcome, the RAND findings implying that the United States was "in deep trouble" and that it was aligned "with the side that was going to lose this war" only confirmed that the road ahead was fraught with perils. The delivery of the findings illustrated one of the problems of research: By the time the results were tabulated, analyzed, and presented, they might have been overtaken by events. The Viet Cong Motivation and Morale Project started when U.S. policy toward Vietnam had not been firmly set, but when the analysts brought their answers to Washington, positions had hardened.

At the time Zasloff and Donnell were making their rounds of presentation in Washington, the situation in South Vietnam had deteriorated further. The Viet Cong now controlled half of the countryside and one-quarter of the rural population. They were on the verge of cutting South Vietnam in half by driving from the Central Highlands to the provinces along the seacoast. The political situation was rife with turmoil. The opposition to Khanh had grown more intense, with Buddhists staging uprisings in major cities and holding protests with strong anti-American overtones. In Hue, the former imperial capital and a city known for its xenophobia, students ransacked the United States Information Service library. In Saigon, Ambassador Maxwell Taylor was under increasing pressure from Washington to get rid of Khanh, but the general refused to relinquish power. By the end of January 1965, McNamara began to press President Johnson to take resolute action to save South Vietnam from "the brink of collapse." McGeorge Bundy concurred with him, telling the president that the "time has come for harder choice" and recommending using American power to "force a change in Communist policy." The alternative, he informed Johnson, would be to "negotiate a withdrawal" in order to salvage "what little can be preserved, with no major addition to our present military risks."

Lyndon Johnson, not wanting to be the president to lose Vietnam, decided to act decisively on the advice of McGeorge Bundy and McNamara. However, he lacked an incident that would give him a legitimate excuse to resume air attacks against the North. In the hope of provoking such an incident, U.S. destroyers were ordered back to patrol the Gulf of Tonkin on February 3. As McGeorge Bundy recalled later, it was "like waiting for a streetcar." On February 7, during McGeorge Bundy's fact-finding mission in Vietnam, the Viet Cong handed Johnson such an excuse. Their sappers infiltrated the U.S. advisor's compound and airfield in Pleiku, in the Central Highlands, and attacked with mortar rounds, causing explosions that killed eight American servicemen, wounded more than 100 others, and burned 20 aircraft parked on the airstrip. McGeorge Bundy, who had previously dismissed U.S. casualties in Vietnam as no more significant than traffic-related deaths in the Washington area, flew to Pleiku with General Westmoreland and reacted emotionally to the scene of death and destruction. The streetcar he had been waiting for "had arrived."[92] Bundy recommended a new policy, with the bombing of North Vietnam as the centerpiece, not because he believed that this would win the war but because, like McNaughton, he was convinced that, without making a valiant effort, the United States would face charges in many parts of the world and in America itself that "we did not do all that we could have done." Although he put the chances for engineering a favorable outcome at 25 percent, he thought that the "value of the effort . . . exceed[s] its cost."

American retaliatory strikes against the North occurred swiftly on February 7, marking the beginning of Operation Flaming Dart I, a limited bombing campaign against carefully selected targets located south of the 19th parallel in North Vietnam. Then, on February 18, the Joint Chiefs of Staff ordered the implementation of Rolling Thunder I, the continuous air campaign that would last for over three years and drop 630,000 tons of bombs on North Vietnam. This sustained bombing campaign was meant as a signal to Hanoi to change its behavior. By inflicting pain, Rolling Thunder would induce the North to lower its support of the insurgency, which, in turn, would allow the GVN to make military progress, boost its morale, and encourage it to increase its effectiveness. The attacks on North Vietnam might have lifted spirits in the South but did little to stiffen the resolve of the GVN or to end instability.

General Khanh narrowly escaped an aborted coup attempt in which Colonel Pham Ngoc Thao, a secret Viet Cong agent, played a central role. The Armed Forces Council, which included senior South Vietnamese generals, lost patience with Khanh and demanded his resignation. He left the country to go into exile on February 25. Ambassador Taylor finally had succeeded in removing this irritant. The insurgency, however, raged on, as Hanoi intensified attacks to destroy the ARVN before the United States could enter the war on the ground. American and South Vietnamese casualties grew alarmingly, morale sank in the South Vietnamese army, and desertions rose to over 350 per day.

At the end of February 1965, President Johnson took another irrevocable step in turning the war into an American war. At the request of General Westmoreland and the Joint Chiefs of Staff, he approved the deployment of a helicopter squadron, as well as two Marine battalions to Danang, just below the Demilitarized Zone (DMZ), to guard the air base that was being used for Rolling Thunder.

In Saigon, Ambassador Taylor opposed the introduction of American combat units, fearing that the political costs would outweigh any military gains. He believed that the presence of American soldiers would evoke memories of French colonialism and provoke a hostile reaction among the Vietnamese population. Besides, American

---

[92] McMaster, *Dereliction of Duty*, 1997, p. 215.

troops were not adept at fighting an insurgency, and their operations would inevitably cause civilian casualties, which would feed anti-American hostility and create the perception that the United States was waging "a white man's war against the brown." He predicted that, instead of stiffening the resolve of the South Vietnamese army and making it more aggressive, the introduction of American troops would induce it to slacken and leave the Americans to shoulder the full burden of the war.

Taylor resisted as long as he could, but finally informed the GVN of the impending landing and arranged for it to put forth a request for the dispatch of the Marines to maintain the fig leaf of South Vietnamese sovereignty. General Westmoreland, on the other hand, had no reservations about bringing in U.S. combat units. In the aftermath of the attack on the Pleiku airfield, he informed General Earle Wheeler, Chairman of the Joint Chiefs of Staff, that U.S. combat forces might be needed to protect American facilities and personnel in Danang, the greater Saigon area, and Nha Trang. He was encouraged by President Johnson's approval of the dispatch of two battalions of Marines and urged more deployment of Marines in the future. On March 9, the Marines landed in Danang.

While the Viet Cong Motivation and Morale Project was proceeding, other Vietnam studies were also undertaken by RAND. They were not part of a comprehensive research plan RAND had developed for Vietnam but, rather, responses to requests from clients, although an attempt was made in November 1964 to set up such an integrated approach. The ad hoc committee[93] created for this purpose by Frank Collbohm and chaired by Charlie Zwick of the Economics Department met frequently between November 1964 and January 1965, and issued its report in February 1965.[94] The committee thought RAND could play a role in research "involving national, policy, doctrine, and techniques related to countering Communist revolutionary warfare," in which it would have a "significant opportunity to influence policy and techniques."[95]

However, RAND had to be selective in choosing areas of research to match its areas of expertise. For this reason, the committee recommended that RAND initiate research in revolutionary warfare, focusing on Vietnam, where RAND had made a heavy professional investment, as a case study of insurgency and counterinsurgency so that it could assess U.S. experience, highlight communist techniques and strategy, and help establish a better analytic framework for addressing other revolutionary problems. Second, RAND should study major policy alternatives the United States could pursue in Southeast Asia. The committee recommended integrating the fragmentary work being undertaken and synthesizing the fragments to deal with the larger issues of secu-

---

[93] The members of the committee were Bill Graham and Jack Ellis from Engineering, Joe Goldsen and Guy Pauker from Social Science, and M. W. Hoag, Charlie Zwick, and Richard Moorsteen from Economics.

[94] See Charles J. Zwick et al., "RAND's Southeast Asia Research Program," Santa Monica, Calif.: RAND Corporation, D-13381, February 5, 1965.

[95] Goldberg, "RAND and Vietnam," 1969, p. 12.

rity and policy in Southeast Asia. The committee recognized that implementing such an ambitious research program implied that RAND would have to double or triple its current effort.[96]

However, RAND's vaunted systems analysis approach was not applied in Southeast Asia, despite the committee's recommendation. There is no evidence that RAND management implemented the report. The main reason was that its clients were not interested in broader syntheses of strategy and policy issues. Either through departmental or individual interest, work continued on some aspects of the two major research areas recommended by the committee, but no grand research scheme was implemented.[97] As the Vietnam War escalated, RAND's major clients—ARPA and the Air Force—focused on short-term, operational studies to address specific technical problems relating to the prosecution of the war, and RAND responded to this need. Such works absorbed the energy and time of RAND's specialists, who otherwise might have devoted their attention to broader studies.

In 1964, RAND's disparate works in Vietnam included the study of a village undergoing pacification. The request, in this instance, came from General William Westmoreland himself, who had put his faith in pacification as a way to win the war—a faith that Ambassador Taylor described as unrealistic in his November 1964 report to Washington. After General Khanh took over the government, he had initiated a new pacification program called *Chien Thang*, or "Victory." It was modeled loosely on the failed Strategic Hamlet Program, but would not resort to forced resettlement and was to have better planning and execution. It, too, was based on the "spreading oil slick" concept—consolidating government control in one area before pushing out into another one—and would secure the countryside through a combination of military, paramilitary, police, and economic activities, and social reforms.

General Westmoreland, after taking over as commander of MACV in June 1964, had himself initiated an accelerated pacification program—called *Hop Tac*, or "Working Together," to indicate that it was a joint program with the GVN, rather than an American undertaking—in six provinces surrounding Saigon, to secure the capital and its environs. He called this a "laboratory experiment in pacification." At this point, Westmoreland was optimistic that the situation was stabilizing and that he could turn it around. As part of his plan to reverse the situation, he requested additional American military personnel, which would grow from 16,000 to 22,000 in the coming months, and initiated *Hop Tac*. The aim was to restore security to the zones closer to Saigon first and then expand government control outward until all six provinces were pacified and the Viet Cong were pushed from the doorstep of the capital. After stalling for a while, *Hop Tac* would eventually achieve some success, but the *Chien Thang* pacification program would do little toward reestablishing GVN control in the countryside.

---

[96] See Zwick et al., "RAND's Southeast Asia Research Program," 1965.

[97] Goldberg, "RAND and Vietnam," 1969, p. 12.

With his interest in and hope for pacification, General Westmoreland asked for a study of a Vietnamese village as it evolved from guerrilla to government control through pacification. His request was relayed to the ARPA R&D Field Unit in Saigon, and AGILE in 1964 sponsored the study with Michael Pearce of RAND. Pearce had been a summer intern at RAND while he was getting a graduate degree at the University of Washington. Jack Ellis hired him after he completed his studies. Ellis remembered that Pearce, a social scientist, "was a real gung-ho, young fellow" who had studied Vietnamese and could apparently speak it fluently. He was, besides, not reluctant to relocate to Vietnam, and he and his wife moved to Saigon in 1963.[98]

For the village study, Mike Pearce chose Duc Lap, about 20 miles west of Saigon, for its relative security and proximity to the city, allowing him to commute in and out safely over a two-month period to observe firsthand the process of pacification and the interaction between the villagers, the GVN, the South Vietnamese army, and the insurgents. Duc Lap was located in Hau Nghia Province, where the Viet Cong were very active. Originally, the project was planned as a short-term study. However, as it progressed, Pearce thought that the evolution of Duc Lap as it went through different phases of pacification was too complex to be adequately examined in one short report. So, to avoid making a superficial survey, he decided to write three reports, covering in succession the conditions before pacification, the situation as it existed at the time, and future prospects for the village. The first report, which dealt with the more timely topic of what Duc Lap had undergone after eight months of pacification, was published in April 1965. It concluded that the results had been mixed, and that pacification had achieved success, as well as meeting with failure. Security was still not ensured, even with the presence of an ARVN battalion during the pacification phase, and the village chief could only move within four of the six hamlets that made up the village. If the battalion were to leave before the village could develop its own local defense force, the Viet Cong would return in a matter of days, or even hours.[99]

The presence of ARVN units in their midst could be more a bane than a blessing for the population. In this first report, Pearce did not mention the problems the ARVN 22nd Division was causing in the area. Seymour Deitchman, who knew Mike Pearce, recalled that during one of his frequent trips to Vietnam, Pearce told him, "The ARVN 22nd Division [units] are inactive and corrupt. The Viet Cong attack a village, they're 500 yards away and they don't come to the rescue, and they bleed the villagers of money and everything else." Deitchman included this story in his trip report, which went to McNamara. Deitchman heard later that McNamara called General Earle Wheeler, the JCS Chairman, and said, "What about this? I thought you told me that was under control." Wheeler apparently gave him an evasive answer along the line

---

[98] Author interview with Jack Ellis, 2003 and 2004.

[99] Michael R. Pearce, *Evolution of a Vietnamese Village, Part I: The Present, After Eight Months of Pacification,"* Santa Monica, Calif.: RAND Corporation, RM-4552-1-ARPA, April 1965.

of "We're working on it"—and the matter went away. According to Deitchman, "Mike found out there was this problem but nothing was done about it. I think that was kind of endemic with regard to observations from outside 'the system.'"[100]

As General Westmoreland increased the number of American military personnel from 16,000 to, eventually, 22,000 (a third of whom served as advisors within the South Vietnamese armed forces), ARPA became interested in how to improve the Americans' relationship with their Vietnamese counterparts and render their performance more effective. As Sy Deitchman explained the problem, American advisors in the field had the responsibility of carrying out policies set in Washington, but had received little training in how to cope with a culture so different from their own. Their stay was usually short and did not afford them the opportunity to learn more about the people they were advising. As an illustration of the cultural problem an advisor might encounter, he cited the example of U.S. Special Forces advisors working with the Montagnards and getting caught in the age-old conflict between the tribes and the Vietnamese. When a tribal chief was asked what he would do with the weapons he had requested from the Americans, he replied that he would not use them to fight the Viet Cong but to push the South Vietnamese out of his land.[101]

RAND asked Gerry Hickey to conduct this study in 1964, and he spent ten months in the field. While gathering data in the Central Highlands, Hickey was caught in an enemy attack against the U.S. Special Forces camp at Nam Dong on July 6, 1964, that killed 250 people on both sides. The attack, which failed to capture Nam Dong, had been carefully planned with the inside support of the Viet Cong, who had infiltrated into the ranks of the South Vietnamese militia stationed in the camp. It was carried out by a 900-man regiment, supported with a battery of mortars. Many of Hickey's field notes were destroyed in the bloody battle. In recognition of his help in moving ammunition and weapons during the fierce attack, the Special Forces gave Hickey a post-action commendation. The surviving commander of the Special Forces at Nam Dong suspected that the attackers had come not from local guerrilla forces but from a regiment that had infiltrated from North Vietnam. In their interview sample, Zasloff and Donnell themselves had come across a number of North Vietnamese infiltrators, as opposed to regroupees returning South, and, as Zasloff recalled later, their appearance indicated that the North was beginning to send its own troops to the South in response to increased American pressure. It was a harbinger of things to come, he would say later.

For his counterpart study, Hickey interviewed a total of 350 American advisors of all categories, both individually and in small groups. He also visited predeployment training sites in the United States. His report, written in collaboration with Phil Davi-

---

[100]Author interview with Sy Deitchman, 2005.

[101] Deitchman, *The Best-Laid Schemes*, 1976, pp. 13–15.

son, another RAND consultant, was published in March 1965.[102] From his interviews and his visits, Hickey found that, in general, relations between U.S. military advisors and their Vietnamese counterparts were not as close and productive as they should be. He identified the main obstacles to understanding and cooperation, and the skills required to overcome those barriers and succeed. Among the keys to success—beyond professional competence—was the advisor's ability to gain rapport with his counterpart, the amount of time he spent with his counterpart, and the extent to which he shared his counterpart's experience: sharing food and bivouac, and even the dangers of combat.

Hickey recommended screening candidates for aptitude in working with foreigners and training advisors in advance of their deployment in language skills, in Vietnamese culture and customs, in the structure of the South Vietnamese army, and in the performance of civic action. He recommended extending the tour of duty beyond six months, since, just as they began to establish a working relationship with their counterparts, the field advisors had to leave. He suggested reducing bureaucratic demands on advisors to a minimum to relieve them of excessive paperwork that required them to supply data that could be gathered elsewhere just as efficiently. He recommended instituting continuity, with departing advisors briefing incoming advisors and leaving behind records about their counterparts and the advice that had been given and rejected so that their successors would avoid repeating mistakes and not waste time learning through trial and error. Sy Deitchman thought Hickey's report was excellent; since it provided what the system was looking for, it was accepted. General Westmoreland made it required reading for the MACV staff, but changes in the selection, training, and assignment of advisors were hard to detect. So, the report had a practical benefit, but its long-term effect was not discernible.[103]

To conduct this project, Hickey returned to Saigon in 1964. He found that the city had changed for the worse. Grenade attacks had forced sidewalk cafes to move indoors, and most of the elegant French shops along the main downtown street had disappeared. He moved into a small apartment that had a telephone, a luxury in Saigon in those days. A true anthropologist, instead of being taken aback by the Vietnamese quarters near the central market in which he found himself and by the people living in the small, poor enclave near his apartment building—some of whom worked as cyclo drivers and sidewalk food vendors—he found this little traditional slice of Vietnam fascinating. Since he spoke Vietnamese, he was able to connect with his neighbors and, in a small measure, become a part of their world. He helped the cyclo drivers by giving them generous fares and money to purchase traditional medicine; his cook occasionally bought him beef noodle soup from one of the vendors—which he found delicious;

---

[102] Gerald C. Hickey and W. P. Davison, *The American Military Advisor and His Foreign Counterpart: The Case of Vietnam*, Santa Monica, Calif.: RAND Corporation, RM-4482-ARPA, March 1965.

[103] Deitchman, *The Best-Laid Schemes*, 1976, pp. 404–405.

he participated in annual rituals honoring the Five Goddesses whom the residents worshipped at an altar set up at the foot of a gnarled banyan tree. And he observed with interest the comings and goings of the people in the neighborhood, and the rhythm of their daily routine. He could tell the hours of the day by the type of food the sidewalk vendors set out to entice customers: noodle soup in the morning; rice and stir-fried dishes at lunchtime; and snacks and beer, rice alcohol, and Chinese brandy in the late afternoon as the residents gathered to relax after a hard day's work.

While the Viet Cong Motivation and Morale Project cut a big swath in Saigon and Washington, Jack Ellis soldiered on with technical research projects. In 1964, through a former fraternity brother at Berkeley who was now working for the Air Force in Vietnam, Ellis was contracted to study the vulnerability of air operations to enemy ground fire as a way of helping pilots set up and carry out their mission. Ellis spent about three months in Vietnam, from May to July 1964, performing the "Aircraft Losses Operations Analysis," which he refers to as "the hit probability" study. The objective of the research was to analyze the effectiveness of Viet Cong anti-aircraft and small-arms ground fire on Vietnamese and U.S. air operations, and to recommend tactics, procedures, and equipment to counteract Viet Cong ground fire. Using after-action reports filed by the Air Force units, they extracted information on how often aircraft got shot at, with how many rounds each time, and at what altitude and speed the planes were flying when they were hit. Then they compiled a database and "massaged" the information to show "where you were vulnerable, where you weren't, and how you could avoid being shot at."[104]

Most of the projects that Jack Ellis supported with his ARPA budget in 1964 were similar to his "hit probability" study in their use of statistics and in their effort to derive meanings from numbers. McNamara and his civilian staff believed in statistics and quantitative analysis, and the American military in Vietnam obliged them with reams of data. As Gerry Hickey pointed out in his advisor study, even American personnel in the field were overburdened with gathering data and sending it in to feed this demand. There was no shortage, then, of statistics for Ellis's team to wade through and, at times, to get tangled up in the numbers.

Perhaps the ultimate statistical-analysis project at this time was the "Factor and Content Analysis" performed by Ron Jones with the assistance of Joel Edelman. Ron Jones, a former helicopter pilot, was a professor of business at the University of Missouri in Kansas City and had accumulated a great deal of experience in doing programming for large research projects. Joel Edelman was a young staff member in RAND's Aero-Astronautics Department who had been newly hired from Columbia University. When Edelman interviewed at Columbia for the job, he was told that his work "might involve travel to Southeast Asia and going to Vietnam."[105] The thought of going to

---

[104] Author interview with Jack Ellis, 2003 and 2004.

[105] Author interview with Joel Edelman, 2005.

Vietnam made him feel adventurous rather than hesitant. Edelman believed that he was hired because RAND was looking for someone with a background in electronics and communications to send to Vietnam. At first, it looked as though he might get to go to Saigon, but things did not work out. Then Ron Jones came on board and Edelman was assigned to work on the "Factor and Content Analysis."

Edelman did not remember how the project started and whether the idea came from ARPA or somewhere else, but there was some discussion "that we started a project [on] which Ron Jones was the lead researcher to draft a computer program that would hopefully be able to tell us what the trends were and make some predictions about how we could predict how things were going—how could we assess progress."[106] In short, the objective was to develop a program that would answer the "ultimate question" of how to measure the progress of counterinsurgency. It was not that there was a dearth of data to provide the answer. In fact, there were data on a host of things—such as combat incidents, number of wounded and killed, number of attacks initiated by the ARVN, and so on—but no one knew for sure what it all added up to. When they looked into what kind of classified and unclassified data they could gather, they quickly found out that they were "awash in data." As he remembered later, "You name it, we had the data for it."[107]

In their program, they included all the data they had access to: political data, such as voting trends; data on combat incidents initiated by both sides; economic data, including rice production and distribution; data on weather; at the suggestion of George Young, data on the correlation between Viet Cong incidents and the phases of the moon; and even newspaper reports on trends in Vietnam that they "found a way to code." According to Edelman, they threw everything into the program, including "the Vietnamese version of the kitchen sink."[108] It was a massive program, on a scale that no one had attempted to do before.

The project ultimately involved many people. According to Edelman, "We took some off-the-shelf computer programs that had been developed by the UCLA medical school, called the Bio-Medical Series, and we adapted them. It turned out to be a real mistake. We would have been better off starting from scratch. Once we were into it that far, it was too late to go back and start again."[109] The lead military person overseeing the progress of the project and to whom they reported was Admiral Harry Felt, the CINCPAC commander. Edelman described him as a small, crusty man, who looked like someone "straight out of central casting of what we would expect an admiral from World War II to be like." For the project, Edelman spent three months in 1965 in

---

[106] Author interview with Joel Edelman, 2005.

[107] Author interview with Joel Edelman, 2005.

[108] Author interview with Joel Edelman, 2005.

[109] Author interview with Joel Edelman, 2005.

Hawaii "running the . . . program on the CINCPAC computers, in this underground [beneath] Sugar Loaf Hill in Pearl Harbor."[110]

The end product, according to Edelman, was a program that "gave precise results" but the team was not sure that they "were accurate." Edelman remembered that, "we had precision without accuracy. We could tell for the second decimal place from the results what was going on, but we had no idea whether it was true. . . . The program worked in the sense that it produced results which we could never truly interpret."[111] Part of the problem was due to the use of the computer programs developed by UCLA, to which the team had to adapt by "tack[ing] things on." The whole reminded Edelman of a 1950s automobile that the Cubans patch up with homemade spare parts to keep it running. Part of the problem was due to the IBM 7090 computer, then the "largest and fastest computer available," which they contracted with TRW to use.

Edelman recalled that the computer failed "most of the time" because of "the errors going from tape to disk, and from the central processor back to tape, back to disk. . . . The computer . . . made a lot of errors. It threw off a lot of our . . . very fine-grained and very sensitive calculations. We had less confidence in the results. . . . We couldn't in good conscience say, 'Well, this says this, and it's true.' We didn't really know because of the errors." So, the program was of very limited value "in terms of being able to make predictions that were useful for either the civilian administration to make plans, or to really assess progress. I don't think it ever really got used as a predictive device." The head of CINCPAC operations research, a former professor at the University of Pennsylvania, was disappointed because the project failed to meet expectations. Edelman remembered that the stress level was so high for him that he stopped using computers for over a decade.[112]

These statistical analyses and technical research projects, such as the earlier ones undertaken under Ellis's management, might have had their place and their use, but they did not add up to a significant contribution. As Frank Collbohm searched for other research areas, besides social science, for which RAND could "pull its weight," he came to the Economics Department and a study of the American aid program in South Vietnam. The study was undertaken at the request of USAID to better align American aid with the counterinsurgency effort.[113] It was put under the direction of Charlie Zwick, Hans Heymann, Dick Moorsteen, and Chuck Cooper. In May and June 1964, the four RAND economists spent six weeks in Vietnam. This project would be the first in a string of studies on the war by Economics. These economists formed a powerful team from one of the most prominent divisions at RAND. Like the Social Science Division, the Economics Division was set up as an outcome of the conference

---

[110] Author interview with Joel Edelman, 2005.

[111] Author interview with Joel Edelman, 2005.

[112] Author interview with Joel Edelman, 2005.

[113] Management Committee Meeting Minutes, April 29, 1964, RAND Archive.

held by RAND in New York in 1948, with Charles Hitch as its first chairman. Hitch was born in Boonville, Missouri, on January 9, 1910. He attended the University of Arizona as an undergraduate, receiving a bachelor's degree with highest distinction after two years of study. He then went to Harvard for a graduate degree in economics. In his first year there, he received a Rhodes Scholarship and left for Oxford, where he was elected a fellow "don" at Queens College in 1935. During World War II, he worked for a time for Ambassador Averell Harriman's lend-lease mission in London. After the war, Hitch returned to teaching at Oxford. In 1947, he went to the University of Sao Paolo in Brazil as a visiting professor, and it was there that he received an invitation to attend the RAND conference in New York in 1948. Subsequently, RAND got in touch with him and offered him the job of setting up the Economics Division as its first chairman.[114]

According to Hitch, he spent most of his time during his first two to three years at RAND hiring people and organizing the division, with units such as Economic Analysis, Logistics, and Cost Analysis. Hitch would recruit a prominent staff, which included Harry Rowen and Alain Enthoven, two other Rhodes Scholars. Hitch would also initiate the base study led by Albert Wohlstetter, which helped establish RAND as a premier strategic research organization. Gus Shubert, who joined the division in the 1960s, said that Economic Analysis in particular provided a lot of leadership, and the economic analysis of defense performed by Hitch and his team was path-breaking. The Economics Division ". . . through the years did much to give RAND work its distinctive character. That is, the Economics Division helped impart an awareness of cost considerations in the broadest sense and their importance in guiding choice under uncertainty—a way of looking at military problems that has come to figure prominently in the RAND research effort."[115] In time, the Economics Division (which would become a department in 1960) would grow to account for 15 to 20 percent of RAND's research staff, second in size only to all the Engineering units combined.

After their stay in Vietnam, the four RAND economists produced a report that they subsequently supplemented with two papers.[116] Considering that ensuring "a better, freer way of life" for the people of South Vietnam was an objective secondary to fighting the insurgency—as McNaughton had said—it is not surprising that the economists stated that the objective of American economic aid in Vietnam was not to develop the economy but to contribute to the war effort. To this end, American aid should be used to win popular support for the GVN. They recommended reorienting aid away from the countryside to the cities and towns, the core areas of the GVN.

---

[114] Collins, interview with Charlie Hitch, February 1988.

[115] Bruce Smith, *The RAND Corporation*, 1966, p. 63.

[116] Charles J. Zwick, Charles A. Cooper, Hans Heymann, and Richard H. Moorsteen, "A Possible Application of the Approach Set Forth in R-430, 'U.S. Economic Assistance in Vietnam: A Proposed Reorientation,'" Santa Monica, Calif.: RAND Corporation, September 16, 1964 (not available to the general public).

Aid should be used to reduce urban unemployment—approaching 40 percent in some areas—and increase welfare as a way of strengthening support for the government and reducing the appeal of the Viet Cong. As the instability in the urban areas deepened, the economists followed up with papers urging measures to alleviate unrest, such as reducing consumer prices for selected commodities, such as kerosene, condensed milk, gasoline, and cigarettes; lowering utility rates; increasing salaries for civil service functionaries; providing mass low-cost public housing; expanding public works to employ more people and improve the quality of life; expanding educational opportunities; and improving the business climate to encourage private businesses and stimulate economic growth. However, these sensible, if not idealistic, recommendations would founder in the realities of Vietnam.

The economists recommended using aid in the countryside as a carrot to induce support for the government. This approach assumed that peasants would make a "rational choice" based on economic benefits alone. In the view of the economists, American-aid benefits should be provided directly and only to people who were cooperating with the government, instead of being extended indiscriminately to the entire population, regardless of their attitude toward the GVN. By helping only those who cooperated, the GVN could create a marked contrast in the living standard between the areas it controlled and those contested by the insurgents. Thus, by implication, the peasants would make a cost/benefit calculation and decide to throw their support to the government to obtain the same benefits. This theme of using economic programs to induce desired population behavior would be picked up later by RAND economist Charlie Wolf. The economists concluded by saying that spending money wisely in the urban and rural areas would be more cost-effective for the United States than escalating the war, which would require sending more troops and which would produce higher U.S. casualties.

The RAND economists' report was well received by Defense Secretary McNamara. In a Cabinet meeting on September 9, 1964, to discuss actions to strengthen the GVN, McNamara endorsed the economists' view that it was important to apply politico-economic measures in the urban areas to dampen student and Buddhist opposition and increase political support for the GVN. The economists' conclusion that spending money on a reoriented aid program would be cheaper than military escalation was also endorsed. Secretary of State Dean Rusk said that money should be no object to achieve victory, and Ambassador Taylor replied that his country team would request whatever amount of money it needed. President Johnson emphasized that the United States should do what it took in Vietnam and that "it was necessary not to spare the horses."[117] However, although the study was well received in Washington and was con-

---

[117] David M. Barret, ed., *President Lyndon B. Johnson's Vietnam Papers: A Documentary Collection*, College Station, Tex.: Texas A&M University Press, 1998, pp. 86–87.

sidered for policy formulation, its benefit in Vietnam was limited due to a change of leadership in the U.S. mission in Saigon.[118]

Seeking more ways to contribute further to the war effort, RAND sent a team made up of William B. Graham, Amrom H. Katz, and Leon Goure to Vietnam "to search for potential problem areas susceptible to RAND analyses."[119] The three formed an impressive team. William Graham was then the head of the Engineering Division. Leon Goure was a Soviet specialist in the Social Science Department and had gained fame as an expert on Soviet civil defense. Amrom Katz was a well-known expert in camera optics, film resolution, and reconnaissance photography.

Of the three, Katz was probably the most prominent. Born in Chicago in 1915, Katz grew up in Milwaukee, Wisconsin, and graduated from the University of Wisconsin at Madison with a degree in physics. After working in mathematical statistics at the U.S. Census Bureau in Washington, Katz went to work in the photo lab at Wright Field in Dayton, Ohio, for the U.S. Army Air Corps (which later became the Air Force) during World War II, specializing in optics and reconnaissance photography. Katz joined RAND in 1954 with no specific assignment in reconnaissance but with an understanding that he would pursue his interests "whatever they turned out to be." He would later say that RAND was intellectually open in those early days, and that its contract with the Air Force allowed for this intellectual freedom. Calling it "the most remarkable thing ever written," Katz said that the essence of the contract could be summarized in one sentence: "Work hard, do good, and if you find something of interest to the Air Force, let us know."[120]

According to Katz, it was this openness that led him to work on Vietnam. Reminiscing later about the circumstance of his recruitment by Collbohm to go to Vietnam with Leon Goure and Bill Graham, Katz said that he was sitting in his office one spring day in 1964 when Frank Collbohm "walked in and asked if we could have some coffee together."[121] Collbohm started the conversation by remarking that the United States "had plenty of weapons and strategies for the problem of nuclear war," but in "limited war, guerrilla warfare, and nation-building," it was having problems devising responses to "the chaos in Southeast Asia." Katz asked him what he "intended to do about this" and Collbohm answered, "I am looking for three senior, imaginative fellows to go over to Vietnam, look at the situation, and help us construct a research program for Washington." Collbohm mentioned Leon Goure and Bill Graham, and Katz "knew immediately" that he was the third person. To prepare for his trip and work, Katz had to brush up on "Southeast Asia, Vietnam, and wars of national liberation," and

---

[118] Goldberg, "RAND and Vietnam," 1969, p. 10.

[119] Management Committee Meeting Minutes, April 29, 1964, RAND Archives.

[120] Collins, interview with Amrom Katz, 1986.

[121] Amrom Katz, "A Cup of Coffee with Frank," in "Early Personalities and Projects," *Alumni Bulletin*, ed. James Digby, Santa Monica, Calif.: RAND Corporation, P-8055, March 2001, p. 18.

remembers that "it was painful . . . getting into a subject like that. It's like running the 100-yard dash."[122]

The three RAND experts would come back with ideas for research, but it was Leon Goure who scored big with his proposal to study the impact of military operations and especially of airpower on the Viet Cong.[123] It was an idea that resonated in Washington as the United States deepened its military intervention. The issue was no longer to find out who the Viet Cong were and what made them tick, but to identify where and how they could be undermined. By the time the Viet Cong Motivation and Morale Project report was published in March 1965 and distributed within the government in Washington, the United States had committed to direct intervention. There was criticism in some quarters that the report was not *actionable*, providing no guidance on ways to hurt the Viet Cong. In response to this criticism and to the shift in American policy, as well as to a client's request, RAND began steering the Viet Cong Motivation and Morale study in a different direction. The new theme, as expounded by Goure in his proposal, was finding and exploiting enemy vulnerabilities to the impact of military operations. Although he was not working in tandem with the economists— and might not have been aware of their recommendations—Goure's proposal in a way complemented them. To their "carrot" he would add the "stick" of U.S. firepower.

Guy Pauker took the opportunity to discuss this new theme and the reorientation of the Viet Cong Motivation and Morale study when he briefed the Joint Chiefs of Staff. Instead of emphasizing enemy strengths as Zasloff and Donnell had done, he focused on vulnerabilities that could be exploited. Going further, he even held out the promise that the fight against the Viet Cong could end favorably. The picture he

---

[122]Katz, "A Cup of Coffee with Frank," 2001, p. 18.

[123]Following their trip to Vietnam with Goure in 1964, Amrom Katz and William B. Graham proposed the development of the Single Integrated Attack Team (SIAT) in their report, *Southeast Asia Trip Report, Part II: The Single Integrated Attack Team* (U), Santa Monica, Calif.: RAND Corporation, RM-4400-PR, December 1964. SIAT called for the combination of small, aggressive ground units attacking the Viet Cong with close air support directed by Forward Air Control (FAC) aircraft, which communicated the coordinates of the target to the aircraft striking the enemy on the ground. The objective of SIAT would be to undercut the military initiative of the Viet Cong and take the offensive to them.

Under this concept, a low-flying reconnaissance team consisting of an American pilot and a Vietnamese observer would stay airborne within an assigned 1,000-square-mile area of operation in order to cover any trouble spot within this territory. On the ground, small, mutually supporting units would go on patrols to harass the enemy as forward forces, and would call in reinforcements if necessary. When the patrols called for help, the "recce-FAC" airborne unit—always in the area and in communication with the ground units—would call for reinforcements and assist in directing the movement of these troops. It would also summon air strikes within minutes—rather than hours as had been the case—and mark the target. According to Alfred Goldberg, the presentation of the SIAT concept to the Air Force "met with little interest and some opposition, possibly because of its emphasis on the primacy of ground operations." Goldberg wrote that "The most consequential outcome was probably increased interest in and assistance to reconnaissance operations in South Vietnam." See Alfred Golberg, *RAND and Vietnam*, 1969, p. 11.

painted of the insurgency could not have been more different from the one presented just two months before by Zasloff and Donnell.

In Pauker's interpretation, the insurgency could be broken because of vulnerabilities that existed among its hard-core elements and among its followers. The ranks of the regroupees—veterans of the war of independence against the French, the irreplaceable "fanatic old timers" who had built and sustained the high morale and cohesion of the Viet Cong movement—were being steadily eroded through attrition. This "steel frame" of the insurgency could conceivably be melted down through protracted warfare. The insurgency could be further undermined by inducing more defections from the ranks of youthful rank-and-file followers. Whereas Zasloff and Donnell had pointed out a complex mix of motives for these young men in joining the insurgency, ranging from anger against social injustice, resentment against the GVN as the lackeys of the Americans and as agents of the rich and the landowners, and a desire to protect their country against American imperialism to a wish to escape from difficult personal situations or to seek adventure, Pauker saw them as people who had been "sweet-talked, drafted, or shanghaied into the Viet Cong," and who, consequently, were not as ideologically committed, had lower morale, and were more prone to defect.

Zasloff and Donnell did not emphasize enemy vulnerabilities or discuss ways to exploit them. Pauker, however, held out the possibility that military operations could sap the spirit of the insurgents and bring counterinsurgency to a "favorable outcome."[124] These operations, through attrition, could "break the backbone of the VC hard core," while "various military tactics and weapons systems" could weaken the morale of the rank-and-file followers and induce more defections. The "judicious exploration" of the psychological effect of these tactics and weapons on these vulnerable Viet Cong held "considerable promise," Pauker told the Joint Chiefs.[125]

Judiciously exploring the psychological effect of military operations and weapons was exactly what Leon Goure was doing at that time in Saigon to take the Viet Cong Motivation and Morale Project in a new direction. Under Goure's leadership, the project would burgeon in scope and influence as Washington policymakers searched for signs that what they were doing was working, but it would also become mired in controversy.

---

[124] Guy J. Pauker, "JCS Briefing on Viet Cong Motivation and Morale," Santa Monica, Calif.: RAND Corporation, D-13507-ISA, March 8, 1965, p. 7.

[125] Pauker, "JCS Briefing," 1965, p. 7.

CHAPTER THREE

Escalation and Airpower

By the time Frank Collbohm tapped him to go to Southeast Asia with Amrom Katz and Bill Graham to look for research opportunities, Leon Goure had become known not only within the American government but also to the U.S. public. Goure was born in 1922 in Moscow, where his father was a member of the Mensheviks, socialists who were allied with the Bolsheviks during the Russian Revolution. After Lenin liquidated the Mensheviks, Goure's family went into exile in Berlin in 1923, only to have to flee to Paris when the Nazis took over Germany. When Paris fell to the Nazis in 1940, they fled Paris on the last train out of the city, eventually settling in Hoboken, New Jersey. Goure would later say that he felt grateful to the United States for giving him and his family refuge from persecution.[1]

During World War II, he joined the U.S. Army as an infantryman and fought in the Battle of the Bulge. Later, he served in the U.S. Army Counter-Intelligence Corps and interviewed Nazis and their collaborators, using his fluency in German, French, and Russian. He obtained a bachelor's degree from New York University in 1949 and received a doctorate in political science from Georgetown in 1961. Before joining RAND's Social Science Department as a Soviet specialist, he worked for the Air Studies Division of the Library of Congress and also taught at Howard and American Universities.

At RAND, Goure was one of five specialists in the Soviet section and, according to some former members of the Social Science Department, did not stand out among his colleagues, some of whom were distinguished scholars in the field. He studied the political vulnerability of Moscow during the battle for that city in World War II, Soviet administrative control during the Nazi siege of Leningrad, the political position of the Soviet Army since Stalin, and Soviet civil defense.

Of these studies, it was his work on Soviet civil defense that garnered the most attention. According to Goure, during the 1950s the Soviet Union had been building a significant and robust civil defense program, which had strengthened it vis-à-vis the United States. The goal of this vast program was to protect the Soviet administration,

---

[1] Author interview with Leon Goure, 2003.

population, and economy against attacks employing all types of weapons, and to allow the country to survive and recover. Its existence might presage a nuclear attack on the United States. The Soviet civil defense program put into question the military doctrine of Mutual Assured Destruction, which posited the theory that neither the United States nor the Soviet Union could survive as a functioning state in a full-scale nuclear exchange and that, therefore, both countries would be deterred from launching a first strike. During a trip to Moscow, Goure had taken pictures of what was purported to be a concealed blast door in a subway station as proof of this program. At a congressional hearing on the state of readiness of U.S. civil defense, Goure was said to have shown this picture during his testimony.

Upon completion of his research on civil defense, Goure embarked on a round of briefings in Washington, presenting his results to an impressive list of Air Force officials, including Secretary Eugene Zuckert, defense officials such as ISA Director Paul Nitzes, SAC Headquarters, congressional committees, the State Department, and civil defense officials. Zuckert was so impressed with Goure's briefing that he wrote a memorandum to Secretary of Defense Robert McNamara praising it. As a result, copies were forwarded to McNamara and to Deputy Secretary of Defense Roswell Gilpatric.[2] The study created a sensation, and Goure was invited to address public gatherings on Soviet civil defense, and to give print, television, and radio interviews, including CBS, the *Huntley-Brinkley Show*; *Time*, *Newsweek*, and *Life* magazines; and *The New York Times* and *The Washington Post*. In its November-December 1961 issue, *RANDom News* said that, when it tried to get a count of Goure's public appearances, "everyone, including Leon, ha[d] lost track of it long ago." All this publicity fueled demand for the book version of his study, which was published by the University of California Press in 1962.

Goure's work on civil defense became embroiled in a public controversy that developed over the issue of whether or not the Soviets had a civil defense capability and his work was "singled out for criticism."[3] Even within RAND, there were people who thought that Goure had exaggerated the Soviet program.[4] The U.S. Air Force was pleased with Goure's work, however, as evidenced by Air Force Secretary Zuckert's reaction, because it painted the Soviets as more perfidious and more dangerous than anyone had thought and—as Gus Shubert remarked—it proved that "the Reds were red . . . and what a real ratty enemy the Soviets were." Since General Curtis LeMay, the SAC commander, believed that the only way to effectively counter the Soviet threat was to build up American military power, Goure's study could be used as a catalyst to obtain a larger budget for more bombers and missiles—"more fuel for the fire," as

---

[2]   Social Science Department, "Social Science Department Progress Report, March 1961," Santa Monica, Calif.: RAND Corporation, D-8545, March 17, 1961.

[3]   Management Committee and Research Council Meeting Minutes, February 13, 1962, RAND Archives.

[4]   Author interview with Gus Shubert, 2004 and 2005.

Gus Shubert put it. Joe Zasloff remembered Guy Pauker telling him that Goure "was a hero in the Air Force because he had discovered the deep protection the Soviets had built [with] underground shelters to protect against an American atomic strike. The discovery for the Air Force meant that the Soviets felt they could withstand maybe the second strike, so this was a great advantage to the Air Force because it was a source of increase in their own budget."[5]

So, by the time Goure made his first trip to Vietnam in 1964 at the behest of Frank Collbohm, he was someone the Air Force knew and liked. Goure, however, was not dispatched to Vietnam along with Amrom Katz and Bill Graham on a vague mission to look for any significant research opportunities. In fact, their trip was in response to a request from the Pacific Air Forces (PACAF) and U.S. Air Force (USAF) Headquarters to assess how counterinsurgency operations could be evaluated and improved, and to determine research programs on counterinsurgency, especially with regard to the role and utility of airpower.[6] Some of Goure's colleagues would later say that, even before his trip, Goure was already "an advocate of airpower as a weapon of counterinsurgency."[7]

In a report written upon his return to Santa Monica from Vietnam, Leon Goure stated that his research was "sponsored by the United States Air Force under Project RAND" and that one of the purposes of the trip to Vietnam "was to gain a better understanding of the role, utility, and problems of employing air power in counter-insurgency conflicts."[8] At a conference on guerrilla warfare held at McLean, Virginia, on September 24, 1985, Goure told the audience that he had made the trip to Vietnam at the behest of the "Chief of Air Force Intelligence" to do a "survey to see what could be done and how we could help the situation."[9] At the time, the request to RAND to look into counterinsurgency operations was prompted by the growing concern at PACAF Headquarters, which had command responsibility for USAF units in Southeast Asia, over the increasing involvement of the U.S. Air Force in Vietnam.[10]

---

[5] Author interview with Joe Zasloff, 2003.

[6] Cited in Goldberg, *RAND and Vietnam*, 1969, p. 11.

[7] Landau, "Behind the Policy Makers," 1972, p. 35.

[8] Leon Goure, "Southeast Asia Trip Report, Part I: The Impact of Air Power in South Vietnam," Santa Monica, Calif.: RAND Corporation, RM-4400-PR (Part I), December 1964, p. iii.

[9] Leon Goure, "The RAND Corporation POW and Defector Debriefing Program," paper presented at conference on *Analyzing Guerrilla Warfare*, Proceedings of a Conference, September 24, 1985, held at SAIC Tower, McLean, Va., Allan Rehm and Brendon Rehm, transcribers, Allan Rehm, ed. p. 7-1.

[10] From the end of World War II, the U.S. Air Force had been emphasizing strategic offense—represented by SAC—and large-scale nuclear conflict. It was only in the early 1960s, when the Kennedy Administration moved to develop a flexible-response strategy, that the Air Force started to restore its capability for fighting conventional and counterinsurgency conflicts. In 1962, several senior Air Force officers asked RAND to explore the role of airpower in counterinsurgency. In response, a group of department heads under the direction of Hans Speier prepared RM-3203-PR in June 1962, entitled *Counterinsurgency and Air Power: Report of a RAND Ad Hoc Group*.

At this juncture, within Air Force circles, there were discussions about how air-power could disadvantage the insurgency in the South and what types of airpower would be most effective. In fact, since 1961, when Air Force units were first sent to Vietnam, the Air Force had wanted to unleash the full potential of airpower in South Vietnam. Goure himself had talked with Air Force officials on the potential effective-ness of airpower against the guerrillas.

In a 1972 interview with David Landau of *Ramparts*, Goure said that he had discussed with Air Force officials "on a number of separate occasions" about "how useful air power might be against the opponent in South Vietnam."[11] In their Viet Cong Motivation and Morale report, Joe Zasloff, John Donnell, and Guy Pauker had touched briefly on the effect of air and artillery strikes on villagers in combat areas. Basing their observations on interviews with Viet Cong defectors and POWs, with peasants, with ARVN and U.S. officers, and with GVN and American officials, they concluded that these strikes had a negative political effect.

Some of the Viet Cong they interviewed maintained that "when a village suffers artillery or aerial bombardment, it becomes a locus of hatred against the ARVN and the Americans."[12] According to these respondents, the Viet Cong usually withdrew before the strikes took place or could hide in shelters and tunnels they had dug. The civilians, on the other hand, were much more vulnerable. They could not afford to leave their villages in the combat zones because they were attached to their homes and land, and because they feared that they would suffer financial hardships if they aban-doned their traditional livelihood. Air and artillery bombardments did not happen in a "political vacuum," the RAND analysts wrote, and when villages were bombed or

---

The research memorandum examined the nature of counterinsurgency and the role of airpower in such conflicts, and recommended ways to improve the effectiveness of airpower in such operations. According to Alfred Gold-berg, a number of discussions with the Air Force took place regarding further research, but then the matter was dropped. Interest picked up in 1964 as the role of airpower grew in Vietnam. Goldberg, *RAND and Vietnam*, 1969, pp. 7–8.

[11] Landau, "Behind the Policy Makers," 1972, p. 35. According to Landau, the discussions Goure held with the Air Force took place at a time—in late 1964—when there was "intense speculation and activity in Air Force circles, because it seemed likely that airpower would soon come to play a prominent role in the exercise of U.S. policy. There were endless discussions about what effect certain types of airpower would have on the insurgent movement, about how reliably bombing and firepower could contain a guerrilla force on the ground." Goure's discussions with the Air Force "sealed" his selection to lead and continue the RAND study in Vietnam. Landau, "Behind the Policy Makers," 1972, p. 35.

[12] Donnell, Pauker, and Zasloff, *Viet Cong Motivation and Morale*, 1965, p. 45. According to Sy Deitchman, prac-tically all the American social scientists doing research in Vietnam who had contact with the population came to the conclusion—based, not on research, but on conversations with villagers and with a number of American advisors—that "more was being lost, in terms of loyalty and respect of the population for the Saigon government and the Americans, than was being gained in hurting the Viet Cong, by bombing and shelling of villages—even where it was known that they were Viet Cong strongholds, or where Viet Cong attacks against allied forces were deliberately based in and mounted from the villages." Deitchman, *The Best-Laid Schemes*, 1976, pp. 340–341.

shelled, the Viet Cong were on the spot to exploit the damage and casualties, to rally popular support, and to enlist new recruits into their ranks.[13]

The team of Leon Goure, Amrom Katz, and Bill Graham made an extensive tour of Asia lasting from July to October 1964, during which they spent one month in South Vietnam. In Saigon, Goure became familiar with RAND's interrogation project. Tela Zasloff remembered the day the three men stopped by the RAND villa at 176 Pasteur. They just walked in, she said, "without introducing themselves or explaining who they were," perhaps thinking that she already knew. Amrom Katz tried to be charming, but she felt uncomfortable during the visit. They asked to see Joe Zasloff, and when Tela told them that he was out, they asked her to show them his office, which she did. Goure started looking through the files of interviews that were on the top of a cabinet. Tela finally summoned up the nerve to tell him, "I think you should wait till Joe comes back."[14] Goure looked at her but then stopped. Although there was tension between Zasloff and Goure, the Zasloffs gave a big cocktail party and a dinner for the RAND group.

Leon Goure would later say that, while in Vietnam, he visited an interrogation center in Saigon and read some of the interrogation documents, and this was how he "got involved in prisoner interrogation."[15] At a conference held at McLean, Virginia, in the fall of 1985 to draw lessons from the Vietnam War, Goure said that, while in Saigon, he looked at some of the interrogation data and "at some of the Air Force reporting on how we were doing."[16] According to Goure's colleagues interviewed by David Landau, "Goure became convinced as a result of that trip that the Vietnamese guerrilla movement could be destroyed from the air."[17] If the Air Force was expecting an endorsement for airpower in Vietnam, Goure certainly delivered. In the report he wrote upon his return to Santa Monica, Goure called for removing restraints from the use of airpower, albeit with the rejoinder that he was not implying that "we should encourage indiscriminate air strikes."[18] Although he used such caveats as "initial impressions," "inferences from limited evidence," "tentative findings," and "tentative conclusions," his message was clear and it was that airpower was hurting the guerrillas

---

[13] Deitchman, *The Best-Laid Schemes,* 1976, p. 47.

[14] Author interview with Tela Zasloff, 2003.

[15] Author interview with Leon Goure, 2003.

[16] Leon Goure, "The RAND Corporation POW and Defector Debriefing Program," presentation given at a conference on *Analyzing Guerrilla Warfare,* included in "Proceedings of a Conference, September 24, 1985," p. 7-1. The five speakers at this conference were people who had served as intelligence or operations analysts during the war, including Leon Goure and George Allen, who had served with the CIA. Paper available at the virtual archive of Texas Tech University, Lubbock, Texas.

[17] Landau, "Behind the Policy Makers," 1972, p. 35.

[18] Goure, "Southeast Asia Trip Report, Part I," 1964, p. vi.

and could hurt them even more if it could be used more fully, without being restrained by the fear of a political backlash from civilians caught in the attacks.

From his initial findings gleaned from the RAND interviews, from captured documents, conversations with Vietnamese intelligence interrogators and with members of U.S. intelligence-collection agencies, he reached a conclusion diametrically opposed to that of Zasloff-Donnell-Pauker. As he explained, all the sources he had studied failed to demonstrate a single case in which a Vietnamese had joined the insurgency directly because of damage or casualties inflicted on civilians by bombing or shelling.[19] His initial findings, therefore, appeared "to challenge the widespread belief that collateral damage to property or the killing of civilians by air attacks inevitably result in 'making more Viet Cong.' Further investigation is urgently needed[,] since the prevalence of this possibly mistaken view has intensified the arguments for strict control of air operations, target selection, and strike authorizations. These controls, in turn, may have contributed to making air power in Vietnam less responsive and effective than it could be."[20] Since ideologically apathetic Vietnamese tended to be neutral with regard to either side of the war, and to *cooperate with whichever authority is in effective control of his area*"[21] [emphasis in original], restraining the use of airpower did not "necessarily increase popular support of the government," and air strikes did not "automatically increase active civilian cooperation with the Viet Cong."[22] Goure went on to say, "If correct, this conclusion suggests that the present restrictions on the employment of air, designed to safeguard civilians, may in fact be too inflexible and to some extent counterproductive."[23]

With regard to the impact of airpower on the insurgents, Goure wrote that, by applying "continuous pressure," "air power could perhaps play a larger role against the Viet Cong."[24] Goure believed that assessing the effectiveness of airpower in counterinsurgency by the casualties and damage inflicted on the enemy—as was then being done—was too limiting. This effectiveness should also be measured by the negative consequences that air operations inflicted on the enemy's mobility, morale, and ability to carry out effective operations and to recruit new members. Measured in these terms, airpower was effective because "the available information indicates that air operations, even under present constraints, have a significant impact on Viet Cong mobility, initiative, plans, operations, and morale."[25] Airpower could reach the insurgents in remote

---

[19] Goure, "Southeast Asia Trip Report, Part I," 1964, p. 3.

[20] Goure, "Southeast Asia Trip Report, Part I," 1964, p. 4.

[21] Goure, "Southeast Asia Trip Report, Part I," 1964, p. 5.

[22] Goure, "Southeast Asia Trip Report, Part I," 1964, p. 5.

[23] Goure, "Southeast Asia Trip Report, Part I," 1964, p. 5.

[24] Goure, "Southeast Asia Trip Report, Part I," 1964, p. 7

[25] Goure, "Southeast Asia Trip Report, Part I," 1964, p. 13.

bases where the ARVN were afraid to venture into; keep the Viet Cong on the run; destroy their crops with chemical spray; inflict hardships and make life more difficult for the Viet Cong; and turn the guerrilla from "the hunter into the hunted."

In fact, according to Goure, available information from captured documents and interrogation reports indicated that the Viet Cong feared "aircraft more than any other weapons system used against them."[26] In view of the impact of airpower on the insurgents, "Attacks causing collateral civilian damage or casualties undoubtedly frighten people, but unless such actions result in driving them to give active support to the Viet Cong they may be justified if they also significantly hurt the Viet Cong or disrupt their plans and activities."[27] In fact, Goure wrote that if airpower was fully employed, it might pave the way for more intensive ground attacks and facilitate pacification. In short, Goure saw a huge potential for airpower in Vietnam—and a bigger role for the Air Force in the war.

Goure suggested that additional information should be gathered to determine ways in which airpower could be exploited "to induce desirable behavior on the part of the population."[28] Since evidence suggested that the villagers tended to blame the Viet Cong presence in their midst for bringing air and artillery attacks, Goure wrote that, "The fear of air attacks and the association of the threat of attacks with the presence of Viet Cong troops might be exploited so as to induce the population to give intelligence about the Viet Cong and to cooperate more with the government forces. At present people are not penalized for withholding information on the Viet Cong; consequently they tend to fear the insurgents more than the government."[29] Actual and threatened air attacks not only could be used to pressure uncooperative villagers and demonstrate superior GVN authority, they could also be exploited to "force civilians to leave Viet Cong controlled areas for government controlled territory, where they could be more effectively screened and administered."[30]

Mao Tse-tung had compared guerrillas operating among the people to "fish swimming in a pond of water." What Goure advocated was a strategy to drain the water by bombing villages and forcing the people to flee into GVN-controlled areas in order to deprive the Viet Cong of popular support and leave them floundering like fish out of water.

Goure emphasized that, to find out the precise effects of air—and artillery—bombardment, there was a need for extending present intelligence efforts in Vietnam, and he sprinkled his report with suggestions for "more exhaustive information," or

---

[26] Goure, "Southeast Asia Trip Report, Part I," 1964, p. 10.

[27] Goure, "Southeast Asia Trip Report, Part I," 1964, p. 17.

[28] Goure, "Southeast Asia Trip Report, Part I," 1964, p. 18.

[29] Goure, "Southeast Asia Trip Report, Part I," 1964, p. 18.

[30] Goure, "Southeast Asia Trip Report, Part I," 1964, p. 18.

"further investigation," or "additional analysis," or "gaining a better understanding," or obtaining "better intelligence," or conducting "a careful study." These steps were urgently needed to confirm his initial findings or to identify more effective uses of air-power in Vietnam. He ended by pointing out that defectors and prisoners of war pos-sessed "much relevant information and experience that might be tapped if appropriate requirements and questionnaires were given to the collection agencies. . . ."[31]

Three weeks after Goure finished this report, William F. Dorrill in RAND's Social Science Department wrote an extensive critique, which he addressed to Joe M. Goldsen, who had replaced Alex George as the head of the Social Science Department on June 10, 1963.[32] George had asked to be relieved of his responsibilities so that he could pursue research full time. Goldsen had joined RAND in January 1948 and sub-sequently served as administrative officer of the Social Science Department in Wash-ington and then in Santa Monica. Before becoming department chairman, Goldsen had served as associate department head and was project leader for studies on the political-legal aspects of outer-space development.[33] David Mozingo, a China expert in the Social Science Department, recalled that, unlike Alex George, who was a "bril-liant intellectual," Goldsen was—without an "academic . . . or a professional scholarly background"—"overmatched" by the staff of social scientists in the department and it was difficult for him be a strong leader.[34]

William Dorrill had joined RAND in 1963 after a stint in the CIA. He was a China specialist and was still working on his Harvard Ph.D. dissertation. Although China was his field of expertise, the situation in Vietnam upset him and he became preoccupied with it. In October 1964, he had prepared a paper on Vietnam for Pennsyl-vania Governor William Scranton, who was running against Senator Barry Goldwater during the Republican primary of 1964, and for whom he had served as a foreign policy advisor.[35]

---

[31] Goure, "Southeast Asia Trip Report, Part I," 1964, pp. 18–19.

[32] Dorrill's memo was not declassified until February 2005, when RAND requested its use in the documentary *Ideas in Action; 60 Years of RAND*, produced for the inauguration of its new Santa Monica headquarters.

[33] *RANDom News,* RAND's internal bulletin, 1963.

[34] Author interview with David Mozingo, 2002. David Mozingo held a doctorate from UCLA, with a disserta-tion on *Chinese Communist Policies in Relations with Indonesia.* He joined RAND in 1962 because, as he said in a 2003 interview, it had great prestige and the reputation as "an organization that cast its views on lots of things and let the chips fall where they may." According to the Social Science Department's "Progress Report, 1964–1965, All Clients, for Calendar Year 1964, with Forecast of Activities for 1965," Santa Monica, Calif., RAND Corpora-tion, D-13198, February 24, 1965, Mozingo's focus at RAND was on the role of Indonesia in Communist China's Southeast Asia strategy, but might also include Chinese policies and objectives relating to North Vietnam, and China's policies toward Southeast Asia as a whole, "in an effort to forecast China's positions in this area in the 1970's."

[35] This paper later became a research memorandum with the title "South Vietnam's Problems and Prospects," Santa Monica, Calif.: RAND Corporation, RM-4350-PR, October 1964.

In his memo to Goldsen, Dorrill said that he was disturbed by Goure's report and wondered "whether this is, in fact, a *bona fide* research proposal or a tantalizing offer . . . to document a case for intensified U.S. air operations in South Vietnam."[36] After saying that Goure's arguments were "loading the dice" to support his conclusions, Dorrill went on to pick them apart and to highlight the flaws in their logic.[37] For example, he pointed out that to claim that air strikes causing property damage or the death of civilians did not push people to join the Viet Cong ignored the fact that, although the toll on civilians—by and of itself—might not be a direct factor in Viet Cong recruitment, it could be a significant contributing factor, coming as it did on top of other brutalities committed by the Saigon armed forces. Dorrill added that markedly increased suffering of the population from an intensification of warfare could have a serious overall outcome by further eroding support for the government among the noncommunist masses. Vietnamese who objected to inflicting more suffering on their own people could make it impossible for the government to pursue the war, even if they did not join the insurgency or support it actively.[38]

In summary, Dorrill wrote that Goure's report "leaves the clear implication that if all the facts were known, the U.S. would greatly intensify its air operations in Vietnam at no great risk of adverse civilian reaction and with the happy prospect of 'a significant and relatively quick improvement in the military situation, which is essential if pacification measures are to succeed.'"[39] Dorrill concluded his memo by writing that, "For the sake of RAND's continued reputation for objective analysis," he sincerely hoped that Goure's paper elicited a more favorable impression than his own from other people at RAND who also read it.[40]

Dorrill's objections had no effect, and copies of Goure's report were distributed in Washington and Saigon. Ambassador Taylor asked for copies. Its findings were distributed through MACV's staff. Copies were also sent to the commander of the Special Air Warfare Center at Eglin Air Force Base. In addition, the "tentative findings" were presented to several senior military officers, including General Glen W. Martin, Deputy Chief of Staff for Plans and Operations at PACAF and his staff; to General Arthur C.

---

[36] William Dorrill, "Critique of RM-4400-PR (Part 1) December 1964," memorandum to Joe M. Goldsen and Guy J. Pauker, January 11, 1965, p. 1.

[37] Dorrill, "Critique of RM-4400-PR (Part 1) December 1964," 1965, p. 1.

[38] In a footnote, Dorrill challenged Goure's contention that, in VC areas, villagers' fears of attacks would motivate them to provide intelligence to and cooperate more with the government. In Dorrill's view, "the history of guerrilla warfare has amply demonstrated that a civilian population cannot be bludgeoned or blackmailed into cooperation with the occupying force. Brutality has inevitably boomeranged to the advantage of the insurgents." Dorrill, "Critique of RM-4400-PR (Part 1) December 1964," 1965, p. 6.

[39] Dorrill, "Critique of RM-4400-PR (Part 1) December 1964," 1965, p. 6.

[40] Dorrill, "Critique of RM-4400-PR (Part 1) December 1964," 1965, p. 7.

Agan, Deputy Chief of Staff for Plans and Operations in the Pentagon; and to General Richard Yudkin, deputy director of Plans for Policy at U.S. Air Force Headquarters.[41]

When he returned from his trip, Goure reported his impressions to the Chief of Intelligence of the Air Force.[42] As they discussed the impact of airpower, Goure suggested that, instead of theorizing about the use of airpower in Vietnam, they should ask the Viet Cong themselves. "'A fine idea', the Air Force Chief of Intelligence told Goure. 'We'll have our people out there do it.'" Goure reminded him that U.S. military officials were not allowed access to Viet Cong captives and defectors, but that RAND already had authorization to conduct interviews. The Air Force Chief of Intelligence was impressed and pulled the necessary strings to ensure that he would be able to continue the Viet Cong Motivation and Morale Project.[43] As a result of Goure's report, Collbohm and Goure held briefings and discussions "with General Jack Thomas, the Assistant Chief of Staff/Intelligence of the Air Force" and, in December 1964, "RAND decided . . . to enlarge the prisoner of war interrogation project and concentrate its analytical efforts on the effects on the Viet Cong of military operations, especially air, and their military vulnerabilities."[44]

Goure would later imply that his selection was casually reached, and that it was almost by accident that he found himself in Vietnam running the project. As he recalled, the Air Force Chief of Intelligence asked, "Do you speak French?" When Goure replied in the affirmative, the Chief said, "You're on your way to Vietnam," and, "It used to be a French colony. Therefore go!"[45] According to Goure, "Frank Collbohm was quite willing to support all this. We were supposed to pick up an ARPA contract . . . and I was given about $100,000 and told to go, which I did."[46] Apparently, most—if not all—the people in important positions at RAND were happy to see Goure continue the Viet Cong Motivation and Morale study as a way for RAND to keep its finger in the pie. There is no written record of any leaders trying to stop Goure's new assignment. The project was funded by ARPA/AGILE but was undertaken for the Air Force.[47] The Social Science Department had overall direction.

---

[41] Social Science Department, "Progress Report for 1964–1965," 1965.

[42] Author interview with Leon Goure, 2003. Goure also recalled in his interview with the author that he briefed John McNaughton as well, and that McNaughton was, at the time, very reluctant to see the United States get involved in Vietnam.

[43] Landau, "Behind the Policy Makers," 1972, p. 35.

[44] Goldberg, "RAND and Vietnam," 1969, p. 13.

[45] Author interview with Leon Goure, 2003.

[46] Author interview with Leon Goure, 2003.

[47] Author interview with Leon Goure, 2003. According to Sy Deitchman, the Air Force could have approved it and then asked ARPA/AGILE to fund it, because the ARPA/AGILE budget had more flexibility. Author interview with Sy Deitchman, 2005.

The deliberate selection of Goure—a supporter of the air-war concept—to continue the project and to take it in a direction desired by the Air Force has been confirmed by two key RAND staff members. Jim Digby, who later replaced Jack Ellis as ARPA/AGILE contract manager, recalled that Frank Collbohm selected Leon Goure to counter the Zasloff-Donnell-Pauker conclusion that airpower was ineffective.[48] After reading Goure's 1964 research proposal "with relish," Collbohm told Guy Pauker in early 1965 that "the motivation and morale program was being reoriented toward air power effectiveness and that Goure would be assuming control."[49]

Collbohm's choice of Goure—someone with no background in Asia and whose expertise had been focused on Soviet civil defense—has even been interpreted as a conspiracy between Collbohm and the Air Force to deliver results that would favor the use of airpower in Vietnam. According to this conspiracy theory—subscribed to by a historian at Carnegie Mellon University who had researched RAND's work in Vietnam—some Air Force generals came to see Frank Collbohm and objected to Zasloff and Donnell as being "much too soft" on the Viet Cong, and suggested that he got rid of Zasloff and Donnell and replace them with a "hardline person" who would say "the right thing" about airpower in order to make "the Air Force look good." Goure was viewed as the right person, and Collbohm selected him.[50] Gus Shubert initially maintained that there was no evidence to support this theory,[51] but he said in 2004 that the theory that there was a deal between Collbohm and the Air Force "is probably right, and if it was, then it was a disgrace."[52] Another senior RAND person, Jim Digby, would later confirm that Collbohm and Goure did in fact decide to go along "with the Air Force interest in the effect of . . . the large bombers" on Viet Cong morale."[53] Joe Zasloff maintained, however, that he was not fired. He did not plan on staying with RAND in Vietnam beyond the completion of his study because he had teaching commitments at Pittsburgh. But the fact is that RAND did not ask him to continue the project. It was handed over to Goure to expand and orient in a new direction.

If Collbohm in fact did choose Leon Goure to give the Air Force the results it wanted, his selection is all the more interesting because there is some evidence that he himself did not believe in indiscriminate bombing of villages. To him, the ideal use of airpower in Vietnam would be to attack with slow-flying planes and helicopters, rather than destroy entire villages with bombs. Other people at RAND also shared his belief

---

[48] Jim Digby, "Frank and Civil Defense," in Jim Digby, ed., "Early Personalities and Projects," *RAND Alumni Bulletin*, Santa Monica, Calif.: RAND Corporation, P-8055, March 2001, p. 13.

[49] Jardini, "The Wrong War," 1998, p. 45.

[50] Author interview with Gus Shubert, 2004 and 2005.

[51] Collins, interview with Gus Shubert, session of May 20, 1992, p. 15.

[52] Author interview with Gus Shubert, 2004.

[53] Author interview with Jim Digby, 2002.

that massive bombing would galvanize popular opposition, rally support for the other side, and motivate them to fight harder, as had happened during the Allied bombing of Nazi Germany in 1944–1945. Hans Speier thought that "the whole idea of bombing civilians was not only distasteful" to him personally, but that it was also inefficient as shown in the Strategic Bombing Survey conducted in Japan and Germany after World War II.[54] Frank Collbohm himself was opposed to the bombing of North Vietnam because he thought that it would not staunch the flow of supplies and that it would stiffen enemy morale instead. According to Collbohm, he was one of the few who had been privy to the secret deliberations in late 1964 leading to the decision to bomb the North, and that he did "everything he could . . . to keep it from starting."[55]

Collbohm's opposition to the bombing of the North and indiscriminate air strikes against villages in the South, and his reputation as someone who would stand up to the Air Force—even to the formidable General Curtis LeMay—made his selection of Goure puzzling. Perhaps he catered to the Air Force in this instance as a way for RAND to stay relevant to Vietnam as Washington decided to intensify and win the war. As one senior RAND person commented about the replacement of Zasloff-Donnell-Pauker with Leon Goure, "You hire an architect to build a bridge from here to San Francisco. He says it can't be done. So you fire him and get someone else. The question, from the President on down, was 'How do we proceed to *win* this war?' RAND, like everyone else, was in the business of getting things done."[56]

According to Goure, when Frank Collbohm initially sent him to Vietnam, "the Management Committee, everybody, Frank, supported the war, nobody objected." RAND was in favor of his going to Vietnam and thought that his project "was supposed to be a great idea, at least I suppose it was meant to be a great idea."[57] David Mozingo, in a retrospective interview, thought that RAND's leaders viewed Vietnam as an opportunity for RAND to shine as it had done in the strategic basing study. "RAND," Mozingo said, "would come in and find ways to win the Vietnam War or make a powerful contribution to the winning of it, and that decision was fatal because it inevitably led to support of policies that the Kennedy and Johnson Administrations were going to do anyway, and made RAND just another nag in the pack of worn out horses trotting down the Vietnam War trail."[58]

With his support assured, Goure returned to Saigon on December 12, 1964, to assume leadership of the project. It would start in January 1965 and would take five to seven man-years to complete, including gathering data in the field, analyzing the

[54] Collins, interview with Hans Speier, 1988, p. 49.

[55] Landau, "Behind the Policy Makers," 1972, p. 35.

[56] Landau, "Behind the Policy Makers," 1972, p. 34.

[57] Author interview with Leon Goure, 2003.

[58] Author interview with David Mozingo, 2003.

findings, making briefings, and preparing reports.[59] Susan and David Morell maintained that Goure came to Vietnam with the purpose of making a case for airpower. Susan, still the administrative assistant for RAND in Saigon, went to pick up Goure at the Saigon airport. As they made their way into town, she tried to make conversation, asking Goure whether he was going to use the existing Zasloff-Donnell questionnaire or start all over again with a new one. Goure patted the briefcase he was carrying and said, "I have the answer right here." She asked him what he meant by that, and he replied, "When the Air Force is paying the bill, the answer is always bombing." His comment left Susan Morell speechless, and she thought, "I'll never forget this moment."[60] David Morell remembered taking Goure to the Rex Hotel in downtown Saigon for a dinner in the rooftop restaurant and hearing Goure say, "I've got all the facts here." He was shocked by this and thought, "How can you have the answers, you haven't asked any questions yet." David Morell, however, did not remember Goure saying something about "the Air Force is paying the bill." Susan Morell insisted that he did, and that she remembered it so vividly because it was like an epiphany for her.[61] At any rate, both Morell stories indicate that Goure already knew what answers he was going to obtain from his study.

Although Susan Morell did not stay in Vietnam for the entire Goure tenure—departing in March 1965—she recalled that Goure proceeded to develop questions that "were directed at providing answers that would lead to a decision to have more military involvement and more air force and more bombing," and that Goure "was trying to make a case that you had to go after them [the Viet Cong] where they were most fearful: If that's what they were most afraid of, then if we do that then they'd stop what they were doing. It was that simple, which of course didn't turn out to be the case." David Morell remembered that he did some work with the Goure study and that he began to see results that were very different from the Zasloff-Donnell findings. He recalled that the focus was on "village reactions to bombing as reiterated presumably by the people we were interviewing—the prisoners, and the *Chieu Hoi*." It appeared to him that Goure was trying to prove that the villagers blamed the bombing on the Viet Cong presence rather than on the Americans, and that the contrast between the Zasloff-Donnell and the Goure studies was like "night and day."[62] It is worth noting that neither Susan nor David Morell had access to the Goure study once they left Vietnam and their respective jobs with RAND and with MACV, and therefore their recollections were based on what they knew at the time.

---

[59] Social Science Department, "Progress Report 1964–1965," 1965.

[60] Author interview with David and Susan Morell, 2004 and 2005.

[61] Author interview with David and Susan Morell, 2004 and 2005.

[62] Author interview with David and Susan Morell, 2004 and 2005.

According to Susan Morell, Goure was "a man with a mission" who "knew what he was there to do," and his mission in Vietnam was to put together a report that would support the policies that the Air Force wanted to implement. If he could produce such a report, "he would be doing a good job."[63] Susan Morell described Goure as belonging to the group of Eastern Europeans who had found refuge in the United States and who harbored a profound dislike and distrust of communism. So, Goure had come to Vietnam, she said, to "fight communism" because in his view "it would be a good thing to have one less Communist country in the world."[64] Goure himself would explain that he wanted to help the United States out of gratefulness for taking him and his family in as refugees. He disliked and distrusted communism because the communists would persecute innocent people—such as a relative in the Soviet Union who had been imprisoned in a gulag prison camp simply for being related to someone whose political stand they opposed. "We're condemned for what our parents do. That's how these people [communists] work," he would later say.[65]

It is difficult to discern Goure's motives, but David Mozingo believed that Goure might have accepted the Vietnam assignment because, "like some other people involved in Vietnam," he saw this as a way to further his career. This seems to be supported by a review of his work following his star turn with Soviet civil defense. After his work on this issue was completed, he did not have a firm assignment and for a while led Project STAR, which was on how to better protect the president of the United States, focusing on "threat assessment" and "election campaign situations."[66] It could be, then, that he was at a crossroads, career wise, and the Vietnam assignment seemed like a great opportunity, especially since it had the backing of the Air Force leadership and of Frank Collbohm. As David Mozingo put it, Goure had "ridden" Soviet civil defense "to a dead end and was quite ready to find something else that may give him a shot at the top."[67]

According to Goure, when he returned to Saigon, he got no cooperation from Joe Zasloff, who was wrapping up his own study and preparing to return to the United States. Goure said Zasloff refused to provide any help, such as finding interviewers, and was unhappy that he was doing a project for the Air Force. Both Zasloff and Goure remembered a confrontation about a week after Goure's return, during which Zasloff accused Goure of pandering to the Air Force. Regardless, Goure was able to staff his project fairly quickly and was off and running. In 1965, he would turn his proj-

---

[63] Author interview with David and Susan Morell, 2004 and 2005.

[64] Author interview with David and Susan Morell, 2004 and 2005.

[65] Author lunch conversation with Leon Goure, 2003.

[66] Social Science Department, "Progress Report, for Calendar Year 1963, with Forecast of Activities for 1964," Santa Monica, Calif.: RAND Corporation, February 10, 1964 (not available to the general public).

[67] Author interview with David Mozingo, 2003.

ect into the largest RAND effort in Vietnam in the resources and attention it would command.

Before leaving Santa Monica for Vietnam, Goure had talked to Joe Carrier, now back in Cost Analysis, and asked him whether he would be interested in coming to Saigon to assemble and lead a team of Vietnamese interviewers. He told Carrier to plan on staying for a year or longer. Goure wanted to hire another person, because he realized that the project would be too big for the two of them to handle. Carrier suggested Tony Russo, also in Cost Analysis, who had expressed an interest in going to Vietnam. Carrier was the first American team leader to arrive in Saigon in January 1965.

Tony Russo, an Italian-American from Virginia, had obtained two master's degrees at Princeton—one in aeronautics engineering and one in public affairs—the second degree because he wanted to get away from aeronautics and move into the field of social science, which, he believed, would get him out into the world and allow him to "hit the road."[68] It was at Princeton that he learned about the RAND interview project in an international affairs seminar given by Klaus Knorr, a well-known and conservative international strategist. Klaus Knorr said that RAND was considering a Viet Cong prisoner interrogation project and had tried to implement it but that Ngo Dinh Diem would not allow Americans to talk to prisoners. When Russo heard about it, he wanted to go work for RAND. In 1964, a professor he was working for gave Russo the responsibility of organizing the Princeton Conference on the space program, to which he invited David Novick, the head of RAND's Cost Analysis Department. Russo talked to Novick about joining RAND and was offered a job.

Russo was determined to go to Vietnam. His overall goal was to get there. He had "a kind of calling," because "that was the public policy problem, and there seemed to be some questions about it."[69] At the same time, he felt ambivalent about Vietnam: On the one hand, he found the image of the Viet Cong as fighting peasants "romantic and appealing," and was inclined to think they were legitimate; on the other hand, President John F. Kennedy was fighting them, and Russo, who admired JFK, thought that the president could not be wrong. The contradiction intrigued him, and he wanted "to get to the bottom" of it. While working in Cost Analysis, Russo heard about the Viet Cong Motivation and Morale Project. He talked to Joe Goldsen, Joe Carrier, and David Novick, but they discouraged him, perhaps because they wanted to make sure that this was what he really wanted to do, and that "it wasn't just a lark." Then he talked to Chuck Thomson, whom Goure had selected to be his deputy, and suddenly he was hired. Russo thinks that was because no one else wanted to go.[70]

Chuck Thomson was then the administrative officer of the Social Science Department, focusing on problems of budgeting, reporting, and personnel, but also working

---

[68] Author interview with Tony Russo, 2003 and 2004.

[69] Author interview with Tony Russo, 2003 and 2004.

[70] Author interview with Tony Russo, 2003 and 2004.

on issues of command and control, and U.S. civil defense. In Saigon, as Leon Goure's deputy, Thomson helped with the development of the questionnaire and with staff issues, and would co-author some of the reports. Whenever Goure returned to the United States, Thomson would fill in as project manager. Tony Russo, who became friends with Thomson, recalled that Thomson admired Leon Goure and thought Goure was "a great talker and a bright guy."[71]

Russo described Thomson as a "craggy, snow-haired man in his 50s" who had the "imperious air of a stern schoolmaster."[72] Gus Shubert, who would later take over the leadership of the Viet Cong Motivation and Morale study, thought that Thomson was reluctant to disagree with people above him and that his general approach was "peace at any price." This was Thomson's attitude toward Leon Goure. Some RAND staff members in Saigon thought that Thomson was quiet when Goure was around and deferred to him. Ardith Betts, who would later join the RAND team in Saigon, remembered that, periodically, when Goure returned to the United States, Thomson would hold forth and preside over 176 Pasteur as the most senior "I know everything" kind of person.[73] Her impression was that Thomson "deferred to Leon, and it was obvious there was no question that he was ever going to challenge him in any way in terms of findings or research results, anything on an intellectual basis. Leon was god—he was the big thing."[74] According to Tony Russo, Thomson, in fact, chafed at being the number-two man, but could not challenge Goure for leadership.

Both Goure and Thomson, Russo said, had no intellectual curiosity about Vietnam and its people. Before leaving Santa Monica, Thomson took Russo to see Leon Goure at his Pacific Palisades home. Russo found Goure warm, affable, and very charming—a handsome man, in his forties, with graying temples and a twinkle in his eyes, "which denoted an unmistakable *joie de vivre*."[75] Speaking with a Parisian accent, Goure projected the image of "the stereotypical continental professor."[76] Russo liked him and "looked forward with excitement to working in Saigon with this man of the world."[77] Russo remembered that, during the visit, Goure said "something about the Air Force being disturbed by [the] Zasloff-Donnell study."[78] On February 22, 1965, Chuck Thomson and Tony Russo boarded a Pentagon flight to Saigon. When he arrived in Saigon, Russo met Steve Hosmer, who would come in and out of Saigon

---

[71] Author interview with Tony Russo, 2003 and 2004.

[72] Anthony Russo, "Looking Backward: Rand and Vietnam in Retrospect," *Ramparts*, July 1972, p. 41.

[73] Author interview with Ardith Betts, 2004.

[74] Author interview with Ardith Betts, 2004.

[75] Russo, "Looking Backward," 1972, p. 41.

[76] Russo, "Looking Backward," 1972, p. 41.

[77] Russo, "Looking Backward," 1972, p. 41.

[78] Author interview with Tony Russo, 2003 and 2004.

intermittently to address administrative issues and later fill in as manager on a temporary basis. Russo remembered that Hosmer talked a lot "about VC terrorism"—a subject that Hosmer would later elaborate on in his own studies—and this made Russo angry at the Viet Cong. He recalled that he thought, "Those sons of bitches, they ought to be put in their place."[79]

At this point in his life, Russo was "just this naive, young guy" for whom war was a concept that still had to be sorted out. "I was at the stage where I thought, 'Why do people make war?'" he would later say. He did not know much about Vietnam, but he believed it to be a primitive and dangerous place. He imagined that he would see people planting corn across the street from the RAND office and that he would find himself in a combat situation and would have to wear "special shoes" to protect himself in case he "stepped on punji sticks."[80] But life in Saigon was not what he had imagined. He discovered that the food was great and that the living was pleasant. He found a nice apartment above a little French restaurant that served delicious steak tartare. It was near downtown, about a block and a half from the RAND villa. As he recalled, "You can go and live in Saigon and never know there was a war going on."[81] Other things made life interesting, such as the convoluted local politics and being able to indulge his love of flying in airplanes that took him all over the country to conduct interviews. All in all, it was a great adventure.

Russo's excitement at living in an exotic place was shared by Leon Goure, who found the incongruous juxtaposition of war and peace mind-boggling and amusing at the same time. When he went on a trip to the seashore town of Vung Tau, known as Cap Saint Jacques under the French, he saw aircraft dropping bombs and firing rockets in the distance. The action continued all day and all night. Flares were dropped to illuminate the darkness and, then, in the morning, the town shook as large bombs began falling again. But out on the beach, kids were playing soccer, American GIs were flirting with their girlfriends, and Leon and his companions lunched on lobster and steak while watching the battle unfolding across the bay: "tracers, black clouds from bombs, flashes of explosion, planes diving, choppers carrying troops and med-evac choppers bringing back the wounded."[82]

As a team leader, Russo's job was to supervise three to four Vietnamese interviewers out of a total of about ten for the entire project and to take them on field trips. Vietnamese could not fly on American planes unless they were accompanied by an American, so a team leader had to travel with them. The presence of an American served as a guarantee that they were not Viet Cong and could be trusted. Every three weeks or so, Russo would take his team to a province town, where they lived like the locals. They

---

[79] Author interview with Tony Russo, 2003 and 2004.

[80] Author interview with Tony Russo, 2003 and 2004.

[81] Author interview with Tony Russo, 2003 and 2004.

[82] Leon Goure, letter to a friend in Santa Monica, May 30, 1965.

Joe Carrier at a Chieu Hoi *center.*

would find accommodation in a hotel, where a room cost on average about fifty cents a night (before inflation raised the price)—and eat in restaurants serving tasty local delicacies and different varieties of rice. They would stay for three or four days to conduct interviews with prisoners, defectors, and refugees. As with Zasloff and Donnell, there was no central file of defectors and prisoners, so the team did not know what sources would be waiting when they arrived at their destination, and they could pick only from whomever were available at the time. It was not possible to select a scientific, statistically valid sample. Upon their arrival at a *Chieu Hoi* center, for example, they would talk with the director to determine which people among the defectors might provide the most interesting information in the interviews.

Depending on the number of defectors kept at a *Chieu Hoi* center, they might see anywhere between ten to one hundred defectors loafing around the central courtyard. Scenes like these gave rise to the impression among many Americans that the *Chieu Hoi* Program was nothing but "rest and recreation" for the Viet Cong, allowing them to sit out the war for a while and recuperate before they went back into action. Since security was lax, the interviewers could take the defectors to a cafe or back to their hotel to sip beer, to build rapport. Russo usually limited his participation in the interviewing, because he thought that his presence might bias the interview. He would leave the interviewers

Steve Hosmer (front) on the front porch of the RAND Saigon villa, with (left to right) Hanh, Que, and an unidentified person.

to do their job and go check out the area or talk with Vietnamese and American officials. The Americans, he thought, were out of touch, "hassled, powerless, and isolated" because "they stuck together in their compounds."[83] To talk to prisoners in the field, the team would head for the provincial jail. Here, they usually found lower-ranking cadres, because higher-ranking prisoners were sent to the National Interrogation Center (NIC) or the Military Interrogation Center (MIC) in Saigon—both sponsored by the CIA.

For the interviews, Russo and his team would apply the questionnaire that Goure had adapted from the one developed by Zasloff-Donnell and reoriented toward the effect of military operations and weapons. For example, there were questions probing what types of weapons the Viet Cong feared the most and what kinds of attacks demoralized them the most. These were questions to which the military would like to get answers. According to Goure, the military would say to him, "Since we're unauthorized to ask questions of these men, could you find out what is the effect of this or that weapon or bomb? . . . We're out here to win the war, and if you want to cut any influence you'll help us do just that."[84] Goure would respond by incorporating questions to elicit the answers. "We didn't do in-depth studies in the fields," Goure would later say, "We didn't do research studies. You designed the questions to get the needed

---

[83] Russo, "Looking Backward," 1972, p. 55.

[84] Landau, "Behind the Policy Makers," 1972, p. 36.

input."[85] As he would recall later, "We were constantly changing the questionnaire, depending on the direction people wanted us to focus on."[86] The direction, Goure said, came from several sources—sometimes it came "from Washington, sometimes from talking to MACV people, sometimes just because it seemed like we'd better find out what goes on, we did it ourselves."[87]

As Goure saw it, his project was supposed to be militarily-oriented and to assist "the war effort." Although he and his team continued to gather information regarding motivation and morale and although eventually several substantive studies did emerge from the data—the project, in his view, was not meant to be a mere continuation of the work of Zasloff and Donnell because that "was not what the chief of intelligence of the Air Force wanted. Of course not, he wasn't interested in that—he wanted to know about the war and the effectiveness of the war, how you fight the war better. The miliary wasn't interested in that kind of [social/political study]. . . . It might have been set up that way originally, but it certainly was not the direction that they asked me to do."[88] By the time he became involved, it seemed to him that the project "was essentially an intelligence thing." This new direction, according to Goure, stemmed from the Air Force's reaction to his briefing following his initial trip in 1964, when he informed them that "there was good intelligence, interesting intelligence that could be gotten from interviews, interrogations, such as offset target marking." He recalled that "that was exactly what Air Force intelligence wanted."[89] Tony Russo remembered that Goure used to say around the RAND office, "We got the best damned intelligence in the war!"[90]

On his first trip, Russo took a team of three Vietnamese interviewers to Qui Nhon, a port town on the central coast. Phan was a worldly pipe smoker with limited English and an imaginative, flowery use of the language, given to writing sentences such as "the wavering ambience wafting from the village."[91] Ninh was a small, quiet man with a quick smile, who would fall asleep at his desk whenever he had had a late evening attending a Vietnamese reformed opera, or *cai luong*.[92] Thang sported a thin

---

[85] Landau, "Behind the Policy Makers," 1972, p. 36.

[86] Author interview with Leon Goure, 2003.

[87] Author interview with Leon Goure, 2003.

[88] Author interview with Leon Goure, 2003. According to David Landau, on occasions when younger members of Goure's American team in Saigon balked, "the military would quickly become annoyed and say, 'Fine, if you people want to be long-hairs, if you want to ask philosophical questions, go ahead. But we're here to win the war. . . .'" Landau, "Behind the Policy Makers," 1972, p. 36.

[89] Landau, "Behind the Policy Makers," 1972, p. 36.

[90] Russo, "Looking Backward," 1972, p. 57.

[91] Author interview with Ardith Betts, 2004.

[92] Ninh came close to being fired by Phil Davison, a Columbia University professor and RAND consultant who came to Saigon in summer 1965 to act as interim manager when both Leon Goure and Chuck Thomson had to

Interviewers Phon Anh, Thang, and Que, eating at a restaurant on a field trip.

mustache and believed that he was projecting the image of a suave playboy. Russo remembered that "Qui Nhon was a ghost town," surrounded by the VC, and that there was hardly anyone around.[93] An official from the provincial USAID mission met them at the airport, took them to their small hotel, and gave them the use of a Land Rover for the duration of their stay. One evening, they came down from their rooms on the second floor to go out to dinner. One of the interviewers walked ahead, opened the door to the car and turned white as a ghost. He said, "Ho Chi Minh piaster!" Somebody had left North Vietnamese currency with the likeness of Ho Chi Minh on one of the car seats. They took this as a warning from the Viet Cong. They also thought that the Land Rover had been booby-trapped, but a search turned up nothing suspicious. The interviewers were frightened. They did not know what to expect next, but the field trip went smoothly. Russo recalled that the visit to Qui Nhon was "one of the scariest field trips. For me, it was trial by fire because here I am just coming to Vietnam and all of a sudden I'm face up against the war, but yet no one is around! That was typical of that war."[94]

A closer brush with the war happened on another field trip, to Rach Gia near the Cambodian border. Russo and his team were walking to a restaurant when they heard a loud explosion. Arriving at the scene, they found that the restaurant had been blown apart and saw the horrible aftermath.

---

return to the United States. Davison decided to let him stay because he was afraid that the firing would demoralize the Vietnamese staff. Author interview with Phil Davison, 2003.

[93] Author interview with Tony Russo, 2003 and 2004.

[94] Author interview with Tony Russo, 2003 and 2004.

To complete his staffing, Goure recruited Bonnie Leib to edit the translated interviews and Roselle Foy to serve as a secretary. It was Rita McDermott, the administrative assistant for Joe Goldsen, who suggested sending the women to Saigon to improve the production quality of the translated interviews and to take care of paperwork. McDermott had joined RAND when it was still part of Douglas Aircraft and was considered an "old RAND hand." She chose Leib and Foy because she thought that they were independent women who "wouldn't cry every night from homesickness." Joe Goldsen resisted the idea of sending the women to a war zone. McDermott told him, "You know it's not a war zone. Saigon is the Paris of the Orient and they have flush toilets out there." Frank Collbohm said, "Why not,"[95] and so Roselle Foy and Bonnie Leib were sent to Saigon after signing a contract to work there for one year. Bonnie Leib would later say that both she and Foy were interested in getting out of the United States for a while for personal reasons.[96] The two women typified a general American attitude at the time. Vietnam was a poor country mired in war, and it did not offer the modern amenities Americans were used to having. Americans themselves were not as attuned to foreign cultures as they are now. So unless an American was very interested in living in Vietnam or had some strong motive to relocate there, he or she would be reluctant to go. Foy left Saigon before her year was over for personal reasons.

Leib, an editorial aide in Santa Monica, was to edit the translated interviews in Saigon and make them more readable, but not to change them textually. She also took care of the payroll. She found out that, in a culture that avoided direct confrontation, the only way to communicate to a Vietnamese staff member that he or she was fired was to withhold the bonus handed out around Tet, the Vietnamese New Year. She also did the banking, depositing the checks from RAND into the account in Saigon, an undertaking that could take half a day because of the cumbersome procedure inherited from the French and because of the lackadaisical attitude of the clerks, who would disappear for hours to go buy a newspaper or to have coffee. She performed other chores, such as going down to MACV to get the mail and to shop at the military Post Exchange, or PX, and handle the domestic staff. She hired a new cook whose specialty was *poulet farci*, or "stuffed roast chicken," which he wanted to serve for all formal occasions, including cocktails.[97]

Gradually, the RAND project became known in Saigon. Although classified, it was common knowledge within the American official circle and the media.[98] Goure would use the frequent small cocktail and dinner parties held at the villa to dispense

---

[95] Author interview with Rita McDermott, 2002.

[96] Author interview with Bonnie Hurwitz, 2003.

[97] Author interview with Bonnie Leib Hurwitz, 2003.

[98] For example, Arthur J. Dommen wrote in "Prisoner Survey: Air Attacks Cause Terror in Viet Cong," *Los Angeles Times*, July 4, 1965, that, "Computerized 'big think' has been recruited for duty in the Vietnam war—with a high-gear research group probing in depth for motivational weaknesses in the enemy Viet Cong morale."

information and his own readings of the Viet Cong. Every night for about a year, a dinner was held at the villa to which such people as George Carver, the CIA expert, Barry Zorthian, the head of the USIA, and some high-ranking military officers were invited. Many senior American officials in Vietnam would stop by 176 Pasteur to get Goure's interpretation of the status of the insurgency. According to Joe Carrier, Goure "had the ear not only of the U.S. military and the American Embassy, he also had the ear of visiting journalists, and we had some of the most prestigious like Joe Alsop come to dinner."[99] The villa became a "prestige stop" for visiting dignitaries and people such as Senator-elect Walter Mondale and Henry Kissinger would drop by, as well as "a curiously in-group place to go for high-level Americans."[100]

The RAND villa was now bursting at the seams with American and Vietnamese personnel, which eventually would include seven RAND staff members and about 20 Vietnamese interviewers, translators, and typists. Joe Carrier's and Chuck Thomson's bedrooms served as office space during the daytime. One morning, Thomson got up late, and when he emerged from the bathroom, he saw the three typists—whom he referred to as "The Three Graces"—already sitting at their desks. He had to ask them to leave so that he could finish getting ready. It was difficult for both the American and the Vietnamese staff to put up with this arrangement, in which office business and personal life were intermixed. To get away from each other once in a while, the Americans would escape to the Cercle Sportif, the elite club that had been set up by the French, to eat, swim, or play tennis. The Vietnamese quietly endured the situation.

In contrast to Zasloff and Donnell, who waited until they had finished collecting and analyzing their data to present their results—and thus risking seeing their findings overtaken by events in the interim—Goure moved fast and presented his findings regularly and in a timely manner. In fact, oral presentations were Goure's main and most effective delivery channel. With the help of Chuck Thomson, he would put a briefing together by taking apart the interviews that had been conducted, through a rudimentary cut-and-paste process. He would pull out various questions, code the answers, sort them into different stacks, see what they added up to, and figure out how things were progressing.

Goure's routine was to start his round of presentations in Saigon, where he would brief the MACV staff—including General Westmoreland on a couple of occasions—the Air Force, and the Embassy. Goure was a skillful, articulate, witty, and dynamic presenter, according to those who heard him. He could project presence and dignity, and it was in his briefings, rather than in his reports, that he made the strongest

---

[99] Author interview with Joe Carrier, 2003. Without citing Leon Goure or RAND by name, Alsop published a column in which he wrote that air strikes, "particularly since B-52 bombings began," had undermined Viet Cong morale and the enemy—even those in the hard-core units—now expected final defeat. Joseph Alsop, "The Viet Cong's Lot Is Not a Happy One," *Los Angeles Times*, October 6, 1965.

[100] Russo, "Looking Backward," 1972, p. 41.

Left to right: Joe Carrier and Leon Goure

From left to right: unidentified American visitor, Tony Russo, Gerry Hickey, and Leon Goure at the RAND villa.

impression. The briefings "appeared to sound a more positive note" than the reports, and that, because they preceded the publication of the written version, "apparently had an earlier and stronger effect."[101] According to those who attended the briefings, both in Saigon and in Washington, Goure was a relentless optimist, "the Joe Alsop of RAND," as one official would later describe him, "one whose message was that all of the military might was working and that additional strength would be even more effective, for the enemy was on the brink of collapse, and one more infusion of force would send him screaming to the peace table."[102] Indeed, in Russo's view, Goure's chief contribution to the air campaign was in linking insurgents' morale to bombing. At the time, there was a big debate among American officials in Saigon regarding the impact of the air war. Some thought that bombing angered the Vietnamese so much that it hardened their resistance. But, using the prestige of RAND and the interview data to support his claim, Goure argued that bombing did not cause an adverse reaction and that, in fact, "it tended to separate the villagers from the NLF."[103]

According to Tony Russo, who attended a few of Goure's briefings in Saigon, U.S. military officers were a receptive audience, unquestioningly accepting his finding that their pressures were pushing back the Viet Cong. Their own lack of knowledge about the enemy and about the impact of their weapons and operations—and, perhaps, also their personal inclination to believe that they were making headway—contributed to this acceptance. The Air Force, for example, had little idea of the effect that its ordnance was having on the Viet Cong, since it dropped most of its bombs in interdiction and harassment operations on targets that it could not observe. Officers would surround Goure after his briefings to ask questions about various topics, such as the effectiveness of anti-personnel weapons. Goure usually came up with answers, and if he did not have the information, he would display a proactive, "can do" attitude that appealed to the military, promising to get back to them in about a week.

According to Goure, he briefed the Air Force regularly in Saigon and relayed "a lot of very useful things" that could be gathered from the interviews about bombing.[104] For example, he told the Air Force people that when a bridge in North Vietnam was knocked out, it could be replaced with a floating bridge, so "you couldn't assume that the bridge was really inoperative." Or instead of bombing a bridge at night, they should drop their bombs a distance away, where enemy soldiers usually massed before crossing. That was the type of information he was giving the Air Force, because "all you could get" from the interview project was just "interesting tidbits" and "impressions."[105] He

---

[101] Goldberg, "RAND and Vietnam," 1969, p. 14.

[102] Landau, "Behind the Policy Makers," 1972, p. 60.

[103] Russo, Tony, "Looking Backward," 1972, p. 53.

[104] Author interview with Leon Goure, 2003.

[105] Author interview with Leon Goure, 2003.

Chuck Thomson (on right) with (from left to right) Hanh, Phan, Thang, Ninh, and Bach (of the Saigon team).

did not find this intelligence-collection aspect of the study objectionable because to him "the idea in principle was that we were military-oriented, at least I thought we were supposed to be military-oriented, in assisting the war effort."[106] In retrospect, he would later say that he did not know whether this information did any good.

The military, in fact, did find his work useful and reassuring. As the first translated interviews under Goure's leadership became available in early 1965, "they were very exciting to the military in Washington, whose contact with events in Vietnam, however frequent, must perforce be limited and fragmentary."[107] For Goure's audiences in Washington—some in the Office of the Secretary of Defense and in particular among the Air Force—his briefings confirmed the views and attitudes they already held, or tended to dispel the doubts they harbored.[108]

---

[106] Author interview with Leon Goure, 2003.

[107] Deitchman, *The Best-Laid Schemes*, 1976, pp. 236–237.

[108] Goldberg, "RAND and Vietnam," 1969, p. 14.

After the rounds of briefings in Saigon, Goure would return to the United States, stopping to brief CINCPAC and PACAF. In February 1965, about two months into his study, Goure briefed Admiral Ulysses Grant Sharp, the CINCPAC Commander. Unlike Zasloff and Donnell, who presented findings that were not actionable, Goure urged exploiting enemy vulnerability to airpower. As Tony Russo indicated, the linkage of enemy morale to bombing was a new message, and it got Sharp's attention. In a memo to General Westmoreland in February 1965, Sharp relayed what Goure had told him about the psychological effect of air strikes, which, in Goure's view, represented a "very promising area for further exploitation." Referring to the first use of U.S. jet aircraft in Phuoc Tuy Province, Sharp expressed the hope that Westmoreland would be able to launch more such missions. He endorsed Westmoreland's position that airpower should be better exploited in South Vietnam and added that he would do all he could to "get restrictions removed."[109] In his reply, Westmoreland told Sharp that he and his staff had also talked to Goure and that they agreed "with the bulk of his conclusions."[110] Although he seemed disappointed that the adverse psychological effect of air strikes—as revealed by Goure—was not as potent as had been expected, Westmoreland agreed with Sharp that airpower should be applied more forcefully, adding that "we are now fully committed to winning the war in Vietnam and we must take the necessary measures to bring this about."[111]

Winning as defined by Westmoreland—and the JCS—was, however, at variance with what Lyndon Johnson's civilian advisors had in mind. McGeorge Bundy and McNamara's objective was to hurt the enemy both in the North and in the South to the point where they became persuaded they could not win and decided to sue for peace.[112] The military, on the other hand, wanted to destroy the North's capacity to pursue the war and at the same time defeat the Viet Cong in the South or make it impossible for them to continue the insurgency. In the strategy advocated by the military, the increased use of airpower was a critical component. In a memo to McNamara, the JCS asked for the relaxation of restrictions on U.S. air strikes within South Vietnam and on other measures, such as hot pursuit of the Viet Cong across the Cambodian border in order to hit them in their sanctuaries. General John P. McConnell, the Air Force Chief of Staff, advocated the deployment of more air squadrons to Southeast Asia, the lifting of restrictions on the air campaign against North Vietnam, and the intensifica-

---

[109] U.S. Grant Sharp, Jr., cable to William Westmoreland, February 1965, William C. Westmoreland Personal Papers, Box 5, Lyndon B. Johnson Library, Austin, Tex.

[110] William Westmoreland, cable to Admiral Sharp, February 1965, William C. Westmoreland Personal Papers, Box 5, Lyndon B. Johnson Library, Austin, Tex.

[111] William Westmoreland, cable to Admiral Sharp, February 1965.

[112] McNamara's other objective was to use airpower to protect U.S. troops, using bombs to destroy enemy forces instead of exposing American soldiers to attacks. As he put it, "We're going to trade firepower for men." Neil Sheehan, "Should We Have War Crime Trials?" *The New York Times*, March 28, 1971.

tion of bombing within the South to destroy Viet Cong concentrations. But although the civilian and military camps differed in the end results they wished to achieve, they both wanted to inflict maximum pain on the enemy. In this environment, Goure's findings on how much the Viet Cong were hurting were well received on both sides.

In March 1965, Goure completed his first interim report, which incorporated what he had presented in his briefings.[113] This report would later be superseded by another one based on a larger sample of interviews. It contained the usual caveats regarding the tentative nature of the findings, which would have to be checked against other evidence. However, despite inaccuracies and distortions that may exist in the answers obtained from the 45 prisoners and defectors interviewed in January 1965, Goure believed that the consistency of the information and the corroboration provided by other intelligence sources indicated that the data were essentially valid. His report essentially reaffirmed the findings in his 1964 proposal regarding the effectiveness of airpower and provided reassurance that bombing did not cause a political backlash among the civilians.

The report's value lay chiefly in the information it provided to buttress the earlier findings that the Viet Cong feared airpower the most of all the weapons deployed against them; that airpower restricted their mobility and hampered their plans and operations; and that it depressed their morale, while failing to cause resentment among the population. For example, as Goure had initially reported, the Viet Cong feared detection and attack by air, even in areas where they felt safe from ground operations. Concretely, Goure cited that some respondents had reported that their units had sustained heavy losses from surprise air assaults. He cited data that showed that the threat of airpower alone was enough to interfere with logistics and operations, disrupt food production and transportation, and force the Viet Cong to keep on the move, thus making their hard life even harder. He specified the types of ordnance the Viet Cong feared the most: napalm, which topped the list; 500-lb bombs and bomb clusters, which inflicted the heaviest damage and highest casualties. With regard to the erosion of morale, Goure added to the earlier finding the sense of vulnerability that the Viet Cong felt in the face of airpower, because they knew they did not have the right weapons to defend themselves against it. In short, Goure took natural human reactions of fear and discouragement in the face of overwhelming force as signs of buckling morale within enemy ranks and saw it as cause, therefore, for optimism for U.S. policymakers.

Goure confirmed the usefulness of air activities that were under way or being planned and, as in 1964, suggested that harassment by ground and air actions be enhanced to exploit Viet Cong vulnerability. In his view, a harassment campaign conducted day and night, reinforced with intensified and continuous air surveillance, would likely inflict more casualties on the Viet Cong, disrupt their attacks, lower their

---

[113] Leon Goure, *Some Impressions of the Effects of Military Operations on Viet Cong Behavior*, Santa Monica, Calif.: RAND Corporation, RM-4517-1-ISA, March 1965.

Interviewer Thang transcribing a taped interview.

morale, and curb their ability to move around, take the initiative, and operate. Such a campaign could create favorable conditions for the GVN to conduct ground operations to attack the Viet Cong—turning them from "hunters to hunted"—and inflict a decisive defeat on the insurgency. Finally, Goure added a suggestion to mount an effective psychological-warfare program—accompanied by credible appeals and promises to the Viet Cong and civilians living in their zones—to exploit the Viet Cong's vulnerabilities and thereby encourage defection.

Providing more-concrete evidence regarding the effect of airpower on the attitude of civilians, Goure noted that none of the respondents reported that civilian damage was a direct cause for people joining the Viet Cong. In fact, several of the captured Viet Cong cadres and regroupees denied outright that attacks on villages was a major motivation for people to join the insurgents.

In fall 1965, the U.S. Embassy in Saigon distributed Goure's study to reporters, identifying it only as a RAND report. Neil Sheehan of *The New York Times* would later write that the study "concluded that the peasants blamed the Vietcong when their hamlets were blasted and their relatives killed. . . ."[114] According to Sheehan, reporters dismissed the study as an illustration of the government's usual ability to find a think tank that would tell it what it wanted to hear.[115]

---

[114] Sheehan, "Should We Have War Crimes Trials?" 1971.

[115] Sheehan, "Should We Have War Crimes Trials?" 1971. The policy of indiscriminate bombing and shelling continued despite the recommendation of a secret study done in the summer of 1966 for the U.S. Embassy and military headquarters on the pacification program: that it be "carefully re-examined." It was conducted by "some of the most experienced Americans" in South Vietnam. "According to the study there was evidence that the practice was driving hundreds of thousands of refugees into urban slums and squalid camps, causing unnecessary death and suffering, and angering the peasantry." However, the recommendation was "vetoed at the highest levels of American authority in Saigon." In so doing, "the American leadership in Saigon was deciding to ordain the practice, to establish a de facto policy" because "devastation had become a fundamental element in their strategy to win the war."

According to David Morell, the MACV staff liked Goure's findings better than those presented by Zasloff and Donnell. March 1965 was a period when there was a lot of excitement at MACV headquarters because "we were first bringing the real [i.e., American] troops in."[116] Their arrival led people to believe that "we're going to clean up this place and be out of here soon."[117] At the same time, American dependents had been ordered to evacuate from Saigon, and the bombing of the North had begun, so there was a sense that the United States had cleared the deck and was really getting down to the business of winning the war. The optimism at MACV was epitomized by a major in J-2 who was convinced that if one good American battalion was put in Ca Mau (the southernmost tip of Vietnam), they would "walk all the way to Hanoi without resistance."[118] Morell remembered that "there was the sense that the American technological prowess and the American fighting man . . . will just take care of this ragtag crowd of Vietnamese—they couldn't stand in our way."[119] In Washington, one senior American official echoed this sentiment, saying privately to a group of subordinates, "These wispy beards and beggars [i.e., Ho Chi Minh and his associates] aren't going to defeat us."

The optimism was shared by Frank Collbohm, who visited South Vietnam toward the end of April. In a report written following his return, he alluded to a future victory and reported that the bombing of North Vietnam had boosted the morale of the South Vietnamese military and civilians—a comment indicating that he saw that at least there was a positive side effect to the air strikes.[120] His optimism also extended to Goure's work, in which he took a personal interest.[121] Making calls on American officials, Collbohm found praise for Goure in some high places. Alexis Johnson, deputy ambassador, "knew about the RAND work in Vietnam and was extremely enthusiastic about the project of uncovering vulnerability to psychological warfare."[122] In addition, some officials told Collbohm that "the RAND interviews are developing more intelligence on more different subjects than the entire intelligence community is delivering. Whenever they are in trouble, they call Leon."[123] As an illustration, Collbohm wrote that the previous Saturday, when they received a request from Washington for information regarding the impact of air strikes on the Viet Cong, they called Goure because "the

---

[116] Author interview with David Morell, May 2004.

[117] Author interview with David Morell, May 2004.

[118] Author interview with David Morell, May 2004.

[119] Author interview with David Morell, May 2004.

[120] F. R. Collbohm, "Trip Report, Part II: South Vietnam, April 29–May 5," Santa Monica, Calif.: RAND Corporation, June 23, 1965 (not available to the general public).

[121] Author interview with Jim Digby, 2002.

[122] Collbohm, "Trip Report, Part II," 1965, p. 2.

[123] Collbohm, "Trip Report, Part II," 1965, p. 9.

only place that information existed was in the RAND building on Rue Pasteur."[124] The RAND team worked all Saturday afternoon, then got a car and delivered the report. Collbohm wrote that he "heard favorable repercussions at CINCPAC. They know it was RAND work and the best they had. The team is getting all kinds of things in addition to what they really started for."[125] According to Collbohm, "RAND's stock in the theater is very high. They really like us. Leon is doing a fantastically good job there."[126] Collbohm's enthusiastic support of Leon Goure would solidify Goure's position and allow him later to withstand serious criticism inside and outside of RAND.

The years 1965–1967 represented an active period for RAND in Vietnam. Besides Leon Goure, various staff members continued to conduct operational research, and one consultant—Ted Britton—was involved in co-opting students and diverting their energy away from political agitation.

During his stay in Saigon, Collbohm had dinner with Britton and later reported only that Britton was "doing a bang-up job,"[127] without specifying what it was. Britton, a professor of education at Cal State Sacramento, had served as a teacher-education advisor to the Diem government from 1959 to 1961 and had assisted it in establishing the secondary-education system. During that time, he also made some documentary films about Vietnam. After the fall of President Diem, George Tanham heard about Britton and his work and suggested that RAND hire him in 1964. This was the period when instability reigned, and Vietnamese students, who had been galvanized by their political activism during the period leading up to the overthrow of Diem, were part of the problem. They formed a volatile segment of the population and were vehemently opposed to the generals' running the country. They often staged antigovernment rallies and were prone to what they called *xuong duong*, or "descending into the streets" to protest, thus contributing to the chaos.

Ted Britton's job in Saigon as a RAND consultant was to conduct a "short unclassified study of the problems presented by youth in Vietnam—their political goals, motivations, attitudes, and probable political involvements."[128] With the support of the U.S. aid mission, Britton had gone to Vietnam in mid-October 1964 to conduct field research, interviewing Vietnamese youths, their leaders, and government officials. Britton was supposed to produce a report, but there is no record at RAND of any analysis written by him.[129] Britton appeared to be more of an organizer than a researcher. He

---

[124]Collbohm, "Trip Report, Part II," 1965, p. 9.

[125]Collbohm, "Trip Report, Part II," 1965, p. 10.

[126]Collbohm, "Trip Report, Part II," 1965, p. 10.

[127]F. R. Collbohm, "Trip Report, Part IV: South Vietnam, May 14–16, 1965," Santa Monica, Calif.: RAND Corporation, June 23, 1965, p. 3 (not available to the general public).

[128]Social Science Department, "Progress Report for 1964–1965," 1965.

[129]According to Tony Russo, by 1968 Britton still had not produced a long-anticipated report. Russo, "Looking Backward," 1972, p. 58.

set up a Summer Youth Program in 1965, with 200 work camps in Vietnam. Ultimately, he attracted more than 8,000 students to this program to engage in a variety of work projects: building roads, housing for refugees, orphanages, schools, and bridges.

This Summer Youth Program was considered an important component of U.S. nonmilitary actions in Vietnam, and McGeorge Bundy cited it in a June 28, 1965, memorandum to President Johnson. He told the president that youths and students remained "volatile and restless" and were "quite capable of making political trouble." To "minimize this prospect and direct their energies along more constructive lines," the U.S. Mission in Saigon had "supported a Summer Youth Program designed to place several thousand urban youth into rural areas to participate in small-scale civic action activities." Bundy added that the program had been "well received by various political and religious groups" and that the CIA had "initiated a supplementary program among student organizations."[130]

Tony Russo described Britton as liberal and easygoing, with "the demeanor of a Scout Master."[131] In that period, Britton was living in a large villa in Saigon, where students frequently gathered. Britton visited the RAND villa often but said little about his work, leading Russo to compare him to the "Quiet American," the principal character in the Graham Greene novel of the same name who was, in fact, an intelligence agent and an "agent provocateur." Britton, Russo said, seemed "to have been something of a second-string 'Ed Lansdale' [i.e., CIA] figure." According to Russo, there was a lot of criticism of Britton among RAND personnel because he had failed to produce a report, but the criticism "was muted by the fact that some people credited him with pacifying the Saigon student movement." The view was that "if he keeps those kids off the streets he will have earned his keep by that alone."[132]

During his stay in Vietnam, Frank Collbohm got VIP treatment. He met with several South Vietnamese and American generals.[133] One of the sights that impressed him the most was a cache of weapons that had been uncovered in the mangrove swamp near Saigon. Infiltrated by sea, the weapons included tons of 70mm Russian Howitzer ammunition, 7.62 anti-aircraft guns, Czech submachine guns, and East German flame throwers—all packed so well that they could be buried in the sand below low-water levels and then dug up in perfect shape for later use. To Collbohm, a quintessential Cold Warrior and anti-communist, the weapons from the Eastern Bloc reinforced his

---

[130] McGeorge Bundy, "The Status of Non-Military Actions in Vietnam," memorandum from the President's Special Assistant for National Security Affairs to President Johnson, June 28, 1965, Foreign Relations of the United States, Johnson Administration, Vietnam, 1964–1968, Volume III, Document 27, State Department Archives, Washington, D.C.

[131] Russo, "Looking Backward," 1972, p. 58.

[132] Russo, "Looking Backward," 1972, p. 58.

[133] One of them was General Nguyen Chanh Thi, I Corps commander, whom Collbohm tried to persuade to stop torturing POWs because it was counterproductive. Collbohm, "Trip Report, Part II," 1965, p. 11.

belief that the United States was fighting global communism in South Vietnam—a view he discussed in a meeting he held with a group of Vietnamese students, telling them bluntly that the United States was fighting in Vietnam out of self-interests to resist the Chinese Communist expansion, and adding "Actually, we don't care whether you're free. It's really no major concern of ours."[134]

The optimism of Frank Collbohm and of the MACV staff was not shared by Lyndon Baines Johnson in this period. Domestic discontent with his escalation of the war was growing in Congress and on university campuses. The first teach-in against the war took place at Michigan State University in March 1965. Johnson also faced international and domestic pressure to stop the bombing of North Vietnam. In the South, the bombing of the North and the dispatch of Marines had done little to improve the situation. In the first week of June 1965, a large force of guerrillas—1,000 strong— overran the district capital of Dong Xoai and attacked a U.S. Special Forces camp 90 miles north of Saigon. South Vietnamese troops counterattacked, but in four days of fighting lost at least 900 men.

General Westmoreland, arguing that the South Vietnamese armed forces were on the verge of collapse, sent a request to CINCPAC for more U.S. troops. He wanted to bring the total to 175,000 for deployment along the coast, as well as inland. In the same cable, he also asked for a change of mission that would allow U.S. ground troops to go on search-and-destroy operations against the enemy, enlarging their role beyond securing American bases. The time had come to "forget about enclaves and take the war to the enemy," he wrote. Westmoreland's plan was to use American troops to fight the growing number of North Vietnamese regulars infiltrated into the South in a war of attrition by killing more of them than could be replaced. As Westmoreland's deputy, General William DePuy, put it, "We are going to stomp them to death." On June 18, President Johnson, fearing that a full-scale buildup would jeopardize his Great Society program, opted for a more gradual approach and partially approved Westmoreland's request, committing a total of 123,000 troops to Vietnam. But he approved the change of mission from defensive to offensive, and McNamara went along with Westmoreland's attrition strategy.

Among Johnson's senior advisors, George Ball, the Assistant Secretary of State, was the lone voice of dissent. Playing his usual role of devil's advocate, he argued against deepening military involvement. In June 1965, at the request of the President, Ball wrote a memo recommending that the United States "cut its losses in Vietnam." Ball started by saying that he wrote his paper "on the premise that we are losing the war in Viet-Nam" and proposed steps to either extricate the United States or to lower its military presence in South Vietnam by reducing U.S. defense perimeters to correspond with limited U.S. deployment capabilities. In his view, even a substantial increase in American commitments with expanded air attacks on the North and larger troop com-

---

[134]Collbohm, "Trip Report, Part IV," 1965, p. 5.

mitments in the South offered no assurance that the United States would achieve its political objectives. Furthermore, enlarging the bombing of the North might risk provoking the Soviet Union and China, and increasing the number of American ground forces in the South and committing them to combat might run grave risks of "bogging down an indeterminate number of American troops in a protracted and bloody conflict of uncertain outcome."[135]

Ball argued that a tactical withdrawal from Vietnam would not lead to disaster: "In our anxiety to build up support for the struggle in South Viet-Nam, we have tended to exaggerate the consequences for US power and prestige of a tactical withdrawal," Ball wrote. A withdrawal "would create short-term problems, especially in Thailand," but the United States could take "prompt and effective defensive and affirmative measures . . . to avoid any serious long-term consequences. By and large, the world knows that the government in Saigon is a joke, and if our withdrawal resulted from an effort to face this problem squarely, friendly nations would not interpret it as a US failure to keep its commitments. More likely most nations would consider that we had more than kept our commitments to Viet-Nam."

Ball went on to contrast the political situation in North and South Vietnam, and cited the Zasloff-Donnell-Pauker study on "Viet Cong Motivation and Morale" to buttress his point : "Politically, South Viet-Nam is a lost cause," he wrote, "The country is bled white from twenty years of war and the people are sick of it. The Viet Cong—as is shown by the Rand Corporation Motivation and Morale Study—are deeply committed. Hanoi has a Government and a purpose and a discipline. The 'government' in Saigon is a travesty. In a very real sense, South Viet-Nam is a country with an army and no government." He concluded by saying that, in his view, "a deep commitment of United States forces in a land war in South Viet-Nam would be a catastrophic error. If ever there was an occasion for a tactical withdrawal, this is it." Ball's position was opposed by Rusk and McNamara, who favored deeper American military commitment. Rusk contended that extrication from Vietnam would damage American credibility and that this, in turn, would "lead to our ruin and almost certainly to catastrophic war."

Whereas General Curtis LeMay had invoked a RAND study to support his argument for bombing North Vietnam, Ball cited another RAND report to support his call for withdrawal. These instances demonstrate the credibility that the name RAND carried in Washington at the time, but they also show how selective Washington officials could be in picking findings that suited their own policy recommendations. In the end, Ball's memo was an exercise in futility.

---

[135] George Ball, "Cutting Our Losses in South Vietnam," memorandum to Sec. of State, Sec. of Defense, M. Bundy, Wm. Bundy, John McNaughton, Leonard Unger, June 28, 1965, National Security File, Troop Deployment History, Box 43, LBJ Library, Austin, Tex., cited in Barrett, ed., *President Lyndon B. Johnson's Vietnam Papers*, 1998.

George Ball's citation of the Zasloff-Donnell study appeared to be the last instance when their report was mentioned in official communication. The stage, as far as the Viet Cong Motivation and Morale Project was concerned, was now occupied by Leon Goure, who would cut a much wider swath than Zasloff and Donnell ever did. Goure's routine was to leave Saigon periodically to return to the United States.[136] Back in Santa Monica, he would give talks to the RAND Management Committee, which was made up of Frank Collbohm and the department heads, and his colleagues. These talks helped him polish his presentation before he headed to Washington to brief the Joint Chiefs and the Secretary of Defense.

According to Goure, the Management Committee never objected to his interpretation of the data or asked him "to change the tenor of his briefing," and he assumed that they approved of it.[137] Some of his colleagues, however, were critical. As early as March 1965, when the first Goure paper appeared, the quality of his work was questioned. According to several of his colleagues, "a fair number of analysts were convinced that Goure was interpreting selectively from the interviews," and believed that his support for airpower was intended to appeal to McNamara's own inclination.[138] Bill Dorrill remembered a "tempestuous" talk given by Goure in a conference room, during which a person in the audience "got so steamed up that Leon himself got angry and gave a tongue-lashing, saying, 'Oh, simmer down.'"[139]

If RAND was hoping that it would acquire influence over Vietnam policy, Goure seemed initially to get it where it wanted to go. Three months after he began his project in Vietnam, Goure was asked to go to Washington to present his findings. Unlike Zasloff and Donnell, whose report never reached Robert McNamara, one of the officials Goure was asked to brief was the Secretary of Defense himself. McNamara had gotten to know about the RAND project earlier, when he was in Saigon on one of his periodic visits. At the time, the Secretary of Defense asked for a paper from the RAND group to be delivered to him by seven o'clock the next morning. His request arrived at 176 Pasteur at 10 p.m. the evening before, and Goure and his staff labored through the night to meet it. After that, McNamara became an enthusiastic supporter of the project. Goure would later say that to the best of his recollection, he told the Secretary of Defense in that briefing that enemy morale had declined because of the bombing, and that North Vietnamese troops were demoralized because "they had been drafted in the

---

[136] According to Tony Russo, Goure *and* Thomson were not interested in broadening their knowledge of Vietnam. Goure spent most of his time shuttling back and forth between Saigon and the United States and talking to Americans. "Thomson spent most of his time in the RAND villa." Russo, "Looking Backward," 1972, p. 53.

[137] Author interview with Leon Goure, 2003.

[138] Landau, "Behind the Policy Makers," 1972, p. 60.

[139] Author interview with Bill Dorrill, 2004 and 2005.

North" and sent South, "and they didn't like the idea," or because "they had been sick" during the arduous march to the South.[140]

Goure said that McNamara asked only a few questions, mainly for clarification. The Secretary of Defense appeared happy and interested, and seemed to find the study useful.[141] To Goure's surprise, McNamara suddenly asked, "What's your budget?" Goure replied, "About one hundred thousand dollars." McNamara then asked, "OK, what can you do with a million?" and Goure said, "I can expand the operation, do much more—more interviews, more write ups." McNamara told him, "You got it."[142] This came as a shock to Goure, because all of a sudden he got a million dollars, which in today's dollars would be equivalent to ten million. Indeed, Goure's briefing did make an impression on McNamara, who would later cite "prisoner interviews" showing that the bombing of the North had hurt enemy morale in the South. As Guy Pauker put it, "McNamara was lapping up Goure's work like good Scotch."[143] In August 1966, John McNaughton on behalf of McNamara would ask for a report each month from Goure showing the trends in changes among the Viet Cong.[144]

After that initial meeting, Goure was required to brief McNamara personally every three to four months, either in Saigon, which the Defense Secretary visited on a number of occasions, or in Washington. Goure was now reaching the highest ranks within the Pentagon. Since he was briefing the Secretary of Defense, other officials wanted to know what he said, especially the Joint Chiefs. For everybody, "It was a must."[145] In addition, he was also distributing his reports widely, along with copies of all POW and defector interviews. They were given to MACV J-2; to the Vietnamese J-2—but with prisoner names removed so that the Vietnamese would not retaliate against those who had been critical of the ARVN; to PACAF; to CINCPAC; to OSD; and to many more places. To Goure, his ultimate boss was McNamara: He was "reporting . . . to the Secretary of Defense."[146]

According to Goure, his influence irked General Joseph A. McChristian, the new head of J-2 at MACV, who tried to take over the project several times because he was upset that Goure was giving McNamara a progress report on the war without

---

[140] Author interview with Leon Goure, 2003.

[141] According to journalist Jack Foisie of the *Los Angeles Times*, during the tenure of McNamara as Secretary of Defense, there was a belief in Washington that "military victory was obtainable for the American Army even though its power was restrained by political considerations." Consequently, briefers had to demonstrate progress and "were honor-bound to be optimistic." Jack Foisie, "Laird to Get Vietnam Briefings with Optimism Toned Down," *Los Angeles Times*, March 9, 1969.

[142] Foisie, "Laird to Get Vietnam Briefings," 1969.

[143] Jardini, "The Wrong War," 1998, p. 46.

[144] Jardini, "The Wrong War," 1998, p. 46.

[145] Author interview with Leon Goure, 2003.

[146] Goure, "The RAND Corporation POW and Defector Debriefing Program," 1985, p. 7-4.

McChristian's participation and without McChristian's control. As the head of J-2, he thought that intelligence should fall under his purview, and tried to control the project, requiring, for example, that RAND's reports and other information go through him.[147] Goure refused to abide by his request, telling MACV, "McNamara wants it. . . . You can't stop it." Once when Goure was giving a briefing at CINCPAC, he looked out and saw McChristian sitting in front among the audience. McChristian had to endure listening to Goure talk about how the war was going, and this "did not go over very well with him."[148] Although this was a very unpleasant situation for Goure, there was little that McChristian could do, because Goure was "fairly well protected at that point."[149]

Goure now became a star of the briefing circuit. He gave so many briefings that he could not recall the total.[150] Goure "would give a briefing at the drop of a hat," some of his staff members would later say, and they would come to refer to those presentations and consultations as "quickies." However, the discussions rarely mentioned the Vietnamese: It was if the Americans "were not advisers at all, but in direct command."[151] In what could be a typical day, Goure described the parade of military advisors and the stream of telephone calls soliciting advice, assistance, or documents. He proudly reported to a friend in Santa Monica that MACV had gotten into "the habit of incorporating our data (statements) into their messages to Washington."[152]

Barry Zorthian, the head of USIS, would send foreign correspondents over to the villa to get "backgrounders" from Goure, and American reporters would cite Goure and RAND without identifying them in their articles.[153] Goure's influence even

---

[147] Gerry Hickey would later recall that "MACV was moving to assert some kind of 'editorial' control over the final drafts of RAND reports in Vietnam." According to him, he was "pleased and somewhat astonished" when Frank Collbohm, who was visiting the country at the end of April 1965, "stated flatly" at ARPA and MACV briefings "that RAND had a policy of hiring well-qualified people for its research and therefore would not accept any MACV censorship. The only reviews of RAND reports in draft would be by the pertinent RAND staff." Hickey, *Window on a War*, 2002, p. 169.

[148] Author interview with Leon Goure, 2003.

[149] Author interview with Leon Goure, 2003.

[150] In its "Progress Report for 1965," RAND D-14389-1, January 26, 1966, the Social Science Department indicated that, "Because the data they have collected cover a wide range of topics of immediate importance to current operations in Vietnam, it has been the practice of the RAND team to make this information available to interested U.S. and Vietnamese personnel in the field as expeditiously as possible. . . . The texts of all our interrogations are distributed to a large number of agencies in Saigon, and on-the-spot analyses are produced frequently, either at RAND's own initiative or in response to special requests from U.S. authorities."

[151] Russo, "Looking Backward," 1972, p. 41.

[152] Goure, Leon, letter to a friend in Santa Monica, May 30, 1965.

[153] Goure's conclusions were conveyed to the press. In "Prisoner Survey: Air Attacks Cause Terror in Viet Cong," 1965, Arthur J. Dommen wrote, without disclosing the identity of Goure and his team, "Preliminary reports from the research group say that Viet Cong live in terror of air and artillery bombardment, and that they are unpopular in many villages because they attract government reprisals. . . . They found 'a major impact' on the

reached the ears of Vietnamese government officials, and he recalled that a group of them contacted him one time to talk about a coup d'etat. They wanted to use him as a channel to the Americans to sound out the acceptability of overthrowing the government. Goure remembered the "weird feeling" of sitting in a house in Saigon discussing all this. He recalled asking them, "What would you do to replace it?" giving them "a lecture on politics," and telling them, "You can't just be against, you have to be for something."[154]

Goure would later say that he found all the attention ridiculous, since he was running a small operation that paled in scale to what the military, the State Department, and the CIA could deploy. When a friend told him that he was bragging about his success, he admitted that he sounded "boastful and self-satisfied," but softened his attitude by saying that he was only pleased with the way the project was going.[155] He relished the opportunity to direct one of the most interesting studies he would "ever have the chance to work on" and told his friend that, if he had to give it up, he would "regret leaving it."[156] However, he also knew that it would be hard for RAND to replace him.

In retrospect, Goure would say that he had not expected all the "hoopla," and that he was not looking for attention from such high places. As he put it, "I wasn't looking for it. I had expected originally that if and when I had to brief somebody it would be the Air Force chief of intelligence who asked me to go out in the first place, that he would be the guy that I would be briefing. . . . I didn't expect to brief the Secretary of Defense or . . . the Secretary of the Air Force." He professed that he found the whole situation baffling, "Why it became that way, why it was, I don't know. I was doing what I pretty much was asked to do, at least I thought I was doing; beyond that, I don't know."[157]

At the time, it struck some people that he enjoyed being in the limelight—not just in Saigon but also in the halls of power in Honolulu and Washington—and that briefing McNamara and the Joint Chiefs elated him. On the way home one time, he was asked to brief CINCPAC. When he arrived, he found "everybody, the entire CINCPAC staff, and the commanding admiral—you name it, they were there, all lined up in this enormous auditorium."[158] Another time, a Navy admiral came to the RAND villa in Saigon and invited Goure and Chuck Thomson to visit the car-

---

Viet Cong largely attributable to the introduction of American jet aircraft strikes against Viet Cong concentration and base areas. . . ." Dommen added, "The findings . . . tend to show that the Viet Cong are increasingly demoralized by constant bombardment and surprise raids; awed by American resources being brought to bear in the war and shaken in their belief in ultimate victory."

[154] Author interview with Leon Goure, 2003.

[155] Leon Goure, letter to a friend in Santa Monica, June 4, 1965.

[156] Leon Goure, letter to a friend in Santa Monica, June 4, 1965.

[157] Author interview with Leon Goure, 2003.

[158] Author interview with Leon Goure, 2003.

rier *Coral Sea* and to brief the pilots who were bombing North Vietnam. When they arrived onboard, the admiral came out on deck to greet them personally. Another time he was flown to Clark Air Base in the Philippines to brief General John Dale Ryan, the SAC Commander, about B-52 strikes. Each of these strategic bombers had wings spanning 185 feet and was capable of carrying 37,000 pounds of nuclear or conventional bombs for 7,500 miles. They had been designed to penetrate and incinerate the Soviet hinterland, but, starting in June 1965, they were unleashed in South Vietnam at the request of General Westmoreland. According to Goure, the Air Force at that time believed that "any area hit by B-52s was neutralized for a month after the attack"; consequently, it would not bomb the same target again during those weeks. The Viet Cong, however, had discerned this pattern and would move into the craters because they knew they would be safe for a while. Goure would later say that he had "a hell of a time telling that to the SAC Commander, that this wasn't quite working the way he thought it was."[159]

Goure's message would extend further, to the highest levels of the U.S. government. Coming from outside official channels and supposedly free of official bias, its validation of Washington policies carried more weight than that provided by sources within the government; consequently, it was welcomed by high-ranking members of the administration. Besides Robert McNamara, Goure also got to brief McGeorge Bundy and Walt Rostow. He did not brief Secretary of State Dean Rusk, but once almost got to brief President Johnson himself. Reading some of the memos that have come to light from officials familiar with Goure's findings, one notices that the obligatory caveats were ignored and that the optimistic readings came through loud and clear: Enemy morale was declining; U.S. military operations especially its airpower—were having an effect; and airpower should be applied even more forcefully to grind down the Viet Cong.

For example, in June 1965, McGeorge Bundy, LBJ's National Security Advisor, cited Goure's study to give the president an optimistic analysis of the effect of airpower in South Vietnam. Bundy told LBJ that, as reported in the RAND study, air attacks, air-envelopment operations that caught the Viet Cong by surprise and inflicted heavy losses, and harassment had severely eroded the morale of Viet Cong units and made them lose faith in victory. Bundy reiterated RAND's suggestion that harassment by air be increased and conducted day and night to reinforce the Viet Cong fear of detection and attack; disrupt their living conditions, movement, and operations; and lower their morale.[160]

---

[159] Author interview with Leon Goure, 2003.

[160] McGeorge Bundy, "RAND Studies of Viet Cong Motivation and Morale," memo to the President, June 28, 1965, National Security Files, M. Bundy Files, Memos to President, Box 3, LBJ Library, Austin, Tex., cited in Barrett, *President Lyndon B. Johnson's Vietnam Papers*, 1998. Also in Foreign Relations of the United States, Johnson Administration, Vietnam 1964–1968, Volume III, Document 27, State Department Archives, with notation indicating that the president saw the memo on June 28.

As the conflict escalated, Washington was anxious to find out how well military pressures were working. Goure's findings became a handy source for officials looking for signs that would justify optimism. In a memo of July 10, 1965, Chester Cooper, deputy to McGeorge Bundy, told his boss that there was ground for encouragement. Summarizing "Rand's Latest Interrogation of Viet Cong Captives and Defectors," Cooper said that RAND had uncovered "some very interesting, possibly very significant findings on VC vulnerabilities." In the first six months of 1965, Chester wrote, intensified GVN and American operations had severely impeded Viet Cong activities and operations and depressed their morale. Cooper credited airpower, which Goure's study had revealed as the most significant weapon in the U.S. arsenal. Citing the RAND study, Cooper said that the threat of air strikes; jet fighter bombers, with their speed and terrifying noise; air reconnaissance; napalm; and helicopters had achieved the most impact. Cooper expected Viet Cong morale to continue to decline, especially as B-52s were unleashed and U.S. forces went on offensive operations. In conclusion, Cooper wrote that RAND's findings could be "regarded with almost certain confidence and can possibly be extended to cover VC attitudes in general." "To an optimist at least," he added, there was ground for optimism.[161]

Within the administration, Goure's message perhaps resonated most with Walt Rostow—an optimist and a hardliner.[162] The day after being briefed by Goure on July 15, 1965, Rostow sent a memo, entitled "The Enemy's Troubles," to Secretary of State Dean Rusk, with copies to McGeorge Bundy and to Bill Moyers—LBJ's press secretary—telling Rusk that he had found Goure's presentation extremely interesting, and pointing out that the Viet Cong vulnerabilities uncovered by Goure represented hopeful signs and, in Rostow's view, provided "substantial encouragement" for the

---

[161] Chester L. Cooper, "Summary of Rand's Latest Interrogation of Viet Cong Captives and Defectors," memo to M. Bundy, July 10, 1965, National Security Files, Memos to President, Box 4, LBJ Library, Austin, Tex., cited in Barrett, *President Lyndon B. Johnson's Vietnam Papers*, 1998. An American reporter, Arthur J. Dommen, "Viet Cong Defections Are a Major Puzzle," *Los Angeles Times*, July 9, 1965, pointed out, however, that the psychological impact of bombing had not translated into enemy decline. He wrote, "During the time the Viet Cong prisoners and defectors in question [among those 250 interviewed by the RAND team] were telling of the terrifying effect of surprise bombing attacks the hardcore strength of the Viet Cong was building up. . . ." Dommen felt that this "major psychological impact" should not give "cause for rejoicing"—as the authors of the research implied—because the air strikes created a civilian backlash, which aided Viet Cong recruiting.

[162] In his article "The Paul Wolfewitz of the '60s," published in the *Los Angeles Times*, September 2, 2007, David Milne, a lecturer in foreign policy at the University of Nottingham and author of a book on Walt Rostow, *America's Rasputin: Walt Rostow and the Vietnam War*, New York: Hill and Wang, 2009, wrote that Rostow, "Enamored of the quality of his own counsel . . . framed a policy of military escalation, manipulated CIA field reports to provide Johnson with a more positive spin on U.S. military prospects and then, through 1967 and 1968, advised Johnson against pursuing a compromise peace with North Vietnam." It was Averell Harriman, the celebrated American diplomat chosen by Johnson to negotiate an end to the war, who called Rostow "America's Rasputin" because of the influence that Rostow's "hard-edged advice exerted on an increasingly beleaguered Johnson."

United States to press forward down the same path and to stick to its objectives.[163] To Rostow, the study was credible because the 250 interviews on which the findings had been based represented a "carefully designed and balanced sample."[164]

Among the findings Rostow reiterated were the stresses and strains the Viet Cong were experiencing in their effort to push the fighting to a higher level in the Central Highlands, where Westmoreland had launched his war of attrition against North Vietnamese troops with the support of fierce airpower. According to Goure, by moving toward a "modified Mao–Stage III offensive"[165] in this region, the Viet Cong were becoming more vulnerable. To advance to this stage—the last stage in revolutionary warfare involving large-scale conventional operations—the Viet Cong had acquired heavy weapons from Eastern Bloc countries, and expanded their forces with increased recruitment in the South and heavier infiltration of troops from North Vietnam. But this push had exacted a heavy price: They had begun to burden themselves with some of the logistical and political problems that had bedeviled the GVN. They had been compelled to use pressure and force to recruit more fighters into their ranks in the South, and as a result had found themselves fighting with large numbers of reluctant and ill-trained troops. To support a larger force, the Viet Cong had to impose higher taxes and requisition more food from the population, and these practices had led to a deterioration in their relationship with the people living in areas under their control.

In addition to these problems of their own making, the Viet Cong were also suffering from the rapidly expanding use of U.S. airpower, beginning in February 1965. Rostow repeated Goure's findings regarding the effect of airpower on Viet Cong operations, as well as the reassuring indication that the bombing, despite its increased ferocity, had failed to cause a political backlash among the population because, in general, the villagers blamed the Viet Cong, rather than the government, for the damage. The increased use of airpower even had a positive outcome, because it had led more villagers to flee into areas under government control, and had induced more Viet Cong to defect or desert back to their home villages. There was potential for turning the recent flood of defectors into "something of a tide,"[166] Rostow wrote, and the seemingly sub-

---

[163] Walt W. Rostow, "The Enemy's Troubles," memo to Secretary of State Dean Rusk, with copies to McGeorge Bundy and to Bill Moyers, July 16, 1965, Walt Rostow Personal Papers, Southeast Asia Folder, Box 13, Lyndon B. Johnson Library, Austin, Tex.

[164] According to Sy Deitchman, busy officials tended to be "indifferent to the methodology" of studies, especially if the results appeared to support their views. "If the results challenged [an official's] intuition, he was likely to dismiss the report as poorly done than to inquire searchingly into the basis of his own beliefs, or ask for a critical review of the report to see whether it might possibly be correct" Deitchman, *The Best-Laid Schemes*, 1976, pp. 390–391.

[165] Rostow agreed with this analysis, since it explained several recent developments, such as the expansion in enemy firepower, the rise in their attacks involving battalion-sized units, and the increase in the number of Viet Cong defectors and refugees fleeing from the areas under their control.

[166] Rostow, "The Enemy's Troubles," 1965.

stantial desertion—undetected to that date—indicated that the VC ranks were being depleted at a greater rate than suspected. To Rostow, the RAND interviews revealed "more vividly" than any other evidence he had seen "the reality of the strains" that the Viet Cong were "feeling in this critical summer campaign."[167]

More importantly, wrote Rostow, the interviews "dramatize[d]" what the United States had to do to "maximize the chance" that Hanoi would "call off the war at this stage and negotiate Americans out of Vietnam, with intent to try again later." To bring this about, Rostow proposed making political warfare a high priority and building it around the insights provided by the interviews regarding "the frame of mind of the Viet Cong, its force, and the population they control." Second, he recommended increasing "to the maximum the application of air power inside South Vietnam." The massive use of airpower aided by "improved spotting and other intelligence techniques . . . may turn out to be a major innovation in modern guerrilla warfare," he wrote.[168] Third, Rostow proposed that the United States "increase the cost to Hanoi of continuing to encourage and support the Viet Cong efforts, by bombing attacks on more vital installations where civilian casualties can be expected to be low." Lastly, Rostow recommended that the RAND materials be made "available to Congressional leaders, Vietnamese military and political officials, and to our allies who are in varying degrees confused about the character of the Viet Cong strategy and the reality of its military and political problems."

---

[167] The stresses and strains on the enemy created by the Viet Cong buildup of military forces in order to move to "a stage three form of guerrilla warfare" beginning in the fall of 1964, and the impact of airpower on the Viet Cong, had also been reported by Lucian W. Pye, in "A View from Vietnam," which had been submitted earlier to Rostow [a handwritten note on the first pages indicates that it was received on January 21, 1965], who circulated it to Dean Rusk. According to Pye, the introduction of American airpower represented the most "critical ingredient in the military picture." Although airpower "cannot yet be declared a decisive factor in shifting the balance," it had thrown the Viet Cong off their timetable and prevented them "from carrying through their strategic pattern of advance." Pye did not make the fact-finding trip to Vietnam or write the report as a RAND consultant, but cited "the RAND study" regarding dissatisfaction among the new recruits who had been transferred to the main force units and the large group defections among "men impressed from particular villages and moved directly to the main forces." Pye's report might have lent added credence, in Rostow's eyes, to Goure's later findings. Personal Papers of Walt Rostow, Southeast Asia Folder, Box 13, Lyndon B. Johnson Library, Austin, Texas.

[168] The importance of visual reconnaissance, as well as of forward air controllers, was recognized by the Air Force. In December 1965, RAND sent Joel Edelman to Vietnam to study these topics. *Visual reconnaissance* was carried out by slow-flying planes looking on the ground for suspicious and unusual signs that deviated from the daily patterns and activities. *Forward air control* spotted targets, communicated the coordinates and descriptions to the attacking aircraft, marked the locations with smoke rockets to direct the ordnance onto the right spot, and then sent confirmation after the targets had been struck. In an actual engagement, instead of marking the target with a smoke rocket, the forward air controller would keep back far enough to stay out of range of enemy fire and would direct the attacking aircraft to hit the right spot. A forward controller also had to communicate with the people on the ground. Sometimes, U.S. army units or American advisors to ARVN units would radio that they were getting mortar fire from certain coordinates and ask for an air strike. The forward air controller would receive the radio call and forward the request to the Air Force to attack that particular location.

In another area of counterinsurgency, Goure also gave encouragement to U.S. authorities aiming to damage the enemy's capacity to pursue the war. Addressing the program to destroy crops with defoliants, Ambassador Maxwell Taylor wrote in a July 5, 1965, cable to the State Department that was also communicated to CINCPAC that a preliminary RAND report had indicated that the spraying had destroyed crops grown by Viet Cong production units, reduced already-scarce food supplies for their combat units, and forced the insurgents to look for food elsewhere.[169] Taylor did not identify the author of the report, but it bore the hallmark of Leon Goure. According to Taylor, since RAND estimated that "one-third to one-half" of the VC manpower was employed in food production, the sprayings had inflicted a heavy blow to this investment in resources. As with airpower, the RAND report found unhappiness among the villagers but no evidence that crop destruction motivated them to join the Viet Cong—despite the fact that the sprayings also killed civilian crops and caused widespread fear among the population that the chemicals harmed their health.

On the basis of the RAND report and MACV's own evaluation of the crop-destruction program in three major VC areas since July 1964, Ambassador Taylor recommended in his cable that the program be expanded to further deny food sources to the Viet Cong. He also recommended amending guidelines to allow crop destruction in less-remote and more-populated areas, if these areas were under strong Viet Cong control and if significant military gain could be achieved from the sprayings. Considering that the alternatives for dealing with VC-controlled areas were to abandon them, to bomb and strafe them, or to attack with ground troops supported by air and artillery strikes, Taylor believed that destroying crops to starve out the VC and the population would pose "comparatively less risk to the civilian population." Taylor accepted that these extensive sprayings would undoubtedly cause some resentment on the part of the population whose crops were also destroyed, but he believed that this resentment could be mitigated with a stronger psychological warfare/civil affairs program to divert this resentment toward the Viet Cong and away from the GVN.

The themes of the effect of airpower on enemy morale and fighting capability would be repeated subsequently and elaborated on by Goure, as well as the recommendation to stay the course and do more of the same to grind down the insurgents and break their will to fight. If anything, subsequent reports showed that the trends were worsening for the Viet Cong and that applying more pressure would push the enemy further toward the breaking point. In a report co-authored with Chuck Thomson, for

---

[169] Maxwell Taylor, Telegram from the Embassy in Vietnam to the Department of State, to CINCPAC for POLAD, Foreign Relations of the United States, Johnson Administration, Vietnam, 1964–1968, Volume III, Document 56, State Department Archives, Washington, D.C.

example,[170] Goure said that not only had enemy morale declined, enemy expectations of victory had also waned.

Difficulties seemed to pile up for the insurgents. In some units, exhaustion from constant moving, digging of shelters and trenches, and short rations had damaged fighting ability. Defoliation and crop spraying were reducing the Viet Cong's ability to obtain food. In villages under partial or complete VC control, popular sentiment was beginning to turn against the insurgents because of their inability to protect the population from GVN air, artillery, and ground attacks. There was a growing feeling among villagers in some areas that the Viet Cong presence was undesirable because it provoked air attacks. Just as Goure had surmised in his 1964 report, the increased use of superior U.S. and GVN firepower and weaponry was changing the behavior of the villagers, driving a wedge between them and the insurgents, and pushing more and more of them into GVN zones where life appeared better and safer. Popular dissatis-faction was also fueled by the large-scale draft of young men and the greatly increased taxes as the Viet Cong attempted to rapidly expand their forces. The quality of some units had declined because "poorly trained and resentful" youths had been drafted into their ranks. Their morale, and even the morale of some veterans, had plunged because the high taxes and their forced prolonged absence from home had impoverished their families.

Goure encouraged doing more to exploit enemy vulnerabilities, affect their morale, and influence the attitude of villagers under their control. In the same report, he urged that "combined military, political, and psychological operations" be mounted to achieve this goal, because if these vulnerabilities were effectively exploited, more Viet Cong would probably desert and defect, and the popular support that was vital to the success of their movement might be undermined.

Goure's encouraging appraisal must have played well in the Office of the Secre-tary of Defense. August 1965 was a time of optimism for Robert McNamara. As he set the machinery of a larger war in motion, he was a figure of confidence. On August 11, he appeared on TV to announce that the body count looked good, that the Viet Cong had lost 7,000 between May and July, whereas the American side had lost only 3,000, and that the enemy had retreated in the past months. His confidence was shared by General Maxwell Taylor, who predicted that the communist offensive would be defeated by the end of the year.

The trends that Goure—and Thomson—detected seemed to indicate that the ground war in the South could bring success—a ground war that was part of the two-pronged, confidential strategy that Westmoreland had outlined to McNamara on July 17, when the Secretary of Defense visited Saigon. This main prong was designed to batter the Viet Cong and North Vietnamese forces and demonstrate to Hanoi that

---

[170] Leon Goure and C. A. H. Thomson, *Some Impressions of Viet Cong Vulnerabilities: An Interim Report,* Santa Monica, Calif.: RAND Corporation, RM-4699-1-ISA, August 1965b.

they could not take over the South by force of arms. The second, or "ancillary prong," was "to reduce Hanoi's will and ability to support the Vietcong and to increase the cost of trying to do so."[171] This two-pronged strategy had been approved by the President, the Joint Chiefs, and senior officials, such as McNamara, as a way for ending the war, out of a belief that it would force a settlement.[172]

Looking back, McNamara would say that this strategy was flawed because it implicitly rested on the assumption that the communists would find it difficult to replace their losses with recruitment in the South and with reinforcement from the North under the double pressure of military operations and air attacks. Another flawed assumption was that the United States and GVN could force the Viet Cong and North Vietnamese regulars "to slug it out on the battlefield in a more or less conventional war." Then, U.S. mobility and firepower, combined with bombing to "choke off supplies and reinforcements from the North," would force the enemy to seek a settlement.[173] The third wrong assumption was that if the Viet Cong and North Vietnamese refused to "fight on our terms and revert to hit-and-run tactics," U.S. and GVN forces "backed by a strong pacification program, could wage an effective anti-guerrilla war."[174] Finally, it was believed that pacification would prevent the enemy from recruiting fighters in the South and finding food supplies for their troops. In mid-1965, however, it appeared as if the strategy was working, and Goure and Thomson's findings at the time seemed to confirm that the trends were working in the allies' favor and to the enemy's detriment.

Goure's briefings and reports unfolded against a backdrop of escalating violence in Vietnam, as the United States poured in more combat forces and intensified the application of its firepower, and Hanoi responded by funneling more troops, weapons, and supplies into the South. In the balance of terror, however, the United States had the upper hand. The destruction it could rain down on South Vietnam soon caught the attention of the American media and people. The first B-52 strikes made headlines, and as civilian casualties mounted, the U.S. press began to report about villages bombed by mistake and about the "unobserved" air strikes where the bombs fell on Vietnamese who might or might not be Viet Cong. In the United States, anti-war sentiment began to grow, although protests remained scattered. On June 26, 1965, an artist group picketed the RAND headquarters to protest its "involvement with American Foreign Policy in Vietnam."[175] On July 7, Brownlee Haydon, RAND's director of

---

[171] Robert S. McNamara, *In Retrospect: The Tragedy and Lessons of Vietnam*, New York: Times Books, 1995, p. 210.

[172] McNamara, *In Retrospect*, 1995, p. 210.

[173] McNamara, *In Retrospect*, 1995, p. 210.

[174] McNamara, *In Retrospect*, 1995, p. 210.

[175] The Artists Protest Committee, handbill on "Dialogue on Vietnam," advertising the debate, provided to the author by Bill Dorrill.

public relations, invited representatives of the Artists Protest Committee to the Santa Monica office to discuss Vietnam.

Joel Edelman, who took part in several teach-ins as a volunteer RAND representative, would later say that Haydon looked the image of an ambassador straight out of central casting. Edelman described him as a "very gracious, very patrician . . . man, who would have been perfectly comfortable at a Boston upper-crust dinner party." Haydon, Edelman said, was also "well-spoken, erudite, knowledgeable . . . very liberal in many ways but supportive," and was "very respected" by "most of the military community, because he understood them and could speak the language, so he could really balance all sides." According to Edelman, Haydon was a "master" at his job and "a great man who did a lot of positive things for RAND."[176]

At this meeting with the artist group, Haydon agreed to a public debate at the Warner Playhouse, on August 3. Haydon asked Guy Pauker, Bill Dorrill, and Bernard Brodie, a renowned professor at Yale, to be part of the panel discussion. They would represent RAND and the progovernment view, and a group of academics would present the opposing view. Dorrill did not know why Haydon asked him to be part of the RAND team, but guessed that it was to balance the voices of Pauker and Brodie. Dorrill actually planned to take the occasion to air his anti-war sentiments and had prepared a statement to this effect. But when William Stewart, who was then the Air Force representative at RAND, overheard him talking in the hallway, he told Dorrill that he could not do so. This injunction only made Dorrill more determined to condemn the war and the U.S. role in it in even stronger terms than he had planned.

The day of the debate, Dorrill arrived at the theater and found it packed with people. He saw many "without shoes[,] sprawling all over the place."[177] The air was redolent with body odor. It was the first time that he had run into the hippies, who represented a new cultural phenomenon. Many Americans at the time viewed their rebellious behavior as threatening to traditional mores. Although intellectually Dorrill agreed with their anti-war stance, culturally he found them appalling. He did think, however, that they were unrealistic and naive in their position. On the whole, he found the boorishness, shabbiness, and obnoxiousness of their supporters in the audience distasteful. He was so repelled that he decided at the last moment not to read the anti-war statement he had brought with him—not to cast his "pearls before the swine"—and to stick to the written position paper, which he had circulated to Joe Goldsen, Guy Pauker, Bill Stewart, and Brownlee Haydon on July 30.[178]

Dorrill told the audience that it may come as a surprise to them that RAND was not a place full of "malevolent Dr. Strangeloves" and that many viewpoints could be found at RAND on most subjects. On the issue of Vietnam, he represented only

---

[176] Author interview with Joel Edelman, 2005.

[177] Author interview with Bill Dorrill, 2004 and 2005.

[178] Author interview with Bill Dorrill, 2004 and 2005.

one viewpoint, but he would speak as "a concerned American citizen," and not as "a spokesman for RAND or for the U.S. government." In this capacity, he stood halfway between "those who would resort to unlimited military escalation to achieve a solution in Vietnam" and "those who favor immediate, unilateral withdrawal." To him, the important issue was how to achieve a negotiated settlement to the expanding war before thousands of additional lives were lost. This settlement would offer some prospect of allowing the Vietnamese to "determine their own future" and, at the same time, "would avoid establishing the pre-conditions for a series of bloody Vietnams throughout Asia, Africa, and Latin-America in the future."[179] According to Dorrill, after the debate "RAND management was very pleased—even ecstatic" over his performance, but he himself felt "humiliated" for not "pulling out all the stops."[180]

The issue of how and whether RAND should take a more public stance regarding Vietnam—as suggested by Guy Pauker in a memo of November 11, 1965, to Frank Collbohm—was debated at the Management Committee meeting of December 1, 1965. In his memo, Pauker recommended that "RAND staff members lecture to reputable university groups on the events leading to the current situation in Vietnam, but not be trapped into public debates which attract the publicity more for their sensationalism than for intellectual content."[181] The Management Committee rejected this recommendation because of the effect this kind of activity might have on RAND's image. In its view, such an "involvement of RAND people in the public advocacy of national issues can smear the image we wish of a sober, responsible, objective, scholarly research organization. Offsetting this advocacy image by scheduling dissenting lectures creates other, obvious problems. Unfortunately, a RAND man's views expressed in public are attributed to RAND, unlike the case for a university representative. History is proving the correctness of our old policy limiting RAND publicity to a minimum." The dilemma was to preserve RAND's image without restricting the intellectual freedom of the staff. The committee concluded that perhaps "the best approach is to create an environment at RAND that does not encourage the staff to publicly pass judgment one way or the other on official U.S. positions, making it clear that RAND serves best when it maintains a state of detached inquiry."[182]

However, this preference for detachment did not seem to apply across the board. According to Joel Edelman, during this teach-in era, requests would periodically come in for RAND to send representatives to speak in support of the administration's position because of RAND's reputation and because of statements made by some RAND people that gave the impression that RAND favored the government's policies in

---

[179] William Dorrill, "Position," paper presented at a public debate at the Warner Playhouse, Los Angeles, Calif., July 1965.

[180] Author interview with Bill Dorrill, 2004 and 2005.

[181] Management Committee Meeting Minutes, December 1, 1965, RAND Archives, Santa Monica, Calif.

[182] Management Committee Meeting Minutes, December 1, 1965, RAND Archives, Santa Monica, Calif.

Vietnam. At this time, Edelman was filled with the patriotic fervor that had imbued America during World War II and after, and he felt that it was his duty to support the government. To the best of his recollection—he would later say—he and Dan Ellsberg were two people who volunteered and were regularly asked to explain what they understood the administration's position to be and what the United States was doing in Vietnam.

They never took part in the same teach-ins, however. Edelman participated in perhaps half a dozen different Vietnam teach-ins—some of which were broadcast on TV. Everything he said at these teach-ins he "believed to be true . . . and to be right" and "so did Dan."[183] He found the teach-ins exciting, interesting, and fun, because most of the audience was often very liberal leaning and anti-war, and he was the subject of so many boos and cat calls that he got used to them.

In summer 1965, CBS held a television debate called "Vietnam Dialogue: Mr. Bundy and the Professors," with Guy Pauker serving on the high-powered panel. According to Joe Zasloff, he was at RAND working on a study when "word came that there was to be a televised debate, with Professor Hans Morgenthau from the University of Chicago on one side, and on the other side was McGeorge Bundy, and each was to have two collaborators."[184] Zasloff was in the hallway in Santa Monica when someone said, "Did you hear that there's going to be a debate on Vietnam, and Guy Pauker's been invited to participate?" In a chorus, everyone present asked, "On which side?" To Zasloff, this question summed up Pauker's position. Pauker, according to Zasloff, could "shift his position to suit the circumstances"[185]—a remark supported by Bill Dorrill, who said that Pauker did not appear to support the war and yet in the televised debate he was arguing in favor of it.

A transcript of the televised debate on Monday, June 21, 1965, showed that it was moderated by CBS news anchor Eric Sevareid, and that the other panelists included Professors Zbygniew Brzezinski and Edmund O. Club of Columbia and John D. Donoghue of Michigan State University. In the debate, Guy Pauker and Brzezinski were on the side of McGeorge Bundy.[186] The debate took place in the wake of a series of nationwide teach-ins in the spring that culminated in a large anti-war demonstration in Washington on May 15th. Sevareid explained that it was "a kind of condensed reprise of that teach-in and confrontation."[187] Explaining the reason he decided to participate, Pauker said that he felt that "one should bring the facts back into the discussion about Vietnam, which had "generated so much emotion on the campuses of

---

[183] Author interview with Joel Edelman, 2005.

[184] Author interview with Joe Zasloff, 2003.

[185] Author interview with Joe Zasloff, 2003.

[186] "Vietnam Dialogue: Mr. Bundy and the Professors," *CBS News Special Report*, as broadcast over the CBS Television Network, Monday, June 21, 1965, 10:00–11:00 p.m. EDT.

[187] "Vietnam Dialogue: Mr. Bundy and the Professors," 1965, p. 3.

American universities that the factual base of this discussion is frequently ignored."[188] He referred to interviews with enemy defectors and prisoners to inject what he felt was a factual basis for his arguments, which were more shaded than those he had made in the 1964 Motivation and Morale report.

Briefly, his argument supported the rationale for U.S. involvement, since he viewed the war in the South as aggression from the North to exploit local grievances, with the ultimate goal of establishing a totalitarian communist rule. Villagers who joined the Viet Cong were misled into believing that they were fighting for national liberation, but their nationalism was being exploited by Hanoi for its own aims. Echoing Goure, Pauker said that the villagers, however, now considered the Viet Cong "a heavy burden," and were getting tired of their high taxes and of what was happening in the villages.[189] On the whole, the debate was dominated by McGeorge Bundy and Hans Morgenthau, and it revolved around the four questions posed by Sevareid: why the United States was in Vietnam; what was the "fundamental nature of the war"; what are the implications of the war in terms of the communist movement in Asia as a whole and of China's "power and aims and future actions"; and what are the alternatives to the present U.S. policy in Vietnam. Pauker dealt mainly with the first question about the nature of the war.

According to David Mozingo, Pauker was able to change his position if called upon to do so because "where the action was was where he'd like to be." Despite "the opportunism that this may show," Pauker, according to Mozingo, was not interested in "trying to peddle a kind of line" on Vietnam but, rather, "to get the facts out on the table."[190] Pauker, Mozingo said, "had no deep intellectual commitment one way or the other," and was not an ideologue. He invited Bernard Fall, the famous French author of *The Street Without Joy*—whose view he seemed to share—to speak at RAND. Mozingo remembered that Fall gave a "magnificent performance," during which he expressed his conviction that the United States would not do any better than the French had in Vietnam and that it would find it impossible to win the war because the situation "had metastasized and was already going in the other direction," and there was nothing "short of destroying the whole country that was going to change it."[191]

---

[188] "Vietnam Dialogue: Mr. Bundy and the Professors," 1965, p. 6.

[189] "Vietnam Dialogue: Mr. Bundy and the Professors," 1965, p. 39. An article in the *Los Angeles Times* identified Pauker as head of the Asia section of RAND. It said that he "supported U.S. Vietnam policy" and that he "rejected arguments by the other side that the rebel movement in Vietnam was primarily nationalistic and an expression of peasant discontent." This is an impression different from the one he had conveyed with Zasloff and Pauker in their report on Viet Cong motivation and morale. See "Bundy Debates Critics over Vietnam Policy," *Los Angeles Times*, June 22, 1965.

[190] Author interview with David Mozingo, 2003.

[191] Author interview with David Mozingo, 2003.

Mozingo was an early critic of the Vietnam War because, to him, it was "wrong war, wrong time, wrong place, wrong enemy."[192] Also, as a China expert, he thought that the war would make it harder for a long period of time for the United States and China to move toward rapprochement. He became best known at RAND for his analysis, which he co-authored with Tom Robinson, a RAND consultant, of a September 2, 1965, speech given by Lin Piao, Communist China's Defense Minister and Marshal of the People's Liberation Army.[193] The speech dealt with people's war and was published in *People's Daily*, the official organ of the Chinese communist regime, and given wide dissemination in China. In this rare official statement, Lin Piao claimed that the strategic revolutionary philosophy enunciated by Mao Tse-tung nearly 30 years ago was still applicable to many situations in the world. He called on the "rural areas of the world" (the developing countries) to rise up and encircle "the cities of the world" (the United States and Western Europe) through revolutionary warfare. Lin held up Vietnam as "the most convincing example of a victim of aggression defeating U.S. imperialism by a people's war" and predicted that although Vietnam was "weak and small," it would render America's technological superiority ineffective and defeat U.S. imperialism.

Most top American officials interpreted Lin Piao's article as a commitment of unrelenting support for Hanoi and as a recognition of the importance of the Vietnamese communist struggle against U.S. efforts to defeat revolutionary war. "The Chinese people will do everything in their power to support the Vietnamese people until every single one of the U.S. aggressors is driven out of Viet-Nam," Lin declared. According to McNamara, senior officials in the Johnson Administration—including him— "interpreted the speech as bellicose and aggressive, signaling an expansionist China's readiness to nourish 'local' forces across the world and to give a helping push when the time came."[194] To them, Lin's remarks seemed to indicate a Chinese commitment to world revolution and, therefore, validated the domino theory. In an interview with Jack Raymond of *The New York Times* at the time, McNamara said that the most important challenge for America was to become more proficient at fighting "wars of national liberation," because it was "perfectly apparent that we will be facing more such wars in the years ahead."[195] To him, the United States was fighting for a just cause, and America had the duty to use its power to contain Chinese expansion.[196]

---

[192] Author interview with David Mozingo, 2003.

[193] David P. Mozingo and Thomas W. Robinson, *Lin Piao on "People's War": China Takes a Second Look at Vietnam*, Santa Monica, Calif.: RAND Corporation, RM-4814-PR, November 1965.

[194] McNamara, *In Retrospect*, 1995, p. 215.

[195] Cited in Deborah Shapley, *Promise and Power: The Life and Times of Robert McNamara*, Boston, Mass.: Little, Brown and Company, 1993, p. 351. McNamara would later tell Shapley that, "We misjudged Chinese geopolitical objectives," and that this misjudgment was a "serious error," p. 318.

[196] Shapley, *Promise and Power*, 1993, p. 359.

Like many of his colleagues, McNamara viewed Lin Piao's speech as something akin to Hitler's *Mein Kampf*: a blueprint for the eventual destruction of the United States. When Prime Minister Pham Van Dong of North Vietnam declared that Hanoi "was ready to fight for twenty years," it looked as though he had been bolstered by Lin Piao's upholding of Vietnam as a model for world revolution. In the same month, Hanoi issued orders to its troops to prepare for a long war, indicating that it was not prepared to give up its aims, despite the American military onslaught, as U.S. policymakers had hoped.

In their report, Mozingo and Robinson gave a different interpretation of Lin's statement. According to them, Lin's article was in the main not a worldwide call to arms but an assessment of the situation in Vietnam following the launching of air strikes against the North and the introduction of 150,000 American troops into the South, and an admonition to the Vietnamese communists to change their tactics to be able to deal more effectively with the new circumstances. Lin's message to the Vietnamese could be summarized as, "Your tactics are wrong and you had better come around to our way of thinking if you expect to win."[197] Lin told the Vietnamese that the main enemy of the Viet Cong was now the United States, not the Saigon government, and the Viet Cong therefore should adopt different political and military strategies. On the political side, they should forge a broad-based alliance with other sectors of South Vietnamese society to defeat the Americans in unison; on the military side, they should abandon mobile warfare and adopt a "strategic defense" posture by retreating into "revolutionary bases in the countryside and carrying on smaller-scale but protracted guerrilla warfare."[198]

Although the assistance of socialist countries was important, the Viet Cong could "win this struggle only if they rely primarily on their own resources and their own revolutionary spirit," because the decisive factor "must be the strength and determination of the Vietnamese Communists." While Lin said that China would offer continuing support, it was the Viet Cong's war to fight and they, not China, "must win this revo-

---

[197] Mozingo and Robinson, *Lin Piao*, 1965, p. 15.

[198] Mozingo and Robinson, *Lin Piao*, 1965, p. vi. Subsequently, Chinese scholar Qiang Zhai in *China and the Vietnam Wars, 1950–1975* (Chapel Hill: University of North Carolina Press, 2000) wrote that the article bore the name of Lin Piao but was in fact written by a group in the General Staff of the People's Liberation Army (PLA) organized by Luo Ruiqing, the PLA chief of staff. According to Qiang, the article may have been "designed mainly to counter Soviet views on war and peace." On the issue of support for Vietnam, Qiang wrote that, between 1964 and 1966, Mao believed that aiding North Vietnam was a way to counter America's policy of encircling China and that a communist success in South Vietnam would "prevent the United States from moving closer to the Chinese southern border." According to Qiang, U.S. attacks on North Vietnam following the Tonkin Gulf incident surprised Mao and led him to perceive the United States "as posing a serious security threat to China." Mao told an associate that "war is coming" and called for preparations for "an early, large-scale, and nuclear war" with the United States. In 1964, Mao took several measures, the most important of which was the launching of the massive Third Front project, to develop an alternative industrial base in remote provinces that "would enable China to continue production in the event of an attack on its large urban centers." China, therefore, was viewing Vietnam with more alarm than the RAND report indicated.

lutionary war."[199] In short, according to Mozingo and Robinson, Lin Piao was saying that the Viet Cong were on their own and that China would not intervene militarily in South Vietnam. China was urging Vietnam on, "rhetorically" only, as Mozingo would later recall.[200]

Indeed, the RAND authors wrote, Lin's statement showed "a striking absence of threats of possible intervention." This omission could "only have been deliberate" and was "consistent with . . . China's understanding that the United States wants to confine the war primarily to South Vietnam, just where Peking also wants it to be fought."[201] This did not preclude intervention, but this intervention would only come "if the North Vietnamese state was on the verge of collapse as a result of U.S. military attack."[202] Although defending the security of North Vietnam would be compelling for China, the revolutionary situation in the South would not be important enough to warrant Peking's intervention. Due to its "industrial weakness" and "American strategic superiority," Peking's preference was to avoid a frontal confrontation with the United States and to continue the proxy war by urging the Vietnamese to keep on fighting—albeit with the correct strategy and tactics as defined by China.

Mozingo recalled that his and Robinson's paper made a "big splash" in 1965 because their analysis refuted the view of Dean Rusk who—like McNamara—believed that Lin Piao's speech represented a communist Chinese blueprint for the conquest of Southeast Asia by using Vietnam to expand in the region.[203] Indeed, Mozingo and Robinson's paper was circulated widely outside of RAND and came to the attention of Murray Marder of *The Washington Post*, who wrote an article in which he pointed out that the RAND analysis showed that Beijing was telling Hanoi to continue the struggle on its own. The report also caught the attention of Colonel Clyde C. Wooten, Assistant Chief of Staff for Intelligence, U.S. Air Force Headquarters, who wrote to Bill Dorrill expressing his skepticism of the accuracy of Mozingo and Robinson's interpretation. In reply, Dorrill wrote that, in his own view, there was no single "central message" in Lin's speech. To him, it served several purposes: as a polemic in the Sino-Soviet dispute; as a "manifesto on world revolutionary strategy"; as a "psychological-conditioning message of reassurance and exhortation to the Chinese people in the face of possible war" with the United States; and as "a general commentary on the conduct of 'People's War'—applicable in Vietnam *and elsewhere*." [204]

---

[199] Mozingo and Robinson, *Lin Piao*, 1965, p. vi.

[200] Author interview with David Mozingo, 2003.

[201] Mozingo and Robinson, *Lin Piao*, 1965, p. vii.

[202] Mozingo and Robinson, *Lin Piao*, 1965, p. vii.

[203] Author interview with David Mozingo, 2003.

[204] William Dorrill, memorandum to Colonel Clyde C. Wooten, AFNINA, Santa Monica, Calif.: RAND L-2620, February 7, 1966.

With regard to Vietnam, Dorrill said that he was most concerned about the report's conclusion that China would intervene directly only if it believed that Hanoi—but not the Viet Cong—was facing collapse. According to Dorrill, Lin Piao actually suggested in the article that if Hanoi—due to American military pressure—could no longer assist the insurgency in the South, China might find herself forced to intervene. Although China "may be hedging" in the belief that it could "come into the war if and when that ever becomes necessary to ensure a favorable outcome—or, at the minimum, to prevent an irrevocable defeat," it was "imperative" that the United States should "take full account of what might happen if and when the Chinese leadership" decided to enter the war directly.[205] Considering that miscalculation could have terrible consequences, the United States ought to consider carefully whether China's threshold of tolerance for "defeat in the South may be much lower than has hitherto been believed." To Dorrill, the key question was what actions China would ultimately take if it became faced with "the reality of imminent and irrevocable defeat" in South Vietnam—such as fomenting armed insurgencies in such vulnerable countries as Thailand and Malaysia, or even launching large-scale attacks in the Taiwan Strait, or in Korea, or on the Indian border.

Dorrill would later say that he took issue with Mozingo and Robinson's interpretation that China was dissatisfied with the strategy of the Viet Cong and warned them not to engage in big-unit attacks. He thought that Lin Piao's statement could be interpreted another way, and that Mozingo and Robinson's analysis could steer the United States toward "recklessness" in South Vietnam out of a conviction that China would not enter the war because it disapproved of the way the Viet Cong were fighting it. Dorrill might have a point in asserting that the report might reassure the Johnson Administration that the Chinese would not intervene in the South. Although it remained cautious in attacking the North, whose security and survival were important to China—keeping the bombing far from the Chinese border and sparing certain targets, such as railway lines leading into China and the dike system in the Red River Delta, to avoid provoking Chinese intervention—the administration seemed to have no such inhibition in the South, where it continued to pursue military escalation without constraint.[206]

If Lin Piao's statement gave McNamara pause, developments in Vietnam starting in fall 1965 would give him cause for concern. Rather than breaking, the enemy was adapting to the presence of a large U.S. force by stepping up recruitment in the South and by increasing the infiltration of men and materiel down the Ho Chi Minh Trail. In response, Westmoreland requested that the number of U.S. troops be increased to

---

[205] Dorrill, memorandum to Colonel Clyde C. Wooten, 1966.

[206] It appears that McNamara was unaware of the Mozingo report and its conclusions. Author Deborah Shapley wrote that, "Had McNamara known better, he might have taken heart from Lin Piao." Shapley, *Promise and Power*, 1993, p. 351.

210,000 by the end of the year; then, in mid-October, he revised his estimate and asked for 325,000 troops by July 1966. Yet the possibility remained that Westmoreland could ask for more later, without any guarantee that the United States would be able to reach its objectives. To McNamara, it seemed that the "momentum of war and the unpredictability of events" were overwhelming the Joint Chiefs' and Westmoreland's predictions of the level of forces needed.[207] He found Westmoreland's new troop request troubling and thought that it could signal "the beginning of an open-ended commitment." McNamara felt that "things were slipping out of control."[208] Later, McNamara would say that it was in this period that his view began to shift gradually "from concern to skepticism to frustration to anguish."[209]

On November 7, 1965, he sent a memo to Johnson, giving the president a gloomy assessment of the situation in South Vietnam. In the memo, he pointed out that the insurgency was continuing "at high intensity" and showing "no signs of abating." The new government headed by Marshal Nguyen Cao Ky and General Nguyen Van Thieu had "accomplished little" and, worst of all, had weakened its hold over the countryside.[210] After presenting alternatives available to the administration, McNamara recommended raising the number of American combat forces in Vietnam to 350,000 by the end of 1966. But he also recommended making "an all-out effort to start negotiations" and instituting a bombing pause in North Vietnam that "would set the stage for another pause, perhaps in late 1966, that might produce a settlement." If the pause proved fruitless, he recommended intensifying air strikes over North Vietnam. However, he told Johnson "that none of these actions assures success," and that they might lead "the Chinese and Russians to escalate the war."[211]

In addition, McNamara told the president, U.S. casualties might climb to between 500 and 800 a month. The odds were that, even with further escalation, the North Vietnamese and the Viet Cong would persist and match every U.S. move, and that, despite all efforts, the United States would be faced "in early 1967 with stagnation at a higher level."[212] President Johnson was skeptical of what another bombing pause—coming after the cessation in May, which had failed—could accomplish, and thought that Hanoi would only view it as a sign of weakness. Other senior officials concurred. The Joint Chiefs thought that North Vietnam would exploit it militarily and interpret it as a sign of weakness. Dean Rusk "doubted that Hanoi would respond positively."[213]

---

[207] McNamara, *In Retrospect*, 1995, p. 213.

[208] McNamara, *In Retrospect*, 1995, p. 213.

[209] McNamara, *In Retrospect*, 1995, p. 207.

[210] McNamara, *In Retrospect*, 1995, p. 219.

[211] McNamara, *In Retrospect*, 1995, pp. 219–220.

[212] McNamara, *In Retrospect*, 1995, p. 220.

[213] McNamara, *In Retrospect*, 1995, p. 220.

Henry Cabot Lodge—reinstalled as ambassador to replace General Maxwell Taylor, now appointed Special Consultant to the president and chairman of the Foreign Intelligence Advisory Board—"believed it would demoralize South Vietnam and drive a wedge between Saigon and Washington."[214]

In November 1965, the first large battle between North Vietnamese regulars and American troops took place in Ia Drang, near the border with Laos, and lasted from the 14th to the 19th. The Americans won on the strength of their fighting skill and airpower. Westmoreland and the JCS were in high spirits over the favorable outcome of this test of combat effectiveness, and General Johnson said, "After the battle of Ia Drang, the worst was behind us." McNamara viewed it differently. Although the kill ratio was favorable, 300 Americans against 1,300 enemy soldiers, the number of U.S. killed in just this one battle indicated to him that cumulative losses would be heavy in the months ahead. Also, the toughness of the People's Army of Vietnam (PAVN) and their willingness to stand and fight impressed on him that the war would be bitter and long. The optimism he had displayed in August 1965 became guarded.

Ia Drang confirmed the intelligence information that MACV had gathered, indicating that the rate of infiltration had greatly increased, that there were now nine North Vietnamese Army (NVA) regiments in action rather than the three that had been reported earlier, and that Viet Cong forces had also grown from five regiments to twelve. In view of the increasing infiltration, Westmoreland on November 23, 1965, asked that the total number of U.S. troops in Vietnam be raised to 410,000 by the end of 1966. According to McNamara, Westmoreland's message "came as a shattering blow" because it meant "a drastic—and arguably open-ended—increase in U.S. forces and carried with it the likelihood of many more U.S. casualties."[215] Westmoreland's request prompted McNamara to make his seventh trip to Vietnam. In Saigon, the MACV Commander mentioned that it might be necessary to ask for another deployment of 200,000 American troops in 1967. While Westmoreland thought that the larger force would allow him to expand the war of attrition and win—through search-and-destroy operations against enemy main forces conducted by American troops, combined with mop-up activities carried out by the South Vietnamese army following in their wake to "pacify and hold"—Prime Minister Nguyen Cao Ky estimated that, after two years of this kind of grinding ground war, his government would control 50 percent of the country—a lower number than the 65 percent Ky had estimated during McNamara's trip in July.

On his return to Washington, McNamara submitted another memo to President Johnson. In it, he told the president that infiltration had increased, and that the enemy which had been avoiding engagements in mid-year were now willing to fight it out with American troops as they had done at Ia Drang. McNamara warned that Hanoi

---

[214] McNamara, *In Retrospect*, 1995, p. 220.

[215] McNamara, *In Retrospect*, 1995, p. 221.

might dispatch 150 battalions to the South by the end of 1966, and that at this rate, the enemy might be able to replace their losses with an "equal input" of manpower, even under bombardment. Although McNamara did not say it outright, this "equal input" meant that the war of attrition that was predicated on killing more enemy soldiers than could be replaced would not lead to the desired results. In his memo, McNamara recommended raising the level of troops to 400,000 by the end of 1966 as Westmoreland had requested, and added that perhaps another 200,000 or more might be needed in 1967. Yet, even these measures would not guarantee success, he told the president. U.S. casualties might rise to 1,000 a month in early 1967, and the United States might be confronted with an even "higher level of violence, destruction, and death."[216]

In Saigon, Ambassador Henry Cabot Lodge thought that the increased infiltration offset the good news that he had been getting from some reports in the field, as well as from the findings Leon Goure had presented him. In his weekly cable to Johnson, dated December 15, 1965, he wrote, "If it were not for the incursion from Hanoi, we could be taking some satisfaction from the progress which has been made with regard to the rank and file Viet Cong."[217] Among the evidence of progress, he cited the highlights of a briefing by Leon Goure. According to Lodge, Goure had told him that interviews with about 180 Viet Cong prisoners and defectors between July and December 1965 had indicated a change from 1964. While 65 percent of the Viet Cong believed in 1964 that victory could be achieved because their movement had the support of the people, now—in 1965—this percentage had dropped to 20 percent. This decline was wrought mostly by jets, B-52s, artillery bombardment, and helicopters. The B-52s in particular, with their tremendous power of destruction, had inflicted a major psychological scar on the Viet Cong because the size of the bomb craters convinced them that the passive-defense measures on which they had been relying would no longer be effective, that they would not survive the bombings, and that "there was no survival by digging" shelters and trenches.

In general, the picture Lodge took away from Goure's briefing was of an enemy that was being ground down by the war. Fear of detection created mistrust. For example, afraid that there might be agents within their ranks, the officers of one main force battalion "made everybody strip off their clothes so as to look for hidden radios." Defoliation made the Viet Cong feel more exposed and reduced their food supplies. In addition, the movement of refugees into government zones aggravated the food situation. The saying among the Viet Cong now was, "The ocean in which we are supposed to swim is receding and drying up. We must depend on the people; but the people are leaving us." Each soldier was given only "one can and a half of cold rice a day," and many units were "down to one hot meal a day at 3 o'clock in the morning"

---

[216] McNamara, *In Retrospect*, 1995, p. 222.

[217] Henry Cabot Lodge, cable to President Johnson, December 15, 1965, State Department Archives, Foreign Relations of the United States, Foreign Relations 1964–1968, Volume III, Vietnam, Document 230.

because they feared that the smoke of their cooking fire would be detected and would bring an attack. Sickness was rampant. "There is much beri-beri. There is also a high rate of malaria in the army of North Viet-Nam," Lodge quoted Goure as saying. The Viet Cong ranks were fraying. Up to 70 percent of the recruits were deserting. Many civilian cadres who had been transferred to military units were deserting. There was a shortage of well-indoctrinated officers, and those who remained tended to leave when they were criticized. Morale was further depressed by the realization that their families were doing poorly back at home.

Two weeks after sending Johnson the memo with the grim assessment, McNamara in mid-December went further, telling Johnson that, "The military solution is not certain," and that "We must perforce find a diplomatic solution."[218] Johnson decided to order a short bombing halt over North Vietnam, beginning Christmas Eve. In public, McNamara gave no hint of his personal doubts. Years after the war ended, questions were raised about why, considering his disillusionment in late 1965, he went on supporting and enlarging a war he knew was unwinnable. In reply to his critics, McNamara said that he recommended escalation because the objective was not to achieve a military victory but to force Hanoi to come to a political settlement.

By the end of 1965, Leon Goure had established himself as an important source of information about how the enemy was faring under American pressure.[219] However, his support for airpower was becoming controversial inside as well as outside RAND. In an editorial on Sunday, November 21, 1965, condemning the use of massive air strikes that killed civilians along with the Viet Cong, *The New York Times* cited RAND's support for intensifying the air war in South Vietnam.[220] Before deciding last winter to deploy American airpower on a massive scale, the editorial pointed out, RAND "carefully studied the advisability of such a move." The RAND study group, "after taking account of the extent to which American-built planes with American pilot-advisors already were being used in Vietnam, concluded: 'We've got the onus. Let's get the bonus.'"[221] The military "bonus" had been significant, and all reports agreed that air strikes had damaged the strength of the Viet Cong. However, the "onus" had also climbed. By September, "about 5 percent of South Vietnam's rural population had fled into the cities and refugee camps." The devastation led General Westmoreland, an advocate of airpower himself, to issue in that month an order for restraints, warning

---

[218] Shapley *Promise and Power*, 1993, p. 364.

[219] Leon Goure seemed to be such a part of the "country team" that, according to the Pentagon Papers, Gravel Edition, Volume 2, Chapter 7, he was invited to a conference in Warrenton, Va., in December 1965 and January 1966, to "review the joint GVN-US pacification/rural construction program" and increase its effectiveness, and also to discuss the organization of the U.S. mission in Vietnam to improve the management of the U.S. effort in Vietnam. The conference was attended by a heavy contingent of mission members, as well as by representatives of ISA, the CIA, the White House, and CINCPAC.

[220] "Bombing South Vietnam," editorial, *The New York Times*, Sunday, November 21, 1965.

[221] According to Goure, Amrom Katz coined this saying. Author interview with Leon Goure, 2003.

that "'unnecessary force' would embitter the South Vietnamese peasantry and make victory more difficult."

Although the editorial did not divulge Goure's name or criticize RAND, it implied that RAND's support had contributed to the "mounting ferocity of American air warfare in South Vietnam and the heavy damage it inflicts on South Vietnamese villages and the people who live in them." The statistics it cited were telling. Sorties had been growing month by month "from about 1,000 in January, before American air units were engaged, to about 7,500 in July. In the past month alone, there have been about 12,000 strike sorties—more than in all 1964—and about 11,000 buildings were destroyed or damaged." More sorties were being flown by U.S. aircraft than in the Korean War. The statistics, however, could not capture the damage and suffering being inflicted on the South Vietnamese countryside because, in a guerrilla conflict, it was not possible to avoid hurting civilians as well as Viet Cong.

The editorial questioned the tactic of wiping out villages far removed from combat areas based often on unreliable reports that the Viet Cong had received shelter there, under the notion that such tactics would discourage villagers from cooperating with the insurgents. The editorial did not ascribe this notion to Goure, but this was a line that he had been advocating. It was a viewpoint that had been challenged by Roger Hillsman, former Assistant Secretary of State for the Far East, who testified to a Senate subcommittee that "bombing the North has been a bad mistake, bombing the South a tragic one." Finally, the editorial called attention to the wider impact of the bombing campaign in South Vietnam. The devastation of the South Vietnamese villages and the destruction of their social structure might give other countries in the region pause regarding the cost of calling for American defense against communist threats.

However, even as questions were being raised about the RAND study, McNamara remained a sponsor, and his support gave Goure continued access to and influence in the halls of power. Despite his concern over developments in Vietnam, the Secretary of Defense's objective was still to compel the Viet Cong and Hanoi to desist. As McNamara would put it later, he was pursuing the war, because he believed that this military pressure would inflict a cost, which, in turn, would spur Hanoi to negotiate. Goure's findings about the cost exacted from the Viet Cong, therefore, would remain of interest to McNamara—and also to other policymakers who, likewise, were looking for signs that the enemy was buckling under the weight of U.S. military might. The year 1966 would see Goure reaching his peak of influence.

CHAPTER FOUR

Controversy

At 176 Pasteur, with the bigger budget granted by McNamara, Leon Goure enlarged the staff to meet the needs of the expanded project. Back in September 1965, Douglas C. Scott had joined the Saigon team to take over administrative and editorial responsibilities, and to act as interim manager whenever Leon Goure and Chuck Thomson made their periodic visits to the United States. Scott was a speechwriter and an aspiring musicals composer, with an outgoing personality, a keen sense of humor, and pride in his creativity. Joe Carrier was astonished by Scott's hiring and could not fathom why RAND had to go out and get someone without the appropriate background—and neither could Doug Scott. Carrier thought that the only explanation was that RAND had difficulty persuading its own Santa Monica staff to go live and work in Vietnam for an extended period of time.

Then, in January 1966, Russ Betts joined the team from the Social Science Department, where he was reporting to Guy Pauker. Betts had a bachelor's degree from Stanford and a master's degree from the East-West Center in Honolulu. His wife Ardith, who also got her bachelor's from the center, was an editorial assistant in the Electronics Department, where she had been hired although she had misspelled 37 out of 50 words in a test. Her intelligence and sharpness of mind trumped her weakness at spelling which could be easily rectified with a dictionary. At the East-West Center, Russ Betts had written the equivalent of a master's thesis on Southeast Asia, and he and his wife had lived in the region, so they were no strangers to this part of the world. In the Social Science Department, Russ Betts worked with Pauker, projecting the future of Southeast Asia and the security arrangements that would be required. He felt that his career was going nowhere because he did not have a doctorate, and he was also chafing under Pauker.

Given Betts's interest in Southeast Asia and his dissatisfaction, Vietnam seemed like a good alternative. At the time, he did not know where else he could go, and he thought that Leon Goure's project would give him a chance to gain a broader knowledge of the dynamics of the war and of the change under way in Southeast Asia.

Since he could not bring his wife, Russ Betts wanted to be in Vietnam for only six months. At the end of this period, RAND created a job for her in order to keep him.

With staff members being barred from bringing their families to Vietnam, it would have been difficult for RAND to find a replacement for him. Ardith Betts was glad to rejoin her husband and to leave her job in the Electronics Department, where she was editing reports dealing with such topics as rockets—about which she knew nothing—and proofreading reports "filled with equations."[1] Besides, she was very curious about Vietnam and wanted to see what it was like. Having been to Southeast Asia, she had no trepidation about relocating to Saigon.

Arriving in August 1966, she was put in charge of quality control, keeping track of interviews to avoid duplication. Duplication had happened on several occasions. Sometimes, captured senior cadres would pass themselves off as low-ranking personnel by using different names and would end up being interviewed more than once. Ardith Betts created a file on all the respondents by making out cards with names, ages, birthplaces, schooling, and other personal information. Without the aid of a computer, this was laborious work. If she read an interview and thought that it sounded familiar, she would "go chase it down."[2] But there were only ten to fifteen cases of duplication during the year she was in Saigon.

Later, her responsibility was enlarged and she began working with translated captured documents, going through them to find information relevant to the interviews and to correlate and verify information that the interviews turned up.

From a personal standpoint, life was pleasant, though circumscribed. With the exception of a few excursions, it was mostly limited to Saigon, which Ardith characterized as a "fantastically interesting place, but plagued with smog and garbage, and filled with American males aged 18–24."[3] One Christmas, she and her husband went to Dalat, the mountain resort, and walked among the pines. After the roar of Saigon traffic, the quiet sound of the wind in the trees was soothing. On a couple of occasions, they drove to My Tho in the Mekong Delta, and she felt exhilarated to see green rice fields and peasants working in them. She and her husband rented an apartment near the main cathedral in the center of Saigon, above a restaurant, and either walked to work or commuted on a motorbike to the RAND office a few blocks away. Sometimes, she would feel frustrated when the hot water did not flow in the apartment or the refrigerator broke down.

Ardith Betts soon discovered that there was "nothing to do in Vietnam except enjoy the company of other people."[4] But the conversation tended to be one-dimensional, revolving around the war, since the Americans tended to "live, eat and

---

[1]   Author interview with Ardith Betts, 2004.

[2]   Author interview with Ardith Betts, 2004.

[3]   Ardith Betts, letter to a friend in Santa Monica, August 2, 1966.

[4]   Ardith Betts, letter to a friend in Santa Monica, October 30, 1966.

RAND staff on the front porch of the RAND villa in Saigon. The American staff includes, front row, Tony Russo (kneeling); second row, Bonnie Leib on left; fifth row, Ardith Betts holding child, Ken Strother in the middle (to the right of unidentified African-American visitor), Shirley Shaffer to the right of Ken Strother; standing in the back, from right to left: Russ Betts, Doug Scott, Jim Carlson, and Chuck Thomson.

Interviewers include, in the second row, Huu (in the middle, behind Tony Russo); third row, from right to left—Que, An (next to Que), and Phuc (wearing glasses); and, farther back, Thang (with pipe, next to Chuck Thomson) and Phan (between Chuck Thomson and Ardith Betts).

sleep the problems of this country."[5] She and her husband became good friends with one of the interviewers, Mr. Phuc, a thin and distinguished-looking man who was a skilled ballroom dancer and a great badminton player. He and his wife, who was a terrific cook, would invite them to their house for meals or they would go out to eat together, and they would play badminton with him at the Cercle Sportif a couple of times a week. His friendship created a personal bond with Vietnam and its people in a way that their stay in other parts of Asia later would not. The ballroom dancing, badminton games, and meals were small ways in which Phuc tried to hang on to a normal life in the midst of war. Russ Betts realized what an effort this must have been for him. He lived with his wife and two teenage children in a house that had sandbags in every bedroom for protection in case there was an attack on nearby Tan Son Nhut Airport.

Until, toward the middle of her stay, rockets began falling into Saigon near where they lived, the war seemed surreal to Ardith Betts. It remained close enough—but still

[5]   Ardith Betts, letter to a friend in Santa Monica, October 30, 1966.

far away—although some nights she could hear the sound of bombing. One evening, she and her husband had dinner in a rooftop restaurant. In the distance, probably several kilometers outside the city, they could tell that a battle was unfolding. They could see guns on helicopters "go off and flash . . . like fireworks," but they could not hear any sound.[6] To them, sitting in the lovely garden and savoring the delicious food, the war seemed abstract, and it was hard to turn their minds to it and to imagine people dying out there. If she had seen body bags, the war would have seemed more real to her.[7] On a couple of occasions, she could see the consequences of the war up close, such as the time she and her husband went out to some areas on the edge of Saigon, close to a military installation. She saw shacks that had been thrown up to cater to the needs of American soldiers: laundry services and bars where prostitutes were plying their trade.

The closest Ardith Betts ever came to the war was when B-52s were dropping a stream of bombs close enough to the city so that the explosions were audible. At first, there was "a rumble in the distance," and then the bombs would get closer and closer, and the glass would rattle and the ground would shake. The whole thing "built up to this crescendo," and then stopped.[8] She felt somewhat frightened because the attack had come a little close. For Russ Betts, the only nerve-wracking time during his many travels in Vietnam was when he and his team had to drive to their destination near the Cambodian border. Suddenly, they saw some roadblocks. The Vietnamese pushed him down on the floor, put a hat on his head and their feet over his body, and covered him with a blanket, saying "This is going to be very bad if anybody knows you're here."[9]

At this point, Russ Betts agreed with the aim of the war but objected to the way it was waged. Above all, he thought the war was a tragedy for the Vietnamese, but he blamed the Viet Cong for creating this social chaos. He tended to see the war through the perspective of the Vietnamese interviewers, for whom a communist victory would spell disaster. Of the 14 to 15 interviewers who worked for RAND at any one time, most came from either the middle or upper-middle class and were convinced that their social background would subject them to oppression—if not elimination—should the communists take over. Many had fled the North with their families before Ho Chi Minh came to power in 1954. As a result, they had a visceral dislike and a profound fear of communism. Many perceived their work for RAND as a way to get to know their enemy better, so that they could fight them more effectively.

For some—living in an urban oasis that the fighting had barely touched—working for RAND made the war more immediate and the sufferings harder to ignore. Through their jobs, they could empathize better with the victims in the countryside. Huu—a naturally elegant interviewer who had studied in Australia—told Ardith Betts that

---

[6]   Author interview with Ardith Betts, 2004.

[7]   Author interview with Ardith Betts, 2004.

[8]   Author interview with Ardith Betts, 2004.

[9]   Author interview with Russ Betts, 2004.

"she was immensely glad" to be working at RAND, because "for the first time in her life, she is directly involved intellectually with the war." Talking with the Viet Cong, she became "involved in their lives and problems," and this made her feel more a part of the war and "less guilty about continuing to live her good life while the rest of the country is torn apart."[10]

In his "User's Guide to the RAND Interviews in Vietnam,"[11] published in 1970, Phil Davison cited a Vietnamese staff member who wrote in 1969 that, for the interviewers, the work for RAND opened their eyes to what was happening. A RAND consultant, Davison was a former member of the Council on Foreign Relations and professor of journalism and sociology at Columbia University. He served briefly as director of the project in the summer of 1965 while Goure made his periodic return to the United States.[12] According to Davison, these interviewers felt discouraged when they heard about the miserable conditions in the countryside from their respondents. However, their hope was that, by bringing these conditions to light, they would induce the GVN to alleviate the situation and thereby lessen the appeal of the Viet Cong to the peasants. Another cited by Davison mentioned that the field trips were usually exhausting but revealing about how the war was being waged and how the villagers felt about it.

Through the interviews, Vietnamese staff members understood better what the strong and weak points of their own noncommunist side were, how the Viet Cong were organized, what the state of their morale was, and the reasons the Viet Cong could attract Vietnamese of all ages, religions, and social backgrounds. They also became more politically concerned. These personal and political motives drove many of the Vietnamese staff to work diligently, often in trying circumstances in the jails and the *Chieu Hoi* detention centers.[13] It should be mentioned that they were probably motivated also by the good salary, which equaled that of a senior Vietnamese civil servant. According to Davison, most of the interviewers were idealistic and had high expectations about the influence of their work on officials in Saigon and Washington. But as time passed, they began to doubt the influence of their reports.

The American staff at 176 Pasteur now included Shirley Shaffer, a secretary, as well as Jim Carlson, a student at MIT who had been referred to RAND by Lucian Pye, one of his professors, and who had been hired to replace Joe Carrier, now back in Santa

---

[10] Ardith Betts, letter to a friend in Santa Monica, Calif., August 2, 1966.

[11] W. P. Davison, "User's Guide to the RAND Interviews in Vietnam," Santa Monica, Calif.: RAND Corporation, D-19904-ARPA, January 29, 1970.

[12] Tony Russo described him as a "tweedy pipesmoker," who was "easy-going and kindly," but who tended to go with the flow. Russo, "Looking Backward," 1972, p. 57.

[13] Not all interviewers worked out. One was let go quickly when it became apparent that he was not temperamentally suited for the assignment. Another quit when the quality of his work was questioned; later, however, investigation into his work indicated that it was fine. A few other interviewers left to take jobs elsewhere, although turnover was slight. Ninety percent of the interviews were conducted by experienced staff members who stayed with the project for a long time.

Monica. Carlson's case illustrates the mixture of motives, ranging from personal to professional, of RAND people who agreed to go work in Vietnam. Carlson had done a two-year stint in the Army in Vietnam, during which he had met Bich and fallen in love. He wanted to return for a variety of reasons, the most important being to see Bich again. Carlson believed that he was the only person among the American staff who had no problem adjusting to life in Saigon. He actually liked being in Vietnam, perhaps because he could lead a close-to-normal life with his wife and infant son in a nice apartment in a quiet neighborhood—despite the frequent power outages and the curfew that began at midnight.[14] During one of the power outages, Bonnie Leib was caught in an elevator between floors when she went to MACV to get the mail. She had to be pulled head first through the two-foot hole at the top—a maneuver that bruised her shin and yanked both of her arms half out of their sockets. Other times, staff members who labored into the night had to work by candlelight.

With the addition of Carlson, the staffing was complete. The villa became overcrowded. Doug Scott, Tony Russo, Russ Betts, and Jim Carlson shared the one office downstairs. Upstairs, Bonnie Leib worked in one of the bedrooms with six typists, and Ardith Betts shared another bedroom with five interviewers and a translator. To relieve the overcrowding, some of the staff eventually shifted to the ARPA complex by the Saigon River. At the beginning, none of the team leaders had any problem working with Leon Goure. In February 1966, Doug Scott and Tony Russo collaborated with him to produce a report.[15] Based on about 450 interviews, it furnished a midterm analysis of trends in Viet Cong vulnerabilities and morale, updating findings on the effect of air and artillery strikes since the last report by Goure and Thomson.

The year 1966 when this report appeared was believed to be a decisive one for the United States, as General Maxwell Taylor, now a presidential advisor, had predicted. This was going to be the year when General Westmoreland's strategy would "take the offense against communist forces" and expand the pacification program to win the hearts and minds of South Vietnam's peasants.[16] This phase would last from January 1 to June 30, 1966. If the communists refused to give up, attacks would be launched "to destroy or render militarily ineffective the remaining organized VC units and their base areas."[17] This phase—the last in Westmoreland's strategy to end the war by convincing the communists that they could not win militarily and forcing them to accept a settlement favorable to South Vietnam and the United States—would run from July 1, 1966, to December 31, 1967.

---

[14] Author interview with Jim Carlson, 2003.

[15] Leon Goure, Douglas Scott, and Anthony Russo, *Some Findings of the Viet Cong Motivation and Morale Study: June–December 1965*, Santa Monica, Calif.: RAND Corporation, RM-4911-2-ISA/ARPA, February 1966.

[16] McNamara, *In Retrospect*, 1995, p. 209.

[17] McNamara, *In Retrospect*, 1995, pp. 209–210.

In this climate of official expectation for ending the war by clobbering the communist forces, Goure's optimistic analysis played well within the Johnson Administration. It is not clear where Goure ended and Russo and Scott began in the February 1966 report, but since Goure called the shots, it would be safe to say that the report bore his personal stamp. Many of the findings had appeared in earlier reports, but now they were bolstered by the larger body of data and seemed, therefore, more authoritative. In general, the report gave confidence that American operations and weapons were eroding the strength and morale of the Viet Cong. According to the report, the Viet Cong had failed to make major headway during their rainy-season offensive of 1965, and this failure therefore had rendered remote the prospect for a much-touted "General Offensive and Uprising," which would bring the war to a successful conclusion. Instead of seeing the war ending soon, the communist forces now realized that they were facing a protracted war, and this prospect demoralized many soldiers and made them war-weary.

In delivering punishing blows on the Viet Cong, B-52s were considered one of the most potent weapons. SAC and other commanders wanted to gauge their effectiveness, and Goure obliged with a new inquiry into these bombers. As Goure had told Ambassador Lodge, B-52s had a huge impact. They could devastate Viet Cong underground bunkers and tunnels, and their awesome power had impressed both the Viet Cong and the villagers, leading them to conclude that they had no adequate means to protect themselves against such attacks. Consequently, villagers in areas that were bombed tended to move to GVN-controlled towns in large numbers. The stealthy arrival of the bombers and their surprise attacks heightened their impact. Rumors and stories about the B-52s spread fear among the Viet Cong and the population, and the mere prospect of getting bombed forced some VC units to move from the base camps in their sanctuaries. Goure's belief in the effectiveness of B-52 strikes became so well known that, during one of his visits to 176 Pasteur, Henry Kissinger asked Russ Betts and Tony Russo, "What's this stuff about B-52 bombing solving things?"[18]

As Westmoreland's strategy anticipated expanding pacification and intensifying a drive to "win hearts and minds" in the first half of 1966, Goure's findings about eroding popular support for the Viet Cong seemed to promise that such attempts might find more fertile ground among the population. By levying heavy taxes, by instituting forced military draft and stricter control measures, and by being unable more and more to protect people in their zones from superior GVN and U.S. firepower, the Viet Cong now appeared increasingly "as ruthless exploiters of the people and as a constant source of danger to them."[19] The Viet Cong had been forced to resort to "intimidation and terror" instead of relying on "persuasion and voluntary cooperation" to control the

---

[18] Author interview with Russ Betts, 2004.

[19] Goure, Scott, and Russo, *Some Findings*, 1966, p. 24.

people.[20] The inability of the insurgents to protect the people had led to a growing flow of refugees to GVN areas, and this loss of population was undermining the economic base of the insurgency and reducing the source of recruits for their army. It had even created concern among the insurgents that their troops would face a food shortage.

As American troops pushed their offensive, Goure added a probe into the effect of their operations. Here, too, there was cause for optimism. The growing tempo of the American attacks had "radically altered the balance of military power," depressed the morale of the VC, dampened their "expectations of victory," and "strengthened the popular conviction that the VC will eventually be defeated."[21] As with bombings, operations by American troops did not provoke popular resentment. Civilians in the GVN areas interviewed by the RAND team tended to approve of the presence of American troops and expressed the hope that this presence "would bring about a speedy victory,"[22] while refugees, "eager to return to their villages . . . welcomed pacification by U.S. forces."[23]

Other conclusions of this paper mirrored those of earlier reports. Among them were the negative impact of airpower and artillery on the morale and combat effectiveness of the Viet Cong; the rising rate of defection and desertion; the lower quality of the units due to draftees who "were predominantly cowardly, uninterested in VC aims and indoctrination, and eager to desert"[24]; and the absence of "widespread or deepseated hatred" among the civilian population against the GVN and the Americans for air and artillery attacks.[25] On this last issue, a qualification was introduced: If the villagers believed that the attacks had been unprovoked by VC activities, they tended to blame the GVN and the Americans for the destruction and casualties, but if they believed that the VC presence and activities had brought on the attacks, the villagers blamed the insurgents. According to the authors, the majority of respondents to the interviews "claimed that the villagers most often blamed the Viet Cong."[26]

The presence of an increasing number of soldiers from the People's Army of Vietnam provided an opportunity to probe their morale and the impact of the air attacks on North Vietnam—a topic of great interest not only to MACV and the U.S. Air Force but also to the Navy, from whose carriers the planes took off to drop bombs. According to PAVN soldiers, the air attacks on the North had produced mixed results. The bombing had interrupted communications, damaged industrial and agricultural

---

[20] Goure, Scott, and Russo, *Some Findings*, 1966, p. 24.

[21] Goure, Scott, and Russo, *Some Findings*, 1966, p. 15.

[22] Goure, Scott, and Russo, *Some Findings*, 1966, p.17.

[23] Goure, Scott, and Russo, *Some Findings*, 1966, p. 18.

[24] Goure, Scott, and Russo, *Some Findings*, 1966, p. 19.

[25] Goure, Scott, and Russo, *Some Findings*, 1966, pp. 10–11.

[26] Goure, Scott, and Russo, *Some Findings*, 1966, p. 10.

production in some areas, and caused commodities' prices to rise. As to the effect on morale, North Vietnamese respondents said that the attacks had stirred up the people of the North, to whom the air raids represented "acts of unprovoked American aggression."[27] Among the Viet Cong, the bombing of the North had provoked "mixed reactions." Some cadres had "come to doubt the strength of North Vietnam and the solidarity of the Communist nations."[28] To most Viet Cong, however, the bombing seemed "very remote," and caused "little concern," since it had not brought about the collapse of North Vietnam or crippled the flow of supplies.[29]

Because American troops increasingly had to battle PAVN soldiers who had infiltrated into the South, the state of their morale evoked interest. The North Vietnamese respondents interviewed by Goure's team turned out to be well indoctrinated and loyal. They believed that their only choice was to continue fighting, since defection or desertion would preclude their returning home and would bring retaliation against their families. Many felt that it was their duty to "help liberate the South Vietnamese from American imperialism and capitalist oppression and to unify the country."[30] However, their morale had been adversely affected by the diseases and privations they had endured during their arduous trek into the South and by the rigors of combat, which had turned out to be more severe than they had expected. Many worried about their families in the North. Others were disappointed that the situation in the South was not as favorable as they had been told and that, contrary to what they had been led to believe, most of the countryside was still in the hands of their enemy, forcing them to fight mainly in the inhospitable jungle.

Following his routine, Leon Goure had presented his findings before the report was issued. Once again, he found a receptive ear in McNamara, who, in turn, found Goure's analysis helpful in soothing an anxious president. In a telephone conversation with Lyndon Johnson in mid-January 1966, McNamara—when asked by the president about enemy desertion and defection—mentioned "an interesting report from a man named Goure, who works for the Rand Corporation."[31] McNamara explained that, "we hired the Rand Corporation to go out there and carry on, over a period of months, an extensive interrogation of Viet Cong prisoners and defectors," and told the president that Goure's report confirmed "what I think you've heard from other sources."

McNamara then went on to reassure Johnson with Goure's encouraging findings. First, McNamara said, there had been a substantial increase in defections, which was

---

[27] Goure, Scott, and Russo, *Some Findings*, 1966, p. 30.

[28] Goure, Scott, and Russo, *Some Findings*, 1966, p. 29.

[29] Goure, Scott, and Russo, *Some Findings*, 1966, p. 29.

[30] Goure, Scott, and Russo, *Some Findings*, 1966, p. 31.

[31] "Telephone Conversation Between President Johnson and Secretary of Defense McNamara, January 14 or 15, 1966, State Department, Foreign Relations of the United States, 1964–1968 Vietnam, Volume IV, Document 26, Washington, D.C.

"on the order of 10,000 for 1965 versus 2,000 for 1964." The number might include "Viet Cong sympathizers as well as members of that force," but still represented a small percentage of a force "that's at least . . . 250,000 in total." Although it was not "a great number," it was "a substantially larger number than in 1964. More significant than the number of defectors—McNamara went on to say—was the fact that their attitude reflected "the morale of those who haven't defected," indicating that he interpreted the small sample of interviews as representing enemy forces at large.

Citing Goure, McNamara said that the defectors revealed that "they're ridden with disease. They're harassed by air. They're constantly forced to move. They have no sanctuary in which they can rest and recuperate." The old bases they had used, with their "deep underground tunnels and caves" were "under constant attack," so that they "never know when they're safe." They had difficulties obtaining hot food and moving from place to place. They were afflicted with diseases but lacked adequate medication. The incidence of "malaria and other diseases, particularly in the Viet Cong in the highlands, appears to run between 24 and 35 percent." Many were disheartened, and many who had believed in victory now questioned whether they would win. McNamara added that he was not saying to the president "that the morale is shot," but that he just wanted "to indicate that the pressure that is being applied to them by air and by constant offensive probing" by the GVN and by U.S. forces was starting to have an effect on morale.

Early in 1966, Walt Rostow, one of Goure's staunchest supporters, was elevated to the more influential position of National Security Advisor, replacing McGeorge Bundy, who had left to become the Ford Foundation president. Goure now had a supporter in the White House itself. Even at this stage in the war, Rostow was not given to the doubts that had begun to infect McNamara. Rostow was a strong advocate of airpower, and his belief in its effectiveness remained undiminished. Richard Moose, one of his assistants in the White House, would later say that Rostow "thought airpower could be used to good effect against the Viet Cong and was in favor of more against the North."[32] Moose said that, although Rostow would not have maintained that the war could be won through airpower, "he certainly wanted more of it, and he looked for a supportive opinion and evidence in that regard." Rostow, who had an academic background and inclination, "believed in research," and was an enthusiast of RAND's work, knew RAND people, and "liked the RAND product, especially that part that tended to confirm his views on things."[33]

Although Rostow was familiar with the Goure material and used it, he "had his own views on things," and was "selective in his use of materials, not only selective among RAND materials but highly selective in the intelligence output," and "tended

---

[32] Author interview with Richard Moose, 2003.

[33] Author interview with Richard Moose, 2003.

to invoke them and use them when they suited him."[34] McNamara described him as "optimistic in nature" and "skeptical of any report that failed to indicate that we were making progress."[35] According to Moose, with President Johnson, Rostow "constantly reinforced the idea that indeed we were winning and you could prove it by body count, you could prove it by the effects of airpower, and therefore he should stay the course."[36] Rostow's influence on Johnson was not decisive "but it reinforced the President's belief that perhaps if he kept after it he could win."[37] Goure's findings, therefore, suited Rostow's frame of mind.

In April 1966, Rostow and McNamara asked Goure to prepare a summary of recent findings. Goure obligedwith a 26-page paper entitled "Some Informal Notes on the 'Viet Cong Morale Study.'"[38] A copy went to General Maxwell Taylor. The roster of senior officials he briefed was impressive and revealed the extent of his access to decisionmakers. Besides Rostow and McNamara, he also briefed Deputy Secretary of State Cyrus Vance, Assistant Secretary of Defense John McNaughton, Assistant Secretary of Defense John S. Foster, Assistant Secretary of Defense Harold Brown, General Westmoreland, the Joint Chiefs, ISA, the Air Staff, Admiral Sharp and the CINCPAC Staff, Ambassador Lodge and Deputy Ambassador William Porter, ARPA, the CIA, the State Department, the Vietnam Coordination Committee, USIA, General Ryan (SAC) and staff, the 3d Air Division (in Guam), and General Hunter Harris, PACAF.[39]

In forwarding a copy to Rostow, Goure attached a letter addressing him as "Walt" and referencing a conversation they had held earlier. This implied a good personal relationship with a very senior official. Rostow and Maxwell Taylor read Goure's analysis and marked it heavily before Rostow forwarded it to the president on May 9, 1966. In his attached note, Rostow told LBJ that he wanted to bring the president's attention to "passages on VC morale that might interest [him], from the latest RAND report on prisoners and defectors."[40] Just as with McNamara, Rostow's objective appeared to be to reassure LBJ with good news from a credible source. The fact that Rostow did not feel the need to elaborate on the RAND project indicated that LBJ was already familiar with it.

By May 1966, the air campaign in the North had been going on for over a year, and Westmoreland's second phase of attacks was supposed to be nearing its end in two

---

[34] Author interview with Richard Moose, 2003.

[35] McNamara, *In Retrospect*, 1995, p. 235.

[36] Author interview with Richard Moose, 2003.

[37] Author interview with Richard Moose, 2003.

[38] Leon Goure, "Some Informal Notes on the 'Viet Cong Morale Study,'" 1966.

[39] Social Science Department Staff, Social Science Department, "Progress Report on ISA and ARPA Projects January–June 1966, Santa Monica, Calif.: RAND Corporation, D-14863-ISA/ARPA, June 1966.

[40] Rostow, Walt, letter to President Lyndon Johnson, May 9, 1966, Santa Monica, Calif.: RAND Corporation, L-8557; copy from LBJ Library, Austin, Tex.

months' time before moving to the third and last stage of his strategy. Washington undoubtedly was trying to gauge the effect of its strategy and tactics. Goure's analysis, as provided to Rostow at his request, gave a positive barometer of progress. Rostow said in his cover letter that the report "was distinctly encouraging" but did not indicate that—as yet—VC morale was approaching the decisive breaking point, thus implying that this breaking point might be reached later.

To call the president's attention to signs that American strategy was working, Taylor and Rostow marked sections of Goure's report on the adverse effect of American military actions on Viet Cong morale and strength. These sections reiterated Goure's earlier findings. The fact that Taylor and Rostow emphasized them for the president underscores their effort to show continuing results in the war. For this reason, it is worth restating these findings, which, when cited in repetition by various senior officials, came to sound like a mantra. Among the signs of progress against the enemy was the damage inflicted by heavy weapons and intensified operations. The other signs included significant casualties; loss of morale; erosion of faith in victory; belief that the GVN and the United States, with their superiority of weapons, equipment, and supplies, would prevail; fear of airpower, especially of B-52 attacks, and of powerful ordnance, such as large bombs and CBUs; and artillery shelling.

Other problems were plaguing the enemy. The number of deserters and defectors had grown, with deserters outnumbering defectors by perhaps a 2:1 ratio—or higher. Some units reported losing 20–40 percent of their men in the year, and others were constantly operating under strength. A higher number of cadres had defected, indicating leadership-morale problems. Food and manpower were increasingly hard to find for their units. A high proportion of new recruits was below the draft age, many as young as 15–17 years old. The food-supply difficulty was exacerbated by the chemical sprayings and the loss of population. Close to a million villagers had fled into GVN zones—driven out by air attacks, but also to some extent by sprayings.

The tremendous flow of people—sometimes consisting of entire hamlets and villages—from contested and VC-controlled zones, and the impact that this evacuation had inflicted on the Viet Cong's food supplies, manpower availability, intelligence gathering, morale, and ability to hide among the people, led Goure to suggest a deliberate program of generating refugees as part of a strategy to wrest control over population and resources. After pointing out that refugees were "a major asset" and that the role they played in "resource control and denial is self-evident," he suggested that "systematic and deliberate manipulation of population movement in critical areas or at critical times could have a major effect on reducing VC food and manpower resources, disrupting VC supply lines and logistic system and undermining VC morale."[41] In view of the facts that population control was a barometer of the war's progress and that greater GVN control would damage enemy morale and their belief in victory, "the

---

[41] Goure, "Some Informal Notes on the 'Viet Cong Morale Study,'" 1966, p. 9.

refugee movement to GVN controlled areas" would be "an important psychological warfare asset."[42]

Furthermore, Goure added, getting refugees to move from VC-controlled and contested zones into GVN areas would be a way to achieve pacification "without the expenditure of military forces."[43] According to the interviews, "as a rule the VC infrastructure does not follow the refugees," and if this was in fact true, "then the refugees are largely 'sanitized' from the VC infrastructure once they move to the GVN area."[44] Rostow/Taylor highlighted for the president Goure's suggestion that "the success of any deliberate program of encouraging and manipulating population movement will obviously depend" on its "integration into a comprehensive, planned military and pacification strategy," and also on "the effectiveness" of refugee "assistance programs."[45] The tactic of using firepower to overcome the civilians' natural reluctance to leave their land and to drive them into refugee camps—and under GVN control—would become highly controversial and draw harsh criticism.[46]

Other signs of progress highlighted by Taylor and Rostow included the problems plaguing the North Vietnamese infiltrators. They noted findings such as deteriorating morale; declining fighting caliber; insufficient training and indoctrination before hasty dispatch into the South (thus implying that North Vietnam was also facing a shortage of combat manpower); prevalent diseases; under-strength units; and inadequate food supplies. However, North Vietnamese soldiers appeared to have retained their discipline and their belief that they had no choice but to go on fighting. In support of the use of heavy weapons by the GVN and the United States, Goure indicated that such weapons remained important in the balance of forces, because the North

---

[42] Goure, "Some Informal Notes on the 'Viet Cong Morale Study,'" 1966, p. 12.

[43] Goure, "Some Informal Notes on the 'Viet Cong Morale Study,'" 1966, p. 12.

[44] Goure, "Some Informal Notes on the 'Viet Cong Morale Study,'" 1966, p. 10.

[45] Goure, "Some Informal Notes on the 'Viet Cong Morale Study,'" 1966, p. 13.

[46] As Goure put it in his draft, "Some Informal Notes on the 'Viet Cong Morale Study,'" 1966, p. 8, "the villagers move only when fear for their lives or deterioration in their economic conditions have made it intolerable for them to remain any longer at home." Correspondent Denis Warner endorsed this strategy in an article in *The Reporter* in December 1965, without identifying Goure or RAND, since the project was supposed to be classified. Echoing "the analyst," he wrote, ". . . to ignore the opportunity [created by refugees abandoning liberated areas] would be to discard the only practicable and immediately available means of dividing the Vietcong from the population. . . ." Also echoing Goure, Warner wrote, "We ought to increase our night-time interdiction of the waterways in the Delta and maintain the B-52 attacks on Vietcong base areas. Interference with mobility will break the Vietcong's back. . . . Don't just kill. Interfere with the Viet Cong." Calling the RAND project of "tremendous importance," Warner ended his article by saying that the work "revealed much more about the Vietcong than we have ever known before . . . there are guidelines for action and a whole body of information on matters that until now have always been either a matter of guesswork or woefully inadequate intelligence. We are getting to know the enemy." Cited in Russo, "Looking Backward," p. 56.

Vietnamesc— as well as the Viet Cong—remained confident that they could match GVN/U.S. troops in combat if the latter were not backed by such weapons.[47]

Goure's report was also delivered to Robert S. McNamara. Subsequently, on May 10, 1966, Goure sent supplemental notes via teletype to Larry Henderson, RAND's Washington office director, for transmittal to Colonel Marshall E. Sanders, USAF, Chief of the Special Projects Division in the Policy Planning Staff of OSD/ISA, and for eventual delivery to the Secretary of Defense.[48] The teletype contained Goure's analysis of the impact of U.S. troops and of the status of popular support for the Viet Cong. Basically, Goure said that the presence of American troops was a positive rather than a negative, and that the Viet Cong were losing more support among the people. Interviewees commented favorably on the American troops' conduct toward and treatment of civilians, as well as toward the prisoners they captured. Villagers seemed to welcome the prolonged presence of U.S. troops, because it improved security and brought benefits. The deployment of more U.S. combat forces had not intensified resentment against the Americans among the population, nor had it bolstered the Viet Cong's propaganda and appeals. Many prisoners and defectors who were interviewed said that they were afraid of American forces and mentioned that their side had suffered heavy losses in battles against the Americans.

Goure repeated other findings, which, once more, showed that the enemy was on a downward spiral. Enemy desertion had increased, and the quality of enemy troops had declined. In the villages, civilian cadres were finding it increasingly difficult to control the population. Popular dissatisfaction over the draft, high taxes, and restrictions on trade and movement had undermined the authority of the cadres and forced them to resort to threats and punishment. When VC troops camped among them, the people would become afraid of air and artillery attacks, and they would refuse to attend indoctrination meetings or to remain in the villages. The morale and performance of cadres in zones undergoing pacification had plummeted as GVN authority was restored. The flow of refugees into GVN zones had caused a drop in agricultural production in the Delta and confronted the Viet Cong with growing finance and food-supply difficulties. Although McNamara's doubts about the war were growing at this time, he nevertheless passed along Goure's encouraging findings at a meeting of the National Security Council on the afternoon of May 10, reading from the RAND

---

[47] In a "backgrounder" organized by the Joint United States Public Affairs Office (JUSPAO) for the American press corps in Saigon, Goure was emphatic, saying that the "question of morale" had disappeared from his interview samples and had been replaced by the question of pure hardware and of military power in leading the VC to believe that they would lose because the GVN had airplanes, artillery, tanks, better supplies, more ammunition, and more mobility. JUSPAO, *Transcript of Leon Goure (Rand Corporation) Backgrounder on Viet Cong Morale*, 1965, document in the Vietnam Archives at Texas Tech University.

[48] Leon Goure, teletype to L. J. Henderson, Washington office, for transmittal to Colonel Marshall E. Sanders, USAF, Chief, Special Projects Division, Policy Planning Staff in OSD/ISA (for submission to Defense Secretary Robert McNamara), May 1966 (not releasable to the general public).

report "on the extensive damage done to the Viet Cong and North Vietnam during the past three months."[49]

Following his schedule of briefings every couple of months, Goure talked to Walt Rostow for an hour on August 2, and on August 3, he briefed McNamara.[50] Right after Goure's briefing, Rostow sent a memorandum to President Johnson on August 2, highlighting some of the points Goure had made.[51] In May Rostow had told LBJ that the enemy had not yet reached the breaking point; now he told the president that the process of enemy disintegration had begun. The most significant finding, Rostow thought, was the "progressive decline in the morale and fighting capacity of the VC," as well as loss of faith in victory within enemy ranks.[52] Rostow told LBJ that when RAND began its interview program, 65 percent of the defectors and prisoners believed that the Viet Cong would win, 25 percent believed that the GVN would win, and 10 percent were uncertain. Now, only 20 percent believed that the Viet Cong would win, whereas 60 percent believed that the GVN would win, and 20 percent were uncertain. To Rostow, the increase in the number of Viet Cong who were "uncertain" was important, as was the growing number of hard-core communists among the defectors. Rostow told the president, "As you said at lunch yesterday to the newspaper men, no one can tell you when this progressive decline will lead to the breaking up of units or to the ending of the war. But the process under way among the VC is clear."

Rostow recommended that the president undertake actions to accelerate this downward trend. Although Rostow told Johnson that it would be "extremely important not to overestimate these trends and develop excessive optimism," he also said that it would be "equally important" to "look at them soberly and, especially, mount the kind of political as well as military operations which will accelerate them." Rostow suggested that Johnson might "like to hear directly from Goure his reflections on the evidence which now . . . included not only interrogations but a mass of captured documents which bear on morale." Rostow mentioned that Goure would be in town for a few more days. At the bottom of his memo, Rostow gave the president two options to mark: "Bring Goure in" and "Not necessary." Records of State Department archives indicate that Johnson read the memo but did not ask to have Goure brought in, and his daily schedule showed that he did not see Goure.

---

[49] State Department, Foreign Relations of the United States, 1964–68, Vol. IV, Vietnam: 135.

[50] For this briefing, Goure used "Some Findings of the Viet Cong Motivation and Morale Study, January–June 1966: A Briefing to the Joint Chiefs of Staff," dated August 1, 1966, which updated earlier findings.

[51] Walt Rostow, "Memorandum from the President's Special Assistant (Rostow) to President Johnson," State Department, Foreign Relations of the United States, 1964–68, Vol. IV, Vietnam: 198.

[52] Jack Foisie of the Los Angeles Times wrote in 1966 that the work of Goure—whom he did not identify by name—"indicated a decline in the morale of the enemy and a belief the communist forces have lost the Vietnamese War. . . . The findings of the survey supported allied military tactics in almost every respect, and gave an encouraging overall picture of progress in the ground war." Cited in Russo, "Looking Backward," 1972, p. 52.

According to Olivier Todd, a correspondent for *Le Monde Diplomatique*, although President Johnson did not talk to Goure directly, he began—reportedly—to carry a summary of Goure's findings in his pocket "like he carries the results of the Gallup Poll on his popularity" because he was "cheered by the conclusions."[53] These conclusions had not been divulged to the public and would "probably remain classified for a long time," but for the Americans, they were "very encouraging." When Todd interviewed Goure for his article, Goure said that the Viet Cong had lost the "fight for hearts and minds," and that "in the past few months more than a million refugees" had left VC zones. According to Goure, this did not mean that these people had switched their allegiance to the GVN, but this outflow meant that the Viet Cong could no longer count on them for support. In addition, Goure told Todd—as he had told senior officials in Washington—the morale of Viet Cong regular units had dropped, they were having "terrible recruitment and food supplies problems," and their forces were "reaching the stage of war weariness which we saw in the Spanish Civil War." According to Goure, "The people . . . in Vietnam want this war to end. And it's us who can finish it off."

Asked about the immediate future, Goure—according to Todd—sounded more circumspect. He told Todd that the Viet Cong had two options: "fight to the finish," which could not be excluded or, possibly, "in the cards," they would try to carry out in the fall "an important military and political escalation." If they failed to achieve a breakthrough and if there was "no turmoil in Saigon," they would "accept to negotiate."

This last "profound thought" of Goure's—that the Viet Cong would "tire out"—was important because it was beginning to emerge in "official American declarations." In Todd's view, this hopeful reading that the enemy was getting exhausted should be kept in mind, because it would explain "the bloody American follies in the coming months," as the "American geo-strategists," for whom the "cherished model" was the defeat of the Malayan insurgency, pursued a policy to crush the communists as the British had done in Malaya.

Indeed, President Johnson was growing optimistic in this period, cheered by cables from Saigon indicating that Viet Cong morale was bad and that the war was "going better than ever for the United States." The president "for the first time, sees light at the end of the tunnel. He figures victory is now within sight and that his firm position will be vindicated."[54]

At this time when Leon Goure, with his unbridled optimism, was riding high, dissatisfaction with his work actually grew inside and outside RAND. In Saigon, Doug Scott, Tony Russo, and Russ Betts became increasingly concerned about Goure's penchant for selecting data from the interviews that would support his own position on the war and his anti-communist perspective. Betts, along with Doug Scott and Tony

---

[53] Olivier Todd, "Ce qui se passe dans le monde depend en partie de ces chercheurs," *Le Monde Diplomatique,* 1966.

[54] Drew Pearson, "President's Confidence in Viet Victory Grows," *Los Angeles Times,* May 27, 1966.

Russo, disagreed with Goure on a lot of his agenda which Betts understood to be, "More bombs, and we're going to win this war," because Goure "very much believed that a stronger application of military force would turn the course of the war and we would inevitably win."[55] Goure would say, "Oh, I talked to Bob McNamara yesterday or the day before, and I said to him these B-52 bombings are really effective to undermine the morale of the North Vietnamese and the Viet Cong, and if we can do it with a little more accuracy so we don't bomb quite so many villages, we can destroy their logistics and we can deny them the support of the people."[56] According to Russ, none of the junior staff "could agree with that. We just couldn't do it." They would sit "around the office for hours at night and talk about what we could tolerate with what Leon was saying and what we couldn't."[57] But as junior staff, there was nothing they could do to challenge or stop Goure, who enjoyed high-level backing inside and outside RAND and was the only person authorized to brief senior officials, whose views could influence policies. Occasionally, when Goure was out of town, the junior staff would get to talk to visiting luminaries, such as Henry Kissinger, or to American reporters. But Kissinger was then outside the government and had no influence in Washington. According to Russ Betts, Kissinger "didn't talk all the time back then" and "asked very insightful questions," which "took a lot of thought" to answer in a balanced way. When Kissinger asked about B-52 bombings as the answer to the war, for example, Russ and Russo told him that there was other evidence. Kissinger said, "You mean, this isn't RAND's perspective?" and they replied, "If Leon says it is, it is, but we don't see it in the data; we can't do that."[58]

Russ Betts would later say that the data from the interviews could "support anybody's perspective on anything." He and the other team leaders knew, because they read and edited the interviews. The prisoners, defectors, and refugees who were interviewed "had every perspective across the spectrum." According to Betts, when Goure came out and said, "Look at this data. It proves that bombing is the effective way to win this war," the junior staff members looked at each other, "just despairing," and said, "It's hopeless. That's wrong. That's not what the data says. You can't prove that with the data. Use statistical analysis, whatever you want to do, just look at how many times they say that and how many times they say the opposite. The weight of the evidence is that that was wrong."[59]

But that did not stop Goure. According to Betts, "Leon already knew. He had his conclusions, and he didn't need the data except to prove what he wanted to prove."

---

[55] Author interview with Russ Betts, 2004.

[56] Author interview with Russ Betts, 2004.

[57] Author interview with Russ Betts, 2004.

[58] Author interview with Russ Betts, 2004.

[59] Author interview with Russ Betts, 2004.

Goure would go to Westmoreland and say, "Look at what this interview says. Question 23, it says that B-52 is really destroying their effectiveness." Next, he would tell McNamara the same thing.

According to Tony Russo, he and Doug Scott "would have these long conversations into the night, figuring things out," and they came to the conclusion that Goure "was not analyzing the interviews in any scientific way, he was just trying to gain points with the Air Force."[60] By this time, the two men had seen enough of the project, absorbed enough of the interview material, acquired enough knowledge, and gained enough experience in Vietnam to become disillusioned with what they perceived as Goure's selective use of the data to push his own line on the war. By about this time, Tony Russo was beginning to change his view, losing his ambivalence and developing more sympathy for the insurgents, whom he believed had more legitimacy than the corrupt and brutal GVN. For his part, Russ Betts thought that when Goure told U.S. policymakers that "more B-52s would eliminate communism in the world . . . he believed it" and that nothing he and his colleagues said could change Goure's mind. The RAND Saigon staff became split between those who sided with Goure—Leib, Shaffer, and Carrier before he returned to Santa Monica—and those who were unhappy with his interpretation of the data—Scott, Russo, and Russ and Ardith Betts. Carlson was oblivious to the tension and did not side with either group.

Sometime in spring 1966, Doug Scott and Tony Russo decided to write to Joe Goldsen. Doug Scott took the lead in drafting the letter, in which he pointed out the deficiencies of the project in leadership, analysis of the data, and the design of the research itself. Russo co-signed. Goldsen did not respond. Russo believed that Goldsen, who was a strong supporter of Goure, just put it away in his files. But while Goldsen ignored their complaint against Goure, others in Santa Monica were growing concerned about his work. According to Alex George, Goure's project became controversial within RAND and, eventually, RAND suffered "a black eye" because of it—"in the judgment of many people."[61] A large number of people at RAND "felt that the quality of the analysis was very questionable" and yet it was being relayed directly to Walt Rostow.[62] Goure "tried very hard to be objective," George would later say, but "the problem of analyzing prisoner of war interviews is not as easy as it might seem" and the information they provided "had to be evaluated very carefully." Goure "could see all the damage that we were inflicting on the Viet Cong and it added up," and he believed that "we were winning the battle of attrition" because interviews "indicated heavy casualties."[63]

---

[60] Author interview with Tony Russo, 2003 and 2004.

[61] Author interview with Alex George, 2004.

[62] Author interview with Alex George, 2004.

[63] Author interview with Alex George, 2004.

Alex George thought that the crucial factor—which Goure failed to grasp—was the ability of the Viet Cong to recoup with their hit-and-run strategy, which made it possible for them to attack, disappear to recuperate from their losses, and then attack again, in an endless cycle, and with reinforcements from North Vietnam.[64] This ability of the enemy to "keep putting forces in was unexpected and went on much longer" than Alex George and others at RAND had originally estimated, and led them to conclude that it would be really important for RAND not to produce results that people inside and outside RAND viewed as "questionable," and analytically and politically biased "because the effect was to support the idea that we were going to win the war of attrition."[65] Steve Hosmer would later confirm that there was disagreement with Goure in Santa Monica. Whereas Goure believed that the enemy was about to collapse, others saw that evidence was lacking to support such a conclusion. Because of these differences in interpretation, it was decided that Goure's perspective should not be the only one.

So, according to Alex George, he himself decided that one thing RAND could do was to bring in Konrad Kellen to evaluate the interviews through "proper, professional analysis" in order "to get a feel for what they really told us."[66] Kellen was born in Berlin in 1913 and, as the son of a successful brewery owner, grew up in wealthy surroundings. He had to give up his law studies in Munich and flee to Paris when the Nazis came to power. His mother and sisters managed to escape, but his father and the rest of the family perished in Germany. Kellen moved to the United States in 1935. For a period of time, he worked in Los Angeles as the personal secretary to the exiled writer Thomas Mann. During World War II, he served as an officer in the U.S. Army, working in an intelligence unit, and remained in Germany after the war as a political officer for the U.S. Office of Military Government. According to Daniel Ellsberg, a close friend at RAND, Kellen had worked with materials derived from interrogation in World War II and with defectors from Eastern Europe. Alex George had gotten to know Konrad Kellen when they were working in the same office and sharing a house in Berlin after the war, and had confidence in him, his knowledge of military operations based on the work that he had done in Germany, his judgment, and his analytic ability. Kellen would win the respect of many people at RAND, including those who

---

[64] Alex George's view seemed to be supported by the pilot studies that the office of Alain Enthoven, a former RAND economist then serving as Assistant Secretary of Defense for Systems Analysis, conducted at the time. Those studies tried to make the point that the war of attrition was a test of staying power and that the Viet Cong and the North Vietnamese had control of their rate of casualties. If they wanted fewer casualties, they would "just stay further back into the jungle and not aggressively attack us." So, the war of attrition was not going to work because the enemy could control the casualties they were going to take "to the level they consider[ed] bearable and then stay[ed] there forever." His office of Systems Analysis did not take these pilot studies any further because the staff did not have expertise on Vietnam. Author interview with Alain Enthoven, 2005.

[65] Author interview with Alex George, 2004.

[66] Author interview with Alex George, 2004.

did not see eye to eye with him. Gus Shubert would later say that he had "great respect for Kellen's intellect," and that Kellen would become "one of the few people at RAND who saw the whole picture" in Vietnam.[67]

According to Kellen, he was living in New York [where he was working for Radio Free Europe and at the Hudson Institute] when RAND hired him. The call from RAND came after *The New York Times* printed a letter he had written criticizing leaflets that some "smart boys" in Washington had dropped over North Vietnam in the millions. The leaflets "told the Vietnamese to lay down their arms because we were good people and their leaders were bad people . . . and that they should stop fighting the war."[68] Konrad had served in World War II as a psychological warfare expert and thought that "it was obvious nonsense to shower [a] large number of soldiers with a leaflet saying 'stop that war.'" So he wrote a letter to the *Times* in which he pointed out that soldiers "don't begin wars" and they "don't stop wars," and therefore "if you want to stop a war you have to do it differently."[69] Kellen did not pay much attention to the letter, but it caught the attention of people at RAND, who called him and asked him to join RAND, and he agreed.

Since the enemy had withstood American military pounding, the question that was of interest to Kellen was how they had managed to bear up under this pressure. So, whereas Leon Goure focused on enemy weaknesses and ways to exploit them, Kellen attempted—as he put it in one of his reports—to evaluate the factors that contributed to cohesion within enemy forces and that had allowed them to maintain control over their actions and their organization. To accommodate Kellen's work, the interviews in Vietnam began to include a questionnaire to elicit data on elements of cohesion within enemy ranks. Gus Shubert would later summarize the gist of Kellen's work as, "There is nothing no how, nowhere, no time that's going to make these guys quit that it's within our power to do or within our will to do."[70] Shubert thought that Kellen "didn't derive from the data any sense that we were having any impact whatsoever on the effectiveness of the VC or NVA operations that would in any way suggest that they would quit, surrender, or do anything else but fight on until they had won or until the last one of them was buried somewhere."[71]

Perhaps because some of his family members had perished during the Second World War, Kellen was sensitive to the sufferings that were being inflicted on the Vietnamese by U.S. military actions that were at times needless and futile. He was particularly incensed by Goure's conclusion that air attacks and artillery bombardments

---

[67] Author interview with Gus Shubert, 2004.

[68] Author interview with Konrad Kellen, 2002.

[69] Author interview with Konrad Kellen, 2002.

[70] Collins, interview with Gus Shubert, session of May 20, 1992, p. 42.

[71] Collins, interview with Gus Shubert, session of May 20, 1992, p. 42.

would not push villagers to join the Viet Cong and therefore could be launched with impunity. In a memo to Goure and some of his colleagues on September 30, 1966, titled "US/ARVN Shelling and Air Bombardment of Vietnamese," Kellen questioned the morality of this stance.[72] Kellen asked whether a "guarantee that villagers will not join the VC when bombed and shelled" would constitute a "hunting license" and whether "tactical considerations" should be "the only criterion" "when it comes to killing people, or engaging in operations that make such killing likely." In his view, even within the narrow confines of whether the peasants would or would not join the Viet Cong as a result, a case could be made that the trade-off of indiscriminate bombing and shelling would be "in our disfavor" because of the large-scale killings, and because such activities would put Americans "in danger of degrading their basic value structure if their calculations in this particular area should come to center merely or mainly around what we can get away with."

Other colleagues of Goure, including Gus Shubert, were critical of "Goure's methods and his conclusions,"[73] and argued that "Goure's findings could be sustained only by an extremely selective use of the interview data," and "denounced him as an opportunist who was willing to sacrifice intellectual honesty to support the interests of the Air Force."[74] They also "warned that the analytical negligence of Goure's research threatened to impugn the scientific validity of systems analysis and thus risked RAND's reputation."[75] Also, as the war took a heavy toll on the Vietnamese, some of Goure's colleagues "felt that by validating the use of overwhelming air power, Goure's work was adding needless death and injury to that U.S. forces were already inflicting on the Vietnamese population."[76] According to Alfred Goldberg, the internal criticism of Goure was generally verbal, and there was "little in the written record."[77]

The controversy that the project sparked within RAND was because it had "received more than the usual attention accorded RAND work in the U.S. national security community" and that it seemed to be "exercising an influence out of proportion to its intrinsic merits."[78] The controversy partially reflected "the basic predilections of the people involved, especially their attitude toward the war," but it also reflected different "attitudes toward the proper role for RAND, the nature of the work that RAND should be doing, and RAND's relationship with the Air Force and other government

---

[72] Konrad Kellen, "US/ARVN Shelling and Air Bombardment of Vietnamese," memorandum to Leon Goure et al., September 30, 1966, provided to David Jardini by Gus Shubert and cited in Jardini, "The Wrong War," 1998, p. 52.

[73] Jardini, "The Wrong War," 1998, p. 49.

[74] Jardini, "The Wrong War," 1998, p. 49.

[75] Jardini, "The Wrong War," 1998, p. 49.

[76] Jardini, "The Wrong War," 1998, p. 49.

[77] Goldberg, "RAND and Vietnam," 1969, p. 15.

[78] Goldberg, "RAND and Vietnam," 1969, p. 15.

agencies."[79] Joe Carrier, who remains a staunch supporter of Goure, has ascribed some of the criticism to professional jealousy and to resentment that Goure was running a big project with a large budget and had the ear of high-level officials in Washington.

According to Gus Shubert, "Goure's line was shoot more, bomb more, because the more you shoot and the more you bomb, the more they [the Vietnamese peasants] blame the Viet Cong."[80] In Shubert's opinion, there was "no validity to that at all" and that Goure had arrived at this conclusion by "selecting among the things that they [the interviewees] said carefully."[81] Shubert would later recall that Albert Wohlstetter and several other people among the "cognoscente" in Washington, who were "suspicious" of Goure's work from the beginning, christened Goure's project the "How I Learned to Love to Be Bombed Study."[82] Another complaint Shubert had was that Goure "would put briefings together and he wouldn't write them down, and it was very difficult to pin him down on what he was really saying."[83] To Shubert, Goure was like a "loose canon,"[84] because he would ignore the criticisms leveled against his presentations in Santa Monica and would fly off to Washington to say whatever he wanted to say without regard to his colleagues' objections.

Despite Kellen's powerful condemnation and despite the persistent criticism of other colleagues, Goure remained secure in his position, as long as Frank Collbohm and Joe Goldsen continued to support him, and as long as he satisfied his Washington clients. Gus Shubert would later recall a visit he made to the Pentagon during which he saw people he knew smiling broadly. He asked a general friend of his, "Johnny, what's going on around here? Why is everybody sitting around smiling?" The general said, "Oh, that's simple. Leon's just been through. It's just like a breath of fresh air to hear how well we're doing in Vietnam. It raises everybody's spirits." Then the general added, "Leon is the only hopeful sign on the horizon."[85] Frank Collbohm himself was aware that some people were questioning the quality of Goure's work, but to him it was fine as attested by the approval of officials, such as General Westmoreland, who told Collbohm during his 1965 visit to Vietnam that Goure's study "supplied helpful intelligence information for U.S. and South Vietnamese ground operations."[86]

Goure's influence was confirmed when Carl Rowan, former head of the U.S. Information Agency, wrote in a syndicated column of August 16, 1966, that the

---

[79] Goldberg, "RAND and Vietnam," 1969, p. 15.

[80] Author interview with Gus Shubert, 2004.

[81] Author interview with Gus Shubert, 2004.

[82] Collins, interview with Gus Shubert, session of May 20, 1992, p. 11.

[83] Author interview with Gus Shubert, 2004.

[84] Author interview with Gus Shubert, 2004.

[85] Collins, interview with Gus Shubert, session of May 20, 1992, p. 15.

[86] Landau, "Behind the Policy Makers," 1972, p. 60.

RAND study lay "at the heart of President Johnson's strategy." Rowan was referring to the Goure report of August 1, 1966, for the Joint Chiefs of Staff—which he did not identify specifically in his column. According to Rowan, the president had "most carefully" read the report, which "indicates that the communist forces are already disillusioned, often hungry and sick, fearful of direct military encounters, and increasingly doubtful of a Viet Cong victory." Rowan added that this study "reportedly has convinced President Johnson that, as long as Hanoi refuses peace talks, he has no alternative to continuing the bombing and the military pressure. The hope is that, sooner rather than later, the communists' morale will descend past the breaking point."[87] The impact Goure was having in Washington, and the powerful backing he enjoyed inside and outside RAND, made his position secure regardless of the criticism being raised against him.

Part of the criticism at RAND was over Goure's interpretation of the data and part was over the quality of his work, which suffered because of his attempt to meet McNamara's demand for periodic updates on changes in trends concerning the Viet Cong. At the beginning, Goure expected that RAND's procedure to ensure quality would be enforced, and that his papers and briefings would be reviewed and scrubbed— a process that usually took several weeks—before he would be allowed to "appear in public" in Washington.[88] As he explained later, when he embarked on the project, he thought that he would have one year between reports "in which he and others could sit back and collect their thoughts, and then circulate drafts of a final study among their RAND colleagues to ensure that responsible intellectual standards would be met."[89]

Initially, when McNamara's request was relayed to RAND, there was opposition to providing such trend reports on the grounds that they would be "too impressionistic and fleeting," but RAND eventually acquiesced with reluctance to McNamara's demand.[90] With the blessing of Frank Collbohm, a paper—which amounted to a "compendium of somewhat refined military intelligence reports"—was churned out every 90 days "to accompany the quarterly briefing tour from Saigon to Honolulu to Santa Monica and on to Washington."[91]

To accommodate this schedule, Goure's work was exempted from RAND's rigorous review process to ensure quality. According to Guy Pauker, "When Goure would return from Vietnam to Santa Monica, he would stay long enough to change his shirts,

---

[87] Carl Rowan, "Defense Dept. Believes Viet Cong Morale Slipping," *Los Angeles Times*, August 17, 1966. Rowan based his column on the Goure report to the Joint Chiefs of Staff, but did not identify Goure or RAND. According to Rowan, the classified study showed "a remarkable decline in the morale" of the Viet Cong.

[88] Leon Goure, letter to a friend in Santa Monica, June 4, 1965.

[89] Landau, "Behind the Policy Makers," 1972, p. 61.

[90] Goldberg, "RAND and Vietnam," 1969, p. 14.

[91] Goldberg, "RAND and Vietnam," 1969, p. 14.

then fly off to Washington to brief McNamara."[92] So, although Goure's reports would be circulated under the RAND imprint, they would not be subjected to the internal scrutiny and critical review that usually took place before papers were distributed outside RAND. A number of people at RAND would later admit that they were "shocked at Frank Collbohm's acquiescence to this breach of normal practice."[93] Collbohm himself would defend his decision, maintaining that "the procedure requested by McNamara was appropriate to wartime, and that RAND had acquiesced in a similar way at the time of the Korean war."[94] As far as Goure was concerned, since RAND's senior management and his Washington clients were not objecting to his work, he assumed that he was doing a fine job and that he could press ahead. He also felt that he was fulfilling RAND's function, which—as he saw it—was to assist the Air Force, MACV, and the military in general.

But, gradually, skepticism of Goure's unrelenting optimism grew outside of RAND. In Vietnam, toward the end of 1965, General Westmoreland had already begun to doubt Goure's optimistic findings. In a diary entry following a briefing, he wrote that Goure was reporting "that earlier guesses as to morale and attitude of the Viet Cong" were "being confirmed."[95] However, Westmoreland noted that he "can't help but get the feeling that Goure's analysis is probably optimistic with respect to the status of morale and attitude of the Viet Cong." Having seen how fiercely the enemy was fighting back, Westmoreland wrote that Goure's findings "seemed to be generally contradicted by the increase in incidents and will to fight that has been evident during recent months." Then, on December 13, 1966, following a briefing by Leon Goure,[96] Westmoreland noted in his diary, "I don't fully accept the Goure report because he has traditionally overplayed the presumed low state of Viet Cong morale."

In Washington, Seymour Deitchman became concerned over Goure's briefings and reports when he started getting the word from a source close to McNamara that they were influencing the Secretary of Defense.[97] So, when this source told him that

---

[92] Jardini, "The Wrong War," 1998, p. 46.

[93] Landau, "Behind the Policy Makers," 1972, p. 61.

[94] Landau, "Behind the Policy Makers," 1972, p. 61.

[95] Westmoreland, William C., Diary, Personal Papers, Box 7, Lyndon B. Johnson Library, Austin, Tex.

[96] For this briefing, Goure took along the Dinh Tuong project leader, David Elliott, and an interviewer, Mai Elliott, then working on a RAND study of Dinh Tuong Province (see Chapter Six for details) to bolster his own interpretation, but Goure did most of the talking. Westmoreland noted that, since he did not trust what Goure had to say, he did not trust what the Elliotts had to say, either.

[97] For example, according to author Deborah Shapley, McNamara said at a press briefing that the bombing of the North was sapping enemy morale in the South, citing prisoner interrogations. In his interview with the author, Deitchman said he could not recall who his source was, but he thought that the information probably came from one of the military assistants to McNamara, or to Harold Brown, or to Johnny Foster, the director of Defense Research and Engineering. Author interview with Sy Deitchman, 2005.

"McNamara was feeling very optimistic about the war as a result,"[98] and that his action on the war was being affected, Deitchman began to worry because he thought that Goure was "giving McNamara a distorted picture of how the war was going,"[99] and that it was a bad idea to have Goure's reports going directly to the Secretary of Defense and a dangerous procedure to let Goure brief McNamara because the results were preliminary and unevaluated.

Although Goure "played it straight," and clarified that the results he was briefing were preliminary and impressionistic, it seemed to Deitchman and some of his colleagues "that the nature of those impressions might possibly be highly misleading."[100] For example, with regard to the effect of the war on the population, the impressions were that the villagers were blaming the Viet Cong, not the Americans, for the death and destruction, because the Viet Cong presence attracted the bombs. Deitchman and some of his colleagues thought that when the results were so close to what one might want to hear, "it pays to be suspicious."[101] Later, more extensive, detailed, and fully analyzed results showed that the preliminary impressions had been distorted and that the peasants blamed all sides in the war for their sufferings. If someone wanted to blame the Viet Cong or the Americans, he could find evidence in the interviews to support either view.[102]

So, Deitchman put a stop to Goure's briefings and delayed the reports from reaching McNamara until he could see whether it was worthwhile to forward the conclusions to McNamara's office. It was a delicate procedure. "I exercised censorship," Deitchman would later admit.[103] As a sponsor of research, Deitchman generally wished that the studies would have more impact on policies than they did. Usually the results came too late to make the system reverse course. Goure's case, however, was one of those times when Deitchman feared the influence of research and wished research results had no influence on events.[104] Besides Deitchman, there were other officials in the Defense Department who were concerned about Goure's work. According to Alex George, those people asked Eugene Webb—a social psychologist of great distinction

---

[98] Author interview with Sy Deitchman, 2005.

[99] Author interview with Sy Deitchman, 2005.

[100] Deitchman, *The Best-Laid Schemes*, 1976, p. 407.

[101] Deitchman, *The Best-Laid Schemes*, 1976, p. 408.

[102] Deitchman, *The Best-Laid Schemes*, 1976, p. 408.

[103] Deitchman said that Brown and Foster knew of his intervention. Deitchman did not recall with whom he worked at OSD to stop Goure's briefings and reports from reaching McNamara. Author interview with Sy Deitchman, 2005.

[104] Deitchman, *The Best-Laid Schemes*, 1976, p. 407.

who was working at DoD at the time—to check Goure's work. Webb performed the review and "was very critical of it."[105]

In Congress, RAND's project had come to the attention of the Subcommittee on International Organizations and Movements back in mid-1965, during a hearing on social science research in foreign countries sponsored by the "Military Establishment." According to Seymour Deitchman, Goure's reorientation of the project toward "current VC operations" and the focus on questions such as "how they organized; how they operated in the field; their methods of recruiting and military training; and their reactions to the increasing American air and ground combat operations" closely resembled "straight military intelligence."[106] In the view of the subcommittee, the military itself should be collecting this kind of intelligence, rather than some highly paid consultants. Some members of the subcommittee expressed skepticism over the value of this huge research effort which General John W. Vogt, Chief of ISA's Policy Planning Staff, tried to explain at the hearing.

General Vogt told the subcommittee that the Pentagon had hired RAND to find out "what kind of an operation on our part would impose extra-heavy burdens" on the enemy.[107] Among the RAND findings he cited was the discovery that the enemy was experiencing many difficulties from having to be constantly on the move. As General Vogt put it, when the Viet Cong were forced out of their bivouac area after having fought all day, they had to dig trenches and work all night to secure their new position before they could go to sleep, and this back-breaking labor exhausted them. Congressman Peter H. B. Frelinghuysen responded that a child could have drawn the conclusion that "it is an effort, in a jungle, to move from one place to another,"[108] and said that taking three man-years of study to come up with this finding disturbed him.[109] Another finding revealing when the Viet Cong ate their evening meals was questioned by Congressman Harold Royce Gross, who said, "We didn't have to send consultants over there to find" this out.[110]

While the subcommittee was skeptical of the value of the RAND research, Senator J. William Fulbright, a vocal critic of the war, questioned the integrity of the findings themselves. After Goure's work came to his attention, Senator Fulbright wrote to McNamara in May 1966 demanding an investigation of the RAND study methods and asking that McNamara report back to the Foreign Relations Committee.

---

[105] Author interview with Alex George, 2004. Webb told Alex George about this after he joined the faculty at Stanford.

[106] Deitchman, *The Best-Laid Schemes*, 1976, p. 236.

[107] Deitchman, *The Best-Laid Schemes*, 1976, p. 238.

[108] Deitchman, *The Best-Laid Schemes*, 1976, p. 239.

[109] Deitchman, *The Best-Laid Schemes*, 1976, p. 240.

[110] Deitchman, *The Best-Laid Schemes*, 1976, p. 239.

Fulbright said in the letter that he had "received reports of recent surveys conducted by the RAND Corporation and others concerning the attitudes of the Viet Cong defectors and prisoners," which suggested "that those in charge of the project may have manipulated the results in such a way as to affect the results."[111] McNamara appointed a high-level Air Force team to examine Goure's operations, "which, not surprisingly, found that Goure's methods were sound and that his findings had been quite useful to the Air Force."[112] To Gus Shubert, this report was "a typical bureaucratic put-off."[113] Fulbright's demand for an investigation unsettled some people at RAND who thought that Goure's work was damaging RAND's reputation.

The internal chorus of criticism, the current of discontent in the Saigon office—which, according to Goure, included a "letter writing campaign to Collbohm" to "cut his throat"[114] —and the external rumblings of dissatisfaction over Goure's work might have prompted Frank Collbohm to finally take action in late 1966. The day Gus Shubert returned to Santa Monica from his NATO assignment in Paris, Collbohm was waiting for him in the hallway and told him—essentially—that RAND was in trouble and that he wanted a reliable person to rectify how things were going with regard to research in Vietnam. Collbohm told Shubert that he was the right person for this job. Shubert guessed that Collbohm's move might have been prompted by "some kind of rebellion or something"[115] that had upset him and perhaps also by the negative feedback from influential people like Andy Marshall, who was still at RAND at the time and was one of the big critics of the study.[116] Marshall grew up in Detroit and received a graduate degree in economics from the University of Chicago. He joined RAND in 1949 and gained prominence as a nuclear strategist, along with Herman Kahn and Albert Wohlstetter. He was—and is—considered a giant in the field of national security, with many ardent admirers and loyal supporters inside and outside the government. Subsequently, President Nixon appointed him to direct the Pentagon's Office of Net Assessment, the Pentagon's think tank.[117]

---

[111] Jardini, "The Wrong War," 1998, p. 48.

[112] Jardini, "The Wrong War," 1998, p. 48.

[113] Jardini, "The Wrong War," 1998, p. 48.

[114] Goure, letter to a friend in Santa Monica, August 16, 1967. In a lunch conversation with the author in 2003, Goure said that he must have been "naïve" not to know that RAND was unhappy with him. He wondered why RAND "picked on him" among the many RAND people working on Vietnam.

[115] Collins, interview with Gus Shubert, session of May 20, 1992, p. 14.

[116] Author interview with Gus Shubert, 2004.

[117] Andrew Marshall is sometimes referred to as the Pentagon's futurist-in-chief. James Der Derian wrote in *The New York Times* ("The Illusion of a Grand Strategy," May 25, 2001) that Marshall has been head of the Office of Net Assessment since his appointment by Nixon, "despite efforts by some defense secretaries to get rid of him." According to Der Derian, his "innocuous-sounding office" actually performs extremely important work: "to assess regional and global military balances and to determine long-term trends and threats." Nicholas Lemann described him in "Dreaming About War" (*New Yorker*, July 16, 2001) as a "small, bald man with wire-rimmed

Later, Collbohm explained to Gus Shubert privately, "We've got this thing going on in Vietnam which is out of control. We want to get somebody in there who will understand the substance and fix it."[118] Shubert said he did not know why Collbohm chose him because the RAND president never gave him an explanation. At first, Shubert resisted the assignment because he had built up his NATO expertise and did not want to veer away from it. Collbohm told him to go to Saigon and find out what was going on—and Shubert agreed. Collbohm did more than selecting Shubert to oversee the Vietnam project; he also appointed him manager of the ARPA/AGILE contract, replacing Jack Ellis. As Collbohm explained to Ellis in a meeting, the problems remaining in Vietnam were social science–related and not engineering or military operations kinds of problems, and that he wanted the "right kind of stewardship" which Gus Shubert, who had the required qualification, could provide.[119]

Shubert spent a lot of time in Vietnam because he wanted to arrive at a fair judgment of the project. What he found in Saigon upset him, but for reasons that differed from Collbohm's. As soon as he set foot in the villa and realized what was going on, he "sensed that it was a mess."[120] He found a general sense of demoralization among the staff—with the exception of Goure. According to him, "Doug Scott and Tony Russo . . . could hardly wait" to sit down with him and tell him how unhappy they were with the way Goure was misrepresenting the data to back conclusions that could not be supported by information coming from the interviews.[121] Tony Russo was the most critical, and what Russo told him greatly influenced the opinion he formed of the project. Russo would later recall that Shubert arrived in Saigon as a kind of investigator and seemed to have a bad impression of Goure.

---

spectacles who dresses in the manner of an unreconstructed nineteen-fifties organization man." He is known as shy and quiet, and Lehman wrote that "in public settings he doesn't say much . . . often mumbling in a low voice, or questioning but not answering, or simply saying he has nothing to add to the discussion." But he retains a strong mystique because of the network of ardent admirers and loyal protégés he acquired as the longest-reigning strategist since the days of the Cold War. This network spans the defense industry, academia, and government. His loyal protégés include people formerly in high places, such as Donald Rumsfeld, former Secretary of Defense; Paul Wolfowitz, former Assistant Secretary of Defense; Richard Armitage, former Deputy Secretary of State; and James Roche, former Secretary of the Air Force. The spate of 2001 articles about him appeared because, in that year, he was appointed by Rumsfeld to guide the strategic review for the Pentagon and draft the plan to upgrade the military for the Bush Administration.

[118] Collins, interview with Gus Shubert, session of May 20, 1992, p. 14.

[119] Author interview with Jack Ellis, 2003 and 2004. Joe Carrier has made the claim—so far unsubstantiated— that Goure's project commanded such a large budget and enjoyed so much visibility that the Economics Department had attempted to get hold of it unsuccessfully until Shubert managed to wrest it away from the Social Science Department.

[120] Author interview with Gus Shubert, 2004.

[121] Author interview with Gus Shubert, 2004.

It appeared to Shubert that the situation in Saigon "was worse than you could even dream," and he knew that something "had to be done."[122] He decided right at that moment that the project had to be terminated because he thought that it could seriously threaten RAND's integrity, reputation, and the quality of its work. What Shubert found in Vietnam was bad news to Collbohm, but the extent of the problem persuaded Shubert that the project should not continue. It was not clear what Collbohm had wanted Shubert to achieve. Shubert guessed that Collbohm might only have wanted him to make cosmetic changes—to improve the project without altering the message—because Collbohm basically agreed with Goure and supported the application of more firepower. If the RAND president expected only cosmetic changes, he picked "the wrong man," because once Shubert completed his review of the way the project had been run, he was determined to terminate it.[123]

First, according to Shubert, he wanted to ascertain that the criticism of Goure's work was well founded, and that he was not missing something. He brought in Paul Berman, a quantitative political scientist from MIT, as a consultant to review the project, asking him, "What do you think of this stuff?" Berman came back with a negative evaluation.[124] In addition, Shubert also asked the people in the Social Science and Economics Departments to review the project and what it had produced. From those reviews, Shubert concluded that "from any way you looked at it," Goure's work was flawed. As far as Shubert could determine, Goure's "only methodology" was to go through the interviews and select information that "would make the Air Force and the military in general look good . . . and ignore everything that contradicted it."[125] Shubert, however, could not remove Goure because Collbohm continued to back him up. Shubert guessed that Collbohm could not fire Goure because if he did "the Air Force"—whoever "the Air Force" was—"would have been all over him."[126] According to Shubert, Goure was getting "a lot of plaudits from the Air Force and from the DoD when he started emitting those positive signals during the darkest days of the war,"[127] which said in essence that "bombing, and to some extent shelling, resulted in increased hatred for the Viet Cong and not for the Americans, and therefore the more, the better," since this would bring the United States "closer . . . to victory."[128]

Goure's selective use of the interview data brought the issue of methodology to the fore, and the people at RAND who were concerned with or about his project lined

---

[122]Author interview with Gus Shubert, 2004.

[123]Author interview with Gus Shubert, 2004.

[124]Author interview with Gus Shubert, 2004.

[125]Author interview with Gus Shubert, 2004.

[126]Author interview with Gus Shubert, 2004.

[127]Collins, interview with Gus Shubert, session of May 20, 1992, p. 33.

[128]Collins, interview with Gus Shubert, session of May 20, 1992, p. 40.

up into a qualitative camp—mostly in the Social Science Department—and a quantitative camp—mostly in the Economics Department. The social scientists believed that the project had its merits and that the problem was with the way Goure was interpreting the data. The economists, such as Gus Shubert, thought that the interviews did not represent a scientific sample. This division was confirmed by Olivier Todd. While researching his article, Todd found that people at RAND, where samples of Goure's work were being submitted to a multidisciplinary "methodological review" at the time, were split over their value. Some thought that the samples were "deficient" and that the interview methods lacked rigor, but others believed that Goure had "obtained good results in difficult circumstances."[129]

Shubert's doubts about the methodology of the project were reinforced on one of his visits to Vietnam, during which he accompanied Tony Russo on a field trip. He was shocked that Russo's "criterion for selecting respondents was to walk into a prison and ask, 'You've got anybody interesting for me today?'"[130] In this instance, however, Shubert and others who joined him in his criticism did not appreciate the conditions for conducting the interviews in wartime in Vietnam and the difficulty of obtaining a scientific sample.

Goure acknowledged—as do former team leaders—that it was impossible to have "statistical control . . . for the simple reason there was no statistics about the total number of prisoners, and no statistics in any given location."[131] Interviewers could talk only to defectors and prisoners whom the local Vietnamese authorities allowed them to see. It was not possible to obtain a statistical sample, Goure said, because he had "no idea what the total sample was or what the people we talked to represented" in the totality.[132] But he pointed out that the interviewers traveled all over the country to get a balance, and that on rare occasions they managed to talk to "a number of people from the same units . . . or from the same village or the same town—especially those recruited in the South."[133] According to Goure, Alex George attempted to explain to him "about statistical samples and how to do statistical samples because that's what they had done in Korea"—where the Americans controlled the POW camps—and he had "a hard time explaining to him it couldn't be done." He "didn't have anything against statistical samples," Goure said, but he "couldn't get statistical samples" in the conditions in Vietnam.[134]

---

[129]Todd, "Ce qui se passe dans le monde," 1966.

[130]Author interview with Gus Shubert, 2004.

[131]Author interview with Leon Goure, 2003.

[132]Author interview with Leon Goure, 2003.

[133]Author interview with Leon Goure, 2003.

[134]Author interview with Leon Goure, 2003.

Shubert was now put in the position of being in charge of a project over which he felt he had little control. The Viet Cong Motivation and Morale Project remained within the domain of the Social Science Department, in which Goure retained the support of Joe Goldsen and Hans Speier—and stayed under Goure's leadership. The conflict Shubert had with Social Science over Goure boiled over in a full Management Committee, presided over by Frank Collbohm, during which the argument between Goldsen and Shubert became so heated that the two men almost came to blows. Shubert and Goldsen were sitting directly across from each other, separated by a table that was wide enough so that they could not make physical contact. Collbohm, who preferred to deal with people privately rather than publicly, did not intervene or utter a word, but got "whiter and whiter" and "his lips got tighter and tighter and tighter,"[135] which was his way of manifesting rage.

Shubert had brought some people who knew him well and who were also familiar with the project, such as Andy Marshall; Burt Klein, the head of Economics; and a couple of other staff members to back him up just in case it became necessary. However, they all kept quiet except for Burt Klein, who spoke up in support—but not forcefully. The others, aware of Collbohm's stand on the issue, remained silent in his presence, although they had been complaining about how absurd the study was and how it had to be ended. Or they demurred when Shubert turned to them, saying, "Oh, don't ask me. I don't know anything."[136] So, all Shubert's support evaporated and he found himself "out on the end of a very long limb."[137] On the other side, Joe Goldsen and Hans Speier defended Goure vehemently. According to Shubert, the meeting came to a close with Hans Speier saying, "three cheers for Leon Goure."[138] To this, Shubert replied that the project was incompetent and devoid of sound methodology, and that this was serious business because it was "getting people killed."[139] According to Shubert, "there was a lot of general shouting," but the argument remained unsettled.[140]

Shubert surmised that Hans Speier's strong defense of Goure stemmed from the fact that Goure was a member of his department and had Collbohm's support. According to Shubert, Speier felt that part of his job was to please Collbohm. Shubert thought that Speier was "meticulous in applying . . . standards of scholarship to himself and to any co-workers that might be working immediately with him" but "got very myopic when he got into areas that he didn't know a lot about, and certainly Southeast Asia was

---

[135] Collins, interview with Gus Shubert, session of May 20, 1992, p. 10.

[136] Collins, interview with Gus Shubert, session of May 20, 1992, pp. 13–14.

[137] Collins, interview with Gus Shubert, session of May 20, 1992, p. 14.

[138] Author interview with Gus Shubert, 2004.

[139] Author interview with Gus Shubert, 2004.

[140] Collins, interview with Gus Shubert, session of May 20, 1992, p. 10.

one of them."[141] Shubert doubted that Speier even read the reports that were being produced, because the project was not as important to him as it was to Goure and Shubert himself. As for Collbohm's failure to back him up, Shubert said that the RAND president was in "the paradoxical position" of giving full support to Goure as well as to him, and this became untenable, and "Something had to give."[142] However, Shubert was careful not to cast aspersions on Goure's motives, because he thought that "it is at least possible, and maybe even probable, that Leon Goure thought he was doing the right professional thing in running that project the way he was running it."[143]

According to Ralph Strauch, then a member of the Mathematics Department, Collbohm at this Management Committee Meeting was supposed to have turned to Ed Quade, who was the head of the Mathematics Department, and said, "You've got all the mathematicians, you figure out who's right" in this debate over methodology.[144] After the meeting, Quade then came to Strauch and asked him to look into the matter. Strauch would later say that, at the time, there were two major camps with regard to the use of the interview data. One was represented by Leon Goure, who performed very subjective analysis, and would read the interviews, make notes, and keep track of "whatever categories he kept track of."[145] According to Strauch, Goure tended to believe in the effectiveness of the U.S. war effort in Vietnam and claimed that the Viet Cong's morale had sunk significantly. On the other side was a group in the Economics Department who tended to derive a much less optimistic view from the data than Goure. In an effort to inject statistical rigor into the interview data, the Economics Department had assigned Frank Denton—author of several quantitative studies on Vietnam[146]—to oversee a group of UCLA graduate students serving as summer interns at RAND to read the interviews, code them, and create a mathematical database, and then run statistical analyses from the data. The actual analysis of the data would be performed by the RAND staff.

Strauch said that "both groups were somewhat derisive of the other group's analysis."[147] For his assessment, Strauch talked to some of the researchers to find out how the interviews were conducted in Vietnam, including Joe Carrier, who happened

---

[141] Collins, interview with Gus Shubert, session of May 20, 1992, p. 12.

[142] Collins, interview with Gus Shubert, session of May 20, 1992, p. 12.

[143] Collins, interview with Gus Shubert, session of May 20, 1992, p. 40.

[144] Author interview with Ralph Strauch, 2004.

[145] Author interview with Ralph Strauch, 2004.

[146] See, for example, "Time Variations in Viet Cong Morale: or 'a VC Fever Chart'" (Santa Monica, Calif.: RAND Corporation, D-14498, February 9, 1966) and "Data on Viet Cong Attacks on RVN Military Units and Facilities" (Santa Monica, Calif.: RAND Corporation, D-1342, February 18, 1965).

[147] Author interview with Ralph Strauch, 2004. According to Alfred Goldberg, the "validity of the data base—the qualitative and quantitative value of the interviews . . . and the methodology by which findings and conclusions were derived from the data" were at the heart of the controversy. In his review of the RAND project,

to be back in Santa Monica. When he completed his research, Strauch concluded that he neither understood nor was competent to comment on what Goure did to reach his conclusions. But he thought that by attempting to code the data and treat the data as if they came from "some kind of sound scientific study"—that is to say, from some well-designed questionnaires "required by well-designed statistical sampling methods"—the economists were using invalid assumptions and applying "the statistical test," which was inappropriate to the interviews.[148]

When he looked at the interview responses themselves and the way they were collected, he concluded that it was very difficult to see how the data could be subjected to this quantitative methodology. In his paper, Strauch pointed out that, despite the fact that the data were not suitable for statistical manipulation, they were still useful for drawing meaningful conclusions. He added that, even if an attempt was made to subject the data to statistical manipulation, any conclusions drawn would still be "based largely on the subjective judgments of the analyst."[149] In other words, subjective interpretation would come into play either way.

When interviewed later about this controversy, Strauch cited, as an illustration, the economists' attempt to treat the responses as if the individual prisoners or defectors had selected answers from a list of multiple choices when, in fact, they were responding to open-ended questions. These multiple choices had been created after the interviews had been conducted. The students then read the interviews and decided which choices the respondents would have likely selected. Strauch remembered that, in some cases, inferences were even drawn based on some of the semantic structures of the interviews—on whether a prisoner or a defector had used *I* or *we*—and that the coders assumed that the words were the very ones that the prisoners and defectors themselves had used. But such inferences were not solid, because the interviews had been translated from Vietnamese into English and it was difficult to know what exactly the original Vietnamese words were. For interviews conducted during the Zasloff-Donnell phase, some had gone through not one but two translations—from Vietnamese to French, and then from French to English—making these inferences even more tenuous. So Strauch concluded that it would be difficult to "assign all the kinds of validity" that the economists were trying to do, and that it would be invalid to treat the responses as "statistically significant."[150]

Goldberg stated that both sides of the debate agreed that "the work was preliminary and tentative," but the critics also "regarded it as lacking in iterative quality." Goldberg, "RAND and Vietnam," 1969, p. 15.

[148] Author interview with Ralph Strauch, 2004.

[149] Ralph Strauch, "Some Views on Interviews," Santa Monica, Calif.: RAND Corporation, D-15172-AGILE/ISA, October 24, 1966, p. 2.

[150] Author interview with Ralph Strauch, 2004. In his "User's Guide to the RAND Interviews in Vietnam," 1970, Phil Davison cautioned that, since the respondents did not represent a random sample, it would be "risky to use statistical methods in analyzing the interview reports." He quoted a RAND analyst who had written in an internal memorandum in October 1966, "It does not appear feasible to draw any useful objective conclusions from

Strauch thought that the paper he wrote following his research into the topic would elicit a big reaction. He was disappointed when he ran into the staff member who was in charge of quantifying the interview data in the hall a few days after the man had received it. The man said, "Great piece of work, Ralph, you raised a lot of questions. Gee, if we can ever get enough time, we ought to think about them; but right now we've got a study to do."[151] So, as far as he could tell, what he did had very little effect. "Both sides went on doing what they did," he said, and the general attitude was, "Oh, well, that's that, we go on with what we're doing."[152]

Tony Russo was one of the critics of the lack of methodology and the absence of a research design in Goure's project for issues such as the extent of flexibility that should be allowed in the questionnaire and how the changes in the responses by defectors, POWs, and refugees collected over the years by RAND should be recorded. To Russo, Frank Denton "provided some science," by coding the interviews and by providing a guide with "a whole list of items, and the percentages of different responses to the questions—'yes,' 'no,' 'don't know'—stuff like that in there."[153] The guide Russo alluded to was a report called *Two Analytical Aids for Use with the Rand Interviews*, published in May 1967.[154] The two aids were described as a code system for converting the verbal answers in the interviews into numerical responses for statistical analysis of trends and relationships, and an index system listing the 15 major categories, or topics, and the 97 subcategories into which the interviews were divided. Each question and answer in each interview was assigned to one or more of the subcategories. The code conventions fell mostly into the "Yes-No or High-Medium-Low variety."[155] Open-ended responses that were deemed codable, because they were unambiguous, were converted into closed answers. For example, an open question of "What did you like in the VC?" was turned into "Did subject indicate a like of: VC aims, VC cadres" and the open-ended response was converted into "Yes" or "No" and assigned a numeral indicator of (1) or (0).[156] To help retrieve relevant original material from the interviews, the index also contained all responses to a given topic, arranged by interview and question.

Over 1,000 interviews were conducted by RAND by January 1967, "varying in length from 2 to 150 single-spaced typewritten pages," with an average length of

---

the available data through the use of statistical inference." In talking to RAND staff members who had used the data, Davison concluded that other analytic methods could be successfully employed instead to mine the rich and diverse data.

[151] Author interview with Ralph Strauch, 2004.

[152] Author interview with Ralph Strauch, 2004.

[153] Author interview with Tony Russo, 2003 and 2004.

[154] Frank Denton, *Two Analytical Aids for Use with the Rand Interviews*, Santa Monica, Calif.: RAND Corporation, RM-5338-ISA/ARPA, May 1967.

[155] Denton, *Two Analytical Aids for Use with the Rand Interviews*, 1967, p. 12.

[156] Denton, *Two Analytical Aids for Use with the Rand Interviews*, 1967, p. 10.

approximately 35 pages. The database covered "more than 35,000 pages covering a multitude of aspects of the war in Vietnam."[157] Of these 1,000 interviews, Denton's report discussed the coding of 700 interviews that had been conducted by Zasloff and his team, by Goure and his team, and by David Elliott and his team in Dinh Tuong Province (see Chapter Six on RAND's project in Dinh Tuong Province). The coding and indexing were completed in fall 1966. It was a massive undertaking.

In his paper, Frank Denton cautioned that limits had to be placed on using these coded materials in any way. To keep the process of coding the interviews manageable, "the number of possible responses must be reasonably small";[158] consequently, "only certain types of data are coded."[159] Therefore, "the coding is partial."[160] In addition, "the categories of possible responses to an open-ended question are not exhaustive,"[161] and a "general category of 'uncodable' is included for all code items. . . . If the written interview material is ambiguous or provides no information on a given code item, it is marked in the uncodable category. . . . Thus, the sample of responses on a given topic is usually much less than the total sample size."[162] On the issue of the reliability of the coding, Denton stated, "To achieve reliability, the coders must understand explicitly what types of statements go into each code category. Yet the nature of verbal responses to very general questions is such that strict comparability from subject to subject is not always possible."[163] So, "The material coded from these interviews must therefore be used cautiously. It is of great importance that the user know the relationship between the coded category and the original material. The short category titles, of necessity, do not always carry a complete description of what this relationship is."[164]

Applying a quantitative approach to the interview data, Denton refuted Goure's findings that peasants in villages that were bombed or shelled tended to blame the Viet Cong for provoking the attacks. Rather than relying on the direct approach and

---

[157] Denton, *Two Analytical Aids for Use with the Rand Interviews*, 1967, p. 10.

[158] Denton, *Two Analytical Aids for Use with the Rand Interviews*, 1967, p. 9.

[159] Denton, *Two Analytical Aids for Use with the Rand Interviews*, 1967, p. 10.

[160] Denton, *Two Analytical Aids for Use with the Rand Interviews*, 1967, p. 10.

[161] Denton, *Two Analytical Aids for Use with the Rand Interviews*, 1967, p. 10.

[162] Denton, *Two Analytical Aids for Use with the Rand Interviews*, 1967, p. 11.

[163] Denton, *Two Analytical Aids for Use with the Rand Interviews*, 1967, p. 9.

[164] Denton, *Two Analytical Aids for Use with the Rand Interviews*, 1967, p. 9. In "VIPS: Vietnam Interview Processing System," (D-17870-ISA/ARPA, October 2, 1968), R. A. Duis, T. K. Sawtelle, and M. Weiner wrote that "The adequacy of the indexing process—the appropriate assignment of particular questions and answers to specific subcategories—was difficult to assess." Since the indexing was so massive, they could conduct only a spot check to gauge its adequacy. They found "some ambiguity and incompleteness," but concluded that the index was still "a useful retrieval tool." Frank Denton himself subsequently completed a few studies based on the computerized data, including RM-4966-ISA/ARPA, *Some Relationships Between the Attitude of the Viet Cong Soldiers and Their Exposure to U.S.-RVN Military Operations*, based on the results of a computer analysis of 167 interviews. For more details on Denton's work, see Chapter Five.

Gus Shubert

asking "directly for causal relationships," Denton employed an indirect approach to measure villager attitude.[165] He concluded that the data "consistently indicate significant (as much as 25 percent of the population in some cases) alienation resulting from attacks."[166] While Goure's direct approach—using data "taken without regard to control"—indicated "some greater 'blame' attachment to VC in *attacked villages*," and resulting loss of popularity for the insurgents, Denton found that the indirect evidence "strongly indicates alienation" against "*the regime in power*" as the result of attacks.[167] This alienation occurred in areas under VC control, as well as in those that were not. And, while Goure noted that peasants seemed to accept damage and to feel that U.S./ GVN attacks were justified as acts of war, Denton thought that it would be reasonable to suppose that the peasants' concern for survival would cause them to resent exposure to possible death.

While the date over Goure's work raged on, Shubert tried to institute some control and went to great lengths to apply the RAND review system to Goure's work. Unable to remove Goure, Shubert exerted pressure to have Goure's presentations reviewed before they were given in Washington. According to Shubert, Goure went along and participated in the review, but when he made his briefings, he would deviate from what had been agreed to at RAND. When Shubert heard through feedback from the Pentagon and other places in Washington that Goure was doing this, he came up with "the very clever device of never letting him go anywhere without a senior RAND colleague

---

[165] Frank Denton, "Alienation of the Peasant in South Vietnam," Santa Monica, Calif.: RAND Corporation, May 4, 1966, p. 2 (not available to the general public).

[166] Denton, "Alienation of the Peasant in South Vietnam," 1966, p. 8.

[167] Denton, "Alienation of the Peasant in South Vietnam," 1966, p. 8. Emphasis in original.

with him."[168] He asked George Tanham to accompany Goure on his rounds of brief-ings, hoping that Tanham's presence would keep Goure from going "off the rails."[169] Shubert said that trying to contain Goure in this manner made him feel like a spy, but there was no other alternative. He would later say that, "we tried everything that we could think of to get this into some reasonable mold"[170]—short of firing Goure.

In retrospect, his failure still rankled because, in his opinion, what Goure was doing "was not fun and games" and because his study "was one of the few RAND projects that really affected people's lives, and it deserved a lot more care than it got."[171] Shubert remembered that "there were people in government like Rowen and his cote-rie who agreed with that, but there was nothing they could do about it either."[172] For him, it was a "battle" that went on until 1967.[173] Looking back, Shubert said, "I still shake with anger and frustration at the thought of my inability to control him" because of "the circumstances."[174] In his view, dealing with the Goure problem was "the only rotten experience he had at RAND" and he said that he met his "own comeuppance" at the hands of Goure.[175] Besides trying to rein in Goure in his briefings, Shubert also had Goure submit his reports for review. Many corrections were forced on Goure in this process, but, in Shubert's view, the process failed to sufficiently dampen the opti-mistic tone that was "consistent with the notion that everything was going well."[176]

Steve Hosmer would later confirm that such efforts to manage Goure were made—subjecting his reports to peer review and his briefings to dry runs. However, he did not know or think that the pressure had come from Gus Shubert and believed that they had been undertaken at the initiative of the Social Science Department itself, and not in response to pressure from ARPA or complaints from other clients.[177] According to him, Social Science also decided to caveat the quarterly reports that McNamara asked from Goure and to call attention to the limited sample and what such a sample could really reveal. Goure resisted such caveating as "undue interference," since McNamara "was asking for his impressions."[178]

---

[168] Collins, interview with Gus Shubert, session of May 28, 1992, p. 41.

[169] Collins, interview with Gus Shubert, session of May 28, 1992, p. 41.

[170] Collins, interview with Gus Shubert, op. cit., session of May 28, 1992, p. 41.

[171] Author interview with Gus Shubert, 2004

[172] Author interview with Gus Shubert, 2004.

[173] Collins, interview with Gus Shubert, session of May 20, 1992, p. 33.

[174] Author interview with Gus Shubert, 2004.

[175] Author interview with Gus Shubert, 2004.

[176] Collins, interview with Gus Shubert, session of May 28, 1992, p. 41.

[177] Author interview with Steve Hosmer, May 2004.

[178] Author interview with Steve Hosmer, May 2004.

According to Hosmer, the corrective measures instituted by the Social Science Department were not surprising, since RAND had a tradition of requiring peer reviews and dry runs of briefings—not just once, but sometimes several times. These RAND procedures were intended to move away "from one person out in Saigon interpreting the data, doing the briefings out there, and representing what the material said" and to broaden the analysis. Goure was consulted, and the Social Science Department held many discussions with him. "The argument was made," Hosmer said, and these changes were imposed on not just Goure. Hosmer admitted that "there was a lot of animosity" toward Goure and that some people from that period who are still at RAND remain upset with Goure. However, he himself believed that Goure did "what he felt was responsible in his own mind."[179]

The Social Science Department instituted other corrective measures, including strengthening the analysis by moving it from Saigon to Santa Monica and limiting the field operation to data collection. At the same time, the interview questionnaire was enlarged and amended to provide data for other types of studies, and an effort was made to inject a more rigorous methodology into the project by expanding the coverage of enemy units in the interrogations and by sharpening the focus of the interviews, which, up to then, had been based on a very broad set of questions that were "all over the waterfront."[180]

It was acknowledged that wider coverage was difficult to achieve in the conditions prevailing in Vietnam, but the hope was that wider access and a larger sample would make it easier to generalize about enemy morale. With a broader database and the involvement of other analysts—such as Konrad Kellen and Frank Denton—RAND tried to strike a balance and provide "a broader base from which to draw inferences about and distinguish trends concerning the Viet Cong."[181] Goure ceased to be the sole voice for RAND as far as the Viet Cong were concerned.

The more cautious tone and the numerous caveats of a RAND report that appeared in January 1967 indicate that the measures were enforced—at least when it came to written documents that were distributed outside RAND. In an analysis bearing the title "Some Impressions Derived from Recent Interviews,"[182] Goure's tone was more cautious than in his earlier reports. Goure emphasized the impressionistic nature of the conclusions and pointed out that the small number of defectors and prisoners interviewed could not be viewed as representative of the Viet Cong and NVA still serving in enemy ranks. The report was limited in the sense that it did not attempt to evaluate

[179] Author interview with Steve Hosmer, May 2004.

[180] Author interview with Steve Hosmer, May 2004.

[181] Goldberg, "RAND and Vietnam," 1969, p. 15.

[182] Leon Goure, *Quarterly Report on Viet Cong Motivation and Morale Project, October–December 1966*, Santa Monica, Calif.: RAND Corporation, January 30, 1967; copy from Lyndon Johnson Archives, Austin, Tex. The document did not bear a report number.

the progress of the war and indicated only some possible vulnerabilities within certain parts of the enemy's organization.

In a departure from past practice and to present a more balanced picture, the findings of vulnerabilities were accompanied by findings on enemy strengths. While confirming earlier conclusions regarding the effects of military operations on enemy morale and effectiveness, Goure's January 1967 report stated that, in spite of growing strains, most of the Viet Cong and NVA regular troops had maintained strong discipline and cohesion and continued to perform their military duties. The power and effectiveness of B-52s was not emphasized and, although the report stated that hamlet, village, and district cadres and soldiers would likely defect if their families moved to GVN areas, either forcibly or voluntarily, it went on to say that prolonged allied operations that could induce these population movements were rare, and that the Viet Cong could reestablish their control quickly if the allied operations caused only temporary setbacks and the people chose to remain in their villages rather than moving to GVN areas. At the village level, the Viet Cong had a well-organized and highly flexible structure and population-control system, which allowed them to "adjust to new situations and recover from temporary setbacks." Using "well-tested techniques of persuasion and coercion," the enemy seemed "to retain a considerable capacity to extract needed support from the villagers remaining in an area."

The report repeated earlier findings that allied operations had caused difficulties for the Viet Cong in securing food supplies and porters, reduced productivity and the tax base, but cautioned that there was "no evidence in the interviews that the Viet Cong's overall capability to secure needed provisions from the countryside has been seriously impaired or that, except for temporary dislocations, they have been unable to provide their men with food supplies." In conclusion, the report repeated the caveat that

> It is important to emphasize once again that this report is based on a small sample of interviews and focuses on selected developments and attitudes within the enemy structure. Limitations of the data and the many uncertainties attached to it make it impossible to determine with any certainty the extent to which these findings generally apply to major elements of the Viet Cong and NVA.[183]

Caveats aside, Walt Rostow, for his part, found the optimistic interpretation more useful for President Johnson's speech to Congress. In early 1967, he instructed Bill Jorden in the State Department's Policy Planning Council to prepare a draft for Johnson's "A Special Message from the President to Congress on the Situation in Vietnam," which Rostow reviewed. In the draft, Jorden wrote, "During the past year, many prisoners and defectors have told of growing hardships resulting from our unrelenting military pressure. North Vietnamese prisoners, in particular, say they were led to believe

---

[183] Goure, *Quarterly Report on Viet Cong Motivation and Morale Project, October–December 1966,* 1967.

that victory would be theirs and would come quickly. They now know better, and many have stopped believing that they can win at all. As this hope diminishes further, and as hardships multiply, we may expect at some stage to see a real weakening of their effort."[184]

In Saigon, as Goure came under pressure, tension grew between him and Doug Scott, Tony Russo, and Russ Betts. According to Ardith Betts, Goure was convinced that anyone on his staff who did not "believe his every word and worship him" were "out to subvert his position" and were deliberately "making life miserable for him," and threatened to do something about these "young Turks."[185] The team leaders, on the other hand, thought that Goure was ignoring "rather than attempting to solve" problems in the office.

The situation came to a head. Steve Hosmer came to Saigon in August 1966 and spent a week talking to the staff. According to Ardith Betts, Hosmer was "a smooth talker," and everyone "bared their soul" to him. He was "very nice . . . moderate and gentle and understanding," seemed to be on "everyone's side" and "promised to solve problems," such as providing more support from Santa Monica, improving communication about what was happening, answering letters promptly, giving immediate attention to requests, and raising salaries.[186] But after Hosmer returned to Santa Monica, nothing was heard from him. For his part, Hosmer said that he got all kinds of reports, was aware of the professional and personal conflicts in Saigon, and was trying to deal with them "in the sense of getting a solid product for the clients."[187]

Despite the tension, the team leaders found a way to perform studies that allowed them to get their points across separately from Leon Goure. According to Russ Betts, RAND had a policy of encouraging team leaders to focus on issues that interested them and that they wished to pursue. Jim Carlson decided to study infiltration and had the interviewers probe conditions along the route, the effect of bombing, and the presence of tracking or warning devices employed by the United States to slow the flow from the North. The information unearthed through the interviews convinced him that the measures that were deployed had little consequence and hardly stopped anyone from coming South. He recalled giving a briefing to an Air Force general at Tan Son Nhut who was unimpressed with his finding that the bombing was ineffective in stopping infiltration and that diseases killed more infiltrators than air attacks.

Doug Scott focused on refugees and, according to Ardith Betts, wrote a good piece about the refugee problem in late 1965. This study grew out of the interviews with civilians who had fled the combat zones into GVN areas, using a newly written questionnaire that Scott had interviewers apply to as representative a sample as

---

[184] William Jorden, draft of Johnson's speech, Lyndon B. Johnson Archives, Box 192, Austin, Tex.

[185] Ardith Betts, letter to a friend in Santa Monica, August 26, 1966.

[186] Ardith Betts, letter to a friend in Santa Monica, January 19, 1967.

[187] Author interview with Steve Hosmer, May 2004.

he could find among the people in refugee villages. According to Ardith Betts, the report was approved by Leon Goure and forwarded to Santa Monica in March 1966. It went through reviews and was returned to Scott in June with suggested changes. Scott incorporated the suggestions and sent the paper back to RAND in July. According to Ardith Betts, Steve Hosmer did not like it "because it was critical of the current refugee program," and it went nowhere. Finally, the last week of December, Hosmer wrote to Doug Scott saying that it was an "excellent paper" but it had become "so thoroughly dated it of course couldn't be an RM"—a full-fledged RAND report.[188]

Doug Scott's report might have been killed in review because of the sensitivity of the issue of refugees. General Westmoreland himself was opposed to a refugee study to determine the true underlying causes driving people into refugee camps—perhaps because it might expose the effect of heavy weapons on civilians. In a report about his trip to Laos and Vietnam in May and June 1967, Gus Shubert wrote that, "there is alleged to be an 'Eyes Only' communication from Westmoreland to Deitchman dating from something like December of last year saying that there is to be no assault on this [refugee] problem at all."[189]

Killing reports with review was a problem that Russ Betts also ran into with his own paper on atrocities committed by South Korean troops. The South Korean forces had come in as part of an effort by the Johnson Administration to create the impression that the fight against communism in South Vietnam was being undertaken by the Free World, rather than by the United States alone. Among the countries that were asked to participate, Australia was the most willing ally and sent about 1,000 troops, mostly stationed in ARVN's III Corps, encompassing the region surrounding Saigon. The Philippines was also asked to contribute a few thousand troops, but, at the time, the newly elected president was amenable to sending only military construction engineers. Combat units were also requested from Germany, but the German chancellor only dispatched a hospital ship. Of the allies, South Korea was asked to contribute the largest contingent of soldiers, a total of about 17,000 men. At General Westmoreland's request, the first South Korean brigade was to land in April 1966, with the rest of the division to arrive in July.

In a telephone conversation on January 17, 1966, with President Johnson—who fretted about allies' contribution to the war—Defense Secretary McNamara reassured him that it was certain that the Koreans would come in and that it was "just [a] matter of price." He told LBJ that, in return for their division, the South Korean government had requested "about $600–$700 million worth of cumshaw."[190] He said that both

---

[188] Ardith Betts, letter to a friend in Santa Monica, January 19, 1967.

[189] Gustave H. Shubert, "Southeast Asia Trip Report," Santa Monica, Calif.: RAND Corporation, August 16, 1967, p. 44 (not available to the general public).

[190] "Telephone Conversation Between President Johnson and Secretary of Defense McNamara," State Department, Foreign Relations of the United States, 1964–1968, Volume IV, Vietnam: 14–29, Document 26, Washing-

the State Department and the Defense Department had refused and had asked the American ambassador in Seoul to make a counter-offer of "something on the order of $70 million worth of extra equipment and payments." After they arrived, the South Koreans were deployed in the central provinces of Tuy Hoa and Binh Dinh, hotbeds of Viet Cong support and activities. According to Russ Betts, the South Koreans' method of operation was to kill villagers in large numbers the first time they came through. When interviewed about these episodes, Betts recalled that there were two or three instances of massacres when South Korean troops lined up "one hundred people out of a village of four hundred," shot them, and let them drop into a trench. The rest of the villagers were so cowed that whenever the South Koreans passed through again, they would obey meekly and would "bow and scrape."[191]

By their ruthless methods, the South Koreans were effective in controlling the people, but to Russ Betts this was not the way to win hearts and minds. Betts would later recall that the information about the South Koreans' abuses surfaced in interviews conducted, not with prisoners and defectors, but with civilians who had fled to refugee villages, when they were asked what they thought of the South Korean forces operating in their areas. These interviews revealed "some pretty significant atrocities that nobody had been reporting."[192] The interviews also probed villagers' reactions to the Australians, but the information in this case was neutral. Russ Betts did not know what happened to the report he wrote on the South Korean atrocities, which—in his recollection—bore a title like "American Partners: Participation in the War." A search of RAND's library catalogue turned up no such paper by him.

Tony Russo claimed that "material on torture of prisoners or brutal treatment of civilians" by Koreans or GVN troops "was removed when the interviews were being typed up in Saigon."[193] According to Russo, this practice had been set by Goure, and although he and some of the staff bitterly disagreed with Goure, "most complied" with his "censorship policies."[194] However, in his "User's Guide to the RAND Interviews

---

ton, D.C., January 17, 1966. *Cumshaw* derives from the Chinese (Amoy dialect) *kamsia*, which means "grateful thanks" and, in Pidgin English, is used to refer to a gratuity.

[191] Author interview with Russ Betts, 2004.

[192] The atrocities became a public controversy in South Korea around the year 2001, when a South Korean student made it the topic of her doctoral dissertation. The Koreans' tactics might have contributed to the high rate of VC defection in their two provinces. In *A Profile of Viet Cong Returnees: July 1965 to June 1967*, RM-5577-ISA/ARPA, published in October 1968, Joe Carrier reported that the two provinces in which the Koreans operated accounted for a "disproportionately large share" of defectors during this period, and that the rate of defection markedly increased with their arrival. Carrier pointed out that prior to operating in an area, the Koreans would send refugees back to the villages to get their relatives to defect. Defectors and their relatives were given money and rice by the Koreans as rewards. It is not clear whether it was the reward or the fear of reprisals that induced defection.

[193] Russo, "Looking Backward," 1972, p. 57.

[194] Russo, "Looking Backward," 1972, p. 58.

in Vietnam," Phil Davison wrote that little was cut in the final interview transcripts, and that "nearly always" only parts that were "incomprehensible" were removed.[195] He did note, however, that one of the team leaders "later reported that he occasionally cut material having to do with mistreatment of prisoners, in order not to jeopardize access to certain police or military installations, but this does not seem to have been a general practice."[196]

The behavior of the South Korean troops came to public light when James Otis of *Ramparts* wrote an article in September 1972, titled "Seoul's Hired Guns," after the Alternative Feature Service (AFS) of Berkeley disclosed "a secret study by the RAND Corporation" that mentioned that RAND interviews had revealed the abominable conduct of Korean troops in the provinces of Tuy Hoa and Binh Dinh in the central region of South Vietnam.[197] According to Russo, the report to which Otis referred was something that had been put together quickly by Leon Goure in December 1966 "in response to a request from General Westmoreland."[198] But Russo wrote that "most if not all the quotations had been censored out of the RAND interviews."[199] Later, when the story resurfaced, a *Los Angeles Times* reporter heard that RAND had produced reports on the "allegations of brutality and atrocities committed by South Korean troops. . . ." When he inquired at RAND, he was told by a "spokesman . . . that Rand was not commissioned to do substantive investigation on the Korean issue as such but collected some data on Korean activity in the course of other investigations."[200]

Joe Carrier, who had a good relationship with Goure, gave him credit for allowing the junior staff to work on issues that interested them. According to Carrier, Goure told him, "Look, I know that you're not trained as a social science researcher, you're an

---

[195] Davison, "User's Guide," 1970, p. 57.

[196] Davison, "User's Guide," 1970, p. 57.

[197] James Otis, "Seoul's Hired Guns," *Ramparts*, September 1972.

[198] Russo, "Looking Back," 1972, p. 58. Korean brutality apparently continued unchecked. In a December 10, 1969, memo to Rear Admiral William E. Lemos, USN, Francis ("Bing") West, a former Marine officer then working as a RAND consultant, mentioned running into refugees during a large ARVN/Korean search-and-destroy operation in Quang Tin Province who told him and Charlie Benoit, another RAND consultant fluent in Vietnamese, of Korean brutality and killings. In his memo on RAND official stationery, West wrote that the ARVN battalion commander engaged in the operation told him that "the Koreans were the cruelest soldiers he had seen in 20 years of warfare." West told Lemos that the stories he picked up might constitute "hearsay evidence," but that "the theme of blood and slaughter was too pervasive, too specific, too immediate, for me to dismiss the terror and grief of those refugees as products of overwrought imaginations." West suggested that if the Koreans were to stay in Vietnam, "an effort" should "quietly be made to determine whether their presence is consonant with U.S. and, hopefully, GVN policy," and their areas of operation—which had been closed to unescorted foreign observers—be opened to such observers. It is not clear whether these recommendations were acted upon. Francis J. West, "Memo to Rear Admiral William E. Lemos, USN, Director, Policy Plans and NSC Affairs," December 10, 1969. Copy obtained from the National Archives.

[199] Russo, "Looking Back," 1972, p. 58.

[200] Murrey Marder, "Terrorism of Viet Civilians Laid to S. Korean Troops," *Los Angeles Times*, January 11, 1970.

economist. I would like you to get involved in some aspect of the project that would interest you. So, you make the selection of what it is that you'd want to work on."[201] Carrier decided to study the *Chieu Hoi* program, and eventually produced two reports, one co-authored with Chuck Thomson and one under his own name. He started collecting the data and took a team of interviewers with him to various *Chieu Hoi* centers to interview Viet Cong and NVA defectors exclusively. In addition, in July 1965 a MACV intelligence officer devised a biographical card that defectors had to complete, to aid in the selection of defectors for interrogation, and Carrier helped him improve it. For his study, Carrier used copies of the cards that had been sent to J-2 MACV by the province American intelligence advisor. The biographical cards provided useful quantitative data to supplement the RAND interviews.

The report Carrier produced with Chuck Thomson used the data obtained from the biographical cards on Viet Cong who had defected between June 1965 and January 1966, as well as from 302 RAND interviews.[202] Carrier and Thomson found that ideological reasons hardly featured in defection. Most of the defectors left the Viet Cong for personal reasons, such as the physical hardships they had to endure in the insurgency, their anxiousness to attend to the economic needs of their families, their desire to evade criticism or punishment, their fear of death as the war grew more ferocious, and their longing to return home. A surprising finding was that few of the respondents mentioned reverses and losses as reasons for defecting, and a large majority saw the *Chieu Hoi* Program as a way for them to return home to their families and to avoid further combat. According to the two authors, a significant number of the defectors expressed disillusionment with the Viet Cong but had not yet come to the view that the GVN possessed political righteousness. The biographical cards that Joe Carrier obtained accounted for only a portion of all defectors, and it was not clear how representative the sample was for the rest of the defectors. One interesting finding derived from the biographical information was that the defectors included a larger number of Viet Cong with two or more years of service and Viet Cong 30 years of age or older—an indication that more-experienced people were defecting. This finding may be attributed to the protracted nature of the war, which increased the number of insurgents with more years of service. On the other hand, it raised the question of why, since the Viet Cong had instituted a systemwide conscription to expand their forces in 1965, there were not a larger number of recent draftees among the defectors. One explanation could be that the Viet Cong may have been successful in retaining draftees or that draftees preferred to desert home rather than defect.

Among the deterrents to defection, the factors most frequently mentioned were fear of mistreatment, difficulty of slipping away from one's unit, fear of reprisals against

---

[201] Author interview with Joe Carrier, 2003.

[202] J. M. Carrier and Chuck Thomson, *Viet Cong Motivation and Morale: The Special Case of* Chieu Hoi, Santa Monica, Calif.: RAND Corporation, RM-4830-ISA/ARPA, 1966.

oneself if the defector failed in his attempt or against his family and friends if he managed to defect; inability to "go home" to a home located in a zone controlled by the Viet Cong; tight surveillance by the VC; and not knowing the terrain. Many potential defectors hesitated to come out, and first sought reassurance from relatives, friends, or people who had already defected, in particular cadres whom they felt they could trust. Since its inception in 1963, the program had become more widely known, and 74 percent of the defectors interviewed by RAND knew of the program before defecting, or, in the parlance of the South Vietnamese government and the American authorities in Vietnam at the time, "rallying" (to the cause of the GVN). However, a sizable portion of the enemy personnel did not know about it, and 26 percent of the defectors in the RAND sample came out, hoping blindly that they would receive decent treatment, or simply to escape dangers and hardships they found intolerable.

The authors found that, among the methods used to reach potential defectors—such as leaflets and radio broadcasts—word of mouth from family, friends, or fellow soldiers often was viewed by enemy personnel as the most credible source. Carrier and Thomson suggested that the GVN tailor the *Chieu Hoi* message to different groups within enemy ranks. For example, in trying to reach North Vietnamese troops, the GVN should emphasize that surrender could be a way of escaping from having to fight a protracted war. The authors recommended that the GVN facilitate defection by providing specific information on the steps to follow in rallying, by reducing the potential defectors' fears of risks to themselves and their families, and by reassuring enemy personnel about the future if they rallied to the GVN side. The report was sent to the National Security Council, and Dick Moorsteen, a former RAND staff member then working in the White House, wrote a note to Carrier telling him that his report had attracted great interest.

Another American official who was interested in the issue of defection was Sam Adams, a CIA analyst who had gone to Saigon in 1966 to research the Viet Cong order of battle. According to Richard Moose, the enemy order of battle "was one of the big running issues" in 1966 and 1967 as the White House staff tried to figure out the size of enemy forces and their composition, and the strength of the Viet Cong relative to that of the NVA, to determine whether the enemy ranks were being reduced by the war of attrition.[203] At the CIA, Adams, as part of a group working on an overall assessment of the war that McNamara had requested, wanted to figure out the true strength of the Viet Cong. A statistic on enemy defection had puzzled him. The Viet Cong were losing men to defection at an astounding rate of 10,000 per year. In addition, they were also sustaining heavy casualties. MACV had reported that the enemy order of battle stood at 285,000 men. If this order of battle was correct, Adams wondered, how could the Viet Cong have managed to continue fighting with such ferocity despite such losses? In Saigon, he was trying to research enemy defection when George Allen, the CIA sta-

---

[203]Author interview with Richard Moose, 2003.

tion chief, told him that, bad as defection was for the Viet Cong, desertion was an even bigger problem for the enemy, and told him to go see Leon Goure. Allen's mention of desertions only added to the puzzle that Adams was trying to solve.

So, Adams went to 176 Pasteur and met with Goure, who told him that, indeed, desertion was "the Viet Cong's biggest problem," and that there were "*many* more deserters than defectors."[204] When Adams asked Goure whether he had figured out a ratio of deserters to defectors, Goure told him that, based on the interviews, there were seven deserters to each defector. Adams calculated that, at this rate, the Viet Cong were losing 80,000 men a year—10,000 as defectors and 70,000 as deserters—and said, "My God! That's on top of all their other losses, too—and from a quarter-million man army." Goure told him, "You're right. Think of the consequences."[205] They discussed the serious consequences for the Viet Cong for thirty minutes, and then Goure introduced him to Joe Carrier, "RAND's expert on VC defection."[206] Adams spent the rest of his visit that morning talking about the unreliable *Chieu Hoi* statistics with Carrier.

Through his own research, Adams discovered that Goure's ratio was correct, perhaps even low. Adams thought something did not add up. If there were 80,000 deserters and defectors a year, and "we were killing, capturing, and wounding VC at the rate of 150,000 a year, as some reports indicated, then "it was hard to see how a 280,000-man army could last much longer."[207] Yet, the Viet Cong seemed able to replenish their depleted units and to go on fighting. The explanation Adams came up with, after further research, was that MACV had underestimated the VC order of battle by underreporting by as much as 200,000 the number of guerrillas and militiamen.[208] These insurgents defended the hamlets and villages and were inflicting—with mines, grenades, and booby traps—a large percentage of the casualties sustained by U.S. forces, and they could be funneled into the regional and main force units.

---

[204]Sam Adams, *War of Numbers*, South Royalton, Vt.: Steerforth Press, 1994, p. 46.

[205]Adams, *War of Numbers*, 1994, p. 46.

[206]Adams, *War of Numbers*, 1994, p. 46.

[207]Adams, *War of Numbers*, 1994, p. 63.

[208]In January 1982, CBS aired a 90-minute *CBS Reports* documentary, "The Uncounted Enemy: A Vietnam Deception," which alleged that U.S. military leaders in South Vietnam underreported enemy strength to mislead the American public, despite CIA estimates to the contrary. According to the Museum of Broadcast Communications Web site, former intelligence officers stated that the U.S. military command in Vietnam set a 300,000-troop ceiling for the enemy order of battle to create the impression that the war was going well. The CBS report characterized this manipulation of information as a "conspiracy" in print ads and at the top of the broadcast. Subsequently, General William Westmoreland filed an "unprecedented $120 million libel suit" against the producer, correspondent Mike Wallace, and others for alleging that he had conspired to mislead the American public. The suit was dropped "with CBS merely issuing a statement saying the network never meant to impugn the general's patriotism."

The implication of this explanation was that the enemy was larger and the war bigger than had been believed and that the cross-over point at which enemy losses surpassed their replacements—the point that President Johnson had asked Westmoreland to reach by December 1966—was far off and perhaps out of reach, according to the CIA. Adams' work had no effect, and his warning that Viet Cong forces were more numerous than estimated was ignored. In November 1966, Robert Komer, then a presidential assistant, wrote McNamara, "I suspect that we have reached the point where we are killing, defecting, or otherwise attriting more VC/NVA strength than the enemy can build up." In May 1967, General Joseph McChristian, the head of J-2 MACV, after careful research, finally revised the order of battle to 500,000, but Westmoreland refused to forward his intelligence estimate to Washington, saying, "If I send that cable to Washington, it will create a political bombshell." Three weeks after submitting the new figure to Westmoreland, McChristian was relieved of his post and sent to Fort Bragg, in Texas.

When he went to Saigon to investigate Goure's project, Gus Shubert also looked at the operational studies that RAND continued to perform in Vietnam and decided to let them continue. This kind of operational research was irrelevant—he thought—because no matter how many sorties you could get out of a plane, as one RAND project was trying to determine, the result would not change the outcome of the war. But, he concluded that, since the work was "sophisticated, the analytical techniques were sound," since it was not large, did not involve many people, and did not carry a big price tag, and since the Air Force, "which was input-oriented throughout the entire war," thought it was useful, it should be allowed to continue "undisturbed."[209]

Such work at that time included the assessment of the F5A aircraft, a fighter plane produced by Northrop that had not yet seen combat and that McNamara wanted to test to see whether it would be a suitable modern aircraft for the nascent Vietnamese Air Force. It also included a logistical study for the Air Force to see whether it could support a wing deployed to Vietnam from the continental United States without having to move field maintenance, organizational maintenance, supplies, and transporting to Vietnam. RAND was also performing a study of Viet Cong logistics, using intelligence reports tracking the movement of a Viet Cong battalion, which indicated how hard it would be to stop the insurgents, since an enemy fighter traveled light, carrying "just a bowl, a length of rope, a rifle, and a tarp to sleep on"—and got rice and ammunition from villages that could be reached through a network of trails.[210]

In January 1967, Frank Collbohm retired as president of RAND and was replaced by Harry Rowen. Born in Boston, Massachusetts, in 1925, Rowen had earned a bachelor's degree in industrial management from the Massachusetts Institute of Technology in 1949 and a master's in economics from Oxford University in 1955. He joined

---

[209]Collins, interview with Gus Shubert, session of May 28, 1992, pp. 39–40.

[210]Author interview with Bob Holliday, 2004.

RAND in 1950 and worked for the Economics Department until 1953. He returned to RAND in 1955, and in 1960 became a research associate at the Harvard Center for International Affairs. From 1961 to 1964, he served as Deputy Assistant Secretary of Defense for International Security Affairs, responsible for European issues. He joined the U.S. Bureau of the Budget in 1965 as assistant director, a position he held until appointed as RAND president in 1967.

Although Rowen had helped secure funding for the Viet Cong Motivation and Morale Project when he was in the Pentagon in 1964, he was "totally out of it" once he moved the Bureau of the Budget in 1965, and was unaware of the Goure controversy because he was "working on health, education, and welfare."[211] According to Gus Shubert, however, Rowen knew about the Goure study from people such as Albert [Wohlstetter]. Rowen never made any public pronouncement, but when he returned to RAND, he had already formed fairly definite views about the Goure study and about the war, which were similar to those held by Daniel Ellsberg, a close friend who had turned dovish. Among the first things he did upon assuming the RAND presidency was to meet with Shubert and say, "That's got to stop and [Goure's] got to go." Shubert replied, "I'm with you. Let's do it."[212] According to Shubert, Rowen thought that what Goure was doing was "harmful to the country," as well as "harmful to RAND," and "was bad work besides." And so Rowen was "very eager to make that change as quickly as he could."[213] According to Jim Digby, Rowen thought that "Goure's work was biased," that it made "the bombings look good," and that it "gave unnecessary weight to the deleterious effects on morale of the bombing raids."[214] In fact, Digby would go further and say that Rowen thought that "it was rather shameful," and "immediately replaced Goure."[215] According to David Landau, Rowen fired Goure because he "was unconvinced" by Goure's findings and thought that the low quality of his work was embarrassing to RAND.[216] Rowen, however, said that he did not remember the firing.

In retrospect, Rowen said that he was not so much opposed to the war as he was skeptical about how it was going, and that he was "trying to figure out a better way of handling things and managing things."[217] He remembered that he agreed with the "correct and very important" point Albert Wohlstetter made at the time, which was

---

[211] Author interview with Harry Rowen, 2005.

[212] Collins, interview with Gus Shubert, session of May 20, 1992, p. 10.

[213] Author interview with Gus Shubert, 2004. Shubert added that Rowen told him, "One of the first things I've got to do is solve the Goure problem, and I'm going to solve it by firing him, in essence."

[214] Author interview with Jim Digby, 2002.

[215] Author interview with Jim Digby, 2002.

[216] Landau, "Behind the Policy Makers," 1972, p. 62.

[217] Author interview with Harry Rowen, 2005.

that as long as the Ho Chi Minh Trail remained "open and effective," the United States had no real way of stopping support from the North. The bombing had failed to shut down the infiltration route, and, unless that "back door" was blocked with ground action extending into Laos—which would necessitate a bigger commitment— "the odds were stacked against us." Therefore, "If one accepted that as a proposition, then the outlook was bleak." He recalled that "there were reasons to not be optimistic," and that the open Ho Chi Minh Trail represented one "important basis . . . for some of us to be concerned about the trend." He said he did not "remember coming to RAND convinced that it was lost," only "that the odds were not good."[218]

In Saigon, the staff got wind that something was afoot. In a letter to a friend in Santa Monica, dated February 16, 1967, Ardith Betts wrote, "There's no doubt that [the project] is highly controversial, especially Leon's work and position." She mentioned that, for the past two weeks, George Tanham had been in Saigon to evaluate "the project and its relation to the on-going conduct of the war as Rowen's personal envoy." Leon Goure had hoped that he would return to Saigon and retain his position, but by February 8th he still had not made his way back from Santa Monica.[219] Ardith Betts speculated that "Rowen won't let Leon back out until Tanham has reported to Rowen and some high-level decision is done." On April 1, 1967, they got the news that Leon Goure had been ousted, and that Bill Jones, a retired Air Force colonel who had joined the RAND staff—accompanied by Chuck Thomson—would be due in in a few days to take over the project. Goure's departure left the staff wondering about the future of the study.

Lee Meyer, who was George Tanham's administrative assistant, remembered in a 2004 interview that, at the time, there was increasing concern over Leon Goure's leadership of the project and growing doubt regarding the objectivity of his research and its quality, which was judged to be below RAND's standards. Meyer recalled seeing Goure, who would come to brief all the high officials in Washington. He seemed "caught up" in his briefings—"sort of intoxicated" by them—she said. She also remembered that there was suspicion that he was using the research to give these officials what they wanted to hear. "He was saying that Viet Cong morale was bad and that the tide was turning," she recalled. According to her, Harry Rowen sent George Tanham to Saigon to fire Goure. "Vietnam brought out the best and the worst in some people," she said, "and with Leon, it seemed, perhaps, to have brought out the worst." For his part, Goure thought that he became the "fall guy" and an embarrassment for RAND— a reminder of its involvement in a failed enterprise—as sentiment about the war soured in the country at large and at RAND.

---

[218] Author interview with Harry Rowen, 2005.

[219] Ken Strother, a retired colonel, was sent from Santa Monica to oversee the Saigon office pending Goure's replacement—not in any substantive manner, but simply to be a senior figure while the project leadership was decided upon. According to Ardith Betts, Strother had no authority and was only "babysitting" the office.

On May 10, 1967, Rowen reported to the Management Committee about the organizational changes, including the appointment of Bill Jones as manager in Saigon and of Chuck Thomson as his assistant. In addition, Major Sam Cochran would help facilitate analysis performed in Santa Monica while Jones was in Saigon. In one of her letters, Ardith Betts wrote that Bill Jones did not get along with Steve Hosmer and, at his insistence, Hosmer was removed, and Major Sam Cochran replaced him as the point person for the project in the United States. Jim Digby, in addition to being the ISA Project Manager, would take over from Gus Shubert as project manager for ARPA/AGILE. Shubert would "continue to coordinate work in the 'field of revolutionary warfare' and would "conduct research on the lessons learned from Vietnam."[220]

Other changes affecting the Viet Cong Motivation and Morale Project also took place. In June 1967, Joe Goldsen resigned as chairman of the Social Science Department. In Saigon, the staff interpreted the departure of Goure, Goldsen, and Hosmer as a defeat for people who believed in a "qualitative" approach and a victory for "quantitative" people, such as Gus Shubert. Although she did not believe that Bill Jones had the required academic credentials to run the project—nor that he had the right academic ideas about what it should produce—Ardith Betts was relieved that Goure was gone because Goure had been critical of her husband Russ, refusing to give him recognition for his hard work and complaining to "anyone who would listen that Russ was irresponsible . . . and had no concept of hard work or the goals of the project."[221]

Ardith and Russ Betts, then, must have been relieved when Bill Jones arrived in Saigon. In a letter to her friend, Ardith Betts wrote that Jones had been a great change. She thought that he was an "honest, fair, and moral person" who was not going to let himself be "pushed about in any way by anyone," and that he was the right person to administer the office. In her view, Jones was "well suited for the job," and he had "no vested interests, no personal ambitions," and was "loyal to RAND and Harry Rowen." Jones himself told her that he was a "logical choice to help out in Saigon," and he believed that Rowen was "smart for picking him." Initially, he did not want to come, he told her, "but finally decided that he could manage for a year."[222] According to Russ Betts, the staff in Saigon in general was relieved that Goure had been replaced and thought that there was now some chance of getting the project back into balance, because Goure, by becoming doctrinaire and resistant to alternative arguments, had lost some of their respect as project leader.

---

[220]Management Committee Meeting Minutes, May 10, 1967, RAND Archives. In March, Shubert had drafted a letter to McNamara asking for OSD funding for research on a number of topics, including "lessons from Vietnam," which would consist of "a series of historical analyses of the pacification programs, military operations, aid activities, and police force operations, etc." Then, in April, Rowen had discussed the idea for a "lessons learned" type of study with General Paul P. McConnell, Chief of Staff of the U.S. Air Force, and Air Force Secretary Harold Brown, who had reacted enthusiastically.

[221]Ardith Betts, letter to a friend in Santa Monica, January 19, 1967.

[222]Ardith Betts, letter to a friend in Santa Monica, May 1, 1967.

According to Jim Digby, Bill Jones was a former Air Force colonel and, being "a very steady" and "very straightforward" man, was "exactly the kind you'd want to replace someone who you thought was doing the wrong things"—someone who would "put things on the right path."[223] Gus Shubert thought that Jones was a "noncontroversial, honest guy who would do his best" in cleaning up what Shubert perceived as the mess in Saigon.[224] Tony Russo, who became friends with Bill Jones, thought that his selection illustrated the difficulty RAND encountered in finding competent leaders to head the project. In Russo's view, RAND "sort of goes off the reservation so to speak to find some kind of leadership to hold the shop together like Bill Jones."[225] The son of Bill Jones, Greg Jones, speculated that Harry Rowen's selection of his father might have been because Rowen might have become acquainted with his father when he was in DoD and Jones was assigned to the office of the JCS Chairman. In retrospect, Russo said that Jones was "a hell of a nice guy," but said that Jones was "an organizational" and a "military" man who would execute orders without question and without "vitriol."[226] Russo, having agitated against Goure in concert with Doug Scott, must have tended to view any change of leadership as a step in the right direction.

Russo had befriended Jones during the transition period when he was briefly back in Santa Monica between his first and second tour in Vietnam. According to Russo, prior to going to Saigon to replace Goure, Jones would stop by his office everyday to discuss the project and educate himself about it. Jones asked him to return to Vietnam with him to run the project. In Saigon, the two men would sit in the living room practically every night, smoking cigarettes and talking for hours. Russo felt that he could express his views openly to Bill Jones without fear of retribution. They remained friends until Russo returned to the United States for good in 1968.

According to Russo, after Bill Jones took over, "The project was going down to just production of the interviews," and there were "no policy recommendations."[227] By that time, Russo had come to believe that the United States should wind down the war as quickly as possible. He had become less reticent about expressing his opposition to the war and his sympathy for the insurgents. His feeling had gradually built up, he said, from an accumulation of things he had picked up in interviews and on his trips to the provinces that led him to believe that the real villains were not the "Front people"—who were "very nice," "accommodating," and helpful to the people—but the government soldiers, who would steal chickens and beat up villagers. It got to the point

---

[223]Author interview with Jim Digby, 2002.

[224]Author interview with Gus Shubert, 2004.

[225]Author interview with Tony Russo, 2003 and 2004.

[226]Author interview with Tony Russo, 2003 and 2004.

[227]Author interview with Tony Russo, 2003 and 2004.

where he blurted out to Ken Strother, the interim project manager, that "the peasants would be better off under the Liberation Front." [228]

With the project winding down to production and, without an authoritative voice to represent it in Saigon—and also without Goure's dynamic personality and articulate analyses—the RAND villa gradually ceased to be a place that military and civilian officials, visiting dignitaries, and correspondents gravitated toward to get the latest prognostication on the war. The social gatherings stopped. Most of the American staff, seeing the writing on the wall, hastened their plans to return to the United States to pursue other options. Russ and Ardith Betts left in June 1967 for MIT. Tony Russo returned to the Economics Department in January 1968, just as the Tet Offensive got under way. Doug Scott joined the RAND New York office, which had recently been opened as part of Rowen's diversification into domestic issues. Bonnie Leib got married to a major and left in July for Germany where her husband was going to be stationed. Shirley Shaffer also left to return to the United States. Joe Carrier who had come back to Vietnam in January 1967 left in July of that year.

In a letter home in July 1967, Bill Jones wrote that "all of the old clique" was gone, possibly referring to Leon Goure and his supporters on the staff—Joe Carrier, Shirley Shaffer, and Bonnie Leib Hurwitz. He also wrote that he had had to deal with them "harshly," and speculated that the pressure on the "old clique" to leave might have stirred resentment in Santa Monica among their supporters.[229] (For good measure, Jones also fired the cook.) For their part, some of the staff members thought that, in contrast to Leon Goure, who was urbane, gregarious, and charming, Bill Jones was an uptight and humorless person, and a man of few words. Some also thought that he was paranoid—perhaps because he was uncertain of his support among the staff in Saigon and because he was navigating in what for him was unfamiliar and uncomfortable terrain in Vietnam.

Soon after taking over as president of RAND, Harry Rowen discussed the future of Vietnam-oriented work and, in answer to questions posed to him at a Management Committee Meeting on January 11, 1967, said that two alternatives should be considered: either to continue the work or replace it with other research topics. Possibly as part of the review leading to a decision of whether to continue the Viet Cong Motivation and Morale Project, Gus Shubert visited Vietnam again in June 1967.

---

[228]Author interview with Tony Russo, 2003 and 2004.

[229]Letters provided by Greg Jones. The harsh treatment might have included trying to get Joe Carrier dismissed from RAND. According to Carrier, when he returned to Santa Monica in July 1967, his department head summoned him and told him that he was fired and that he would have two months to find another job. According to Carrier, Bill Jones and Gus Shubert had a hand in this episode. In his interview with the author, he recalled that Steve Jeffries, the RAND corporate secretary, read him a letter from Bill Jones that was used as the basis for his dismissal. After Carrier threatened legal action, he was retained until he left in 1969.

In a trip report written following his return to Santa Monica, Shubert gave a discouraging picture of both Saigon and the prospects for continuing the project.[230] The sense of excitement and optimism that David Morell and others had felt in 1965—as American troops were pouring into the country and American planes were beginning to pound North Vietnam continuously—was gone. Saigon had become tense and more dilapidated, Shubert wrote, and had the appearance of a military enclave. Things had deteriorated, and there was a general sense of degradation. The influx of American wartime money had created widespread corruption, which had reached the Americans themselves, some of whom—according to a rumor—were engaged with Vietnamese officials in shady schemes and getting rich. But the Americans themselves, by spending freely, were also corrupting the city. On the political front, he found that the GVN was not genuinely interested in political reforms and was only playing games—for example, by holding elections—to placate the Americans.

The first day he arrived in Saigon, on June 1, Shubert spent most of the evening discussing the project with Bill Jones. It seemed to both him and Jones that "unless there's a worthwhile analytical effort set in motion in Santa Monica, it's by and large useless to continue the field effort out here."[231] They concluded that the interviews were adding little value, because the interviewers were "very repetitive" and remained "unfocussed."[232] It seemed to Shubert that "all we're doing is piling more and more trivia on an ever-increasing pile of trivia."[233]

Considering the large and immediate problems in Vietnam, the difficulties of operating in the country, and the bad "intellectual atmosphere" prevailing there, Shubert doubted that RAND should continue the project "unless we can focus both existing work and our new work on either long-run implications of Vietnam to the U.S., or on problems of mid- to long-range planning for Vietnam."[234] In his view, "the interview study, as presently continued, probably no longer has a useful role in Vietnam. If our efforts to refocus the project (on pacification, for example) are unsuccessful, then we ought to face up to terminating the project."[235] During his stay in Vietnam, Shubert met with ARPA and USAID representatives to scout for other research projects, but nothing came out of those sessions.

By summer 1966, McNamara's doubts about the war had grown, especially about the efficacy of bombing North Vietnam, after the JASON study he had commissioned from the Pentagon's Institute of Defense Analyses concluded that the air

---

[230]Shubert, "Southeast Asia Trip Report," 1967.

[231]Shubert, "Southeast Asia Trip Report," 1967, p. 44.

[232]Shubert, "Southeast Asia Trip Report," 1967, p. 44

[233]Shubert, "Southeast Asia Trip Report," 1967, p. 44.

[234]Shubert, "Southeast Asia Trip Report," 1967, p. 73.

[235]Shubert, "Southeast Asia Trip Report," 1967, p. 73.

attacks had been ineffective. In May 1966, following a trip to Vietnam, he gave a pessimistic evaluation of the situation to President Johnson that hardly reflected Goure's optimistic findings. The enemy had adjusted to American strategy and maintained its morale, McNamara wrote. He added that pacification had retrogressed: GVN control of the countryside had hardly grown; the number of guerrillas and regional forces had increased, as had their attacks; the Viet Cong political organization was thriving in most of the country; and full security did not exist anywhere in South Vietnam.

In 1967, as Gus Shubert was talking about terminating the project, McNamara's thinking was turning more and more toward limiting American military involvement and getting a settlement. In March 1967, Westmoreland broke the agreement on the troop ceiling and requested 210,000 more troops and ten more tactical air squadrons to make incursions into Cambodia and Laos and to increase the war tempo in the Mekong Delta. McNamara opposed his request, on the grounds that acceding to it would add $10 billion to the ballooning defense budget, deepen the political division within the United States, and create a national disaster of major proportion. His deputy, John McNaughton, who had turned "dovish," also opposed the request and urged McNamara to strongly oppose what he called "the philosophy of the war," which amounted to "trying to impose some US image on distant peoples we cannot understand. . . ."[236]

On May 19, 1967, McNamara submitted to the president "an explosive twenty-two page single-spaced" memo rejecting the troop request and expressing more openly his pessimism.[237] The Defense Secretary gave a disheartening picture and wrote that there appeared to be "no attractive course of action" in Vietnam.[238] Although American troops were making gains against North Vietnamese regulars in the big-unit war, these had not been translated into gains in the "other war" of pacification. He cited pervasive corruption—the "rot in the fabric"—within the GVN; lack of government control; moribund political structure; apathetic population; and a "tired, passive, and accommodation-prone" army.[239] Neither had the military gains broken the morale of the enemy in the South—a statement indicating that by this time Goure's conclusion that the breaking point was near would not have been convincing to the Secretary of Defense. On the diplomatic front, Hanoi continued to show no interest in a settlement and seemed determined to match any effort by the United States to escalate the conflict. This last assessment showed that McNamara had moved away from his previous faith in Thomas Schilling's "signaling-and-bargaining" theory.[240]

---

[236]Shapley, *Promise and Power*, 1993, p. 418.

[237]Shapley, *Promise and Power*, 1993, p. 418.

[238]McNamara, *In Retrospect*, 1995, p. 266.

[239]Shapley, *Promise and Power*, 1993, p. 419.

[240]Shapley, *Promise and Power*, 1993, p. 419.

McNamara recommended giving Westmoreland 30,000 additional troops at the most, prohibiting incursions into Cambodia and Laos, limiting interdiction bombing of the infiltration route to the "funnel" below the 20th parallel, and "adopting a more flexible bargaining position while actively seeking a political settlement."[241] These steps would not "win the Vietnam war in a military sense in a short time," but it would avert a larger war.[242] On August 3, 1967, the White House accepted his recommendation. In his May memo, McNamara also recommended a drive to settle the war by "clarifying" U.S. aims as only preventing outside interference with South Vietnamese self-determination but not ensuring a "free and independent South Vietnam."[243]

Therefore, in 1967, the thinking in OSD was turning to getting negotiations started. In an interview in 2004, Les Gelb, former director of Policy and Planning in the Pentagon from 1967 to 1969, said that, in that year, the focus of his office was on how to get negotiations going, on the effectiveness of the bombing of the North, and "what do you have to do with respect to the bombing" in order to get the peace talks off the ground? Acting like "a hired gun for the Secretary of Defense and for the Assistant Secretary of Defense for ISA," his office produced a large number of memos on Vietnam, including the weekly memos, in collaboration with Systems Analysis, to the president from McNamara. Gelb remembered that there were "all sorts of memos questioning the efficacy of the military war effort, and questioning whether or not there was any such thing as a military victory in the war, questioning whether the bombing was really having anywhere near the effect on the battlefield that it was having in terms of adverse opinions of America around the world."[244]

By June 1967, McNamara had come to the conclusion that "we had failed" in Indochina and that "our policies and programs . . . had evolved in ways we had neither anticipated nor intended, and that the costs—human, political, social, and economic—had grown far greater than anyone had imagined."[245] He asked John McNaughton to begin "collecting documents for future scholars to use"[246] to explore the reasons for this failure and the lessons that could be drawn from the American experience in Vietnam to avoid similar failures in the future. The project would produce what became known as the Pentagon Papers.

As McNamara grew more disillusioned with and more pessimistic over the course of the war, he might have lost interest in Goure's reports, with their depictions of enemy decline that had failed to materialize in the field. This could explain why Deitchman

---

[241] McNamara, *In Retrospect*, 1995, p. 270.

[242] Shapley, *Promise and Power*, 1993, p. 420.

[243] Shapley, *Promise and Power*, 1993, p. 420.

[244] Author interview with Les Gelb, 2004.

[245] McNamara, *In Retrospect*, 1995, p. 280.

[246] McNamara, *In Retrospect*, 1995, p. 280.

could stop Goure's briefings and reports without McNamara noticing. In a telephone interview in 2004, McNamara could not recall the name of Leon Goure, nor could he remember any of his quarterly briefings and reports. This lapse might indicate that, as soon as Goure's usefulness as an outside validation of McNamara's own interpretation of the war's progress dissipated, he was quickly forgotten. It has to be recognized, however, that McNamara was so deluged with data and information, not just about Vietnam but also about a host of other pressing issues, that the memory of Goure might have simply become hazy after Goure stopped appearing in the office of the Secretary of Defense. It could be that by 2004 McNamara's memory had been weakened. However, in his memoir *In Retrospect*, published in 1995, he did not mention either RAND or Goure. Be that as it may, the decline of Goure's influence in Washington seemed to have coincided with McNamara's own loss of interest. In his review, Alfred Goldberg wrote that, "By 1967, doubts about the desirability and feasibility of seeking answers to current operational and policy problems in the interview data . . . impelled RAND Management" to reorient the program away from a focus on the morale of the Viet Cong and toward other subjects—such as "small unit actions, pacification, and revolutionary development."[247] Concurrently, the Saigon interview effort was cut back; it was finally stopped in early 1969.

Goure's shortcomings aside, the interview project was generally judged to be useful for producing a large body of unique data on the Viet Cong that served as an important resource for other studies on Vietnam. In his "User's Guide," Phil Davison quoted a RAND analyst who had used the interview data as saying,

> We are, of course, conscious that any interview program, especially under the conditions prevailing in Vietnam, is bound to be imperfect and that the results will contain a variety of distortions. We believe, however, that the internal consistency of the answers, and the fact that much of the data tie in with information obtained from other sources, indicate that much of the collected information is, on the whole, credible and usable for purposes of analysis.[248]

The ultimate value of the interviews, in Davison's view, is that they gave the rural people of South Vietnam the chance to tell the story of their lives in a time of violent warfare and unprecedented turmoil. They were "the people at the bottom of the pyramid . . . who brought in the harvests and bore the brunt of the fighting, the hardworking, hopeful, discouraged, terrified people"[249] whose voices—seldom heard—came through clearly in the RAND interviews.

---

[247] Goldberg, "RAND and Vietnam," 1969, p. 16.

[248] Davison, "User's Guide," 1970, p. 2. According to Sy Deitchman, the knowledge derived from the Viet Cong Motivation and Morale Project was used to produce a "VC Manual" in English and Vietnamese about Viet Cong organization and methods. This manual became a reference book and a training aid, but there is no way to determine whether it made much difference in the struggle against the Viet Cong in the villages.

[249] Davison, "User's Guide," 1970, p. 11.

CHAPTER FIVE

The Many Aspects of the War

The near-demise of the Viet Cong Motivation and Morale Project ended whatever cohesiveness Vietnam research had achieved. With the shifting of analysis to Santa Monica, more researchers dove into the data and the many aspects of the conflict, either in pursuit of their own interests or in response to clients' requests, most of which dealt with the immediate requirements of the war. More analysts of the Vietnam situation emerged, supplementing or replacing the interpretation of Leon Goure, who had more or less served as RAND's major voice on Vietnam.

One area of immediate concern to the Pentagon was infiltration and interdiction, and Leon Goure was tapped once again. Shortly after Goure's forced departure in 1967, George Tanham—whom Harry Rowen had sent to Saigon to fire Goure—put Goure in touch with Army Lieutenant General Alfred D. Starbird to secure another project. According to Goure, Tanham told him to go talk to General Starbird, saying, "you might be able to work something out."[1] Starbird, then head of a group with the innocuous name of "Defense Communications Planning Group" (DCPG) to hide its true objective—had turned to RAND in mid-1967 and made a "forceful request" for assistance.[2] Starbird had learned of the RAND interview project in Vietnam and thought that a similar endeavor would provide him with the information on infiltration he needed to meet an urgent deadline set by McNamara. Since Leon Goure had extensive experience running the RAND interview project, he seemed a logical choice. So, not long after his removal as head of the Viet Cong Motivation and Morale Project, Leon Goure reappeared in Saigon—to the dismay of Bill Jones.

The infiltration project, under the sponsorship of ARPA and the Air Force, was limited. It was to last for 60 days—from August 14 to October 12, 1967—and involved Goure and three interviewers. It paled in scale and importance relative to the Viet Cong Motivation and Morale Project, but it gave Goure a contract funded by ARPA and the Air Force, which secured his position at RAND. Even if Rowen was unhappy

---

[1] Author interview with Leon Goure, 2003.

[2] V. J. Croizat, J. A. Carlson, and L. Goure, *Final Report on the Interdiction-Evaluation Project*, Santa Monica, Calif.: RAND Corporation, D-18355-ARPA/AGILE, January 14, 1969, p. ii.

with Goure, he could not fire him because, as Goure would recall later, "you don't push the Air Force around too much."[3]

General Starbird, a research and engineering officer, had been appointed by Defense Secretary McNamara in September 1966 to head a secret task force charged with developing a barrier to check infiltration from North Vietnam. A group of MIT and Harvard faculty members had originally suggested the idea to McNamara in late 1965. The concept for a barrier appealed to McNamara because, as the proposal explained, it would transform the "contest from one of will (in which the DRV [Democratic Republic of Vietnam] and VC have as much reason to outlast us as we do to outlast them) to a contest of physical capability in which we are superior."[4]

McNamara reacted favorably, but the idea did not gain impetus until 1966, when it was endorsed by the JASON scientists at the Institute of Defense Analyses. McNamara had asked the JASON group to assess the effectiveness of the bombing of North Vietnam. In its August 1966 report to McNamara, it concluded that the air attacks had produced "no measurable direct effect" on Hanoi's ability to support and conduct military activities in the South, and it supported the building of an electronic barrier as an alternative.[5] McNamara, searching for different ideas as his strategy was failing, renewed his enthusiasm for the concept.

So, although the Joint Chiefs of Staff was unenthusiastic about the proposal, McNamara went ahead with the project. In a memo to President Lyndon B. Johnson in October 1966, McNamara wrote that the infiltration barrier "would lie near the 17th parallel—would run from the sea, across the neck of South Vietnam (choking off the new infiltration routes through the DMZ), and across the trails in Laos." He added that, "This interdiction system (at an approximate cost of $1 billion) would comprise to the east a ground barrier[6] of fences, wire, sensors, artillery, aircraft, and mobile troops; and to the west—mainly in Laos—an interdiction zone covered by air-laid mines and bombing attacks pinpointed by air-laid acoustic sensors." The barrier, McNamara told Johnson, "would be persuasive evidence . . . that our sole aim is to protect the South from the North." The Defense Secretary gave General Starbird until November 1, 1967, to make this barrier operational.

---

[3] Author interview with Leon Goure, 2003.

[4] Cited in Shapley, *Promise and Power*, 1993, p. 363.

[5] Stanley Karnow, *Vietnam: A History; The First Complete Account of Vietnam at War*, New York: Penguin Books, 1997, p. 513.

[6] Work on this part of the barrier on the eastern coastal plain of Vietnam began secretly in summer 1967. Since the Marines had responsibility for the area in which the barrier was supposed to be built, they were assigned the job. The Marines, who strenuously opposed the barrier concept, had to divert troops and resources to this task. In January 1968, the sensors and other equipment intended for the barrier along the DMZ were diverted to the defense of the Marine outpost at Khe Sanh, which was besieged by the NVA. When the siege was lifted in April, work on the barrier did not resume. By this time, McNamara had left the Defense Department to head the World Bank. This part of the barrier became known derisively as the "McNamara Line."

In a memo to General Westmoreland, dated September 16, 1966, General Starbird requested assistance and asked for the assignment of six officers from the theater, including someone who could provide knowledge about the methods and requirements for airpower to counter infiltration, about available intelligence applicable to this type of operation, and on the latest infiltration tactics.[7] Subsequently, Westmoreland had a couple meetings with Starbird, but he remained skeptical of the benefits of the project and suspected that certain groups believed that, if an effective barrier could be established, the United States could stop bombing North Vietnam. He noted in his diary at the time that such thinking was unrealistic. In his memoir, *A Soldier Reports*, Westmoreland wrote, "As any experienced military man would know, the concept had a basic flaw in that no fence—electronic or otherwise—would be foolproof without men to cover it by fire, which raised the specter of tying down a battalion every mile or so in conventional defense."[8] By January 1967, however, as he noted in his diary, Westmoreland had come around to view the concept of a barrier more favorably. In one of his entries, he indicated that the concept was gelling because it had become more realistic. "Like most problems," he wrote, "logic and capabilities prevail in the end."[9]

Westmoreland was right in detecting an effort to substitute the barrier for the air attacks against the North. Part of the concept was that Marines manning the strong points strung along the barrier lying near the DMZ, aided by sensors, "could kill anything that came across."[10] They would not stop infiltration all together but they could inflict a punishment that was severe enough to render the bombing redundant. The air war could then be stopped, which would induce Hanoi to negotiate. Meanwhile, the United States could continue to check infiltration into the South. Privately, McNamara was hoping that the bombing could be turned off one day if the barrier "worked to limit infiltration" and "America could fight on without an expensive and politically costly air war."[11] Despite misgivings on the part of top military leaders, the White House gave the project the highest national priority in January 1967.

Starbird's approval of Goure to collect information on infiltration was not welcomed by Bill Jones in Saigon, for whom Goure represented an unpleasant burden to deal with. For his part, Goure was rankled that Bill Jones did not ask for any input from him regarding the ongoing but reduced Viet Cong Motivation and Morale Project. Jones wanted Goure "out completely," Goure would later recall, and made "no

---

[7] General Alfred D. Starbird, memo to General William Westmoreland, Personal Papers of William Westmoreland, Lyndon B. Johnson Library, Austin, Tex.

[8] William C. Westmoreland, *A Soldier Reports*, Garden City, New York: Doubleday, 1976.

[9] Westmoreland, Diary, entry of January 1, 1967.

[10] Shapley, *Promise and Power*, 1993, p. 363.

[11] Shapely, *Promise and Power*, 1993, p. 432.

request for assistance, no request for information, no request for interpretation."[12] In fact, according to Leon Goure, he had a confrontation with Bill Jones after he arrived in Saigon during which Jones told him to his face, "Don't mess with my operation," and warned that he would not tolerate any attempt by Goure to reinsert himself. Goure recalled that he was dismayed and offended.[13] Goure, who had maintained a high profile for himself and the project, thought that Jones was keeping what was left of the Viet Cong Motivation and Morale study "unnoticed and quiet" out of caution.[14]

At this time, with Frank Collbohm gone, Goure felt vulnerable at RAND. He also found out from Bill Jones that several people at RAND and at ARPA objected to his return to Vietnam. He realized that there had been disagreements over his briefings and accusations of bias against him at RAND, and that ARPA was still unhappy over the fact that it had been forced by McNamara to give the Viet Cong Motivation and Morale Project more money than it had wanted to. Goure also knew that he had made mistakes, but he thought that Jones's attitude toward him was unjustified. However, he also realized that he was walking "on eggs" because he was apparently on "probation" and Jones could "wreck" his current project and his position at RAND if he crossed Jones.[15] He wished things had not gotten to this point and wondered whether it would be worth his while to stay at RAND. But he had a job to do, so he left Saigon for Danang, where he based his infiltration project, taking three interviewers with him.

For 60 days, his team interviewed North Vietnamese infiltrators, using a questionnaire that included questions raised by the Defense Communications Planning Group, RAND, the Air Force, and MACV J-2. From this work, Goure prepared three preliminary reports that were distributed to the DCPG, MACV J-2, Headquarters 7th Air Force, III Marine Amphibious Force, CINCPAC, PACAF, ARPA, and RAND. In order to provide Starbird with information quickly, Goure prepared these reports by debriefing the interviewers rather than waiting for the full-length interviews to be produced. In the first report, Goure stated that his project—sponsored by ARPA and the Air Force—resulted from interest in "some Air Force and DoD agencies, notably the Defense Communication Planning Group" about the impact of U.S. interdiction efforts.[16] According to Goure, the objective of the interview program was to get more detailed information than was currently available on "the organization of the infiltration, the character of the infiltration routes, and the patterns of behavior of

---

[12] Author interview with Leon Goure, 2003.

[13] Author interview with Leon Goure, 2003.

[14] Leon Goure, letter to a friend at RAND, August 16, 1967.

[15] Leon Goure, letter to a friend at RAND, August 16, 1967.

[16] Leon Goure, "Some Preliminary Observations on NVA Behavior During Infiltration," Santa Monica, Calif.: RAND Corporation, D-16339-PR, November 3, 1967, p. ii.

the infiltrators."[17] Such information would improve knowledge of how the enemy was infiltrating forces into the South as well as aid in the evaluation of how effectively U.S. interdiction methods were working.

At the conference on "Analyzing Guerrilla Warfare" in McLean, Virginia, on September 24, 1985, Leon Goure recalled that knowing this pattern of behavior was crucial to being able to correctly interpret what the sensors picked up. For example, it was necessary, he told his audience, to know answers to questions such as, "How did the infiltrating units march? How and when did they talk? How and when did they get off the trail? What noises did they make?"[18] Such questions about enemy activities in Laos and North Vietnam were not being asked by U.S. Army and Air Force interrogators, who limited themselves to eliciting information about activities inside South Vietnam only.

In three reports, based on 63 interviews with North Vietnamese prisoners and defectors who had infiltrated through the DMZ, Laos, and Cambodia, Goure provided information to answer such questions.[19] The information was akin to operational intelligence, but it was asked of him by the project sponsors. He wrote that the infiltrators had been warned to watch for mines during their march and had received instructions on the types of American mines being used and on ways to deal with them. They had also been cautioned about sensors that Americans had placed or parachuted along trails and campsites to listen for noises made by the troops on the march or in camp, and then send signals to nearby aircraft to launch attacks. Consequently, the infiltrators were under strict orders not to make noises, such as raising their voices when speaking, cutting down trees, singing, laughing loudly, or coughing. They were also prohibited from picking up things that looked like radios along the route. If they spotted any unfamiliar or unusual object, they should alert the unit's cadres or officers, who would destroy them or make them inoperative.

Regarding the conditions of the trails, Goure reported that the infiltrators followed old, heavily used routes that were concealed from view. However, it was not possible to pinpoint the location of the trails in Laos from the description given by the respondents. Infiltration usually took place during the dry season, there was no set rule for organizing a march, and the infiltrators usually walked single-file. In Laos, the infiltrators were guided by communication-liaison agents, who would take them from one

---

[17] Goure, "Some Preliminary Observations on NVA Behavior During Infiltration," 1967.

[18] Goure, "The RAND Corporation POW and Defector Debriefing Program," 1985, p. 7-2.

[19] See Goure, "Some Preliminary Observations on NVA Behavior During Infiltration," 1967, based on 25 interviews; and "Additional Preliminary Observations on NVA Behavior During Infiltration," Santa Monica, Calif.: RAND Corporation, D-16340-PR, November 3, 1967, based on 11 interviews. See also "Some Further Preliminary Observations on NVA Behavior During Infiltration," October 10, 1967, Santa Monica, Calif.: RAND Corporation, D-16341-PR, based on 27 interviews and contained in Croizat, Carlson, and Goure, *Final Report*, 1969. Goure's three reports were originally issued as "letter reports" and dated September 6, September 21, and October 10, 1967 (see Croizat, Carlson, and Goure, *Final Report*, 1969, p. 2).

way station to another. If they crossed the DMZ, they were guided by their unit's own reconnaissance elements, who had gone a day or several days ahead to scout the route. The unit's commander always marched with the guide or with the reconnaissance element at the head of the lead company. For a battalion, the unit's staff was dispersed so that at least one staff officer marched with each of the companies.

The march was well disciplined. Each soldier, camouflaged with branches and leaves, carried a load between 25 and 35 kilograms—and marched in silence. Orders were passed by word of mouth or by runners, and radios were used only in emergencies. In Laos, the infiltrators marched during the daytime, except when they had to cross a river, a road, or a defoliated area. The DMZ was usually crossed at night. The troops marched for 8 to 10 hours—sometimes up to 12 hours a day—with breaks for rest and meals. After every four to five days of march, the troops were given one to two days of rest. On average, they covered about 20 kilometers of ground daily, but if the terrain was difficult, they could cover only about 3 kilometers a day. Cooking was done in underground ovens so that the smoke could not be spotted from the air. Infiltrators usually were issued 7 to 14 days' rice ration at the last stop as a food reserve, in case the way stations to which they were headed were destroyed or they were delayed in their march. The number of infiltrators who got sick on the trails was small, and few deserted. There was no active anti-aircraft defense, but only two of the respondents said that their groups had been attacked by aircraft during the march—an indication that encounters with air interdiction were rare.

Although Goure made Danang his base of operation, Bill Jones was wary of what he might be up to. In one of his letters home, Bill Jones intimated that he kept an eye on Goure's moves through what he called his "spy network," and he wrote that "Leon is working like a beaver and apparently staying out of trouble." Jones complained that, whenever Goure came to Saigon, he had to spend an inordinate amount of time taking care of him and his needs, and that Goure commandeered the use of the car, leaving Jones without transportation. When Goure announced in October 1967 that he was returning to the United States, Jones was relieved, writing to his family, "I can't say I'm sorry" about his departure. Before leaving, however, Goure gave Jones a bit of a shock when he announced that he might stay for another six months: Admiral James R. Reedy, who liked Goure's reports, wanted to recommend that the project be extended. However, Harry Rowen wrote Goure, telling him that the issue had become politically sensitive and instructed him not to "speculate or express personal opinions" or "embarrass RAND."[20] Goure replied that, if Rowen felt uncomfortable, he should come out and tell him so, and he would alter his plans. While the proposal was being debated vigorously in Washington and at RAND, Goure had to leave because his theater authorization was running out.

---

[20] Leon Goure, letter to a friend in Santa Monica, September 1967.

In the end, Starbird approved a six-month extension. Bill Jones and Vic Croizat, who replaced Jones, oversaw the continuation of the project. Over 100 additional interviews—for a combined project total of 147—were conducted until March 1968, and two more reports were prepared by Jim Carlson in December 1967 and May 1968. These were combined with those done by Leon Goure in a final report that was published in January 1969.[21] The additional interviews did not reveal any new information and Carlson wrote that the results meshed substantially with those indicated in Goure's reports. He concluded that the infiltration was well organized and rarely disrupted by interdiction activities.

The failure to interdict infiltration led Secretary Harold Brown to look for ways to improve the situation. On November 16, 1967, Goure met with him and Colonel Fred W. Vetter, his military assistant, to discuss this subject. Subsequently, Goure solicited ideas from a number of people at RAND and compiled them in an informal paper, "Some Unevaluated and Tentative Suggestions for Harassment of NVA Infiltration into South Vietnam" (D-164 81-PR, December 14, 1967). As the title indicates, the list represented a mix of suggestions that were untested for their technical and cost feasibility. The suggestions included many novel ideas, such as creating roadblocks with craters and landslides; using illumination at night to force enemy trucks into hiding; improving night air-attack capability using the latest techniques in nighttime vision and armed reconnaissance sorties; using the chemical agent CS2 (a replacement for tear gas), which irritated the eyes, mucous membranes, and lungs; obscuring the trails with chemical smoke bombs to slow down enemy movement during the daytime; using very short, highly intense light flashes to cause temporary blindness or permanent retinal damage; and using steady illumination of an area occupied by the enemy to expose him to detection. It is not clear whether any of these suggestions was implemented.[22]

---

[21] J. Carlson, "Preliminary Observations on NVA Behavior During Infiltration," December 14, 1967, Appendix D; and "Preliminary Observations on NVA Infiltration," May 21, 1967, Appendix E, in Croizat, Carlson, and Goure, *Final Report*, 1969.

[22] A major concern of the Air Force was bombing in North and South Vietnam. Among the efforts to improve the impact of bombings in the South was a computer modeling program called FAST-VAL, or Forward Air Strike Evaluation, which RAND had developed for the European theater. As part of the Tactical Air Study RAND undertook in 1964, FAST-VAL was designed to calculate air sortie requirements in attacks against enemy ground forces in large-scale limited war. For Vietnam, this model was modified to fit the requirements of the local theater. It was retooled to measure not just the impact of airpower but also that of other ordnance, such as artillery and mortars, on the outcome of a firefight. The study was conducted by a team headed by Jack Lind. They used Marine records for a firefight at the Marine base at Khe Sanh in 1967 for their simulation and found that their model produced results comparable to the outcome of the actual firefight. The simulation indicated that a new weapon (such as the CBU-24) or alternative use of existing weapons could change the outcome when added to air and artillery bombardments. Subsequently, the team traveled to Okinawa and Vietnam to collect more data, in December 1968.

Although the military seemed interested enough to attend FAST-VAL briefings and cooperate in the data collection, it is not clear that the computer model was ever adopted. One reason might be that the RAND team's suggested level of firepower was below what the Air Force and Army were already employing in Vietnam. At one briefing in Vietnam, for example, their suggestion for as many as ten to 20 sorties for close air support for certain

At the request of General Starbird, Goure did return later, to Danang, to assess the effectiveness of air attacks on infiltration. He was assigned a small team of Americans from Detachment 66499, which was the Air Force intelligence operation in Southeast Asia. Goure was in charge of the interrogation program. The Americans assigned to his team—five or six officers and enlisted men—were professional interrogators, and they worked with Vietnamese translators.

Goure and his team lived in a little villa on the outskirts of Danang, "very near a *Chieu Hoi* camp, in the flight path of the rockets that wanted to hit the airfield."[23] The day the team arrived in Danang, Goure went to meet them at the airfield and found them dressed for war: with full uniforms, helmets, flak jackets, hand grenades, and rifles. The first night, at about three or four o'clock in the morning, there was a rocket attack. The men rushed out in their underwear—*sans* uniforms, helmets, flak jackets, and weapons—but with their cameras. The team had a good relationship with the Marines operating in the area, who would supply them with steaks for lunch.[24] Before turning prisoners they had captured over to the Vietnamese, the Marines would hand them over to the team for interrogation.

Although Goure had fallen down in stature and importance, he did not let this bother him. He enjoyed his stay in Danang and his team's company. What his clients wanted was information on infiltration, and that was what Goure supplied. His project boiled down to finding out how vulnerable the trails and the groups of infiltrators were, where they stopped along the way, what role the guides played in taking them down the trail from station to station, and how they dealt with the sensors, and to obtaining answers to such questions as, "How did you travel down the trails?" "Were you attacked?" "What did you do when you saw the aircraft?" Goure would later recall that he made some recommendations, such as seeding the trails not only with sensors but also with "what was called a dragon's tooth": a very small plastic bomb that resembled a sensor and that could blow "a hole in your heel."[25] His idea, he said, was not to cause harm so much as to make the infiltrators afraid to pick up the sensors and dispose of them, out of fear that what they picked up may explode. According to Goure,

---

situations did not faze General George Scratchley Brown, the commander of the 7th Air Force, who had been advocating using the whole air fleet to knock out North Vietnamese assembly points in the South. At another briefing, the team's suggestion that 2,000 to 4,000 rounds of artillery be used in attacking a dug-in North Vietnamese company did not impress their audience, since more than 20,000 rounds of artillery were used daily in I Corps alone—80 percent of them in harassment and interdiction missions. See J. Lind, K. Harris, S. Spring, and M. Yanokawa, "Trip Report: FAST-VAL Data Collecting and Briefing Visit to Vietnam and Okinawa," Santa Monica, Calif.: RAND Corporation, D-18905-PR, June 2, 1969.

[23] Author interview with Leon Goure, 2003.

[24] Note that the Vietnamese found the comforts American troops enjoyed astonishing.

[25] Author interview with Leon Goure, 2003.

his recommendations were not followed.[26] He said that he did not know whether what he uncovered was useful or not, but that was the kind of information the Air Force wanted.

From this second study, Goure produced a paper, "Some Factors Affecting Infiltration Across National Boundaries" (D-18288-ARPA, October 31, 1968). This paper was more substantive than his previous papers in the sense that it addressed the broader issues affecting infiltration across national boundaries, with Vietnam as a prime case, instead of focusing solely on the details of infiltration. Goure identified several factors relevant to infiltration, such as the distance traveled by infiltrators, the terrain of the frontier zones they had to cross, the nature of the defenses they had to breach, the availability of logistical support, the feasibility of concealment to avoid detection, the attrition rate in crossing, the attitude toward the infiltrators of the people living in the frontier zones, and the safety of the regions lying between the crossing point and the target area that the infiltrators had to traverse.

For Vietnam, Goure concluded that none of these factors posed insurmountable barriers. The distance from the point of departure in North Vietnam to the crossing into the South—through the DMZ, Laos, or Cambodia—was formidable and the march on foot was slow, but Hanoi was not deterred. Infiltrators on foot took one month to reach the DMZ, and two to six months to reach the crossing point into South Vietnam from Laos or Cambodia. Because of the long distance (it varied widely, but could reach up to 700 miles) and the many difficulties of the trip, the infiltrators usually traveled not individually but—at the minimum—in small groups to achieve greater efficiency and to provide mutual aid. The size of the infiltration groups varied from a few men to battalions averaging some 350 men.

To provide security for infiltration, the North Vietnamese seized control of the area in Laos bordering Vietnam and got the Cambodians to at least let them pass through without hindrance. To facilitate infiltration, they developed an elaborate system of trails, roads, guides, and supply points, and the numerous trails leading from Laos and Cambodia gave them flexibility in selecting which crossing points to use for entering the South. The terrain along the infiltration route presented difficult but not impossible obstacles. There was no continuous barrier, and no large rivers or incredibly tall mountains that could not be crossed. The triple-canopy jungle concealed their movements, making it safe for them to march in daytime. When concealment was not

---

[26] According to Sy Deitchman, *gravel mines*—"explosives that looked like little tea bags but could blow the leg off someone who stepped on one"—were supposed to be dropped along the trails. "The idea," he said, "was [the infiltrators] could sweep them off the trails if they saw them but this would keep them from going off the known and targeted trails to make new ones." When the Air Force attempted the first drop, a mechanical failure prevented the dispenser from opening and scattering the mines, and the Air Force decided, "We don't want to do that any more." The real reason might be that the Air Force feared that the North Vietnamese would pick up the gravel mines and turn them into booby traps against South Vietnamese and American troops—as they were wont to do. Author interview with Sy Deitchman, 2005.

possible, they traveled at night, using trails known by the guides to be safe. There was attrition due to exhaustion and disease, but apparently these losses were tolerable and, as the trail and supply system were improved, the attrition rates would gradually drop. This last finding by Goure was less encouraging than the picture of demoralized and disease-stricken infiltrators he had painted in his Viet Cong Motivation and Morale study.

The infiltrators depended completely on guides to lead the way and on preestablished logistics support. Initially, Laotian and Montagnard guides in Laos and along the Laos–South Vietnamese border were used, but eventually they were replaced by North Vietnamese who had learned the trail network lying between their way station and the next ones, where other guides would take over. Infiltrators crossing into South Vietnam were rarely detected, ambushed, or attacked. The available information indicated that the infiltrators were somewhat concerned over detection and air attacks, but were not worried about mines or other hidden defenses. The infiltrators had great confidence in their leaders and guides, and expected that they would avoid unwanted contacts with defending forces. Once they crossed into the South, the infiltrators entered zones sparsely inhabited by ethnic minorities, who were either neutral or under overt VC control or would cooperate with them under pressure or out of hostility toward the GVN. In general, this population—regardless of which side they supported—did not pose any difficulties for the infiltrators and, in the early years of the war, even cooperated with them willingly. This cooperation appeared to be continuing in many of the frontier zones in which the population had not moved away to safe areas under government control.

In most cases, these border zones were remote from the more populated, more resource-rich areas that were the targets of the infiltrators. These intervening areas often had inhospitable terrain covered with dense jungle, and they were sparsely populated. To survive and to move through these areas, the infiltrators "had to rely on an elaborate logistic support system including guides, food dumps, base camps, medical facilities, native porters, etc." Movement across these areas often required an additional month of marching before the infiltrators could reach their zone of operation. However, the infiltrators could take advantage of these inaccessible areas near the border "to establish their bases, training centers, and supply points, . . . and use them as strongholds and safe zones from which they could launch attacks against the more densely inhabited areas."

The existence of these vast undefended areas, where the infiltrators could hide while they built up their strength, provided them with a major advantage and made it more difficult for the government to protect the more densely inhabited areas. Food supply represented a problem, and the infiltrators—as well as the local VC—had to depend heavily on an intricate logistical support system, using South Vietnamese, North Vietnamese, Cambodian, and Laotian resources. The NVA main force units were encouraged to grow some of their own food to reduce dependence on resupply from the outside. They also relied heavily on outside resupply of ammunition, weapons, equipment, medicines, etc., and a large portion of the infiltrators, supplemented by South Vietnamese porters, were used exclusively or occasionally to transport food, ammunition, and other supplies.

Goure concluded that all these factors—the control the North Vietnamese held over the trail network in eastern Laos, the political attitudes of the population in South Vietnam, and the existence of large, remote border areas that were outside of government authority and that provided infiltrators with relative safety and concealment—made it possible for North Vietnam to infiltrate men and supplies into the South on a large scale. On the whole, the analysis Goure presented in his various reports indicated that the measures used to counter infiltration were ineffective in checking the flow of men and supplies.

Although the Air Force had contemplated keeping the team and the project Goure had built, it terminated the operation—to Goure's chagrin—in June 1968. It was time for Goure to return home. Rowen had told him to leave Vietnam, saying in essence "no more you," as Goure put it.[27] Also, Goure's wife was unhappy with him for having been gone so long. But Goure worried about what would happen to him when he returned to RAND, wondering, "What am I going to do there?"[28] since RAND was going through a wrenching redirection under Rowen as it moved to diversify itself.[29] "With so many people leaving and all sorts of strange guys running things," he thought that it was "a bit scary" to contemplate his return.[30] He said to a friend, "What I need is a new war. . . . Should I start one?"[31] Goure hung on until 1969, when Fred Iklé, the new chairman of the Social Science Department, called him into his office and told him that he had to leave RAND, giving him no reason.[32] But Goure had received the signal that RAND was unhappy with him—even embarrassed by him—because, by this time, Rowen and RAND wanted to minimize RAND's connection with Vietnam and "hide" it.[33] Goure did not want to leave RAND, because he enjoyed working there and because he felt he had done what RAND had wanted him to do. Goure managed to obtain a position at the University of Miami in 1969, and he left RAND feeling bitter over what he viewed as unfair treatment.

---

[27] Leon Goure, letter to a friend in Santa Monica, June 1, 1968.

[28] Goure, letter to a friend in Santa Monica, June 1, 1968.

[29] For more details on RAND's diversification, see the Epilogue.

[30] Goure, letter to a friend in Santa Monica, June 1, 1968.

[31] Goure, letter to a friend in Santa Monica, June 1, 1968.

[32] According to a RAND staff member at the time, Fred Iklé was a man not known for his communication skills. After Goure emerged from Iklé's office, he went to talk to her, repeating what Iklé had told him and wondering what it really meant. She told Goure, "You've been fired."

[33] Author interview with Leon Goure, 2003.

Unbeknownst to Goure—and perhaps to others at RAND—the interviews that his Viet Cong Motivation and Morale teams had conducted in Vietnam served a novel purpose in the U.S. attempt to check infiltration. According to Sy Deitchman, as an offshoot of the JASON recommendation to set up a barrier, the question was raised regarding the topography of the trail network meandering through the border area in Laos. ARPA solicited information from the military and others, but the usual reply was, "Well, it's a bunch of trails down the jungle. I don't know what it looks like."[34] In trying to come up with an answer, a German geologist at the Research and Analysis Corporation who had studied the geology and terrain of Laos read the RAND prisoner interviews and, culling bits and pieces of description of the trails from them, developed a picture of what the trail system was like and how the infiltrators operated on them.

The information was used to devise the barrier scheme in Laos, where the known or suspected trails were seeded with acoustic and seismic sensors, dropped mostly by Navy and Air Force planes, to detect troop movement and truck vibration. Those sensors broadcast to an orbiting airplane—a specially equipped Lockheed EC-121—which relayed the signal to the Infiltration Surveillance Center at Nakhon Phanom Air Base in Thailand, across the Mekong River. The plan was that, the moment the infiltrators were detected, air strikes would be launched against them. This operation, dubbed Igloo White, gained in importance when Rolling Thunder, the air bombardment of North Vietnam, ended in 1968 with the start of peace negotiations and the focus of the bombing campaign shifted to interdiction of the Ho Chi Minh Trail.[35]

---

[34] Author interview with Sy Deitchman, 2005.

[35] A network of some 20,000 sensors was dropped in strings of five or six to ensure that at least three sensors in each string would survive and be activated. The sensors operated on batteries, which ran down after a few weeks, so replacement sensors had to be dropped. The acoustic sensors could hear both voices and vehicles. The seismic sensors sensed earth motion to detect people and vehicles. The difficulty in using the sensors was in separating the false alarms generated by wind, thunder, rain, earth tremors, and animals—especially frogs. Other kinds of sensors were used as well, including the "people sniffer," which chemically sensed sweat and urine. Besides picking up the sensors—some of which are now on display at the history museum in Hanoi—to render them inoperative, the North Vietnamese took other countermeasures, such as destroying the sensors or inducing false signals by driving animals up the trail and hanging buckets of urine in the trees. Igloo White failed to stop infiltration, and the trail system in Laos became known as "Sullivan's Highway"—after William Sullivan, the U.S. ambassador to Vientiane—because of the ease with which North Vietnamese soldiers and trucks could move through it to reach South Vietnam. One limitation was that many of the trails were not known, so that not every one of them was wired. According to an online article of the *Journal of the Air Force Association*, "even at the peak of Igloo White, the North Vietnamese were building one or two miles of new road a day. In 1972, North Vietnamese tanks appeared in South Vietnam, having come all the way down the trail without being detected, much less stopped." Igloo White operations on the trail diminished in 1972, when the full-scale bombing of North Vietnam resumed under President Richard Nixon, and then stopped all together. The computers at Nakhon Phanom were removed and shipped back to the United States. See John T. Correll, "Igloo White," *Journal of the Air Force Association*, Vol. 87, No. 11, November 2004.

Goure's studies of infiltration and interdiction represented a continuation of previous RAND research projects on the subjects. RAND's research in these areas began with Vic Sturdevant's 1964 study of border control, which examined the cost-effectiveness of such interdiction methods as barrier control and patrol ships. Joe Zasloff's RM on the role of North Vietnam as a sanctuary called attention to the problem of infiltration in July 1964. However, it was only in 1966 that RAND analysts began to focus more seriously on interdiction and bombing of the North "because it was the major concern of the Air Force."[36] In December 1965, following his trip to Vietnam in which he had seen a cache of weapons infiltrated from the North, Frank Collbohm directed that "interdiction be given top priority" among important problems "relating to Vietnam that seemed to require research."[37] Collbohm "suggested that a small group of analysts, headed by Edward H. Sharkey in the Electronics Department, examine the feasibility of creating the equivalent of a no-man's-land across South Vietnam."[38] Over the next 18 months, beginning in January 1966, "as many as a dozen people produced papers on different aspects of interdiction in connection with this project."[39] The results were compiled in a report published in November 1967.[40]

The study found deficiencies in the air operations and recommended remedies. It concluded that air operations had failed to achieve their primary objectives, which were to choke off the movement of supplies and troops into South Vietnam and, combined with the strategic bombing of the North, to weaken Hanoi's will to pursue the war in the South. Interdiction had been ineffective because, although it had drastically reduced the flow of supplies, enough supplies still got through to meet the enemy's needs, which were small to begin with and which they could calibrate by choosing when to initiate ground actions that consumed heavy quantities of materiel.[41] To sup-

---

[36] Goldberg, "RAND and Vietnam, II," 1969, p. 17. Considering RAND's "preoccupation with air strategy and tactics," it was surprising that—prior to 1965—it did not "give much thought or devote any effort to the major problems of air strategy and tactics that might develop in Vietnam."

[37] Goldberg, "RAND and Vietnam," 1969, p. 19.

[38] Goldberg, "RAND and Vietnam," 1969, p. 19.

[39] Goldberg, "RAND and Vietnam," 1969, p. 19.

[40] E. H. Sharkey and G. C. Reinhardt, *Air Interdiction in Southeast Asia*, Santa Monica, Calif.: RAND Corporation, RM-5283-PR, November 1967.

[41] The RAND findings regarding the bombing campaign's effectiveness against North Vietnam and infiltration were echoed by a pilot study performed by the Office of Systems Analysis in DoD. According to Alain Enthoven, the head of Systems Analysis at the time, the study conducted by his office indicated that the bombing had done little to reduce or limit the flow of men and supplies from the North, raise the costs to the North for continuing the war, and induce Hanoi to negotiate. Enthoven thought that perhaps 10 percent of the men and supplies sent into the South were destroyed by the bombing. At the same time, the bombing did not have noticeable effects on enemy activities in the South, despite a fourfold increase in U.S. attack sorties against North Vietnam between 1965 and 1968. During that period, the enemy augmented its main force strength by 75 percent, increased its attacks fivefold, and raised its overall activity level ninefold. See Alain Enthoven and K. Wayne Smith, *How Much Is Enough? Shaping the Defense Program, 1961–1969*, New York, Harper & Row, 1971.

port 300,000 troops in South Vietnam, the enemy required only about 40 tons of supplies per day, which could be brought by a fleet of about 400 trucks spread out along routes from Hanoi to the border of South Vietnam. Interdicting such sparse traffic was difficult, because the trucks traveled at night, were concealed by jungle cover, and were heavily defended along parts of their routes. Even if his supply chain was disrupted temporarily, the enemy could continue operating with stockpiled materials.

As to troop infiltration, airpower made little difference in stopping the flow of soldiers marching to South Vietnam under heavy jungle cover. The strategic bombing of North Vietnam was hampered by heavy air defense—considered unprecedented in the history of warfare—around primary targets in Hanoi and Haiphong . That defense was made up of guns, surface-to-air missiles, and MiG aircraft, as well as of frequent bad weather, which rendered visual bombing attacks difficult.

Nevertheless, the report said, the attacks had played an essential role in limiting what the enemy could do militarily in South Vietnam and in forcing him to move covertly and to cut back on the flow of supplies. It pointed out that these operations would not achieve success unless drastic improvements were made in bombing accuracy in any weather condition and with any degree of visibility, and in nighttime detection of targets. Even such improvements could not guarantee that the movement of troops and supplies could be cut off, or that Hanoi would be compelled to alter its policies, but they could greatly increase by an order of magnitude the effectiveness of air attacks and would help the war effort by discouraging or defeating the enemy's operations in Vietnam.

The solutions the report proposed for remedying deficiencies were presented in briefings "at RAND and to Air Force audiences in Washington, Vietnam, PACAF, and elsewhere."[42] According to Ed Sharkey, they made little impression on the Air Force audience. Although Secretary Brown reacted favorably, the Air Staff's reaction was unfavorable. Several reasons were given to explain this reaction. The Air Force was skeptical that the necessary equipment could be developed in a timely enough manner to be used in Vietnam, and even if it could be developed in time "it would be too complex for effective use and maintenance in the field."[43] There was also concern that improving effectiveness by an order of magnitude would alter the force structure. Finally, the Air Force was disinclined to believe that "the interdiction campaign was not doing well and that improvements were urgently needed."[44] So, Sharkey and the other RAND analysts "could make little headway" in the face of such "skepticism and inaction."[45]

---

[42] Goldberg, "RAND and Vietnam," 1969, p. 19.

[43] Goldberg, "RAND and Vietnam," 1969, p. 20.

[44] Goldberg, "RAND and Vietnam," 1969, p. 20.

[45] Goldberg, "RAND and Vietnam," 1969, p. 20. According to David Jardini, Ed Sharkey "had become disillusioned" while working on the project, and in October 1967 wrote "a thought-piece expressing the deep frustra-

At the same time that Ed Sharkey and his associates were conducting the study on interdiction, Burt Klein, the head of the Economics Department, tried to initiate several important studies that he believed would be of interest to the Office of the Secretary of Defense and the White House. The idea that garnered the most attention right from the beginning was research on the bombing of North Vietnam. Several economists looked at the possibility of studying different aspects of the air campaign. But the only study that came to fruition was the one performed by Oleg Hoeffding on the economic and political effects of the bombing on North Vietnam. Gus Shubert recalled that he himself suggested that Hoeffding "take a look at the vulnerability of the North Vietnamese economy and other less-developed countries' economies to force and intervention from the outside."[46] According to Shubert, he had a hard time persuading Hoeffding to undertake the study; however, a week later Hoeffding came back and said that he had taken a look at the bombing's effect on North Vietnam. When Shubert asked him what his conclusion was, he said, "There's nothing there. All we're doing is making holes in the ground. There's no economy, in the conventional sense, for us to go up there and destroy."[47]

Hoeffding would later publish a report assessing the economic and political effects of the air war against the North,[48] using materials in Hanoi publications and in the American, French, and Soviet press. He also consulted classified intelligence material for background, but did not draw directly from it. The report attempted to evaluate the U.S. air offensive against North Vietnam in terms of its effects on the physical and organizational functioning of the North as an economic and political entity, and its efficacy in inducing the Hanoi government to agree to negotiations on terms that would be initially acceptable to the United States. The study did not address the direct and primary objective of the campaign, which was to reduce the level of infiltration or to substantially increase the cost of infiltration of men and equipment from the North to the South. Hoeffding stated that he simply proceeded on the premise supported by available information that the bombing in North Vietnam and Laos, while raising the

---

tions felt by RAND analysts." (See E. H. Sharkey, "Some Thoughts on RAND's Tactical Warfare Programs," Santa Monica, Calif.: RAND Corporation, D-16251-PR, October 1967.) In spite of the "massive efforts" the United States had marshaled in Vietnam, "no victory or solution was in sight." Sharkey criticized the Air Force for refusing to employ tactics more suited for Vietnam while providing inexact information about its performance to the government. He made fun of an analysis that the Air Force had given to the Stennis Committee (the Senate Armed Services Preparedness Investigating Subcommittee) in which it claimed that the bombing activities had saved the United States about $75 billion in expenditures and the deployment of 800,000 more troops "by crippling the North Vietnamese economy and interdicting south-bound supplies." See Jardini, "The Wrong War," 1998, pp. 52–53.

[46] Collins, interview with Gus Shubert, session of May 20, 1992, p. 17.

[47] Collins, interview with Gus Shubert, session of May 20, 1992, p. 17.

[48] Oleg Hoeffding, *Bombing North Vietnam: An Appraisal of Economic and Political Effects,* Santa Monica, Calif.: RAND Corporation, RM-5213-1, December 1966.

cost of infiltration, had not reduced it sufficiently to prevent the North from maintaining a force in the South strong enough to make it unlikely that the United States could achieve a decisive military victory in the near future.

Hoeffding concluded that, although the bombing—and the cost of sustaining the war in the South—had imposed severe strains on the North's physical, administrative, and organizational resources, he found no evidence that it had critically disrupted the economy of North Vietnam or set it on a course of gradual deterioration. Through dispersal and decentralization, Hanoi was able to place beyond the reach of air attacks a significant portion of its small manufacturing capability, which was essential to its war effort. To hit these dispersed facilities, the United States would have to engage in the utmost in indiscriminate and wasteful air attacks. There were few industrial targets for the United States to hit to begin with; through dispersal, Hanoi was able to reduce the number even more. With expanded military and economic aid from its allies, Hanoi could import the essentials. Hanoi's determination and strategy could be explained by its expectation that, even if the bombing escalated further, the military and economic aid would continue unabated. The U.S. failure to block imports—out of a desire to avoid risking a confrontation with China and the Soviet Union and, perhaps also, out of uncertainty of the effectiveness of such an effort—appeared to be a significant loophole in its strategy to coerce North Vietnam into calling off the war. Hoeffding believed that even a substantial intensification of air operations against the North would not achieve the desired political (or military) objectives unless the United States were willing to abandon the major limitations imposed on its operations to date, including the crucial constraint against direct maximum interdiction of imports into the DRV. Even if the constraint were lifted, the question would still remain: "Would the physical and political effects on the DRV make themselves decisively felt within a time frame acceptable to the United States?" A graver question would also arise: "What would be the Soviet and Chinese reactions to such an escalation?"

Hoeffding concluded that, leaving aside the issue of interdiction, as long as the existing constraints on "objectives and operations" remained unchanged, and in view of the fact that halting the bombing had increasingly become an indispensable precondition for negotiations, "the potential gains from cessation or, at least, drastic and demonstrative de-escalation," would outweigh "the advantages" of continuing or intensifying the raids.[49] Copies of Hoeffding's draft RM were circulated to officials in Washington in summer 1966, including to Walt Rostow, who scribbled on the cover of the White House copy, "This is interesting." However, Hoeffding's study did not seem to have influence. It was the JASON scientists' study that persuaded McNamara that the bombing of the North was not producing the desired outcome.[50]

---

[49] Hoeffding, *Bombing North Vietnam,* 1966, p. 32.

[50] The JASON study echoed some of Hoeffding's findings. It pointed out, for example, that the bombing had not heavily damaged the North Vietnamese economy, which was overwhelmingly agricultural and offered few rich

Interest in assessing the effect of the bombing received a boost as a result of the hearings held by the Senate Preparedness Subcommittee of the Senate Armed Services Committee in August 1967. Chaired by Senator John C. Stennis, focusing on the air war. In a letter to Harry Rowen, dated September 15, 1967, Air Force Secretary Harold Brown, who had assumed the position of Secretary of the Air Force, asked RAND to conduct a joint study with the Operations Analysis office of the Air Staff in Washington on the effect of airpower on North Vietnam, as well as on interdiction and infiltration. Brown's request represented the only instance in which higher-level authorities within the Air Force asked for a major study on airpower in Vietnam. Brown wanted a comprehensive undertaking that would last as long as required, from six months to a year. He requested a "quantitative assessment, insofar as possible, of the effectiveness of the air campaign" in terms of resources expanded and the effects achieved.[51] The joint study would focus first on the bombing of the North; in a subsequent phase, it would "consider alternative forces, equipment, and tactics for the use of air power in interdiction."[52]

Known as the RAND/AFGOA group, the project team undertook the largest, single, non–field study effort on Vietnam. Headed by Edward P. Oliver of RAND's Washington office and made up of 16 to 18 staff members, drawn equally from RAND and from the Air Force Operations Analysis, this project represented the "largest single study effort on Vietnam" for RAND.[53] The group worked out of the Pentagon and reported to Brown and to General Bruce K. Holloway, the Vice Chief of Staff of the Air Force. It began work in October 1967, and in September 1968, it presented its Summary Report, backed up by ten volumes of supporting materials. Its basic conclusion was that "the costly campaign in the North may not be buying us very much," and that "the interdiction campaign had not achieved its major objective of cutting off the Viet Cong from the North Vietnam lifeline."[54] Brown reacted favorably to the report, but the Air Staff "disagreed with some of the findings and recommendations," out of concern "about the effects of the study on the force structure and levels of the Air Force."[55] As a result, only a very limited number of copies was distributed and circulation was limited to the Air Force.

---

targets for air attacks, and that whatever damage was inflicted could be made up by aid from Communist China and the Soviet Union.

[51] Goldberg, "RAND and Vietnam," 1969, p. 22.

[52] Goldberg, "RAND and Vietnam," 1969, p. 22.

[53] Jardini, "The Wrong War," 1998, p. 36.

[54] Jardini, "The Wrong War," 1998, p. 23.

[55] Jardini, "The Wrong War," 1998, p. 23. According to David Jardini, the report caused "a vitriolic reaction from the Air Force and a near collapse in RAND–Air Force relations." See Jardini, "The Wrong War," 1998, p. 36. According to Goldberg, two committees were formed, under Harold Brown's prodding, to examine the study's recommendations "thoroughly and critically." One of the committees oversaw the development of a "coor-

To address what remained the main concerns of the Air Force, a variety of projects on interdiction and infiltration continued at RAND during 1966–1968. The majority of these studies dealt with technical issues, such as improving bombing accuracy or navigation, emplacing sensors, and interdicting supply trucks. However, no attempt was made "to look at the air campaign against the North as a whole—in a broad context that would search out the military and political implications and state the case for and against it."[56] According to Alfred Goldberg, "RAND could and probably should have taken positions—not necessarily institutional positions—on ways of using airpower and overall military power in Vietnam and on important aspects of air warfare."[57] Such topics represented the primary area in which RAND had demonstrated the analytic competence of its research. Part of the problem was that, under the pressure of the war, the military in general and the Air Force in particular were primarily concerned with solving short-term problems—mainly technical and operational—and were not inclined to pursue answers to long-term issues, anticipating that the recommendations would come too late to be of use.

Typical of the technical studies was the one on anti-infiltration barrier systems for South Vietnam, coordinated by Marv Schaffer.[58] The findings were presented to the Air Force, but Schaffer "heard nothing about the effects of the study or any further use of it by the Air Force."[59] According to Marv Schaffer, in 1971 he produced, in collaboration with co–project leader Milt Weiner at RAND, a study on border security in South Vietnam.[60] It was a technical, countrywide study, which examined the issue at both the micro and macro levels, using the information that Schaffer had gathered on a trip to Vietnam in 1968. Schaffer contributed one chapter, and the other chapters were written by various RAND staff members. On a micro level, the study considered "the kinds of defenses that were necessary to prevent the border from being infiltrated." Then, on the macro level, it assessed "whether this was feasible—whether there were enough forces, whether there was enough infrastructure, enough weaponry to prevent

---

dinated action plan" for implementation of decisions that might arise from the report's recommendations. The other was to "determine how the Air Force could speed decisions on which of its adopted engineering projects deserved special treatment and how to ensure that they received such treatment."

56 Goldberg, "RAND and Vietnam, II," 1969, p. 17.

57 Goldberg, "RAND and Vietnam, II," 1969, p. 17.

58 Before joining RAND, Marv Schaffer had worked at the Picatinny Arsenal in New Jersey and had helped develop the CBU, the anti-personnel cluster bomb.

59 Author interview with Marv Schaffer, 2004. See Milt Weiner et al., "Infiltration and Invasion Project: Activities in Study of Counter-Infiltration Program for South Vietnam," Santa Monica, Calif.: RAND Corporation, D-18538-ARPA/AGILE, March 4, 1969.

60 Schaffer, Marvin B., and Milton G. Weiner, *Border Security in South Vietnam*, Santa Monica, Calif.: RAND Corporation, R-0572-ARPA, February 1971.

the North Vietnamese and their associated forces from entering the country."[61] According to Schaffer, they gave extensive briefings in the Pentagon and in the Department of the Army. By that time, the strategy of Vietnamization—withdrawing U.S. forces from Vietnam and letting the South Vietnamese troops assume the full burden of the war—was being implemented, and the general reaction was, "we're not interested," and words were uttered along the line of, "The South Vietnamese are no longer our allies," which Schaffer interpreted as indicating that American policy to support the South Vietnamese had ceased. Although this policy change was not apparent to people at lower levels or to people at RAND, this "was apparent to people at higher levels."[62]

♧ ♧ ♧

As Goure moved on to research infiltration and interdiction, three key controversial issues that had surfaced during his tenure as head of the Viet Cong Motivation and Morale Project lingered on: whether the crop destruction program was hurting the Viet Cong; whether civilians blamed the GVN and the United States for casualties they suffered in bombing and shelling; and whether the enemy was weakening with the decline in morale and strength, as Goure had maintained.

The effectiveness of crop destruction was researched by Russ Betts and Tony Russo. Betts would later recall that he and Russo initiated the studies. The reports they produced indicate, however, that their research was undertaken at the request of ARPA and OSD. *Crop destruction* was a program aimed at denying food to the Viet Cong; it differed from *defoliation* operations to clear vegetation for tactical military purposes. To obtain the required data, Betts and Russo instructed interviewers to explore the ramifications of the crop destruction program whenever and wherever the topic arose during talks with prisoners, defectors, and refugees. They added questions to the standard questionnaire to ferret out relevant information, such as the experiences of people whose crops had been sprayed; the effect of the chemicals on their health; the effect on their relationships toward the ARVN, the Viet Cong, or NVA forces; and the effect on their feelings toward the Americans. The issue was pursued for several months, and teams of interviewers were specifically taken to the areas where the sprayings had been extensive.

According to Ardith Betts, her husband had been assigned to conduct the project "because the subject was too sensitive and none of the senior researchers—Konrad Kellen, Chuck Thompson, and George Tanham, etc.—would touch it with a ten foot pole."[63] From the data gathered by the interviewers, Russ Betts produced a draft that was submitted to Steve Hosmer in early September 1966. The comments did not come

---

[61] Author interview with Marv Schaffer, 2004.

[62] Author interview with Marv Schaffer, 2004.

[63] Ardith Betts, letter to a friend in Santa Monica, January 19, 1967.

until November and were given orally to Leon Goure. They said, in essence, that Russ Betts "was incompetent" and "must not be allowed to finish the paper," which would be "given to someone else to finish."[64] This "someone else" turned out to be Frank Denton, who would produce the final report in collaboration with Russ Betts. The decision, naturally, upset Ardith Betts and her husband. Ardith Betts believed that her husband's analysis reflected the data truthfully "but would make some people in high places unhappy because it admits that the herbicide program, as currently being run, is not totally effective," and surmised that this was the reason why he was not allowed to continue.[65] She felt that this episode made her husband feel that his work was not appreciated and that he was not allowed to think independently.[66] For his part, Russ Betts would later say that he "may have needed some help" in developing the report, either because he was "too emotional about it" or he "couldn't write it well," and Frank Denton "was dispassionate" and could provide assistance.[67]

In sponsoring the study, ARPA asked for a specific focus on the attitudes of the rural population toward the United States and GVN as a result of the crop destruction program, the effects on the peasants and on the Viet Cong, and ways to lessen the negative reaction among the peasants. Crop destruction was first undertaken in 1962, when the chemicals were tested against VC sanctuaries in Phuoc Long Province.[68] Since that date, the crop spraying had grown in scale: from 936 acres of agricultural land in 1962 and 1963 to 113,335 acres in 1966. During the first four months of 1967 alone, 37,600 acres of crops were sprayed to deny food to the Viet Cong. The chemicals were dispensed from specially fitted C-123 transport aircraft. The potential for destruction was substantial, because, in ideal conditions, an airplane could practically wipe out, with one sortie, the vegetation, including crops, growing in a 300-acre area.[69]

Since the program was initiated, the Viet Cong had grown from a relatively small group self-sufficient in food to a large organization that controlled, or at least had access to, major portions of the countryside. In addition, the number of affected civilians had increased as the spraying expanded. Considering that the insurgents did not seem to have starved, and considering that more civilians were now affected, questions

---

[64] Ardith Betts, letter to a friend in Santa Monica, January 19, 1967.

[65] Ardith Betts, letter to a friend in Santa Monica, January 19, 1967.

[66] Ardith Betts, letter to a friend in Santa Monica, January 19, 1967.

[67] Author interview with Russ Betts, 2004.

[68] According to William A. Buckingham, Jr., in *Operation RANCH HAND—The Air Force and Herbicides in Southeast Asia, 1961—1971*, Washington, D.C.: Office of the Air Force Historian, 1982, the seed for the program began when a military hardware research and development team went to Vietnam in 1961, at the suggestion of Walt Rostow, then a foreign affairs advisor to President John F. Kennedy, to explore the usefulness of various techniques and gadgets against the insurgents. Aerial defoliation became one of these "techniques."

[69] At the same time, defoliation operations to deny cover to insurgents or to clear a field of fire were also expanded. In 1964, a total of 63,500 acres was sprayed by defoliation sorties. "This increased to 751,100 acres in 1966, and to 547,400 acres in the first four months of 1967."

arose about what damage—if any—the crop destruction operations had inflicted on the VC food supplies and whether the program was serving a useful purpose in view of its political cost.

In their report, published in October 1967,[70] Denton and Betts concluded that the program was ineffective. Based on over two hundred interviews conducted in 1966[71] that had been coded, and using the frequency of responses, they wrote that the crop destruction program had not achieved its goal of denying food to the enemy, although it provoked hostility among the peasants whose crops were destroyed and increased support for the Viet Cong. The key reason for failure was the Viet Cong's easy access to resources so that they could get the food supplies they needed. Accounting for a fraction of the population—about 1.5 percent—the Viet Cong required only about 3 percent of the food consumed in the country, a quantity they could easily obtain from the population. They grew very little of what they needed, and, consequently, most of the crops destroyed by the chemicals belonged to the population. When necessary, the Viet Cong would resort to coercion to get the supplies they required; if a region was sprayed, the Viet Cong would transfer the deprivation to the local people, rather than going without food for their troops. This fact was illustrated by the correlation between the rice rations of Viet Cong troops in different regions of the country with the quantity of chemicals sprayed. Denton and Betts found that, even in hard-hit areas, the average Viet Cong seemed to be eating the same amount of food as the local people. In short, the Viet Cong who operated in resource-rich regions ate relatively well and those in regions that were short of rice ate less well, and the level of intensity in the spraying did not seem to affect their rice rations.

In view of this situation, Betts and Denton concluded that it would be exceedingly difficult to use crop destruction to deny food to the enemy, and that the program, in fact, may well be harmful, because the Viet Cong continued "to feed themselves while the peasant bears the brunt of the deprivation, and he doesn't like it."[72] Interview respondents almost unanimously reported that the sprayings provoked hostility among the peasants toward the United States and the GVN. The alienation seemed to spring from several causes. First, the chemicals ruined the major source of livelihood and security for the peasants. Second, a significant percentage of the respondents expressed the fear—stemming from firsthand experience or from hearsay—that the chemicals were poisonous to humans.[73] Third, the villagers did not always view the crop spraying

---

[70] Russell Betts, and Frank Denton, *An Evaluation of Chemical Crop Destruction in Vietnam*, Santa Monica, Calif.: RAND Corporation, RM-5446-1-ISA/ARPA, October 1967.

[71] The interview data were supplemented with materials collected up to June 1967, with MACV-captured document files, and interviews conducted by various U.S. and GVN agencies with POWs and defectors.

[72] Betts, and Frank Denton, *An Evaluation of Chemical Crop Destruction in Vietnam*, 1967, p. xiii.

[73] Agent Orange, which accounted for over 60 percent of the total 19.4 million gallons of herbicides sprayed over Vietnam, contained relatively high levels of an exceedingly poisonous contaminant known as dioxin.

operations as necessary or useful for attacking the Viet Cong, and, in many instances, came to believe that the sprayings were directed as much at them as against the Viet Cong—or that the GVN was not averse to sacrificing them to strike at the Viet Cong. This feeling reinforced the perception that the United States and the GVN were indifferent to their welfare, making them receptive to Viet Cong appeals. All this could stymie pacification.[74]

Denton and Betts did not recommend a cessation of crop spraying, but they suggested a few steps to reduce civilian's alienation if crop spraying were to continue, such as educating peasants about the chemicals' effects on humans and ways to cope with exposure; reducing the concentration of chemicals to lessen toxicity without sacrificing effectiveness; communicating the government's concern for the villagers' welfare; and providing meaningful assistance to alleviate the deprivation of those whose crops were destroyed.

Concurrently with Denton and Betts, Tony Russo also published his own report in October 1967,[75] focusing on the effects of crop destruction on the Viet Cong. As he would recall later, when he, Denton, and Betts were assigned to write the studies, they decided "to split the work." Russo would do a separate study using his model "because there was enough complication in my model to take up a lot of space." Russo credited Frank Denton with being "the spark plug" and with helping him and Betts "organize their work."[76]

Russo's report, based on RAND's interviews with defectors and prisoners, on USAID statistical abstracts, and on official crop-destruction operations data, measured the effect of the program on Viet Cong rice consumption. Using regression techniques, his empirical model strongly indicated that Viet Cong consumption of rice was closely related to economic variables in the regions where Viet Cong operated, and was only marginally, if at all, affected by the chemical crop sprayings. For example, his model showed that in "the area hardest hit in 1966 (approximately 23 percent of the crop was destroyed)," there was "a decrease in average rice ration of approximately 5 percent

---

[74] This conclusion was supported by a 1965 MACV/ARVN assessment of crop spraying. According to Buckingham, a few months after Goure, Scott, and Russo published a report (RAND RM-4911) in which they noted that crop spraying had forced the Viet Cong to abandon their fields and move to new locations, MACV and the Vietnamese Joint General Staff, through their Combined Intelligence Center (CICV) "produced a more extensive evaluation," using the RAND interviews but also citing from captured documents and U.S. and ARVN files. This evaluation "favored crop destruction" but "found more problems of adverse impact." The CICV analysts "noted that in 1965 herbicides had destroyed enough food to feed about 245,000 people for one year." They concluded that, "In many instances . . . the local civilians suffered more than the Viet Cong." However, citing the Viet Cong's own reports of "food shortages and other adverse effects," the analysts concluded that "the crop destruction program had significant potential which justified expansion."

[75] Anthony J. Russo, *A Statistical Analysis of the U.S. Crop Spraying Program in South Vietnam,* Santa Monica, Calif.: RAND Corporation, RM-5450-1-ISA/ARPA, October 1967.

[76] Author nterview with Tony Russo, 2003 and 2004.

(from 660 grams per VC per day to 627)."[77] At the same time, civilians suffered significant losses, and seemed "to carry very nearly the full burden of the results of the crop destruction program," with "over 500 civilians experienc[ing] crop loss for every ton of rice denied the VC."[78] He estimated that, in 1966 alone, at least 325,000 people in the VC-controlled areas that tended to be the targets of crop destruction were affected by crop spraying.

As did Betts and Denton, Russo pointed out that the VC represented a tiny percentage of the population, and the quantity of rice they needed represented only a small portion of the entire crop. Since they controlled or had access to the population and to almost all of the crop grown, they should experience no serious difficulty in obtaining the amount of rice they needed. The results of his study, Russo wrote, "strongly imply that the relationship between the VC and the rice economy is so intimate and pervasive" that "a major proportion (perhaps 50 percent or more) of the rural economy" would have to be destroyed with measures such as crop spraying in order to cripple or significantly reduce VC rice consumption.[79] To do so, however, "would very likely be self-defeating."[80] Looking back, Russo would later say that "the thrust" of his report was that "the individual combatant rice rations in a given area were positively correlated with rice production in that area, which showed that they were being supported by the people."[81] In his report, Russo concluded that, "In terms of denying food to the VC, the returns from the crop destruction program seem insignificant at best, and the costs to the villager seem disproportionately high."[82] On the basis of the results of his study and of his opinion shaped by his own experience in Vietnam, he recommended that the program be reviewed and discontinued.

According to Russo, after he completed his study, he looked forward to briefing people in Saigon. Finally, a presentation was arranged for him in a room at Tan Son Nhut. He went out there and waited, but no one showed up. After about an hour, Bruce Griggs of UCLA, who was then serving as Westmoreland's scientific advisor, walked in. Griggs "belittled" him, Russo would later recall, and maintained that, since the Viet Cong "were up in the mountains, growing their rice up there . . . we had to wipe out the rice." Griggs told Russo that the program worked because "he had flown over" the VC areas up in the mountains and had seen "how spraying was wiping out the rice." According to Russo, Griggs "never sat down, he just took a copy, threw it down, and said, 'in World War II, we had some good operational research, but this

---

[77] Russo, *A Statistical Analysis*, 1967, p. ix.

[78] Russo, *A Statistical Analysis*, 1967, p. ix.

[79] Russo, *A Statistical Analysis*, 1967, p. ix.

[80] Russo, *A Statistical Analysis*, 1967, p. 32.

[81] Author interview with Tony Russo, 2003 and 2004.

[82] Russo, *A Statistical Analysis*, 1967, p. 32.

is not good research, this is crap.'" Then he walked out. Russo said, "Well, thank you very much."[83] Griggs would not be the only person reacting negatively to Russo's report. According to Gus Shubert, Russo's study was one of the "good and competent" works that came out of Goure's interview project, but it provoked a lot of controversy at RAND."[84]

The RAND findings were controversial in Washington and in Vietnam as well. MACV and the Seventh Air Force strongly disagreed. However, after reviewing the results, Alain Enthoven's staff in the Office of Systems Analysis issued their own conclusions in November 1967, agreeing with the RAND reports "that the existing wholesale crop destruction program . . . was counterproductive because it alienated the affected population without denying food to the Viet Cong."[85] Citing the results of the RAND studies, McNamara on November 21, 1967, directed the JCS Chairman "to review RAND's work and report to him within a month whether or not the objectives of crop destruction . . . were being met, and whether changes should be made in the program."[86]

CINCPAC Headquarters then sent a civilian advisory group to Vietnam in 1967 to review crop destruction activities. Using captured documents and an analysis of crop-spraying sorties in 1967, the group gave a divergent assessment of the program, contending that it had inflicted "a significant adverse effect on VC/NVA food supply, logistical requirements, and combat effectiveness," and concluded that crop destruction was a vital element of economic warfare and an "integral, essential and effective part of the total effort in South Vietnam."[87] This disparity led the Air Force Chief of Staff to order still another evaluation by the Seventh Air Force, which also found that the program was "carefully organized, tightly controlled, and very effective."[88] The Seventh Air Force study admitted that the crop destruction program was directed at civilians, as well as at the Viet Cong, since one of its objectives was to "force people to move away from VC-controlled areas" to deny the Viet Cong access to the population for support.[89]

On December 29, 1967, the Joint Chiefs sent their reply to McNamara, using the information contained in these CINCPAC and Seventh Air Force reports, as well as from MACV. The Chiefs attacked the validity of the RAND studies and concluded

[83] Russo, *A Statistical Analysis*, 1967, p. 32.

[84] Collins, Martin, interview with Gus Shubert, session of May 28, 1992, p. 41.

[85] Buckingham, *The Air Force and Herbicides*, 1982, p. 135.

[86] Buckingham, *The Air Force and Herbicides*, 1982, p. 135.

[87] Paul Frederick Cecil, *Herbicidal Warfare: The RANCH HAND Project in Vietnam,* New York: Praeger, Praeger Special Studies, 1986, p. 108.

[88] Cecil, *Herbicidal Warfare*, 1986, p. 108.

[89] Cecil, *Herbicidal Warfare*, 1986, p. 108.

that the program was meeting its objectives of denying food to the Viet Cong, forcing the enemy to divert manpower to grow food, weakening enemy strength, inducing civilians to move from VC areas and thus depriving the guerrillas of manpower. They concluded that crop destruction was effective and important to the war effort, and that no changes were required. The program continued until it was terminated in early 1971, after considerable public controversy.[90]

The issue of whether civilians who were bombed and shelled blamed the GVN and the United States or the Viet Cong reemerged briefly within RAND. It arose with Jack Ellis and Marv Schaffer, who were proposing using tactical airpower to enhance rural security in provinces undergoing full pacification. In those provinces, after the regular army troops had cleared villages of insurgents and had forced the insurgents presumably to revert to small-unit actions of platoon size or smaller, security would be handed over to the Regional Forces and Popular (or Self-Defense) Forces. Ellis and Schaffer maintained that these forces, by themselves, would probably be inadequate and therefore would need to be able to summon air support quickly and at a level they required.[91] Under their proposal, these village/hamlet forces would acquire the capability to communicate directly with Forward Air Controllers that would maintain 24-hour patrols, and to call for support from artillery, armed helicopters, heliborne troop reinforcements, flare ships, and heavy air strikes. Procedures would be put in place to relay requests and ensure fast response. Proposed ordnance included 100-lb bombs, CBUs, 2.75-inch rockets, miniguns, and 40mm grenades. Ellis and Schaffer did not discuss the possibility that the Regional and Popular Forces would misuse or abuse such firepower—or overrely on it—beyond saying that they should be trained in the proper use of tactical air support. According to Ellis and Schaffer, air support could be delivered with precision and would inflict low collateral damage, and such a low rate of destruction would show the villagers that these tactics of defense were beneficial.

To provide support down to this level of small-unit actions, whereby an attack on a hamlet outpost or a village ground-patrol contact could bring heavy firepower, implied an intensified—not to mention disproportionate—use of weapons and the concomitant rise in civilian casualties, which could cause adverse popular reaction against the GVN and the United States. To address this potential problem, Marv Schaffer, in collaboration with colleague Greg Carter, issued a paper that concluded that villagers were "generally understanding of the air/ground support" and by a ratio of more than 2:1 tended to "blame the VC, rather than the GVN, for civilian damage."[92] They reached

---

[90] According to Russ Betts, a Harvard professor used the RAND studies for his testimony at a congressional hearing that led to recommendations that the program be terminated. Author interview with Russ Betts, 2004.

[91] J. W. Ellis, Jr., and M. B. Schaffer, *Improving Tactical Air Support to Regional and Popular Forces in South Vietnam*, Santa Monica, Calif.: RAND Corporation, RM-5483-PR, May 1968.

[92] G. A. Carter and M. B. Schaffer, "On Some Counterproductive Aspects of Tactical Force Employment in South Vietnam: Interviews with Vietnamese Prisoners and Civilians," Santa Monica, Calif.: RAND Corporation, D-16278-PR, October 19, 1967, p. 2.

this conclusion using 25 RAND interviews and the results of a CBS Public Opinion Survey of 1,413 Vietnamese civilians of voting age and living in secure areas. According to Schaffer and Carter, if the Viet Cong were at the site when an attack occurred, an overwhelming majority of the people—76 percent—blamed the Viet Cong. Even if the Viet Cong were not present, almost half the people still blamed them. In short, "even though the people do not *like* the bombing it is not at all clear that the bombing is counterproductive in the sense that it alienates more Vietnamese than it befriends."[93] The results, the RAND analysts wrote, indicated that the majority of Vietnamese exposed to attacks were "willing to accept the hardships of war in preference to being overrun by the Viet Cong. (At the very least, they appear to be understanding of the circumstances which caused their misfortune)"—as evidenced by the results of the CBS poll, which showed that 37 percent of the people said Americans should continue to bomb and burn when necessary, whereas 46 percent said they should stop.[94]

This statistic provoked a rebuttal by Tony Russo, who feared that the conclusions could mislead people into thinking that the entire Vietnamese rural population felt that way.[95] Using data from 189 RAND interviews conducted as of January 1967, which provided "blame" data, Russo showed that the majority of the people did not always blame the Viet Cong, as Schaffer and Carter had indicated. Rather, there was a relationship between "blame" and the side that controlled a village that had been attacked. In areas controlled by the Viet Cong, the people blamed the Americans and the government, whereas in contested areas, villagers may see the Viet Cong as intruders and tended to blame them for bringing about the attack. And as Schaffer and Carter had indicated, if the Viet Cong were not present, a substantial number of people—almost half—blamed the government. In view of these findings, Russo said, "I do not know how one can imply that attacks on civilians are *not* counterproductive" if such a large segment of the population blamed the attacker.[96] In the final analysis, according to Russo, the United States and the GVN still "got the 'majority blame,'"[97] and may appear like "a big impersonal juggernaut" that was willing to ignore the effect on the civilians as long as it could injure the Viet Cong.[98] Leaving aside the issue of whether "one VC 'blame' cancels out one U.S./GVN 'blame,'" Russo believed that there were

---

[93] Carter and Schaffer, "On Some Counterproductive Aspects of Tactical Force Employment in South Vietnam, 1967, p. 9.

[94] Carter and Schaffer, "On Some Counterproductive Aspects of Tactical Force Employment in South Vietnam, 1967, p. 50.

[95] Anthony Russo, "Attitudinal Reactions of Vietnamese Civilians to Allied Attacks: Some Comments on D-16278-PR," Santa Monica, Calif.: RAND Corporation, D-16478-PR, December 14, 1967.

[96] Russo, "Attitudinal Reactions of Vietnamese Civilians to Allied Attacks," 1967, p. 11. Emphasis in original.

[97] Russo, "Attitudinal Reactions of Vietnamese Civilians to Allied Attacks," 1967, p. 2.

[98] Russo, "Attitudinal Reactions of Vietnamese Civilians to Allied Attacks," 1967, p. 3.

some compelling arguments for minimizing civilian casualties from "a moral stand-point alone—no matter who gets the blame."[99]

By far, the issue that had provoked the most controversy under the Goure tenure of the Viet Cong Motivation and Morale Project was whether the enemy was buckling under U.S. military pressure, as Goure claimed. Since Goure's optimism had been belied by the tenacity of the Viet Cong and the NVA, Alex George had brought Konrad Kellen to RAND to look at the interviews and see whether another perspective on the issue of enemy morale and vulnerability might be warranted.

Kellen in fact did see the enemy's state of morale under a different light. When he read the interviews, he was struck by what he would describe in his reports as elements of cohesion within their camp. Unlike Goure, he did not see a weakening adversary but rather one who was keeping popular support, holding its ranks together, and maintaining its spirit in the face of many challenges that tested its psychological and physical mettle. According to Daniel Ellsberg, a friend of Kellen's at RAND, Kellen, "who had dealt with prisoner interrogation material in World War II and Korea and defectors from Eastern Europe," was impressed with the RAND interviews. He told Ellsberg that "he had never seen" such interviews. He said to Ellsberg, "Prisoners and defectors tell you what they think you want to hear. These people, you can't get them to say anything critical of their regime."[100] Kellen concluded that "this was one adversary whose leadership and population simply 'could not be coerced'" and asked Daniel Ellsberg to pass along this conclusion to Henry Kissinger when Kissinger became National Security Advisor to President Nixon after Nixon's election in 1968.[101]

So, while Goure focused on what made the enemy weak and vulnerable, Kellen would focus on what made the enemy strong and cohesive. However, rather than emphasizing such factors as nationalism and organizational structure in explaining the Viet Cong's strength—as Zasloff and Donnell had done—Kellen explained elements that motivated the Viet Cong and North Vietnamese and allowed them to maintain their momentum and combat effectiveness against an adversary possessing vastly superior firepower and resources.[102]

Using interviews conducted in 1966 and 1967, Kellen concluded that enemy cohesion, combat strength, and tenacity seemed to stem from a variety of factors that may continue to motivate them indefinitely. According to Kellen, North Vietnamese and Viet Cong troops alike were sustained by a sense of mission and seemed united in the belief that their cause was just and in the conviction that their war against the Americans had to be fought to save their nation. They were also sustained by a trust in their

---

[99] Russo, "Attitudinal Reactions of Vietnamese Civilians to Allied Attacks," 1967, p. 3.

[100] Daniel Ellsberg, *Secrets: A Memoir of Vietnam and the Pentagon Papers*, New York: Viking, 2002, p. 290.

[101] Ellsberg, *Secrets*, 2002, p. 290.

[102] Konrad Kellen, *A View of the VC: Elements of Cohesion in the Enemy Camp in 1966–1967*, Santa Monica, Calif.: RAND Corporation, RM-5462-1-ISA, October 1967.

leaders; by the relationship forged with the local people; by the widespread expectation that the United States and GVN were not going to win; and by the sporadic nature of combat, which made the war bearable, even though the soldiers realized that hostilities would last a long time.

As to whether the enemy was nearing the breaking point at which he would abandon the fight, Kellen did not detect that this was going to happen soon. As to whether the United States could push the enemy toward disintegration, Kellen thought that the more pressure was brought to bear, the more it would stiffen the enemy's back and make him feel even more deeply obligated to fight to defend his country and his own life in it. According to Kellen, it seemed unlikely that present strategies could bring about a collapse of the VC—either as an entire movement or as individual units unless they were faced with annihilation. He could not detect a weakest link, because the VC movement functioned more like an organism than a chain, with the various components of strength and cohesion playing an equally important role, reinforcing each other and interacting with each other to sustain the entire group. Kellen concluded that the VC might not have a breaking point and, if this were so, then they could, within the realm of possibility, force the United States not only to accept higher and higher losses of its own but also to kill an increasing number of them and of the Vietnamese civilian population—which would not be in the national interest of the United States. If future studies validated his conclusion and solidified it, then the most logical recommendation that could be drawn from his own report would be to search for alternative strategies in the conduct of the war.

While Kellen attempted to explain the insurgency's staying power as the war dragged on, Ed Mitchell, a professor of economics at the University of Chicago and consultant to the RAND Economics Department, set about to examine the other side of the coin—the GVN's pacification and control—to determine through statistical analysis the various factors that might explain why it had failed in certain areas while succeeding in others. For his study, Mitchell used linear regression analysis with six independent variables.[103] When his findings indicated that variables measuring the inequality of land-tenure arrangements provided a powerful explanation for control, he shifted focus to "the relationship of inequality and insurgency."[104] This change produced a report that became one of RAND's most influential—and most controversial—works.

---

[103] Edward J. Mitchell, *Land Tenure and Rebellion: A Statistical Analysis of Factors Affecting Government Control in South Vietnam*, Santa Monica, Calif.: RAND Corporation, RM-5181-ARPA, June 1967. For his study, Mitchell used a number of variables "measuring social, economic, topographic, and ethnic factors" (p. v). See also Mitchell's *Land Tenure and Rebellion in South Vietnam*, RAND D-15176-ARPA/AGILE, October 1966; *Inequality and Insurgency: A Statistical Study of South Vietnam*, RAND P-3610, June 1967; and *Relating Rebellion to the Environment: An Econometric Approach*, RAND P-3726, November 1967.

[104] Mitchell, *Land Tenure and Rebellion*, 1967, p. 1.

From his study, Mitchell arrived at conclusions that contradicted the impression left by "the popular literature and implicitly from U.S. and GVN policy statements" that the success of the insurgents was due to their "ability to attract poorer, primarily landless peasants" with the promise of land redistribution.[105] According to Mitchell, greater GVN control was "associated with greater inequality"—rather than the reverse.[106] It seemed natural, Mitchell wrote, "to expect poorer peasants to be more land-hungry and therefore more sympathetic to the VC cause."[107] Consequently, one could expect that "ceteris paribus . . . the VC have been most successful in areas of greater inequality where few peasants own their own land and where land reform has been ignored."[108] However, Mitchell's statistical findings showed that it was in these areas of greater inequality that the GVN exercised the greatest control. He concluded that the ideal province for government control would be one in which "few peasants operate their own land, the distribution of land holdings is unequal, no land redistribution has taken place, large French holdings existed in the past, population density is high, and the terrain is such that mobility or accessibility is low."[109]

The areas with inequality in land tenure were more stable and less prone to insurgency because of the landlords' power and the tenants' docility. With greater wealth, the landlord could acquire greater political influence with the central government and could keep his tenants submissive in return "for the favors he is able to provide, such as security of tenure and provision of credit."[110] Therefore, when a government disrupted this relationship with land redistribution, it could create a dangerous situation. The tenants, on the other hand, had been conditioned by a lifetime of obedience and tended to support "the existing order merely from the habit of following their superiors."[111] In addition, poor peasants had low aspirations "due to overwhelming preoccupation with merely making a living."[112]

Destabilization occurred when economic conditions changed. When a peasant became more prosperous, he began to entertain higher aspirations, and the gap between his aspirations and the reality of his condition produced discontent and induced a disposition toward rebellious activities. A change in condition, therefore, could be unset-

---

[105] Mitchell, *Land Tenure and Rebellion*, 1967, p. 1.

[106] Mitchell, *Land Tenure and Rebellion*, 1967, p. 2. However, Mitchell cautioned that, since his results "were derived from an essentially static model, one must be cautious in drawing dynamic inferences" (see p. iii).

[107] Mitchell, *Land Tenure and Rebellion*, 1967, pp. 1–2.

[108] Mitchell, *Land Tenure and Rebellion*, 1967, p. 2.

[109] Mitchell, *Land Tenure and Rebellion*, 1967, p. 33. According to Mitchell, "little or no formerly French-owned land has been redistributed" and was intended to be "converted into state farms" instead (p. 15).

[110] Mitchell, *Land Tenure and Rebellion*, 1967, p. 29.

[111] Mitchell, *Land Tenure and Rebellion*, 1967, p. 29.

[112] Mitchell, *Land Tenure and Rebellion*, 1967, p. 29.

tling because "asymmetry between rise and decline from a customary position could result in increasing discontent from *any* change in position. This is consistent with the notion that social and economic change *per se* whether upward or downward is generally destabilizing."[113] U.S. policymakers believed that, if the GVN improved the condition of the peasants with a land-reform program, it would undermine the appeal of the Viet Cong and enhance its own influence. However, in Mitchell's view, land redistribution would be an unwise policy because of the relationship between land tenure, which would bring a change in economic conditions, and rebellion. He wrote, "In Vietnam, the VC's considerable aptitude in political matters makes it not unlikely that the vacuum of authority wrought by redistribution will be filled by the rebels, rather than by the GVN."[114] According to Mitchell, the relationship between inequality and rebellion had many historical precedents, such as the English Civil War and the French Revolution.[115]

In a telephone interview with Hedrick Smith of *The New York Times,* Mitchell suggested that "large landowners might help provide a cohesive political and social system on the local level, and that when their authority is destroyed, the Vietcong can move into the vacuum."[116] Mitchell told Smith that he was not "arguing for or against land reform, but simply discussing its actual impact in Vietnam during war and civil turmoil." He added, "Quite possibly, when you redistribute land, you change the structure of authority, you eliminate the kinds of people who have been running things up till then, and essentially you create chaos" unless the government could "step in and provide the kinds of services that landlords provide." Otherwise, "you're in trouble," because a vacuum would be created, and this would be "ideal for the Vietcong because they've got an organization to fill the vacuum."

Mitchell's study, with its counterintuitive conclusion, was controversial inside RAND. Tony Russo recalled that Gus Shubert thought it was nonsense and asked him to write a rebuttal, telling him, "Go out there and see if you can refute that study."[117] Russo would later say that Mitchell was a member of what he called "the

---

[113] Mitchell, *Land Tenure and Rebellion*, 1967, pp. 27–28.

[114] Mitchell, *Land Tenure and Rebellion*, 1967, p. 29.

[115] Mitchell cited Alexis de Tocqueville, who wrote in *L'Ancien Regime* that "It is not always by going from bad to worse that a society falls into revolution. It happens most often that a people, which has supported without complaint, as if they were not felt, the most oppressive laws, violently throws them off as soon as its weight is lightened. . . . The evil, which was suffered patiently as inevitable, seems unendurable as soon as the idea of escaping from it is conceived" (see p. 23). In *Inequality and Insurgency*, Mitchell said that, according to de Tocqueville, "The centers of revolution . . . were the very districts in which social reform and progress had been most visible, whereas resistance to the revolution sprang up in areas where the old order had been most completely retained" (see p. 1).

[116] Hedrick Smith, *The New York Times,* "Study Challenges Vietnam Reform: Rand Analyst Says Dividing of Estates May Aid Foe," October 15, 1967.

[117] Author interview with Tony Russo, 2003 and 2004.

Chicago boys" due to their association with the University of Chicago, which included Charlie Wolf—now promoted to head of the Economics Department—and Albert Wohlstetter. Mitchell's paper, he said, indicated "the correlation between provincial control and land tenure," and "purported to show that the poor were the ones who supported the Americans' war rather than the richer peasants."[118] According to Russo, Mitchell was saying that "the richer peasants were the ones who resisted because their value capabilities were farther away from their value expectations than the poor," but he went "way out into left field to make these inferences."[119] Russo said that it was "the worst kind of culture shock" for him to listen to this "nonsense" when he returned to Santa Monica. He added, "When you've been to Vietnam, you know damn well that it's the poor who are the ones who suffer more and who fight harder, who have nothing to lose."[120]

While Shubert was critical of Mitchell's study, Charlie Wolf and Wohlstetter supported him. According to Russo, Wohlstetter would make comments like, "From Tocqueville to Mitchell"—a reference to Mitchell's citation of Tocqueville's analysis of the French peasantry's behavior during the Revolution in *L'Ancien Regime*.

When Russo wrote his rebuttal of the Mitchell report, he was back at work in the Economics Department in Santa Monica. Russo left Vietnam in January 1968 and when he got home, Gus Shubert, who had been assigned by Harry Rowen to manage RAND's diversification into domestic issues, arranged for a position for Russo in this department. In retrospect, Russo said that he should have studied Charlie Wolf more before he joined Economics. At the time, he liked the idea of working there because he saw Economics as a "star department"—a place where he could do work that produced important findings. But Wolf turned out to be a man with whom Russo found difficult to get along because of conflicting political views.[121] Furthermore, when Russo critiqued Mitchell's work, Wolf became unhappy. Russo said that Wolf suppressed his work and refused to publish it. The paper finally appeared in December 1968.[122]

At the end of that year, Wolf terminated Russo's employment at RAND. Although Wolf mentioned a budget crunch and told him, "This is not politics or anything, this has nothing to do with political difference," Russo believed that the firing was political, because he was the only one who "took the crunch" despite the fact that in his

---

[118] Author interview with Tony Russo, 2003 and 2004.

[119] Author interview with Tony Russo, 2003 and 2004.

[120] Author interview with Tony Russo, 2003 and 2004.

[121] Author interview with Tony Russo, 2003 and 2004.

[122] Anthony J. Russo, "Economic and Social Correlates of Government Control in South Vietnam, Santa Monica, Calif.: RAND Corporation, D-18288-ARPA, December 1968.

view, he had done good work at RAND. By then, Russo said, he had become "one hundred percent radicalized"—not by his firing—"but by all the lies" he had seen, and "by the longest war costing 1,000 dollars a second, [which was] based on lies." He was "very cynical about everything," he said, and thought that Wolf was really doing him a favor, "because working for RAND is not good for one's reputation" as far as he was concerned.[123]

The circumstances of Russo's firing were confirmed by Dan Ellsberg, who said that he tried—unsuccessfully—to get Wolf to rescind the firing, telling Wolf that "it was a mistake and a real loss for the department." Wolf "insisted that the decision was only for budgetary reasons," but Ellsberg noticed that Russo "seemed the only one affected." Ellsberg believed that Wolf, the "hawkish" department chairman, did not like Russo's works on herbicides and land tenure, and his exposure in a classified study of "the widespread practice of beatings and torture of VC prisoners by ARVN captors and jailers, often with American advisers observing."[124] According to Ellsberg, others at RAND at the time worried about the Air Force's reaction to Russo's studies.

By the time he wrote his critique of Mitchell, Russo had developed a deep sympathy for the insurgents, whom he viewed as poor peasants fighting injustice. In his paper, he said that he undertook the work because he felt "that the root cause of the war . . . had been widely ignored and misunderstood" by Americans.[125] The fact that Mitchell's study—with its results, which Russo found "incredulous"—received any acceptance at all reflected "the rather extreme lack of understanding that . . . Americans have with regard to, not only Vietnam, but also, all other Third World revolutions."[126] Russo explained that his "feelings and impressions" had evolved over a period of 18 months in South Vietnam and admitted that he had developed some "very strong impressions and some heavy biases," because "one cannot stay uninvolved" and "detachment becomes an abstract idea."[127] In fact, there had been times when he wondered whether "there could be such a thing as a value-free study of the Vietnam situation,"[128] which was an "issue highly charged with passions and emotion in all its aspects."[129]

When he undertook the study, he "felt rather strongly, that the war in Vietnam was very much a class war" and that—communist ambitions and ideology aside—"the forces which sustained hostilities and increasing levels of violence came directly as a

---

[123]Author interview with Tony Russo, 2003 and 2004.

[124]Ellsberg, *Secrets*, 2002, p. 291.

[125]Russo, "Economic and Social Correlates," 1968, p. 1.

[126]Russo, "Economic and Social Correlates," 1968, p. 1a.

[127]Russo, "Economic and Social Correlates," 1968, p. 1.

[128]Russo, "Economic and Social Correlates," 1968, p. 1.

[129]Russo, "Economic and Social Correlates," 1968, p. 1.

result of the enormous economic and social cleavages within Vietnamese society."[130] The GVN, in his view, consisted of people "who were richer, from urban backgrounds, had formal educations, and were highly influenced by the past French colonial presence."[131] The Viet Cong, on the other hand, "were peasants, had a strong Vietnamese identity, and had inherited the legacy of the Viet Minh."[132] However, he tried to be "objective and dispassionate" in his analysis, and he believed that his paper showed a high degree of objectivity.[133] In a retrospective interview, Russo would say that he could not "criticize the Mitchell study too much." To him, what Mitchell did "was very, very poor reasoning . . . [and] the parameters were not the correct ones."[134]

Russo's findings differed markedly from those of Mitchell, and he found nothing to support the conclusion that poorer areas were likely to provide more support for the GVN. Mitchell arrived at this finding by implicitly equating "inequality and poverty (or relatively low income)."[135] But when Russo used mean household income, he found that a different picture emerged: that income level and, hence, welfare, was positively correlated with GVN control. Mitchell assumed that the poorer peasants lived in areas in which inequality in land distribution was high; however, this was not true, because this inequality was relative. In his own analysis, Russo found, for example, that a province such as Quang Tri in the central region, which had low inequality in land tenure, could be poorer than a province such as An Giang in the more prosperous Mekong Delta, which had relatively high inequality in land tenure. In Central Vietnam, within-province variations in farm sizes were small, but the mean farm size was also very small—in short, "everyone is fairly equitably poor."[136] On the contrary, in the southern region, within-province variation in farm sizes was relatively greater, but the mean farm size was larger, and since the soil was more fertile, the rice yields were roughly twice what they were in Central Vietnam. In the central region, the 1964 mean household income for rural residents was around 15,000 Vietnamese piasters, whereas in the richer southern region it was around 25,000 piasters—a difference of 67 percent. It was not surprising, therefore, that Mitchell found "a positive correlation between his measure of [land distribution] inequality and GVN control, because within-province inequality is higher where the peasant is generally better off."[137] Russo's study, then, could explain why the Viet Cong were stronger in a province such as Quang Tri, with

---

[130] Russo, "Economic and Social Correlates," 1968, p. 1a.

[131] Russo, "Economic and Social Correlates," 1968, p. 1a.

[132] Russo, "Economic and Social Correlates," 1968, p. 1.

[133] Russo, "Economic and Social Correlates," 1968, p. 1.

[134] Author interview with Tony Russo, 2003 and 2004.

[135] Russo, "Economic and Social Correlates," 1968, p. 3.

[136] Russo, "Economic and Social Correlates," 1968, p. 43.

[137] Russo, "Economic and Social Correlates," 1968, p. 43.

low inequality in land tenure but greater poverty, whereas the GVN was stronger in a province such as An Giang, with greater inequality of land tenure but with higher income. In short, mean household income variables offered a more powerful explanation of government support, and "in areas where income is relatively high, GVN control is relatively strong."[138]

Russo also refuted Mitchell's conclusion that poorer peasants tended to be docile and had low aspirations. This was "misleading if we consider the poor peasant in an isolated way, or if we speak of him in a sense which portrays him as being somehow entrenched in a 'steady-state' mode of docile existence."[139] In a Third World revolution, propaganda and agitation by revolutionaries could change the dynamics of the situation, because the goal of revolutionaries was precisely to "change aspirations" among the poor "in order to recruit support for the cause of change."[140] In situations in which there was no revolutionary agitation, or in which it had not grown significantly, or in which the government could compete with the revolutionaries in attracting the support of the poor, aspirations were influenced more by the peasants' position on the standard-of-living scale. In such situations, peasants were likely to prefer the status quo. In situations in which poor peasants had high aspirations, the change was likely to have been caused by "agit/prop activity."[141] In such cases, the poor peasants were likely to believe that their aspirations would be realized by supporting and cooperating with the revolutionaries. In Vietnam, it was well known that the Viet Cong focused on the poor for support, whereas the GVN could not match the insurgents in access or appeal.[142]

Russo would later recall that, when Mitchell published his paper in the journal *World Politics* at Princeton University, it "set off fireworks throughout the literature."[143] People who saw it were in disbelief. Subsequently, about seven studies were performed to check Mitchell's analysis. Russo's work, which he said was suppressed by Charlie Wolf, later appeared in the book *Anger, Violence and Politics*, edited by Ted Robert Gurr, a professor at Johns Hopkins and an expert in this area, and the husband-and-

---

[138] Russo, "Economic and Social Correlates," 1968, p. 2.

[139] Russo, "Economic and Social Correlates," 1968, p. 44.

[140] Russo, "Economic and Social Correlates," 1968, p. 44.

[141] Russo, "Economic and Social Correlates," 1968, p. 46.

[142] Another RAND analyst, Paul T. Schultz, wrote a critique of Mitchell in "Modeling of Complex Political Systems: Mitchell's Government Control Model for Vietnam," Santa Monica, Calif.: RAND Corporation, D-18923-ARPA/AGILE, June 1969. In Schultz's view, Mitchell's study "is marred by statistical defects, and moreover, does not support the policy implications attributed to it." He found that others at RAND were also "disturbed by the inappropriate application of statistical tools of analysis to complex, poorly-understood, behavioral systems."

[143] Author interview with Tony Russo, 2003 and 2004. Mitchell's paper appeared under the title of "Inequality and Insurgency: A Statistical Study of South Vietnam," *World Politics*, Vol. 20, No. 3 (April, 1968, pp. 421–438).

wife team of Ivo and Rosalind Feierabend.[144] The book was a five-volume compilation of the authoritative papers in the subfield of political violence and was "supposedly the leading work" in this area.[145] Russo was very proud to be included in the book and felt vindicated. He said that "years after that, if you look at the literature you'll find all kinds of commentaries" on his work.[146] Then, in 1974, Jack Nagel, the author of an article in *World Politics* that reviewed four critiques of Mitchell's study, considered Russo's critique "the clearest and most powerful revision of Mitchell."[147] Ted Robert Gurr used Russo's study for years in his graduate seminars.

Nevertheless, Mitchell's work had a great influence on American policymakers. Congressmen and others in the U.S. government interpreted Mitchell's work as indicating that bringing prosperity to the peasants and performing land reform would destabilize the situation and erode GVN control.[148] In early 1967, high-level Washington officials told Robert L. Sansom, a Rhodes Scholar performing research for his doctoral dissertation at Oxford University on the economics of the Vietnamese insurgency, that a RAND study "had found that land reform was not an important source of Viet Cong support."[149] According to Sansom, Mitchell's results implying that "the Viet Cong had made their inroads in owner-farmed rather than tenant-farmed areas," and the corollary flowing from his study that "land tenure issues were not important grievances, or at least that such grievances had not served as the basis for the support gained by the Viet Cong in the areas they controlled" were immediately accepted by high-level U.S. officials in Saigon and Washington.[150] To him, the reaction typified American officials' "readiness to accept academic and other concoctions as substitutes for reforms in Vietnam."[151]

On close examination of Mitchell's work, Sansom concluded that his methodology was flawed and his understanding of the conditions in Vietnam poor, as evidenced

---

[144] Ivo K. Feierabend, Rosalind L. Feierabend [and] Ted Robert Gurr, *Anger, Violence, and Politics: Theories and Research*, Englewood Cliffs, N.J.: Prentice-Hall, 1972.

[145] Author interview with Tony Russo, 2003 and 2004.

[146] Author interview with Tony Russo, 2003 and 2004.

[147] Jack Nagel, "Inequality and Discontent: A Nonlinear Hypothesis," *World Politics*, Vol. 26, No. 4 (July, 1974), pp. 453–472. Nagel concluded that, ". . . stability in the long run is most likely to be ensured by the policy least likely to preserve order in the short run—radical, egalitarian land redistribution. See p. 471.

[148] See Schultz, "Modeling of Complex Political Systems," 1969, p.ii.

[149] Robert L. Sansom, *The Economics of Insurgency in the Mekong Delta of Vietnam*, Cambridge, Mass.: MIT Press, 1970, p. 230. Sansom was able to read this report when it was published in June 1967 as an unclassified document.

[150] Sansom, *The Economics of Insurgency,* 1970, pp. 230–231.

[151] Sansom, *The Economics of Insurgency,* 1970, p. 230.

by his "specification of the independent variables employed."[152] Through Sansom's own field research in Vietnam, he found that it was the land redistribution implemented by the Viet Minh and the Viet Cong that accounted for disparities in land ownership between GVN- and non-GVN-controlled areas. Therefore "properly specified, Mitchell's model would explain the inequality of distribution by the extent of Viet Cong as opposed to GVN control, not the other way around."[153] Sansom compared Mitchell's mistake "to that of one who, after observing that all who had the flu had been visited by doctors, concluded that the doctors caused the flu."[154] In Sansom's view, "The fact that land was more inequitably distributed in GVN than in Viet Cong areas did not mean that the Viet Cong gained control in areas of equitable land distribution but that, in the areas they controlled, the Viet Minh and the Viet Cong, through their land reform programs, caused the land to be more equitably distributed."[155] Sansom wrote that, in view of its shortcomings, Mitchell's analysis "must be rejected."[156]

Sansom suggested some possible explanations for the U.S. reluctance to recognize the importance of land reform and "their readiness to accept . . . doubtful analytical substitutes," such as that of Mitchell.[157] The basic reason was that "U.S. officials did not believe that land-based grievances were important." Also, there was opposition among the political section of the U.S. Embassy staff in Saigon out of concern that a land reform would undermine the Vietnamese government and cause it to fall, because so many members of the GVN and of the Constituent Assembly were landowners. This was why, after pressuring President Diem to carry out land reforms in 1955 and later, the United States in the 1960s did not make land reform a central part of its policy in Vietnam.

Another reason Sansom offered was that Americans, coming from a "capital-intensive economy," could not grasp the significance of land in a traditional economy

---

[152] Sansom, *The Economics of Insurgency,* 1970, p. 231. According to Sansom, even if Mitchell had overcome the problems stemming from his poor knowledge of Vietnam, "his model as specified could not possibly have shown what he purports to have demonstrated." Mitchell's model "completely ignores what is known in econometrics as the identification problem. He assumes that causation in his equation runs from his independent variables to the dependent variable of GVN control." Sansom's findings showed the reverse, "That is Viet Cong presence, and before that Viet Minh presence, led to institutional changes that redistributed land." Sansom also pointed out that "Mitchell's effort to argue that in Vietnam the conditions of revolution are analogous to those in eighteenth-century France or elsewhere, where the middle class rather than the peasant class revolted, is unconvincing. He fails to establish that insurgent revolutions are similar to those of Western Europe, nor does he establish that the predominantly rural societies of Asia resemble those of Western Europe in the eighteenth or nineteenth centuries, where the revolutions were urban led."

[153] Sansom, *The Economics of Insurgency,* 1970, p. 232.

[154] Sansom, *The Economics of Insurgency,* 1970, p. 232.

[155] Sansom, *The Economics of Insurgency,* 1970, p. 232.

[156] Sansom, *The Economics of Insurgency,* 1970, p. 232.

[157] Sansom, *The Economics of Insurgency,* 1970, p. 233.

and society that were based on rice cultivation.[158] In Vietnam, land ownership meant more than having a piece of property under one's own name; it meant the ability to survive by one's own work, the possibility of escaping from a life of servitude to the landlord, and therefore the chance to achieve dignity. Unless the Vietnamese peasant could achieve his aspiration for survival and dignity, he could not aspire to a free society, a democracy, or a constitution. In the struggle in Vietnam, "the Americans offered the peasant a constitution; the Viet Cong offered him his land and with it the right to survive."[159] The reason Americans showed a lack of understanding of the role of land in Vietnam was that few stayed in Vietnam longer than the usual twelve-month tour or worked in the rural areas without delving into the situation. As one moved higher in the American bureaucracy in Saigon and in Washington, the land issues were rarely considered.

Another RAND study that was circulated in early 1967 at the U.S. Mission in Saigon and that received widespread attention, according to Sansom, was Charlie Wolf's "Insurgency and Counterinsurgency: New Myths and Old Realities."[160] According to Wolf, when his paper was circulated internally at RAND in the early 1960s, he got a compliment from Frank Collbohm. After reading it, the RAND president called him and said, "Sounds right . . . I hadn't thought of it this way. Maybe you should develop it further." Wolf took this as "high praise" from the RAND president, who was known as a man of few words.[161]

---

[158] Sansom, *The Economics of Insurgency,* 1970, p. 234.

[159] Sansom, *The Economics of Insurgency,* 1970, p. 234. Sansom wrote that the appeal of this land reform "was especially strong from 1960 until late 1964 when the Viet Cong enjoyed the accelerating success in the rural areas that gave credence to their claims to govern South Vietnam. The peasants were excited about the prospect of owning their own land; they were told they would become owners if the Viet Cong succeeded, and, by all appearances, through late 1964 the Viet Cong were succeeding." In Sansom's estimation, 8 million of the Delta's 10 million people received economic benefits from Viet Cong land reform measures. "Much of the rural support for Viet Cong policies can be attributed to the direct economic benefits or the promise of potential long-run gains that Viet Cong success offered. In contrast, the tenant had little incentive to support the Vietnamese government's policies because of the GVN's complicity with the landlord." According to him, "Whatever path self-interest forced the farmer to choose, Viet Cong land redistribution and, of broader significance, the Viet Cong's role as a rent depressant were clear factors in the farmer's favor."

[160] Wolf's study appeared in the *Yale Review,* Vol. LVI, Winter 1967. Copies of this article were circulated at the U.S. Mission in Saigon. In 1970, Wolf also published his work as a monograph with Nathan Leites as co-author and with the title of *Rebellion and Authority.* The original paper written by Charles Wolf was *Insurgency and Counterinsurgency: New Myths and Old Realities,* Santa Monica, Calif.: RAND P-3132-1, July 1965. Wolf would later summarize the gist of his paper as saying that "the 'new myth'—the 'hearts and minds' explanation for the ripening setbacks in Vietnam's resistance to the Vietcong—was a less robust explanation for shifting loyalties than the ruthless effectiveness of the Vietcong's dispensation of penalties and rewards to motivate compliant behavior—the "old reality." Charles Wolf, Jr., in "Frank: Few Words, Strong Character," in Digby, ed., "Early Personalities," 2001.

[161] Wolf, "Frank: Few Words, Strong Character," 2001.

Wolf's paper contained the kind of "counterintuitive" conclusions that Russo thought Wolfe often reached and with which Russo disagreed. The paper essentially assumed that, like Westerners, the populace in underdeveloped countries going through an insurgency would weigh the costs and benefits of their behavior and action and make a rational choice. It did not take into consideration the issues of values, history, and culture that might influence this choice. Because of this assumption, Wolf proposed that the established government institutes military, economic, and social programs to reward and punish the populace in order to induce the behavior and action it wants to promote and discourage the behavior and action that would benefit the insurgents.

Wolf argued that, in a transitional society, grievances and animosities against the government were too ingrained to be altered in the short run; therefore, the main thrust of counterinsurgency should be to induce the population to change their behavior and action rather than try to influence their loyalties and attitudes. This was the case, because, contrary to the then–currently accepted doctrine on insurgency, popular support was central neither for the insurgency nor for the government. In Wolf's view, "popular attitudes and popular support" did not play "the decisive role in enabling insurgent movements to get started, gain momentum, and erupt in 'liberation war'"; therefore, to successfully combat an insurgency, a government would not have to make winning popular support a central requisite of its efforts.[162] Indeed, because of lingering "discontent and grievance" among the population of a transitional society, a counterinsurgency program that emphasized winning popular support would have little chance of succeeding.[163]

The way to attack the insurgency was not to view it as a movement that was built on or expanded from popular support—or, as Wolf put it, as "an inscrutable and unmanageable force grounded in the mystique of a popular mass movement"[164]— but as a coherent operating system that took inputs from the local environment (such as food, recruits, and information) through coercion or persuasion, or from foreign sources (cadres, organization, materiel, and funds) and produced the outputs characteristic of an insurgency. *Counterinsurgency* could be divided into two parts: The first part would be "to raise the costs and reduce the availability of the inputs that the system requires," and the second part would be "to curtail the outputs of the system by interfering with the process by which inputs are converted into outputs, and by directly blocking or destroying the outputs."[165]

---

[162] Wolf, "Insurgency and Counterinsurgency," *Yale Review*, pp. 225–226. See also Wolf, *Insurgency and Counterinsurgency*, 1965, p. 1

[163] Wolf, *Insurgency and Counterinsurgency*, 1965, p. 9.

[164] Wolf, *Insurgency and Counterinsurgency*, 1965, p. 25.

[165] Wolf, *Insurgency and Counterinsurgency*, 1965, p. 11.

Operationally—in view of the above conclusions—Wolf proposed an alternative approach to counterinsurgency that would use military measures as the principal means to directly meet and curtail "the system's outputs," as well as economic, social, and political programs "to impede the supply of inputs to the system."[166] However, these latter nonmilitary policies would have to be selective to avoid facilitating guerrilla operations by making the inputs more readily available to the insurgents—for example, "policies that would increase rural income by raising food prices, or projects that would increase agricultural productivity through distribution of fertilizer or livestock, may be of negative value in an on-going insurgency."[167] In all programs, "the primary consideration should be whether the proposed measure is likely to increase the cost and difficulties of insurgent operations and help to disrupt the insurgent organization rather than whether it wins popular loyalty and support, or whether it contributes to a more productive, efficient or equitable use of resources."[168]

Some countermeasures Wolf suggested would include buying up rural food supplies to deny them to the insurgents; reducing the supply of recruits by improving the flow of information to the government so that guerrilla units would be more effectively harassed and so that the prospect of service in the insurgency would be rendered less attractive; making defection a more attractive option; buying up weapons to reduce the firepower of the insurgents; providing cash incentives to the population to obtain better intelligence and treating with severity those who had informed on government forces and units while providing security to those individuals and villages that gave useful information on the insurgents; tightening the discipline of the government's military forces and eliminating wanton abuses "so that such harshness as [is] meted out by government forces is unambiguously recognized as a penalty deliberately imposed because of behavior by the populace that contributes to the insurgent movement."[169]

Finally, Wolf recommended economic and social improvement programs, such as the building of schools, dispensaries, roads, and other social services that would improve the government's ability to maintain surveillance and to control the flow of inputs to the insurgency over more-productive projects that would, for example, develop agriculture.[170] The choice would be based on "providing rewards for the kind of behavior

---

[166] Wolf, *Insurgency and Counterinsurgency*, 1965, p. 11.

[167] Wolf, *Insurgency and Counterinsurgency*, 1965, p. 12.

[168] Wolf, *Insurgency and Counterinsurgency*, 1965, p. 25.

[169] Wolf, *Insurgency and Counterinsurgency*, 1965, p. 21.

[170] These kinds of projects were already being carried out in Vietnam, but, according to George Tanham, who headed the Rural Affairs Program as associate director of the U.S. aid mission in 1964, the Viet Cong would destroy the schools and health centers, or sometimes "induct or subvert the teachers." He thought that the problem was that the United States was too focused on "building things" rather than on "training and motivating officials to serve honestly the people." Tanham's comments indicate, then, that—rather than occurring in a vacuum—the government's countermeasures usually provoked a reaction on the part of the insurgents and that

the government is trying to promote and, by withholding benefits and projects, providing penalties for the kind of behavior that the government is trying to discourage."[171] The selection of projects would also be based on their potential for restricting "the flow of inputs to the insurgency." With regard to the outside source of input—North Vietnam—since attempting to seal the long, contiguous border with South Vietnam would be operationally difficult and bombing carried other problems of an operational or political nature, Wolf suggested sabotaging North Vietnam with counterfeit money, fake ration and identity cards, and leaflets and newspapers disseminating rumors or hints that some officials were conspiring against others.

Interest in Wolf's paper among U.S. government officials, as well as Sansom's belief that RAND was exerting influence on U.S. policy both among Washington decisionmakers and through former employees now occupying high-level government positions, led Sansom to conclude that Wolf's "'revisionist' attack on the accepted doctrine of insurgent movements" deserved attention, although Wolf had presented "no evidence" to support his view.[172] Policymakers, whether they agreed or disagreed with Wolf, carefully studied his paper, and his view of insurgency as an operating system taking in inputs and converting them into outputs was echoed by such officials at Douglas Pike at JUSPAO, who believed that organization was "the essence" of the Viet Cong.[173] It was also reflected in the comments often expressed by Americans in Vietnam who believed that defeating the insurgency was a matter of rooting out the Viet Cong infrastructure. To Sansom, it was "wishful thinking" to believe that the Viet Cong movement—"to which peasants have generously made even the most extreme sacrifices"—was in a major sense "merely an organization or communications accomplishment."[174] In Sansom's own view, important as organization was to the Viet Cong's successes, it could not have gotten the Viet Cong the support they gained in the Delta, where he focused his research, "without the major economic, political, and social grievances the movement sought to and actually did ameliorate."[175] The Viet Cong movement itself vindicated "the conventional view that a successful insurgency can be and probably usually is a grievance-based movement. The 'new myths' of organization and so on, cannot obscure the 'old realities' of the Delta economy that served

---

the bedrock problem for counterinsurgency in Vietnam remained the absence of an efficient and noncorrupt government.

[171] Wolf, *Insurgency and Counterinsurgency*, 1965, p. 24. Charlie Zwick and Chuck Cooper et al. had earlier recommended limiting economic and social programs to government-controlled areas as a way to reward people living there and withholding them from Viet Cong–controlled areas as a penalty.

[172] Sansom, *The Economics of Insurgency*, 1970, p. 242.

[173] Sansom, *The Economics of Insurgency*, 1970, p. 242.

[174] Sansom, *The Economics of Insurgency*, 1970, p. 243.

[175] Sansom, *The Economics of Insurgency*, 1970, p. 243.

as the basis for the success of the Viet Cong movement."[176] His own evidence, in short, clearly supported the so-called accepted doctrine.[177]

Sansom also opposed the revisionist view of economic and social improvement programs as tools to promote the kind of population behavior favored by the government, as well as Wolf's suggestion that projects providing social services, such as schools, dispensaries, and roads, may be more effective than those promoting agricultural development, for example. From his own research, Sansom concluded that "this view of aid is untenable."[178] According to him, the counterinsurgent policy should be to give aid to people living in the zones controlled by the insurgents, because, "to the extent that grievances are the source of discontent, and the insurgents gain support by appealing to these grievances, then policies to raise the incomes of the poor who are caught in the vicious circle of indebtedness and landlord control will tend to ameliorate the grievances and lessen insurgent support."[179] Therefore, the government should allow anything that could help improve the living conditions of the peasants—such as fertilizers, motor pumps, tractors, and land reform—to be pushed into Viet Cong zones by market forces that operated regardless of security considerations.

♧ ♧ ♧

The year 1967, when the Mitchell and Wolf studies appeared, saw one of the biggest changes in the prosecution of the war. On August 9, 1967, Senator John C. Stennis, Chairman of the Armed Services Committee, opened hearings on the air war against North Vietnam. Stennis, a strong supporter of the armed forces, belonged to the group of powerful senators who were arguing that restraints imposed by civilian leaders on the military were causing the United States to lose the war. The pressure prompted President Johnson to intensify the air campaign and expand it to more and more-sensitive targets. A few days after the hearings began, planes hit the Paul Doumer Bridge, inside Hanoi itself for the first time, and attacked inside the zone near the Chinese border that had been kept off-limits. *The New York Times* warned that the dikes could be targeted next, to inundate the rice paddies and flood the civilian population. "There was a sense in those weeks of August that all-out war was imminent."[180] It was in this atmosphere that Defense Secretary McNamara was called to testify.

McNamara appeared on August 25, after Stennis had called the senior military commanders—who opposed Johnson's and McNamara's restraints—to testify.

---

[176] Sansom, *The Economics of Insurgency*, 1970, p. 245.

[177] Sansom, *The Economics of Insurgency*, 1970, p. 242.

[178] Sansom, *The Economics of Insurgency*, 1970, p. 244.

[179] Sansom, *The Economics of Insurgency*, 1970, p. 244.

[180] Shapley, *Promise and Power*, 1993, p. 428.

The hearing would be a "kangaroo court."[181] McNamara had kept his doubts and misgivings about the war private. Now, under intense pressure, he decided to lay out his case to the American public. He argued against widening the air war against the North, which he declared had never been intended as a substitute for the ground war in the South. According to McNamara, the United States was dropping almost as many bombs over the North as it had during World War II in Europe. Yet the enemy needed such a low volume of supplies to sustain the war in the South that a few trucks could meet his requirements. In McNamara's view, the bombing had damaged and was continuing to hurt North Vietnam's capability to sustain the war, but there was no basis "to believe that any bombing campaign, short of one which had population as its target, would by itself force Ho Chi Minh's regime into submission."[182] Showing that restraint had spared only trivial targets, he spent a great deal of time going over those targets on the list that had not been hit, such as a plant that produced 30 tires a day and a vehicle repair shop that was smaller than an American garage. Finally, McNamara opposed widening the bombing to include the ports, because the risks of hitting Soviet and other foreign ships were high and because the North needed very little incoming fuel to continue the war.

At the hearing, when pressed, McNamara maintained that the United States was winning the war. However, his testimony did imply that "the bombing had virtually no impact on the struggle in South Vietnam" and "that the North could fight on indefinitely and that escalating the bombing would be dangerous."[183] As some editorial writers noted with insight, McNamara's real message at the hearing was not to make a case against bombing more targets in North Vietnam but to gain support for more bombing halts and to move toward a negotiated settlement. His testimony infuriated President Johnson, and the tension between the two men intensified. When McNamara told Johnson bluntly that "no reasonable military means" would lead the administration to achieve its objective in Vietnam and that it should, therefore, seek negotiations with Hanoi, Johnson refused to accept his judgment.[184] According to McNamara, it became clear to both him and Johnson that, since neither he nor the president would change his position, "Something had to give."[185] It was time for McNamara to leave. Richard Moose would later say that after McNamara told Johnson that "he no longer believed that we could win the war within the parameters that we were going to fight

---

[181] Shapley, *Promise and Power*, 1993, p. 428.

[182] Shapley, *Promise and Power*, 1993, p. 429.

[183] Shapley, *Promise and Power*, 1993, p. 432.

[184] McNamara, *In Retrospect*, 1995, p. 313.

[185] McNamara, *In Retrospect*, 1995, p. 313

it," it became inappropriate for McNamara to stay on as Defense Secretary. From that moment on, the question was, "how does McNamara go?"[186]

If McNamara had resigned, Moose said, his departure would have been used by the peace movement as a vindication of their own stand—something that Johnson did not wish to happen. According to Moose, "McNamara never felt he was in a position to resign in protest to the war because he was so responsible for having encouraged the President to believe that he could win it, so the President had to find a way out for him."[187] Moose said that, "It took them a while to arrange that, and it was a very elegant ballet that went on, how they finally did it. It wasn't that the President forced him to leave, by any matter of means, it was how can he leave and not do any damage one way or the other. I think that was really the issue."[188] The arrangement was made in November, when Johnson appointed McNamara as president of the World Bank. McNamara would later say that, "To this day I don't know whether I resigned or was fired."[189]

To replace him, President Johnson appointed Clark Clifford, the quintessential insider and a leader of the country's political establishment. A consummate lawyer, with an office across the street from the White House, Clifford was the man whose advice politicians and business leaders often sought. Clifford had a sterling resume, having served as special counsel to President Harry Truman and as the leader of John F. Kennedy's transition team. He also had unequaled familiarity with the problems facing the country, and he had helped determine the policies for the reconstruction of Europe after World War II, and devise the legislation setting up the CIA and the Defense Department. He often played the part of Washington "wise man" in addressing crises that arose within the inner circle of government. This was the role that President Johnson wanted him to assume in dealing with the Vietnam problem as his new Secretary of Defense.

---

[186] Author interview with Richard Moose, 2003.

[187] Author interview with Richard Moose, 2003.

[188] Author interview with Richard Moose, 2003.

[189] Shapley, *Promise and Power*, 1993, p. 439. According to historian Arthur Schlesinger, Jr., McNamara did not know that his appointment as president of the World Bank was imminent and learned of his firing from the press (see Karnow, *Vietnam: A History*, 1983, p. 511).

The Mekong Delta and the Central Highlands

The Mekong Delta, the rice basket of South Vietnam, was the locus of what became an in-depth study of the insurgency in Dinh Tuong Province. Crisscrossed by streams, canals, marshes, and swamps, the Delta is a low-lying region with an average elevation below 50 feet. During the rainy season, which lasts from June to November, about 70 percent of the terrain is inundated, making the dry season the preferred time for offensive operations. Besides being the main rice-producing area, with over 5.4 million inhabitants, the delta was also the population center of South Vietnam. The Viet Cong and the GVN were evenly matched in the Delta: The insurgency had a total force of 30,000; the Saigon government had 35,000 when the project began in 1965.

According to David Elliott, the Dinh Tuong project manager, initially the study was directed at detecting vulnerabilities among the cadres so that the cadres could be persuaded to defect. He believed that RAND—or Leon Goure—sold it to MACV as a way to uncover a different and more cost-effective approach to dealing with the enemy. If Goure had told MACV that the project would show them how to fight the war better, the military would not have been interested, so instead it was presented as a way to devise a political strategy against the Viet Cong, "as opposed to the military strategy of attrition which aimed at killing them off."[1]

In June 1965, General Westmoreland requested that the project be undertaken to uncover the vulnerabilities of the Viet Cong to psychological warfare, as well as to determine the kinds of programs that should be formulated to exploit their weaknesses and ways to measure the effectiveness of such programs. Besides Westmoreland, General William E. DePuy, the operations chief for MACV, was also enthusiastic because he wanted an in-depth study that he hoped would yield information about the Viet Cong so that the military could fight them more effectively.[2] To conform to Westmoreland's interest, Leon Goure defined the project's objective as helping to improve

---

[1] Author interview with David Elliott, 2006.

[2] Author interview with Steve Hosmer, 2004 and 2005. At this time, according to Hosmer, General DePuy had not turned against counterinsurgency in favor of all-out conventional warfare against the enemy.

"the Psychological Warfare effort in that province."[3] Goure envisaged the project as an operation that would unfold in three stages. At the beginning, the focus would be on "uncovering vulnerabilities" among enemy military and civilian ranks.[4] Afterward, psychological themes and appeals would be developed by the GVN, with advice from American officials to target these vulnerabilities. Finally, the effectiveness of these operations would be measured through the interviews.

As the research evolved, however, Elliott shifted the focus and expanded the scope so that the study encompassed the insurgency's organization, strategy, tactics, reaction to pacification, and then the entire revolutionary movement itself.[5] As a first step in analyzing vulnerabilities among the cadres, Elliott sought to understand who the cadres were and how they related to one another within the organizational context of the insurgency. In this first phase, he concluded that the district-level cadres formed the key link between the top leadership and the rank-and-file at the bottom. Since it was not possible to go after the top leaders and since it was not as rewarding to go after the "small fry," he recommended targeting the mid-level cadres who represented a vulnerable link in the chain of leadership.[6]

Then, in order to understand the organizational context itself, he shifted his attention to the Viet Cong system to find out how the various links interacted with each other to create synergy and make the whole stronger than its individual parts. The focus, as with the cadres, was to identify the critical junctures that linked the top to the bottom and target them to weaken the system. The defect of this focus on organizational dynamics, Elliott would later say, was that it attributed the strength of the insurgency to its organization and did not address the larger social and political context of the Viet Cong movement itself.

When Elliott returned to Vietnam in 1971 to pursue the third phase of the project, he would shift his focus away from organization and individuals to these larger issues. He summarized the progression of his research as moving from "individual cadres, to organization, and to the movement itself," and said that the project began as a "practical task" but in order to perform that task, it became necessary to scrutinize the underlying assumptions.[7]

---

[3]   Leon Goure, "Summary Outline of the Dinh Tuong Project," no date (memorandum provided to the author by David Elliott; not available to the general public).

[4]   Goure, *Summary Outline of the Dinh Tuong Project*, no date. Emphasis in original.

[5]   David W. P. Elliott, *The Vietnamese War: Revolution and Social Change in the Mekong Delta, 1930–1975*, two volumes, Armonk, New York, and London, England: M. E. Sharpe, 2003. The book used materials from the Dinh Tuong interviews. Elliott wrote that he was thankful to RAND for having given him a great deal of freedom to research the communist revolution in the province.

[6]   Author interview with David Elliott, 2006.

[7]   Author interview with David Elliott, 2006.

The product of prep school and Yale, Elliott grew up in the intellectual atmosphere of Harvard, where his father was a prominent professor of political theory. While in graduate school majoring in political science with an area focus on Brazil, he volunteered for the Army, in which he became a sharpshooter. He was assigned to the Defense Language Institute in Monterey, California, to study Vietnamese and subsequently was sent to Vietnam with the Army Security Agency, or Signals Intelligence Branch. He lost his security clearance when he married a Vietnamese national,[8] and MACV assigned him to its Translation Section. He became familiar with the Viet Cong movement as a result of overseeing teams of Vietnamese translating reams of captured enemy documents. His academic credentials, his fluency in Vietnamese, and his knowledge of the insurgency made him an ideal candidate to head the project when his military service ended in 1965. According to Tony Russo, Elliott's name came up when he was flying to Saigon with Chuck Thomson to begin work under Leon Goure, and recalled that Thomson talked a lot about Elliott, telling Russo that Elliott was a "manner-born fellow" and "very bright."[9]

Elliott at first commuted to My Tho, the provincial capital, from Saigon, traveling on frequently mined Highway 4, the only major route linking the capital to the Delta. Since the commute was dangerous, his wife, who was working as an interviewer for Goure's project, joined him in My Tho. At the time Elliott began his work for RAND, he was in favor of the U.S. involvement but had seen enough in Vietnam to realize that the American strategy was not working. He accepted the RAND job because, as a political scientist, he wanted to understand the Vietnamese communist revolution that began in August 1945 (when the Viet Minh came to power and declared independence from the French) and the Viet Cong movement better, and also because he thought he could make a positive contribution to the U.S. efforts. My Tho, a quiet but nondescript city, offered no cultural attractions and few entertainment opportunities. Elliott and his wife rented a two-story house, built with more sand than cement, with walls stained by tropical dampness and painted a lurid blue. The house adjoined two other houses, so there were no side windows. The gloomy interior was illuminated by long fluorescent tubes emitting a milky light. Water had to be pumped by hand into a tank on top of the roof for use on the second floor. An irascible cook prepared barely edible meals on a kerosene stove and made feeble attempts at cleaning the place.

As the only interracial couple in town, Elliott and his wife attracted curiosity. Prying eyes followed them if they ventured out together into the streets. Elliott, however, was totally absorbed in his research and took his physical surroundings in stride, accepting the living conditions as a small price to pay for obtaining a close look at the insurgency. With high-level backing, he was able to secure access to defectors and prisoners quickly and to get his project under way. Since he spoke Vietnamese fluently, he

---

8   It should be disclosed that "a Vietnamese national" refers to the author of this work.

9   Author interview with Tony Russo, 2003 and 2004.

Interviewer Cau (left, second row), David Elliott, and interviewer Phuoc (on right).

hired interviewers who normally would have been screened out for lack of English fluency and inability to communicate with the project leader, and thus was able to open the field to people of high caliber who might have been overlooked otherwise. Of the three interviewers, only one spoke a little bit of English. But they possessed superior knowledge of the communist movement, of the South Vietnamese countryside, and of the GVN. David Elliott credited them for the quality of the Dinh Tuong interviews. He said that it was they who added the most value to the project. "They saw the issues emerging and pursued them," he would recall later.[10]

Dinh Xuan Cau was a writer, journalist, and political activist who had been thrown in jail twice. During the war against the French, he opposed the Viet Minh and was incarcerated in a reeducation camp for noncommunist intellectuals. Later, his political opposition to President Diem landed him in jail once more. Also a journalist, Vuong Van Bach was the brother of Colonel Vuong Van Dong, who led the abortive 1960 coup d'etat against President Diem. As the coup was unfolding, Diem telephoned his brother from the presidential palace. Bach happened to pick up the receiver, and it was he who told Diem to surrender because he was surrounded. After the coup failed, Bach was jailed by Diem and then released by the military junta that overthrew him. Unlike Cau and Bach, who were refugees from North Vietnam, Nguyen Huu Phuoc was a native southerner. As a landowner, he had deep roots in the countryside and understood rural conditions well. A colonel in the ARVN and a Catholic, he was an ardent supporter of President Diem, who appointed him deputy mayor for the security of Saigon. After Diem was toppled, Phuoc was thrown in prison by the military junta. Despite the interviewers' opposing political

---

[10] Author interview with David Elliott, 2006.

Cau (on right) and Phuoc (on left) with pacification cadres of the GVN.

beliefs, all came from a genteel background, and civility reigned among them. The quality of the interviews, Elliott said, reflects the interviewers' training as journalist and writer, their knowledge of the South Vietnamese countryside and its people, and their desire to understand the communist movement so that they could fight it better.

Elliott sometimes conducted the interviews himself. His wife, who did an occasional interview, spent most of her time translating the Vietnamese interview transcripts into English. The special circumstances of the project, in Elliott's view, gave the data a higher level of reliability than those interviews conducted for the countrywide Viet Cong Motivation and Morale Project.

Elliott rented a house in My Tho for his team of interviewers, and they would spend the week there. Sometimes, they would bring defectors from the *Chieu Hoi* center to the house for interviews. Generally, each respondent was interviewed for about one week and, in that time, contradictions would likely surface and be noted. The prolonged stay in the province by Elliott and his team made them experts of Dinh Tuong, and their in-depth knowledge of the local situation alerted them to falsehoods, contradictions, and exaggerations in the interviews. As an added level of caution, Elliott employed a defector with four years' experience in the insurgency to go over all the transcripts. The man was quick to spot false information.[11] A very knowledgeable American correspondent

---

[11] Sy Deitchman opined that, in the study, "in a Mekong Delta province . . . to piece together the interlocking patterns of VC political and military activity in an area straddling one of their main supply routes, the effects of bias were easier to fathom and rectify," because "there were other data in the records of the war and the military

Interviewer Bach (on right) in front of RAND office in My Tho.

who read the Dinh Tuong interviews said he was "impressed by the skill and fairness of the interviewers"[12] and found the interviews "totally absorbing" and revealing about "Vietnamese and Viet Cong daily life."[13] To him, this was "the real thing."[14] After reading interview after interview, he concluded that the materials shed light finally on an enemy who had "remained in the shadows" despite years of U.S. efforts to fight them,

---

operational system, and the memories of some of that system's members, against which to check." Deitchman, *The Best-Laid Schemes*, 1976, pp. 375–376.

[12] David Halberstam, "Voices of the VietCong" *Harper's Magazine*, January 24, 1968, p. i. Since the project was classified, Halberstam did not identify the province by name, or RAND, or David Elliott, whom he interviewed and referred to as, "One extremely knowledgeable young American who worked on these interrogations."

[13] Halberstam, "Voices of the VietCong" 1968, p. i.

[14] Halberstam, "Voices of the VietCong" 1968, p. i.

Dinh Tuong Province, 1954–1975

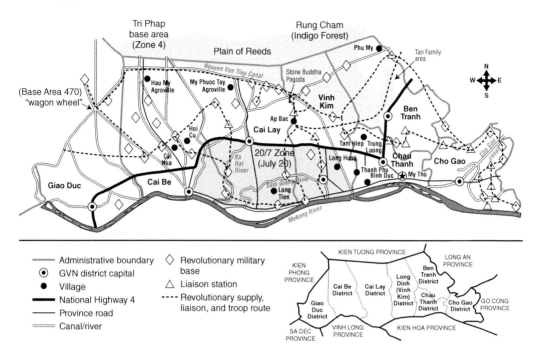

kill them, and propagandize against them, and that "for the first time we are seeing into the darkness, seeing their faces, often hearing their voices, sensing how they live."[15]

The province of Dinh Tuong was chosen not only for its proximity to Saigon and for its accessibility, but also for its geopolitical importance to both the Viet Cong and the GVN. The province was located at the junction of two strategic lines of communication: One axis was National Highway 4, which bisected almost the entire length of the province and served as a crucial link between Saigon and the rice-producing areas in the southern Mekong Delta. Six of the province's seven districts lay along this conduit of rice to Saigon. The other axis was the upper branch of the Mekong River, which bordered the province to the south and connected to the Plain of Reeds, the VC sanctuary on the edge of Cambodia; and to the coast, where supplies were infiltrated by sea.

The first reports to emerge from the Dinh Tuong project were based on data extracted from interviews conducted during the last half of 1965 and early 1966, and on information derived from captured documents and from interviews conducted by Goure's teams in Saigon. Elliott produced two draft reports. Chuck Thomson was assigned to edit and merge them into one. Goure urged Thomson to steer the report toward an emphasis on

---

[15] Halberstam, "Voices of the VietCong," 1968, p. i.

enemy vulnerabilities. In a February 25, 1966, letter to Chuck Thomson, Goure told him to highlight the cadres' "problems, weaknesses, stresses, and strains." He wrote to Thomson, "What should come out of it is a paper showing that the VC cadres are neither monolithic nor always pure, that they have problems and weaknesses, exploitable ones, and that a careful examination of them shows all cracks and fissures." He also urged Thomson to ". . . indicate that data from other parts of Vietnam show this situation is not unique to Dinh Tuong." Beyond his propensity to emphasize vulnerabilities, it appeared that Goure's intention was to reinforce his reputation as a key player in exploiting enemy weaknesses through psychological warfare, and he expressed his pleasure over the fact that ". . . for whatever it's worth, we (i.e., RAND) are still the cadres of psywar here and they [Americans in charge of psywar, such as General Fritz Freund] all come for help, advice, or just to cry."

However, Elliott, as head of the Dinh Tuong project, which was separate from Goure's Viet Cong Motivation and Morale Project and which was not under Goure's purview, controlled the substance of his own findings. He did not go along with Goure's idea, and his report described a more nuanced picture of the enemy in Dinh Tuong.[16] The Viet Cong had suffered reverses, but they remained resilient, he pointed out, and the cadres continued to keep their commitment and their faith in eventual victory, because they felt their movement had the support of the people. It was a movement that had grown and strengthened itself despite the fact that Dinh Tuong was the seat of the ARVN 7th Division—one of the GVN's best units.

The National Liberation Front, as the Viet Cong called their movement, dominated over a fourth of the villages, 24 of the province's 93, and controlled over 40 percent of the population of half a million, counting those living in their zones and those living in contested areas. However, the NLF's military strategy in Dinh Tuong—as in the rest of the Mekong Delta—was not to make the province a center of military operations, but to maintain it mainly as a source for recruits and economic resources. As a result, insurgent military activities in Dinh Tuong, and elsewhere in the Delta, were limited relative to those in the Central Highlands. They were aimed mainly at securing lines of communication to allow access to the rice and manpower of the Delta and to permit arms and ammunition infiltrated by sea to reach the Plain of Reeds. The NLF's other objectives in the province were to interrupt or block supplies to Saigon and other large cities, tie down ARVN forces, and generally derail GVN economic, political, and social efforts.

In the 1965–1966 period, the NLF in Dinh Tuong suffered some of the same reverses that were afflicting it elsewhere. GVN military pressures had strained its manpower supplies and economic resources, and had forced it to place increasing demands on the population—a move that intensified popular resentment. Yet, despite these

---

[16] D. W. P. Elliott and C. A. H. Thomson, *A Look at the VC Cadres: Dinh Tuong Province, 1965–1966*, RAND-RM-5114-1-ISA/ARPA, March 1967.

challenges, which were compounded by defections and desertions, Elliott concluded, the Viet Cong cadre ranks, especially those at the upper levels, had been relatively unaffected by the erosion of strength and by the dimmer prospects. They continued to show their resilience and determination to fight for as long as it took, regardless of the costs. Their steadfastness stemmed from their commitment for their cause and from their belief that victory would come eventually, because the NLF enjoyed popular support. Despite difficulties and hardships, they attended to their tasks with efficiency, recruiting and retaining control in the Viet Cong zones, as well as in most contested areas.

Elliott grouped the cadres into three categories: the "movers," who performed important functions at the district level or above; the "enforcers," Village Party Chapter Secretaries or their deputies, or those responsible for such functions as tax collection at the village level; and the "little brothers," so called among the Viet Cong, at the lowest level who had direct contact with the population and carried out orders. According to the analysis, the "movers" and "enforcers" may respond to U.S./GVN appeals, but it was the "enforcers," the key links at the village level, who could be the most susceptible because they had a tough job to perform. Regardless of the difficulties they faced—desertions, reassignments, or casualties inflicted by GVN sweep operations—they were expected to come up with the quotas for manpower demanded by their superiors. Often criticized for failures, which they ascribed to difficult circumstances, and blamed by those above, who had no knowledge of local conditions, enforcers could become prone to resentment, and their dissatisfaction could provide a wedge for the GVN to induce them to defect.

Those cadres who wavered and began to take stock of their situation—because they felt either disgruntled or threatened by internal conflicts—could be open to appeals for defection, particularly if they could be convinced that popular support, the bedrock of their belief in the movement, was eroding. Such a reassessment might pierce the psychological protective barrier they had built against GVN blandishments, and this vulnerability could be exploited with dissemination of information about the war's progress, declining popular support, the safety of defecting, and employment prospects under the GVN.

Sounding a new note that set his apart from other RAND reports, Elliott recommended that the *Chieu Hoi* Program be offered to the cadres, not just as an alternative to continuing warfare but also as a way to achieve national reconciliation. When it was distributed, the report was well received by General Westmoreland. In a letter to Chuck Thomson, dated October 12, 1967, Elliott wrote, "The cadre paper, as you have probably heard by now, got raves from Westmoreland and 300 copies have been ordered printed."

Living in My Tho removed David Elliott from the controversy and tension surrounding Leon Goure and his team in Saigon. As Elliott would later recall, "It was a drag to have to live in My Tho but it was also a blessing" because he was "out of sight and out of mind" of Goure and therefore "was left alone."[17] In one of her letters back to Santa Monica, Ardith Betts wrote with envy of Elliott's position. She told her friend that "Dave, if you haven't guessed, is about the most informed and most valuable person out here."[18] Working in My Tho, she said, "he isn't under Leon's thumb," and "Leon can't control his every move." According to her, since Elliott just did not care about a career at RAND, "he does as he pleases," and Goure was afraid to stop him "for fear he'll quit." But Goure was also interested in "showing off" Elliott as an informed RAND staff member. Once he flew down to My Tho with the columnist Joseph Alsop. Elliott remembered that in his usual bullying manner, Alsop pressed him to give what amounted to intelligence. Elliott refused, saying that he was not in the intelligence business. Alsop got testy and rude. Subsequently, Elliott recalled, Goure arranged a dinner with the two of them to smooth Elliott's ruffled feathers, and Alsop apologized to Elliott for his behavior. Elliott was also the only team leader whom Goure took to see General Westmoreland.[19] Bill Jones' takeover as project manager in Saigon did not affect Elliott in any way, and he carried on as he had before—until Jones shut down the project in 1967.

The next work Elliott produced was an extensive draft that William Stewart, the assistant to Joe Goldsen, edited down to a RAND-sized study. Bill Stewart was a former Air Force colonel who had been assigned to RAND in 1962, and then became a permanent staff member in 1964. Stewart would later recall that when Harry Rowen was in ISA, he kept urging Stewart to spend time at RAND. When Stewart came to Santa Monica in 1962, he was one of three Air Force representatives. According to him, these representatives had no clear-cut responsibilities at RAND. Their main function was "to advise about the classification of materials" because "you had to have a military guy available for that."[20] He recalled that this was "about the only job they had." Their other function was "to help the RAND people find their way back to the Air Force to get information and to advise RAND people on things they might be doing or not be doing."[21] For example, they could suggest that researching a certain problem might

---

[17] Author interview with David Elliott, 2006.

[18] Ardith Betts, letter to a friend, January 19, 1967.

[19] Since Elliott's father was a well-known Harvard professor with many contacts, Elliott was used to visiting with important figures. When he was still in the Army in Saigon, Henry Cabot Lodge summoned him to the Embassy. General Maxwell Taylor called him in for a meeting when he became U.S. ambassador to Vietnam. These summons surprised the MACV staff, who wondered why these two eminent figures wanted to see a lowly corporal. Henry Kissinger sought him out during one of his visits to Vietnam, and on his return to the United States made a point of telling Elliott's mother about the meeting. During one of Elliott's trips to the United States, his father arranged a meeting for him with Walt Rostow at the White House. Elliott remembered that Rostow spent the entire time telling him how the war was going in Vietnam.

[20] Author interview with William Stewart, 2005.

[21] Author interview with William Stewart, 2005. Stewart recalled, for example, the time Arnold Horelick performed a study of the Cuban Missile Crisis, and someone in the Pentagon wanted to classify it "Secret." Stewart

be difficult. Or, if RAND people wanted some information, they "were encouraged to provide it" if possible. He remembered that the Air Force representatives' assignment "was just a liaison job of not much importance, but a lot of fun. . . . It was just a nice tour of duty."

Then, in 1964, Stewart was assigned to go to Vietnam. He had opposed American involvement from the start, believing that Vietnam was of no strategic importance to American national interest. He told his superiors, "Well, I don't believe that that war is important. We shouldn't be in it, so I don't want to go out there and serve, besides I know the intelligence general out there and he's a jerk, I don't want to work for him. Do I have the option of not going?" They said, "Well, you can always retire." According to Stewart, the Air Force liked to encourage a colonel to retire "because that means one less guy battling for promotion to general." So he resigned from the military and went back to RAND and was offered a job. He recalled that he had no intention of retiring at RAND, and planned to get a doctorate degree at UCLA and teach later.

At the time, RAND was hiring former senior military people who seemed bright and aware, and whom the staff had gotten to know in the Pentagon. Once an officer got to RAND, however, it would take him six or seven years "to get out of his military stance and become creative—start thinking more independently," Stewart said.[22] For example, a RAND person would meet a general in the Pentagon and "he would seem very bright . . . informed and aware" because he was surrounded by staff people who prepared work for him. But a general "tended to be shaped by the people they got around them," and was not "necessarily capable of doing the thinking for himself." At RAND, an ex-general would lose all this support and would have to be an independent thinker, and it would take him years to adapt. Stewart advised Frank Collbohm to stop hiring retired military people because it usually took them so long "to do anything productive at RAND." Stewart said that he fit this mold: "I didn't know what . . . I was going to do. It took me about seven years to become intellectually active. I was passive, I just sat around and encouraged other people to do better work." At RAND, the retired military people were hired mainly as "just resources. . . . People would go to them and say, 'How does it work?' They were never as a group creatively important at RAND."[23]

When Stewart arrived in the Social Science Department, he thought that "it was out of this world." Alex George, whom he admired greatly, was there, and Nathan Leites, another person he considered "a giant in Political Science," was there half the time. Stewart became Joe Goldsen's assistant and friend. Stewart remembered that

---

read it and decided that everything in it was in the public domain. He recommended declassifying it, and the Pentagon followed his suggestion. Stewart said that until this happened, "Arnold always thought that I was a right-wing reactionary."

[22] Author interview with William Stewart, 2005.

[23] Author interview with William Stewart, 2005.

Goldsen was not "a hugely creative thinker" but was "a compulsive worker" who did good work because he labored so hard. Goldsen was also good at "organizing things . . . and . . . could lay out in a period of a few days what the program for the whole department was." As Goldsen's assistant, Stewart did anything Goldsen asked him to do. In general, his main duty was to spend as much time as he could with the younger staff, "giving initial reviews of their work and suggesting to them directions in which to take their research or ways to improve it." Stewart recalled that the department " had some awfully bright and active young guys."[24]

Stewart had had no involvement with the Vietnam research projects when Dave Elliott's lengthy report on pacification in Dinh Tuong arrived in the Social Science Department in 1967. Stewart could see that it contained "great insights," but he knew that the length would deter people from reading it.[25] He decided to edit it down to a manageable size. He said that he "always felt embarrassed" for putting his name on it as a co-writer, but he also felt that he put a lot of work into it. While working on the report, David Elliott had come down with Hepatitis A, demonstrating the danger of living in a small town with questionable sanitation, and Bill Jones had had to arrange for his evacuation to Clark Air Base in the Philippines for treatment. He spent several weeks recovering from the disease, and did not return to work until July 1967.

That summer, Bill Jones came down to My Tho to inform David Elliott that the Dinh Tuong project would be terminated. Elliott asked Jones to let the interviewers continue their work after his departure, to maintain continuity. However, Jones adamantly refused. In an October 12, 1967, letter to Chuck Thomson, Elliott wrote that he tried to keep the Dinh Tuong interviews going after he left, but Bill Jones thought it would be too expensive. Elliott had the feeling that Jones also thought that it could not be "effectively supervised" after his departure, even though Elliott was attempting to make "arrangements to return to Vietnam every two months or so" from Taiwan, where he was going to learn Chinese. In a subsequent letter to Thomson on November 10, 1967, Elliott wrote that Jones had told him "upon his return, after a long party and much booze, that he is going to cut off the My Tho project in three months for 'lack of funds.'" Elliott, however, felt that Jones's "real objection is not money but lack of direct control." Elliott wrapped up his work, and he and his wife departed for Taiwan to study Chinese and then for Cornell University, where he would pursue a doctorate. However, they stayed on as RAND consultants for part of 1968.

While in Taiwan and at Cornell, Elliott would exchange frequent and lengthy correspondence with Stewart over the editing of his report, because Stewart was not familiar with Vietnam and even less with Dinh Tuong, pointing out, for example, errors and distortions that he wanted to correct.[26] On the whole, Elliott found that the

---

[24] Author interview with William Stewart, 2005.

[25] Author interview with William Stewart, 2005.

[26] David Elliott, letter to Bill Stewart, May 15, 1968.

Bill Jones (on left) and David Elliott (on right) in front of RAND office in My Tho before its closing.

editing made the report more digestible, but at the same time he also felt that much was lost in the compression. Dan Ellsberg, whom Stewart had asked to read the original and the edited versions of the report, himself liked the original version, telling Stewart that the final report was "a decent piece of work," but that he preferred the "bigger version." Stewart would later say that he picked Ellsberg as a main critic because "he was more likely to oppose it than anybody else."[27]

The report was finally published in January 1969.[28] The long interval between Elliott's submission of his report and its publication made Elliott think that RAND had lost interest in Vietnam in general—and therefore in his own study—after the January 1968 Tet Offensive led to the initiation of peace talks in Paris and the focus shifted to a negotiated settlement. Elliott believed that his report was dusted off and published after it became clear that President Nixon, who succeeded Lyndon Johnson, would continue to pursue the war and that Vietnam—and pacification in particular—would remain an important issue. Stewart thought that this might have been the reason, but he also pointed out that the editing, rewriting, reviewing by internal and external critics, clearing through official channels, and publishing, took several months. According to him, the review process, although lengthy, did not produce any strong objections or critical comments. The reviewers, he said, "just came back and said that they thought

---

[27] Author interview with Bill Stewart, 2005.

[28] David W. P. Elliott and W. A. Stewart, *Pacification and the Viet Cong System in Dinh Tuong: 1966–1967*, Santa Monica, Calif.: RAND Corporation, RM-5788-ISA/ARPA, January 1969.

it was a clear characterization of what was happening in that period of time. Dave's research was good; it was solid, everything was documented."[29]

The report represents the second phase in the evolution of the Dinh Tuong project, as Elliott shifted his focus toward studying the Viet Cong movement as an organization. It was based on more than 250 interviews conducted before his departure from Vietnam in 1967 and on his extensive field experience—living among Vietnamese in the province and working with them over a long period of time. The interviews were done during a period when Dinh Tuong was going through two big developments: the deployment of a brigade of the U.S. 9th Division, the first American unit to be stationed in the populous Mekong Delta, and the pacification operations launched in 1966–1967 to secure the area in which a base for this brigade was going to be constructed and to target Viet Cong lines of communication and the region adjacent to the Plain of Reeds. The objective of the study was to provide an understanding of how the Viet Cong were organized, how their system functioned, what their strategy and tactics were, as well as how their system had reacted to the pacification operation and the presence of the brigade of the U.S. 9th Division.[30] In view of the way the Viet Cong

---

[29] Author interview with William Stewart, 2005. However, although the final version sailed through the reviews, it got bogged down in the clearance process. In a letter to Elliott dated January 9, 1969, Stewart told him that the State Department required that a passage be deleted because the language "could be interpreted as suggesting that the Viet Cong have a humanitarian interest in the local population." The original passage mentioned a captured Viet Cong document instructing their forces to avoid provoking attacks on heavily populated "liberated areas" in order to limit "the damage caused to the people," and to "build mock-up houses near the treelines, where airstrikes are frequently directed" to spare the people from destruction. Stewart recommended accepting the change because, by this time, he was feeling "terribly ground down by the interminable wait for clearance" and did not see any point "in delaying publication while we put in a reclama on this issue." Consequently, he had instructed the Publication Department to print the piece with the required changes, and "with all haste."

[30] The potential advantages and disadvantages of stationing U.S. troops in the Mekong Delta had been discussed briefly by Vic Croizat, a former Marine colonel who had joined RAND following his retirement from the corps, in a paper dated October 11, 1966—a few months before they were actually deployed. Croizat had written the paper in response to a request from the Defense Department regarding a MACV proposal to dispatch American combat troops to the Mekong Delta. His paper was forwarded to Walt Rostow by Amrom Katz. There was no indication of how Rostow reacted to Croizat's arguments and recommendations, or whether he passed the information to others in the White House, in the Pentagon, or at the State Department. However, the fact that U.S. troops were later deployed in the Delta would indicate that Croizat's paper had produced no effect. Croizat cautioned against putting American troops in the Delta because their large-scale operations in this densely populated region to counter a local guerrilla war would cause undesirable destruction and alienate the peasants. Croizat, therefore, suggested two alternatives. The first was using the 9th Infantry Division in the northern and western parts of South Vietnam to extend U.S. areas of operation and interdict North Vietnamese lines of communication. Such a deployment might relieve ARVN units, which could then be reassigned to the Mekong Delta. A second alternative would be to base the 9th Division at Baria and to conduct heliborne search-and-destroy missions over a major part of the Delta without actually basing U.S. Army units in this region on a permanent basis. As a former Marine, Croizat suggested that these missions could be supported by U.S. naval forces in amphibious operations. Victor Croizat, "Problems Relating to the Deployment of U.S. Ground Combat Forces to the Mekong Delta Area of South Vietnam," Santa Monica, Calif.: RAND Corporation, October 11, 1966 (not available to the general public), with cover letter from Amrom H. Katz, dated October 17, 1966, LBJ Archives, Austin, Tex.

system functioned, the report suggested tailoring counterinsurgency efforts to target the key links to weaken it.

The report provided insights into how the Viet Cong movement operated in a Mekong Delta province, where the more open topography had forced the enemy to adopt tactics more suited to the terrain, and it described their strategy, which was geared more toward securing resources and manpower to meet the military needs of other regions. To achieve their aims, the Viet Cong structured their movement as "a balanced, well-coordinated, closely interrelated, political-military organization in which each element supports every other element and multiplies its effectiveness."[31] Within this system, political and military activities were carefully calibrated to reinforce each other so that control could be gained over both territory and people.[32]

Politically, a mutually supporting balance was maintained among Viet Cong organizations at the hamlet, village, and district levels. Within this system, the cadres who formed the link between district and village operations played an essential role in sustaining its effectiveness. These were "the organizers, activists, and operatives," in whom the Viet Cong had invested heavily in training and experience.[33] They moved from place to place to carry out face-to-face contacts with the population, to collect taxes, recruit laborers for various tasks, hold mass propaganda meetings, and conduct a whole host of other support activities—such as communication and intelligence—that bolstered the effectiveness of the movement.

These key cadres were shielded by Viet Cong forces, whose hovering threat formed a protective umbrella that deterred GVN military incursions and provided the security and freedom of movement they needed to fulfill their tasks. Consequently, any GVN/U.S. activity that undermined the feelings of personal security of these cadres might inhibit their ability to perform the functions that were essential to maintaining the effectiveness and cohesion of the system. For example, the performance of these key cadres, whose effectiveness depended on frequent and intensive face-to-face communication, could be disrupted by GVN/U.S. military operations that drove major protective VC units from an area. Other activities to slow the movement's momentum could include random patrols by small units, ambushes carried out by commandoes, and arrest followed by release of the people the cadres contacted to arouse suspicion.

Militarily, the Viet Cong's effectiveness depended on a carefully maintained balance among its three types of units: guerrillas, provincial Local Force, and regional Main Force. These units interacted with one another for mutual support and protection, as well as with the political side of the system, which they shielded and which, in turn, gave them logistical support and manpower. The guerrillas relied on Local Force

---

[31] Elliott and Stewart, *Pacification and the Viet Cong System*, 1969, p. 1.

[32] Elliott and Stewart cautioned, however, that the conditions and situation in Dinh Tuong might be unique and that the description of the Viet Cong system and its strategy and tactics might not apply elsewhere.

[33] Elliott and Stewart, *Pacification and the Viet Cong System*, 1969, p. 101.

and Main Force units to protect them from the hazard of running into unexpected ARVN troops. The Local Force, in turn, depended on the Main Force, whose likely presence in an area ensured that GVN units would dare to venture into the zone only if they were large enough to take it on. The approach of such large groups of men would, however, give Local Force units plenty of warning. For their part, before entering an area, the Main Force needed the Local Force and guerrillas to give logistical support, store supplies, check out the structure of fortified resting places, collect intelligence, and provide security. Within this interdependent and mutually reinforcing military system, the Local Force represented the key link. Therefore, driving the Local Force from an area would disrupt this balance. The guerrillas would become vulnerable, and the Main Force units would—without the Local Force shield—become more exposed and less effective as a combat group.

The mutually reinforcing military forces enabled the Viet Cong to expand their zones of control in a careful interplay of roles. First, the guerrillas, backed by Local Force units, moved into an area to clear the way for the larger units. When the area was secured, the Main Force units moved in to deter GVN encroachments and threaten adjacent government zones. From this stepping stone, or base, the guerrillas and Local Force moved forward to the next contested or government-controlled area and repeated the process. Their forays were meant to demoralize and undermine GVN forces and allow political cadres to come in and organize. The cadres, in turn, created the control system that sustained and supported further military activity. The expansion of VC territory achieved another purpose: It pinned down GVN troops in static defense of areas that were or could be threatened by Viet Cong attacks.

Expansion of territory was also a strategic necessity for the Viet Cong; without it, their core areas would be in greater danger. However, the open topography in parts of the province forced the Viet Cong to restrict their operations to areas bounded by the Plain of Reeds to the north and the Mekong River to the south. The Plain of Reeds itself—overgrown with the vegetation that gave it its name—provided the only terrain suited for a major base. The Viet Cong used it as a sanctuary, as a base from which their Main Force could launch military forays, and a safe haven into which the VC could retreat. If the GVN gained control of the zones bounded by the Plain of Reeds and the Mekong River, within which the Viet Cong had to restrict their operations, it could create reverberations in other regions and other provinces.

The narrower focus of the study provided the opportunity to take an in-depth look at how the Viet Cong reacted to pacification in a province located in the critical Mekong Delta. Since their main objective in Dinh Tuong—as elsewhere in the Delta—was simply to hold on to siphon off manpower and resources for II and III Corps, the main theaters of the war, their strategy was to hunker down. Faced with an enemy possessing greater manpower and firepower, their response to pacification was to increase self-reliance among the villages and to return to guerrilla-warfare tactics.

Politically, they created organizational links between villages to minimize the need for communication with the more distant district level. Cadres in charge of these links—called *sectors* and *clusters*—were given enhanced authority to make decisions without having to refer to the district. They were chosen for their skill, training, and experience to ensure that the system's effectiveness would be sustained to a high degree, despite the disruption caused by pacification operations. Militarily, the VC strategy was to avoid direct confrontations with U.S. troops, even by Main Force units, and to strike at areas that were lightly defended, forcing their opponents to spread themselves thin and take away their offensive initiative. Concurrent with this strategy, the Viet Cong attempted to shift the fighting to areas controlled by the government, and accelerated attacks on urban areas in 1967. These moves culminated in the Tet Offensive, which began at the end of January 1968.

In conclusion, the report pointed out that, since the military strategy of the Viet Cong in Dinh Tuong was to create "psychological pressures" on GVN-controlled areas and to deter GVN operations from entering their own zones, the conventional yardsticks of American military operations, such as the body count and the ability to launch offensive actions against VC regular force units, would not be useful indicators of success.[34] Elliott recommended that, in light of the Viet Cong's sophisticated and interconnected organization, a systematic approach be taken in dealing with the Viet Cong movement in Dinh Tuong. His recommendations for a more effective pacification included applying pressure on sensitive links in the system simultaneously—in particular, against the key-level cadres and the Local Force units to weaken it, and avoiding targeting marginal adherents or participants who were "expendable and replaceable."[35] Punishing these players on the margin would be counterproductive, since it might embed them even more deeply in the system by convincing them that the only course of action would be for them to stay with the Viet Cong. Finally, the report recommended a systematic approach to disrupt the balance of Viet Cong forces and interfere with the insurgents' lines of communication leading from the Plain of Reeds to other important bases, such as the one in the Iron Triangle near Saigon, and to exploit certain Viet Cong characteristics—such as their fears of the mobility of U.S. forces, and "their preoccupation with maintaining communications and providing leadership, and their concern over loss of control of areas they viewed as strategically important."[36]

According to Bill Stewart, the report was well received by Robert Komer, who had been appointed special assistant to President Johnson for pacification in March 1967 as part of the president's efforts to push the program forward. Impatient with the lack of progress, Johnson directed Komer to oversee the program from Washington

---

[34] Elliott and Stewart, *Pacification and the Viet Cong System*, 1969, p. 65.

[35] Elliott and Stewart, *Pacification and the Viet Cong System*, 1969, p. 102.

[36] Elliott and Stewart, *Pacification and the Viet Cong System*, 1969, p. 105.

and instructed William Porter, the deputy ambassador to Vietnam, to consolidate the U.S. Mission's pacification activities into a single organization. Komer's responsibility was to direct, coordinate, and supervise all these efforts. According to Ambassador William Leonhart, Komer's deputy, these changes reflected Johnson's determination to speed up the pacification programs, give them the same priority as military operations, and conduct them with the sense of urgency required in wartime.

After Richard Nixon's election to the presidency, Komer lost his White House post and joined RAND as a consultant. Stewart recalled that Komer was very enthusiastic about the report, declaring "this is the way we should have fought this war all along."[37] According to Stewart, Komer took the report "to all the military he knew" and told them, "This is how we should fight the war out there in Vietnam."[38] So many people in the military were interested, Stewart said, that the report became a "best seller"—because the military "weren't hearing anything fresh about Vietnam, and this was fresh" and because the report "described the way the Viet Cong acted in a specific province in a fairly clear-cut way and that made interesting reading" for them.[39] However, they were not highly placed and did not have the influence to change the way the war was fought. Besides, according to Stewart, "The military are very flat headed . . . once they're doing things a certain way, they're not going to change it." Stewart believed that the report "was potentially a very valuable thing," but it came out after the Tet Offensive, and by then "the idea of changing the way we fought the war was just very unpopular in the Pentagon building."[40]

Later, a former U.S. captain came to RAND and told Stewart how a group he had commanded in Dinh Tuong used the report to adjust their operations. The report had indicated that the way to affect the Viet Cong in the province was to intercept their routes to and from the Plain of Reeds. Those routes were "carefully detailed" in the interviews and provided "a clear road map," Stewart said. The captain told Stewart that a volunteer squad of American draftees—"from various universities who were just going crazy . . . out there doing the kind of pointless things that the 9th did," such as "charging into the villages"—would go out at night into the Plain of Reeds and intercept the Viet Cong "while they were sneaking around." These Americans, according to Stewart, "were some of the happiest soldiers around because they were finally doing something they could understand instead of going out and destroying a village and everybody in it."[41]

---

[37] Author interview with William Stewart, 2005.

[38] Author interview with William Stewart, 2005.

[39] Author interview with William Stewart, 2005.

[40] Author interview with William Stewart, 2005.

[41] Author interview with William Stewart, 2005.

While Elliott was more interested and more focused on studying the Viet Cong system as a whole, he was drawn back to address psychological warfare—a bread-and-butter issue for RAND in Vietnam at that time. In a lengthy memo to George Tanham, who had asked for his comments on current operations, Elliott said that he was not qualified to comment, since he was not an expert in the field, and offered only to address the broader problems with psywar as he perceived them from activities in Dinh Tuong.

According to Elliott, psychological warfare in Vietnam had been equated, among its practitioners, with posters, broadcast missions, and propaganda teams—"the advertising approach." The effort directed at the ranks of the Viet Cong themselves had been unsystematic and inadequate. The concentration of personnel in Saigon, and the lack of training among those charged with psychological warfare in the field, produced overreliance on guidance from the capital, as well as on materials prepackaged there. Those materials neither contained "compelling arguments" to persuade the Viet Cong ranks, nor exploited local situations for effect. There was also a tendency to follow general guidance rigidly. Elliott cited, for example, the "phased leaflet drop" followed by U.S. combat units, in which a series of leaflets containing sequential arguments was dropped at regular intervals to guide the Viet Cong to a logical conclusion that the United States was strong and that they therefore should defect. The assumption, Elliott wrote, was that the Viet Cong picking up the leaflets would respond "to the desires of the propagandist," and would follow "his argument chronologically, step by step, to the inescapable conclusion."

Elliott recommended that "the scope and concept of psychological operations" be reexamined, that psychological operations go beyond "mass propaganda and leafleteering," and that intelligence-gathering and psywar programs be coordinated. He suggested that messages be geared to the factors that could have an effect on rural Vietnamese in general and rural Viet Cong in particular. Consideration should be given to the way information was disseminated, since rural Vietnamese, and especially the Viet Cong themselves, were leery of impersonal, outside sources. Therefore, "The persuasive appeal of impersonal media . . . should be very closely examined." Elliott recommended that—in lieu of a centralized approach—a program encouraging local initiative be instituted and sustained to produce results. Instead of using leaflets written in Saigon by urban Vietnamese, Elliott suggested, for example, using personalized messages handwritten by local defectors, accompanied by their photos, which would be distributed on the ground, possibly by troops going on operation through the hamlets or villages of the authors of the leaflets. Lastly, Elliott recommended using former Viet Cong in armed propaganda teams and in the Province Reconnaissance Units to maximize psywar operations and advertise the *Chieu Hoi* Program. However, Elliott confessed that he tended "to be somewhat pessimistic about the possibilities for remedial action of an enduring nature." In the memo to Tanham, Elliott also discussed using the presence of the 2nd Brigade of the U.S. 9th Division for psychological impact. At that juncture, Dinh Tuong was serving as a base from which American troops were launching operations to all regions in the upper Delta in support of pacification operations undertaken by the ARVN. Elliott thought that using U.S. troops to support pacification carried many pitfalls, and suggested using the presence of U.S. troops as a deterrence to neutralize "the protective umbrella" that VC units offered to civilian cadres—a protection that was more psychological than military. The mere threat that VC forces might be present transformed VC zones into safe havens in which the cadres could operate with impunity, knowing that the ARVN would dare enter only with a large and noisy operation, which would give them plenty of warning to melt away. Instead of the 9th Division jumping around in pursuit of targets and accumulating body counts, Elliott suggested that its operational elements maintain a constant physical presence "within easy striking distance" of the complex of VC bases, to inhibit the cadres' activities and push their infrastructure into a more exposed position.

The ability of American troops to enter the VC safe zones at will would increase the likelihood of intrusion, inject greater uncertainty, and undermine the cadres's sense of security. With their own speed, mobility, firepower, and frequency of operations, the U.S. 9th Division could counter the Viet Cong's own strategic advantages of unpredictability and credibility of force. However, although the constant counterthreat posed by the continual, physical presence of an operational U.S. force could do much "to neutralize the VC safe haven strategy," it could not "eliminate it." To achieve elimination, the concentrated VC units would have to be destroyed or pushed out of their areas of operation. Destroying these VC forces or forcing them out would require adopting "a continuing, geographically focused counter effort" to replace the current scattershot strategy of pursuing "suitable military targets" wherever they appeared—a strategy that spread thin the offensive capabilities.

If these capabilities were focused geographically and sustained, they could produce more lasting, "if less spectacular, success." In conclusion, Elliott recommended that the immediate goal of U.S. forces in the Delta should be to interdict "specific safe haven base areas" and that the ultimate goal should be to completely destroy VC concentrated units operating in those areas. In this strategy, U.S. troops would not engage in pacification per se, but would simply provide psychological support for it by posing a "poised threat against VC units within a defined geographical area." For these reasons, Elliott recommended that "psychological planning" form the "point of departure" for military planning.

♣ ♣ ♣

Elliott's recommendations might or might not have been passed along by Tanham. Even if they had been forwarded to the U.S. Army leadership, they had no effect. The fact remains that the 9th Division's 2nd Brigade continued its aggressive tactics.[42] During its operations, the brigade netted sackfuls of captured enemy documents, Elliott remembered. By chance, on a visit to the headquarters of the 9th Division, Elliott came across documents belonging to a Viet Cong demolition platoon of the 514th Battalion. The demolition platoon was an elite unit that played a crucial role in this battalion's offensive operations. The 514th relied on it to spearhead its attacks by clearing the way and removing obstacles with explosives. Usually, captured documents provided disparate records, giving a fragmentary view of Viet Cong organization and activities. When an intelligence officer showed the documents to him, Elliott noticed that they formed a complete and unique set, offering

> a detailed and comprehensive picture of a military unit that, although limited in size, reflects the organizational principles and problems of the larger force to which it is attached. At the same time, the smallness of the unit allows the important factor of personality to come into clear focus, thus complementing the recitation of abstract organizational details.[43]

The officer told Elliott that the division had extracted tactical information from the documents and had no further use for them. Elliott seized the opportunity and took the documents, with the idea of translating them to provide an in-depth look at a Viet Cong unit.

In June 1967, when Gus Shubert came down to My Tho during his tour of Vietnam to assess whether or not to wind down all the RAND projects, Elliott proposed the translation and Shubert was amenable. On this visit, Shubert met with Lt. Colonel Royal B. Brown, the U.S. province military advisor, who told him that Elliott had given him invaluable information and that he appreciated the help RAND had provided.[44] At the end of the meeting, Brown said that he hoped that Elliott's project could continue indefinitely. Shubert, however, deferred the decision to Bill Jones, who opted to terminate it—much to Elliott's unhappiness. Elliott believed that, considering the time and resources that had been sunk into the project, the study could continue to reap benefits, with the only costs being the relatively low salaries of the Vietnamese staff.

---

[42] The aggressive tactics culminated in Operation Speedy Express, launched in the aftermath of the Tet Offensive in 1968. See details of this offensive in Chapter Seven.

[43] David W. P. Elliott and Mai Elliott, *Documents of an Elite Viet Cong Delta Unit: The Demolition Platoon of the 514th Battalion, Part One: Unit Composition and Personnel*, Santa Monica, Calif.: RAND Corporation, RM-5848-ISA/ARPA, May 1969, p. iv.

[44] Shubert, "Southeast Asia Trip Report," 1967.

A few interviews were conducted in early January 1968, but, essentially, by the end of 1967, the project was finished.

Later, RAND accepted Elliott's translation proposal. The work was completed while he and his wife lived in Taiwan, and the five-volume set was published in mid-1969, with extensive prefaces by Elliott.[45] The documents covered the demolition platoon's history from the beginning of 1966 to mid-May 1967, when they were captured. The first volume in the translation series described the unit's composition and personnel; the second dealt with Party organization; the third, with military organization and activities; the fourth, with political indoctrination and military training; and the fifth presented personal letters belonging to the platoon members. This was the last project that David Elliott and his wife conducted for RAND in this period.

The value of the documents lay in the fact that, with the exception of the personal letters, they were written for internal rather than external consumption, and certainly not for the elucidation of the Americans or the GVN. Therefore, they revealed a more candid and more reliable picture of what it was like to live and operate within a Viet Cong unit. Through the documents, the platoon members emerged as real people, with their strengths and their foibles. They wrote about battles and forced marches, recounted self-evaluations given in criticism sessions, confessed their misconduct, reaffirmed their dedication, told their life histories, and explained the reasons they joined the insurgency. "They are all here," Elliott wrote, "The braggart soldier, the repentant sinner, the roisterous but able leaders, the quarrelsome true believer, the romantic revolutionary," and together their "personal accounts afford unusual insights into Viet Cong practices and habits of mind."[46]

The pervasive role of the Communist Party within the unit—as leader, indoctrinator, motivator, and disciplinarian—emerged very clearly. As Elliott put it, Party control over military affairs was "an axiomatic principle of Communist leadership."[47] As did other Viet Cong concentrated units, the 514th Battalion had Party representation throughout its hierarchy. The demolition unit was unusual in that it had a Party Chapter, rather than a Party cell, due to the large Party membership within its ranks. The importance of the Party Chapter was reflected in a document that stated that ". . . the Party Chapter is the nerve center directing all our activities."[48] The Party Chapter meeting was the mechanism through which the Party controlled its members.

---

[45] David W. P. Elliott, and Mai Elliott, *Documents of an Elite Viet Cong Delta Unit: The Demolition Platoon of the 514th Battalion Part One: Unit Composition and Personnel*, Santa Monica, Calif.: RAND Corporation, RM-5848-ISA/ARPA, May 1969; *Part Two: Party Organization*, RM-5849-ISA/ARPA, May 1969; *Part Three: Military Organization and Activities*, RM-5850-ISA/ARPA, May 1969; *Part Four: Political Indoctrination and Military Training*, RM-5851-ISA/ARPA, May 1969; and *Part Five: Personal Letters*, RM-5852-ISA/ARPA, May 1969.

[46] Elliott and Elliott, *Documents of an Elite Viet Cong Delta Unit, Part One*, 1969, p. x.

[47] Elliott and Elliott, *Documents of an Elite Viet Cong Delta Unit, Part Two*, 1969, p. 1.

[48] Elliott and Elliott, *Documents of an Elite Viet Cong Delta Unit, Part Two*, 1969, p. 4.

During these meetings, problems were brought out, discussed, and resolved collectively. Exhortatory examples of personal conduct were also held up to encourage and motivate the members. In short, Elliott wrote, the documents indicated "an elaborate and effective organizational mechanism of control and motivation. It is clear that the Party apparatus is much more than just a surveillance mechanism."[49] Between surveillance and exhortation, it seemed that persuasion and example played a more "positive and dynamic role" in the execution of Party policy than the "check of the surveillance and disciplinary mechanism."[50]

The war was not an unending succession of firefights, and as for many Viet Cong units in the Delta, the 514th Battalion had long stretches of time when it was not engaged in military operations. As for any combat unit anywhere, these lulls were problematic for the soldiers, as well as for their commanders. To keep the troops from falling into laxity during these intervals, the cadres engaged the platoon in a long succession of Party activities, instructing the soldiers in both political and military matters, coaching them in the "usual arts of war," explaining the unit's immediate military goals and the enemy's presumed intentions, inculcating in them "a firm Communist ideological stand," arousing their hatred of the Americans, and convincing them "that the Party is the supreme leader in all things."[51]

The last volume in the translation series contained letters that had passed between the demolition unit members and their families and friends back home. These were the only unofficial documents among those captured and gave a valuable glimpse into the state of mind of these Viet Cong soldiers—a rare look into their "personal lives . . . [and] their hopes and fears during the trials of war." Readers of these letters, Elliott wrote, would "discover nothing . . . resembling the 'scholar at war.'"[52] Rather, they would find "the private and simple annals of the obscure." But therein lay their value "for they succeed . . . in showing the enemy to be like soldiers everywhere."[53] Fear of censorship probably inhibited the spontaneous expression of personal feelings, but the contents of the messages and poems seemed sincere. Even in their muted and simple way, many were poignant: They brought news of the desolation of war and of death, and talked of loneliness, of the pain of separation, and of the longing for home and companionship. The admonitions and encouragements the letters contained were "probably no more than the conventional formulae of letter writers everywhere," but they imparted "a strong feeling of group solidarity and social cohesiveness."[54]

---

[49] Elliott and Elliott, *Documents of an Elite Viet Cong Delta Unit, Part Two*, 1969, p. 10.

[50] Elliott and Elliott, *Documents of an Elite Viet Cong Delta Unit, Part Two*, 1969, p. 10.

[51] Elliott and Elliott, *Documents of an Elite Viet Cong Delta Unit, Part Four*, 1969, p. ix.

[52] Elliott and Elliott, *Documents of an Elite Viet Cong Delta Unit, Part Five*, 1969, p. ix.

[53] Elliott and Elliott, *Documents of an Elite Viet Cong Delta Unit, Part Five*, 1969, p. ix.

[54] Elliott and Elliott, *Documents of an Elite Viet Cong Delta Unit, Part Five*, 1969, p. 2.

☙ ☙ ☙

Elliott was not the only RAND analyst who made use of the rich materials he and his team collected. Back in Santa Monica, the richness of the Dinh Tuong interviews attracted the attention of Melvin Gurtov, who used them to produce a couple of reports. Gurtov, a China expert, was recruited by RAND in 1966. When RAND contacted him, Gurtov was studying Chinese in Taiwan after completing his master's degree at Columbia. He had written his thesis on the war of independence fought by the Viet Minh against the French, which was about to be published as a book, and this fact made him appear like a good candidate to work on Vietnam. It was the height of the war, and "RAND, like everybody else, was scrambling around for supposed experts on Vietnam."[55] When RAND inquired at Columbia, it was told that "there is a guy who just graduated from our School of International Affairs; he's out in Taiwan." Gurtov interviewed at RAND and was hired by the Social Science Department. That was his first job, and he was delighted with the salary offer of $10,000 dollars a year, which "seemed like a mountain of money at the time."[56]

As someone fresh out of graduate school interested in doing research, he was also attracted by the prospect of working in a think tank. RAND gave him an ideal setting in "sunny, golden California," a welcome change from "the depths of New York," where he had spent his entire life, and gave him access to all kinds of materials he wanted. Gurtov recalled that it was "heaven"—money was available, and the staff was given the freedom to do whatever they liked. He felt that RAND had a "very trusting relationship" with its analysts and assumed that whatever they produced would be useful.[57] He was productive at RAND, and said that he would never "look unfavorably on that experience." To him, those days are probably gone forever. Gurtov fit right into Social Science, where Vietnam was a big priority. There were people working on other areas, such as China and Europe, but "if you put it all together there was more work being done on Vietnam than anything else."[58]

Gurtov expected to return eventually to his real expertise and to do research on China. For the time being, he was needed specifically to work on Vietnam. He had been told nothing about the Viet Cong Motivation and Morale study or any other RAND studies. When he arrived at RAND, he was put in a trailer in a parking lot, and was given a stack of interviews, along with the latest studies that had come out of the Vietnam projects, and anything relevant to Vietnam that RAND was doing. At the time, he was in favor of the U.S. involvement and believed that the war was "an unfor-

---

[55] Author interview with Mel Gurtov, 2004.

[56] Author interview with Mel Gurtov, 2004.

[57] Author interview with Mel Gurtov, 2004.

[58] Author interview with Mel Gurtov, 2004.

tunate but necessary thing."[59] He took a classic Cold War view of the conflict, and viewed the communist movement in Vietnam "in a very undifferentiated way"—as the "typical kind of organizations that Moscow and Beijing typically had a strong hand in sponsoring."[60] However, he thought that the execution of U.S. policies was flawed, and he took issue with the bombing of North Vietnam and the excessive use of firepower in South Vietnam.

Neither Gurtov nor RAND had any idea of what to expect of him. Nobody asked him to study this or that aspect of the war. RAND just believed that, as an analyst with Asia experience, he would produce some intelligent works out of the documents. It was up to him to choose his own research projects, and so he did. He received very little direction, and he set his own pace. He was given a large pile of interviews "in no particular order, just whatever was available at the time," and as time went on, more and more interviews kept arriving. So, he just started to read, not knowing what he was going to find, and without the foggiest notion of what the project in Vietnam was about. It was left to him to figure out how to make sense out of all the information that was thrown at him.

Within a few weeks, he began to form some impressions that would change his attitude toward the war. He thought that the interviews gave a "very personal view of the war—one that you would never ordinarily get reading newspapers or studies about the war at the time or any other time." From reading the interviews, Gurtov appreciated better the reasons "why people fought, what prompted their involvement," and he saw that in the case of the Vietnamese communists, the reason "had nothing to do with ideology, but had everything to do with nationalism and issues very closely connected with home and village—land especially."[61] The war had little to do "with the larger, global struggle that the American government had tended to put it in."[62] The evolution of his view was "counter-intuitive," he said, because "you would think that working in a place like RAND under government contract would strengthen my commitment to the war, any war." But, in fact, the opportunity to read materials such as those from the Vietnam projects, "more so than any esoteric classified information," the immersion in RAND's "information-flooded environment," and the time for reflection, "profoundly changed" his assessment.[63]

As he became more familiar with the data and the Vietnam projects, he decided to focus on the Mekong Delta. The quality of the interviews facilitated the studies that he, as well as other analysts in Santa Monica, would eventually produce about this

---

[59] Author interview with Mel Gurtov, 2004.

[60] Author interview with Mel Gurtov, 2004.

[61] Author interview with Mel Gurtov, 2004.

[62] Author interview with Mel Gurtov, 2004.

[63] Author interview with Mel Gurtov, 2004.

region. As Elliott put it, the only thing the analysts in Santa Monica had to do was "to pick out" what was already contained in the interviews that had been produced by the Vietnamese interviewers who "labored in obscurity" and were to him the "unsung heroes" of the RAND Vietnam projects.[64] In September 1967, Gurtov published a study of three regular force battalions operating in and around Dinh Tuong Province during the 1965–1966 period, before American troops were deployed in the region: two regional Main Force units—the 261st and the 263rd—and one provincial Local Force unit—the 514th—which David Elliott had written about.[65] In looking for openings to induce the insurgents to defect, Gurtov found also what made them resilient. As were Elliott and Konrad Kellen, he was struck by the ability of the Viet Cong to sustain combat effectiveness, despite setbacks that were plaguing the movement here and elsewhere: difficulty in recruiting and villagers' apathy or hostility toward military service in the NLF; doubt about imminent victory; frustration over the prospects of a long war; nascent doubts about the wisdom of serving in an army that had been misleading its troops with talks of impending successes while being unable to regain the initiative; lack of benefits accorded to the families of the soldiers and cadres; and fear of being transferred elsewhere.

Gurtov found that each battalion was able to remain cohesive and effective because it was organized as a "closed society" and "a complex molecule whose many atoms join together only for the march and the battles."[66] The battalion was atomized into cells consisting of three to five men: three cells per squad and three squads per platoon. The squads sometimes moved and camped separately, coming together only when they moved around or when they engaged in battle. The glue that held each cell together was the cadre who lived with the troops and fought alongside them, sharing the hardships of daily life and the rigors of combat. Discipline and morale was sustained through the *kiem thao*, which Joe Zasloff and John Donnell had found was the key mechanism for control, and information was limited to news of victories and enemy losses. Each day, the cell members met for 10 to 15 minutes for criticism and self-criticism to reinforce one another and to bring out problems and weaknesses that should be addressed.

This lid on information, the "fragmented structure and compartmentalization," and the "pervasive control and surveillance system" helped maintain cohesion in the ranks "despite highly adverse developments which, under a different military system,

---

[64] Author interview with David Elliott, 2006.

[65] Melvin Gurtov, *The War in the Delta: Views from Three Viet Cong Battalions*, Santa Monica, Calif.: RAND Corporation, RM-5353-1-ISA/ARPA, September 1967. It covered the 1965–1966 period and was based on RAND interviews with 39 former members of these battalions, and also on interviews done by the Military and National Intelligence Centers in Saigon.

[66] Gurtov, *The War in the Delta*, 1967, pp. x, 40.

might have prompted widespread demoralization."[67] Also, members of the battalions believed that they did not have any safe alternative to remaining with their units, and fear of maltreatment by the GVN or retaliation by the NLF deterred defection and seemed to have held the ranks together. As one assistant squad leader put it, "Once you sit on the back of a tiger you have to ride it."[68] When they did leave, it was out of personal resentment toward the NLF, or out of fear of dying in combat, or unwillingness to endure continued hardships.

❧ ❧ ❧

Absorbed in his work, Gurtov did not pay attention to or wonder about the effect or lack of effect of what he produced on Dinh Tuong—or other topics he tackled, such as China.[69] When asked about how the reports he wrote on Dinh Tuong were circulated and what reaction he got, Gurtov remembered that they were distributed to clients as a matter of course but that he never got any feedback. As he put it, a report just "goes out there somewhere into deep space and who knows if anybody's reading it, and for that matter who knows if someone isn't influenced by it." He was not disturbed because this was the case in academe also. As he said, "you write academic books and articles and you never get any feedback either."[70]

The Dinh Tuong interviews also attracted the interest of a team of analysts in the Economics Department who produced a study on the Viet Cong military system's ability to adapt to the challenges posed by an environment that had turned hostile.[71] The study, performed by M. Anderson, M. Arnsten, and Harvey Averch, focused on the ability of Viet Cong Local and Main Force units in Dinh Tuong to solve problems they encountered. The main instruments used by the units to learn and adapt were the self-criticism session and the after-action report. The authors could not predict whether this impressive Viet Cong organization could adapt to the presence of American troops. However, in their view, the Viet Cong organization was designed to observe and analyze carefully how U.S. troops behaved, and to note any weaknesses, in order to react accordingly.

---

[67] Gurtov, *The War in the Delta*, 1967, p. ix.

[68] Gurtov, *The War in the Delta*, 1967, p. 48.

[69] Among Gurtov's other works on Dinh Tuong, see "Viet Cong Cadres and the Cadre System: A Study of the Main and Local Forces," Santa Monica, Calif., RAND Corporation, December 1967 (not available to the general public). See also *Riding the Tiger: A Study of Regular Force Viet Cong Cadres*, Santa Monica, Calif., RAND Corporation, March 1967 (not available to the general public).

[70] Author interview with Mel Gurtov, 2004.

[71] See M. Anderson, M. Arnsten, and H. Averch [of the Economics Department], *Insurgent Organization and Operations: A Case Study of the Viet Cong in the Delta, 1964–1966*, Santa Monica, Calif.: RAND Corporation, RM-5239-1-ISA/ARPA, August 1967.

Gerry Hickey and Joe Carrier on a field trip.

In conclusion, the authors stated that U.S. counterinsurgency programs had been based on the belief that the insurgency was an organization pursuing an automatic three-phase course of action [moving from guerrilla warfare to mobile warfare to general offensive]. However, in the authors' view, the insurgents were very adaptable; therefore, in making plans and in carrying out counterinsurgency activities, the United States should think of the Viet Cong as people adept at learning and adjusting to new developments.

Unlike Gurtov, the authors of this report got a reaction. According to an Economics Department "ISA Semiannual Progress Report—Economics Department, January–June 1967," dated July 3, 1967, this report was briefed at ARPA, ISA, OSD Systems Analysis, Defense Intelligence Agency, CIA, and the Combined Intelligence Center in Vietnam; by the end of 1967, it was reported to be widely circulated at the request of MACV and "used widely in the field," and was drawing "considerable attention."

Besides the project in Dinh Tuong, another focused, in-depth RAND study was carried out by Gerry Hickey in the Central Highlands of South Vietnam. Hickey's Montagnard study would become the longest-running RAND project in Vietnam, lasting from 1965 to 1972. It put Hickey in an enviable position. He was the unchallenged RAND expert on these ethnic minorities inhabiting a strategically important region—perhaps even the only American expert—and he had the field to himself. In Vietnam, he was his own boss and had complete freedom to do whatever he wanted.

Gerry Hickey with Montagnards.

He came and went as he pleased, and no one at RAND questioned what he was doing, or how he went about doing it, or challenged his findings.

As he investigated the conditions of the highlanders, Hickey developed a deep sympathy for them and came to embrace their cause, becoming their intermediary: communicating their aspirations and interceding on their behalf with the U.S. Mission and American military, and with the Saigon government. In this regard, he was unique. He was the only RAND staff person in Vietnam who was both researcher and advocate within the American government apparatus—not just for a set of ideas and programs, but for a group of people he had come to study as an anthropologist. In the view of a former senior ARPA/AGILE official, Hickey earned the respect of both the American Mission and South Vietnamese authorities for his role with regard to the Montagnard while nevertheless maintaining "his detachment, to the point where he could remain aloof at appropriate times and yet not jeopardize their liking and respect for him."[72]

Hickey had been a strong supporter of President Ngo Dinh Diem, whom he viewed as a nationalist misunderstood by American leaders out of ignorance of Vietnam's history and culture. When he first arrived in Vietnam as part of the advisory Michigan State University group in 1956, he "felt strongly that American economic support of the Ngo Dinh Diem government was justified because South Vietnam showed promise of becoming a viable state within the new post-colonial order of Southeast Asia."[73] He recalled the enthusiasm and hope he sensed in South Vietnam at the time. Subsequently, Diem's overthrow and assassination appalled him. But he remained in favor

---

[72] Deitchman, *The Best-Laid Schemes*, 1976, p. 381.

[73] Hickey, *Window on a War*, 2002, p. 349.

of the United States' continued involvement, although he decried the policies—in particular, the military strategy, which he believed was ill-suited for Vietnam.

RAND's hiring of Gerald Hickey—as well as of John Donnell and Joe Zasloff—was originally a response to AGILE's decision to engage "anthropologists, political scientists, etc., who would learn about how we can better understand and influence native attitudes," as captured in the minutes of a Management Committee Meeting held on November 16, 1962. At the time Hickey embarked on his highland study, the concept of an anthropologist performing research to aid counterinsurgency was not controversial. When asked by RAND to return to Vietnam to study the highlanders, Hickey hesitated, not because he had reservations about the assignment but because he wondered whether he should accept or stay in academe, moving from his temporary appointment in the Southeast Asia Program at Yale to other academic possibilities. Paul Mus, the foremost French sociologist, was then at Yale and told him that his decision should be based on whether or not he wanted to participate "in the events of history."[74] Hickey joined the RAND Washington office in 1963.

Hickey's work in the Central Highlands was to gather information about tribal groups to be used "in trying to effect a reconciliation of the ancient enmity between those groups and the ethnic Vietnamese."[75] The volatility of the situation in the Central Highlands made Hickey's expertise even more valuable and sought after. As the war escalated and the Central Highlands gained in importance for American strategy, his stature would grow among U.S. decisionmakers in Vietnam. While Hickey was in Vietnam in 1964 to conduct his counterpart study, a revolt by the CIDG, or Civilian Irregular Defense Group—locally recruited paramilitary units trained, armed, and advised by the U.S. Special Forces—erupted in five camps in the Central Highlands on September 20. At this time, the highland CIDG, composed of ethnic minorities, numbered about 20,000, and their relatively large number meant that they could cause serious trouble. George Tanham, then working with USAID in Saigon, arranged for Hickey to meet with Ambassador Maxwell Taylor and General William Westmoreland, who asked Hickey to go to the Central Highlands. In the course of his stay, he learned that the rebels had revived a 1958 movement called FULRO—an acronym for the French name that meant "United Struggle Front for the Oppressed Races"—and that their aim was to push the Vietnamese out of the highlands and take back the land that they said the Vietnamese had stolen from their people. The revolt was eventually put down by the GVN, but the FULRO remained a force, and clashes with the government would continue.

The revolt disturbed Americans in Saigon and in Washington, because it happened at a time when American involvement was growing and the United States was attempting to stabilize the political situation in South Vietnam, which had been plunged into

---

[74] Hickey, *Window on a War*, 2002, p. 104.

[75] Deitchman, *The Best-Laid Schemes*, 1976, p. 342.

a state of chaos following the overthrow of President Ngo Dinh Diem. After Hickey finished his counterpart study in late 1964, he was free to focus on the highlanders and their leadership. He returned to Saigon in February 1965, after the bombing of North Vietnam had begun and American dependents were being evacuated. War was beginning to take a toll on Saigon, now swollen with thousands of refugees who had fled the intensified fighting in the countryside. As more and more Americans arrived, bars—bearing such names as "Liz Bar" and "Number One Bar"—were mushrooming and taking over what used to be elegant shops on the main downtown street. Hickey recalled that as soon as bland, new buildings were hastily erected, they were immediately turned into lodgings for U.S. military personnel. Saigon streets were jammed with cars, buses, and American military trucks and Jeeps.

The inhabitants of the Darlac Plateau in the Central Highlands whom Hickey was about to study included several ethnic groups. Numbering about 1 million, they were distinct from the Vietnamese in the lowlands, spoke languages that were different from Vietnamese, and lived mainly in the two provinces of Kontum and Pleiku in the military region called II Corps by the South Vietnamese government. According to Hickey, although these groups had had contacts with Vietnamese, Laotians, Cambodians, Thais, and French over the course of history, they remained untouched and uncivilized. Often referred to as "tribes," these ethnic groups in fact had no tribal organization, and their society centered on the village. However, they had no political organization or leadership beyond the village. Each village was self-sufficient economically, producing what it needed and consumed. The Montagnards practiced "slash-and-burn," or swidden, agriculture, planting dry rice after they had burned the vegetation and relying on the ashes as fertilizer for their crops. They supplemented their diet with vegetables and domestic animals they raised, and by hunting and fishing. Contrary to perception, they were not nomadic.

By mid-July 1965, with American troops stationed in the highlands, U.S. interest in the region grew. The Political Section of the U.S. Embassy formed a Montagnard Committee made up of representatives from the Political Section, MACV, CIA, the aid mission USOM (United States Operations Mission), and the U.S. Information Service. Hickey was invited to be the only nongovernment member. According to him, the role of the committee was to serve as a forum for the exchange of information regarding developments in the highlands and to make recommendations to the American Mission on ways to ameliorate relations between the Montagnards and the GVN. Thus began Hickey's dual role as researcher and intermediary.

In December 1965, Hickey met with a group of FULRO leaders who complained that the life of their people had become difficult with the intensification of the war. They told Hickey that their people were being increasingly caught in military operations and in bombings by American and Vietnamese planes. In addition, communists were going into villages to demand tax payments and to forcibly recruit young men, and South Vietnamese soldiers were entering the communities to steal. The government had kept few of the promises it had made to the highlanders.

In January 1966, General Westmoreland invited Hickey to his office.[76] Westmoreland wanted Hickey to meet General Nguyen Huu Co, who had expressed to Westmoreland his concern for the Montagnard problem and his desire for "a new approach."[77] Westmoreland hoped that "this contact might lead to a development of a more enlightened program by the government toward the Montagnard and perhaps an organization to guide and assist in this effort. Such a program is important for short and long range security."[78] Westmoreland's concern came after a second FULRO revolt and in the face of GVN intransigence. The Vietnamese government leaned toward repression and blamed the Americans for the problem because they had armed the highlanders. Ambassador Henry Cabot Lodge did not want to push the GVN toward a more benign stance, since relations between the United States and Vietnam were already strained.

Hickey himself recalled that he met with Westmoreland to discuss solutions to the escalating conflict between FULRO and the government. He told the general that some of the programs that had been promised to the highlanders could be carried out, in spite of wartime conditions, to alleviate the situation—such as giving them political representation at the central-government level, granting them land titles, and slowing assimilation by allowing them to teach in their groups' languages in the schools and reviving tribal laws. Hickey said that Westmoreland seemed uncomfortable discussing these political solutions and asked him to meet with General Co in the prime minister's office. Subsequently Hickey sent Westmoreland a letter, dated January 10, telling the general that the meeting with Co had gone reasonably well. In the letter, Hickey wrote that General Co was genuinely interested in some new ways to cope with the worsening situation in the highlands, and that "there was a note of desperation" in his voice. Hickey informed Westmoreland that he was preparing some suggestions, including the

---

[76] Westmoreland, Diary, entry of January 5, 1966.

[77] Westmoreland, Diary, entry of January 5, 1966. On April 7, 1966, the Department of Defense awarded Hickey the Medal for Distinguished Public Service. The ceremony was held in Westmoreland's office. A citation signed by Robert S. McNamara was read, which mentioned Hickey's "ethnographic studies," "contributions to the enhancement of U.S. Advisor/Vietnamese Counterpart relationships," and "presence and counsel during periods of attack by Viet Cong forces and Montagnard uprisings." Westmoreland pinned the medal on Hickey's lapel and shook his hand. "It was a good moment" for him, Hickey wrote, but after he left RAND and was applying for a job at the University of Chicago, his alma mater, he was advised not to mention it. By this time, anthropological research for counterinsurgency purposes—directly or indirectly—had taken on a sinister connotation in some academic circles.

[78] Westmoreland, Diary, entry of January 5, 1966. Gerald C. Hickey, *Notes on a Meeting with General Nguyen Huu Co, Vice Chairman of the Central Executive Committee at the Prime Minister's Office, Commissioner General for War and Construction, and Minister of Defense*, Saigon, January 7, 1966, Personal Papers of William Westmoreland, LBJ Archives, Austin, Tex.

"use of our military presence in aiding GVN programs for the Montagnards."[79] Hickey would later give a less diplomatic description of the meeting with Co, saying that the meeting was "non-productive," with Co observing that the Montagnards were like "big children" who had to be dealt with firmly; otherwise, they would take advantage.[80] Co's comments hardly showed that he was interested in a new approach.[81] General Co's reaction reflected the attitude of the Vietnamese government, whose policy toward the highlanders had been high-handed, a mixture of oppression, disdain for their lack of "civilization," and efforts at forced assimilation. The Vietnamese generally shared this attitude and had been encroaching on land belonging to the tribes. All this fed the highlanders' grievances and created a volatile situation in a strategic region.

These conditions called out for ways to reduce discontent and to improve security. In a paper published in September 1967, Hickey set out to recommend a range of social and economic development programs for the highlands that could serve as guidelines for the U.S. aid mission.[82] He believed that such programs would ameliorate the lives of the people and win support for the government. In his view, if these programs were implemented, the government would reap many benefits, such as obtaining better intelligence, enlisting the service of men familiar with the terrain and skilled in jungle combat, reducing the likelihood for protest and the appeal of autonomy, and—above all—diminishing the attraction of the Viet Cong, who would find it more difficult to operate in the highlands. Hickey thought that these programs would give the highlanders a definite place and role on the national scene while allowing them to make social and economic contributions to South Vietnam and to retain their own identity.

The programs Hickey recommended reflected the desire of FULRO and other highland leaders to win guaranteed freedom to preserve their language and customs, greater participation in the nation's political life, more direct control over the administration of the highlands, and the right for their people to hold clear title to their land. Among the programs deemed desirable, agricultural development was viewed as critical to the ethnic minorities' advancement from their current economy, since their livelihood depended entirely on agriculture. For example, cash crops could be introduced, and the highlanders could be instructed on new farming techniques, marketing, organization of transport, and the development of rudimentary economics and petty commerce. The highlanders' progress could be aided by an expansion of the

---

[79] Hickey, *Notes on a Meeting with General Nguyen Huu Co,* 1966.

[80] Hickey, *Window on a War,* 2002, p. 182.

[81] After a second FULRO revolt erupted, the American Embassy succeeded in pressuring Prime Minister Nguyen Cao Ky to set up, on February 21, 1966, a new position of Commissioner for Highland Affairs, headed by a local leader. In his memoir, *Window on a War,* 2002, p. 182, Hickey wrote that this brought "the first meaningful highlander presence in Saigon and it marked a new phase in the development of ethnonationalism among the highlanders."

[82] Gerald C. Hickey, *The Highland People of South Vietnam: Social and Economic Development,* Santa Monica, Calif.: RAND Corporation, RM-5281/1-ARPA, September 1967.

education system to spread literacy at the primary-school level, to teach needed skills and techniques at the secondary-school level, and to train the future highland elite at the university level, where ready access should be provided. Finally, settling the land-tenure issue would be crucial to improving the economic well-being of the highlanders. Clearly defined and formulated laws should be enacted to grant the highlanders unambiguous title to their land so that they could reap the benefits of their labor.

Before Hickey's paper was published in final form, copies of the draft were distributed in February 1967 to American Embassy and U.S. aid officials concerned with highland affairs. Then, in March, Hickey was summoned to Westmoreland's office to discuss the draft, and they spent an hour talking about the economic and social blueprint. Westmoreland said that it had given him ideas, which he would take to an upcoming meeting in Guam with President Johnson, Defense Secretary McNamara, and Generals Nguyen Van Thieu and Nguyen Cao Ky. Major General Richard M. Lee, deputy senior advisor of II Corps, also reacted favorably to the report. And the study got Hickey an invitation to dinner with Ambassador Ellsworth Bunker, who had acquired a keen interest in the highlanders as a result of his study of anthropology at Yale University in 1916.

However, Robert Komer, now responsible for pacification in Vietnam as head of the Civil Operations and Revolutionary Development Support, or CORDS, ignored it, as did his staff. No one from the CORDS headquarters contacted Hickey, and he doubted that anyone there even read it. According to Hickey, Komer's indifference was due to his belief that the highland people represented an insignificant group among the population.

Hickey did not have a favorable impression of Komer, who had come to Vietnam to head up CORDS after it was set up in May 1967 to place the entire American pacification effort under MACV control, reporting directly to General Westmoreland. Hickey thought that Komer, a graduate of the Harvard Business School, was ill-suited for the job because he was misapplying his business managerial skills and running CORDS as if it was "a large corporation instead of an ill-defined effort with a history of failure under various names": Strategic Hamlet Program in 1962; Rural Life Program in 1963; Rural Construction in 1966; and Revolutionary Development Program in 1967.[83] Hickey would later recall that, like a corporate executive, Komer had created a computerized system called the Hamlet Evaluation System, or HES, to measure rural security and quantify military and political progress in South Vietnam by using statistics indicating the degree of government and Viet Cong control in the countryside. It became operational in July 1967 and was adopted by the American Mission in Saigon; by August, the White House had begun using it to track results, and the statistics HES provided came to be viewed almost as a proxy for pacification progress.

---

[83] Hickey, *Window on a War*, 2002, pp. 208–209.

HES attempted to measure the status of pacification in each South Vietnamese district by using "uniform quantitative data" collected by American district advisors. Each month, those advisors evaluated "the military, political, economic, and social situation in each hamlet in their area."[84] To maintain the integrity of what they reported, "Regulations prohibited anyone, including superior officers, from tampering with the adviser's rating."[85] The advisors ranked hamlets into one of six categories: A, B, or C hamlets denoted different levels of government control; D or E hamlets were considered contested; and those rated as V were viewed as under Viet Cong control. The ratings were based on tracking progress in each hamlet in six areas:

> Viet Cong military activity; subversion and political activities; defensive and security capabilities of friendly forces; administrative and political activities of the government; health, education, and welfare activities; and economic development.[86]

For each of these areas, there were three indicators or questions, giving a total of 18 indicators per hamlet. Then, "For each indicator, the advisor selected the rating that he felt best described the circumstances in the hamlet."[87] The advisor, therefore, had to use standards that had been arbitrarily set to evaluate the conditions of each hamlet. Hickey recalled that American pacification advisors were required to fill out monthly questionnaires asking such questions as, 'Are the children of the hamlet friendly?' and 'Does the hamlet chief sleep in the hamlet?'"[88]

Having his work on the Montagnards ignored by Komer and his staff at CORDS displeased Hickey. However, his research was generally well received. A senior ARPA/AGILE official thought that, on the whole, Hickey's studies of the Montagnards, as with the Viet Cong Motivation and Morale Project, fell into the category of projects that were conducted successfully in Vietnam because, in his view, they "fit the pattern of operations and philosophy for prosecution of the war that were common among the military and civilian authorities in both Washington and Saigon."[89]

At that time, GVN insensitivity to the highlanders' plight was only one factor contributing to Hickey's unhappiness. As someone who had seen South Vietnam in more peaceful days, he was appalled by the havoc wrought by the war and by the destruction of the local society. In the Central Highlands, the large presence of American troops transformed such places as Kontum and Pleiku into honky-tonk towns. Kontum became the Rest and Recreation center for American troops serving in the

---

[84] Hunt, *Pacification*, 1995, p. 95.

[85] Hunt, *Pacification*, 1995, p. 95.

[86] Hunt, *Pacification*, 1995, p. 95.

[87] Hunt, *Pacification*, 1995, p. 95.

[88] Hickey, *Window on a War*, 2002, p. 209.

[89] Deitchman, *The Best-Laid Schemes*, 1976, p. 342.

region. Cheap bars and restaurants—in fact, disguised brothels—sprang up to cater to their needs. The transformation was most profound in Pleiku after the U.S. 4th Division arrived in the province in October 1966. Huge construction projects were launched for military installations, air bases, and roads, and private American construction firms brought in workers, many of whom were Vietnamese. The town's population grew, and a whole new large section sprang up with "dismal shacks and flimsy shops." The main part of Pleiku was turned into a "G.I. town," with bars, snack shops, steam baths, and "soul brother" bars that catered to black American soldiers. The streets were jammed with Jeeps, military trucks, bulldozers, and seemingly endless convoys. It was not unusual to see—along the edge of sidewalks thronged "with American soldiers, prostitutes, pimps, vendors, shoeshine boys, and petty thieves"—groups "of Jarai men in their loincloths, clutching bush scythes, followed by women with backbaskets and children." Outside of towns, the highland landscape was also transformed, and "the undulating green plateau became filled with American and Vietnamese military cantonments, fire bases (artillery), airstrips, helipads, and truck parks. On some hills, large antennas swung about like strange windmills."[90]

As 1967 drew to a close, Saigon was bursting at the seams with refugees and rural people flocking to the city to find employment in the booming wartime economy. Slums sprang up everywhere, even in affluent sections of town. The city's boundaries expanded past Tan Son Nhut Airport. An American surfeit of consumer goods spilled from the military Post Exchange into the downtown streets, where vendors displayed stands filled with pilfered goods—expensive stereo sets, tape recorders, canned food, detergents, and alcohol—which were quickly snapped up by residents who had prospered in the new economy. As Tet, the Vietnamese lunar new year, approached in January 1968, Saigon's inhabitants prepared to celebrate the occasion in what they believed would be a respite from war, since a cease-fire usually took hold at this time of year to allow the population to enjoy their most important holiday in peace.

---

[90] Hickey, *Window on a War*, 2002, p. 196.

CHAPTER SEVEN

The Tet Offensive

Yogi Ianeiro was a RAND security guard in Santa Monica when Steve Hosmer recruited him in May 1967 to go to Saigon for two years. Ianeiro hesitated, but two colleagues told him that he should stop being a guard and go do something different. It was a decision he did not regret. According to Jim Digby, Ianeiro had been a bartender at a bar that he and some RAND security guards owned in Westwood, "so he was very affable and a very active person."[1] Ianeiro said that, in Saigon, he "helped a lot of people get things done."[2] Essentially, he was a "fixer," and this role came naturally to him. He liked people, had a good sense of humor, maintained a positive attitude, and endeared himself to most people he worked with.

Digby said that Ianeiro fit right in as an office manager in Saigon. He quickly mastered the many challenges of dealing with the Vietnamese bureaucracy. Ianeiro's work was varied and centered on taking care of details so that others could do their jobs. Ianeiro was RAND's liaison with ARPA,[3] through which he arranged Air America flights for team leaders and interviewers to various parts of the country. He got along well with the staff at Air Vietnam, the domestic airline, as well as people at the Vietnamese National Police Headquarters, where he obtained entry visas for RAND staff and visitors. He made friends with the guards at Tan Son Nhut Airport, which was well guarded for security reasons, and he could go in and out without difficulty to pick up and drop off people. Sometimes he would fly with the interview teams to different places, drive rented cars to interview facilities, sit around and wait, and—being his gregarious self—get to know people there.[4] Another part of his job was to ship

---

[1] Author interview with Jim Digby, 2002.

[2] Author interview with Yogi Ianeiro, 2003.

[3] Yogi's popularity at ARPA was enhanced by his friendship with Bruce Arnold, the son of Hap Arnold, one of the founders of RAND. Eventually, ARPA gave Ianeiro a citation commending him for his work as RAND liaison, and Harry Rowen handed it to him.

[4] Ianeiro remembered that, on one of the field trips, he visited a POW camp. He saw a young Vietnamese girl who was kept in a low, small, bamboo cage, with barbed wire. She had seduced a South Vietnamese soldier and was going to get him to bomb the camp. Ianeiro recalled vividly that every time she shifted, she would get cut by the barbed wire.

interviews, MIC [Military Interrogation Center] and NIC [National Interrogation Center] captured documents back to Frank Denton in Santa Monica for input into the computer. He picked up and dropped off the mail at MACV, shopped for supplies for the villa at the military PX, and took checks to the bank for deposit into the RAND account. At the PX, he was so popular that he was allowed to purchase quantities of liquor beyond the limit.

Ianeiro reported to Bill Jones, who, as he would later recall, gave him complete freedom and never interfered. Digby gave Ianeiro credit for making things go smoothly and for facilitating Jones's job in Saigon. Leon Goure, no fan of Bill Jones, gave a different picture of the relationship, calling it one of manipulation, with Bill Jones using Yogi "as his whip[,] or heavy" with the rest of the staff. This ran counter to Ianeiro's natural congeniality. He fretted that the staff disliked him, and felt frustrated and "unloved."[5] Gradually the staff began to change. Some of the Goure "old guard," such as Joe Carrier, Shirley Shaffer, and Bonnie Leib, left. Russ and Ardith Betts also departed, along with Doug Scott, who joined the newly opened RAND office in New York.

In mid-1967, Kay O'Bligh came to replace Shirley Shaffer as administrative assistant. Ianeiro described O'Bligh as a tall, lanky blonde who was a sensation wherever she went, especially since American women were a rare sight in Saigon. According to Leon Goure, O'Bligh, Ianeiro, and Jones socialized after work, and in a city that offered few entertainment options, their idea of relaxation was to go to a bar and drink.[6] Ianeiro remembered that RAND people would come from Santa Monica to visit. They enjoyed "hanging out" with him, perhaps because they could relax in his company and not have to impress with incisiveness of mind or authority.[7]

In early December 1967, Vic Croizat came to Saigon to replace Goure as manager of the infiltration interview project after it was extended for six months and after the decision was made to replace Goure as project leader—following discussions in Santa Monica and Washington. Then, toward the end of January 1968, Croizat began the transition as Bill Jones's replacement. In one of his letters home, Jones wrote that he was "boss" until Croizat took over in mid-February. But since he and Croizat were on friendly terms, he would consult with Croizat on decisions that might affect the office after his departure. Vic Croizat, a French-American former Marine colonel, had served in the Navy section of the Military Assistance Advisory Group (MAAG) in Saigon as a liaison officer with the French Army in 1954.

By the time he reached Saigon back then, Dien Bien Phu had fallen and, as the flow of refugees from the north to the south swelled following the armistice, he was assigned to assist with their evacuation from Haiphong, the point of embarkation.

---

5   Leon Goure, letter to a friend in Santa Monica, August 22, 1967.

6   Leon Goure, letter to a friend in Santa Monica, September 23, 1967.

7   Among the senior RAND people visiting Saigon was Gus Shubert, whom Ianeiro tried to teach how to drive his motorcycle. Before Ianeiro could finish his instructions, Shubert took off and crashed into the metal gate.

Afterward, he stayed on as a member of the joint American-French Training Relations and Instructions Mission, or TRIM, which had been created in 1955 to transfer responsibility for the organization and training of the South Vietnamese armed forces from the French to the American military. In the course of this duty, he also served as interpreter for Lieutenant General John W. O'Daniel, the MAAG commander, in meetings with President Ngo Dinh Diem.

Upon returning to the United States in 1956, Croizat served in various posts and, in 1961, was assigned to Bangkok as the U.S. military representative at the Southeast Asia Treaty Organization (SEATO), the formal alliance between the United States and friendly countries in the region. From SEATO, he was assigned to the Marine Corps camp at Pendleton, California, where he commanded a regiment. In 1965, the Marines conducted a big exercise to capture the essential elements of insurgency, in which his regiment played the role of the insurgents—"the bad guys," as he would later recall.[8] It was then that he met Bill Graham and a group of people from RAND who had been invited as observers. After his year with the regiment, Croizat was moved up to Chief of Staff of the division, but he also found out that he was not going to be promoted to general. "So that was the end of that," he recalled. "If you weren't promoted you were automatically retired."[9]

He joined RAND in 1966 as a consultant. Coming from the military where everyone had a clear role within a well-defined organization, he found RAND confusing. "RAND was not structured like the military," he recalled. He could find no one at RAND he knew who had a table of organization. Even if there had been charts "showing boxes with people's names," this would not have meant anything because "you were free to do pretty well whatever you wanted."[10] Left to choose what to focus on, Croizat decided to translate a volume of the "lessons learned" that the French Army had compiled from its experience in Indochina.[11]

Croizat thought he could not stay at RAND with just a bachelor's degree, so he enrolled in UCLA to obtain a doctorate in geography. After he got his master's degree, RAND assigned him to Saigon to replace Bill Jones. When asked why RAND pre-

---

[8]   Author interview with Vic Croizat, 2004.

[9]   Author interview with Vic Croizat, 2004.

[10]   Author interview with Vic Croizat, 2004. Another bewildering aspect of the civilian world of the RAND Corporation was the difficulty of telling who was who. Croizat said that, in the military, "you look at a man's uniform and you know exactly where he's been, what he's done . . . how much money he earns. You know whether you should be polite to him or he should be polite to you. His decorations tell you whether he's brave, how brave he is, where he's been, what battles he's fought in." But in civilian life, "you'd have to find out who you're talking to." Croizat remembered that he did not feel comfortable at RAND, especially when he came into contact with "the young operations research types who wore sandals, let their toe nails grow long, and had an answer to everything."

[11]   This became *A Translation from the French: Lessons of the War in Indochina, Vol. 2*, Santa Monica, Calif.: RAND Corporation, RM-5271-PR, May 1967.

ferred retired military people, such as Ken Strother, Bill Jones, and Vic Croizat, to run the office in Saigon, Jim Digby said that the reason was that RAND management believed Vietnam to be "a rather dangerous environment and that somebody needed to be there who understood the military and military dangers, and could actually organize local defense if need be, or organize an evacuation."[12] Looking back, Croizat would say that accepting this invitation to go to Saigon was "about the stupidest thing" he had ever done.

He said that his motivations at the time were very difficult to understand, even to himself. Psychologically, he was "a mess." He was having trouble adjusting to his retirement from a 26-year career in the Marines. He thought going to Vietnam, where he had served, would give him a chance to continue what he had done and to make a contribution, although he had been taken aback by the U.S. involvement when America jumped into the war. He still remembered vividly what a French officer had told him as they shook hands when the French finally departed from Vietnam for good, "Well, it's all yours now, and I can't tell you how sorry I feel for you."[13] These words stayed with him for years, he said. When he accepted to go to Saigon, he thought that the United States was doing the wrong thing by sending so many troops over and turning the insurgency into an American war.

When Croizat returned to Saigon, the city shocked him. Back in 1954, Saigon was a pleasant, French colonial city, with nice gardens and clean streets, and a population of about 200,000. It was quiet and peaceful, although technically it was still at war because the armistice between the French and the Viet Minh became effective in a staggered fashion, at different dates depending on the region. He saw people strolling in the streets and stores with their doors open. The French military presence was not evident, and the only sign of war was "the wire screens outside the cafes to keep grenades from being thrown in among the customers[,] which happened sometimes."[14] When he came back in December 1967, Saigon had become bloated with a million inhabitants. The streets were crowded, and the little motorcycles were polluting the air with their foul-smelling exhaust fumes. He found the American presence overwhelming and a bit bewildering. The U.S. military was supposedly engaged in a war, and yet it had Post Exchanges where its personnel could purchase refrigerators and household items. A lot did not make any sense to him, he said, especially the way Americans were lavishing money on problems and shoving the Vietnamese aside and taking over the job out of impatience with people who did not do things the same way they did.

As Tet, the Vietnamese New Year, approached, things slowed down and RAND had to suspend its interviews. This gave Croizat time to read some of the interview transcripts. He found many of them quite different from military interrogations and a

---

[12] Author interview with Jim Digby, 2002.

[13] Author interview with Vic Croizat, 2004.

[14] Author interview with Vic Croizat, 2004.

bit baffling, dealing as they did with "social motivations and things of that nature."[15] To his disappointment, he discovered that his job as office manager lacked substance, because he had "nothing to do with the projects."[16] Croizat moved in with Bill Jones, who was living in the RAND villa by himself after the three remaining team leaders— John Harbut, Tony Russo, and Jim Carlson moved out to be on their own. Then Tet arrived. In one of his letters home, Bill Jones noted that Tet started at midnight on January 30th, with "blasts of firecrackers, big and small." The noise continued all night without abating. For the Vietnamese, the sound of firecrackers was joyous—blasting away the troubles of the old year and ushering in the promises of the new year. To an ex-military man like Bill Jones, however, the racket of explosions—too akin to gunfire was "abominable."[17]

The evening of the 30th, Vic Croizat was a dinner guest in the quarters of Joe Donohoe, a Marine colonel who was Westmoreland's Deputy Public Information Officer. Croizat remembered that the dinner conversation was free-ranging, yet no one mentioned the possibility that something out of the ordinary was going to happen, and Croizat got the impression that in fact everything seemed to be going well. After dinner, Croizat drove through Saigon, back to the villa ahead of the new midnight curfew. He found the city deserted, with only policemen in the streets, and no one seemed to expect anything. In Washington, the White House noted enemy buildup around Saigon and Hue, but no one predicted the attack, "although there was a lot of nervousness, uneasiness about it."[18] When it began, the offensive took everyone by surprise. At about 3:00 o'clock in the morning of the 31st, the Tet Offensive erupted in Saigon and all over the country.

That night, David Elliott and his wife happened to be in the RAND villa, having come back from Taiwan to Saigon to celebrate the new year with her family. They were sound asleep in one of the bedrooms with a window that opened toward Thong Nhut, the boulevard that ran past the U.S. Embassy toward the presidential palace, when they were awakened by loud banging on their door. Groggily, they instinctively switched on their bedside lamp and heard the military barking of Vic Croizat, "Turn off the light. We're under attack." They listened for a while, and since there was nothing they could do, they turned over and went back to sleep. In a letter to his family describing what he knew of the offensive, Jones wrote that the RAND villa was located within a triangle formed by the presidential palace, the American Embassy, and the Vietnamese Navy Headquarters, all of which came under attack. These structures were far enough away, however, so that the villa was out of the line of fire. Croizat tried to catch a glimpse of the attack on the embassy by standing on the toilet and looking

---

[15] Author interview with Vic Croizat, 2004.

[16] Author interview with Vic Croizat, 2004.

[17] Bill Jones, letter to his family, January 30, 1968.

[18] Author interview with Richard Moose, 2003.

through the ventilation window near the ceiling, but all he could see was the top of the building. Unlike the Elliotts, who slept comfortably in their bed, Jones wrote that he and Croizat hunkered down and "spent the rest of that night taking cover in case the house was hit by a stray bullet—which it was not."[19]

The next days, while his wife returned to her family to spend time with them, David Elliott joined some American correspondents he knew and went around town to check out what was happening as the attacks continued. Jones, meanwhile, was "taking all precautions." The two ex-military men, Croizat and Jones, taking no chances, armed themselves and locked themselves in the villa, which they blacked out each night. Jones found it comforting that the villa was close to "an American, well armed BOQ [Bachelor Officers Quarters]," and felt reassured by the thought that they could "always move into the BOQ if things get more tense."[20] Jones admitted that he and Croizat were being careful "to the point of being considered cowardly by some of the brasher types here." He "couldn't care less what people might think," however, and would continue to minimize his exposure.[21]

By arming themselves, Croizat and Jones violated a RAND stricture. Jim Digby recalled that "RAND people were not supposed . . . to carry arms," because "if they had been caught" by the Viet Cong "they might have been executed."[22] The stricture did not stop Yogi Ianeiro from keeping a carbine, an M16 grenade, and a flak jacket. During the attacks, John Harbut, who had joined RAND in Saigon, was the only RAND casualty. Harbut was staying at the house of Thuyet, his Vietnamese girlfriend, near the airport when the offensive began. As communist soldiers infiltrated the area and went around looking for Americans, Harbut hid on a ledge next to a wall and was severely wounded when it was hit by a mortar round. Thuyet braved the fighting in the street and bicycled to a Catholic church to get help. Harbut was moved to the American 3rd Field Hospital, where—according to Gerry Hickey—he "underwent surgery to remove the small finger of his right hand and close a large hole in his lower abdomen." When Hickey paid a visit a few days later, he found Harbut lying in a crowded ward and feeling "depressed by the doctor's news that mending the broken nerves controlling muscles in the left leg would be a long process." Hickey noted that "John, who was already very thin, seemed to have shrunk."[23]

Tony Russo counted himself lucky for managing to leave ahead of the offensive. He got the next-to-last seat on a Pan Am flight out of Saigon just before Tet. He had decided to leave because he had had enough, and because he felt that he was wasting

---

[19] Bill Jones, letter to his family, February 5, 1968.

[20] Bill Jones, letter to his family, February 6, 1968.

[21] Bill Jones, letter to his family, February 5, 1968.

[22] Author interview with Jim Digby, 2002.

[23] Hickey, *Window on a War*, 2002, p. 238.

his time. The only hope, he thought, for putting an end to the war was for him to return home, get involved, and "start speaking out [against the war]."[24] He heard of the attack while sitting at the Bangkok airport, waiting to board a flight to Tokyo. As his plane flew over Danang Airfield, he looked down and saw aircraft that were "all broken up—it was a wing here, a fuselage cracked in two. And it was all over the place, it wasn't just here and there."[25] When he arrived in Tokyo, he checked the news and found out what had happened. He said to himself, "Oh my God, I've just barely gotten out of there."[26]

The Tet Offensive was a daring, simultaneous countrywide series of attacks. It was put in place in mid-1967, as the war reached a stalemate, by the leaders in Hanoi. The objectives were complex—a mixture of military, political, and diplomatic goals—and the final plan envisaged a range of outcomes. In accordance with revolutionary warfare principles, the emphasis was on political more than on military goals. Militarily, the objective was not to inflict a direct defeat on U.S. forces, but to demonstrate to Washington that the war had reached a stalemate and could not be won militarily, and to force the United States to choose between escalation and disengagement. By moving the war to the towns and cities, the communists also wanted to take pressure off the liberated areas in the countryside. Politically, their objective was to right the balance of terror. The United States had been inflicting death and destruction on the countryside and driving the population into the urban areas to seek safety, and this massive flow of refugees had deprived the insurgency of manpower, tax revenue, and resources. By attacking the towns and cities, the insurgents aimed to bring the terror of war to the urban areas, rendering them as insecure and as inhospitable as the villages, and, it was hoped, driving the people to leave. The assault on the urban areas, the communists hoped, would also trigger an insurrection against the Americans and the GVN by "weary government soldiers, dislocated peasants, frustrated religious factions, fractious youths and other unhappy elements of the southern population."[27] Diplomatically, the aim was to force the United States to seek a settlement on terms favored by the communists.

The planners of the offensive envisaged a range of outcomes. Militarily, the first scenario was a definitive victory, which would not defeat the United States but would force it to begin peace talks. The second scenario was victory in many areas; however, the other side would regroup and, reinforced from outside, would recapture important locations—particularly Saigon to continue the war. The third and most pessimistic scenario—but also the one deemed least likely—was that the United States would send

---

[24] Author interview with Tony Russo, 2003 and 2004.

[25] Author interview with Tony Russo, 2003 and 2004.

[26] Author interview with Tony Russo, 2003 and 2004.

[27] Karnow, *Vietnam*, 1983, p. 549.

more troops and escalate attacks in North Vietnam, Laos, and Cambodia to change the direction of the war and bolster its weakened position.

Politically, the maximum outcome was the collapse of the GVN and the formation of a neutralist but pro-VC coalition government that would eject the Americans and begin the process of reunifying Vietnam under communist control. Diplomatically even if the communists failed to topple the Saigon government they believed that the outcome would lead President Johnson to halt the bombing of the North and initiate negotiations on their terms. Once peace talks began, the negotiations would drive a wedge between Washington and Saigon: GVN senior officials would become apprehensive and suspicious that the United States might abandon them.

The offensive actually began in September 1967, when the communists staged a series of attacks in remote areas to draw South Vietnamese and U.S. forces from the cities. Among their targets was Dak To in the Central Highlands. Delighted that the enemy was finally choosing to fight a conventional battle in a remote, sparsely populated area where he could unleash his superior weaponry, Westmoreland responded with massive firepower. B-52s flew 300 missions, and more than 2,000 fighter-bombers carried out assaults; together, they rained bombs on enemy positions. Seventy thousand artillery shells were fired, and chemical warfare operations were launched to destroy what little was left of the vegetation. Estimates of communist casualties during the three months leading up to Tet boosted Westmoreland's optimism, and he declared on a visit to Washington in November that "the enemy's hopes are bankrupt."[28]

By far, the biggest diversionary attack staged by the communists was their siege of Khe Sanh, a small Special Forces camp along Route 9 leading into Laos that Westmoreland had begun to enlarge in the summer of 1967 to target communist sanctuaries in Laos and supply lines from the North. In late 1967, reports indicated that the North Vietnamese had amassed a force of 40,000 men, consisting of four infantry divisions reinforced by two artillery regiments and armored units, near Khe Sanh. Westmoreland interpreted the move as a communist plan to stage a climactic battle on the scale of Dien Bien Phu as part of a larger scheme to wrest control over South Vietnam's northernmost provinces, thereby boosting their bargaining position prior to peace talks, as they had done at Dien Bien Phu before the Geneva Conference in 1954.

Westmoreland moved 6,000 U.S. Marines to the area. His plan of counterattack included massive bombing and the potential use of tactical nuclear weapons. The battle erupted on January 21, 1968. By the time the NVA withdrew and the Marines secretly abandoned Khe Sanh two months later, the North Vietnamese had paid a heavy price, losing 10,000 men while killing fewer than 500 Marines.

---

[28] Karnow, *Vietnam*, 1983, p. 552.

Map of Tet Offensive

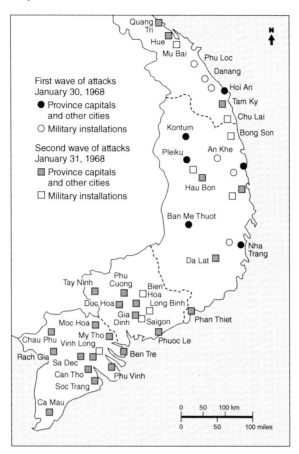

However high the cost to the NVA, the feint at Khe Sanh and the diversionary attacks elsewhere worked. As U.S. troops were moved to the northern region, the security of the Saigon area was transferred to ARVN forces—out of necessity, but also as a gesture of confidence in the Vietnamese military. Exploiting the lax security, Viet Cong attack teams moved arms, ammunition, and explosives into the city from a base 30 miles north of Saigon. Then, as Tet approached, more than one-half of the ARVN forces were given leave in late January to celebrate the holiday with their families.

On January 31, 1968, the full-scale offensive began, with simultaneous attacks by the communists on five major cities, 36 provincial capitals, 64 district capitals, and numerous villages. The ferocity and scope of the offensive caught Westmoreland and other U.S. military leaders in Vietnam off guard. In a review in March 1968, American intelligence experts concluded that the surprise was the result of intelligence failure, but also of "the false sense of security" created among U.S. officers by illusory reports on North Vietnamese and Vietcong casualties, infiltration, recruitment, and morale, which had led military leaders to underestimate the strength of the enemy.

The gunfire audible at the RAND villa in the early morning hours of January 31st emanated from the attack on the American Embassy—the symbol of American power, located in the safest, central part of the capital, and one of the key targets of the offensive. At three o'clock that morning, a team of Viet Cong commandos pulled up in front of the building in a truck and a taxicab. They blasted the building with anti-tank rockets and rushed inside, firing their automatic weapons and killing five GIs in the melee. The embassy was hardly the only target. Viet Cong commandos also took over the main radio station, a key communications facility, while another team tried to break into the presidential palace. When they failed, they barricaded themselves in an apartment building nearby. The Viet Cong also attacked Westmoreland's MACV headquarters and the South Vietnamese general staff offices, both located near the Saigon airport. Meanwhile, a Viet Cong division attacked the U.S. base at Bien Hoa, blocked American and South Vietnamese reinforcements from reaching the capital, and blew up an ammunition dump near Saigon with rockets. Inside the city, police posts, army barracks, prisons, and other installations also came under attack. It took the Americans six-and-a-half hours to secure the U.S. Embassy.

Saigon was thrown into turmoil, and an extensive curfew was imposed even during daytime hours. Communication with Santa Monica was cut off, and Bill Jones attempted by every means possible to send messages to RAND, all the while not knowing if any got through. Slowly, the city returned to a semblance of normality. With a small force attacking so many targets, the Viet Cong were spread thin and were subdued in a withering counterattack by American and South Vietnamese forces. Saigon fared much better than Hue, the former imperial capital, which was seized and held for three weeks by an estimated force of 12,000 communist troops. During the occupation, the communists were reported to have executed 2,000 to 3,000 government and police officials, and other residents they accused of being "counter-revolutionaries." After weeks of arduous fighting, carried out mainly by three U.S. Marine battalions backed by South Vietnamese troops and artillery—the communists were driven from the city. They suffered heavy casualties, losing an estimated 5,000 men; the Marines lost 150 men and the ARVN, 400.

Gerry Hickey recalled that, in Saigon, the Tet Offensive

> ushered in a long nightmare of street fighting, bombings, and rocket attacks that set off huge fires in thatched poor sections. Bunkers and trenches were dug in parks and gardens. Sandbags were piled in front of public buildings and houses . . . in living rooms, and on apartment building balconies. Barbed wire was ubiquitous. All glass windows were taped. Strict curfews were enforced.[29]

ARPA began to hand out weapons to American civilians, including Hickey, who asked for a carbine despite RAND's injunction to its staff members not to carry arms.

---

[29] Hickey, *Window on a War*, 2002, p. 248.

In the days following the initial attacks, things quieted down in the area around the RAND villa, although, as Jones informed his family, there were still "scattered fights every night in the outer parts of the city." By February 5, only four of the interviewers had checked in at the office. Since it had become impossible to continue interviewing prisoners and defectors, Bill Jones assigned them to conduct "a public opinion surveying-type of operation" by interviewing Saigon residents, who were asked to evaluate whether the Tet attack was "a failure or a psychological success" and to reveal what they expected the GVN to do in the current situation. Between February 5 and 9, the teams conducted about 50 interviews. Then, much to his relief, the time came for Jones to leave Vietnam, on February 19. In a letter home, he wrote, "I can't say that I will be sorry to leave."

In Santa Monica, David Mozingo had written a paper anticipating Hanoi's offensive. He recalled that Guy Pauker, who had been impressed by his analysis of Lin Piao's speech and who had agreed with its conclusions, approached him about writing an analysis of North Vietnam's diplomacy and strategy, using open texts, such as translated captured documents and radio intercepts contained in Foreign Broadcast Information Services (FBIS) reports of statements by Hanoi's military on the war. In his paper, Mozingo concluded that Hanoi was going to "go to higher level–sized engagements, from guerrilla warfare to mobile warfare," and that they would use these engagements to create favorable political conditions. By going on the offensive and sustaining heavy military pressure, the communist forces could potentially bring about the collapse of the GVN and confront the United States with the prospect of an endless war, which in turn would create intense political pressure within the United States to withdraw—as the French had done. This, to Mozingo, would be standing "Maoism on its head," because Maoism dictated that it was "the political" that created "the military" rather than the other way around.[30]

According to Mozingo, the communist leadership viewed the GVN/ARVN as the chink in the U.S. armor, as "the delayed action bomb in the lap of the United States."[31] This army had been defeated, and the war had already been lost, when the United States entered the war in 1965. Although the United States had poured troops into the South, it could only delay the disintegration of the GVN/ARVN. No matter how many troops the United States sent to the South, it could not achieve numerical superiority over the insurgents in order to defeat them, because its troop increases had been matched by those of the insurgents and their allies in the North. This balance of forces was not about to change in the future, since economic, political, and military realities would make it very difficult for the United States to dispatch more and more

---

[30] Author interview with David Mozingo, 2003.

[31] David Mozingo, *Hanoi on the War in South Vietnam*, Santa Monica, Calif.: RAND Corporation, D-15182, October 27, 1966, p. 27.

troops. Mozingo's predictions were borne out by the communist Tet Offensive and its aftermath.

However, at the time he wrote his paper, his analysis ran counter to the conventional wisdom that the enemy was hurting and on the ropes—a line taken by such people as Leon Goure and some hawks in the Economics Department, Mozingo remembered. Mozingo gave Guy Pauker credit for not attempting to "gag" him or "change the scope of the paper." Instead of criticizing him, Pauker encouraged him just as he was encouraging "anybody . . . that wanted to do work on Vietnam." The Social Science Department, however, "gagged" him for two years before the Tet Offensive. "They couldn't very well have objected," he recalled, "because I was simply reporting what the Vietnamese [were saying]." Nonetheless, they practically reviewed it to death, and it was not published as a research memorandum, or RM. The paper went through a couple of drafts and, although "some of the criticism was well taken," it was clear that "they didn't want it to get out."[32] It was not even circulated informally to DoD. The paper remained as a D (draft)—a less formal, less polished, less authoritative, and less prestigious designation than RM.[33]

For Mozingo, this was the only time he had anything that was killed with review. "They couldn't say no," he remembered, because "they didn't want me to leave, I guess," but, on the other hand, "they didn't want to go on." According to Mozingo, after the Tet Offensive, Joe Goldsen asked him to come back in the summer of 1968—from Cornell University, where he had gone to teach—to revise his paper for publication as an RM "so that RAND could show that it knew all along." Mozingo came back, but by that time Fred Iklé had replaced Joe Goldsen as chairman of the Social Science Department. Mozingo said that he would have revised the paper but his meeting with Iklé went badly so he told RAND "to buzz off."[34] At that point, he was working on something else anyway, and so the would-be RM died.

In Vietnam, as conditions remained too unsettled for the RAND team to travel around the country, the interviewers were instructed to continue interviews on the Tet Offensive in and near Saigon. Eventually, a total of 425—called Tet A interviews— were conducted with middle- and upper-middle-class noncommunist Vietnamese, a group that had not featured in RAND studies. This research would last from February to April 1968. These Tet A interviews were used by Victoria Pohle, a former staff

---

[32] Author interview with David Mozingo, 2003.

[33] Mozingo, *Hanoi on the War in South Vietnam*, 1966.

[34] Author interview with David Mozingo, 2003.

member who had become a RAND consultant, for a report[35] on Viet Cong political actions during the attacks and the reactions of the respondents to the offensive. She concluded that the offensive reinforced the uneasiness of the middle-class regarding the intention of the United States, and speculated that fear of eventual NLF control might lead some to seek accommodation with the Viet Cong.

Consistent with their mode of operation, the Viet Cong combined military and political activities in the attacks. The political actions were designed to instill fear and erode the "confidence, morale, and cohesion" of the people and of members of the GVN, ARVN, and police, to neutralize the GVN security apparatus, seize control of some hamlets in the vicinity of Saigon, and compromise the local population in the eyes of the GVN to eliminate potential support for the government—using propaganda, and threats; forced draft; destruction of GVN-issued identification cards; arrest and assassination of government officials, police personnel, and ARVN officers; and other terrorist acts.[36] They succeeded to a certain extent, given that the interviews indicated that the offensive reinforced the fear of the middle- and upper-middle class Vietnamese that the United States would one day withdraw and leave them to the mercy of the communists. Doubts about U.S. commitment grew during and following the Tet Offensive. People speculated about the reasons for the Viet Cong attack, and rumors circulated that the United States had "collaborated with the Viet Cong" and allowed it to take place, and that it was part of a scheme by the United States to "sell out" South Vietnam: a pretext that would allow the Americans to impose a coalition government or to withdraw.[37] Pohle's analysis indicated, therefore, that one of the enemy's aims in launching the Tet Offensive was achieved: to sow distrust of the United States among elements of the population who supported American involvement in the war.

Class background and affiliation with the government and/or the Americans influenced the attitude of the respondents. Those who believed the rumors tended to be people who feared the communists the most—refugees from the North; upper-middle class and wealthy citizens; Catholics; members of the GVN, ARVN, or police; employees of U.S. agencies; and adherents of various religious sects—and who had the most to lose if the Viet Cong could secure a favorable outcome to the war. Some of the most active anti-VC elements among them were greatly concerned and frightened that the Tet Offensive might bolster the Viet Cong's position and lead to their eventual takeover of the South. Out of concern for their ultimate survival, they opposed peace negotiations and would rather see the GVN and, they hoped, the United States

---

[35] Victoria Pohle, *The Viet Cong in Saigon: Tactics and Objectives During the Tet Offensive*, Santa Monica, Calif.: RAND Corporation, RM-5799-ISA/ARPA, January 1969.

[36] However, acts of terror were directed mainly at government personnel. Among the general population, acts of terror were "*not* randomly carried out," and were generally directed only "against selected groups of people—usually those known to be hostile to the Viet Cong" (emphasis in original), Pohle, *The Viet Cong in Saigon*, 1969, p. 21.

[37] Pohle, *The Viet Cong in Saigon*, 1969, p. x.

as well, continue the war either at the same pace or escalate it further. They feared that negotiations would ultimately lead the United States to accept a political coalition in the South and to begin withdrawing its troops.

In contrast, poor and middle-class Buddhists said that they did not care which side won, because the continued fighting was destructive and served no purpose.[38] Of these, two-thirds favored peace negotiations either because there was no hope that the GVN could defeat the Viet Cong or because the war was exacting too high a cost. During the fighting, they were generally more concerned with their personal safety than with the issues dividing the two sides of the war. They did not actively provide support to either side and did not volunteer to fight or provide information. They usually tried to avoid contact and confrontation with the Viet Cong as much as possible. If contact was unavoidable, they generally acceded to demands for food and shelter and complied as little as possible without risking a confrontation with the Viet Cong. The analysis led Victoria Pohle to conclude that the general population of Saigon and, possibly, other urban areas would remain uncommitted in the conflict and refrain from actively supporting either side.

Pohle also saw danger for the government. Peace talks and Viet Cong pressure on the cities and towns—if it continued—might induce some urban residents who were leaning toward the GVN and the United States to hedge and "accommodate" in some fashion to the Viet Cong. If and when this accommodation began, it would probably gradually motivate others in the GVN and ARVN to do likewise. In her view, accommodation made either publicly or privately, whether limited or extensive, would not only embarrass the GVN politically but might also lessen its ability to deal with the Viet Cong's military threat and implement its political and social programs. She warned that such disintegration "from the bottom up" would at the very least bolster the Viet Cong's political leadership and, at the worst, "might create intolerable pressures on the GVN, thereby weakening its bargaining position in any negotiations, and lead to the collapse of the present government."[39]

While Pohle's report seemed to have passed without creating a ripple of objection, another RAND paper related to the Tet Offensive provoked controversy. It was based on interviews conducted with lower-class refugees who had poured into Saigon during the offensive and in the American/GVN counterattack that followed. Unable to travel around the country, team members—to fill the vacuum—conducted about 200 interviews with these refugees between February and March 1968. From the information collected, Len Ackland produced a report revealing the effect of firepower on civilians during the offensive and counterattacks: a sensitive topic. General Westmoreland him-

---

[38] Some people in the poorer sections openly showed their pro-VC sympathies: They greeted and talked with enemy troops, invited them into their homes, and even "offered them food and a hiding place from the ARVN," Pohle, *The Viet Cong in Saigon*, 1969, p. 31.

[39] Pohle, *The Viet Cong in Saigon*, 1969, p. 63.

self had opposed research on refugees for fear that it would bring this effect to light, and RAND had stayed away from this subject, even going so far—according to Ardith Betts—as to bury a report done by Doug Scott.

Ackland, a Vietnamese-speaking former member of the International Voluntary Services in Hue, had been hired in Saigon by RAND to be a team leader/analyst.[40] In June 1968, Ackland sent to Santa Monica his paper on the refugees' reaction to the bombing and shelling of their former home villages. Titled "Observations Concerning the Political Dimensions of the Refugee Situation in the Saigon Area." It was intended as an "in-house" memorandum for RAND staff members to use.

However, the paper was not reproduced and circulated at RAND, because, as Ackland was told, it was considered too controversial. Ackland worked for RAND in Saigon for a few months. In 1970, while studying at the Johns Hopkins School for Advanced International Studies as a graduate student and working as a research assistant at the Brookings Institution, Ackland talked to Robert M. Smith of *The New York Times* and provided him with a copy of his paper.[41] According to Smith, when he inquired at RAND about the suppression of Ackland's paper, a RAND official who had been present in Saigon in 1968 denied that he had said the reason the report was not reproduced and circulated was that it was too controversial. But he could not give Smith an explanation of "why the report had not been reproduced." A RAND official in Santa Monica told Smith that "such memorandums were usually printed for internal distribution as a matter of course and said he was trying to learn what happened to Mr. Ackland's report."

In his paper, Ackland reported that the sufferings inflicted on refugees by excessive and indiscriminate bombings and shellings had provoked resentment against the government, undermining its efforts to enlist popular support. In its counterattacks, the GVN had overrelied on airpower and artillery, using heavy weapons even against "small bands of VC spread out in large, populated areas," with the consequence that more than half of the refugees interviewed had seen or heard about air or artillery strikes, and most of these had themselves been victims of such strikes, including a woman whose children had been killed in a bombardment. Not all the victims were willing to assign blame for their sufferings, since—as Ackland pointed out to Smith—they knew they were talking to interviewers working for the Americans. Still, as Ackland wrote in his RAND report, it was striking that of those who were willing to assign

---

[40] Ackland, at the time of this writing a journalism professor at the University of Colorado at Boulder, refused to grant an interview with the author because he could not be assured that her report would be made available to the public by RAND. As a journalist, Ackland has fought to make information public, and he felt that he could not participate unless the book would be released. The interviews Ackland did for his RAND report were conducted in refugee camps in Saigon/Gia Dinh and were called "Tet B" interviews, as opposed to the "Tet A" interviews with middle- and upper-middle-class Vietnamese.

[41] Robert M. Smith, "Report Compiled in '68 Says Excessive Allied Bombing in South Vietnam Stirred Hostility to Regime," *The New York Times*, January 22, 1970.

blame, more than half blamed the government out of anger over the "heavy-handed response that showed so little concern for their welfare." As one respondent who, while acknowledging that the GVN had to respond to Viet Cong provocations, put it, "I wish the Government could have found some other means to defeat the enemy [other than bombings and shellings], which would have saved many lives."

The conduct of some government soldiers further aggravated the situation. Refugees reported that South Vietnamese soldiers had stolen their possessions. Although there were less than a dozen reports of such looting, the news was spread by market gossip and created resentment against the government and the ARVN soldiers who came "to save" but "also came to steal."

The refugee problem had become serious with the change of command from General William Westmoreland to General Creighton Abrams, an "aggressive tank commander from the General Patton school."[42] In pursuing what became known as a "clear and hold strategy," Abrams employed heavy firepower in populated regions, with "devastating consequences for many civilians," especially in many Mekong Delta provinces."[43] Abrams's strategy, however, was not a drastic departure from what Westmoreland himself was contemplating before being replaced; Abrams's "clear and hold" operations in effect were implementing Phase III of Westmoreland's plan to extend and expand "clearing and security operations . . . throughout the entire populated area of the country."[44]

Before the Tet Offensive, Westmoreland had tried to minimize civilian casualties. Partly out of concern about the effect on civilians as U.S. troops substituted "firepower for American lives," Westmoreland "preferred to fight in remote areas." "To build safeguards against the consequences of unrestrained military operations in heavily populated areas," Westmoreland devised "careful and legalistic 'rules of engagement.'"[45] Such restraint, however, did not apply to "free fire zones," where civilians were considered Viet Cong supporters and therefore viewed as legitimate targets. Nor were these rules observed for harassment and interdiction fire, which was designed to keep the Viet Cong off balance but which could wound or kill civilians. The GVN, for its part, was not bound by any such restrictions.

Just before the Tet Offensive, however, Westmoreland had become "frustrated with the high costs and slow progress of pacification" and began to consider "the relative merits of a depopulation strategy." In a memorandum dated January 4, 1968, on "The Refugee Problem," he discussed the dependence of the insurgents on their control of the population, and mentioned that, to thwart their efforts, "it is necessary to eliminate the 'fish' from the 'water,' or to dry up the 'water' so that the 'fish' cannot survive."

---

[42] Elliott, *The Vietnamese War*, 2003, p. 336.

[43] Elliott, *The Vietnamese War*, 2003, p. 335.

[44] Elliott, *The Vietnamese War*, 2003, p. 336.

[45] Elliott, *The Vietnamese War*, 2003, p. 335.

There were only two options: "either the communists and their political control must be driven from the populated areas and security provided to keep them out, or the people must be relocated into areas that will facilitate security and prevent communist control apparatus from re-entering the community." The first option, Westmoreland wrote, was "preferred" but it would be "time consuming." The second option, he added, "can be carried out relatively quickly and is not as expensive in security troops as the first course of action." He concluded, "In summary, there are two basic ways of eliminating communist influence: one, by tediously catching the 'fish' (the VC) and letting the 'water' (the people) remain in place; two, by draining off the 'water' and recapturing it at another location and allowing the 'fish' to strangle. Discrimination must be exercised in choosing the method to be employed. The relocation of the population should not in all practicability be disallowed, since it can save lives, destruction, and time. However, the refugee care must be anticipated and sympathetically planned."[46]

❧ ❧ ❧

While the RAND interviewers were kept busy with research on the Tet Offensive and the refugee situation, Vic Croizat found himself with a lot of time on his hands. After Bill Jones left, Croizat lived by himself in the RAND villa. With the early curfew, he would sit around in the evening, with "absolutely nothing to do," and found this state of affairs "most unpleasant."[47] Tet had disrupted the routine of the office and imposed a long hiatus for RAND's main program of defector and prisoner interviews. It also caused a lot of turmoil, and he could not predict what was going to happen next. Communication was problematic. He felt isolated and unable to communicate with RAND because he could not just "pick up the phone and call anybody." Fortunately, he had some friends who kept him "from going completely nuts." One was General John Chaisson, an old friend from the Marine Corps who was serving as director of the Combat Operations Center for Westmoreland. Chaisson allowed him "to read the classified message traffic which was very important, very interesting" and to send messages to RAND.

But the most unpleasant aspect of his stay in Saigon, according to Croizat, was that he was not performing any substantive work. To give himself something to do, Croizat made out an office organization chart, with a list of personnel and a definition of their duties, and assembled it all in March 1968 into *Organization, Personnel Policies and Operating Procedures*. Croizat now laughs at that effort as "typical of a Marine" who, upon taking up a new assignment, immediately checks out the organization chart and, if one does not exist, hastens to make one up. To keep himself occupied, he also contacted people he knew, such as those in the CIA who were working on the Phoenix

---

[46] Elliott, *The Vietnamese War*, 2003, pp. 335–336.

[47] This and the other quotes in this paragraph are from the author's interview with Vic Croizat, 2004.

program. This covert intelligence operation had been set up by the CIA in 1967—in close collaboration with GVN intelligence—to identify, target, and "neutralize" the Viet Cong infrastructure through capture, kidnapping, assassination, or torture, or by induced surrender, or disruptive actions. Croizat said that he was disturbed by Phoenix because, from a mere interpretation of "various bits of evidence," people could be dealt with in a "definitive way." To him, "A profile [of a person] is not an objective thing. Somebody's got to draw it up" and, to his mind, "no matter how honest you are when you do these things, there's got to be an element of uncertainty." He recalled that what he learned left a "very bad taste" in his mouth, because he hated "the thought of people being killed with an element of uncertainty."[48]

Croizat might have compiled *Organization, Personnel Policies and Operating Procedures* out of boredom, but it is a useful, historical document about office procedures and about the American and Vietnamese staff at 176 Pasteur at the time. Calling himself "Director, Vietnam Program," Croizat wrote that he was assisted by a "Manager, Vietnam Field Operations," a position then occupied by Tom Kiley. Kiley was given the title of Deputy Program Director, and in this capacity he was "the executive agent specifically responsible for carrying out all incountry activities" relating to the interview project. The description makes Kiley's position sound important, but some of the American staff members could not recall exactly what he was doing administratively. David Elliott said that the only interaction with Kiley he could remember was a brief exchange during which Kiley asked him about RAND's retirement-benefits package. Elliott recalled that he was dumbfounded by the question because he was not thinking about retirement at age 30 in the middle of a war.

Croizat listed three team supervisors—John S. Harbut, Jim Carlson, and Len Ackland—and 17 interviewers.[49] According to Croizat, the three teams took turns going into the field—if and when conditions allowed. While one team was off conducting interviews, a second one would get ready to take a field trip, and the third would be in Saigon transcribing and translating the interviews. Personnel policy for the American staff included a 30-day home leave for those who had served one year and agreed to extend for another year, and Rest and Rehabilitation (R&R) every three months to Thailand, Malaya, Singapore, or Hong Kong. The Vietnamese staff was expected to work 44 hours a week, including a half-day on Saturday, and were entitled to seven days of annual leave and five days for sick leave. They got a bonus at Tet, equivalent to one month's pay.

Croizat also enumerated emergency procedures in the event of "uprising, attack, or other disturbance." When such events occurred, Croizat instructed that the RAND staff remain inside if they happened to be indoors and avoid standing by windows or on roof terraces. If there was small-arms fire, they should stay close to the floor. If there

---

[48] Author interview with Vic Croizat, 2004.

[49] According to Carlson, Harbut later moved to Alaska with his Vietnamese wife.

was mortar fire, they should not go to the upper stories of buildings, and should shield themselves from debris by covering themselves with a mattress. If they happened to be outdoors, they should stay away from crowds or gatherings and then make their way to the nearest safe haven. He told the staff they should keep an emergency kit consisting of candles and matches, two days' supply of canned food, two days' supply of drinking water, a first-aid kit, a flashlight with good batteries, and a battery-powered radio. Practically no one among the staff paid any heed to these instructions. Jim Carlson's reaction to Croizat's style was perhaps typical. He found Croizat "kind of military," and recalled that Croizat was attempting to "put a lot of structure" into a rather loose-knit operation.

As Croizat soon discovered, the nature of the RAND operation itself and the disruption of the Tet Offensive would ensure that procedures he wanted to put in place, such as weekly meetings, could not be applied. The atmosphere changed, and a feeling of stagnation settled over the villa. In a letter to Joe Carrier, Le Thi Que, one of the veteran interviewers, wrote that the team spirit, the pride of working for RAND, and the satisfaction derived from believing that one was doing something worthwhile were gone. Despite what Croizat wrote in his personnel manual regarding the interview program, Que told Carrier that she had not gone on a field trip for more than a year.

❖ ❖ ❖

The sense of uncertainty that bothered Croizat and kept RAND from resuming normal activities lingered on. According to Gerry Hickey, a month after the Tet Offensive began, calm returned to Saigon but anxiety remained high due to Red Alerts, which were issued occasionally to put the residents on guard about anticipated enemy attacks. "The city began to take on the aura of an armed camp," he recalled, and a 7 p.m. curfew was imposed.[50] Then, in May 1968, another communist offensive began with a new series of attacks, called "Mini Tet."

On the morning of May 6, explosions were followed by flares, mortar and artillery fire, and airstrikes. Rockets—the first to hit Saigon—fell into the downtown area and into the vicinity of the central market. Reports circulated that the communists would fire more mortars and rockets into the city to try to knock out police stations. Shops began to close at noon. When the decision was made that the American staff should all move into the villa, Gerry Hickey took Joan Allen back to her apartment on Ham Nghi Boulevard near a market and the Saigon River so that she could pack some clothes. Allen had arrived in Saigon in early 1968 to replace Kay O'Bligh. Allen was no stranger to Vietnam, having worked in the Foreign Service there for two years. After joining RAND, she worked for Albert Wohlstetter. When O'Bligh's position opened in Saigon, someone in Personnel who knew that she had spent time in Viet-

---

[50] Hickey, *Window on a War*, 2002, p. 242.

nam asked whether Joan would like to take the assignment. Her job would entail doing such things as coordinating car transportation for the RAND staff in Saigon —since everyone had to share one car and one driver—typing RAND reports, and answering the phone.

When Hickey and Allen arrived at her apartment, they saw American helicopters flying low over houses across the Saigon River and strafing and firing rockets. While they were waiting for Yogi Ianeiro to come and pick them up, Allen brought iced gin and tonics to the terrace, and they sipped the cocktails while watching the helicopters. Ianeiro was dumbfounded to find them, cocktails in hand, as though nothing was going on. They were in no hurry to leave and told him that they wanted to finish their drinks first. They said that this was better than rushing around in a state of panic, so he told them, "Make me one, then."[51] They stood on the balcony and watched, but, although they heard shots, they did not see anything. The picture of the three standing on a balcony drinking cocktails and watching the military action captured the incongruous nature of the war: It could be deadly and a spectacle at the same time. Since American F-105 jets began to dive over the area across the river to drop bombs, Gerry Hickey decided to move into the villa as well.

Jim Carlson remembered that during the last couple of months he and his wife were in Saigon, after Tet, life was not secure, because the Viet Cong would occasionally fire rockets into the city. On at least two occasions, the rockets landed close to his apartment building, sending debris from the ceiling, and he and his wife had to go downstairs to take shelter with their infant son. Rockets even fell on Tu Do Street, right in the heart of Saigon.[52] At night, the sound of helicopters, the flares, and the occasional bursts of gunfire and explosions frightened residents into thinking that another communist attack might be in the offing.

Ianeiro was in his element during this period. Armed with a carbine, he drove around town in the station wagon he had purchased from Japan to pick up RAND staff members and ferry them to the villa. He kept the staff well-supplied with food when the markets were not open regularly, and even managed to obtain a large store of eggs and steaks from a military friend. As Joan Allen would say in retrospect, Ianeiro was very good at taking care of people.

While Ianeiro seemed to thrive in these conditions, in which his skills and services as a "fixer" were more vital than those of anyone else's at the villa, Vic Croizat found himself further disturbed by the turn of events. Ianeiro recalled that Croizat spent most of his time at the Cercle Sportif, and that, "The moment [he] heard an

---

[51] Author interview with Yogi Ianeiro, 2004.

[52] According to Gerry Hickey (*Window on a War*, 2002, p. 254), "When fighting flared between Saigon and Cholon along Boulevard Tran Hung Dao, watching the war from rooftops became a Saigon pastime. People gathered on roofs of hotels to drink and point at the jets diving to discharge bombs . . . and tanks firing down streets lined with smashed and burning shops and houses. Choppers were sweeping in[,] firing machine guns and rockets. Jets seemed to come from nowhere to drop bombs that shook the hotel."

explosion, he wanted to move to Bangkok."[53] Joan Allen remembered Croizat saying that "he didn't intend to get killed" in Saigon.[54]

Croizat did cut short his stay and move to Bangkok after the May Offensive, which to him was like the last straw. His decision might have been prompted by a rocket attack that happened one evening after dinner. The explosions shocked Croizat and the staff out of their post-dinner torpor and drinks, and they all rushed into the yard, violating Croizat's own instruction to stay indoors in an attack. Yet, according to Allen, after this episode, the RAND staff got a commendation, praising them for their "heroism." According to Croizat, he decided to leave for Bangkok because he believed that, with the interview project still in a state of suspension due to lack of access to prisoners and defectors—and with no indication of when POWs and defectors would be made available again—he could leave the management of the Saigon office in the hands of Ianeiro and Allen. He did not want to remain in Saigon, he would later say—living "under tight wartime restrictions," with "nothing to do and little chance of finding gainful occupation."[55] After arriving in Bangkok, he visited—on his own initiative—some of his former associates at SEATO to explore the possibility of RAND performing analyses on some issues SEATO was researching, but apparently nothing resulted from his efforts. Shortly thereafter, he returned to the United States, "saddened" that his Saigon assignment "had been a waste of time." He left RAND for good in fall 1968.[56]

The diplomatic breakthrough that the communists attempted to create with their Tet Offensive materialized in 1968. Pressure on President Johnson to seek a settlement grew as the scope and ferocity of the attacks, coming after months of rosy reports and optimistic predictions about the course of the war, stunned his administration and the American public watching the fighting on their television evening news. The attack on the U.S. Embassy and the assault on the towns and cities were beyond anything President Johnson could have imagined. The embassy attack in particular—the symbol of

---

[53] Author interview with Yogi Ianeiro, 2004.

[54] Author interview with Joan Allen, 2003.

[55] Author interview with Vic Croizat, 2004.

[56] In October 1969, Vic Croizat's paper, *The Development of the Plain of Reeds: Some Politico-Military Implications* (Santa Monica, Calif.: RAND Corporation, P-3976), which he had written earlier, was published. He recalled that he had written it at the request of ARPA, which wanted to see how this strategic area could be developed and denied to the communists who were using it as a transit zone to move supplies into the Mekong Delta. According to Croizat, the problems for developing the Plain of Reeds were complex. The biggest obstacle would be to take away control of the area from the Viet Cong. The second problem would be to secure Cambodia's cooperation for managing the floodwaters that flowed from Cambodia and inundated the area during the rainy season. Croizat concluded that the Vietnamese themselves could initiate the development, but that, eventually, any meaningful development project would have to be implemented as part of an international effort involving Cambodia.

American power in the heart of the South Vietnamese capital—had a powerful psychological impact. The offensive shocked Johnson and plunged his eroding popularity to a new low. Even opinion leaders—"business executives, media commentators, educators, clergymen and other 'elites' whose voices resonated more forcefully in Washington than those of Middle America"—began to abandon the president, isolating him further in a year when he was planning to seek reelection.[57] Clark Clifford, the new Secretary of Defense, would later recall in his 1991 memoir that military and civilian officials alike were "profoundly affected by the Tet offensive," and that "there was, for a brief time, something approaching a sense of events spiraling out of control."[58]

The toll of the offensive was lopsided. By early March 1968, the communists had lost 50,000 men, compared with 2,000 American and 4,000 South Vietnamese casualties. The communist losses decimated the native, southern insurgents, who had borne the brunt of the fighting. To replace them, more North Vietnamese forces were sent South, and their growing presence even down into the Mekong Delta gave the insurgency a new military and political cast. But the communists achieved one of their objectives: forcing Washington to either escalate or start negotiating. Clark Clifford had assumed office with a reputation as a hardliner. By early March 1968, however, he had come to the conclusion that "all we were going to do was waste our treasure and the lives of our men out there in the jungles," and this had led him to "quietly" oppose the war.[59] From that date onward, he became convinced that the United States should limit its involvement and begin to withdraw gradually.

To change Johnson's thinking about the war, Clifford proposed to convene the group of elder statesmen: Dean Acheson, Secretary of State under Truman; Arthur Goldberg, the president's envoy to the United Nations; George Ball; McGeorge Bundy; Henry Cabot Lodge; Averell Harriman; Cyrus Vance; and Douglas Dillon, a banker from New York who had served both Presidents Eisenhower and Kennedy. These were the "wise men" of the Eastern establishment who moved with ease between prestigious positions inside and outside government and who had great influence over the president. With Johnson's approval, the group met in Washington in March 1968. Although the "wise men" had supported the president's policies five months before, they now unanimously leaned toward withdrawal, in one way or another, from Vietnam.

Dean Acheson, the senior statesman of the group, summarized for Johnson that the majority of the group felt that "we can no longer do the job we set out to do in the time we have left and we must begin to disengage"[60] Acheson proposed what would later become known as a "decent interval": a face-saving period of sufficient

---

[57] Karnow, *Vietnam*, 1983, p. 559.

[58] Cited in Karnow, *Vietnam*, 1983, p. 560.

[59] Karnow, *Vietnam*, 1983, p. 568.

[60] A. J. Langguth, *Our Vietnam: The War 1954–1975*, New York: Simon and Schuster, 2000, p. 491.

duration between a U.S. disengagement and the GVN's final defeat at the hands of the communists.

Johnson would later say that the "wise men" had a profound influence on him. In an address to the nation on the evening of March 31, 1968, Johnson announced that he was limiting U.S. airstrikes against the North to the area below the 20th parallel—thus putting 90 percent of North Vietnamese territory off limits to bombardments—and that he would begin peace negotiations with the communists.[61] Faced with voter rejection in the New Hampshire primary and with the candidacy of Robert Kennedy, he also announced that he would not seek reelection. In May, responding to overtures from Hanoi, Johnson dispatched diplomat Averell Harriman to Paris to meet with North Vietnam's Foreign Minister Xuan Thuy to discuss a settlement of the war. More meetings—known as the Paris peace talks—between U.S. and North Vietnamese delegates would be held, but a settlement would not be reached until 1973.

The man who worked the hardest at turning Clark Clifford around was Paul Warnke, a partner in the prestigious law firm of Covington and Burling. Warnke had been appointed Assistant Secretary of Defense for ISA following John McNaughton's death in a plane crash. Warnke saw that the war had reached a stalemate in which the lives of American soldiers would be wasted because, no matter how "many battles they won, they could not win the war."[62] His perception was shared by his staff, "composed mostly of young civilian and military officials frustrated by the futility of the war."[63]

Even before the Tet Offensive brought matters to a head, Paul Warnke was searching for options. According to Gus Shubert, in late 1967 a time when there was "unbounded US optimism"—Warnke asked RAND to "examine alternatives to the strategy of attrition in Vietnam." He left it up to RAND to come up with the alternatives for analysis, but it was apparent that Warnke and many of his colleagues believed, as did many analysts at RAND, that victory was not imminent and that, unless a less costly strategy could be initiated, domestic pressure would force the United States to "withdraw . . . under unfavorable conditions."[64] At the time, a debate was raging in the country, in the universities, and at RAND about what the United States ought to do in Vietnam, and Shubert himself had thought of doing a major RAND study on the alternative courses of action that the United States could pursue. The request from Warnke provided the impetus for him to implement his idea. Shubert's work in a very

---

[61] According to Alfred Goldberg ("RAND and Vietnam," 1969, p. 23), the RAND/AFGOA group study in February–March 1968 for Harold Brown on the effectiveness of an "interdiction campaign limited to the area below the 20th Parallel," might have been among "the materials made available to the President by the Department of Defense in connection with his announcement of the bombing limitation on March 31."

[62] Karnow, *Vietnam*, 1983, p. 566.

[63] Karnow, *Vietnam*, 1983, p. 566.

[64] Shubert, "Summary Briefing on Vietnam Alternatives," Santa Monica, Calif.: RAND Corporation, DRU-1819, February 1998 (originally published in November 1968), p. 1.

generalized way marked a departure for RAND. Before the failure of the war of attrition became starkly evident, the focus of most of RAND's works was on how to make U.S. strategy in Vietnam produce better results. As the attrition strategy faltered, some of the works shifted to a focus on how to get the United States out of a quagmire.

For the study for Warnke, Shubert recruited Konrad Kellen and Dick Rainey of the Economics Department. Shubert thought that Rainey—"the biggest hawk" at RAND—was "qualified and knew what he was talking about."[65] Rainey and Kellen headed two teams of experts who held diametrically opposed views regarding what would constitute an appropriate policy for the United States. The sharp divergence in opinion reflected the divided positions on the war within RAND. Shubert orchestrated the effort and did not interfere. The analysts read each other's works and these, in turn, were checked by outside reviewers.

Team 1 was headed by Dick Rainey, who believed that the United States had to stay the course in Vietnam and "win the war in some sense."[66] Team 2 was headed by Konrad Kellen, who had become convinced, from his own work, that a military victory was impossible. Shubert asked them to base their analyses on the overall question, "If you had your way, what would you recommend to the President or the Defense Department or the Congress that the United States should do, at what resource level, to make your position a reality?" The result was "one rather lengthy and one fairly brief study on staying or going."[67]

The staying option, or "population protection strategy," written by Dick Rainey and his team, discussed the steps that would have to be taken if the United States were going to remain in Vietnam for the long haul and the resources that would have to be invested to implement this strategy. The cost was substantial, because the option "involved the expenditure of huge amounts of resources, the potential loss of many, many more American lives, not to mention Vietnamese lives, which nobody ever seemed to think about during this period, at least not many of my colleagues did."[68] Shubert did not argue with the conclusions, but only "tried to make sure that the method was as sound as it could be, that all the numbers were right and the calculations of effects were reasonable."[69]

---

[65] Collins, interview with Gus Shubert, session of May 20, 1992, p. 44.

[66] Collins, interview with Gus Shubert, session of May 20, 1992, p. 43.

[67] For the project, the two sides consulted several RAND documents, including Kellen's "Lessons Learned: An Inventory of Thoughts on a Forthcoming Study," December 10, 1968 (not available to the general public); his "Alternative Vietnam Strategies: The Extrication Option," October 8, 1968 (not available to the general public); and M. Gurtov, O. Hoeffding, Arnold Horelick, and Konrad Kellen, "Extrication from Vietnam: A Memorandum for the Record," Santa Monica, Calif.: RAND Corporation, D-19252-ISA, August 24, 1969, which was revised from an earlier paper published on August 6, 1968, under the title "Extrication from Vietnam: Problems and Implications" (not available to the general public).

[68] Collins, interview with Gus Shubert, session of May 20, 1992, p. 43.

[69] Collins, interview with Gus Shubert, session of May 20, 1992, p. 43.

The getting-out option, called the "withdrawal strategy," was written by Kellen. Arguing that the cost in lives and resources had reached such a level that it would not be worth pursuing the war, Kellen recommended extrication. He started out with the memorable line, "If you want to get out, the only thing you have to do is decide to get out."[70] In essence, Kellen maintained that the absolute-minimum condition under which the United States would withdraw from Vietnam would be "the return in good shape of all our prisoners of war."[71] The difference in terms of money and lives between the two options was such that Shubert concluded there was "no way the United States was going to spend the resources or the time or the lives that would be required to sustain the win option, and that therefore we'd better get busy about deciding how we're going to get out of there," but he never stated that this was his inference and let his audience at the Pentagon draw their own conclusions.[72] Shubert recalled that Kellen's extrication study "was a very unorthodox RAND study," and the statement that, "If you're going to get out . . . you'll have to decide to get out," was "very radical." It was "not a scientific statement" but, rather, "a proposition or . . . an assertion" and "in a sense . . . a tautology." Although it was a departure from the usual RAND analysis, Shubert believed that it was "correct."[73]

The briefing given to Paul Warnke and his ISA staff in November 1968 was subsequently published as a summary report in the same month.[74] In their oral presentation, the RAND team explained that the alternatives they were suggesting were based on their assumption that the objective of the United States at that juncture was to reach a settlement that would permit the National Liberation Front to join in the political process, run for office, vote, and "otherwise to participate in government."[75] Gus Shubert gave an introduction, then Dick Rainey presented the population protection strategy. Under this option, the United States would continue its military intervention, but at a reduced pace, to lower American human and financial costs and to allow the withdrawal of some—but not all—American troops, leaving about 200,000 in the country. At the same time, the option would aim at strengthening and motivating the GVN and its forces to shoulder the major responsibility for the war and at achieving enough security to allow the GVN to carry out its activities in the cities as well as in the countryside.

In terms of tactics, the "stay option" would use small patrols in the villages to hinder Viet Cong access to the population and to protect GVN police and other offi-

---

[70] Author interview with Gus Shubert, 2004 and 2005.

[71] Collins, interview with Gus Shubert, session of May 20, 1992, p. 44.

[72] Collins, interview with Gus Shubert, session of May 20, 1992, p. 44.

[73] Collins, interview with Gus Shubert, session of May 20, 1992, p. 51.

[74] Shubert, "Summary Briefing on Vietnam Alternatives," 1998.

[75] Shubert, "Summary Briefing on Vietnam Alternatives," 1998, p. 5.

cials in the performance of their duties. Effective coordination of all forces in an area would be achieved by integrating village defense units into a larger system. Police actions would attack the NLF infrastructure, and strike teams would penetrate the territory of VC Main Force and NVA units, and massive artillery and tactical air support would be brought to bear if contact was made. Meanwhile, South Vietnamese forces would be upgraded at all levels to take the place of American troops as soon as possible. Assuming that this strategy met its goals, it would reduce American financial and human costs, thereby relieving domestic political pressure on the United States. Finally, by weakening the enemy's political organization and eroding his base of support among the South Vietnamese population, it would "make clear to the enemy . . . that he will be better off negotiating a settlement of the war on any given day than he will be on any succeeding day."[76]

In the last part of the briefing, Konrad Kellen presented the withdrawal strategy, assuming that the current U.S. objective would be discarded in favor of extrication in a manner that would limit damage because of three developments: the population protection strategy had proved ineffective; Vietnamization had failed; and the Paris peace negotiations had stalled. The extrication strategy would unfold in stages. First, Hanoi was notified that the United States had decided to disengage militarily from South Vietnam fully and rapidly, provided that Hanoi agreed to, and subsequently adhered to, minimum American demands. The minimum conditions would be: release of American prisoners; commitment by the enemy not to interfere militarily with the U.S. withdrawal; guarantee by the enemy to adhere to a decent interval: an acceptable time lapse between the cease-fire and the U.S. withdrawal of troops and a communist attempt to take over the government of South Vietnam by force. The RAND team estimated that "an interval of a year following the withdrawal of US forces would be adequate for the US to adjust to the new situation at home and abroad; one or more years might be obtainable."[77]

Three possible scenarios were advanced for the interval period. Under the first one, the GVN would remain in power, but its constitution would be amended to allow all South Vietnamese—regardless of political affiliation—to take part in countrywide, free elections that would be held before the cease-fire expired. Under the second scenario, a provisional government would be established in Saigon that would include representatives of the NLF as well as important, sizable noncommunist groups, and elections would be scheduled. Under the third scenario, fighting would resume after the cease-fire expired, and the GVN would be left to survive as best it could, "presumably with continued American economic and military assistance, but without direct US involvement."[78] Ultimately, the peace accords signed in Paris in 1973 would include

---

[76] Shubert, "Summary Briefing on Vietnam Alternatives," 1998, p. 6.

[77] Shubert, "Summary Briefing on Vietnam Alternatives," 1998, pp. 13–14.

[78] Shubert, "Summary Briefing on Vietnam Alternatives," 1998, p. 15.

elements detailed in Kellen's second scenario, and events from 1973 to 1975 would unfold along the lines described in his third scenario.

In Kellen's opinion, the enemy would accept this settlement, even if it did not amount to total victory, because he knew that he could not defeat the United States militarily or force it out, and because rejecting the withdrawal offer would leave him exposed to continued—and perhaps even intensified—American military pressure. In Kellen's estimation, the enemy, worn out from heavy losses and high costs, would be amenable to this option, since a U.S. departure would leave him "in a much better position to achieve his ultimate objectives of communist control in the South followed by reunification at much lower cost."[79] To "bolster the durability of the interval, " the United States could offer the carrot of economic aid to both sides, and hold the threat of air and naval attacks to deter violations of the agreements and to induce compliance.[80]

By the time Shubert took the two RAND teams to present their analyses in the Pentagon in November 1968, some of their ideas might not have appeared as original as they probably had hoped. Dean Acheson had proposed disengagement and the concept of a decent interval—although he had not spelled out the details. Other ideas had been espoused by Warnke's staff. In a review in early March, done at President Johnson's behest, of General Westmoreland's post-Tet request for 260,000 additional troops to press his military advantage and "materially shorten the war,"[81] Warnke's staff had recommended that, rather than committing more forces and escalating the war—steps that could be matched by the communists and that would prolong the conflict—American units be redeployed to defend the more populated coastal areas, a proposal that echoed the "population protection strategy" of the RAND team.[82] Arguing that more American troops would encourage the GVN to sit back, bicker, and engage in corruption, Warnke's staff recommended upgrading and improving the South Viet-

---

[79] Shubert, "Summary Briefing on Vietnam Alternatives," 1998, p. 15.

[80] Shubert, "Summary Briefing on Vietnam Alternatives," 1998, p. 15.

[81] Regarding his troop request, Westmoreland would later say that he was manipulated by General Earle Wheeler, the JCS Chairman, into asking for more troops. Wheeler wanted to use the Tet Offensive as an opportunity to press Johnson to mobilize the reserves. Wheeler planned to send only half of the troops to Vietnam and to use the other half "to fulfill America's security obligations elsewhere in the world." Although Westmoreland exuded confidence in public, he was in private "dispirited, deeply shaken, almost a broken man," according to Richard Holbrooke, then a young U.S. foreign service officer, who met with him during a trip to Saigon to assess the situation. Westmoreland's request for more troops would be rejected by a presidential commission headed by Defense Secretary Clark Clifford. Colonel Herbert Schandler, who served at the time as assistant for Southeast Asian Affairs, Policy Planning Staff, ISA, recalled that Clifford concluded that there was no JCS strategy behind the troop request, other than the usual one of killing more enemy soldiers.

[82] The enclave strategy had been proposed as early as 1965 by General James Gavin, a retired lieutenant general and former ambassador to France. Gavin urged that the United States radically change Westmoreland's attrition strategy, hold American forces to "defensive enclaves," halt the bombing of North Vietnam, and "seek a political settlement in Geneva or at the U.N." See Langguth, *Our Vietnam*, 2000, p. 419.

namese forces into a more effective army, a recommendation similar to that of the RAND briefers. Also, in timing, the RAND briefing came too late. By November 1968, Richard Nixon had won the presidential election and the Johnson Administration was on its way out.

At one point during the discussion following the presentation by the Shubert team, Mort Halperin, a member of Warnke's staff, said,

> The message is clear, but you're preaching to the converted. We know we've got to get out of there. There's just nothing we can do to make that decision. We'll use the study as we can for the few weeks we have remaining to us in office, and we'll try to pass it along to the next administration, because we think it's very good work and very useful work.[83]

Warnke himself said, "There isn't anybody in the room who doesn't agree with you. I see that you're trying to be neutral, but it doesn't take a genius to figure out which of these strategies you prefer and you think is preferable. We would all agree with you, but there's nothing we can do. We're all captives."[84]

Warnke also told Shubert that, although LBJ secretly wanted to get out of Vietnam, he did not want to "even discuss the idea [of extrication]," and added that in view of Johnson's position and his desire not to be the first American President to lose a war, there was absolutely nothing that could be done to implement the disengagement strategy recommended by Kellen. According to Shubert, the briefing to Warnke was "as high as" they ever got. After that, the whole LBJ "crew was thrown out on its ear after the election, and we had a whole new set of officials to deal with."[85]

Konrad Kellen's extrication option was certainly a radical idea, but in November 1968 it was not a popular one.[86] Kellen, along with other RAND co-authors, had advocated it in a previous paper issued in August 1968 that was classified "Secret."[87] The authors would later say that their document had received a "mixed reaction" in and out of RAND when it appeared. The key objections were that the situation in Vietnam was not as dire as portrayed and therefore extrication was not necessary; that the United

---

[83] Collins, interview with Gus Shubert, session of May 20, 1992, p. 44.

[84] Author interview with Gus Shubert, 2004 and 2005.

[85] Collins, interview with Gus Shubert, session of May 20, 1992, p. 44.

[86] Frank Denton also believed that withdrawal would be inevitable. In his "A Vietnam Alternative" (D-17118-ISA/ARPA, May 10, 1968), he argued that the GVN would remain ineffective and that the United States eventually would have to withdraw. After the U.S. departure, the GVN would probably survive for two years, "at which time the NLF would take over." Such an outcome, Denton believed, would not have a major effect on Southeast Asia.

[87] Kellen's co-authors were Melvin Gurtov, Oleg Hoeffding, Arnold Horelick, and Paul Langer. The document was later revised and published as "Extrication from Vietnam: A Memorandum for the Record," Santa Monica, Calif.: RAND Corporation, D-19252-ISA, August 24, 1969.

States could not afford to abandon its objectives because of likely foreign and domestic repercussions; and that even if the U.S. government wanted to withdraw, the American people would not accept it—an argument also made by Paul Warnke. Other strong objections were that the minimum compliance demanded of the enemy in the extrication option would be "unobtainable or unenforceable," and that the United States after withdrawing would—contrary to the authors' claim—lose its leverage to steer "the course of political events in Vietnam" in the desired direction.[88]

Les Gelb would later recall that, "Not a single . . . soul" in the government—other than Townsend Hoopes, the then–Undersecretary of the Air Force—"was saying at that point, 'Get out.'" Although most people later would claim that "they had views at the time that were very strongly anti-war—get out now, whatever. They didn't."[89] According to Gelb, at the end of 1968, beginning of 1969, "all the talk . . . was focused on limiting and reducing American involvement in the war, turning over more responsibility to the South, and beginning what everyone understood would be a long process of negotiation. That's where people were." He remembered that, when Bobby Kennedy started to talk about withdrawal during the period he was running against Lyndon Johnson, "we all criticized him."[90] Everybody would later remember that they agreed with Kennedy, but this was not the case. According to Gelb, "People's views evolve very slowly, and if you work inside the government, they were slower still. Any effort to move outside a certain box at that time was very dangerous, personally, politically."[91]

As an example, Gelb cited the time when he was part of the interagency working group preparing for negotiations—"in theory because negotiations had not started." The group "wanted to look at various levels of U.S. interests and objectives in the negotiations." But when Dean Rusk found out that "we wanted to look at alternative objectives," he "came down like a ton of bricks, saying, 'We're looking at no alternatives. The only objective of negotiations is an independent, noncommunist South Vietnam—can't look at any other possibility.'" According to Gelb, "that was the atmosphere and the climate. And when people say that they were opposing the war, and they had this plan to get out, and the rest of it, I never heard of any such thing. Including our group [in ISA] which was the most advanced inside the government, in terms of thinking about diminishing American involvement, we were not talking about just getting out—it was not on the horizon at that point, in 1968 and early '69. [It was] only later in 1969 that people began to entertain more cosmic possibilities."[92]

---

[88] Gurtov et al., "Extrication from Vietnam," 1969, pp. 1–2.

[89] Author interview with Les Gelb, 2004.

[90] Author interview with Les Gelb, 2004.

[91] Author interview with Les Gelb, 2004.

[92] Author interview with Les Gelb, 2004.

As RAND analysts such as Konrad Kellen argued for extrication as a way for solving the problem of Vietnam, others at RAND had earlier come up with different suggestions. Over the years, the intractable situation in Vietnam had led some of them to suggest ways to deal with it. As far back as February 1965, as the South plunged into chaos in the wake of Diem's overthrow, Guy Pauker argued that the United States should dispatch combat troops to South Vietnam, not to fight the Viet Cong but to take over the task of governing the country.[93] According to Pauker, the South had never had a popular or legitimate government, nor would it acquire one in the near future; therefore, the first step in pursuing a successful struggle against the Viet Cong would be to do away with the fiction that the United States was dealing with such a government and to simply step in and take over. In a confidential memo to William Graham, with copies to Frank Collbohm, Joe Goldsen, George Tanham, and Charlie Zwick, Pauker compared the situation to that of a Wild West movie, filled with "bad guys," which needed a courageous and efficient sheriff "to rally the solid citizens and reestablish law and order."[94] That sheriff, of course, would be the United States, because, if the United States really wanted to keep South Vietnam from falling into communist hands, it should place the country under American military occupation, probably for as long as it would take to successfully combat the insurgency.

Pauker advocated that, once in control, the United States could use its authority to impose the rule of law and reestablish order. Troublemakers—such as obdurate Buddhist monks and students and opportunistic politicians and military officers who conspired against the central government—should be rounded up, detained, arrested, and deported to one of the island penal colonies for as long as the counterinsurgency operations lasted. After clearing the deck, an American military administration would run the country with the aid of senior Vietnamese advisors, government functionaries, and members of the armed forces, and it would institute meaningful reforms to benefit the population, such as land redistribution, urban development (as had been proposed by Charlie Zwick and his colleagues), and better pay and prospects for the rank-and-file soldiers. Counterinsurgency should consist as much as possible of police action; military operations would be directed precisely against enemy targets, rather than against the whole population with free-fire zones and destruction with napalm and widespread and indiscriminate bombardment. In taking over, the intention of the United States was not to turn South Vietnam into a colony but to act temporarily on behalf of the Vietnamese masses so that it could be handed back to them and their descendants, a healthy country free of revolutionary war.

---

[93] Guy J. Pauker, "Where Do We Go from Here? A Few Unanswered Questions and Controversial Proposals Concerning the War in Vietnam," March 3, 1966 (not available to the general public).

[94] Guy J. Pauker, memo to William Graham, dated February 1, 1965, with copies to Frank Collbohm, Joe Goldsen, George Tanham, and Charlie Zwick; provided courtesy of Mrs. Tanham and Lee Meyers.

Joe Zasloff remembered attending a public seminar at RAND held by Pauker to discuss his proposal. Zasloff recalled that Pauker said, "We ought to consider the insurgency in Vietnam something like a cowboy movie, there are the good guys and the bad guys, the Viet Cong are the bad guys, and the sheriff comes in in a white hat, and he takes over the town and clears it out by himself or with his own forces, and gives it back to the people afterwards, and that's what we ought to do." Zasloff said that Pauker played the role of the cowboy with great skill, and with his "Romanian accent," was "very interesting and provocative." Pauker's message, Zasloff remembered, was that "the American colonialists ought to take over and clear out the place and give it to the Vietnamese after we got rid of the Viet Cong."[95]

The chaos and internal strife that alarmed Pauker worsened in 1966, when the Buddhists mounted a powerful struggle with the backing of the military commander of I Corps against the government headed by Air Marshal Nguyen Cao Ky. As South Vietnam appeared on the verge of degenerating into civil war among the noncommunists and even heading toward secession by the I Corps commander, a Soviet expert in the Social Science Department, Arnold Horelick,[96] argued that the United States should begin thinking through how it could disengage from Vietnam. In Horelick's view, the strife indicated a failure by the South Vietnamese to create viable political structures. This failure might lead to the collapse of the current regime, generalized civil war even among the noncommunists in the south, warlordism, and a complete breakdown of the political order in which no individual or group possessing the symbols, let alone the substance of political power in the country, would exist. Or this breakdown might lead to the emergence of a government determined to end the war on terms unacceptable to the United States. Any of these possibilities would confront the United States with the unpleasant choices of taking over (as advocated by Guy Pauker) or disengaging and eventually withdrawing.[97] (As it turned out, however, the central government crushed the Buddhist "Struggle Movement," and the I Corps commander was forced into exile. Thus, the civil war among the noncommunists and warlordism did not materialize—as had been feared—and the Saigon government remained "whole" until it was defeated by the communists in 1975.)

Considering the unpleasant contingency of a complete breakdown of the political order, Horelick suggested in his paper that the United States begin thinking through disengagement/withdrawal and the way disengagement might be carried out. Horelick acknowledged that "heavy costs would attend any decision to disengage and with-

---

[95] Author interview with Joe Zasloff, 2003.

[96] Arnold Horelick was an alumnus of Rutgers University, where he was a member of Phi Beta Kappa and from which he graduated magna cum laude in 1948. He obtained a master's degree from Harvard. He joined RAND's Social Science Department in 1958 as a Soviet expert.

[97] Arnold L. Horelick, "'Sour' Contingencies and U.S. Policy in Vietnam," Santa Monica, Calif.: RAND Corporation, July 26, 1966 (not available to the general public).

draw without achieving declared US objectives," but said the question was "how heavy would these costs be compared with the price that would have to be paid and the risks that would have to be assumed to support further efforts . . . increasingly without prospects . . ." and how these costs might be reduced by skillful use of instruments of power and influence still available.[98] In his paper, he envisaged such instruments as covering a "whole range of U.S. military, political actions and policies ranging initially from cessation of offensive military operations against the VC and North Vietnam, and perhaps regroupment in defensive 'enclaves,' to withdrawal of part or all of U.S. military forces from Vietnam under conditions that fall short of the minimum ones now held to be acceptable."[99] Withdrawal as a result of a military defeat would be dangerous, but would not be the case in Vietnam. Nonetheless, disengagement under conditions postulated in his paper "would have to be carried out in a most deliberate, phased manner, and certainly not under enemy fire" to avoid "the danger that U.S. forces might be made to appear to be pulling out under attack."[100] This condition would require the tacit or explicit cooperation of the enemy, which, in Horelick's view, could be secured if the United States made clear its intention to take punitive action in case of attack or interference with its disengagement.

Regarding the oft-repeated pledges by the U.S. government to defend South Vietnam, Horelick argued that, in light of the increasingly "sour" internal South Vietnamese contingencies, it would be well for U.S. leaders to make clear that the commitment presupposed, and was based on, the existence of a viable functioning central political authority in Saigon to which assistance could be rendered effectively. With regard to the rest of Asia, the United States could—in concert with its friends and allies in the region—develop policies that would soften the effect of its disengagement or withdrawal. Horelick ended by stating that his paper sought to stimulate the exploration of "the range of possible policies and actions that might be implemented to shore up the position of noncommunist Asian countries and to protect American interests in Asia" in the event of disengagement.[101]

Later in 1966, Gerry Hickey waded in with his concept of accommodation. He first discussed this idea in a talk he gave in December 1966 in Santa Monica.[102] In introducing Hickey to the Social Science audience, Steve Hosmer said that Hickey would discuss the aspirations of the Montagnards and his proposals for social-economic-political development to win their support for the war effort. Hickey, however, seized the opportunity to talk instead about accommodation—a concept he said

---

[98] Horelick, 1966, p. 6.

[99] Horelick, 1966, p. 6.

[100] Horelick, 1966, p. 11.

[101] Horelick, 1966, pp. 25–26.

[102] Gerald Hickey, "Talk on Vietnam 12/16/66," Santa Monica, Calif.: RAND Corporation, March 15, 1967 (not available to the general public).

he had been thinking about for several months. His basic premise was that a complete military victory was not possible, and that, therefore, a political settlement would be in order. Under this concept—which Hickey admitted he had not completely thought through—the GVN would accommodate and share power with the various ethnic, political, social, and religious groups—such as the Buddhist Hoa Hao and the syncretic Cao Dai[103]—and even with the Viet Cong.[104]

Hickey's key, underlying assumption was that the GVN would be willing to share power and that the Viet Cong would accept to give up their military struggle to become one of several interest groups within a kind of coalition government in which the GVN—and its army—would retain dominance. Another assumption was that this amalgamation would not create the danger of a Viet Cong takeover because the communists would be checked and stymied by the other groups within the coalition. In Hickey's vision, the GVN stood to gain much if it accommodated the various noncommunist groups within Vietnamese society. Assuming that these groups, such as the Hoa Hao and the Cao Dai religious sects, would be willing to subordinate their interests to the national interests, and assuming that they favored the GVN over the Viet Cong, the GVN would indirectly extend its hold over the territory and the population that these groups controlled.

A very lively discussion ensued after his presentation, and some Social Science analysts suggested how he could improve his concept so that it might be better received in Washington. Subsequently, the RAND office in Washington arranged a briefing for Hickey with members of the State Department, Defense Department, USAID, U.S. Information Agency, and the CIA, on January 5, 1967. According to Hickey, Richard Holbrooke, whom he had "known in Vietnam as one of the young bright lights of the American embassy," was the first to raise his hand at the conclusion of the talk. He said, "What you're saying, Gerry, is that we're not going to win a military victory in Vietnam." Hickey responded that Holbrooke could draw his own conclusions, but that

---

[103] The Hoa Hao sect was established in 1939 and now claims 2 million followers in Vietnam, mostly farmers in the Mekong Delta. It emphasizes worship in the home and deemphasizes temple worship and the ordination of monks. It considers farming the pursuit most likely to lead to self-improvement. The Cao Dai sect was established in 1926 in Tay Ninh Province. It combines elements of Taoism and Buddhism, but its members worship a pantheon of saints, including Buddha, Jesus Christ, Mohamed, Joan of Arc, and Victor Hugo. It has a hierarchy akin to that of the Catholic Church, with a Pope and a Holy See in Tay Ninh City.

[104] The concept of *accommodation* would concede dominance to the religious sects over the areas they controlled. Permitting them to continue controlling their zones of influence would weaken the central government and make it harder for it to assume the burden of the war following the eventual departure of American combat troops. The French experimented with this concept when they allied themselves with the Hoa Hao and Cao Dai sects to create a unified front against the Viet Minh. However, when they attempted to Vietnamize the war, they found that, by condoning the existence of these "states within a state," they had fragmented the Vietnamese government and weakened it in its fight against the Viet Minh.

his own "major premise was that the war in Vietnam was a political struggle that could only be resolved in political terms."[105]

According to Hickey, accommodation—unfortunately—"was viewed around Washington as heresy" at the time.[106] Nevertheless, RAND published his concept in a report in October 1967.[107] However, the report was circulated in Saigon a whole year later—in January 1968—to no effect. Hickey recalled that there was "no reaction to the report from either the embassy or Pentagon East" (MACV headquarters).[108] It probably got lost in the turmoil caused by the Tet Offensive. During a leave to return to the United States, Hickey gave another talk on political accommodation at RAND in Santa Monica on June 12, 1968. He recalled that it "was well received and stimulated interesting discussion." A week later, Alice Hsieh, a China expert in the Social Science Department, wrote to William F. Bundy, Assistant Secretary for East Asian and Pacific Affairs at the State Department, telling him that Hickey "was in the process of developing further some very interesting ideas on political 'accommodation' which people in State may find of interest insofar as they might have at least an indirect bearing on the U.S. negotiation position." Since Bundy was in Paris to attend the peace talks, Hsieh asked his secretary to direct Hickey to an appropriate person to contact, adding that Hickey was "an extremely modest individual who is not inclined to promote his ideas aggressively." However, according to Hickey, there was no follow-up by the State Department.[109]

As the prosecution of the war faltered and a settlement became more likely, there was speculation about how negotiations would take place: under what form and in which forum. Prior to the Tet Offensive and the beginning of peace talks in Paris in May 1968, Melvin Gurtov reviewed the Geneva Conference that had been convened in 1954 to settle the war between the Viet Minh and the French. He concluded that it would be unlikely that a similar conference that included the participation of many countries, such as the Soviet Union and China, would be held because the multinational format of Geneva had created many complications, none of which neither the United States nor North Vietnam would want to see recur.[110]

Drawing lessons from Geneva for the United States, Gurtov recommended that Washington refrain from displaying eagerness to begin the peace talks, since this would lead the communists to believe that it was desperately seeking a settlement that

---

[105] Hickey, *Window on a War*, 2002, p. 201.

[106] Hickey, *Window on a War*, 2002, p. 201.

[107] Gerald C. Hickey, *Accommodation in South Vietnam: The Key to Sociopolitical Solidarity*, October 1967.

[108] Hickey, *Window on a War*, 2002, p. 221.

[109] Hickey, *Window on a War*, 2002, p. 257.

[110] Melvin Gurtov, *Negotiations and Vietnam: A Case Study of the 1954 Geneva Conference*, Santa Monica, Calif.: RAND Corporation, TS-3157, January 3, 1968.

would not harm its prestige and would encourage them to act on this belief. Another possible lesson of the Geneva experience would be for the United States to concede nothing in advance to the communists. The French had pursued this strategy successfully in 1954 by refusing to acknowledge Viet Minh military gains in Vietnam, as well as in parts of Laos and Cambodia. As the conference unfolded, these gains became negotiable.

Gurtov believed that the Viet Minh's own experience in Geneva continued to influence Hanoi's attitude toward negotiations. At the 1954 peace talks, the Viet Minh had failed to use their gains on the battlefield to obtain guarantees for post–cease-fire political arrangements, and this failure had taught Hanoi to aim for military victory—or at least to achieve an outcome close to it—before engaging in negotiations. Also, learning from mistakes in 1954, Hanoi would not again, presumably, be offering a cease-fire "in exchange for promises of a future political settlement." For Hanoi, "[f]ighting and talking simultaneously is the only acceptable tactic," because "when the fighting stops, the talking will have reached the point of agreement eminently favorable to them."[111]

♧ ♧ ♧

Overarching possible solutions to the Vietnam problem were the attitude and likely reactions of the Soviet Union and China—Vietnam's superpower supporters. As a China expert, Mel Gurtov turned his attention to the China aspects of the equation in a paper published in 1967, in which he examined developments in Hanoi's relations with its Chinese ally since the Tonkin Gulf incidents.[112] He wrote this paper following a visit to the Pentagon in June 1967, during which Lieutenant General Glen W. Martin, Deputy Chief of Staff for Plans and Operations, U.S. Air Force, asked him to provide copies of a study he was preparing on Communist China's policy toward the Vietnam War since the Tonkin Gulf incident, part of a larger study of China's relations with the whole of Southeast Asia that Gurtov planned to issue at a later date.

In Gurtov's view, China's policy had evolved from alarm over U.S. intentions following the Tonkin Gulf incidents in August 1964 to "minimal risk-taking, increasing caution, and carefully qualified commitments" toward Vietnam beginning in early 1966.[113] This change occurred after what appeared to be a "tacit understanding" between Washington and Peking that, at the very least, the United States would invade neither China nor North Vietnam.[114] As long as the United States limited its objec-

---

[111] Gurtov, *Negotiations and Vietnam*, 1966, p. 191.

[112] Melvin Gurtov, "Communist China's Policy Toward the Vietnam War Since Tonkin," Santa Monica, Calif.: RAND Corporation, D-15960-PR, August 10, 1967.

[113] Gurtov, "Communist China's Policy," 1967, p. 71.

[114] Gurtov, "Communist China's Policy," 1967, p. 72.

tivcs to South Vietnam and its attacks to the areas below the border between Vietnam and China, it seemed reasonably certain that a clash with China would not occur. The more cautious tone was also the result of internal developments, because the onset of the Cultural Revolution preoccupied the Chinese leadership and led to a desire to avoid a direct confrontation with the United States over Vietnam.

However, Gurtov cautioned that overt Chinese intervention could not be entirely ruled out in certain eventualities. For example, if China perceived that U.S. actions threatened the survival of North Vietnam or the lifelines of its economy, it could drastically change its attitude. Therefore, it would be in the United States' best interest to keep the Chinese role in the Vietnam War from going "beyond that of faithful supporter."[115]

With regard to negotiations, China appeared much more inflexible than North Vietnam. According to Gurtov, Peking viewed negotiations as "absolutely unnecessary except to put a *pro forma* close to a U.S. defeat."[116] For China, the central issue was the withdrawal of U.S. forces from the South, and, as long as American combat troops remained, negotiations would be out of the question. Hanoi, however, had asserted that the bombing of the North was the real impediment to peace talks and that, once all forms of aggression against it were halted, negotiations could begin. In the meantime, as it vied with the Soviet Union for leadership of world communism, China kept up its support as a way of deepening Hanoi's dependence on Peking and also as a way of increasing its influence over Hanoi's military and diplomatic planning. The onset of the Cultural Revolution in China and the chaos it engendered could limit Chinese aid to the North. However, China would be unlikely to suspend support because, as had the United States, it had "so broadly defined the importance of the Vietnam war" that withdrawing assistance to Hanoi "would seriously impair its image of benefactor to socialist neighbors and revolutionary movements."[117]

As the Cultural Revolution raged in China, Konrad Kellen detected—in a 1966 paper written with consultant Tom Robinson—a more flexible Chinese attitude toward a negotiated settlement of the Vietnam War.[118] According to Kellen and Robinson, the Cultural Revolution [which swept over China in the summer and fall of 1966] was causing chaos and, with the Red Guards getting out of control, the Chinese leadership wanted to keep the army ready throughout the country to restore order. Realizing that their country was going to be beset with serious internal difficulties for years, Chinese leaders believed that it would be "prudent to keep the foreign scene reasonably

---

[115] Gurtov, "Communist China's Policy," 1967, p. 73.

[116] Gurtov, "Communist China's Policy," 1967, p. 53.

[117] Gurtov, "Communist China's Policy," 1967, pp. 70–71.

[118] Thomas W. Robinson and Konrad Kellen, "Protracted War or Negotiation Now? Some Thought on China's Changing Vietnam Strategy," Santa Monica, Calif.: RAND Corporation, September 13, 1966 (not available to the general public).

quiet."[119] Hence, Marshal Chen Yi, the Chinese Foreign Minister, had been quoted as saying that China wanted to avoid war with the United States and that there was "room" for discussions with Washington on the Vietnam War.[120]

Kellen and Robinson thought that the Chinese might be very interested in working toward a settlement. Among the reasons, the more important one seemed to be that the Chinese might believe that, if present trends continued, a direct military confrontation with the United States would become unavoidable. Such a conflict would severely damage large segments of Chinese industry and inflict heavy casualties on the Chinese army. In view of these possibilities, the Chinese "may have concluded that it is best to prevent Hanoi from pulling them to the brink, settle for whatever they can get for their Vietnamese quasi-allies [the Viet Cong], and lose some face now rather than a great deal more, as well as much blood and treasure."[121] In the view of Kellen and Robinson, Chen Yi's declaration—if it had been reported correctly might herald "a fundamental change in Chinese policy," and might be "the opening gambit in a process leading to a negotiated settlement of the Vietnam conflict."[122] Chen Yi's statement, therefore, should be viewed as a significant chance for the United States to "find a way to extricate . . . from continual involvement in the Vietnam conflict."[123]

China's policy toward Vietnam would evolve further and its support for its Vietnamese allies would decrease from the height achieved in 1964 following the Tonkin Gulf incidents, when it began sending engineering troops to build and maintain critical facilities, such as defense structures, airfields, roads, and railways; dispatching Chinese anti-aircraft units to defend important strategic targets; and providing large amounts of military equipment, as well as of civilian materials. From 1966 onward, the Chinese leadership felt less disposed to provide Vietnam with the same level of support because of the ravages of the Cultural Revolution and also because Hanoi—which had drawn closer to Moscow—found itself caught in the rivalry and conflict between the Soviets and the Chinese, which eventually climaxed in a border clash between the two powers in March 1969. The clash led to a strategic reevaluation by China, whose leaders began to perceive the "Soviet social-imperialists" as their "most dangerous enemies," to reassess China's relationship with the United States, and to consider the role that America could play as a counterweight to the Soviet Union for Chinese security.[124] This strategic

---

[119] Robinson and Kellen, "Protracted War or Negotiation Now?" 1966, p. 4.

[120] Robinson and Kellen, "Protracted War or Negotiation Now?" 1966, p. 1.

[121] Robinson and Kellen, "Protracted War or Negotiation Now?" 1966, p. 3.

[122] Robinson and Kellen, "Protracted War or Negotiation Now?" 1966, p. 7.

[123] Robinson and Kellen, "Protracted War or Negotiation Now?" 1966, p. 8.

[124] Chen Jian, *Mao's China and the Cold War*, Chapel Hill, N.C.: University of North Carolina Press, 2001, p. 233.

reassessment would lead to President Nixon's visit to China in 1972 and détente with the United States.

At RAND, the Soviet dimension of the Vietnam War received little attention relative to other, more fundamental and significant aspects of the Cold War. Arnold Horelick was perhaps the only Soviet expert who wrote on the subject, but even his output on the issue was small. In a paper published in April 1965, he examined what Vietnam meant to the Soviet Union.[125] According to him, the Soviet stake in Vietnam was chiefly a function of the relationship between the war there and the dispute with China for leadership of the world communist movement, on the one hand, and the maintenance of the USSR policy of detente with the United States, on the other hand.

The Chinese viewed détente as "a conspiracy between the American 'imperialists' and the Russian 'revisionists' to domesticate the world revolution."[126] Consequently they had embraced "a militant . . . strategy that argues for reliance on direct, violent, revolutionary struggle."[127] In Vietnam, they wanted the communists to achieve total victory so that they could validate their position that "violent revolution and terrorist subversion can succeed, even in the face of armed opposition by the United States," and confirm their contention that they—not the Soviet Union—should assume the mantle of leadership of the communist world.[128]

The Soviet Union, on the other hand, saw "competition between the Soviet bloc and the advanced capitalist countries of the West as the central and decisive arena of conflict" and "peaceful coexistence and avoidance of thermonuclear war" as the "overriding requirement" of this fundamental struggle.[129] To the Soviets, "violent conflict and revolutionary war on the peripheries" could jeopardize the success of this "central struggle . . . either by creating the danger of escalation to nuclear war, or, in lesser ways, by galvanizing Western political and economic opposition to communist designs."[130] The Soviet leaders' main concern at this juncture was to deepen their rapprochement with the United States in order to maintain Soviet security and sustain the high growth rates of their economy.

In this situation, Horelick suspected that if the Soviet leaders could dictate events in Vietnam, they would "prefer to see the Viet Cong take only half a loaf, or, even less, postponing the final victory of the communist revolution in the South for many years,

---

[125] Arnold L. Horelick, "Sino-Soviet Relations and the Crisis in Vietnam," Santa Monica, Calif.: RAND Corporation, D-13608-PR, April 15, 1965. This paper was a revised transcript of a talk he had given to the Hughes Management Club at the Biltmore Hotel in Los Angeles on March 11, 1965.

[126] Horelick, "Sino-Soviet Relations," 1965, p. 8.

[127] Horelick, "Sino-Soviet Relations," 1965, p. 8.

[128] Horelick, "Sino-Soviet Relations," 1965, p. 8.

[129] Horelick, "Sino-Soviet Relations," 1965, p. 9.

[130] Horelick, "Sino-Soviet Relations," 1965, p. 9.

if necessary, rather than risk new, more dangerous escalation that could severely strain Soviet relations with the United States and perhaps even involve the Soviet Union in hostilities."[131] But Moscow, largely out of concern about its competition for world communist leadership with China, also did not wish to see escalation in Vietnam and had warned the United States not to push the war to a dangerous level.

It was in the area of negotiations that the differences between Moscow and Peking would have the strongest bearing. Whereas Peking had insisted that American forces pull out of South Vietnam before any peace talks could begin, Moscow maintained that the United States had to cease its air attacks on North Vietnam in order to create conditions for negotiation. Caught in the rivalry between his two main, vital supporters, President Ho Chi Minh of North Vietnam had skillfully managed to keep a delicate balance. Resisting pressure to choose sides, he had carefully remained neutral for as long as he could. On the issue of negotiations, as on most other sensitive matters over which China and the Soviet Union differed, Hanoi had refused to commit itself. However, as Melvin Gurtov indicated, Hanoi's position on peace talks, by 1967, had edged closer to that of Moscow. Also, Gurtov pointed out, because North Vietnam needed more-sophisticated weapons to cope with U.S. intervention, Moscow's influence had grown: It was able to give Hanoi heavy military equipment, including missiles, launch facilities, and radar, and train the Vietnamese in a program established near Moscow in the use of that equipment.[132]

Horelick concluded by saying that the evolution from a bipolar world, in which the United States and its Western allies confronted a monolithic Communist Bloc, to a multipolar world was complicating the task of U.S. decisionmakers. Back then, Western decisionmakers knew, at least, that if they could "exert sufficient influence and pressure on a small circle of leaders in the Kremlin, reasonably predictable consequences would follow in whatever part of the world Western and communist interests happened to be in conflict."[133] The picture had become complicated, and, in Vietnam, the Viet Cong—the main targets of the United States—were several times removed from American military and diplomatic pressure on the Soviet Union and China. In this situation, the United States had to carefully orchestrate and conduct its diplomacy and policy so that the president was able to "apply just enough pressure at one point without pressing too hard in another; to induce one communist opponent [the Soviet Union] to urge moderation on the others; to punish still another opponent [North Vietnam] severely enough to make 'sitting it out' an unrewarding strategy, yet not to

---

[131] Horelick, "Sino-Soviet Relations," 1965, pp. 9–10.

[132] According to author Chen Jian, on a visit to Moscow in March 1966 as the head of a North Vietnamese delegation to attend the Twenty-Third Congress of the Soviet Communist Party, Le Duan, General Secretary of the Vietnamese Lao Dong, or Communist Party, "reportedly described the Soviet Union as his 'second motherland.'" When the Chinese leaders "learned this, they were 'angrily shocked.'" Jian, *Mao's China,* 2001, p. 232.

[133] Horelick, "Sino-Soviet Relations," 1965, p. 19.

damage it so precipitately that it places itself completely in the hands of its powerful big neighbor [China]."[134]

A Russian analysis, based on Soviet-era archives, of Soviet-Vietnam relations indicates that Soviet policy toward Vietnam in general favored a negotiated settlement, because one of Moscow's objectives was to avoid being drawn into the war. While it provided North Vietnam, within limits, with all the military aid it needed to fight the war, the Soviet Union also viewed the escalating conflict as a dangerous threat to global security. After Moscow's relations with Peking deteriorated, Soviet leaders feared that Washington would play the "China card" against it through rapprochement with its communist rival. Starting in late 1968, Moscow would help Washington get the peace talks under way as part of an effort to forge an alliance with the United States against China. However, it would do so with a "low profile . . . acting behind the scenes and rendering indirect services, avoiding publicity in their diplomatic activities."[135] The signing of the peace accords between Washington and Hanoi in 1973 was greeted with a sense of relief in Moscow, because it eliminated a great impediment to détente with the United States and opened the way for greater flexibility in its dealings with China.

As events in Vietnam and developments in China and the Soviet Union began to push the war toward a negotiated settlement, and sentiments in the United States favored reducing American direct involvement, the RAND presence in Vietnam began to wind down further in tandem with the decline in American intervention. After the Tet Offensive, the once-high-profile operation with policy impact and implication was reduced to a study of the mechanics of Viet Cong organization. To reflect the change, and reduced role, the Viet Cong Motivation and Morale Project was renamed the Communist Organization and Operations Study and placed under Sam Cochran.[136] The emphasis on Viet Cong infrastructure was reflected in another project that RAND agreed to undertake for ARPA and MACV CORDS, the agency in charge of pacification in Vietnam.

Called broadly "Pacification and Revolutionary Development Studies," the project was in fact focused on enemy organization. A small staff continued to conduct interviews specifically to address clients' interests, rather than to study the fundamental issues of the war, and personnel in Saigon were reorganized. Only one interview

---

[134]Horelick, "Sino-Soviet Relations," 1965, p. 20.

[135]Ilya V. Gaiduk, *The Soviet Union and the Vietnam War*, Chicago, Ill.: Ivan R. Dee, 1996, p. xi.

[136]Economics Department, RAND Corporation, "ARPA/ARGILE Progress Report of 21 August 1968."

team would be retained, and "all US personnel not directly required for support of this project [would] be returned to Santa Monica."[137]

In addition, some staff members were farmed out to whomever would pay their salaries. At this juncture, loaning employees was a way for RAND to stay involved without having to assume responsibility. Charlie Benoit would be one of the RAND staff members hired out to other projects. Benoit was hired by Vic Croizat as a team leader to replace John Harbut, who had returned to Santa Monica. A graduate of Yale University, where he was a varsity football player and captain of the lacrosse team, Benoit was solidly built and had a neck that someone said was at least 20 inches thick. He was bright and articulate, and could pick up foreign languages with ease (at last count, he speaks fluently Vietnamese, Chinese Mandarin, and Thai). He had a good sense of humor and a cheerful demeanor, and connected easily with people.

Benoit attended graduate school in 1966, but, after a year, the world beckoned. And, as he would recall later, he wanted "a big piece of it."[138] In 1967, "Vietnam was echoing." He knew that he might be drafted and sent there. He had "nothing against Vietnam as such," but he did not want to go there as a soldier. He told himself, "There must be a better way." A friend came to see him one day and said, "Did you see the advertisement in the *Boston Globe*?" It was a full-page ad by USAID "looking for people with some sort of language facility." USAID's plan "was to recruit Americans who could learn [Vietnamese], train them for nine months, and then send them to Vietnam" to work because "we couldn't trust the Vietnamese." Benoit was feeling "rambunctious," so he decided to sign up. He was among the first group recruited.

Benoit worked for USAID in Vietnam for over a year-and-a-half, mostly as an assistant district advisor in III Corps. During this time, he spent nine months living alone in a hamlet. Thrust into a situation in which he had to use the language daily, he developed fluency in Vietnamese and got to know the customs so well that he could fit easily into the local society. He was comfortable with Vietnamese and they with him. Benoit remembered that somehow he heard about the RAND office in Saigon and about a job opening there, so he paid a visit to the RAND villa, where he met Joan Allen and Vic Croizat. He vaguely recalled that he met Croizat again when he went to Santa Monica after he accepted the job, but he could not say who was in charge of the Vietnam operation or how the decision to hire him was made.

While in Santa Monica, Benoit read some RAND reports on Vietnam as well as "very brown, tattered, raw interviews that had been translated and typed up and were just lying in piles." He thought that "anybody who read [these reports and interviews] would say, 'Enough already,' . . . [and] would come away with a tremendous sense of respect for the self-sacrifice and the dedication and the motivation of the people we were fighting." Benoit recalled that "the morale and motivation was so high that sud-

---

[137] Economics Department, RAND Corporation, "ARPA/ARGILE Progress Report of 21 August 1968."

[138] This and the other quotes in this paragraph are from the author's interview with Charlie Benoit, 2005.

denly you realized that those guys were going to win because they really believed that they were on the right side. . . . There wasn't anybody who was going to quit." Reading the materials, he also realized the depth of the anguish and pain that the war inflicted, not only on the Viet Cong but also on the civilians caught in the fighting. What he read changed his position on the war—not "180 degrees" but at least "165 degrees"—from being supportive of the aims of the war to opposing it as futile and disastrous for the Vietnamese.[139]

Benoit never worked for Vic Croizat. By the time he returned to Saigon in about August 1968, Croizat was gone. He recalled that he felt fortunate. Of his employment by RAND, he said, "It was one of those things, you scratched yourself and wondered, 'What happened here? Was I lucky or what?'"[140] His surprise was compounded when he was granted a Top Secret clearance. He remembered that the first time he was handed a Top Secret document, his hands shook when he received it from Yogi Ianeiro.

Benoit said that when he came on board in Saigon, the Viet Cong Motivation and Morale Project was almost defunct. It appeared, although he is not sure about this, that "Someone had piggy-backed on that project and had sold something to the CIA, to the Phoenix-related CORDS, saying 'You're interested in infrastructure, we can conduct some interviews based on our previous interview schedule. Same thing, we'd go to the *Chieu Hoi* and POW camps and we would interview people.'" Benoit thought that the project was probably funded by CORDS or possibly by the CIA, but he was not certain. He recalled that it was different from "the original RAND [Viet Cong Motivation and Morale] work, which . . . was to interview prisoners and defectors and try to understand better their morale and motivation—why after we've dropped so many bombs on your head did you refuse to quit or to surrender?"[141] Benoit thought that his boss might have been Andy Sweetland, whom he rarely saw. Benoit did not know Sweetland's background and recalled only that Sweetland did not speak Vietnamese. In fact, Sweetland had been assigned to take charge of the fieldwork in Saigon.[142] Besides Ianeiro, Allen, and Sweetland, Benoit remembered that the Saigon operation included Gerry Hickey and Tom Kiley, whom he believed was a holdover from the previous Viet Cong Motivation and Morale Project.

When Benoit arrived in Saigon, RAND was maintaining an office at the villa and another one at the ARPA compound where he ended up working. By that time,

---

[139] This and the other quotes in this paragraph are from the author's interview with Charlie Benoit, 2005.

[140] Author interview with Charlie Benoit, 2005.

[141] Author interview with Charlie Benoit, 2005.

[142] Economics Department, RAND Corporation "ARPA/AGILE Progress Report, July–December 1968, February 4, 1969. Yogi Ianeiro remembered that Sweetland loved to play the piano and that he had to rent one for him. Whenever he came in, Sweetland would play the theme song from the movie *Alfie*—his favorite piece of music—and sometimes Ianeiro would just sit and listen. Ianeiro believed that Sweetland was working on village security [the Hamlet Evaluation System]. (Author interview with Yogi Ianeiro, 2003.)

according to Joan Allen, the RAND operation seemed to be in limbo. RAND staff members spent very little time at the villa, and mostly came and went. Not much work was being done, and Allen had little to do, beyond answering the phone and typing up some of Gerry Hickey's reports or helping Charlie Benoit with some work. Few memos or administrative documents were exchanged between the Saigon office and RAND in Santa Monica. After the "mini Tet" offensive in May 1968, things began to wind down at the villa. RAND stopped sending prominent people to Vietnam, although a few still came once in a while. After Vic Croizat left, Arnold Mengle, a Navy veteran, was dispatched to Saigon to replace him because—in Jim Digby's words—RAND "thought somebody with military experience needed to be there."[143]

No one had explained to Benoit what his job entailed, but he himself thought that it was "to manage, oversee, and somewhat motivate a group of interviewers."[144] For Benoit, the job was strange because he did not have any real work to perform, except to serve as a passport to get the interviewers into the camps and prisons. The routine had not changed from that of the previous Viet Cong Motivation and Morale Project. The eight to eleven interviewers did all the work. They would make the appointments, and Benoit would go with them to the interview sites all over the country, where he would talk to the people in charge and get them through the gate. Once inside, the interviewers would interview people they had selected from a list.

Benoit also served as a conduit of information to the interviewers, but even in this capacity he was sometimes made superfluous by Kim Vinh, Andy Sweetland's girlfriend. Kim would get the scoop and pass it along to the interviewers. "I would be the last guy to find out," he recalled, and as a result he felt as though he was a fifth wheel.[145]

Unlike the more free-flowing format of the interviews conducted under Goure, the interviewers adhered to "a series of questions that were asked of every person so that it could be consistent, and one person's answer could be measured against [those of] others."[146] According to Benoit, the questionnaire was mostly designed to ferret out information from defectors and prisoners about the Viet Cong infrastructure, "who reports to whom . . . and things of that sort."

While the interviewers were busy, Benoit was sitting around, free and with nothing to do. So he told himself, "Why don't I do my own interviews?" With his mastery of the Vietnamese language, this posed no problem. He did not have to adhere to the questionnaire and could talk about anything he wanted. From these free-ranging conversations, he developed clear views of what was happening in the country. To this day, he can still remember the faces of many of the people he interviewed and most of what

---

[143] Author interview with Jim Digby, 2002.

[144] Author interview with Charlie Benoit, 2005.

[145] Author interview with Charlie Benoit, 2005.

[146] This and other quotes are from the author's 2005 interview with Charlie Benoit.

they told him. Although he cannot recall the conversation with Vic Croizat that got him hired, he can remember vividly the talk he had with a girl in Binh Dinh who told him her life story "in tears for an hour-and-a-half."

Benoit's project lasted about four or five months. After it was completed, another attempt was made "to write a proposal piggy-backing on the one we had just finished—to extend it," but he believed it never got funded. Then Don Marshall, who had heard about him, asked him to collaborate on what would become known as the Marshall Study for General Creighton Abrams, the new MACV commander. Don Marshall was a lieutenant colonel with a doctorate in anthropology from Harvard, a very erudite man who was a mentor for Benoit: someone who seemed "more like a thesis advisor . . . than a boss." Marshall had been teaching at Harvard but had failed to get tenure and, according to Benoit "was very bitter about that and went back to the military as a solution to his stymied academic career." RAND was willing to lend its employees as long as their salaries were paid for, so Benoit joined Marshall's staff.

The day Benoit went to meet Marshall, he found him sitting in a small conference room in the company of Herman Kahn, whom Benoit described as "this huge guy from the Hudson Institute." While Kahn carried on about all sorts of issues, Benoit just kept quiet. The big man "was going on about Vietnamese being as cruel as he'd ever encountered to each other, and he told the story about how one Vietnamese turned to another Vietnamese, remarking about the napalm that had just been dropped, saying that it doesn't appear as hot as it used to be." Benoit was offended and said something, but Kahn just "chewed me up and spat me out into little pieces." Then, as Kahn left, he said sarcastically, "I have to rush now because I'm leaving my driver out there in the hot sun and if I don't get there soon he'd become a VC"—referring to some remark Benoit had made. Later, Marshall told another person that he had been impressed by Benoit's composure in such a difficult situation. But all Benoit wanted to do was to avoid arguing with Kahn—this "behemoth" of an opinionated man.

At the meeting, Marshall asked Benoit whether he would be interested in joining his project, which Marshall traced back to General Creighton Abrams himself. Marshall told Benoit proudly that Abrams had given him complete freedom, and that his purpose was to devise a *tabula rasa* strategic plan for Vietnam—as if the United States was starting from zero, as if no commitment whatsoever had been made. Or as Marshall put it, "What would be the ideal thing we would do . . . if there were no sacred cows." In fact, Marshall had been selected by Abrams to head the Long-Range Planning Task Group (LORAPL) in July 1968. Marshall had worked on the Army's 1966 PROVN, or "Program for the Pacification and Longer-Term Development of Vietnam," study, which had advocated "more pacification and less attrition"—an approach also favored by General Abrams.[147]

---

[147] Richard A. Hunt, *Pacification: The American Struggle for Vietnam's Hearts and Minds*, Boulder, Colo.: Westview Press, 1995, p. 212.

Peace talks might have begun in Paris in 1968, but the United States still had a war to fight. How to wage this war became the responsibility of General Creighton Abrams. Searching for a different strategy, Abrams created the Long-Range Planning Task Group to help him change the way that the U.S. Army was fighting the war. Abrams wanted to reorient the Army from search-and-destroy operations in unpopulated areas toward support for pacification, in order to take advantage of the communists' retrenchment in the wake of heavy losses suffered during and after the Tet Offensive and to push them out of contested areas. During the accelerated pacification drive of 1968–1969, Abrams would devote almost half of American ground operations to clear the contested areas and provide a modicum of security and a "shield" for the GVN to move in and reestablish its control. His strategy—which became known as "clear and hold"—was a response to the communists' retrenchment, but it also reflected his view that the war was both military and political: that the "big-unit war and pacification were 'one war.'" In a message to his regional commanders in October 1968, he told them they should make pacification and rural development top priorities, while at the same time intensifying their "offensive against infrastructure, guerrillas, and local force units."[148] However, "clear and hold"—by combining "big-unit war and pacification" into "one war" in populated, contested areas—relied on the use of heavy weapons and aggressive operations, which increased civilian casualties.

To Benoit, Marshall's project was somewhat unique. Many people were recruited for it, mainly from the military. Because of this military cast, Benoit wondered "how fresh a look this [study] could really be." However, Marshall at the time told him with pride that Abrams had given him complete freedom to "reach any conclusions that [he] felt were justified." Benoit did not know what the other people on the project were doing. He could not relate to it, and did not ask to be involved. He did not have a good relationship with the rest of the staff, including a couple of SP4s—Specialists Fourth Class in the U.S. Army, equivalent in rank to Corporals, who perform special tasks and who have no command authority over enlisted men—serving as typists. Benoit did not know how to type—"nobody had a computer back then"—so he would write in longhand, laboriously, and then give the papers to the SP4s. However, on one occasion, they thought what he had written "was propaganda," and refused to type it up until Marshall ordered them to do so.[149]

---

[148] Hunt, *Pacification*, 1995, p. 212.

[149] Gerry Hickey, who was also recruited by Marshall for the project, recalled that General Creighton Abrams had ordered this "Long Range Planning Project" to thoroughly examine American strategy in Vietnam, make an in-depth "Appraisal of Current Strategy," and project "future strategy based on the geographical, historical, economic, socio-psychological, and political . . . perspectives." According to Hickey, Marshall's "broad conceptual framework (which reflected the anthropological 'total culture' approach) was badly needed to lend a multidimensional perspective to American strategy." According to Hickey, the Marshall Group included "some very capable young American military officers of varied background" and also "wisely contacted some Vietnamese officers with expertise dating back to the Indochina War. Hickey agreed to do the "Montagnard and the FULRO Context" for Marshall, which he completed in March 1969. Hickey, *Window on a War*, 2002, p. 260.

Marshall gave Benoit a broad mandate. He could "go anywhere and do anything." All he had to do was to travel to distant places for a couple of days and then return to Saigon to pull his field notes together into a report to capture "what I saw, what I felt, and what I thought about what I saw and what I felt." No one on Marshall's staff had that kind of mandate and, because of this, what Benoit produced was unique compared with what the others were doing. Marshall thought that what Benoit did provided an important perspective and found some of the things Benoit wrote "very different"—"things that weren't being said by anyone else."

(Of the trips he made in Vietnam, Benoit remembered most vividly his visit to a village that was contested even though it was near an American firebase that was adjacent to a secure district capital. Benoit knew the village and had written about it for Don Marshall who was intrigued by the lack of security in the village despite its location. The day Benoit was there in 1972—during a field trip made either at the behest of RAND or in his capacity as a reporter, which he had become by 1972—the village was napalmed. Suddenly, a little girl—her clothes burned off and her skin scorched by the napalm—ran past him. The trauma of seeing her knocked him "right to one knee." Subsequently, a picture shot by Vietnamese journalist Nick Ut, showing Kim Phuc, the little girl Benoit had seen running down the road, screaming in utter anguish, would epitomize to the world the suffering being inflicted on the Vietnamese.[150])

After Benoit submitted a trip report that Marshall liked, Marshall asked him to develop a profile of the Viet Cong, trusting that he would "come up with something that would be interesting." Without a background in this area, Benoit found the assignment difficult. He remembers that he "struggled and struggled" and that Marshall helped him a great deal. In the end, Benoit wrote "as though there was this young fellow who was a farmer" and about "what he might have seen which would have led him to decide to join the NLF, etc." It was, Benoit said, a sympathetic profile. However, he believes that his piece probably ended up being "relegated to an appendix in the total study." Besides these assignments, sometimes Marshall would ask him "to write this or do that." He worked for Marshall for five or six months.

Benoit did not know what final conclusions Marshall reached or what recommendations he made to Abrams, because he never received a copy of the report. However, he believed that the report made little difference, although at the outset Marshall honestly believed that "he was doing work that had never been done before and . . . should have been done from the beginning." In fact, Marshall submitted the report to Abrams in November 1968, which concluded that "security was critical to victory" and recommended that "U.S. resources should be devoted to three main functions: popula-

---

[150]Charlie Benoit left RAND in 1969, but he accepted brief assignments with RAND until around 1973. He became a reporter in 1972. In 1973, he joined the Ford Foundation in Saigon. He stayed in Vietnam for the Ford Foundation until 1975 and made a dramatic last-minute evacuation in 1975 when Saigon fell to the communists.

tion security . . . support of pacification, and national development."[151] The report, in essence, confirmed Abrams's own thinking about how the war ought to be fought at that point.

The report laid the foundation for the MACV strategic plan, which was approved in March 1969. The main departure from MACV's previous strategy was the emphasis on support for pacification and protection of the population by American and South Vietnamese forces, with the goal of expanding the secure areas within which the government could establish sound institutions, carry out economic-development programs, and institute meaningful social change. As it evolved, pacification was achieved mainly through depopulation with firepower.[152]

Benoit did have one memorable briefing with General Creighton Abrams, who had been a classmate of his father at the Agawam High School in Massachusetts. In 1969, Bud Collins, a reporter for the *Boston Globe* and a friend of Benoit, came to Saigon and, knowing that his father and Abrams had gone to school together, set up a briefing with Abrams. Collins thought that Benoit should talk to Abrams because he had a different perspective and could back it up with facts and figures. Collins showed up one day and said, "Charlie, it's on. Let's go. . . . I have a meeting in half an hour with General Abrams." They went into Abrams's office and sat down. Abrams asked how Benoit's father was doing, and then "broke out the cigar, bit off the end and spat it out on the rug," and then they started talking.

Benoit figured he did not have much time, and told Abrams "a lot of factual things that he'd never heard before," and Abrams "harumphed about seven times." Abrams asked Benoit three or four questions, which showed he did not appreciate Benoit's more nuanced perspective on the Viet Cong and which betrayed the standard military view that the enemy the United States was fighting in Vietnam were "terrorists." The questions were in the vein of, "But what about the guys who put plastique in bicycles in front of schools and blow them up?" Abrams, according to Benoit, also displayed a lack of understanding of how the local population could perceive American military actions. This side of Abrams that he was introduced to that day led Benoit to conclude that there was no major difference between Abrams and Westmoreland. The new MACV commander was reputed to have changed the U.S. military and to be doing things differently, but this was not what Benoit saw at the meeting.

♣ ♣ ♣

As Abrams pounded the enemy with his "clear and hold" strategy, the search continued for a political settlement to the war at the meetings in Paris between the United

---

[151] Hunt, *Pacification*, 1995, p. 212.

[152] According to Hunt (*Pacification*, 1995, p. 192), "U.S. Army support for pacification" at times still "seemed closer to attrition than to a pacification-oriented strategy."

States and North Vietnam. Since the prospects for a political solution seemed to have brightened with the continuation of the Paris talks, Gerry Hickey updated his paper on political accommodation within South Vietnam in the hope that it would have more of an effect. On November 19, 1968, Hickey presented his ideas to the Marshall Group, which he had been invited to join. However, the American embassy had passed word in December to Marshall that they were "lukewarm" about accommodation because it carried the connotation of "giving in." Also, Vietnamese and American officials thought that extended gains in the countryside through "clear and hold" would make accommodation unnecessary. Hickey felt disappointed over his lack of impact. Not only had his ideas been ignored by American officials in Saigon and in Washington, he had also failed to make headway at RAND, where few of the "physicists, political scientists, and economists who held sway in Santa Monica" were "reflective people."[153] He then took his ideas to the press, discussing them with some reporters and columnists, including C. L. Sulzberger of *The New York Times*, telling them his view that the inclusion of the Viet Cong in the political arena would galvanize the other noncommunist political groups into coming together so that the Viet Cong could be kept from achieving dominance and taking over. According to Hickey, Sulzberger called the approach "venturesome," and the reaction reinforced Hickey's feeling that he was a voice in the wilderness.[154]

The post-Tet situation in South Vietnam—with huge dislocations created by the communist offensives and the counterattacks by GVN and American forces—intrigued Bing West, a former Marine officer who had joined RAND. West had spent many years in the Marine Corps and served with the Corps in Vietnam as a captain and a commander. His job with the Marine Corps in Vietnam "was to go into combat with different small units and write it up, and [General Lewis W. Walt, the Marine commander in Vietnam] sent that back to Washington to be used to train the lieutenants coming out."[155] After the Marines, West attended the Woodrow Wilson School at Princeton and graduated in 1967. From his Marine experience West wrote *Small Unit Action in Vietnam*.[156] Sir Robert Thompson, then a consultant to RAND, recommended that RAND hire him as an analyst on counterinsurgency. West joined the Social Science Department in September 1967 and stayed for about three years.[157] In November 1967, he asked to go back to Vietnam, and RAND agreed. He traveled

---

[153] Hickey, *Window on a War*, 2002, p. 281.

[154] Hickey, *Window on a War*, 2002, p. 265.

[155] Author interview with Bing West, 2004.

[156] Francis J. West, "*Small Unit Action in Vietnam, Summer 1966*, Washington, D.C.: Historical Branch, G-3 Division, Headquarters, U.S. Marine Corps, 1967.

[157] West subsequently served as Assistant Secretary of Defense for International Security Affairs in the Reagan Administration. West has written six well-received books on Vietnam and Iraq and has been called a "warrior-scholar." He is also a respected journalist covering the war in Iraq.

through the countryside and subsequently filed a special trip report for RAND, focusing on what was happening in scores of hamlets and districts in a dozen provinces scattered throughout Vietnam in the period leading up to the Tet Offensive.

In the summer of 1968, West returned to Vietnam to revisit many of those hamlets, some of which he had known for years. He decided to get out into the countryside because what he learned in Saigon from data, briefings, and formal reports did not tell him much about what was really happening. West thought that Benoit's fluency in Vietnamese and his knowledge of the countryside would make him an ideal colleague for these trips. West asked Benoit if he would join him, and Benoit agreed—adding his knowledge and taking West to locations he had known for a long time. They were on their own, because they were going "where they were shooting."[158] After they returned to Saigon, West would write what "in essence became a series of field reports about how the war looked if you were out in the countryside fighting it."[159] Benoit recalled that the deal he worked out with West was that "we'd go out into the field and we'd come back in two or three weeks; we'd sit and write up what we saw, heard, and make some sense out of it, draw some conclusions."[160]

According to Benoit, West wrote most of the conclusions that were submitted to generals, since he "had some sense of what they were interested in." Benoit "didn't have a clue," and never attended any of the briefings West gave to the generals, not because West neglected to invite him but because he was not interested.[161]

Benoit said that when he met Bing West he did not know what work West was performing for RAND. He himself was just beginning a career, and was impressed by how West was able to make himself visible by delivering "what a lot of people were interested in." Benoit recalled that he "stood in awe" of West's ability to turn his data—even limited data into interesting briefings. West, Benoit said, was willing to go out into the field and put himself in danger, "in trenches and on night patrols and things of that sort" to get a feel of what was happening. But what distinguished him from plenty of other people in the military who were doing the same thing was his ability to write about it and make it interesting.[162] In enlisting Benoit, West added another dimension to his reporting. Benoit said that when they met, West saw that Benoit "could give him more breadth and take him to places that he wouldn't otherwise have gotten

---

[158] Author interview with Bing West, 2004.

[159] Author interview with Bing West, 2004.

[160] Author interview with Charlie Benoit, 2005.

[161] Author interview with Charlie Benoit, 2005.

[162] In the Foreword to West's *The Village: Fifteen Walked In. Eight Walked Out* (New York: Pocket Books, 1972), former Secretary of Defense James Schlesinger, who had known West when they were both at RAND, wrote that the papers West produced at RAND were "different from the torrent of Vietnam analysis." They were "descriptive and concrete—simple vignettes that hinted at, but did not state, larger conclusions. . . . West left the theorizing about grand strategy to others."

to." Benoit added that West was "extremely fair," and made sure that he got an equal amount of exposure. He enjoyed working with West, and felt that their partnership was "a good match up" and that "it's kind of nice to work with a guy . . . who makes sure that he takes you along right with him."[163]

At the end of December 1968, Benoit and West published a report condensing their observations and suggestions. It covered their three months of travel and the approximately 60 districts and hamlets in 15 provinces they had visited.[164] This report provided an overview of the situation in the countryside post-Tet, along with a recommendation for a strategy to deal with the changes that had occurred. Although their evaluation was based on their talks with local Vietnamese officials and troops and some villagers they encountered, the bulk of the information for their reports came from visits and conversations with American small units that operated closer to the scene on the ground and among the population. As Charlie Benoit put it, these American units provided an "institutional arrangement" into which they "could plug to find out what was going on in the hamlets."[165] On the whole, the picture they presented of rural security had a sense of déjà vu and few bright spots.[166]

Their overall assessment was that, in the period after the Tet Offensive, the Viet Cong seemed weaker than in the previous year, but the GVN had been unable to take advantage of this development. Too often, the Viet Cong were able to maintain their psychological grip over the countryside because their organization made their power "appear ubiquitous."[167] The result was that the South Vietnamese Regional and Popular Forces units would defend only the hamlets where their families lived, conceding the others to the enemy. Except for the occasional disruption caused by "token sweeps," the insurgents could safely inhabit these sanctuaries.[168]

---

[163] Author interview with Charlie Benoit, 2005. Benoit said that they remain friends and had traveled back to Vietnam together and revisited some of the old sites.

[164] F. J. West and Charles Benoit, "A Brief Report from Rural Vietnam," Santa Monica, Calif.: RAND Corporation, D-18011-ARPA, July–October 1968, which they later incorporated into "Pacification: View from the Provinces—Part II (July–October 1968)," Santa Monica, Calif.: RAND Corporation, D-18082-1-ARPA, Revised December 13, 1968—a follow-up to Part I (November–December 1967) that Bing West had written and published in January 1968.

[165] West and Benoit, "Pacification—Part II," 1968, p. 85.

[166] One of the bleak anecdotes concerns the behavior of South Korean troops. Even in this post-Tet era, the South Koreans had not changed their mode of operation. In the southern sector of Quang Nam Province, West and Benoit learned about the brutality of South Korean troops. They reported that the behavior of the South Koreans embittered many Marines, who thought they were "excessively cruel in their treatment of the Vietnamese people and defensive in their tactics." Villagers were afraid of the Koreans and wanted to know why the Marines did not kill the Koreans instead of the Viet Cong. The irony was that, according to most Americans in the area, the Koreans' brutality did nothing to enhance their military effectiveness.

[167] West and Benoit, "Pacification—Part II," 1968, p. 116.

[168] West and Benoit, "Pacification—Part II," 1968, p. 116.

American forces, focusing on keeping enemy Main Force units from massing for offensives, rarely influenced this local balance of power. The influence of the Americans had been mainly in preventing the "organizational cement of the Viet Cong" from hardening in the countryside, and they appeared more "to hold things in a state of suspended animation."[169] Morale among both the Americans and the South Vietnamese was low. Americans at lower levels did not see the prospect for victory and were disenchanted with the statements from higher echelons claiming that progress was being made. Local Vietnamese officials dreaded the prospect of Americans pulling up stakes and going home because, if this came to pass, "they would then have lost the war."[170] The Viet Cong reinforced their fear with the oft-repeated threat that the Americans would leave.

Despite efforts to undermine it, the enemy infrastructure—the target of pacification—did not appear near collapse or neutralization. While its ranks might have been depleted somewhat in 1968, the losses might have been reduced by replacements. Moreover, those that were eliminated were often not important figures. Elimination of cadres active in GVN areas addressed only part of the issue. The real problem came from cadres in contiguous areas, who occasionally infiltrated at night to collect taxes, reconnoiter the defenses, and tell the villagers that the Viet Cong were coming back. These cadres could be eliminated only if GVN control was gradually pushed into the VC regions. Other difficulties afflicted the GVN effort to eliminate the Viet Cong infrastructure, such as "bribes, threats, lack of evidence, poor training, arbitration rather than adjudication, and an outlandish penal code."[171]

According to West and Benoit, the Hamlet Evaluation System (HES)—mentioned in Chapter Six—measured the degree of GVN control fairly accurately. However, it did not measure the intangible factor of allegiance: the "hearts and minds" of the people.

$$\clubsuit \quad \clubsuit \quad \clubsuit$$

In their travels, West and Benoit found that some American units were switching to guerrilla-type tactics as the big-unit war of attrition had fallen out of favor. As someone who had operated with the Marines engaging in small-unit action, West was more suited than anyone at RAND to assess the effectiveness of this tactical change. West and Benoit found that many American officers and soldiers were using such guerilla tactics as "engaging and maintaining contact" with the enemy only when they had the advantage; moving "in small bands, cutting their visibility (and so, vulner-

---

[169] West and Benoit, "Pacification—Part II," 1968, p. 120.

[170] West and Benoit, "Pacification—Part II," 1968, p. 116.

[171] West and Benoit, "Pacification—Part II," 1968, p. 117.

ability) by using the bush and the night[;] relying on the ambush to engage[;] and [engaging in] sudden withdrawal by helicopter or boat to avoid taking casualties."[172] By adopting such tactics, these units were ahead of American military doctrine, which still espoused conventional warfare tactic. Nonetheless, ever flexible, the enemy had responded to increased U.S. patrolling by using American-made mines, which exacted "a terrible physical and psychological toll," lowered morale, and deterred U.S. forces from going into certain areas. Many GIs expressed "bitterness about the amount of U.S. mines in enemy hands," the authors indicated.[173]

Operating in small units and fighting like guerrillas might represent an innovation in the U.S. Army, but these tactics had been pioneered by the Marines as far back as 1965, with what they called "Combined Action Platoons" or CAPs. West had commanded a CAP in Binh Nghia Village in Quang Tri Province, despite the fact that his rank as captain was too high for that assignment. He was given the assignment to help the Marine command determine whether it would make sense to leave the Marines in small units in villages to face the Viet Cong.[174] Because of his background with the CAPs, West was keen in checking on them and finding out how they were doing in the post-Tet situation.

The CAP program was started in August 1965 by accident and by necessity. A Marine battalion in I Corps first experimented with the concept when it found itself short of replacements as the war intensified and its tactical area of responsibility grew.[175] It turned to the Popular Forces in the hope of enlisting them to defend the area. Squads of Marines were assigned to live and fight in the villages, alongside the Popular Forces (PFs)—militiamen who occupied the lowest rung in the South Vietnamese army. Badly paid, and poorly trained and equipped, they were for the most part unmotivated. Some made accommodation with the Viet Cong; others would go on leave without permission. However, General Lewis W. Walt believed the PFs could be turned into a good fighting force because each militiaman had a stake in defending his home, relatives, and neighbors, and knew the local terrain intimately.

The Marines adopted the CAP concept when it proved to be effective in countering Viet Cong influence and control in the villages. General Walt expanded the program because he believed that the "struggle was in the rice paddies . . . in and among the people, not passing through, but living among them, night and day."[176] While

---

[172] West and Benoit, "Pacification—Part II," 1969, p. 118.

[173] West and Benoit, "Pacification—Part II," 1969, p. 118.

[174] Bing West, *The Village*, New York: Pocket, 2002, p. xiii.

[175] Bruce R. Brewington, *The Combined Action Platoons: A Strategy for Peace Enforcement*, CSC 1996, Marine Corps Warfighting Laboratory, Wargaming Division, Small Wars Center of Excellence.

[176] Lt. Gen Lewis Walt, *Strange War, Strange Strategy*, cited in Web site of Weider History Group, HistoryNet. Com, on the Marine CAP Program. In "We Are All Alone in Indian Country" published on the U.S. Marines Combined Action Platoons Web site, Tim "CAPVet" Duffie says that the CAPs felt alone and vulnerable

General Westmoreland believed that the key to success was to look for and destroy the NVA and Viet Cong Main Force units and to leave pacification to the ARVN, General Walt—to Westmoreland's displeasure—devoted only a third of his force to search-and-destroy operations and used the remainder to eradicate Viet Cong influence from the villages.

Under the CAP program, a squad of Marines and one Navy Corpsman were placed in villages in I Corps from Chu Lai to the DMZ. The Marines, all volunteers, lived in the villages, trained the local militia, and conducted patrols and ambushes, both day and night. Their mission was to destroy the Viet Cong infrastructure, provide security, protect the bases and lines of communication between the village and the hamlets, organize local intelligence networks, train the Popular Forces, and perform civic action. Their mission would be considered accomplished when the local officials and Popular Forces could stand on their own without their help. The program expanded as Marine volunteers were trained and organized for this kind of assignment, and by the end of 1968 the number of CAPs had reached 114.

Benoit thought that West viewed the Marines and the CAPs favorably—even affectionately—because he was a former Marine captain and CAP commander. But Benoit had to agree with West that the Marines and their CAPs were special and were doing "something different."[177] Benoit attributed the Marines' innovativeness to their smaller size as a force, which made them more willing to employ different tactics to fight the war, whereas the U.S. Army—in his view—remained more rigid in its approach. Benoit remembered that Army officers above the rank of lieutenant colonel frequently remarked, "Look, there are a lot of wars in the world. We're not going to change the US Army for Vietnam, because then we would lose the next war."[178]

Judging from the anecdotes in the report by West and Benoit, the success of the CAPs depended on the makeup of the group of Marines and the attitude of the local Vietnamese with whom they worked. In some areas, the relationship was good; in others, it was either indifferent or bad. But even where it was good, the CAPs—as Bing West and Charlie Benoit pointed out—were isolated teams working without an overall strategic framework and without a linkage to other teams to form a system for

---

as they stood for the first time in an isolated Vietnamese village, surrounded by jungle, terrifying booby-traps, and thousands of supposedly hostile Vietnamese civilians. Images of fanatical Viet Cong pouring out of the jungles and rice paddies hovered in the minds of each of us as we hunkered down for our first night of sleep in such hostile territory. That first night, each new Marine and Corpsman counted the friendly faces of as few as 7 Americans, then looked with mixed emotions at a poorly equipped platoon of Vietnamese Popular Forces, the local village 'militia.' Each Marine or Corpsman certainly pondered the distance to the nearest American military base. Each calculated how long it would take for help to arrive. Each knew that, when needed, help would probably not arrive in time.

[177] Author interview with Charlie Benoit, 2005.

[178] Author interview with Charlie Benoit, 2005.

securing and pacifying the countryside, and they had no program to bring the Popular Forces in to replace the Americans as tactical leaders. When the CAPs were effective, their success surprised Benoit, because, in his view, they were just a small group of men plunked down in the middle of the Vietnamese countryside—an alien presence in villages where the locals distrusted foreign intruders.[179]

According to an evaluation of the CAPs, the program had successes and failures.[180] However, even where they succeeded, the effect of the CAPs was short-lived. After they left in May 1971, the situation reverted to what it had been before. The failures were due to language barriers; cultural misunderstanding; lack of motivation on the part of the Popular Forces; Marine distrust of the militiamen, believing that they were afraid of the Viet Cong and were making deals with them; lack of cooperation from the villagers, who were reluctant to provide intelligence either out of fear of the Viet Cong or out of sympathy for them; and Marine disinterest in civic action, which was a part of their mission to improve the life of the villagers. On the whole, the CAPs did bring security to the villages—if only because their presence protected these places from becoming free-fire zones.[181]

The lack of progress they perceived in the countryside led West and Benoit to suggest that the United States adopt what they called an "area security" strategy, which would pull together GVN and U.S. efforts in the rural areas by optimizing the use of existing resources. The long-term goal of area security would be to induce the majority of villagers who were not committed to either side to change their attitude toward the GVN. The immediate focus, however, would be to reinforce the local forces and officials who were already committed to the Saigon regime but who had been left to

---

[179] Author interview with Charlie Benoit, 2005. Bing West ultimately wrote a book called *The Village*, 2002, chronicling the lives and deaths of the Marines in the CAP that was stationed in Binh Nghia Village, located in the middle of Quang Tri Province. In 2002, Bing West asked Benoit to return with him to this village to see what it was like 35 years later. Benoit was amazed, surprised, and impressed by the number of people "who came up asking by name about one of the soldiers that had been in that camp," and he thought to himself, "How many American soldiers died in Vietnam, and what percentage of them are remembered by even one Vietnamese? All those Marines who died in that village had dozens of people who knew who they were and remember them by name. Kind of touching, really." An encounter with a local villager reminded Benoit how long ago these events had taken place. During the visit, an older woman approached him and spoke to him in "GI lingo." With astonishment, he realized that, 35 years ago—when she was in her youth—this woman might have known the Marines and might have even flirted with them. He felt like he had just landed on the moon.

[180] Brewington, *The Combined Action Platoons*.

[181] The CAP concept was not expanded beyond the Marines' area of operation, because the South Vietnamese military thought that it encouraged the PF to "sit back and let the Marines do the work"—as a Vietnamese general put it. Robert Komer, who assumed leadership of the pacification efforts in May 1967, was not enthusiastic about the CAP concept either. In lieu of the CAPs, the U.S. Army created Mobile Advisory Teams (or MATs), who moved from unit to unit to improve the Regional and Popular Forces with material support and training in the use of weapons and small-unit tactics, such as night operations, ambushes, and patrols. Since the MATs did not stay in one place, the South Vietnamese—it was hoped—would not become dependent on them. The MATs were eventually assigned to all districts in South Vietnam and totaled 354 teams.

fight their own little wars separately, without cohesion and coordination with other localities, and without the support—material or psychological—from their government. These people had to be "brought into some sort of area-security system; and they must be convinced by actions that it is going to work."[182] It was only through convincing action and aid that the government could demonstrate to them that it cared and that victory could be achieved. The role of the Americans would be to provide ideas and information, to push and supervise efforts to get things done, and to train the Vietnamese to gradually take over with the guarantee that they would be able to count on American support.

Area security could be accomplished through surveillance, patrolling, defense, reaction, and pursuit—techniques that had been employed, but in an uncoordinated and sporadic manner. Intelligence provided by the small number of villagers who were either anti-VC or pro-GVN would aid surveillance. Active patrolling could make the people more confident in their government and, when undertaken consistently over time, could keep the Viet Cong from infiltrating. A defensive system could defeat attacks, and "preplanned reaction forces" could boost defense.[183] Pursuit would return the initiative to local forces, because the enemy would be exposed as he sought to disengage. With the "mobility and skill" at their disposal, U.S. and GVN forces could "integrate these components into an interlaced area-security system which would be flexible and responsive to various enemy attack levels."[184]

The authors urged that Americans join the Vietnamese in village and district units to make area security a reality. By being with these units, the Americans—as "hostages"—gave confidence to the Vietnamese, who knew that help would be forthcoming if the situation demanded it. The Americans, in return, would get to know the terrain and the enemy, while giving the Vietnamese firepower and combat skill. In addition, the presence of the Americans shielded the villagers from indiscriminate shelling and bombing.

For this system to work, Americans who were recruited for this type of assignment would have to be people who liked the Vietnamese. "Once area security becomes institutionalized," the authors wrote, "and the Vietnamese become confident in their ability to hold, the ratio of American encadrement can be lowered, but always with the guarantee of return when needed."[185] West and Benoit concluded by saying that area security "would require a conceptual change," and its implementation would require "bureaucratic and tactical changes."[186] There could be no guarantee that area security

---

[182] Brewington, *The Combined Action Platoons*, p. 122.

[183] Brewington, *The Combined Action Platoons*, p. 121.

[184] Brewington, *The Combined Action Platoons*, p. 121.

[185] Brewington, *The Combined Action Platoons*, p. 121.

[186] Brewington, *The Combined Action Platoons*, p. 122.

would lower American casualties significantly, and it was not certain how many years it would take to achieve demonstrable progress. They suggested that this alternative strategy be compared with existing procedures, and tested.

Charlie Benoit was not the only RAND staff member Bing West recruited to travel with him through the countryside. West liked taking Saigon-bound RAND people along to give them a taste of adventure if they were curious and wanted to have some excitement. As a former Marine, West was not reluctant to go where the action was. On one of his field trips, West took Yogi Ianeiro, whom he disguised under the name of Jeff in his report. West later extracted this portion of the trip report for a separate RAND document—with a few modifications—under the title *Yogi Goes to War.* Jim Digby remembered that when West took Yogi on this trip, "they both had M16's." He said that "it was easy to get arms in Vietnam," and that Bing West, being a former Marine, was "accustomed to carrying an M-16 or other arms when he went out into the country." Digby thought that *Yogi Goes to War* was interesting because "Bing was an excellent writer." However, the trip "was in complete violation of policy," and Digby had "the document withdrawn so nobody would find out."[187] To West, however, it was better to carry arms and "stay alive first and work out those details later."[188]

In *Yogi Goes to War*, Bing West wrote that he preferred to wander through the countryside by himself because he did not want to impose too much on those he met and because he had found that people would talk to him more freely in private if he was by himself. However, when Ianeiro told him that he was tired of Saigon and wanted to see the war in the countryside before going home, West invited him to come along on a trip to I Corps. As someone living in the midst of the war, Ianeiro's request to see it up close might sound astonishing. But the fact was that his brushes with the war had been few—limited to the sighting of helicopters, or the sound of distant bombardment or shelling, or the explosion of rockets landing somewhere in town. He had experienced the war mostly as an inconvenience: observing a curfew or ferrying RAND staff members into the villa for safety, for example. He had not been shot at, nor had he had to shoot at someone. To him, as to other RAND staff members in Saigon, the war was so close and at the same time so far.

West thought that Ianeiro deserved a break, having labored month after month supporting the work of the researchers. Ianeiro was "hard to fit into an organizational slot," West wrote, but "he was definitely a man the RAND research effort in Vietnam could ill afford to be without."[189] Ianeiro did his job so well "that it was easy to over-

---

[187] Author interview with Jim Digby, 2002.

[188] Author interview with Bing West, 2004.

[189] Bing West, *Yogi Goes to War*, provided by Yogi Ianeiro, p. 1.

look the knack he had for acquiring what the researchers needed" and for his ability to deal successfully with the Saigon bureaucracy. Arnold Mengle, the successor to Vic Croizat, gave permission to West to take Ianeiro along, and said, "Make sure nothing happens."[190]

At a CAP compound in I Corps, which had eight Marines and 20 Popular Force soldiers led by an American sergeant, Ianeiro had a taste of the war. He learned to handle his M-16 and a grenade launcher. He joined a night patrol of five Americans and six Vietnamese Popular Force soldiers, and walked fifth in the column. After two hours on patrol, they settled in for the night in a thatched hut. Ianeiro was too nervous to get much sleep. The second night, they joined a CAP on an island that the Viet Cong had controlled for two years and where they still had an edge. The Viet Cong moved freely on the island and sometimes would shout taunts at the Marine CAP at night. The night before West and Ianeiro arrived, a Viet Cong squad had walked into an ambush, and the blood trails were still visible. Ianeiro was assigned to man a bunker along with a Marine, and received instructions from the sergeant on how to use a machine gun, a grenade launcher, claymore mines, and tear-gas dispensers. West was manning a machine gun in another bunker. That night, the Viet Cong attacked with satchel charges and B40 rockets. The sergeant called in an artillery barrage. Three helicopter gunships arrived right after the attack began, and the red tracers from their guns looked as comforting to the defenders of the compound as lights on a Christmas tree. No one was hurt, but a section of the trench and of the barbed wire near Ianeiro's bunker was badly damaged.

On another occasion, West and Benoit took Arnold Mengle along on a trip to Hau Nghia, a province in which both NVA and VC units were active. Mengle wanted to go with them in part to reassure himself that they were taking risks that were connected to their research and not unnecessary. While driving down a side road toward a district, a Viet Cong machine gun opened up. A tank that was guarding an Army bulldozer and grader widening the road opened fire. A Huey helicopter came, made a few high passes to stay out of the range of the machine gun, and flew away. Then two helicopters came, one blaring music and broadcasting a call to the Viet Cong to rally to the just cause of the government. The three RAND staff members departed. Mengle was sorry that he had forgotten to take a picture of the scene, because no one in Santa Monica would believe what he had seen.

As the research by West and Benoit indicated, small-scale projects like theirs were still being undertaken by RAND even as its presence diminished. They did not fit into a defined research program but instead were performed ad hoc at the request of clients

---

[190] Bing West, *Yogi Goes to War*, provided by Yogi Ianeiro, p. 2.

or out of personal interest—as was the case with Bing West. Marv Schaffer and John Dudzinsky were two RAND analysts who were among the last to come to Vietnam: Schaffer to work on the HES and Dudzinsky to work on loan for MACV.

Marv Schaffer returned to Saigon in the summer of 1968—for the last time. He remembered going to the areas of the city six months after they had been overrun by the Viet Cong during the Tet Offensive and finding them still "spooky."[191] He and the people he was with felt frightened. At the time, the Viet Cong were shooting rockets into downtown Saigon, killing people and blowing up buildings. After staying at the President Hotel for a few days, Schaffer had to choose where to live, so he visited the *Saigon Daily Post* to obtain all the back issues. From the articles, he made a list of the locations that had been hit and then "plotted them on a map, and they made a very nice ellipse of where the impact points were, with the Catholic church at the center." Schaffer realized that the church was the tallest building in Saigon, visible from across the river, and that the Viet Cong had been using it as a reference point to aim their rockets. That made his choice of where to live easier: He decided to move to an apartment, which he shared with Andy Sweetland, in a building located "miles away from the rocket impact area."

Schaffer and Sweetland were both working on the Hamlet Evaluation System, but independently. With the help of Ted Serong, Schaffer had gained access to the entire HES database and had brought it back with him to Saigon. He "analyzed it in great detail," he said, to see "whether or not the criteria they were evaluating for security had any relation to common sense." He concluded that HES "did and didn't" make sense. According to him, the HES employed "arbitrary" measures "of goodness" in military and nonmilitary categories, which were rated on a scale of one to ten. Then, for each of the thousands of hamlets, the results were averaged and a score was assigned. Schaffer thought that HES was "better than nothing," but that unless there was security "the non-military factors had no validity." He thought that what HES should do was "to get a good handle [on] what the security measure of goodness is, and then develop a more complicated evaluation of the non-military measures." He said that he made his findings available to Robert Komer, but without effect. Komer "duly noted" his recommendation "with thanks," but nothing came of it and what Schaffer suggested "disappeared in the depth of [Komer's] brain."

John Dudzinsky arrived after Schaffer, in the fall of 1968. After he obtained his doctorate at Carnegie Mellon University in electrical engineering in 1965, Dudzinsky interviewed at many places. One of his classmates had been a summer intern at RAND and had told him glowingly about it as a place to work and Santa Monica as a place to live. Dudzinsky applied at RAND but was rejected. He went to work for a subsidiary of North American Aviation for slightly more than a year. He did not like his boss and

---

[191] Author interview with Marv Schaffer, 2004. This and the following quotes from Schaffer are from the same interview.

went back to RAND in 1967 and applied again. By this time, RAND had just landed some big contracts, including one with NASA to perform studies on satellite systems. Dudzinsky was hired into the Engineering Sciences Department. He remembered that he enjoyed working at RAND and that he stayed for almost 15 years.[192]

At RAND, Dudzinsky met many people, including Bill McMillan, a physical chemist and full professor at UCLA, in the Physics Department at RAND. McMillan subsequently was appointed scientific advisor to General Westmoreland. Dudzinsky knew several RAND people who had gone to Vietnam to do different things, and they had regaled him with stories when they came back. At the time, he understood little of what was going on in Vietnam. "I didn't know a Viet Cong from an NVA, from anything," he said. "The war was pervasive in the United States," he remembered, "it created so much hate, so much protest. People with placards, and Jane Fonda, that kind of thing." He knew about the domino theory, but he could not figure out what was really happening from the newspapers, so he decided to go to Vietnam to "find out more about the war." Dudzinsky went to talk to McMillan, who hired him.

Dudzinsky arrived in Vietnam in September 1968. He remembered paying a visit to the RAND villa, where he met Andy Sweetland and Yogi Ianeiro. He found Ianeiro "funny" and "different" and in possession of a cabinet full of weapons. Ianeiro told him to pick out what he wanted, and Dudzinsky chose a .45. After carrying it around for a month, he realized that he really did not need it in Saigon. However, he took it with him whenever he went out into the field. Eventually, Dudzinsky made two trips to Vietnam.

McMillan's staff lived in the Star Hotel on Tu Do Street, two to a room. Every day, a chauffered, four-seat black Ford Crown Victoria came to pick them up in the morning and took them to the office and back again around five o'clock. In the evening, they had dinner together, either at some Chinese restaurant nearby or at the Rex BOQ. "It was a group that had a lot of camaraderie," Dudzinsky said. If they had to go out into the field, they would have to wear Army uniforms, and frequently they would have to spend the night wherever they happened to be. Dudzinsky flew all over the country in "Hueys, Jolly Green Giants, [and] these little Bell helicopters."

The office of the scientific advisor was set up to solve engineering and technical problems that were troubling the military. Bill McMillan had about 20 technical people on his staff—"engineers, scientists, and medically oriented people" who "worked on all kinds of problems, from how to prevent GIs from getting jungle rot in their feet to working on technical problems with firearms and . . . communication problems and radars and all kinds of things." Dudzinsky was the only RAND person on the staff. Technically, he was on leave from RAND and working for ARPA, which paid him the same salary. MACV's hope was that the engineers and scientists could provide advice on how to solve problems or devise helpful innovations. If the Army ran

---

[192]Author interview with John Dudzinsky, 2004. The subsequent quotes are from this interview.

into problems, they would communicate those to McMillan "to see whether there were technical solutions that could be put into place maybe back in a laboratory somewhere in the US or in a manufacturing plant to mitigate or make those problems go away." Or MACV would ask them to test the effectiveness of some weapons. Every week, McMillan would brief Westmoreland.

Mostly, the group worked on technical problems and on testing equipment. For example, they conducted tests to determine whether the 0V2—a Navy plane that had two jet engines and two propeller engines and was equipped with forward- and downward-looking infrared—would be effective in interdicting boat traffic at night. "They would fly up and down the rivers and look with this infrared and they could see the boats . . . at night," he said, "and if they were in a free fire zone or if they suspected something was not right, they had these grenade launchers in the belly of the airplane and they could launch 80 or 100 grenades at a time, straight down, and just blow up a whole big area." Another weapon they were testing was Banish Beach, a substance akin to napalm that was contained in 55-gallon drums that were "rolled off the back of a C130." The plane would fly around with its cargo door open to areas where enemy troops were suspected of being present and the crew would push these drums off. When the drums fell down to about 50 feet or so above the ground, they detonated with a huge fireball.[193]

McMillan assigned him to find out "whether there was any way to prevent the Viet Cong from blowing the bridges on Route 1," which was the only main line of communication from the DMZ to the Mekong Delta. Army trucks hauling supplies and ammunition had to go over those bridges, and whenever the Viet Cong blew up a bridge, this "shut down everything." Dudzinsky visited the bridges and figured out that Viet Cong sappers "would get some plastique and they'd take it with them and they'd float down the river and attach it to the bridge and blow [it] up." Americans had come up with all sorts of schemes to prevent this from happening. For example, "they put lights on the bridges looking down and they put soldiers to try to see these guys and if they saw them they'd shoot them. But . . . the rivers there had a lot of debris, trees and stuff floating down, because things got blown up and there was a lot of junk in the rivers." The sappers "would just attach themselves to a floating piece of bush or something, and the guys couldn't see them."

Then the Americans "started dropping grenades in the water at almost random intervals to try to stop" the Viet Cong. Then, "they . . . had big generators and they

---

[193] Another project was to improve the M-16, which had "around the periphery . . . these grooves [which were] probably some kind of flash suppression system or something." However, these grooves "would always hook on trees when the guys were trying to walk through the bush. It was a big problem for them—it's dark at night, and these things get hooked on the trees and pull their M-16s away from where they want to go." The solution was to put "a ring around [the grooves]" so that the M-16 would not get snagged. Another staff member—either a biologist or someone with a specialty related to biology—"was trying to figure out a way . . . to prevent the GIs' feet from getting rotten" in their boots as they slogged through rainy weather or paddy fields.

generated electrical currents flowing through the water and they tried to electrocute these guys swimming." To see whether this would be effective, "They experimented with pigs; they took pigs and threw them off the bridge, but it didn't really work." Dudzinsky concluded that "it was virtually impossible to stop" the Viet Cong. The solution was to have the Army Corps of Engineers build a two-lane pontoon bridge and set it up next to the one that had been blown up. It was not a bad solution, Dudzinsky said, although "it slowed the traffic down because they had to slow down to go on that thing."

Dudzinsky then moved on to other problems, including a radar system built by MIT that could detect the movement of troops. Set on a tall tower, it sent radio waves toward the ground. The problem was that it could only pick up "a lot of people [coming] through in a group," but it did not work well "if it was just a few people trying to go through the jungle." The other problem was that it would also pick up the movement of animals, but could not discriminate between them and people passing by. After this, Dudzinsky worked on communication problems, because "communication was a big thing there." The military had installed communications towers "on any kind of high points they could find, especially in the mountains." Dudzinsky experimented with "how those communications systems could work for various radio wavelengths."

After nine months in Saigon, Dudzinsky returned to the United States. When McMillan asked him to come back to Vietnam, he agreed without understanding why he would want to do this. By this time, General Abrams had replaced Westmoreland, and McMillan left. The new scientific advisor set about dismantling McMillan's group. Just as Dudzinsky was getting ready to go home, Finn Burke in the Engineering Sciences Department sent him a cable from Santa Monica asking him to participate in a study on the effectiveness of ground sensors in detecting vehicles and troops. These ground sensors were of many types: Some were acoustic sensors; some could detect smell; some could detect light; some could detect vibration. They could be emplaced by soldiers who went into an area to put them in the ground or hang them in trees, or they were dropped by planes. According to Dudzinsky, Finn Burke "was doing some theoretical study on the distribution of these sensors physically—how they lay down on the ground and what they could detect, and how the mathematics of it worked."

Burke asked him to stay in Vietnam and gather information, and Dudzinsky agreed. He spent a great deal of time at Tan Son Nhut, "talking to the Air Force guys who were involved in dropping these things." Then he went to Nakhon Phanom in Thailand, on the border of Laos, just across from Vientiane, where the United States maintained an air base with a single airstrip. The Information Surveillance Center was located there. Dudzinsky recalled that it "was a very interesting place . . . a huge war room . . . in the middle of nowhere." The center was about 80 to 100 feet wide and featured a map with the Ho Chi Minh Trail. This was where Americans monitored all these different sensors. According to Dudzinsky, "They had a code so they knew what was what, and so you could see the Ho Chi Minh Trail, you could see these sensors where they were on the board." At night, they sent a Beechcraft Bonanza—a remotely piloted plane—to fly over the Ho Chi Minh Trail "in a racetrack type pattern." The plane had many receivers, and it would receive signals from these sensors and send them to the Information Surveillance Center. Controllers sitting in the ISC looking at the sensors could give vectors to attack jets already in the air to drop the bombs on the trucks.

Dudzinsky found out that there were many problems, because pilots could not see well at night or the trucks would go hide under the jungle vegetation.[194] Dudzinsky spent six months gathering data. He concluded that the system was inefficient because "trying to blow up people on the ground, in trucks or walking, using high-performance jet airplanes was not a very good way of using the equipment." He gave a briefing upon his return to Santa Monica, and Finn Burke performed his analysis, "which was sort of theoretical." Dudzinsky did not know whether the analysis "really panned out to anything" and whether all the effort they put into the work was worthwhile.

Of his tours in Vietnam, he said that the most interesting thing for him was not the job but the opportunity to travel all over the country, from the DMZ to the Mekong Delta, visiting a lot of towns and villages, and to see what was going on. He particularly enjoyed Cam Ranh Bay with its beautiful scenery and the hill resort city of Dalat, with its cool temperatures and serenity. The scariest experience was the time he was sitting in a movie theater right in the center of Saigon when two rockets landed close by. One of his most vivid memories is of the B-52 arc strikes that dropped 500-pound bombs over "a big swath across the whole country," making "these big craters and blowing everything up." He remembered that "you could see flashes" from the explosions miles away and that the scene was very dramatic. When he flew over those craters, he felt as though he was looking down at a moonscape.

What he saw and learned in Vietnam changed his perspective on the war. When he went to Vietnam, he thought it was important to fight communism and he believed the United States was doing the right thing. He had heard about the domino theory, and thought that "we got to stop those Chinese communists from taking over the whole of Southeast Asia." However, after he had been in Vietnam for a while, he changed his mind: "I thought it was a bad war," he remembered, "and that we shouldn't be getting our people killed there. It was virtually impossible to fight that kind of an enemy, if you

---

[194] In the "Batcats and Big Computers" section of an article titled "Igloo White" (*Journal of the Air Force Association*, Vol. 87, No. 11, November 2004), author John T. Correll says that

> The darkened war room contained rows of scopes. Its walls featured large situation displays. Two IBM 360-65 computers—the most powerful then available—collated and processed the sensor data for use by the target analysts. The computers also contained extensive electronic maps of the Ho Chi Minh Trail and knew the precise locations of the sensors. When something tripped one of the sensors, the computers knew instantly where it had happened. The sensor signals were too weak to reach [Nakhon Phanom] directly, so aircraft orbited the trail, 24 hours a day, monitoring the sensors on their radio receivers and relaying the information [to the surveillance center].

will—I don't see them as enemies, but they were enemies because they were trying to kill our guys—on their home turf, under their conditions, with their determination." American soldiers, on the other hand, were not quite clear about what they were fighting for, and their hearts and souls were not in the war. There might have been some determined Marines and SEALs, but many only cared about finishing their tours of duty and going home. Soldiers had charts that they colored to track when they could return to the United States. In retrospect, he says he does not know what the U.S. government should have done differently. However, he thinks that it should not have fought the war and that "it would have been better if they could have negotiated it somehow rather than fought, even if negotiations took forever and nothing ever got settled, it would have been a better way to go."

The sense of futility that Dudzinsky felt was taking hold among a large segment of the U.S. population and within the Johnson Administration as it phased out to make way for the Nixon Administration. The Tet Offensive was bringing the era of American escalation to an end. American disengagement would be the order of the day. Among the Vietnamese interviewers at RAND, a sense of unease about the future descended like a pall. Their apprehension was no doubt sharpened when Jim Carlson—one of their team leaders—predicted during a field trip to Danang that they would be abandoned by the United States. Carlson might have felt sympathetic for their plight, but by mid-1968, as he was about to return to graduate school in Illinois, he, like many Americans, no longer believed that the war was worth fighting.

The prospect of American withdrawal led RAND to wind down what was left of its operations in Vietnam further. RAND was "reading the handwriting on the wall," Marv Schaffer would later say. Schaffer himself stopped making field trips to Vietnam. The staff became smaller and smaller. One by one, those that were left departed: Len Ackland, Tom Kiley, Jim Carlson, Charlie Benoit, and Yogi Ianeiro. Jim Digby subsequently closed down the office on Rue Pasteur in late 1968. When asked why RAND closed down the villa, Digby said, "Because we thought the American aspect of the war was phasing out, and it did." According to Joan Allen, an American demolition unit moved in after RAND vacated the villa.

The remaining American staff—Joan Allen, Andy Sweetland, and Gerry Hickey—moved to the ARPA compound by the river. The pace slowed even more. Allen recalled that there was very little going on. Hickey came in every day when he was in Saigon to get his mail and to give Allen things to type. There was a sense of suspended animation as the scene of action shifted to Paris, where the peace-talks wrangling riveted worldwide attention, and to Washington, where the administration of Richard Nixon charted a new course for Vietnam.

CHAPTER EIGHT

Pacification and Vietnamization

Just as, with the waning of the Johnson Administration, Vietnam was receding in importance at RAND, the advent of the Nixon presidency revived interest in it for a short while as an issue worth pursuing. The appointment of Henry Kissinger as National Security Advisor seemed to promise access to the White House and a chance to influence Vietnam policies at the highest level. Cold since RAND criticized him for advocating "limited nuclear wars as instruments of U.S. policy" in 1957, Kissinger's relationship with RAND had warmed as a result of efforts by Fred Iklé.[1] Following his appointment, Kissinger paid a visit to Santa Monica. Gus Shubert seized the opportunity to brief Kissinger on the strategic alternatives for Vietnam that had been presented to Paul Warnke, telling Kissinger, in essence, that the United States was unlikely to win the war, and so Kissinger—as National Security Advisor—ought to do everything in his power to disengage the country from Vietnam.

As Shubert recalled, Kissinger kept "nodding and nodding, and every once in a while he'd shake his head." When the briefing ended, Kissinger said, "I hear what you're saying. I hear what you're saying. But there's just no way we can lose that war. There's no way we can lose that war." According to Shubert, "On that note, amid murmurs and complaints and gripes and so on, the meeting ended." The message was clear, and Kissinger was not "stupid," so Shubert knew that Kissinger "saw the logic of what we were saying. . . . But it just brought him up against a wall, which had nothing to do with our logic and nothing to do with our arguments. It was simply, 'We cannot lose this war. . . .' As you know from history, that's what he believed and that's what he acted on."[2]

Kissinger's reaction probably reflected more his own perception of his role as an agent of Nixon rather than his personal thinking about the war at that point. He himself had argued in an article written before he joined the Nixon Administration, which appeared in the January 1967 issue of *Foreign Affairs*, that victory was not possible and that a negotiated settlement would be unavoidable. In the article, he criti-

---

[1] Ellsberg, *Secrets*, 2002, p. 228.

[2] Collins, interview with Gus Shubert, session of May 28, 1992, p. 48.

cized Westmoreland's attrition strategy as ineffective because the guerrillas could go on absorbing more casualties than the United States could inflict and that, therefore, they would "win" as long as they did not "lose." Since a settlement of the war had become unavoidable—because the impact of the Tet Offensive on American public opinion would restrict further U.S. escalation—he proposed a diplomatic roadmap for negotiation that would delink the military and the political. The United States and North Vietnam would settle military issues, such as an armistice and the mutual withdrawal of their forces from the South, while the GVN and the Viet Cong would be left to work out a political arrangement. Later, Kissinger would say in private that, under his scenario, a "decent interval" would be secured to give the GVN a "reasonable" chance to survive.

Kissinger's rejection of Shubert's extrication option in Santa Monica did not shut the door, and he went on to commission RAND to prepare a paper on strategic alternatives for him to present at his first national security meeting. For this prestigious assignment, Harry Rowen chose Daniel Ellsberg, a close friend and an analyst known for his brilliance. Born in Detroit in 1931, Ellsberg graduated summa cum laude from Harvard in 1952 with a bachelor's in economics. After studying for a year at King's College in Cambridge University on a Woodrow Wilson Fellowship, Ellsberg joined the Marine Corps, where he served for three years, from 1954 to 1957, as rifle platoon leader, operations officer, and rifle company commander. Following his stint in the Marines, he became a Junior Fellow in the Society of Fellows at Harvard University, where he earned his doctorate in economics in 1962. Ellsberg joined RAND in 1959 as a strategic analyst, "specializing in problems of the command and control of nuclear weapons, nuclear war plans, and crisis decision-making."[3]

According to Bernard Brodie, one of America's premier civilian strategists, RAND at this time was a place where "it was not only permissible but popular to be a cold warrior," and Ellsberg—as a "gung-ho former Marine Corps officer, a man who was 100 percent for the American policy on Vietnam"—fit right in.[4] Ellsberg would later say that RAND was the perfect milieu for him, because it gave him a great deal of freedom, with minimal supervision, to choose the issues he wanted to research. Ellsberg was a protégé of Albert Wohlstetter, and Wohlstetter's praise made Ellsberg, then 28 years old, a prized catch and "a golden boy when he arrived at RAND."[5] According to Guy Pauker, Ellsberg was considered "the brightest person at RAND" and its "pride and joy."[6]

---

[3] Daniel Ellsberg, Daniel Ellsberg's Web site.

[4] Muriel Dobbin, "Rand Corporation Still Feels Pentagon Papers' Aftereffects," *Baltimore Sun,* February 15, 1973.

[5] Tom Wells, *Wild Man: The Life and Times of Daniel Ellsberg,* New York: Palgrave, 2001, p. 206.

[6] Wells, *Wild Man,* 2001, p. 206.

Ellsberg's star began to rise at RAND and within defense intellectual circles. In July 1964, at the recommendation of Harry Rowen and Tom Schelling of Harvard, Assistant Secretary of Defense John McNaughton recruited him to be his special assistant.[7] McNaughton had been asked by Defense Secretary McNamara to help him manage Vietnam, and he told Ellsberg to focus most of his attention on this issue. Ellsberg at the time was not interested in Vietnam, but McNaughton persuaded him that, as a student of crisis decisionmaking, Vietnam would be a good case study of "how crises arose, how mistakes got made, and what crises were really about."[8] He told Ellsberg, "Vietnam is one crisis after another; it's one long crisis."[9] Ellsberg would not just be a researcher, he would be "living the history of it."[10] McNaughton also assured him that he would have access to all documents on Vietnam in his office, including memos and cables "for his eyes only" that went directly to him. He told Ellsberg that he would have to exercise great discretion, but Ellsberg felt there would be no problem because he had demonstrated his talent for "sensitive secret keeping."[11]

Ellsberg accepted the offer. This assignment would lead to what Ellsberg would later call his obsession with "the problem of U.S. policy in Vietnam."[12] He would spend "nights and days and weekends for a year reading cables from Saigon."[13]

Those who worked with Ellsberg in this period described him as a hawk on the war, someone who believed in bombing North Vietnam and in committing ground forces in South Vietnam. Guy Pauker, who consulted for ISA at the time and talked to Ellsberg on many occasions, said that Ellsberg was "an ultrahawk," and Gus Shubert called him "an ardent hawk."[14]

---

[7]   According to Tom Wells (*Wild Man*, 2001, p. 200), Alvin Friedman, Deputy Assistant Secretary of Defense at the time, was then probably McNaughton's top aide on Vietnam—and not Ellsberg. Contrary to Ellsberg's claim later, he was not "extensively involved in Vietnam planning" at the time (*Wild Man*, 2001, p. 201). Ellsberg told Tom Wells that McNaughton already knew him and that a recommendation from Harry Rowen did not add "a tremendous amount" (*Wild Man*, 2001, p. 197).

[8]   Ellsberg, *Secrets,* 2001, p. 36.

[9]   Ellsberg, *Secrets,* 2001, p. 36.

[10]   Ellsberg, *Secrets,* 2001, p. 36.

[11]   Ellsberg, *Secrets,* 2001, p. 36.

[12]   Daniel Ellsberg, "Some Prospects and Problems in Vietnam," transcript of informal briefing to the RAND Board of Trustees, November 11, 1967, Santa Monica, Calif.: RAND Corporation, D-16722-ARPA/AGILE, February 15, 1968, p. 1.

[13]   Ellsberg, "Some Prospects and Problems in Vietnam," 1968.

[14]   Wells, *Wild Man*, 2001, pp. 204–205. But Ellsberg was not "a crude hawk." Stanley Hoffman, a Harvard professor who had debated Ellsberg about Vietnam in 1965, thought that, "He was the only hawk I'd heard who made any sense at all. . . . There was something extremely genuine and human in him that I didn't see in other hawks. He was not a government mouthpiece or an intellectual adding machine, but a human being you could argue with" (*Wild Man*, 2001, p. 206).

Ellsberg's memory of his position at the time differed from that of his critics. According to him, the "preoccupation" in McNaughton's office in 1964 was to get the bombing of the North started, and in 1965 it was "getting the [American] troops on the way."[15] However, although he worked on these issues, he opposed the bombing and, like McNaughton, was against the commitment of American troops.[16] However, once the bombing began, he was no longer against sending troops, because he thought "the bombing won't do any good but if we're in the war already then the troops are at least relevant to what's going on, . . . [they] will make some difference."[17] He did not have a clear limit on how many troops to send. He would later say, "I wish I could remember that I was in favor of sending 50,000 troops, or 100,000 troops, but not 500,000—but I don't recall having any opinion on that."[18] But once the United States began to dispatch combat troops to Vietnam, the move was "basically all right" with him.[19]

In an informal briefing given to the RAND Board of Trustees on November 11, 1967, Ellsberg said that, in the spring of 1965, when he was working in the Pentagon, he had been among people who favored dispatching American combat troops to Vietnam. This move, Ellsberg conceded, "clearly tied our interests and prestige deeply and irrevocably" to the war in Vietnam. Ellsberg explained that he was in favor of committing U.S. troops, because he thought that "nothing less would avert imminent defeat" and because he believed that it was crucial for the United States to buy the necessary time for the GVN to make "fundamental changes in character and operation that would lead to the ultimate defeat of the communists." This time was bought, but "at the price of ever-higher stakes and commitment" for the United States.[20]

The relationship between Ellsberg and McNaughton eventually soured, because Ellsberg did not measure up to McNaughton's expectations for productive work and discretion.[21] In August 1965, Ellsberg joined a team led by General Edward Lansdale

---

[15] Author interview with Dan Ellsberg, 2004.

[16] Author interview with Dan Ellsberg, 2004. In his memoir, *Secrets* (2002, p. 62), Ellsberg explained that he opposed the bombing because, from his study of bombing in Word War II and Korea, he "agreed with the civilian intelligence analysts of the CIA and the State Department that conventional bombing would simply fail either to cut off the relatively small flow of infiltration [at the time] to sustain the guerrilla war in the South or to induce the Hanoi leadership and its people to give up the armed struggle."

[17] Author interview with Dan Ellsberg, 2004.

[18] Author interview with Dan Ellsberg, 2004. In a radio interview on July 28, 2008, Ellsberg recalled that, as an assistant to McNaughton, he worked "on the escalation of the war in Vietnam, the secret decisions to get us involved in a big way under President Johnson." Transcript of "Interview with Daniel Ellsberg," "Salon Radio with Glenn Greenwald," Monday, July 28, 2008.

[19] Author interview with Dan Ellsberg, 2004.

[20] Ellsberg, "Some Prospects and Problems in Vietnam," 1968, p. 1.

[21] Wells, *Wild Man*, 2001, pp. 222–223.

that was heading for Vietnam.[22] Lansdale, a retired Air Force major general who had done extensive work for the CIA, had earned a reputation as the foremost American counterinsurgency expert by helping defeat the Huks in the Philippines in the early 1950s. He had been instrumental in securing U.S. support for Ngo Dinh Diem at the beginning of his presidency. In 1965, he was selected by President Johnson to go to Vietnam as head of an interagency group to do work with the South Vietnamese government on political matters. Ellsberg volunteered to be on Lansdale's team, because he wanted to go to Vietnam and see the war for himself; he was accepted, despite the fact that he had no background in counterinsurgency.[23] Ellsberg did not know why Lansdale took him: He was the only person on the team who had not worked with Lansdale in situations similar to the one in Vietnam. In his November 1967 informal briefing to the RAND Board of Trustees, Ellsberg said that he went to Vietnam with Lansdale in the hope of helping "build a victory." He also wanted to learn about the war and "help the United States learn how to win this kind of war." In addition, he expected "to be in the front lines of the political conflict, in an exposed position."[24]

According to Ellsberg, none of the team members—including Lansdale—had clear-cut responsibilities. Ellsberg did not know what President Johnson had instructed Lansdale to do. Ellsberg's own status on the team was low; he had been, in effect, taken on "as an apprentice" so that he could learn how to conduct political warfare as practiced by Lansdale.[25] Ambassador Henry Cabot Lodge assigned Lansdale a special role in pacification, and Ellsberg's job was to attend meetings of the American Mission Council, take field trips, and report his observations. Comments from some people who knew Ellsberg and his work in this period, and Ellsberg's own writings at the time, indicate that Ellsberg was a "fervent believer in the American cause . . . a genuine enthusiast of counterinsurgency," and that he only questioned "means and results

---

[22] According to people who talked to Tom Wells, McNaughton might have engineered this transfer to Lansdale's team to get rid of Ellsberg. Lansdale told Gus Shubert that he did not initially want Ellsberg on his team. Shubert thought that the team was engaged in "counterterrorist" actions. Collins, interview with Gus Shubert, session of May 28, 1992, p. 54. According to Tom Wells, the mission that was given was the vague task of building democracy and winning hearts and minds through pacification in order to defeat the insurgency. In Saigon, they encountered mistrust within the U.S. Mission. Wells, *Wild Man*, 2001, p. 230.

[23] Interview with Dan Ellsberg, 2004.

[24] Ellsberg, "Some Prospects and Problems in Vietnam," 1968, p. 1. In his July 2008 Salon Radio interview with Glenn Greenwald, Ellsberg said that, when he went to Vietnam, he was "certainly a Cold Warrior. That was my profession, trying to defeat communist expansion as I understood it, not very well, at that time. I went to Vietnam having been there very quickly in1961 and perceived it as a losing proposition, very much, under the dictator we had installed, President Ngo Dinh Diem. We clearly had no prospect of defeating the communist-led liberation front, which had the prestige in Vietnam of having defeated the French in the northern part of Vietnam. So I saw it as not the place to plant our cold war flag, if possible, but when the President did do that I thought it was my duty, responsibility, to get into the war to do the best I could to make something out of it, without much hope."

[25] Ellsberg, *Secrets*, 2002, p. 103.

rather than the ultimate goal" of U.S. involvement.[26] Robert Komer, for example, said that Ellsberg was "very pro–Vietnam War, very pro-government, very anti-VC, anti-Hanoi."[27]

Joe Zasloff remembered a meeting with Ellsberg in 1967 in Saigon during which Ellsberg insisted on telling him about Viet Cong atrocities committed against South Vietnamese troops. Zasloff had to dash to another appointment, but Ellsberg insisted that he listen to the horrific details. Zasloff asked, "Dan, why are you telling me all this? I've got to go." Ellsberg replied, "You made us listen when you did the briefing in '64 [to John McNaughton in ISA about Viet Cong Motivation and Morale], you've got to listen, you've got to hear this." Zasloff recalled that, "It was as if he was paying me back for having given the story that made the Viet Cong look so selfless."[28]

Another person recalled that Ellsberg was "just totally gung-ho in everything that he said and did."[29] Lieutenant Colonel Tran Ngoc Chau, a GVN province chief whom Ellsberg admired and befriended, recalled that Ellsberg was "very, very aggressive" about the war and believed that it could be won.[30] In an October 1965 memo, Ellsberg "theorized" that "if the United States escalated its operations in Vietnam, including its airstrikes over the North, that might strengthen the U.S. position in any peace talks."[31] Ellsberg himself admitted that he was in favor of escalation. As he said in his briefing to the RAND board, "After ten years as a cold warrior, at RAND and in the Marines before that, I had a personal desire to beat the communists, this once, this place."[32] Bernard Brodie, a RAND analyst known as the dean of American civilian strategists, said that Ellsberg was a "gung-ho former Marine Corps, a man who was 100 percent for the American policy on Vietnam."[33]

Gus Shubert and George Tanham were among the RAND people who met Ellsberg in Saigon. They described him as belligerent when it came to the Viet Cong. Shubert recalled running into a well-armed Ellsberg in the streets of Saigon.[34] Tom

---

[26] Wells, *Wild Man*, 2001, p. 256.

[27] Wells, *Wild Man*, 2001, p. 257.

[28] Author interview with Joe Zasloff, 2003.

[29] Wells, *Wild Man*, 2001, p. 257.

[30] Wells, *Wild Man*, 2001, p. 258.

[31] Wells, *Wild Man*, 2001, p. 258. Wells added, "All this from the same man who later claimed that he considered the U.S. bombing campaign against the North criminal."

[32] Ellsberg, "Some Prospects and Problems in Vietnam," 1968, p. 1.

[33] Dobbin, "Rand Corporation Still Feels," 1973.

[34] Wells, *Wild Man*, 2001, p. 254. In the interview with the author (2004), Daniel Ellsberg said that Shubert's recollection was not correct, and that he only carried weapons when he went out into the field to protect himself. Yet, a State Department staff member recalled to columnist Joseph Kraft that once "on a routine [J]eep trip around Saigon, Mr. Ellsberg made him keep his head under cover and carry and even cock a gun." Joseph Kraft, "Ellsberg: Unlike the Others, He Was 'A Man Driven,'" *The New York Times*, July 4, 1971.

Schelling of Harvard recalled that ". . . it was clear [from Ellsberg's letters] that he enjoyed tramping around with a gun in one hand" and to show that he was in danger, "right in the thick of things."[35] Ellsberg said that he did not carry weapons while he was in Saigon, and only armed himself for self-protection when he went out into the field—like other American civilians. However, he had no wish to personally fight the Viet Cong. When he took part in an operation with American troops and they came under attack, he would shoot his weapon if they were firing all around him—only to avoid attracting "unfavorable attention," because otherwise someone would come over and check.[36]

In an effort to learn more about Vietnam, Ellsberg stopped by the RAND villa, where he met Tony Russo. Russo recalled talking extensively with Ellsberg about the Viet Cong Motivation and Morale Project. Ellsberg also sought out people reputed to be experts on Vietnam. The one whom he most admired and who would have a great influence on his view of the war was John Paul Vann, a former army officer with a reputation—within the American media, in particular—as a strong critic of U.S. policies, of the GVN, and of the ARVN, and as someone not afraid to speak truth to power. At the time, Vann was a USAID province representative for pacification. Vann took Ellsberg under his wing, and Ellsberg started driving around the countryside with him to learn firsthand what was going on. According to Gus Shubert, Ellsberg "worshipped" Vann. Ellsberg admired Vann's "idealism, knowledge of the war, and his brashness, toughness, and courage."[37] Under Vann's tutelage—and from his own observations—Ellsberg became more critical of U.S. policies and more pessimistic about the prospects for pacification. He came to see that the ultimate impediment to U.S. goals was the very foundation on which U.S. policies were built: the political system and social structure of South Vietnam itself.

The knowledge Ellsberg gained about conditions outside Saigon caught the attention of Deputy Ambassador William Porter, who was spearheading and coordinating American support for pacification. When President Johnson asked the embassy, in spring 1966, for regular reports on the "other war," beginning with a report on what level of progress could be expected in pacification in that year, Porter asked that Ellsberg be assigned from the Lansdale team to collect data from the III Corps area around Saigon. Ellsberg became a special assistant to Porter, with the primary responsibility for making "field evaluations . . . of programs and operations, particularly those that deal with pacification and other joint military and civilian operations."[38] For this eval-

---

[35] Wells, *Wild Man*, 2001, p. 255.

[36] Ellsberg, *Secrets*, 2002, p. 152. Fred Haynes, a Marine commander in Vietnam, who met Ellsberg a few times, told Tom Wells that Ellsberg "liked to be seen as a guerrilla fighter, as the guy who was out with the boys and out in the bush" (*Wild Man*, 2001, p. 249).

[37] Wells, *Wild Man*, 2001, p. 244.

[38] Wells, *Wild Man*, 2001, p. 143.

uation, Ellsberg drove through every province of the corps area and concluded that, "In most of III Corps national priority area, odds are against achieving even modest goals for hamlet pacification in 1966."[39] Later, he would say that, during those extensive travels, he became disturbed by what he witnessed: for example, the burning of a hamlet by South Vietnamese rocket and mortar fire, and the bombing and strafing by American planes of people who might or might not be Viet Cong.[40]

Subsequently, Ellsberg came down with hepatitis and was hospitalized for weeks. Ellsberg took this time to write memos on what he had learned "about why we weren't going anywhere and how we might conceivably do better."[41] Believing in the influence of his ideas, he held back on making suggestions on how to find a way out of Vietnam, saving his recommendations for Washington officials who could act on his advice. Instead, he focused on the reasons the United States should stop supporting military candidates—such as Generals Nguyen Van Thieu and Nguyen Cao Ky— in the upcoming elections and start encouraging or allowing their replacement by civilian leaders who could win popular allegiance. Unless the top leadership changed, there would be "no real prospect of any sort of lasting progress in South Vietnam, civil or military," he stated.[42] Indeed, the reality of Vietnam that he had witnessed firsthand had transformed Ellsberg. As Gus Shubert, who met Ellsberg during periodic visits to Vietnam, recalled, Ellsberg "was having his eyes opened as to what was going on around him, and he was losing the faith," and "his resolve was being sapped."[43] Ellsberg would join the ranks of other RAND people who went to Vietnam as supporters but returned as skeptics—if not opponents—of the war.[44]

As he was recuperating in the hospital, Ellsberg learned that his friend Harry Rowen had been appointed president of RAND in January 1967.[45] Rowen admired

---

[39] Wells, *Wild Man*, 2001, p. 126.

[40] In *Secrets* (2002, p. 138), he wrote that he felt a "great sense of unease at the thought that all over Vietnam humans were being hunted like animals from the air" because they were wearing black pajamas. At his Pentagon Paper trial in April 1973, he was seized by emotion when he described the scene of the smoking hamlet. During the lunch break, he went to "the room assigned to the defense team" and sat by himself and "cried for most of the lunch period" (Ellsberg, *Secrets*, 2002, p. 132).

[41] Ellsberg, *Secrets*, 2002, p. 176.

[42] Ellsberg, *Secrets*, 2002, p. 177.

[43] Collins, interview with Gus Shubert, session of May 28, 1992, p. 62.

[44] In his Salon Radio interview, 2008, Ellsberg recalled feeling that the war was tragic and fruitless, and that the question became how to end it. He told Greenwald, ". . . people were being killed and we were losing Americans to no justifiable purpose or effect. And that was seen, I think, by most people who went to Vietnam. I can't speak for them. Three million of them went. I think within months or a year—I was there two years—most people came to realize there was going to be no success and that the war should really be ended. The question really was, what to do about that?"

[45] In the 2004 interview with the author, Ellsberg said that Harry Rowen and John Paul Vann were his best friends "on earth." He felt that "John is my best friend in Vietnam, and Harry is my best friend in the U.S." They

Ellsberg and, according to Alex George, "was not reluctant at all to convey to others—on more than one occasion—that he felt that Dan Ellsberg was a superior person, and the kind of person RAND should give power to."[46] Charlie Wolf would later recall that, when Rowen was designated as president of RAND, Ellsberg sent Rowen a cable from Saigon, saying that he was available. Rowen cabled back asking him to return to RAND.[47] Wolf, who would later fire Ellsberg, said that "Rowen had a great respect for keen minds, no matter how distorted."[48] Wolf's comment is probably influenced by the fact that he and Ellsberg clashed on many issues, including the Vietnam War.

According to Ellsberg, he decided to go to RAND rather than return to the Pentagon, because he thought that, at RAND, he would have the freedom "to tell what I knew and what I believed about our Vietnam policy to officials across the board in government agencies without having to worry if I was contradicting the position of a boss or a department."[49] After three years in Vietnam, "largely listening and learning," he believed that he "knew things about the situation" that would be worthwhile to convey to people responsible for making or advising on national security policy.[50] In his briefing to the RAND board following his return to RAND, Ellsberg said that he "did not beat the communists" in the two years he had spent in Vietnam—as he had wanted to do when he signed on with the Lansdale team.[51] However, he did learn the reasons that American efforts and the successive South Vietnamese governments the United States was assisting had failed to defeat the communists in the 1950s and would be unlikely to defeat them in the 1960s.

In July 1967, Ellsberg was back at work in the Economics Department at RAND in Santa Monica. Many saw a changed man, "worn out" and "depressed." Rufus Phillips, a member of the Lansdale team who saw Ellsberg in this period, thought Ellsberg seemed to be "struggling" over what the United States should do in Vietnam. Phillips recalled that Ellsberg was "beginning to make arguments . . . about the fact that what we were doing out there was futile."[52] Ellsberg got his chance to have an effect in Washington when Henry Kissinger asked Harry Rowen for a study on

---

were "professional friends" as well as "personal friends" who respected each other. He thought that Rowen would open up and share his views with him "more than with anybody else I can think of," and that their views on the war "ran in the same vein."

[46] Author interview with Alex George, 2004.

[47] Author interview with Charlie Wolf, 2003. The cables the two friends exchanged had a playful tone. According to Tom Wells, Rowen showed Ellsberg's cable to some people at RAND. It said something like, "Harry—Take me. I'm yours." Charlie Wolf recalled that Rowen replied, "Yes, you're mine. Come back."

[48] Author interview with Charlie Wolf, 2003.

[49] Ellsberg, *Secrets*, 2002, p. 181.

[50] Ellsberg, *Secrets*, 2002, p. 181.

[51] Ellsberg, "Some Prospects and Problems in Vietnam," 1968, p. 2.

[52] Wells, *Wild Man*, 2001, p. 271.

Vietnam options to prepare for his first National Security Council meeting in January 1969. Ellsberg recalled that Harry Rowen proposed that he lead the project, that Kissinger approved but had a message relayed by Fred Iklé, expressing his concern about Ellsberg's discretion.[53] Also, according to Ellsberg, Kissinger did not want it to be known that Ellsberg was involved in the study, because Ellsberg had the reputation as a critic of American involvement and because RAND by this time had become known as a relatively "dovish" group—at least from a Republican perspective—within defense circles.[54]

According to Guy Pauker, Kissinger actually contacted him—an old friend from Harvard—and Pauker flew to New York for a meeting at the Pierre Hotel, which was being used by Nixon and his staff as their transition headquarters. According to Pauker, Kissinger told him, "I need a study from you on how to extricate from Vietnam" in an honorable manner, because Richard Nixon did not want to be the first American president to lose a war. Pauker remembered that he went to Rowen, "who immediately pulled Dan into this."[55] The move was interpreted by Pauker as Rowen trying to do a favor for his friend Ellsberg, who was delighted to be picked for this high-profile assignment.[56]

---

[53] Morton Halperin told Tom Wells that if Kissinger had objected to Ellsberg's participation, as Ellsberg said, "it wouldn't have happened" (*Wild Man*, 2001, p. 312). According to Ellsberg, Kissinger visited RAND—at Fred Iklé's invitation—on November 8, 1968, three days after the presidential elections and before he was appointed National Security Advisor to President-elect Richard Nixon. Ellsberg recalled that, in a talk that day, Kissinger repeated what he was reported to have said at the Republican National Convention: "Richard Nixon is not fit to be president." But this did not "stop Kissinger from accepting Nixon's invitation a few weeks later" to be his National Security Advisor (*Secrets*, 2002, p. 228).

[54] Ellsberg, *Secrets*, 2002, p. 232.

[55] Wells, *Wild Man*, 2001, p. 311. Edged out, Pauker would later make a preemptive move by sending Kissinger his own memo on strategic options two days before the Ellsberg team was due to meet Kissinger to brief him on their paper. In his memo, Pauker proposed the neutralization of South Vietnam "under some form of international guarantees" that would be enforced by an Asian Peace-Keeping Force for South Vietnam. Pauker pointed out that this option had several advantages. It would give South Vietnam "a genuine 'last chance'" to get its house in order so that it would be able to compete politically with the communists, following an immediate cease-fire negotiated in Paris. It would also appeal to the American public, since fighting would cease and American troops would be withdrawn in 12 to 18 months—"or even sooner"—without leaving the South Vietnamese "to the mercy" of the communists. By making American withdrawal "not only credible but certain," this plan would also shock the South Vietnamese elites and regime—who were only concerned about their self-interests and about exploiting the American presence for their own benefits—into action. Yet, at the same time, it would protect South Vietnam for a period of three years to allow them to prepare for political competition with the communists.

Pauker did supply copies of his memo to Rowen, Shubert, Ellsberg, Wolf, Kellen, and a few other people at RAND. In a short letter, dated December 27, 1968, Kissinger told Pauker that he had just received his "Vietnam Options" paper, but informed him that he had not yet had a chance to read it, since he was getting ready to fly to Key Biscayne [where Nixon was staying with his close friend Bebe Rebozo]. Kissinger reassured Pauker that he would go over the paper "with real interest" later.

[56] Wells, *Wild Man*, 2001, p. 312.

Some people at RAND said that, at that point, Ellsberg seemed to have stalled in his career and was having difficulty producing works that would truly express his brilliant potential. According to Gus Shubert, despite Ellsberg's "problems," Rowen continued to have faith in him and to believe that "this mystique of potential was going to suddenly blossom."[57]

Rowen's choice of Ellsberg for the options study proved his faith in his friend. However, Rowen supervised the work. It was possible that Rowen selected Ellsberg because the project played to his forte. As Ellsberg put it, he "was a logical choice," because "[d]efining strategic alternatives reflecting various objectives and points of views—in ways that would be accepted by their respective advocates as expressing their perspectives accurately—had long been a professional specialty of mine, at Rand and in the government."[58]

Ellsberg had met Kissinger in Saigon when Kissinger visited Vietnam as a consultant to Ambassador Henry Cabot Lodge. From the discussions they had on Vietnam, Ellsberg was favorably impressed. Ellsberg recalled that Kissinger had become "realistically skeptical and pessimistic, especially about the character and prospects of the Saigon regime."[59] Later, in 1967 and 1968, at conferences on Vietnam that Ellsberg also attended, Kissinger was articulating a viewpoint that was ahead of what other prominent political figures were expressing at the time, arguing that the key objective for the United States should be to get "some sort of assurance of . . . a 'decent interval' between our departure and a communist takeover, so that we could withdraw without the humiliation of an abrupt, naked collapse of our earlier objectives."[60] Ellsberg thought that Kissinger's "practical objective of a decent interval seemed less ambitious and more realistic" and "went well beyond encouragement of a coalition government . . . to stipulate acceptance of a communist government in Saigon, not immediately but within a couple of years."[61] Kissinger had not made his proposal public, but Ellsberg presumed that he was advocating it with Nelson Rockefeller, the Republican candidate to whom he served as foreign policy advisor.

When Nixon chose Kissinger as his National Security Advisor, the appointment was perceived by "a wide circle of nonhawkish insiders and academics" as confirmation that Nixon was inclined to extricate the United States from Vietnam.[62] Perhaps this perception was based on the Republican platform for the 1968 presidential campaign being "very close to the Johnson-supported plank of the Democrats," and that Nixon's

---

[57] Wells, *Wild Man*, 2001, p. 296.

[58] Ellsberg, *Secrets*, 2002, pp. 231–232.

[59] Ellsberg, *Secrets*, 2002, p. 229.

[60] Ellsberg, *Secrets*, 2002, p. 229.

[61] Ellsberg, *Secrets*, 2002, p. 230.

[62] Ellsberg, *Secrets*, 2002, p. 230.

staff had resisted "the more hawkish position of Governor Ronald Reagan."[63] In fact, the impression that Nixon endorsed Kissinger's ideas was erroneous, since—according to Ellsberg—Nixon did not accept a communist takeover after a "decent interval or ever." Indeed, Nixon was "prepared not only to prolong the war indefinitely but to expand it to prevent" such an outcome.[64]

By the end of 1967, as reconstructed by a number of historians, Nixon saw the war as a stalemate and realized that a military victory was not possible. In the aftermath of the Tet Offensive, he—like others in the Johnson Administration—became committed to *Vietnamization*: letting the South Vietnamese shoulder the increasing burden of the war while the United States gradually withdrew its forces. Parallel to Vietnamization, Nixon would escalate the war in other ways to pressure Hanoi and prevent a communist victory in the South. In fact, he thought that he could frighten the North Vietnamese into believing that he "might do *anything* to stop the war," including using nuclear weapons. He called this the "Madman Theory."[65] As he explained to his White House Chief of Staff H. R. "Bob" Haldeman, Nixon would "just slip the word" to the enemy that, "Nixon is obsessed about communists. We can't restrain him when he's angry—and he has his hand on the nuclear button."[66] As Nixon envisaged it, the specter of nuclear annihilation would spur the North Vietnamese to abandon their "fight and talk" tactics, stalling in Paris while trying to bolster their bargaining position with successes in the ground war in the South. "Ho Chi Minh himself will be in Paris in two days[,] begging for peace," Nixon told Haldeman.[67]

On the diplomatic front, Nixon contemplated using the Soviets and the Chinese to pressure North Vietnam into accepting a settlement—in moves that would be referred to as triangular diplomacy.[68] He thought that the Soviets, having been forced

---

[63] Ellsberg, *Secrets*, 2002, p. 230.

[64] Ellsberg, *Secrets*, 2002, p. 231.

[65] Cited in Jeffrey Kimball, *Nixon's Vietnam War*, Lawrence, Kan.: University Press of Kansas, 1998, p. 76. The threat of using atomic weapons to move negotiations forward had been used successfully by President Dwight Eisenhower with the Chinese communists and North Koreans. Later, in 1972, Nixon was heard talking about using nuclear weapons in Vietnam. Taped recordings of conversations he had with Henry Kissinger in that year—reviewed by David Usborne of *The Independent* in London in "Nixon Wanted to Drop Nuclear Bomb on Vietnam," March 2, 2002—showed that Nixon was "musing about dropping a nuclear bomb on North Vietnam." In one segment released by the National Archives, "Nixon is heard discussing an extension of bombing raids over North Vietnam with Henry Kissinger. . . . Then, rather abruptly, he says: 'I'd rather use the nuclear bomb.' Whether Nixon was serious or trying to provoke Mr. Kissinger is not clear. In his baritone voice, his adviser replies: 'That, I think, would just be too much.' But Nixon then goes on: 'The nuclear bomb. Does that bother you? I just want you to think big.'"

[66] Kimball, *Nixon's Vietnam War*, 1998, p. 76.

[67] Kimball, *Nixon's Vietnam War*, 1998, p. 76.

[68] According to Jeffrey Kimball (*Nixon's Vietnam War*, 1998, p. 98), Nixon had already outlined his Vietnam strategy by August 1968 and set in place its basic elements. It consisted of five parts: "Vietnamization" of the war; "pacification" of the countryside of South Vietnam; "diplomatic isolation of North Vietnam"; "gradual

to divert massive resources to aid Vietnam at the expense of their own economic development, would be open to peace overtures, especially if such overtures were sweetened with economic incentives. As for the Chinese, he thought that Chairman Mao might be interested in rapprochement with the United States to counterbalance the Soviet Union and that, in return, China might be prepared to push North Vietnam toward a settlement. So, contrary to Ellsberg's perception, Nixon was recruiting Kissinger to implement his own—rather than Kissinger's—plan for Vietnam. As Nixon would later put it, he did not want—no more than Johnson did—to be "the first president of the United States to lose a war."

❧ ❧ ❧

During the Republican primary campaign, Nixon had declared in March 1968 that—if elected president—he would "end the war and win the peace" in Vietnam. He did not present a detailed plan, and public anticipation was high regarding what he would do as he prepared to enter office. To outsiders not privy to Nixon's already-formulated strategy for Vietnam, it looked like matters were still fluid and that Nixon could be swayed during the transition period, before his policies were set. For RAND, then, Kissinger's request for an options paper seemed a golden opportunity to influence policies at a turning point in the war. Harry Rowen himself recalled that, at the time, he thought

> the idea was a good one because it was in the interregnum between the two administrations and there might be an opportunity to change course and we should consider that and have some people work on that. Ellsberg wanted to do that very much and I thought that was a good idea to do it, a kind of basic options. And that was done, it was worked on.[69]

Kissinger's request would also give RAND the opportunity to achieve what it had strived for without success. According to Ellsberg, RAND had wanted for years to operate at a level above the Air Force and the Defense Department. Kissinger's request not only would give RAND a first-ever chance to work directly for the White House but might, it was hoped, open doors in the new administration.

Ellsberg seized the chance to work on this prestigious assignment. As he pondered how to approach his task, he though that—as Kissinger assumed his post—the new National Security Advisor obviously wanted to present alternative options

---

withdrawal of U.S. troops"; and "peace negotiations." Subsequently, Nixon defined "peace negotiations" as "diplomatic efforts coupled with irresistible military pressure," which would be applied mainly through bombing because he believed that bombs could bring the war to an end: "close the whole thing down." Only the details of implementation needed to be worked out after he took office.

[69] Author interview with Harry Rowen, 2005.

without prejudicing one over another, to project objectivity and balance. Although the project would not allow Ellsberg to inject his own views into the paper, he believed that—as team leader—he could at least make sure that arguments against escalation and those favoring less hawkish alternatives would be presented more completely and with force. As an example of his ability to exert some influence, Ellsberg recounted that, during one of the initial exploratory meetings he chaired, it was suggested that, to be comprehensive, the options should mention at least the use of nuclear weapons. Ellsberg rejected this suggestion and stated that he would not be party to a paper that raised the possibility of using nuclear weapons in Vietnam.

Ellsberg spent a week in Washington to consult with Mort Halperin, Les Gelb, and other officials, and to read government documents. On Christmas Day in 1968, Harry Rowen, Fred Iklé, and Daniel Ellsberg checked into the Pierre Hotel in New York. They gave the 27-page draft to Kissinger to read overnight, and Ellsberg was scheduled to discuss it with him the next day. The following day, in the hotel room that Kissinger used as his office, Ellsberg reviewed the draft page by page. Rowen and Iklé were absent, but Tom Schelling of Harvard was there. Schelling, who was close to Kissinger, raised more questions than Kissinger. He pointed out that the draft contained no strategy for winning the war. Ellsberg replied that victory was not feasible. Kissinger, according to Ellsberg, was silent, because he had come to that conclusion himself. Schelling then commented that the paper contained no threat tactic, and Kissinger said, "How can you conduct diplomacy without a threat of escalation? Without a threat, there is no basis for negotiations."[70] Ellsberg told Kissinger that he would include a threat option in the next draft. He worked on it that day and the next, submitting it in the afternoon. Later, as Ellsberg embarked on another project for Kissinger, Fred Iklé would prepare the final version.

The December 27th options paper contained "alternative strategies proposed by agency heads and staff" and defined *victory* as

> The destruction or withdrawal of all NVA units in South Vietnam, the destruction, withdrawal, or dissolution of all (or most) VC forces and apparatus, the permanent cessation of infiltration, and the virtually unchallenged sovereignty of a stable, non-Communist regime . . . with no significant communist political role except on an individual, 'reconciled' basis.[71]

Although there was agreement regarding the definition of *victory*, Ellsberg and his team found systematic and distinct differences of opinion between two groups, which

---

[70] Ellsberg, *Secrets*, 2002, p. 235.

[71] Kimball, *Nixon's Vietnam War*, 1998, p. 91. Kimball was given a copy by Dan Ellsberg.

they designated "Group A" and "Group B," about "the current status of the Saigon regime, the military balance on the field of battle, and the prospects for victory."[72]

Whereas Group A recommended military and diplomatic strategies to achieve a "Communist 'fade-away' or negotiated victory," those strategies recommended by Group B were aimed at bringing about a "compromise settlement" with the other side.[73] Ellsberg—and Iklé—noted a third strategy: the unilateral withdrawal of all U.S. forces in one to two years, even if a settlement could not be reached. No one within the U.S. government was advocating this option, but it "might become necessary if some of the other alternatives failed."[74]

Group A included top leaders in JCS, MACV, State, and the U.S. Embassy in Saigon, and a number of CIA analysts, who believed that enemy forces were in "strategic retreat" and that Hanoi had agreed to peace talks out of "weakness and failure."[75] The United States, therefore, should insist that the communists withdraw their forces from South Vietnam, Laos, and Cambodia. The group maintained that, although the GVN was growing stronger, the United States should retain a large military presence and, until victory was assured, it should not unduly pressure Saigon to carry out reforms, thereby avoiding destabilizing it.

According to Group A, if U.S. and South Vietnamese forces resumed the same level of operation they were undertaking before the Tet Offensive, the war could be brought to an end in a year or two. If the tempo were escalated, victory would come faster and more decisively. The escalation options they recommended included "air and ground operations in Cambodia and Laos; unrestricted bombing and mining of North Vietnam; limited invasions of North Vietnam and Laos; full-scale invasion of North Vietnam; or any combination of these."[76] The United States would have to expand its force levels in Vietnam and mobilize the Reserves; casualties and financial costs would rise; and the Soviet Union and Communist China might respond to American actions. Group A believed that, nonetheless, the American public would accept the higher costs and that the risk of a Soviet and Chinese reaction would be low. However, in the group's estimation, the United States might not have to resort to any of these options, because "the credible threat, explicit or tacit, of unrestricted bombing or limited invasion of North Vietnam might well cause the DRV to accept our conditions for victory immediately."[77]

---

[72] Kimball, *Nixon's Vietnam War*, 1998, p. 91.

[73] Kimball, *Nixon's Vietnam War*, 1998, p. 91.

[74] Kimball, *Nixon's Vietnam War*, 1998, p. 91.

[75] Kimball, *Nixon's Vietnam War*, 1998, p. 91.

[76] Kimball, *Nixon's Vietnam War*, 1998, p. 92.

[77] Kimball, *Nixon's Vietnam War*, 1998, p. 92.

Group B, made up of the Secretary of Defense and most of his staff, a few high-level officials at State, and some CIA analysts, disagreed with Group A, because "they had become convinced that Group A's bankrupt strategy would result in crisis or defeat."[78] Group B did not believe that Hanoi had agreed to attend the peace talks in Paris out of "weakness or desperation," and thought that it would take longer than Group A anticipated to reach a settlement or to end U.S. involvement. Group B maintained that resuming pre-Tet operations or escalation would be unlikely to bring success while imposing higher costs and risks; it recommended, therefore, that the United States reach a diplomatic compromise that would allow for the formation of a coalition government in Saigon, the initiation of a cease-fire, or the withdrawal of American and North Vietnamese forces from South Vietnam. Although a compromise would fall "short of victory," it would avert "defeat" and salvage "credibility," and allow an "honorable exit" for the United States.[79]

In the evaluation of author Jeffrey Kimball, the RAND strategic-options paper probably played a role in the formulation of a plan of action to implement the strategy that Nixon and Kissinger already had in mind, because it gave Nixon and Kissinger "an early and . . . timely assessment of the difficulties they faced in Vietnam," as well as "the range of options" that government agencies considered feasible during the transition period.[80] Ellsberg did not say what impact the paper might have had. Kissinger himself did not mention Ellsberg, RAND, or the options paper in his memoir *White House Years*. In a brief note to Guy Pauker following the meeting at the Pierre Hotel, he said only that "Rowen and company" had "performed superbly as usual" during the briefing.[81]

The process of putting the options paper together highlighted to Ellsberg the sharp and systematic split of thinking within government circles about the war. According to Ellsberg, he decided that what Nixon needed most of all was to be made aware of these profound differences. At a second meeting with Kissinger at the Pierre on December 27, he suggested what would become known as NSSM-1, or National Security Study Memorandum-1—the first of many studies Kissinger would later order from various agencies. In an appendix to the strategic-options paper, Ellsberg had included a set of questions modeled after the list of questions that Robert McNamara had sent

---

[78] Kimball, *Nixon's Vietnam War*, 1998, p. 92.

[79] Kimball, *Nixon's Vietnam War*, 1998, p. 93.

[80] Kimball, *Nixon's Vietnam War*, 1998, p. 97. In Kimball's view, this was not "a finished plan in the sense of a blueprint—a complete diagram of specific events and time lines. It was a plan in the making, some parts complete, some in the drafting. But those sections of the design that were drawn up from time to time were based on an overall concept—a strategy of key principles that guided their ever-evolving specific plans of action." Kimball, *Nixon's Vietnam War*, 1998, p. 100. Ellsberg would later say that the attitude of Nixon and Kissinger at the time was, "We will do it better—and more savagely" (quoted in Strober and Strober, *Nixon: An Oral History of His Presidency*, New York: HarperCollins, 1994).

[81] Kissinger, note to Guy Pauker, December 27, 1968, National Archives, Washington, D.C.

to various offices within the Defense Department when he assumed his position as Secretary of Defense. McNamara's questions were designed not only to solicit information but also to establish his authority in DoD by showing that he and his deputies knew about the controversies within the Pentagon bureaucracy and that it would be ill-advised to try to mislead him by hiding these disputes from him.

Ellsberg suggested that the list of questions be sent to each agency separately, to bring out the controversies. A short deadline would make coordination among them difficult, so that "divergent and well-informed 'rogue' opinions" that usually would not percolate to the highest level of government would be presented to the new president.[82] Ellsberg convinced Kissinger that this process would allow Nixon to obtain answers from many government sources other than the agency ordinarily responsible for handling a particular issue, since the responsible agency would tend to provide answers that would frequently turn out to be wrong or less reliable than the information he could obtain from somewhere else. Such surfacing of conflicting assessments of the same issue "might be disconcerting to the White House, but . . . would be a valuable warning of the uncertainties."[83]

Ellsberg told Kissinger that the controversies and the challenges to the positions taken by some agencies would embarrass the bureaucrats and put them "off-balance and on the defensive" vis-à-vis Kissinger, who had posed the questions—an argument much to Kissinger's liking.[84] Later, Ellsberg would realize that this argument fit in with Kissinger's own design. Nixon had instructed Kissinger to take over control of foreign policy, including Vietnam, and by keeping the bureaucracy busy for weeks providing answers to the lengthy list of questions, Kissinger was able to put arrangements into place to consolidate his control of foreign policy.[85] At the end of the meeting, Kissinger told Ellsberg to detach the list of questions from the strategic-options paper and expand them for Kissinger to issue as a separate directive. Kissinger asked Ellsberg to work full-time on this task right away, and so Fred Iklé took over the drafting of the final version of the strategic-options paper.

Kissinger issued the list of questions to key national security agencies and their leaders on January 21, with a request for their response by February 10. In mid-February, Mort Halperin, whom Kissinger had recruited to be his assistant, asked Ellsberg to come to Washington to review the answers that had come in from the agencies, totaling more than 500 pages. Halperin had assigned his assistant, Winston Lord, to coordinate the answers and to compare and summarize them for Nixon.

---

[82] Ellsberg, *Secrets*, 2002, p. 236.

[83] Ellsberg, *Secrets*, 2002, p. 237.

[84] Ellsberg, *Secrets*, 2002, p. 237.

[85] Kissinger was reported to have told one aide, "I'm tying up the bureaucracy . . . and buying time for the new president."

Ellsberg helped Lord draft the final summary, but most of the writing was done by Lord.[86] The answers revealed an acute split of opinion. According to Ellsberg, one group, made up of the Joint Chiefs, MACV, CINCPAC, and the U.S. Embassy in Saigon, was optimistic, but was unable to say with certainty when victory could be achieved. The other group, comprising the CIA, ISA, and Systems Analysis in OSD; the intelligence section of the State Department; and civilian analysts in Washington, was more conservative or more pessimistic, seeing no progress in pacification, and greater VC overall strength and influence in the rural areas.

According to Ellsberg, the two groups converged on several points: They agreed that the GVN and other noncommunist groups might not be able to compete with the NLF for political power after peace was restored and, therefore, might not survive; that the South Vietnamese armed forces could not resist North Vietnamese and Viet Cong forces "now, or in the foreseeable future"; that the enemy—despite heavy losses—retained enough strength to pursue his objectives; that the attrition strategy had failed because the enemy could replenish his forces faster with recruitment and infiltration than the United States could destroy.[87] According to Ellsberg, MACV and the JCS had to admit that the enormous casualties inflicted on the Viet Cong and the NVA could be replaced easily with recruitment in the South and infiltration from the North, and that unless the enemy launched more offensives on the scale of the Tet attacks, the United States could not impose a rate of attrition that would be beyond their capability to replenish.

Ellsberg found the agreements more meaningful than the disagreements. All sides agreed that enlarging and strengthening the South Vietnamese forces to Vietnamize the war would not make them capable of holding their own against NVA forces without U.S. support with airpower, helicopters, artillery, logistics, and some ground forces. All the agencies also downgraded the domino theory and did not believe that an unfavorable settlement in Vietnam would inevitably lead to communist takeovers outside Indochina.

Ellsberg then suggested more topics for research, including an examination of what "accommodations" and "adjustments" by Southeast Asian countries might mean concretely if Vietnam turned communist and of how damaging these would be to American security, as well as "the actual extent of civilian damage from artillery and bombing in Vietnam." However, Kissinger rejected Ellsberg's proposals when Mort Halperin presented them to him, saying, "We've had enough questions for now."[88]

---

[86] Author Tom Wells (*Wild Man*, 2001, p. 312) concluded that Ellsberg's questions "were searching, penetrating, pointed," and that the paper he helped Winston Lord write showed his "enormous knowledge of the war and critical skills," and that it "was brilliant work that few people could have pulled off."

[87] Ellsberg, *Secrets*, 2002, p. 240.

[88] Ellsberg, *Secrets*, 2002, p. 241.

In his memoir *White House Years*, Kissinger did not credit Ellsberg with coming up with the questions for NSSM-1. He wrote that when the Nixon Administration took office, the first thing they felt they needed was a dependable evaluation of the situation in Vietnam, because their "desire to develop a coherent strategy immediately ran up against the paucity of facts," and their "attempt to modify established practice against the inertia of conventional wisdom."[89] Their need for information led to NSSM-1.[90] Departments and agencies were asked to respond to a list of "twenty-eight major and fifty subsidiary questions." Kissinger's staff analyzed and summarized the responses, and the report was "circulated to the members of the NSC [National Security Council] Review Group on March 14." It was subsequently revised for a March 26 meeting of the National Security Council.

Kissinger's own summary of the agreements and disagreements that surfaced mirrored that of Ellsberg. However, while Ellsberg was impressed by the agreements between the various agencies regarding the dismal prospects for South Vietnam, Kissinger concluded that the answers provided no guidance, since "there was no consensus as to facts, much less as to policy."[91]

Apparently, "Kissinger had deliberately had the disparate estimates compiled in order to dramatize to Nixon the divisions among the Vietnam specialists. Implicitly, Nixon could now feel free to act without reference to the bureaucrats, and he did."[92] However, by the time the final version of NSSM-1 was submitted to the National Security Council at its March 26 meeting, Nixon and Kissinger had already begun to implement their strategy. So, other than implying to Nixon that he could ignore the bureaucrats, NSSM-1 had little influence on Nixon's and Kissinger's Vietnam strategy—and therefore did not achieve the same level of influence as the RAND options paper.[93]

The copious volume of answers to the questions for NSSM-1 contained information that Ellsberg was certain would be of interest to his colleagues at RAND who were performing research on Vietnam. Before Ellsberg left, Mort Halperin took him aside and told him, "I'm going to ask you not to show any of this material to anybody at Rand or to take any copies back with you." Halperin added, "Dan, this *really* can't go back. I mean it. I'm counting on you not to do it; and that means not to Harry Rowen,

---

[89] Henry Kissinger, *White House Years*, Boston, Mass.: Little, Brown, and Company, 1979, p. 237.

[90] Kissinger's description of the process of obtaining answers for NSSM-1 is similar to Ellsberg's.

[91] Kissinger, *White House Years*, 1979, p. 239. Later, according to Tom Wells, Ellsberg expressed anger that the Nixon Administration had "largely disregarded the lessons of NSSM-1." Wells, who generally portrayed Ellsberg in an unflattering manner, as an egomaniac, ascribed this anger to personal pique that Kissinger had not listened to him or let him be his strategist.

[92] Karnow, *Vietnam: A History*, 1983, p. 604.

[93] Kimball, *Nixon's Vietnam War*, 1998, p. 97.

not to Fred Iklé, not to anybody."[94] Ellsberg interpreted this as a pro-forma warning from Mort Halperin, who simply wanted to go on the record that he was not authorizing the transfer of the materials to RAND or knew about it, and as a signal that word should not "get back to the White House that Rand had this material." Ellsberg believed that the information was "not that sensitive" and proceeded to duplicate the documents himself "in the copying alcove of the NSC."[95]

Upon his return to Santa Monica, Ellsberg held a meeting with about a dozen analysts who were doing work on Vietnam. He handed out copies and repeated Halperin's warning, stressing that "no word should reach the White House that we had them." According to Ellsberg, it was not unusual for RAND people to bring back documents "that were obtained 'under the counter.'" RAND analysts therefore were familiar with this kind of warning, "though it had perhaps never involved the White House before."[96] Ellsberg claimed that later he checked back with Halperin to make sure that he had understood Halperin's warning correctly, and that it was "OK" with Halperin that he had copied the documents and given them to his RAND colleagues along with the warning that Halperin should not be told about this by Ellsberg or anyone else. According to Ellsberg, Halperin replied that, "Of course," he had been correct in making that assumption.[97]

According to Haldeman, at the start of his presidency, Nixon expected that he would be able to reach a negotiated settlement—which would be "acceptable, if not totally satisfactory"—within the first six months in office.[98] Kissinger shared Nixon's optimism that the war could be settled in "a matter of months," as he told his Harvard colleagues.[99] Nixon wanted to end the war so that he could have the freedom to deal with pressing domestic and international issues. Also, he did not want to "end up like LBJ"—as he had observed after his victory in November 1968—"holed up in the White House afraid to show my face on the street. I'm going to stop that war. Fast."[100]

Nixon believed, as did such senior officials as Defense Secretary Melvin Laird and Henry Kissinger, that if he did not settle the war by the end of his six- to nine-month honeymoon with the American public, Vietnam would become "his war," as Haldeman observed. If Nixon failed to achieve peace by then, antiwar demonstrations would erupt anew. Kissinger himself felt that they were wedged between "the hammer of anti-

---

[94] Ellsberg, *Secrets*, 2002, pp. 241–242.

[95] Ellsberg, *Secrets*, 2002, p. 242.

[96] Ellsberg, *Secrets*, 2002, p. 242.

[97] Ellsberg, *Secrets*, 2002, p. 243.

[98] Ellsberg, *Secrets*, 2002, p. 101.

[99] Ellsberg, *Secrets*, 2002, p. 101.

[100] Ellsberg, *Secrets*, 2002, p. 101.

war pressure and the anvil of Hanoi."[101] The strategy adopted by Nixon and Kissinger in this situation was, as Kissinger put it, "to walk a fine line . . . between withdrawing too fast to convince Hanoi of our determination and withdrawing too slowly to satisfy the American public."[102]

Nixon and Kissinger did not believe that the public four-party negotiations in Paris—involving the United States, North Vietnam, the GVN, and the National Liberation Front—would lead anywhere and, therefore, favored direct, secret talks with Hanoi, which commenced in August 1969. Meanwhile, on the ground in South Vietnam, their strategy was to increase pressure on the enemy to induce them to settle. By January 8, 1969, Nixon believed that, as a first order of business, the United States should begin bombing enemy bases in Cambodia to apply unbearable pressure on Hanoi and push it to accept a settlement on terms favorable to the United States.

In response, Kissinger ordered the compilation of a list of targets to be hit in Cambodia. General Creighton Abrams cabled General Earle Wheeler that hard intelligence and information provided by a defector had revealed the location of the Central Office for South Vietnam (COSVN) headquarters under the jungle canopy along the Cambodia–South Vietnam border, in what was known as Base Area 353. COSVN was the nerve center that directed NLF operations in the South, and Abrams believed that a B-52 attack on those facilities would destroy them and prevent the enemy from planning possible future offensives. MACV's intention in proposing the bombing was to destroy enemy troop concentrations, interdict supply lines, deter attacks, and, in general, weaken the enemy in preparation for the planned withdrawal of American troops, which began in August of that year. Nixon was receptive to Abrams' recommendation when it was relayed to him, because it fit in with his own desire to pressure Hanoi, showcase his personal resolve, and demonstrate his madman theory.

On February 18, 1969, Abrams sent two colonels from Saigon to meet with Kissinger, Laird, and Wheeler. The two officers gave the assurance that even if COSVN was not located there, the base complex would be a good target, since it contained enemy forces, hospitals, and substantial stores of supplies. Because the briefing took place over breakfast, this became the code name for the air attack. Kissinger would later claim that the officers assured him that no civilians lived in the area. Kissinger then wrote a memo, relaying this information and urging the attack, but recommended delaying the attack until the end of March or until the enemy provided a pretext with some provocation.

That pretext came with enemy attacks on February 22, 1969, which were designed to expand NLF control of rural and urban areas and thwart pacification and Vietnamization, and therefore force Nixon to rethink his plan and take another look at the situ-

---

[101] Ellsberg, *Secrets*, 2002, p. 101.

[102] Ellsberg, *Secrets*, 2002, pp. 101–102.

ation.[103] Nixon and Kissinger decided to launch the air attacks in Cambodia in secret, to avoid congressional, media, and public reaction to the expansion of the war. On March 17, 60 B-52s dropped their bombs during the night on Base Area 353 in what is known as the "Fish Hook" region of Cambodia. Other B-52 attacks would follow—bearing the code names of Lunch, Snack, Dinner, and Dessert—and the entire operation would be known as Menu. Over a period of 14 months, "from the first raids in March 1969 to May 1970, 3,825 B-52 sorties dropped 103,921 tons of bombs on six of the 17 border base camps."[104] Even after Menu ended, the bombing would continue and expand farther into the interior of Cambodia. Airpower became "Nixon's primary war-making weapon,"[105] and he used it to achieve the "negotiated victory" desired by Group A in the RAND options paper and not the "compromise settlement" urged by Group B.

Since resuming the bombing of North Vietnam was politically unacceptable, bombing Cambodia became a substitute. By March 1973, B-52s had dropped 212,678 tons of bombs on a country that had tried to remain neutral and stay out of the war that was consuming its neighbor. At the same time, air attacks in Laos were intensified against villages and communist military units in the Plain of Jars and against the Ho Chi Minh Trail. In South Vietnam itself, B-52 sorties increased from 1,000 in 1967 to 3,000. The tonnage of bombs dropped over Indochina rose sharply and reached over 4 million tons.

♧ ♧ ♧

Journalist David Landau believed that RAND played a role in these aggressive moves of the Nixon Administration. On February 25, 1969, about a month before the air attacks were launched in Cambodia, Fred Iklé wrote a memorandum under the title "U.S. Responses to Enemy Escalation in Vietnam: A Checklist of Issues."[106] This paper probably represented the "threat options" that Schilling thought were missing from the original draft of December 1968. As Ellsberg described how the options were arrived at, Iklé might not have originated these options himself but simply distilled the views gathered from within official circles. Nonetheless, in his *Ramparts* article, Landau saw

---

[103] According to Kimball (*Nixon's Vietnam War*, 1998, p. 128), Kissinger called the enemy offensive "an act of extraordinary cynicism" but did not note that the U.S. and South Vietnamese had also launched extensive attacks of their own—such as Operation Dewey Canyon in I Corps, which began on January 22 to disrupt enemy logistics and bases threatening the former imperial capital of Hue, and Operation *Toan Thang* ("Total Victory"), launched in III Corps on February 17 to maintain continued pressure on the NLF.

[104] Kimball, *Nixon's Vietnam War*, 1998, p. 135.

[105] Kimball, *Nixon's Vietnam War*, 1998, p. 137.

[106] Cited in Landau, "Behind the Policy Makers," 1. The Iklé Memorandum, 1972. When asked about this memo in a brief phone interview, Iklé said he was not dealing with Vietnam strategic issues at this time and that his focus was on domestic issues.

the Iklé memo as the blueprint for the Nixon Administration's aggressive moves: suspending the peace talks and reescalating the war in subsequent years. Landau pointed out, for example, that the invasions of Laos and Cambodia took place in 1970 and 1971; in 1972, following intelligence reports indicating that the North Vietnamese had built up massive forces north of the 17th parallel, Nixon ordered the American representative at the peace talks in Paris to walk out.[107]

Then, as the situation worsened on the ground for Saigon in 1972, the U.S. bombed the North, first above the DMZ and then at Hanoi and Haiphong, mined the harbors, and attacked the dikes. According to officials serving in the White House during this period whom Landau interviewed, the scenario described by Iklé was "unusual" and "far from commonplace at the time it was written."[108] Although Landau acknowledged that the Nixon Administration had already established "the larger policy framework on Vietnam," he accused Iklé of being willing to go along with Washington in order to maintain access to policymakers—"like any good RAND consultant."[109]

Excerpts from the memo showed that some of the actions subsequently undertaken by the Nixon Administration were indeed discussed in the Iklé memo as options the United States might implement if the enemy stepped up operations in Vietnam while the peace talks unfolded in Paris, either by launching a major new offensive; by intensifying rocket (or mortar) attacks on cities; by increasing or committing "particularly dramatic assassinations of U.S. or senior Vietnamese officials"; infiltrating more forces from the North; or carrying out other kinds of attacks. Among the responses available to the United States, Iklé listed bombing of North Vietnam, ground operations "immediately North of the DMZ," ground military incursions into Laos, and operations carried into Cambodia. Another option was suspending the peace negotiations in Paris to reinforce U.S. pressure on Hanoi. As Iklé wrote, "To coerce an enemy, the threat of punitive action is sometimes more effective than the action itself—and cheaper." Just resuming the bombing of the North would not be "any more threatening . . . than it is today" and so, besides making "visible military preparations," the United States could render this threat more credible by *suspend[ing] the Paris talks* (emphasis in original).[110]

In discussing the repercussions of resuming bombing, Iklé pointed out that doing so could presumably trigger a negative political reaction in the United States. However, Hanoi had presented the bombing halt to its own population as a great victory, so a resumption would represent a setback for Hanoi. The memo proposed a more aggres-

---

[107] Landau, "Behind the Policy Makers," 1972, p. 28.

[108] Landau, "Behind the Policy Makers," 1972, p. 26.

[109] Landau, "Behind the Policy Makers," 1972, p. 28

[110] In *White House Years,* 1979, Henry Kissinger wrote that the threat of resuming bombing and scuttling the peace talks had been implied by Averell Harriman, Lyndon Johnson's chief negotiator in Paris, on November 4, 1968, in a warning to the North Vietnamese to deter future major attacks.

sive bombing campaign in case air bombardment of the North was resumed. It pointed out that, in case of resumption, the issue of targeting would have to be addressed. Adhering to the same restrictions—i.e., steering clear of the 19th parallel, the Chinese border, and the Hanoi-Haiphong area—would give the "impression that the same old ladder was being climbed" and might have an adverse political effect in the United States while not applying optimal coercion on Hanoi. Although the resumption of bombing could "clearly establish that there are limits" that Hanoi could not cross, the decision about what would trigger this response would depend on "whether on balance a bombing or non-bombing posture is preferred." Finally, before renewing the bombing, it "may be desirable to consider the degree of success or other conditions that would permit stopping it again."

The memo cautioned that, as the 1965–1968 period had shown, being able to inflict "substantial costs and hardships on the enemy" was not the same as being able to coerce him. Besides, U.S. escalation might cause the Soviet Union to step up its aid so that—as in the past—North Vietnam would emerge "stronger than before." If the United States carried out major incursions into Cambodia, such operations could lead that country to seek Soviet assistance and expand its collaboration with North Vietnam. In terms of cost, the resumption of bombing of North Vietnam would add about half a billion dollars to the annual budget and cause about 50 to 250 pilot losses per year, and "any substantial and continuing increase in costs would run counter to the U.S. objective of making the war more sustainable by reducing casualty and dollar costs." Also, increased "U.S. military activities outside South Vietnam," even if "thoroughly provoked," would "likely exact some diplomatic cost" in terms of opposition from foreign governments—even from sympathetic allies. Before resuming bombing, therefore, "a decision should be made whether to give a full and explicit interpretation of the bombing halt agreement" that had been presented in a "vague and general" fashion, so that the public would become aware "that certain actions by the other side might not only be deemed unacceptable by the U.S., but in fact violate an explicit agreement."[111]

Considering that Nixon had already formulated his strategic concept, the Iklé memorandum served mainly as an articulation of the options available and the consequences to be considered in carrying them out, rather than as a blueprint for the Nixon Administration's subsequent escalation of the war in Vietnam, intensification of air attacks in Laos, and expansion of the conflict to Cambodia both on the ground and in the air. Nonetheless, the memo could be seen as one of the most influential works RAND produced on the war.

---

[111] In *White House Years,* 1979, Kissinger wrote that there had been only "an 'understanding'" between the LBJ Administration and Hanoi that, in return for the bombing halt, North Vietnam would refrain from carrying out "indiscriminate attacks on the major cities," launching artillery shells, rockets, or mortars from across and within the DMZ, moving troops from across or within the DMZ, massing or moving forces near the DMZ "in a manner threatening to the other side." Hanoi "never agreed to these provisions but, rather, 'assented by silence.'"

The studies done for Kissinger and the White House represented the last major projects on Vietnam for RAND. In fall 1969, Kissinger set up his own Vietnam Special Studies Group, an interagency committee, to provide input on Vietnam issues, and his own Vietnam Working Group within the National Security Council to perform research and analyses, thus reducing, if not negating, the need to obtain external assistance for policy formulation. In an internal paper published on January 29, 1970, Iklé recognized the difficulty of landing this kind of work.[112] He wrote that, while it would seem "inappropriate for Rand not to conduct any research on overall Vietnam [military and political] policy—the Government's most pressing problem abroad," RAND faced the impediment of finding itself "too far from the field and too outnumbered by MACV and innumerable Washington task forces, teams, and specialists."[113] A possible opening would be for RAND to evaluate "systematically future enemy options" because it "would have practically no competition" in this area, and so a "Red Team" project was proposed for this purpose. For a "variety of reasons" it had gotten off to a slow start. The plan, however, was to "wrap up and deliver" the results in early March.[114] It appears that this project did not get implemented.

Although unable to secure projects that could influence policy formulation at the highest levels in Washington—on the scale, scope, and prestige of the options paper and NSSM-1—RAND continued to devote some attention and resources to two pillars of Nixon's strategy—besides intensifying military pressure—for extricating the United States from Vietnam: pacification and Vietnamization. But even in these areas, with the exception of the Dinh Tuong project, which was revived in 1971 in response to interest within the National Security Council, the works were not in-depth studies.

In the field of pacification, RAND relied on the work of Robert Komer, a consultant who had been General Westmoreland's civilian deputy for pacification as head of Civil Operations and Revolutionary Development Support. CORDS was set up in 1967 to improve pacification results by unifying civilian and military efforts under MACV—a move that Komer had advocated when he was White House special assistant for pacification for President Johnson. Komer wanted CORDS placed under Westmoreland because he thought that, of all the U.S. organizations in Vietnam, MACV had the largest budget and personnel, and could, with its military operations, provide

---

[112] F. C. Iklé, "Enemy Options in Vietnam, 1971–1972: First Working Notes," Santa Monica, Calif.: RAND Corporation, January 29, 1970 (not available to the general public).

[113] Iklé, "Enemy Options in Vietnam, 1971–1972, 1970, p. ii.

[114] Iklé, "Enemy Options in Vietnam, 1971–1972, 1970, p. ii. The variety of reasons included RAND's move to diversify its research into domestic issues, which absorbed most of its energy and resources, but also the turmoil caused by the growing dissent within RAND over Vietnam. (See Chapter Nine.)

the security needed to achieve lasting pacification in a "semiconventional war."[115] Unifying pacification management would end the confusion caused by the split in responsibilities between the U.S. Mission and MACV.

In Washington, Komer had earned the nickname "Blowtorch" for his reputation as a man who knew how to twist arms and get things done.[116] Komer did not lack confidence, and before he left Washington for Saigon to head CORDS, he wrote to Johnson, "I believe that by this time next year we can break the back of the VC in South Vietnam—even if the war continues." His optimism was epitomized in his reply to Gus Shubert. One or two weeks before the Tet Offensive took place, Shubert asked Komer whether RAND could perform a study on pacification, and Komer answered, "Before you can get geared up to study pacification, we'll have Vietnam pacified."[117] However, Komer's public optimism might have masked private doubts. At a press conference given at the Saigon airport after he disembarked on the day he arrived to assume his new post, Komer was extremely confident about improvements in Vietnam and expressed high expectations for pushing pacification to success. Subsequently, Daniel Ellsberg, who had known Komer at RAND, paid him a visit at the U.S. Embassy. When Ellsberg asked him, "Bob, did you believe any of that stuff you were saying at the airport?" Komer "leaned forward with his elbows on the desk and held his head in his hands. He looked down at the desk and closed his eyes. He seemed exhausted. He said softly, 'Dan, do you think I'm crazy?'" Ellsberg asked him why he had taken the job, and Komer told him, "When the president of the United States says he wants you to do something . . . you've got to do it, no matter how hopeless it is."[118]

With support from President Johnson, Komer, who carried the rank of ambassador, was able to build CORDS into a powerful and large organization, absorbing under his leadership practically all facets of pacification, such as the National Police, *Chieu Hoi,* Revolutionary Development, civic action and civil affairs, and reporting and evaluation. CORDS also gained control over the training and improvement of the Regional and Popular Forces. CORDS's senior pacification advisors were drawn from both military and civilian ranks.

---

[115] Robert Komer, "The Current Pacification Program in Vietnam," Santa Monica, Calif.: RAND Corporation, December 23, 1969, p. 3 (not available to the general public). In Komer's view, the kind of "Malaya-type police action" advocated by Sir Robert Thompson, which would have been appropriate in the early stage of an insurgency, would not be relevant to Vietnam, where large-unit attacks were taking place. In such conditions, pacification could not begin until American and South Vietnamese offensive operations succeeded in clearing out enemy Main Force units.

[116] Komer, according to Daniel Ellsberg, loved his nickname of "Blowtorch." Ellsberg writes that Komer was "loud and optimistic." It was easy to tell when Komer had arrived at the embassy: ". . . you could hear him barking greetings on the lower floor. . . . He shook hands and slapped the backs of people" as he burst into his outer office and filled the room with "energy and enthusiasm." Ellsberg, *Secrets,* 2002, p. 178.

[117] Author interview with Gus Shubert, 2004 and 2005.

[118] Ellsberg, *Secrets,* 2002, p. 178.

Although Komer liked to reiterate that the GVN retained primary responsibility for pacification, it was clear that CORDS was the force that drove pacification. It was Komer who pressured General Nguyen Van Thieu, the new president of South Vietnam, to act quickly and decisively, and to prod the lethargic GVN bureaucracy into motion. Under Komer's vigorous leadership, an accelerated pacification campaign, or APC, was finally launched in November 1968, just as he left Saigon to be replaced by William Colby as head of CORDS, to exploit the weakened state in which the enemy found himself in the aftermath of heavy losses suffered during and after the Tet Offensive. APC would end just as President Nixon took office in 1969—but pacification itself would continue.

Komer, along with General Creighton Abrams and William Colby, hoped that APC would help convince critics back in the United States that pacification could succeed and that the war could be won. Colby himself hoped to impress the Nixon Administration with its results. Following his return to the United States, Komer temporarily took a position at RAND.[119]

When Komer reviewed the results of APC at a three-day seminar at RAND in November 1969, statistics indicated that APC had achieved impressive results. As the author of APC, Komer was justifiably proud. Also, since one of the goals of this accelerated drive was to demonstrate that pacification could work, Komer was personally motivated to demonstrate how successful it had proven to be. Referring to APC as "the new model" of pacification,[120] Komer pointed out that one of the features setting APC apart from past pacification efforts, such as the Strategic Hamlet Program, was that it brought "protection to the hamlet" itself rather than moving villagers to more defensible areas.[121] Taking obvious pride in this "new model," Komer called it "the most imaginative and innovative major program that a hidebound U.S. sponsored in Vietnam."[122] To him, it was "one of the most productive if not the most productive . . . major program"—one that was better suited to the political-military conflict in South Vietnam than the massive military effort undertaken by the United States.[123] "For the first time," he said, "we had managed to give [pacification] some top level status, some unified central management and above all some U.S. backing on a scale that it had

---

[119] In a letter to Colby dated August 8, 1969, Colonel Robert M. Montague, who had been Komer's executive officer at CORDS, wrote that Komer was at RAND in Santa Monica temporarily while he weighed what job to take next. According to Montague, Komer told him he was going to become "a captain of industry" and leave the government.

[120] The seminar contents were later published as "The Current Pacification Program in Vietnam," December 23, 1969, and were then expanded and restructured into "Organization and Management of the 'New Model' Pacification Program—1966–1969" (D-20104-ARPA), which was published in May 1970. See "The Current Pacification Program," 1969, p. 2.

[121] Komer, "The Current Pacification Program," 1969, p. 4.

[122] Komer, "The Current Pacification Program," 1969, p. 20.

[123] Komer, "The Current Pacification Program," 1969, p. 21.

never enjoyed before."[124] While he said that it remained to be seen how lasting a result pacification had achieved, he felt that it had greatly improved conditions in the rural areas.

Komer's optimism was confirmed by none other than Sir Robert Thompson, now serving as a RAND consultant. Thompson had been hired by President Nixon in November 1969 to assess the situation in South Vietnam, because American withdrawal—which had begun in August—was due to continue. Thompson was to provide expert outside advice to Nixon to complement National Security Council staff reports as part of the president's reappraisal of strategy. Nixon had met Thompson in October, and Thompson had told him then that Vietnamization could succeed within two years.[125] Encouraged by Thompson's assessment, Nixon began to think about accelerating Vietnamization while keeping the tempo of the war at the existing level—as he would later recall in his memoir *RN*[126]—to prepare the GVN to continue fighting after American troops were completely withdrawn.[127] In November, Nixon decided to send Thompson to Vietnam to confirm his October evaluation firsthand.

Upon his return to Washington, Thompson reported that the GVN was in a "winning position" and would continue to hold the upper hand unless the United States withdrew its military and economic aid too precipitously.[128] *Time* magazine in its December 12, 1969, issue reported that Sir Robert Thompson—"a Rand . . . consultant"—had told Nixon that "things felt much better and smelled much better over there" in Vietnam. *The Washington Post* issue of December 17, 1969, quoted Thompson—to whom it referred as "consultant to Rand Corporation and to President Nixon"—as saying that, "They [the Americans and South Vietnamese] can win. . . . We—meaning the West—have not understood how badly they [the North Vietnamese] have been hurt." To support his own assessment, Thompson arranged a meeting between Nixon, Kissinger, and John Paul Vann, now serving as the senior CORDS official in the Mekong Delta. Vann, who had squired Thompson during his Delta visit, "not only assured Nixon that pacification would continue to succeed but also argued that the South Vietnamese could be trained to fight as well as Americans," provided they were equipped with heavy weapons, artillery, and air support.[129] He predicted that

---

[124] Komer, "The Current Pacification Program," 1969, p. 8.

[125] Kimball, *Nixon's Vietnam War*, 1998, p. 179.

[126] Richard M. Nixon, *RN: The Memoirs of Richard Nixon*, New York: Grosset & Dunlap, 1978.

[127] Kimball, *Nixon's Vietnam War*, 1998, p. 179.

[128] Kimball, *Nixon's Vietnam War*, 1998, pp. 179–180. In his report, Thompson added, "The year 1970 could . . . end decisively in our favour so that, if President Thieu is re-elected in 1971, the VC revolutionary movement within the South should be reduced to a negligible threat" ("Visit to Vietnam—October 28th–November 25th, 1969, Report by Sir Robert Thompson," signed by Thompson and dated December 3, 1969, National Archives, Washington, D.C.).

[129] Kimball, *Nixon's Vietnam War*, 1998, p. 180.

this kind of support would give them the capacity to even fight off an NVA offensive from the North after American combat troops left.

Heavy pressure "from the top to produce encouraging reports" meant that Thompson's evaluation was endorsed by the Vietnam Special Studies Group, despite their general skepticism of rosy assessments.[130] Some committee members actually doubted that the favorable pacification trends could be sustained after American withdrawal, questioning whether the GVN would be able to establish permanent control in the countryside. They also wondered whether the enemy retrenchment was due to pacification or to a strategic decision by Hanoi to scale back operations for the time being.

Besides the work of Robert Komer, RAND's output on pacification and Vietnamization in 1969–1970 rested also on the reports of Bing West. Among West's reports on pacification was the one he produced with Charlie Benoit's assistance in November 1969—at the same time that Sir Robert Thompson himself was in the country to assess the situation for Nixon. The report was very much in West's style, based as it was on observations obtained at the ground level rather than on information available in Saigon. West and Benoit's report supported the skepticism of the Vietnam Special Studies Group and gave a perspective that differed markedly from that of Thompson and Robert Komer.

West and Benoit concluded that progress on pacification had been achieved with firepower and depopulation; that pacification, in fact, was more a case of "occupation"; and that the reported gains had been distorted by efforts to improve HES scores and by flaws in the HES system itself. Whatever progress had been achieved, West reported, was being undermined by the government itself and by American troops' insensitivity toward the rural population and indiscriminate use of firepower. West and Benoit concluded that the situation did not look promising for achieving the pacification goal of upgrading security for 90 percent of the population by the end of 1970 so that they would live under some form of government control in B hamlets. To West, this goal was "preposterous" with the Americans still around, and it would become "absolutely absurd" with them gone.

Written following extensive field trips,[131] West and Benoit's paper represented the third in a series of field reports and was written in the form of a letter dated December 10, 1969—actually addressed to Rear Admiral William E. Lemos, USN. It

---

[130] Kimball, *Nixon's Vietnam War*, 1998, p. 180.

[131] Francis J. West and Charles Benoit, "Pacification: View from the Provinces—Part III (November 1969)," Santa Monica, Calif.: RAND Corporation, January 20, 1970 (not available to the general public). In addition, Charlie Benoit wrote "Conversations with Rural Vietnamese," Santa Monica, Calif.: RAND Corporation, D-20138-ARPA-AGILE, April 1970, to describe his trips through the outlying regions of four provinces, his open-ended interviews with over 100 Vietnamese along the way, and his observations on pacification. In the Preface, Benoit wrote that his document, along with Bing West's companion report, *Pacification: View from the Provinces—Part III*, were submitted to MACV. Bing West's companion report incorporated many anecdotes and observations from "Conversations with Rural Vietnamese," 1970, p. ii.

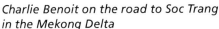

Charlie Benoit on the road to Soc Trang   Bing West
in the Mekong Delta

contained a summary followed by a narrative giving details of the trips and extended
conversations and observations, along with specific illustrative examples. Many of the
examples were collected by Charlie Benoit during trips through the outlying regions
of four provinces and during his open-ended interviews with many Vietnamese along
the way about what he called "that amorphous concept called *pacification*."[132] According to Benoit, what he and West reported did not enhance their "popularity" within
American official circles in Saigon.

In one respect, Bing West agreed with Komer, Thompson, and reports submitted
by MACV to Washington. As did they, West thought that the enemy had been weakened. According to him, the war of attrition, combined with the losses inflicted during
and after the Tet Offensive, had heavily damaged the native southern Viet Cong. This
weakening of the VC position and the perception that they were not going to win
the war were common themes running through the random conversations West and
Benoit had with villagers and local government troops in IV, III, and I Corps. Another
difficulty facing the Viet Cong was that, in trying to replace their losses, they had promoted out of the villages many of the old, dedicated, cadres who had won the respect
of the villagers, replacing them with men of lesser quality. Thus, the military defeats,
the lessening of popular support, and higher taxes had "diminished the VC in the eyes
of the villagers," who no longer held them "in awe" and were less willing to lend them
"psychological and material support." Many areas that the government had taken back
from enemy control had not turned out to be "hotbeds" of communist support, and

---

[132] Benoit, "Conversations with Rural Vietnamese," 1970. In the Preface (p. ii), Benoit wrote that his document,
along with Bing West's companion report, "Pacification: View from the Provinces—Part III," were submitted to
MACV. According to Benoit, their observations about the two provinces in the northern region were "attentively
received at the headquarters of . . . I Corps."

the people had reacted to the GVN return with a "wait-and-see attitude" rather than with "sullen hostility."[133]

However, pacification gains were being undermined by the government itself, through its corruption and through the predatory behavior of its troops. When its soldiers moved into pacified outlying areas considered traditionally supportive of the Viet Cong, they victimized the villagers, whom they perceived as pro-VC. Their behavior could be partially explained by the inflation that was then afflicting the South Vietnamese economy: The ARVN soldiers, and the Regional and Popular Forces, were on fixed salaries and, stuck at the bottom of the heap, they had been hard hit by the inflation; meanwhile, officials in the upper ranks of the GVN, who engaged in corruption and could simply pass the burden to those below, were unaffected.

The result was that the troops who were fighting to perpetuate the "Establishment" had become more disaffected toward it. Their economic distress—and the poor example set by their own leaders—had made them more predatory toward people living in areas previously considered VC. West related a conversation with an assistant district chief, who told him, "All the VC are poor and are expected to make sacrifices; on the GVN side, the higher-ups are rich, and it is the workers who are poor, and with the new round of inflation, are expected to make additional sacrifices. With the leaders setting a poor example, why should the troops sacrifice?"[134] West concluded that, "It was not poverty itself which generated resentment and rebellion; it was inequality."[135]

Pacification gains were also undermined by the insensitivity of U.S. troops. What the villagers feared from the Americans was not "thievery" but "bullying, [and] thoughtlessness."[136] West narrated incidents that illustrated such behavior—for example, American troops destroying personal property while searching for Viet Cong in villages or treating peasants with disrespect: "The trooper who shoves aside a farmer in order to look inside his house ('hootch') for a lurking VC who is never there; the knife nicks in furniture which is junk in the trooper's eyes and irreplaceable to a poor family."[137] Above all, the villagers feared the Americans' indiscriminate use of firepower, such as "the H&I [harassment and interdiction] artillery round which destroys 5% of a one-hectare crop; the terrible swift helicopter which shoots anyone who runs."[138] Unless

---

[133] West, "Pacification: View from the Provinces—Part III," 1970, pp. 4–5.

[134] West, "Pacification: View from the Provinces—Part III," 1970, p. 11.

[135] West, "Pacification: View from the Provinces—Part III," 1970, p. 11.

[136] West, "Pacification: View from the Provinces—Part III," 1970, p. 6.

[137] West, "Pacification: View from the Provinces—Part III," 1970, p. 6.

[138] West, "Pacification: View from the Provinces—Part III," 1970, p. 6.

the "piracy" of the GVN soldiers and the indiscriminate use of firepower ceased, *pacification* became *occupation*, West wrote (emphasis not in original).[139]

In evaluating the causes for pacification progress, West said that it had been achieved by firepower and depopulation. Playing devil's advocate, West listed what he called "heretical causes." He believed that the rapid rise in pacification was due—in addition to enemy weakness—to a few factors that were not captured in HES statistics.

First, the population shift toward government areas was caused by the use of indiscriminate U.S. firepower and H&I fire in free-fire zones, which had pushed the people to flee. According to him, ". . . it would be a phenomenon if the VC population had not decreased due to evacuation."[140] Komer had declared that an innovative feature of the "new model of pacification" was taking security to the people instead of moving them to secure areas, as the Strategic Hamlet Program had done. In West's view, however, there were many instances in 1969 in which "pacification has not gone to the people . . . ; the people have come to pacification. Some might say surrendered."[141] West cited specific examples of areas that had been depopulated by indiscriminate firepower: Trang Bang district in Hau Nghia, Binh Son district in Quang Ngai, and Dien Ban district in Quang Nam. When West and Charlie Benoit visited a refugee hamlet that was baking in the sun for lack of shade and where the "roofs glitter sun which parches the crops," the inhabitants "reluctantly admitted to Charlie that the main impetus to their resettlement had been American firepower, particularly by the random artillery and the preying helicopters."[142]

There was another HES statistic that failed to capture the reality on the ground, and this concerned what West described as a "floating population," whose hamlets were destroyed in order to pacify them. Once their hamlets were abandoned, the HES

---

[139] West, "Pacification: View from the Provinces—Part III," 1970, p. 8. In his "Conversations with Rural Vietnamese" (1970, p. 23), Benoit wrote that overwhelming firepower was used to avoid putting the lives of American soldiers at risk. In Vietnam, where it was difficult to separate the enemy from the people, often the firepower was directed at an entire VC village rather than at "individual VC's." To Benoit, while the purpose was laudable, the results were counter to the ideal of saving the South Vietnamese from communism. His conclusions echoed those reached by Len Ackland in his own report about refugees' reactions to indiscriminate bombing and shelling.

[140] West, "Pacification: View from the Provinces—Part III," 1970, p. 7.

[141] West, "Pacification: View from the Provinces—Part III," 1970, p. 7. In his "Conversations with Rural Vietnamese" (1970, p. 43), Charlie Benoit acknowledged that, in terms of "daytime access," the GVN had expanded its nominal control into areas "where for years only VC had dared tread." However, Benoit concluded, it would be impossible to bomb the entire population out of the VC areas and force them to flee to zones where the GVN could maintain security. In such outlying areas, unless the GVN could find a more constructive way of dealing with the population, the Viet Cong would always have "a constituency" and would remain "a force that cannot be exterminated."

[142] West, "Pacification: View from the Provinces—Part III," 1970, p. 13.

map stopped showing them as Viet Cong–controlled.[143] By day, "under huge GVN flags to ward off preying helicopters they will farm their outlying fields and by night retreat to temporary homes in the . . . GVN hamlets" to avoid harassment and interdiction shelling.[144]

Judging from West's report, pacification gains might not be as solid as Komer had indicated. West cited a district that was classified by HES as totally pacified in 1969, with all the hamlets being categorized as either B or C. However, the American senior advisor in the district told West that "the situation would fall apart if (when) the US units left." He also told West that he felt the current situation was "a case of occupation more than pacification."[145] West agreed with this assessment, stating that "I believe that occupation is a better word than pacification for the current phenomenon of countryside progress." In his view, "It will take a social revolution of enormous dimensions to beget true pacification—i.e. 80–90% of the people united in defense of their government, so that they act with . . . dedication, organization, and fervor. . . . As it stands today, pacification relies on armed might, not moral right."[146]

Second, the impressive progress in pacification was due to a concerted effort by U.S. and GVN commanders to improve HES scores. In September 1967, 15 percent of the total U.S. infantry resources were allocated to area security. In September 1969, this proportion had grown to 40 percent. On the GVN side, more resources had been devoted to pacification—mainly to the expansion of Regional and Popular Forces units. However, whereas Komer thought that the GVN had gotten better, West concluded that it had not improved either politically or militarily.

West reported that the GVN was playing games with HES statistics. The GVN had "flatly ordered radical statistical upgrading."[147] At the same time, local officials were interested in upgrading HES scores to obtain funds for village development. West mentioned a conversation he had with the U.S. senior district advisor in Trang Bang, who told him that the Vietnamese hamlet chiefs were reluctant to share "adverse information with him" because they "had positive monetary and political incentives to upgrade the HES rating."[148] For example, they did not inform him that an NVA unit had passed through the area, nor did they tell him that the Viet Cong were collecting

---

[143] West, "Pacification: View from the Provinces—Part III," 1970, p. 7. In "Conversations with Rural Vietnamese" (1970, p. 10), Benoit wrote that, "Such migrations enable us to consider these people as being pacified. Were they resident in their hamlet, it would be difficult to consider them under GVN control." The hamlets, in fact, were not "abandoned" since the people returned to farm there during the day. They were just afraid to spend the night in their homes.

[144] West, "Pacification: View from the Provinces—Part III," 1970, p. 7.

[145] West, "Pacification: View from the Provinces—Part III," 1970, p. 11.

[146] West, "Pacification: View from the Provinces—Part III," 1970, p. 8.

[147] West, "Pacification: View from the Provinces—Part III," 1970, p. 7.

[148] West, "Pacification: View from the Provinces—Part III," 1970, p. 12.

taxes from the people. The GVN was also engaged in "gerrymandering" to improve HES ratings. When Charlie Benoit asked this district advisor why "several hamlets he had known from 1968 were not on the 1969 HES map," the advisor replied that "the GVN had changed some village and hamlet boundaries, a form of gerrymandering which ruled out of existence by fiat some VC hamlets."[149]

Third, West gave less credit to pacification in securing the countryside. In his view, it was the war of attrition that was pushing pacification, not the other way around. Pacification encroachment on Viet Cong areas had contributed to the weakening of the enemy, but it had not been the primary reason for that weakening. Rather, it was conventional clashes that had weakened the Viet Cong; the degradation of enemy capabilities, in turn, had allowed pacification to expand. For the moment, the GVN and the United States had "the momentum," because the VC/NVA had not seriously impeded pacification growth. One reason for this state of affairs, according to West, was that the Viet Cong and the North Vietnamese believed the "results would not be worth the cost."[150]

One question West posed was whether the GVN, in the long run, would be able to take the place of the Americans in areas that the enemy had abandoned for the moment and operate at the same level of effectiveness. West believed that the ARVN would not be able to defeat the NVA now or in the future. The low level of enemy activity should not be equated with its lack of capability. The ARVN had improved and the NVA had been weakened; nevertheless, West concluded that, in an even match, the NVA could defeat the ARVN.

West cited an operation he took part in in I Corps with an ARVN battalion that MACV had rated in the first quintile. The operation was a success. However, neither the commander nor his experienced advisor believed that the unit could defeat an NVA battalion in an even match. The commander said that he had no intention of putting this to the test, and added that "even if he were to win such a battle," the heavy casualties he would suffer would force many of his men to desert, rather than having to fight "that way against the NVA again."[151] His philosophy was to outlast the NVA and to hold onto key areas, rather than to look for the enemy wherever they might be located and drive them out. West concluded that the ARVN as a whole was performing well within its frame of reference, in which incentives encouraged selfish behavior, concern for personal interest, and political consideration, rather than fighting spirit, initiative, commitment, and a desire for victory from the top to the bottom. So, the challenge was not in reforming the ARVN's tactics but in changing this frame of reference and the behavior it engendered.

---

[149] West, "Pacification: View from the Provinces—Part III," 1970, p. 12.

[150] West, "Pacification: View from the Provinces—Part III," 1970, p. 7.

[151] West, "Pacification: View from the Provinces—Part III," 1970, pp. 9–10.

On the issue of American withdrawal, West said that this information was held in tight secrecy and not shared at the lower rungs of a district or a rifle company, so that there was no sense of urgency. West saw "too many examples of egregious incompetence, selfishness and corruption" for him to believe that the GVN was taking "radical remedial steps" to acknowledge that it was the "eleventh hour."[152] West urged that the South Vietnamese be told that, after Americans left "the entire job is yours," in order to induce anxiety within GVN circles.[153] He would like to see "the pressure put on all the way up and down the line," and the message conveyed to the GVN: "Shape up because we're shipping out."[154]

The finding by Bing West and Charlie Benoit that pacification had been achieved by depopulation was echoed by Gerry Hickey's research in the Central Highlands and by David Elliott in his follow-up study in Dinh Tuong Province. According to Hickey, as the South Vietnamese armed forces began to assume greater responsibility in the Central Highlands, they began to engage in large-scale, forced relocation of the ethnic minorities. General Ngo Dzu, the new commander of II Corps, issued an order directing that, by October 31, 1970, there be no "D or C hamlets"—meaning those not under government control in the HES rating—in his region. A massive relocation of villagers was undertaken. Given short notice—usually a few days—villagers had to abandon their possessions, which were looted by the troops. In some cases, villages were burned to the ground. The relocated people were moved to dismal resettlement centers, where they lacked housing, water, and health care. By April 1971, from 100 to 150 villages had been relocated. Hundreds died after being forced to relocate. Hickey managed to bring this matter to the attention of President Thieu, who told General Dzu to discuss it with Hickey, but the relocations proceeded apace. Hickey then met with William Colby, the head of CORDS, and subsequently, through American pressure, the relocations were halted.

♣ ♣ ♣

While Bing West and Charlie Benoit pursued their own field research on pacification and Vietnamization, the question remained of what to do with what was left of RAND's operations in Vietnam. In June 1970, Robert Komer became program manager for defense studies, replacing Jim Digby. In this capacity, Komer assumed responsibility for ARPA/AGILE contracts, which included the RAND projects in Vietnam. In July 1970, Komer returned to Vietnam for a two-week visit, accompanied by

---

[152] West, "Pacification: View from the Provinces—Part III," 1970, p. 4.

[153] West, "Pacification: View from the Provinces—Part III," 1970, p. 3.

[154] West, "Pacification: View from the Provinces—Part III," 1970, p. 4.

Digby.[155] The news that Komer was now in charge was not welcomed by Gerry Hickey in Saigon. Hickey knew too well that Komer would not look favorably on his study of the Montagnards, believing as he did that these ethnic minorities were an insignificant segment of the population. He viewed research on these people as "a waste" for someone like Hickey, who had done work on the Vietnamese village, which was a more topical issue in view of the emphasis on pacification.[156]

After his arrival, Komer held a meeting with Hickey and the small RAND staff of Joan Allen, Charlie Benoit, and Andy Sweetland. Hickey recalled that Komer began by saying that research budgets were being reduced, but added that there were still possibilities for RAND to perform research focused at the village level. Komer mentioned a village survey that had been performed recently by another research group and said that this was the type of research that was needed. In the discussion that ensued, Komer suggested that "RAND could contribute more than it had thus far." Hickey informed Komer and Digby that RAND reports and memos were distributed to American decisionmakers but they went unread. To Hickey's surprise, Komer admitted that this was the case and said that "when he was at CORDS he did not make use of the expertise and valuable reports of research groups in Vietnam such as RAND."[157]

Hickey interpreted Komer's call for village studies as part of a basic problem that had occurred with the change in leadership at RAND following the retirement of Frank Collbohm in 1967. In Hickey's view, Collbohm had maintained RAND's independence in research; however, under his successor, Harry Rowen, this spirit had given way to "a posture of pleasing the client."[158] While in Saigon, Komer had approached William Colby about research on village government, and they both agreed that Hickey would be the right person for this project. Later, Komer told Hickey about this in a letter from Santa Monica, saying that he had tried hard to fund Hickey's continued work in Vietnam for another man-year. Yet, because of budget cuts, "it goes without saying that the more immediately useful work you have under way, in response to specific field requests, the better we can defend your case."[159] For Hickey, Komer's letter advising him to do "more immediately useful work" was "the handwriting . . . on the wall."[160] He had not anticipated that Vietnamization would place him in a posi-

---

[155] During this visit to Saigon, William Colby invited Digby, along with Gerry Hickey, to a dinner at his villa. The affair drew "a large VIP group of all the high-ranking Vietnamese generals and American CORDS officials." Digby and Hickey were seated "at a fringe table." During the dinner, Digby "sniffed at the 'middling cuisine' and rosé wine, which he whispered tasted like 'something that should be served with ham sandwiches at a picnic.'" Hickey, *Window on a War*, 2002, p. 284.

[156] Hickey, *Window on a War*, 2002, p. 283.

[157] Hickey, *Window on a War*, 2002, p. 284.

[158] Hickey, *Window on a War*, 2002, p. 283.

[159] Hickey, *Window on a War*, 2002, p. 285.

[160] Hickey, *Window on a War*, 2002, p. 285.

tion where he had to reemphasize to RAND the importance for him of finishing his research on highland leadership in order to keep from getting pulled into research that would aid pacification.

Hickey's frustration over being heard but not listened to was reinforced by his testimony in Congress. On May 1, 1971, Hickey received an invitation from Senator J. William Fulbright to appear as a witness before his U.S. Senate Committee on Foreign Relations to be held on May 13 in conjunction with the McGovern-Hatfield Bill (Vietnam Disengagement Act of 1971), which called for a "safe and systematic withdrawal" of remaining U.S. forces by December 31, 1971. In Washington, Hickey had a cool reception at the RAND office because, according to him, he was advocating his accommodation-coalition concept. At the hearing, after Hickey read a statement, Fulbright asked how accommodations were implemented. Hickey responded that "it is a process of bargaining between two parties with mutual compromises to arrive at an agreement from which both sides benefit."[161] The hearing represented the last time Hickey "publicly advocated accommodation-coalition" as a means to end the war.[162]

During his trip to assess what RAND should be doing in Vietnam, Komer took the opportunity to travel around the country to check the progress of pacification. After he returned to the United States, Komer hastily put together the impressions he had gathered and sent them to a number of American officials in Washington and Saigon who had expressed an interest in getting his assessment of the situation.[163] His report brimmed with optimism. Returning to Vietnam 20 months after his depar-

---

[161] Hickey, *Window on a War*, 2002, p. 295.

[162] Hickey, *Window on a War*, 2002, p. 296. Although Hickey expressed frustration, his accommodation concept did provoke debate. In May 1969, Guy Pauker wrote a letter to Chuck Benoit, with a copy to David Elliott, in which he mentioned that Hickey's views on accommodation had been discussed at length within American official circles in Saigon. Pauker also said that, "There is much talk in Washington today of 'accommodation' as part of the settlement that will terminate the war in Vietnam." Pauker himself doubted that the Viet Cong would accept "the role of a permanent minority" and agreed with Elliott, who felt that "the probable question will be one of non-communist groups accommodating to the NLF rather than the reverse" and had expressed skepticism that "the Viet Cong will at some point find it in their interest to abandon coercive military action and agree to play out the rest of the game politically under rules that have been largely shaped by the GVN." However, since "the accommodation thesis persists," Pauker wanted to enlist Benoit to conduct research that would answer the question, "What does accommodation mean and how can this concept be translated into operationally meaningful negotiating points?" Elliott himself did not want to be part of this accommodation study—although he was willing to talk to Benoit—because, as he told Guy Pauker, "It seems to me to be totally impossible to [divine] the political intentions of non-communist individuals and groups . . . not only because Vietnamese don't talk to strangers about these things, but also because of the apparent assumptions on which it rests." However, Pauker's accommodation study did not appear to get off the ground.

[163] Komer later published his impressions in an internal RAND paper entitled "Vietnam Revisited," Santa Monica, Calif.: RAND Corporation, July 30, 1970 (not available to the general public).

ture in November 1968, Komer was struck by the remarkable physical improvements. Accompanied by Jim Digby, he traveled without escort to many places he had been unable to visit before. Together, they visited 20 provinces (out of over 40) from North to South, bypassing only the Central Highlands. They talked to a wide range of South Vietnamese military and civilian officials, from President Nguyen Van Thieu, Prime Minister Tran Thien Khiem, and corps commanders, to the chiefs of hamlets and leaders of Popular Forces platoons.

From this tour and official contacts, Komer concluded that the United States and the GVN had achieved military superiority over the enemy and had gained control over most of the population. Weakened by the heavy losses inflicted during and after the Tet Offensive, Hanoi had been forced to shift to a less costly strategy of protracted war, laying low and waiting for the United States to withdraw. The main problem confronting the United States at this juncture, therefore, was to find a way to secure and enhance the progress that had been achieved as the withdrawal gathered momentum. While he enthusiastically listed the achievements of pacification, Komer cautioned that the political struggle—to destroy the clandestine Viet Cong infrastructure and to consolidate the GVN position before Hanoi shifted from its strategy of protracted war or attempted to reach its goals through negotiations—was still far from being won. In his view, unless the United States changed its strategy and programs to respond to the enemy's own shift in strategy and unless it could win the political struggle, it may yet lose the gains that had been obtained at such high costs.

Overall, Komer went away with favorable impressions of the situation in South Vietnam. He noted a more quiescent enemy. The war was not finished, but its intensity had clearly dropped dramatically in most regions of Vietnam, with the exception of a few northern areas. Infiltration from the North had significantly declined from that of the year before, which was already low compared with 1968. At the same time, Viet Cong recruiting in the South had been reduced by pacification and by the expansion of the GVN's Regional, Local, and Self-Defense Forces—as well as by the GVN general mobilization [instituted under U.S. pressure after the Tet Offensive], which had absorbed most of the available rural manpower. The marked decrease in the strength of the Viet Cong Main Force and guerrilla forces led Komer to conclude that the military side of the Viet Cong insurgency had been basically defeated and that the war had become a war fought mainly by the North Vietnamese regular army.

As matters now stood, the GVN had a larger military force than that fielded by the Viet Cong, whose order of battle, including guerrillas, numbered only about 230,000. Although Komer attributed the improvement in the situation to U.S. and ARVN operations, which had pushed enemy Main Force units out of many rural areas, and to the exhaustion of the VC/NVA, he also gave credit to pacification. The contribution of pacification to this success was even more significant than he had "dared hope" when he left in November 1968.[164]

Throughout his travel in Vietnam, Komer saw many positive changes. According to him, the GVN had brought the majority of the rural population—over 91 percent—under varying degrees of control between November 1968, when he launched the accelerated pacification campaign, and July 1970. The establishment of security was allowing people to return in huge numbers to their former homes in areas that had been contested or controlled by the Viet Cong—in particular, in III Corps and the Mekong Delta. Even more significant, the VC now controlled only 1.4 percent of the population in the countryside, which meant that the Viet Cong had been denied a rural base from which they could draw recruits and political strength. The Regional, Popular, and People's Self-Defense Forces had come into their own as a "clear and hold" force and were denying the countryside to the enemy's local forces and guerrillas. Komer concluded, "Their notable expansion since Tet 1968 has made them the true nucleus of a People's Army."[165]

In the economic sphere, a true revolution was taking place in the countryside, mainly as a by-product of the war. Komer pointed out that agricultural production was being rapidly mechanized and noted that the number of tractors, trucks, water pumps, and boat motors had risen enormously; likewise, the use of fertilizers and miracle rice seeds was growing. The prosperity of the Delta farmers had turned them into the "new rich" of the South. The massive repair, building, and reconstruction of roads and waterways had facilitated pacification and brought economic benefits to the people in the countryside. The number of schools, health facilities, and markets had grown, and a wider range of services was being provided to the rural population. Village self-government had been revived. However, Komer cautioned that this trend was still uneven and that the military district chiefs—jealous of their own power—were loathe to grant autonomy to the villages.

Lastly, Komer called the government cabinet under Prime Minister Tran Thien Khiem "the most administratively competent yet."[166] Admitting that this was not saying much, Komer pointed out that at least the government was functioning "marginally better" and that there was a higher level of confidence among most officials he encountered.[167] To support his own optimistic assessment, Komer cited with approval what Bob Kaiser of *The Washington Post* had written on pacification. Kaiser argued that pacification gains could no longer be called "fragile," and that the saturating presence of the ARVN in the countryside and other improvements would make it unlikely that a weakened enemy could do no more than "perturb" the situation. Nevertheless,

---

[164] Komer, "Vietnam Revisited," 1970, p. 2.

[165] Komer, "Vietnam Revisited," 1970, p. 5.

[166] Komer, "Vietnam Revisited," 1970, p. 6.

[167] Komer, "Vietnam Revisited," 1970, p. 6.

Komer reported, American and South Vietnamese pacification authorities, fearing a slowing in momentum, had launched on July 1 a four-month special campaign to expand government control "into the last remaining VC-held populated areas."[168]

On the negative side of the ledger, Komer cited ineffectiveness in the Phoenix program and the need for the government to improve its image among the population by pushing land reform, helping veterans, and reducing corruption. Worrisome signs included wartime inflation, which had accelerated in 1970 and could destabilize the country. Komer found that ordinary Vietnamese in Saigon and in the provinces were more preoccupied with rising costs than ever before. The striking paradox, in Komer's view, was that while the threat to the GVN was becoming less military and more political and economic, the United States continued to expend most of its energy and resources on the military war. He lamented that, "We literally fire more ammo and drop more bombs in one day than the cost of our entire investment in *Phung Hoang* [Phoenix] for a solid year."[169] To him, it was this "strange discontinuity between our priority needs and our resource inputs" that had impeded progress in Vietnam.[170]

With regard to Vietnamization, Komer felt that the United States was "over-Americanizing" the South Vietnamese army and was creating a force that would be beyond the country's ability to sustain over the long haul. He advocated, instead, a militia-type "'People's Army,' backed by a much smaller professional force," which in his view might be the best solution for South Vietnam.[171] Finally, Komer noted that the United States was over-emphasizing material and logistics support and was not focusing enough on "improving leadership, training, and performance" of the South Vietnamese armed forces. There were some improvements, but desertion rates remained too high and the core problem of poor ARVN leadership persisted. Komer emphasized that, ultimately, better leadership within the ARVN, rather than money or material, would be key to making Vietnamization a success.

In conclusion, Komer recommended that the United States shift its priorities and resources to deal with the political/economic war; increase its support for economic stabilization; apply its decreasing leverage as it withdrew to improve GVN and ARVN leadership at key levels; make Phoenix a top priority; push land reform ("Land to the Tiller" program); resolve the growing conflict between the district chiefs and the

---

[168] Komer, "Vietnam Revisited," 1970, p. 9.

[169] Komer, "Vietnam Revisited," 1970, p. 3.

[170] Komer, "Vietnam Revisited," 1970, p. 3.

[171] Komer, "Vietnam Revisited," 1970, p. 4. The communists use the concept of a people's army (as in People's Army of Viet Nam [PAVN], the army of North Vietnam) to indicate that their army belongs to and serves the people, protecting and respecting them and not engaging in predatory behavior. Such a people's army includes main force units as well as guerrillas. Komer was advocating borrowing the name but he was not advocating duplicating the organization. The purpose of a South Vietnamese "people's army," as expanded later by Brian Jenkins, was mainly to reduce the size of the South Vietnamese army to make it more affordable for the South Vietnamese government to sustain—not necessarily to make the army serve the interests of the people better.

village administration; and upgrade the military and paramilitary forces—by paying them more and improving their living conditions, for example. He concluded by reiterating the two main points of his report: The situation in Vietnam had improved much more than many in the United States yet realized; and "timely and imaginative shifts in priority" to address current needs would contribute greatly to the consolidation of the gains that had been achieved.[172]

Komer's optimism was not unfounded. Between 1969 and 1970, statistics indicated that pacification had achieved impressive and unprecedented security gains throughout the country and contributed to the further weakening of the Viet Cong. At the end of 1969, for example, over 1,000 contested hamlets came under varying degrees of government control, and almost half of them were located in the critical Mekong Delta. With improved security, the GVN was able to hold elections of local officials, begin economic development, open roads, and increase the number and operations of its police, Regional/Local Forces, and militia. In the country at large, two-thirds of the population now lived in relatively secure areas. Such gains could bolster the GVN's claim that it had sovereignty over the territory and population of South Vietnam as it jockeyed with the Viet Cong and their North Vietnamese allies at the Paris peace talks and as it prepared for a cease-fire that would be based on the conflicting claims advanced by both sides regarding their control of the population in the countryside. At the same time, popular support seemed to increase with the implementation of the Land to the Tiller land reform, which had turned a large number of South Vietnamese into landowners with a bigger stake in the GVN's survival.

Meanwhile, weakened by losses, the enemy forces were unable to stop pacification. They opted to lie low, reverting to small-unit attacks and to political subversion and terrorism, thereby conserving their strength and waiting for the day when American troops completed their withdrawal. In February 1969, they tried to roll back pacification by launching an offensive, but the effect was limited. Between 1968 and 1972, then, prospects could not have appeared brighter for the South Vietnamese government.

Despite these impressive statistics, Komer failed to convince critics that pacification gains were real and solid and that the war was winnable. At the conclusion of APC, an assessment by the Nixon Administration concluded that the results were "inflated," because questions were raised about the reliability of the data used to show progress.[173] Officials in Washington also concluded that the improvements were "fragile," since they suspected that the GVN would not measure up and would be unable to consolidate its gains after the departure of American troops, who had been—as

---

[172] Komer, "Vietnam Revisited," 1970, p. 12.

[173] Hunt, *Pacification*, 1995, p. 202. Bing West and Charlie Benoit had reported how the HES data had been manipulated to indicate progress. After the war, William Colby himself would say that some of the statistics used to show results "were fairly soft, to put it mildly" (Hunt, *Pacification*, 1995, p. 206).

General Abrams put it, "bashing down the VC" so that the GVN could "raise its head up."[174] Some critics thought that the GVN lacked "the skills and resources" necessary to improve pacification and to cope with the political threat of the Viet Cong organization. Even Ambassador Ellsworth Bunker in Saigon thought that the GVN remained "plagued by inefficiency and corruption," and that it was still "not strong enough."[175] In the view of Washington critics, the achievements of the APC had been aided by circumstances that might not recur again: "heavy dependence on U.S. Army operations to keep enemy forces at bay and the absence of a strong challenge from the enemy."[176] They feared that the gains could be "gradually eroded" and could be "erased" if the communists chose to challenge the GVN with another offensive on the scale of Tet.

In another respect, Komer, along with Colby and Abrams, had also failed. They had hoped that APC achievements would convince the Nixon Administration that pacification could work and that the war could be won. But the Nixon Administration, desirous to put the war behind to focus on domestic issues, was not aiming for a military victory. Nixon did not wish to use pacification to win the war. He wanted to use pacification only to "press the enemy hard and force it to negotiate" and "to help America withdraw."[177]

Washington's critical assessment of the APC might have dampened Komer's optimism. In a September 1970 speech given at the Sixty-Sixth Annual Meeting of the American Political Science Association held at the Biltmore Hotel in Los Angeles,[178] he offered a more tempered view of pacification. He repeated the conclusions he had drawn earlier, but softened them with stronger qualifications. The "new model" pacification had contributed to short-term improvements in the GVN's position and ability to deal with the insurgency. However, Komer admitted that the degree of popular commitment to the government and the durability of the changes in the countryside were less apparent and far more difficult to measure than the physical changes, since no amount of data could quantify how the physical changes were affecting the hearts and minds of the rural population. There was no adequate way to infer answers to questions such as, "To what extent are any positive effects of pacification (improved security, economic revival, etc.) offset by the negative effects of how the GVN and U.S. have conducted the war? To what extent have coercion, corruption, or arbitrary use of power by GVN administrators taken the bloom off the rose?" It is worth noting that, in their own report, Bing West and Charlie Benoit provided some disheartening answers to such questions.

---

[174] Cited in Hunt, *Pacification*, 1995, p. 193.

[175] Hunt, *Pacification*, 1995, p. 202.

[176] Hunt, *Pacification*, 1995, p 203.

[177] Hunt, *Pacification*, 1995, p. 213.

[178] The text prepared for his speech was published in August 1970 as *Impact of Pacification on Insurgency in South Vietnam*, Santa Monica, Calif.: RAND Corporation, P-4443.

Komer cautioned that, although the insurgency was faltering under the pressure of pacification, the Viet Cong remained a potent force. Furthermore, it was difficult to infer whether pacification could in the long run create a social and political environment that could preclude the insurgency from rising again in the future. Meanwhile, the North Vietnamese regular units remained a threat that could be supported for an indefinite period with infiltration from the North. With regard to the upsurge in population under GVN control, Komer admitted that a high percentage of the growth in the "relatively secure" population in 1965–1967 happened not because of "increased security in the countryside" but, rather, "as a result of refugee movements and the accelerated urbanization taking place"—tacit acknowledgment by Komer that pacification progress had been gained at the cost of depopulation.[179]

Even in the short term, Komer said, "it is hard to assess the *relative* extent to which undoubted changes in the countryside can be properly attributed to the *pacification* program"[180] [emphasis in the original]. The big-unit war that drove the VC/NVA Main Forces from the most populated areas and the exhaustion of the enemy contributed largely to an environment in which pacification could achieve rapid gains from late 1968 to 1970. Other factors, such as the villagers' alienation from the VC because of harsh policies and their perception that the insurgents were not winning the war, also helped change the situation. Therefore, it would be hard to determine how much pacification had achieved relative to the effect of these other factors. Such developments as new NVA offensives, or political changes in Saigon, or the terms of a negotiated settlement might influence the final outcome in Vietnam.

At RAND, Guy Pauker—who had exhibited pessimism regarding South Vietnam's prospects over the years—found encouragement in the vastly improved situation. With the GVN appearing more in control and more able to take over the burdens of the war, Pauker thought that Vietnamization, one of the key components of President Nixon's strategy, held promise for American disengagement. In a paper published in March 1971, Pauker admitted that his new position represented a "drastic change" in his assessment of the outlook for the war and for the GVN.[181] Pauker had held a jaundiced view of the South Vietnamese elites and their political regime, believing that they lacked "civic morality" and would never be able to build a viable government and

---

[179] Komer, *Impact of Pacification on Insurgency in South Vietnam*, 1970, p. 13. However, even after factoring this in, the increase in population living in "relatively secure" areas was still significant. In "U.S. Strategy in South Vietnam: Extrication and Equilibrium" (Santa Monica, Calif.: RAND Corporation, D-19736-ARPA, December 15, 1969), Gerry Hickey wrote that, as of the end of 1969, there were 3-and-one-half million refugees out of a total population of 17 million. A large number of these refugees had moved into the cities, and this mass migration had created many problems. Hickey feared that these problems would be exacerbated if any kind of national crisis were to occur.

[180] Komer, *Impact of Pacification*, 1970, p. 11.

[181] Guy Pauker, *Essay on Vietnamization*, Santa Monica, Calif.: RAND Corporation, R-604-ARPA, March 1971.

nation. Now, Pauker believed that, after pouring resources into the country for five years, the United States may have succeeded in transforming the GVN into a regime that could survive if the United States continued to provide massive assistance.

Of the two options available to the United States to end its involvement in the war—negotiation and Vietnamization—Pauker believed that the GVN had a better chance of surviving under Vietnamization than under a negotiated settlement. Under a settlement, the communists would be allowed to participate in free elections, and being more organized and united, they would likely win over the fractious noncommunist groups. Under this scenario, then, the GVN would not survive political competition. Under Vietnamization, the GVN would stand a greater chance for survival, since it had become viable enough to withstand communist military pressure and, with continuing American military and economic aid, would be capable of keeping the communists from taking over by force. Several reasons gave cause for optimism. The South Vietnamese armed forces had grown to over 1 million men, four times the size of the communist forces, and they were now better equipped, with modern weaponry, artillery, and support helicopters, than the Viet Cong and the NVA. The massive pacification campaign had improved rural security and, by the end of 1970, had put 95 percent of the population in A, B, and C hamlets. Lastly, U.S. attacks in Cambodia and in Laos had boosted the self-confidence of the South Vietnamese military so that it might acquire the resilience to withstand severe blows that heretofore would have shattered it.

In Pauker's view, Vietnamization could work if U.S. and GVN policymakers understood and implemented the complex requirements for it to succeed. Pauker went on to list the prerequisites "in decreasing order of urgency in the short run but of increasing importance in the long run." First, the South Vietnamese armed forces should be trained and equipped well enough—but "not in accordance with abstract standards of perfection"—to prevent the NVA/VC from scoring substantial military successes in the future. Second, the government of President Thieu should consolidate its power, "not in accordance with Western political standards but in line with Vietnamese experience and capabilities." Third, the United States should support the economy of South Vietnam "probably for at least a decade," with policies that would be "compatible with the present political needs of the system." Finally, the GVN should make a genuine effort "to implement promised reforms and to combat flagrant cases of brutality and corruption" in order to nurture the hope "for social justice or at least the rule of law."[182]

According to an article in the *Los Angeles Times*, which appeared 18 months after RAND published Pauker's paper, the report was unclassified but was never released publicly after it was submitted to the Pentagon "for routine security review" in March

---

[182] Pauker, *Essay on Vietnamization*, 1971, p. 80.

1971.[183] A copy was later obtained by the Associated Press. Sources familiar with Pauker's study told the *Los Angeles Times* that it had attracted the attention of Washington officials, including Henry Kissinger. It is not clear, however, what Kissinger and other officials thought of it. At the time (the *Times* article was written in 1972), peace negotiations and Vietnamization continued to be the two main elements of Nixon's strategy for disengagement from Vietnam, so Pauker's assessment that a negotiated settlement would undermine Vietnamization was of interest to the author of the article. However, Pauker's conclusion that Vietnamization could succeed now appeared problematic, since events in Vietnam seemed to put the government of President Thieu in a more precarious situation: The communists had launched a major offensive, and Thieu had cracked down on political opposition, suspended elections in the provinces, and closed down several newspapers. Thieu was consolidating his power, a move that Pauker had endorsed, but he was not enacting the reforms that Pauker thought would be necessary.

One aspect of Vietnamization that Komer had mentioned—but not elaborated upon—was the reorganization of the South Vietnamese Army in order to strengthen it to fight the Viet Cong and North Vietnamese on its own. Komer had ventured the idea of turning the South Vietnamese armed forces into a People's Army—a military concept employed by the communists in North Vietnam and China. It was Brian M. Jenkins who picked up this notion and developed it into a report.[184] Borrowing a page out of the communist's book had been a frequent recourse as Americans tried to improve the GVN so that it could better compete with its enemy. Under American prodding, the GVN had used land reform to win popular support, hired former Viet Minh to apply communist political tactics, and borrowed aspects of communist organization—such as the creation of revolutionary development cadres who wore VC-like black pajamas and underwent communist-like training to inculcate in them zeal and dedication out of a belief that organization was what was driving Viet Cong success.

Jenkins was a doctoral candidate in history at UCLA and a former captain in the U.S. Special Forces when he was introduced by Gerry Hickey to RAND in Saigon. After serving in the military from December 1966 to December 1967, Jenkins had worked as a civilian member of Don Marshall's Long Range Planning Task Group at MACV, from October 1968 to July 1969. The concept of a People's Army for South Vietnam grew out of Komer's view, which was widely shared, that in building a South

---

[183] "Rand Study Calls Peace Talks and Vietnamization Incompatible," *Los Angeles Times*, October 17, 1972.

[184] Brian M. Jenkins, *A People's Army for South Vietnam: A Vietnamese Solution,* Santa Monica, Calif.: RAND Corporation, R-897-ARPA, November 1971.

Vietnamese army in its own image, the United States was creating an armed forces that would be too expensive for South Vietnam to sustain. The Preface to Jenkins' own report stated that he had spent the first four months of 1971 performing research for this study, as a member of the Social Science Department. It added that the South Vietnamese themselves, realizing that they could not afford to replicate the American army, had increasingly discussed the creation of a People's Army as a possible solution to cope with a protracted war and to prepare themselves for the day when American support declined. In his acknowledgment, Jenkins did not credit Komer with the concept, but wrote that he had played an active role in the development of the research and of the final report.

According to Jenkins, many South Vietnamese civilian officials and military officers were considering the concept of a People's Army as an organization more appropriate to their country's requirements and resources, and there were indications that the South Vietnamese were moving toward creating such an army because they had no other alternative.[185] However, two colonels—Quynh and Nhan—of the ARVN joint general staff told Don Marshall that they were uncomfortable with the term "People's Army" and with its ideological implications, since the only people's armies in existence belonged to communist countries. Furthermore, they told Marshall that the People's Army was a good concept but that South Vietnam "cannot and will not apply the full aspects of the communist system" and that the South Vietnamese army must have the mobility and firepower of a modern army and not just the rifles of a People's Army.[186] Nevertheless, Jenkins gave extensive briefings about this concept to representatives of NSC, JCS, Joint Staff, ISA, the Army Staff in Washington, CINCPAC, and U.S. Army of the Pacific (USARPAC) headquarters in Honolulu. That a People's Army for South Vietnam never came to pass indicates that the concept was found to be unworkable and that a People's Army—that of the communists—already existed in the country.

The objective of Jenkins' report was to examine the concept, suggest how it could be implemented, and estimate the costs and savings from its implementation. As constituted at the time, the South Vietnamese army was beyond the country's ability to

---

[185] Jenkins had discussed the concept in earlier papers. In "The Politics of a People's Army," D-20531-ARPA, dated July 20, 1970, Jenkins wrote that the concept of a People's Army had been advanced by a number of people with different political motives. For President Thieu, it was to "counterbalance" the power of the Corps commanders. For Senator Tran Van Don, an advocate of the "third force"—an alternative between the NLF and the GVN—a People's Army would be an alternative to the ARVN and the communist forces. For Colonel Nguyen Be, a former Viet Minh recruited to command the training school for Revolutionary Development cadres, a People's Army would consist of highly motivated cadres who would "build and defend their communities as well as fight against the corruption on the government side." Jenkins acknowledged that senior ARVN commanders opposed the concept of a People's Army as an attempt to intrude into their *satrapies* [areas under their command] and to cut back their authority and power. (Jenkins also discussed the People's Army for the South in "Vietnamization: Divergent Views," February 17, 1970.)

[186] This conversation was recorded in a memo of July 8, 1970, of the Long Range Planning Group.

sustain in the long run. Created originally by the United States to fight what it feared would be an invasion from the North, it was a conventional army that had become over-reliant on lavish, expensive, and destructive artillery and air support. The war would continue long after American troops went home, and, fighting in the manner to which it had become accustomed, this army would exhaust the country's resources in a protracted conflict. It had been kept afloat by American aid, but the U.S. Congress might not keep giving South Vietnam $3 billion a year to pay for the war and subsidize the economy. Even with this massive aid, South Vietnam was facing serious economic problems, and unless this army was reorganized to require fewer resources, it could threaten the country with collapse.[187]

In his report, Jenkins harked back to Vietnamese history, rather than to communist organization, as the source of inspiration for the concept of a People's Army, to avoid the communist connotation, which bothered the South Vietnamese higher command. Among the historical precedents he invoked was Admiral Tran Hung Dao of the thirteenth century, who built an army based on popular support to repel an invasion from China, then under Mongol rule. So, centuries before Mao Tse-tung formulated the concept of a people's war, the Vietnamese had recognized that winning the people to their side was crucial to victory in warfare. To gain popular support in the current context, Jenkins recommended a "territorial force" with the responsibility for defending their own local areas. In addition, to ensure popular support for operations—at least for those of smaller size—village defense committees that included local military and civilian leaders and notables should be set up to give advice for or against certain military operations in their areas, explain the goals, and obtain the support of the people. Other historical precedents Jenkins invoked were the concepts of a rotational active-duty reserve and the establishment of military colonies in abandoned strategic areas.

The People's Army that Jenkins proposed would consist of lightly armed soldiers tasked with defending their own local areas. As Komer had pointed out, South Vietnam already has an "incipient" people's army in the guise of the People's Self-Defense Forces, Popular Forces, and Regional Forces, which together numbered about 4 million part-time or full-time local soldiers. Jenkins suggested a three-phase program to

---

[187] In a July 1969 speech, Jenkins criticized the U.S. Army, the model for the ARVN, for using doctrine, tactics, organization, and weapons more suited to conventional warfare in Europe than to Vietnam. His talk was later issued as *The Unchangeable War*, RM-6278-1-ARPA in September 1972 because—as the Preface stated—the topic remained relevant. In his view, the Army resisted changes because it believed that they might not work; that current strategy was working; that change was unnecessary because *more* was available; that organizational changes were impossible in the midst of war; that the Vietnam War was "an aberration" and did not "represent the future"; and that new doctrines were "exotic" and of "marginal importance." Additional inhibiting factors included the commanders' performance review, which was still based on the orthodox criteria of a conventional army fighting a conventional war—in Vietnam, the number of enemy killed was used as a criterion for effectiveness, particularly at the battalion level; and institutional loyalty, which rejected external pressure for change. According to the Preface, his paper elicited both favorable and critical responses in the defense establishment.

combine these forces, make them more effective, and turn them into a People's Army that would be inexpensive to support and stay within the country's means. Eventually, the people's army would assume most of the burden of defending South Vietnam and, therefore, allow the regular armed forces to be reduced in size. It is in the first phase that these three types of forces would be combined immediately under a single command and renamed officially the People's Army. In Jenkins's view, even just changing the name would be symbolically important, since it would force people to view the People's Army as something distinct from the ARVN.

In a People's Army, the local soldiers would defend their own territory under the command of local officers, rather than officers who came from the urban areas, as they were at the moment. At the same time, the fighting capabilities of the People's Self-Defense Forces would be improved by encadreing them with a small number of veterans drawn from the ARVN, by providing them with better training, and by supplying them with more small arms and weapons, such as light machine guns and small mortars. Measures would be taken to prepare for the day when parts of the regular army would be demobilized, such as the creation of a reserve to be attached to existing Regional and Popular Forces units and the establishment of *don dien*, or military-agricultural colonies in strategic areas, a concept that the Vietnamese had used in their history. Volunteer soldiers would be grouped in units of company size and would settle with their families in these colonies to farm. However, they would continue to bear arms and be placed under military command. By using the *don dien*, South Vietnam could avoid complete demobilization while keeping parts of its army engaged in productive agricultural work.

In the second phase—probably sometime in 1973—as the People's Army could shoulder a larger defensive burden, the ARVN army could start to demobilize soldiers who could readily find employment. The rest should be given vocational training part-time to acquire employable skills, so that they could find jobs once they were demobilized, to lessen the likelihood of high unemployment and social unrest as thousands of them were released into the economy. At the same time, an urban auxiliary militia of part-time soldiers could be created to take over some of the regular tasks usually undertaken by full-time soldiers, so that more could be demobilized. To avoid heavy reliance on heavy air and artillery support, which would become necessary in only rare large attacks, the South Vietnamese would have to change their tactics to rely more on maneuvering small units.

The People's Army would mature in the third phase, possibly around 1975, at which point ARVN ranks could be substantially reduced. When it became fully formed, the People's Army would include a large People's Self-Defense Force reinforced with veterans from the ARVN, supported by a territorial force of 300,000–400,000 full-time local soldiers, and backed by a much smaller regular army. By maintaining a presence in all the populated areas, the People's Army would be able to prevent an enemy buildup for a large, Tet Offensive–scale campaign against population centers.

Meanwhile, as the People's Army freed it from static defense, the mobile, highly professional regular army could be sent into the most vulnerable areas of the country should the enemy mount an offensive there. In addition, the South Vietnamese might revert to a rotational system for the reserves, which they had used in their history. Under this system, the reserves would be divided into units that would take turns going on active duty. Those not on active duty would engage in seasonal agricultural production.

As the People's Army grew in strength, the regular army could gradually be reduced to 300,000 men—a goal mentioned by President Thieu. The downsizing would save $640 million a year. These savings would not end South Vietnam's dependence on U.S. assistance, but demobilization would allow thousands of men to resume productive roles in the South Vietnamese economy, thereby reducing the country's reliance on American economic aid. Jenkins thought that opposition would likely come from the regular army, particularly senior South Vietnamese officers, who might regard the People's Army as a threat to their military authority and political power, which they derived from their command of large units. Beyond intensifying a sense of urgency among the South Vietnamese, the United States should play a restrained but constructive role in the formation of the People's Army by providing material support and nudging the South Vietnamese in this direction.

A footnote was added later to the Preface of the report to update it in view of the changed circumstances in Vietnam. It mentioned that, in the nine-month interval since Jenkins wrote the paper and briefed its conclusions to government officials, the North Vietnamese had launched a major conventional attack across the DMZ.[188] In view of this development, the footnote added that the most pressing defense problem for South Vietnam at the time was clearly not protracted war. However, even if the North Vietnamese forces could be driven back, Hanoi and the Viet Cong would be unlikely to completely give up their attempt to conquer South Vietnam. The South would, therefore, continue to confront threats that ranged from conventional attacks to low-level guerrilla warfare, and would still have to face the underlying problem of defending themselves with reduced American support—a problem that could become even more severe.

---

[188] The offensive the footnote alluded to was called the Spring Offensive by the communists, but became known as the Easter Offensive because of the time of the year when it took place in 1972. It began in March, after a massive artillery barrage, followed by attacks across the DMZ into Quang Tri Province carried out by an estimated 15,000 North Vietnamese troops supported with armored vehicles, artillery, and mobile anti-aircraft guns. In addition, a reinforced PAVN division pushed toward Hue. Several PAVN divisions advanced from Laos and Cambodia into the Central Highlands. There were also attacks in III Corps and in the Mekong Delta. Within a week, half of Quang Tri Province fell into the hands of the PAVN, as did Loc Ninh in III Corps, and the South Vietnamese positions near Hue came under heavy pressure. The performance of ARVN officers and troops was mixed: "Whole units surrendered, others were defeated, large numbers fought poorly or joined refugees fleeing the advance, but many also held their ground." Only massive American bombings, especially those by B-52s, saved the day for the South Vietnamese. In addition, President Nixon ordered air attacks in the North against several targets, including those near Hanoi. U.S. official analysts thought that, had it not been for massive American air intervention in the South, the communists could have won the war at the time.

In the end, however, the topic of a People's Army would not be pursued.[189] Indifference to the concept within the U.S. military and resistance from the South Vietnamese armed forces, as well as the reversion to large-unit attacks by the enemy, effectively torpedoed the idea.

In 1969, as some RAND analysts discussed facets of pacification and Vietnamization, the Nixon Administration had to confront the reality that the president's strategy of gradual troop withdrawal and continued negotiation with Hanoi was not bringing the United States closer to ending the war. In Paris, North Vietnamese negotiators remained opposed to the Nixon Administration's demands that both the United States and the DRV withdraw forces from the South; that the NLF abandon "the use of force" as a precondition for participation in South Vietnamese politics while allowing the Thieu regime to remain in power; and that elections held after mutual troop withdrawal be supervised by an international body—a measure the NLF rejected as undue "foreign interference."[190] At the same time, the DRV's insistence on the removal of the Thieu regime—in its counter-proposal—was unacceptable to the United States on the grounds that the United States could not overthrow an allied government.

Since North Vietnam had remained—in Henry Kissinger's view—intransigent at the Paris talks, Kissinger thought the United States should push Hanoi toward a "rapid negotiated compromise" with intense military action.[191] At the order of Nixon and Kissinger, a military contingency plan known as "Duck Hook" was developed in September 1969 from an earlier plan devised in April 1969, when Nixon began to contemplate a "program of mining Haiphong to look tough."[192] At a September meeting with his staff to whom he gave the task of developing the contingency military plan, Kissinger told them that their assignment was to "examine the option of a savage, decisive blow against North Vietnam, which would push North Vietnam—"a little fourth-rate power"—to the breaking point.[193]

"Duck Hook" called for the resumption of the bombing of North Vietnam, targeting important military and economic sites, and the mining of ports and harbors.[194]

---

[189] It was raised again in March 1972 by Jim Digby and John P. White, RAND's vice president, as a possible topic of study for the CIA. Digby and White were looking for an additional source of revenue for RAND after the Defense Department cut $3 million from a budget of $25 million following congressional reduction of "certain Defense appropriations." William Colby, now CIA director, turned down their proposal, saying that the agency was also experiencing budget cuts and that "from time to time we do have need for external research on a technical level but that on an over-all analytical and substantive level we probably would be inclined to do most of our work in-house." See proposal attached to a letter of March 31, 1972, from John P. White, RAND's vice president, to William Colby, and Colby's "Memorandum for the Record" of February 25, 1972.

[190] Cited in Kimball, *Nixon's Vietnam War*, 1998, p. 147.

[191] Kimball, *Nixon's Vietnam War*, 1988, p. 159.

[192] Kimball, *Nixon's Vietnam War*, 1988, p. 159.

[193] Kimball, *Nixon's Vietnam War*, 1988, p. 163.

[194] Cited in Kimball, *Nixon's Vietnam War*, 1998, p. 164.

Duck Hook also included contingency planning for "an invasion of North Vietnam, the bombing of Red River dikes, and the blockading of Sihanoukville."[195] Some of these planned actions, such as the resumption of bombing of the North and the mining of the port of Haiphong, had been mentioned as options in the Iklé memo of February 1969. Under the Duck Hook scenario, after a four-day attack, a pause would be instituted to allow the DRV to respond. If Hanoi failed to accede to U.S. peace terms, another four-day attack would follow. The pattern would repeat until Hanoi agreed to diplomatic concessions. Kissinger envisaged that Duck Hook would commence on November 1—hence it was also referred to as the "November Option." However, Nixon decided against Duck Hook in October, fearing that it would inflame domestic and world opinion and damage his diplomacy with the Soviet Union and Communist China without fundamentally changing the military and political situation in South Vietnam.

By October 1969, the month in which he asked Sir Robert Thompson to visit Vietnam and assess the situation, Nixon had become more anxious about his ability to end the war quickly before it became "his war." He felt that time was running out. As he told Haldeman, he had "bought nine months" and "kept the doves at bay," but he did not "expect to get any more time."[196] He was caught in a dilemma. He felt that he had to withdraw U.S. troops in large enough numbers to placate American public opinion, but not in too large numbers to undermine Vietnamization and Hanoi's incentive to negotiate.[197] He thought he needed Duck Hook to quickly end the war, yet he also believed that if he implemented it he would be unable to "hold the government and the people together."[198]

The death of Ho Chi Minh on September 2, 1969, at the age of 79 briefly gave Nixon the hope that Ho's passing would bring a change of attitude in Hanoi. However, subsequent speeches and a statement made by General Vo Nguyen Giap, victor over the French at Dien Bien Phu, seemed to dispel this notion. Kissinger interpreted what Giap had said as an indication that Hanoi was not going to give up its struggle, and that it retained its faith in a protracted struggle as an efficient strategy to defeat the United States and its technological superiority. In January 1970, Kissinger sent President Nixon a report summarizing Giap's message and pointed out that the enemy

---

[195] Cited in Kimball, *Nixon's Vietnam War*, 1998, p. 164.

[196] Cited in Kimball, *Nixon's Vietnam War*, 1998, p. 169.

[197] By April 1970, the number of U.S. troops withdrawn would reach 115,500. See Kimball, *Nixon's Vietnam War*, 1998, p. 182.

[198] Kimball, *Nixon's Vietnam War*, 1988, p. 169.

the United States faced remained determined. Kissinger wrote, "the North Vietnamese cannot have fought for 25 years only to call it quits without another major effort."[199]

At RAND, Mel Gurtov analyzed Giap's speeches and statement, concluding that there actually had been some wavering within the DRV leadership regarding the level of support for the South, and that Giap's objective, in fact, was to argue for continued commitment to a protracted-war strategy—at a time when some leaders were favoring reducing material support for the South and devoting more resources to rebuilding the North after the cessation of U.S. bombing.[200] Giap insisted that a protracted-war strategy in the South and North would be viable, and called on the North to remain alert and to prepare for a resumption of U.S. attacks by modernizing the army and by reinforcing air defense in particular, because, in his view, the U.S. threat was ever-present.

Giap argued that the war efforts waged by the North and South had "shattered American belief in the infallibility of modern weapons and air and naval power" and forced the United States to admit that it had failed in its "limited-war strategy," to enter into negotiations with the National Liberation Front, and to de-Americanize the war.[201] It was American failure that had forced the United States to negotiate and to begin disengagement. Whereas some American observers believed that the communists in the South were retreating into guerrilla warfare because they had lost the Main Force war, Giap believed that guerrilla warfare was only one element in a flexible military strategy for the South. Far from retreating, Giap said, in the future, it would be critical to maintain initiative on the battlefield and remain on the offensive to adhere to the ideology of revolutionary warfare and to sustain troop morale.

The flexible strategy he called for involved attacking by using all types of forces (Main, Regional, and guerrilla) in all areas (mountains, Delta, cities), and carrying out operations of all scales (small, medium, and large). By fighting "relentlessly, resolutely, continuously, comprehensively, and with every force available," the strategy of "opposing a maximal force with a minimal force" could bring success.[202] To successfully pave the way for "the regular war to defeat the enemy,"[203] Giap called for developing guerrilla war "to a very high level"; in other words, according to Gurtov, the emphasis was on "guerrilla warfare as the key to protracted resistance and a war of attrition."[204] Giap added, "We can defeat the enemy in a protracted war . . . provided military and politi-

---

[199] Cited in Kimball, *Nixon's Vietnam War*, 1998, p. 182.

[200] Melvin Gurtov, "Some Recent Statements by North Vietnamese Leaders: General Giap," which was published on March 10, 1970, as D-20026-ARPA/AGILE.

[201] Gurtov, "Some Recent Statements by North Vietnamese Leaders," 1970, p. 1.

[202] Gurtov, "Some Recent Statements by North Vietnamese Leaders," 1970, pp. 1–2.

[203] Gurtov, "Some Recent Statements by North Vietnamese Leaders," 1970, p. 2.

[204] Gurtov, "Some Recent Statements by North Vietnamese Leaders," 1970, p. 3.

cal struggle are coordinated, attacks are continuous and widespread, and the communist forces retain the initiative."[205] Finally, Giap voiced the belief that "Protracted resistance will eventually compel the Americans to abandon their latest strategy."[206]

In his January 1970 report to Nixon, Kissinger also questioned recent optimistic assessments of the fighting capabilities of the South Vietnamese armed forces. At Kissinger's recommendation, Nixon sent a team of analysts to evaluate the situation in Vietnam. The team, led by General Alexander Haig, Kissinger's military assistant, toured several key provinces for ten days in January and reported that "There is no sign that the enemy has given up" and that U.S. troop withdrawals might lead to "a deterioration of territorial security force performance and a loss of popular support for the GVN."

The fact that the enemy had not given up led Konrad Kellen and Brian Jenkins to try to discern the reasons they kept on fighting. In a paper prepared for delivery at the Southeast Asia Development Advisory Group meeting in New York on May 8, 1971,[207] Konrad Kellen reiterated his belief that North Vietnam was totally committed and was unlikely to abandon its efforts, and he provided an analysis of why it would keep on fighting. Kellen concluded that what had sustained the enemy was the strength and confidence of the leaders, as well as "the extraordinary cohesion, resilience and apparently unwavering dedication on the part of the people, soldiers and civilians, and their firm conviction that they had absolutely no choice but to endure the hardships of what seemed [to] them an entirely defensive war against a foreign invader. . . ."[208]

According to Kellen, the confidence of the Hanoi leaders was fueled by their past successes and their interpretation of Marxist-Leninist theories, which—in their view—showed "incontrovertibly that the war will end, if not in formal victory, at least in a departure of the Americans, followed by a united though not altogether unified Vietnam."[209] This outcome would materialize because of the "contradictions" that were diluting the power of the United States and undermining its efforts in Vietnam: the contradiction between the American imperialists and Vietnamese national liberators; the contradiction between the American people and their government; and the contradiction between Washington and Saigon, where the government was weakened and compromised by its association with a foreign power.

To Brian Jenkins, the reasons Hanoi kept fighting were rooted not only in the leaders' adherence to communist ideology but also in their Confucian background, their unwillingness to give up a mission that had inspired them for decades, and their

---

[205]Gurtov, "Some Recent Statements by North Vietnamese Leaders," 1970, p. 4.

[206]Gurtov, "Some Recent Statements by North Vietnamese Leaders," 1970, p. 1.

[207]Later published in June 1971 as *1971 and Beyond: The View from Hanoi*, Santa Monica, Calif.: RAND Corporation, P-4634-1.

[208]Kellen, *1971 and Beyond*, 1971, pp. 16–17.

[209]Kellen, *1971 and Beyond*, 1971, p. 4.

country's historical resistance to foreign domination. Whereas Kellen believed that Marxist-Leninist theories gave the Hanoi leaders confidence in a final favorable outcome, Jenkins thought it was the belief that they possessed the "Mandate of Heaven"—the Confucian concept of legitimacy and the right to rule—that provided the source of this confidence.[210] The Hanoi leaders combined their belief in their "Mandate of Heaven" with a strategy taken straight out of Vietnamese tradition, which relied on protracted warfare, persistence, and time, to fight opponents who were stronger either in number, such as the Chinese, or in technology, such as the French.

In warfare, the Vietnamese ignored their own losses and kept on fighting, depriving their enemy of victory and forcing them to keep winning until they decided that they could not reasonably continue to incur losses themselves and withdrew. The Vietnamese might agree to negotiate, but negotiating to them was just part of fighting: to obtain a truce to regroup in order to fight another day. In Jenkins's view, the U.S. belief that North Vietnam's enormous losses would make it give up its objective in the near future should be carefully examined.

With the enemy persisting in fighting for what they perceived as a just cause and refusing to accept the peace terms that Nixon was willing to propose, Nixon's hopes of ending the war in 1969 evaporated. Although the war remained one of America's most pressing national security issues, it became less and less the subject of study at RAND. The strategic options paper and NSSM-1 done by Daniel Ellsberg for Kissinger at the beginning of the Nixon Administration marked the last high point of RAND's output on Vietnam. Works that were produced by analysts familiar with Vietnam—Komer, Kellen, Gurtov, Pauker, Jenkins, and West—began to decline in frequency and significance. Part of the reason pertained to RAND's own internal situation and dynamics, but the main reason was lack of interest from DoD clients as the war wound down from its height under the Johnson Administration, when RAND's research was most in demand. On the civilian side in Washington, while Vietnam remained a pressing issue for the White House, Kissinger, now at the center of policy, had set up his own Vietnam Working Group within the National Security Council soon after coming into office to provide him with the analyses he needed to formulate strategies, thus obviating the need to go outside for expert research—let alone, advice. The one exception was the revived Dinh Tuong project, which the Vietnam Working Group commissioned from David Elliott, now pursuing his doctorate degree at Cornell University, with RAND acting as a facilitator.

---

[210] See Brian M. Jenkins, *Why the North Vietnamese Keep Fighting*, Santa Monica, Calif.: RAND Corporation, P-4395, August 1970.

The Vietnam Working Group was headed by Larry Lynn, who had been one of the top deputies to Alain Enthoven in Systems Analysis. Robert Sansom, a Rhodes Scholar who worked for Larry Lynn at the time, recalled that the entire focus of his group was to try to figure out what was happening at the ground level in the country-side in Vietnam—in particular, with respect to the *war of local control*, a new descriptor for *pacification*, to meet Kissinger's interest right after assuming his post.[211] Lynn's job was to analyze Vietnam for Kissinger. "We spent a whole lot of time trying to analyze the war," Sansom said, "and who was winning, and what our chances were." By this time, General Creighton Abrams had assumed command of MACV and the war of local control—"hearts and minds, and all that stuff"—was no longer controversial. The military, Sansom said, "had internalized it as part of the strategy, how it related to Vietnamization."[212]

According to Sansom (mentioned previously in Chapter Five), the period from 1969 to 1971, when he left the National Security Council, was very intense and Vietnam was a burning issue. He made repeated trips to Vietnam with Lynn or with General Alexander Haig. His Vietnam Working Group produced numerous papers that, in his view, captured the situation in Vietnam. Sansom himself was familiar with Vietnam, having spent time there on several occasions during the Johnson years to conduct his own research for a doctoral dissertation on the economics of insurgency in the Mekong Delta. Also, Sansom had numerous contacts in Vietnam, people whom he felt confident understood the situation well, such as John Paul Vann or USAID province advisors, and he would talk to them directly during trips he made with Lynn or with Haig. "We knew so many people," he recalled, and whenever they came to Washington, "we'd talk directly with them." Kissinger, for his part—according to Sansom—"had his own set of individuals" who would drop by the White House to talk to him about Vietnam. So, Sansom felt that they were getting not just institutional positions but individual viewpoints, as well. He said, "We obviously felt we were experienced, we knew the people in Vietnam, we knew who to reach out for."[213]

Sansom had become familiar with the RAND interviews conducted by David Elliott and his team in Dinh Tuong when he was performing his doctoral research. To him, those interviews were "the gold standard." He remembered that reading the interviews, "You had the feeling that you can get the fine grain of what was going on. You get these people to describe their lives. It wasn't just the military component, it was the economic component, the social component."[214] To him, the interviews provided "an introduction to the reality of it, what's on the ground," and he remembered "how utterly mesmerized" he was "by the facts and the details and the lives of the Viet

---

[211] Author interview with Robert Sansom, 2005.

[212] Author interview with Robert Sansom, 2005.

[213] Author interview with Robert Sansom, 2005.

[214] Author interview with Robert Sansom, 2005.

Cong."[215] Now, assigned the responsibility of figuring out the situation in the country-side, Sansom became interested in sponsoring David Elliott's return to Dinh Tuong to perform a follow-up study.

By this time, Elliott had finished his course work at Cornell and had obtained a grant to go to Vietnam to conduct research for his dissertation—a comparative analysis of the Chinese and Vietnamese communist revolutions—by interviewing North Vietnamese defectors who could shed light on conditions in the North. To do so, however, Elliott needed to get theater clearance, which could be obtained only with official sponsorship. Elliott had approached Guy Pauker and Bill Stewart at RAND in 1969, but had been turned down by Frank Hoeber, Fred Iklé's deputy in the Social Science Department. In a letter to Elliott, dated April 11, 1969, Hoeber explained that, "The cutback in our interviewing efforts and work in this area does indeed appear to preclude this enterprise at this time."

So, Elliott approached Bob Sansom about doing a six-month study that would be a follow-up to his 1965–1967 Dinh Tuong project. Elliott's plan was to stay on after he completed this project, to conduct his doctoral research. Sansom was very interested in the follow-up study and commissioned it with the understanding that, after its completion, Elliott would pursue his own research. Through Sansom, the National Security Council arranged for RAND to administer the project. Elliott recalled that, "This was not a project that RAND had proposed or in any of their priority studies. RAND was simply selected as an organization of convenience to manage this project for the NSC—for Sansom."[216] With the National Security Council expressing support, Fred Iklé gave his endorsement.[217]

To finalize the study, Elliott submitted a proposal to Sansom, who wrote back on July 9, 1970, that it looked "superb" and that he could not add anything to it. However, the project could not get off the ground, because MACV denied the theater clearance and rejected the study.[218] As Elliott recalled, "MACV's position was that it knew everything that was going on in Vietnam, that this study would duplicate existing efforts, wouldn't add anything to American understanding of the situation, and would tax

---

[215] Author interview with Robert Sansom, 2005.

[216] Author interview with David Elliott, 2006.

[217] In response to an April 5, 1970, letter from Elliott describing the two studies, Iklé wrote that, "Both are of great interest and could turn into excellent projects." He added, "We are right now trying to line up support . . . and will be in touch with you shortly. I am fairly confident that one of these studies, if not both, can be undertaken more or less along the lines you propose."

[218] Telegram of December 7, 1970, from Col. E. M. Gershater, Director, OSD/ARPA RDFU-V to RUEKJCS SEC/DEF, stating that "MACV had disapproved the ARPA proposal for the Elliott study of the NLF structure and policies in the Dinh Tuong Province."

MACV's over-strained administrative resources to deal with it, so they didn't approve it. That was their reasoning."[219]

The logjam was finally broken when General Alexander Haig delivered a message from the National Security Council to MACV, asking that the project be approved. A memo found in the National Archives indicated it was Wayne Smith—Larry Lynn's replacement on the National Security Council after Lynn resigned over the Cambodia invasion in 1970—who had intervened to get the project going by asking Haig on one of his trips to Vietnam to carry his message to Saigon.[220] The memo to Haig, dated December 11, 1970, carried a notation in bold letters, "**Urgent Action for Your Trip**," and addressed the subject of "David Elliott's Study of the Viet Cong in Dinh Tuong."[221] Smith mentioned that Elliott had produced "some of this government's best analytical work on the Viet Cong in his RAND studies of 1965–67." Smith added that Elliott had "proposed to update his earlier work" and that the Vietnam Special Studies Group had "strongly urged him to do so." Smith emphasized that Elliott's study would be "an important contribution to our current knowledge on VCI [Viet Cong Infrastructure] strength and activities" and concluded by asking Haig to raise the issue with General Abrams, stressing that, "If we don't get this turned around ASAP, we will lose Elliott and the study."

The theater clearance came through, and Elliott and his wife returned to Vietnam in February 1971. Although an interim report Elliott later produced stated that Elliott was a RAND consultant working in Vietnam under the auspices of ARPA, Elliott got no assistance whatsoever to get his project under way, beyond being allowed to use the RAND office at the ARPA compound and getting limited administrative support. Elliott had to "essentially organize this thing more or less" by himself, since there was no RAND presence on the ground. To set up the project, Elliott had to rely on Vuong Van Bach, one of his interviewers, and Bach's Vietnamese contacts, who got Elliott access to the *Chieu Hoi* center in My Tho. If he had had to rely on MACV or the embassy, "we probably would still be waiting," Elliott would later recall.[222]

---

[219] Telegram of December 7, 1970, from Col. E. M. Gershater, Director, OSD/ARPA RDFU-V to RUEKJCS SEC/DEF. Elliott recalled that "I didn't know until later how serious the problems were, and eventually the request for theater clearance was denied." Elliott subsequently saw—probably at RAND—a stack of correspondence about an inch thick "comprised mainly of cables between MACV and ARPA, or somebody in ISA" regarding his theater clearance.

[220] Elliott heard that Haig delivered the message right upon his landing in Saigon, to a "MACV person" on the tarmac of Tan Son Nhut Airport. Telegram of December 7, 1970, from Col. E. M. Gershater, Director, OSD/ARPA RDFU-V to RUEKJCS SEC/DEF.

[221] Wayne Smith identified Elliott as the son of Henry Kissinger's mentor and former Harvard professor, William Y. Elliott. Smith pointed out that DoD supported the study, but MACV had just "turned down the proposal after dragging out their review for months (in the hope, undoubtedly, that Elliott would give up)," without giving any reasons for their rejection. The refusal "was signed by Chief of Staff Dolvin."

[222] Author interview with David Elliott, 2006.

Elliott reassembled his old team of interviewers and eventually conducted 100 interviews covering over 40 villages out of the 96 in the province, representing each district, as well as several extensive interviews conducted with cadres operating in the urban areas. He concluded his field research in early September 1971. Using information gathered from the first batch of 70 interviews and HES data, Elliott produced an interim report in August 1971,[223] which RAND distributed, even though it had not gone through the usual review procedure, because, as the Preface explained, the trends that it detected "should be of immediate interest to policymakers involved in assessing the progress of the pacification program."[224]

In November, Elliott sent a final draft report to Frank Hoeber, who had been assigned as his contact in Santa Monica. Then, on January 27, 1972, Elliott wrote an extensive memo to Major Smith, MACV's liaison to ARPA, summarizing his six-month research from March to August 1971. This memo incorporates the conclusions he had reached in the interim paper, as well as in his final draft report, which was never published due to internal developments at RAND. In his memo to Major Smith, Elliott described and analyzed the changes that had occurred since he completed his previous research in 1965–1967, and he attempted to "assess the prospects of the NLF" in Dinh Tuong Province. According to Elliott, the introduction of U.S. combat forces into the Delta and the Tet Offensive had drastically altered the situation in the province. However, the NLF was hanging on and, with latent popular support, might be able to recover and revive their movement after the withdrawal of American troops.

The most profound changes had been wrought by the U.S. 9th Division. With their aggressive tactics and mobility, American troops had inflicted heavy casualties on the Viet Cong. However, the U.S. operations had also brought suffering to the civilian population caught in the war zones. To seek safety, villagers fled Viet Cong areas, which became "largely depopulated during the most intensive and destructive phase of operations in 1968–1969."[225] Consequently, "At a tragic cost in civilian lives and property, the separation of fish and water was achieved, and the NLF sources of materiel and manpower sharply diminished."[226]

---

[223]David W. P. Elliott, "Dinh Tuong Revisited: First Impressions of Viet Cong Responses to Pacification," Santa Monica, Calif.: RAND Corporation, WN-7534-ARPA, August 1971.

[224]Elliott, "Dinh Tuong Revisited," 1971, p. ii.

[225]David Elliott, memo to Major Smith, January 27, 1972, p. 3.

[226]Elliott, memo to Major Smith, January 27, 1972, p. 3. In this period, the 9th Division launched a major operation—SPEEDY EXPRESS—to support the APC. SPEEDY EXPRESS, with its use of excessive force, bore the hallmark of its commander, General Julian Ewell, who believed that "maximum pressure on the enemy boosted pacification more than anything else, that 'the only way to overcome VC control and terror is by brute force.'" Ewell used the body count to measure the success of this operation. See Richard Hunt's *Pacification*, 1995, p. 189. SPEEDY EXPRESS relied on the heavy use of airpower, artillery, and helicopter gunships. The casualty ratio, according to the division, was favorable: 10,883 enemy soldiers killed versus only 267 casualties for the division. However, since the division captured fewer than 800 enemy weapons, the discrepancy led some people to

(In his interim report, Elliott pointed out that the GVN practiced another "... variant of 'removing water from the fish'" to depopulate hamlets.[227] Villagers who had moved to the middle of rice fields from the orchards and treelines—the targets of bombings and shellings—were given four or five days on average to move into New Life Hamlets near GVN military posts. If the villagers failed to comply, their houses and all the contents would be summarily burned. With this policy of forced removal, the GVN intended to cut cadres off from the civilian population in order to starve or paralyze the cadres. Its calculation was reminiscent of the thinking underlying the failed Strategic Hamlet Program. Besides showing a lack of humanitarian concern for the peasants and fomenting adverse political repercussions, this policy—in the consensus of the interview respondents, most of whom were defectors—had little effect on the ability of the cadres to survive. Considering that forced relocation had not brought about the demise of the cadres, this policy did not appear to be productive for the GVN.)

Despite the pounding it had received, the NLF was clinging tenaciously. While its infrastructure had suffered heavy casualties and recruitment was at a "standstill," a nucleus of the movement, consisting of hard-core elements, continued to exist from the province to the village level. These cadres had devised heavily defended "mini bases," where they were hiding. After the study was concluded, the GVN began to launch operations against these cadre hideouts. However, according to Elliott, the collected evidence suggested that the GVN would be unable to completely eliminate these bases.

According to Elliott, in the future, some of the military factors that had contributed to the success of pacification would disappear. Foremost among these was the presence of American troops, which broke the stalemate that had existed between the NLF and GVN forces and caused the dislocation of civilians and the depopulation of Viet Cong areas. Another factor was the large expansion of the Regional, Local, and Self-Defense Forces, which allowed the GVN to occupy the areas that had been cleared of Viet Cong units. The departure of the U.S. forces might drive the GVN to divert this manpower to other areas and thereby weaken its position in the province.

On the military side, the Tet Offensive had caused heavy losses for the NLF, with some battalions suffering up to 80-percent casualties, "while others which preserved their forces were ground down in the subsequent US-GVN counter-offensive."[228] Although the Tet Offensive was a "psychological and diplomatic success for the NLF,"

---

doubt the favorable kill ratio and questioned whether most of the casualties were civilians caught in the onslaught. "According to some accounts, many noncombatants—Viet Cong supporters and innocent bystanders—were probably eliminated in addition to enemy personnel bearing arms." Richard Hunt, *Pacification*, 1995, p. 189.

[227] Elliott, "Dinh Tuong Revisited," 1971, p. 6.

[228] Elliott, memo to Major Smith, 1972, p. 3.

it delivered a severe military blow "from which the NLF forces have not recovered."[229] However, the research also revealed that the degree of popular enthusiasm for the Tet Offensive was "astonishing."[230] According to many cadres interviewed, about 70 to 80 percent of the rural population in the province took part in the Tet Offensive, with great enthusiasm, although they were "mobilized on less than twelve hours' notice."[231] However, this outpouring of support in the countryside passed unnoticed "as the main attention shifted to the cities."[232] In retrospect, high-level NLF cadres were "bitter that they did not press their advantage in the countryside instead of chewing up their troops in the cities. Had they done so, the current situation might have been quite different."[233] Once the offensive lost momentum and the prospect for victory dimmed, popular enthusiasm quickly subsided. However, there appeared to be "a considerable reservoir of latent sympathy for the NLF," which might be revived if "circumstances change, and the dangers of actively supporting the NLF are diminished."[234]

(In his interim report, Elliott elaborated further on the outpouring of popular support for the Tet Offensive, saying that it was due to the "fervent peasant desire for peace." However, the peasants seemed to favor "peace NLF-style" more strongly than "peace GVN-style," and their attitude might reflect "a calculation that the GVN military superiority at the moment cannot be translated into political victory." Consequently, although the NLF had been weakened, the peasants had "remained aloof and indifferent to the GVN bandwagon," or had become "sullenly hostile toward the GVN because of the repellent behavior of the GVN soldiers . . . and the bitterness and hatred caused by bombings and forced relocation." Even "the natural base of support" for the GVN was being "systematically eroded," because local village officials were being alienated by the corruption of the military district chiefs.[235])

Although it was difficult to predict what the future would bring, the weight of history seemed to favor the NLF. In the past, there had been instances when the great strides in pacification in the Delta were reversed by NLF (or Viet Minh) successes elsewhere. If the NLF and the NVA were able to reconsolidate their position in other areas, if the GVN suffered setbacks in another region or was rent by a political or economic crisis, conditions might arise that would allow the NLF to reactivate its latent support. Pacification in many places was "little more than a military occupation of a

---

[229] Elliott, memo to Major Smith, 1972, p. 3.

[230] Elliott, memo to Major Smith, 1972, p. 4. Charlie Benoit reported that the same phenomenon also occurred in Mo Cay District, Kien Hoa Province, in the Delta, where many peasants supported the Tet Offensive. Benoit, "Conversations with Rural Vietnamese," 1970, p. 27.

[231] Elliott, memo to Major Smith, 1972, p. 4.

[232] Elliott, memo to Major Smith, 1972, p. 4.

[233] Elliott, memo to Major Smith, 1972, p. 4.

[234] Elliott, memo to Major Smith, 1972, p. 4.

[235] Elliott, "Dinh Tuong Revisited," 1971, p. 8.

depopulated countryside."[236] If and when the population went back to their villages, their return would provide the remaining cadre infrastructure with the opportunity to rebuild their movement in the province—"even in the absence of major changes elsewhere." In conclusion, Elliott wrote that it would be "premature to count out the NLF in Dinh Tuong," in view of "the continuing tenacity of the NLF cadre infrastructure," "the degree of latent support suggested in the interviews," and "contingencies" that might arise outside the Delta. If the National Liberation Front managed to overcome its current weakness, the Delta would "almost certainly not be the cutting edge of such a reversal." However, "it may follow the lead of other areas much faster than many people suspect."[237]

(In his interim report, Elliott indicated that the relative quiescence in the Delta might have been a mixture of the NLF's lack of capacity and a desire to conserve forces for more opportune times. Recently, there had been signs of a more aggressive guerrilla strategy to regain lost territory—at least in the Delta; defend the cadres' areas; and force the GVN to expand its resources in defending this region. These developments suggested that the stand-down of 1970 might be coming to an end. Elliott added that, ". . . if (as the preliminary interview data suggest) sympathy for the NLF is still widespread, success in the GVN pacification program may be only temporary. In this case, returning the people to their hamlets may simply mean delivering them back in to the hands of the NLF cadres."[238] So, while officials like Komer were encouraged that peasants were returning "in droves" to their former hamlets, Elliott's analysis indicated that this reverse migration might re-create a popular base for the NLF.)

Elliott's analysis was cited in an article written by Fox Butterfield of *The New York Times* on November 5, 1972, under the title "Core of Viet Cong Surviving War." In his article, Butterfield also mentioned the view of many "well-informed Vietnamese and American officials," which agreed with Elliott's conclusion about the tenacious survival of the insurgents' core of dedicated cadres despite many years of arduous fighting. These officials estimated that the Viet Cong still had from 40,000 to 60,000 committed cadres, and feared that this core political organization would pose a formidable threat to the GVN under a cease-fire. Butterfield also noted Elliott's point that a large measure of "latent support" for the Viet Cong still existed among the villagers, as well as his prediction that this sympathy—which was not apparent when the GVN was strong—could reemerge should the government weaken, as had happened at the time of the 1968 Tet Offensive. Before the offensive, many Vietnamese and Americans believed that the Viet Cong were on the verge of defeat in Dinh Tuong Province. But when the communists issued the sudden order to attack, "almost the entire rural population in the province was mobilized and coordinated in support" of the offensive.

---

[236]Elliott, memo to Major Smith, 1972, p. 5.

[237]Elliott, memo to Major Smith, 1972, pp. 5–6.

[238]Elliott, "Dinh Tuong Revisited," 1971, p. 1.

At the request of Frank Hoeber, Elliott also prepared a seven-page memo, dated July 12, 1971, giving his comments on the Phoenix program.[239] In it, he pointed out many of its abuses. Elliott was careful to note that he was presenting his own personal observations, but he added that his view of the program stemmed from the analytic work he had performed for the Dinh Tuong project. However, he thought that many of his comments could be supported by data in other areas of the country. To Elliott, the most telling comment he frequently heard from the Vietnamese with whom he spoke was the comparison of Phoenix to President Diem's disastrous "*To Cong*," or "Anti-Communist Denunciation," campaign in 1957–1959, which victimized many Vietnamese, created resentment, and built popular support for the insurgents. In his cover letter, Elliott added that "at best" the Phoenix program contributed marginally to pacification because it had not led to the capture of cadres who played a vital role in the Viet Cong village infrastructure. In the long run, Phoenix would increase popular hostility among the common people and turn those who were arbitrarily arrested into NLF sympathizers.

According to Elliott, as with the *To Cong* Campaign the *Phung Hoang* program suffered "from the political weakness of the GVN."[240] The premise of Phoenix was accurate identification and location of NLF cadres; to be successful, it needed the cooperation of the people to provide it with good information. However, the GVN had been unable to elicit enthusiastic popular response to its regime, and the populace had remained indifferent to its appeals to turn in the cadres. This left the government with three alternatives for targeting the Viet Cong infrastructure: relying on its own police, military, or other official organs; relying on defector and prisoner information; and relying on financial rewards. Probably because it was recognized that financial rewards would "inevitably lead to abuses," this form of incentive had not been used.

Nevertheless, through extortion, the Phoenix program had turned into "a great source of income for policemen and GVN officials." The usual method was "to arrest an innocent person or one with some remote connection with the NLF and then have his relatives buy his freedom." Elliott had met people to whom this had happened.[241] Deprived of the cooperation of the villagers, the GVN had to fall back on its military and its police, which relied on information provided by prisoners and defectors. Prisoners were usually uncommunicative and gave sketchy, unreliable information, but defectors, eager to demonstrate their bona fides, were often willing "to return to their villages and round up those whom they consider accomplices of the NLF."

---

[239] David W. P. Elliott, memorandum to Frank P. Hoeber, "Comments on the Phung Hoang program," July 12, 1971.

[240] Elliott, memorandum to Frank P. Hoeber, 1971, p. 2.

[241] Elliott, memorandum to Frank P. Hoeber, 1971, p. 3. There was another kind of ransom, and this involved releasing high-ranking cadres caught in the net in return for a large sum of money. According to Elliott, it had been reliably reported to him "that several important province cadres" had bought their freedom in the past two years.

The contribution of the defectors had been mixed. Defectors were usually afraid to lead GVN security forces into the heavily fortified areas in which the cadres were hiding. But even if they were willing to do so, the local security forces would likely be reluctant to follow them. Consequently, the defectors generally denounced ordinary villagers, who were "variously accused of 'paying taxes to the Viet Cong,' 'buying cloth for the Viet Cong,' or simply of being 'a good (NLF) citizen.'" According to Elliott, most of those denounced by the defectors were probably sympathetic to the NLF, but, in his view, "the wisdom of allowing defectors to arbitrarily indict villagers to get themselves off the hook is open to serious question." Besides, very few leading cadres could be captured by this method. Those who did get apprehended in the past three years had been caught in "the intensive military pacification operations of 1969–70."[242]

The problem was aggravated by the pressure on the police to fill "arbitrary quotas," which had led to the expansion of arrests of innocent people or "marginal figures" with tenuous relationships with the NLF. Those arrested were usually sentenced to imprisonment for a period ranging from three months to two years, or they were released for ransom. According to Elliott, by combining "the corruption and the oppressiveness of the GVN in a single program, *Phung Hoang* has been a major contribution to the alienation of the civilian population, including, significantly, many potential GVN supporters who have had relatives snared in its web."[243] The blurred line between guilt and innocence that cut deeply into the civilian population did not bode well for the success of pacification.

In Elliott's view, the extension of National Police operations to the village level was "in fact, a recognition of the failure to enlist the cooperation of the population" and—even more significantly—the collaboration of village officials. Elliott had known some cases in which village officials not only withheld cooperation but were even alienated by "the arbitrary arrest of friends and relatives for the purpose of extracting ransom." Elliott stressed that his experience in this area was "limited and possibly not representative," and he could not say how widespread this practice was, "but the potential for it is built into the program and the probabilities that it will take place are multiplied by the numerical quotas assigned."[244] According to Elliott, people such as Sir Robert Thompson had advocated "police and more police" to increase village security, but the extension of the National Police system to the village level did not appear to have had much of a good influence. In fact, it was the military and paramilitary forces that were providing the people with whatever level of security they currently enjoyed. But even these forces would not take the extra step of rooting out the cadres. They preferred

---

[242]Elliott, memorandum to Frank P. Hoeber, 1971, pp. 4–5.

[243]Elliott, memorandum to Frank P. Hoeber, 1971, p. 3.

[244]Elliott, memorandum to Frank P. Hoeber, 1971, p. 7.

"to co-exist" with them "rather than to risk death or mutilation by invading their strongholds."[245]

Another problem affecting the Phoenix program was the corruption of the GVN military bureaucracy at district level. Many village chiefs who should be at the forefront of the effort to destroy the NLF infrastructure had been alienated by the ARVN district chiefs. These military officers treated them like lowly subalterns or forced them to collect "contributions" from the villagers. Elliott knew of four village chiefs in one critical district—out of a total of 11—who had resigned or been dismissed in the past year. According to him, these were not "isolated cases."[246]

Steve Hosmer passed the letter Elliott addressed to Hoeber and his memo to William Colby on August 5, 1971, as well as to Robert Komer on August 6, 1971. In his cover letter to Colby, Hosmer wrote, "Given Mr. Elliott's unique expertise on the Viet Cong in Dinh Tuong, we feel his views should be taken seriously," even though—as Elliott pointed out himself in his letter to Hoeber—the comments he offered on the Phoenix program were "impressionistic" and based only on his "own personal experience." In his own cover memo to Colby, Komer wrote that "Dave is a most perceptive young Vietnamese speaker," and added that his conclusions were disturbing. Komer asked Colby to pass along Elliott's papers to Colonel George Jacobson, the Chief of Staff for Ambassador Ellsworth Bunker and the Mission Council coordinator, whom Komer was certain would be interested. Recognizing the sensitivity of Elliott's conclusions and his position in Vietnam, Komer wrote that Jacobson would know how to handle the documents, adding that, "The last thing we want is MACV's clamping down on Elliott."

From Elliott's memo on Phoenix, Komer drew three "operational conclusions." The first was that the government in Saigon should instruct the district chiefs in no uncertain terms to stop harassing and interfering with the village chiefs. The second conclusion was that Phoenix quotas had led to widespread abuses. Komer suggested that the GVN issue a directive that only genuine Viet Cong be arrested, that inspections be carried out to enforce this, and that quotas be reduced sharply and maybe even abolished. Komer urged the banning of arbitrary arrests of marginal adherents and communicating these reforms to the population. The third conclusion was that Komer recommended a major effort to root out corruption at the local level. It is not clear whether Komer's suggestions were followed. It is clear, however, that corruption and abuses were not eliminated.

Elliott recalled that, through his own research afterward, he discovered that "the impressive appearance of pacification . . . as it turned out was not as impressive as we thought." The Viet Cong movement, compared to that in the 1965–1967 period "was very, very weak," but the North Vietnamese troops had moved into the Delta by this

---

[245] Elliott, memorandum to Frank P. Hoeber, 1971, p. 7.

[246] Elliott, memorandum to Frank P. Hoeber, 1971, p. 4.

time and they had "guerrilla-ized themselves to the point where they were almost as effective as the old Viet Cong."[247] As Elliott predicted in his reports and memos, the tide did turn for the NLF in Dinh Tuong as a result of events elsewhere. In the wake of the Easter Offensive of 1972, the guerrilla movement in the Mekong Delta experienced a resurgence, and latent popular support was reactivated once conditions changed. The revived NLF movement relied on a level of popular support that was much lower than before, but the war was "a comparative game," and NLF's recouped strength was sufficient to allow it "to carry it off."[248] In retrospect, Elliott sees that the years 1970–1971 represented a crucial transition period for the NLF. "The time of trouble"—as the cadres his team interviewed called it—was the period of "greatest weakness" for the NLF, but it also revealed "some of the most tenacious strengths of the movement."[249]

After official sponsorship ended in September 1971, Elliott kept the interviewing going in Dinh Tuong with his own funds, and he had Bach continue the interviews for a while even after he and his wife returned to the United States. In November 1971, Elliott completed the draft of his final report. According to Elliott, he asked Frank Hoeber several times what he intended to do with the draft and whether he wanted to go through the regular process to turn it into an official RAND report. However, he never "got a clarification or response." His impression was that it was sent to Steve Hosmer and possibly somebody else for review, but "nothing further was ever heard about it."[250] When asked about this, Hosmer said he did not have any recollection. In Elliott's estimation, his follow-up Dinh Tuong project ended "with a whimper and not a bang."[251] He does not know whether the draft of his final report was transmitted to the National Security Council or what the response was. According to Bob Sansom, he left the National Security Council in April 1971 and consequently never saw Elliott's report—even if it was circulated to the NSC.

The timing of Elliott's final report was unfortunate. By June 1971, the Pentagon Papers controversy had erupted and RAND was reeling in its wake. With its own survival at stake, RAND's attention was focused elsewhere. The last major field project conducted in Vietnam simply got lost in the turbulence.

---

[247] Author interview with Dave Elliott, 2006.

[248] Author interview with Dave Elliott, 2006.

[249] David W. P. Elliott, *The Vietnamese War: Revolution and Social Change in the Mekong Delta, 1930–1975*, Concise Edition, Armonk, New York: M. E. Sharpe, 2007, p. 356.

[250] Author interview with Dave Elliott, 2006.

[251] Author interview with Dave Elliott, 2006.

CHAPTER NINE

The Pentagon Papers

During a visit to Harvard in fall 1966, at the invitation of Professor Richard Neustadt, McNamara discussed an idea with him and some other faculty members that would later be transformed into the Pentagon Papers. As he recounted in his memoir, he told them over dinner that, since the war was not going well, scholars would undoubtedly want to know why. He thought that their scholarship ought to be facilitated, to help avoid similar errors in the future. By mid-1967, McNamara had reached the conclusion that U.S. policies in Indochina had failed, and the realization led him to wonder why the United States had not succeeded, whether this failure could have been prevented, and what lessons could be learned to prevent similar experiences in the future. Increasingly, he began to think that, after the war, scholars would undoubtedly be interested in exploring these questions.[1]

In June 1967, McNamara decided to ask John McNaughton to begin collecting documents for this purpose. He told McNaughton "to cast his net wide" and to gather relevant papers, not just from the Department of Defense but also from the State Department, the CIA, and the White House. Since he wanted the work to be objective to the extent possible, he told McNaughton that he would not be personally involved and that McNaughton should tell his researchers "not to hold back. Let the chips fall where they may."[2] But McNamara did not mention the project to President Johnson or to Secretary of State Dean Rusk. He explained in his memoir that it never occurred to him to do so, perhaps because he was driven by "the same impulse" of wanting to keep the study objective.[3] But, in his view, the project could not have been a secret, since,

---

[1] Harry Rowen recalled that he talked with McNamara over lunch one day about such an undertaking. He said, "I'm not sure I'm the only one but I'm one of the people who said we should really get a record of this thing which has turned out so badly, and that some of this might be fleeting material, and so we ought to collect it. I don't know whether this prompted him to do it or not, but in any case in due course a team is assembled." Author interview with Harry Rowen, 2005.

[2] McNamara, *In Retrospect*, 1995, p. 280.

[3] McNamara, *In Retrospect*, 1995, p. 280. Les Gelb would later recall that McNamara "did not want the collecting and weighing of the documents to be influenced by anyone." Cited in John Prados and Margaret Pratt Porter, eds., *Inside the Pentagon Papers*, Lawrence, Kan.: University Press of Kansas, 2004, p. 18.

ultimately, it involved 36 researchers and analysts. Years later, when Rusk asked him why he had not told him or the president, McNamara "felt chagrined" and thought that he should have done so.[4]

According to McNamara, the collection of documents began on June 17, 1967—one month before John McNaughton was killed in an airplane crash—under the direction of Leslie H. Gelb. After McNaughton's death, the project continued under Paul Warnke, his replacement as head of ISA. Les Gelb would later say that, initially, he was asked to answer 100 questions handwritten by an Army lieutenant colonel and John McNaughton.[5] Gelb believed that the story of what happened subsequently got confused "by the town criers."

Originally, Mort Halperin was asked to set up a small group to answer the questions, but then it was decided that Halperin should stay with Policy and Planning and that Gelb should direct the study half-time, "staying in policy and planning half time and doing this half time." Halperin became project manager while Gelb took over as study director. According to Gelb, "Most of the questions had a decidedly political cast to them," and this led some people to speculate at the time that McNamara was preparing these questions for his friend Robert Kennedy, who was running against Lyndon Johnson in the Democratic primary.[6] Gelb said that he did not know what was on McNamara's mind when he commissioned the study. In his memoir, McNamara recalled that, "Wild rumors circulated about why I had started the project. One report even alleged I had done so at Robert Kennedy's behest, to undermine LBJ and help Bobby's 1968 campaign. That was nonsense."[7]

Gelb recalled that the project initially "had nothing to do at that point with the history of the Vietnam War—nothing."[8] Among the 100 questions, there were "about 12 historical questions," whereas "most were about contemporary issues—body count, and pacification, and the like."[9] There was an administrative file for the project, but "it disappeared," and Gelb could never find it again. He remembered that he was asked to assemble "six people to work for three months to answer the 100 questions—and

---

[4] McNamara, *In Retrospect*, 1995, p. 282.

[5] Author interview with Les Gelb, 2004. The officer was Army lieutenant colonel Robert Gard, a military assistant to McNamara, who—according to *Inside the Pentagon Papers* (Prados and Porter, 2004, p. 15)—brought in Les Gelb to head the study.

[6] Author interview with Les Gelb, 2004.

[7] McNamara, *In Retrospect*, 1995, p. 282.

[8] This quote and those following are from the author's interview with Les Gelb (2004), unless otherwise indicated.

[9] As reported in *Inside the Pentagon Papers* (Prados and Porter, 2004, p. 15), Gelb remembered that the questions were the kinds "that would be asked at a heated press conference. Are our data on pacification accurate? Are we lying about the number killed in action? Can we win this war? Are we lying to the civilian leaders? Are the civilian leaders lying to the American people? . . . There were about eight or so questions that were directly historical," such as "Could Ho Chi Minh have been an Asian Tito?"

about that, my memory is absolute. Six people—three months—but that's not the history of the Vietnam War, is it?" According to Gelb, as the group studied the questions, they felt they "couldn't answer them adequately without going back into the files." After about four or five months, Gelb wrote a memo to McNamara saying that "if you really want serious answers to these questions, you'll have to get involved in a longer project and we'll need to go back and do studies, and if we do these studies, then we can answer your questions better."

Gelb proposed a two-phase project: "First to do about 23 studies, and then answer the questions. That expanded to 45 or whatever the depth was, and then we never answered the questions. That's how it happened." The Pentagon Papers eventually would include analyses and summaries, as well as documents: a total of 7,000 pages covering 23 years of U.S.–Vietnam relations, from 1945 to 1968.

Gelb disputes reports that the study group tried to keep the project secret, especially from Walt Rostow, out of fear that Rostow would attempt to squelch it. Although McNamara did not inform Rostow, Gelb called Richard Moose, Rostow's assistant, right away to tell him about the project and to ask for documents. Moose then told Rostow, so "Rostow knew about it and everybody on Rostow's staff knew about it."[10] McNamara did not inform Rusk, but he told Richard Helms, the CIA director, and set up Dixon Davis as a liaison for Gelb. Gelb contacted Ben Reed, the State Department's executive secretary, to ask for diplomatic material, so Rusk found out immediately. "I called them all for documents," he said. In the end, the group "got the least documents from the White House."[11] In his memoir, McNamara quoted Gelb, who told a researcher years later that, "All I had to do was call up and say: 'McNamara asked' . . . I would go see people, explain the study, and say I wanted the following kinds of material. . . . They all said: 'Yeah, sure.' No one refused a thing."[12] McNamara recalled that Gelb and his task force "assembled memos, position papers, cables, and field reports stretching back more than twenty years." In the end, however, the Pentagon Papers were mostly based on John McNaughton's and McNamara's files.

Gelb added staff as the project expanded. About two-thirds of the 36 analysts had acquired Vietnam experience. Half were from the military. Among the remaining half, only nine were professional scholars; the others were civilian employees of the federal government. After the unauthorized release of the Pentagon Papers, McNamara was reported to have said that he considered Les Gelb a dove on the war and a biased

---

[10] *Inside the Pentagon Papers* (Prados and Porter, 2004, p. 15) reports that, according to Mort Halperin, originally the intention was to restrict the study to Pentagon documents and to give it a Top Secret classification in order to keep Walt Rostow from finding out. Rostow's continuing optimism contrasted with the growing doubts in the Defense Department, and "Pentagon officials feared that if Rostow knew of the project, he would intercede with the president to cancel the study, whose conclusions might well jar LBJ. Rostow would later say that he was vaguely aware of a project under way at the Pentagon but had no detailed knowledge of the Pentagon Papers."

[11] Author interview with Les Gelb, 2004.

[12] McNamara, *In Retrospect*, 1995, p. 281.

historian. McNamara's criticism stung Gelb, because he "had tried to make the narratives and summaries unbiased and nonaccusatory, and he particularly intended the write-ups to be 'neutral.'"[13] At the height of the Pentagon Papers controversy, Gelb said that, "We were not a flock of doves working our vengeance on the Vietnam War. . . . I would say about one-fourth [of the authors] were basically supporters of administration policy, a handful were highly critical of the U.S. commitment, and the bulk did not question the commitment so much as the means for meeting the commitment. No one was ever asked his views before being signed on."[14]

After McNamara authorized the expansion of the project to 23 studies, Mort Halperin told Gelb, "Why don't you get Dan Ellsberg involved in it. He's back and he's got nothing to do right now."[15] Later, Ellsberg claimed that the task force was anxious to hire him. However, Halperin said that they were asking "anybody who we thought was likely to be willing to participate and had sort of basic skills."[16] Ellsberg happened to fit the requirements: someone with academic training, knowledge of Vietnam, a security clearance, and freedom to spend several months working on the project. According to Halperin, the task force was asking "anybody who fit that bill," and although Ellsberg would have been highly qualified in all these aspects, "It wasn't that we sort of searched the whole country and said, 'Dan Ellsberg is the one.'"[17] Gus Shubert recalled that Gelb was glad to have Ellsberg on board and subsequently wrote a letter to Harry Rowen thanking him for making some RAND analysts available for the study. "It was a letter which was full of praise for Ellsberg," because Gelb knew that Rowen and Ellsberg were best friends and that his letter would "get good reception" if he had nice things to say about Ellsberg. According to Shubert, "The rest of the people who worked on the Papers just got a mention as X, Y, and Z, but Dan glowed."[18]

Gelb says that Ellsberg looked at the list of studies and decided to focus on the year 1961 of the Kennedy Administration. A number of RAND people, including Gus Shubert, Mel Gurtov, William R. Simons (a former Air Force colonel who had joined the RAND staff following his retirement), and Hans Heymann, also took part in the project. Shubert described them as people who were interested in Vietnam or had expertise and experience with the issue. Simons was recruited to work on the year 1964,[19] and Heymann wrote the sections for early 1965.

---

[13] Shapley, *Promise and Power*, 1993, p. 490.

[14] Cited in Prados and Porter, *Inside the Pentagon Papers*, 2004, p. 18.

[15] Author interview with Les Gelb, 2004.

[16] Wells, *Wild Man*, 2001, pp. 280–281.

[17] Wells, *Wild Man*, 2001, pp. 280–281.

[18] Author interview with Gus Shubert, 2004 and 2005.

[19] Simons recalled having had "access to papers from McNamara's safe, a good set of cable traffic, State Department material from William P. Bundy, but precious little from the Joint Chiefs of Staff and no National Security Council documents. On the highly controversial events of the Tonkin Gulf affair, Simons never had access to

Gus Shubert recalled that Harry Rowen was "very eager" to have RAND participate in the study, and that he discussed the pros and cons with Rowen on a number of
occasions.[20] The advantages would be to induce the government to take some favorable
actions, set the record straight, and get access to all those documents. The disadvantages would be not being able to control your own final write-up. However, "Nobody
envisioned the potential complications that ensued."[21] On one occasion when Shubert
went to Harry Rowen to discuss the pros and cons, he said, "Do you think this is a
good idea?" Rowen replied, "I don't think it's worth wasting time thinking about it.
You ought to just get in there and learn all you can, and get hold of all the inside dope
that you can." Shubert said, "Well, I can see that point of view, but on the other hand,
there are risks involved."[22] At the end of the conversation, Rowen told him, "Gus,
what's the matter with you? Why aren't you like Dan? Just say 'yes' and get in there
and do it."[23]

With regard to Vietnam, Gelb remembered that Ellsberg at that point was critical
of "how things were being done, not critical of the war itself"—a position consistent
with that of RAND in general.[24] RAND, Gelb recalled, had earned a reputation by
making recommendations on how to improve the way the United States was fighting the war, "but being critical of the ways in which the war was being fought does
not mean that you're critical of the war itself. In fact, it could have meant just the
opposite—that we needed to do a better job of fighting the war in order to win it."[25]
Gelb remembered that Ellsberg was "critical of various programs, but I do not remember him being critical of the war itself to the point where he said we had to get out."
Gelb did not recall that Ellsberg had developed a dovish reputation at the time. If he
had, "Kissinger would never have chosen him to do the NSSM study—never would
have done it."[26] Kissinger, Gelb said, thought that "Dan was basically a kindred spirit

---

National Security Agency intercepts of North Vietnamese communications that were central to the events of the
day." Simons wrote three studies for the year 1964, which later were combined into a single volume. Prados and
Porter, *Inside the Pentagon Papers*, 2004, p. 19.

[20] Collins, interview with Gus Shubert, session of May 28, 1992, p. 59.

[21] Collins, interview with Gus Shubert, session of May 28, 1992, p. 59.

[22] Author interview with Gus Shubert, 2004 and 2005.

[23] Author interview with Gus Shubert, 2004 and 2005.

[24] Author interview with Les Gelb, 2004.

[25] In his memoir, Ellsberg recalled that, in the fall of 1967, he was still a Cold Warrior "looking for lessons in
our Vietnam experience that could help the United States defeat Communist insurgencies *elsewhere* in the world
where circumstances were different and our chances of success were better." However, he also thought that it was
urgent to "avoid further escalation" in Vietnam and to end the war "somehow" before frustration with the stalemate led the president to expand the war into North Vietnam, "right up to the border of China, and probably
beyond it." Ellsberg, *Secrets*, 2002, p. 198.

[26] Author interview with Les Gelb, 2004. This refers to NSSM-1, for which Kissinger hired Ellsberg as a
consultant.

at that point. If he didn't think he was a kindred spirit, he would not have let him play such an important role and do this study, I guarantee you."[27]

Ellsberg belongs to Gelb's generation, and Gelb remembered that it was a "very confusing time" for people their age. They had been brought up to believe in the domino theory—and even now Gelb finds that it holds "a lot of psychological power."[28] Practically all of them supported the war in Vietnam from the beginning. Those who joined the defense establishment did not examine the issue of Vietnam in "a very critical and sophisticated kind of way." They had no Vietnam expertise, and hardly any of them knew the history of the country. The knowledge they acquired "was force-fed," he recalled, "[a]nd the tenet of the expertise focused on the conduct of the war rather than on history." Events forced them to "look deeper," and since they were not placed in top government positions and were not decisionmakers, they could spend time studying the issues at greater depth. "Because we were looking through the keyhole at the war," he said, "we had a chance to examine our views more carefully than our superiors who were making the decisions. It's harder when you make the decisions to examine what you're thinking."[29]

Thus, they began to embark on "this very slow process of change, and it was a slow one because this was our education. In order to change your view about Vietnam, you have to rethink what you thought America's role was in the world, you have to rethink what you thought the consequences of a military defeat would be—unthinkable before—or less than military victory—what that would be. And for all of us who had started out on another path, that was a very difficult and slow process."

According to Gelb, "The one who got there first was Paul Warnke because he was not a foreign policy expert, he was a lawyer—an incredibly smart man. But he jumped ahead of the whole pack in reaching that conclusion; the rest of us were very slow to get there. The RAND people, like the rest of us, were part of that process. We were all, I would say, very much establishment thinkers—all of us. It was events that forced us to examine our assumptions, and it was happening for the RAND experts as well as for those of us in government."[30]

In the process of developing the Pentagon Papers, an author would join the Vietnam Task Force, study the available material, and produce his piece about three months later. "This put a premium on analysts who could take temporary assignment[s], making think tanks natural and fertile recruiting grounds," such as the Institute for Defense Analyses and RAND.[31] Les Gelb would typically ask the analysts to interpret the

---

[27] Author interview with Les Gelb, 2004.

[28] Author interview with Les Gelb, 2004.

[29] Author interview with Les Gelb, 2004.

[30] Author interview with Les Gelb, 2004.

[31] Prados and Porter, *Inside the Pentagon Papers*, 2004, p. 20.

documents and write "a narrative that would not only connect the materials but also aid in understanding them."[32] Gelb explained later that, if an author did not follow his instructions, he had "no recourse but to accept the study." He could rarely extend their service on the task force, since most of the analysts were "moonlighters" and had other assignments to perform.[33]

Those working on the project were specifically ordered not to try to seek interviews with participants in the events they were researching, perhaps to maintain secrecy and objectivity. Howard Margolis, one of the outside analysts who rewrote the portion Ellsberg was supposed to have produced, recalled that he could have talked to General Maxwell Taylor but did not, because he did not want "to either be bound by Maxwell Taylor's interpretation of the Taylor mission" for Kennedy or "be in the awkward position of telling my boss he was wrong on something that was a big part of his life."[34]

After the Pentagon Papers became public, Les Gelb would say that he did not feel "we were writing the definitive history" of the Vietnam War to explain why they did not cover all the grounds in their research.[35] Later, Gelb would characterize the study in his letter of transmittal to McNamara as "not so much a documentary history, as a history based solely on documents—checked and rechecked with ant-like diligence."[36]

Mel Gurtov recalled that, in 1967, he got a call—perhaps from Mort Halperin—asking if he "would agree to be detached from RAND in order to participate in a Vietnam history project" within the office of the Secretary of Defense. The objective, he was told, was "to inform the secretary of the origins and evolution of U.S. involvement in Indochina."[37] Gurtov was asked to work on U.S. involvement during the years following World War II—the topic of his master's thesis at Columbia. RAND was willing to let him join the Vietnam Task Force, and Gurtov happily agreed. Gurtov believed that he was probably the first outside person brought into the task force. All he knew

---

[32] Prados and Porter, *Inside the Pentagon Papers*, 2004, pp. 20–21.

[33] Prados and Porter, *Inside the Pentagon Papers*, 2004, p. 21.

[34] Prados and Porter, *Inside the Pentagon Papers*, 2004, p. 30.

[35] In a review of the Pentagon Papers, Professor George McT. Kahin of Cornell University, a prominent critic of the war, wrote that the papers did not "provide a comprehensive or balanced account of U.S. involvement in Indochina. Much significant documentation has been left out, particularly that relating to the political side of American intervention, and in a number of important instances coverage of the covert level of U.S. operations—military as well as political—is absent. The narrative and analyses in some of the sections are unbalanced and occasionally rest on faulty scholarship." See George McT. Kahin, "*The Pentagon Papers*: A Critical Evaluation," *The American Political Science Review*, Vol. 69, No. 2, June 1975. Ellsberg thinks that the Pentagon Papers were limited also because the study was only at the Top Secret level and not at the "code-word level higher," and because the CIA only supplied estimates that made them look relatively good and held back documents about their covert operations. Prados and Porter, *Inside the Pentagon Papers*, 2004, pp. 32–33.

[36] Prados and Porter, *Inside the Pentagon Papers*, 2004, p. 18.

[37] Prados and Porter, *Inside the Pentagon Papers*, 2004, p. 23.

was that it was going to be a "private study for the Secretary of Defense . . . a kind of diplomatic history starting with the early years after World War II." Gurtov presumed that McNamara had ordered the study, "because he was, hopefully, re-thinking . . . the war and wanted to know an answer to the fundamental question of how did we ever get in so deep."[38] Since McNamara had authorized the study, Gurtov assumed that it would be taken "seriously," and that it might influence his thinking on the war, over which he was beginning to waver.

Gurtov expected to spend one month at the Pentagon but ended staying for three. As time went on, other people joined the project and, "naturally, like all Washington projects," the study "kept getting extended and extended," and the materials got "richer and richer," so that in the end it encompassed more than 40 volumes.[39] Gurtov read all the relevant materials, and what he found only reinforced his belief "that the United States needed to end its involvement and get out of there"—a sentiment increasingly embraced by many among the American public. Gurtov recalled that the project was located in one of the offices that was part of McNamara's suite in the Pentagon. From time to time, he would look out the window and see anti-war demonstrations. By then, he was "very much with them in spirit," and a few people on the task force also shared this feeling.[40] He found it fascinating and exciting to be part of the project, and he enjoyed the opportunity to meet many researchers, such as some of the military people in the Pentagon, who were detached to work on the study, and Henry Kissinger, who was serving as a consultant.

After about three months, Gurtov finished his piece covering the period from the French return to Indochina after the end of World War II to the Geneva Conference of 1954, and returned to RAND. He had thought "perhaps naively" that his piece would undergo the usual editing and would become the lead into the final document. When the Pentagon Papers was published, however, he saw that only some of his work was retained and that "much had changed as the study's director, Les Gelb, added questions and refocused answers."[41] Moreover, some of what Gurtov had written was modified. For example, his depiction of Ho Chi Minh as a dedicated nationalist—as well as a committed socialist—was "shaded . . . toward the 'responsible center' so as not to offend higher-level people who might read the study," because the official American view of Ho was that he was a communist.[42]

---

[38] Author interview with Mel Gurtov, 2004.

[39] Author interview with Mel Gurtov, 2004.

[40] Author interview with Mel Gurtov, 2004.

[41] Prados and Porter, *Inside the Pentagon Papers*, 2004, p. 25.

[42] Prados and Porter, *Inside the Pentagon Papers*, 2004, p. 25.

Besides Gurtov, Gus Shubert also spent several months in Washington working on the French period, on U.S.–French relations, and on the role of the U.S. Military Advisory Group. Most of the materials he used were common knowledge—unclassified data that he could take back with him to RAND when he finished. As did Gurtov, Shubert remembered that it was the height of the anti-war protests and he could see demonstrations from his office window. He recalled that Ernie May from Harvard was part of the task force, along with a number of very distinguished historians. But the group never jelled as a team because people came and went and passed each other "like ships in the night."[43]

Ellsberg, for his part, recalled that he agreed to join the task force in fall 1967 in the hope that his participation would eventually allow him access to the entire study, so that he could perform a comparative analysis and look for patterns—things in which he was truly interested. There is a disagreement about whether Ellsberg would be given access to the entire study when it was completed. According to Ellsberg, Les Gelb promised to let him read the whole study later, and that he was "the only researcher in the country with authorized access to the entire study."[44] Warnke, Gelb, and Halperin, would later dispute this claim. Warnke said that Ellsberg "has the tendency to lay it on a bit thick at times," whereas Gelb remembered that he did not "in any way either say or imply that Dan would have access." Halperin pointed out that they were not "in a position to do that," because they had "no idea what would happen to the studies."[45]

Ellsberg chose to work on decisionmaking in the Kennedy Administration in 1961, a period about which he had scant knowledge and wanted to learn more. Both Gus Shubert and Hans Heymann remembered that Ellsberg did little work. Shubert never saw any product by Ellsberg and recalled that Ellsberg played the role of "kibitzer-in-chief" and of "gadfly critic," and that as far as he could make out, Ellsberg "never wrote a thing, but he probably read everybody's stuff."[46] While Shubert was grinding away at his part of the project, Ellsberg was busy talking to people and digging through the files to find nuggets of information that seemed to occupy him. According to Hans Heymann, Ellsberg behaved in a curious manner—endlessly collecting information in an "unhealthy and emotional probing into the failures of U.S. policy," with the notion that "there was a gigantic deception."[47]

Army lieutenant colonel Robert G. Gard—a military assistant to Defense Secretary Robert McNamara—recalled that Ellsberg's lack of production was the only problem encountered by the task force. Gelb went into Gard's office one day to tell him

---

[43] Collins, interview with Gus Shubert, session of May 28, 1992, p. 59.

[44] Wells, *Wild Man*, 2001, p. 281.

[45] Wells, *Wild Man*, 2001, p. 281.

[46] Collins, interview with Gus Shubert, session of May 28, 1992, p. 57.

[47] Wells, *Wild Man*, 2001, p. 282.

about his concern that "Ellsberg was reading everything but not doing any writing." Ellsberg was about to return to RAND soon and Gelb wanted him to finish his portion before leaving. Gard called Ellsberg into his office, "fixed him with a steely gaze, shook his finger in Ellsberg's face, and remonstrated with him."[48] Ellsberg explained that he had been trying to "find patterns" in the materials he had been reading and "promised to finish the study" after he returned to RAND if necessary. But, according to Les Gelb, Ellsberg in the end "did not do his work."[49] Howard Margolis was brought in to finish what Ellsberg had not done. Margolis said that Ellsberg had written only four or five pages, so Margolis told Gelb that the entire paper had to be redone and he would just start over. Ellsberg claims that he in fact had written four hundred pages, but neither Gelb nor Margolis recall seeing this lengthy draft. In the end, the volume on the 1961 period would be entirely written by Margolis and would contain none of Ellsberg's work. As Margolis recalled, he was "quite sure" that he "didn't use any material [Ellsberg] wrote."[50]

When Clark Clifford replaced Robert McNamara in March 1968, he did not put a stop to the project, which was completed in January 1969, 18 months after McNamara had commissioned it. The study was given the official title of "The History of U.S. Decision-Making in Vietnam, 1945–1968." In all, 15 sets were produced.[51] By this time, McNamara had become president of the World Bank. As soon as the study was completed, Les Gelb went to Melvin Laird, the new Secretary of Defense for Richard Nixon, and told him that he wanted to bring a set over to McNamara. He also gave Laird a distribution list, which Laird approved. So Gelb and a military officer brought the set in two boxes to the World Bank. McNamara opened the boxes, took one look, and said, "Take them back."[52] The visit lasted about five minutes.

McNamara's reaction reflected his "ahistorical nature" but also his determination to distance himself from the war.[53] It also showed his insensitivity and his failure to realize that he could hurt the feelings of Les Gelb and his task force, "who had labored in the belief that McNamara, having invented the study, would care about the result and share their pride in it."[54]

---

[48] Prados and Porter, *Inside the Pentagon Papers*, 2004, p. 21.

[49] Prados and Porter, *Inside the Pentagon Papers*, 2004, p. 21.

[50] Wells, *Wild Man*, 2001, p. 283.

[51] Robert M. Smith, "Laird Increases Security on Papers at Rand Corp.," *The New York Times*, July 3, 1971.

[52] Author interview with Les Gelb, 2004.

[53] Shapley, *Promise and Power*, 1993, p. 486.

[54] Shapley, *Promise and Power*, 1993, p. 486.

Adhering to the distribution list for these documents—classified Top Secret—Gelb delivered a set to Clark Clifford, who kept it in his office safe.[55] One set was kept for Paul Warnke and another one for Gelb and Mort Halperin. These last two sets were stored at RAND, with the approval from Laird's office, and Halperin called Harry Rowen to make the arrangement. Paul Warnke would later say that he did not have secure storage for his own copy and thought RAND would be a safe place and would provide easier access for him now that he was out of government than the Defense Department or any other government agency. Gelb had joined the Brookings Institution by this time and no longer had a security clearance that would allow him to keep them in his office. Gelb recalled that, "The terms of their being lodged at RAND were that people could have access to these two sets only if two of the three of us—Warnke, Halperin, and Gelb—said 'yes,' and then RAND researchers could have access to them."[56] At the Pentagon Papers trial in 1973, Mort Halperin would testify that "the documents were to be outside the Rand top secret control system . . . to insure access on our own authority" and prevent them from being widely distributed at RAND. However, according to him, they would be kept in a top-secret safe.[57] As a result, "Jan Butler and her Top Secret Control counterpart in RAND's Washington office were not informed of it." Butler would later say, "We were circumvented completely."[58]

Evidence introduced by the government during the Pentagon Papers trial indicated that the Defense Department delivered the documents to the RAND Washington office on January 21, 1969.[59] Rowen himself said that it was natural that RAND got a copy, because it had participated in the study. However, he did not remember that it was not logged into RAND's top-secret system.[60] He would testify to this effect at the Pentagon Papers trial in 1973. By this time, Rowen had become a professor of public management of Stanford. In court, he "denied he agreed that a set of the Pentagon Papers received by the Rand Corp. in 1969 were to be kept outside the top-secret control system."[61]

---

[55] Under this distribution list, copies were given to "about a half dozen Johnson administration officials, Henry Kissinger, and several official repositories." Wells, *Wild Man*, 2001, p. 313.

[56] Author interview with Les Gelb, 2004. This arrangement was confirmed during the Pentagon Papers trial, when the Ellsberg defense introduced a December 18, 1968, memo from Warnke, Halperin, and Gelb to Harry Rowen, stating that "access to and distribution of the Pentagon task force study and related papers on the Vietnam War shall be approved by any two of the signators." Gene Blake, "Ellsberg Given Access to Files, Defense Claims," *Los Angeles Times*, February 14, 1973.

[57] Gene Blake, "How Ellsberg Got Access to Files Disclosed," *Los Angeles Times*, March 22, 1973. The trial did not deal with how many sets were sent to RAND and was concerned only with the set Ellsberg copied.

[58] Wells, *Wild Man*, 2001, p. 314.

[59] Gene Blake, "Unaware of Pentagon Data Probe—Haldeman," *Los Angeles Times*, May 3, 1973.

[60] Author interview with Harry Rowen, 2005.

[61] Blake, "Unaware of Pentagon Data Probe—Haldeman," 1973.

This lack of retention for such administrative details might be ascribed to Rowen's reputed less-than-stellar management of RAND's affairs and also to his preoccupation with a host of challenges in this period. Gus Shubert recalled that Rowen was facing a myriad of problems in 1969, "dealing with diversification into the domestic field, dealing with an increasingly discontent Air Force, which was cutting the budget and was very angry with Harry and was saying so. So he had a lot of things on his mind."[62] Also, according to Gus Shubert, Larry Henderson was the senior official in Washington who handled the storage of the Pentagon Papers when they arrived at RAND. It was like someone had handed him a "red-hot poker," Shubert said. Henderson's reaction was, "Oh, my God, what am I going to do with this?" So, instead of putting the volumes in the security system, he said, "This is too hot for the security system. This will have to remain under my personal surveillance."[63]

The issue of how the papers were stored was just a technicality, in Shubert's view, because, although they were not entered into the top-secret control system, they were kept in a top-secret safe and given "maximum security."[64] It should be noted that RAND was strict in granting access, and only two RAND analysts were authorized to read the documents under permission given by Gelb and Halperin: Daniel Ellsberg and Dick Moorsteen, a former White House aide now working as an analyst at RAND. At the Pentagon Papers trial, Mort Halperin testified that the arrangement with RAND was private, because it was between RAND and three individuals: Halperin, Warnke, and Gelb. Under this private arrangement, the documents given to RAND were not to be treated as materials "received under a contract" with the Defense Department, because they were not from the Defense Department but from files that he, Gelb, and Warnke maintained in their own offices.[65] Therefore, they were not to be entered into the formal top-secret security system, thereby providing easy access to the three former government officials. Technical violations of security regulations by Washington officials were apparently not uncommon. Halperin said at the trial that he was only following a standard practice among many government officials when he took classified information with him upon leaving the Defense Department and later the National Security Council. He denied that this represented a violation of security regulations.[66]

---

[62] Collins, interview with Gus Shubert, session of May 28, 1992, pp. 64–65.

[63] Collins, interview with Gus Shubert, session of May 28, 1992, p. 67.

[64] Collins, interview with Gus Shubert, session of May 28, 1992, p. 67. Another issue during the trial was whether the papers deserved the Top Secret classification. Gelb said in court that the "classification was done routinely, with little discussion," while General Gard testified that they were given the classification because most of the source materials were classified as such. Martin Arnold, "Ellsberg's Attorney Contradicted by F.B.I. Agent," *The New York Times*, April 25, 1973.

[65] Blake, "How Ellsberg Got Access to Files Disclosed," 1973.

[66] Gene Blake, "Ellsberg Leak Feared in 1969," *Los Angeles Times*, March 24, 1973.

According to Gelb, "Soon after Ellsberg called Halperin and asked for access to it." Halperin called Warnke, who said, "No, I don't trust him." Mort called Gelb who said, "No, I don't trust him." Gelb does not remember whether Rowen then called him, or Warnke, or Halperin, to put a lot of pressure to have Ellsberg gain access. Rowen said, "Why do you store the documents here? He worked on the study, how can you deny him access?" Gelb denied access for the second time through Halperin, but Halperin came back to him and said, "We just can't say 'no.' Harry wants him to do it, and the documents are there." So, Gelb said, "Alright."[67] The two decided not to tell Warnke, because, as Halperin recalled, "We decided not to burden him with that decision. And we were pretty sure he would say no anyway."[68] Warnke would later say that he turned down everybody because he thought the granting of access would have to come from McNamara.

According to Halperin, the reason Rowen gave him was that Ellsberg was working, under contract for the Defense Department, on a RAND study on the lessons of Vietnam and should have access, and that he had agreed to have the volumes stored at RAND "with the understanding that RAND would benefit from them."[69] Since the Defense Department was giving Ellsberg access to very sensitive documents, Rowen asked, "How can you guys make an independent judgment that he should not be trusted with these documents?" They were putting him in an "awkward position, he told Haleprin" because "he was sitting on a document of very great relevance to what Ellsberg was doing *officially* for the government."[70] At the Pentagon Papers trials, Halperin would testify that "there was some fear the 'sensitive' information might be disclosed, perhaps in a magazine article, if Ellsberg were given access."[71] However, Halperin testified, "Rowen persisted in his request, pointing out that Ellsberg had top-secret clearance and was working at Rand on a Vietnam study under a Defense Department contract."[72] Gelb then agreed with Halperin to grant Ellsberg access.

A progress report of RAND's Economics Department at the time indicates that Ellsberg was working on a study jointly with Charlie Wolf on "Lessons of Rebellion and Insurgent Forces," and makes an oblique reference to the Pentagon Papers.[73] The study states that, "The record of American experience in Vietnam over 25 years offers a wealth of data that can be used to extract useful lessons. Yet there seems to be little

---

[67] Author interview with Les Gelb, 2004.

[68] Wells, *Wild Man*, 2001, p. 315.

[69] Wells, *Wild Man*, 2001, p. 314.

[70] Wells, *Wild Man*, 2001, p. 314. Emphasis in original.

[71] "Ellsberg Leak 'Feared' in 1969, Witness Says," *Los Angeles Times*, March 24, 1973.

[72] "Ellsberg Leak 'Feared' in 1969, Witness Says," 1973.

[73] Economics Department, "Report of 9 February 1970, ARPA/AGILE, July–December 1969." A search of RAND's library catalogue did not turn up such a report. Probably, the study did not materialize.

current response in the research community either to the need or to the opportunity." In an indirect reference to the Pentagon Papers, the study reveals that "a major historical analysis of US decision-making in Vietnam from 1940 to 1968" was undertaken in 1968–1969 "in the Office of the Assistant Secretary of Defense (International Security Affairs), with excellent access to DOD and State files," but comments that this study, "although unprecedented in scope and access, did not attempt to derive generalizations from a range of similar experiences."

The report says that "Ellsberg participated in that study (as did several other RAND researchers), drafting one volume on decisionmaking in 1960–61, and commenting on several others." However, "Most of the studies covered one or a few years, and no comparative analysis of different periods, or of a given problem over the whole period, was attempted." It is this gap that the Ellsberg/Wolf study would seek to fill, since these "are precisely the outputs most relevant to future policy."

There might have been another reason why Gelb was willing to grant Ellsberg access. The same progress report states that,

> Recently a project with a similar purpose has been launched at The Brookings [Institution] under Leslie Gelb, who managed the DOD study mentioned above. Gelb's study has a panel of advisors who will meet to discuss successive chapters of his work. Ellsberg and Moorsteen are members. Gelb has recently visited RAND to consult with Moorsteen and Ellsberg, and the two projects should benefit by close consultation. As currently planned, the projects are closely complementary in subject matter, with little overlap. Gelb proposes to concentrate on the very early period, and on more recent themes, including the bombing campaign and negotiations, that are not specific subjects of the RAND study.

The progress report goes on to say that,

> Work by Ellsberg on this project is currently directed toward producing a book, to be completed by the summer of 1970, which will deal with political factors in revolution and counter-revolution, and analytical models for dealing with them; 'revolutionary judo;' alternative approaches to pacification; and alternative political strategies. It will also address US perceptions of political/administrative/military complexities in Vietnam, and limitations revealed in our response to them.

But the big study that Ellsberg was supposed to produce for RAND on "Lessons of Vietnam" that would become a book—as well as lead to a series of RMs along the way—never materialized. Ellsberg would later testify at his trial that he was going "to draw conclusions for the help of the executive branch and of the president at the highest level," and that he was "the only man at RAND—actually in the whole country—who was on government funds, spending full time doing research drawing lessons from our

Vietnam experience."[74] Albert Williams, a White House staffer for Vietnamese issues who later joined RAND, said that people at RAND were aware that Ellsberg "had taken upon himself to do a big thing, and it wasn't getting done."[75] Ellsberg would later explain that the reason for his lack of productivity was depression over the war.[76] The papers that he did produce were, in the view of some people at RAND, below expectations. He put out a series of ten papers called "Working Notes on Vietnam,"[77] which were supposed to be incorporated later into the book.

The first Working Note appeared in June 1969. In the Preface, Ellsberg acknowledged that these D's were "unpolished or incomplete," but he was putting them out in the interests of "communication, stimulation . . . feedback of thoughts and reactions" to him. He stated that this series of papers contained the reflections and comments that had occurred to him over recent years, "especially the last." He had filled many notebooks with them, and now he was grouping them by subject and presenting them "hastily filled out and edited." Rather than "polish[ing] them or, more importantly, follow[ing] through the analysis in any one paper," he had decided to put out "a fair number of these notes"—in no particular order—"as quickly as possible toward readers who might be moved to comment; for my benefit, and perhaps, in some cases, for

---

[74] Wells, *Wild Man*, 2001, p. 292.

[75] Wells, *Wild Man*, 2001, p. 294.

[76] Wells, *Wild Man*, 2001, p. 292.

[77] The Working Notes were: "US Aims and Leverage in Vietnam, 1950–65" (D-18963); "Critical Postures on US Decision-Making in Vietnam: Multiple Choice" (D-18958); "US Policy and the Politics of Others" (D-19129); "Vu Van Thai on US Aims and Interventions in Vietnam" (D-19127); "Confucians and Communists: Hoang Van Chi on the Relation of Marxist to Confucian Concepts, and Cultural Susceptibility to Communism" (D-19135); "On Pacification: Comments by Thai and Ellsberg" (D-19136); "Communists and Vietnamese: Comments by Hoang Van Chi" (D-19134); "US Support of Diem: Comments by Vu Van Thai" (D-19128); "Infeasible Aims and the Politics of Stalemate" (D-19205); and "Revolutionary Judo" (D19807). Vu Van Thai and Hoang Van Chi were friends of Ellsberg whom he had brought in as consultants to RAND. Thai was an economist and former South Vietnamese ambassador to the United States. Chi was the author of *From Colonialism to Communism*, New York: Praeger, 1964. In the words of the Economics Department's progress report of September 28, 1970, Ellsberg was going to turn his "Revolutionary Judo" into RM-6386-ARPA for external distribution. The progress report summarizes his paper as follows:

> This study analyzes the tendency of an existing authority to cooperate suicidally with insurgents by actions that alienate the public. Using, 'judo,' the rebels (R) act as the controller in a servo system in which A (Authority) and P (Public) are the main energy sources. Small energy inputs from R (assassinations, sniper fire, small attacks) evoke large energy responses from A, such as air strikes on the snipers' villages. These responses, in turn, cause significant shifts in P's support away from A. One of the most useful aids to the insurgents is for A to suppress the non-communist opposition. If A won't cooperate, if it suppresses any tendency to alienate the population under R's stimulus, R's efforts alone cannot arouse P to overthrow A.

In his interview with the author, Ellsberg said that RAND had second thoughts about publishing his "Revolutionary Judo" as an RM in 1971, after his unauthorized release of the Pentagon Papers, because it did not want to be associated with him. "It was a very good paper," he said. Author interview with Ellsberg, 2004.

theirs."[78] The last Working Note, "Revolutionary Judo," appeared in January 1970. Albert Williams said that, at RAND, "people were looking at those Ds and saying, 'Oh? What's this?'" and described these papers as "rambling" and not "sharply focused."[79]

Although Ellsberg felt depressed about the war, he was still not at the point where he wanted the United States to pull out of Vietnam. In his memoir, he recalls that, in spring 1969, the questions of "How could we have won in Vietnam?" and "What might the United States have done to improve the odds of success?" still "held an intellectual attraction" for him.[80] He addressed these questions in a paper dated August 1969—the ninth in the series of ten papers at RAND.[81] What is noteworthy about this paper is not the non-novel arguments that the aim the United States pursued in Vietnam—"the *permanent exclusion of the Communist Party of Indochina from open politics, and ultimately, its total destruction as an organization*" [emphasis in original][82]—was infeasible from the start and that stalemate occurred because neither side was strong enough to dominate, but the emotional tone and the admission of pain for having participated in the costly failure. It was painful for people like him, Ellsberg wrote, to recognize that "one's own, and the country's, effort, was wasted, hopeless, *from the start*" [emphasis in original] and to see that the failure had exacted many lives, destroyed Vietnamese society, damaged American prestige, and brought "bad things . . . to our own country."[83] The emotional hint presaged the turnabout that was going to occur.

The questions Ellsberg addressed in this paper revealed his continuing American preoccupation with winning. But his perspective on the war was about to change drastically in the summer of 1969 with his reading of the earliest volumes of the Pentagon Papers stored at the RAND office in Washington. Instead of seeing the war only "as an involvement that should be ended and that above all must not be escalated," he began to feel that the war was illegitimate and morally wrong.[84] This feeling had emerged following a talk in April 1969 that he gave on South Vietnamese politics to a class at the University of Ohio, during which he tried to define South Vietnamese political opinion by explaining that "most of the people of South Vietnam have preferred that the war be over—with a victory by *either* side—than that it should continue at anything

---

[78] Ellsberg, "US Aims and Leverage in Vietnam, 1950–65," Working Notes on Vietnam No. 1, Santa Monica, Calif.: RAND Corporation, D-18963-ARPA/AGILE, June 1969, p. ii.

[79] Wells, *Wild Man*, 2001, p. 294.

[80] Ellsberg, *Secrets*, 2002, p. 246.

[81] Ellsberg, "Infeasible Aims and the Politics of Stalemate," Working Notes on Vietnam No. 9, Santa Monica, Calif.: RAND Corporation, D-19205-ARPA/AGILE, August 1969.

[82] Ellsberg, "Infeasible Aims and the Politics of Stalemate," 1969, p. 3.

[83] Ellsberg, "Infeasible Aims and the Politics of Stalemate," 1969, p. 3.

[84] Ellsberg, *Secrets*, 2002, p. 256.

like the present scale."[85] Afterward, he pondered the implication of what he had said. If the majority of South Vietnamese wanted the war to end no matter who won, "What did that say about the legitimacy of imposing our will to continue the war?"[86] He concluded that the United States did not have the right to prolong a war it could not win in a country that did not pose a threat to America, against "the intense wishes of most of the inhabitants of that country." To continue to do so would be "morally wrong."[87]

His conclusion was reinforced by his reading of the Pentagon Papers. "[B]eginning in the summer of 1969, and definitively by the end of September," he stopped believing, as did many of his colleagues in Washington, that the war was "a worthy effort gone wrong or gone too far, as a case of good intentions that failed [short] of their legitimate, though perhaps infeasible, aims."[88] At the end of August, he brought back to RAND Santa Monica from Washington the volumes covering the period from 1945 to 1960. He recalled when he brought these and subsequent volumes to Santa Monica that "they were not to be put in the RAND Top Secret system."[89] This was not his idea, he said, but "that was the condition on which they were given," and personally he did not care "whether they were in the system or not."[90]

As a result, not even Charlie Wolf, his boss, knew that he had the volumes and was reading them and taking notes. According to Ellsberg, "Harry Rowen knew that, he was the only person at RAND who knew that because he was the only person at RAND then qualified to know the Pentagon Papers were there. No one else must know." Ellsberg recalled that, "Later, Dick Moorsteen was brought in on it, and one or two other people," including Ernie May, who "came and read some stuff there."[91] Ellsberg said that he wanted to get more people access because he wished to be able to discuss the papers with them and allow them to learn from the study as well. He was always telling Rowen, he recalled, "Let's get this acquisition list wider," and Rowen would approach Gelb or Halperin, who always said, "No, it ought to be kept to the minimum."[92]

---

[85] Ellsberg, *Secrets*, 2002, p. 248.

[86] Ellsberg, *Secrets*, 2002, p. 248.

[87] Ellsberg, *Secrets*, 2002, p. 249.

[88] Ellsberg, *Secrets*, 2002, p. 256.

[89] Author interview with Dan Ellsberg, 2004. At the Pentagon Papers trial, Richard Best testified that, since the documents had not been entered into RAND's Top Secret Control System, they were not "given a control number and were not assigned a cover sheet listing the persons authorized to have access to them. When Ellsberg picked them up to take to Rand's Santa Monica office, there was no top-secret register of the transmittal made." Gene Blake, "Lax Handling of Pentagon Papers Alleged," *Los Angeles Times*, February 16, 1973.

[90] Author interview with Daniel Ellsberg, 2004.

[91] Author interview with Daniel Ellsberg, 2004. Moorsteen was granted access by Gelb and Halperin in a letter dated October 6, 1969, to Harry Rowen. Blake, "Lax Handling," 1973.

[92] Author interview with Dan Ellsberg, 2004.

As Ellsberg read these Pentagon Papers volumes in August and September 1969, "The belief that we had *ever* had a right to try to 'win' in Vietnam, to impose our political preferences by military means, died for me."[93] What impressed him was a "fundamental sense that there never had been any legitimacy in our involvement or our war in Vietnam, or any legitimate claim to authority for any of the regimes we backed, either under the French or later. . . . Realistically seen, it was *never* a 'just cause.'"[94] The reading of official Secret documents led him to believe that, since the war "had been wrong from the start," prolonging it seemed to him "a wrong of the highest degree imaginable. A crime. An evil." and "Mass murder."[95] The United States, therefore, must cease the war, "as quickly as possible."[96]

Bernard Brodie thought that the change in Ellsberg's attitude toward the war might have been prompted as well by what he had seen in Vietnam. "What had been an abstraction to him before became the sight of people being hurt or killed," he said, and this led Ellsberg to undergo "a kind of Saul of Tarsus thing—a complete swing from far right to far left."[97]

Another factor that influenced Ellsberg's thinking was that he had learned in mid-August 1969 through Mort Halperin, now serving as an assistant to Henry Kissinger on the National Security Council, that Nixon was not "getting out" of Vietnam. To Ellsberg, this was "horrible" news because he thought that meant Nixon would expand the war. Ellsberg was not surprised by this information, because to him the new president was doing exactly what four predecessors had done before him—as revealed in the Pentagon Papers.[98] Later that summer, when Ellsberg was staying at Halperin's home, Halperin told him that Nixon was not prepared to see "Saigon under a Vietcong flag after a 'decent interval' of two or three years—or ever. Not, at least, while he was in office. That meant not through 1976, if he could help it, as he believed he could."[99] He would accomplish this goal by withdrawing U.S. combat forces slowly while building up the ARVN and continuing to provide air support indefinitely, and even perhaps by keeping a large American residual force and resuming bombing of the North. Ellsberg saw that Nixon's campaign promise that he would end the war was "a hoax," and the war for all intents and purposes would get even bigger and would go on indefinitely.[100]

---

[93] Ellsberg, *Secrets*, 2002, p. 249.

[94] Ellsberg, *Secrets*, 2002, p. 256.

[95] Ellsberg, *Secrets*, 2002, p. 257.

[96] Ellsberg, *Secrets*, 2002, p. 257.

[97] Dobbin, "Rand Corporation Still Feels," 1973.

[98] Ellsberg, *Secrets*, 2002, p. 257.

[99] Ellsberg, *Secrets*, 2002, p. 258.

[100] Ellsberg, *Secrets*, 2002, p. 258.

Halperin also told him about the secret bombing of Cambodia that Nixon had begun in February to show the enemy that he would not abide by the limits observed by the Johnson Administration, such as "mining harbors and blockading, hitting dikes, population, bombing" and even using "nuclear weapons."[101] According to Halperin, Nixon would not go into the 1972 election "without having mined Haiphong and bombed Hanoi."[102] Although he was horrified, Ellsberg thought it "might not be too late to deflect" Nixon from an "essentially foolish course" by inducing him to "think again, to postpone decision."[103]

After leaving Washington, Ellsberg—"no longer a committed counter-revolutionary"[104]—went to Haverford, a Quaker college near Philadelphia, to attend a meeting of the War Resisters League. There, he met Bob Eaton, who was going to go to jail for resisting the draft. In retrospect, Ellsberg would realize how isolated he and his RAND colleagues had been from the anti-war movement, even after they had become profoundly critical of the war. One of the draft resisters gave a speech about members of the War Resisters League who had chosen imprisonment to protest against the war and also because, to stay true to their principles, they did not want to be part of a war they considered wrong.

The power of their action hit Ellsberg. He was so moved that he broke down crying. He went to the men's room, slid down on the floor, and sobbed "convulsively, uncontrollably." A thought kept recurring in his head: "We are eating our young." It had come to this in his own country, so that "The best thing that the best young men of our country can do with their lives is to go to prison."[105] After an hour of sobbing, he thought of what he could or should do to help end the war. Neil Sheehan of *The New York Times* would later write of Ellsberg that, "Zealotry is a constant in the character of a man" even when his opinions change.[106] The former hawk was now determined to bring the war to a close. To Gus Shubert, it appeared clear that Ellsberg "had not only lost the faith, he had found a new faith, and he became, to the surprise of everyone, an advocate of ending the war."[107] Shubert recalled that Ellsberg was ardent in his opposition to the war: "Dan has never been one to hide his light under a bushel. . . . He was extremely vocal."[108]

---

[101] Ellsberg, *Secrets*, 2002, p. 259.

[102] Ellsberg, *Secrets*, 2002, p. 260.

[103] Ellsberg, *Secrets*, 2002, p. 261.

[104] Ellsberg, *Secrets*, 2002, p. 262.

[105] Ellsberg, *Secrets*, 2002, p. 272.

[106] Cited in Shapley, *Promise and Power*, 1993, p. 487.

[107] Collins, interview with Gus Shubert, session of May 28, 1992, p. 62.

[108] Collins, interview with Gus Shubert, session of May 28, 1992, p. 62.

On his way back to RAND, Ellsberg stopped at its Washington office to pick up another eight volumes of the Pentagon Papers. What he read dissipated in his mind the "quagmire myth"—the notion that presidents "had been misled at critical turning points" by the "unrealistic optimism" of their "civil and military advisers."[109] Rather, each president had chosen to continue the war—despite warnings from knowledgeable advisors—that their policies would lead to stalemate and would at the most delay withdrawal and defeat—while lying to the public about their action and keeping secret what their advisors had told them about the prospects for success.[110]

Ellsberg thought that the only way to change Nixon's course was to get the public and Congress to pressure him. Ellsberg did not possess documents revealing Nixon's preferred course of action in Vietnam, so he thought that the next best thing was to present the American people with "public recommendations by former officials with great authority or second-level analysts who could claim access to classified information."[111] Among those second-level analysts were some of Ellsberg's RAND colleagues who had been calling for unilateral withdrawal from Vietnam. He thought that perhaps by publicly declaring their views, they might be able to persuade these former senior officials to join them in calling for disengagement. In mid-September, Ellsberg told Konrad Kellen that he was ready to join his colleagues in going public with their recommendation for U.S. withdrawal.

Kellen brought the other members of this small group—Mel Gurtov; Paul Langer, who was a Laos expert; Arnold Horelick; and Oleg Hoeffding—to the first meeting to discuss what action to take. Mel Gurtov had become close to Kellen, Langer, and Horelick soon after joining the RAND staff in 1966. Even back then, while many people at RAND believed that the war was worth fighting and that the problem lay in the way it was being fought, these analysts were already convinced that the United States had no business being in Vietnam and that American involvement was a bad idea that was "likely to get worse."[112] These colleagues, along with what he learned while working at RAND, convinced Gurtov that the war was "a terrible mistake" and that something had to be done about it.[113] Kellen thought that the war was "criminal" because "it killed so many people for no good purpose," and he began to oppose it.[114]

As the group discussed what action to take, they became more and more inclined toward something that would be dramatically different from a memo that would be circulated internally and discarded. They settled on submitting a letter to the news-

---

[109] Ellsberg, *Secrets*, 2002, p. 274.

[110] Ellsberg, *Secrets*, 2002, p. 275.

[111] Ellsberg, *Secrets*, 2002, p. 276.

[112] Author interview with Mel Gurtov, 2004.

[113] Author interview with Mel Gurtov, 2004.

[114] Author interview with Konrad Kellen, 2002.

paper calling for the United States to withdraw unilaterally from Vietnam, since a letter would allow them to publish their views as private citizens without having to go through a cumbersome clearance process. They believed that their status as researchers and consultants on defense issues would lend credibility to their public statement.

At that time, calls for unilateral withdrawal were coming only from leftists and radicals—although Senator Charles Goodell—a Republican from New York—was beginning to reach that conclusion. Arnold Horelick recalled that it was an option that was beginning "to be taken seriously, but only privately," and that no respectable scholars and researchers were making a good case for it. "It was not yet a public option," he said.[115] The group decided to write the letter "because there was a powerful analytical argument that was not being made."[116] According to Ellsberg, they also thought that their letter would encourage influential voices in the media and Congress—who agreed with this stance but were reluctant to call for it—to come out in support.

Ellsberg instead favored a study that would allow the group to lay out the facts and their arguments more completely, but the others said, "It's a letter or nothing."[117] According to Mel Gurtov, they wanted "to do something that might really make a splash and cause some heads to turn." They were angry enough and frustrated enough about the way the war was going to want to do something out of the ordinary.

It was an anger borne out of "policy convictions" and "moral concerns." They had all written critically about the war, "whether through the Motivation and Morale Project, or through some other topic," and it was evident that what they had written had been ignored. Gurtov recalled that Washington officials typically would allow "a throw away alternative . . . on the menu for study, just in order to be able to say 'Well, you see, we considered all points of view.'" But the reality was that "only certain points of view really stood any chance of getting attention, and ours stood no chance." Gurtov said that, for years, he had labored onward, probably out of a sense of misplaced idealism, believing that if he did a good job, his work would stand on its own intellectual merits, "but the truth of the matter is that it was discounted . . . from the very outset." The only options that "were really ever being considered during the war were those that varied only in terms of how much force, how much deeper should the U.S. effort be because the aim was always victory."[118]

As the Nixon Administration was coming in, some in the group had contributed to the paper calling for extrication from Vietnam, which was presented to Paul Warnke. But, "Predictably that option never got very far and wasn't seriously considered."[119]

---

[115] Author interview with Arnold Horelick, 2004.

[116] Author interview with Arnold Horelick, 2004.

[117] Ellsberg, *Secrets*, 2002, p. 281.

[118] All quotes are from the author's interview with Mel Gurtov, 2004.

[119] All quotes are from the author's interview with Mel Gurtov, 2004.

Having gone through all these exercises, "we deeply believed that something else needed to be done." Gurtov said that Ellsberg provided the spark, and he surmised that Ellsberg's frustrating experience with trying to change policies might have had a good deal to do with his attitude that they should do something "much sharper" or they "might as well forget about it and go on and study African affairs or something." Indeed, Ellsberg had concluded that providing private counsel, as RAND had been doing, was enabling the president—no matter who he was—to act without being challenged publicly by expert opinions.

Publishing a letter in the newspaper was a radical deviation from RAND's practice of keeping dissent internal and limited to clients. Gurtov and Kellen volunteered to draft the letter, and the group agreed to meet again to review it. They wrote and rewrote, looking for the best way to express their views. While they were drafting and redrafting the letter, Ellsberg decided to do something even more drastic. The trigger was an article he read in the *Los Angeles Times* on the morning of September 30, 1969. It recounted the murder of a Vietnamese committed by the U.S. Green Berets in Vietnam. The victim had been employed by the Special Forces, but when they suspected him of being a double agent, they shot him—after interrogating him with lie detectors and injecting him with truth serum. They then put his body in a weighted bag and sank it in the South China Sea. The Army field commander charged eight Green Berets suspected of the murder, but Stanley R. Resor, Secretary of the Army, dismissed the charges on the grounds that the CIA had refused to produce witnesses for the trial.

The details of the story revealed to Ellsberg the lying that had occurred up and down the chain of command, civilian and military, from the officers in the field to Commander in Chief Nixon, to conceal murder. They were part and parcel of the system that he had worked for and had been part of for 15 years, since his days in the Marine Corps: a system that lied automatically. The story encapsulated what that system had been doing in Vietnam on an "infinitely larger scale, continuously for a third of a century" and what it was still doing. He decided that, "I'm not going to be part of this lying machine, this cover-up, this murder, anymore."[120] The thought occurred to him that in his safe at RAND he had "seven thousand pages of documentary evidence of lying, by four presidents and their administrations over twenty-three years, to conceal plans and actions of mass murder."[121] He made up his mind to stop hiding this information and to—somehow—make it public. This meant he would have to copy the Pentagon Papers. But he could not possibly do it at RAND or at a copy shop. He thought of leasing a copy machine and called his close friend Tony Russo.

The two had struck up a friendship shortly after Russo returned to RAND in 1968. It began the day Ellsberg walked into Russo's office and asked to be briefed on the Viet Cong Motivation and Morale Project. Ellsberg was then working on his

---

[120]Ellsberg, *Secrets*, 2002, p. 289.

[121]Ellsberg, *Secrets*, 2002, pp. 289–290.

"Lessons of Vietnam" and wanted to know about a study that, as Ellsberg told Russo, evoked controversy wherever he went in Washington. Russo said, "Sure, sit down." Ellsberg sat down and pulled out his steno pad and started taking notes. Russo briefed him "continuously for the next year," about the project, about his readings on Vietnam, and lent him some books.[122]

According to Ellsberg, Russo had an office down the hall from his. Russo often shared with him what he had learned from the interviews and showed him a number of the transcripts. Russo was impressed by the patriotism, dedication, and conviction of many of the defectors and prisoners he had interviewed, and he told Ellsberg that many of the defectors left the Viet Cong ranks for personal reasons or because they could no longer put up with the hardships, and had nothing disparaging to say about the cause or their top leaders.[123] Ellsberg saw that Russo, who had gone to Vietnam as a Cold Warrior, had returned changed by his encounters with the North Vietnamese and Viet Cong and by their stories. He had come back with admiration for them and with a conviction about the justice of the cause they were fighting for. Ellsberg, however, did not share Russo's views, having not had Russo's experience with members of the NLF.

According to Ellsberg, Russo was subsequently fired by Charlie Wolf, the perceived pro-war chairman of the Economics Department, for having written a critical analysis of the herbicide program in Vietnam; for having exposed in a classified study the widespread mistreatment and torture of Viet Cong prisoners by the ARVN— "often with American advisers observing"; and for having written a rebuttal of Ed Mitchell's study on land tenure and rebellion. There was also concern among some people at RAND that the Air Force would react negatively to Russo's herbicide and prisoner mistreatment studies. Ellsberg was impressed with Russo's work, so when Russo told him that he was being fired, Ellsberg told Wolf that "it was a mistake and a real loss for the department." Wolf insisted to Ellsberg that "the decision was for budgetary reasons," although Ellsberg noticed that Russo seemed to be the only one who was cut off.[124] By this time, Russo had become "very cynical about everything," and thought, "[Well,] he's really doing me a favor,' because working for RAND is not good for one's reputation as far as I am concerned."[125]

After Russo left RAND at the end of 1968, Ellsberg started to see him after work and they became close friends. Ellsberg found Russo funny and thought that he had "a

---

[122]Author interview with Tony Russo, 2003 and 2004.

[123]Konrad Kellen, who had read hundreds of the interviews, had gone away with the same impression: that the prisoners and defectors had nothing critical to say about their regime. Kellen had urged Ellsberg to pass along to Henry Kissinger his conclusion that "this was one adversary whose leadership and population . . . could be annihilated but not coerced." Ellsberg, *Secrets*, 2002, p. 290.

[124]Ellsberg, *Secrets*, 2002, p. 291.

[125]Author interview with Tony Russo, 2003 and 2004.

very original and creative mind, and not just about the war."[126] Russo and Ellsberg held the same view about the war, and believed that "it was time for acts of resistance."[127] On September 30, as Ellsberg made up his mind to photocopy the Pentagon Papers, he did not have any doubt that Russo was "one friend, the only one, I could tell what I wanted to do."[128] Russo, for his part, was fond of Ellsberg, whom he found to be different from the "robots" and "automatons" with "zero consciousness" who worked at RAND. Russo had heard of the McNamara Vietnam Task Force before he left for his second tour in Vietnam. Russo said he remembered "exactly" that he urged Ellsberg in his office at RAND, "Dan, you should leak that," and that Ellsberg looked up at the wall "with a slight smile on his face," rolled his eyes, and said, "My God, that would be something." Afterward, Russo would frequently ask Ellsberg, "Dan, have you leaked it yet?"[129]

Ellsberg, on the other hand, disputes Russo's recollection because the volumes were not at RAND in 1968. Ellsberg points out that the study was not completed until 1969 (although the cutoff date for the history of the war was March 1968, after the Tet Offensive), and Ellsberg brought the volumes to RAND in August of that year. "This is a total mis-memory of his," Ellsberg said, "There was very little to copy actually in early '68, except what I had done on '61."[130] Also, Ellsberg said that, at the subsequent Pentagon Papers trial, Russo testified under oath "that the first time he knew that I had worked on the study was September 30, 1969, the day I asked him for a copy machine. That was the first time he knew that I had worked on it or that [it] existed [at] RAND."

Russo had heard about the study and had asked Ellsberg if he knew anything about it, and Ellsberg was evasive. Russo also asked Gus Shubert, who was evasive as well. Ellsberg insists that it was not Russo who "got me to copy the Pentagon Papers." To him, Russo's recollection is "just the way a lot of people mis-remember things that put them in the center of things which they weren't part of."[131]

Ellsberg, however, does give Russo credit for having planted a seed in his mind. A week or two before they started copying the Pentagon Papers, Russo talked about the "lying that he knew from the Motivation and Morale Study," and Ellsberg said he had read a study—without mentioning the Pentagon Papers and without saying that it was at RAND—"Well, that's true at the highest level, too, and I read a study that showed that there was a great deal of lying at the highest level." Russo told him, "Whatever you

---

[126] Ellsberg, *Secrets*, 2002, p. 291.

[127] Ellsberg, *Secrets*, 2002, p. 294.

[128] Ellsberg, *Secrets*, 2002, p. 291.

[129] Author interview with Tony Russo, 2003 and 2004.

[130] Author interview with Dan Ellsberg, 2005.

[131] Author interview with Dan Ellsberg, 2005.

know, you should put that out."[132] Ellsberg recalls that "this was a significant moment," because although he had "decided to do anything that was worthwhile to do," he had not "particularly focused on putting out the Pentagon Papers." What Russo suggested was very unusual, and what Russo said "might well have been working in my mind a week or two later when I did decide to put it out, as something to do," and that "it did have an influence." However, Ellsberg said that "the idea that he'd been pressing me on this for a year previously just has no relation to reality whatever."[133]

Ellsberg also acknowledged that perhaps if Russo had not planted the idea in his mind, he might not have copied the Pentagon Papers at all in September 1969, and if he had waited, he might have concluded that it would be futile to do so because, on November 3, 1969, Nixon gave a speech that indicated that he was not going to get out of Vietnam—the speech marking the turning point at which Vietnam became Nixon's war. In the speech, Nixon essentially told the American public that the United States would stay in Vietnam until peace on American terms was achieved through Vietnamization, de-Americanization, negotiation, and escalation should Hanoi rev up the tempo of the war.

When Ellsberg got to Russo's apartment, he told his friend, "You know the study I told you about a couple of weeks ago? I've got it at Rand, in my safe, and I'm going to put it out." As Ellsberg had surmised, Russo did not ask for an explanation and simply said, "Great! Let's do it."[134] Ellsberg told him that it would take a long time to copy the volumes and asked whether Russo could locate a Xerox machine. Russo told Ellsberg, "I'm pretty sure I can," because his girlfriend ran an ad agency on Melrose and Crescent Heights that had a Xerox machine—which was relatively new at the time.[135] In the early evening of October 1, 1969, Ellsberg took out the 1964–1965 volumes of the McNamara study, which filled two drawers of his office safe at RAND, to photocopy. He thought this Johnson period had parallels with the Nixon era: "a president making secret threats of escalation, and secret plans to carry them out if they didn't work, as was almost certain; a war on the way to getting much larger and longer, with the public wholly unaware."[136] He had not thought through how and when he would release them, but he wanted this to happen before anti-war demonstrations took place on October 15 all across the United States as part of a nationwide campaign given the designation of "Moratorium." Time was of the essence.

Gus Shubert later speculated that the volumes were kept in Harry Rowen's office safe and that Rowen let Ellsberg have access—although Shubert acknowledged that

---

[132] Author interview with Dan Ellsberg, 2005.

[133] Author interview with Dan Ellsberg, 2005.

[134] Ellsberg, *Secrets*, 2002, p. 295.

[135] Author interview with Tony Russo, 2003 and 2004.

[136] Ellsberg, *Secrets*, 2002, p. 300.

it was "a very complicated business" and that his memory might not be accurate.[137] It could be that Ellsberg would take the volumes from Rowen's safe as he needed them and keep them in the safe in his office while he was using them, because the set had not been entered into RAND's security control system. If it had, he would have had to either read them in the Top Secret Office or borrow them and return them when he left his office. At his trial in 1973, Ellsberg would admit under cross-examination that "on two occasions in 1969, he stored the volumes in the safe of Harry Rowen . . . so they would not be discovered in inventories by the top secret control officer. This was because of an agreement to keep them out of Rand's top secret control system. . . . "[138] Ellsberg took the volumes that night, put them in his briefcase, and walked out of the RAND building. He was nervous, but he knew that the guards would not check his briefcase. As expected, the two security guards on duty who knew Ellsberg simply said, "Good night, Dan."[139] He went into the parking lot and drove to Tony Russo's apartment. Russo's girlfriend was there, and the three of them drove to her office, located on the second floor above a flower shop.

With Russo's help, Ellsberg Xeroxed the pages, and then worked alone until 5:30 the next morning. He waited until 8:00 before going to his office, walked past the security guards to his office, and put the volumes back in his safe. He would repeat this process: taking the volumes out at the end of the work day, Xeroxing them, and then putting them back in his office safe the next morning.[140] He knew that publishing highly classified documents without authorization was a crime and that he could get a life sentence, but he did not dwell on the consequences for himself, or for his family, or for others who might be implicated He even enlisted his son Robert, who was 14 at the time, to help him Xerox the volumes. Later, he would say that—like most people—he did not know then that the United States does not have an Official Secrets Act under which unauthorized disclosure of top-secret information would be prosecuted as a crime.[141] At the same time, however, he also knew that he would not be revealing secret codes in official documents because the Pentagon Papers were not at

---

[137] Author interview with Gus Shubert, 2004 and 2005.

[138] Gene Blake, "Ellsberg Admits He Violated Pledge on Pentagon Papers," *Los Angeles Times*, April 18, 1973. Ellsberg conceded in court that he had signed "in good faith" the "promises not to copy the top-secret Pentagon Papers on the Vietnam war." He admitted that "no one had given him permission to remove the documents from Rand Corp. and reproduce them."

[139] Ellsberg, *Secrets*, 2002, p. 300.

[140] At his trial later, Ellsberg would testify that he "always returned the Papers to RAND the next working day." However, author Tom Wells considered this "unlikely, given his disorganization and the greater risks that would have involved. Ellsberg's testimony was probably designed to help beat the criminal charge he faced that he had 'converted' the documents to his use; he had not deprived anybody of the material, he was effectively saying." Wells, *Wild Man*, 2001, p. 325.

[141] Glenn Greenwald, Salon Radio interview with Daniel Ellsberg, 2008.

the "code-word level"—a higher classification than Top Secret.[142] Revealing such secret codes would certainly have landed him in jail for life.

For his part, Russo knew that "he was getting involved in something extremely serious." He also recalled that Ellsberg reassured him—several times—that he would "take the heat for the whole thing," and that Russo would be "free and clear." Russo, however, knew that "when something like that goes down, I would be the first one they'd come to. Because people had associated us at RAND."[143] Ellsberg thought that Russo and his girlfriend were incurring a legal risk, but they were helping him voluntarily. Besides, according to him, he did not believe then that he was putting them at great risk. As for his best friend and supporter, Harry Rowen, Ellsberg knew that his action would damage his career, but he thought that such damage was unavoidable if he were to achieve his objective. Apparently, Ellsberg felt that his cause was "bigger than Rowen, bigger than RAND."[144]

Given that Ellsberg is a complex man, it is hard to detect his true motivation in copying and ultimately releasing the Pentagon Papers. He himself thought it was moral outrage, but others ascribed various motives to his action: a love of adventure and excitement; his guilt over his participation in the prosecution of the war and his need for atonement; his disappointment over his lack of brilliant accomplishments and, therefore, his desire to make a big splash to make up for his failure to meet expectations; his anger and frustration for having had his advice ignored by those in power; his need to impress Patricia Marx, the anti-war activist who would become his second wife; his desire for publicity; his ambition to make it big; his egomania. Gus Shubert thought that Ellsberg did it "for two reasons: the greater glory of Dan which is always a big motivation for him, and because he really believed it."[145] According to Shubert, after Ellsberg was identified as the source of the leak, Albert Wohlstetter said,

---

[142] Prados and Porter, *Inside the Pentagon Papers*, 2004, p. 33

[143] Wells, *Wild Man*, 2001, p. 321. Gus Shubert remembered running into Tony Russo at a small social gathering at Dan Ellsberg's house at Malibu Beach around the time the two were secretly photocopying the Pentagon Papers. Russo had adopted the counterculture look and "the hirsute appearance of the sixties. . . . He was so shaggy, you could hardly see his face, and he wore a cap" pulled down almost to his eyes, "so there was nothing but hair and eyes." When Shubert asked Russo what he was doing, Russo smiled and said, "Oh . . . a little bit of this and a little bit of that." Shubert asked whether he was enjoying doing it, and Russo said, "I love it. It's really something I can't describe to you, but some day you'll know about it." Collins, interview with Gus Shubert, session of May 28, 1992, pp. 66–67.

[144] Wells, *Wild Man*, 2001, p. 345.

[145] Author interview with Gus Shubert, 2004 and 2005. Joseph Kraft ("Ellsberg: Unlike the Others," 1971) wrote that Ellsberg had an inclination toward "dramatization and self-dramatization." Ellsberg, according to Kraft, "loved to run covert operations and once demonstrated the possibilities by leaving a dinner party only to return five minutes later disguised as an Arab." A colleague of Ellsberg's, discussing his motivation, told a reporter, "People keep looking for some key to Dan. . . . Why can't the story be a fine mind finding out the truth, and acting on it." Paul L. Montgomery, "Ellsberg: From Hawk to Dove," *The New York Times*, June 27, 1971.

RAND's presidents: Donald B. Rice (1972–1989), Franklin R. Collbohm
(Director 1948–1956, President 1956–1967), and Henry S. "Harry" Rowen (1967–1972)

"The only way he would have liked to have done it better is to swing upside down . . . from the chandelier."[146] It is probable that his action was motivated by a combination of feelings.

♧ ♧ ♧

While Ellsberg was engrossed in Xeroxing, the anti-war letter was drafted. The group did not plan to either use RAND stationery or identify that they worked for RAND; they would simply state that they were "professional researchers and analysts on Vietnam, by implication working for the government."[147] They had agreed early on that they would show the letter to Harry Rowen before mailing it, but they thought that it would not be possible for him to stop them from sending it as private individuals. He could, however, fire them or take other punitive measures. Kellen said that, if Rowen forbade it, they would not go ahead, and the rest of the group agreed.[148] Ellsberg

---

[146] Montgomery, "Ellsberg: From Hawk to Dove," 1971. Ellsberg denies that he released the Pentagon Papers to attract publicity. He says that he was "a backroom boy," and "an anonymous bureaucrat," and that he was "happy with that." He also says that he expected bad publicity and condemnation from what he was going to do, and that he anticipated being called a "traitor," a "madman," and a "terrible guy." See Wells, *Wild Man*, 2001, p. 342. Ellsberg also denies that he was motivated by a need for atonement. However, in a lecture given "shortly *before* [emphasis in original] the Papers were published . . . he stated, 'As I look back at my own role in the last eight years, it is with a heavy sense of guilt.'" Wells (*Wild Man*, 2001, p. 344) claims that Ellsberg later cut this statement out of the published version of his lecture.

[147] Ellsberg, *Secrets*, 2002, p. 311.

[148] Arnold Horelick recalls that the group knew that they were putting their jobs on the line, but agreed that they would resign if Harry Rowen thought that it would unacceptably damage RAND. Author interview with Arnold Horelick, 2004.

suspected that Rowen was opposed to continuing the war and would sympathize with the letter privately, but he also thought that Rowen—as president of RAND—would find it difficult to approve it. Therefore, making the publication of the letter dependent on Rowen's blessing was unrealistic, he thought. At the same time, he could understand why the others were reluctant to proceed without Rowen's approval: They were concerned about retaining their jobs and their security clearances, whereas he himself was past that point. Ellsberg was not an active participant in the drafting of the letter, because he was exhausted from spending every night Xeroxing the Pentagon Papers so that he could get the information to Congress or the public by the Moratorium Day called by anti-war groups for October 15.

The analysts' plan was to show the letter to the heads of their respective departments, Fred Iklé in Social Science and Charlie Wolf in Economics, if Rowen approved the letter. They suspected that Iklé and Wolf would oppose it, but if Rowen had cleared it for RAND, they could not possibly stop it. They finished the letter on Wednesday, October 8, obtained an appointment with Rowen, and walked into his office as a group. Rowen read it attentively but did not appear to disapprove of what he was reading. He told them that it was going "to cause a good deal of trouble for Rand from its sponsors" but he did not dwell on this idea.[149] Then he asked why the letter was not typed on RAND letterhead. They explained that they did not wish to associate RAND with it, and he said that it would transpire anyway that they worked for RAND and this "would look as though we were trying to hide it." He asked them to use RAND letterhead, but to make it clear that they were speaking as individuals and not for RAND or for its employees. He tried to look at the bright side and said, "We'll get heat for this, but there's a good side to it too; it will show we encourage a diversity of views here."[150]

For his part, Rowen recalled that he did not tell the group, "Look, this is inconsistent with your work here," and so the letter was sent.[151] He also said that, "In hindsight, I probably should just have let them sign without identifying RAND, let the press figure it out, which would have taken them very little time. Probably that would have been the way to handle it, I imagine, in hindsight. But I didn't, and that was that."[152] Ellsberg says that he respected Rowen—and still respects him—for his decision. Subsequently, a RAND vice president told Ellsberg that Rowen had made a significant mistake and should have solicited the opinion of the Board of Trustees. However, Newton Minow later said that even if the issue had been presented to the Board of Trustees, the Board would not have interfered. He was not chairman at the time, but if he had been and if he had been asked, he would have said, "That's fine. People can

---

[149] Ellsberg, *Secrets*, 2002, p. 311.

[150] Ellsberg, *Secrets*, 2002, p. 311.

[151] Author interview with Harry Rowen, 2005.

[152] Author interview with Harry Rowen, 2005.

say what they think," and privately, he would have said, "Congratulations."[153] Gurtov guessed that Rowen did not attempt to stop the group because he might have thought that the damage would be limited and that the letter "would just be another voice in the wind and it would pass after a day or two."[154]

The letter called for complete U.S. withdrawal within one year, and for this disengagement not to be contingent upon "agreement or performance by Hanoi or Saigon"—that is to say, without making it "subject to veto by either side." The writers made clear that they had worked on government projects and that, therefore, they were insiders who nevertheless were calling for unilateral withdrawal from Vietnam. They expressed the view that, "apart from persuasive moral arguments," there were four factors that precluded continuing U.S. involvement in the war: (1) enemy forces could not be eliminated by military means, unless the United States was prepared to destroy the whole country and its population; (2) past promises to the people of Vietnam were "not served by prolonging" an "inconclusive and highly destructive military activity"; (3) the importance of the future political arrangement in South Vietnam to American national interest had been "greatly exaggerated"; and (4) "[a]bove all, the human, political, and material costs of continuing our part in the war far outweigh any prospective benefits, and are greater than the foreseeable costs and risks of disengagement." The letter ended by declaring, "We do not predict that only good consequences will follow for Southeast Asia or South Vietnam (or even the United States) from our withdrawal. What we do say is that the risks will not be less after another year or more of American involvement, and the human costs will surely be greater."

The group sent a copy of the letter to Fred Iklé and made an appointment to see him. Ellsberg does not recall whether they also showed the letter to Charlie Wolf. According to Ellsberg, the meeting with Iklé was difficult. Four of the signers belonged to the Social Science Department, and they kept silent during the meeting, leaving it up to Ellsberg to respond to Iklé's challenges. Since Ellsberg's name came first in the alphabetical listing of signers, Iklé assumed that Ellsberg was the one who had instigated it and written it, so he aimed his objections at him. Ellsberg had been Iklé's colleague for ten years. He did not know him well, but they liked and respected each other. Ellsberg describes him as a Swiss who was "very reserved in manner and speech," and "not an easy person to get close to."[155]

According to Ellsberg, Iklé did not argue much with the contents of the letter, because he probably did not find much to disagree with. But he was dismissive and patronizing, referring to their "letter to the editor" in a contemptuous tone. The approach "did not make any sense," Iklé told them. "A letter to the newspaper! How could that possibly accomplish anything?" He doubted that it would have much of

---

[153] Author interview with Newt Minow, 2005.

[154] Author interview with Mel Gurtov, 2004.

[155] Ellsberg, *Secrets*, 2002, p. 313.

an effect on high government officials, who probably would not even read it and with whom they could communicate directly through their privileged position.

As to other audiences that the letter could reach, Iklé dismissed them as unimportant.[156] When Ellsberg mentioned that the letter might be published in *The New York Times*—which Ellsberg had contacted—Iklé became "distraught," saying that publication would damage RAND. He suggested what he considered a more effective and productive alternative, which was to write a classified study on the budget costs of the war and transmit it to the SAC commander with a letter pointing out how the cost of continuing the war was "cutting into his budget for modernization." Then he turned to Ellsberg and said, "This letter is no way to operate in Washington." Ellsberg pointed out that he knew better than Iklé how to operate in Washington, and said, "I think this is worth doing." Iklé looked glum as the group left his office; it would be 22 years before Iklé would speak to Ellsberg again.[157] In the hall, the group confirmed that they would still go through with the letter, although several of the group who were on Iklé's staff looked gloomy.[158]

Ellsberg had contacted Steve Roberts, the *New York Times* Los Angeles bureau chief, who was waiting in the parking lot. Ellsberg gave him the letter, and Roberts told him that it would appear the next day. The next morning, Thursday, October 9, the *Times* published a by-line by Roberts in an inside page with the headline, "Six RAND Experts Support Pullout: Back Unilateral Step Within One Year in Vietnam." The *Times* did not publish the letter but treated it as part of a news story, saying that it was written "by men of considerable expertise who normally shun publicity," and said that the letter "provided new impetus to the growing public demand for swift disengagement from Vietnam." The story identified them as RAND analysts who had performed research on Vietnam for the U.S. government—but pointed out that they were speaking for themselves as individuals and not as employees of RAND. It added that Ellsberg had worked in Saigon for the State Department for two years. Ellsberg was not entirely happy with the story, because he thought that a few points he considered important were omitted, but, on the whole, he was pleased that it reflected the gist of their position.

Since *The New York Times* had not published the entire letter, the group offered it to *The Washington Post,* which published it in the center of its editorial page on Sunday, October 12, with the heading "A Case Against Staying in Vietnam," but juxtaposed it with an op-ed letter by Henry Owen, formerly head of the State Department's Policy Planning staff, and an editorial on the Moratorium, both pieces denouncing their call for unilateral withdrawal within one year. The signers of the letter were attacked as "hard-core critics" and once as "extreme critics." *The Washington Post,* however, also

[156] Ellsberg, *Secrets,* 2002, pp. 313–314.

[157] Ellsberg, *Secrets,* 2002, p. 314.

[158] Ellsberg, *Secrets,* 2002, p. 314.

carried a column by Joe Kraft in the same issue with the headline "Breaching the Code: RAND Analysts' Protest on Vietnam Policy Raises Basic Question of Responsibility." The column was based on Kraft's interviews with Ellsberg and some of the other signers. It focused on the moral issue raised by the public dissent of people who performed work for the government, rather than on the substance of the letter.

Kraft's column began with the statement, "When six analysts from the Rand Corp. drop their slide rules and open their mouths to protest about Vietnam, something important has happened." To Kraft, the protest went "beyond the issue of Vietnam to the central moral problem of American public life" and raised the "question of the responsibility borne by officials and analysts for the action and policies they serve." Kraft pointed out that RAND's existence depended on funding and a good relationship with the federal government, and that RAND's analysts traditionally had only "questioned prevailing government policies behind closed doors." By protesting publicly against a government policy with which they disagreed, the six signers of the letter had breached this tradition, and they had done so "over strong opposition from some of Rand's chief executives" and at some risk to the future of their careers.

To Kraft, there was "nothing shocking in the views" expressed by the letter signers, because such views were also held by many senior officials in the present and previous administrations. However, only a few of these officials had expressed their thoughts publicly, preferring to "play inside politics." By adhering to "the basic Washington mystique that fidelity to a President transcends fidelity to convictions on even the most critical issues," they had "followed the code of the apparatchik." For Kraft, the letter's main importance was as "a repudiation" of this code. He concluded his column with the statement that, by making a public protest, the signers had breached "bureaucratic tradition of mute service even when policy conflicts with conscience." This concluding sentence was particularly satisfying for Ellsberg, who was contemplating another, even more spectacular, public protest with the release of the Pentagon Papers.

The letter—and the subsequent unauthorized release of the Pentagon Papers—encapsulated the fraying of the Cold War consensus within RAND. As Arnold Horelick recalls, prior to Vietnam, debates within RAND occurred within a very strong consensus, and there was no ideological split. This also held true for the United States at large. Many people at RAND were of the World War II generation, and, to them, the United States was automatically on the side of right. At the beginning of the Vietnam War, the common assumption was that the war was a legitimate effort and that it was doable. The purpose of RAND was to help the United States prosecute the war more successfully, and the debate was on what the best way to fight the war was. As the war began to get bogged down, there was genuine disagreement within RAND, which became split between people who were hawks and people who were moderate and wanted to find more-effective and sustainable ways to conduct the war.

At the same time, there were a number of people who were not as engaged with the issues of the war. Outside of the Social Science Department, people who paid close attention to Vietnam were skeptical that the war was going anywhere, but they believed it would be too costly for the United States to withdraw because of their faulty understanding of the Soviet Union and China, believing that they were allied in a plan to dominate the world. According to Horelick, by 1968–1969, people should have understood that China and Vietnam were not great allies, and that the Soviet Union was only helping Vietnam because it was competing with China and because it thought the war was tying down the United States—and not out of any grand scheme for world domination. Besides, neither could really tell Vietnam what to do.

When things began to go badly in Vietnam, most RAND people were reluctant to conclude that U.S. policies could be as wrong as they turned out to be. It was harder still for them to go into opposition. Then, as the war broke up the country and domestic costs became unacceptable, some people concluded that the effort was not sustainable. Some looked for ways for the United States to stay, but at lower costs. A smaller number of people concluded that the war was not winnable. An even smaller number of people looked for ways for the United States to withdraw. A tiny number, such as the signers of the letter to *The New York Times* and *The Washington Post,* advocated unilateral withdrawal. That just six analysts at RAND signed the letter was indicative of the prevailing attitude at RAND, according to Bernard Brodie.[159]

Bob Levine, an analyst in the Economics Department at the time, remembered that RAND was split over Vietnam, and that the letter illustrated that division.[160] It was a division that Ben Bagdikian—who had joined RAND as guest consultant at Harry Rowen's invitation and was later to become an assistant managing editor of *The Washington Post*—picked up on at social gatherings of the Cold War generation. There were those who said, "You've got to stay the course" or who thought that, "You've got to be tough." To them, "the only problem was the peaceniks who are hampering" the effort "to defeat the enemy in Vietnam."[161] Bagdikian recalled that there were a lot of anti-war demonstrations at the time, and at parties he would hear some people muttering, "What they need is for the cops to shut them down." Bagdikian said that the hardliners were angered by the anti-establishment scene, and he remembered that they were upset and bitter over the burning of the American flag in the counterculture *Aquarius* musical, or over what they perceived as the "glorification of the peaceniks" in the movie *Jesus Christ Superstar.*

He recalled going to a performance of *"Aquarius"* with some of these people. They became so angry that, after the performance "they drove their cars out of the parking lot at 50 miles an hour." In contrast, there were people at RAND who saw Vietnam

---

[159] Dobbin, "Rand Corporation Still Feels," 1973.

[160] Author interview with Bob Levine, 2004.

[161] Author interview with Ben Bagdikian, 2003.

"as a failed enterprise." According to Bagdikian, "The whole country was divided," and so was RAND.[162]

Gus Shubert recalled that about 65 to 70 percent of the RAND staff "carried over all their Cold War thinking into Vietnam," believing in the domino theory and subscribing to the fear that the communists were "going to get us."[163] At the same time, between 30 to 35 percent—like the "silent majority" of Americans—"not only questioned but contested those assumptions."[164] RAND was in a turmoil over Vietnam, but the differences between hawks and doves were not so much due to political orientation, "because . . . there were Democrats who wanted to go over and pave the place, and there were Republicans who wanted to get out," but to different perspectives on how to examine "reality and alternatives." People saw that the war was not the same as the U.S. confrontation with the Soviet Union, and this "raised a whole host of different questions, and blind loyalty or blind dedication to a principle, it was quickly seen by many, didn't get you anywhere. You really had to do some thinking backwards instead of forwards, and that thinking backwards raised a lot of troublesome questions."[165] This examination and questioning led some to recognize that the war was a tragic mistake.

Commenting on the aftermath of the publication of their anti-war letter, Gurtov says that it turned out to be "another voice in the wind." Although the letter had no effect, "it felt good."[166] Internally, however, the letter caused a furor, because the signers had crossed a line and were perceived as people who were putting the organization at risk. Before this incident, civility reigned at RAND. Konrad Kellen remembered that RAND was a very polite place, and hawks and doves got along, "I mean I could go

---

[162] Author interview with Ben Bagdikian, 2003.

[163] Collins, interview with Gus Shubert, session of May 28, 1992, p. 46. According to Daniel Ellsberg, most people within the Social Science Department and Economics Department—with the exception of Charlie Wolf, Chuck Cooper, and consultant Ed Mitchell—agreed on the war. Engineering, however, included "a lot of right wing Republicans and general hawks" who "didn't know anything about the war to speak of, but . . . probably supported it." Author interview with Dan Ellsberg, 2004.

[164] Collins, interview with Gus Shubert, session of May 28, 1992, p. 46.

[165] Collins, interview with Gus Shubert, session of May 28, 1992, pp. 47–48.

[166] Author interview with Mel Gurtov, 2004. Senator Goodell entered the letter into the *Congressional Record* on October 13, 1969, declaring on the floor of the Senate that it was "extremely significant" when such experts from "one of the oldest and most respected research institutions" specializing in national security urged unilateral withdrawal. Their letter represented "one of the most cogent pieces of reasoning . . . on why it is essential that the United States disengage its troops from this terrible war within the next year" and provided "another piece of evidence that swift disengagement from Vietnam is the only policy that makes sense." See "Statement by Rand Corp. Staff Members Favoring Total Withdrawal of U.S. Troops from Vietnam Within 1 Year," *Congressional Record*, Senate, introduced by Mr. Goodell, October 13, 1969, S12395.

Senator George McGovern also quoted from the letter in a speech in the Senate and entered it into the *Congressional Record* in its entirety on October 13, 1969. See "The Only Way out of Vietnam," *Congressional Record*, Senate, October 13, 1969, S12377.

out to lunch if I wanted to with the greatest hawk and he with me."[167] However, Mel Gurtov said that this civility and tolerance of diversity of views existed up to a point. As long as dissent was kept "within the boundaries of secrecy and privacy"—and the dissenters "weren't going out demonstrating" against the war, for example—and as long as it was stated in papers in a non-outrageous way, it was tolerated. "So, the whole discourse was kept within proper boundaries," he said, "and as long as that happened, why, I guess it was OK."[168]

The civility evaporated after the letter was published, and Gurtov recalled that there were a lot of memos attacking them for having jeopardized RAND. According to him, these colleagues "were concerned that they'd lose their jobs, and that in some ways government support would be cut back, and that we had no right to do that." He adds, "they were more upset about that aspect than about the contents. Nobody questioned our right to believe what we did about US policy but the manner in which we did it was threatening and was inappropriate, and should not have been done." At the same time, the doves "appreciated our courage in doing that, and wished us well and all that."[169] Gurtov said that despite what happened, the group had no regret.

Arnold Horelick's recollection was that the letter hit RAND "like a bombshell." A strong majority expressed animosity toward the signers and were vociferous in condemning them for having violated the privileged relationship between RAND and the government—a relationship they viewed as akin to that between a lawyer and his client. Horelick, for his part, thought that he was only behaving like a private citizen expressing his strong conviction that the Vietnam War was damaging the country. He thought that RAND as an institution should be examining the full range of alternative options for dealing with the Vietnam War, including withdrawal, as well as strategies for sustaining continued struggle. According to Gus Shubert, most people at RAND thought that the letter writers were "simply gutless bastards." It was "strong language," he said, "but there was a lot of strong language around the halls."[170] Many at RAND still believed that the United States could succeed if it would just "try something else," or that more bombing would "do the trick," or that the Viet Cong were buckling under the U.S. military onslaught. So, according to Shubert, these people found it galling that some of their colleagues would go out and say publicly the opposite, and they were very angry.[171]

Ellsberg said that he had never seen such a deluge of memos coming from all corners of the corporation. Somehow people thought that the group had used the RAND

---

[167] Author interview with Konrad Kellen, 2002.

[168] Author interview with Mel Gurtov, 2004.

[169] Author interview with Mel Gurtov, 2004.

[170] Collins, interview with Gus Shubert, session of May 28, 1992, p. 66.

[171] Collins, interview with Gus Shubert, session of May 28, 1992, p. 66.

letterhead on their own and this pushed them into "a frenzy of memo writing." With few exceptions, the memos were all "negative, often very hostile, angry, reproachful, disdainful, accusatory," calling the letter writers' behavior "reprehensible" and attacking them for their "lack of professional ethics."[172] What surprised Ellsberg was that those who bombarded the group with memos hardly questioned the substance of the letter. Generally, each wrote that he [nearly all the professional staff at RAND were male] opposed continuing the war as well, but condemned them for having behaved irresponsibly toward RAND, its staff, and possibly toward the country itself. Ellsberg had expected to be criticized for damaging national security and RAND's credibility and effectiveness vis-à-vis the Air Force. He thought those who objected would say, "We're doing important work for the military and you're undermining that because you're hurting our relations."[173] He would have accepted that as a reasonable concern and substantive objection, but, instead, everyone said, "You're jeopardizing my job, my income." Their reaction to a letter addressed to newspaper editors, which, after all, expressed views held by most of the American public, as well as by many people at RAND in private, disappointed Ellsberg, who had expected them to be more idealistic.[174]

An example is a memo, dated October 14, 1969, written by Ed Sharkey in the Engineering Department, condemning the letter. It was strongly supported by some other critics. Sharkey sent copies to many influential people at RAND, including Harry Rowen, Vice-President Goldstein, Bill Graham, Fred Iklé, and Charlie Wolf.[175] In it, Sharkey wrote that he too favored withdrawing U.S. combat forces from Vietnam—although for "more cogent reasons" than those expressed by the letter writers—but he felt that he had no right as a RAND professional to go over RAND and its clients into the national media to influence someone with his individual views. The professional obligation for the RAND staff was to present the best remedies for critical national problems to government agencies, and to persevere at persuasion no matter how discouraging this could be at times, instead of "moaning loudly in public that things are in dreadful shape, and suggesting unilateral national retreat from problems." If this task of persuasion became too burdensome for some, they had the option of resigning from RAND and then going out to make their views public.

However, the most compelling reason for Sharkey's condemnation appeared to be the potential threat that he thought the letter might pose to RAND's existence. He pointed out that, in the past year, the Air Force had developed a great lack of sympathy for RAND and had cut its contract with RAND by $3 million. Within DoD,

---

[172] Ellsberg, *Secrets*, 2002, p. 317.

[173] Author interview with Dan Ellsberg, 2004.

[174] Author interview with Dan Ellsberg, 2004.

[175] Edward Sharkey, "Your Letter to *The New York Times* and *Washington Post*," Santa Monica, Calif.: RAND Corporation, Memo M-7193, October 14, 1969.

there had been some sympathy for restoring the cut, but the letter might cause adverse reactions within the parts of government that were more favorable toward the continued existence of RAND than the Air Force. There was no reason why the Executive Branch, Congress, or the Defense Department would be happy with the letter and, by their action, the letter writers had put the future of RAND at stake and jeopardized everyone who worked at RAND. In Sharkey's view, RAND was the only organization that had the potential for leading the way toward correcting the many military and political problems facing the government, and therefore it was "inexcusable" for the letter writers to weaken this crucially important institution. His conclusion was that their letter and interviews with the press bordered on complete irresponsibility toward their colleagues, RAND itself, "and quite possibly, the welfare of the country."

Merritt W. Olson, also of Engineering, agreed with Sharkey, but added that he deemed the action of the letter signers "reprehensible" because it was "a complete and offensive violation of the recognized rules of conduct" associated with their special status as RAND employees, and because they had "jeopardized the idea, the concept, and the existence of the RAND Corporation." H. H. Bailey, also of Engineering, opined that they may put their jobs on the line, but they did not have "the right to lay" his on the line as well. Jack Ellis wrote that RAND had been betrayed by "a flagrant attempt to use its professional image and strength in the public press to further the individual views of a few staff members" and that its image and reputation had been jeopardized. In his view, RAND staff should abide by a code of behavior similar to that of "client and lawyer," but if they felt their views were not receiving a proper hearing within the accepted channels, they should resign "before speaking out as individuals." D. H. Lewis said in his memo that being a RAND employee located at the Pentagon when the letter was published was a "unique experience." He believed that "the confidences and trusts" that had been built up in the Air Force had been badly damaged, and hoped "that the six authors get exactly what they deserve."[176]

Many of the memos originated in Engineering. However, John Mallett of that department was actually encouraged by the letter. He wrote that perhaps RAND had not been "dead" but only "sleeping," and there was hope for RAND because its people

---

[176] Merritt W. Olson, "Your Behavior and Your Letter to *The New York Times* and *Washington Post*," Santa Monica, Calif.: RAND Corporation, WM-1302, October 25, 1969; H. H. Bailey, "Your Letter to *The New York Times* and *Washington Post*," Santa Monica, Calif.: RAND Corporation, M-7308, October 17, 1969; Jack Ellis, "Your Letter to *The New York Times* and Its Aftermath," Santa Monica, Calif.: RAND Corporation, M-7290, October 17, 1969; D. E. Lewis, memo to E. H. Sharkey, "Your Memo M-7193 Regarding the Letter to the Editor of *The New York Times*," Santa Monica, Calif.: RAND Corporation, WM-1315, October 23, 1969.

While many of the critics worried about an adverse Air Force reaction, at least one Air Force colonel, Eugene F. Calafato, seemed to show a balanced attitude. He wrote to Paul Langer that he respected "those who have the courage of their convictions," although he had "unresolved doubts . . . concerning the wisdom" of the course advocated by the letter. But he believed that the articulation of the authors' views represented "a valuable input" to the national decision process. See Eugene F. Calafato, Colonel, USAF, letter to Paul Langer, October 15, 1969.

were starting to voice their opinion on not just one side of an important issue. He wondered why this had not happened sooner. When it came to Vietnam, it was mostly the young in America who had "turned the tide" and "pointed the way," rather than RAND and its experts. They were the ones who had "deposed a powerful president and set the wheels in motion to question our society, our goals and our military involvement." RAND's charter was broad, and it spoke of "national interest, not dedication to client," and if RAND compromised and became an apologist for its clients, then it would not be RAND. He thanked the letter signers for having awakened the RAND staff and RAND's management for "grappling with the task of nurturing a Rand that not only eats but is responsive to its Charter."[177]

The controversy prompted Kathy Archibald, one of the handful of female professionals at RAND, to write a memo expressing her view that RAND professionals should be grateful to the letter writers for forcing them to examine their role as analysts vis-à-vis their government clients.[178] If it was similar to that of a lawyer giving advice to a client, then no one should make any public statement supporting certain alternatives. However, at times, some analysts had spoken out "loudly on public platforms" when their work produced conclusions that were "consistent with client policies or desires"; but when their studies suggested that "the client may be seriously in error," they remained "silent in public debates." This had been true especially with regard to defense policies, the consequences of which could be most serious, creating the perception that "professional expertise" was "overwhelmingly lined up [on] one side of the issue." It would be difficult to come up with arguments, she wrote, that "could convince anyone that this effect contributes to democratic decision-making or to the national welfare."

The publication of the letter gave rise to an intense debate within RAND regarding the legitimacy and propriety of airing views in the media that contradicted government policies.[179] To clarify this issue, Harry Rowen addressed a memo to RAND

---

[177] John D. Mallett, memo to Harry Rowen, "Better Late Than Not at All," Santa Monica, Calif.: RAND Corporation, M-7283, October 17, 1969.

[178] Kathy Archibald, "Issues Behind the Vietnam Letters," Santa Monica, Calif.: RAND Corporation, M-7630, October 30, 1969.

[179] At the same time, expression in the media of opinions that supported government positions did not usually provoke outrage at RAND. Ben Bagdikian pointed out in his memo of October 28, 1969, that he could not recall any outrage when some RAND staff members who supported weapon development or the "outlook of particular agencies" of government succeeded in getting their views into the media. There was no criticism, although they too identified themselves as RAND employees who were speaking only for themselves and not for the organization, and although they publicized their views "precisely to influence public opinion on a subject under debate"— as the six letter writers had done. Ben Bagdikian, memo to Harry Rowen, "The Vietnam Letters," Santa Monica, Calif.: RAND Corporation, M-7573, October 28, 1969.

employees, stating that they had the right—as the writers of the letter to *The New York Times* and *The Washington Post* had—to air their personal views in public, as long as they did not divulge classified or proprietary information or violate contractual agreements regarding the public release of information.[180] He pointed out that management advised against sending the letter, but felt that the authors had the right to do so, and insisted that the signers identify themselves as RAND staff members speaking as individuals and not for RAND or for their colleagues, since not mentioning RAND could have led the newspapers to charge that RAND was resorting to "covert action."

But the issue of public expression of opinion became less clear-cut when what was involved was not "the right of a staff member to express himself, but the propriety and likely effect of such expression." Many of the issues over which members of the professional staff may want to state their position publicly were also questions over which other staff members differed. On some of these issues, expressing one's view in public "may make more difficult the private and more effective conduct of research and presentation of research results. In such circumstances, the propriety as distinct from the right of any particular public expression is itself bound to be subject to differing and sometimes intensely held views. This problem raises difficult questions not unlike those affecting the relationship between lawyer and client."

Although "[n]o machinery or procedure is likely to make" decisions easier, Rowen announced that he was establishing a "Committee on Professional Standards," chaired by Roger Levien, to advise the professional staff on how to proceed in cases that were not clear-cut. Rowen urged members of the professional staff to consult with this committee "in any case in which they believe that a proposed public expression or activity raises substantial questions of propriety, or of probable effect on Rand." Rowen concluded that, in the end, "responsibility for a personal statement must remain with the individual, but he must bear a corresponding responsibility for its consequences. And the Rand management has a responsibility not only to see that contractual commitments to clients are observed but also to judge the propriety of the actions of members of the staff."

Along with his memo, Rowen issued a "Policy Statement—Public Expression of Personal Views" that attempted to delineate personal freedom of expression versus responsibility to clients. RAND encouraged intellectual independence among its research professionals working on issues of public policy, and its vitality and usefulness to its sponsors depended "crucially upon this independence." Professional staff members had the "fundamental right of any American ultimately to decide, as responsible citizens, whether, when, and how to state their personal views in public discussion," even when they "might be controversial or contradict current Government policy." However, RAND was neither a university nor a part of the U.S. government, and RAND

---

[180]Harry Rowen, memo to "Everyone at Rand" and "Policy Statement—Public Expression of Personal Views," Santa Monica, Calif.: RAND Corporation, M-7357, October 21, 1969.

researchers had "special responsibilities" that must dictate their decision whether to publicly voice their opinions. RAND's objective was "to help decision-makers choose among policy alternatives by providing them with careful, objective analysis as to the consequences of these alternatives." To achieve this objective, RAND had to maintain trust with its clients. Therefore, there was a tension between the requisites for RAND's success: "freedom of expression and participation; personal concern for public well-being and national interest; and Rand's responsibility to its clients and to the public." How each professional dealt with this tension could affect the ability of others to function, and so he must weigh these considerations and expect his colleagues, "along with Rand management—whose special responsibility it is—to judge the propriety of his action."

The division over the Vietnam War within RAND that Gus Shubert and others had observed became public with the printing of a letter written by four other RAND professionals opposing the position taken by the signers of the letter calling for unilateral withdrawal. On Tuesday, October 14, 1969, *The Washington Post* published a letter signed by Ellsberg's colleagues in the Economics Department: Chuck Cooper, Hans Heymann, Albert P. Williams, and Charlie Wolf. To Bernard Brodie, these four pro–Vietnam War letter writers were probably more representative of the "hundreds of other Rand workers" than the six anti-war letter signers.[181] In their counter-letter, the four RAND analysts wrote that they wanted to make clear that "there are others at Rand with equivalent professional experience in Vietnam and Southeast Asia who, as individuals, hold different views as to what U.S. policy should be." They fundamentally disagreed with their colleagues, who they thought had underestimated "the continued relevance and importance of the basic principles that underlie the war in Saigon"—namely, resisting aggression and thwarting the "use of force to change political boundaries."

Instead of calling for unilateral withdrawal, the group advocated an unconditional "responsible reduction in U.S. military support" that would make it possible for the South Vietnamese to increase the effectiveness of their government and armed forces—which were "showing signs of continuing improvement"—to better defend themselves. Although they agreed with their colleagues that the North Vietnamese had demonstrated "resiliency, determination, and effectiveness," they felt that it would be a grave mistake for the United States to base its policy either on an "overly optimistic view" of the enemy or on an "over[ly] pessimistic view" of the South Vietnamese allies' ability to survive on their own. If the United States pulled out "precipitously" and left behind a military vacuum, and if it withdrew with "the expectation of only

---

[181] Dobbin, "RAND Corporation Still Feels," 1973.

half-hearted political support in the future," it would put a "crushing, not stimulating, pressure on the Saigon government."

The letter was also submitted to *The New York Times*, and on Saturday, October 18, 1969, Steve Roberts published another article with the headline "Four at Rand Ask Gradual Troop Cuts." Unlike the *Post*, which published the letter in its entirety, Roberts treated it as part of a news story, with extensive excerpts. Roberts identified the four as experts on Vietnam and Southeast Asia and wrote that their letter called for a "responsible reduction" in the number of combat troops, which would "allow the South Vietnamese gradually to assume a larger burden of the fighting." Roberts mentioned that the first RAND letter advocating unilateral withdrawal had "caused considerable upset within Rand," which was doing "76 percent of its work for the Defense Department" and had "recently received several lucrative research contracts from the White House." According to Roberts, some RAND staff members feared that the letter would "jeopardize the company's confidential relationship with Henry A. Kissinger. . . ." In comparing the two letters, Roberts wrote that they "differed primarily on their assessment of the South Vietnamese government and army." The second letter did not seem to cause a ripple at RAND, proving Ben Bagdikian's point that public expression of views supportive of government policies rarely, if ever, provoked outrage among the staff.

Because of the "considerable upset" they had caused, the six signers of the letter calling for unilateral withdrawal came under intense pressure at RAND. Years later, Konrad Kellen would tell Dan Ellsberg that they held on to their jobs by their fingernails and that an effort was made to get rid of all of them. Arnold Horelick, for his part, recalled that signing the letter did not have an adverse effect on his position at RAND. The issue of his security clearance came up briefly, but he retained it. He went on eight years later to serve in the U.S. Intelligence Community and was awarded the Distinguished Intelligence Medal when he left government service.

Mel Gurtov recalled that the pressure on him to leave RAND did not arise until 1971. It came from Fred Iklé, who told him "to start thinking about something else."[182] The message was "never couched in terms of 'the letter,'" but the implication of what he said was "pretty obvious." Gurtov remembers that Iklé, whom he describes as "a difficult person to deal with . . . a very unemotional guy and not someone who had much of a personality," came into his office and said "in his own particular way . . . that the opportunities for further work would be limited. I think that's close to the way he put it." However, in the end Gurtov left on his own because he wanted to start a teaching career at UC Riverside in June of that year. By this time, he had been at RAND for

---

[182] This quote and the following ones in this paragraph are from the author's interview with Mel Gurtov, 2004.

five years and had written a lot, and he was beginning to feel that he did not want to devote the rest of his life "to that kind of work." Also by this time, he had obtained his doctorate degree and he was ready to leave and go into teaching. So, "two things did come together: my interest in finding something else to do and RAND's interest in having me go."

On October 13, 1969, the day after the letter appeared in *The Washington Post*, Senator William Fulbright sent Ellsberg a letter asking him and two other signers to testify at hearings before the Foreign Relations Committee on a number of resolutions dealing with Vietnam, beginning on October 27. When Charlie Wolf heard that Ellsberg had accepted Fulbright's invitation, he summoned Ellsberg into his office and asked him to resign before he testified. Ellsberg refused, and Wolf told him, "You're only being asked because you're from Rand. You're exploiting the name of Rand, its reputation for objectivity and high-level access. You should dissociate yourself from Rand by resigning, so you can speak as an individual. Otherwise, you're using the name of Rand to give your opinions an authority they wouldn't have otherwise."[183] Ellsberg argued that he would not be speaking for RAND, but he had earned the right to speak from RAND. As to exploitation, RAND had obtained its reputation from the work of people like him. "Who's exploiting whom?" Ellsberg asked, "Rand uses *our* objectivity, our honesty, our names, or rather our work."[184] Wolf had been unhappy with Ellsberg for some time over his lack of productivity, and Ellsberg's activism simply worsened an already-frayed relationship. Ellsberg, however, says that, since he had to keep the existence of the Pentagon Papers at RAND secret, he could not tell Wolf that he was reading and taking notes from them for his study on the lessons of Vietnam, and so Wolf got the impression that he was not productive.

Ellsberg refused to resign, telling Wolf, "You can fire me, Charlie. But I'm not going to resign. You'll have to fire me if you feel that strongly."[185] Ellsberg did not want to resign because he wanted to appear before the committee with all the authority he could command, "as a past official of Defense and State, with two years' service in Vietnam, and a past and current Rand analyst."[186] Later that day, he told Rowen about Wolf's attempt to force him to resign. Rowen immediately replied, "Well, I'm not asking you to do that. In fact I don't want you to do that. That would look bad for us."[187] Fulbright's invitation meant that Ellsberg would not have enough time to finish copying the Pentagon Papers before the Moratorium on October 15 and prepare for his appearance in the Senate at the same time. This meant that he would have to delay

---

[183] Ellsberg, *Secrets*, 2002, p. 321.

[184] Ellsberg, *Secrets*, 2002, p. 321.

[185] Ellsberg, *Secrets*, 2002, p. 321.

[186] Ellsberg, *Secrets*, 2002, p. 321.

[187] Ellsberg, *Secrets*, 2002, p. 321.

his schedule for leaking the papers. However, being in the Senate might give him an opportunity to pass along all the documents he had managed to copy by the time he appeared for the hearings.

In Washington, Ellsberg told Jim Lowenstein, the aide to Fulbright who had invited him, and Norvil Jones, Fulbright's legislative assistant, about the McNamara study and explained how it could be used for hearings. They thought that Fulbright should hear this himself, so they took Ellsberg to his office. It was late in the afternoon, and Ellsberg was carrying the portions of the Pentagon Papers that he had Xeroxed in a couple of briefcases. He briefed Fulbright and the aides about the study and told them the reasons that Congress and the public ought to know the contents, which showed a pattern of deception by four previous presidents very similar to that now being practiced by Nixon. He believed that, by revealing this pattern of deception, Congress could act to stop Nixon from escalating the war. Ellsberg said that he had thought of giving the documents to the press, but it seemed to him that congressional hearings would be the best platform for revealing them. The documents were classified Top Secret, but "much of the information had been wrongfully withheld from Congress and was highly relevant to what was going on now."[188] Ellsberg thought that Congress could "subpoena witnesses, in both closed and open sessions, and force them to explain the discrepancies between these documents and what they had told the public."[189] According to Jones, Ellsberg thought that "it would be dynamite" if the papers were released and that the information might push Congress "to take strong action to end the war." Jones, who had long experience working in Congress, was skeptical.[190]

According to Ellsberg, Fulbright was enthusiastic and told him to give the materials to Jones to prepare for the hearings. Ellsberg asked not to be disclosed as the source because he was not eager to go to jail, and Fulbright said that he did not think that they would have to attribute their acquisition of the papers to him. Release of the papers through the Foreign Relations Committee would protect Ellsberg against prosecution; as he would later say, "I thought I was much safer . . . if they came out in a hearing."[191] As they were about to leave, Ellsberg asked Fulbright whether he would like to see the volume on the Tonkin Gulf incidents. Ellsberg knew that Fulbright would be interested, since Fulbright felt that Lyndon Johnson had deceived him about these incidents. Indeed, Fulbright said that he would like to see it. Ellsberg then handed him an

---

[188] Ellsberg, *Secrets*, 2002, p. 326.

[189] Ellsberg, *Secrets*, 2002, p. 326.

[190] Wells, *Wild Man*, 2001, p. 351. Subsequently, the course of events made Jones feel that he had been correct. Weeks after the Nixon Administration provided a set of the Pentagon Papers to the House and Senate, Jones found out that only one senator had taken the trouble to look at the set for a few minutes. Also, the publication of the papers did not affect the Senate vote on the McGovern-Hatfield Amendment to cut off war funding for all of Indochina by the end of 1971.

[191] Wells, *Wild Man*, 2001, p. 349.

extra copy he had made. It was a deliberate act by Ellsberg so that he would be able to say in court later, if it came to it, that he had given the classified material to the chairman of the Senate Foreign Relations Committee in front of witnesses.

After they left Fulbright's office, they went to the next room, where Ellsberg emptied his briefcases on Norvil Jones's desk. Ellsberg promised Jones that he would send him the rest of the study later.

Once back in Santa Monica, Ellsberg resumed his routine of taking the classified materials out of his office at night and driving to the office of Russo's girlfriend to Xerox the documents. He was now photocopying by himself, because Russo and his girlfriend had stopped coming to help. As he finished copying sections of the study, he shipped them to Norvil Jones, who would later say that he did not know then how Ellsberg got hold of the Pentagon Papers. "This was all a mystery," he would recall.[192] Jones locked the papers in his safe. Fulbright, meanwhile, was not inclined, out of political caution, to release Top Secret documents. Instead, Fulbright asked Jones to write to Defense Secretary Melvin Laird to obtain the McNamara study officially. Their effort would fail repeatedly. In April 1970, the FBI got wind that Ellsberg had copied Top Secret documents and given them to Senator William Fulbright—as well as to Senator Charles Goodell, who had introduced legislation asking for a complete withdrawal by December 1970. Ellsberg learned this through his former wife after agents had come to see her. He thought, "The jig was up," and presuming that they would come to RAND next to see him or Harry Rowen, he decided to leave because he did not want to be arrested at RAND or to make things difficult for Rowen.[193]

Ellsberg's resignation might not have been as voluntary or as altruistic as he made it out to be. According to one account, when two FBI agents came to see Rowen, the RAND president told them that Ellsberg was leaving, that he had been "encouraged to look for another position," and that it had been agreed "he should leave in April."[194]

In fact, as far back as January 1970, the FBI had gotten wind that Ellsberg was copying the Pentagon Papers.[195] Throughout the spring of that year, as part of its extensive investigation, the FBI interviewed RAND's senior officials, among others. The meeting with Rowen was part of that investigation. However, the RAND officials "were under the impression" that they should do nothing to tip off Ellsberg or "to take any action that might interfere with the investigation."[196] Ellsberg, consequently, was not stripped of his Top Secret clearance.[197] For his part, Rowen neither alerted Defense

---

[192] Wells, *Wild Man*, 2001, p. 351.

[193] Ellsberg, *Secrets*, 2002, p. 333.

[194] Wells, *Wild Man*, 2001, p. 359.

[195] Peter Schrag, "The Ellsberg Question," *The New York Times*, June 17, 1974.

[196] Schrag, "The Ellsberg Question," 1974.

[197] Schrag, "The Ellsberg Question," 1974.

Department security officials—an omission that would later anger those people—nor did he instruct RAND to launch its own investigation.[198]

Charlie Wolf would later say that Ellsberg was not pressured to leave, but that his performance evaluations were not encouraging because of lack of productivity, missed deadlines, and unfulfilled commitments, and that these evaluations might have hastened Ellsberg's departure, since their message was that RAND was not the place for him.[199] Besides, Ellsberg's colleagues had turned unfriendly, because, as Konrad Kellen said, "he was a very vocal dove . . . [and] his whole way of doing things was too flamboyant for RAND."[200] At any rate, Ellsberg called Everett Hagen, an economics professor and head of the Center for International Studies at MIT, who had invited him to the campus for a year as a senior research fellow. Ellsberg had turned him down when the invitation was extended, but now wanted to find out whether it still stood. Hagen told him that he could start immediately.

Ellsberg then went to see Harry Rowen and told him that he was leaving RAND. Rowen did not try to talk him out of it, and Ellsberg surmised from Rowen's quick acceptance that, after the tension of the past few months, Rowen was relieved to see him depart. Rowen, in his usual understatement, said only, "It's too bad it has to end like this."[201] When Ellsberg informed Charlie Wolf of his decision, Wolf asked him to leave RAND by April 15—before his second Senate testimony on May 13. However, Wolf wanted Ellsberg to stay on as a consultant so that he could finish his paper on "Revolutionary Judo" by June—a deadline Wolf later extended to July. Ellsberg would depart at the end of the summer, when RAND terminated his consultancy.

On April 13, Ellsberg flew to the East Coast to sign the contract at MIT. When he returned to Santa Monica, he had to move to a small office on the fourth floor, where he worked on "Revolutionary Judo." The FBI did not appear, and the danger of being exposed seemed to recede for Ellsberg. Apparently, the investigation was dropped in fall 1970, after the Justice Department and the FBI decided that it did not warrant pursuing.[202] When Ellsberg's consultancy was ended, Richard Best and his assistant repeatedly requested that Ellsberg sign RAND's and the Department of Defense's "Security Termination Statements," "certifying that he was not retaining any classi-

---

[198] Wells, *Wild Man*, 2001, p. 359.

[199] Ellsberg denied that he was pressured to leave because of his lack of productivity. He claims that he was "one of the most valuable and distinguished people . . . that RAND had," that he was "a terrific asset," whether he "produced for them this month or that month. . . ." So Wolf could not fire him. Besides, Harry Rowen had no desire to fire him. Wells, *Wild Man*, 2001, p. 360.

[200] Wells, *Wild Man*, 2001, p. 360.

[201] Ellsberg, *Secrets*, 2002, p. 334.

[202] Wells, *Wild Man*, 2001, p. 359.

ficd information and would not disclose any to those not cleared for it."[203] However, Ellsberg refused to do so.

Events in 1970 convinced Ellsberg further of Nixon's plan to escalate the war. In that year, Nixon began to lean toward bold military actions that would, as Henry Kissinger put it, "persuade Hanoi to negotiate."[204] To the mix of diplomatic triangulation, Vietnamization, and "madman threats," Nixon and Kissinger would add military attacks, which Kissinger conceived mainly in terms of "air operations."[205] As Nixon told Melvin Laird, his Defense Secretary, "we must play a tough game."[206] That "tough game" would extend beyond the secret bombing of Cambodia to include the invasion of this country. In March 1970, the deposition of Prince Norodom Sihanouk of Cambodia by General Lon Nol in a coup d'etat offered Nixon the chance to ratchet up the pressure on Hanoi and demonstrate Nixon's "madman theory."[207]

Sihanouk had been performing a balancing act to keep his country from being engulfed in the war next door, by adopting a neutral stance while tolerating the presence of communist sanctuaries and troops on his soil, and allowing them to purchase supplies in Cambodia and to use the port of Sihanoukville. Sihanouk was out of the country when the coup took place. In response, he flew to Beijing and declared support for the communist Khmer Rouge insurgents—whom he had been trying to eliminate. The new Lon Nol government immediately ordered Vietnamese communist troops to leave, canceled agreements with Hanoi, and asked South Vietnam for assistance in attacking the sanctuaries. Washington welcomed Sihanouk's overthrow and, as the coup plotters had hoped, the United States extended diplomatic recognition, channeled weapons and money to Lon Nol's government, and authorized the South Vietnamese to conduct operations against the sanctuaries.

---

[203]Wells, *Wild Man*, 2001, p. 363. Best would later testify to this effect at the Pentagon Papers trial. Gene Blake, "Pentagon Papers Jury Told of Security Pacts," *Los Angeles Times*, February 13, 1973. Best also read "acknowledgments by both Ellsberg and Russo that they understood it would be a violation of law to copy or disclose to unauthorized persons any top-secret materials." Blake, "Pentagon Papers Jury Told of Security Pacts," 1973.

[204]Kissinger, *White House Years*, cited in Kimball, *Nixon's Vietnam War*, 1998, p. 184.

[205]Kissinger, *White House Years*, cited in Kimball, *Nixon's Vietnam War*, 1998, p. 184.

[206]Cited in Kimball, *Nixon's Vietnam War*, 1998, p. 183.

[207]No evidence of direct U.S. involvement in Sihanouk's overthrow had been uncovered. But some degree of encouragement was probably extended. As author William Shawcross wrote in his book *Sideshow: Kissinger, Nixon, and the Destruction of Cambodia* (New York: Simon and Schuster, 1987), Kissinger declared in 1977 that the United States was not involved, "at least not at the top level." Shawcross added, "It was clear . . . that Americans in Vietnam were aware of its planning and were indirectly in touch with the plotters. In some circumstances, there is only a fine line to be drawn between foreknowledge and complicity." Cited in Kimball, *Nixon's Vietnam War*, 1998, p. 199.

B-52 raids prepared the ground for the incursion, which began on March 27 and continued into April. Some operations penetrated ten miles into Cambodia, and some were joint attacks with the Cambodian military. Hanoi responded by attacking Cambodian troops and positions to cover their evacuation from the border areas and protect existing and newly established bases, communication lines, and weapon and ammunition caches. They also declared support for the Khmer Rouge, who were gaining strength among the population in areas devastated by secret U.S. bombings. The Vietnamese communist attacks, combined with the emboldened Cambodian insurgency, threatened the existence of the Lon Nol regime, whose support was narrow and confined to the middle class and elite in the capital of Phnom Penh, and to the army. The rural masses, still loyal to Prince Sihanouk, were hostile to the new regime. The director of the CIA, Richard Helms, reported to Nixon that the new government appeared fragile.

In this context, Nixon's meeting in Honolulu on April 19 with Admiral John McCain—whose son was a POW in Hanoi—inclined him more toward an idea he had been considering for some time. McCain argued for an invasion to save the Cambodian government, thereby protecting South Vietnam's western flank as U.S. troops withdrew and permitting Vietnamization to succeed. Nixon had been thinking about invading two border areas jutting into South Vietnam—known as the Fish Hook and the Parrot's Beak—with American and South Vietnamese forces, to attack communist sanctuaries. Kissinger recalled in *White House Years* that this joint invasion had been a strategic option favored by Ambassador Ellsworth Bunker, General Creighton Abrams, the Joint Chiefs, and Richard Helms.

According to White House aide Bob Haldeman, Nixon and Kissinger believed that the incursions launched by the South Vietnamese army had only "crippled" the North Vietnamese but could not destroy their sanctuaries.[208] This, they thought, could be achieved only with an invasion carried out mainly by American troops. The invasion fit Nixon's desire to make bold moves in Laos and Cambodia, out of a belief that, if he could maintain enough pressure on Hanoi he could wind up the war in 1970. Nixon expected that the invasion would send "a symbolic, threatening message to Hanoi" and, at the same time, save the government of Lon Nol; close the port of Sihanoukville; destroy enemy sanctuaries and troops; capture the NLF's command headquarters COSVN, which American intelligence believed was located in this region—and protect Vietnamization.[209]

With Nixon's approval, the operation was launched on the morning of April 29, Saigon time. Phase I consisted of 8,700 South Vietnamese troops—12 infantry and armored battalions—attacking the flanks of the Parrot's Beak. On the morning of May 1, 1970, Saigon time, Phase II began. U.S. armored and heliborne units pen-

---

[208] Kimball, *Nixon's Vietnam War*, 1998, p. 206.

[209] Kimball, *Nixon's Vietnam War*, 1998, p. 206.

etrated into the Fish Hook from the south and east, supported by a smaller South Vietnamese force attacking from the north. Artillery, B-52s, and fighter bombers prepared the ground for the invading force, numbering 15,000 men. Ultimately, the total invading force would number 31,000 American and 19,000 South Vietnamese troops. Fighting was heavy during the first two days but tapered off as enemy units moved away. Search-and-destroy operations continued through May and June. The invasion eventually spread over a large swath of Cambodian territory and was reinforced by naval vessels outside Sihanoukville and aircraft bombing supply depots north of the DMZ. To drive home his point, Nixon poured a large number of troops and heavy firepower into Cambodia.

At 9:00 p.m. Washington time on April 30, one-and-a-half hours after the U.S. invasion of the Fish Hook had begun, Nixon appeared on national television to inform the American people, blaming the enemy for necessitating the action. However, he did not mention the secret bombing or the previous incursions. Across the country, many campuses erupted in protests, and demonstrators rallied in the streets to oppose the invasion. On May 4, National Guardsmen called to the campus of Kent State University in Ohio fired into a group of protesters, killing four students and wounding another nine. The shooting sparked widespread protests nationwide against the killing and against the invasion of Cambodia, at over 1,300 universities and colleges in the month of May. The day after Kent State, Nixon, feeling under pressure, promised that he would pull troops out of Cambodia by the end of June.[210]

On April 30, Ellsberg watched Nixon announce the invasion on television. For Ellsberg, the invasion was proof of Nixon's plan for escalation, and he tried to convince various people of Nixon's secret and dangerous machinations. Traveling to Washington on May 9 to appear on a public television program, *The Advocates*, as an opponent of the war, Ellsberg found the capital shrouded in tear gas and its streets filled with over 100,000 students who had gathered from universities and colleges that had been shut down all across the country. He also found Congress very angry at the president for having invaded another country without making a pretense of consulting with the House and the Senate. Appearing with Ellsberg on the program was Senator Charles Goodell, who was calling for American withdrawal from Vietnam and Cambodia.

On May 13, Ellsberg testified before the Senate Foreign Relations Committee, during which he spoke about U.S. support for a succession of unpopular governments in Vietnam and mentioned specifically the case of his friend Tran Ngoc Chau, who

---

[210] The protests did not deter Nixon from sending South Vietnamese troops into southern Laos for Operation Lam Son 219 on January 1971, to disrupt North Vietnamese supply lines on the Ho Chi Minh Trail. The operation, slated to last for 90 days, ended in a debacle after 60 days, and ARVN troops were driven back into South Vietnam.

had been put on trial in March by President Thieu, allegedly because of his secret contacts with his brother in North Vietnam. The real reasons, John Paul Vann had told Ellsberg, were that Chau had been denouncing the corrupt dealings of the government and advocating negotiations with the NLF. The arrest had affected Ellsberg deeply and strengthened his opposition to the Saigon regime. But Ellsberg did not take this opportunity to reveal the Pentagon Papers, even when Fulbright questioned him at length about his knowledge of the Tonkin Gulf incidents.

It was in that same month, May 1970, that RAND finally entered the Pentagon Papers into its security control system. This fact was revealed during the Pentagon Papers trial. As reported by journalist Martin Arnold of *The New York Times,* RAND conceded in court on February 15, 1973, that the Pentagon Papers had been "in its hands for 16 months before they were entered into the corporation's top secret control system."[211] Richard Moorsteen, who had become a manufacturer in San Diego by this time and was appearing as a witness for the prosecution, testified that this happened after Ellsberg walked into his RAND office on May 20, 1970—Ellsberg's last day as a full-time employee at RAND—and put the papers on his desk. Moorsteen said he took one quick look and called Harry Rowen, and "within an hour 'the Rand top secret control officer came with a little cart and picked them up' and gave him a receipt." Earlier on the same day, Richard H. Best said "under cross-examination that the failure to put the papers into the control system for so many months was unusual, and that he had no explanation for it."[212] Rowen himself told the court that "he learned they were not in the system when Ellsberg was about to leave the Rand Corp. and asked what he should do with the volumes."[213] He admitted, "This was an irregular procedure," and "conceded he did not report Ellsberg for security violations."[214] Jan Butler, RAND's Top Secret Control Officer, subsequently logged them into the system. She also removed all Top Secret documents from Ellsberg's office safe on May 20, 1970.[215]

In 1970, Ellsberg was still trying to influence the policies of the Nixon Administration. In August of that year, Ellsberg met with Henry Kissinger at his office in San Clemente. Ellsberg thought he would encourage Kissinger to read at least sections of the Pentagon Papers so that he would learn that hopes for escalations in the past had been dashed and draw some lessons. Kissinger, who had a copy in the White House, asked, "Should I?" Ellsberg told him he should "at least . . . read the summaries" at the beginning of each volume: about 60 single-spaced pages in all. "They make a very

---

[211] Martin Arnold, "Rand Concedes Delay in Putting Pentagon Papers Under Control," *The New York Times,* February 16, 1973.

[212] Arnold, "Rand Concedes Delay," 1973.

[213] Blake, "Unaware of Pentagon Data Probe," 1973.

[214] Martin Arnold, "Rand Concedes Delay in Putting Pentagon Papers Under Control," *The New York Times,* February 16, 1973.

[215] Wells, *Wild Man,* 2001, p. 361.

readable story. You really should make the effort," he told Kissinger, who asked, "But do we really have anything to learn from this study?" Ellsberg's "heart sank," but he went on to say, "Well, I certainly do think so. It's 20 years of history, and there's a great deal to be learned from it." Kissinger said, "But after all, we make decisions very differently now."[216] Ellsberg realized that he was not getting anywhere with Kissinger and concluded that Kissinger was seeing him only so he could say that he was listening "to everyone, the whole range of opinions."[217]

By December 1970, it seemed clear to Ellsberg that Fulbright was not going to release the papers or use them. By this time, Ellsberg had supplied Norvil Jones with almost the entire documentation. However, the war was receding in importance in public opinion and there was no support within the Foreign Relations Committee for hearings that might provide an opportunity to divulge the existence of the papers. Besides, Fulbright was not about to take the risk of disclosing highly classified information. In a meeting that month, Fulbright had asked him, "Isn't it after all only history?" When Ellsberg replied that it was "quite important history," and a history "that wasn't over yet," Fulbright said, "But does it really matter? Is there much in there that we don't know?" Fulbright asked him to give an "example of a revelation that would make a big splash." Ellsberg said that "it was not any individual page or revelation, or even a small set of them, that was very important." He added, "It was the overall detailed documentation of our involvement over the years and the repetitive patterns of internal pessimism and of desperate escalation and deception of the public in the face of what was, realistically, hopeless stalemate."[218] Following this meeting, Norvil Jones suggested that Ellsberg "might just give the study to *The New York Times*."[219]

Next, Ellsberg offered the papers to Senator George McGovern, a strong war critic, in January 1971, but McGovern turned him down. McGovern would later recall that he "wasn't about to break the law" by releasing the papers, and told Ellsberg to do so himself and "take whatever risk," since he had control of the papers. McGovern said he was "indignant" that Ellsberg thought that "it was fine for a United States senator to break the law, but not for him."[220] McGovern suggested that he hand the papers over to *The New York Times*. Ellsberg also tried senator Charles Mathias, who turned him

---

[216] Ellsberg, *Secrets*, 2002, p. 347.

[217] Ellsberg, *Secrets*, 2002, p. 349.

[218] Ellsberg, *Secrets*, 2002, p. 357.

[219] Ellsberg, *Secrets*, 2002, p. 357.

[220] Wells, *Wild Man*, 2001, pp. 390–391. McGovern disliked Ellsberg. He recalled that "There was a certain arrogance that I saw in him that turned me off. And a kind of an implication, 'Well, now that I have decided that the war doesn't make sense, everybody else ought to immediately turn off on it.' You know, I'd turned off on it years before then. I just kind of resented the lack of appreciation for people who had been opposing him and other advocates of the war all those years."

down. Mathias asked for papers on the Nixon Administration, and Ellsberg gave him a copy of the classified NSSM-1.

The New York Times was also suggested by Dick Barnet, Mark Raskin, and Ralph Stavins of the Institute for Policy Studies, a left-leaning think tank. Staff of the institute were writing a book "analyzing U.S. involvement in Vietnam in relation to war crimes," and Ellsberg lent them parts of the Pentagon Papers for background research.[221] In February 1971, Ellsberg met with them during a trip to Washington for a speaking engagement at the National War College. When they learned that Ellsberg had failed with Fulbright and McGovern, they told him that it was very important for him to publicly release the papers so that they could refer to the documents in their book, which was due to be published by June.

Since disclosure by Congress was not an option, Ellsberg thought that, among the newspapers, the *Times* looked like the "obvious choice."[222] He had met Neil Sheehan, one of its reporters, in Vietnam and had leaked Top Secret information to him in 1968. Sheehan had just written an article on war crimes for *The New York Times Book Review.* Ellsberg called Sheehan and asked to spend the night at his house. They talked all night, and Ellsberg was struck by Sheehan's "passionate involvement with the war, his feeling that it had been a terrible mistake and waste of lives on both sides, his intense desire to see it over."[223]

Sheehan had done extensive coverage of Vietnam and would likely appreciate the significance of the Pentagon Papers. Also, his experience suggested that *Times* editors would take his recommendation seriously. During the conversation, Ellsberg mentioned the Pentagon Papers and said that he had the entire study in his possession. Sheehan was keenly interested in reading it. He said he could not promise that the *Times* would use it, but if the study was as Ellsberg described, he believed it would. Ellsberg said that he would show the study to him in Cambridge, and they made a date for Sheehan to come to Boston.

A week before, Ellsberg had given an interview to Tom Oliphant of *The Boston Globe*, during which he mentioned the secret McNamara study to support his analysis that "Nixon's secret threats fitted into a pattern of failed threats and escalations that had lasted over twenty years" and his warnings about Nixon's war policies "were based on more than intuition."[224] Ellsberg also said that Les Gelb and Mort Halperin, who had "read this whole history had drawn much the same policy conclusions."[225] Oliphant subsequently interviewed Gelb and Halperin, and published an article on

---

[221] Ellsberg, *Secrets*, 2002, p. 365.

[222] Ellsberg, *Secrets*, 2002, p. 365.

[223] Ellsberg, *Secrets*, 2002, p. 368.

[224] Ellsberg, *Secrets*, 2002, p. 369.

[225] Ellsberg, *Secrets*, 2002, p. 369.

March 7, 1971, with the headline, "Only 3 Have Read Secret Indochina Report; All Urge Swift Pullout." The article quoted Halperin as saying, "I think the President is not getting out. I think the present policy runs grave risks of further escalation, and I think it's splitting the country apart."[226] The article quoted Ellsberg as saying that the secret study had affected his views enormously and admitting that, as he looked back on his involvement in Vietnam, he realized he was "participating in a criminal conspiracy to wage aggressive war." It ended with Ellsberg's comment that Nixon's current strategy was "a criminal policy."[227]

The revelation of the study concerned Ellsberg, who feared that the FBI might come to his apartment and take away the copies he had made of the Pentagon Papers. With the help of his wife, he got additional copies made at a commercial shop on Harvard Square, then stored the sets at the homes of friends and relatives. Oliphant's article pushed Ellsberg to release the papers before—he believed—the FBI would come and seize them. When Sheehan came to Cambridge on March 12, Ellsberg showed him a copy of the papers. Sheehan, according to Ellsberg, immediately saw that the papers "lived up to my description."[228] Sheehan said that, to convince the *Times*, he would have to read most of the volumes, which would obviously take time. He asked to make a copy, but Ellsberg turned him down. According to Sheehan, Ellsberg agreed to let *The New York Times* publish the Papers if it would subsequently print the entire study in book form. Ellsberg would say later that he set two conditions which he wanted Sheehan to convey to the newspaper: that the *Times* publish a great portion of the Papers, and that it did so with the actual documents. Ellsberg thought that if this was done, the documents would have become public knowledge in the event his copies were subsequently confiscated by the authorities. Ellsberg told Sheehan he wanted a "'big story' with a great deal of space allowed to it—that it would not be just a single day's story, large or small, but a multi-part project that could do justice to the text and documents, pages and pages of print."[229] Ellsberg agreed to let Sheehan take extensive notes, and Sheehan spent a couple of days doing so before returning to New York.

On his next trip to Boston, he told Ellsberg that "his editors were definitely interested, but that—unsurprisingly—there was a lot of debate, uncertainty, and qualms about the project."[230] The editors wanted to learn more about the contents, so Sheehan took more notes in order to better convince his editors. However, in subsequent phone calls from New York in the next few weeks, Sheehan informed Ellsberg that the *Times*

---

[226]Ellsberg, *Secrets*, 2002, p. 369.

[227]Ellsberg, *Secrets*, 2002, p. 370.

[228]Ellsberg, *Secrets*, 2002, p. 372.

[229]Ellsberg, *Secrets*, 2002, p. 373.

[230]Ellsberg, *Secrets*, 2002, p. 374.

editors were "having trouble deciding and not moving very fast toward a resolution."[231] He asked whether he could make a copy to keep with him in New York so he could work "nights and weekends on it" in preparation for the eventual publication. By now, the unceasing escalation in Vietnam had made Ellsberg feel "even more pressed to get the papers out," so Ellsberg agreed.[232]

Unbeknownst to Ellsberg, Sheehan had already made a copy of the McNamara study over a weekend, when he was in Cambridge taking notes while Ellsberg and his wife were out of town. Ellsberg would later learn that work was already under way at *The New York Times*. For more than a month, using the set of the Pentagon Papers Neil Sheehan had obtained, a team from the newspaper had been working feverishly in several suites the *Times* had rented in the New York Hilton to maintain secrecy, writing commentaries and choosing documents and sections of the text for publication. Sheehan had begun writing a series of articles based on the study, with the collaboration of Hedrick Smith, another veteran *Times* correspondent who had spent time in Vietnam. The *Times* team worked in the suite, guarded by security guards to maintain secrecy.

According to Hedrick Smith, the copy of the Pentagon Papers that the *Times* obtained, minus the volumes on diplomacy, were so massive that he spent two whole weeks reading just to get a sense of the contents. He and Neil Sheehan decided to use a historical approach, breaking the information down in sections for their articles, which eventually numbered about 12. Accompanying the articles were reprints of official cables, memoranda, and position papers.[233]

As the *Times* prepared to bring out the first issue with articles on the Pentagon Papers, it moved Sheehan and Smith along with the documents into its building, so that they would, in theory, be protected under the First Amendment. It shut down its building and checked everyone coming in and out, afraid that the FBI would arrive with an injunction before it could go to print. Word, however, leaked out. In Washington, Les Gelb and Mort Halperin knew about the impending leak when Hedrick Smith phoned Gelb to question him about the study, and they both concluded that Ellsberg was the source. Gelb contacted Warnke, who then contacted Robert McNamara. They all felt betrayed by Ellsberg. At the White House, Al Haig had also gotten wind of the impending publication. He called Walt Rostow—then in Austin, Texas—who told him that "it is a guy named Ellsberg" who had leaked them.[234]

The Washington Post also learned that something was afoot at the office of its competitor. The day before the publication, Ben Bagdikian, who had joined the *Post* as assistant managing editor, phoned Harry Rowen. Bagdikian said, "We hear that the

---

[231] Ellsberg, *Secrets*, 2002, p. 375.

[232] Ellsberg, *Secrets*, 2002, p. 375.

[233] The four volumes on diplomatic negotiations, which Ellsberg had withheld in 1971 as being too sensitive to divulge, were finally released by the government in May 2002 under the Freedom of Information Act.

[234] Wells, *Wild Man*, 2001, p. 408.

Times has something that's supposed to be very hot, and it's something to do with a RAND report"—bearing on Cuba, according to rumors. Rowen said he did not know anything about that and wanted to find out what Bagdikian knew. When Bagdikian said, "Well, do you know anything about any other subject matter?" Rowen replied, "No."[235] Rowen would later recall that he did not know anything was amiss until he read the Sunday edition of *The New York Times*.[236]

♧ ♧ ♧

Anticipating strong demand, the *Times* published a much larger run than usual of its Sunday issue of June 13, 1971. The story carried the headline: "Vietnam Archive: Pentagon Study Traces 3 Decades of Growing U.S. Involvement." Ellsberg was not revealed as the source of the leak. The publication surprised and angered Ellsberg, who had not been told by Neil Sheehan. However, he soon became exhilarated that the papers were out. At the same time, he was also apprehensive about the effect the publication would have on him personally.

At RAND, Harry Rowen immediately guessed that Ellsberg was the source. According to Gus Shubert, he and Albert Wohlstetter were in Rowen's office when the news came in. Rowen said, "It's got to be Dan[;] it's got to be Dan." Shubert asked, "How do you know that?" and Rowen replied, "I just know it."[237] Rowen would later say that, "As soon as it was published, of course, it didn't take long to figure out who it was."[238] Shubert recalled that Wohlstetter, who had been a mentor to Ellsberg, thought that "Ellsberg was a traitor who had committed a despicable act and was thus now a despicable person," and "came to detest Ellsberg and felt betrayed."[239]

According to Shubert's account, the publication was "a total surprise and total shock" for Rowen.[240] He could not believe that Ellsberg would "treat their friendship and their institutional relationship" in this manner. Rowen, Shubert recalled, "was bent by this act." He remembered being in Rowen's office when the phone was ringing off the hook. Calls were coming from "this part of the Pentagon, that part of the Pentagon, the State Department, the White House." As he fielded the calls, Rowen's voice would get "'weaker and weaker." At the end of one call, Rowen turned around to look at them and said, "I don't need this. I don't need this. I don't want this."[241] George

---

[235]Wells, *Wild Man*, 2001, p. 408.

[236]Author interview with Harry Rowen, 2005.

[237]Author interview with Gus Shubert, 2004 and 2005.

[238]Author interview with Harry Rowen, 2005.

[239]Wells, *Wild Man*, 2001, p. 418. Wells thinks that Wohlstetter "may have worried about how this debacle would affect his own reputation and influence at RAND."

[240]Collins, interview with Gus Shubert, session of May 28, 1992, p. 68.

[241]Collins, interview with Gus Shubert, session of May 28, 1992, p. 68.

Tanham, who had come to Santa Monica, recalled that, "They were all glum. . . . They were in a state of shock and knew it was goddamn serious."[242] Richard Best remembered that Harry Rowen called him on June 14, when he had arrived at his office early in the morning. When Best reached Rowen's office, Larry Henderson, RAND's vice president in Washington was there, and they wanted him to collect all copies of the Pentagon Papers and gather information "on the antecedents of this disaster." To Best, it appeared that, "Damage control has started." He also thought that they were looking for scapegoats.[243]

At the time of the release, Mel Gurtov had left RAND. He later said that he would never forget the day the first *New York Times* installment appeared. It was a Sunday afternoon and he was at the home of a colleague from the Political Science Department of UC Riverside. Before they sat down for lunch, his colleague handed him a copy of the newspaper and said, "By the way, do you know anything about this?" Gurtov was surprised but did not immediately "grasp the significance of it," and he was not "ready to think about what does this all mean." He simply said, "You know, I worked on that study. That's really interesting." Then the thought hit him, "Wow, something's really strange here[;] how did this happen?"[244]

When Tony Russo heard the news on his radio, he said, "*Oh, my God. It has hit.*"[245] He tried unsuccessfully to reach Ellsberg. He began waiting for the FBI. In Cambridge, Ellsberg and his wife—also anticipating a visit from the FBI—moved out of their apartment and, although they did not go into hiding, they made themselves scarce. By June 15, the FBI had identified Ellsberg as the "prime suspect" and gotten on his trail.

By Tuesday, the *Times* printed its third installment. Attorney General John Mitchell wrote to the *Times*, asking it to suspend publication on the grounds that it violated the espionage laws and to hand over the copy of the study. When the *Times* declined, the Justice Department asked a federal district court in New York to issue an injunction, and the judge issued a temporary restraining order while he considered the demand.

The injunction would turn the release of the Pentagon Papers into a huge controversy, because it represented the first government effort in U.S. history to stop a newspaper from publishing a story with a federal court order for national-security reasons. Initially, the public and other journalists found the massive amount of informa-

---

[242]Wells, *Wild Man*, 2001, p. 417.

[243]Wells, *Wild Man*, 2001, p. 419. Best believes that, as was Harry Rowen, "Larry Henderson had been intimately involved in the storing of the Pentagon Papers outside RAND's Top Secret Control system, and in allowing Ellsberg access to them." Apparently one RAND official wanted to fire Best. He would later say, "If they fired me, I was going to blow the front office apart."

[244]Author interview with Mel Gurtov, 2004.

[245]Wells, *Wild Man*, 2001, p. 415. Emphasis in original.

tion overwhelming, and the television networks and wire services did not take notice for nearly a day after the first *New York Times* installment appeared.[246] But when the government charged that the publication would irreparably damage the security of the United States and obtained the restraining order, it turned the publication into a test case of freedom of the press under the First Amendment and attracted worldwide attention to the story.

Since the *Times* had ceased publication, Ellsberg decided to give the Pentagon Papers to *The Washington Post*.

Afraid that he was under FBI surveillance, Ellsberg called *The Washington Post* from a pay phone, using a fake name, and Ben Bagdikian flew to Boston to meet with him. According to *Post* correspondent Don Oberdorfer, Bagdikian already knew that Ellsberg was the source of the leak, even before the revelation was made. Ellsberg agreed to provide Bagdikian with the classified materials, on condition that the *Post* refrain from divulging information about the code system embedded in the documents, because such disclosure could bring a longer prison sentence for Ellsberg. To Bagdikian, this showed that Ellsberg "had very well researched" the issue.[247] The *Post* began publishing the papers on Friday, June 18, but soon it too got a court injunction to stop publication. The story about the leaked papers began appearing in all major newspapers, including the *Los Angeles Times*. Ultimately, the case went to the Supreme Court, which decided that the newspapers could not—under the Constitution—be stopped.

By June 16, a radio station identified Ellsberg as the source of the leak. The revelation stunned the RAND staff. Kathy Scoffield, who was an administrative assistant at RAND at the time, recalled that when it became known that Ellsberg was the culprit, everyone was shocked, and Jan Butler was very "nervous and worried."[248] According to her, people were saying, "This is going to have a very big effect on RAND."[249] Bob Levine remembered that the RAND staff, who had been divided over Vietnam and over the anti-war letter to *The New York Times*, were united in their outrage at what Ellsberg had done, "no matter which side they were on" on the war.[250] Gus Shubert said that 97 percent of the people at RAND wanted to "hang" Ellsberg "from the highest tree in town." To most, Ellsberg was "a loathsome traitor."[251] Employees believed that the publication would damage RAND's relationship with the Pentagon and, hence, RAND's future; they were frightened at the prospect of losing their jobs, their income, and their

---

[246]"Cover Story: Pentagon Papers: The Secret War," *AllPolitics*, online article, June 28, 1971.

[247]Wells, *Wild Man*, 2001, p. 424.

[248]Author interview with Kathy Scoffield, 2004.

[249]Author interview with Kathy Scoffield, 2004.

[250]Author interview with Bob Levine, 2004.

[251]Wells, *Wild Man*, 2001, p. 453.

pensions. Jan Butler recalled that everyone was "stunned," and people "became more and more paranoid and fearful and angry."[252]

In a *New York Times* article dated November 16, 1971, journalist Steve Roberts described the "traumatic" effect the release had on RAND. According to him, "One reason was that staff members feared the corporation would lose the trust of the Defense Department, and thus its major source of funds."[253] Moreover, the majority of RAND people remained "devoted to the value of defense research, and to an unwritten code of conduct that stresses secrecy, anonymity and 'going through channels.'" Ellsberg's action was viewed by the staff as a violation of the rules of this conduct. In the same article, Roberts said that Harry Rowen was bitter about what his friend had done, quoting Rowen as saying in a July 1971 public statement that, "There can be no excuse or proper reason for the violation of trust and confidence by any person who has received a high security clearance from the Government."

However, not everyone at RAND condemned Ellsberg and his action. Gus Shubert said that some people thought that Ellsberg had done a good thing. Bob Holliday counted himself among those people. He thought that Ellsberg "did make a big sacrifice."[254] However, he recalled that he did not "come out firmly for or against" Ellsberg. In the atmosphere of anger reigning at RAND, he became "a bad guy" among some people because he did not condemn Ellsberg. He said, "You had to really condemn him for violating security and all that." People were aware that he knew Ellsberg from the time they were both in Vietnam, and he speculated that his lack of condemnation marked him as a friend of Ellsberg. In retrospect, Holliday thinks that his lack of condemnation "sort of marked the end of my days," and speculated that this probably explained the attitude of Peter Greenwood, his last boss at RAND, who "wasn't very nice" to him when he "got ready to leave."[255]

The unauthorized release naturally had the greatest effect on Harry Rowen. From the start, Harry Rowen probably feared that his job was on the line—especially since he was aware that Newt Minow was not "a fan."[256] According to Richard Best, Rowen "appeared uncommunicative, withdrawn, numb."[257] Patrick Sullivan, who was a RAND psychologist, recalled that Rowen was "extremely angry and anxious," although he appeared outwardly calm and in control. He knew he had a lot of explain-

---

[252] Wells, *Wild Man*, 2001, p. 453.

[253] Steve Roberts, "Rand Chief Quitting; Reason Disputed," *The New York Times*, November 16, 1971.

[254] Author interview with Bob Holliday, 2004.

[255] Author interview with Bob Holliday, 2004.

[256] Wells, *Wild Man*, 2001, p. 417.

[257] Wells, *Wild Man*, 2001, p. 417.

ing to do to the Board, since he had been "Ellsberg's chief defender and protector at RAND, sticking his neck out for him, even extolling him."[258] Above all, he had helped Ellsberg gain access to the Pentagon Papers.

Gus Shubert remembered that Rowen was "absolutely crushed . . . to think that someone as close to him, someone he knew as well as Dan, would do that. . . . He was really down. Done in by one of his very best friends." Another analyst said that Rowen was stunned and "felt betrayed in every possible way."[259] Robert Komer recalled that, "The general opinion of those RANDsters who were in-the-know was that Ellsberg had done a terrible thing to his good friend."[260] Rowen himself would later say that, "There was a big fuss, of course. And I knew that RAND was in trouble, and I was in trouble, but I was more concerned about whether RAND was in trouble." He tried to calm people at RAND, "but it wasn't so easy. . . . Everybody was upset, and they were upset with me."[261]

The publication of the papers sent RAND management and the Board of Trustees into a tailspin. Around the day the papers were published, Jim Gaither—RAND's outside counsel—got a call from Harry Rowen giving him a very cursory description of what had happened and asking him to come to Santa Monica. By the time he met with Rowen, "everybody knew that it was Dan Ellsberg—nobody had any doubt who had done it." They called James Schlesinger and Henry Kissinger, who told Rowen, "Don't worry about it. Everybody knows Dan's kind of lost it. Nobody is going to blame RAND for what happened."[262] Newton Minow, who had just assumed the position of chairman of the Board of Trustees at RAND, got a phone call from Harry Rowen one morning at six o'clock Chicago time, or four o'clock California time. It was highly unusual, since Rowen rarely contacted him. He immediately knew something important had happened. Rowen told him, "You're probably going to read it in the paper today or hear on the news that what are called the Pentagon Papers are going to appear about the history of the U.S. involvement in Vietnam."[263] Minow said, "Yeah." Rowen then said, "We think maybe those papers were stolen from RAND." Minow said, "Oh, my God," and Rowen added, "We're not sure yet, but I wanted to alert you to this." Minow's first thought after the phone call was, "What a time to become chairman." Later, Minow found out what it was all about: "*The New York Times* broke the story of the Pentagon Papers . . . then it appeared that, in fact, the Papers came from RAND, from a man who was working at RAND named Daniel Ellsberg." Minow

---

[258] Wells, *Wild Man*, 2001, p. 417.

[259] Wells, *Wild Man*, 2001, p. 417.

[260] Wells, *Wild Man*, 2001, p. 453.

[261] Author interview with Harry Rowen, 2005.

[262] Author interview with Jim Gaither, 2005.

[263] This and the following quotes in this paragraph are from the author's interview with Newton Minow, 2005.

could recall meeting Daniel Ellsberg only once: when he gave a briefing to the Board in which "he was clearly in favor of the U.S. involvement and wanted the U.S. to be more deeply involved." At the time, Minow thought that "there was something strange," because Ellsberg "seemed obsessed somehow," and very emotional.

The RAND board—along with RAND employees and management—were right in anticipating the negative ramifications of Ellsberg's disclosure of the Pentagon Papers. The reaction in Washington was quick and sharp as soon as the *Times* article appeared on June 13. According to the transcript of a White House telephone conversation between Nixon and Alexander Haig that day, Haig alerted Nixon to the *"New York Times* exposé of the most highly classified documents of the war." Haig told Nixon that the study had been done for McNamara by "the peaceniks" over at the Pentagon, that it had been "stolen" during the transition period, that the leak was "a devastating . . . security breach . . . of the greatest magnitude of anything I've ever seen," and that the study had been released deliberately to affect the vote on the Hatfield-McGovern amendment to cut off funding for the war. Haig's description that it was a massive security leak made an impression on Nixon, and the president wanted to know what action Defense Secretary Melvin Laird was going to take.[264] Nixon was at first inclined to view the leak as "no skin off my back"—as he would later write in an affidavit filed in 1975.[265] Then he began to look at the publication by the *Times* in a different light: as a challenge to his presidential authority. As he wrote in the affidavit, "the way I saw it was that far more important than who the Pentagon Papers reflected on, as to how we got into Vietnam, was the office of the Presidency of the United States. . . ."

When Henry Kissinger called later that same day, Nixon raised the subject of *The New York Times* publication of the Pentagon Papers. Kissinger at first seemed to play down the significance of the disclosure, saying that the leak "if anything will help us a little bit" in public opinion "because this is a gold mine of showing how the previous administrations got us in there," and summarized to the president that the papers indicated "massive mismanagement" and that they pinned the blame for the war on Kennedy and Johnson, rather than Nixon, because "no one reading this can then say . . . that this president got us into trouble, this is an indictment of the previous administra-

---

[264]Transcript of telephone conversation of June 13, 1971, 12:18 p.m., reproduced in Prados and Porter, *Inside the Pentagon Papers*, 2004, pp. 90–91. According to Seymour Hersh (*The Price of Power: Kissinger in the Nixon White House*, New York: Summit Books, 1983, p. 389), Haig believed that Ellsberg was "a traitor whose goal was to see the United States defeated in South Vietnam."

[265]Anthony Lewis, "More Than Fit to Print," Review of Prados and Porter, *Inside the Pentagon Papers, The New York Review of Books*, Vol. 52, No. 6, April 7, 2005. The notes H. R. Haldeman, Nixon's chief of staff, made of the meeting with Nixon indicated that Nixon was pleased that the leak might damage the reputation of Presidents Kennedy and Johnson, and Defense Secretary McNamara, and make Walt Rostow look like—as he put it—the "key villain." Cited in Prados and Porter, *Inside the Pentagon Papers*, 2004, p. 75.

tions." The president, however, took a harsher view, saying, ". . . this is a treasonable action on the part of the bastards that put it out" and added that "people have gotta be put to the torch for this sort of thing, this is terrible." Kissinger, sensing Nixon's mood, changed his attitude and went along with the president, telling him, "it's treasonable, there's no question—it's actionable, I'm absolutely certain that this violates all sorts of security laws."[266] Kissinger would later write in *White House Years*, "I not only supported Nixon in his opposition to this wholesale theft and unauthorized disclosure; I encouraged him."[267]

When *The New York Times* published its second installment on Monday, the leak had become, according to Charles Colson, Nixon's presidential assistant and "hatchet man," "a full-scale government crisis."[268] In his memoir, President Nixon would later write that "defense and intelligence agencies raced to obtain copies of the study in order to assess the impact of its disclosure."[269] The National Security Agency was concerned that "some of the more recent documents could provide code-breaking clues. . . . The CIA was worried that past or current informants would be exposed. The State Department was alarmed because the study would expose Southeast Asia Treaty Organization contingency war plans that were still in effect."[270] Colson saw Kissinger pacing the floor and heard him say angrily that the leak would make it difficult to conduct foreign policy.[271] Kissinger told Haldeman that "the President must act—today. There is a wholesale subversion of this government underway."[272] Nixon ordered that *The New York Times* be cut off from White House access. At this point, the president

---

[266]Transcript of telephone conversation between Nixon and Kissinger, June 13, 1971, 3:09 p.m., reproduced in Prados and Porter, *Inside the Pentagon Papers*, 2004, pp. 95–100.

[267]Kissinger, *White House Years*, 1979, p. 730.

[268]Cited in Prados and Porter, *Inside the Pentagon Papers*, 2004, p. 79.

[269]Nixon, *RN*, 1978, p. 508.

[270]Nixon, *RN*, 1978, pp. 508–509. However, Ellsberg had withheld the four volumes on diplomatic negotiations, which contained information that could be damaging to U.S. foreign policy. According to Sanford J. Ungar of *The Washington Post*, the four diplomatic volumes remained "top secret-sensitive" in 1973 during the Pentagon Papers trial. When Senator William Fulbright asked to see them at the time, he was told by the State Department that their release would compromise their secrecy. The other volumes of the Pentagon Papers, however, were available at the U.S. District Court clerk's office in Los Angeles for anyone to read "no matter who you are." See Sanford Ungar, "'Secrecy' of Pentagon Papers Depends on Where You Look," *The Washington Post*, February 11, 1973.

[271]Kissinger would write in his memoir that he was concerned that the leak would undermine the administration's effort to reach out to China. The Pentagon Papers were released after "we had struggled for months to establish a secret channel to Peking, having overcome many obstacles and suspicions." So, "the sudden release of over 7,000 pages of secret documents came as a profound shock to the Administration." The "nightmare at that moment was that Peking might conclude our government was too unsteady, too harassed, and too insecure to be a useful partner." *White House Years*, 1979, pp. 729–730. Kissinger was also concerned about the effect on the Strategic Arms Limitation Talks (SALT) negotiations with the Soviets and peace talks with the North Vietnamese.

[272]Cited in Prados and Porter, *Inside the Pentagon Papers*, 2004, p. 79.

suspected that Les Gelb at the Brookings Institution was the source of the leak. He told Haldeman to "charge Gelb" and to "smoke out Brookings."[273] His instructions on June 14 would lead to the hatching of a weird plot to use White House operatives disguised as firemen to firebomb Brookings and raid its safes. Nixon told John D. Ehrlichman to find out what legal options were available, and Ehrlichman referred the matter to the Justice Department.[274] Ehrlichman also began to "hold daily crisis meetings on the Pentagon Papers."[275] Haldeman seemed to fan Nixon's anger, telling the president at one point that what the Pentagon Papers revealed to the "ordinary guy" was that "you can't trust the government; you can't believe what they say; and you can't rely on their judgment; and the implicit infallibility of presidents, which has been an accepted thing in America, is badly hurt by this."[276]

When Ellsberg was identified as the source of the leak, Kissinger became alarmed—more so than the president, according to Charles Colson. He feared that his past association with Ellsberg would damage his standing in the eyes of Nixon, who was paranoid about leaks and had already been upset over leaks from Kissinger's staff in the NSC.[277] To distance himself from Ellsberg, Kissinger described him in unflattering terms, as someone who was "always a little unbalanced" and who had switched "from hawk to peacenik" because of drug abuse.[278] Kissinger was even more concerned that Ellsberg might release other classified materials more damaging to current national-security matters. Erhlichman would recall that Ellsberg was thought to be "in knowledge of very critical defense secrets of current validity, such as nuclear deterrent targeting."[279]

At one point, Kissinger told Nixon that if he did not act, this would show that he was weak.[280] Nixon, who was already angry over what he perceived as collusion between his enemies and the press, became even more indignant. After a Kissinger

---

[273] Prados and Porter, *Inside the Pentagon Papers*, 2004, p. 79.

[274] Nixon wanted to prosecute the persons who gave the papers to *The New York Times* rather than the *Times* itself. As he told Ehrlichman, "Hell, I wouldn't prosecute the *Times*. My view is to prosecute the . . . that gave it to them." Prados and Porter, *Inside the Pentagon Papers*, 2004, p. 80.

[275] Prados and Porter, *Inside the Pentagon Papers*, 2004, p. 80.

[276] Transcript of telephone conversation between Nixon and Haldeman, June 14, 1971, 3:09 p.m., cited in Prados and Porter, *Inside the Pentagon Papers*, 2004, pp. 100–104.

[277] Some historians have maintained that Kissinger was motivated by the fear that "the Pentagon study indirectly indicted him, because of his previous role as a consultant to the Johnson Administration, and that his past association with Ellsberg and other former aides and RAND employees who had turned against the war now undermined his standing with Nixon. His tirades against Ellsberg in the Oval Office . . . were attempts to distance himself from liberals, leakers, and the study itself." Kimball, *Nixon's Vietnam War*, 1998, p. 254.

[278] Hersh, *The Price of Power*, 1983, p. 384.

[279] Hersh, *The Price of Power*, 1983, p. 384.

[280] Langguth, *Our Vietnam*, 2000, p. 588.

tirade, Nixon was extremely angry and, according to Colson, the president "was pounding his desk and using colorful language."[281] Nixon told his Cabinet, "We're going to go forward with Ellsberg and prosecute him."[282] According to Erhlichman, "Without Henry's stimulus . . . the President and the rest of us might have concluded that the Papers were Lyndon Johnson's problem, not ours."[283] Kissinger's aggressive stance undoubtedly goaded Nixon into action, but the president himself was disposed from the beginning to adopt quick and hard measures. Kissinger might have thought that the best thing for him to do was to match the president's virulence or he would fall out of favor with Nixon.[284]

Apparently, the White House then became interested in learning more about Ellsberg and might have asked the CIA to perform a psychological study of Ellsberg in August 1971. However, the CIA study—according to *The New York Times*, which obtained a copy—was "rejected by the White House investigating unit" because it described Ellsberg in laudatory terms.[285] The CIA document called Ellsberg a "brilliant, success-oriented man"—someone who was "motivated by 'what he deemed a higher order of patriotism'" and "saw himself as 'having a special mission, and indeed as bearing a special responsibility' toward the Vietnam War."[286] It was later revealed that the White House then asked the CIA to conduct another study of Ellsberg, but the contents were never disclosed.[287] To look for incriminating evidence against Ellsberg, the White House investigating unit subsequently burglarized the office of Ellsberg's psychiatrist in Los Angeles.

The White House did not believe that Ellsberg had acted alone and suspected a conspiracy. Besides Les Gelb, the list of possible conspirators included Mort Halperin and Paul Warnke. It also worried that Ellsberg would release more secret documents embarrassing to the administration for publication in newspapers, so State and Defense officials wanted to stop him by indicting him as soon as possible. The White House had learned by this time that Ellsberg had given Senator Charles Mathias a copy of the Top Secret NSSM-1.[288] Gordon Liddy would recall, "We knew he had a lot of stuff." However, no one knew exactly what Ellsberg had and where he was keeping the materials, since RAND "had been particularly lax in keeping track 'as to what went in,

---

[281] Wells, *Wild Man*, 2001, p. 460.

[282] Wells, *Wild Man*, 2001, p. 460.

[283] Prados and Porter, *Inside the Pentagon Papers*, 2004, p. 86.

[284] Kimball, *Nixon's Vietnam War*, 1998, p. 254.

[285] "CIA Ellsberg Study Reported as Laudatory," *Los Angeles Times*, August 4, 1973.

[286] "CIA Ellsberg Study Reported as Laudatory," 1973.

[287] "CIA Ellsberg Study Reported as Laudatory," 1973. The revelation came during a Senate hearing about the burglary of a Democratic Party's office at the Watergate complex that was linked to the White House.

[288] Hersh, *The Price of Power*, 1983, p. 383.

what went out, and what have you.'"[289] Senior officials were unhappy with RAND over its lapse, and Fred Buzhardt, the Defense Department legal counsel, wondered "why we continue to do business with Rand, knowing all that we do about them."[290]

In his memoir, Nixon wrote that he wondered how many hypersensitive documents Ellsberg might have obtained during the years he worked in the Defense Department and at RAND, and worried about what other documents Ellsberg might give the newspapers next.[291] Jim Gaither said that the concerns over further leaks by Ellsberg were legitimate. He recalled that at RAND, "We were worried . . . that Dan had access to the most sensitive information that the United States government had. All of the nuclear stuff, Dan knew. We thought the next thing he was going to do was to disclose that kind of stuff. He never has. But we were worried. And we had no control. Nobody had any control over Dan."[292]

Apparently, Buzhardt and the Justice Department were convinced that Harry Rowen and other people at RAND were misleading with or withholding information from investigators.[293] Nixon himself had expressed anger with RAND, telling Haldeman, "We've got to get our enemies out of the clearance business. I mean, Rand."[294] Rowen himself recalled that, in an attempt at damage control, he talked to the White House legal counsel, who was "trying to figure out whether I was part of a plot and I told him that there wasn't."[295] He remembered that he went over the history of the events, and in the end the conclusion "must have been that I was not part of a plot."[296] In the meantime, White House operatives—who would later become known as "the Plumbers," along with officials from Defense and Justice—met with members of the House Armed Services Committee to try to get them to begin an investigation of the Pentagon Papers release. And by late July, they reported to Ehrlichman that "only the FBI is disposed to thinking that Ellsberg is the sole prime mover." The White House operatives "claimed substantial evidence could be gathered for criminal indictment of Leslie Gelb, Morton Halperin, Paul Warnke, and RAND Corporation executives as well," and referred to the release of the papers as "their" project.[297]

At RAND, Jim Gaither and others were unaware that "Haldeman and Ehrlichman were in fact working with the president, believing that RAND was at fault, that

---

[289]Wells, *Wild Man*, 2001, p. 467.

[290]Wells, *Wild Man*, 2001, p. 467.

[291]Nixon, *RN*, 1978, p. 512.

[292]Author interview with Jim Gaither, 2005.

[293]Wells, *Wild Man*, 2001, p. 467.

[294]Wells, *Wild Man*, 2001, p. 467

[295]Author interview with Harry Rowen, 2005.

[296]Author interview with Harry Rowen, 2005.

[297]Prados and Porter, *Inside the Pentagon Papers*, 2004, p. 87.

there was a conspiracy going on here, in the liberal media and RAND," and that there was a link between Rowen and Ellsberg, and Harvard, MIT, *The New York Times,* and *The Washington Post.* Gaither only learned that the government suspected a plot when FBI agents showed up to ask Rowen questions about a conspiracy. Gaither immediately put a stop to the questioning, telling the agents, "Wait a minute, this is really serious stuff that you're talking about. This is not fair to ask somebody to wing it. If you have a bunch of questions, write the questions up, and let us think about it and make sure that we respond carefully to you. This is too serious a charge to just do it off the cuff." The FBI acquiesced, and Gaither's intervention saved Rowen from having "to sit there for five hours just talking off the cuff." Gaither thought that the FBI must have been working under orders from somewhere in the government—probably from the White House. Subsequently, RAND answered all of the questions that the FBI posed.[298]

At the Pentagon, Defense Secretary Melvin Laird—feeling embarrassed by the publication of secret documents from his department and probably under White House pressure to take action—condemned RAND for its "deficiencies in the security system and practices," in a July 1 memo to Robert C. Seamans, Secretary of the Air Force.[299] In the same memo, he instructed the Air Force to take custody of all classified documents at RAND. Air Force personnel to be stationed at RAND would take custody of all secret documents and make an inventory to determine whether RAND would need them for its work.[300] Later that July, the Air Force "disclosed . . . that RAND had more than 170,000 confidential documents" at its Santa Monica and Washington offices, which—as they were inventoried—"would be transferred to the Air Force."[301] All Top Secret and "most special-access documents" would be placed in "one central repository with an adjacent reading room," and RAND personnel would no longer be allowed to take documents to their offices. Any staff member who wanted to have access to the documents had to be cleared beforehand by the Air Force personnel. An Air Force officer, instead of a RAND official, would be stationed "in the central reading and storage rooms" at each of the RAND offices.[302]

In Washington, according to Lee Meyer, the Air Force took over the security system in the RAND office and "ran it for a couple of years."[303] A captain and a sergeant were assigned to the office to assume oversight of classified documents and control access. RAND people had to put in many hours of overtime work to check and make sure that everything was properly handled according to security standards. RAND

---

[298]Author interview with Jim Gaither, 2005.

[299]Robert M. Smith, "Laird Increases Security," 1971.

[300]Robert M. Smith, "Laird Increases Security," 1971.

[301]"Air Force Guards RAND Secret Data," Special to *The New York Times,* July 22, 1971.

[302]"Air Force Guards RAND Secret Data," 1971.

[303]Author interview with Lee Meyer, 2004.

analysts thought that the crackdown was "an indignity, and an embarrassment." Hans Heymann recalled that five investigators descended on his Santa Monica office, and the visit "was very intimidating."[304] In addition, Jim Gaither recalled that there was also "a request or an order to terminate all of RAND's contracts."[305] However, this cancellation did not come to pass, thanks to John Mitchell, the Attorney General, who "took the position . . . that the government doesn't have the right to do that, and so ultimately RAND's contracts were not cancelled."[306] Gaither had expected his stay in Santa Monica to be short but "all hell broke loose," and he ended up spending a week helping RAND figure out what it was going to do. When Nixon heard of the Pentagon's crackdown on RAND, he approved the move and said, "Let them squeal."[307]

Among the measures the Air Force adopted, Jim Gaither remembered that it assumed physical custody of the RAND building—which had been cleared as a place where classified documents could be stored—thus "denying RAND the ability to run an independent facility."[308] In place of RAND guards, there were now Air Force guards to ensure that "all the classified information at RAND was protected. When people left, when they went by the guards' desk at RAND, there was an Air Force officer who was checking what they were taking out." But even before the Air Force took action, RAND had already clamped down, and "anybody who wanted to take a briefcase out had to open up and show them what they had."[309] Gaither said, "The government was quite upset. We didn't know where it was coming from."[310] To him, it was "mind-boggling" that a "Republican administration would go after" RAND, which had a prestigious board, with members such as Bill Hewlett and Walt Wriston—"big business executives who ran really impressive organizations"—but "it happened."[311]

According to some RAND staff members, the fall out of the security crackdown on RAND employees themselves appeared varied. With regard to individual clearances at RAND, some apparently were affected while others were not. According to Jim Gaither, the government threatened to take away the security clearances of some senior people at RAND, such as Harry Rowen, but relented in the end, concluding

[304]Wells, *Wild Man*, 2001, p. 454.

[305]Wells, *Wild Man*, 2001, p. 454.

[306]Wells, *Wild Man*, 2001, p. 454.

[307]Wells, *Wild Man*, 2001, p. 467.

[308]Author interview with Jim Gaither, 2005.

[309]Author interview with Jim Gaither, 2005.

[310]Author interview with Jim Gaither, 2005.

[311]Author interview with Jim Gaither, 2005.

"that they had done nothing wrong."[312] In the RAND Washington office, apparently no one lost his or her security clearance.[313] However, according to a *Baltimore Sun* article written at the time of the Pentagon Papers trial, "more than 800 Rand employees lost their top-secret clearance."[314]

Among those 800 were Bob Paulson and Dave Dreyfus, who were on special assignment in Washington at the time of the crackdown, working on a project reviewing ARPA operations in Vietnam. Sent by RAND at the request of a former Army Ordnance colonel who was looking for "a Cost man and a Systems man,"[315] they went to Washington in 1971 and worked in the ARPA building located in Arlington, Virginia, near Key Bridge. Their job was to check "every contract issued . . . everything that ARPA had done with respect to Vietnam" from the start of the Kennedy Administration to the end of the Johnson Administration. They had to look at "who got the contract, what it was for, how much money was involved, and whether or not we could judge whether it was successful or not." The project was performed for "President Nixon's office," and the men in charge were "an attorney named Buzhardt," and RAND's vice president in the Washington office—Paulson could not remember whether it was Larry Henderson or his successor. Paulson thought that the research "had a political purpose" and that the White House was "looking for corruption in the Johnson Administration."

One day, four men came in while they were eating lunch and asked them to leave the ARPA building, telling them, "Don't take your papers, don't take your notes, leave your briefcases, leave everything." Then they escorted them to the ground entrance and told them to leave. "We'd lost our security clearances because of the Pentagon Papers," Paulson said. "It was a traumatic experience," he recalled.[316] Paulson and Dreyfus called up RAND's vice president in Washington, and said, "Could we go home?" He told them, "No. Stay where you are," and contacted Buzhardt, who said, "No, leave them where they are. I'll get their clearances back so they can finish this work." So, they spent a week waiting for their clearances to be restored. Finally, they were told, "Your clearances are back, go back to work."[317] According to Paulson, "The rest of RAND was shut down—they couldn't do anything with classified information at all, and it took them about three months to get their clearances back." Paulson and Dreyfus ultimately finished their analysis and produced a 300-page Top Secret report. They made two copies, one of which they sent to the Office of President, but never heard back. The

---

[312] Author interview with Jim Gaither, 2005.

[313] Author interview with Jim Gaither, 2005.

[314] Dobbin, "Rand Corporation Still Feels," 1973.

[315] Author interview with Bob Paulson, 2003.

[316] Author interview with Bob Paulson, 2003.

[317] Author interview with Bob Paulson, 2003.

other copy went to Don Rice, Harry Rowen's successor as president of RAND. The Top Secret report was never published.

The crackdown sent the RAND board into damage-control mode. According to Newt Minow, when the Defense Department "took away RAND's security clearance," it was "devastating because if the institution did not have a security clearance, it would in effect be out of business, everybody would lose their jobs. It was a disaster."[318] So, he consulted with Ed Huddleson and Jim Gaither, RAND's legal counsels in San Francisco and two of the best lawyers he had ever known. As an attorney himself, he knew how important it was to have good lawyers in situations like this. Huddleson had been a RAND trustee for a long time, and Gaither's father had helped set up RAND. Together, they tried to come up with a strategy, and immediately obtained an appointment with David Packard, who was then Deputy Secretary of Defense.[319]

Minow remembered "very clearly" walking into the office of Packard, whom he did not know, and saying, "Mr. Secretary, I bring you greetings from one of our RAND trustees whom you know very well."[320] Packard asked, "Who's that?" Minow replied, "Bill Hewlett." Packard said, "Bill is on the board of RAND?" and Minow told him, "Yes, Mr. Secretary. You just took away his security clearance." Minow did not know whether individuals at RAND had lost their clearances or not, but he wanted to get Packard's attention. "The minute I got his attention," he said, "I realized that he knew how important this was." Packard said, "We did that?" Minow replied, "Mr. Secretary, we got an official notice that RAND's security clearance is gone. Now, we're here because there's something you know and I know that the public does not know. As chairman of this not-for-profit institution where hundreds and hundreds of people are going to lose their jobs and their careers, I feel obligated to have a press conference to tell the country about it." Packard said, "What's that?" Minow told him, "We didn't invent Daniel Ellsberg, we got him from you. You're the one that cleared him, you're the one that sent him to us, so I think that the country ought to know that he's not a product of RAND, he's a product of the Department of Defense." Packard said, "Don't get excited. Keep your shirt on. Don't get excited." Minow said, "I'm not excited. I just don't want there to be a misunderstanding between us, because if we don't straighten this out, that's what I feel obliged to do." There was kind of a pause for a few minutes.

Then Packard said, "Just a minute," and went to his phone and pressed the buzzer. A man entered from the office's back door, and Packard introduced him as his lawyer. It was Fred Buzhardt, who later became President Nixon's lawyer during the Watergate scandal. Packard told Minow, "I want you to talk to Mr. Buzhardt. You're all lawyers.

---

[318] Author interview with Newt Minow, 2005.

[319] However, Jim Gaither said that he did not attend the meeting with David Packard and that only Ed Huddleson went with Minow. Author interview with Jim Gaither, 2005.

[320] This and the quotes from Newt Minow are from the author's interview.

See how we can work this out." "So, in effect, he delegated this to Mr. Buzhardt," Minow recalled. Buzhardt—who knew all about the case—said, "You should understand, this was not a decision of the Department of Defense." When asked who it was, he said, "A higher authority, namely the President of the United States. . . . When this thing broke, and the President learned that the Papers had been from RAND, he instructed that RAND's security clearance should immediately be removed." He then told them, "Give me a day or so to work this out." Minow told him, "If you don't work it out within a day or so . . . there's going to be a lot of fireworks involved. Clearly, we'll give you that time but it's not going to be very long."

Minow repeated to Buzhardt that "we didn't invent Daniel Ellsberg but he was sent to us from the Department of Defense." Then he left. Huddleson stayed behind to work with Buzhardt, "and within a day RAND's security clearance was restored." Minow later said that he believed that "the Department of Defense very quickly recognized that Daniel Ellsberg was not RAND and that RAND's work for the Department of Defense would be seriously jeopardized and would be a loss to the national interest." Buzhardt himself might have been well-disposed toward RAND because of the work that Paulson and Dreyfus were doing—looking for instances of corruption in ARPA contracting under the two previous Democratic administrations—on behalf of the president's office. Also, Laird himself probably felt he shared some of the responsibility, since—as Les Gelb said—he had approved the distribution list and his office had approved the storing of the volumes at RAND.

According to Gus Shubert, "RAND's board of trustees was prepared to intervene at the highest levels [of government] if necessary."[321] All the board members—in particular, General Lauris Norstad, former Supreme Allied Commander Europe and Commander-in-Chief U.S. European Command, who was chairman of Owens-Corning Fiberglass—were asked by Newt Minow to call government officials. Whether he did so or not, the matter was resolved so quickly that his intervention would have been unnecessary. Minow gave Huddleson a lot of credit for this resolution through his work with Buzhardt at the Pentagon.

Meanwhile, in RAND's Washington office, many meetings were held to strategize how RAND was going to respond to the crisis. George Tanham told Lee Meyer, his administrative assistant, that it was "a tough time" because some people in Congress, in the Air Force, and elsewhere in the government wanted to shut RAND down.[322] Meyer was convinced that RAND was not going to survive and would go out of business. According to her, Tanham, who had many good contacts within the Air Force, worked hard to keep RAND from going under. Meyer later said that he believes that his efforts helped keep RAND afloat.

---

[321] Collins, interview with Gus Shubert, session of May 28, 1992, p. 71.

[322] Author interview with Lee Meyer, 2004.

Although RAND managed to fend off the most fatal blows, "the relationships with the Pentagon absolutely went down hill, and the access to the White House was very restricted," Gaither said. He recalled that "They were very distrustful of Harry Rowen and the senior management" and "very unhappy with RAND" simply because the Pentagon Papers were "now all over the world." It was left to John White, the senior vice president, and Gaither to deal with the Pentagon to maintain access and rebuild trust.[323] According to Gaither, "They really didn't want RAND people around there." However, since White was well respected and was serving as RAND's advisor on "the compensation work at the highest levels of the Air Force and the promotion work," he "had wonderful access." While Gaither and White worked to rebuild the relationship with the Pentagon, Ed Huddleson was ironing out the major issues with Fred Buzhardt and other senior Pentagon officials. Among those issues, according to Gus Shubert, was whether there was a crime "if indeed a crime it was . . . what the nature of this crime . . . was, how it ought to be specified and dealt with."[324] Shubert thought that Huddleson "was a very constructive influence on the whole outcome," since, in the end, it was determined that RAND had not committed a crime.[325]

Keeping RAND from being cut off by the government was "the immediate issue," Minow recalled. As a governance obligation, the next issue for the board was to determine "what had happened: how did those Papers get removed? How they got there in the first place? Who were responsible, and what we should do about it?" He had a "frank talk" with Rowen—whom he did not know well—who told him, "I'm the one that asked Daniel Ellsberg to come here. I never authorized anything like this, and I'm shocked by it, but I'm the one that brought him here."[326] Minow called a special meeting of the board, which was held at the Hyatt Hotel near O'Hare Airport in Chicago—an equidistant location for board members from the East and West Coasts. All the board members came. Unfortunately, a convention of rock 'n' roll disc jockeys was taking place at the hotel at the same time, and the noise kept the board members awake all night. The board discussed the release of the Pentagon Papers and, according to Gus Shubert, there were "a lot of inquiries," and questions were raised about what had happened—such as, "What was So-and-so's role?"—and about what actions should be taken—for example, "What should be done about the security person?"[327] At the end, the board decided to launch an independent review of "what does the record

---

[323] According to Gus Shubert, while he was senior vice president for domestic issues, John White was his counterpart "on the military side" for RAND. Author interview with Gus Shubert, 2004 and 2005.

[324] Collins, interview with Gus Shubert, session of May 28, 1992, p. 71.

[325] Collins, interview with Gus Shubert, session of May 28, 1992, p. 71.

[326] Author interview with Newt Minow, 2005.

[327] Collins, interview with Gus Shubert, session of May 28, 1992, pp. 71–72.

really show?"[328] and to appoint a subcommittee of the board, consisting mainly of Ed Huddleson and Jim Gaither, "to make a thorough investigation."[329]

As part of his research, Gaither went to the RAND library and asked for a list of all the books Ellsberg had checked out. Ellsberg had made statements that he had released the papers "as a matter of conscience" and that he "was prepared to go to jail."[330] The library circulation list showed that Ellsberg had carefully "studied the various books on how to make sure that you wouldn't go to jail for releasing classified information." Gaither recalled, "There was a book that made it clear that the government's ability to enforce those rules, criminally, was very limited. So, while he said he was prepared to make the ultimate sacrifice, he knew that it would be very hard for the government to convict him." This was the reason Gaither "urged the Justice Department to bring a civil suit, not a criminal suit, because we could clearly enforce his agreement to honor the classification, that we could sue him and put an injunction on him and get all the documents back and everything else."

Ultimately, the Justice Department brought a criminal suit, and, according to Gaither, "They made a big mistake. . . . it was a bad case from the start."[331] Ellsberg would later say he did not know at the time that the United States did not have an Official Secrets Act, "which criminalizes any unauthorized disclosure of classified information," and that he fully expected to be prosecuted and sentenced to life imprisonment.[332] At his trial, he would demur "when shown a statement he had signed stating he had read portions of the espionage laws dealing with disclosure of classified information."[333] He told the court, "There are no portions of the espionage laws applying to people at Rand which refer to classified information."[334]

Shubert was involved in the investigation and worked "day and night" for two months. Along with other RAND people, he had to prepare a lot of records, "shuffling papers and rationales, and creating chronologies and working with our lawyers." He

---

[328] Collins, interview with Gus Shubert, session of May 28, 1992, pp. 71–72.

[329] Author interview with Newt Minow, 2005.

[330] Author interview with Jim Gaither, 2005.

[331] Author interview with Jim Gaither, 2005. Among the difficulties for the government case against Ellsberg that would later surface during the trial was the burden of producing enough evidence to prove that a conspiracy existed, as well as the question of whether there was a theft, since Ellsberg only copied the documents and then brought them back to RAND. In addition, proving that the release of the documents damaged national security would be another hurdle for the prosecution. Gene Blake, "Chance of Ellsberg Acquittal Indicated," *Los Angeles Times*, May 10, 1973.

[332] Salon Radio interview with Daniel Ellsberg, 2008. In this interview Ellsberg said that he was "the first person to ever be prosecuted for leaking unauthorized documents."

[333] Blake, "Ellsberg Admits He Violated Pledge," 1973.

[334] Blake, "Ellsberg Admits He Violated Pledge," 1973.

was engaged in what he called an attempt "to create instant history."[335] After spending six months reviewing what "exactly [had] happened," Gaither produced a report for the board that basically showed that "RAND was not involved in any conspiracy" and that "RAND did not do anything wrong."[336] The report described the release of the Pentagon Papers as the act of a single, unstable person. It went into Dan Ellsberg's background, recounting his "incredible transformation from being a hawk on the war even to the point of carrying weapons in Vietnam" to being a dove.[337] Ellsberg had become "extremely agitated and went to the absolute other extreme about the war." It pointed out that Ellsberg's instability was well known, to the point that nobody was surprised when he turned out to be the source of the leak. Even government people at the level of Schlesinger and Kissinger knew how unstable he was and how strongly he felt about the war.

Another evidence of Ellsberg's psychological problem was the "very difficult personal situation" that he experienced after his return from Vietnam. Ellsberg was a brilliant and articulate man who had accumulated "an incredible record" at Harvard and at RAND, where he had performed research on extremely sensitive national-security issues, such as nuclear policy—topics that were at a level of classification to which few people could have access. But "all of a sudden he lost the capacity to do research, and he literally could not produce a written piece of material." Harry Rowen and others at RAND tried for a long time to help him. They got him medical assistance and tried to figure out why he could not "produce anything in written form." In the end, they concluded that "there really wasn't a place for him at RAND and he went to MIT," and it was while he was at MIT that he released the Pentagon Papers.

On the issue of RAND's share of responsibility for the duplication of the Pentagon Papers, Gaither says that the report tried to answer the question, "How much fault do we ascribe to the other people at RAND?" His conclusion was "none," because "you cannot control this kind of individual behavior." Certainly RAND could have tightened its security system, but in fact it was following the same procedure as the Pentagon: that staff members who held security clearances were not subjected to searches when they left the building. Consequently, it was very easy for Ellsberg to smuggle the volumes out in his briefcase when he left work at night, Xerox them, and bring them back the next day. Gaither cites the more recent cases of John Deutch, former CIA director and Deputy Secretary of Defense, and Samuel Berger, President Clinton's National Security Advisor, both of whom took classified documents with them when they left meetings. Bernard Brodie, who had worked at the Pentagon on national-security studies, thought that RAND's security control—even before the Pentagon

---

[335] Collins, interview with Gus Shubert, session of May 28, 1992, p. 70.

[336] Author interview with Jim Gaither, 2005.

[337] Author interview with Jim Gaither, 2005. This and the subsequent quotes from Jim Gaither are taken from the author's interview with him.

Papers episode —was better than that at the Pentagon itself. In his opinion, "Ellsberg could have leaked secret documents from the Pentagon with less risk of discovery than at Rand."[338]

Gaither presented his report to the board at its meeting in New York around November 1971, when the weather had turned very cold. To him, the occasion was "a big deal" because it was early in his legal career. The report was "very sensitive stuff because it was a very objective presentation of everything that happened." Gaither also delivered a copy to David Packard and described to him what his conclusions were. Packard did not say anything, which was appropriate because he had not had the chance to read it. "He was respectful," Gaither recalls, "but he didn't try to deal with it without going back and doing his homework." Packard afterward was "very helpful in getting the matter resolved within the Pentagon, concluding that there was no fault of RAND."[339]

At the Hyatt meeting, the board also began to ask unofficially, "Should we be required here to change the president since he was the one ultimately in charge and he was the one that brought Ellsberg?"[340] According to Gus Shubert, another major question, besides the replacement of Harry Rowen, was the restructuring of RAND. At one point, RAND's Vice President Goldstein suggested that all RAND corporate officers resign, including Shubert, so that the board would be free to choose which ones it would reappoint and which ones it would not. Minow also suggested this to Shubert, so Shubert resigned. This resignation would "make it easier for the board to deal with [w]hat they saw was the problem of Harry. . . . It's traditional that when any government changes, that the whole team changes. A secondary reason, maybe even a primary reason, would be to provide the new guy, when they found one, with the freedom not to renew some of these people." The resignations, however, were pro-forma and did not change anything.[341]

Gaither recalls that the board also wanted to reorganize RAND, with Rowen playing a role similar to that of "a provost with responsibilities for the departments" and "for the intellectual quality of the organization," and with Dick Goldstein assuming "responsibilities for the programs and for relationships with all of the customers." Gaither was invited to the board meeting during which this reorganization was discussed. Afterward, he was asked to go explain it to RAND's management and then come back and report their reaction. According to him, "The management basically said, to a person, everybody, if the board wants to do this, we're out, we will leave, that it was crazy" because "you can't split the responsibilities for running a complex organization." Consequently, the board decided not to proceed with the plan, and "it was

---

[338] Dobbin, "Rand Corporation Still Feels," 1973.

[339] Author interview with Jim Gaither, 2005.

[340] Author interview with Newt Minow, 2005.

[341] Collins, interview with Gus Shubert, session of May 28, 1992, p. 72.

not too long after that that Harry decided that the problems weren't going to go away as long as he stayed so that he ought to step down."[342]

The issue of Rowen's position at RAND had come up even earlier—almost immediately in the wake of the release of the Pentagon Papers. As early as during the trip to Washington to see Dave Packard, Minow told Huddleson, "We'd better have a Plan B here. We'd better look around for somebody who could be the president in case it's decided that we have to make the change."[343] After the meeting at the Hyatt, another one was held during which Rowen was asked to come and talk to the board members. It was concluded that Rowen would have to leave and that the board would look for a new president. Harry Rowen realized that his "situation at RAND was untenable."[344] He would later say, "It didn't take me long to decide that I could not go on and the board came to that view quickly, I'm sure, that I had to leave."[345] This conclusion was confirmed by Jim Gaither, who said that, "it became clear that the problem had been so closely associated with Harry that we concluded we weren't going to be able to solve it with him continuing to serve as president, and he decided to step down."[346] Part of the impetus for Rowen's replacement might have originated with the Air Force. Lee Meyer remembered that the Air Force told Tanham, "Look, something's got to happen." Subsequently, Tanham went to the chairman of RAND's board and said, "Our clients are standing firm. RAND has to show some responsibility." According to Meyer, "The buck stops at the top and Rowen finally resigned."[347]

Newt Minow does not recall any pressure from the Air Force or the Department of Defense, and said that he "never got any official word" from them that Rowen had to leave. Replacing Rowen was a decision that the board reached on its own, because it felt that "given the enormity of this risk to the institution and the fact that Ellsberg was really Harry's responsibility," Rowen had to leave.[348] If there had been pressure from the Air Force, "it was certainly subtle," Jim Gaither said. The suggestion was certainly made in the Pentagon at that time, that he and John White were in a better position than Harry Rowen to rebuild the relationship. In Gaither's view, however, the pressing issue at the time with regard to people in government was not so much about Harry

[342]Author interview with Jim Gaither, 2005.

[343]Author interview with Newt Minow, 2005.

[344]Author interview with Harry Rowen, 2005.

[345]Author interview with Harry Rowen, 2005.

[346]Author interview with Jim Gaither, 2005.

[347]Author interview with Lee Meyer, 2004.

[348]Author interview with Newt Minow, 2005.

Rowen as it was about RAND. He said, "It was at such a crisis level. They were just going to cut RAND off."[349]

According to Gus Shubert, the board "certainly put pressure" on Rowen to resign and Newt Minow had a strong hand in the matter.[350] Shubert was not a member of the board at the time, but he attended all their meetings and could see what was going on. To him, it was like "a mob scene," to the point that Jim Gaither became upset and said, "What the hell's going on here? How can anybody be so mean to Harry? He would never be like that to anybody else." According to Shubert, Gaither "was very aggravated at the way Rowen was treated; he thought it was totally unjustified." Shubert, however, thought "RAND did have to do something."[351] Apparently, Rowen took it well. According to Minow, Rowen "was a gentleman throughout this" because he "realized what had happened."[352] When asked whether he felt the board was too hard on him, Rowen replied, "No . . . I said to Jim [Gaither] 'I think I'd better leave,' and he said, 'Yes.' I wasn't trying to stay there, it was clear that I'd have to move on."[353] He adds, "The Navy has a rule that if a ship goes aground, there's never any excuse. . . . So that rule seems to be the right rule in this case, it's an applicable rule. And I did actually have some responsibility for it. . . . And trusting Dan was a bad mistake."[354]

According to Newt Minow, one of the factors in Rowen's departure was the violation of security rules. The Pentagon Papers "were never logged into the system at RAND," he said. The board "felt that was Harry's fault," and this represented "a very significant factor in our analysis of why Harry had to be replaced."[355] Minow said that, beyond Rowen's responsibility for the release of the Pentagon Papers, there was the issue of Rowen's management style, which some people found wanting. Another concern, as Minow recalled, was the reaction in the Pentagon to Rowen. While in the Defense Department, Minow picked up indications of unhappiness with Rowen in general, not only from the Air Force but also from many people in the Department of Defense. However, Minow could not tell what had caused those bad feelings, although he heard comments about Rowen being "too academic" and a poor listener.[356]

---

[349] Author interview with Jim Gaither, 2005.

[350] Author interview with Gus Shubert, 2004 and 2005.

[351] Author interview with Gus Shubert, 2004 and 2005.

[352] Author interview with Newt Minow, 2005.

[353] Author interview with Harry Rowen, 2005.

[354] Author interview with Harry Rowen, 2005.

[355] Author interview with Newt Minow, 2005.

[356] Author interview with Newt Minow, 2005.

Gus Shubert recalled that Rowen "annoyed the Air Force."[357] He remembered—
long after Rowen had left RAND—asking Ed Huddleson, the head of the search
committee for Frank Collbohm's replacement, why Rowen had been hired. He said to
Huddleson, "What were you thinking of? Why did you want to bring Rowen back?
Tell me off the record. Didn't you know that the Air Force was just waiting to get
him?" Shubert remembered telling Huddleson, "You could have gone out and picked
a thousand different people—none of whom would have had this baggage. Why did
you pick this guy?" Huddleson said, "You want to know the real truth?" Shubert said,
"Yes, of course," and Huddleson told him, "I didn't look; I didn't ask; I didn't ask the
Air Force what they thought about Rowen." Shubert said, "Well, everybody knows
that the Air Force just didn't like the choice." He said, "That's news to me," and added
"You can't check everything." To Shubert, this would have been "the obvious thing to
do if this guy is going to be heading the organization." At any rate, Huddleson—who
"was a great trustee" and "loved RAND"—"didn't have all the facts when Harry came
to RAND, that the Air Force hated him—whatever the Air Force is, the Old Guard,
no doubt."

According to Shubert, Rowen had "built up a record when he was in DOD which
was viewed as the worst thing that had ever happened to the Air Force. From the word
go, they were just waiting for him and they knew they'd get him on something, and
they did on Ellsberg." Shubert did not know what Rowen had done to antagonize the
Air Force, but he was viewed as anti–Air Force—"whatever that means."[358] At the Pentagon, Shubert had picked up complaints that Rowen was arrogant, because he seemed
to go out of his way "to step on the Air Force's toes every time he could from his new
position which nominally [put] him above the Air Force." General John Vogt—an
Air Force general in ISA and a good friend—commented to Shubert about the choice
of Rowen to head RAND: "You know, there are good selections and bad selections,
this one comes under the category of stupendously bad."[359] Gaither, too, remembered
that, as one of McNamara's Whiz Kids, Rowen had antagonized the military, which
resented being told by these civilians what to do. As a result, he says, "It was not easy
for Harry to deal with the Pentagon but it never reached the point where it was hurting
RAND, until Ellsberg."[360]

When asked about the antagonism he had created within the Air Force as one of
the Whiz Kids, Rowen expressed surprise, saying, "Me? I had nothing to do with the
Air Force, I worked NATO matters, I didn't work Air Force matters. Maybe somebody
took offense at something, but really I don't know what it would have been. . . . I really

---

[357] Author interview with Gus Shubert, 2004 and 2005. The following quotes from Shubert in this paragraph
come from the same interview.

[358] Author interview with Gus Shubert, 2004 and 2005.

[359] Author interview with Gus Shubert, 2004 and 2005.

[360] Author interview with Jim Gaither, 2005.

wasn't working with any of the services; I was working on Berlin questions, on NATO questions to a large extent."[361] To Shubert, this response demonstrates Rowen's insensitivity or inability to pick up on how people were reacting to him, which probably gave rise to the perception that he did not listen or was arrogant. Shubert said, "Whether this is true or not, the Air Force felt that he did anything he could to screw them. That hurts." Rowen, Shubert remembered, was "like a corporal coming out of the ranks" who was given a position of authority that allowed him to do "bad things" and who actually did those "bad things" in the eyes of the Air Force.[362] According to Gaither, another source of the Air Force's unhappiness with Rowen was his diversification into domestic research. There were "tensions about RAND starting in 1969 to do domestic work," and Rowen's decision to take RAND in that direction "was not well received," he said.[363]

Rowen resigned in November 1971. In a *New York Times* article dated November 15, Steven Roberts wrote that "well-informed sources said that his departure had been caused partly by Pentagon dissatisfaction with Rand's role in the release of the Pentagon Papers."[364] These sources told Roberts, "Officials of the Defense Department, which supplies three-quarters of Rand's $27-million budget, were increasingly critical of Mr. Rowen after the disclosure of the top-secret papers and made their views known to the corporation's board members."[365] By this time, Ellsberg had conceded that he had duplicated RAND's copy of the Pentagon Papers and released them to the press. A RAND spokesman—citing Rowen and Minow—denied that Rowen's departure had anything to do with the Pentagon Papers and indicated that Rowen's resignation had come from his own initiative. Rowen had issued a statement saying that, "Maintaining vitality in institutions and in people is brought about by change—Rand and I are no exception."[366] RAND's announcement mentioned that Rowen would remain as president for up to 18 months to allow the board time to choose a successor, but Senior Vice President Dick Goldstein would assume day-to-day responsibilities in the interim.

Sources within RAND told Roberts that the reasons for Rowen's departure were more complex than the official announcement had made them out to be, and that

---

[361] Author interview with Harry Rowen, 2005. When Harry Rowen was appointed RAND president in 1966, journalist Peter Bart wrote in a *New York Times* article ("Economist Named New Head of Rand Corporation") dated July 27, 1966, that Rowen "joined the Defense Department in 1961, specializing in problems relating to the North Atlantic Treaty Organization. He is credited with having contributed to the establishment of the Defense Plans Working Group, which has sought to rejuvenate NATO's long-term planning in dealing with non-nuclear threats in Europe."

[362] Author interview with Gus Shubert, 2004 and 2005.

[363] Author interview with Jim Gaither, 2005.

[364] Roberts, "Rand Chief Quitting," 1971.

[365] Roberts, "Rand Chief Quitting," 1971.

[366] Roberts, "Rand Chief Quitting," 1971.

for some time "both the board of directors and the corporation's clients have been unhappy with Mr. Rowen's managerial performance."[367] One of the sources explained that, "Some of Rand's military clients objected to Mr. Rowen's growing interest in domestic issues." The source told Roberts, "They felt that such projects would collect people on the staff who were antimilitary and reduce Rand's effectiveness as an organization for the military." The release of the Pentagon Papers "was the last straw" and "brought matters to a decisive point." It gave people who had been unenthusiastic about Rowen more ammunition. The source added, "In this business it is very important to maintain high mutual confidence between people in government, in the White House . . . and particularly in the Defense Department and the leadership and Rand." RAND had lost this confidence as evidenced by Secretary of Defense Melvin Laird's order to the Air Force in July to take custody of all classified documents at RAND. Roberts revealed that, "As part of a Government campaign to limit access to classified material, Rand recommended recently that top secret clearance be removed from more than 1,000 staff members and consultants."

According to Gus Shubert, tension over the release of the Pentagon Papers lingered at RAND, but in the long run did no great harm. In his opinion, "the long-term impact . . . was zero." The security crackdown did not reflect inherent hostility on the part of the Air Force and was carried out to comply with orders. It did this with "a big wink" and "really didn't mean it." After "about four or five years, all the fuss was over, except internally among the staff which Ellsberg sort of lit off with his spectacular acrobatics."[368] Jim Gaither shared the view that the Air Force had to crack down because of political pressure, and said he would agree that, in the long run, the Pentagon Papers episode left no scarring on RAND, but it certainly created a crisis at the time. He said, "We went through the crisis, but then once we got through it, they didn't impose any sanctions, they didn't fire anybody, and they didn't take away the clearances, and we ultimately put the thing back together. But it was very serious."[369] Ultimately, according to him, people in the government accepted that the blame for the Pentagon Papers rested solely with Dan Ellsberg acting on his own, and this made it possible for RAND to work its way out of its trouble. Looking back, he said that "those were very bad days. . . . RAND got as close as you can to falling off a cliff without doing so. There were real questions as to whether RAND could survive that. That's why I was there almost full-time for six months."[370] According to him, it took RAND

---

[367] All quotes in this paragraph are from Roberts, "Rand Chief Quitting," 1971.

[368] Author interview with Gus Shubert, 2004 and 2005.

[369] Author interview with Jim Gaither, 2005.

[370] Author interview with Jim Gaither, 2005.

a long time to get over the crisis, and "it was not until after Don Rice arrived that we got back in good graces and began building RAND again."[371]

To find a replacement for Rowen, a search committee was set up, headed by Newt Minow, and Gaither was asked to do the search. Ultimately, Gaither and Huddleson recommended Don Rice as the next president of RAND. Rice had been recommended by George Schultz, then the head of the Office of Management and Budget. Rice, a graduate of Notre Dame, with a doctorate from Purdue University, had been assistant to Schultz but had also worked in the Pentagon as Deputy Assistant Secretary of Defense for Resource Analysis, and had earned respect within government domestic and defense circles.[372] According to Gaither, the selection of Rice was supported by John Foster, the head of ARPA. Newt Minow recalled that he told the board before it voted that he would present to the members all of Rice's credentials except for one fact. After the board completed its review, they asked him what that "one fact" was. Minow replied that it was Rice's age: He was 31 at the time. Minow said, "If I had told you his age before you met him, you would have been troubled. But I knew that once you met him, you would see that he was a mature, experienced person."[373]

According to Gus Shubert, the board selected Don Rice quickly, and on his first visit to Santa Monica, Rice was brought not as a candidate but as the person who was going to be president. "So they wanted to move very fast and they didn't want any arguments," he said. Rice was the "new broom" who took "a lot of exciting actions" to address the problems he saw. Shubert thought that Rice "was a great benefit to RAND, especially in his first years here."[374] Gaither considered Rice's appointment the turning point for RAND. Don Rice was president of RAND for 20 years, and then left to become Secretary of the Air Force. He remains a trustee of RAND.

In the aftermath of his release of the Pentagon Papers, Dan Ellsberg was charged with conspiracy, espionage, and theft of government property. On Sunday, June 20, 1971, his former wife Carol testified before a federal grand jury, providing information about Ellsberg's duplication of the Top Secret documents; on June 25, she signed an affidavit that, along with those signed by Jan Butler and Richard Best at RAND, was attached to a warrant for Ellsberg's arrest. Ellsberg became a media sensation, and while keeping his whereabouts secret, he gave an interview to Walter Cronkite at CBS, which was broadcast on June 23. On June 28, Ellsberg surrendered to the authorities

---

[371] Author interview with Jim Gaither, 2005.

[372] Author interview with Jim Gaither, 2005.

[373] Author interview with Newt Minow, 2005.

[374] Collins, interview with Gus Shubert, session of May 28, 1992, p. 73.

at the U.S. Attorney's office in Boston.[375] The FBI flew Richard Best to Boston to positively identify Ellsberg, who then posted a $50,000 bond. On that same day, a grand jury in Los Angeles indicted him on one count of theft of government property and one count of unauthorized possession of documents and writings related to national defense in violation of the Espionage Act. He became the first person in American history to be charged under this act "without being formally accused of passing official secrets to a foreign power."[376]

On June 22, Tony Russo was subpoenaed by the FBI to appear before the "supersecret" federal grand jury as a witness.[377] He refused to testify, despite the grant of immunity, because he did not want to provide incriminating information about a friend. According to Russo, if he had testified, Ellsberg would have been "nailed."[378] Ellsberg, however, was unhappy, since this meant that Russo would also be indicted and he would no longer be the sole protagonist in what promised to be a sensational trial. "I was horning in on his thing," Russo would later say.[379] Also, according to Russo, Ellsberg and his wife viewed him as "a wild-eyed radical" and feared that Russo "was going to blow it for Dan."[380]

By then, Russo had joined the counterculture and had adopted hippie attire and hairstyle, wearing his hair long and letting his sideburns grow bushy. While Ellsberg appeared in court in elegant suits, Russo at times looked unkempt. Russo had also become a vocal radical who talked about American imperialism and revolution.[381] This kind of talk would drive Ellsberg "up the wall."[382] For his refusal to testify, Russo spent 47 days in jail. During his imprisonment, he went on a hunger strike for 23 days. Just before Christmas in December 1971, a federal grand jury issued a new and harsher 15-count indictment against Ellsberg that added conspiracy to the previous criminal charges. If convicted, Ellsberg would face a maximum of 105 years in prison. Russo

---

[375] On June 29, 1971, Senator Mike Gravel of Alaska read aloud for hours in front of his Subcommittee on Buildings and Grounds from his copy of the Pentagon Papers, which had been provided to him by Ben Bagdikian, in a filibuster against the renewal of the legislation authorizing the Selective Service System, which he opposed. Gravel read past midnight and then had "the balance of the Pentagon Papers entered into the public record." Prados and Porter, *Inside the Pentagon Papers*, 2004, p. 60. Senator Gravel subsequently arranged for the publication of the Pentagon Papers, and Beacon Press published *The Senator Gravel Edition: The Pentagon Papers* in fall 1972. The *New York Times* and the Government Printing Office ultimately also published versions of the Pentagon Papers.

[376] Wells, *Wild Man*, 2001, p. 470.

[377] Gene Blake, "U.S. Grand Jury in LA Probing War Data Leaks," *Los Angeles Times*, June 24, 1971.

[378] Author interview with Tony Russo, 2003 and 2004.

[379] Wells, *Wild Man*, 2001, p. 451.

[380] Wells, *Wild Man*, 2001, p. 451.

[381] Wells, *Wild Man*, 2001, pp. 527–528.

[382] Author interview with Tony Russo, 2003 and 2004.

Daniel Ellsberg and Anthony Russo during the Pentagon Papers trial period.
(Associated Press)

was also charged with conspiracy and three counts of theft and espionage, with a possible sentence of 35 years in jail.

During the trial, RAND provided most of the evidence for the case and most of the witnesses, including Harry Rowen, Richard Best, and Dick Moorsteen. Mel Gurtov remembered that, among Ellsberg's former colleagues, he was the only person who appeared to testify in Ellsberg's defense and support. "Nobody at RAND stood up and said a word," according to him.[383] His testimony was not "terribly significant," but Gurtov says that he is proud of it.[384]

Even before the case went to trial, tension mounted between Ellsberg and Russo, who became split over legal strategy. Russo wanted to be confrontational, to set up a

---

[383] Author interview with Mel Gurtov, 2004.

[384] Author interview with Mel Gurtov, 2004. According to a *New York Times* article on September 24, 1971, when the Pentagon Papers controversy erupted, Mel Gurtov joined Ellsberg in denouncing "Washington's Vietnam policy as designed to deceive the American public." In the wake of this denunciation, RAND asked the publisher of Gurtov's book *China and Southeast Asia—The Politics of Survival: A Study of Foreign Policy Interaction* (Lexington, Mass.: Heath Lexington Books, 1971) "to remove all traces of its sponsorship," although it had earlier asked the publisher to rush it into print with the notation on the jacket and title page that the book was "a Rand Corporation research study." Henry Raymond, "Rand Seeks to Dissociate Itself from Book on China by Ex-Aide," *The New York Times,* September 24, 1971.

defense committee, and to use the courtroom as a forum to "mount a struggle" against the war, because the fighting was still going on in Vietnam and "people were dying every day" over there.[385] For this reason, he wanted to call radical anti-war activists as defense witnesses, whereas Ellsberg preferred establishment figures, such as McGeorge Bundy and Theodore Sorensen from the Kennedy Administration.[386] Russo was disappointed, since it seemed to him that Ellsberg, who had talked about going to jail, now just wanted to stay out of prison. Russo recalled Ellsberg telling him, "We've already got the Pentagon Papers out; we have accomplished our task. Now our job is to get off, even on a technicality or whatever."[387] In the end, Ellsberg and his wife hired and paid for the lawyers, and controlled the legal maneuvers.[388] To Russo's resentment, Ellsberg had little to do with him and tried to "wall" him off.[389] Russo also resented the fact that the spotlight shone on Ellsberg while he himself was ignored. Later, Russo would say that Ellsberg "abandoned" him and "betrayed" him.[390]

The prosecution of the two men went on until May 11, 1973, when Judge Matthew Byrne dismissed the charges because of "improper Government conduct." The conduct referred to was the Nixon Administration's admission in April 1973 that two members of the White House Plumbers had broken into Ellsberg's psychiatrist's office on September 3, 1971, to rifle the safe, looking for incriminating files on Ellsberg,[391] and to the wiretapped conversations between Mort Halperin and Ellsberg in the spring of

---

[385] Author interview with Tony Russo, 2003 and 2004.

[386] Elaine Woo, "Rand Staffer Encouraged Pentagon Papers Leak," obituary of Tony Russo, *Los Angeles Times*, August 8, 2008.

[387] Author interview with Tony Russo, 2003 and 2004.

[388] Russo claimed that Ellsberg raised $1 million for the defense. According to Russo, even before he was indicted, he talked to Ellsberg about a defense committee. Ellsberg said this would not be necessary, because his wife would pay for the lawyers. When he heard this, Russo said, he "ran quickly to the restroom and threw up." Author interview with Tony Russo, 2003 and 2004.

According to a *Baltimore Sun* article of February 13, 1973—with the title of "Ellsberg-Russo Defense Paying High Price for Cause; Trial Budget Runs $100,000 in the Red"—by 1973 the legal costs had exceeded $600,000. The cost was running at $60,000 a month, and the defense was facing a deficit of $100,000. Russo and Ellsberg were making efforts to raise money—giving lectures and writing articles. Public appeals had brought in about $20,000—mostly in small donations. Russo, who had "allegedly" been subsisting on $500 a month, had "twice petitioned the court for financial assistance and been denied."

[389] Wells, *Wild Man*, 2001, pp. 530–531.

[390] Wells, *Wild Man*, 2001, p. 531. Russo would later say that the "only support" he had during the trial was "the Black Panthers who came in off the street." Author interview with Tony Russo, 2003 and 2004.

[391] The White House created the Plumbers unit because it was upset that J. Edgar Hoover, the FBI director, was less than zealous in pursuing Dan Ellsberg's leak. Nixon recalled that Ellsberg's success in "using the press, television talk shows, and antiwar rallies" to rally support for his cause made Hoover reluctant to "pursue the case vigorously," because he was concerned that "the media would automatically make Ellsberg look like a martyr, and the FBI like the "heavy." Nixon, *RN*, 1978, p. 513. Nixon said he wanted to discredit Ellsberg's "efforts to justify unlawful dissent," and therefore "urged that we find out everything we could about his background, his motives, and his co-conspirators, if they existed." Nixon, *RN*, 1978, p. 513.

1969 and summer of 1971, during electronic surveillance of Halperin's home.[392] In addition, Byrne had been identified in the press as having met with Ehrlichman, while he was presiding over the trial, to talk about his prospects of becoming FBI director. Byrne did not mention his conflict of interest in dismissing the charges, but ruled that Ellsberg and Russo should not be tried again on charges of stealing and duplicating the Pentagon Papers.

The long trial, the disagreements over legal strategy, Russo's resentment over what he perceived as Ellsberg's monopolizing of the limelight, the fact that he was the only one going to jail for 47 days for refusing to answer grand jury questions—while Ellsberg served no time in prison—and the stress of it all destroyed the friendship between the two men. Russo would later say that the whole experience had been "*horrendous*" for him and that he "was sitting on his anger" every day.[393] Toward the end of the trial, Russo told a journalist apropos of Ellsberg, "To tell you the truth, I really don't want to ever see him again."[394] It appeared that up until Tony Russo's death in 2008, Russo and Ellsberg were not on speaking terms.

After the trial, Ellsberg became a hero for many in the anti-war movement and a lecturer who was much in demand, until the glow began to wear off. Russo, on the other hand, was remembered only for his supporting role in the Pentagon Papers affair, and the perception that he had been "'just a Xeroxer'" rankled him until his death.[395] Because the creation of the Plumbers unit later led to the break-in of the Democratic Party headquarters at Watergate and ultimately to Nixon's near impeachment and actual resignation, both men believed that their action helped bring down Nixon and contributed to the end of the war, since his removal from office ensured that America would not intervene again after U.S. troops were withdrawn.

The publication of the Pentagon Papers did not affect Nixon's Vietnam policies or change the course of the war. The fighting continued until the North Vietnamese achieved victory in April 1975. The Pentagon Papers episode is now remembered less for the contents of the study and more for the Nixon Administration's attempt to silence the press and for the controversy that ensued. The leak of the papers did reinforce distrust of government among an American public already skeptical of official pronouncements, because of the "credibility gap" created by the Johnson Administration over Vietnam.

At RAND, the aftertaste lingered for a long time among the staff. According to Gus Shubert, people in general continued to view Ellsberg as "a traitor" who "ought

---

[392]"Ellsberg Case Dismissed," *Los Angeles Times*, May 11, 1973. Halperin's telephone was wiretapped because he had been suspected of leaking information while serving on the National Security Council.

[393]Wells, *Wild Man*, 2001, p. 533.

[394]Wells, *Wild Man*, 2001, p. 533.

[395]Woo, "Rand Staffer Encouraged," 2008.

to be dealt with accordingly."[396] Shubert himself did not agree with this sentiment and felt that he was perhaps the only person who did not believe that "Ellsberg should be drawn or quartered or hung in a public place."[397] Rowen is still not on speaking terms with his old friend Ellsberg, and thinks that the release of the Pentagon Papers had no impact on the war. Shubert concurs, saying that the effect was "zilch, zero."[398]

About a year-and-a-half after the publication of the Pentagon Papers, journalist Muriel Dobbin of the *Baltimore Sun* found that RAND was still reeling from the impact, psychologically and financially. In "Rand Corporation Still Feels Pentagon Papers' Aftereffects," she wrote in February 1973—three months before the case against Ellsberg was dismissed—that, "What Daniel Ellsberg did to Rand, the think-tank by the sea, was enough to make even one of its computers shudder." She added, "More than 800 Rand employees lost their top-secret clearance," and those who kept theirs had to peruse classified documents in a "closely guarded control room." There was nostalgia for the pre-Ellsberg era, and people viewed Ellsberg as "a man who let his side down." The staff, now peering "from beneath [a] new and thicker security blanket"— imposed by the Air Force—longed for the day when "We were all in the vault together, and nobody had to put things under lock and key."

By far, the most severe impact was on RAND's funding. According to Dobbin, "The House Appropriations Committee slashed proposed spending for Rand and similar institutions by 25 percent," and "to add to Rand's sudden load of sorrows, its chief client, the Air Force . . . had reduced its contract funds by at least 30 percent." So, as Ellsberg stood trial in a courtroom in Los Angeles, RAND "30 miles away in Santa Monica, is still quivering from the repercussions of the most painful and most publicized incident in its 27-year history."

---

[396]Author interview with Gus Shubert, 2004 and 2005.

[397]Author interview with Gus Shubert, 2004 and 2005. According to Shubert, over the years, Ellsberg had expressed through third parties any chance he could "his continuing admiration for RAND and his hopes that he did not in any way damage the institution and, in particular, his esteem and affection for Harry and his sorrow at having caused him the trouble that he caused him." Collins, interview with Gus Shubert, session of May 28, 1992, p. 70. Nobody at RAND wanted to have any contact with Ellsberg after the release of the Pentagon Papers. The first person to see Ellsberg was Konrad Kellen, whom Ellsberg arranged to meet in the early 1990s. Ellsberg asked Kellen how people at RAND had reacted to his release of the Pentagon Papers. According to Kellen, Ellsberg "'had this fantasy' that people had applauded him." Kellen told him, "But Dan, how naive can you get? You think that people at RAND are going to cheer? . . . You mystify me." Wells, *Wild Man*, 2001, p. 521.

[398]Author interview with Gus Shubert, 2004 and 2005. Few of the decisionmakers in Washington bothered to read the voluminous study, Mel Gurtov concluded at a three-day panel discussion sponsored by "17 congressmen on the significance of the . . . papers." For this reason, Gurtov thought it was "ludicrous" to have "spent so much time and effort studying U.S.–Vietnam policy decisions." Thomas J. Foley, "Author Says Very Few Read 'Pentagon Papers'," *Los Angeles Times*, July 28, 1971.

CHAPTER TEN

The End of the War

A year before the Pentagon Papers affair erupted, another controversy embroiled RAND in a heated public debate about an issue often referred to as the "bloodbath theory." To stave off critics who were urging faster or unilateral withdrawal of U.S. combat troops from Vietnam and to rally support for his policy, President Nixon repeatedly warned that precipitous disengagement would lead to communist massacres of South Vietnamese. As Robert J. Donovan of the *Los Angeles Times* wrote in his column, "Bloodbath—Fantasy or Realistic Fear?" on Sunday, June 28, 1970, which recapped the debate, this question was fraught with emotion. It asked, in essence, "whether an early pull-out of U.S. troops would condemn America's allies and friends in South Vietnam to extensive massacre by the Communists." The basic assumption was that the South Vietnamese government would collapse and that the communists would take over.

In a press conference at the White House on May 8, 1970, President Nixon declared, for example, ". . . if we withdraw from Vietnam and allow the enemy to come into Vietnam and massacre the civilians there by the millions, as they would—if we do that, let me say that America is finished insofar as the peacekeeper in the Asian world is concerned."[1] Donovan reported that shortly after the president made this assertion, Douglas Pike, considered one of the government's leading experts on the Viet Cong, suggested that the communists "might murder perhaps 3 million people if they 'should win decisively' in South Vietnam." The fundamental question of whether the communists would have the wherewithal to win a decisive victory was not discussed in this debate. On the other side of the debate were political leaders, such as former Secretary of Defense Clark Clifford and Senator William Fulbright, Chairman of the Senate Foreign Relations Committee, who did not believe that the danger existed for a massacre.[2] Also, various scholars and many critics with similar viewpoints maintained that Nixon was trying to frighten Americans into supporting his Vietnam policies by

---

[1] Robert J. Donovan, "Bloodbath—Fantasy or Realistic Fear?" *Los Angeles Times*, June 28, 1970.

[2] The former Defense Secretary had predicted instead, in a *Life* magazine article, "When it becomes apparent that the Americans are in fact leaving, all parties seeking power in South Vietnam will have a strong incentive to negotiate a compromise settlement." Cited in Donovan, "Bloodbath," 1970.

painting the communists as fiends who would treat their vanquished foes brutally if his goals were not achieved.[3]

In the middle of this debate, RAND published a report by Steve Hosmer, *Viet Cong Repression and Its Implications for the Future* (R-0475-ARPA, April 1970). In his study, Hosmer stated that repression was not simply a tactic or a policy for the Viet Cong but part of their doctrine of "crime and punishment."[4] By calling repression a doctrine, Hosmer implied that it was and would be implacable. Although he discussed the different forms of repression the communists might adopt after they won control of the South, he concluded that they would execute at least 100,000 of their former foes. In his view, although the communists might adopt a conciliatory policy as a political expediency, he believed that they would decide to treat their former enemies harshly, and "the number of *executions alone* could well total many tens of thousands."[5] He added, "One can only guess at what the *minimum* would be," but, given the number of South Vietnamese blacklisted by the communists, "this author finds it difficult to believe that the number would be much less than 100,000. Indeed, it might well be considerably higher."[6] According to Hosmer, the culture of revenge of Vietnam itself rendered such a bloodbath even more likely. By using terms such as "bloodshed" and "bloody," Hosmer made his prediction sound more ominous.

The longest portion of the report, which was based on captured documents, was devoted to demonstrating that repression—through elimination, demoralization, and subversion of GVN personnel at all levels—had been a critical component of Viet Cong political and military activities in South Vietnam for over a decade. Under the organization and direction of the Viet Cong Security Service, repression played a vital role in the VC efforts to extend control over the population and to bring about the collapse of the GVN. Through repression, the Viet Cong sought to gradually undermine the government and, eventually, to make it impossible for the GVN to administer and maintain security in areas it controlled, as well as to stymie its efforts to expand into areas that were contested or held by the Viet Cong.

It follows, therefore, that the people the Viet Cong targeted were GVN officials, from Saigon down to hamlet level; officers of the ARVN and of paramilitary forces; intelligence and counterintelligence operatives and the informers who worked for them; security and police personnel; defectors; and psychological-warfare and revolutionary-development cadres. The blacklists the Viet Cong established to target such people also included members of political parties considered adversaries of the social and political change the Viet Cong advocated; anti-communist religious leaders; and other people whose activities the Viet Cong viewed as damaging to their movement. Targeted

---

[3] Donovan, "Bloodbath," 1970.

[4] Hosmer, *Viet Cong Repression*, 1970, p. v.

[5] Hosmer, *Viet Cong Repression*, 1970, p. 186. Emphasis in original.

[6] Hosmer, *Viet Cong Repression*, 1970, p. 186.

people were classified as "tyrants," "reactionaries," "counterrevolutionaries," "spies," or simply "opponents." As such, they were "criminals with blood debts to the people" and deserved the harshest punishment. Hosmer wrote that the communists, therefore, considered the "assassination, execution, or long-term imprisonment" of such people appropriate acts of justice. Also, to the communists, these measures represented practical ways to disrupt and paralyze the government apparatus and reduce potential support for the GVN.[7]

According to Hosmer, this repression was not random but, for the most part, had been carefully thought out and implemented to achieve defined political and military objectives. Up until the Tet Offensive of 1968, the communists tended to use repression flexibly, to fit the political situation prevailing in each area. They were aware that if repression was misused, it could lead to loss of popular support; so, they were careful to keep it under control out of political expediency. To avoid indiscriminate repression that might harm innocent people and provoke popular hostility, the communists exercised tight control from the center.

This flexibility and restraint were abandoned in favor of greater violence during the Tet Offensive of 1968. In the hope of bringing about a quick disintegration of the government, the communists vastly intensified their repression "(virtually declaring 'open season' on many government persons and establishing quotas for the number to be killed by individual units)."[8] During their occupation of Hue, the communists—according to reports—killed 3,000 people and buried them in mass graves.[9] Elsewhere, they made a determined effort to get the population to help track down and eliminate government officials, "spies," and "reactionaries," but failed. Likewise, their effort to enlist popular support in their offensive and to instigate popular uprisings were unsuccessful.

---

[7] Hosmer, *Viet Cong Repression*, 1970, pp. v–vi.

[8] Hosmer, *Viet Cong Repression*, 1970, p. vi.

[9] The number of people killed by the communists during their occupation of Hue was disputed at the time, and some people argued that many of the dead were victims of American bombing and shelling during the U.S. retaking of the city. In his postwar interviews in Vietnam, Stanley Karnow wrote that he could get "little credible evidence from the communists to clarify the episode." One communist official claimed that "the exhumed bodies were mostly of Vietcong cadres and sympathizers slain by the South Vietnamese army after the fight for the city." But this official also acknowledged that the communists were responsible for some of the killings, explaining that "the 'angry' citizens of Hue had liquidated local 'despots'" so as to prevent them from committing "further crimes." This explanation echoed what Hosmer had found in Viet Cong captured documents. Stanley Karnow concluded that, "Balanced accounts have made it clear, however, that the Communist butchery in Hue did take place—perhaps on an even larger scale than reported during the war." See Karnow, *Vietnam: A History*, 1983, p. 543. Hosmer did point out that some of the indiscriminate and "more brutal" killings in Hue were probably carried out not by security cadres but by North Vietnamese and other military forces, and that they seemed uncharacteristic of the VC Security Service. Nevertheless, the communists considered this repression as "both necessary and generally successful," he wrote. Hosmer, *Viet Cong Repression*, 1970, p. 76.

The basic tool for repression was the "blacklist," containing information about government civilian and military personnel in the rural as well as the urban areas, including the "crimes" each had allegedly committed.[10] According to Hosmer, the blacklist was extensive but mostly included lower-level GVN personnel in hamlets and villages, and it had been compiled with information provided mostly by informants but also by prisoners and defectors, secret agents, captured or stolen documents, and surveillance of government installations. The information, however, was cursory and, often, provided only basic information, such as the names, positions, and addresses of the people targetd.[11] Each blacklist supposedly contained information about pro-GVN personnel who were to be tracked down and "dealt with" after the Viet Cong gained control of an area.[12] However, up to date, such "master rosters" had not been found. The majority of the lists—captured by American and GVN forces—were not "master rosters" but rather "operations lists" which were limited and targeted persons living—not in a wide area—but in a specific location or working for a particular GVN agency or a political party.

The method of repression varied with the accessibility of the targets. In GVN areas, the communists resorted mainly to assassination or abduction. Those who were kidnapped were taken to Viet Cong areas to be interrogated, after which they might be executed, or incarcerated in prison camps, or subjected to indoctrination and then freed. Warnings could be issued to GVN civilian and military personnel, along with an offer of clemency, to induce them to perform a service for the Revolution—such as providing intelligence information. In regions they controlled or in contested areas, the communists used a range of punishments, including execution; confinement to "thought-reform camps"; arrests; "reduction in prestige"; "home surveillance"; "in place reform"; and "the warning"—the "mildest and probably the most common form of repression"—intended to impress the victim with both the "strict viewpoint" and "the tolerance" of the Revolution.[13]

According to Hosmer, "The number of those killed and abducted is large." The best available official estimate was "44,000 for 1966–1969, of whom about 4,000 were government officials or employees."[14] Nevertheless, Hosmer believed that these totals were significantly lower than the actual number of murders, because they excluded

---

[10] Such a list was used in Hue by the Viet Cong, who, according to Karnow, "conducted house-to-house searches" to arrest and kill people they categorized as "cruel tyrants and reactionary elements—a rubric covering civilian functionaries, army officers and nearly anybody else linked to the South Vietnamese regime as well as uncooperative merchants, intellectuals and clergymen." Karnow, *Vietnam: A History*, 1983, p. 543.

[11] Hosmer, *Viet Cong Repression*, 1970, pp. 52–57.

[12] Hosmer, *Viet Cong Repression*, 1970, p. 49.

[13] Hosmer, *Viet Cong Repression*, 1970, pp. 86–87.

[14] Hosmer, *Viet Cong Repression*, 1970, pp. vii, 66.

"those killed in military attacks and other actions" not considered assassinations.[15] The number of assassinations and abductions could have been higher if the communists had better access to their targets. Hosmer wrote, "When one compares the stated intentions of the Viet Cong (as reflected in the large target categories, the number of persons on blacklists, the high quotas assigned to individual units, etc.) with the numbers of persons actually repressed, one may wonder why the Communists do not kill, abduct, and incarcerate more persons than they do."[16] The most important reason was "quite simply: that *the Viet Cong want to assassinate or abduct many more people than they are able to*,"[17] because "the vast majority of all targets are comparatively well defended."[18] Many lived in secure towns and cities or, if they resided in the countryside, they usually spent the night in military outposts. Others carried arms.

After laying out the Viet Cong's patterns of repression, Hosmer discussed what the future might hold for their opponents. He argued that, in view of the history of repression on both sides, accommodation was not feasible. GVN officials undoubtedly knew that they were targeted by the communists. The bloody repression of the Land Reform campaign in North Vietnam in 1953–1956 and the brutal extermination of GVN officials and those connected with the government during the occupation of Hue only served to reinforce their fear of reprisals if the communists seized power in South Vietnam. These perceptions helped explain why GVN leaders were adamantly opposed to sharing power with the communists in a coalition government, which to them was nothing more than a pathway for the communists to gain complete control. Former President Nguyen Cao Ky epitomized their attitude toward reconciliation with the communists when he said, "I regard the Communists as traitors and they regard me as a traitor. If I catch them I'll shoot them, and if they catch me they'll shoot me."[19] On the Viet Cong side, memories of repression by the South Vietnamese government, such as President Ngo Dinh Diem's large-scale and harsh persecution of former Viet Minh adherents, led many Southern Viet Cong cadres to doubt GVN's promises of amnesty and to fear for their fate if their side lost.

It was the report's last section, "Some Thoughts on the Likelihood of Repression Under a Communist Regime," that attracted the most attention and provoked the most controversy. In it, Hosmer examined the implications "in the melancholy contingency that a Communist regime were to assume power in South Vietnam."[20] Since the

---

[15] Hosmer, *Viet Cong Repression*, 1970, p. 69.

[16] Hosmer, *Viet Cong Repression*, 1970, p. 112.

[17] Hosmer, *Viet Cong Repression*, 1970, p. 113. Emphasis in original.

[18] Hosmer, *Viet Cong Repression*, 1970, p. 114.

[19] Hosmer, *Viet Cong Repression*, 1970, p. 149. Ky fled to the United States in 1975 but has moved back to Vietnam, where he is now living in retirement.

[20] Hosmer, *Viet Cong Repression*, 1970, p. 175.

Viet Cong leadership envisaged a series of General Offensives and General Uprisings—similar to those attempted in the Tet Offensive of 1968—as the most likely ways for them to defeat the GVN, their present doctrine would "necessitate the systematic hunting down and annihilation of many thousands of government officials, civil servants, military leaders, 'spies,' and 'reactionaries'" should they achieve control in this manner.[21] In addition, they might attempt to incite the masses to help track down and exterminate the groups that they targeted. If the communists were to gain power in this way, they could resort to large-scale killings while they were consolidating their power in order to eliminate people who might oppose their government.

If the communists were to take over by other means—for example by gradually subverting and taking over a coalition government established under international auspices—then the scope of the violence might be less widespread, at least in the initial stages of the coalition, when they were trying to win the support of their opponents. If they managed to achieve final control without resorting to widespread violence, their behavior might be tempered.[22] Other considerations might influence their conduct. The disintegration of the GVN would mean that government civilian and military officials would now be stripped of power and would no longer be in a position to threaten and undermine the Revolution, as they had done during the war. The need to administer and rehabilitate the war-torn country might lead the communist government to eschew actions that might impede efforts to unite the people and mobilize their support after decades of divisive warfare.

In particular, it would induce them to avoid mass reprisals that might alienate the majority of South Vietnamese, or lead to pervasive passive resistance, or push religious and ethnic groups to mount an insurgency.[23] The communists might decide that being tolerant and lenient—especially toward former rank-and-file military and civilian personnel—would be the best policy.[24] Finally, the communists might be deterred by the fear of an international backlash if they carried out a bloodbath.[25]

On the other hand, the communists might view repression as essential for the establishment of their control of the South, especially in areas formerly under GVN domination. They might consider it necessary to eliminate people whom they viewed as "hard-core" supporters of the GVN, because such people might constitute "a dangerous source of potential opposition" and might sabotage the regime and its programs to achieve the socialist transformation of the South.[26] In such a case, a substantial

---

[21] Hosmer, *Viet Cong Repression*, 1970, p. 176.

[22] Hosmer, *Viet Cong Repression*, 1970, p. 178.

[23] Hosmer, *Viet Cong Repression*, 1970, p. 179.

[24] Hosmer, *Viet Cong Repression*, 1970, p. 179.

[25] Hosmer, *Viet Cong Repression*, 1970, p. 180.

[26] Hosmer, *Viet Cong Repression*, 1970, p. 181.

number of people from all levels of the GVN civilian and military structure could be lumped into this category and might be eliminated physically, or incarcerated for extended periods of time in "thought-reform camps," or brought before the population in "public denunciation sessions" in a "ritual of condemnation, confession, and trial by a People's Court. . . ."[27]

Beyond these practical considerations, the Viet Cong might be guided by their belief that anyone who perpetrated a serious crime against the Revolution or the people had to be punished or had to perform a service to atone for this crime.[28] For this reason, once the communists gained control of the South, thousands of people who had been labeled as "criminals" could expect to be executed or imprisoned for a long time.[29]

It is at this point in the report that Hosmer came up with the prediction that a minimum of 100,000 people—or perhaps even more—would be executed.[30] Hosmer would go further, adding that if the communists should embark on a rapid socialist transformation of the South, including collectivization and the use of "grass-root violence" similar to that employed in the Land Reform campaign of the 1950s in the North, the number of potential victims could "swell" and "the likelihood of an extensive bloodbath would be very great indeed."[31]

♧ ♧ ♧

Hosmer's report on repression was criticized within RAND by Michael E. Arnsten of the Economics Department.[32] Arnsten disclosed that Hosmer's study had been declassified immediately by the Defense Department in May 1970, a month after it had been published as a "Confidential" report in April 1970—presumably because it reinforced the "bloodbath theory"—and released to the media. Then, on June 3, it was decided that the report would be published as a book, and, on June 9, D.C. Heath Co. agreed to print it. The speed with which this process happened astounded and disturbed Arnsten: "Rarely, if ever," he pointed out, "has Rand achieved instant communication with a mass audience; up to now this has never happened to any Rand publication on Vietnam."[33]

Arnsten focused on the concluding section of Hosmer's report, which contains Hosmer's "ominous forecast" that the communists, once in power, would murder at

---

[27] Hosmer, *Viet Cong Repression*, 1970, p. 182.

[28] Hosmer, *Viet Cong Repression*, 1970, p. 183.

[29] Hosmer, *Viet Cong Repression*, 1970, p. 183.

[30] Hosmer, *Viet Cong Repression*, 1970, p. 186.

[31] Hosmer, *Viet Cong Repression*, 1970, p. 187.

[32] Arnsten, Michael E., *A Review of the Bloodbath Report and a Note on Some Shortcomings of the Rand Review Procedure,* IN-21039-ARPA/AG, August 1970.

[33] Arnsten, *A Review of the Bloodbath Report*, 1970, p. 3.

least 100,000 of their former foes, and that this minimum number might turn out to be much higher. To Arnsten, the sheer number of the killing and the use of words such as "bloodbath, bloodshed, etc." implied that the United States should not allow this tragedy to take place,[34] and since Hosmer offered no policy alternatives to the continuation of support for the GVN, this left only one "moral choice," which would be to acquiesce to the policies of the Nixon Administration.[35] In short, the choice as implied by Hosmer, was "defeat and mass killings or continued American defense of the South," but without specification of the duration or cost of such a commitment.[36] To Arnsten, this prediction of the dire consequences for a U.S. defeat in South Vietnam, combined with the implicit message, had been invoked and would continue to be invoked to justify the current pace of withdrawal, to blunt the arguments of critics who urged that disengagement be accelerated.[37]

In Arnsten's view, "The purpose of many Rand studies is to help policy planners and decision makers to deal with an uncertain future; the uncertainties associated with the future behavior of the adversary are a crucial element in the analysis. . . . Study of contingency plans for an uncertain future is the most important contribution of Rand studies."[38] However, Hosmer "ignores this completely." He "should have addressed himself to the question: If this 'melancholy contingency,' that is, the loss of the South, were to come about, what could the United States do to influence the victorious side's policy toward repression?"[39] It could be that, if a promising policy in this regard could have been recommended, it "would have made the Report less useful as a justification of the present policy" and "might have turned it into a weapon that could be used by critics of the war."[40]

Arnsten questioned the arbitrary figure of 100,000 executions Hosmer had used, writing that he did not believe in the feasibility of projecting the number of victims that would be harmed by the Viet Cong at some point in the future. In analyzing Hosmer's report, Arnsten concluded that this "magic" number seemed to be plucked out of nowhere and appeared "to be based solely on the author's sheer, undifferentiated, personal belief . . . there are no calculations."[41] In fact, Arnsten determined that this figure did not appear in the original draft Hosmer submitted to RAND reviewers and was inserted in the final report.

---

[34] Arnsten, *A Review of the Bloodbath Report*, 1970, p. 1.

[35] Arnsten, *A Review of the Bloodbath Report*, 1970, p. 1.

[36] Arnsten, *A Review of the Bloodbath Report*, 1970, p. 5.

[37] Arnsten, *A Review of the Bloodbath Report*, 1970, p. 5.

[38] Arnsten, *A Review of the Bloodbath Report*, 1970, p. 4.

[39] Arnsten, *A Review of the Bloodbath Report*, 1970, pp. 4–5.

[40] Arnsten, *A Review of the Bloodbath Report*, 1970, pp. 4–5.

[41] Arnsten, *A Review of the Bloodbath Report*, 1970, p. 6.

Arnsten suggested an alternative way. He wrote, "Instead of professing one's personal belief in a magic number, one can calculate explicitly—necessarily arbitrarily—minimum and maximum numbers of deaths and, using the Delphi process, show the distribution of opinions of a number of Rand experts on communism."[42] To arrive at a total number, Hosmer could have estimated the number of people in each category and subcategory who were the most vulnerable to Viet Cong reprisals—something he failed to do—and then estimated the percentages of each category that might be killed. To Arnsten, the arbitrariness of the 100,000 figure was demonstrated by Hosmer's selection of minimum figures: "many thousands of Vietnamese could expect death or at least long prison terms"; "executions alone could well total many tens of thousands"; and then "not much less than 100,000"; and, finally, "it [the minimum] might well be considerably higher than the 100,000."

Arnsten wrote that he had not taken sides in the bloodbath controversy. He believed neither President Nixon's predictions of a bloodbath nor North Vietnamese Premier Pham Van Dong's assurances that there would be no reprisals. In his view, both parties in the war had displayed cruelty, and so the possibility existed that, if either side won, it would be merciless toward its former enemies. Therefore, the United States should be concerned about the fate of the losers—no matter which side they happened to be on. Arnsten believed that, "If the bloodbath controversy is about the welfare of the Vietnamese it would focus on another question: What could the United States do to influence the victorious side's policy [whether Viet Cong or GVN] toward its former adversaries?"[43]

If Hosmer was concerned about the fate of the people he predicted would be executed in the event of a communist victory, he should have suggested policy options that the United States could follow. According to Arnsten, Hosmer should have "addressed himself to two questions: What could the United States do to help the members of the ex-A [GVN] to leave the South and to influence the new A's [communist regime] policy toward their former adversaries who remain in Vietnam?"[44] The United States could help members of the GVN escape, and the "degree of our responsibility for the survival of Vietnamese who remain and our ability to take some Vietnamese with us, as we depart, will vary from scenario to scenario."[45] These scenarios might include a GVN that survived after the American withdrawal—made unilaterally or as part of a peace settlement—or a GVN that agreed "to a coalition government or even to an outright takeover."[46] For example, Arnsten pointed out, under one of the scenarios

---

[42] Arnsten, *A Review of the Bloodbath Report*, 1970, p. 6.

[43] Arnsten, *A Review of the Bloodbath Report*, 1970, p. 3.

[44] Arnsten, *A Review of the Bloodbath Report*, 1970, p. 13.

[45] Arnsten, *A Review of the Bloodbath Report*, 1970, p. 17.

[46] Arnsten, *A Review of the Bloodbath Report*, 1970, p. 17.

that Hosmer postulated—"gradual subversion" of a coalition government—that some former GVN officials, "especially those with Swiss bank accounts," could leave the country.[47] To moderate the behavior of the communist victors, the United States could offer economic aid on the condition that they refrained from engaging in reprisals that violated a "predetermined threshold of violence."[48]

Hosmer's use of the word "*doctrine*" bothered Arnsten, because it suggested that repression had a moral imperative that may have a greater influence on a communist regime's postwar policies than "all of the practical considerations" that it might weigh for self-preservation.[49] Hosmer discovered this doctrine through evidence he had gleaned from "captured security directives and blacklists." Arnsten argued that "all of this evidence is found in captured documents written during the war. During a 'Revolutionary' war convincing one's enemies of 'assured destruction,' unless they abstain from undesirable acts or change sides, is a form of deterrence, coercion and persuasion."[50] However, it did not necessarily follow that the same would apply in a time of peace.

Arnsten wrote, "In short, there is a distinction between the tactics of intrawar 'repression' and the alleged postwar 'doctrine.' Can one derive the latter from the former?"[51] He argued that, "A side, after it comes to power, may behave differently because its objectives change and become more complex, and because it acquires a wider spectrum of instruments that can be used to coerce, reward, and persuade."[52] Citing the killings in Hue, he wrote that the Viet Cong and the North Vietnamese troops probably had only two choices before they withdrew during the Tet Offensive: They could either release their prisoners or kill them. After the war, however, they would have the additional option of sending them to prison or "re-educating" them. Arnsten thought that the title of the report, *Viet Cong Repression and Its Implications for the Future*, takes this implication for granted. He suggested that, "A non-prejudicial title might have had the following form: *Viet Cong Wartime Repression. Does It Have Implications for the Postwar Future?*"[53]

Arnsten believed that, after the war, a communist regime might be driven less by "an inner voice saying 'you shall be punished,' and more inclined—at least tem-

---

[47] Arnsten, *A Review of the Bloodbath Report*, 1970, p. 14.

[48] Arnsten, *A Review of the Bloodbath Report*, 1970, p. 16.

[49] Arnsten, *A Review of the Bloodbath Report*, 1970, p. 18. Arnsten thought that Hosmer "stresses the Vietnamese character of the doctrine, presumably, because he knows that it cannot be found in the communist literature of other countries."

[50] Arnsten, *A Review of the Bloodbath Report*, 1970, p. 18.

[51] Arnsten, *A Review of the Bloodbath Report*, 1970, p. 18.

[52] Arnsten, *A Review of the Bloodbath Report*, 1970, p. 20.

[53] Arnsten, *A Review of the Bloodbath Report*, 1970, p. 20.

porarily—to ignore past crimes if this suits its postwar interests."[54] Furthermore, citing Robert Jay Lifton's work on China and Nathan Leites' work on Vietnam,[55] Arnsten argued that "the Chinese and Vietnamese Communists have a strong penchant for re-educating their former enemies."[56] After stating that "anyone who has committed a serious crime 'must either submit to the punishment of the Viet Cong or atone for his past actions by performing a concrete service for the Revolution,'" Hosmer proceeded—in subsequent discussions—to ignore this option, which, if the Communist Party permitted, each person could choose. Thus, Hosmer left execution and other harsh measures as the only alternatives.

Arnsten also questioned why Hosmer did not address the issue of GVN repression and its implications. He wrote, "If wartime VC 'repression' 'implies' a red bloodbath, does not wartime GVN repression 'imply' a white bloodbath? There are many parallels between communist and nationalist patterns of repression."[57] He found it "difficult to believe that the number of names—of the VC infrastructure—stored on the Phoenix blacklist is much less than 100,000." He also found it "difficult to believe that in the last few years the annual total Phoenix 'eliminations' does not approximately equal the yearly total of VC 'repressions.'"[58]

The handling of Hosmer's report led Arnsten to suggest a more rigorous review process for controversial papers. He thought that, for Hosmer's study and for Ed Mitchell's report,[59] such a procedure would have corrected some deficiencies prior to

---

[54] Arnsten, *A Review of the Bloodbath Report*, 1970, p. 18.

[55] Arnsten did not specify these authors' works, and only wrote, "See Lifton on China and Leites on Vietnam." However, in the case of Robert Lifton, Arnsten must have referred to *Thought Reform and the Psychology of Totalism: A Study of 'Brainwashing' in China*, first published in 1961 and reprinted by the University of North Carolina Press, Chapel Hill, N.C., in 1989. In the case of Leites, Arnsten must have referred to *The Viet Cong Style of Politics*, Santa Monica, Calif.: RAND Corporation, RM-5487-1-ISA/ARPA, 1969.

[56] Arnsten, *A Review of the Bloodbath Report*, 1970, p. 18. Following the communist victory of 1975, hundreds of thousands of former civilian and military officials of the Saigon regime were incarcerated for different lengths of time—ranging from a few months to over ten years—in "re-education camps." The harshest camps were located in the North. The number who died during incarceration is unknown. During the accelerated socialist transformation of the South—the "smash the bourgeoisie" campaign—thousands of merchants were stripped of their assets and sent to "New Economic Zones," where they were forced to produce food and eke out a living with little financial and material support from the government. It is not known how many died in the process.

[57] Arnsten, *A Review of the Bloodbath Report*, 1970, p. 20.

[58] Arnsten, *A Review of the Bloodbath Report*, 1970, p. 21. According to author Marilyn B. Young in *The Vietnam Wars 1945–1990* (New York: HarperCollins, 1991, p. 213), Robert Komer, when he was head of CORDS "set a quota of three thousand VCI to be 'neutralized' each month." However, "[f]rom 1968 to mid-1971, 28,000 VCI were captured, 20,000 assassinated, 17,000 persuaded to defect (though whether all these people were in fact VCI is doubtful . . .)." On the issue of land reform, Arnsten cited as an example of a "white bloodbath" the 1965 killing in Indonesia of 300,000 to 500,000 "poor or landless farmers who had been organized by the Indonesian Communist Party" during the government's anti–land reform campaign.

[59] Arnsten did not specify Mitchell's work, but probably referred to Edward Mitchell's *Inequality and Insurgency: A Statistical Study of South Vietnam*, Santa Monica, Calif.: RAND Corporation, P-3610, June 1967, which was

publication. As a departure point for discussion, he called for a "Special Review Proce-dure." When an author or members of his department were aware of the controversial nature of a paper, they—or the department—should notify someone in the adminis-tration vested with the responsibility for deciding when the special procedure should be applied. The draft then should be issued as an internal paper and circulated widely among those who had the expertise to comment on its contents. This apparently did not happen with Hosmer's report. The reviewers should hold one or several seminars to discuss the draft and then read the report before it went into final publication.

For Hosmer's report, this additional check might have forestalled the inclusion of the prediction that at least 100,000 people would be killed. After all these steps were taken, if serious points of disagreement remained, a corporate appendix could be added in which "the reviewers, perhaps with the cooperation of the author, should summa-rize why, in view of insufficient data or limitations of methodology, certain questions cannot be conclusively resolved. . . ."[60] With regard to Hosmer's report, some of the reviewers stated that "they would have insisted on additional changes in the text, if they had anticipated the instant declassification of the text."[61] Therefore, because some reviewers were "less stringent in reviewing reports they believe will be classified,"[62] RAND should have the right—if a report was going to be declassified—to make final changes before the printing of the declassified version that would reach an audience that would include Congress, the media, and the general public.

When asked about Arnsten's critique, Hosmer said that he wanted "to straighten out what happened."[63] He recalled that the report had been reviewed by his peers at RAND and that, in the initial draft, he did not have "any estimates as to the number of people who might be executed." Since the reviewers had "strongly suggested" that he "come up with a hard number," he "worked out with a specialist . . . what was a reasonable estimate as to the number of people who were at serious risk of execution." However, he did not want to reveal who this specialist was.

Hosmer recalled that, at the time, "Vice President Agnew was saying it was going to be three million, and that was the Administration's number." In the report, he sug-gested "that it was going to be more like 100,000 or perhaps more." He remembered the controversy his report provoked at RAND and ascribed it to the fact that "it was at the point where anybody who was against the war was against anything that might suggest prolonging U.S. involvement." As to Arnsten's criticism that he should have used the Delphi method, Hosmer said that doing so "would have been absolutely use-

---

published under the same title in *World Politics*, Vol. 20, No. 3 (April 1968).

[60] Arnsten, *A Review of the Bloodbath Report*, 1970, p. 23.

[61] Arnsten, *A Review of the Bloodbath Report*, 1970, p. 23.

[62] Arnsten, *A Review of the Bloodbath Report*, 1970, p. 23.

[63] Author interview with Steve Hosmer, 2004.

less" because the people he might have consulted with about a likely number had not studied the issue. Hosmer also said that he had produced the report "at no one's direction," and that he had simply written it because the data were there, and "there were captured documents talking about repression." The report was a classified document because "all the interviews were confidential."[64]

Hosmer remembered that, "It was a complete surprise to ARPA" when he circulated the draft in the government. When he came back from a trip to Vietnam, he was asked to meet "immediately" with the head of ARPA at the time, who said, "We want to declassify this report." Hosmer replied, "Fine, we'll send it through the regular declassification procedure." The ARPA chief said, "No, you don't understand, we want to declassify it now." Hosmer asked, "Who's going to determine this?" and the ARPA official said, "You are. You're going to tell us, and we'll do it." Hosmer agreed to perform this task. Then, he was told, "We'd like you to write a *Reader's Digest*–length summary." Hosmer thought that by this they meant that he "should write an article which would be suitable for publication in the *Reader's Digest* about Viet Cong repression." He replied, "That, I will not do, because I do not want to become an advocate on the issue of the war. However, you're entitled to [do so] . . . There's a summary already in it, but if you want a longer summary, I'll be happy to write you a longer summary but it will not be something the *Reader's Digest* will be interested in publishing." He was met with silence, and then the ARPA official said, "OK." After that, Hosmer went down "to another office and we went through the document and I said, 'This out, that out,' and they declassified the document on the spot."[65]

According to Hosmer, this happened because of White House interest. Then "they ordered 4,000 copies of this thing—it was a huge printing. I may be wrong, but it was a very large printing, and a copy was given to every member of the House of Representatives and of the U.S. Senate. They were handing them out like candy." Hosmer believed that the good reception of his repression report within the Nixon Administration would later help RAND when "the Ellsberg affair took place." He was told that "at one point Nixon was saying, 'Let's close RAND down,'" but someone told the president, "Wait, RAND also does some good work," and cited Hosmer's study. Hosmer said that, later, a RAND staff member who was doing work at the Nixon Library, decided to check "out of sheer curiosity" which RAND reports had been retained by Nixon. He told Hosmer that when he went through the RAND file he found "only one thing" in it: Hosmer's report on Viet Cong repression."[66]

Hosmer remembered that many newspapers carried front-page stories about his report. He was asked to give interviews, but he refused because he thought that his "credibility as an advisor to the U.S. government" would suffer if he became a "public

---

[64] Author interview with Steve Hosmer, 2004.

[65] Author interview with Steve Hosmer, 2004.

[66] Author interview with Steve Hosmer, 2004.

advocate." He felt that his report had been written and made available for everybody to read, and that "there was nothing I could say to embellish it in the personal interviews." His report, he recalled, was used by people on both sides of the Vietnam War issue in the United States. According to him, "The anti-war people took umbrage with it. [But] . . . Senator [Edward M. "Ted"] Kennedy[,] who was a war critic[,] used it in the debate in terms that we must have planning to evacuate a sufficient number of the high-risk people[;] this was not an unmanageable task because we were talking about 100,000 or so people. So it was used by both sides if you will, [by] those who said this is a reason to keep us in the war, and by those who said, 'No, this is not a reason to keep us in the war. This is a manageable number.'"[67]

Hosmer felt that his estimate "was not far off" because the United States evacuated . . . maybe less than 100,000" South Vietnamese at the end of the war, and that of these many were "on the list." He also cited two UC Berkeley faculty members who did an analysis "based on interviews with Vietnamese refugees in Europe and elsewhere [on] whether they knew people who had been executed, and they came up with the number that at least 65,000 people were executed for political reasons between 1975 and 1983. This figure does not include people who died from accidents, clearing minefields for example, from malnutrition, diseases, exhaustion, etc."[68] Following the communist victory in South Vietnam in 1975, U.S. observers—such as the State Department, the Senate Refugee Subcommittee, and journalists—agreed that there had been "no indication of anything resembling a massacre by the victorious North Vietnamese."[69]

The study Hosmer referred to was "A Methodology for Estimating Political Executions in Vietnam: 1975–1983," by Jacqueline Desbarats and Karl D. Jackson, a paper presented at the annual meeting of the Asian Studies on the Pacific Coast, June 22–24, probably in 1987 in Los Angeles. The paper was based on interviews the two authors had conducted with 615 Vietnamese refugees in Chicago and California in 1982, who provided 47 names of people whose executions they claimed to have witnessed. Of these 47, the authors discarded 16, or 34 percent, because the names were duplicates. From these 31 names of alleged eyewitness executions provided by the 615 refugees, they extrapolated that this figure would translate into 65,000 political executions among the entire South Vietnamese adult population. From interviews with refugees worldwide, they projected that there had been a total of 95,000 names of execution victims.

---

[67] Author interview with Steve Hosmer, 2004.

[68] Author Interview with Steve Hosmer, 2004.

[69] George C. Wilson, "No Vietnamese 'Bloodbath' Is Found: 100 Days After Fall, U.S. Fear of Massacre Unrealized," *The Washington Post*, August 1975.

Their methodology was reviewed and criticized as invalid by authors Gareth Porter and James Roberts.[70] Porter and Roberts wrote that "the methodology used by Desbarats and Jackson to turn 31 names into a bloodbath of this magnitude is indirect, convoluted and dependent on several assumptions, each of which can be shown to be invalid." Using computer simulation and following the same flawed methodology, the authors concluded, for example, that 94,700 of the 95,000 names of victims they had come up with would be duplicates. Generally, there have been no credible reports of a "bloodbath" in South Vietnam in the decade following the end of the war. Such organizations as Amnesty International and the U.S. State Department faulted the communist regime for the detention and inhumane treatment of prisoners in reeducation camps but did not allege that a "bloodbath" had occurred.[71]

As Hosmer recalled, many newspapers carried stories about his declassified report. The media was mainly interested in it for the role it played in the "bloodbath" debate, and articles tended to focus on his estimate that 100,000 or considerably many more South Vietnamese would be executed—because of what President Nixon himself had predicted to justify his policy—rather than on the entirety of the report about Viet Cong repression. For example, in "Bloodbath—Fantasy or Realistic Fear?" in the *Los Angeles Times* issue of June 28, 1970, Robert J. Donovan, the chief of the *Times'* Washington bureau, reviewed the bloodbath debate and the challenges to President Nixon's "dire forecast." The bloodbath scenario was based on the assumption that the communists would be able to massacre South Vietnamese at will, and this—to Donovan—raised the question, "Assuming they were not totally conquered or frightened away," what would the highly armed South Vietnamese forces, numbering about one-and-a-quarter-million men—if police and civil defense forces were included—and armed with the most modern American equipment, be doing "while the communists were setting out for a massacre?"[72] Citing from a recent article by Les Gelb and Mort Halperin, Donovan wrote that predictions about a bloodbath "can be nothing more than speculation and hence could prove futile." In Donovan's view, this futility was shown by "the variance between the Rand Corp.'s prediction of at least 100,000 executions and the President's estimate of 'millions' of deaths." The remainder of Donovan's column was devoted to the controversy surrounding the number of people estimated to

---

[70] See Gareth Porter and James Roberts, "Creating a Bloodbath by Statistical Manipulation," *Pacific Affairs,* Vol. 61, No. 2, Summer 1988.

[71] Likewise, among this author's own circle of acquaintances, there have been no reports of executions although there have been many reports of imprisonment, harsh treatment, and, in undetermined instances, deaths, in reeducation camps.

[72] Donovan cited these figures from an unspecified article by Les Gelb and Morton Halperin, which pointed out that this large South Vietnamese army would continue to receive American military aid following the withdrawal of U.S. troops and would face a "combined North Vietnamese and Viet Cong force of about 220,000 backed up by a North Vietnamese army of approximately 400,000." It should be pointed out that, at the end of the war, the South Vietnamese armed forces were ordered to surrender by the last president of South Vietnam.

have been killed in the land reform in North Vietnam and in the Viet Cong attack on Hue during the 1968 offensive, and to the question of whether these were good predictors of a bloodbath as claimed by the Nixon Administration.

Taking a different tack, Stephen Rosenfeld, in his column "Vietnam Reprisals Theory Disputed," in *The Washington Post* issue of June 19, 1970, thought Hosmer's report agreed with a statement made by North Vietnamese Premier Pham Van Dong regarding the unlikely prospect of reprisals in South Vietnam. Dong had told Richard J. Barnet, co-director of the Institute for Policy Studies, during Barnet's visit to Hanoi that there would be "no reprisals" in South Vietnam because national reconciliation would be necessary to "avoid the disintegration of South Vietnamese society."

Barnet had relayed this statement in a memo to Senator Ted Kennedy of Massachusetts. In his column, Rosenfeld wrote, "To the list of expert witnesses who dispute President Nixon's insistent claim that only his own policy will avert a 'bloodbath' in South Vietnam, add North Vietnamese Premier Pham Van Dong and—look here—social scientist Stephen T. Hosmer, author of a new Pentagon-commissioned Rand Corp. Study of 'Vietcong Repression and Its Implications for the Future.'" Although these experts, as well as Hosmer and Dong, diverged in their interpretation of what North Vietnam had done in the past, they used striking similar arguments that said in effect that, after the United States withdrew, the Viet Cong would—out of political expediency—adopt a less repressive policy in the South.[73]

According to Rosenfeld, as did President Nixon, Hosmer assumed that the GVN's million-man-strong army would somehow melt away and that the communists would gain complete power. If the communists took over through force of arms, Hosmer expected a major bloodbath. But Hosmer surmised that, if the communists gained control by gradually subverting a coalition government, they would be less likely to engage in large-scale reprisals—at least during the period when they were taking over power. The reasons that would lead them to be more lenient—as explained by Hosmer—were: The GVN, after its disintegration, would no longer pose a threat; the

---

[73] Part of the debate about Hanoi's past record dealt with the issue of land reform in North Vietnam in the early 1950s. The polemics centered on whether a bloodbath occurred during this campaign in reprisal against former opponents. Anita Lauve Nutt, a RAND consultant, subscribed to the argument that extensive killings did take place. In *On the Question of Communist Reprisals in Vietnam*, Santa Monica, Calif.: RAND Corporation, P-4416, August 1970, she took issue with those who criticized President Nixon's prediction that Hanoi would inflict a bloodbath on South Vietnam if U.S. troops were withdrawn precipitously—similar to the one it had committed during the land reform. She concluded (p. 15) that, "a belief in the Communist reprisals that took place in North Vietnam after the 1954 cease-fire is a necessary first step in the prevention of similar Communist reprisals after the next cease-fire." The argument on whether or not a bloodbath had occurred during the land reform was later clarified by Professor Edwin E. Moise of Clemson University, who wrote what can be considered the most objective and credible study of North Vietnam's land reform. In *Land Reform in China and North Vietnam: Consolidating the Revolution at Village Level*, Chapel Hill, N.C.: University of North Carolina Press, 1983, he put the figure of those labeled as landlords who were executed at around 5,000. According to him, the land reform was also used as an opportunity by the Hanoi regime to purge its own cadres whose loyalty it doubted, and their persecution decimated the Party in the countryside.

need to run a country would lead the communists to avoid alienating large segments of the population; and the fear of international condemnation should the communists resort to excessive repression. Rosenfeld questioned why in view of these arguments, Hosmer in the end stated that it was his personal belief that the communists, out of a temptation to consolidate control and out of what he says is a peculiarly Vietnamese taste for revenge, would execute upwards of 100,000 people." In Rosenfeld's view, Hosmer failed to explain "why this belief should be given more weight than his argumentation, which goes mostly in the opposite direction."

Rosenfeld thought that Hosmer's argumentation that the communists would lean toward leniency paralleled the argument of Pham Van Dong "in its important aspects." Rosenfeld wrote, "What the North Vietnamese official contends and what the Rand scholar concedes come out quite the same: There would be important political considerations pressing upon the Vietcong to conciliate rather than to kill their erstwhile political foes. Whether these considerations would finally govern the policy of the Vietcong is, of course, necessarily a matter of judgment and conjecture." Finally, Rosenfeld criticized President Nixon for making the bloodbath argument while ignoring the bloodshed caused by the ongoing war. It was "a tactic unworthy of a President whose stated objective is a negotiated settlement to the war to pass over the several hundred thousand *actual* deaths of Vietnamese civilians—a great many of them victims of American bombs and shells—and to raise the *prospect* of an enemy massacre of civilians 'by the millions,' as though it were a certain thing." If President Nixon were "truly interested in deterring a bloodbath," he should be pressing for a negotiated settlement, as well as for "pledges and guarantees against reprisals, sanctuaries for especially frightened people, international observers—which could be of practical value in limiting repressions against any Vietnamese." Rosenfeld concluded, "To stay on the military track alone, as Hanoi and the Rand study agree, is to assure the bloodiest outcome of all."[74]

Tom Wicker of *The New York Times* criticized the interpretation of Hanoi's past record to predict a bloodbath and justify the stay-the-course policy by President Nixon, in his column of May 12, 1970. Citing two studies by scholars familiar with Vietnam, Wicker wrote that there had been no extensive reprisals in North Vietnam after 1954 and characterized Nixon's prediction of a bloodbath as a "historical hobgoblin." He charged the president with using an "emotional argument" that "seems to stem from

---

[74] Senator Edward Kennedy inserted the column by Rosenfeld in the *Congressional Record* for the Senate on June 23, 1970, after declaring on the Senate floor that he was "deeply skeptical" of the bloodbath argument, especially as it was "phrased by administration spokesmen." Senator Kennedy thought that this argument was being used by the Nixon Administration to "win support for the short-term military plans of the President" and "to evade the hard issues involved in reaching a political settlement in Vietnam—a negotiated peace—that will end once and for all the military bloodbath that is going on today."

something stronger than evidence. It is as though he *wills* it to be true, even though it isn't. . . ."[75]

Following the Pentagon's release of Hosmer's study, *The New York Times* picked up the story and carried an article with the title of "Reprisals Predicted in Vietcong Victory." While Rosenfeld focused on Hosmer's arguments that the communists would lean toward leniency after victory, the *New York Times* article emphasized his speculation that "reprisal killings" could reach at least 100,000 or easily higher. According to this article, Hosmer's report "is at the heart of the United States['] plans for withdrawal from Vietnam and central to the 'blood bath' arguments for not deserting the South Vietnamese Government." The article mentioned that RAND's study concluded that, "Lenience by the Vietcong toward adversaries would be inconsistent with history," and that Hosmer said he believed "that a Vietcong regime in South Vietnam would go through with the killings."

As Hosmer recalled, his report was also used by politicians on both sides of the argument regarding U.S. disengagement from Vietnam. For its part, the Nixon Administration found Hosmer's report, and its association with the authoritative name of RAND, useful to ward off calls for speedier withdrawals. In August, Vice President Agnew seized upon Hosmer's prediction of a bloodbath to attack Senator Mark O. Hatfield for sponsoring an amendment, along with 24 other Senators, to bring all American ground combat troops home by December 31, 1970. Citing the RAND study and Douglas Pike, Agnew declared that, if the United States withdrew too fast, hundreds of thousands of Vietnamese "who placed their faith in us will die for that error in judgment."[76] However, in his riposte to Agnew, Hatfield also found ammunition in Hosmer's report to counter Agnew's attack. In a speech on the Senate floor on August 18, Hatfield responded that "the Rand Corporation report which the Vice President referred to also maintains that a new coalition or even an all-Communist government would have decisive political reasons for holding down the level of political reprisals."[77]

While debates about American Vietnam policies continued unabated in the United States, back in Saigon, RAND's staff was reduced to one anthropologist: Gerry Hickey. By now, the Pentagon Papers episode, the reorientation of RAND research toward internal American issues, and the winding-down of the United States' military involvement in Vietnam, had combined to ring the death knell for RAND's presence

---

[75] Tom Wicker, "In the Nation: Mr. Nixon's Scary Dreams," *The New York Times, May 12, 1970.*

[76] "Excerpts from Hatfield's Senate Speech Replying to Agnew," Special to *The New York Times*, August 19, 1970.

[77] "Excerpts from Hatfield's," 1970.

in Saigon. Aware of that knell, Hickey applied for a position at the University of Chicago, but he was turned down because of his association with RAND and his Defense Department–sponsored research. As the mood over Vietnam soured in the United States, and as distaste grew for what U.S. military activities had inflicted on the Vietnamese, such associations were perceived as sinister. Anthropologists such as Hickey, who had done work for the U.S. government, came under a cloud, suspected of using their research to serve the counterinsurgency policies of the United States.[78]

Rebuffed, Hickey continued to wrap up his work for RAND. It was an uneasy time in the Central Highlands. By now, security had begun to crumble in the northern provinces in the wake of the withdrawal of U.S. troops, and the refugee problem among the highlanders worsened. In these circumstances, highland leaders feared that the GVN might abandon their region, especially since one of them had heard retired Australian colonel Francis P. [Ted] Serong, then a lecturer at the National War College in Saigon, discuss this possibility in 1971. Serong was strongly advocating that the GVN withdraw its forces from the highlands and concentrate them along the coastal areas. In 1975, President Thieu would follow a similar strategy—with disastrous results.

As Hickey was completing a long report for RAND on highland leadership, he found out that support for his work would soon end. Late in 1971, he had asked for more time, but the response from RAND had not been encouraging. One reason might have been that, as American forces withdrew from the highlands, interest in the region began to decline significantly. Hickey thought another reason for RAND's discouraging stance was his refusal to perform research on pacification in the villages. This refusal, in his view, had eroded his position at RAND. Another reason was that, as budget cuts were made at the Pentagon in December 1971, "RAND was shifting with the Washington winds" and refocusing on "longer-range problems of tactical, limited war and deterrence under the Nixon doctrine."[79] Hickey felt less and less appreciated, especially when a friend at RAND wrote to him in January 1972 that RAND was giving him little or no credit for the "direct advice and consulting" he had provided to the Embassy and Vietnamese government and was mainly focused on the number of reports that he had produced.[80]

Hickey subsequently received a letter, dated January 18, from Fred Iklé, chairman of the Social Science Department, with whom he had never managed "to attain any rapport whatsoever"—"stating bluntly" that his support from RAND would be cut off on March 30, 1972.[81] To Hickey, this letter was "a far cry from the letter of

---

[78] According to one of Hickey's supporters in academia, his peers believed that he had shown "bad judgment" for having chosen "to work for several years for the RAND Corporation." Hickey, *Window on a War*, 2002, p. 304.

[79] Hickey, *Window on a War*, 2002, p. 313.

[80] Hickey, *Window on a War*, 2002, p. 313.

[81] Hickey, *Window on a War*, 2002, p. 314.

24 May 1968" that he had received from Harry Rowen, which said, "As an early 'set-tler' in Vietnam, and one who has made an outstanding contribution to our work there, we owe you a larger debt of appreciation than I can express. So I'll just say thanks."[82] Hickey decided to stay on, using his own savings and a gift from a friend. On March 30, 1972, his deadline, Hickey sent his nearly finished manuscript to Iklé. He also sent a copy to George Tanham—who had been "a very good friend at RAND"—along with a letter saying, "Sad to say that in the long run my peers were quite correct—it was bad judgment on my part to have come to Vietnam to do research for the RAND Corporation. The bad judgment was in my believing that the RAND Corporation was serious about doing depth research."[83]

On April 25, 1972, John P. White, vice president of RAND, wrote to Hickey, offering to "enter into a letter of agreement" with him which would provide him sup-port to complete his highland leadership report.[84] When the letter of agreement arrived in June, Hickey signed it and returned it to Santa Monica. But events in this period, such as the communist attacks in Kontum, Quang Tri, and An Loc, which is within 50 kilometers of Saigon, distracted and sidetracked him. Hickey recalled the crisis atmosphere at the time. In Quang Tri, ARVN units fled after burning the city, and refugees streamed into Hue and Danang. In Kontum, soldiers started to loot the city's downtown and homes abandoned by owners who had fled. Ninety percent of the pop-ulation of Pleiku fled toward the towns of Qui Nhon and Nha Trang. President Thieu proclaimed martial law, and the draft age was changed to make men between 17 and 43 years of age subject to call-up. Prices were rising, and people rushed to buy basic staples. All bars, nightclubs, and other places of amusement were closed. Hickey tried to get transportation to move highland refugees to Pleiku and then to Ban Me Thuot.

The plight of the highlanders distressed Hickey. He reckoned that, by August 1972, the war had exacted a heavy toll on the ethnic minorities. There were 150,000 highland refugees and estimates put the number of highlander deaths since 1965 at 200,000. At least 85 percent of villages had, for one reason or another, been displaced.

At the ARPA R&D compound, only one typist, an American army corporal, was left, and he was swamped with work. Hickey sent the final version of his report to RAND on October 13, 1972. Fortunately, as his RAND employment was terminating, Cornell University's Southeast Asia Program came through in December 1972, offer-ing Hickey a position as visiting associate professor for the academic year 1973–1974. The invitation resulted from a meeting that Hickey had held with Professor George Kahin, "an eminent Southeast Asia scholar who had been critical of the American position in Vietnam."[85] In the atmosphere at the time, this appointment was highly

---

[82] Hickey, *Window on a War*, 2002, p. 314.

[83] Hickey, *Window on a War*, 2002, p. 321.

[84] Hickey, *Window on a War*, 2002, p. 321

[85] Hickey, *Window on a War*, 2002, p. 338.

Sequence of the Collapse of South Vietnam

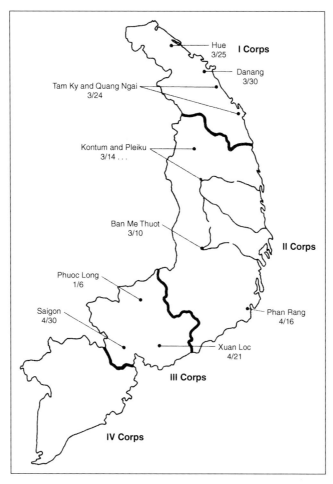

unusual, especially since it had come through the intervention of one of the most ardent critics of American policies in Vietnam. On January 23, 1973, at eight o'clock in the morning, the cease-fire agreed upon in Paris went into effect. When Hickey returned from a trip to the highlands, he went to check his mail at the R&D compound. He was "surprised to find the few American personnel gone." The incredulous Vietnamese staff in the compound told Hickey that "Sergeant Booker was fixing his usual lunch when a telephone call informed the Americans that a vehicle was coming to take them to the airport. They already had their bags packed, so when the vehicle arrived, Booker turned off the gas under the pots of food and they all departed." Since Hickey had not eaten all day, he went into the kitchen and ate "some of the excellent soul food Booker had prepared."[86] Hickey sailed from Saigon on April 1, 1973. As the ship departed, he had a feeling of "finality—a mingling of sadness with a curious sense of relief." When

---

[86] Hickey, *Window on a War*, 2002, pp. 341–342.

his ship sailed in a northeastern direction within sight of the central coast, Hickey's last glimpse of Vietnam was the two mountain peaks called "Mother and Child"—in the highland region inhabited by the Rhade minority.[87]

Reflecting upon his sojourn in Vietnam, he recalled how, when he first arrived in the country as part of the Michigan State University group, he had "felt strongly that American economic support of the Ngo Dinh Diem government was justified because South Vietnam showed promise of becoming a viable state within the new post-colonial order of Southeast Asia."[88] From that promising beginning, American leaders had blundered by deposing him, misjudging him out of "invincible ignorance" of the Vietnamese, their culture, and their history, and especially of Vietnamese national-ism.[89] The military strategy that the United States adopted subsequently was ill-suited for Vietnam and brought considerable death and devastation, and destroyed Vietnam-ese society.

The Paris peace agreement that sent the ARPA personnel abruptly to the airport in January 1973 had come as a result of secret negotiations between the American and North Vietnamese delegations in Paris. These secret talks were held to bypass the South Vietnamese parties—the GVN and the National Liberation Front—who were more intransigent and less prone to compromise because they would have to live with any agreement that was reached. The breakthrough came on October 8, 1972, when Hanoi offered a proposal under which the United States and North Vietnam would together arrange a cease-fire, American troop withdrawal, prisoner exchanges, and other mili-tary matters. Political issues would be left to the opposing South Vietnamese sides to address. A transitional "council of national reconciliation" would be formed, consist-ing of the Saigon government, communist and "neutral" representatives, to supervise eventual elections and achieve permanent peace. In the interim, the Saigon regime and Vietcong would continue to exist as distinct entities. Their respective armies would retain the areas they each controlled—in a "leopard spots" pattern. To strengthen President Thieu in advance of a cease-fire, the United States rushed $2 billion worth of military equipment to South Vietnam. In the process, the South Vietnamese air force became the fourth largest in the world.

After the North Vietnamese approved the accord on October 21, Kissinger flew to Saigon to obtain President Thieu's consent. Thieu, however, objected that North Viet-namese troops would be permitted to stay in the South and feared that the transitional council of reconciliation would turn into a coalition government that would legitimize

---

[87] Hickey, *Window on a War*, 2002, p. 347.

[88] Hickey, *Window on a War*, 2002, p. 349.

[89] Hickey, *Window on a War*, 2002, p. 350.

the Viet Cong. Although Thieu refused to sign, Kissinger announced that "peace is at hand." Following his landslide reelection, President Nixon directed Kissinger on November 14 to present to the North Vietnamese peace delegation 69 amendments. Believing that the United States was attempting to rewrite the draft that had been agreed upon, the North Vietnamese balked and their chief negotiator, Le Duc Tho, returned to Hanoi. Nixon then directed the Joint Chiefs of Staff to prepare massive air attacks against targets that had been placed off limits to American bombers, such as railroads, power plants, radio transmitters, and other installations around Hanoi, as well as docks and shipyards in Haiphong.

Operation Linebacker Two began on December 18. For 11 days, with the exception of Christmas Day, B-52s and other American attack aircraft flew nearly 3,000 sorties, most of them over the heavily populated 60-mile stretch between Hanoi and Haiphong, dropping "some forty thousand tons of bombs in the most concentrated air offensive of the war against North Vietnam."[90] The North Vietnamese "shot down twenty-six U.S. aircraft, among them fifteen B-52s and ninety-three pilots and crew members were lost, thirty-one of them captured."[91]

In the wake of the air campaign, which became known as the Christmas bombing of North Vietnam, Kissinger and Le Duc Tho met again in Paris on January 8, 1973. President Thieu, after what the United States had done on his behalf, acquiesced—in the face of President Nixon's ultimatum that "You must decide now whether you desire to continue our alliance or whether you want me to seek a settlement with the enemy which serves U.S. interests alone."[92] The peace agreement was formally signed in Paris on January 27, 1973. It was not much different from the draft that had been forged in October. Nixon's objective in bombing the North was not intended to pressure the North, but was meant to reassure President Thieu and to warn the communists that he would resume the bombing of the North, without hesitation, if the armistice collapsed.

The Paris Agreement basically established a truce during which a political solution might be hammered out. The Saigon government was given a "decent interval" to organize to resist the communists, but the communists did not fade away and were

---

[90] Karnow, *Vietnam: A History*, 1983, p. 667.

[91] Karnow, *Vietnam: A History*, 1983, p. 668.

[92] Karnow, *Vietnam: A History*, 1983, pp. 668–669. Bui Diem, a former South Vietnamese ambassador to the United States, recalled that President Thieu signed the agreement after strong arm-twisting by Nixon. According to Bui Diem, some of Nixon's messages "were couched in the toughest language that diplomatic practice has ever seen," such as "I am firmly convinced that the alternative to signing the present agreement is a total cut-off of funds to assist your country," and "If you cannot give me a positive answer by 1200 Washington time, January 21, 1973, I shall authorize Dr. Kissinger to initial the agreement even without the concurrence of your government." See Steve Hosmer, Konrad Kellen, and Brian Jenkins, *The Fall of South Vietnam: Statements by Vietnamese Military and Civilian Leaders*, Santa Monica, Calif.: RAND Corporation, R-2208-OSD (HIST), December 1978, p. 5. (This report is discussed at length below.)

allowed to remain in the areas they controlled—a situation described by a communist commentator as "half war and half peace." President Nixon proclaimed that he had achieved "peace with honor," but for him and for the majority of Americans, the war would not be over until American prisoners of war held in North Vietnam returned home. Beginning in 1961, "nearly nine thousand U.S. airplanes and helicopters had been lost in action over Cambodia, Laos and the two Vietnams. Some two thousand pilots and crew members had been killed, more than a thousand were missing and the captives in communist hands numbered close to six hundred."[93] The first American POWs were released February 12, 1973, under the terms of the cease-fire agreement. When the last of them left Hanoi in March, "the prevailing sentiments in the United States were relief that the war had ended and revulsion toward the very subject of Vietnam. American news organizations closed their offices or drastically reduced their staffs in Saigon, exorcising Vietnam from newspaper headlines and television screens."[94]

With the POWs home, Congress began to enact legislation to ensure that the United States would not be ensnared again in Southeast Asia. On March 15, President Nixon had indicated that the United States might reenter the war to prevent communist violations of the cease-fire. On June 4, however, Congress preempted such action by passing a bill, sponsored by Senators Clifford Case of New Jersey and Frank Church of Idaho, to prevent the U.S. government from using funds to finance any American military activities in Indochina. This congressional move, as well as the subsequent cut in appropriation of funds for South Vietnam to $700 million a year from a ceiling of $1 billion, would later be blamed by Henry Kissinger and some others for the collapse of South Vietnam in 1975. However, in view of the public's opposition, the U.S. government would have found it difficult to enlist support for rescuing the Thieu regime at the time. Congress was only carrying out the will of the American people, who opposed more aid to South Vietnam.

Some American commentators have called the Paris Agreement a "fig leaf" that allowed the United States to disengage without the appearance of a defeat. The accord did not solve the situation on the ground and left the two hostile armies in place to face one another yet again. Both Hanoi and Saigon knew that fighting would erupt in the future. Both sides began to prepare for such an eventuality, and violations of the agreement occurred immediately.

When the truce went into effect, President Thieu was in a strong position: His army of over one million men was well-equipped with modern American weapons; he continued to receive American aid; and he controlled about two-thirds of South Vietnam's territory and about 85 percent of its people. Thieu perceived the truce as simply a lull; to prepare for the renewal of hostilities, he launched military operations to seize terrain controlled by the North Vietnamese and Viet Cong in the Mekong

---

[93] Karnow, *Vietnam: A History*, 1983, p. 669.

[94] Karnow, *Vietnam: A History*, 1983, p. 670.

Delta and along the Cambodian border. These land-grabbing operations stretched his army thin and bogged them down in static defense. However, since Nixon had written to him in January with the reassurance that "we will respond with full force should the settlement be violated by North Vietnam," Thieu was confident that, should the situation deteriorate, the United States would come in and rescue him from defeat.[95] His confidence led him to be inflexible and to reject any accommodation with the communists—as called for in the Paris Agreement—through a policy of the "Four No's": no negotiation, no communist activity in the country, no coalition government, and no ceding of territory to the communists.

The communists, for their part, were using the truce to rebuild their forces for the expected renewal of fighting. In March 1973, communist leaders held a meeting in Hanoi to discuss future plans. At this meeting, they received a disturbing assessment of their situation in the South. General Tran Van Tra, one of the top commanders in the South, told the North Vietnamese leaders that they faced grave problems while Thieu was retaking key areas. In a book written in March 1982, Tra revealed that, at that time, their troops "were exhausted and their units in disarray." He wrote, "We had not been able to make up our losses [incurred in the massive 1972 spring offensive]. We were short of manpower as well as food and ammunition, and coping with the enemy was very difficult." In addition, cadres were "confused" and passive because they thought they had to abide by the truce even in the face of attacks by the Saigon troops.[96] On top of this disturbing assessment, communist spies inside the GVN had conveyed to the Hanoi leaders the unsettling information that President Thieu was planning to continue taking territory for the next two years and that he would not authorize elections until he felt secure and confident enough that the elections would make him the "sole authority" of South Vietnam.[97] Once he had won the elections, he would abandon the cease-fire agreement and eradicate the communists from the South—turning the clock back to the "dark days of the 1950s" when President Diem hunted down the remnants of the Viet Minh.[98] The assessment of their own weakness and the information about what Thieu had in store for them made the communist leadership realize that, if they let things proceed as they were, they would be staring disaster in the face. However, while sobered by the situation, the communist leaders were also heartened by the fact that the GVN had its own weaknesses: It would no longer be able to count on B-52s and American advisors, and would have to rely on poorly trained soldiers.

The communist leadership decided to go on a limited offensive and try to tip the situation in their favor. They ordered their troops to attack—but only when they had a decisive military advantage. At the same time, they began to embark on an enormous

---

[95] Karnow, *Vietnam: A History*, 1983, p. 672.

[96] Cited in Karnow, *Vietnam: A History*, 1983, p. 673.

[97] Karnow, *Vietnam: A History*, 1983, p. 673.

[98] Karnow, *Vietnam: A History*, 1983, p. 673.

logistical buildup to prepare for a large-scale offensive to be launched eventually. They constructed an all-weather highway from Quang Tri Province on the central coast to the Mekong Delta so that they could move and position equipment—large trucks, tanks, and armored vehicles—to attack Saigon. They also began to build a 3,000-mile-long oil pipeline, from Quang Tri to the town of Loc Ninh, their main headquarters, located 75 miles northwest of Saigon. They also established a modern radio network, centered in Loc Ninh, to communicate directly with Hanoi and with their units operating in the field. For these huge undertakings, the communists could not rely on new supplies from their Soviet and Chinese allies, who had rejected Premier Pham Van Dong's request for more aid in October 1973. Chinese Prime Minister Zhou Enlai, in fact, told Pham Van Dong, "It would be best for Vietnam and the rest of Indochina to relax for, say, five or ten years."[99] Under these circumstances, the North Vietnamese had to use supplies they had amassed in the North and which American bombings had failed to destroy.

In the South, in fall 1973, Viet Cong units began to attack the GVN's weak targets, such as "small airfields, remote outposts and storage facilities."[100] By late spring 1974, General Tra estimated that they had retaken all the territory in the Mekong Delta that the GVN had seized after the cease-fire. Meanwhile, the situation was starting to unravel for President Thieu and his government. The South Vietnamese economy crumbled with the departure of the Americans. Millions of people who had earned their living catering to the needs of the Americans—secretaries, maids, tailors, cleaners, laundry washers, etc.—lost their jobs. Prices soared, partly because of the Arab oil embargo imposed as a result of the Yom Kippur War in 1973. Army morale crumbled. In a survey conducted in the summer of 1974, the U.S. Mission in Saigon found that more than 90 percent of the South Vietnamese soldiers were not getting paid enough to support their families.

The economic disintegration was exacerbated by the endemic corruption, which had become even more excessive. For example, quartermaster units frequently exacted bribes before delivering food and other supplies to the troops; sometimes, they even demanded payments in exchange for supplying soldiers in the field with ammunition, gasoline, and spare parts. To raise funds, officers, in turn, squeezed money out of villagers, and some even traded with the communists. The American report "cautioned that the 'deterioration' had to be halted 'if the South Vietnamese military is to be considered a viable force.'"[101]

In 1974, the resignation of President Nixon removed the staunchest supporter of President Thieu. The prospect that the United States would reenter the war to save him and his regime grew dimmer. The unraveling of Nixon's presidency originated with

---

[99] Karnow, *Vietnam: A History*, 1983, p. 674.

[100] Karnow, *Vietnam: A History*, 1983, p. 674.

[101] Karnow, *Vietnam: A History*, 1983, p. 675.

the burglary of the offices of the Democratic National Committee in the Watergate building on the night of June 18, 1972. The burglars were later revealed to be operatives from a clandestine unit—called derisively "the Plumbers"—which was ultimately traced back to the White House and Nixon's reelection committee. Nixon tried to cover up his involvement, but White House conversations that he had secretly taped and was forced by Supreme Court order to hand over to the special prosecutor charged with the investigation revealed that he had indeed played a role. On August 9, 1974, President Nixon resigned from office to avoid impeachment proceedings for his role in the Watergate break in and its cover up.

After he took over as president, Gerald Ford reassured Thieu that the United States would continue to provide adequate support to the GVN. The U.S. resolve was tested early in 1975. In January, the communists captured Phuoc Binh, the capital of Phuoc Long, a mountainous province about 60 miles north of Saigon. The taking of Phuoc Binh did not provoke an American response. The lack of American reaction and the loss of the town stunned the GVN. Encouraged, Hanoi decided to push ahead and prepared for a general offensive, in 1976. They discussed whether the United States would intervene again, but thought that American planes might return, but not American ground troops—and only these troops could change the situation. Hanoi's decision was made easier by the Soviet Union's fresh pledges of support given in December—in competition with the Chinese, who were increasing their aid to the Cambodian Khmer Rouge.

On March 1, 1975, General Van Tien Dung, appointed to lead the offensive in the South, feigned an attack on Pleiku, the headquarters of II Corps. Then, on March 10, he launched a surprise attack on Ban Me Thuot in the Central Highlands, his main target, using tanks and artillery. As one senior officer of the South Vietnamese Joint General Staff would later describe it, this attack created a domino effect, which led to the disintegration of the entire country. The defenders of Ban Me Thuot were outnumbered, isolated—and easily defeated. Many South Vietnamese troops abandoned the town to flee to safety with their families, who usually lived with them to stretch their meager salaries. President Thieu, who had proclaimed that he would not cede an inch of land to the communists, reversed his strategy by ordering General Pham Van Phu, the II Corps commander, to evacuate the towns of Pleiku and Kontum. Thieu's new strategy was to abandon the sparsely populated, marginal, and mountainous regions so that he could concentrate his forces on defending the more important coastal areas.

The withdrawal was botched and turned into a rout. General Phu left Pleiku to fly to Nha Trang on the coast. His leaderless troops, along with a mass of civilians—a total of 200,000 people—fled down a narrow and difficult mountain road to the coast, under communist shelling. The South Vietnamese never recovered from this precipitous and badly implemented withdrawal from the Central Highlands. The communists then pressured Nha Trang, which, overflowing with civilian refugees and evacuated military personnel by this time, had descended into chaos. On April 1, the II Corps staff, including General Phu, the corps commander, fled and abandoned the city.

Meanwhile, the communists were pressing their attacks in I Corps. On March 10, President Thieu ordered the redeployment of the Airborne Division—considered the best in the ARVN—to Saigon. The redeployment; the loss of Ban Me Thuot, Pleiku, and Kontum; and the rumor of a new partitioning, with the northern provinces going to the communists, triggered a panic, and refugees began to pour out of Hue and Quang Tri. The panic was induced by memories of the killings in Hue, as well as by the prediction of a major bloodbath: Former Premier Tran Van Huong had said that upward of 5 million people would be killed. The prediction of a bloodbath had been used to delay American departure and to motivate South Vietnamese to fight harder against the communists. But in the face of the crumbling of South Vietnamese defenses, this prediction had the opposite effect. Instead of resisting, average citizens and army and government personnel took off in flight. Hue was abandoned on March 25, after the situation had gotten out of hand, with commanders unable to control their troops, who were deserting. The commander of I Corps, General Ngo Quang Truong, withdrew to Danang, which soon descended into anarchy with the arrival of 2 million refugees, including a large number of leaderless GVN soldiers. With the communists massing forces to attack the city, General Truong decided to evacuate Danang on March 29. General Truong would later say that, at the end, he was alone in his command post, after all his troops and staff had fled. Thus, with desertions of troops and commanders alike, Hue and Danang fell. About two weeks after they began their offensive, the communists had gained control of the whole of I and II Corps without the South Vietnamese putting up major resistance.

The rapid disintegration of the South Vietnamese army surprised the Hanoi leaders. Seeing an opportunity, they decided to accelerate their timetable and to "liberate" the South before the monsoon rains began in May and before the South Vietnamese could regroup their troops to defend Saigon. Their plan was to launch the offensive against Saigon by the last week of April. The United States now faced the possibility of having to evacuate the 6,000 Americans still in Saigon, and more than 100,000 Vietnamese current and former employees of American agencies. When the relatives of these people were included, the total would swell to nearly a million people. The magnitude of the task was daunting, and no evacuation plan was made. In Saigon, Ambassador Graham Martin also resisted evacuating early, out of fear that doing so would provoke panic in Saigon. On April 22, the U.S. Justice Department finally announced plans to waive immigration restrictions to allow up to 130,000 refugees from Indochina, including high-ranking members of the Saigon government, to enter the United States.

As the communists massed their forces for an attack, President Thieu resigned under pressure on April 21, to be replaced eventually by General Duong Van Minh, an advocate of neutralism for South Vietnam, who Saigon hoped would be able to work out a political accommodation with the communists in the eleventh hour. But it was too late. In the last week of April, under intense pressure from Washington, the U.S. Embassy began to evacuate Americans and Vietnamese. Then, on April 29, as communist rockets began to slam into Saigon airport, the United States launched a massive evacuation by helicopter. Over 18 hours, a fleet of 70 Marine helicopters flew back and forth from U.S. aircraft carriers stationed offshore to Saigon to carry over 1,000 Americans and close to 6,000 Vietnamese out of the city.

Of these, 2,000 alone were plucked from the U.S. Embassy compound. Saigon was in the grip of panic. The U.S. Embassy was mobbed by panicking Vietnamese seeking evacuation while thousands of others streamed toward evacuation sites, clamoring to be taken out.[102] Ambassador Martin waited until the very end to board a helicopter. By dawn on April 30, communist tanks entered the capital. General Minh surrendered and ordered what remained of the South Vietnamese army to lay down their arms. The long war was over, and the communists were now in control of the entire country in the space of about six weeks.

In the final days of Saigon and following the fall of their country, thousands of South Vietnamese fled to the United States. Among them were many former South Vietnamese military and civilian leaders. At the request of the Historian, Office of the Secretary of Defense, Steve Hosmer, Konrad Kellen, and Brian Jenkins interviewed 27 of them regarding what they perceived as the causes of this sudden collapse. The objective was to obtain the recollections of these eyewitnesses and participants in the final events before memories faded and mythology replaced history. The respondents were selected for their knowledge of the events, either as witnesses or participants, or as high-level officials with an overall view of what had transpired. Of the 27 respondents, 23 were senior officers and four were civilians. The military people included former Premier and Air Force Marshal Nguyen Cao Ky, 13 officers holding the rank of general, and nine colonels. About half had commanded troops in combat; the remaining half had occupied senior staff positions. One had been Minister of Defense in the final days of the war; one was a I Corps commander; one was commander of the Capital Military District; one was the Chief of Staff for II Corps; and one general was in charge of the Artillery Command. Civilian officials included an ambassador to Washington, a speaker of the House of Representatives, and an Assistant Secretary of Defense.

Their statements, oral and written, were collected from February 1976 to January 1977 and summarized in a report issued in December 1978, without evaluation

---

[102] The exodus of refugees would continue unabated following the fall of Saigon, leading Senator Edward Kennedy to say, "I'm convinced that . . . the bloodbath scare resulted in a much greater number of South Vietnamese leaving their country than would have done so otherwise." Wilson, "No Vietnamese 'Bloodbath,'" *The Washington Post*, 1975.

and without cross-checking by the authors for accuracy or validity because the purpose of the exercise was to present the views of the Vietnamese respondents and what they perceived as the reasons for the collapse.[103] The authors cautioned readers to bear in mind that, "Despite the apparent candor with which the interviewees responded, they did not, presumably, respond without *bias*. On the whole, this bias—as would be expected—runs in the direction of exonerating themselves and placing the blame" on their top leaders and on the United States.[104]

As perceived by the respondents, the collapse could be traced to several causes that were linked, as well as to the serious shortcomings in the country's political and military leadership and weaknesses in planning and organization.

The most fundamental cause was the pervasive corruption, which led to the rise of incompetent leaders, destroyed army morale, and created a vast gulf of social injustice and popular antipathy. Although they put a great deal of blame on the United States for the collapse, they were also critical of "their own institutions and behavior" in the period before and during the collapse.[105] Most of them agreed that no "single calamitous event or mistake" led to the fall of South Vietnam, and none "stated that the enemy's military power was so overwhelming that all resistance was futile." Some of the respondents admitted that they "defeated themselves."[106]

The respondents ascribed the mistakes committed by the United States to misunderstanding of the situation in Vietnam. Among the mistakes the respondents blamed on the Americans was the tendency to rely on corrupt and incompetent but cooperative leaders, such as President Thieu, whom the United States backed to the end. The other mistake was to foster dependency and passivity within the South Vietnamese leadership. Some of the respondents said that "The inherent power and omnipresence of the United States, coupled with South Vietnam's situation of dependency, reduced South Vietnam's own leaders to submissive order takers."[107] One respondent claimed that the Americans "guaranteed" this submissiveness by choosing leaders who "were willing to be cooperative."[108] One respondent observed that "in Thieu's mind the Americans were responsible for everything and they [the South Vietnamese leaders] didn't need to do anything. And everyone just sit down and wait because they think the American[s] are responsible for everything."[109] Former ambassador Bui Diem said that Thieu "always considered the American factor the most important element—if not the vital one—in

---

103 Hosmer, Kellen, and Jenkins, *The Fall of South Vietnam*, 1978.

104 Hosmer, Kellen, and Jenkins, *The Fall of South Vietnam*, 1978, p. xvii.

105 Hosmer, Kellen, and Jenkins, *The Fall of South Vietnam*, 1978, p. v.

106 Hosmer, Kellen, and Jenkins, *The Fall of South Vietnam*, 1978, pp. xvii–xviii.

107 Hosmer, Kellen, and Jenkins, *The Fall of South Vietnam*, 1978, p. 28.

108 Hosmer, Kellen, and Jenkins, *The Fall of South Vietnam*, 1978, p. 28.

109 Hosmer, Kellen, and Jenkins, *The Fall of South Vietnam*, 1978, p. 29.

every problem that he had to solve, whether it was concerning the future of the country or his own political future."[110]

The promise by President Nixon that the United States would re-intervene had a deleterious effect. Nixon might have intended this reassurance as a way to induce Thieu to sign the Paris Agreement and to motivate the South Vietnamese to resist, but, instead, it induced complacency on the part of GVN leaders. Although they thought the United States had "abandoned" them through the Paris Agreement—thus dealing them a severe psychological blow by discarding them as no longer "worth saving"—they also persisted in believing that Washington had invested too much financial and human resources in South Vietnam to walk away at the last moment. GVN leaders, the respondents included, kept their faith that the United States would take some action if the communists committed grave cease-fire violations that might jeopardize the continued existence of South Vietnam. Their faith was reinforced by the assurances given by a succession of American presidents, but also by their belief that the United States, out of self-interest, would not tolerate a communist victory and would reenter the war at least with airpower—especially B-52s—if reentry should become necessary. In retrospect, the respondents perceived that their faith in the United States "actually contributed to the sudden collapse," because it had "led them to conduct their military and civilian affairs with considerable complacency."[111]

Another key mistake by the United States that contributed to the collapse was in structuring the South Vietnamese army to resemble the American army.[112] The respondents blamed the United States for having burdened them with a military organization that was too expensive for South Vietnam to maintain. The American lavish use of airpower and artillery in combat had trained South Vietnamese soldiers to rely on such support. The troops had also become used to air and ground transport, and had "forgotten how to walk."[113] With the Americans gone, South Vietnam did not have the resources to provide its soldiers with the level of support to which they had become accustomed. All these problems were compounded by the lack of "a viable command and planning structure." These functions had been "dominated" by the Americans, and their departure left a leadership vacuum. The respondents acknowledged, how-

---

[110] Hosmer, Kellen, and Jenkins, *The Fall of South Vietnam*, 1978, p. 29.

[111] Hosmer, Kellen, and Jenkins, *The Fall of South Vietnam*, 1978, p. v.

[112] Hosmer, Kellen, and Jenkins, *The Fall of South Vietnam*, 1978, p. v. There had been intermittent talk about creating a "People's Army" during the war (see discussion in Chapter Eight). The concept, however, was rejected by many. One idea, advanced by the commander of the First Infantry Division, was to reduce the number of personnel in support units and assign them to the Regional and Popular Forces, which would be restructured as "Rice Producer Units." These units would produce rice when the situation permitted and fight when the enemy was active. One respondent thought the idea was not suitable for Vietnam, because the "Rice Producer Units" would be living in proximity to the Viet Cong in the countryside, where they could easily be targeted and harassed by the enemy night and day, and prevented from growing food.

[113] Hosmer, Kellen, and Jenkins, *The Fall of South Vietnam*, 1978, p. vi.

ever, that the absence of competent military leadership could not entirely be blamed on the Americans. Many among the top military leaders were incompetent, having been appointed for their political loyalty or for their linkage to the network of corruption, rather than for their leadership and ability. Yet, according to one military respondent, nobody within the South Vietnamese leadership worried very much about such short-comings, because, again, they expected that the Americans would bail them out if things went wrong. Without the Americans to back them up, the South Vietnamese armed forces were unable to fight the war on their own after the United States with-drew its forces.

According to the majority of the respondents, it was corruption—this "funda-mental ill" plaguing the Saigon regime—that, in the end, "was largely responsible for the ultimate collapse of South Vietnam."[114] Summarizing the answers, the authors of the RAND report wrote that, "there was not one high-ranking person in the Saigon government who was not accused by at least some of the respondents as having par-ticipated in the corruption and profited from it."[115] They added, ". . . to benefit from corruption was . . . the principal motivation of a substantial part of the military and civilian leadership."[116] One respondent even said that South Vietnamese leaders were not interested in resisting the communists in 1975 because they had so enriched them-selves that "it made more sense" for them "to take [their] winnings and run."[117] Former Premier Nguyen Cao Ky claimed that even before the fall of Danang, President Thieu and some top generals were preparing to flee the country. However, the respondents maintained that the dismal caliber of the leadership was partially the responsibility of the United States, which stuck with Thieu until the bitter end.

According to the respondents, corruption manifested itself in one of four ways: "racketeering in scarce and often vital goods"; engaging in bribery; buying and sell-ing important positions and appointments; and pocketing the payroll of nonexistent (ghost) soldiers or soldiers who "appeared only for roll call" and who "yielded their salary to their superiors in return for being permitted to be absent from duty."[118] The money collected for ghost soldiers alone was enormous, since casualties were heavy and about 100,000 soldiers deserted each year. Because of this corrupt practice, many units were seriously under strength.

Corruption had a corrosive effect on the army. It destroyed the leadership, since it allowed men to obtain military commands for which they were unqualified. It also ruined the morale of the soldiers. As one respondent put it, the pervasive corruption

---

[114] Hosmer, Kellen, and Jenkins, *The Fall of South Vietnam*, 1978, p. 31.

[115] Hosmer, Kellen, and Jenkins, *The Fall of South Vietnam*, 1978, p. 30.

[116] Hosmer, Kellen, and Jenkins, *The Fall of South Vietnam*, 1978, p. 31.

[117] Hosmer, Kellen, and Jenkins, *The Fall of South Vietnam*, 1978, p. 31.

[118] Hosmer, Kellen, and Jenkins, *The Fall of South Vietnam*, 1978, p. 31.

"created a sense of social injustice," which, in turn, weakened the will to resist the communists. According to this former South Vietnamese commander, "Corruption had created a small elite which held all the power and wealth, and a majority of middle-class people and peasants who became poorer and poorer and who suffered all the sacrifices." It was these people "who sent their sons to fight and die for the country while high government officials and wealthy people sent theirs abroad."[119] The draft itself was discriminatory and onerous. Those South Vietnamese who could not evade the draft with bribery or emigration, or through social connection, had to join the army for a lifetime of military service, from which they could escape only if they were killed or if they reached old age. In return for their military service, soldiers were paid little. One respondent said bitterly that, while soldiers and subalterns knew that their families did not have enough to eat, the wealthy people in Saigon "had food, liquor, they have money, they relax, have a good time." Why should the troops "fight to the death" for this elite? he asked.[120]

One former commander related the story of an army doctor who once told him that "he was disheartened to see that all the wounded, all the amputees who crowded his hospital came from the lower class, from the peasants' families, and they had suffered and sacrificed for a small class of corrupt elite."[121] Social and economic reforms could have given the people "a cause worth fighting for" but were never enacted.[122] As a result, the population remained detached from the war. As a respondent put it, "They were not involved in the fight. It was the opposite of a 'people's war.' The way we conducted the war, we should have realized that in the long run we had to lose it."[123] Other respondents, when discussing "the corruption, lethargy, and gross mismanagement of human, economic, and military resources," said that the South Vietnamese basically caused their own downfall.[124]

By the time the communists launched their offensive in 1975, "national will and military morale" in South Vietnam were at a very low ebb, sapped by the pernicious effect of corruption and by high inflation. Politically, the situation was chaotic, if not anarchic. The pervasive corruption alienated most of the population and further narrowed President Thieu's base of support. It angered the staunchly anti-communist Catholics to the point that they organized into a major opposing force. One of the respondents called the loss of this strongly anti-communist base the "most catastrophic" development for Thieu and his government. At the same time, the Buddhists increased

---

[119] Hosmer, Kellen, and Jenkins, *The Fall of South Vietnam*, 1978, p. 31.

[120] Hosmer, Kellen, and Jenkins, *The Fall of South Vietnam*, 1978, p. 57.

[121] Hosmer, Kellen, and Jenkins, *The Fall of South Vietnam*, 1978, p. 31.

[122] Hosmer, Kellen, and Jenkins, *The Fall of South Vietnam*, 1978, p. 17.

[123] Hosmer, Kellen, and Jenkins, *The Fall of South Vietnam*, 1978, p. 20.

[124] Hosmer, Kellen, and Jenkins, *The Fall of South Vietnam*, 1978, p. viii.

their resistance to the Saigon regime, and the Hoa Hao religious group in the Mekong Delta, as well as the ethnic minorities in the Central Highlands, withdrew their support for Thieu. One respondent said that, "in 1975 most people not only failed to support the government, they opposed it—strongly."[125]

Thus, on the eve of the communist offensive, South Vietnam—as summed up by a respondent—was on the verge of a "psychological collapse" that infected "every South Vietnamese, be he top leader or regular citizen, military or civilian, commander or private soldier."[126] There was a profound sense of pessimism, even among the leaders, who, according to one former official, expected that, "Sooner or later, South Vietnam had to fall into communist hands."[127] In the view of the report's authors, if South Vietnamese leaders expected that the communists would win in the end, the war then "was lost from its inception."[128]

President Thieu, not surprisingly, bore the brunt of the respondents' ire. They thought he was a "mediocre" general; an inept political and military leader; a man preoccupied with staying in power; a leader who appointed "incompetent and corrupt men to high military positions"; a man with "a virtual passion for inaction" who "trusted nobody and was not trusted by anybody" and who "was involved in the extensive corruption plaguing the country."[129] His "Four No's" strategy which he enunciated after the signing of the Paris Agreement encapsulated his propensity for inaction, since it, in effect, boiled down to waiting out his enemies. At the same time, it expressed his intransigence in dealing with the communists. One former general said that this refusal to work out an accommodation provided the communists grounds to accuse the government of failing to implement the terms of the Paris Agreement and use them as justification for their violations of the accord.

Other leaders in the GVN also came in for severe criticism. The respondents "spoke of incompetent generals . . . of cowardly commanders who avoided enemy action; of blatantly corrupt military and civilian leaders in Saigon and in the provinces."[130] According to some of the respondents, these leaders were indifferent to the plight of the people, who, in turn, held them in contempt for their venality, incompetence, and also for their close links with the Americans. One former general said that "the dependence

---

[125] Hosmer, Kellen, and Jenkins, *The Fall of South Vietnam*, 1978, p. 18.

[126] Hosmer, Kellen, and Jenkins, *The Fall of South Vietnam*, 1978, p. 20.

[127] Hosmer, Kellen, and Jenkins, *The Fall of South Vietnam*, 1978, p. 21.

[128] Hosmer, Kellen, and Jenkins, *The Fall of South Vietnam*, 1978, p. 21.

[129] Hosmer, Kellen, and Jenkins, *The Fall of South Vietnam*, 1978, pp. 22–23. One respondent said that as the situation deteriorated, Thieu spent more of his time playing tennis and water-skiing on the Saigon River.

[130] Hosmer, Kellen, and Jenkins, *The Fall of South Vietnam*, 1978, p. 27. Field commanders remained remote from their troops and, as one respondent said, "It was common . . . that, in case of heavy fighting, the commanders took off in their helicopters, leaving the fighting to the troops on the ground. This had a very negative effect on troop morale" (Hosmer, Kellen, and Jenkins, *The Fall of South Vietnam*, 1978, p. 57).

and subordination of the Vietnam government" to the Americans was so profound and obvious that the South Vietnamese population "could not refrain from viewing their government as a puppet deprived of all national prestige, lacking in national mandate and thus being untrustworthy."[131]

Although South Vietnamese leaders expected their country to fall into the hands of the communists eventually, they were stunned by the speed with which their nation—which possessed one of the strongest armies in Asia—collapsed. The respondents ascribed this sudden meltdown to several factors.

One was the military edge that North Vietnam had acquired through its unchallenged buildup of a logistical network that made it possible for it to quickly assemble troops and equipment—including armor and artillery—to target weak South Vietnamese positions freely. On the other side, high casualties, desertions, and reduced supplies caused by the cut in American aid had weakened the ARVN.[132] The South Vietnamese armed forces, furthermore, had to spread themselves extremely thin to defend extensive territories. The result was that they were "nailed to their places." Redeploying forces, as President Thieu tried to do at the last moment, therefore led to a debacle because the ARVN, which had no "strategic reserves," also had no "strategic mobility."[133]

Surprise was another factor working in favor of the communists. Lulled into complacency, South Vietnamese leaders thought that the enemy would not be able to stage such a large-scale offensive because the United States would not allow it to happen. They made no defense plans—especially plans for strategic retreats—and this failure led to the debacle following the fall of Ban Me Thuot, and to enormous military losses and the destruction of morale.

Another major weakness was the "virtual absence of a functioning general staff; inadequate leadership; and insufficient technical training on the part of local commanders."[134] At crucial moments, commanders in the field got no guidance from the Joint General Staff. In short, there was a "breakdown in military and political leadership," which the respondents laid at the feet of President Thieu.[135]

---

[131] Hosmer, Kellen, and Jenkins, *The Fall of South Vietnam*, 1978, p. 28.

[132] The cut in aid was not entirely responsible for shortages of materiel. For example, deliveries of spare parts and ammunition were hampered by corruption. Despite complaints of shortages of artillery shells, a *Los Angeles Times* correspondent reported excessive and unnecessary firing of artillery by corrupt commanders to obtain brass casings for sale in Singapore. Also, respondents to the RAND study mentioned enormous amount of ammunition and equipment being abandoned by the South Vietnamese armed forces in their rush to get out of I and II Corps.

[133] Hosmer, Kellen, and Jenkins, *The Fall of South Vietnam*, 1978, p. 43.

[134] Hosmer, Kellen, and Jenkins, *The Fall of South Vietnam*, 1978, p. vii.

[135] Hosmer, Kellen, and Jenkins, *The Fall of South Vietnam*, 1978, p. vii.

The respondents also blamed Thieu's "irresolution and violent reversal of strategy at the top" for the disaster. Up until the beginning of the offensive, "Thieu's strategy had been to hold on to every outpost, even though this had dispersed and chewed up his forces." Now, in the wake of the communist attack on Ban Me Thuot, he "reversed himself in a series of sudden strategic redeployments that virtually precluded organized defense." According to the respondents, Thieu "sacrificed too much, too fast, handing the enemy the entire northern part of South Vietnam and thereby making their victory inevitable."[136] The quick withdrawals led to rumors that a "deal" had been struck between Hanoi and Saigon, and maybe between the United States and the Soviet Union, to draw a new line of partition further south. The retreat, coupled with the widely believed rumors, "triggered a massive flight of civilian refugees that disrupted military movements and further induced the soldiers not to fight."[137]

Another important factor cited by the respondents was the presence of dependents of soldiers in I and II Corps. Concerns about their families' safety pushed the soldiers to desert en masse to protect them or at least be at their side, leading to a total breakdown of discipline, morale, and resistance, as happened in Danang, where some elite troops not only failed to fight but even mutinied. Finally, the desertion of commanders who abandoned their troops in the crisis aggravated "disorganization and panic."[138]

Paralysis at the national and corps levels, was another major factor contributing to the collapse. In the words of the respondents, this "paralysis of inactivity" led to a situation in which "no one was in charge of anything . . . no one did anything."[139] The paralysis stemmed, in part, from the expectation and hope—entertained by leaders including Thieu until the very end—that the United States would come in and save them from disaster.

According to the respondents, the South Vietnamese air force did not acquit itself well, either. Afraid of being hit by communist anti-aircraft gunfire and SAM-7 missiles, pilots flew high and missed targets at critical moments during the offensive—or even dropped ordnance on their own troops, thus further eroding their morale. Pilots were not willing to take the risk of flying low, because they did not see the point of sacrificing themselves for the regime in Saigon. Former Air Marshal Nguyen Cao Ky, for example, mentioned the comment of a squadron leader, who told him, "You know, now I drop a bomb at 35,000 feet because I don't want to go down and be hit by Communist antiaircraft. What for?"[140] In the debacle, helicopter pilots took off in panic with their families and then ditched their planes on the tarmac of airfields, where no

---

[136] Hosmer, Kellen, and Jenkins, *The Fall of South Vietnam*, 1978, p. vii.

[137] Hosmer, Kellen, and Jenkins, *The Fall of South Vietnam*, 1978, p. vii.

[138] Hosmer, Kellen, and Jenkins, *The Fall of South Vietnam*, 1978, p. vii.

[139] Hosmer, Kellen, and Jenkins, *The Fall of South Vietnam*, 1978, p. vii.

[140] Hosmer, Kellen, and Jenkins, *The Fall of South Vietnam*, 1978, p. 71.

one would take care of them, the mechanics themselves being busy attending to the welfare of their own families. Reviewing the comments regarding the South Vietnamese air force, the authors of the report wrote that this air force, which had more than 1,000 planes, should have given the GVN an edge. However, no such edge materialized, despite the fact that the communists did not have any aircraft in the South.

As one former South Vietnamese general put it, these factors combined led to "a rout unprecedented in the annals of military history."[141] As for what might have been done in the final period to prevent the collapse, the respondents thought that South Vietnam could not, on its own, either disrupt the enemy buildup or stop the offensive when it began, without direct military assistance from the United States. Wishfully, they said that if they had been able to hold out for a few months, the United States would have "been more likely" to reenter the war because they had "proved" themselves.[142] Most believed that, had the United States not "abandoned" South Vietnam and had it reintervened with airpower—in particular, by unleashing B-52s—defeat would have been prevented in 1975.[143] However, the authors pointed out that none of the respondents "would contend that continued air or renewed intervention would have ended the war or brought victory—significantly, the word 'victory' does not appear in the interviews."[144] Interestingly enough, quite a few respondents thought that the collapse of South Vietnam was "inexorable."[145] The enemy, they felt, had "an unlimited willingness to endure" and would never stop fighting, whereas the United States abandoned South Vietnam out of a lack of patience.[146]

Another question the authors raised was whether the respondents thought there were changes the South Vietnamese might have enacted to avoid collapse. Here, the respondents' answers became "more diffuse and complex," and the authors could only infer what these reforms could have been from the reasons the respondents gave for the collapse.[147] These changes might have included the following: the removal of Thieu, which, by extension, would imply the dismissal of "the corrupt and incompe-

---

[141] Hosmer, Kellen, and Jenkins, *The Fall of South Vietnam*, 1978, p. vii. This general added that the "closing days of the Vietnam War" were unique in other aspects: "five billion dollars worth of equipment was lost, a country with nineteen million people collapsed and joined the ranks of the Communist countries." Hosmer, Kellen, and Jenkins, *The Fall of South Vietnam*, 1978, p. xv.

[142] Hosmer, Kellen, and Jenkins, *The Fall of South Vietnam*, 1978, p. viii.

[143] Hosmer, Kellen, and Jenkins, *The Fall of South Vietnam*, 1978, p. 129.

[144] Hosmer, Kellen, and Jenkins, *The Fall of South Vietnam*, 1978, p. 129.

[145] Hosmer, Kellen, and Jenkins, *The Fall of South Vietnam*, 1978, p. viii.

[146] Hosmer, Kellen, and Jenkins, *The Fall of South Vietnam*, 1978, p. 131.

[147] Hosmer, Kellen, and Jenkins, *The Fall of South Vietnam*, 1978, p. 129.

tent people he appointed"; the consolidation of South Vietnamese territory "to make it more defensible"; adoption of a "style of fighting" more suitable to South Vietnam's resources; modification of manpower policies and the activation of more divisions; the development of a "coherent strategy for conducting the war," as well as "more viable contingency plans" in case the enemy launched an all-out offensive; harassment of the enemy's lines of communication; and an attempt to resist longer. However, the South Vietnamese leadership, the respondents included, "did none of these things."[148] One reason they gave for this failure was that they lacked the power to act without U.S. acquiescence. Another reason given was the apparent conviction of the leaders that "such painful reforms were in fact unnecessary, because the Americans could be counted on to bail out the South in an emergency."[149]

The fundamental reason that "discouraged reforms" was the respondents' belief that, by themselves, they could not have made a difference because the causes for the collapse "were so 'inextricably interwoven' that no single change in the conduct of the war on their part alone would have affected the outcome and, in any case, they considered most reforms to be difficult, if not impossible to realize."[150]

The fundamental causes for the collapse encompassed a wide range of "military, social, political, and international factors" that interacted "upon one another" and "left South Vietnam vulnerable to an enemy superior in will and power."[151] One of several examples cited to illustrate the vicious circle confronting South Vietnam was the risk of removing Thieu from power. Since he alone enjoyed the support of the United States, getting rid of him would have left South Vietnam bereft of American support, without which it could not continue the war.

One theme that emerged emphatically from the interviews was that the South Vietnamese did not move events but were instead "moved" by outside forces—in particular, by the United States. Some respondents saw the war as not just a fight between the South and the North but as part of a larger struggle between the Communist Bloc, led by the Soviet Union and China, and the West, led by the United States. In this struggle, real power was in the hands of the Americans, and the South Vietnamese were powerless to influence the outcome. In the end, America's desire for detente with the Soviet Union and rapprochement with China, combined with the effects of Watergate and American impatience, led to South Vietnam's downfall. So, ultimately,

---

[148] Hosmer, Kellen, and Jenkins, *The Fall of South Vietnam*, 1978, p. 129.

[149] Hosmer, Kellen, and Jenkins, *The Fall of South Vietnam*, 1978, pp. 129–130.

[150] Hosmer, Kellen, and Jenkins, *The Fall of South Vietnam*, 1978, p. 130.

[151] Hosmer, Kellen, and Jenkins, *The Fall of South Vietnam*, 1978, p. 130.

South Vietnam could not control its own destiny. As one respondent concluded, "Fate was not on our side."[152]

In conclusion, the authors of the report wrote that, "Regardless of what the respondents saw as the causes of the collapse, they tended to stress that an unsuccessful U.S.–South Vietnamese interaction had been largely responsible for it," and they left no "doubt that in their view the alliance between the biggest and most powerful nation of the West and the small, technologically undeveloped Asian nation had been a failure."[153]

The RAND report was published by Crane, Russak and Co., in 1980, under the title *The Fall of South Vietnam*. In a CIA review of the book, the reviewer considered the RAND work as meaningful and significant "far beyond 'instant history,'" because it revealed the "difficulties that seem inherent in maintaining an alliance between a small state and a great power." In this regard, the book should "therefore, appeal to a broader audience than those interested in reliving the fall of Saigon." In addition, the reviewer lauded the authors for contributing "an intimate and revealing portrait not only of the Vietnamese" but also of how Americans were "perceived in Vietnam." The reviewer, who had had personal experience in Vietnam, was shocked by "the deep and abiding faith" that the Vietnamese respondents had in the United States and by their firm belief that "the US would not allow Saigon to fall to the Communists." One answer in particular made him sit "bolt upright." To the question posed by one of the RAND interviewers—"When did this belief start to erode?"—came the reply, "The last day."[154]

♧ ♧ ♧

With the fate of Vietnam resolved, Americans preferred not to be reminded of the trauma of the war. Vietnam would occasionally surface, but only as a cautionary tale for the United States: as the kind of military involvement that the country should avoid, one in which American national interests were not truly at stake, and that had no exit strategy and little popular understanding and support. At RAND, work on Vietnam, which never represented a significant portion of its total budget and manpower, practically disappeared. When it appeared in major RAND works at all, it would be studied—not as a topic by and of itself but as a case study for broader

---

[152] Hosmer, Kellen, and Jenkins, *The Fall of South Vietnam*, 1978, 131.

[153] Hosmer, Kellen, and Jenkins, *The Fall of South Vietnam*, 1978, pp. viii–ix.

[154] CIA review of *The Fall of South Vietnam*, approved for release December 2, 2003, CIA-RDP81B00401R002500070015-5.

Modern-day location of RAND building at 176 Pasteur.

issues.[155] The report by Hosmer, Kellen, and Jenkins, *The Fall of South Vietnam*, would be the last major work on the Vietnam War.

Gerry Hickey's departure in 1973 marked the end of the RAND presence in Vietnam. Long before that, RAND's visibility and influence had peaked under the tenure of Leon Goure as project manager, during a period when policymakers, such as

[155] See, for example, Robert A. Levine, *The Arms Debate and the Third World: Have We Learned from Vietnam?* Santa Monica, Calif.: RAND Corporation, R-3523, 1987; Benjamin C. Schwarz, "The Influence of Public Opinion Regarding Casualties on American Military Intervention: Implications for U.S. Regional Deterrence Strategies," Santa Monica, Calif.: unpublished RAND research, 1993; Eric V. Larson, *Casualties and Consensus: The Historical Role of Casualties in Domestic Support for U.S. Military Operations*, Santa Monica, Calif.: RAND Corporation, MR-726, 1996; Stephen T. Hosmer, *Psychological Effects of U.S. Air Operations in Four Wars 1941–1991*, Santa Monica, Calif.: RAND Corporation, MR-576, 1996; and William G. Rosenau, *Special Operations Forces and Elusive Enemy Ground Targets*, Santa Monica, Calif.: RAND Corporation, MR-1408, 2001. A few deal more closely with issues raised by the war, such as Mark A. Lorell, *Casualties, Public Opinion, and Presidential Policy During the Vietnam War*, Santa Monica, Calif.: RAND Corporation, R-3060, 1984; Douglas F. Zatzick, *Post-Traumatic Stress Disorder and Functioning and Quality of Life Outcomes in a Nationally Representative Sample of Male Vietnam Veterans*, Santa Monica, Calif.: RAND Corporation, LRP-199712-05, 1997; and Douglas F. Zatzick, *Post-Traumatic Stress Disorder and Functioning and Quality of Life Outcomes in Female Vietnam Veterans*, Santa Monica, Calif.: RAND Corporation, LRP-199710-03, 1997.

Robert McNamara and Walt Rostow, thought American military strength—especially airpower—could make a difference in Vietnam. The building at 176 Pasteur, practically synonymous with RAND's intellectual prowess in Saigon for many years, was transformed into a kindergarten following the communist victory in 1975. As Vietnam sank into economic stagnation, the villa was left in its original state to deteriorate with time and weather.

Later, as reforms launched the Vietnamese economy into fast-development mode, it would be remodeled and rebuilt into an unrecognizable large structure, with the kindergarten being expanded to encompass the building next door. The generation of children attending the school were born long after the war ended. To them, the Vietnam War will undoubtedly appear like old history—as it already is for RAND. Even for the RAND staff members who labored over studies of the Vietnam War, memories of that period have dimmed with the passage of time. However, the passion of the war—although long dissipated—is not entirely forgotten.

CHAPTER ELEVEN

Laos and Thailand: Sideshows

Laos, the sleepy, landlocked kingdom bordering Vietnam and Thailand, emerged as a crisis early in the presidency of President John F. Kennedy. The crisis began in 1959, when the cease-fire between the communists and noncommunists, negotiated at the Geneva Conference in 1954, broke down. By December 1960, supplied by the Soviet Union and backed by neutralist forces and North Vietnamese troops, the communist Pathet Lao were on the verge of taking over half the country. Prior to leaving office, President Dwight "Ike" Eisenhower told President John F. Kennedy that "Laos was the key to the entire area of Southeast Asia," and that the United States might have to dispatch combat troops to stop communist expansion. The Pathet Lao advance unnerved Thailand and South Vietnam, which was facing a growing insurgency. Most important of all, with the United States and the Soviet Union backing opposite camps in the civil war, the two superpowers appeared to be on a collision course toward an unwanted military confrontation.

The communist movement in Laos dated back to the French period, when the Pathet Lao allied themselves with the Viet Minh to liberate their country from colonialism. They set up a Provisional Resistance Movement headquartered in Sam Neua Province, and by March 1951 had expanded their guerrilla resistance along the entire length of the border with Vietnam: from Phong Saly in the north to the Bolovens Plateau in the south. Under U.S. pressure, France granted Laos autonomy within the French Union in 1949. In 1954, as part of their struggle for independence, Viet Minh forces moved into Laos, advancing as far as to threaten the Royal capital of Luang Prabang and the Mekong Valley. At the Geneva Conference of 1954, convoked to settle the conflict between the French and the Viet Minh, a cease-fire was agreed upon. Under the terms of the agreement, French forces and Viet Minh troops would withdraw from Laos. In exchange for the neutralization of Laos, China and its allies agreed to accept the integration of the Pathet Lao forces into the government army. National elections were slated for August 1955. While the terms of the integration were being ironed out, Pathet Lao troops would regroup to the provinces of Sam Neua and Phong Saly.

It was after the 1954 Geneva Conference that the United States began to get deeply involved in Laos. Starting in 1955, the United States attempted to turn Laos into an anti-communist bastion on the fringes of China and Vietnam. It tried to do so by unifying all noncommunist political groups and strengthening them with military and economic support. The policy was flawed because it was based on the erroneous assumption that Laos had adequate national unity and leadership, as well as political and social cohesion, to use American aid effectively to resist the Pathet Lao. But—except in name—Laos was not a country. Historically, ethnically, and geographically, Laos was divided into separate regions having little in common. The heterogeneous population included a diversity of ethnic groups who practiced different religions and who regarded each other with fear and hostility. The elite was made up of rival clans practically devoid of national allegiance, for whom government and public service were simply means through which they could acquire power and influence in order to accumulate wealth.

Economically, Laos was underdeveloped in every respect. It had a limited road network that linked the main towns along the Mekong River but that generally bypassed the rugged hinterland of hilly jungles and limestone peaks. The economy was so rudimentary that it was insufficient to support the small army and bureaucracy that a country with 3 million people would normally require, and certainly was woefully inadequate to sustain these institutions now enlarged by the requirements of warfare. In such conditions, U.S. resources were soaked up without producing results. The army, paid for by American money, was ineffectual, and economic aid was siphoned off by corruption and blatant stealing. Politically, the noncommunist groups remained divided, despite concerted American persuasion and pressure to get them to unite in the fight against the Pathet Lao.

In 1956, Prince Souvanna Phouma, a neutralist, became prime minister in Vientiane, and in 1957 he crafted an agreement for national reconciliation with his half-brother, Prince Souphanouvong, a Pathet Lao leader. Souphanouvong and Phoumi Vongvichit, another prominent Pathet Lao leader, would become ministers in a coalition government under the leadership of the Lao king residing in Luang Prabang. In addition, the Neo Lao Hak Sat (NLHS), the political front of the Pathet Lao, was allowed to take part in the elections for the National Assembly scheduled for 1958 under the clauses of the existing constitution. The two communist-controlled provinces of Sam Neua and Phong Saly would be absorbed into the national government, and about a quarter of the Pathet Lao troops would be integrated into the Royal Army in two battalions.

To the dismay of the noncommunists, the Neo Lao Hak Sat won nine seats out of 21. With their political allies, who controlled another four seats, the NLHS commanded the majority of the votes in the National Assembly. In August 1958, a right-wing government hostile to the communists came into power under Phoui Sananikone. The United States stepped up its aid, delivering new equipment, including trucks and tanks—which proved to be more useful in staging a coup d'etat in Vientiane than in fighting the Pathet Lao—and dispatched American and Filipino military advisors to help expand the Royal Army from 25,000 to 29,000 men. Laos began to forge links with the Southeast Asia Treaty Organization.

Strengthened by American support, the Lao military began to meddle heavily in politics. China accused the United States and the Lao government of violating the terms of the Geneva agreement, which had called for the neutralization of Laos, of fomenting tension in Indochina, and of threatening its security. In Washington, there was fear that the Chinese might invade Laos and also concern that the United States might have to engage in a ground war in Laos. Consequently, a standby combat force and logistics support were created in Okinawa to intervene in Laos if necessary.

In the face of these developments, the Pathet Lao became more and more apprehensive over the growing influence of the United States, the increasing role of the Lao military in politics, and the developing links to SEATO. Furthermore, they were appalled by the corruption that American aid was fueling within the army and the government. In May, the Royal Army surrounded the two Pathet Lao battalions and tried to disarm them, capturing a part of one battalion. The remaining Pathet Lao troops fled to North Vietnam. The Royal Police also arrested the Neo Lao Hak Sat leaders, including the deputies who had been elected to the National Assembly. After about a year of imprisonment, in May 1960 these leaders, including Prince Souphanouvong, bribed their way out of jail and escaped back to their base in the two provinces near Vietnam. These moves by the Royal Lao Government, or RLG, effectively destroyed any prospect for national integration.

As hostility grew, the Pathet Lao responded by initiating a series of attacks in July 1959 against Royal military outposts in northeastern Laos. By this time, their forces had grown from a few hundred poorly armed guerrillas at the time of the 1954 armistice to several thousand. Aided by North Vietnamese troops, whose presence was kept secret by the Democratic Republic of Vietnam to avoid accusations of violating Lao neutrality, the Pathet Lao regained control of the two provinces that had been returned to the government. These territorial gains served the purpose of Hanoi at a time when it wanted to secure its infiltration route running through the Lao panhandle into South Vietnam to increase its aid to the Viet Cong.

To complicate matters further, in the summer of 1960, Captain Kong Le, a paratroop commander, staged a coup and brought back Prince Souvanna Phouma as prime minister with the objective of neutralizing Laos once again. When the United States cut off aid to Laos, Phouma turned to the Soviet Union for assistance. Beginning in December 1960, Soviet aid began to arrive through North Vietnam to Kong Le, who had allied himself with the Pathet Lao. A large part of that aid would be funneled by Hanoi to the Pathet Lao. With Soviet equipment and weapons, as well as with the American arms and supplies Kong Le had given them from captured Royal Lao Army caches, the Pathet Lao troops were now transformed from guerrillas to regular forces.

Toward the end of 1960, right-wing General Phoumi Nosavan, who had connections with the CIA, staged a countercoup. Backed by the United States, Nosavan launched an offensive, driving Prince Souvanna Phouma to flee to Cambodia and then to the Plain of Jars—a region of rolling grassland littered with half-buried ancient jars—which controlled a strategic junction of roads in northern Laos. There, the prince set up his headquarters. Kong Le and his crack paratroopers had settled there after retreating from Vientiane. The large jars, covered in lichen, stand "as high as a man's chest" and resemble a "giant's tea set," which can only be moved with a crane. No one has figured out "what ancient civilization made them or what it used them for."[1] The plain is less then ten miles across, but it is the largest region in northern Laos that is somewhat level. It is surrounded by mountains with limestone peaks that occasionally rise above the canopy of forest trees.

While Washington quickly recognized the new government under Prince Boun Oum, which was installed in the wake of the Nosavan coup, Peking and Moscow continued to back the Souvanna Phouma government and to provide aid to its army under the command of Kong Le. The combined neutralist and communist forces pushed on with their offensive and overran almost half of the country. Their steady advance—and concern about their final objective—confronted President Kennedy with a crisis.

To prevent the communists—aided by the neutralists—from thrusting into the Mekong Valley, the United States attempted to strengthen the Phoumi forces by sending six AT-6 aircraft equipped with machine guns and capable of firing rockets and dropping bombs, and by dispatching the White Star Mobile Training Team of 400 Special Forces personnel to strengthen the Royal Lao Army. Phoumi forces proved ineffective and unmotivated; so, Washington had to consider other alternatives. Direct military involvement was ruled out, and, to avoid a potential confrontation, the United States agreed with the Soviet Union in April 1961 to defuse the situation by arranging a cease-fire and by convoking an international conference to again neutralize Laos, thereby removing it from the Cold War conflict. China, another power with a stake in Laos, also agreed to the arrangement, to avoid the possibility that American sol-

---

[1] Roger Warner, *Shooting at the Moon: The Story of America's Clandestine War in Laos*, South Royalton, Vt.: Steerforth Press, second paperback edition, 1999, p. 20.

diers might be introduced into a country on its southern border. Kennedy's decision to accept neutralization implicitly acknowledged that the Eisenhower Administration's policy of building up a strong anti-communist bastion in Laos had failed.

♧ ♧ ♧

For RAND, Laos never afforded the opportunity for in-depth research that it found in Vietnam. Even early in the Kennedy Administration, when Laos became a foreign policy crisis, RAND only produced a number of studies on this country. These studies were done only as part of Project REDWOOD, the limited war game conducted by RAND's Mathematics Department. Later, as the war intensified in Laos along with the escalation of the war in Vietnam, RAND would produce a few additional reports that were more in-depth. The paucity of research on Laos in general meant that a couple of these RAND reports would be groundbreaking by providing valuable information and analysis about the little-known country. Since Laos was an extension of the battleground in Vietnam, the RAND research would focus on the role and activities of the two main adversaries—the United States and North Vietnam—and their proxies, the Hmong mercenaries fighting on behalf of the Americans and the Pathet Lao allies of the North Vietnamese. However, since Laos would remain a sideshow to the U.S. involvement in Vietnam, thus attracting less official attention and fewer resources, RAND's output on Laos would never match the volume and the scope of the research it produced for Vietnam; nor would its Laos studies attain the level of influence, limited as it was, that its work on Vietnam was able to achieve.

From time to time, RAND would dispatch analysts to Laos but it never maintained an official presence in Vientiane like it did in Vietnam. Occasionally, a few RAND visitors came to the country on a detour from Vietnam, their main destination—more for a quick check on the situation than to acquire knowledge about a pressing national-security issue facing the United States or to ferret out research opportunities. For RAND, as for the United States, Laos would remain a sideshow.

The first RAND study on Laos was done in June 1960. As part of Project REDWOOD, Abraham M. Halpern used Laos as a case study of limited war and analyzed the political and military situation leading up to hostilities in summer and fall 1959. He concluded that, contrary to expectations, the noncommunist side backed by the Free World had the initiative, whereas the communists, supported by their allies, were only reacting to the actions of their enemies.[2] Both sides operated under severe constraints, and the fighting was kept to a minimum. The combat ended in a stalemate, with a status quo, to the dissatisfaction of both sides. Halpern predicted that, under certain conditions, hostilities could resume.

---

[2] Abraham M. Halpern, *Communist Strategy in Laos*, Santa Monica, Calif.: RAND Corporation, RM-2561, June 1960.

A few more in-depth studies on Laos would follow. For example, in November 1960, Joel Martin Halpern of the Social Science Division produced a report which examined the Lao elite, their composition, and their relationship with other population segments, as well as the strains within Lao society and the pressures for change.[3] In his view, the elite's traditional control of the political machinery was not in danger, unless the Pathet Lao gained power through a coup d'etat. Although the stress on Lao society was apparent, it was not serious enough to cause the elite's control to collapse. At the same time, while the elite was tradition-bound, it was also capable of change and could be encouraged to move in the right direction. By understanding the cultural attitudes and social values of the elite, the United States might be able to help transform it into a group that could provide effective leadership and direct Laos toward goals compatible with Western interests and values.

Then, in February 1961, in a joint paper, Anne M. Jonas and George Tanham analyzed the Lao revolution, which, in their view, was part of the warfare carried out by the international Communist Bloc to exploit national liberation movements.[4] For the Soviet Union, this technique of conflict minimized the danger of a confrontation with the United States while allowing it to avoid putting its avowed policy of peaceful coexistence in jeopardy and enabling it to negotiate with the United States at the highest level. As these works indicated, research on Laos at RAND was as disparate as that being conducted by RAND analysts on Vietnam in the same period (see Chapter One).

In March 1962, RAND produced a report that—as events unfolded—turned out to be by far the most influential RAND report on Laos at the time: *The Military Geography of Laos: A Barrier to Communist Aggression*. Produced as background material for Project REDWOOD by R. E. Koon of the Mathematics Department and Ken C. Strother,[5] the report provided the Kennedy Administration with information about the terrain of Laos as it made plans to stop what it feared was the communist thrust toward the Mekong Delta in 1962. According to the RAND report, the Laos terrain had four dominant features: its contiguous border with all continental countries in the region with the exception of Malaya which gave Laos a strategic location in Southeast Asia; the inaccessible Annamite Mountain chain; the Mekong Valley lowlands; and the narrow passes leading from the mountains into the lowlands. Although the rugged Annamite Mountains, located to the east and north of the country, bordering North Vietnam and extending into southern China, could constitute a physical barrier to

---

[3]   Halpern, Joel Martin, *The Lao Elite: A Study of Tradition and Innovation*, RAND RM-2636-RC, November 1960.

[4]   Anne M. Jonas and George Tanham, *Laos: The Current Phase in a Cyclic Regional Revolution*, Santa Monica, Calif.: RAND Corporation, P-2214, February 1961.

[5]   R. E. Koon and Ken C. Strother, *The Military Geography of Laos: A Barrier to Communist Aggression*, Santa Monica, Calif.: RAND Corporation, RM-2986, March 1962.

impede aggression from these two countries, the report pointed out that the communists had built truck routes through three mountain passes, which could lead them to the strategic Mekong Valley and onward to Thailand and South Vietnam. This RAND report would be cited by officials in the Kennedy Administration as they contemplated responses to communist advances in 1962.

♣ ♣ ♣

The communist advance took place while the Geneva Conference convened in May 1961 was still unfolding. As talks continued in Geneva, General Phoumi rejected the formation of a coalition government as part of a settlement, and fighting continued. In January and February 1962, the Pathet Lao and North Vietnamese troops inflicted a resounding defeat on Phoumi's troops at Nam Tha, a town of 1,800 in northern Laos close to the Chinese border. North Vietnam's rout of Phoumi's 5,000-man force was intended to force the rightists to come to terms at Geneva and also to keep them out of the area in which China was building a road from its southern border into northern Laos. In Washington, the Kennedy Administration was unsure where the communist forces might be headed next and what their final objective was. One possibility was that the Nam Tha debacle was a prelude to communist penetration into the critical Mekong Valley. President Kennedy, concerned about the security of Thailand, sent 5,000 U.S. troops to northeast Thailand, from which they could be dispatched to Laos at short notice if necessary. The presence of American troops was also meant as a warning to Hanoi and Peking. In Washington, President Kennedy declared that there were only two courses of action the United States could take: diplomatic negotiations or military intervention. In his view, the United States did not have a good third alternative.

Contingency planning went into high gear in Washington to determine what options were available to the United States if the situation worsened, and what communist responses might be to each U.S. move. The RAND report on the military geography of Laos was consulted and used in discussing the feasibility of occupying the strategic Mekong Valley as an option to stop potential communist advances. A summary of the RAND report, prepared by Roger Hilsman, director of the Bureau of Intelligence and Research at the State Department, was attached by Mike Forrestal, a member of the National Security Council staff, to a memo addressed to President Kennedy in June 1962.[6] In his memo, Forrestal distilled the views of the State and Defense Departments, and pointed out that, given the strategic importance of the Mekong Valley as described in the RAND report, its loss would worsen the situation in Laos, aggravate the security threat to Thailand, and facilitate North Vietnam's infiltration into South Vietnam. Consequently, State and Defense recommended that the United

---

[6] Michael V. Forrestal, Memorandum of June 4, 1962; Memorandum of June 5, 1962; and Memorandum of June 6, 1962, Foreign Relations of the United States, State Department Archives, Kennedy Administration, 1961–1963, Volume XXIV, Laos Crisis.

States not only occupy the Mekong River areas but also launch ground and air attacks against the Pathet Lao and North Vietnamese forces inside Laos, as well as in North Vietnam if the communists reacted to a U.S. occupation of the Mekong Valley by intensifying their military activities to a degree unacceptable to Washington.

Subsequently, however, McNamara and the Joint Chiefs of Staff backed away from the offensive option, and the agreement between State and Defense—concerning the recommendations to be made to the president regarding the "Phase Line" approach to Laos—evaporated.[7] McNamara now rejected the recommendations and argued that planning for Laos must be based on two stark options: Either the United States intervened militarily to decisively engage North Vietnamese troops or stayed out of Laos completely. The reason was the Pentagon's dislike of the prospect of U.S. troops being forced to remain in the Mekong Valley for an indefinite period of time if they were dispatched to occupy this region, and the apprehension that an occupation could lead to a wider war.

Alexis Johnson, Deputy Undersecretary of State for Political Affairs, used the RAND report to argue that the Mekong Valley was defensible and implied that this region could be held without having to resort to a bigger war.[8] He wrote that the RAND study indicated that, if U.S. forces occupied the "dominant geographical features of the terrain" in the Mekong Valley currently held by the Royal Lao Government, they would be able to control this region. As the RAND report pointed out, whereas the densely forested mountains of the north and east of Laos favored guerrilla activities, the more open and level terrain of the Mekong Valley did not. An occupation of the Mekong Valley would provoke the communists into intensifying their guerrilla warfare; however, the terrain of this region would make such warfare difficult while providing natural advantages to the American forces defending it.[9]

Johnson argued that, if control of the Mekong Valley was "ceded" to the communists, this event would create a "political shock" in Thailand and South Vietnam. In addition, from a strategic point of view, the loss of the valley would allow the North Vietnamese to increase their infiltration of troops and equipment into South Vietnam, as well as into Thailand and Cambodia. Consequently, it would become even more

---

[7]   Alexis Johnson, Memorandum to Dean Rusk, June 6, 1962, Foreign Relations of the United States, State Department Archives, Kennedy Administration, 1961–1963, Volume XXIV, Laos Crisis. The "Phase Line" approach included six anticipated steps: "Phase I: Further buildup outside of Laos; Phase II: Occupation of the Mekong Valley; Phase III: Air action within Laos outside of the Mekong Valley; Phase IV: Offensive ground operations within Laos; Phase V: Air action against North Vietnam; and Phase VI: Amphibious operations against North Vietnam."

[8]   Johnson, Memorandum to Dean Rusk, 1962.

[9]   Johnson, Memorandum to Dean Rusk, 1962. Another option under consideration at the time was occupation of the southern panhandle. However, Johnson thought that, in view of the RAND study's conclusion that its terrain was more conducive to guerrilla activities, occupation of this region would present the United States with a more serious guerrilla war and would necessitate a much bigger military effort.

difficult to defend South Vietnam. Furthermore, as the RAND study pointed out, "[i]f the Communists obtained full control over the east bank of the Mekong, with its relatively good north-south road, the defense of Thailand would be much more difficult." Such an eventuality would make it more challenging for the United States to hold all of Southeast Asia, and would require U.S. forces to remain in Southeast Asia for a long period of time—as was the case in Korea—to buy time for the governments in the region and keep those governments from falling into communist hands.

After careful consideration of the options and their ramifications, President Kennedy decided to pursue a settlement to the crisis and to neutralize Laos as the best alternative. Also, the conditions in Laos that had undermined the Eisenhower Administration's policy to build a strong anti-communist government were still there: an undeveloped economy, a feeble administration, a divided population, a corrupt elite, and an ineffective leadership. These weaknesses of Laos convinced Kennedy to change course in Laos. The rout of Phoumi's forces at Nam Tha and U.S. pressure broke Phoumi's resistance to a coalition government. At a summit in the Plain of Jars the three princes—neutralist Phouma, rightist Boun Oum, and Communist Souphanouvong—agreed to form a coalition government, under the leadership of Prince Souvanna Phouma.

On June 12, 1962, the king of Laos formally approved the new government. An international agreement was finally reached and signed in Geneva on July 23, 1962. Under the terms of the settlement, a cease-fire went into effect—between the rightist Royal Lao Government on one side and the Pathet Lao and their neutralist ally on the other. Foreign powers committed themselves not to intervene in the internal affairs of Laos, and foreign troops and military personnel were scheduled to leave Laos by October 1962. The integration of the three factions and their armies remained to be settled. The United States complied with the settlement by withdrawing U.S. and Filipino personnel who had been fighting on the side of the Royal Lao Government. The North Vietnamese, who had always concealed the presence of their forces, withdrew some but not all of their troops.

The Lao settlement simply maintained the status quo. The factions continued to control and administer their own areas. The neutralist forces under Kong Le consisted of about 10,000 men: almost half in the Plain of Jars under his direct command and the rest dispersed in fortified positions in the central region and along the road from the Royal capital of Luang Prabang to Vientiane. By now, the Pathet Lao had an army of 19,500 men and controlled most of the highlands of Laos, or about half the territory, including the area of the Ho Chi Minh Trail and the northern provinces bordering Vietnam. These regions were sparsely populated, however, accounting for only 20 to 30 percent of the total population. The rightists numbered about 48,000 men, mostly stationed in the Mekong Valley, and included detachments of CIA-supported Hmong guerrillas deep within Pathet Lao territory. The tribal Hmong, also called the Meo—a term the Hmong consider pejorative—had migrated from southern China about a century and a half before into Laos and had settled at an altitude above 3,000 feet to grow rice, maize, and opium as a cash crop. They were considered the best fighters in Laos.

The CIA had begun building this Hmong guerrilla force in the strategic Plain of Jars in 1961 to fight the Pathet Lao and North Vietnamese, a job that the regular Lao army could not shoulder, given their lack of military skills and leadership, and their traditional fear of the North Vietnamese. This region was inhabited by minorities, of which the Hmong represented the largest ethnic group; consequently, the Agency turned its attention to them. The tribe traditionally followed a strong leader, so the CIA began searching for someone who could win the allegiance of the guerrillas. They found him in the person of Vang Pao, a Hmong officer with proven toughness and leadership, who already had a nucleus of Hmong fighters under his command. Vang Pao had collaborated with the French in their war against the Viet Minh, and joined the Royal Lao Army after Laos gained independence. He eventually reached the rank of colonel and rose to become commander of Xieng Khouang Province and then of Military Region (MR) II, which bordered North Vietnam.

Vang Pao thought that the scattered Hmong communities in the upland valleys of the Plain of Jars could be organized into a guerrilla force. To build up Vang Pao's army, his officers and CIA agents "leapfrogged" among the scattered Hmong villages around the "western and northern perimeter of the Plain of Jars" in helicopters and light Helio-courier aircraft, and offered "guns, rice, and money in exchange for recruits."[10] According to one Hmong leader, the recruiters used "threats as well as inducements," and his people had "no choice" but to join Vang Pao's forces, because the recruiters "came to the village and warned that if we did not join him he would regard us as Pathet Lao and his soldiers would attack our village."[11] The CIA used Thai police commandos and Green Berets to train Vang Pao's forces. To link the Hmong villages to Vang Pao's and CIA's headquarters in the Plain of Jars, the agency hacked airstrips on the mountain ridges. Air America, the Agency's own airline, was used to deliver weapons, ammunition, food, medication, and other supplies to the Hmong. Vang Pao's forces grew to between 14,000 and 18,000 men at the time the Geneva Accords were signed in 1962, thus making his army as large as that of the Pathet Lao.

Less than a year after the 1962 accords were signed, the Pathet Lao's Prince Souphanouvong and Phoumi Vongvichit left Vientiane to return to Sam Neua, contending with some justification that their lives were in danger in the capital. The coalition government dissolved in April 1963. In the same year, open warfare broke out between the Pathet Lao and their one-time ally, the neutralists. Captain Kong Le retreated from the Plain of Jars to Vientiane, leaving his forces under the control of Colonel Deuane Sispaseuth, his rival and enemy.

---

[10] Alfred W. McCoy, *The Politics of Heroin in Southeast Asia*, New York: Harper & Row, 1972, p. 274.

[11] McCoy, *The Politics of Heroin*, 1972, p. 274.

Completely dependent on the communists, Deuane became, in essence, an appendage of the Pathet Lao. Kong Le, no longer able to rely on Soviet aid, had to turn to the United States for support.[12] Washington, anxious to prevent the Lao situation from becoming polarized once again, was willing to oblige. By May 1964, as the Pathet Lao military pressures continued without letup, Washington decided to expand the number of the guerrillas on the CIA's payroll. By fighting a proxy war through these mercenaries, the United States could avoid the appearance of violating the peace and neutrality of Laos to which it had agreed in Geneva and, at the same time, resist the Pathet Lao. The military confrontation between the Pathet Lao and a combination of noncommunist rightists and neutralists—and Hmong guerrillas—was still going on when Frank Collbohm, the president of RAND, made a side trip to the country in 1965 after visiting South Vietnam.

On his stop in Vientiane, Collbohm was struck by its smallness and backwardness. It did not look like a capital city, he would write in his subsequent trip report.[13] The streets had no names, the houses bore no numbers, and one could see bullock carts passing by and water buffaloes lying in mud puddles. However, the unusual thing about Vientiane that set it apart from its noncommunist neighbors was that, as the capital of a neutral country, it had diplomatic representations from both the Eastern and Western blocs. This was why Collbohm found a Communist Chinese Embassy in Vientiane. Also, although the coalition government had long fallen apart, he was able to locate the Pathet Lao headquarters building. He discovered that the United States was deliberately maintaining a small presence with an ambassador; one Air Attache; one Army Attache; and a USAID chief, because William Sullivan, the head of the U.S. Mission, wanted to maintain a minimal staff as a way of encouraging the Laotians to do more for themselves and prevent them from becoming dependent on the Americans.[14]

From conversations with American officials in the capital, Collbohm gathered that the United States was adhering to the Geneva Accords of 1962 but fighting a covert war at the same time. Over lunch at the U.S. Embassy with a political officer,

---

[12] Kong Le eventually became army chief in the Lao government. In 1964, the Pathet Lao ejected his forces from the Plain of Jars. Kong Le was ousted from his post as army chief in November 1966 and went into exile.

[13] Frank Collbohm, "Trip Report, Part III: Laos, Thailand, Malaysia, Singapore, May 5–13, 1965," Santa Monica, Calif.: RAND Corporation, June 23, 1965, p. 6 (not available to the general public).

[14] Collbohm, "Trip Report, Part III," 1965, p. 1. Collbohm complained that American military advisors were spending too much time sitting in Vientiane and writing reports to meet an OSD requirement. They had "no time to go out and see things themselves," he wrote, and just accepted what the Lao told them. Intelligence gathering seemed haphazard: There was no cataloguing, no indexing of captured documents, and military interrogation reports were filed under the name of the prisoner.

Collbohm asked him about the restrictions on U.S. operations in Laos. The officer "made it very clear that he is following the policy established in 1962" and that the embassy did not want "to do anything that would force the Russians to react."[15] Covert action, the officer told Collbohm, gave the United States more freedom of action, because it did not "involve the prestige of the President," thus making it easier to "back down."

Covert action gave the American Mission "multiple means of doing things." For example, the political officer said, they were using "Air America, and Bird and Sons, and three other contractors," and if any of these were compromised, "we still have four more." The policy of the embassy was to talk about "peaceful help" but to keep quiet about operations that went well.[16] It preferred to let Souvanna announce the successes. One of the quiet operations that went well was related to Collbohm by Douglas S. Blaufarb, then the CIA station chief.

According to Collbohm "the people on the ground everywhere seem to want napalm," so he questioned the political officer about the prohibition of its use. The officer said that using napalm would have adverse political repercussions. He told Collbohm that air commanders had requested napalm, but that he had directed them to Souvanna. If the prime minister requested it, this would mean that he was in favor of it, but so far Souvanna had not asked for it. A Cold Warrior determined to fight communism, Collbohm asked whether the new napalm—which "has some kind of plastic jell that . . . will stick to things instead of running off" and which "will be in the theater pretty soon"—would "make a difference—especially if it has a different name." The officer said that "he might reconsider if it had a different name, but if it's called napalm, no."[17]

An aircraft and airpower enthusiast, Collbohm spent part of his visit discussing their use in Laos. He found that political constraints restricted the use of airpower. In a conversation with the American Army Attache, Collbohm wondered whether control of the Plain of Jars could be extended if air support was provided to ground forces in the area. The attache replied that gaining control of the entire Plain of Jars was possible if air support was available, but they were prohibited from doing as much as they

---

[15] Collbohm, "Trip Report, Part III," 1965, p. 2.

[16] Collbohm, "Trip Report, Part III," 1965, p. 2.

[17] Collbohm, "Trip Report, Part III," 1965, pp. 2–3. Collbohm wrote that he later discussed this matter with General William Westmoreland. The general told him the new weapon had been given the name of Napalm II, and that he was unhappy about this. In Japan, Collbohm raised the issue with Ambassador Edwin Reischauer, who told him that "it could make a difference if you gave it a different name." When Collbohm saw Admiral Ulysses S. Grant Sharp at CINCPAC, he again discussed the issue. Sharp told him that "they have had a big hassle and were worried about whether a new name would mean we were introducing a 'new massive weapon,' and that would be bad, so they decided it would be worse to have a new name than to call it napalm B instead of 2. They have decided to call it napalm B. At the moment that is where it stands." Collbohm wrote in his trip report that he intended to bring up the issue in Washington, as well. Collbohm, "Trip Report, Part III," 1965, pp. 3–4.

could. The Air Attache told Collbohm that the U.S. Air Force could help push back the Pathet Lao, but it had to rely on the tiny Lao Air Force, which had only 25 pilots organized into two units, each of which was supplied with 20 T-28 aircraft equipped with very limited ordnance. Nineteen more pilots were being trained.

In Collbohm's meeting with William Sullivan, the ambassador told him that, "What is happening [in Laos] is supposed to be very covert. Unlike in South Vietnam and most other places in the world where we are fighting insurgency, in Laos we are conducting insurgent operations" and supplying the guerrillas. In Sullivan's view, the operation was "doing everything insurgents do normally" against the Pathet Lao, and that the Hmong had been "very effective" in ambushing the Pathet Lao and targeting their supply line. The ambassador disclosed to Collbohm that the operation was "run by the Agency." While the CIA could "draw upon military support, sometimes for air support . . . most of the work is done under contract by people like Air America, Bird and Sons, and so on."[18] Douglas Blaufarb would later write in a RAND report he produced after becoming a RAND consultant that the CIA support of the Hmong guerrillas was closely controlled by the American ambassador and from the State Department, in order to avoid overextending resources and overcommitting the United States.[19]

During his stay, Collbohm was invited to go "up country" to check out the camps that had been set up for families of the Hmong guerrillas. The visit gave him a close look at how the clandestine war was affecting this ethnic minority. The camps were within one day's walking distance from the area in which the guerrillas were operating so that they could come and see their families from time to time. To sustain the families initially, they were given enough land to set up a little village, rice seeds to plant their crop, and enough rice to eat until the harvest. Everything else they had to do for themselves. For example, they had to grade their own property and build their own homes. The Hmong were self-sufficient people. Collbohm found that they did not want to use American tools and insisted on making their own. He watched as they made these tools in little forges they had built, using scrap iron supplied by the Americans. They were also resourceful, using as bed covers the small parachutes that Air America employed to drop rice supplies.

The Hmong were supplied by air, so the country was "just dotted with small airstrips," each "built on a hillside—flat on the top, and the hill comes down, then flat again."[20] Helios and porters would land and take off on these airstrips. Collbohm watched a Bird and Sons C-47 land with some supplies and take off empty. Typically, the Helios and Porters would roll downhill "almost to the bottom" before taking off.

---

[18] Collbohm, "Trip Report, Part III," 1965, pp. 2–3.

[19] Douglas S. Blaufarb, *Organizing and Managing Unconventional War in Laos, 1962–1970*, Santa Monica, Calif.: RAND Corporation, R-919-ARPA, January 1972.

[20] Collbohm, "Trip Report, Part III," 1965, pp. 4–5.

Aerial view of Pha Khao in Hmong territory.

From the first village, Collbohm flew in a little Helio to another village that had just been set up and was still awaiting its first rice crop. Collbohm and his party reached it on foot after the aircraft landed. The first thing they had to do was to visit the village chief in his house and share some tea and rice wine—a local alcohol that was kept in earthen jars and drunk communally through long thin straws. In talking to the locals, Collbohm found out that this was the fourth village that the guerrilla families had set up as they moved to keep close to the fighters. The practice was that, "When the guerrillas get more than a day's walk away, they abandon the village and build another one." Collbohm learned that the village was overcrowded, with about 3,000 people, including refugees it had taken in. It was the village of "legal camp followers—the families—women, children, and old men." The able-bodied males "were all away," and the villagers "had nothing to fight with."[21]

During his visit, Collbohm met with Vang Pao, now holding the rank of general, whom Collbohm described as "the head of the insurgent operation" as well as the chief of the Hmong tribe "and Province Chief." Vang Pao was in the village because Kong Le and some other generals had come in for a surprise meeting. Collbohm thought that Vang Pao was "a pretty smart fellow"[22]—an impression that was confirmed by Gerry Hickey, who accompanied Collbohm on this trip. Hickey revealed that the meeting occurred in Long Cheng (also called Long Tieng), Vang Pao's headquarters, located in the mountains with limestone peaks reminiscent of Chinese paintings. Hickey talked

---

[21] Collbohm, "Trip Report, Part III," 1965, p. 6.

[22] Collbohm, "Trip Report, Part III," 1965, p. 5.

to Vang Pao in French about articles that had been written about the culture of the Hmong; the general surprised him by displaying a good knowledge of these articles.

The Hmong commander Collbohm and Hickey met in Long Cheng was linked with the narcotics trade. Opium was the Hmong's traditional cash crop, and they were the largest producers in Laos because the strain they grew did exceedingly well at the high elevation at which they had settled. After slashing and burning vegetation, a farmer could grown opium in the same field for about ten years. Cultivating and harvesting were carried out mostly by women; they did not require the labor of men, so the absence of men during the war did not affect production—unless a field became exhausted and new land had to be cleared for cultivation. It was legal to possess opium in Laos, and the trade was not forbidden. The Hmong kept some to use as medication, and they sold the rest. Abuse and addiction were rare, so opium did not create social problems for them. During the colonial period, the French had helped the Hmong in their opium trade as a way to win and retain their loyalty, realizing that the Hmong's wish to defend their own region against the Viet Minh had a lot to do with a desire to defend their opium. The CIA saw this same motivation, although it referred to it as a wish by the Hmong to retain their way of life.

General Vang Pao was open about his trade in opium, and at one point "was storing about a ton of opium under his house" in Long Cheng.[23] Vang Pao did not smoke it himself, and he did not allow his soldiers to use it because "it made them too lethargic."[24] His goal was to sell it to outsiders. For him, "[i]t was like an emergency bank account, in case the Americans left entirely,"[25] and a means to win the loyalty of his subordinates. The CIA was aware of this trade but turned a blind eye, preferring to condone it as a traditional tribal practice because the Hmong were proving to be excellent mercenaries.[26] Before 1965, Chinese caravans would arrive at Hmong settlements at harvest time to buy up the opium supplies. However, when the fighting became heavy, they stopped coming to collect opium. It was alleged that starting in 1965, Air America began flying the opium to Vang Pao's headquarters in Long Tieng from villages north and east of the Plain of Jars. By this time, the CIA had built a 30,000-man Hmong army, which was assisting the United States in protecting radar installations crucial for the bombing of North Vietnam, rescuing American pilots shot down by the enemy, and fighting Pathet Lao forces. According to this allegation, Air America

---

[23] Warner, *Shooting at the Moon*, 1999, p. 81.

[24] Warner, *Shooting at the Moon*, 1999, p. 81.

[25] Warner, *Shooting at the Moon*, 1999, p. 81.

[26] The CIA, in general, did not attempt to change the ways of the Hmong. In a review of Operation MOMENTUM—as the support for the guerrillas was called—that he wrote after assuming his post as station chief in Vientiane, Douglas Blaufarb credited the success of the program to Vang Pao's leadership, but also to the Americans' respect for the tribal customs, including some that might strike Western observers as extremely superstitious. See Blaufarb, *Organizing and Managing*, 1972.

"was known to be flying Meo opium as late as 1971."[27] Also according to this allegation, the U.S. Embassy in Vientiane "adopted an attitude of benign neglect toward the opium traffic."[28] The allegation that Air America aided in the transportation of opium on Vang Pao's behalf has been denied by former covert American personnel working with the Hmong.

However, the big traffic in drugs was not in opium but in heroin—from refined opium—and it was centered in the northwest. General Ouane Rattikone, the Royalist commander in chief, dominated the heroin trade and got his supplies from major Burmese sources in the Golden Triangle—a major opium producing region that includes mountainous areas overlapping Thailand, Laos, and Burma, and bordering Yunnan Province in China. The heroin was smuggled into South Vietnam, which was viewed as a huge potential market because of the presence of half a million American servicemen. Over the years, accusations were leveled against the CIA that it was using profits from the narcotics trade—and from arms smuggling—to finance its proxy war in Laos and other operations. However, according to one account, such accusations were a myth, because the agency had no trouble getting all the funds it needed from Congress.[29]

On their brief visit, Frank Collbohm and Gerry Hickey saw Vang Pao only as the genial host. They did not see the other side of the Hmong leader. Vang Pao, in fact, "had a violent, brutal side." He kept "prisoners in sleeved 55-gallon barrels in holes in the ground and was not averse to summarily executing prisoners or even miscreants from his own tribe." However, this cruel trait could be ascribed to the culture of a people who "had survived in a harsh environment by being brutal." He was also "stubborn"—a characteristic he shared with his people.[30] At the same time, Vang Pao was a "tactically brilliant" man who held simplistic views of politics. To him, "capitalism was good, communism bad, period. The world was divided into good guys and bad guys . . . and if you were smart you went along with what the good guys said."[31] In the recollection of a former CIA agent who had worked with him, Vang Pao "had enough tricks up his sleeve tactically that he would play like a cat with a mouse, in terms of how to do this and that in a given campaign."[32]

For a man with only five years of formal education, Vang Pao was also extremely ambitious. He did not just want to be a great general: He wanted to be "the big man of Laos." Considering that he was the member of a tribal minority and that the lowland

---

[27] McCoy, *The Politics of Heroin*, 1972, p. 263.

[28] McCoy, *The Politics of Heroin*, 1972, p. 263.

[29] See Warner, *Shooting at the Moon*, 1999.

[30] Warner, *Shooting at the Moon*, 1999, p. 81.

[31] Warner, *Shooting at the Moon*, 1999, p. 81.

[32] Warner, *Shooting at the Moon*, 1999, p. 81.

Lao elite feared and despised him, this was an "astonishing ambition."[33] But American praise and support made him believe he could succeed. He reveled in his influence: the power to call in air support—he was the only Lao general who could tell American planes where to bomb—and the access to huge sums of money that he dispensed in "fistfuls . . . to people who humbly petitioned him."[34] The funds came from the CIA to pay the guerrillas. Each month, boxes and boxes of money arrived by plane at Long Cheng, from which Vang Pao and other commanders would take 10 to 20 percent off the top. This was considered "normal" by Asian standards, and "not 'graft' in the Western sense."[35] The CIA tolerated this corruption, viewing it as insignificant compared with the graft among the lowland Lao, because of the usefulness of Vang Pao and his tribal guerrillas.

Besides the Hmong, the CIA also recruited among the Lao Theung, ethnic minorities living at mid-elevation, below the Hmong. Many of these tribes and sub-tribes lived in the north of Laos and in the southern panhandle. It was among one of these ethnic groups that Steve Hosmer landed with Chuck Cooper, then working for USAID in Laos. They flew in one of the small aircraft that could "tuck their flaps way down so they could slow down" for landing uphill on a very short runway high up in the mountain, Hosmer recalled.[36] They were coming to visit the headquarters of a tribal chief in a typical tribal village, "with women and children and pigs." The chief had "all kinds of equipment." Cooper and Hosmer were taken down into a large go-down that looked like a big warehouse, to meet the chief. They found him sitting at a desk, and behind him they saw cases of Coca-Cola stacked up "from floor to ceiling" and going back as far as the eye could see. The Coca-Cola had been brought in by Air America, along with food and other supplies, and the chief personally kept it like "gold ore" to dispense to his people as a reward.[37]

The growth of the Hmong forces and their fierce resistance against the Pathet Lao did not deter the latter from gaining in strength, thanks to the assistance provided by North Vietnam. Yet, little was known about this support. In 1966, Ambassador William Sullivan asked RAND to conduct research on the Pathet Lao, their relationship with the North Vietnamese, and the role Hanoi was playing in Laos. In

---

[33] Warner, *Shooting at the Moon,* 1999, p. 277.

[34] Warner, *Shooting at the Moon,* 1999, p. 277.

[35] Warner, *Shooting at the Moon,* 1999, p. 120. In addition, "there were 'ghost' soldiers on the payroll, kick-backs aplenty, unequal levels of pay between units, and other peccadillos" (Warner, *Shooting at the Moon,* 1999, p. 120).

[36] Author interview with Steve Hosmer, 2004.

[37] Author nterview with Steve Hosmer, 2004.

response, RAND dispatched Joe Zasloff, who had initiated the Viet Cong Motivation and Morale Project in Vietnam in 1964, and Paul Langer, a Japan specialist in the Social Science Department. To Zasloff, his selection reflected recognition for the quality of his work in Vietnam. Zasloff took another leave of absence from the University of Pittsburgh and moved to Vientiane with his wife, Tela, to conduct what turned out to be the most important RAND work on Laos.

They were referred to USAID for logistics support and, with its help, they got a house, a car, and occasionally interpreters when they needed them. Zasloff and Langer had a "cozy relationship" with the embassy, and were provided with an office in the USAID compound and invited to sit in on the meetings of the USAID staff.[38] As the study progressed, they briefed Ambassador Sullivan frequently about the results of their research. In all, the two analysts spent eight months in Laos, from December 1966 to August 1967.

Zasloff recalled that Laos was much less developed than Vietnam. It was "laid back and rural . . . even Vientiane was a cluster of villages."[39] As "a sleepy backwater," it had a "much less active, much smaller, modern sector." Even in the modern sector, he said, "the intellectuals don't have the vibrancy of the Vietnamese intellectual community. You don't have this striv[ing] for literacy that you have in Vietnam. . . . On the other hand, the Lao people are sweet, gentle, and lovable, and everybody who goes to Laos warms to the people." Tela Zasloff remembered that she and her husband rented a newly built house on a street so new that no local had heard of it. In letters home, she wrote that she found Vientiane lovely, with wide streets and little traffic, and relaxed because the war was still remote. It had "none of the sadness and tensions [that] agitated the air of Saigon."[40]

The project was semi-secret. Tela was project administrator and researcher, and one of her main tasks was to clip information from the Foreign Broadcast Information Service that was relevant to the study her husband and Paul Langer were conducting. She worked surrounded by Lao communist documents, such as leaflets and manifestoes, which would have to be translated into English. Interviews of defectors and prisoners provided the main data on the Pathet Lao and the North Vietnamese. Zasloff recalled, however, that there were far fewer prisoners and defectors in Laos, compared with Vietnam, and that consequently the pool of respondents for him and Langer to draw upon was small. Interviews that were done had to be transcribed from tapes, and then processed and coded. The staff included several transcribers, one secretary, a few translators, and occasional interpreters.

The office consisted of a set of rooms in one of the air-conditioned buildings of the USAID compound. One dusty street ran through the compound, and along it stood

---

[38] Author interview with Joe Zasloff, 2003.

[39] Author interview with Joe Zasloff, 2003. The following Zasloff quotes are from this interview.

[40] Letters provided by Tela Zasloff.

Paul Langer on a field trip in Laos.

low yellow buildings housing, among other things, the post office, a restaurant, a movie house, a supply building, a commissary, and a carpool. Tela was based in Vientiane and did not travel to the province towns and mountain areas with her husband and Paul Langer.

For their research, Zasloff and Langer supplemented the data from documents with interviews with Laotians who knew the history of the communist movement, and prisoners and defectors.[41] They did not hire any interviewers, conducting the interviews themselves. Sometimes, Zasloff conducted the interviews in French with French-speaking respondents and other times he used an interpreter recommended by the U.S. Mission to translate from Lao to English, or the Vietnamese wife of an American U.S. aid employee to translate from Vietnamese to English. Zasloff remembered that Langer was "better at talking than listening." The focus of the study was different from that of the Viet Cong Motivation and Morale Project, in that it looked mainly at the "history and political sociology" of the Lao communist movement. Zasloff recalled that the obscure role of the Lao Communist Party was the issue that interested him

---

[41] Later, as they expanded their research to existing Western literature about Laos, they would find that there was a dearth of information about modern Laos and the Lao communist movement. This was in marked contrast to the situation in Vietnam, where the U.S. research effort had invested enormous resources in studying the Viet Cong and their organization, policies, and operations. In Laos, no similar effort had been undertaken to study the Lao revolutionary movement, with the result that little was known about how the Pathet Lao came into existence, how the movement evolved, and how it was organized and led.

Joe Zasloff in Sayaboury.

the most at the time. There was a secret Lao People's Revolutionary Party headed by Pathet Lao leaders, but he and Langer were not sure whether this was in fact the Lao Communist Party itself. Zasloff recalled that "it was hard to get any information on this secret party," because the Pathet Lao "had a deliberate policy of keeping it secret." According to him, even Prime Minister Souvanna Phouma, who was "a sophisticated politician," was not aware of what it was. When Zasloff asked him, "Is Souphanouvong a member of this Party?" Souvanna "just passed it off." Zasloff concluded that, "modern political organizations" did not interest the Lao as much as family ties in political interaction.

The Pathet Lao had originated in the Lao *Issara*, or "Free Lao" independence movement under the French, so Zasloff and Langer interviewed former members of this group, including such prominent personalities as Prince Souvanna Phouma, the prime minister. They found that at the beginning, the Lao *Issara* was a united group but later was sundered into different factions. The split was epitomized by the political paths taken by the three most prominent members of the group, who were brothers from an aristocratic family: Prince Phetsarath, the leader of the Lao *Issara*; Prince Souvanna Phouma; and Prince Souphanouvong. Prince Phetsarath remained in the middle of the political spectrum; Souvanna Phouma became a neutralist, and Souphanouvong, a communist. "So, there's a whole story to tell about the origins of this movement," Zasloff said. Since the members of the Lao *Issara* had grown up during the colonial period, there were many people who spoke French and were available—and willing—to talk about it.

The case of the three princes also illustrated the nature of the Lao elite. Through the political officer at the U.S. Embassy, a "very voluble" man who knew the gossip of Laos, Zasloff and Langer picked up valuable insight into this elite, which comprised "a series of big families around the country." To understand the politics of Laos, one had to understand family relationships, he recalled. An illustrative example was the relationship between Prime Minister Souvanna Phouma and Prince Souphanouvong, nicknamed the Red Prince because of his communist affiliation. Zasloff remembered Prince Souvanna Phouma telling him at one point that he and Prince Souphanouvong dined together when his half-brother was in Vientiane. When Zasloff asked him, "Do you have political trouble with him?" Souvanna replied, "Politics has nothing to do with family ties." These bonds were so strong that they prevented "complete alienation" among relatives belonging to competing political groups.[42]

In the report Zasloff and Langer produced from their research, they wrote that practically all the Pathet Lao leaders had close relatives in the Royal Lao Government. These family ties tended to remain unbroken, except during times when fighting became intense. Among the older generation, friendly relations with family members who were political enemies were not frowned upon among the upper ranks. For example, during the period when he was residing in Vientiane following the 1962 Geneva Accords, Prince Souphanouvong would visit his mother who was living with a close relative whose husband would attack him on the floor of the National Assembly in the morning and invite him to a family dinner in the evening. Talking to such members of the Lao elite provided Zasloff and Langer with information about the origin of the Pathet Lao. But for information about what North Vietnam was doing in Laos, they had to turn to defectors and prisoners.

When Zasloff arrived in Vientiane in 1967, the truce established by the 1962 Geneva Accords was still officially in effect, and Laos was still partitioned de facto into two zones. The Royal Lao Government controlled the valleys next to the Mekong River, from Luang Prabang to Vientiane. The Pathet Lao controlled the border area with Vietnam. The military situation seesawed with the weather. In the dry season, the North Vietnamese would push forward; in the wet season, they would pause. Everybody at the time, however, knew that the Pathet Lao—or, more precisely, the North Vietnamese—if they wished to make the effort, could take any target in Laos fairly quickly. But it was not in their interest to do so, because their primary objective in Laos was to maintain access to South Vietnam through the Ho Chi Minh Trail. Consequently, they were content to live with a stalemate.

The best source about the role North Vietnam played in Laos came from a defector Zasloff and Langer interviewed. Mai Dai Hap was a North Vietnamese captain

---

[42] Author interview with Joe Zasloff, 2003.

who had served as a military advisor to a Pathet Lao battalion in Nam Tha Province in northern Laos from February 1964 until he defected in December 1966. Through an interpreter, Zasloff and Langer interviewed him in April and May 1967, in ten sessions lasting three to four hours each. They found him intelligent and articulate, with solid analytic skills, a good command of the Lao language, and knowledge of military matters, along with sensitivity to political issues. The transcript of the interview ran to 100 pages. At their request, Hap also provided written answers to a set of questions and wrote a 70-page account describing his experiences as a military advisor. His testimony provided valuable insight into the role of North Vietnam in Laos, which Zasloff concluded was akin to the one played by the United States in South Vietnam.

Using excerpts from his testimony, Langer and Zasloff produced a report in which they let Mai Dai Hap speak for himself, so that they could show how he—an advisor to a Pathet Lao battalion—viewed the problems he had to confront and how he attempted to solve them.[43] The authors noted that Hap's account was confirmed by evidence found in documents and by the testimony of Pathet Lao defectors and other North Vietnamese military personnel who deserted their posts in Laos.

To put the captain's account into context, the authors preceded the excerpts with a section on the historical relationship between the Vietnamese and the Pathet Lao, starting in the colonial period, when Vietnam, Cambodia, and Laos were combined to form French Indochina. It was in those colonial days that the Vietnamese community in Laos expanded with the influx of civil servants and immigrants. The bureaucrats were recruited by the French from Vietnam—the most advanced and the most populous among the three Indochinese countries—to help them run Laos. At the same time, Vietnamese immigrants flocked to Laos in search of economic opportunities. The majority settled in towns along the Mekong River and, together with the overseas Chinese, they dominated Laotian crafts and trade. When World War II ended, about 50,000 Vietnamese were living in Laos. Vietnamese influence grew, and, in time, several Pathet Lao leaders would develop personal ties with Vietnam.

The Lao *Issara* independence movement was stimulated by the example of the Viet Minh, from whom they obtained encouragement as well as support. The Viet Minh provided money, weapons, advice, and personnel for the establishment of small resistance bases in the mountainous region bordering Vietnam. In 1949, the Lao independence movement split. While some within the Lao *Issara* accepted the French offer of autonomy within the French Union, another group, led by Prince Souphanouvong, chose to continue the struggle for complete independence alongside the Viet Minh.

The Pathet Lao evolved from the merger of Souphanouvong's group with several small Lao guerrilla forces located in eastern Laos and North Vietnam. As in Vietnam, a front, the Neo Lao Hak Sat—was set up to present a "public face" to the world, but

---

[43] Paul F. Langer and Joseph J. Zasloff, *The North Vietnamese Military Adviser in Laos: A First Hand Account*, Santa Monica, Calif.: RAND Corporation, RM-5688-ARPA, July 1968.

real power was invested in the Phak Pasason Lao (or "Lao People's Party"), a semi-clandestine organization with Marxist-Leninist leanings. The secretary general of this party was Kaysone Phoumvihane. The historical relationship between Vietnam and the Pathet Lao had left a distinct Vietnamese imprint on their organization. The ties with Vietnam were also evident in the personal bonds the three most prominent Pathet Lao leaders had with their neighboring country: Kaysone was half-Vietnamese, and both Souphanouvong, the chairman of the NLHS, and Nouhak Phoumsavan, perhaps the second most powerful figure in the movement, had Vietnamese wives.

In 1953–1954, Viet Minh forces, assisted by a small number of Pathet Lao, launched a military offensive that swept through northeastern, central, and southern Laos, took the provinces of Phong Saly and Sam Neua, and led to the Viet Minh's victory over the French at Dien Bien Phu. This pattern of operation, with the North Vietnamese troops assuming the brunt of the attacks, would be continued by North Vietnam later in Laos. After the Geneva Conference of 1954, most Vietnamese forces withdrew, but North Vietnamese military and political cadres stayed behind in Phong Saly and Sam Neua to advise the Pathet Lao, fill certain technical posts, and provide military and political training. When hostilities resumed, it was the North Vietnamese troops who gave the Pathet Lao the military edge to expand the region under their control, so that by the time the 1962 Geneva Conference established an unofficial cease-fire line, about half of the territory of Laos was in their hands.

Since that time, North Vietnam had continued to maintain its presence in Laos through its own units operating separately and through its advisors and support personnel assigned to the Pathet Lao. Mai Dai Hap was one of these advisors. Hap came from a peasant family in a village of Thanh Hoa Province, in the coastal lowlands of North Vietnam. He joined the Viet Minh at age 20 and became a member of the Lao Dong (Communist) Party two years later. He was promoted steadily and spent most of his army service in the Northwest Military Region in North Vietnam, a highland area close to Laos. In early 1964, he, along with 29 other military personnel, was assigned to serve in Laos.

North Vietnam used two organizations to run its advisory effort in Laos. Group 959, located near Hanoi, provided political guidance and administrative support to the Pathet Lao and received instructions from the Central Committee of the Vietnamese Communist Party and from the Commander in Chief of the North Vietnamese forces. Purely military matters were handled by the Northwest Military Region Headquarters in Son La in North Vietnam, which coordinated North Vietnamese military activities in northern Laos. Personnel of these headquarters stayed in close touch with advisors in Laos, and also dispatched inspectors to check their work.

The North Vietnamese advisors were embedded at critical echelons throughout the Pathet Lao political, military, and administrative organization to provide guidance, training, logistics support, medical and technical aid, and communications. On the civilian side, North Vietnamese advisors operated at the province level. The political advisors functioned through the Lao Communist Party, and the administrative advisors worked through the Neo Lao Hak Sat political front in such fields as communications, economic affairs, and police. On the military side, an advisory mission operated in each province to give military advice to the Lao provincial leadership and direct the Vietnamese military advisors assigned to Pathet Lao units in the province. Usually, each Pathet Lao battalion had one military advisor and one political advisor.

The day before Hap and his contingent left for Laos, their brigade commander gave a farewell address in which he told them that serving in Laos was the same as serving at home. It was noteworthy that Hap and his group made their journey to Laos through southern China. Active North Vietnamese involvement was demonstrated by the fact that, along the way, they met the first battalion of the 316th NVA Brigade, which was also heading for Laos, and were joined by the battalion commander and the executive officer of the 408th Pathet Lao Battalion, returning home from training in Hanoi. Subsequently, Hap and his group crossed into Laos and reported for duty with the 408th Pathet Lao Battalion, which operated in the northern area of Nam Tha Province, along the border with China.

In his assignment with the Lao battalion, Hap trained its personnel and planned and guided its operations. Without such vital support, the Pathet Lao forces would find it difficult to sustain their insurgency against the Royal Lao Government. As Hap put it, "Generally speaking, everything is initiated by the North Vietnamese advisors, be it important or unimportant. If the North Vietnamese advisory machinery were to get stuck, the Pathet Lao machinery would be paralyzed."[44] Like other North Vietnamese advisors and cadres, Hap had internalized the admonition that he should consider the Pathet Lao battalion to which he was assigned as his own unit, and in helping the Pathet Lao carry out their duties, he must act as if those duties were his own. As an advisor, he was "like a helmsman" and the Pathet Lao were "like the crew," and it was the job of the helmsman to "guide the boat to its port."[45] The advisor should eschew action that might undermine "the friendship and solidarity between Laos and Vietnam." If anything damaging happened, "the North Vietnamese advisers must bear the major responsibility, no matter who is right or wrong."[46] This meant, in practice, that the military advisor had to get to know the Pathet Lao organization thoroughly, including "the state of the unit's equipment, food supplies, arms, and ammunition." In addition, he had to obtain "all the information about the enemy's situation [and] the population."[47] He had to design his military plan according to what he had learned. Another function of the military advisor was to provide training. Besides Hap, the bat-

---

[44] Langer and Zasloff, *The North Vietnamese Military Adviser in Laos*, 1968, p. vi.

[45] Langer and Zasloff, *The North Vietnamese Military Adviser in Laos*, 1968, p. 19.

[46] Langer and Zasloff, *The North Vietnamese Military Adviser in Laos*, 1968, p. 19.

[47] Langer and Zasloff, *The North Vietnamese Military Adviser in Laos*, 1968, p. 19.

talion also had a Vietnamese political advisor to assist in matters dealing with ideology and morale.

The frustrations that Hap encountered were reminiscent of those encountered by American military advisors in South Vietnam. He complained that the Pathet Lao troops were inferior to those in North Vietnam. They lacked discipline and did as they liked. They had little sense of responsibility and carried out only a portion of the activities that had been planned. Soldiers would get drunk or chase girls, or they would disappear into the woods to "shoot birds or hunt deer."[48] The Pathet Lao soldiers were "poor fighters and poor shots."[49] The Pathet Lao forces were "weak," and if they were sent somewhere, a Vietnamese unit had to go with them. If they took part in a joint attack, the North Vietnamese troops had to shoulder the brunt of the fighting.[50]

Hap thought that the Lao military leadership was poor. Lao cadres "worked when they liked; when they were depressed, they would do nothing. If their pride was hurt, they would refuse to listen to the adviser."[51] During combat, they could not control the soldiers when things got tough. Between operations, they "cared very little about their units."[52] The battalion's morale went up and down with successes and reverses. Hap revealed that "whenever we won a victory, or whenever the enemy eased his pressure, the Pathet Lao troops became careless. If we met with defeat or faced a difficult situation, they lost their fighting spirit and were discouraged and confused."[53] Relations with his counterpart, the battalion commander, could be rocky at times. Hap described one incident during which the battalion commander got drunk and became impatient and testy with his Vietnamese political advisor.

Hap lived in the field with the battalion. Although he could live separately and eat better with the daily stipend he received from his government, Hap chose to share the hardships of his battalion. "It was wartime," he said, and he and the political advisor "did not feel right eating separately." Each day, they contributed eight kip of Lao money to the unit for food—the same amount each Lao received per day. Eating with the Lao was hard "but we just closed our eyes and ate the way the Lao did."[54] At the beginning, however, the unit was stationed in Muong Sing, a populous and prosperous settlement, from January to September 1965, and things were relatively peaceful, so his living conditions were better. Hap described Muong Sing as a place with "animated

---

[48] Langer and Zasloff, *The North Vietnamese Military Adviser in Laos*, 1968, p. 24.

[49] Langer and Zasloff, *The North Vietnamese Military Adviser in Laos*, 1968, p. 32.

[50] Langer and Zasloff, *The North Vietnamese Military Adviser in Laos*, 1968, p. 32.

[51] Langer and Zasloff, *The North Vietnamese Military Adviser in Laos*, 1968, p. 23.

[52] Langer and Zasloff, *The North Vietnamese Military Adviser in Laos*, 1968, p. 23.

[53] Langer and Zasloff, *The North Vietnamese Military Adviser in Laos*, 1968, p. 23.

[54] Langer and Zasloff, *The North Vietnamese Military Adviser in Laos*, 1968, p. 29. Just as American advisors found Vietnamese food difficult to get used to, Vietnamese in general found Lao cuisine crude.

market activities, a clear communications line to China, an adequate supply of food and commodities, and rather low market prices." Food was ample, and the Vietnamese could organize their own mess. At that time, "the life of a battalion adviser was quite 'high class,'" and Hap "had no thought other than to fulfill my task."[55]

In December 1965, however, things began to change for the worse. His unit took part in dangerous operations and suffered reverses. In late 1965, Vietnamese forces, which had been stationed nearby, were sent elsewhere, leaving Hap's battalion to face the enemy on their own. Although the Pathet Lao managed to drive the Royal Lao Government forces out of the area, Hap was apprehensive, because his battalion would no longer enjoy the support of the Vietnamese units. As were the men in his battalion, Hap was pessimistic and discouraged but had to show enthusiasm and courage to set an example. By this time, he had begun a liaison with a Lao woman, although he had a family back in Vietnam. He had to keep the relationship secret, because, as an advisor on mission in Laos, he had to adhere to strict behavior and to abstain from chasing after women and marrying a local Lao. As a Vietnamese officer, if his conduct became known to his superior, he would be disciplined. On home leave in 1966, he requested to be reassigned but was told to return to his post in Nam Tha. He decided that he had to somehow escape this situation, and in December 1966, he and his wife defected.

Hap's testimony was included in the final report Zasloff and Langer prepared, which they presented to Ambassador Sullivan.[56] Zasloff remembered that they got positive feedback from the ambassador and from the head of USAID, but could not recall whether they gave briefings in Washington. The report was based on field research; interviews with defectors and prisoners; existing literature; and interviews conducted in Laos and in Washington with people knowledgeable about Laos. Of these knowledgeable people, a number had attended school during the French colonial period, with Lao and Vietnamese classmates who would later become their enemies. Others were linked to these adversaries through family ties, or had belonged to the same political groups, or had sat on opposite sides of the negotiation table.

The defectors and prisoners provided the most revealing information about the role of the Vietnamese in Laos. Some among them were officers with experience and knowledge regarding the relationship between the Pathet Lao and North Vietnamese forces. In addition, the authors also studied reports issued by the Royal Lao Government from interrogations of North Vietnamese prisoners and defectors, which allowed them to assemble a composite picture of North Vietnamese operations in Laos. Langer and Zasloff also used captured Lao and Vietnamese documents—including diaries and internal communications, textbooks, newspapers, propaganda literature, and posters—and radio broadcasts.

---

[55] Langer and Zasloff, *The North Vietnamese Military Adviser in Laos*, 1968, p. 29.

[56] P. F. Langer, and J. J. Zasloff, *Revolution in Laos: The North Vietnamese and the Pathet Lao*, Santa Monica, Calif.: RAND Corporation, RM-5935-ARPA, September 1969.

Despite the large amount of data collected, Zasloff and Langer felt that their research had been hindered by a number of factors, such as the paucity of information; the secrecy that surrounded communist operations; the lack of prominent defectors from the communist ranks; and the inaccessibility of communist decisionmakers residing in communist zones. The average defector they interviewed, being far removed from the inner circle where important policy and organization issues were decided, had a limited perspective and were unable to place events in a broader context. Finally, researching the North Vietnamese role in Laos was made all the more difficult by Hanoi's efforts to hide what it was doing. In spite of these difficulties, Zasloff and Langer thought that they had managed to gather a body of data that was large and reliable enough to piece together the complex role the North Vietnamese played in the Lao revolution. Since their work was groundbreaking in shedding light on this topic—and remains unique in its scope and depth to this day—it would be worthwhile to examine it at some length.

Zasloff and Langer explained that the objective of the study was to track the development of the relationship between the Pathet Lao and the North Vietnamese and to determine the precise nature of this relationship—a relationship that had turned the Pathet Lao from a movement commanding little standing at the 1954 Geneva Conference into a formidable player in the current struggle in Laos. On the whole, they found that this relationship was historical, strong, and, above all, critical for the Pathet Lao. North Vietnam had played a significant, remarkable, and pervasive role in not only creating but also shaping the Pathet Lao into a replica of the DRV. It had chosen and molded the Lao leadership into a cohesive, stable, and dedicated group that had served the movement well for over two decades, providing political and ideological training to practically the entire Pathet Lao cadre structure and helping these cadres build and control an army, a bureaucracy, a Communist Party, and mass organizations. It had given direction and cohesion to the movement, without which the Pathet Lao would have been fractured by the ethnic, cultural, social, and economic differences prevalent in the zones under their control. Without the military assistance of North Vietnam, the Pathet Lao would have been unable to expand their territory. Yet, North Vietnam was able to achieve all this progress without provoking resentment on the part of their allies—by relying on a political and military advisory system it had developed and honed over decades. In conclusion, Zasloff and Langer wrote that "the Lao revolutionary movement owes its existence to the direct initiative, guidance, and support of the Viet Minh," and that since 1954 it had remained "heavily dependent on Vietnamese assistance and direction."[57]

---

[57] Langer and Zasloff, *Revolution in Laos*, 1969, p. v.

Zasloff and Langer began with a review of the geographical, ethnic, social, and political conditions of Laos that had shaped the Pathet Lao, and then proceeded to focus on the history and scope of their relationship with the Vietnamese. Their analysis indicated that, from the outset, the natural and social environment of Laos posed formidable obstacles for the Lao revolutionaries and pushed them to turn toward Vietnam for protection and sustenance. In researching the topography, the authors concluded that, even if political considerations had not thrust the Lao revolutionary movement into an alliance with the Vietnamese communists, the need to survive for the Pathet Lao—or any Lao group that was competing for power from a base in the eastern region—would have driven them to seek the support of their more powerful neighbor. This area was mountainous, sparsely inhabited by ethnic minorities, accessible only via trails not suited for cars and trucks, and lacking in natural and human resources. While the region offered an ideal terrain for insurgents to conceal themselves and to survive despite the pressure from a government that controlled the greater resources in the Mekong Valley and that was aided by Thailand and the Western powers, the low level of economic development left the Pathet Lao without the requisites for sustaining their struggle: a trained military and civilian personnel, production facilities, good communications, and organizational skills to direct their affairs.

Yet the heavy reliance of the Pathet Lao on the Vietnamese was not marred by the hostility characteristic of the relationship between those who gave aid and those who received it. In view of the prevalence of nationalism in Asia, one would expect that Vietnamese involvement would provoke nationalistic antagonism among the Pathet Lao, but this had not been the case. One possible reason was that Vietnamese domination was the extension of a historical relationship. Under the Vietnamese monarchy, Lao kings had to accept the suzerainty of the Vietnamese court and send tribute. The Vietnamese continued to dominate Laos during the French period, when the French brought in civil servants from Vietnam to administer the country and the Vietnamese immigrant community grew and began to assume a leading economic role. The domination had provoked little resentment among the lowland Lao, except for a segment within the elite who feared Vietnamese aggressiveness, organization, and drive. Such apprehension, however, did not deter frequent intermarriage between the Lao and Vietnamese elite. The absence of the fierce nationalism and resentment of foreign influence commonly evident in contemporary Asia thus eased the Pathet Lao acceptance of Vietnamese guidance and support.

Nonetheless, this state of affairs was a detriment for the Pathet Lao, since they could not exploit nationalism—a potent force for other political groups in Asia—to build their movement: all the more so, because the lack of nationalistic feelings was even more pronounced among the ethnic minorities living in the mountainous areas where they maintained their bases. As a substitute, to appeal to the population, they had to stoke opposition to American and Thai imperialism. But this appeal was not as attractive in Laos because xenophobia was milder than elsewhere in Asia. Neither could the Pathet Lao invoke social injustice as a cause since gaping inequities, uneven land distribution, or abject poverty existing side by side with great and conspicuous wealth, or oppression by government officials, or widespread exploitation of the poor by the rich did not exist in Laos—as they did in Vietnam.

In addition, the Laotians' political apathy made it difficult for the Pathet Lao to mobilize popular support. The average person in the rural areas—and even in the few towns in the country—had a limited horizon and was not concerned with affairs beyond his own interests. The population did not participate much in national life, partly because communications were poor and illiteracy was widespread. The Lao, even the educated elite, showed little interest in intellectual attainment and in ideology. Even among the Lao revolutionaries, ideology hardly played a role. Lastly, the Pathet Lao could not lay claim to traditional leadership. In the lowlands, the Lao traditionally looked to a small elite for leadership, but in the highlands, the Pathet Lao leaders could not count on this tendency. Here, the allegiance of the ethnic minorities was claimed by the chief of each tribe. Under such prevailing social, political, historical, and economic conditions, the Lao revolutionaries by necessity had to turn to North Vietnam.

Psychologically also, their long association with Vietnam, starting in the French period, had conditioned them to accept dependence on and advice from Vietnam. But other ties existed to bind them to the Vietnamese, for beyond these practical considerations, the Lao communists shared the Vietnamese opposition to the French in the past and opposition to the United States at the present time. In addition, they also shared the same world view and a belief in the kinds of solutions best suited to solve its problems. This affinity was in some instances reinforced by family relations or marriage bonds with Vietnamese.

The prototypical Lao revolutionary was Prince Souphanouvong, who was married to a Vietnamese follower of Ho Chi Minh. Prior to his return to Laos in 1945, Souphanouvong had spent most of his adult life outside of Laos, largely in Vietnam as a student and then as an engineer. He had more interaction with Vietnamese than he did with the Lao of his generation. He spoke fluent Vietnamese and may have felt more of an intellectual affinity with the educated Vietnamese than with the Lao from his upper class. In general, he deplored the political passivity of the Lao and their disinclination to take action, and he admired the dynamism of the Vietnamese. However, his cooperation with the Vietnamese may well have stemmed more from pragmatic than from ideological considerations. He was ambitious, but in family hierarchy, he was the younger brother to two famous aristocrats: Prince Phetsarath, a leader of the Lao nationalist independence movement; and Prince Souvanna Phouma. His lack of seniority would make it difficult for him to reach the top leadership position. Besides, during the colonial era, his brothers could count on the support of Thailand, so he believed that only by securing Vietnamese assistance would he be able to compete and climb to the highest leadership position.

For the Vietnamese, the alliance with the Pathet Lao served their purpose. During the colonial period, the Viet Minh's primary goal was to expel the French, so it was in their interest to help create and nurture a Lao organization that would work in tandem with them toward this goal. No matter how small, whatever contribution the Lao could make to weaken the French would be useful for the Viet Minh's struggle. Since then, self-interest continued to motivate North Vietnam in guiding and supporting the Pathet Lao. Through its involvement, North Vietnam was pursuing three objectives: protecting its borders, maintaining access to South Vietnam, and establishing a friendly political regime in a neighboring country.

By keeping the Pathet Lao zone as a buffer, the DRV could reduce the danger that the United States and its allies might undertake hostile activities—such as fomenting unrest among the ethnic minorities living on both sides of the border—to threaten its security. Furthermore, Pathet Lao control allowed the DRV to secure its access to South Vietnam via the Ho Chi Minh Trail. As the war in the South intensified, control of the infiltration route was so crucial that North Vietnam practically took over the portion of the corridor that ran through southern Laos, a move that was facilitated by Pathet Lao control of the area. Apart from self-interest, there was an additional reason that explained the Vietnamese support for the Pathet Lao: Vietnamese communists, out of proletarian international solidarity, would naturally feel well-disposed to helping the Pathet Lao—their revolutionary comrades—fight the pro-West, corrupt, and feudal Lao government.

The DRV had been supremely adroit at concealing its real role. This secrecy was partly due to the usual way in which communist insurgents operated—and partly to a wish to avoid international scrutiny. North Vietnamese intervention was accomplished through its advisory personnel, as well as through its own troops. Hanoi maintained a force of about 40,000 fighters in Laos to accomplish three missions: protect the border, operate the infiltration route, and strengthen the Pathet Lao. The majority of this force, about 25,000 soldiers, was assigned to maintain and protect the Ho Chi Minh Trail. The rest included about 700 advisors, whose role had been discussed in the report of Mai Dai Hap, and about 7,000 troops assigned to several provinces to operate with the Lao People's Liberation Army (LPLA). However, they remained in their own units, received orders from their own officers, and lived and fought separately.

In addition, North Vietnam kept mobile units that could be dispatched wherever required in Laos. It also maintained an efficient operation serving both North Vietnamese and Lao troops, including heavy weapons and anti-aircraft guns, a medical system, a communications network, logistics operations, and transportation units. Compared with South Vietnam, the DRV enjoyed two advantages in stationing troops in Laos: It faced a much weaker enemy in the Royal Lao Government, as opposed to the GVN, and it could supply and communicate easily with its troops just across the border.

Besides securing the border, North Vietnamese troops in Laos had the mission of contributing to the DRV's primary objective: to bring the war in South Vietnam to a successful conclusion by keeping the pipeline to the South open. The presence of the troops acted as a deterrence and sent a clear signal to the United States and Thailand that Hanoi would fight aggressively to defend this vital artery and would overrun other regions of Laos if the United States and its allies made inroads into the border area and disrupted the infiltration route. If it had wanted to, North Vietnam could have used its forces in Laos to break the stalemate that had prevailed since the 1962 Geneva Accords. But it had not done so because it feared that expanding the Lao conflict would risk American and Thai intervention, forcing North Vietnam to divert previous resources from its primary objective, which was to win the war in South Vietnam. In the meantime, both sides in Laos were content to hold the line while waiting for a resolution to the Vietnam War, which would, in turn, dictate the future of Laos.

The other mission of North Vietnamese troops was to strengthen the Lao People's Liberation Army by coordinating military efforts, often by operating alongside them. The usual pattern was for special shock troops sent from North Vietnam to weaken RLG defense positions. After the attack, the commandos withdrew and let Lao and Vietnamese troops move in to take their place and consolidate the gains. The presence of the NVA was also meant to deter the RLG. For example, in 1967–1968, a *Forces Armees Royales* (FAR), or Royal Armed Forces, commander in southern Laos undertook an ambitious pacification drive in the Sedone Valley. NVA troops with LPLA support attacked an important post and put pressure throughout the region, wiping out the pacification gains that had been achieved. The attack was intended to demonstrate how fragile the FAR were and to warn the RLG not to challenge the DRV and its Lao ally. Overall, North Vietnam had succeeded in forging a successful military partnership between its troops and those of the Pathet Lao, who respected them for their leadership, organization, and fighting spirit. Even in their rare dealings with the local people, North Vietnamese troops had avoided provoking antagonism by adhering to a strict code of conduct.

Next to stationing troops, North Vietnam used a military and political advisory system developed over the years to bolster and influence the Pathet Lao, as Mai Dai Hap's account indicates. In general, Vietnamese advisors were effective and kept resentment to a minimum. They succeeded by being tactful in dealing with their counterparts suggesting rather than demanding, maintaining an unobtrusive presence and circumspect role, avoiding offending the sensitivities of their Pathet Lao counterparts, and working through the appropriate channels. Within the Pathet Lao forces, the North Vietnamese advisors were able to forge close bonds by sharing the forces' hardships: living among them, wearing the same clothes, and eating the same food. On the civilian side, political advisors, embedded at key points in the organization of the Neo Lao Hak Sat and the Lao Communist Party, assisted the Pathet Lao in controlling their political and military structure. This access to decisionmakers at critical junctures in the Pathet Lao movement would give North Vietnam a variety of options, regardless of its future aims in Laos.

But the advisory effort was not without its problems, mainly because of cultural differences, as Mai Dai Hap had attested. The contrast in styles, for example, was quite stark. The easygoing Lao were astounded by the austere habits of the Vietnamese, and although they respected them for their self-control, they were not inclined to emulate them. The Vietnamese, for their part, had plenty of bad things to say about their allies, complaining about the Pathet Lao's lack of organization and ideological commitment, and lackadaisical attitude. They frequently felt frustrated, and many wished that their country would intervene more directly. However, the Hanoi leaders had found it desirable to keep things the way they were.

Lastly, Zasloff and Langer attempted to predict the long-range objectives of North Vietnam in Laos and to answer the question: Beyond the basic goals of keeping its border safe, securing its infiltration route, and helping to create a friendly regime in Laos, did North Vietnam harbor expansionist designs over Laos? Their answer was, "Yes." One reason was the historical relationship. From the past to the present, Vietnam had viewed Laos as part of its sphere of influence; therefore, Hanoi might find it natural to retain its domination over Laos in the future. Ultimately, what the North Vietnamese would choose to do in Laos depended on what happened in South Vietnam. But regardless of the outcome in Vietnam, Zasloff and Langer believed that North Vietnam would continue to view the border region—in particular, the provinces of Phong Saly, Luang Prabang, Sam Neua, and Xieng Khouang—as critical to its own national security and would endeavor to keep these areas from falling under the control of forces inimical to its interests.

Paul Langer and Joe Zasloff's report was unique in elucidating the secret role North Vietnam played in Laos. The report was subsequently published as a book under the title *Partners in the Struggle for Laos* by Harvard University Press in 1971. In a review of their book in *The New York Times* on February 21, 1971, David K. Wyatt, a professor of history at Cornell University, lauded the authors for their substantial contribution to the knowledge of the little-understood involvement of North Vietnam in the chaos that was Laos. The other contribution of their work, Wyatt wrote, was to remind readers that the situation in Laos had evolved too far to bring it back to what it had been in 1954 or 1962. Long-standing interests and recent developments had turned Laos into "an even more explosive scene of conflict in Southeast Asia than it was a decade ago," and there was no way one could "turn back the clock," no matter how much one wished to do so. This study by Zasloff and Langer represented the only important field research project for RAND in Laos.[58]

---

[58]   Later, Zasloff would supplement the data with further research for a book on the organization and leadership of the Pathet Lao. It was an elaboration of themes already touched on in the RAND report. Langer would write a couple of short papers on Laos, such as *Search for Peace in the Midst of War*, P-3748, December 1967; *Preparing for a Settlement in Vietnam*, P-4024, February 1969; and *Education in the Pathet Lao Zone*, P-4726, 1971.

♣ ♣ ♣

While Zasloff's and Langer's research looked at the communist side of the Lao struggle, consultant Douglas Blaufarb's report provided a perspective on the activities of the other major protagonist in the Lao conflict: the United States.[59] His paper served to bookend the report by Zasloff and Langer. Blaufarb's work dealt with the four-and-a-half-year tenure of Ambassador William Sullivan, from 1964 to 1969, and provided an insider's view of the economic and military assistance—including air support—the U.S. Mission provided the Hmong guerrillas to fight a proxy war against the Pathet Lao and North Vietnamese.

In analyzing the U.S. Mission's tribal program, Blaufarb concluded that the most critical factor contributing to its success was the sole control exercised by Sullivan—without interference from outside authorities—and the cohesion that control brought to the effort. Sullivan had a broad sweep of responsibilities. He made all decisions pertaining to Laos, civilian and military; controlled U.S. military and paramilitary personnel and activities in the country; and directly coordinated with military commands outside of Laos on important policy matters. Such power over military and paramilitary activities was unusual for a diplomatic envoy. But Sullivan enjoyed a broad mandate that made him Chief of Mission, as well as Director of Operations for all U.S. government programs in Laos. The wide range of responsibilities for the ambassador to Laos dated from the Kennedy Administration, when the president was unhappy over the division and indecisiveness in the U.S. Mission there and wanted to put power in the hands of one individual. More importantly, the Geneva Accords of 1962 ruled out the presence of an American military command in Laos, so Washington had to rely on the Chief of Mission to direct and control its military involvement. "Thus," Blaufarb reported, "by dint of special circumstances, Laos has become the setting for an organizational arrangement, somewhat unusual in U.S. experience, in which a civilian official wields significant wartime military authority" in the style of a proconsul.[60]

In an interview with Blaufarb after he left Vientiane in 1969, William Sullivan explained why the Chief of Mission came to enjoy so much authority over military activities in Laos. First, it was easy for the ambassador to keep a grip on the paramilitary war because it was limited in scope and in territory. Second, since this proxy war was more than a military operation, and since so much of it was controlled by the CIA rather than the Pentagon, it "became a simpler proposition for the ambassador to keep a grasp on it."[61] Third, "the situation in Laos was so confused and confusing, so unattractive that the Joint Chiefs really didn't want to take it on. They were never quite sure that it wouldn't all collapse the day after tomorrow, and they didn't really want to

---

[59] Blaufarb, *Organizing and Managing*, 1972.

[60] Blaufarb, *Organizing and Managing*, 1972, p. 58.

[61] Blaufarb, *Organizing and Managing*, 1972, p. 59.

get themselves in the position of being responsible for a fiasco, so I don't think there was any great thrust of urgency to take it over."[62] Indeed, the JCS was not interested in assuming military responsibility for Laos, because the Geneva Accords would restrict their freedom of action.

Another reason was that Sullivan had a direct line to senior officials with whom he had worked—such as McNamara, McGeorge Bundy, Bus Wheeler, and John McCone—and could get in touch with them if necessary. His staff knew that, "so that was a factor in giving a certain amount of cohesion to our operation," he told Blaufarb.[63] Finally, by the time Sullivan arrived in Vientiane in late 1964, "everyone in Washington who might have concerned himself with sending instructions or otherwise dabbling in the affairs of Laos was so preoccupied with South Vietnam that . . . we got practically no instructions whatsoever from Washington." Sullivan recalled that, during the four-and-a-half years he was in Laos, he received no more than three instructions. Since "nobody had time to bother about Laos, they were perfectly willing to leave it in the hands of the people who were sitting out there."[64]

Thus, Blaufarb wrote, Sullivan had the authority "to insist that the military chain of command consult with him and submit its proposals to him for approval."[65] Before undertaking any military actions, they had to convince him that what they proposed was needed or, at the least, would not damage American objectives in Laos. In addition, the military had to respond to Sullivan's proposals for military activities he wanted carried out to further U.S. goals in Laos; these could be his own initiatives, or they could be requests that had come to him from the Laotian government.

All these constraints suited Sullivan. They worked to his advantage, since Sullivan liked to control what went on in his bailiwick. In fact, Sullivan found the Geneva Accords convenient, because they gave him a justification for keeping U.S. ground forces from being introduced into Laos.[66] Under White House orders, he had to allow limited reconnaissance missions and raids on the North Vietnamese infiltration routes in southeast Laos, but he drew the line there. He refused to let American ground troops be stationed in Laos, or military planes to be based in the kingdom; so the aircraft had to fly from Thailand or South Vietnam or from carriers at sea.

Sullivan's military authority enabled him to initiate and control the secret bombing campaign in northern Laos—called BARREL ROLL—to support the tribal mercenaries soon after assuming his post in Vientiane. It was the first air operation carried

---

[62] Blaufarb, *Organizing and Managing*, 1972, p.60.

[63] Blaufarb, *Organizing and Managing*, 1972, p. 60.

[64] Blaufarb, *Organizing and Managing*, 1972, pp. 60–61.

[65] Blaufarb, *Organizing and Managing*, 1972, p. 61.

[66] Roger Warner, author of *Shooting at the Moon*, thought that Sullivan also had a personal interest in salvaging what was left of the accords, which he had helped negotiate as deputy to Averell Harriman in Geneva. The accords represented a high point in his diplomatic career.

out by the U.S. Air Force directly in support of the guerrillas on the ground. According to Blaufarb, up to this point, U.S. Air Force involvement in Laos had been indirect. The Air attache office in Vientiane advised and supported the Royal Lao Air Force (RLAF) in its combat operations, such as providing air support for the guerrillas with T-28 aircraft. Additional air support came from Thai pilots based in Udorn, Thailand, whom the U.S. Air Force trained and briefed. A U.S. Air Commando wing stationed in northern Thailand maintained and armed the T-28 planes—bearing RLAF markings—flown by the Thais. In addition, the U.S. Air Force provided forward air control for close combat support, and collected and prepared target information.

These limited USAF activities were expanded after the United States launched ROLLING THUNDER, the sustained air bombardment of North Vietnam. Sullivan, who wanted to preserve what was left of the Geneva Accords, fought hard to keep these air attacks within bounds. To aid its bombartment, the Air Force in 1966 installed a sophisticated radar system over Phou Pha Thi, a mesa about 5,000 feet high located near the border with North Vietnam. In 1967, President Lyndon B. Johnson directed Sullivan to allow the installation of a new, more sophisticated bombing system on Phou Pha Thi that could guide jet fighters and bombers to their targets, even through heavy cloud cover, and electronically release the bombs at the exact moment. Sullivan, however, drew the line at stationing American Special Forces to defend the installation. U.S. Air Force personnel assigned to Phou Pha Thi had to resign from the service to comply with his requirement that only unarmed American civilians be brought into Laos. Defense of the site was given to the Hmong guerrillas. North Vietnam considered this installation close to its border a threat to its security, and in 1968 the NVA overran Phou Pha Thi and destroyed it.

To gather target information for its enlarged bombing campaigns in Laos and over the Ho Chi Minh Trail, the U.S. Air Force secretly stationed a contingent at Long Tieng. Vang Pao's military headquarters was a good source of intelligence, which could be collected by debriefing commanders and guerrillas returning from the field, and by interrogating prisoners. The U.S. Air Force also stationed large helicopters, called "Jolly Green Giants," at Long Tieng and other bases in northern Laos to rescue pilots shot down during their bombing runs over North Vietnam. The most intense bombing campaigns were STEEL TIGER and TIGER HOUND, to interdict infiltration through the Ho Chi Minh Trail in southern Laos. However, they did not have a direct bearing on the war in Laos itself. These two programs were controlled and commanded from Saigon, but all operations against targets inside Laos had to be approved in advance by Ambassador Sullivan. The Embassy had to be consulted before B-52s could engage in bombings. Other types of aerial activities, such as armed reconnaissance, close air support, and photographic reconnaissance, also had to be approved by the ambassador. For continuing programs of interdiction, rules of engagement were established with the consent of the Embassy. For preplanned strikes, targets also had to be approved in advance by the Embassy.

To coordinate with the U.S. Mission in Saigon, Sullivan held a series of meetings with its representatives. Blaufarb reported that, at these sessions, the policy of supporting the neutrality of Laos was intensely discussed and modifications agreed upon. Several times, military representatives from MACV pressed Sullivan to relax restrictions on a number of activities, such as the bombing of the Ho Chi Minh Trail, the infiltration of U.S. Special Forces into this area, and the location of navigational devices in northeast Laos. Sullivan often took a firm stand against the proposals, thus pitting himself against senior military officers. Without American ground troops in Laos, the military could not use the argument that his interference would jeopardize the lives of American soldiers to pressure the ambassador. Military authorities had resorted to this argument elsewhere to justify the use of maximum firepower, regardless of the ramifications of such firepower.

The commitment at the highest level in Washington to observe the Geneva Accords gave Sullivan clout in insisting that the military follow the ground rules demanded by this policy. Afterward, he would keep tabs to make sure that the military commands adhered to the decisions and to the agreements that had been reached, and he would insist on strict compliance. Sullivan believed that such steps were necessary to preserve the neutrality of Laos, but his insistence on putting political considerations above military requirements made him controversial among senior military circles. Officers in Southeast Asia and the Pacific viewed him as a civilian who deluded himself into thinking that he had a grasp of military strategy and interfered in military matters. However, they could not ignore him.

Blaufarb thought that Sullivan's aggressive protection of the U.S. policy of maintaining the neutrality of Laos kept it from getting eroded by military exigencies. But the Ho Chi Minh corridor running through Laos held such strategic importance for the war in Vietnam that Sullivan had to accede to some of the military demands. A "clearly demarcated" section of Laos—the operational area of the STEEL TIGER bombing campaign—was ultimately treated as part of the Vietnam War theater. However, Sullivan retained the power to scrutinize and veto American activities in this region, and "any projected departures from agreed practice were generally submitted to Souvanna beforehand."[67]

The bombing campaign that had a direct effect on the conflict in Laos was BARREL ROLL. It struck enemy road traffic, depots, and other military installations, and provided U.S. combat air support to ground paramilitary forces. According to Blaufarb, for preplanned BARREL ROLL strikes, targeting was based on information provided by the irregulars, who conducted patrols and interrogated prisoners. The ambassador personally reviewed each of the proposed targets, and he would continue to do so even after the sorties multiplied. The targets were then forwarded to Udorn and Saigon to be placed on target lists for the 7th and 13th Air Force to strike. In the

---

[67] Blaufarb, *Organizing and Managing*, 1972, p. 73.

case of close support for ground troops, a forward air control (FAC) aircraft maintained contact with a ground controller, and airstrikes were called in on enemy positions. The use of USAF supersonic aircraft to support primitive tribesmen was "a novelty" in the history of warfare, Blaufarb wrote.[68]

BARREL ROLL was a tightly controlled program when it was initiated in 1964, but restrictions were loosened when sorties multiplied as more aircraft became available after the bombing of North Vietnam was halted to start peace negotiations. Another contributing factor was the North Vietnamese buildup of forces in Laos. By 1970, after Sullivan had left Laos and been replaced by Ambassador G. McMurtrie "Mac" Godley—the number of USAF sorties in Laos, including those targeting the Ho Chi Minh Trail, soared to about 170,000.[69] BARREL ROLL itself increased from about 15,000 sorties in 1969 to over 42,000 in 1970.

Civilian casualties rose as the number of sorties multiplied. As Blaufarb wrote, "The bombing of military installations in or close to important centers came to be judged acceptable by the Mission in view of increased NVA pressure, at the same time that many more aircraft sorties became available." Towns such as Xieng Khouangville, Phongsavan, Khang Khay, and Ban Ban in the Plain of Jars, and others in Tchepone and Mahaxay, were obliterated. "Of course," Blaufarb added, "such destruction did not stem from a deliberate decision but was a consequence of relaxed ground rules, permitting heavy attacks on military targets in or near these towns, and of a huge increase of available sorties."[70]

However, for all his power, Sullivan did not have complete control over aerial activities. According to Blaufarb, the ambassador could *request* attacks against various targets, and he could withhold or grant approval for air operations proposed by military commands outside of Laos. But he could not *determine* air activities, and he had to accept the decisions of the 7th or 13th Air Force and MACV on how resources were going to be committed, because these decisions were based on overall requirements for the war in Vietnam, not on the needs of Laos. Sullivan's biggest problem was controlling the secret U.S. airstrikes in Laos to interdict North Vietnamese infiltration into South Vietnam, which at times would hit the wrong targets. Despite his authority, Sullivan could not solve this problem, nor could he make the Air Force and the Navy, which owned the planes, march to his drumbeat. While he had the authority to accept or reject the military's preplanned bombing targets, and while he could also ask for air attacks against certain targets, the Air Force and the Navy had the ultimate power to comply or not, and they did not always want to play by his rules.

---

[68] Blaufarb, *Organizing and Managing*, 1972, p. 51.

[69] The bombing in southern Laos expanded until it became bigger than the bombardment of South Vietnam and Cambodia. In 1971, more than 400,000 tons of ordnance were dropped on Laos, almost twice the quantity dropped over South Vietnam.

[70] Blaufarb, *Organizing and Managing*, 1972, p. 51.

Sullivan had greater control over the tribal resistance run by the CIA in his own backyard—the centerpiece of the U.S. effort in Laos.[71] Blaufarb considered it flexible, unconventional, and innovative. In the tribes, especially the Hmong, the Agency found a people willing to fight the Pathet Lao for reasons that had to do with their dislike of the communists for demanding rice and men from the villages, and for allying themselves with North Vietnam—a feared enemy. The tribes' resistance against the communists was not a standard insurgency, since it was not aimed at restoring security and government control in the countryside. Because of the strictures of the Geneva Accords, to which the United States government continued to profess adherence, the CIA simply used this resistance as a convenient mechanism to stop the Pathet Lao and to pin down North Vietnamese troops that could otherwise have been sent to South Vietnam as the war there escalated.[72] Besides their hatred of the Pathet Lao and the North Vietnamese, the tribes were also motivated by their belief that the United States would be willing and able to supply them with the weaponry they needed to fight their enemies and to give them the material goods to improve their lives.

Although the CIA ran the tribal war, it did not have a free hand. Each incremental expansion of the tribal forces had to be specifically approved by the ambassador and by the State Department, "within guidelines laid down at the highest interagency level and approved by the White House."[73] The supply of powerful weapons was reviewed and authorized by the ambassador, who also scrutinized the movements of CIA personnel in Laos. On several occasions when Vang Pao proposed expanding his operations, Sullivan rejected the requests because he thought they would "imply excessive and unwise commitments."[74] From time to time, Vang Pao would propose to retake the Plain of Jars, but the ambassador would turn him down.

---

[71] To set down guidelines for paramilitary and military activities, the U.S. Embassy issued a paper in 1967 that carried the title of *U.S. Policy with Respect to North Laos*. The document concluded that, "From the U.S. standpoint, expansion should only be undertaken when it can clearly be shown that: a) our war effort in Vietnam would be substantially helped, b) the security of Thailand and of presently held territory in North Laos would be significantly enhanced, or c) our relations with the RLG would be significantly enhanced, or that our failure to support expansion in North Laos would result in substantial deterioration in our relations." In terms of actual military operations, the most important courses of action laid out were, "Continue to take areas in North Laos which will increase our ability to damage NVN vehicular and personnel traffic. Enhance protection of Thailand and of friendly-held territory in North Laos by . . . [closing] existing gaps between friendly positions in east and west Luang Prabang province. Continue to engage in small-scale harassment operations to keep the enemy off balance . . . Refrain from actions which could provoke serious enemy retaliation." See Blaufarb, *Organizing and Managing*, 1972, p. 37.

[72] According to Roger Warner, some former CIA agents who operated in Laos believed that the arrival of Theodore Shackley, Blaufarb's replacement as CIA station chief in 1966, marked "the point when the United States started using the locals almost purely for American ends in Vietnam . . . The priority changed to using Laotian '"assets"' to tie down North Vietnamese divisions in Vang Pao's area and to making the Ho Chi Minh Trail more expensive for the North Vietnamese to use." Warner, *Shooting at the Moon*, 1999, p. 189.

[73] Blaufarb, *Organizing and Managing*, 1972, p. 37.

[74] Blaufarb, *Organizing and Managing*, 1972, p. 37.

The CIA was able to keep its proxy war secret, because the northern region was remote and accessible only by planes that belonged either to its own airline, Air America, or to contractors it hired.[75] Being able to locate operational headquarters in Udorn, Thailand, also allowed the CIA to maintain a low profile. Thailand's supply of personnel to participate in the paramilitary war—including Thai parachutists in the Police Aerial Reinforcement Unit, or PARU, and, later, the Thai Special Guerrilla Unit (SGU)—made it possible for the CIA to keep its staff to a few hundred, including those stationed in Thailand. Staff from other countries, such as the Philippines and Taiwan, also enabled the U.S. Mission to keep its personnel small and the costs low. The CIA operations cost less than $100 million, and the "outside total—*excluding USAF bombing*" was estimated at $260 million for fiscal year 1970.[76] These expenditures were large for a country the size of Laos, but still considerably lower than the tens of billions being spent in Vietnam.

☘ ☘ ☘

After paramilitary activities, the most important undertaking for the U.S. Mission was USAID's Refugee Relief Program. The name implies a humanitarian endeavor, but, in fact, the program was an integral and essential part of the effort to enlist tribes in the paramilitary war. Members of the tribes did not join the war per se; rather, they joined to follow a leader, such as Vang Pao, into war. The decision was not made by individuals but by the entire village. The problem was that, once the men left, the village would be defenseless against enemy attacks. Unless the United States made the commitment that it would move their families to safety if necessary, the men would not join the resistance; or, if they did join, they would flee with their families to safety at the first sign of trouble—regardless of orders to the contrary. Consequently, the Embassy had to commit itself to evacuating the villages if they became threatened, taking the families to a safe location, and supplying them with food until they could produce two successive rice crops. Even if the villages did not have to be evacuated, supplying the inhabitants was still a necessity. Often, after all the able-bodied males left to join the guerrillas, the village would lack the necessary manpower to produce enough food to survive. In these cases, USAID would have to air-drop rice and other food items to feed the families. The American commitment to provide protection and care for their families, therefore, was an important factor in persuading tribesmen to join the resistance.

Among the tribes, the Hmong accounted for the majority of the fighters, and their resistance represented the backbone of the tribal program. USAID, therefore, maintained a strong field presence at Sam Thong, the civil headquarters of the Hmong.

---

[75] Air America was dissolved on June 30, 1976.

[76] Blaufarb, *Organizing and Managing*, 1972, p. 55.

USAID field representatives participated closely with Vang Pao and the CIA in military operations. With the assistance of a staff of USAID personnel and Lao employees, the field manager kept abreast of the refugee population, their location, and needs, and prepared a daily schedule for air delivery of supplies. For air transport, USAID used the same aircraft available to the CIA.

Another USAID contribution to the tribal program was the medical care it provided through its Public Health Division, which built a 200-bed hospital at Sam Thong, as well as primitive dispensaries in over 100 locations. The Public Health Division also trained over 1,000 medical personnel to work mainly with refugees. Related to this contribution was the treatment of war casualties at the dispensaries and at the hospital in Sam Thong. People injured in the war were evacuated by helicopter or small aircraft for treatment. By providing medical care to the war-wounded, the dispensaries and the field hospital played a crucial role in reassuring the tribesmen that those injured in combat would be cared for.

USAID also undertook other projects that increased the position and prestige of the tribal guerrilla leaders and strengthened the appeal of the resistance. For example, it established informal schools and provided textbooks to the students; helped agricultural development by supplying improved strains of crops, such as corn; enlarged the airstrips at Sam Thong and Long Tieng; and built a road connecting these two Hmong centers.

In summary, many USAID projects not only supported the guerrillas but also contributed to the appeal of leaders, such as Vang Pao, who could point to benefits such as the road and the schools as proofs of the advantages enjoyed by the Hmong under his command.

The costs of all these civilian and paramilitary operations were low for the United States. Overall, the unique situation in Laos made this possible. First, the United States' limited objectives in Laos and the Geneva Accords obviated a costly military buildup.[77] Second, the simple standards of living of the minorities meant that supporting them with rice and a few other essentials did not entail huge expenditures. The weakness of

---

[77] The U.S. Mission also provided support to the Lao regular army by supplying it with military supplies. Military advice in Laos was supplied by the Air and Army Attaches and their deputies, but these officers were not assigned to Lao units and were not authorized to go into combat. Other military assistance, such as the training, was handled by the Deputy Chief, Joint U.S. Military Advisory Group Thailand, located in that country. Most of the military assistance to the Lao regular army was in ammunition and equipment—especially aircraft and ordnance for the Lao air force—as well as upgrading the Lao army. However, the Lao armed forces continued to perform poorly in combat with the North Vietnamese. In general, the Lao army suffered from an absence of commitment and even from a lack of military knowledge. The leadership provided by the Lao officers was poor, and even catastrophic in some instances. Consequently, the United States was unable to make much headway. Blaufarb, *Organizing and Managing*, 1972, pp. 45–47.

the Lao government justified keeping it out of programs, thus eliminating an additional layer of bureaucracy, as well as added costs, because it prevented resources from being drained by corruption.

In Blaufarb's view, Sullivan's approach contributed to the efficiency of the U.S. Mission. His style was informal, and he favored administrative simplicity and personal contact over paperwork. Senior Mission personnel tried to deal face-to-face with one another and with the Laotians. Sullivan liked to be decisive and to move quickly. Formal arrangements or an elaborate bureaucratic structure was absent.

The cohesion of the U.S. programs was achieved through the "daily operations meeting," attended not just by the country team but also by representatives of all American agencies. The daily meeting was not a decisionmaking mechanism but a forum to review the status of current operations and discuss operations planned for the future, as well as to facilitate the sharing of information.[78] Sullivan insisted on unity and a team approach, and those who did not abide by this policy had to leave Laos. He attended the meetings regularly to reinforce the point that he was not only the Chief of Mission but also the operations manager.

In view of the dismal performance and poor leadership of the Royal Lao Army, as well as the animosity between the minorities and the Lao, the U.S. Mission kept the government out of the tribal resistance. The fear was that, if the Lao General Staff assumed control, Vang Pao and his fighters would lose their morale because, in their view, this change in command would expose them to the exploitation of the Lao. For these reasons, the CIA strongly opposed getting the Royal army involved in the tribal war. Details of the program were not discussed with the army leadership in advance. Whenever Lao military leaders asked for details, the U.S. Mission suspected that their request was a bid to assume control, and would keep them at arm's length by providing generalized information or would tell them only after action had been taken.

The hostility toward the Hmong was shared even by Prince Souvanna Phouma, who looked down on them as "aggressive and untrustworthy savages"—a view he developed after participating in an operation to suppress a Hmong rebellion against the French.[79] Souvanna was at first indifferent when the idea of enlisting the Hmong in the war was discussed in 1962, in part because he suspected that the United States and Vang Pao might be maneuvering toward independence for the Hmong. But, over time, he became more favorably disposed toward the program after the Hmong dem-

---

[78] William Sullivan viewed the daily meeting as a device through which everyone could find out what was going on: for all the representatives to know what each agency was doing, and for him to know what everyone was doing. In this way, he said, "there was no excuse for anyone being out of step through ignorance of the facts" (Blaufarb, *Organizing and Managing*, 1972, p. 67). Another quality in Sullivan's management of the paramilitary war, in Blaufarb's view, was the delegation of responsibility to the field representatives, which gave them the flexibility to develop and improvise solutions to deal with unexpected contingencies—regardless of bureaucratic norms.

[79] Blaufarb, *Organizing and Managing*, 1972, p. 78.

onstrated their effectiveness against the North Vietnamese and after he was convinced that the Hmong were loyal to the king and to Laos.

However, Vang Pao was not disposed to submit to Lao domination, and the future relationship between the Hmong and the government remained to be ironed out. The dilemma for the United States was that, by denying the government the control of such a program on its own soil, it was violating the independence of Laos as well as contravening its long-range objective of fostering the self-reliance that would permit the Lao to deal with their problems on their own.

By 1967, the total number of tribal irregulars rose to 30,000. The majority, 22,000 men, were under Vang Pao's authority. In addition, as the head of Military Region II, Vang Pao also commanded 7,000 regular Lao troops. By 1969, restrictions were loosened because of the escalation of fighting and Vang Pao's forces had come under great pressure in their own heartland. In that year, Vang Pao—whose proposal to take over the Plain of Jars had been regularly turned down by the ambassador—was granted permission to undertake this operation. Vang Pao began the campaign in March and captured the Plain of Jars in September, aided by sustained USAF bombardments, which reduced the town of Xieng Khouangville to rubble. Eventually, with the constraints removed by the new American ambassador, Mac Godley, the air force would carry out "some of the heaviest bombing anywhere since World War II" and leave "not a single structure . . . standing on the plain anywhere."[80] An unknown number of civilians were killed. A CIA agent who flew over the plain after its capture wrote to his family that nothing was left in the area, and everything had been "blown up or burnt."[81] During the bombardment, civilians in the plain had to move into caves or live in ditches propped up with lumber, and could only go out at night. After the capture of the plain, they were herded onto American cargo planes and forcibly moved to the Vientiane valley. The capture of the Plain of Jars marked the high point of Vang Pao's career.

Despite Vang Pao's success, by 1970, the military situation in Laos remained mired in a stalemate. The conflict continued to swing back and forth within the marginal area bordering the zones controlled by the Royal Lao Government on one side and the Pathet Lao on the other. Neither side was willing to incur the consequences of striking into their enemy's heartland. Although the stalemate had not been broken, the war had intensified. In 1969, the communists began to gain the military edge through an expansion of their capabilities in response to the American buildup of the Hmong. By this time, Vang Pao had become stronger, thanks to American airpower and to the

[80] Warner, *Shooting at the Moon*, 1999, p. 293.

[81] Warner, *Shooting at the Moon*, 1999, p. 292.

supplies of heavy weapons that he had received: 105mm and 75mm howitzers, 4.2-inch mortars, 75mm recoilless rifles, and propeller-driven T-28 planes. The Hmong had also become tougher fighters, because they knew they could call upon extensive air support and get their forces extricated by helicopters if they became encircled. If they felt they had to hang on to a particular terrain, either because of its significance in their spirit world or because it was vital for their resupply by air, without which they could not survive, they would stand and fight.

To counter the strength of the Hmong, the Pathet Lao and the North Vietnamese were obliged to operate in larger units dependent on secure lines of communication and truck transport to supply their operations. They also had to boost their firepower with anti-aircraft guns and artillery, and to dig in to hold their ground, further reducing their mobility. Consequently, they usually went on the offensive during the dry season, when the roads were passable, and then retreated to rest and regroup when the monsoon rains began. The Hmong, meanwhile, would step up their attacks during the wet season, to take advantage of the reduced mobility of their enemies. Then, as dry weather returned, the communists resumed their offensive.

The back-and-forth attacks by both sides suggested that the fighting in Laos had been deliberately left inconclusive, because neither the United States nor North Vietnam was seriously seeking to solve the problem of Laos. Ultimately, the fate of Laos would be settled in Vietnam; in the meantime, both sides believed that it would be unwise to encourage activities, such as attacks on critical targets, that would completely undermine the Geneva Accords. The U.S. Mission, therefore, discouraged the Lao government from launching attacks on communist positions that might provoke a sharp response. Its justification was that abstaining from such attacks would prevent the politically and militarily weak RLG from venturing into ill-conceived operations and therefore keep the United States from having to intervene to bail it out of trouble.

Indeed, with the exception of the Ho Chi Minh Trail area, the United States preferred to pursue a defensive policy in Laos, a theater it considered secondary in importance to the war in South Vietnam. Although they showed less restraint than before, the communists on the whole continued to avoid risky probes to test the tolerance thresholds of the United States, and to eschew activities that would destroy the Geneva Accords, because it afforded the Trail area a measure of protection from ground attacks by the United States. Thus, the communists had refrained from taking the principal towns, which were under government control.

With the exception of Vientiane, they could reach these towns within a two days' march or less from their advance positions, and it would be relatively easy for them to capture these targets. The North Vietnamese probably did not see the advantage of pressing for more gains, since they were already achieving their minimal objectives: controlling the infiltration route and helping the Pathet Lao retain control of a territory and a population large enough to grow their movement. Keeping the war quiet was not only in the best interest of Hanoi, it was also in the best interests of the United States and the Soviet Union. All three parties favored maintaining the fiction of Lao neutrality, because none wanted to have to engage in a costly, full-scale war as the conflict escalated in Vietnam.

In Blaufarb's tentative assessment, the tribal resistance had been a qualified success in the period from 1962 to 1970, since it helped achieve the primary objective of preserving the RLG and enabling it to retain control of most of the Mekong Valley. This success was due in part to the North Vietnamese decision not to press forward with a takeover. The U.S. intervention nevertheless did raise the costs for the North Vietnamese in Laos. Ambassador Sullivan himself acknowledged that the constraints on North Vietnam came from external factors rather than from the U.S.-backed proxy war, but he believed that the U.S. effort "made it infinitely more difficult for them and much more costly, and therefore brought them up against constraints perhaps at a lower threshold than they would have otherwise."[82] The proxy war, in Sullivan's view, also bought space and time for the noncommunists. As he put it, "I think we bought a considerable degree of space during most of the time we were there," with the Hmong holding on to their terrain, and ". . . we bought a considerable amount of time, permitting the lowland Lao structure to survive until the rest of the situation in Indochina developed to a point where . . . this whole war may be settled in one composite effort."[83]

Elaborating on Sullivan's statement, Blaufarb wrote that it implied that the North Vietnamese had been forced to "settle for a good deal less in Laos than they would have obtained without the U.S. involvement there."[84] The second achievement of the U.S. effort was the preservation of the Geneva Accords—although it remained precarious. Another payoff was the toll that it exacted from North Vietnam in the corridor and in the northern part of Laos in terms of men and resources. Year after year, the North Vietnamese had been forced to throw in fresh forces to retake the same terrain they had lost time and again before, thus draining their resources with these repeated efforts. Finally, the U.S. involvement reassured Thailand that a buffer zone would remain between it and the communist forces.

Blaufarb believed that, while the costs for the United States in Laos had been low, the costs to the Lao had been significant, "both in terms of human suffering and in the destruction of towns and villages caused by bombing."[85] During the course of the war, perhaps as many as 700,000 people out of the roughly 1,900,000 under the control of the government had been forced to flee their homes—several times, in many cases—to resettle permanently or temporarily elsewhere. Civilian and military casualties had been disproportionately high for a small country such as Laos. The toll was borne most

---

[82] Blaufarb, *Organizing and Managing*, 1972, p. 84.

[83] Blaufarb, *Organizing and Managing*, 1972, p. 85.

[84] Blaufarb, *Organizing and Managing*, 1972, p. 85.

[85] Blaufarb, *Organizing and Managing*, 1972, p. 86.

heavily by the Hmong. By 1970, the casualties suffered by this tribe had been variously estimated at between 40,000 to 100,000—or roughly from 9 to 20 percent of a total population of 450,000. Blaufarb wondered whether, considering these "grim statistics," the Hmong would have chosen to side with the United States had they known beforehand of the devastation that would befall them and their communities. Unfortunately, "the final balance cannot be struck while the conflict still goes on, the outcome as uncertain as ever."[86]

In addition to heavy casualties, many Hmong communities had also been devastated by displacement. The Hmong refugee problem began in 1968, when the CIA evacuated all the Hmong under Vang Pao's control in a massive airlift out of northeastern Laos, after Vang Pao began losing control of Sam Neua, in order to deny the population to the communists. Since USAF bombing of this region had become heavy starting in 1967, the tribesmen left willingly. Air America evacuated over 9,000 people in less than nine weeks. In the following three years, communist offensives drove tens of thousands of Hmong to become refugees. Eventually, over 100,000 villagers were resettled in the territory between Long Cheng and the Vientiane Plain. In 1971, the communists attacked Long Cheng, forcing the CIA to evacuate some 50,000 dependents of the Hmong mercenaries to a resettlement south of Long Cheng. Often Air America could not cope with the large number of villagers fleeing enemy attacks; consequently, the villagers had to embark on long, arduous marches to safety.

In the wake of the bombing halt over North Vietnam and the initiation of peace talks with Hanoi, U.S. military involvement in South Vietnam began to wind down, bringing a decreasing American commitment to Laos as well. In 1969, the director of USAID in Laos and the director of the USAID Office for Southeast Asia Affairs in Washington asked RAND to study the relevance and validity of its rural development program in Laos, and to consider "desirable future directions" for the program in light of the changing political and strategic context. Reflecting the uncertainty of American commitment, USAID asked the RAND team to limit the scope of their recommendations to a two-year time frame.

In June and July 1969, Hans Heymann of the Economics Department and John Donnell of Temple University flew to Laos to begin their field research. The results were published in a report in February 1970.[87] In their report, Heymann and Donnell

---

[86] Blaufarb, *Organizing and Managing*, 1972, p. 86.

[87] Hans Heymann and John C. Donnell, *Rural Programs in Laos: A Mid-1969 Reassessment*, RAND RM-6120-AID, February 1970.

briefly reviewed a classified study that RAND had done in September 1965.[88] This project took two man-years of research, had a broader scope, and was conducted in a vastly different strategic context in Southeast Asia in the first half of 1965. Then, the United States was hugely expanding its security commitment in Vietnam and in the region. In this situation, the 1965 study urged that the United States make a long-term investment in Laos and that it undertake a range of actions to improve and strengthen the Royal Lao Government, develop a better relationship between the central and regional authorities, and foster a national identity. However, even under the favorable circumstances of that period, the U.S. Mission considered the adoption of such programs and the measures that would be necessary to implement them infeasible.

By the time Donnell and Heymann arrived for their own research, conditions in Laos had changed drastically. Security had deteriorated—not only in upland areas but also in the Mekong Valley itself. Major RLG routes of communication had been cut, and important towns, such as Attopeu and Saravane had been isolated. Vang Pao's guerrillas, once the only effective fighting force, had suffered from steady attrition and declining morale. As things stood, airpower was the only weapon capable of protecting the Royal Army from the determined enemy assault, and the prospects for long-term viability of the government appeared very dim. In these conditions, one could hardly expect that the rural programs that USAID had been pursuing in Laos since 1963, with some modifications along the way, would be able to help advance overall U.S. objectives in Laos. The deteriorating security conditions in the countryside caused development efforts to be retrenched to the resource-rich and strategic Mekong lowland, the heartland of the RLG. Donnell and Heymann supported this retrenchment, since it fit strategic realities, the absence of effective Lao local leadership, and the likelihood that fewer experienced American personnel would be available in the future.

Consequently, they recommended that near-term expectations be scaled back to the minimum goal of maintaining RLG presence in this region. The U.S. rural assistance program should be modest in scope and simple in design to avoid overstraining the capabilities of the RLG and to enhance the prospects that the RLG would be able to take over the program in the long run. Their recommendation reflected not only their assessment of the security conditions but also their basic belief that rural development programs in Laos could not act as catalysts for social and political change—as expected by the earlier 1965 RAND report—because of the weakness and inefficiency of the RLG, which remained family-based, faction-ridden, urban-oriented, and elitist —and thus unable to forge any true political link with the outlying regions.

By the time Heymann and Donnell published their report in early 1970, the "grim statistics" Blaufarb wrote about were taking their toll, and the Hmong were no longer so eager to fight for Vang Pao. The Hmong were bitter about Vang Pao's willingness

---

[88] Chuck Cooper, Paul Langer, Richard Moorsteen, and Charles Zwick, *Security and Assistance in Laos* (U). Not available to the general public. The author could not gain access to this report.

to take excessive casualties; his cruel treatment of his soldiers, such as executing them himself; and his growing affluence. Indeed, by Hmong standards, Vang Pao was doing well. Long Cheng, his military headquarters, had grown to become the second-largest city in Laos after Vientiane. The transformation started in mid-1965. As former CIA agents recalled, in that period the Americans began to expand Long Cheng with comfortable housing for a larger American contingent, a new airstrip with a broad cargo ramp, and a road linking Long Cheng and Sam Thong. There were also warehouses, trucks, and jeeps.[89] Personally, Vang Pao was benefiting from his alliance with the United States. He now lived in a two-story stone house that the Americans had built for him—a luxury in the eyes of Hmong tribesmen, who traditionally lived in flimsy huts. Vang Pao also bought homes for his wives in Vientiane, where they conducted business ventures. Then, at his insistence, Vang Pao got his own Xieng Khouang Airways, whose planes were used mainly to carry supplies and his relatives. American dignitaries flew in to sing his praises. By the standard of other corrupt Lao generals, Vang Pao was not wealthy, but to his destitute tribesmen, he appeared rich enough—and they believed he had become a rich man on the back of their own suffering.

Above all, it was the horrendous casualties that turned the village elders against Vang Pao. From 1967 to 1971, more than 3,000 of his army were killed and more than 5,000 wounded in combat, out of a total of 30,000–40,000 fighters. Vang Pao was forced to recruit from other tribes, and by April 1971, the Lao Theung in northern Laos made up 40 percent of his troops. From the Hmong population itself, many of the new recruits Vang Pao was able to extract were young boys. In 1968, Edgar Buell, the USAID field manager, told a *New Yorker* correspondent that among a batch of 300 new recruits, "Thirty per cent were fourteen years old or less, and ten of them were only ten years old. Another 30 per cent were fifteen or sixteen. The remaining 40 per cent were forty-five or over." The ones in between, Buell said, were "all dead," and in two weeks 90 percent of the new recruits would be killed.[90]

There were teenage company commanders leading fighters who were little more than children. The less-experienced troops took heavier casualties, making it necessary for Vang Pao to press more tribesmen into service with threats, intimidation, and other strong-arm tactics, because few Hmong families were willing to have their sons fight for him. Those in Vang Pao's army were less willing to go into combat: With so many American jets in the sky, they preferred to let them do the job. America's favor changed Vang Pao. One former CIA agent recalled that he became less of a guerrilla leader. He was spending less time with his troops in the field and more time at his headquarters,

---

[89] One CIA agent lamented that the Hmong had become too dependent on the Americans. "They didn't need T-shirts," he said, "or transistor radios or motorcycles on the runway. They didn't need Xieng Khouang airways to haul goods to the Long Cheng market. They didn't [need] Long Cheng at all" (Warner, *Shooting at the Moon*, 1999, p. 250).

[90] Warner, *Shooting at the Moon*, 1999, p. 245.

"meeting bigwig Americans on Tour, and believing their flattery," and "building up Long Cheng even more."[91]

After paying a heavy price in casualties, Vang Pao lost the Plain of Jars to the communists in 1970. His young soldiers fled at the sight of North Vietnamese tanks. "Tribal leaders denounced him to his face," telling him "he was destroying the Meo race for the sake of his own power and for the sake of the Americans."[92] It was the beginning of the disintegration: His army was falling apart, and his tribesmen were frightened and had lost their morale. When the North Vietnamese approached Sam Thong and Long Cheng, the Hmong fighters fled into the hills with their families, to hide. The tribal elders mutinied. Vang Pao had to fly to Vientiane to ask Prime Minister Souvanna Phouma to immediately evacuate 100,000 of his people to Sayaboury, near the Thai border. USAID said this could not be done because all the air charter companies were already flying at full capacity to supply refugees whose numbers had now swelled to half a million. Besides, the U.S. Mission did not want to remove all the Hmong, because they were crucial for the defense of Vientiane: They were the only thing that stood between the communists and the capital.

Sam Thong fell to the communists without a fight in March 1970, because all the inhabitants had fled by the time they arrived—including the soldiers, who left to be with their families. The Hmong fighters, according to the USAID field manager, would "never fight again like they have in the past. They wonder what they fought and died for."[93] With the American withdrawal from Vietnam, the Air Force began to cut back its sorties. Meanwhile, the North Vietnamese were building up their forces, bringing in 130mm artillery with a range of 28 km, and North Vietnamese MiGs appeared over Laos. On January 16, 1971, Vang Pao met with about 400 tribal elders. He admitted to them that they were losing the war, and there was no prospect for their returning to their own villages once the fighting stopped. When the North Vietnamese increased their pressure on Long Cheng, most of the Americans left, including Air America pilots and the forward air controllers. Bombings by American jet aircraft and B-52s and the arrival of the Thai Special Guerrilla Unit, or SGU, gave Long Cheng a temporary respite.

With American disengagement from Vietnam, the Hmong were no longer as useful as they had once been. Air support dropped to 32 sorties a day as American withdrawal proceeded apace in Vietnam. When Nixon went to China on February 21, 1972, Vang Pao knew, as he later said, that "he was going to lose the war."[94] In June 1972, he flew secretly to the United States and went to Missoula, Montana. Vang Pao was already thinking of leaving Laos and settling here with his six wives and 25 chil-

---

[91] Warner, *Shooting at the Moon*, 1999, p. 250.

[92] Warner, *Shooting at the Moon*, 1999, p. 298.

[93] Warner, *Shooting at the Moon*, 1999, p. 301.

[94] Warner, *Shooting at the Moon*, 1999, p. 329.

dren. He knew that if the communists won, they would kill him. But he did not tell anyone. Americans who knew him, however, "assumed that Vang Pao had arranged for his own private exit from the Laos war, and that if need be he would abandon his people."[95]

Following the signing of the Peace Accords between the United States and Vietnam, National Security Advisor Henry Kissinger flew to Vientiane on February 9, 1973, to force Souvanna Phouma to sign an agreement stipulating that Laos would return to neutrality. To pressure Souvanna, Kissinger's envoys, William Sullivan and Alexander Haig, had pointed out to Souvanna Phouma on an earlier visit that American air support of Laotian troops would soon end, and without such support, the Royal Army would not be able to withstand a communist offensive.[96] Kissinger got what he wanted: Although the agreement did not require North Vietnamese troops to withdraw, Souvanna had no choice but to acquiesce.

On February 21, 1973, the Vientiane government signed the Agreement of the Restoration of Peace and Reconciliation in Laos with the Pathet Lao. Neither the United States nor North Vietnam affixed their signatures because to do so would have been an admission that they had been fighting in Laos in violation of the 1962 Geneva Accords. The cease-fire provision prohibited paramilitary forces, so Vang Pao's fighters were merged into the Royal Army. On July 1, 1973, most of the CIA advisors in the tribal program left Laos, as did the 15,000 Thai SGUs who had been brought in by the United States to defend Long Cheng when it was threatened by the communists. "By August 1973 . . . parts of the Long Cheng Valley were overgrown with brush."[97] In November, 1,500 Pathet Lao troops arrived in Vientiane. Their presence was now accepted as Laos reverted to being a neutral country—one that would not take sides in the Cold War. Then, on April 3, 1974, Prince Souphanouvong arrived in the capital, where he was enthusiastically greeted by the largest crowd the city had ever seen. Two days later, the coalition government was formed, with Cabinet posts evenly shared between the Royalists and the Pathet Lao.

---

[95] Warner, *Shooting at the Moon*, 1999, p. 332. In his assessment of Vang Pao, Warner wrote that he was "a talented but uneducated man who had risen to an organizational level beyond his competence. He excelled at short-term tactics—at capturing a hill from the enemy—the kinds of skills majors and colonels needed. But he had never been good at long-term strategic planning, which is part of what major generals are meant to do" (Warner, *Shooting at the Moon*, 1999, p. 308). In the end, he thought the only alternative for him was to flee from a complex situation that entrapped him.

[96] In 1972, Sullivan became Henry Kissinger's deputy to the secret peace talks with the North Vietnamese in Paris. Sullivan was in favor of settling the war in Vietnam. In his long-range strategic thinking, the Soviet Union was the biggest threat to the United States—not North Vietnam. To change the balance of power between the United States and the USSR, the alliance between the Soviet Union and China—already eroded—would have to be sundered. But as long as the Vietnam War lasted, the relationship between the Soviet Union and China would not be broken completely, and the Soviet Union could not be isolated. He believed, therefore, that it was important to solve the Vietnam War in order to solidify the rapprochement with China.

[97] Warner, *Shooting at the Moon*, 1999, p. 353.

☘ ☘ ☘

The cease-fire that enabled Souphanouvong and his troops to return to Vientiane left unanswered the question of how the Pathet Lao would fare in Laos's political arena and compete for power with the Royal Lao Government. Overarching this question was what role North Vietnam itself would play in Laos. In a report issued after the cease-fire, Joseph Zasloff attempted to anticipate this role as well as to determine the extent of popular support the Pathet Lao could muster in a political contest with the Royal Lao Government.[98]

There were no definitive answers to these crucial questions, and Zasloff could only offer some speculation. With regard to the role of North Vietnam and its relationship with the Pathet Lao, Zasloff thought that Pathet Lao leaders—who had been conditioned to accept dependence on the Vietnamese and who had probably come to view this relationship as mutually beneficial—would not feel inclined to modify it. Besides, considering that the RLG was receiving assistance from the Americans, and also from the Thais, the Pathet Lao leaders must feel that they had no other choice but to rely on North Vietnam.

On the question of popular support for the Pathet Lao, Zasloff wrote that it was extremely difficult to give an assessment because of limited information. But he surmised that the people who remained in the Pathet Lao zones must be committed to the movement and its leaders. It was clear that life in the communist zone had been tragic. American bombings had driven thousands to flee to safety. In some areas, people had to stay in damp caves and underground dugouts during the day, and only came out at night to conduct their necessary activities. The devastation had been widespread, and those who remained had to bear enormous hardship and danger.

The Pathet Lao had made life more difficult. It had conscripted most able-bodied men, and some women, into military service; levied heavy taxes; and imposed onerous duties of porterage and other corvée labor on the population. The devastation and the demands of the Pathet Lao must have had an effect, but it was not clear how the people had reacted as a result. There was reason, however, to believe that those who stayed, and perhaps even some of those who had fled, were committed to the Pathet Lao, either because they had sons serving in the Pathet Lao forces or because the bombings and other acts of war may have motivated them to rally around their leaders and to fight an enemy that seemed determined to bomb them into surrender. On the question of how the flight of almost half of the population to the RLG areas had affected the Pathet Lao and the inhabitants who stayed behind, Zasloff could provide no answer.

The cease-fire agreement had ushered in a new phase in the history of Laos. In the coming period, Zasloff concluded, foreign intervention would likely decline, but exter-

---

[98] Zasloff, Joseph J., *The Pathet Lao: Leadership and Organization*, Santa Monica, Calif.: RAND Corporation, R-949, in July 1973. For this report, Zasloff supplemented his research with data collected during his two visits to Laos in 1972 while he was a Fulbright professor in Southeast Asia.

nal powers would continue to influence internal Lao politics. As the struggle shifted to the political arena, the Pathet Lao movement, with a parallel government controlling two-thirds of the country and one-third of the population, would vie vigorously for control of Laos. However, events would unfold very differently, and the political competition Zasloff anticipated never materialized. Once the North Vietnamese took over South Vietnam in 1975, Laos could not escape falling into communist hands.

About a week after the fall of Saigon, Prime Minister Souvanna Phouma summoned Vang Pao to his office on May 5, 1975, and told him that "the time for fighting was over."[99] In anger, Vang Pao resigned his army commission and flew back to Long Cheng. But he had lost his power, and there were people who wanted to kill him: infiltrators, people who had switched sides, and people who were angry at him. The United States told Vang Pao it was time for him and his top aides to leave the kingdom. By May 8, Vang Pao had already flown his wives and younger children to Thailand.

On May 12, 1975, the evacuation to Thailand began at Long Cheng. Gathered near the runway were 5,000–7,000 people, and about 50,000 others were hiking in from the valley in small groups, hoping to get seats on the planes. There was no panic yet, but a few officers threatened to shoot the pilots if their families were not let on board. The Americans planning the evacuation agreed that if Vang Pao was seen leaving in an aircraft, his own people would go wild and kill him, so they decided to sneak him out of Long Cheng. Vang Pao was flown out secretly on a helicopter and then transferred to a plane for the flight to Thailand. At Long Cheng, when people found out that their leader had deserted them, they began to leave en masse, some by motorcycle but most on foot. Hmong soldiers and officers took off their uniforms and changed into civilian clothes. The Pathet Lao entered Long Cheng a day or two later.

The U.S. ambassador and the head of USAID left a few days after Vang Pao. However, unlike Vietnam, the United States did not withdraw completely and a small staff remained at the U.S. Embassy. Anti-U.S. feelings rose to a pitch, but—despite angry anti-American protests, the occupation of the USAID compound in Vientiane, and the placing of Americans under house arrest—no American was killed. This ending of the American role in Laos contrasted with the more dramatic evacuation of U.S. personnel in neighboring South Vietnam.[100]

Eventually crossing the Mekong by boat or raft into Thailand were 10,000–20,000 other Hmong. There, they lived in squalid refugee camps without any assistance from the Thais, who did not want them in their country. The 2,500 people evacuated from Long Cheng were taken to an empty Thai air base near Udorn. At a mass meeting there with Vang Pao, they angrily condemned him and told him that he had led his people

---

[99] Warner, *Shooting at the Moon*, 1999, p. 357.

[100] See Warner, *Shooting at the Moon*, second paperback edition, 1999, p. 366.

to death and destruction, and that they would never follow him again.[101] The U.S. government refused to let Vang Pao enter the country, and the CIA had to intervene to obtain permission for him to emigrate to Montana. Vang Pao flew to the United States in June 1975.[102] In December 1975, the Pathet Lao took over the government and established the Lao People's Democratic Republic to replace the monarchy. As Zasloff and Langer had found out in their research, Kaysone Phoumvihane, the head of the Lao People's Revolutionary Party, the secret communist party they had studied, was the real power holder in the Pathet Lao. He, not Prince Souphanouvong, became the leader of the government.[103]

The epitaph of the tribal program was offered by Ambassador Mac Godley. Long after he had retired from the diplomatic service, Godley admitted that, "We used the Meo. . . . The rationale then, which I believed in, was that they tied down three first-rate North Vietnamese divisions that otherwise would have been used against our men in South Vietnam. . . . It was a dirty business."[104]

In the end, Thailand benefited the most from the proxy war for which the Hmong paid such a high price. Initially, Operation MOMENTUM—the tribal resistance—was conceived to stop the Pathet Lao advance into the Mekong Valley, not only to save the Royal Lao Government but also to keep the communists away from the border with Thailand, which was nervous about its own nascent insurgency in the northeast.

---

[101] Warner, *Shooting at the Moon*, 1999, p. 366. At the height of his power in Long Cheng, when he was doing America's bidding, Vang Pao had looked like a charismatic leader. After his evacuation to Thailand, when he went to meet one of the CIA operatives who had worked with him in Long Cheng, the CIA agent thought that Vang Pao—now out of his element—seemed "uninspired and generic . . . just another short, overweight Asian ex-warlord, like the right-wing leaders and generals from Cambodia and South Vietnam" (Warner, *Shooting at the Moon*, 1999, p. 368).

[102] The CIA intervention, according to Warner, was useful because Vang Pao was "after all, a known polygamist with a history of involvement in the opium trade" (Warner, *Shooting at the Moon*, 1999, p. 367). A few years after arriving in Montana, Vang Pao migrated to Santa Ana, where he lived on an annual pension of $35,000 from the U.S. government. In June 2007, he was arrested and accused of plotting the violent overthrow of the Lao government. However, on October 2, 2009, a federal grand jury in California dropped charges against Vang Pao.

[103] After the war, as Zasloff and Langer had predicted, Laos became a client-state of Vietnam. However, China has muscled in to challenge Vietnamese influence.

[104] Warner, *Shooting at the Moon*, 1999, p. 380. Unlike Douglas Blaufarb, who wrote the RAND report at a time when the war was still unresolved and the ultimate price for the Hmong was not yet apparent, author Roger Warner had the benefit of knowing how it all came to an end in Laos. In his view, it was clear that once the Hmong were no longer needed to serve American objectives in Vietnam, they were abandoned (Warner, *Shooting at the Moon*, 1999, p. 380).

The communist movement in Thailand began as an offshoot of the Chinese Communist Party.[105] Originally an urban organization, it focused mainly on activities among the Chinese community of Thailand. In 1949, it severed its affiliation with the Party in China, but the leadership remained Sino-Thai, and most of the members were still ethnic Chinese. After General—later Field Marshal—Sarit Thanarat gained power in a coup d'etat in 1958 and established a military, authoritarian regime, he began to crack down on the communists, and his suppression drove the party out of Bangkok to seek refuge in the remote forested and mountainous areas in the northeast, near the border with Laos, where it forged links with other opposition groups. In this region, the communists found conditions that they could exploit to grow their movement.

The soil here was arid, and people on average earned 50 percent less in per capita income than Thais in the rest of the country. Nearly three-quarters of the families lived below the poverty line. The inhabitants of the northeast were ethnic Lao, who shared the culture and language of the Lao across the Mekong and felt great kinship with them. General Sarit himself was half Lao and was related to one of the right-wing leaders in Vientiane. Since the government in Bangkok had done little to alleviate their social and economic conditions, the people of the northeast felt discriminated against and neglected—and resentful as a result. Those who joined the communists were not committed to ideology but were persuaded by the Thai or Sino-Thai cadres that, unless they fought against the government to change their lots, they would continue to endure hardship and suffering. The cadres promised that if they joined the fighters in the forest, they would receive money, get trained for a good job, obtain land and tractors, and have schools and hospitals—all the things they did not possess and aspired to have. The communists were careful to resort to violence only sporadically, to avoid alienating the people and inviting powerful government reprisals.[106]

David Morell, formerly MACV project officer for the Viet Cong Motivation and Morale Project (see Chapter Two)—who spent several years performing research for the Research and Analysis Corporation (RAC) in Thailand—described the situation as "internal colonialism," perpetrated by the central government, which was dominated by the elite. Both the government and the elite maintained a very arrogant attitude toward the northeast in particular. Government officials assigned to such areas looked down on the poor villagers, treated them as second-class citizens, and were "more inter-

---

[105] For further details, see John L.S. Girling, *Thailand: Society and Politics*, Ithaca and London: Cornell University Press, 1981.

[106] The communists were also successful among the hill tribes in the north of Thailand. Among the tribes, the Hmong had been the most responsive to the blandishments of the communist organizers, unlike their cousins in Laos, who joined cause with the United States against the Pathet Lao. The Hmong in northern Thailand were resentful of land-grabbing by the Thais and of the contempt and indifference of Thai military and civilian officials, who looked down on them as "savages." Armed rebellion by the Hmong did not occur until 1967, after a Hmong village was burned by local government officials in retaliation for their refusal to pay bribes. In the south, the Bangkok government also faced a rebellion among Muslims.

ested in . . . being corrupt than caring for people and encouraging development."[107] As a result, growing popular resentment against the central government was feeding the insurgency. Unlike in Vietnam, however, there was no foreign intervention to exacerbate the problem.

Considering the proximity to Laos, the ethnic composition of the northeast, and the restive situation there, Sarit was afraid that communist subversion would spread into the region from Laos. He favored the right-wing faction in Laos and was displeased when President Kennedy decided to support the neutralization of Laos and accept neutralist Prince Souvanna Phouma as head of a coalition government in 1962. The Thai acquiesced to the terms of the Geneva Accords of 1962 only after the United States made a clear commitment to defend Thailand with or without SEATO concurrence; station American troops on Thai soil; and increase significantly economic, as well as military, aid designed to cope with the insurgency in the northeast and build the Thai armed forces in response to the developments in Laos and Vietnam.

At Sarit's death in 1963, General Thanom Kittikachorn succeeded him as prime minister. It was during Thanom's tenure that Thailand became increasingly entangled in Laos, to maintain a friendly, noncommunist, and anti-Vietnamese government in Vientiane, as well as in Vietnam, to assist the United States with counterinsurgency. By mid-1964, the Thai allowed the United States to base aircraft at Takhli Airfield in Nakhon Sawan. After the Tonkin Gulf incident, in August 1964, they allowed additional aircraft to be based at Korat, and then Nakhon Phnom, to target the Ho Chi Minh Trail. The American military presence grew, and eventually about 45,000 American military personnel, mostly from the Air Force, were stationed in Thailand, along with about 600 aircraft, including B-52s based at U Tapao.

From these and other facilities in Thailand, the United States conducted air bombardments over North Vietnam and Laos, aerial reconnaissance and supply missions, electronic warfare and intelligence collection, and radar surveillance, and dispatched covert ground teams into Laos and beyond. According to David Morell, although the United States would use large bases, such as Korat, Thakhli, Nakhon Phnom, Ubon, and Udorn, these bases served as "aircraft carriers," and the American presence did not saturate and disrupt the countryside.[108] In addition, the Thais also sent troops into Vietnam and Laos, and allowed the CIA to base personnel on its border to run the paramilitary war in Laos.

It was in 1962, when Sarit was concerned about the neutralization of Laos and the participation of the Pathet Lao in the coalition government in Vientiane, that RAND staff member Jack Blakeslee went to Thailand for a two-year assignment. Whereas the RAND analysts in Vietnam generally came to the country out of intellectual curiosity or out of a desire to assist the war efforts, Blakeslee, as well as other people from

---

[107] Author interview with David Morell, May 2004.

[108] Author interview with David Morell, May 2004.

RAND who went to Bangkok, were motivated more by the desire to spend time in an exotic place and were not as attracted by the nature of the work itself. The projects they engaged in, for the most part, were of the kind that did not require the application of the sophisticated analytic skills for which RAND was famous.[109] Unlike in Saigon, RAND did not maintain an official, direct presence in Bangkok. It did not have an office under its name, and the few RAND staff members who came to Bangkok were attached to the equivalent of the ARPA R&D Field Unit in Saigon and answered to its management. The number of projects in which they participated was small.[110] The output was even less significant than that undertaken by RAND in Laos, and certainly paled in significance when compared with the studies produced in Laos.[111]

The main reason RAND never developed a significant field presence in Thailand was because this country did not become an important U.S. national-security issue that RAND felt it would need to address or for which Washington might want to enlist its help to clarify policy choices. Despite fears to the contrary, the insurgency did not grow into a significant threat to Thailand's security; consequently, U.S. involvement remained limited. David Morell recalled that RAND was little involved in research in Thailand, in contrast to organizations such as RAC and SRI, which were "big players." There were a number of other American defense research institutes performing studies in Bangkok, but RAND was invisible. RAND, he said, was Tony Russo coming into town to visit his wife.[112]

---

[109] The studies RAND performed in Thailand fell into the category of "technical projects," that Gus Shubert thought were "unsuitable" for RAND because, in his view, they were minor, non–policy-oriented studies, and represented a misuse of RAND talent.

[110] Prior to this period, a few pieces of research were written at RAND as background information for the limited war games conducted by the Mathematics Department: R. F. Rhyne in Missiles, *A Hypothetical War in Thailand*, December 7, 1955; SIERRA Project personnel in Mathematics, *Limited War in Thailand, Thai-2: Guerrilla Operations*, D-3731, July 11, 1956, which was withdrawn; and *Limited War in Thailand, Thai-2: Ground Combat*, D-3734, July 11, 1956, which was also withdrawn. Another work that could have been produced for the same purpose is David Allen Wilson of Logistics, *Thailand 1962*, P-2685, December 1962, which concluded that Sarit's tight control was holding political conflict "in a state of suspense." Wilson also wrote *Political Tradition and Political Change in Thailand*, P-2592, June 1962, in which he discussed the makeup of Thai society, the character of Thai political groups, and the problems brought on by the change that they were facing.

[111] Some work on Thailand had been performed earlier in Santa Monica. For example, in September 1963, Herbert P. Phillips of the Social Science Department and D. A. Wilson of Logistics produced *Certain Effects of Culture and Social Organization on Internal Security in Thailand*, Santa Monica, Calif.: RAND Corporation, RM-3786/ARPA. In this report, the authors took up the argument that measures to strengthen security were likely to succeed if they took into account the motivations and attitudes of the Thai people and the traditions of Thai society. Phillips and Wilson argued that, since the communist threat was "nebulous," security measures should not be aimed only at this threat. An exclusively anti-communist approach would be unlikely to attract the villagers' interest or cooperation, but a program that met some of their existing needs—through traditional means wherever possible—would have a better chance at success.

[112] Author interview with David Morell, May 2004.

At the time, ARPA/AGILE had an arrangement with the Thai Military Research and Development Command (MRDC) in the Ministry of Defence to establish a research and test center. This was the equivalent to the test center in Saigon and was organized along the same lines. Each unit of the MRDC was headed by a Thai military officer and a U.S. military officer, and was staffed with Thai and U.S. military personnel. The center had three or four American contract civilian employees. Perhaps as a result of a visit to Thailand made by Jack Ellis in 1962 to explore research opportunities, RAND agreed to assist the test center, and Jack Ellis worked out an arrangement with ARPA. It was after a conversation Jack Blakeslee had with Jack Ellis that he obtained the assignment to the MRDC. Blakeslee had never been to an Asian country and he thought that it would be interesting to live in an exotic locale such as Thailand. Besides, he believed he could make a contribution to the work that ARPA/AGILE was doing.

Blakeslee had joined RAND as an aeronautical engineer from United Aircraft in Connecticut. At the time, the RAND Aero-Astronautics Department performed analyses, studies, predictions, and preliminary conceptual designs of what airborne and spaceborne vehicles might be used in the future in the Cold War. There was a group called the Aircraft Design Group, and there was another group called the Propulsion Group, which dealt with "rocket engines and all kinds of special engines for . . . aircraft."[113] Blakeslee was hired to work in the Aircraft Design Group as an aeronautical engineer "to sort of work up the performance characteristics and other features of airborne systems that didn't exist but that might be used some day—it's sort of a futuristic look at what might be available for the Air Force to use in defense against the Soviet Union's activities and their systems."[114]

He first worked on things such as "air-to-air missile systems from bombers that might be penetrating the Soviet Union in a nuclear war situation," and "on special basing systems for bomber aircraft and so on." Then he went into work "that dealt with the overall characteristics of systems that would use these aircrafts and missiles that we were conceptualizing." RAND in those days did not compartmentalize its staff, which was still relatively small. As Blakeslee recalled, "You were even encouraged to try an idea for a while, and if you came up with something, you could go with it. So individual members didn't have many constraints in working up an idea, even if it was not specifically in our academic background and expertise."[115] It was in this environment of relative freedom that Blakeslee thought of joining the ARPA/AGILE group in Thailand.

This assignment was very different from what he had done, but it was hardly unusual for RAND employees in those days. Blakeslee recalled that there were econo-

---

[113] Author interview with Jack Blakeslee, 2004. Blakeslee could not remember when he joined RAND.

[114] Author interview with Jack Blakeslee, 2004.

[115] Author interview with Jack Blakeslee, 2004.

mists "whose experience didn't necessarily have to do with . . . the cost effectiveness of military systems at all"—people like Alain Enthoven and Harry Rowen "who lent their mental abilities which were considerable to working out not the strictly economic features of systems but working out the military cost effectiveness of these future systems that we were working with." Blakeslee insisted that it was not "as loose" as he made it sound. "Our division heads weren't about to waste our time, or RAND's time, or our military supporter's time at all," he said. "We had to show that we were going to accomplish something, if we wanted to do something different. But if we could show that, then we had a lot of latitude—not a free rein—to do whatever work we were interested in. That worked well. That was something that gave RAND a boost to become the eminent organization that it is today."[116]

Blakeslee remembered that it was up to him to decide what to do once he got to Thailand. The agreement was simply that he would work for a couple of years and make the contribution that RAND had promised under its ARPA/AGILE contract, and that once he got to Bangkok he would just do whatever he could. He knew that the work would be technical, because what the Military Research and Development Command did was technology-oriented rather than policy-oriented, such as testing vehicles and radio propagation. Blakeslee was the first RAND person to be assigned to the test center. He had a RAND secretary, Kathy Taylor, working for him. Later, Viv Pickelseimer came to replace her. Then Jim Wilson arrived the second year Blakeslee was in Bangkok. Together, they formed the RAND group, although there was no RAND office. Blakeslee remembered that the Thais gave them some desks and a place to work, and that was the extent of it.

Blakeslee brought his family along, and rented a plain wooden house on stilts over a canal, like most houses in Bangkok at the time. It was located in Sukhumvit, an eastern suburb of Bangkok, on a street called Soi Klong, and belonged to a middle-level functionary in the Economics Ministry who had built it to rent to foreigners. Blakeslee thought that his life in Bangkok was "plush" and relatively cheap. RAND had a "no win and no loss" policy, which meant that it would reimburse him for whatever expenses he and his family incurred above normal costs in the United States. RAND had adopted this policy because it had confidence in its employees and trusted that they would not abuse it, which turned out to be the case, due to the closeness between the staff and the corporation. The cost of living in Bangkok was low, however, and Blakeslee needed no reimbursement. Although they had not lived in Asia, he and his family experienced no culture shock, and kept themselves busy with visits to such sites as Buddhist temples and with various other activities.

For his research, Blakeslee came up with the idea of doing a visual surveillance project. Then, in his second year, he was asked to participate in a rural security study. Blakeslee remembered that concern over the expansion of the insurgency in the

---

[116] Author interview with Jack Blakeslee, 2004.

northeast— and to some extent in the south—was the main impetus behind the activities conducted by ARPA/AGILE and the MRDC. The work that he and other researchers performed was intended to prepare for such an eventuality.

His objective in conducting the airborne visual surveillance tests was to determine how successful aerial observers could be at identifying insurgents on the ground. He characterized it as "a scientifically-oriented project that would try to measure the ranges" at which this aerial reconnaissance could spot insurgents and the scope of their activities.[117] The project took six months, and a great deal of the time was spent in obtaining from the U.S. Air Force aerial photography of the Ubon area, about 150–200 miles east of Bangkok, and of the Cambodian border region. From that photography, Blakeslee would pick different sites, such as a field with bushes, or a forest area, or a paddy field area, and then design "the pattern of locations of individuals who would be standing up behind the bushes, carrying rifles or not carrying rifles— different situations like that."[118]

The field tests were conducted in the dry season in a rice-growing area typical of Southeast Asia. For each test, a Thai Royal Air Force crew would fly over the site in a helicopter and Blakeslee would determine the distance at which they could detect a person, how long it took them to do so, and at what distance they could identify whether or not the person was carrying a weapon. The "insurgents" were Thai Army people dressed in coolie pajamas and assuming different postures. Using a timing device and a tape recorder, Blakeslee would sit with the tape recorder in the open door of the helicopter while an observer sitting in the copilot seat would tell Blakeslee when he saw something or when he could identify it. From the timing and the location of the helicopter as indicated on the route they were flying, Blakeslee could tell how far away they were from that individual. These empirical tests allowed him to determine how well the airborne observers could perform and how far away they could detect a target and identify it. He would analyze the time and distance data, along with the kind of target being tested, and then present the results using "curves and this kind of thing," to show how far away the airborne observers could successfully identify these targets.[119]

Blakeslee found out that the airborne observers were successful to some extent, but if the target was well hidden, they could not see it or identify it. He concluded that

---

[117] Author interview with Jack Blakeslee, 2004.

[118] The ad hoc nature of Blakeslee's work could be seen in his participation in an effort to measure the propagation of radio transmissions through jungle canopy in Korat, about 60 miles north of Bangkok. The project was carried out by a corporation under contract to the MRDC. Vehicles that were being designed and tested were used to see how well they could travel through muddy trails and swamps to penetrate into the jungle and perform the measurements. In the worst time of the year, the rainy season, the vehicles could not get through. So, a group was organized to go in on elephants, and Blakeslee was asked to go along. Traveling on the backs of elephants was uncomfortable, but the group managed to reach the camp to look at their radio-propagation test data.

[119] Author interview with Jack Blakeslee, 2004.

this kind of airborne surveillance was feasible, but would not yield results if the insurgents on the ground were clever about concealment. The project "just showed how well you could do—good or bad. If it was relatively easy, then you could get some information. If not, then you couldn't." In the end, the six observers identified 211 out of 287 targets. After he collected his data, it took him a while to figure out how to display the information so that people could get answers. According to him, the study "left a lot to be desired in terms of the statistical accuracy of the whole thing, but it had never been done before." He and everybody he knew thought that it was "well worthwhile doing even though it did not satisfy a rigorous statistical analysis standard," which he was not trying to meet.[120] The results were published in a RAND paper that was eventually incorporated into a report issued by the Joint Thai–U.S. Military Research and Development Center in Thai and English versions.

The second project Blakeslee participated in was the rural security pilot study conceived and led by Lee Hough, then a senior ARPA staff member, and was conducted in the northeast because the team was familiar with this region and because it seemed reasonable to assume that an insurgency would likely develop in an area that was remote and economically depressed like the northeast. The study encompassed 40 villages in Udorn Province, 569 kilometers north of Bangkok, and the team visited all of the villages in February and March 1964. The team included an anthropologist; a forester, to inventory the kinds of trees and determine how they might be used as fortification; an operations analyst; a political economist; a military officer; an engineer; an interpreter; and two vehicle drivers.

Blakeslee's responsibility was to determine the geometry of the village, since "that would have much to do with how well the villages could be defended against any insurgent activity."[121] The project was to collect and describe information rather than to analyze the data, and the database was meant to provide information to people in charge of making plans to protect villages in remote areas. It was inspired by the experience in Vietnam, where the ongoing war made field studies of village and hamlet security difficult, and where lack of good information about villages hampered efforts to devise security arrangements. It was therefore deemed productive to determine ways to protect villages before hostilities broke out, so that the Royal Thai Government would be more prepared to provide such protection if the situation demanded.

---

[120] D. J. Blakeslee, *Low-Altitude Visual Search for Individual Human Targets: Further Field Testing in Southeast Asia*, Santa Monica, Calif.: RAND Corporation, D-13353-ARPA, January 29, 1965. Blakeslee (p. vi) explained that, "An analytical relationship between identification slant range, velocity, search strip width, and visual performance factors was used with the test data to provide a speculative framework for assumption of a velocity-strip width effect on observer performance." He concluded that "limiting velocities for effective search for more difficult targets" would "lead to high aircraft vulnerability," while "increasing the velocity can mean very narrow search strip widths and therefore many search passes for complete coverage of large areas, again compromising vulnerability."

[121] Author interview with Jack Blakeslee, 2004.

The situation in this area was representative of the far northeastern region at the time. In addition to insurgent activities, there was also some banditry—a long-standing problem. However, the general level of violence was low. But it was difficult to separate banditry from insurgency. According to Blakeslee, at times it was difficult to tell whether "somebody is just a casual bandit out to steal from somebody or cause some violence or somebody who has a political agenda."[122] In talking to villagers, the team discovered that an insurgency did not exist in the area in which they were conducting research, but that there was cattle rustling, thievery by individuals or small groups coming from neighboring villages, and robbery of homes and stores. Nevertheless, there was fear that insurgency would develop and pose a real threat in the future.

The villages studied were generally located in a flat forest and rice paddy region, in the Korat Plateau, an arid region with chronic water shortage characteristic of the northeast. There were no large rivers in the area, and most of the lakes, ponds, small streams, creeks, and irrigation canals dried up after the rainy season. Villagers were preoccupied with the water problem, which, if left unattended by the government, could lead to popular discontent and feed an insurgency. The principal means of livelihood included rice cultivation and cattle raising. Since there was no water-conservation system, the land was dry for a greater part of the year, and rice production consequently provided a very unstable source of income.

Blakeslee recalled that it was extremely hot and uncomfortable to live in the field, but not strenuous. Lee Hough and the local advisors planned the itinerary so that the group would usually arrive at a village in the evening, clean up, and then find a Buddhist pagoda, or *wat,* where they would spend the night. A village *wat* was usually just a raised platform with a tile roof over it, but it was a nice shelter and a better alternative than lying on the ground in a sleeping bag. Blakeslee remembered that one of the villages they visited had a nice-looking pool, and they took quick dips in it. However, one of the team members luxuriated and relaxed in it for a long time. That night in the *wat,* they were awakened by loud screaming, and saw the man sitting up, looking terrified. It turned out that he was covered with leeches, which were tiny when they attached themselves to him but had gotten big after gorging themselves with blood. The local Thai guide lit a cigarette and burned them off. The team made so many trips into the villages that they got very tired of native food—some of which they could not identify.

The results were published in "agonizing details" in a report by the MRDC in 1965, with a description and diagram of each village,[123] including details such as building materials, soil, and tools; utilities and fuel; village distances and travel times; popu-

---

[122]Author interview with Jack Blakeslee, 2004.

[123]D. J. Blakeslee, "Collection of Author's Contribution: Thailand Rural Security Pilot Study Report," Santa Monica, Calif.: RAND Corporation, D-13434-ARPA, February 22, 1965. This report was later incorporated in *A Village Security Pilot Study: Northeast Thailand,* issued by the MRDC in May 1965.

lation and census data; village officials; village specialists—i.e., doctors, healers, midwives, spirit mediums, carpenters, brick makers, policemen, teachers, veterans, and mechanics; village industries; recent movements of people in and out of the villages; and security.

In Blakeslee's assessment, the security study was "the first of its kind and it should have served somebody well."[124] It gave the Thais the information on how best to defend the villages against the insurgents, but no situation arose that could put such information to use.

After completing his tour of duty, Blakeslee moved to Washington, where he became RAND liaison to the Air Staff. He met Lee Hough, now also back in Washington, a couple of times, but Hough never mentioned whether the report had been disseminated or what effect it might have had. By this time, Blakeslee had put it well behind him and moved on.

The second RAND person to arrive in Bangkok was Bob Holliday. In 1962, ARPA funded a study of roads in Thailand at the behest of CINCPAC J-2. At that time, the Chinese were building a road into northern Laos, and there was fear that they might embark on an invasion of Southeast Asia. The purpose of the research was to estimate, if there was an invasion, how many troops the Chinese could funnel through and how much logistical support the Chinese could give to these troops, given the road capacity. Besides the concern about a Chinese invasion, there were other reasons for the American interest in a road system, according to David Morell. Partly, a good road network would facilitate the trucking of ammunition to the air bases more effectively. "A good road network into the northeast was necessary to truck in all the bombs," he said. In addition, there was interest in the ports. For example, "the improvement of the port in Bangkok was designed to get more military weapons in as well as more commercial goods."[125]

Holliday's specialty was logistical support for ground forces. He had just come back to RAND after spending seven years with another firm, and suddenly he found himself in Thailand, riding in trucks loaned by the Thai government, "running experiments on all kinds of roads . . . from paved to gravel to dirt that went through little villages."[126] On his first trip to Thailand in 1962, Holliday was accompanied by John Greene, a RAND staff member from the Mathematics Department. They obtained a Land Rover and a Thai driver and explored a number of roads all over Thailand for a week, then they went back to Santa Monica to design the experiment. After that, Holliday returned with Roland Morrison, a civil engineer from the U.S. Army Pacific Headquarters in Hawaii, who knew a great deal about roads. Because of his work, Holliday was called a "roads scholar." He was the only RAND person assigned to

---

[124]Author interview with Jack Blakeslee, 2004.

[125]Author interview with David Morell, May 2004.

[126]Author interview with Bob Holliday, 2004.

Bob Holliday

this project. He and Morrison ran the tests in 1963, then they reduced the data and developed formulas to compute road capacity. When he returned to Santa Monica, he used the data he had gathered "to try to find a better way of predicting road capacity in underdeveloped countries to replace what the Army was using then which is just multiplying a bunch of factors together. . . . The multiplier is not a good way, so we developed ways of predicting capacity."[127] According to Holliday, he and Morrison "figured out that our Department of Defense was off by a factor of 2, on the low side, so the threat was twice as much as what they thought because of their erroneous way of computing road capacity."[128]

Holliday explained the new methodology in a report published in November 1963. It looked at each factor differently, instead of basing the road-capacity calculation on the successive multiplication of factors, and concluded that the basic factors were speed and lead.[129] In Holliday's estimation, the results of the study could have been fairly important, because they showed that it would have been "twice as easy for the Chinese to support their troops with truckloads of supplies than our planners thought."[130]

---

[127] Author interview with Bob Holliday, 2004.

[128] Author interview with Bob Holliday, 2004.

[129] L. P. Holliday, *A Method for Estimating Road Capacity and Truck Requirements*, Santa Monica, Calif.: RAND Corporation, RM-3331-ARPA, November 1963.

[130] Holliday, *A Method for Estimating Road Capacity*, 1963. In 1968, Holliday delivered a paper on the subject at a conference sponsored by the Engineer Strategic Studies Group, U.S. Army Map Service, in Washington, D.C. In his paper, *Experience and Evaluation of a Testing Program in an Underdeveloped Area as a Means of Developing a Road Capacity Estimating Method,* RAND P-3913, he discussed multiple correlations between such factors as speed, terrain, condition, surface, day/night, and empty/loaded. He concluded that condition and surface had the most effect on speed and that width and terrain had much less effect. Another work on road capacity was produced by J. W. Higgins in Logistics, from Santa Monica, in December 1966. In *Interdiction and Resupply: Transportation Networks in Thailand and Laos, and the Effect of Network Degradation* (Santa Monica, Calif.: RAND Corporation, RM-5176-PR), Higgins applied the RAND interdiction model of transportation to a hypothetical invasion of Thailand from the communist-controlled zones in Laos by the Pathet Lao and North Vietnamese and by China from Yunnan Province.

For the road tests, Holliday and Morrison used Thai drivers who were engineering students from Chulalongkorn University and spoke a little English. RAND had arranged for Holliday to take some Thai lessons, so he spoke a bit of the language. Some of the field trips were memorable. One night, the driver arranged for them to sleep on the front porch of a local house. The owners of the house gave them knives, and said, "Here, keep these knives because at night there are liable to be bandits that come up here."[131] Holliday hardly slept that night. On another trip, during a stay in a hotel, monkeys came into their rooms and took some of their belongings.

The tests in November 1962 were conducted after the rainy season. So, Holliday undertook more tests during the monsoon season to determine what restrictions the rains could impose. In his report published in 1963, Holliday explained that, during the rainy season, roads that were not adequately drained and equipped with well-designed bridges and culverts, or that were elevated above flood level, could be subject to washouts.[132] He recommended that the highway program financed by U.S. aid be expanded to include improvement of a secondary road system that should be properly drained. These secondary roads, in his view, would serve "Thailand's interests more, from both an economic and a defense standpoint, than a lesser system of paved roads built at the same cost."[133] He also suggested that bridges in areas prone to flooding be modified to prevent erosion and washouts. Since the RAND road-capacity project had "re-established the importance of roads for the support of military operations," he urged that resource allocation be reevaluated with regard to the road systems.[134] The road studies were the only projects Holliday conducted in Thailand.

While Blakeslee was in his second year in Bangkok, Jim Wilson arrived. After returning from Vietnam, Wilson heard through Jack Ellis that there was an opening in Thailand, and rushed over to tell him, "Jack, I want to go."[135] Ellis arranged for the posting, and Wilson, his wife, and their children moved to Bangkok in 1963 for two years. They rented a newly built house, owned by a high-ranking, wealthy Thai official in the government. Living in Thailand was an interesting experience for his wife and children, because they had never been exposed to foreign countries. They immersed themselves in the local culture, and the children attended Thai schools and learned the language. Wilson recalled that the Thais were nice but impossible to hurry. He said, "One thing you don't want to do is get frustrated in Thailand. You've got to be a bot-

[131] Author interview with Bob Holliday, 2004.

[132] L. P. Holliday, *Report on Wet Season Truck Test and Comments on the Thailand Road Program*, Santa Monica, Calif.: RAND Corporation, D-11775-ARPA, October 17, 1963.

[133] Holliday, *Report on Wet Season Truck Test*, 1963, p. 8.

[134] Holliday, *Report on Wet Season Truck Test*, 1963, p. 9.

[135] Author interview with Jim Wilson, 2004.

tomless pit of patience. You ask for something that you need and you sit back and wait. You never push them because they don't like that."[136]

Wilson remembered that he worked out of an office in the Ministry of Defence building, as a RAND representative in the ARPA R&D Field Unit.[137] His job was to survey Thai airfields and to find out how many of the airstrips built by the Japanese during their occupation of Thailand were still discernible and usable. The objective was to locate the airfields for future use, just in case they were needed, and what kind of traffic they could bear. The team looked at things such as facilities and supplies—in short, they tried to determine whether the airfields could "support our troops—can it do this, can it do that—that sort of thing."[138] He remembered getting a call one day from someone in the U.S. Air Force who wanted to know about one airfield in particular. Wilson told him, "Yes, you can use it but you've got to let some air out of your tires, because if you put too much weight on that runway, it will collapse." He added, "You'll never know—there might be a big hole in that runway and then you'd be in big trouble."[139] Wilson wrote several reports in which he simply described what he found. His job was not to make recommendations but to put the data together so that the decisionmakers could "make up their minds." It was not his job "to tell them—you don't tell them anything."[140]

It took a little while to get organized, and then he began flying around the country with a military team to see what could be found. Usually, he relied on the Thais to take him to his destination. If the team had to spend the night somewhere, they would sleep in a school house on a cot. For meals, they ate in local restaurants. He remembered one lunch in particular. By the time the helicopter landed in a police post, Wilson was famished. The commander brought out "this big bowl of rice and this brown stuff," which Wilson thought was gravy. He started eating it and "all of a sudden bells and whistles—it was hot, and I was on fire." He flew back with his tongue "hanging out the door of the helicopter so he could cool it."[141]

When he first got to Bangkok, he heard that there were about 180 airfields in Thailand, but it turned out that this information was incorrect. Most of the "airfields"

---

[136]Author interview with Jim Wilson, 2004.

[137]The administrative assistant at the time was Vivian Pickelseimer, who had taken over from Kathy Taylor. Pickelseimer's reason was simple: She just wanted to see Thailand. She served as typist, and took care of all the office chores, such as arranging transportation in-country. She recalled that some RAND people came through occasionally, but she could not remember their names and what they did, except that it had something to do with "terrorism." She enjoyed her stay in Bangkok, although she found Bangkok still primitive, with many putrid *klong*s, or "canals." She cut short her stay after eating food in a market that made her gravely ill. Author interview with Vivian Pickelseimer, 2004.

[138]Author interview with Jim Wilson, 2004.

[139]Author interview with Jim Wilson, 2004.

[140]Author interview with Jim Wilson, 2004.

[141]Author interview with Jim Wilson, 2004.

were actually just helicopter sites near border outposts. After such a long passage of time, many of the airfields built by the Japanese had deteriorated, but their outlines were still visible in the jungle. The team usually tried to locate the oldest living inhabitants, who might know where the airstrips were. He remembered a very old woman they had as a guide on one of his field trips. When one of the Thais asked her, "Where do we find this airfield?" She said, "Come with me." She found the stakes and said, "There they are."

A typical trip report was the one he filed in August 1963. In it, he described visits to a couple of airfields by H-34 helicopter belonging to Air America.[142] The first airfield could not be found. The second one looked like it had not been used for some time—and there were grass and buffalo-cart tracks on the strip. Another had not been used for some time, but with some leveling and stabilization could become a short-takeoff and landing (STOL) airstrip. One near a Border Police site had a clay and sand surface with low-growing weeds, and was very soft. The last four airfields could not be found.

At the end of his assignment, in 1965, Wilson returned to the United States, where he worked on another project surveying airfields. He remembered that, "At that time, we were having problems with the Russians, and we were using our airfields to disperse aircrafts to save them. We had something like 4,000 airfields across the United States we could disperse the aircrafts to, provided they could support the aircrafts."[143] Bangkok was his last brush with Southeast Asia.

After Jack Blakeslee left to return home, Bob Crawford came to replace him, as the last and main RAND staff member assigned to the MRDC.[144] His departure in 1966 would mark the end of RAND's presence at the R&D Field Unit. Crawford's job was to research target marking in the featureless jungle and to study the vulnerability of air bases in Thailand so that steps to improve protection against enemy attacks could be recommended. RAND had performed a similar study for NATO air bases many years before. This new study would apply the lessons gleaned in Vietnam, where the Viet Cong usually relied on surprise, force concentration, and the use of sapper units or suicide squads in their attacks.

---

[142] Report included in J. A. Wilson, "Trip Reports: Surveys of Long-Vacant Airstrips, Thailand, July–August 1963," Santa Monica, Calif.: RAND Corporation, D-11694-ARPA, September 12, 1963.

[143] Author interview with Jim Wilson, 2004.

[144] At the end of 1964, Kathy Scoffield arrived to replace Vivian Pickelseimer. Scoffield had asked Jack Ellis to post her to Bangkok, because she wanted to travel in the region and the assignment seemed like a great opportunity. She recalled that it was an exciting but also a terrible time to be in that part of the world, and "everybody was living in sort of a heightened state." The spouses of Tony Russo and Mike Pearce were living in Bangkok while their husbands worked in Vietnam, and together they formed with Scoffield a kind of social network. She left Bangkok when the RAND employees left and the office closed down, in 1966. Author interview with Kathy Scoffield, 2004.

Jack Ellis joined him in the project, and together they visited several main air bases to determine the different ways in which an enemy force could breach the defenses of an air base and the tactics that could be adopted to make an attack less effective and more costly for the enemy.[145] Using the experience in Vietnam, Crawford and Ellis recommended that, where feasible, the air bases in Thailand adopt countermeasures, such as patrol aircraft in the immediate vicinity of the air base, especially at night, when the enemy was likely to attack; a ground alert system; fixed-wing aircraft or armed helicopters to provide rapid reactive firepower support; and ground security and defense forces using Air Police units, and sentry dogs to detect early the presence of potentially hostile elements; civic action in and pacification of the surrounding areas to build a security screen; informant net in the same areas to procure information on enemy intentions; dispersal of equipment and revetment to mitigate against the impact of mortar or recoilless-rifle fire; shelters for personnel; simple observation towers or platforms near the outer perimeter of the air base; illumination to detect enemy attackers; fences, preferably made up of a triple arrangement of concertina barbed wire; radar; defoliation to clear the defense perimeter of obstruction; and training and motivation of the security forces.

They recommended that a comprehensive and detailed defense and security plan be put in place, in collaboration with the Thais to avoid confusion, with clearly assigned responsibilities, established routine and emergency procedures, defined command and control relationships, and frequently held training exercises on steps to be taken in an alert. In addition, a Joint Defense Operation Center should be organized and fully manned at all times to handle issues of command and procedures. Threats to the air bases could be reduced by combining active and passive defense and security measures, such as ambush patrols and an airborne alert team. In addition, an infantry company should be assigned to defend each important air base in an area where insurgents were active; this company would complement the security functions of the Air Police and would be responsible for keeping the insurgents from penetrating the outer defense to threaten the vital resources of the air base.

Bob Crawford's departure marked the end of RAND's presence at the R&D Field Unit in Bangkok. However, as the Vietnam War escalated further and Thailand became the launching pad for U.S. air operations, RAND sent a small group of researchers to Thailand in 1967 to participate in a project called Rapid Roger. Among the researchers was John Lu, who had joined RAND in 1964 from IBM. Lu had a doctorate in economics statistics and agriculture economics from Michigan State University, and was recruited by Murray Geisler into RAND's Logistics Department, which at the time was studying Air Force logistics and applying operations-research methods

---

[145] John Winthrop Ellis and Robert Crawford, "Airbase Defense and Security with Application to Thailand," Santa Monica, Calif.: RAND Corporation, D-15350-ARPA/AGILE, December 1966.

to devise a more cost-effective supply system that provided spare parts and equipment in support of Air Force operations.

Rapid Roger was sponsored by the Air Force and was intended to partly resolve a debate between the Air Force, which wanted to obtain more planes to meet contingencies and to have flexibility, and other people in the government, who favored buying fewer aircraft to limit costs and applying more resources instead to maximize the number of flights. The question that was raised by the Air Force hierarchy, and for which RAND was enlisted to provide the answer, was, If more resources were devoted to an aircraft, such as maintenance and spare parts, could more sorties be made per day? The job of the RAND team was to observe how many sorties were being flown by an airplane, and what kind of logistics support was being given, to estimate and project the relationship between the number of sorties and the logistics resources.

John Lu flew into Bangkok and then was taken by military aircraft to Ubon, where the data for Rapid Roger were going to be collected. At this time, the United States had taken over this Thai air base and turned it into a major site for sorties against North Vietnam. With the arrival of the American Air Wing, the base had become very crowded and was very active at all hours, because "the air war had no particular time."[146] Occasionally, a plane or two were shot down, and everyone turned somber. For the project, the RAND team members rotated, spending a month-and-a-half or a couple of months, at the air base. They made their observations and then left, to be replaced by someone else. Lu remembered that he came back to Santa Monica to analyze the data, and then his successor did the same thing to make sure that the data were collected properly. He supposed that RAND wanted "more staff members to be there for the experience and expose themselves to the wartime environment."[147]

At any given time, there were about four members in the team, who came either from the Logistics Department or the Computer Department. He remembered Dick Nelson from Engineering, and the team leaders Irv Cohen, then Chauncey Bell. As civilians, they could not live on the base and had to rent homes in Ubon, which Lu described as a peaceful little town located about 500 miles northeast of Bangkok and about 100 miles from the border with Vietnam. Lu remembered that he and Nelson rented a beautiful small house raised about nine feet off the ground. It had running water, but no hot water. Living in such a small town was a novel experience for both of them. The weather at that time of the year was considered moderate by the Thais, but it was still too hot and too humid for John Lu. He stayed for six weeks and was glad to get home to his family.

The RAND team obtained data the Air Force had collected to track such information as the kinds of spare parts requested and the number of maintenance people assigned. They then expanded these data to determine the type and level of resources

---

[146] Author interview with John Lu, 2004.

[147] Author interview with John Lu, 2004.

that would have to be provided to generate certain numbers of sorties. When the data collection was completed, the group came back to the United States and wrote a classified report. Lu could not recall the numbers they came up with to determine "the relationship between the amount of money you spent to support and the number of sorties you could mount." However, there was "a limit on what you can do," and the maximum you could wring out of each aircraft was probably two or three sorties per day per plane.[148]

✥ ✥ ✥

Just as in Vietnam, analysts in Santa Monica were also producing reports on Thailand in this period of the 1960s. However, these were far fewer and did not reach the level of importance or visibility of those on Vietnam.[149] In November 1967, concern that the incipient insurgency would become a serious problem led USAID and ARPA to sponsor a seminar at RAND to explore how economic development could strengthen Thailand's security. The seminar examined the nature of the insurgency in Thailand and its implications for the development of U.S. aid programs. Its conclusion was that, if the linkage of economic development and security was accepted, the United States should focus on setting priorities, selecting activities that would have a long-range effect, and concentrating on a few key areas.[150]

Although the communist insurgency never developed into a serious national-security threat, the Communist Party of Thailand did make a major effort during the period from 1968 to 1970 to mobilize in the villages, and the insurgency grew. But even in those peak years, RAND did not get involved in research on Thailand in a major way. When research was performed, it was done by RAND analysts in the United States, rather than in the field. Among the more important works was a report by John Enos, published in January 1970,[151] that used the northeast of Thailand as a case study of an underdeveloped economy's growth prospects for a 25-year period by applying a simulation model with over 100 equations. Computer runs were made to determine the likely effect of several sets of conditions and policy alternatives on

---

[148] Author interview with John Lu, 2004.

[149] See, for example, J. W. Higgins, G. S. Levenson, and W. E. Mooz, *A Study of In-Theater Logistic Support of a Large Ground Force by Air*, Santa Monica, Calif.: RAND Corporation, RM-5127-PR, June 1967. The authors considered a hypothetical situation in which 4-1/3 Army divisions had to be deployed and supplied by air. They determined the various types of aircraft capable of supplying the ground troops, their costs, and the operational problems encountered in five basic logistics missions: initial deployment, in-theater redeployment, rear-area supply, forward-area supply, and air assault. The performance of the fleets was evaluated for these missions.

[150] See Hans Heymann, *Seminar on Development and Security in Thailand: Part I, The Insurgency*, Santa Monica, Calif.: RAND Corporation, RM-5871, 1969; and Hans Heymann, *Seminar on Development and Security in Thailand: Part II, Development-Security Interactions*, Santa Monica, Calif.: RAND Corporation, RM-5872, 1969.

[151] John Enos, *Modeling the Economic Development of a Poorly Endowed Region: The Northeast of Thailand*, Santa Monica, Calif.: RAND Corporation, RM-6185-ARPA, January 1970.

development objectives. The conclusion was that population growth would outpace the capacity of the labor market to absorb and would create needs that food production would be unable to meet. According to Enos, subsistence by itself could pose a threat to stability and should be met with a massive, sustained national effort in all sectors.

Besides economic issues, the security threat that attracted some attention at RAND in this period was the renewed possibility that China might invade Thailand. In a paper published in December 1970, Richard Wise of Systems Sciences discussed the hypothetical scenario of a counteroffensive by the United States and Thailand.[152] He envisioned four communist infantry divisions advancing into northeast Thailand, where allied forces stopped them 20 miles north of Khon Kaen. The allied forces had two alternatives: attacking the enemy head on and piercing the defensive positions they had set up, or enveloping them and forcing them to fight in a new direction. In his view, this latter maneuver would be the better of the two alternatives, providing that the enemy disposition offered an assailable flank and the counter forces had superior mobility.

❧ ❧ ❧

Perhaps the RAND person with the most influence on the U.S. counterinsurgency effort in Thailand was George Tanham. David Morell recalled that Tanham made this influence in 1970, when he was detached from RAND and came to Bangkok as Ambassador Graham Martin's special assistant for counterinsurgency (SACI)—replacing Peer de Silva, a very senior CIA executive who had been head of station in Vienna and Saigon. Graham Martin had given a great deal of authority to the SACI position, stating in essence in a memo to the American agency heads, which Morell had access to, that he was delegating all counterinsurgency matters to the SACI.

According to Morell, Tanham changed the approach to counterinsurgency. De Silva had emphasized military and classic intelligence techniques. The main instrument he had relied on was the Border Patrol Police, which was operating not just along the border but "internally as a special kind of para-military force."[153] It was more trained by the Central Intelligence Agency than the military, had better weapons than the military, and had better mobility with greater access to helicopters, for example. Essentially, the Border Patrol Police was the elite force and the main counterinsurgency instrument, operating against the Communist Party members in the villages. The approach worked well as long as intelligence correctly identified these Party members, but problems sometimes arose when communist suppression got tangled in local politics and feuds over land or other issues.

---

[152] Richard Wise, *An Operational Setting for the Comparison of Alternative Tactical Mobility Systems for Ground Forces*, Santa Monica, Calif.: RAND Corporation, IN-21319-PR, December 1970.

[153] Author interview with David Morell, 2004.

Tanham's approach emphasized not only security but also village development as essential in dealing with the insurgency. To integrate efforts, Tanham adopted the approach William Sullivan had employed in Laos, enforcing tight coordination between the various elements of the American counterinsurgency support. Consequently, Tanham, according to Morell, was able to avoid the fragmentation that was common in Saigon. Tanham held a meeting every Tuesday—the Tuesday Group—to bring officials from different agencies together to discuss their weekly strategy. He also coordinated closely with the Thais, something that was missing in South Vietnam, where the Americans tended to take over. This coordination was possible partly because the Thais, who had never been colonized, were much more self-reliant, and were unwilling to cede control to foreigners. Tanham's effort was facilitated greatly by the Thais, who were more successful than the South Vietnamese in integrating their own counterinsurgency efforts with their creation of the Communist Suppression Command (CSOC), which brought the Air Force, the Army, the Special Forces, and the Police together to work more effectively. In Morell's estimation, "to some degree Tanham . . . had a role to play in the success" of counterinsurgency in Thailand—if *success* was defined "as keeping the royal government in place."[154]

The Thai and American effort was successful mainly because the insurgency stalled, and China and North Vietnam did not invade, as feared. North Vietnam had other objectives and limited means, and China—engulfed in the Cultural Revolution—turned inward. In a paper published in October 1970, Robert L. Solomon of the Social Science Department, an expert on Thailand, offered an analysis of why the insurgency did not grow into a security threat after a decade of struggle.[155] According to him, the insurgents suffered from internal dissension and an inability to build an effective grass-roots infrastructure based on strong popular support. Beyond the marginal areas of the northeast, the north, and the extreme south, Thai society in general did not offer fertile ground for their movement to grow. The conditions that allowed a minor insurgency to spread elsewhere and persist, such as sufficient popular grievances, porosity of the borders, and government ineffectiveness and lack of penetration, were either absent in other regions or did not exist to the same extent as in the marginalized areas. Thailand's symbols of authority—the monarchy and the Buddhist religion—continued to enjoy popular support, and the government carried on the day-to-day administration of the country with a level of efficiency that at least met the expectations of the people.

In addition, the guerrillas were afflicted with skill, logistics, and morale problems, and lacked generous external support. According to Solomon, as matters stood, it seemed unlikely that North Vietnam and China would increase their assistance, since

---

[154] Author interview with David Morell, 2004.

[155] Robert L. Solomon, *Thailand in the 1970's: The Regional Context for United States Policy*, Santa Monica, Calif.: RAND Corporation, IN-21191-ARPA, October 1970.

they were both beset by their own problems and preoccupations. Also, neither country was willing to expend more resources in Thailand, considering that the guerrillas were poorly organized and lacked the capacity to absorb the aid and use it effectively.[156] All these weaknesses had limited the expansion of the insurgents and prevented them from destabilizing the situation with mass violence or terror, or economic disruption, or enlarging their zone of control. Having lost the element of surprise, time was not an advantage for them. From such indications, Solomon concluded, it would appear that the insurgency did not pose a threat to Thailand's security.

Yet, the insurgency persisted, because the Thai government had not eradicated the small number of guerrillas, estimated at between 2,800 and 3,500. It had undertaken some countermeasures, such as military operations and economic development, but they were moderate in scope and had left the guerrilla leadership intact and their base areas secure. The standoff resulted from the view that the situation was not alarming enough to necessitate a determined counterinsurgency campaign to wipe out the insurgents. No Thai regime, including those dominated by the military, had considered the insurgency a threat to the stability and territorial integrity of the country or subscribed to the notion that the guerrillas' safe havens near their bases or located in the remote, hilly regions posed enough of a threat to justify investing resources and taking political risks to solve the insurgency problem once and for all. Although it had solicited aid from the United States, the government preferred to cope with the insurgency itself, believing that it alone—and not a foreign power—could deal with the problem.[157] The United States, for its part, had chosen to respect the Thais' decision to handle matters on their own and to assist them only with financial and development support, and advice.

Solomon believed that, even if external support to the insurgents increased, it would not alarm the Thai government or lead it to prepare for a worst-case scenario. If the RTG remained unwilling to devote its full resources to meet the challenge posed by the insurgents—even with the eventuality that the insurgents managed to overcome their problems and inefficiency—then the infusion of more U.S. resources would not

---

[156] Solomon addressed this issue further in "A Model of External Support for Insurgency and Absorptive Capacity of Insurgent Organizations," Santa Monica, Calif.: RAND Corporation, WN-7070-ARPA, September 1970. For this paper, Thailand served as an illustration for the model. The aid donor would judge the recipient's ability to use the aid effectively by assessing his political reliability, as reflected in his doctrine, goals, and maturity of judgment; his effectiveness, as shown by the adequacy, training, and discipline of his manpower and leadership; the soundness of his organizational structure, and his military viability; and his resource needs. Considering that the Thai insurgents fell short of such standards, it would appear unlikely that they would receive additional external support.

[157] Solomon wrote that the Thai preference for handling their own problems might also be attributed to their loss of confidence in the United States. In 1965, the Thai concluded that the United States was going to pursue military victory in Vietnam. However, when this turned out not to be the case, they became uneasy. They became briefly optimistic when the United States invaded Cambodia in April 1970; however, when they learned that the operation was going to be limited in scope and duration, their disappointment returned.

make a difference. If additional American support was provided, further study would be required beforehand, because Thailand was of marginal value to vital U.S. economic, security, and strategic military interests. From a global perspective, a threat to the security of Thailand would not jeopardize the security of the United States and that of its other allies, nor would it weaken the U.S. position in Asia and endanger U.S. global interests as a result.

As events unfolded, however, neither the RTG nor the U.S. commitment was put to the test. The communist movement in Thailand had a brief period of growth with the influx of radical students from major universities fleeing into the hills following right-wing suppression and a military coup d'etat in October 1976. However, in the end, the communist movement was weakened by internal and external factors.

The chain of events leading to the coup began in September 1976, when two student activists in Nakhon Pathom province west of Bangkok were arrested and hanged after distributing posters calling for the departure of Prime Minister and Marshal Thanom Kittikachorn, the successor to strongman Sarit, who had returned on September 19, 1976, from exile in Singapore following his ouster in 1973. The Thai police involvement in the hanging was disclosed by a Thai newspaper. The hanging of the two activists occurred in the aftermath of violent student unrest demanding the arrest or expulsion of Thanom, Thai independence from American imperialism, American withdrawal from Thailand, and a social revolution to improve the lot of the rural poor. Coming in the wake of communist victories in Vietnam, Laos, and Cambodia in 1975, the radicalism of the students unnerved the Thai population and a government uneasy about communist expansion. To them, the radical students' message carried a communist tinge. The general population worried that a U.S. withdrawal would expose them to a communist takeover. Military and civilian leaders were concerned that the student unrest might aid the communist design on the country.

In response to the hanging of the two activists in Nakhon Pathom, protesting students held a mock hanging at Thammasat University in Bangkok on October 5 to dramatize their deaths. The makeup applied to one of the two young actors made him look like Crown Prince Vajiralongkorn, an offense of *lese-majeste* in a country in which the monarchy was revered. The offense sparked popular outrage. A rightist mob converged on the campus of Thammasat University in the evening of October 5. They were joined the next day by armed policemen and several units of heavily armed Border Patrol Police. As the mob tried to storm through the locked gates of the campus, the Border Patrol Police and policemen and other armed individuals opened a barrage of fire on the students. At least 46 students were killed and hundreds were injured. In addition, over 3,000 were arrested in a city-wide roundup. The evening of October 6, under the pretext of restoring law and order and protecting the country from the communist threat, the army staged a coup d'etat to oust the civilian government and reproclaimed martial law.

To escape repression and police roundups, hundreds of students—as well as leftist politicians and intellectuals, and labor and farmer leaders, fled into the hills to join the insurgents—most acting for survival rather than out of ideological conviction. This was the first time that the communist movement was able to attract young, urban intellectuals who were ethnic Thais, rather than ethnic Chinese. It was estimated that over 1,000 students joined the armed struggle following the 1976 coup. The Communist Party of Thailand (CPT) put them in some of the 250 liberated villages under its control, where the hardships were less severe than life in the jungle.

Although it remained a scattered and uncoordinated movement with low-level intensity, the insurgency by 1976 had spread into some districts and provinces, with over 40 of Thailand's 71 provinces considered "sensitive areas" by the Thai government.[158] Despite the government's efforts, the movement had proved resilient and had grown to about 10,000 armed guerrillas—from the approximately 3,000 at the time Solomon published his RAND paper in 1970. These were supported by about 7,000 armed civilian activists within the infrastructure of the CPT. In the northeast, armed insurgents could circulate with relative ease in many areas, and the government was unable to shut off access to supplies in Laos, across the Mekong River.

In 1978–1979, the military government granted amnesty to those who had gone into the hills. By this time, many of them had become disillusioned with the communist movement, and hundreds began to return to Bangkok. Their departure and the worsening dissension within the ranks of the CPT weakened the movement. The division was brought about by the split within the larger communist camp in Asia, after Vietnam invaded Cambodia in 1978 to overthrow the murderous Khmer Rouge regime, which had aligned itself with China. In a riposte, China invaded Vietnam in 1979.

The CPT was caught in this internal strife. Fundamentally, it was closer to China than to Vietnam or the Soviet Union. Most of its leaders were of Chinese ancestry, and its revolutionary strategy followed the Maoist model. At the same time, it also had ties to the Vietnamese. Many Thai revolutionaries—especially those from the northeast— had received training in North Vietnam and Laos. In addition, the CPT had used sanctuaries in Laos and Cambodia and had relied on the North Vietnamese and the Pathet Lao to survive and expand their movement. Following the Chinese invasion of Vietnam, the CPT's pro-Chinese stance cost it the support of Vietnam and Laos. This position also caused it to lose support among some of the student leaders, who were disturbed by its Chinese domination.

By early 1980, the CPT was in "severe disarray" and had become "a victim" of the split in the communist camp. It was torn by "factionalism and confusion over competing revolutionary ideologies and external allegiances." This development was

---

[158] David Morell and Chai-anan Samudavanija, *Political Conflict in Thailand: Reform, Reaction, Revolution*, Cambridge, Mass.: Oelgeschlager, Gunn, and Hain, 1981, p. 295.

a "welcome gift" to the Thai government and gave it time to deal with their country's crises of "legitimacy, participation, and equity" brought on by the reversion to military rule and rapid modernization.[159] In the end, the Thai domino did not fall as a result of communist victories in Indochina, as had been feared. In the post–Vietnam War and post–Cold War era, Vietnam and Laos—the two countries whose conflicts Thailand had helped the United States wage—would become its partners in the Association of Southeast Asian Nations (ASEAN), a regional power bloc of which Thailand is a long-standing member.

---

[159] Morell and Samudavanija, *Political Conflict in Thailand,* 1981, pp. 305–306.

Diversification

The RAND Corporation that emerged at the end of the Vietnam War looked very different from the one that entered it. In 1965, when RAND expanded its presence in Saigon, it was an organization dedicated to serving the needs of the Air Force and to planning for Cold War confrontation with the Communist Bloc. By the time the war ended in 1975, RAND had become less dependent on the Air Force for support and had turned into a diversified organization, as much devoted to domestic issues as to national-security issues.

RAND's diversification occurred with the advent of Harry Rowen's presidency. It coincided with new opportunities in the domestic arena as the United States began to disengage from Vietnam and refocus resources on internal problems besetting the country. According to some people at RAND, however, the decision to diversify—and to accelerate diversification—had less to do with the desire to exploit new opportunities and much more to do with the Air Force cut in funding, which deepened in the aftermath of the Pentagon Papers. Gus Shubert, who was instrumental in taking RAND into the new fields, believed that the budget cut was not as instrumental in pushing RAND to diversify as was the perception that RAND was underutilizing its talent, which could be applied to help solve domestic issues confronting the nation.

But he also acknowledged that diversification earned RAND some breathing room and was a good, cautious move, considering the ups and downs in the relationship between RAND and the Air Force. If RAND had continued to rely entirely on the Air Force for funding, this dependence would have given the Air Force much more latitude "to turn the valve all the way shut instead of just three-quarters of the way shut" if it got really upset with RAND.[1]

As long as he was president, Frank Collbohm had rejected diversification. To Collbohm, RAND was a mission-dedicated organization, and this mission was to protect the United States by supporting the Air Force and to contribute to winning the Cold War. Although Collbohm gave in to internal pressures and external realities and expanded RAND's clients to include other defense agencies, such as ARPA and DoD,

---

[1]   Collins, interview with Gus Shubert, session of July 17, 1992, p. 77.

he disliked doing so and would have preferred to stay with the Air Force and Project RAND—as Gus Shubert recalled. According to Shubert, Collbohm believed that "RAND was its most effective when it was working on future-oriented, quantitatively analyzable, therefore scientifically recreatable problems that were coincidental with the concerns of the Air Force. I think he was pleased when it also turned out that the results were favorable to the interests of the Air Force."[2]

As Collbohm saw it, RAND should maintain this focus, and any diversion from its mission would undermine the basic purpose of the corporation and destroy its coherence—a view shared by Frederick (Fritz) Sallagar, a former special assistant to Secretary of the Air Force Thomas Finletter and a member of the Social Science Department, who had Collbohm's ear on this issue. Gus Shubert recalled that Sallagar predicted that, if RAND diversified, it would "sign its own doom," because it would become fractured, and analysts would begin to compete for resources in order to preserve their jobs rather than to research the right subjects.[3] When Ed Barlow, Director of Research and former head of the Engineering Division, suggested in 1960 that RAND diversify, Frank Collbohm dismissed his recommendation.[4]

But the idea of diversification was kept alive by a number of people at RAND who were interested in doing a different kind of work, and by a small flow of RAND-sponsored research funds and some foundation money to study topics that fell outside the national-security field. One prime example was the urban transportation study undertaken by Charlie Zwick in the Economics Department with a grant from the Ford Foundation.[5] In the 1960s, the Board of Trustees itself was beginning to discuss the idea of diversifying RAND's work. According to Newton Minow, from the board's perspective, "one of the big questions was, should RAND now limit itself to military things, or should RAND try to apply its talents and its methods to health issues, to crime issues, to other issues" and to secure more funding.[6] The board began to realize that perhaps the Planning, Programming, and Budgeting system that RAND had developed could be applied to other problems.

---

[2]   Collins, interview with Gus Shubert, session of January 17, 1991, p. 62.

[3]   Collins, interview with Gus Shubert, session of July 17, 1992, p. 185.

[4]   Gus Shubert recalled that, right after he was hired at RAND, he went to see Ed Barlow and asked why RAND was focusing all its talent on military issues while there were "so many other things to look at." Barlow agreed that RAND was making a mistake and thought of calling the Ford Foundation to seek support for diversification into nonmilitary areas. Author interview with Gus Shubert, 2004 and 2005.

[5]   According to Shubert, the Zwick study "came out with very controversial conclusions" and, "for the first time . . . exposed RAND to some of the wrath that is so common when one discusses domestic issues." RAND analysts were for the first time "held up to this kind of scrutiny" and had their motivation questioned. RAND was accused of being "the tools [sic] of the Ford Foundation, which was the tool of the Ford Motor Company, and that what we were doing, in essence, was selling cars, new and used." Collins, interview with Gus Shubert, session of July 17, 1992, p. 75.

[6]   Author interview with Newt Minow, 2005.

In 1968, the challenges facing many big cities grew worse. "You had some serious riots. You could see the burgeoning healthcare problems," Minow recalled. He became one of the strongest advocates on the board for deviating from purely military issues. According to Minow, Gus Shubert was a big proponent of diversification, as well. According to Shubert, however, the decision to diversify had little to do with getting more money and expanding RAND—although he admitted that there was expectation that some growth might occur.

When he was approached to replace Frank Collbohm in 1967, Harry Rowen, with whom some RAND people had discussed the concept of diversification, sought from the Board of Trustees the freedom to move into nonmilitary areas. Rowen remembered that diversification was his "big thrust" when he came to RAND, and that his idea was "not to give up on the defense issues, obviously, but to add to the RAND portfolio [and to] work on domestic questions."[7] This recollection is confirmed by the minutes of the Management Committee Meeting on February 8, 1967, during which Rowen stressed that he and the board believed that, although it was "desirable for RAND to do fundamental work in important non-defense areas, this should not be at the expense of our national security work—our emphasis and concentration should be on doing better and better work on DoD problems." He told the committee that it was "too early to predict" where RAND was heading in the domestic arena, but he expected that the new clients would be federal agencies—in particular, Housing, Education, and Welfare (HEW)—and that the work would start slowly, "at a rate of something like one million dollars per year."[8]

The board agreed to let Rowen build a domestic program that would be consistent with RAND's resources, but it was not in complete agreement. Shubert recalled that its split reflected the strains within RAND itself, whose staff was divided over the issue. According to him, "There were people on the board who just thought this was a very bad idea, did not want to see RAND leave the shelter of the Pentagon and get out into these other areas. There were others who were 100 percent gung-ho for it. And then there were more sensible people who were in the middle and were willing to be convinced either way. . . ."[9] A *New York Times* article about Harry Rowen's appointment as RAND chief mentioned that it came "at a time when there is widespread speculation about the future course of Rand. Some staff members believe the company should channel more of its research energies on social issues and welfare problems."[10]

---

[7]   Author interview with Harry Rowen, 2005. As Shubert explained to Martin Collins, diversification can fit in with RAND's history and tradition if trying to solve "contemporary social problems, including national security and international affairs problems, at the highest standard of excellence and with the greatest degree of integrity and understanding, is our goal." Collins, interview with Gus Shubert, session of August 13, 1992, p. 188.

[8]   Minutes of RAND Management Committee Meeting of February 8, 1967, RAND Archives.

[9]   Collins, interview with Gus Shubert, session of July 17, 1992, p. 80.

[10]   Peter Bart, "Economist Named New Head of Rand Corporation," *The New York Times*, July 28, 1966.

Among the RAND staff, some were enthusiastic about diversification; others were adamantly opposed. The division was wrenching and the tension almost reached the breaking point, and—as Shubert recalled—RAND "came within an ace, within a couple of years, of dissolving into two separate and distinct organizations, not necessarily affiliated one with the other."[11] There was also resentment in the Air Force "because of the feeling that we were diverting our best people . . . and we were turning our attention away from the Air Force, national security, the national interest as perceived in those terms."[12]

Diversion of talent turned out not to be the case, because more new people were brought in than were diverted. RAND went through a difficult transition phase lasting for six months to a year—before the domestic side was organized—when there was no coordination, no plan, and no definition of research areas. It was a period when the only strategy was what Harry Rowen described as "everybody out for a pass."[13] RAND staff would approach different government agencies or foundations on their own. As Shubert recalled, "One would approach people one knew, or one would get introduced to people, or one would walk in cold off the pavement and try to drum up interest. Naturally, that didn't work very well."[14] The result was confusion, not diversification, and little new revenue was brought to the corporation.

While this was going on, Rowen asked Shubert to organize the domestic work and put a plan together to determine the kinds of research RAND should undertake and to estimate where RAND would likely find new sources of funding, including exploring the possibility of setting up an endowment. In around 1968–1969, Shubert was promoted to vice president to take charge of these responsibilities. He consulted with colleagues and drew up a five-year plan, which was approved by the board. The goal was to have nonmilitary work account for half of RAND's revenue in five years; military and national-security work would account for the other half. The goal was reached in six years, because the national-security research budget shrank, which made it easier for the domestic side to hit its target. As Shubert recalled, "Congress got very agitated with RAND and reduced the military spending at RAND, so my half didn't have to be as big anymore."[15]

---

[11] Collins, interview with Gus Shubert, session of July 17, 1992, p. 78.

[12] Collins, interview with Gus Shubert, session of July 17, 1992, p. 78. At a Management Committee Meeting on October 25, 1967, Vice President J. Richard Goldstein relayed the Air Force's unhappiness over the fact that "our better people were being transferred to other contracts" and because "we had not talked with the Air Force before entering into contracts with new clients." Minutes of RAND Management Committee Meeting of October 25, 1967, RAND Archives.

[13] Collins, interview with Gus Shubert, session of July 17, 1992, p. 78.

[14] Collins, interview with Gus Shubert, session of July 17, 1992, p. 78.

[15] Collins, interview with Gus Shubert, session of July 17, 1992, p. 83.

RAND had pushed for foundation support, and had hoped that this would pay for half of the work in the new areas. Back in March 1967, at a Management Committee Meeting, Burt Klein of the Economics Department was urging that RAND obtain foundation grants to finance 15–20 people working for two years or so in nondefense fields, to develop competence in such areas. Rowen agreed. Subsequently, at a meeting of the Management Committee in July 1968, Rowen disclosed a letter he had written to McGeorge Bundy, Ford Foundation president, dated June 20, 1968, in which he renewed a proposal he had submitted in October 1967, asking for support for work on "some of the key issues of American society." In his letter to Bundy, Rowen stated, "We are in fact more convinced than ever that it is important for the country and essential for the health of Rand, to put our work on domestic policy on a firm and permanent basis."[16]

Rowen told Bundy that RAND was receiving about $2 million a year from New York City, HEW, and other agencies for work on domestic issues. However, such work was "short run and operationally oriented." RAND's board had supplemented this budget with about $1 million from RAND's own funds. RAND was living "close to the margin," Rowen told Bundy, because it had no endowment and its working capital was sufficient only "to meet about six weeks of current expenditures." Rowen mentioned that RAND was about to embark on a private fund-raising campaign to get $2 million a year to work on important social issues on a long-term basis—five years or more. In conclusion, Rowen asked the Ford Foundation for $5 million to be spent over five years to provide "the continuity and scale of research needed."

However, RAND's expectation for foundation support was unrealistic, and such financing did not materialize. As Shubert discovered, the federal government became the primary source of money. Shubert's five-year plan contained about half a dozen programs, and, in 1971, the Domestic Division was established and became a "well-defined" entity in RAND.[17] Its staff moved to another building at RAND, where they worked separately from the national-security people. In time, more and more board members became supportive. When Don Rice replaced Harry Rowen as president, he wanted to further develop the domestic work. He asked Shubert to retain complete charge of the domestic area. By this time, the board had become more favorably disposed to diversification.

Eventually, the domestic side grew to become a very strong half of the corporation, but "the funding didn't come from where we had planned to have it come from, and the programs didn't turn out to be exactly the ones we thought would be the most successful."[18]

---

[16]   Minutes of RAND Management Committee Meeting of July 3, 1968, RAND Archives.

[17]   Collins, interview with Gus Shubert, session of July 17, 1992, p. 83.

[18]   Collins, interview with Gus Shubert, session of January 17, 1991, p. 109.

Among the most important programs were the work for the Department of Housing and Urban Development (HUD), and those carried out by the New York City–RAND Institute and the Institute for Civil Justice. All three illustrated the rewards and the perils of doing work for clients other than the Air Force.

The work for HUD was suddenly terminated during the Reagan Administration, when defense spending was emphasized and the budget allotted for research of domestic issues was cut. RAND had been assured of continuing HUD support for a large research program in the housing area, and it was "totally unprepared for HUD's walking away from the table . . . and with no notice."[19] This caused financial havoc, because this work accounted for such a large part of the activities on the domestic side, and sapped staff morale. The episode illustrated the difficulty in developing long-term relationships, similar to the one RAND enjoyed with the Air Force. "Domestic agencies just didn't seem to do business that way," Gus Shubert would later say, "so that while we've achieved relatively long-term relationships (up to five years), none of them has ever rested on the presumption of continuity that exists with the Air Force."[20]

The collaboration between RAND and the City of New York was also marred by unsatisfactory episodes. It was initiated by John V. Lindsay, the then–mayor of New York. He and his emissaries asked RAND to help address some of the problems plaguing the city and to set up an office in New York to do work for the police, fire, housing, health, welfare or human resources, and corrections. In September 1967, Lindsay announced that New York had struck "a partnership adventure" with RAND, but the initial contract was announced in January 1968 at a news conference held at City Hall by Lindsay and Harry Rowen. The contract would last six months and carry a budget of $607,000. However, both men said that it was expected that it would be extended to cover other departments in July.[21]

The New York City–RAND Institute was created as a joint-venture membership corporation. The New York mayor or his representative was a member, and the president of RAND or his representative was the other member. They chose a board of trustees numbering about 20 prominent New Yorkers. Peter Szanton, a member of RAND's Economics Department, was appointed head of the office, which began with a small group and then grew to close to 20.[22] According to Shubert, "The agreement was that we would have relatively free rein within the constraints of the functional

---

[19] Collins, interview with Gus Shubert, session of July 17, 1992, p. 89. According to Shubert, the situation improved with the advent of the Nixon Administration, which had more "program planners." Collins, interview with Gus Shubert, session of July 17, 1992, p. 96.

[20] Collins, interview with Gus Shubert, session of July 17, 1992, p. 90.

[21] Richard Reeves, "City Hires Rand Corp. to Study Four Agencies," *The New York Times*, January 9, 1968.

[22] Szanton was described as a "37-year-old research associate" in RAND's Economics Department, who was a graduate of Harvard Law School and had served as a consultant for the Defense Department and as "deputy director of the program-evaluation staff of the United States Bureau of the Budget." Reeves, "City Hires Rand Corp.," 1968.

area."[23] Shubert's description dovetailed with the statement made by Harry Rowen at the January 1968 news conference, when he said that the contract with New York "was more specific and restrictive than its agreements with the Air Force" but that "Rand would have enough freedom to do what made it famous—make broad and radical recommendations."[24] The institute, it was announced at the January 1968 news conference, would include "economists, sociologists, engineers, cost analysts and other researchers working full or part time on city problems."[25]

The institute thrust RAND into the realm of domestic politics, unions, and bureaucracy. According to Shubert, New York was a "contentious city," and everybody was always "fighting everybody about something." For the RAND analyst, life there was "just one big brawl," and RAND became "a political-union-bureaucratic football from the very beginning."[26] The unions found RAND's work threatening and were nonsupportive. In general, "there was an absolutely hostile, adverse reaction to having data laid out, or having facts exposed, when decisions were going to be made on political grounds, in any case."[27]

The project with the Fire Department was to address the problem of false alarm rates that were skyrocketing and threatening to bring down the system. Shubert remembered that this work was very successful. But when a RAND recommendation to increase pumping efficiency led to the possibility of personnel reduction, the union organized rallies at City Hall denouncing RAND as a "persecutor of the poor" who was "anti-black, anti-Hispanic" and was "depriving the citizens of the city of New York their rightful quantity of fire protection."[28] Newton Minow recalled another project to determine how to best schedule fire fighters. In analyzing the data, RAND saw that "most fires occurred certain times, certain hours, certain days of the week." Consequently, it recommended that the Fire Department reschedule the firemen so that there were more on duty during those times. Although the Fire Department accepted the logic of the recommendation, it refused to implement it for the simple reason that the union would not go along with it.

---

[23] Collins, interview with Gus Shubert, session of July 17, 1992, p. 115.

[24] Reeves, "City Hires Rand Corp.," 1968.

[25] Reeves, "City Hires Rand Corp.," 1968. At the news conference, Rowen announced that a meteorologist would be assigned to the staff. Lindsay asked him what the meteorologist was going to do. "Mr. Rowen smiled and said, 'We'll explain that later.'" Reeves, "City Hires Rand Corp.," 1968. Lindsay told reporters that RAND would assist municipal employees in the departments involved "in instituting program budgeting—a long-range financial planning system in which appropriations are made on the basis of broad objectives rather than for the purchase of items." Reeves, "City Hires Rand Corp.," 1968.

[26] Collins, interview with Gus Shubert, session of July 17, 1992, p. 121.

[27] Collins, interview with Gus Shubert, session of July 17, 1992, p. 94.

[28] Collins, interview with Gus Shubert, session of July 17, 1992, p. 121.

Both Shubert and Minow recalled the difficulties in dealing with the police. One project Minow remembered was how to determine the best way to schedule policemen's shifts. RAND "figured out that most violent crimes occurred around 1 to 4 am, Sunday morning, and were usually a drug group that had moved into another drug group's neighborhood, and it was a jurisdictional fight that occurred usually between 1–4 am on Sunday morning." RAND showed its finding to the Police Department, and its reaction was, "Well, what's the moral of the story?" RAND replied, "Well, the moral of the story is have more policemen go to these areas" during those hours. But the union said, "Are you crazy? We're not going to do that."[29] According to Minow, these political problems made RAND realize that it was dealing with a system that was very different from the military, in which those in charge could simply make those below follow orders.

Shubert recalled that the work with the police took place at the time when the Knapp Commission was investigating corruption in the department. The police chief did not want RAND around his department gathering information about his personnel. Shubert remembered that RAND used the human resources data on police for one project called "Patrol Car Allocation Analysis" to match deployment to crime location and rate of crime. Another problem RAND tried to address was "cooping"— a practice whereby a police officer would drive his cruiser to a secluded spot, park it, and nap for up to several hours, while nobody knew where he was or what he was doing. In response, RAND proposed a car-locator system that would let headquarters know where every car was "every minute of every day." The police department "threw up their hands in absolute horror" because they did not want to keep track of the cars and get "involved in all kinds of things" they did not want to know.[30] RAND's recommendation was not implemented. The institute was disbanded when New York City developed financial difficulties that resulted in a budget crisis. "Needless to say, we were not asked to do any further work for the city," Shubert said.[31]

The Institute for Civil Justice (ICJ) became embroiled in controversies, as well. It was set up as an independent entity at RAND, and the Board of Trustees approved its charter in November 1979. It had its own Board of Overseers and was the only part of RAND that had private funding: The insurance industry paid more than half of the costs in the early years, and the rest of the funds came from "manufacturers, service industries . . . and private foundations."[32] Shubert left the Domestic Division to head this new institute for six months and get it up and running.

---

[29] Author interview with Newt Minow, 2005.

[30] Collins, interview with Gus Shubert, session of July 17, 1992, p. 119.

[31] Collins, interview with Gus Shubert, session of July 17, 1992, p. 125.

[32] Collins, interview with Gus Shubert, session of July 17, 1992, p. 150. At the time of the Collins interview in 1992, the institute got "significant" funding from the government. Collins, interview with Gus Shubert, session of July 17, 1992, p. 162.

The ICJ was created at the initiative of the property casualty insurance industry, which, at the time, had become alarmed by what it perceived as the medical malpractice crisis, with juries handing out "more and more money in the form of verdicts to less and less deserving people."[33] The trend was hurting the industry's profits, and the industry wanted to learn more about what was happening. No U.S. institution was devoted "to the kind of empirical objective research" to shed light on the questions that were bothering the industry: ". . . what is happening to the civil justice system, what does it look like, whom is it serving, at what cost, with what kind of outcomes, and where is our road map to [lead us to] continue to exist."[34] So, the industry turned to RAND. According to Shubert, "The ICJ was started on the premise that it would not, itself, take policy positions, but that it would produce empirical data, analyze those data, and present them in such a way that they could be used by the various parties engaged in this system to improve that system."[35] Law students under the direction of George Priest, a law professor at UCLA and a RAND consultant, began to gather jury data, focusing on "tort law and tortious contract disputes."[36]

RAND was no stranger to controversies, but whereas controversies with clients within the national-security officialdom tended on the whole to be private, the controversies and attacks encountered by the ICJ were public and seemed more heated precisely because they took place publicly. According to Shubert, RAND "had terrible struggles with the plaintiffs' bar at the beginning," who thought that RAND was an agent of the insurance industry and was out "to do them in."[37] The data RAND collected showed, however, that the insurance industry's perception was incorrect because, in 1979 "one was getting essentially the same [median] compensation as one had been getting in 1959," controlling for variables such as inflation, and that the argument that the system was out of control was not valid."[38] However, the average award, "was rapidly being dragged away from the median, up from the median, by about the top 10 percent of cases" called "new litigation"—complex cases that the courts were not used to handling, such as medical malpractice.[39]

The vagaries of domestic research deepened RAND's appreciation of its unique relationship with the Air Force, which gave RAND a great deal of flexibility and freedom to choose what research to pursue. The flexibility was built into the budget, which paid for labor input, facility depreciation, and all overhead costs, but also included a

---

33 Collins, interview with Gus Shubert, session of July 17, 1992, p. 139.

34 Collins, interview with Gus Shubert, session of July 17, 1992, p. 136.

35 Collins, interview with Gus Shubert, session of July 17, 1992, p. 143.

36 Collins, interview with Gus Shubert, session of July 17, 1992, p. 141.

37 Collins, interview with Gus Shubert, session of July 17, 1992, p. 151.

38 Collins, interview with Gus Shubert, session of July 17, 1992, p. 144.

39 Collins, interview with Gus Shubert, session of July 17, 1992, pp. 144–145.

fee—usually 6 percent of the Project RAND budget—that RAND could use as it saw fit. Over the years, this fee was used mainly to finance new research, such as the Latin America program; to invest in new people; and to produce RAND books.

Furthermore, the Air Force recognized and appreciated the quality of RAND's research. In Shubert's view, of all the clients that he had dealt with, the Air Force was "the most enlightened and intelligent sponsor of research." According to him, the Air Force was "the most tolerant, the most eager to see new ideas, the most eager to have new ideas, and the most willing to be criticized. . . . to have RAND around and speak up when RAND thinks they're doing wrong."[40] Besides giving RAND freedom to choose what issues to pursue, it also encouraged RAND to look at long-term rather than short-term problems. This stance contrasted with the attitude of the nonmilitary bureaucracy he dealt with when RAND first engaged in domestic research. People in these agencies had no experience working with a research organization and did not understand or know how to appreciate the quality of research.[41]

The relationship with the Air Force did not always go smoothly. For example, when the Air Force got upset over what RAND was doing, or at someone at RAND, it would question RAND's actions. Then, there were the times when—under congressional pressure—the Air Force would take action to rein RAND in, to demonstrate that the Air Force was managing its research contract with RAND and other research organizations. Despite all this, the Air Force—by and large—remained "no doubt the most broad-minded and accepting and the most tolerant of policy disagreement, substantive disagreement."[42]

Even at the start of diversification, Harry Rowen was well aware of the challenges in forging a relationship with clients on the domestic side that could match the one RAND had developed with the Air Force. At the Management Committee Meeting of February 8, 1967, he emphasized how difficult it would be to obtain satisfactory Project RAND–like relationships with other clients and mentioned that RAND would have to deal with "the nit picking, the narrowly defined studies, the small projects, the tasking of problems and people, etc." Such constraints would make it difficult for RAND "to develop and keep a competency."[43]

---

[40] Collins, interview with Gus Shubert, session of July 17, 1992, p. 180.

[41] Shubert recalled the comment of an assistant secretary of HEW who told him, "Gus, don't tell me about quality research. I can't tell the difference, and nobody else in this agency can, either" (Collins, interview with Gus Shubert, session of July 17, 1992, p. 181).

[42] Collins, interview with Gus Shubert, session of July 17, 1992, p. 91.

[43] Minutes of RAND Management Committee Meeting of February 8, 1967, RAND Archives.

The intellectual freedom RAND enjoyed in its relationship with the Air Force did not exist to the same extent on the domestic side, for which RAND had to bid on contracts. "When you get involved in the whole world of separate contracts and grants," Shubert said, "you very quickly get into the world of defined research areas, in some cases at the project level."[44] Whereas the Air Force Division and the National Security Division each had essentially one contract, the Domestic Division came to have well more than 100, and probably as many as 150 contracts and grants at any given point in time, "and trying to make a silk purse out of [a] sow's ear was no mean feat."[45] According to Shubert, "once you got into a mode of a contract-by-contract, grant-by-grant operation . . . you're right on the edge of becoming a job shop, and you have people who are increasingly concerned with survival instead of substance."[46]

Shubert thought that some of Fritz Sallagar's predictions had been borne out, because "the down side of this [diversification], of course, was division of labor, division of sponsorship, competition for job security, competition for grants and contracts."[47]

Another negative aspect was that the staff was no longer united by a common vision of RAND and of their role in it. Having lost this vision, RAND had become a "fractionated" organization in which the dominant concern was "who's going to support me to do what tomorrow," and "the quest for revenues and the quest for support" had become "a very important force," as RAND managers confronted the "tradeoffs between independence and survival."[48] So, in diversifying, RAND could run the risk of becoming like "ordinary study houses . . . with people doing 'special orders' research and turning the place into a job shop" out of anxiety about short-term financial realities.[49] But there was also a bright side. The need to survive in the new competitive environment—in which the military services and government agencies could field analysts as competent as those at RAND—was forcing the RAND staff to work harder and to demonstrate their "brightness."[50]

Despite all the negative aspects brought about by diversification, Shubert believed that, if RAND had continued to follow the advice of Sallagar and stayed exclusively with the Air Force, "We would have just dwindled away as the Air Force's influence dwindled away, as good people left RAND."[51] If RAND had not changed as the out-

---

[44] Collins, interview with Gus Shubert, session of July 17, 1992, p. 97.

[45] Collins, interview with Gus Shubert, session of July 17, 1992, p. 97.

[46] Collins, interview with Gus Shubert, session of July 17, 1992, p. 101.

[47] Collins, interview with Gus Shubert, session of July 17, 1992, p. 77.

[48] Collins, interview with Gus Shubert, session of July 17, 1992, p. 182; Collins, interview with Shubert, session of January 17, 1991, p. 92.

[49] Collins, interview with Shubert, session of January 17, 1991, p. 92.

[50] Collins, interview with Shubert, session of January 17, 1991, p. 93.

[51] Collins, interview with Shubert, session of January 17, 1991, p. 90.

side world changed, it would have shrunk or even gone out of existence. So, in the final analysis, the Vietnam-related events that led to the Pentagon Papers episode and Air Force pressure in its wake might have pushed RAND further along on the road to becoming—not the "job shop" feared by Gus Shubert and some other RAND people—but the strong, competitive, and complex organization that it is today—with many more clients and a presence not only in the United States but in many other countries.

Bibliography

Ackland, Len, *Observations Concerning the Political Dimensions of the Refugee Situation in the Saigon Area*, cited in Robert M. Smith, "Report Compiled in '68 Says Excessive Allied Bombing in South Vietnam Stirred Hostility to Regime," *The New York Times*, January 22, 1970. [Report not reproduced by RAND for circulation.]

Adams, Sam, *War of Numbers*, South Royalton, Vt.: Steerforth Press, 1994.

"Air Force Guards RAND Secret Data," Special to *The New York Times*, July 22, 1971.

Alsop, Joseph, "The Viet Cong's Lot Is Not a Happy One," *Los Angeles Times*, October 6, 1965.

Anderson, M., M. Arnsten, and H. Averch, *Insurgent Organization and Operations: A Case Study of the Viet Cong in the Delta, 1964–1966*, Santa Monica, Calif.: RAND Corporation, RM-5239-1-ISA/ARPA, August 1967. As of May 6, 2009:
http://www.rand.org/pubs/research_memoranda/RM5239-1/

Anderson, Mary E., Richard Benjamin Rainey, L. A. Rapping, and J. R. Summerfield, *Support Capabilities for Limited War Forces in Laos and South Vietnam*, Santa Monica, Calif.: RAND Corporation, June 1962 (not available to the general public).

Archibald, Kathy, "Issues Behind the Vietnam Letters," Santa Monica, Calif.: RAND Corporation, M-7630, October 30, 1969.

Arison Lindsey H., III, *Executive Summary: The Herbicidal Warfare Program in Vietnam, 1961–1971*, Operations Trail Dust/Ranch Hand, paper posted online by Arison, n.d. As of May 6, 2009:
http://www.utvet.com/agentorange2.html

Arnold, Martin, "Rand Concedes Delay in Putting Pentagon Papers Under Control," *The New York Times*, February 16, 1973.

Arnold, Martin, "Access to Papers at RAND Outlined," *The New York Times*, February 17, 1973.

Arnold, Martin, "Ellsberg Backed on Access to Data: Halperin, Head of Pentagon Papers Study, Denies U.S. Owns Copy Cited in Trial," *The New York Times*, March 22, 1973.

Arnold, Martin, "Ellsberg's Attorneys Contradicted by F.B.I. Agent," *The New York Times*, April 25, 1973.

Arnsten, Michael E., *A Review of the Bloodbath Report and a Note on Some of the Rand Review Procedure*, Santa Monica, Calif.: RAND Corporation, IN-21039-ARPA/AG, August 1970 (this document has not been approved for distribution outside the RAND Corporation and is available only online on the RAND intranet).

Arnsten, Michael, and Nathan Leites, *Propaganda and Reforms in Rural Vietnam* (later changed to *Land Reform and the Quality of Propaganda in Vietnam*), RAND RM-5764-ARPA, 1970.

Bagdikian, Ben, memo to Harry Rowen, "The Vietnam Letters," Santa Monica, Calif.: RAND Corporation, M-7573, October 28, 1969.

Bailey, H. H., "Your Letter to the New York Times and Washington Post," Santa Monica, Calif.: RAND Corporation, M-7308, October 17, 1969.

Ball, George, memorandum to Sec. of State, Sec. of Defense, M. Bundy, Wm. Bundy, John McNaughton, Leonard Unger, "Cutting Our Losses in South Vietnam," June 28, 1965, National Security File, Troop Deployment History, Box 43, Lyndon B. Johnson Library, Austin, Tex. Cited in David M. Barrett, ed., *President Lyndon B. Johnson's Vietnam Papers: A Documentary Collection*, College Station, Tex.: Texas A&M University Press, 1998.

Barrett, David M., ed., *President Lyndon B. Johnson's Vietnam Papers: A Documentary Collection*, College Station, Tex.: Texas A&M University Press, 1998.

Bart, Peter, "Economist Named New Head of Rand Corporation," *The New York Times*, July 27, 1966.

Benoit, Charles, "Conversations with Rural Vietnamese," RAND D-20138-ARPA-AGILE, April 1970. As of May 6, 2009:
http://www.rand.org/pubs/documents/D20138/

Berger, Marilyn, "Clark Clifford, Key Adviser to Four Presidents, Dies," *The New York Times*, October 11, 1998.

Betts, Ardith, letters to a friend in Santa Monica, various dates.

Betts, Russell, and Frank Denton, *An Evaluation of Chemical Crop Destruction in Vietnam*, Santa Monica, Calif.: RAND Corporation, RM-5446-1-ISA/ARPA, October 1967. As of May 6, 2009:
http://www.rand.org/pubs/research_memoranda/RM5446-1/

Blair, Anne, "'Get Me Ten Years': Australia's Ted Serong in Vietnam, 1962–1975," Lubbock, Tex., Texas Tech University, Symposium, 1996.

Blair, Anne, *There to the Bitter End: Ted Serong in Vietnam*, New South Wales, Australia: Allen & Unwin, Crows Nest, 2001.

Blake, Gene, "U.S. Grand Jury in LA Probing War Data Leaks," *Los Angeles Times*, June 24, 1971.

Blake, Gene, "Pentagon Papers Jury Told of Security Pacts," *Los Angeles Times*, February 13, 1973.

Blake, Gene, "Ellsberg Given Access to Files, Defense Claims," *Los Angeles Times*, February 14, 1973.

Blake, Gene, "Lax Handling of Pentagon Papers Alleged," *Los Angeles Times*, February 16, 1973.

Blake, Gene, "How Ellsberg Got Access to Files Disclosed," *Los Angeles Times*, March 22, 1973.

Blake, Gene "Ellsberg Leak Feared in 1969," *Los Angeles Times*, March 24, 1973.

Blake, Gene, "Ellsberg Admits He Violated Pledge on Pentagon Papers," *Los Angeles Times*, April 18, 1973.

Blake, Gene, "Unaware of Pentagon Data Probe—Haldeman," *Los Angeles Times*, May 3, 1973.

Blake, Gene, "Chance of Ellsberg Acquittal Indicated," *Los Angeles Times*, May 10, 1973.

Blakeslee, Jack, "Low-Altitude Visual Search for Individual Human Targets: Further Field Testing in Southeast Asia," Santa Monica, Calif.: RAND Corporation, D-13353-ARPA, January 29, 1965.

Blakeslee, Jack, *Village Security Pilot Study, Northeast Thailand*, Joint Thai-U.S. MRDC, 65-016, May 1965. (Incorporates "Collection of Author's Contribution: Thailand Rural Security. Pilot Study Report," Santa Monica, Calif.: RAND Corporation, D-13434-ARPA, February 22, 1965.)

Blaufarb, Douglas S., *Organizing and Managing Unconventional War in Laos, 1962–1970*, Santa Monica, Calif.: RAND Corporation, R-919-ARPA, January 1972. As of May 7, 2009:
http://www.rand.org/pubs/reports/R919/

Bower, John L., memorandum to Harry Rowen, "The RAND Position on 'Six Rand Experts Support Pullout,'" Santa Monica, Calif.: RAND Corporation, M-7300, October 17, 1969.

Brewington, Bruce R., *The Combined Action Platoons: A Strategy for Peace Enforcement*, CSC 1996, Marine Corps Warfighting Laboratory, Wargaming Division, Small Wars Center of Excellence. As of April 13, 2009:
http://www.smallwars.quantico.usmc.mil/search/Papers/brewington.pdf

Brush, Peter, "Civic Action: The Marine Corps Experience in Vietnam, Part I and Part II," *The Viet Nam Generation*, Vol. 5, Nos. 1–4, March 1994, pp. 127–132. Library Science, the University of Kentucky, made available online by the Sixties Project. As of May 6, 2009:
http://www.library.vanderbilt.edu/central/brush/civic-action-marine-corps-vietnam.htm

Buckingham, William A., Jr., "Operation RANCH HAND—The Air Force and Herbicides in Southeast Asia, 1961–1971," Washington, D.C.: Office of the Air Force Historian, 1981.

Buckingham, William A., Jr., *The Air Force and Herbicides in Southeast Asia, 1961–1971*, Washington, D.C.: Office of Air Force History, United States Air Force, 1982.

Bundy, McGeorge, memorandum to the President, RAND Studies of Viet Cong Motivation and Morale, June 28, 1965, National Security Files, M. Bundy Files, Memos to President, Box 3, Lyndon B. Johnson Library, cited in David Barrett, ed., *President Lyndon B. Johnson's Vietnam Papers*, 1998. Also in Foreign Relations of the United States, Johnson Administration, Vietnam 1964–1968, Volume III, Document 27, State Department Archives, Washington, D.C., with notation indicating that the president saw the memo on June 28.

Bundy, McGeorge, memorandum from the President's Special Assistant for National Security Affairs to President Johnson, "The Status of Non-Military Actions in Vietnam," June 28, 1965, Foreign Relations of the United States, Johnson Administration, Vietnam, 1964–1968, Volume III, Document 27, State Department Archives, Washington, D.C.

"Bundy Debates Critics over Vietnam Policy," *Los Angeles Times*, June 22, 1965.

Busch, Peter, "Killing the 'Vietcong': The British Advisory Mission and the Strategic Hamlet Programme," *Journal of Strategic Studies*, Vol. 25, No. 1, March 1, 2002, pp. 135–162.

Butterfield, Fox, "Core of Viet Cong Surviving War," *The New York Times*, November 5, 1972.

Calafato, Eugene F., Colonel, USAF, letter to Paul Langer, October 15, 1969.

Carrier, Joseph M., *Vietnamese Army Communication Support Requirements and Practices*, Santa Monica, Calif.: RAND Corporation, RM-3622-ARPA, 1963. (Provided courtesy of Joe Carrier.)

Carrier, Joseph M., *A Profile of Viet Cong Returnees: July 1965 to June 1967*, October 1968 (not available to the general public).

Carrier, Joseph M., and Charles Thomson, *Viet Cong Motivation and Morale: The Special Case of Chieu Hoi*, RAND RM-4830-2-ISA/ARPA, 1966. As of May 6, 2009:
http://www.rand.org/pubs/research_memoranda/RM4830-2/

Carter, G. A., and M. B. Schaffer, "On Some Counterproductive Aspects of Tactical Force Employment in South Vietnam: Interviews with Vietnamese Prisoners and Civilians," Santa Monica, Calif.: RAND Corporation, D-16278-PR, October 19, 1967.

Cecil, Paul Frederick, *Herbicidal Warfare: The RANCH HAND Project in Vietnam*, New York: Praeger, Praeger Special Studies, 1986.

Central Intelligence Agency, *The Fall of South Vietnam*, review of the book of this title published by Crane, Russak and Co., New York, 1980, approved for release December 2, 2003, CIA-RDP81B00401R002500070015-5.

Chen Jian, *Mao's China and the Cold War*, Chapel Hill and London: The University of North Carolina Press, 2001.

Chi, Hoang Van, *From Colonialism to Communism*, New York: Praeger, 1964.

"CIA Ellsberg Study Reported as Laudatory," *Los Angeles Times*, August 4, 1973.

Clark, Paul G., *Military Assistance Policy in an Underdeveloped Country: Iran*, Santa Monica, Calif.: RAND Corporation, April 1959 (not available to the general public).

Clifford, Clark, interview in *Life*, quoted in Robert J. Donovan, "Bloodbath—Fantasy or Realistic Fear?" *Los Angeles Times*, June 28, 1970.

Cline, Ray S., Letter of November 20, 1964, to William F. Dorrill. Copy provided to author by William Dorrill.

Colby, William E., Central Intelligence Agency, "Memorandum for the Record," February 25, 1972.

Collbohm, Frank, "Trip Report, Part II: South Vietnam, April 29–May 5, 1965," Santa Monica, Calif.: RAND Corporation, June 23, 1965 (not available to the general public).

Collbohm, Frank, "Trip Report, Part III: Laos, Thailand, Malaysia, Singapore, May 5–13, 1965," RAND D-13816, 1965.

Collbohm, Frank, "Trip Report, Part IV: South Vietnam, May 14–16, 1965," June 23, 1965 (not available to the general public).

Collins, Martin J., "RAND's Oral History Project (RAND)," Department of Space History, National Air and Space Museum, consisting of interviews with 29 RAND individuals and covering the period from 1945 to the early 1960s. Interview with Frank Collbohm in 1987; with Charles Hitch in 1988; with Amrom Katz in 1986; with Gus Shubert in 1986, 1988, 1991, and 1992; with Hans Speier in 1988; with George Tanham in 1987; with Lawrence J. Henderson, Jr., in 1989.

Cooper, Chester L., memorandum to M. Bundy, "Summary of Rand's Latest Interrogation of Viet Cong Captives and Defectors," July 10, 1965, National Security Files, Memos to President, Box 4, Lyndon B. Johnson Library, Austin, Tex. Cited in David M. Barrett, ed., *President Lyndon B. Johnson's Vietnam Papers*, 1998.

Cooper, Chuck, Paul Langer, Richard Moorsteen, and Charles Zwick, *Security and Assistance in Laos* (not available to the general public). The author could not gain access to this report.

Correll, John T., "Igloo White," *Journal of the Air Force Association*, Vol. 87, No. 11, November 2004. As of April 13, 2009:
http://www.airforce-magazine.com/MagazineArchive/Pages/2004/November%202004/1104igloo.aspx

"Counterinsurgency and Air Power: Report of a RAND Ad Hoc Group," Santa Monica, Calif.: RAND Corporation, RM-3203-PR, June 1962. Cited in David Jardini, *The Wrong War: RAND in Vietnam, 1954–1969*," paper presented at Carnegie-Mellon University Colloqium on "Cold War Science & Technology," 1998. Jardini presented this paper at a colloqium panel on "Policymaking in a Cold War Quagmire: RAND and Vietnam, 1954–1972," with Gus Shubert of RAND as a discussant, November 5, 1998.

"Cover Story—Pentagon Papers: The Secret War," *AllPolitics*, online article, June 28, 1971. As of April 29, 2004:
http://www.cnn.com/ALLPOLITICS/1996/analysis/back.time/9606/28/index.shtml

Croizat, Victor, "Problems Relating to the Deployment of U.S. Ground Combat Forces to the Mekong Delta Area of South Vietnam," October 11, 1966 (not available to the general public), with cover letter from Amrom H. Katz dated October 17, 1966, Lyndon B. Johnson Archives, Austin, Tex.

Croizat, Victor, *A Translation from the French. Lessons from the War in Indochina*, Vol. 2, Santa Monica, Calif.: RAND Corporation, RM- 5271-PR, May 1967. As of May 7, 2009: http://www.rand.org/pubs/research_memoranda/RM5271/

Croizat, Victor J., "Organization, Personnel Policies and Operating Procedures," Saigon, March 1968.

Croizat, Victor J., *The Development of the Plain of Reeds: Some Politico-Military Implications*, Santa Monica, Calif.: RAND Corporation, P-3976, October 1969. As of May 7, 2009: http://www.rand.org/pubs/papers/P3976/

Croizat, V. J., J. A. Carlson, and L. Goure, *Final Report on the Interdiction-Evaluation Project*, Santa Monica, Calif.: RAND Corporation, D-18355-ARPA/AGILE, January 14, 1969.

Daniel Ellsberg's Web site. As of April 20, 2009: http://www.ellsberg.net/

Davison, W. Phillips, "User's Guide to the RAND Interviews in Vietnam," Santa Monica, Calif.: RAND Corporation, D-19904-ARPA, January 29, 1970.

Deitchman, Seymour J., *The Best-Laid Schemes: A Tale of Social Research and Bureaucracy*, Cambridge, Mass., and London, England: The MIT Press, 1976.

Denton, Frank, "Data on Viet Cong Attacks on RVN Military Units and Facilities," Santa Monica, Calif.: RAND Corporation, D-13428-ARPA/AGILE, February 18, 1965.

Denton, Frank, "Time Variations in Viet Cong Morale: or 'a VC Fever Chart,'" Santa Monica, Calif.: RAND Corporation, D-14498, February 9, 1966.

Denton, Frank, "Alienation of the Peasant in South Vietnam," Santa Monica, Calif.: RAND Corporation, May 4, 1966 (not available to the general public).

Denton, Frank, *Some Effects of Military Operations on Viet Cong Attitudes*, Santa Monica, Calif.: RAND Corporation, RM-4966-1-ISA/ARPA, November 1966 (formerly *Some Relationships Between the Attitude of the Viet Cong Soldiers and Their Exposure to U.S.-RVN Military Operations*, RM-4966-ISA/ARPA). As of August 17, 2009: http://www.rand.org/pubs/research_memoranda/RM4966-1/

Denton, Frank, *Two Analytical Aids for Use with the Rand Interviews*, Santa Monica, Calif.: RAND Corporation, RM-5338-ISA/ARPA, May 1967. As of May 7, 2009: http://www.rand.org/pubs/research_memoranda/RM5338/

Denton, Frank, "A Vietnam Alternative," Santa Monica, Calif.: RAND Corporation, D-17188-ISA/ARPA, May 10, 1968.

Der Derian, James, "The Illusion of a Grand Strategy," *The New York Times,* May 25, 2001.

Desbarats, Jacqueline, and Karl D. Jackson, "A Methodology for Estimating Political Executions in Vietnam: 1975–1983," paper presented at the Annual Meeting of the Asian Studies on the Pacific Coast, Los Angeles, Calif., June 22–24, ca. 1987.

Digby, Jim, "Frank and Civil Defense," in Jim Digby, ed., "Early RAND: Personalities and Projects as Recalled in *The Alumni Bulletin*," Santa Monica, Calif.: RAND Corporation, P-8055, March 2001. As of May 7, 2009: http://www.rand.org/pubs/papers/P8055/

Dobbin, Muriel, "Rand Corporation Still Feels Pentagon Papers' Aftereffects," *Baltimore Sun*, February 15, 1973.

Dommen, Arthur, *Conflict in Laos: The Politics of Neutralization*, New York: Frederick A. Praeger, 1964.

Dommen, Arthur J., "Prisoner Survey: Air Attacks Cause Terror in Viet Cong," *Los Angeles Times*, July 4, 1965.

Dommen, Arthur J., "Viet Cong Defections Are a Major Puzzle," *Los Angeles Times*, July 9, 1965.

Donnell, John C., and Gerald C. Hickey, *The Vietnamese "Strategic Hamlets": A Preliminary Report*, Santa Monica, Calif.: RAND Corporation, September 1962 (not available to the general public).

Donnell, John C., Guy J. Pauker, and J. Joseph Zasloff, *Viet Cong Motivation and Morale in 1964: A Preliminary Report*, Santa Monica, Calif.: RAND Corporation, RM-4507/3-ISA, March 1965. As of May 7, 2009:
http://www.rand.org/pubs/research_memoranda/RM4507.3/

Donovan, Robert J., "Bloodbath—Fantasy or Realistic Fear?" *Los Angeles Times,* Sunday, June 28, 1970.

Dorrill, William F., *South Vietnam's Problems and Prospects: A General Assessment,* Santa Monica, Calif.: RAND Corporation, RM-4350-PR, October 1964. As of May 7, 2009:
http://www.rand.org/pubs/research_memoranda/RM4350/

Dorrill, William, memorandum to Joe M. Goldsen and Guy J. Pauker, "Critique of RM-4400-PR (Part 1) December 1964," Santa Monica, Calif.: RAND Corporation, January 11, 1965.

Dorrill, William, "Position," paper presented at a public debate at the Warner Playhouse, Los Angeles, Calif., July 1965.

Dorrill, William, memorandum to Colonel Clyde C. Wooten, AFNINA, Santa Monica, Calif.: RAND Corporation, L-2620, February 7, 1966.

"Doubts Cast on Vietnam Incident, but Secret Study Stays Classified," *The New York Times,* October 31, 2005.

Duis, R. A., Sawtelle, T. K., and Weiner, M., "VIPS: Vietnam Interview Processing System," Santa Monica, Calif.: RAND Corporation, D-17870-ISA/ARPA, October 2, 1966.

Economics Department, RAND Corporation, "ISA Semiannual Progress Report—Economics Department: January–June 1967," Santa Monica, Calif., D-15812-ISA, July 3, 1967.

Economics Department, RAND Corporation, "ARPA/ARGILE Progress Report of 21 August 1968," Santa Monica, Calif., August 21, 1968.

Economics Department, RAND Corporation, "ARPA/AGILE, July–December 1968, Report of 4 February 1969," Santa Monica, Calif., February 4, 1969.

Economics Department, RAND Corporation, "ARPA/AGILE, Jan–June 1969, Report of 12 August 1969," Santa Monica, Calif., August 12, 1969.

Economics Department, RAND Corporation, "ARPA/AGILE, July–December 1969, Report of 9 February 1970," Santa Monica, Calif., February 9, 1970.

Economics Department Staff, "Economics Department Progress Report (ARPA), July 1–December 31, 1962," Santa Monica, Calif.: RAND Corporation, January 8, 1963.

Economics Department Staff, "Economics Department Progress Report (ARPA), January 1–June 30, 1963," Santa Monica, Calif.: RAND Corporation, D-11407-ARPA, July 5, 1963.

Economics Department Staff, "Economics Department Progress Report, 1963–1964: RAND-Sponsored Research Projects," Santa Monica, Calif.: RAND Corporation, D-11952-RC, December 20, 1963.

Edelman, Joel, "A Trip Report on Activities Related to Forward Air Controllers in South Vietnam: The Text of a Briefing," Santa Monica, Calif.: RAND Corporation, 1966 (not available to the general public).

Elliott, David W. P., correspondence with George Tanham, William Stewart, and Chuck Thomson, personal documents of David Elliott.

Elliott, David W. P., "Dinh Tuong Revisited: First Impressions of Viet Cong Recent Responses to Pacification," Santa Monica, Calif.: RAND Corporation, July 1971 (not available to the general public).

Elliott, David W. P., letter to Guy Pauker, May 10, 1969.

Elliott, David W. P., letter to Robert Samson, May 12, 1969.

Elliott, David W. P., letter to Bill Stewart, March 10, 1969.

Elliott, David W. P., memorandum to Frank Hoeber, "Comments on the Phung Hoang Program," July 12, 1971.

Elliott, David W. P., memorandum to Major Smith, January 27, 1972.

Elliott, David W. P., *The Vietnamese War: Revolution and Social Change in the Mekong Delta, 1930–1975*, two volumes, Armonk, New York, and London, England: M. E. Sharpe, 2003; concise edition, 2007.

Elliott, David W. P., and Mai Elliott, *Documents of an Elite Viet Cong Delta Unit: The Demolition Platoon of the 514th Battalion—Part One: Unit Composition and Personnel*, Santa Monica, Calif.: RAND Corporation, RM-5848-ISA/ARPA, May 1969. As of May 7, 2009:
http://www.rand.org/pubs/research_memoranda/RM5848/

Elliott, David W. P., and Mai Elliott, *Documents of an Elite Viet Cong Delta Unit: The Demolition Platoon of the 514th Battalion—Part Two: Party Organization*, Santa Monica, Calif.: RAND Corporation, RM-5849-ISA/ARPA, May 1969. As of May 7, 2009:
http://www.rand.org/pubs/research_memoranda/RM5849/

Elliott, David W. P., and Mai Elliott, *Documents of an Elite Viet Cong Delta Unit: The Demolition Platoon of the 514th Battalion—Part Three: Military Organization and Activities*, Santa Monica, Calif.: RAND Corporation, RM-5850-ISA/ARPA, May 1969. As of May 7, 2009:
http://www.rand.org/pubs/research_memoranda/RM5850/

Elliott, David W. P., and Mai Elliott, *Documents of an Elite Viet Cong Delta Unit: The Demolition Platoon of the 514th Battalion—Part Four: Political Indoctrination and Military Training*, Santa Monica, Calif.: RAND Corporation, RM-5851-ISA/ARPA, May 1969. As of May 7, 2009:
http://www.rand.org/pubs/research_memoranda/RM5851/

Elliott, David W. P., and Mai Elliott, *Documents of an Elite Viet Cong Delta Unit: The Demolition Platoon of the 514th Battalion—Part Five: Personal Letters*, Santa Monica, Calif.: RAND Corporation, RM-5852-ISA/ARPA, May 1969.

Elliott, D. W. P., and W. A. Stewart, *Pacification and the Viet Cong System in Dinh Tuong, 1966–1967*, Santa Monica, Calif.: RAND Corporation, RM-5788-ISA/ARPA, January 1967. As of May 7, 2009:
http://www.rand.org/pubs/research_memoranda/RM5788/

Elliott, D. W. P., and C. A. H. Thomson, *A Look at the VC Cadres: Dinh Tuong Province, 1965–1966*, Santa Monica, Calif.: RAND Corporation, March 1967 (not available to the general public).

Ellis, John Winthrop, and T. Green, "Viet Nam and Thailand Trip Report February 1 to March 1, 1962," RAND D-9817-ARPA, 1962.

Ellis, J. W., Jr., and T. E. Green, "Vietnam and Thailand—Trip Report, 1 February–1 March 1962," Santa Monica, Calif.: RAND Corporation, D-9835-ARPA, March 14, 1962.

Ellis, J. W., Jr., "Trip Report—Southeast Asia, 30 Dec–3 Feb 1963," Santa Monica, Calif.: RAND Corporation, D-11393-ARPA, June 21, 1963.

Ellis, Jack, "Progress Report on Project AGILE—XI," Santa Monica, Calif.: RAND Corporation, D-12990-AGILE, October 22, 1964.

Ellis, J. W., Jr., R. D. Jones, A. H. Peterson, and C. V. Sturdevant, "Future Research Possibilities for Project AGILE," Santa Monica, Calif.: RAND Corporation, D-13092-ARPA, November 13, 1964.

Ellis, Jack, "Progress Report on Project AGILE—XII—1 November through 13 December 1964," Santa Monica, Calif.: RAND Corporation, D-13216-ARPA, December 23, 1964.

Ellis, Jack, "Progress Report on Project AGILE—XIII, 1 January through 28 February 1965," Santa Monica, Calif.: RAND Corporation, D-13446-ARPA, February 24, 1965.

Ellis, Jack, "Progress Report on Project AGILE—XVI 1 July through 31 August 1965," Santa Monica, Calif.: RAND Corporation, D-14138-ARPA October 7, 1965.

Ellis, John Winthrop, and Robert Crawford, "Airbase Defense and Security with Application to Thailand," Santa Monica, Calif.: RAND Corporation, D-15350-ARPA/AGILE, December 28, 1966.

Ellis, J. W., Jr., "The Case for USAF Support to RD Security Operations," Santa Monica, Calif.: RAND Corporation, August 3, 1967 (for RAND use only).

Ellis, J. W., Jr., "Some Notes on the Paramilitary War in III Corps, October 1966–March 1967 Inclusive," Santa Monica, Calif.: RAND Corporation, November 1, 1967 (not available to the general public).

Ellis, Jack, "Your Letter to the New York Times and Its Aftermath," Santa Monica, Calif.: RAND Corporation, M-7290, October 17, 1969.

Ellis, J. W., and M. B. Schaffer, "Three Months in Vietnam—A Trip Report: The Paramilitary War," Santa Monica, Calif.: RAND Corporation, D-16004-PR, August 16, 1967. As of May 7, 2009: http://www.rand.org/pubs/documents/D16004/

Ellis, J. W., Jr., and M. B. Schaffer, *Improving Tactical Air Support to Regional and Popular Forces in South Vietnam*, Santa Monica, Calif.: RAND Corporation, May 1968 (not available to the general public).

Ellsberg, Daniel, "Some Prospects and Problems in Vietnam," Santa Monica, Calif.: RAND Corporation, D-16722-ARPA/AGILE, February 15, 1968.

Ellsberg, Daniel, Working Notes on Vietnam:

No. 1: "U.S. Aims and Leverage in Vietnam, 1950–65," Santa Monica, Calif.: RAND Corporation, D-18963, June 1969.

No. 2: "Critical Postures on U.S. Decision-Making in Vietnam: Multiple Choice," Santa Monica, Calif.: RAND Corporation, D-18958, June 1969.

No. 3: "U.S. Policy and the Politics of Others," Santa Monica, Calif.: RAND Corporation, D-19129, July 1969.

No. 4: "Vu Van Thai on U.S. Aims and Intervention in Vietnam," Santa Monica, Calif.: RAND Corporation, D-19127, July 1969.

No. 5: "Confucians and Communists," Santa Monica, Calif.: RAND Corporation, D-19135, July 1969.

No. 6: "On Pacification: Comments by Thai and Ellsberg," Santa Monica, Calif.: RAND Corporation, D-19136, August 1969.

No. 7: "Communists and Vietnamese: Comments by Hoang Van Chi," Santa Monica, Calif.: RAND Corporation, D-19134, August 1969.

No. 8: "U.S. Support of Diem: Comments by Vu Van Thai," Santa Monica, Calif.: RAND Corporation, D-19128, August 1969.

No. 9: "Infeasible Aims and the Politics of Stalemate," Santa Monica, Calif.: RAND Corporation, D-19205, August 1969.

No. 10: "Revolutionary Judo," Santa Monica, Calif.: RAND Corporation, D-19807, 1970.

"Ellsberg Case Dismissed," *Los Angeles Times*, May 11, 1973.

"Ellsberg Leak 'Feared' in 1969, Witness Says," *Los Angeles Times*, March 24, 1973.

Ellsberg, Daniel, *Secrets: A Memoir of Vietnam and the Pentagon Papers*, New York: Viking, 2002.

"Ellsberg-Russo Defense Paying High Price for Cause; Trial Budget Runs $100,000 in the Red," *Baltimore Sun*, February 13, 1973.

Enos, John L., *Modeling the Economic Development of a Poorly Endowed Region: The Northeast of Thailand*, Santa Monica, Calif.: RAND Corporation, RM-6185-ARPA, January 1970.

Enthoven, Alain, and K. Wayne Smith, *How Much Is Enough? Shaping the Defense Program, 1961–1969*, New York: Harper and Row, 1971.

Etzioni, Emitai, "Knowledge and Power," a review of Bruce Smith's book, *THE RAND CORPORATION: Case Study of a Nonprofit Advisory Corporation*," *The New York Times*, July 31, 1966.

"Excerpts from Hatfield's Senate Speech Replying to Agnew," Special to *The New York Times*, August 19, 1970.

Farmer, James, "Counter-Insurgency: Viet-Nam 1962–1963," Santa Monica, Calif.: RAND Corporation, D-11385-ARPA, June 19, 1963.

Feierabend, Ivo K., Rosalind L. Feierabend and Ted Robert Gurr, *Anger, Violence, and Politics: Theories and Research*, Englewood Cliffs, N.J.: Prentice-Hall, 1972.

Foisie, Jack, "Laird to Get Vietnam Briefings with Optimism Toned Down," *Los Angeles Times*, March 9, 1969.

Foley, Thomas J., "Author Says Very Few Read 'Pentagon Papers,'" *Los Angeles Times*, June 28, 1971.

Forrestal, Michael V., Memorandum, June 4, 1962, Memorandum of June 5, 1962, and Memorandum of June 6, 1962, Foreign Relations of the United States, State Department Archives, Kennedy Administration, 1961–1963, Volume XXIV, Laos Crisis.

Gaiduk, Ilya V., *The Soviet Union and the Vietnam War*, Chicago, Ill.: Ivan R. Dee, 1996.

Gardner, Lloyd C., *Pay Any Price: Lyndon Johnson and the Wars for Vietnam*, Chicago, Ill.: Ivan R. Dee, 1995.

Gershater, Col. E. M., Telegram, December 7, 1970.

Girling, John L. S., *Thailand: Society and Politics*, Ithaca and London: Cornell University Press, 1981.

Gogerty, D. Calvin, "Rapid Roger Supply Data," Santa Monica, Calif.: RAND Corporation, D-16030-1-PR, May 1968.

Goldberg, Alfred, "RAND and Vietnam," Santa Monica, Calif.: RAND Corporation, April 23, 1969 (not available to the general public).

Goldberg, Alfred, "RAND and Vietnam II: Some Questions from the Record," Santa Monica, Calif.: RAND Corporation, May 12, 1969 (not available to the general public).

Goure, Leon, "Summary Outline of the Dinh Tuong Project," no date (memorandum provided to the author by David Elliott; not available to the general public).

Goure, Leon, *Southeast Asia Trip Report, Part I: The Impact of Air Power in South Vietnam,* RAND Corporation, RM-4400/1-PR, December 1964. As of May 7, 2009: http://www.rand.org/pubs/research_memoranda/RM4400.1/

Goure, Leon, letter to a friend in Santa Monica, May 30, 1965.

Goure, Leon, *Some Impressions of the Effects of Military Operations on Viet Cong Behavior*, Santa Monica, Calif.: RAND Corporation, August 1965 (not available to the general public).

Goure, Leon, letter to Chuck Thomson, February 25, 1966.

Goure, Leon, "Some Informal Notes on the 'Viet Cong Morale Study,'" Santa Monica, Calif.: D-14813-ISA-ARPA, April 28, 1966; attached to letter RAND L-8557 addressed to Walt Rostow, copy from Lyndon B. Johnson Library, Austin, Tex.

Goure, Leon, teletype to L. J. Henderson, Washington Office, for transmittal to Colonel Marshall E. Sanders, USAF, Chief, Special Projects Division, Policy Planning Staff in OSD/ISA (for submission to Defense Secretary Robert McNamara), RPN-9992, May 1966 (not releasable to the general public).

Goure, Leon, letter to Walt Rostow, Santa Monica, Calif.: RAND Corporation, L-8557, May 2, 1966; located at the Lyndon B. Johnson Library, Austin, Tex.

Goure, Leon, "Some Findings of the Viet Cong Motivation and Morale Study, January–June 1966: A Briefing to the Joint Chiefs of Staff," August 1, 1966.

Goure, Leon, *Quarterly Report on Viet Cong Motivation and Morale Project, October–December 1966*, Santa Monica, Calif.: RAND Corporation, January 30, 1967; copy from the Lyndon B. Johnson Library, Austin, Tex.

Goure, Leon, "Some Preliminary Observations on NVA Behavior During Infiltration," Santa Monica, Calif.: RAND Corporation, D-16339-PR, November 3, 1967.

Goure, Leon, "Additional Preliminary Observations on NVA Behavior During Infiltration," Santa Monica, Calif.: RAND Corporation, D-16340-PR, November 3, 1967.

Goure, Leon, "Some Unevaluated and Tentative Suggestions for Harassment of NVA Infiltration into South Vietnam," RAND D-164 81-PR, December 14, 1967.

Goure, Leon, "Some Factors Affecting Infiltration Across National Boundaries," Santa Monica, Calif.: RAND Corporation, D-18008-ARPA, October 31, 1968.

Goure, Leon, "The RAND Corporation POW and Defector Debriefing Program," presentation, in Allan Rehm, ed., *Analyzing Guerrilla Warfare*, Proceedings of a Conference, Allan Rehm and Brendon Rehm, transcribers, held at SAIC Tower, McLean, Va., September 24, 1985.

Goure, Leon, Douglas Scott, and Anthony Russo, *Some Findings of the Viet Cong Motivation and Morale Study: June–December 1965*, Santa Monica, Calif.: RAND Corporation, RM-4911-2-ISA/ARPA, February 1966. As of May 7, 2009:
http://www.rand.org/pubs/research_memoranda/RM4911-2/

Goure, Leon, and C. A. H. Thomson, *Some Impressions of Viet Cong Vulnerabilities: An Interim Report,* Santa Monica, Calif.: RAND Corporation, RM-4699-1-ISA/ARPA, September 1965. As of May 7, 2009:
http://www.rand.org/pubs/research_memoranda/RM4699-1/

Graham, W. B., and A. H. Katz, *Southeast Asia Trip Report, Part II—SIAT: The Single Integrated Attack Team (A Concept for Offensive Military Operations in South Vietnam)*, Santa Monica, Calif.: RAND Corporation, RM-4400-PR (Part 2), December 1964. As of May 8, 2009:
http://www.rand.org/pubs/research_memoranda/RM4400.2/

Gray, Colin S., "What Rand Hath Wrought," *Foreign Policy*, No. 4, Autumn, 1971.

Green, John, and L. P. Holliday, "Road Reconnaissance in Thailand—A Trip Report," Santa Monica, Calif.: RAND Corporation, D-10716-ARPA, November 26, 1962.

Greene, Terrell E., "Notes on the Thompson Report on South Vietnam, and Discussion with R. G. K. Thompson," Santa Monica, Calif.: RAND Corporation, April 9, 1962 (not available to the general public).

Gurtov, Melvin, *Forced Withdrawal from Vietnam and U.S. Alternatives*, Santa Monica, Calif.: RAND Corporation, September 22, 1966 (not available to the general public).

Gurtov, Melvin, *Riding the Tiger: A Study of Regular Force Viet Cong Cadres*, Santa Monica, Calif., RAND Corporation, March 1967 (not available to the general public).

Gurtov, Melvin, "Communist China's Policy Toward the Vietnam War Since Tonkin," Santa Monica, Calif.: RAND Corporation, D-15960-PR, August 10, 1967.

Gurtov, Melvin, *The War in the Delta: Views from Three Viet Cong Battalions*, Santa Monica, Calif.: RAND Corporation, September 1967 (not available to the general public).

Gurtov, Melvin, *Viet Cong Cadres and the Cadre System: A Study of the Main and Local Forces*, Santa Monica, Calif.: RAND Corporation, December 1967 (not available to the general public).

Gurtov, Melvin, *Negotiations and Vietnam: A Case Study of the 1954 Geneva Conference*, Santa Monica, Calif.: RAND Corporation, RM-5617-ISA/ARPA, January 3, 1968. As of May 7, 2009:
http://www.rand.org/pubs/research_memoranda/RM5617/

Gurtov, Melvin, "Some Recent Statements by North Vietnamese Leaders: General Giap," Santa Monica, Calif.: RAND Corporation, D-20026-ARPA/AGILE, March 10, 1970.

Gurtov, Melvin, *China and Southeast Asia—The Politics of Survival: A Study of Foreign Policy Interaction*, Lexington, Mass.: Health Lexington Books, 1971.

Gurtov, Melvin, Oleg Hoeffding, Arnold Horelick, Konrad Kellen, and Paul Langer, "Extrication from Vietnam: A Memorandum for the Record," Santa Monica, Calif.: RAND Corporation, D-19252-ISA, August 24, 1969.

Halberstam, David, "Voices of the VietCong" *Harper's Magazine*, January 24, 1968.

Halpern, Abraham M., and H. B. Fredman, *Communist Strategy in Laos*, Santa Monica, Calif.: RAND Corporation, RM-2561, June 14, 1960.

Halpern, Joel Martin, *The Lao Elite: A Study of Tradition and Innovation,* Santa Monica, Calif.: RAND Corporation, RM-2636-RC, November 15, 1960.

Harms, Erik Lind, "Vietnam, Anthropology, and Ethnographic Authority Through Time and War," paper delivered at the symposium on "Encountering Violence in Southeast Asia," Cornell University, Wednesday, March 22, 2000.

Hayes, J., "Your Letter to the New York Times," memorandum to P. Langer, M. Gurtov, D. Ellsberg, K. Kellen, O. Hoeffding, and A. Horelick, October 16, 1969.

Hersh, Seymour, *The Price of Power: Kissinger in the Nixon White House*, New York: Summit Books, 1983.

Heymann, Hans, *Seminar on Development and Security in Thailand: Part I, The Insurgency*, Santa Monica, Calif.: RAND Corporation, RM-5871-AID/ARPA, March 1969a. As of May 7, 2009: http://www.rand.org/pubs/research_memoranda/RM5871/

Heymann, Hans, *Seminar on Development and Security in Thailand: Part II, Development-Security Interactions*, Santa Monica, Calif.: RAND Corporation, March 1969b (not available to the general public).

Heymann, Hans, and John C. Donnell, *Rural Programs in Laos: A Mid-1969 Reassessment*, Santa Monica, Calif.: RAND Corporation, February 1970 (not available to the general public).

Heymann, Hans, and Albert P. Williams, *United States Options in Thailand: A Prologue to Program Budgeting,* Santa Monica, Calif.: RAND Corporation, December 1968 (not available to the general public).

Hickey, Gerald C., *The Major Ethnic Groups of the South Vietnamese Highlands*, Santa Monica, Calif.: RAND Corporation, RM-4041-ARPA, April 1964. As of May 7, 2009: http://www.rand.org/pubs/research_memoranda/RM4041/

Hickey, Gerald C., *The American Military Advisor and His Foreign Counterpart: The Case of Vietnam*, Santa Monica, Calif.: RAND Corporation, RM-4482-ARPA, March 1965. As of May 7, 2009: http://www.rand.org/pubs/research_memoranda/RM4482/

Hickey, Gerald C., "Notes on a Meeting with General Nguyen Huu Co, Vice Chairman of the Central Executive Committee at the Prime Minister's Office, Commissioner General for War and Construction, and Minister of Defense," Saigon, January 7, 1966. Personal Papers of William Westmoreland, Lyndon B. Johnson Archives, Austin, Tex.

Hickey, Gerald C., Letter to General William C. Westmoreland, January 10, 1966, Personal Papers of William Westmoreland, Lyndon B. Johnson Archives, Austin, Tex.

Hickey, Gerald C., "Talk on Vietnam 12/6/66," Santa Monica, Calif.: RAND Corporation, March 15, 1967 (not available to the general public).

Hickey, Gerald C., *The Highland People of South Vietnam: Social and Economic Development*, Santa Monica, Calif.: RAND Corporation, RM-5281-1-ARPA, September 1967. As of May 7, 2009: http://www.rand.org/pubs/research_memoranda/RM5281.1/

Hickey, Gerald C., *Accommodation in South Vietnam: The Key to Sociopolitical Solidarity*, Santa Monica, Calif.: RAND Corporation, P-3707, October 1967. As of May 7, 2009: http://www.rand.org/pubs/papers/P3707/

Hickey, Gerald C., "U.S. Strategy in South Vietnam: Extrication and Equilibrium," Santa Monica, Calif.: RAND Corporation, D-19736-ARPA, December 15, 1969. As of May 7, 2009: http://www.rand.org/pubs/documents/D19736/

Hickey, Gerald C., *Window on a War*, Texas Tech University Press, Lubbock, Tex., 2002.

Higgins, J. W., *Interdiction and Resupply: Transportation Networks in Thailand and Laos, and the Effect of Network Degradation*, Santa Monica, Calif.: RAND Corporation, December 1966 (not available to the general public).

Higgins, J. W., G. S. Levenson, and W. E. Mooz, *A Study of In-Theater Logistic Support of a Large Ground Force by Air*, Santa Monica, Calif.: RAND Corporation, June 1967 (not available to the general public).

Hoeber, Frank, letter to David Elliott, RAND L-6882, April 11, 1969.

Hoeffding, Oleg, *Bombing North Vietnam: An Appraisal of Economic and Political Effects,* Santa Monica, Calif.: RAND Corporation, RM-5213-1, December 1966. As of May 7, 2009: http://www.rand.org/pubs/research_memoranda/RM5213-1/

Holley, Joe, "Leon Goure, 84, Sovietologist and Civil Defense Expert," obituary in *The Washington Post*, April 5, 2007.

Holliday, L. P., *Report on Wet Season Truck Test and Comments on the Thailand Road Program*, Santa Monica, Calif.: RAND Corporation, D-11775-ARPA, October 17, 1963.

Holliday, L. P., *A Method for Estimating Road Capacity and Truck Requirements*, Santa Monica, Calif.: RAND Corporation, RM-3331-ARPA, November 1963.

Holliday, L. P., *Experience and Evaluation of a Testing Program in an Underdeveloped Area as a Means of Developing a Road Capacity Estimating Method*, RAND P-3913, 1968.

Horelick, Arnold, "Sino-Soviet Relations and the Crisis in Vietnam," Santa Monica, Calif.: RAND Corporation, D-13608-PR, April 15, 1965.

Horelick, Arnold, "'Sour' Contingencies and U.S. Policy in Vietnam," Santa Monica, Calif.: RAND Corporation, July 26, 1966 (not available to the general public).

Hosmer, Chairman S. T., and S. O. Crane, *Counterinsurgency: A Symposium*, Santa Monica, Calif.: RAND Corporation, R-412-ARPA, November 1962. As of May 7, 2009: http://www.rand.org/pubs/reports/R412-1/

Hosmer, Stephen, *Viet Cong Repression and Its Implications for the Future,* Santa Monica, Calif.: RAND Corporation, April 1970 (not available to the general public).

Hosmer, Stephen, letter to William Colby, August 5, 1971.

Hosmer, Stephen, Konrad Kellen, and Brian Jenkins, *The Fall of South Vietnam: Statements by Vietnamese Military and Civilian Leaders*, RAND R-2208-OSD (HIST), December 1978. As of May 8, 2009: http://www.rand.org/pubs/reports/R2208/

Hosmer, Stephen, Konrad Kellen, and Brian Jenkins, *The Fall of South Vietnam: Statements by Vietnamese Military and Civilian Leaders*, New York: Crane, Russak and Co., 1980.

Hosmer, Stephen, *Psychological Effects of U.S. Air Operations in Four Wars 1941–1991: Lessons for U.S. Commanders*, Santa Monica, Calif.: RAND Corporation, MR-576-AF, 1996. As of May 7, 2009: http://www.rand.org/pubs/monograph_reports/MR576/

Hung, Luu, "Dinh Tuong Province: A General Survey," Santa Monica, Calif.: RAND Corporation, June 9, 1966 (not available to the general public).

Hunt, Richard A., *Pacification: The American Struggle for Vietnam's Hearts and Minds*, Boulder, Colo.: Westview Press, 1995.

Iklé, Fred, "Enemy Options in Vietnam, 1971–72: First Working Notes," Santa Monica, Calif.: RAND Corporation, January 29, 1970 (not available to the general public).

Iklé, Fred, correspondence with David Elliott, letter of February 17, 1970 (L-3397), and letter of April 13, 1970 (L-7381).

Jardini, David R., *Out of the Blue Yonder: The RAND Corporation's Diversification into Social Welfare Research, 1946–1968*, Doctoral Dissertation, Carnegie-Mellon University, College of Humanities & Social Sciences, Pittsburgh, Pa., 1996.

Jardini, David, *The Wrong War: RAND in Vietnam, 1954–1969,* paper written in 1998 and presented at Carnegie-Mellon University for a panel on "Policymaking in a Cold War Quagmire; RAND and Vietnam, 1954–1972," November 5, 1998, at a conference on "Cold War Science and Technology," Fall 1998.

Jenkins, Brian M., "Vietnamization: Divergent Views," Santa Monica, Calif.: RAND Corporation, February 17, 1970 (not available to the general public).

Jenkins, Brian M., "The Politics of a People's Army," Santa Monica, Calif.: RAND Corporation, D-20531-ARPA, July 20, 1970.

Jenkins, Brian M., *Why the North Vietnamese Keep Fighting*, Santa Monica, Calif.: RAND Corporation, P-4395, August 1970.

Jenkins, Brian M., *A People's Army for South Vietnam: A Vietnamese Solution,* Santa Monica, Calif.: RAND Corporation R-897-ARPA, November 1971. As of May 8, 2009:
http://www.rand.org/pubs/reports/R0897/

Jenkins, Brian M., *The Unchangeable War*, September 1972 (not available to the general public).

The Johnson Administration and Pacification in Vietnam: The Robert Komer–William Leonhart Files, 1966–1968, Lexis-Nexis, 1996. As of May 8, 2009:
http://academic.lexisnexis.com/upa/upa-product.aspx?pid=3479&type=IS&parentid=3478

Johnson, Alexis, memorandum to Dean Rusk, June 6, 1962; memorandum to Dean Rusk, June 9, 1962, Foreign Relations of the United States, State Department Archives, Washington, D.C., Kennedy Administration, 1961–1963, Volume XXIV, Laos Crisis.

Johnson, Robert H., Oral History, John F. Kennedy Presidential Library, Boston, Mass.

Joint United States Public Affairs Office (JUSPAO), *Transcript of Leon Goure (Rand Corporation) Backgrounder on Viet Cong Morale,* ~1965, document in the Vietnam Archives at Texas Tech University, Lubbock, Tex.

Jonas, Anne M., and George Tanham, *Laos: The Current Phase in a Cyclic Regional Revolution*, Santa Monica, Calif.: RAND Corporation, P-2214, February 2, 1961.

Jones, Bill, letters home, 1967–1968 (provided courtesy of Greg Jones).

Jorden, William, memorandum to Walt Rostow, July 18, 1966, Foreign Relations of the United States, Vietnam, Vol. IV, document 180. Notes on Jorden's draft of LBJ speech were taken at the Lyndon B. Johnson Library, Austin, Tex., from box 192.

Kahin, George McT., "The Pentagon Papers: A Critical Evaluation," *The American Political Science Review*, Vol. 69, No. 2, June 1975, pp. 675–684.

Karnow, Stanley, *Vietnam: A History: The First Complete Account of Vietnam at War*, New York: Penguin Books, 1983.

Katz, Amrom, "Early RAND: Personalities and Projects as Recalled in *The Alumni Bulletin*," Santa Monica, Calif.: RAND Corporation, P-8055, March 2001. As of May 7, 2009:
http://www.rand.org/pubs/papers/P8055/

Kellen, Konrad, "A Profile of the PAVN Soldier in South Vietnam: A Psywar-Oriented Study," Santa Monica, Calif.: RAND Corporation, February 18, 1966 (not available to the general public).

Kellen, Konrad, *A Profile of the PAVN Soldier in South Vietnam*, Santa Monica, Calif.: RAND Corporation, June 1966 (not available to the general public).

Kellen, Konrad, "Outline of a Study of Cohesion and Disintegration in the VC," Santa Monica, Calif.: RAND Corporation, July 29, 1966 (not available to the general public).

Kellen, Konrad, memorandum letter to Leon Goure et al., "US/ARVN Shelling and Air Bombardment of Vietnamese," September 30, 1966; document in possession of Gustave Shubert, cited in David Jardini, *The Wrong War*, 1998.

Kellen, Konrad, "Alternative Vietnam Strategies: The 'Extrication Option,'" Santa Monica, Calif.: RAND Corporation, October 8, 1968 (not available to the general public).

Kellen, Konrad, "Vietnam: Lessons Learned: An Inventory of Thoughts on a Forthcoming Study," Santa Monica, Calif.: RAND Corporation, December 10, 1968 (not available to the general public).

Kellen, Konrad, *A View of the VC: Elements of Cohesion in the Enemy Camp in 1966–1967*, Santa Monica, Calif.: RAND Corporation, November 1969 (not available to the general public).

Kellen, Konrad, *Nineteen Seventy One [1971] and Beyond: The View from Hanoi*, Santa Monica, Calif.: RAND Corporation, P-4634-1, June 1971. As of May 8, 2009:
http://www.rand.org/pubs/papers/P4634-1/

Kennedy, Edward, Senator, *Congressional Record,* Senate, June 23, 1970.

Kershaw, J. A., "The Research Program of the Economic Department," Santa Monica, Calif.: RAND Corporation, February 28, 1961 (not available to the general public).

Kimball, Jeffrey, *Nixon's Vietnam War*, Lawrence, Kan.: University Press of Kansas, 1998.

Kissinger, Henry, letter to Guy Pauker, December 27, 1968.

Kissinger, Henry, *White House Years*, Boston, Mass.: Little, Brown, and Company, 1979.

Koch, Jeannette A., *The Chieu Hoi Program in South Vietnam, 1963–1971*, Santa Monica, Calif.: RAND Corporation, R-1172-ARPA, January 1973. As of May 8, 2009:
http://www.rand.org/pubs/reports/R1172/

Komer, Robert, "The Current Pacification Program in Vietnam," Santa Monica, Calif.: RAND Corporation, December 23, 1969 (not available to the general public). Later expanded and restructured into "Organization and Management of the New Model Pacification Program: 1966–1969," Santa Monica, Calif.: RAND Corporation, D-20104-ARPA, May 7, 1970. As of May 8, 2009:
http://www.rand.org/pubs/documents/D20104/

Komer, Robert, "Vietnam Revisited," Santa Monica, Calif.: RAND Corporation, July 30, 1970 (not available to the general public).

Komer, Robert, *Impact of Pacification on Insurgency in South Vietnam*, Santa Monica, Calif.: RAND Corporation, P-4443, August 1970. As of May 8, 2009:
http://www.rand.org/pubs/papers/P4443/

Komer, Robert, letter to William Colby, August 6, 1971.

Koon, R. E., and Ken C. Strogher, *The Military Geography of Laos: A Barrier to Communist Aggression*, Santa Monica, Calif.: RAND Corporation, March 1962 (not available to the general public).

Kraft, Joseph, "Breaching the Code: Rand Analysts' Protest on Vietnam Policy Raises Basic Question of Responsibility," *Washington Post*, October 12, 1969.

Kraft, Joseph, "Ellsberg: Unlike the Others, He Was 'A Man Driven,'" *The New York Times*, July 4, 1971.

Kuss, Kurt, "An Introduction to the Edward D. Britton Collection," in *Floor to Floor*, Special Collection, University Archives Department, California State University, Sacramento, Vol. 8, No. 4, April 26, 2004.

Landau, David, "Behind the Policy Makers: RAND and the Vietnam War," *Ramparts*, November 1972, pp. 26–39, 60–64.

Langer, Paul, *Laos: Search for Peace in the Midst of War*, Santa Monica, Calif.: RAND Corporation, P-3748, December 1967. As of May 8, 2009:
http://www.rand.org/pubs/papers/P3748/

Langer, Paul, *Laos: Preparing for a Settlement in Vietnam*, Santa Monica, Calif.: RAND Corporation, P-4024, February 1969. As of May 8, 2009:
http://www.rand.org/pubs/papers/P4024/

Langer, Paul, *Education in the Communist Zone of Laos,* Santa Monica, Calif.: RAND Corporation, P-4726, December 1971. As of May 8, 2009:
http://www.rand.org/pubs/papers/P4726/

Langer, Paul, and J. J. Zasloff, *The North Vietnamese Military Adviser in Laos: A First Hand Account*, Santa Monica, Calif.: RAND Corporation, RM-5688-ARPA, June 1968. As of May 8, 2009:
http://www.rand.org/pubs/research_memoranda/RM5688/

Langer, Paul, and J. J. Zasloff, *Revolution in Laos: The North Vietnamese and the Pathet Lao*, Santa Monica, Calif.: RAND Corporation, RM-5935-ARPA, September 1969. As of May 8, 2009:
http://www.rand.org/pubs/research_memoranda/RM5935/

Langguth, A. J., *Our Vietnam: The War, 1954–1975*, New York: Simon & Schuster, 2000.

Larson, Eric V., *Casualties and Consensus: The Historical Role of Casualties in Domestic Support for U.S. Military Operations*, Santa Monica, Calif.: RAND Corporation, MR-726-RC, 1996. As of May 8, 2009:
http://www.rand.org/pubs/monograph_reports/MR726/

Leites, Nathan, *The Viet Cong Style of Politics*, Santa Monica, Calif.: RAND Corporation, RM-5487-1-ISA/ARPA, 1969.

Lemann, Nicholas, "Dreaming About War," *New Yorker*, July 16, 2001.

Levine, Robert A., *The Arms Debate and the Third World: Have We Learned from Vietnam?* Santa Monica, Calif.: RAND Corporation, R-3523–FF/CC/RC, 1987. As of May 8, 2009:
http://www.rand.org/pubs/reports/R3523/

Lewis, Anthony, "More Than Fit to Print," review of *Inside the Pentagon Papers*, in *The New York Review of Books*, Vol. 52, No. 6, April 7, 2005.

Lewis, D. E., memorandum to E. H. Sharkey, "Your Memo M-7193 Regarding the Letter to the Editor of the New York Times," Santa Monica, Calif.: RAND Corporation, WM-1315, October 23, 1969.

Lifton, Robert J., *Thought Reform and the Psychology of Totalism: A Study of 'Brainwashing' in China*, Chapel Hill, N.C.: University of North Carolina Press, 1989.

Lind, J., K. Harris, S. Spring, and M. Yanokawa, "Trip Report: FAST-VAL Data Collecting and Briefing Visit to Vietnam and Okinawa," Santa Monica, Calif.: RAND Corporation, D-18905-PR, June 2, 1969.

Lodge, Henry Cabot, cable to President Lyndon Johnson, December 15, 1965, State Department Archives, Foreign Relations of the United States, Foreign Relations 1964–1968, Volume III, Vietnam, Document 230.

Logevall, Frederick, *Choosing War*, Berkeley and Los Angeles, Calif.: University of California Press, 1999.

Long Range Planning Group, MACV, memo of July 8, 1970, quoting Colonels Quynh and Nhan of the joint general staff of the Republic of Vietnam Armed Forces (RVNAF) responding to Don Marshall about the concept of a People's Army, Santa Monica, Calif.: RAND Archives, Brian Jenkins file.

Maitland, Terrence, *Contagion of War*, Boston, Mass.: Boston Publishing Company, 1983.

Mallett, John D., memo to Harry Rowen, "Better Late Than Not at All," Santa Monica, Calif.: RAND Corporation, M-7283, October 17, 1969.

Management Committee and Research Council Meeting Minutes, February 13, 1962, RAND Archives.

Management Committee and Research Council Meeting Minutes, November 16, 1962, RAND Archives.

Management Committee Meeting Minutes, April 29, 1964, RAND Archives.

Management Committee Meeting Minutes, December 1, 1965, RAND Archives.

Management Committee Meeting Minutes, January 11, 1967; February 8, 1967; March 24, 1967; April 19, 1967; May 10, 1967; October 25, 1967, RAND Archives.

Management Committee Meeting Minutes, May 15, 1968; July 3, 1968, RAND Archives.

Marder, Murrey, "Terrorism of Viet Civilians Laid to S. Korean Troops," *Los Angeles Times*, January 11, 1970.

Martin, R. H., and D. E. Oyster, "Trip Report: SEATO Exercise Air Cobra in Thailand, Counter-Insurgency Discussions in Saigon, Vietnam," Santa Monica, Calif.: RAND Corporation, D-10124-PR, June 11, 1962.

McCoy, Alfred W., *The Politics of Heroin in Southeast Asia*, New York: Harper & Row, 1972.

McMaster, H. R., *Dereliction of Duty: Johnson, McNamara, the Joint Chiefs of Staff, and the Lies That Led to Vietnam*, New York: Harper Collins, 1997.

McNamara, Robert S., *In Retrospect: The Tragedy and Lessons of Vietnam*, New York: Times Books, 1995.

Military Research and Development Center, *Souvenir in Commemoration of the Opening Ceremony*, January 29, 1965.

Milne, David, "The Paul Wolfewitz of the '60s," *Los Angeles Times*, September 2, 2007.

Milne, David, *America's Rasputin: Walt Rostow and the Vietnam War*, Hill and Wang, 2009.

Mitchell, Edward, "Land Tenure and Rebellion in South Vietnam," Santa Monica, Calif.: RAND Corporation, D-15176-ARPA/AGILE, October 1966.

Mitchell, Edward, *Inequality and Insurgency: A Statistical Study of South Vietnam*, Santa Monica, Calif.: RAND Corporation, P-3610, June 1967. As of May 8, 2009:
http://www.rand.org/pubs/papers/P3610/

Mitchell, Edward, *Land Tenure and Rebellion: A Statistical Analysis of Factors Affecting Government Control in South Vietnam,* Santa Monica, Calif.: RAND Corporation, RM-5181-ARPA (Abridged), June 1967. As of May 8, 2009:
http://www.rand.org/pubs/research_memoranda/RM5181/

Mitchell, Edward, *Relating Rebellion to the Environment: An Econometric Approach*, Santa Monica, Calif.: RAND Corporation, P-3726, November 1967. As of May 8, 2009:
http://www.rand.org/pubs/papers/P3726/

Mitchell, Edward J., "Land and Rebellion: Econometric Studies of Vietnam and the Philippines: General Background Paper for Board of Trustees Meeting April 1968," Santa Monica, Calif.: RAND Corporation, D-16894-ARPA/AGILE, March 25, 1968.

Moise, Edwin E., *Land Reform in China and North Vietnam: Consolidating the Revolution at Village Level*, Chapel Hill, N.C.: University of North Carolina Press, 1983.

Montague, Robert M., letter to William Colby, August 8, 1969.

Montgomery, Paul L., "Ellsberg: From Hawk to Dove," *The New York Times*, June 27, 1971.

Morell, David, and Samudavanija, Chai-anan, *Political Conflict in Thailand: Reform, Reaction, Revolution*, Cambridge, Mass.: Oelgeschlager, Gunn & Hain, 1981.

Mozingo, David, *Hanoi on the War in South Vietnam*, Santa Monica, Calif: RAND Corporation, D-15182, October 27, 1966.

Mozingo, David P., and Thomas W. Robinson, *Lin Piao on "People's War": China Takes a Second Look at Vietnam*, Santa Monica, Calif.: RAND Corporation, RM-4814-PR, November 1965. As of May 8, 2009:
http://www.rand.org/pubs/research_memoranda/RM4814/

Murrow, R. B., "Damn the Torpedos . . . ," Santa Monica, Calif.: RAND Corporation, M-7236, October 15, 1969, RAND Archives.

Nagel, Jack, "Inequality and Discontent: A Nonlinear Hypothesis," *World Politics*, Vol. 26, No. 4, July 1974.

Neese, Harvey, and John O'Donnell, eds., *Prelude to Tragedy: Vietnam 1960–1965*, Annapolis, Md.: Naval Institute Press, 2000.

Nichols, R. T., "Economics Department Progress Report," Santa Monica, Calif.: RAND Corporation, D-9236-1-PR, September 21, 1961.

Nutt, Anita Lauve, *On the Question of Communist Reprisals in Vietnam*, Santa Monica, Calif.: RAND Corporation, P-4416, August 1970. As of May 8, 2009:
http://www.rand.org/pubs/papers/P4416/

Oberdofer, Don, *Tet!*, New York: Avon Books, 1971.

Oliver, E. P., "Joint RAND–Air Staff Study for Secretary Brown: The Effectiveness of Air Power in Vietnam," Seminar Background Paper for Board of Trustees Meeting, April 1968, Santa Monica, Calif.: RAND Corporation, D-16860-PR, March 15, 1968.

Olson, Merritt W., "Your Behavior and Your Letter to the New York Times and Washington Post," Santa Monica, Calif.: RAND Corporation, WM-1302, October 25, 1969.

"The Only Way out of Vietnam," *Congressional Record*, Senate, S12377, October 13, 1969.

Otis, James, "Seoul's Hired Guns," *Ramparts*, September 1972.

Pauker, Guy J., "Treatment of POWs, Defectors, and Suspects in South Vietnam," Santa Monica, Calif.: RAND Corporation, D-13171-ISA, December 8, 1964.

Pauker, Guy J., memorandum to William Graham, dated February 1, 1965, Eyes Only, with copies to Frank Collbohm, Joe Goldsen, George Tanham, and Charlie Zwick; provided courtesy of Mrs. Tanham and Lee Meyers.

Pauker, Guy J., "JCS Briefing on Viet Cong Motivation and Morale," Santa Monica, Calif.: RAND Corporation, D-13507-ISA, March 8, 1965.

Pauker, Guy J., "Where Do We Go from Here? A Few Unanswered Questions and Controversial Proposals Concerning the War in Vietnam," Santa Monica, Calif.: RAND Corporation, March 3, 1966 (not available to the general public).

Pauker, Guy, "Vietnam Options," addressed to Henry Kissinger, M-8896, December 23, 1968.

Pauker, Guy J., memorandum to Henry Kissinger, December 27, 1968.

Pauker, Guy, letter to Chuck Benoit (L-9941), May 22, 1969, with copy to David and Mai Elliott and cover letter (L-10121) of May 26, 1969.

Pauker, Guy, *Essay on Vietnamization*, Santa Monica, Calif.: RAND Corporation, R-604-ARPA, March 1971. As of May 8, 2009: http://www.rand.org/pubs/reports/R0604/

Pauker, Guy J., in James Digby, ed., "Early RAND: Personalities and Projects as Recalled in *The Alumni Bulletin*," Santa Monica, Calif.: RAND Corporation, P-8055, March 2001.

Pearce, R. Michael, *Evolution of a Vietnamese Village—Part I: The Present, After Eight Months of Pacification*, Santa Monica, Calif.: RAND Corporation, RM-4552-1-ARPA, April 1965. As of May 8, 2009: http://www.rand.org/pubs/research_memoranda/RM4552-1/

Pearce, Michael R., *Evolution of a Vietnamese Village—Part III. Duc Lap Since November 1964 and Some Comments on Village Pacification*, Santa Monica, Calif.: RAND Corporation, RM-5086-1-ISA/ARPA, February 1967. As of May 8, 2009: http://www.rand.org/pubs/research_memoranda/RM5086-1/

Pearson, Drew, "President's Confidence in Viet Victory Grows," *Los Angeles Times,* May 27, 1966.

Pentagon Papers, Gravel Edition, Volume 2, Boston, Mass.: Beacon Press, 1971.

Peterson, A. H., "Trip Report—Work with OSD/ARPA R&D Field Unit, Vietnam," Santa Monica, Calif.: RAND Corporation, D-12378-ARPA, April 17, 1964.

Peterson, A. H., "Your Letter to the New York Times and Washington Post," Santa Monica, Calif.: RAND Corporation, M-7284, October 17, 1969.

Phillips, Herbert, *Certain Effects of Culture and Social Organization on Internal Security in Thailand*, September 1963 (not available to the general public).

Pohle, Victoria, *The Viet Cong in Saigon: Tactics and Objectives During the Tet Offensive*, RAND RM-5799-ISA/ARPA, January 1969. As of May 8, 2009: http://www.rand.org/pubs/research_memoranda/RM5799/

Porch, Harriet, *Economics Department Publications, 1960–1965: An Author Index of the Open Literature, with Abstracts*, Santa Monica, Calif.: RAND Corporation, RM-2800-1 (Supplement), January 1966.

Porter, Gareth, and James Roberts, "Creating a Bloodbath by Statistical Manipulation," *Pacific Affairs*, Vol. 61, No. 2, Summer 1988, pp. 303–310.

Prados, John, and Margaret Pratt Porter, eds., *Inside the Pentagon Papers*, Lawrence, Kan.: University Press of Kansas, 2004.

Pye, Lucian, *Observations on the Chieu Hoi Program*, enclosure 2 to L-18082, August 30, 1965. Later published as RM-4864-1-ISA/ARPA, January 1969. As of May 8, 2009:
http://www.rand.org/pubs/research_memoranda/RM4864-1/

Pye, Lucian W., *A View from Vietnam*, date unknown, but handwritten note on the first page indicates that it was received on January 21, 1965, Personal Papers of Walt Rostow, Southeast Asia Folder, Box 13, Lyndon B. Johnson Library, Austin, Tex.

Que, Le Thi, letter to Joe Carrier; courtesy of Joe Carrier.

RAND Corporation, biographical sketch of Leon Goure.

RAND Corporation, "Project AIR FORCE: Air Force Oversight," Web page, 2009. As of August 17, 2009:
http://www.rand.org/paf/about/steering.html

RANDom News, December 1961.

RANDom News, January 1962.

RANDom News, 1963.

RANDom News, May 1965.

"Rand Study Calls Peace Talks and Vietnamization Incompatible," *Los Angeles Times*, October 17, 1972.

Raymond, Henry, "Rand Seeks to Dissociate Itself from Book on China by Ex-Aide," *The New York Times,* September 24, 1971.

Reeves, Richard, "City Hires Rand Corp. to Study Four Agencies," *The New York Times,* January 9, 1968.

Rehm, Allan, ed., *Analyzing Guerrilla Warfare*, transcribed by Allan Rehm and Brendon Rehm, Proceedings of a Conference, held at SAIC Tower, McLean, Va., September 24, 1985.

"Reprisals Predicted in Vietcong Victory," *The New York Times,* June 16, 1970.

Rhyne, R. F., "A Hypothetical War in Thailand," Santa Monica, Calif: RAND Corporation, December 7, 1955 (not available to the general public).

Rich, Michael D., *Guy Pauker: A Eulogy*, Santa Monica, Calif.: RAND Corporation, P-8073, September 21, 2002. As of May 9, 2009:
http://www.rand.org/pubs/papers/P8073/

Roberts, Steve, "Six RAND Experts Support Pullout: Back Unilateral Step Within One Year in Vietnam," *The New York Times*, October 9, 1969.

Roberts, Steve, "Four at Rand ask Gradual Troop Cuts," *The New York Times*, October 18, 1969.

Roberts, Steve, "Laird Increases Security on Papers at Rand Corp.," *The New York Times*, July 3, 1971.

Roberts, Steve, "Rand Chief Quitting; Reason Disputed," *The New York Times*, November 16, 1971.

Robinson, Thomas W., and Konrad Kellen, "Protracted War or Negotiation Now? Some Thought on China's Changing Vietnam Strategy," Santa Monica, Calif.: RAND Corporation, September 13, 1966.

Rosenfeld, Stephen, "Vietnam Reprisals Theory Disputed," *The Washington Post,* June 19,1970.

Rostow, Walt W., "The Enemy's Troubles," memorandum to Secretary of State Dean Rusk, with copies to McGeorge Bundy and to Bill Moyers, July 16, 1965, Personal Papers, Walt Rostow, Southeast Asia Folder, Box 13, Lyndon B. Johnson Library, Austin, Tex.

Rostow, Walt W., memorandum to Leonard Unger, January 20, 1966, Personal Papers, Walt Rostow, Southeast Asia Folder, Box 13, Lyndon B. Johnson Library, Austin, Tex.

Rostow, Walt, letter to President Lyndon Johnson, May 9, 1966, Lyndon B. Johnson Library, Austin, Tex.

Rowan, Carl, "Defense Dept. Believes Viet Cong Morale Slipping," *Los Angeles Times*, August 17, 1966.

Rowen, Harry, memorandum to "Everyone at Rand" and "Policy Statement—Public Expression of Personal Views," Santa Monica, Calif.: RAND Corporation, M-7357, October 21, 1969.

Russo, Anthony, *A Statistical Analysis of the U.S. Crop Spraying Program in South Vietnam,* Santa Monica, Calif.: RAND Corporation, RM-5450-1-ISA/ARPA, October 1967. As of May 9, 2009: http://www.rand.org/pubs/research_memoranda/RM5450-1/

Russo, Anthony, "Attitudinal Reactions of Vietnamese Civilians to Allied Attacks: Some Comments on D-16278-PR," Santa Monica, Calif.: RAND Corporation, D-16478-PR, December 14, 1967.

Russo, Anthony J., "Economic and Social Correlates of Government Control in South Vietnam," Santa Monica, Calif.: RAND Corporation, D-18288-ARPA, December 1968.

Russo, Anthony, "Looking Backward: Rand and Vietnam in Retrospect," *Ramparts*, July 1972.

Sansom, Robert L., *The Economics of Insurgency in the Mekong Delta of Vietnam,* Cambridge, Mass., and London, England: The M.I.T. Press, 1970.

Schaffer, Marvin B., and Milton G. Weiner, *Border Security in South Vietnam*, Santa Monica, Calif.: RAND Corporation, R-572-ARPA, February 1971. As of May 9, 2009: http://www.rand.org/pubs/reports/R0572/

Schrag, Peter, "The Ellsberg Question," *The New York Times,* June 17, 1974.

Schultz, Paul T., "Modeling of Complex Political Systems: Mitchell's Government Control Model for Vietnam," Santa Monica, Calif.: RAND Corporation, D-18923-ARPA/AGILE, June 10, 1969.

Seminar on Development and Security in Thailand: Part I, The Insurgency—see Heymann.

Seminar on Development and Security in Thailand: Part II, Development-Security Interactions—see Heymann.

Shapley, Deborah, *Promise and Power: The Life and Times of Robert McNamara,* Boston, Toronto, London: Little, Brown, and Company, 1993.

Sharkey, Edward, "Your Letter to the New York Times and Washington Post," Santa Monica, Calif.: RAND Corporation, M-7193, October 14, 1969.

Sharkey, E. H., and G. C. Reinhardt, *Air Interdiction in Southeast Asia*, Santa Monica, Calif.: RAND Corporation, RM-5283-PR, November 1967.

Sharp, U.S. Grant, Jr., cable to William Westmoreland, February 1965, Personal Papers, William C. Westmoreland, Box 5, Lyndon B. Johnson Library, Austin, Tex.

Shawcross, William, *Sideshow: Kissinger, Nixon, and the Destruction of Cambodia*, Rev. ed., New York: Simon and Schuster, 1987; cited in Kimball, *Nixon's Vietnam War*, 1998.

Sheehan, Neil, "Should We Have War Crimes Trials?" *The New York Times*, March 28, 1971.

Sheehan, Neil, *A Bright Shining Lie: John Paul Vann and America in Vietnam*, New York: Random House, 1988.

Shubert, Gus, "Southeast Asia Trip Report," Santa Monica, Calif.: RAND Corporation, August 16, 1967 (not available to the general public).

Shubert, Gustave H., "Summary Briefing on Vietnam Alternatives," Santa Monica, Calif.: RAND Corporation, DRU-1819, February 1998 (originally published in November 1968). As of May 9, 2009:
http://www.rand.org/pubs/drafts/DRU1819/

SIERRA Project personnel in Mathematics, "Limited War in Thailand—THAI-I," Santa Monica, Calif., D-3652, May 21, 1956. Superseded by RM-2027.

Smith, Bruce L. R., *The RAND Corporation*, Cambridge, Mass.: Harvard University Press, 1966.

Smith, Robert M., "Report Compiled in '68 Says Excessive Allied Bombing in South Vietnam Stirred Hostility to Regime," *The New York Times*, January 22, 1970.

Smith, Robert M., "Laird Increases Security on Papers at Rand Corp.," *The New York Times*, July 3, 1971.

Smith, Wayne, memorandum to General Alexander Haig, December 11, 1970.

Social Science Department, "Social Science Department Progress Report, March 1961," Santa Monica, Calif.: RAND Corporation, D-8545, March 17, 1961.

Social Science Department, "Social Science Department Progress Report, September 1, 1961," Santa Monica, Calif.: RAND Corporation, D-9221, September 21, 1961.

Social Science Department, "Social Science Department Progress Report, September 1–February 28, 1962," Santa Monica, Calif.: RAND Corporation, D-9732, February 22, 1962.

Social Science Department, "Progress Report 1963–1964: For Calendar Year 1963, with Forecast of Activities for 1964," Santa Monica, Calif.: RAND Corporation, February 10, 1964 (not available to the general public).

Social Science Department, "Social Science Department Progress Report for 1964–1965, All Clients for Calendar Year 1964, with Forecast of Activities for 1965," Santa Monica, Calif.: RAND Corporation, D-13198, February 24, 1965.

Social Science Department, "Social Science Department Progress Report for 1965, All Clients, with Forecast of Activities for 1966," Santa Monica, Calif.: RAND Corporation, D-14389-1, January 26, 1966.

Social Science Department Staff, "Social Science Department Progress Report on ISA and ARPA Projects January–June 1966," Santa Monica, Calif.: RAND Corporation, D-14863-ISA/ARPA, June 1966.

Solomon, Robert L., "A Model of External Support for Insurgency and Absorptive Capacity of Insurgent Organizations," Santa Monica, Calif.: RAND Corporation, WN-7070-ARPA, September 1970.

Solomon, Robert L., "Thailand in the 1970's: The Regional Context for United States Policy," Santa Monica, Calif.: RAND Corporation, IN-21191-ARPA, October 1970 (this document has not been approved for distribution outside the RAND Corporation and is available only online on the RAND intranet).

Solomon, Robert L., "United States Security Assistance to Thailand: Case Studies in Military Interaction," Santa Monica, Calif.: RAND Corporation, November 1971 (not available to the general public).

Starbird, memo to General William Westmoreland, Personal Papers of William Westmoreland, Lyndon B. Johnson Library, Austin, Tex.

State Department, Foreign Relations of the United States, Kennedy Administration, 1961–1963, Volume XXIV, Laos Crisis.

"Statement by Rand Corp. Staff Members Favoring Total Withdrawal of U.S. Troops from Vietnam Within 1 Year," introduced by Mr. Goodell, *Congressional Record*, Senate, S12395, October 13, 1969.

Stevenson, Charles A., *The End of Nowhere*, Boston, Mass.: Beacon Press, 1972.

Strauch, Ralph, "Some Views on Interviews," Santa Monica, Calif.: RAND Corporation, D-15172-AGILE/ISA, October 24, 1966.

Strauch, Ralph, "A Possible Bias in the Coded VC Interview Data," Santa Monica, Calif.: RAND Corporation, D-17060-ARPA/AGILE, May 1, 1968.

Strober, Deborah N., and Gerald S. Strober, *Nixon: An Oral History of His Presidency*, New York: HarperCollins, 1994.

Sturdevant, C. V., "Selected Papers on Border Control, Vietnam, 1962," Santa Monica, Calif.: RAND Corporation, D(L)-10095-ARPA, May 28, 1962.

Sturdevant, C. V., "The Border Control Problem in South Vietnam," Santa Monica, Calif.: RAND Corporation, D-10959-1-ARPA, Revised March 8, 1963.

Sturdevant, C. V., J. M. Carrier, and J. I. Edelman, "An Examination of the Viet Cong Reaction to the Vietnamese Strategic Hamlet Program (12 December 1962 through 2 September 1963)" (Draft for Proposed RM), Santa Monica, Calif.: RAND Corporation, D-11871-ARPA, November 19, 1963 (never issued).

Tanham, George, "Some Observations on the United States Experience in Vietnam," unpublished paper provided courtesy of his widow and Lee Meyer.

Tanham, George K., "Trip Report: Vietnam," Santa Monica, Calif.: RAND Corporation, October 6, 1961 (not releasable to the general public).

Tanham, George K., "Trip Report: Vietnam, January 1963," Santa Monica, Calif.: RAND Corporation, March 22, 1963.

Tanham, George K., "Defeating Insurgency in South Vietnam: My Early Efforts," in Harvey Neese and John O'Donnell, eds., *Prelude to Tragedy: Vietnam, 1960–1965*, Annapolis, Md.: Naval Institute Press, 2001.

Taylor, Maxwell, letter to Walt Rostow, May 9, 1966, Lyndon B. Johnson Library, Austin, Tex.

Taylor, Maxwell, telegram from the Embassy in Vietnam to the Department of State, to CINCPAC for POLAD, Foreign Relations of the United States, Johnson Administration, Vietnam, 1964–1968, Volume III, Document 56, State Department Archives, Washington, D.C.

Taylor, V. D., "A Simple Model of the Economy of Northeast Thailand," Santa Monica, Calif.: RAND Corporation, D-17566-ARPA/AGILE, 1968.

"Telephone Conversation Between President Johnson and Secretary of Defense McNamara, January 14 or 15, 1966," Foreign Relations of the United States, Vietnam, 1964–1968, Volume IV, Document 26, State Department Archives, Washington, D.C.

Thayer, Thomas, "War Without Fronts," Conference on "Analyzing Guerrilla War," transcribed by Brendon Rehm, McLean, Va., September 24, 1985.

Tilford, Earl H., Jr., *Setup: What the Air Force Did in Vietnam and Why*, Maxwell Air Force Base, Ala.: Air University Press, June 1991.

Time magazine, December 12, 1969.

Todd, Oliver, "Ce qui se passe dans le monde depend en partie de ces chercheurs," *Le Monde Diplomatique,* 1966.

The Uncounted Enemy: A Vietnam Deception, U.S. Documentary, Museum of Broadcast Communications Web site. As of May 8, 2009:
http://www.museum.tv/archives/etv/U/htmlU/uncountedene/uncountedene.htm

Ungar, Sanford, "'Secrecy' of Pentagon Papers Depends on Where You Look," *The Washington Post*, February 11, 1973.

U.S. Embassy, *U.S. Policy with Respect to North Laos*, 1967.

Usborne, David, "Nixon Wanted to Drop Nuclear Bomb on Vietnam," *The Independent* (London), March 2, 2002.

"Vietnam Dialogue: Mr. Bundy and the Professors," *CBS News Special Report*, as broadcast over the CBS Television Network, Monday, June 21, 1965, 10:00–11:00 p.m. EDT.

Walt, Lt. Gen. Lewis, *Strange War, Strange Strategy: A General's Report on Vietnam*, Funk & Wagnall's Company, June 1970.

Warner, Roger, *Shooting at the Moon: The Story of America's Clandestine War in Laos*, South Royalton, Vt.: Steerforth Press, second paperback edition, 1999.

The Washington Post, "A Case Against Staying in Vietnam," Letters to the Editor, October 12, 1969.

"We Are All Alone in Indian Country," U.S. Marines Combined Action Platoons Web site. As of April 13, 2009:
http://www.capmarine.com/

Weiner, Milton, Michael E. Arnsten, T. T. Connors, E. Dews, G. Schilling, "Infiltration and Invasion Control Project: Activities in Study of Counterinfiltration Program for South Vietnam," Santa Monica, Calif.: RAND Corporation, March 4, 1969 (not available to the general public).

Wells, Tom, *Wild Man: The Life and Times of Daniel Ellsberg*, New York: Palgrave, 2001.

West, Francis J., *Small Unit Action in Vietnam, Summer 1966*, Washington, D.C.: Historical Branch, G-3 Division, Headquarters, U.S. Marine Corps, 1967.

West, Francis J., "Memo to Rear Admiral William E. Lemos, USN, Director, Policy Plans and NSC Affairs," December 10, 1969. Copy obtained from the National Archives.

West, Francis J., *Fifteen Walked In. Eight Walked Out*, New York: Pocket Books, 1972.

West, Francis J., *The Village*, New York: Pocket Books, 2002.

West, Francis J., and Charles Benoit, "A Brief Report from Rural Vietnam," Santa Monica, Calif.: RAND Corporation, October 1968 (not available to the general public).

West, Francis J., and Charles Benoit, "Pacification: View from the Provinces—Part II (July–October 1968)," Santa Monica, Calif.: RAND Corporation, December 13, 1968 (not available to the general public).

West, Francis J., and Charles Benoit, "Pacification: View from the Provinces—Part III (November 1969)," Santa Monica, Calif.: RAND Corporation, January 20, 1970 (not available to the general public).

Westmoreland, William C., Diary, Personal Papers, Box 7, Lyndon B. Johnson Library, Austin, Tex.

Westmoreland, William, cable to Admiral Sharp, February 1965, William C. Westmoreland Personal Papers, Box 5, Lyndon B. Johnson Library, Austin, Tex.

Westmoreland, William C., "Historical Briefing, Dr. Hickey, February 25, 1967," History Files, 27 January–25 March 1967, Personal Papers, Lyndon B. Johnson Archives, Austin, Tex.

Westmoreland, William C., *A Soldier Reports*, Garden City, New York: Doubleday, 1976.

White, John P., letter to William Colby, Central Intelligence Agency, March 31, 1972, with attached proposal, "Suggestions of Possible RAND Study Projects for the Central Intelligence Agency."

Wicker, Tom, "In the Nation: Mr. Nixon's Scary Dreams," *The New York Times*, May 12, 1970.

Wikipedia, "Insurgency," Web page, 2009. As of August 21, 2009: http://en.wikipedia.org/wiki/insurgency

Wikipedia, "Operations Research," Web page, 2009. As of August 21, 2009: http://en.wikipedia.org/wiki/Operations_research

Wilson, David Allen, *Political Tradition and Political Change in Thailand*, Santa Monica, Calif.: RAND Corporation, P-2592, June 1962.

Wilson, David Allen, *Thailand 1962*, Santa Monica, Calif.: RAND Corporation, P-2685, 1962. As of May 9, 2009: http://www.rand.org/pubs/papers/P2685/

Wilson, George C., "No Vietnamese 'Bloodbath' Is Found: 100 Days After Fall, U.S. Fear of Massacre Unrealized," *The Washington Post*, August 1975.

Wilson, J. A., "Trip Reports: Surveys of Long-Vacant Airstrips, Thailand, July–August 1963," Santa Monica, Calif.: RAND Corporation, D-11694-ARPA, September 13, 1963.

Wise, Richard, *An Operational Setting for the Comparison of Alternative Tactical Mobility Systems for Ground Forces*, Santa Monica, Calif.: RAND Corporation, IN-21319-PR, December 1970. Wolf, Charles, Jr., *Economic Development and Mutual Security: Some Problems of U.S. Foreign Assistance Programs in Southeast Asia*, Santa Monica, Calif.: RAND Corporation, RM-1778-RC, 1956. As of May 9, 2009: http://www.rand.org/pubs/research_memoranda/RM1778/

Wolf, Charles, Jr., *Economic Development and Mutual Security: Some Problems of U.S. Foreign Assistance Programs in Southeast Asia*, Santa Monica, Calif.: RAND Corporation, RM-1778-RC, 1956.

Wolf, Charles, Jr., *Foreign Aid: Theory and Practice in Southern Asia*, Princeton, N.J.: Princeton University Press, 1960.

Wolf, Charles, Jr., *Evaluation of Military Assistance in Underdeveloped Countries: A Case Study of Vietnam*, Santa Monica, Calif.: RAND Corporation, RM-2571-PR, April 13, 1960.

Wolf, Charles, Jr., *Insurgency and Counterinsurgency: New Myths and Old Realities*, RAND P-3132-1, July 1965 (as of May 9, 2009: http://www.rand.org/pubs/papers/P3132-1/); subsequently published in *Yale Review*, Vol. 56, Winter 1967.

Wolf, Charles, Jr., "Frank: Few Words, Strong Character," in Jim Digby, ed., "Early RAND: Personalities and Projects as Recalled in *The Alumni Bulletin*," Santa Monica, Calif.: RAND Corporation, P-8055, March 2001. As of May 7, 2009: http://www.rand.org/pubs/papers/P8055/

Woo, Elaine, "Rand Staffer Encouraged Pentagon Papers Leak," obituary of Tony Russo, *Los Angeles Times*, August 8, 2008.

Wyatt, David K., "North Vietnam and the Pathet Lao," *The New York Times*, February 21, 1971.

Wyatt, David K., *Thailand: A Short History*, New Haven, Conn.: Yale University Press, 1982.

Young, G. B. W., "Notes on Vietnam," Santa Monica, Calif.: RAND Corporation, D-11629-1-ARPA, August 16, 1963 (revised August 28, 1963).

Young, Marilyn B., *The Vietnam Wars: 1945–1990*, New York: Harper & Row, 1991.

Zasloff, Joseph J., *The Role of North Vietnam in the Southern Insurgency*, Santa Monica, Calif.: RAND Corporation, RM-4140-PR, July 1964. As of May 9, 2009: http://www.rand.org/pubs/research_memoranda/RM4140/

Zasloff, Joseph J., *The Pathet Lao: Leadership and Organization*, Santa Monica, Calif.: RAND Corporation, R-949, July 1973.

Zasloff, Tela, letters home from Laos, 1967.

Zasloff, Tela, *Saigon Dreaming: Recollections of Indochina Days*, New York: St. Martin's Press, 1990.

Zasloff, Tela, "Viet Cong Motivation and Morale," *RAND Alumni Bulletin*, Summer 1994.

Zwick, Charles J., Charles A. Cooper, Hans Heymann, and Richard H. Moorsteen, *U.S. Economic Assistance in Vietnam: A Proposed Reorientation*, Santa Monica, Calif.: RAND Corporation, R-430-AID, July 1964. As of May 9, 2009: http://www.rand.org/pubs/reports/R430/

Zwick, Charles J., Charles A. Cooper, Hans Heymann, and Richard H. Moorsteen, "Notes on Current U.S. Problem Areas in Vietnam," Santa Monica, Calif.: RAND Corporation, D-12731-AID, August 7, 1964.

Zwick, Charles J., Charles A. Cooper, Hans Heymann, and Richard H. Moorsteen, "A Possible Application of the Approach Set Forth in R-430, 'U.S. Economic Assistance in Vietnam: A Proposed Reorientation,'" Santa Monica, Calif.: RAND Corporation, September 16, 1964 (not available to the general public).

Zwick, Charles J., and J. W. Ellis, "RAND's Southeast Asia Research Program," Santa Monica, Calif.: RAND Corporation, D-13381, February 5, 1965.

Author Biography

Mai Elliott, a native of Vietnam and a writer, is a graduate of Georgetown University. She worked for the RAND Corporation during the war in Vietnam, interviewing defectors and prisoners-of-war as part of RAND's research on insurgency and counter-insurgency: the Viet Cong Motivation and Morale Project from 1964 to 1965, and the Dinh Tuong project in the Mekong Delta from 1965 to 1966 and from 1971 to 1972. Her family memoir, *The Sacred Willow: Four Generations in the Life of a Vietnamese Family*, published in 1999 under the name of Duong Van Mai Elliott, was nominated for the Pulitzer Prize by Oxford University Press.

Index

A

Abductions, 503

Abrams, Creighton, 300, 328, 329, 331, 369, 403

Accelerated pacification campaign (APC), 375, 390

Accommodation, 316–318, 332, 366, 385n162

Acheson, Dean, 306–307, 311

Ackland, Len, 298–300

Adams, Sam, 193–195

Adjustments, 366

Advanced Research Projects Agency (ARPA), 14, 17
   and American-Vietnamese relationships, 81
   and early research on Vietnam, 50
   funding for Leon Goure from, 100
   and Steve Hosmer, 511
   and Yogi Ianeiro, 285
   RAND's contract with, 12
   and Strategic Hamlet Program, 28
   and support for AGILE, 19–21
   Thailand research sponsored by, 596
   weapons distribution by, 294

Africa, 15

AFSG (Air Force Steering Group), 23

Agent Orange, 32, 225n73

AGILE, 17, 19, 20, 50, 100

Agnew, Spiro, 510, 516

Agreement of the Restoration of Peace and Reconciliation in Laos, 589

Agriculture, 387, 396

Aid, 85–87

Aid, economic. *See* Economic aid

Air America, 550, 554–556, 585

Air Force Steering Group (AFSG), 23

Airpower, 94–103, 117–120, 125
   in Cambodia, 370
   effectiveness of, 96–97, 206, 221–222
   expanding use of, 131, 132
   hearings on, 245–247
   in Laos, 372

   psychological effect of, 117
   results of, 156–157
   and SIGMA I, 69
   tactical, 229
   and Viet Cong recruitment, 97, 99

Allen, George, 95n16, 193–194

Allen, Joan, 303–305, 327, 347

Alsop, Joseph, 113n99, 258

"Alternative Vietnam Strategies" (Konrad Kellen), 308n67

Ammunition, 215

Anger, Violence and Politics, 238–239

An Giang province, 237–238

Anthis, Rollen, 35–37

Anti-Communist Denunciation campaign, 410

Anti-war sentiment
   demonstrations of, 447
   development of, 135
   and Nixon, 368–369
   and Pentagon Papers, 433, 495
   and public debates, 138–139

Ap Bac, battle of, 37

APC. *See* accelerated pacification campaign

Aquarius (musical), 447

Arab oil embargo, 524

Archibald, Kathy, 452

Area security, 338–340

Armed Forces Council, 77

Army of the Republic of Vietnam (ARVN), 18
   and airpower, 97
   drafting for, 71
   and escalation, 94
   leadership of, 388
   and pacification, 80, 382, 387
   salaries of soldiers in, 379
   and Tet Offensive, 293
   and Viet Cong zones, 268

Arnold, Bruce, 285n3

Arnold, H. H., 1, 3

Arnold, Martin, 463

Arnsten, Michael E., 505–510

ARVN. *See* Army of the Republic of Vietnam